DATE DUE	
GAYLORD	PRINTED IN U.S.A.

BAUER'S
PRECIOUS STONES

1. Diamond, crystal in matrix (Brazil).   2. The same (South Africa).   3. Diamond (Bort).
4. Diamond (Carbonado).   5. Ruby, crystal.   6. Ruby, cut.   7. Sapphire, crystal.   8. Sapphire,
cut.   9. Spinel (Balas-ruby), crystal.   10. Spinel (Ruby-spinel), crystal.   11. Zircon (Hyacinth), crystal.   12. The same, in basalt.   13. Zircon, cut.

PRECIOUS STONES

A POPULAR ACCOUNT OF THEIR CHARACTERS, OCCURRENCE,
AND APPLICATIONS, WITH AN INTRODUCTION TO THEIR
DETERMINATION, FOR MINERALOGISTS,
LAPIDARIES, JEWELLERS, ETC.

WITH
AN APPENDIX ON PEARLS AND CORAL

BY
DR. MAX BAUER
PRIVY COUNCILLOR, PROFESSOR IN THE UNIVERSITY OF MARBURG

TRANSLATED FROM THE GERMAN WITH ADDITIONS BY
L. J. SPENCER, M.A. (CANTAB.), F.G.S.
ASSISTANT IN THE MINERAL DEPARTMENT OF THE BRITISH MUSEUM

AND WITH
NEW APPENDICES ON SYNTHETIC GEMS AND THE CULTURED PEARL

with 20 plates and 95 figures

CHARLES E. TUTTLE COMPANY: PUBLISHERS
RUTLAND, VERMONT & TOKYO, JAPAN

Representatives

Continental Europe: BOXERBOOKS, INC., *Zurich*
British Isles: PRENTICE-HALL INTERNATIONAL, INC., *London*
Australasia: PAUL FLESCH & CO., PTY. LTD., *Melbourne*
Canada: M. G. HURTIG LTD., *Edmonton*

Published by the Charles E. Tuttle Company, Inc.
of Rutland, Vermont & Tokyo, Japan
with editorial offices at Suido 1-chome, 2-6
Bunkyo-ku, Tokyo, Japan

Copyright in Japan, 1969 by Charles E. Tuttle Co., Inc.

Library of Congress Catalog Card No. 69–12082

First Tuttle edition published 1969

PRINTED IN JAPAN

TABLE OF CONTENTS

FIRST PART

GENERAL CHARACTERS OF PRECIOUS STONES

SECOND PART

SYSTEMATIC DESCRIPTION OF PRECIOUS STONES

THIRD PART

DETERMINATION AND DISTINGUISHING OF PRECIOUS STONES

APPENDIX

APPENDICES TO THE NEW EDITION

INDEX

CORRIGENDA

Page 75, line 9 from bottom, *after* " half-brilliant " *insert* " (Plate II., Fig. 8*a*)."

,, 94, line 1, *for* " Frémy " *read* " Fremy."

,, 110, column 2, line 2, *for* " Chlorastolite " *read* " Chlorastrolite."

,, 280, lines 11, 37, 47, and Fig. 58, *for* " Frémy " *read* " Fremy."

,, 482, line 30, *after* " Amethyst crystals " *insert* (Plate XVIII., Fig. 1*a*)."

,, 511, line 3, *after* " Heliotrope " *insert* " (Plate XVIII., Fig. 6)."

PUBLISHER'S FOREWORD

THE business of publishing books in the final third of the 20th century is, like most other businesses, dominated by contemporary demand. Everything that can conceivably be written about finds its way into book form. Why, then, does a publisher reach back to the turn of the century to reprint a voluminous work on a specialized subject?

In the case of *Precious Stones,* the answer lies in a recent poll taken among out-of-print book sellers who were asked to list those books which they would most like to see appear in new editions. Startlingly enough, *Precious Stones* which first appeared in 1896 in Germany and was later translated and published in England in 1904, appeared high on the list. We use the word startling because there have been enormous advances in the technology applicable to gems in the past sixty years. Nevertheless, the basic information on characteristics and occurrence of precious stones remains valid; this is perhaps the most comprehensive book on gems ever to be published.

In reissuing *Precious Stones* we have retained all of the plates and drawings. In addition to the original appendix on pearls and coral, we have included new material on synthetic gems and the cultured pearl. The English edition of the book was originally published in 1904 by Charles Griffin and Co., Ltd., London.

NOTE BY TRANSLATOR

Since the publication of Professor Max Bauer's " Edelsteinkunde," in 1896 (first issued in parts during 1895 and 1896), many new facts concerning precious stones have appeared in mineralogical literature. They relate mainly to new localities and to modes of occurrence, but also to the chemical composition of stones, the work, in particular, of Professor S. L. Penfield, of Newhaven, having shown that the generally accepted chemical formulæ of several minerals used as gems required revision.

References to the more important papers published since the appearance of his book have been kindly supplied by Professor Bauer. These and many other memoirs have been consulted, while free use has also been made of the valuable Annual Reports on precious stones, compiled by Dr. George F. Kunz, and published in the volumes of the United States Geological Survey.

The translation has thus been brought up to date, and several additions made to the original, notably under Corundum (ruby and sapphire). Under Diamond a short account of the newly discovered deposits in British Guiana has been given, but very little has been added to the original account of the South African diamond-mines—the most important of all gem-mines—since it was found impossible to incorporate much new matter with this section without rewriting the whole.

Among additions to the work will also be found references to some of the more noteworthy specimens of precious stones in the Mineral Collection of the British Museum (Natural History).

Having these and many other additions of minor importance to incorporate, the translation must necessarily be a somewhat free one, and certain portions of the original have been slightly modified or abridged in deference to the needs of English readers. In the original scarcely enough importance is attached to the optical characters of minerals, to their examination in convergent polarised light and to the measurement of refractive indices, which are of the greatest practical value in the determination of faceted stones. It was felt, however, that the addition of such matter would considerably alter the scope and plan of the work, which it has been the aim of the translator to preserve unaltered throughout.

The text-figures and plates have been reproduced directly from the original with such alterations in the spelling of names on the maps as were necessary. A new figure (Fig. 51) is given of the largest diamond yet found, the " Excelsior," a photograph for this purpose having been kindly supplied by Dr. George F. Kunz.

I could not have undertaken the large amount of work involved in this translation had I not been assured of the assistance of my wife, E. M. Spencer. The actual rendering in English is hers, and she has also carefully revised the whole of the proofs; I feel, therefore, that the work is as much hers as it is mine.

L. J. S.

December 1903.

PREFACE

THE desire of the publishers to present, to the German public, a work on precious stones similar in character to that admirably supplied in American literature by George Frederick Kunz's " Gems and Precious Stones of North America" gave the initiative to the writing of the present book. In this case, however, all precious stones had to be dealt with, and an introduction to the methods employed in their determination had also to be given. For the latter the excellent and exhaustive instructions given by C. Doelter in his " Edelsteinkunde" may serve as a model. These, however, have been somewhat modified and simplified. In particular the examination in convergent polarised light has been dispensed with, since it is unusual for gem-merchants and jewellers to be sufficiently well acquainted with the theory of the subject to make practical use of this method, while information of this description would be superfluous to a trained mineralogist. It has been considered advisable, however, to preface the systematic description of precious stones with a general survey of the related sciences, especially those of physics and mineralogy, in so far as they assist in the understanding of the nature of precious stones.

The reader is assumed to be neither a specialist in science nor wholly without scientific knowledge. It has been sought to treat the subject in such a way that it may be intelligible to any one possessed of a good general education. It is therefore hoped that the book will suffice for those who take a general scientific interest in precious stones, and that it will be specially useful to those engaged in the buying and selling of precious stones and in their application to purposes of ornament, namely, to gem-merchants and jewellers.

It was at first considered that pearls and coral, being not minerals but products of the animal kingdom, could not properly find a place in this work. In deference, however, to the wishes of the readers of the earlier parts of the book, an appendix dealing with these important subjects has been added. In writing the section on pearls, the works of Möbius and von Martens, among others, have been consulted, and for coral, those of Lacaze-Duthiers and of Canestrini.

The author has taken especial pains to treat of the mode of occurrence and the localities of each stone with as much detail as the size of the volume allowed; and the distribution of stones in the most important of the countries in which they are found is graphically shown by small sketch-maps in the text. Many new facts relating to this subject have been communicated by the author's colleagues, but even the latest mineralogical literature shows that inaccuracies still abound. Only those who have themselves gone into this branch of mineralogy and have realised how widely scattered are the accounts which deal with the occurrence of precious stones, and how prevalent errors, uncertainties and mistakes are, can appreciate the difficulties connected with such studies. The difficulty of arriving at the necessary facts in the preparation of the sketch-maps was particularly great, and these are therefore less numerous than was originally intended. Many of my colleagues have helped me in this matter by communicating their personal observations or by sending publications bearing upon the subject; to each of them I return sincere thanks.

The methods employed in the working of precious stones, and the purposes to which the latter are generally applied, have been gone into in some detail, since these stand in the closest relation to the natural characters of the stone. The general part, therefore, includes sections dealing with the forms of cutting, the process of grinding, &c., the information relating to each particular stone being repeated with the special description of that stone.

In the execution of the work the publishers have as far as possible carried out the wishes of the author. The originals of the coloured plates have been painted by the artistic hand of Herr E. Ohmann of Berlin. Most of the specimens figured are preserved in the mineralogical collection of the Natural History Museum at Berlin. For permission to use these, I return my most grateful thanks to the Director of the collection, Professor C. Klein, Privy Councillor of Mines, as also to the Curator, Professor C. Tenne, for the time and trouble he devoted to work connected with the production of the water-colours. No small part of the success of these coloured plates must be ascribed to his active co-operation in their production. Thanks are also due to Director A. Brezina of Vienna for permission to reproduce the well-known picture preserved in the Mineralogical Department of the Natural History Museum, and representing the Kimberley mine, the richest and most famous of the Cape diamond mines, here published for the first time.

The references to the literature are few, as such references appear out of place in a work primarily intended for general readers. To the narrower circle of mineralogists the author would fain have given more precise and scientific information on innumerable points. For the majority of readers it is desirable that each section should be, as far as possible, complete and independent in itself, so that there is little or no necessity for referring to other parts of the book. This has necessitated the repetition of many statements, but without, it is hoped, the reiteration becoming tiresome.

The alphabetical index has been made as complete as possible, and includes many terms not to be found in the text; the meaning of each is given together with the page reference.

The author has attained his object if he has succeeded in giving to gem-merchants and jewellers, as well as to admirers of gems, a clear representation of the natural characters and occurrence of precious stones, of the methods according to which they are worked, and of the purposes to which they are applied. If, then, in the pages which follow, the description of certain remarkable minerals should awaken in wider circles a more lively interest in mineralogy as a whole, of which the subject of precious stones is but a part, the author will be gratified, and will consider that he is amply repaid for his trouble.

MAX BAUER.

MINERALOGICAL INSTITUTE OF THE UNIVERSITY, MARBURG,
Autumn 1896.

EXPLANATION OF PLATES

LIST OF TEXT FIGURES

INTRODUCTION

Certain minerals occurring in the earth's crust are distinguished by special beauty, and have therefore been used since the earliest times for personal ornament and for decorative purposes generally. The beauty of such minerals depends upon their transparency, lustre, or colour, or in some cases upon a play of colour, due to the modification of rays of light reflected from the surface or transmitted through the stone. This beauty is not manifested to its fullest extent until the stone is cut and polished, when these features become more conspicuous. In some cases, for example in the rarely occurring diamonds of a beautiful red or blue colour, all these features are present in the same stone; in others, as in the ruby, the play of colour is absent, and the effect of the stone depends upon its transparency, lustre, and colour. In a stone such as precious opal, the beauty of the mineral depends solely upon a play of colour, which is independent of the colour of the stone itself. Opaque minerals, like turquoise, with but little lustre, owe their beauty to their fine colour; finally, colour may be completely absent, and the beauty of the stone due to its transparency, lustre, and play of colour, as in the purest colourless diamonds.

Those minerals which, through the possession of some or all of the features enumerated above, lay claim to beauty of appearance are not all equally suitable for gems. Besides the possession of undeniable beauty, which for its use as a gem-stone is naturally a *sine quâ non*, a mineral must also possess a certain degree of hardness, for otherwise a very small amount of wear will suffice to dim its beauty. Even should it successfully resist the effect of contact with the moisture of the skin, a comparatively soft stone will succumb to the action of grit and dust, which for the most part consist of particles of the mineral quartz. It is desirable, therefore, that all minerals used for personal ornament should possess at least the hardness of quartz, and a still greater hardness, the so-called gem-hardness, is an advantage. Some discretion should be exercised in the setting of stones of different degrees of hardness; thus a comparatively soft stone may be quite suitable for the ornamentation of a brooch, but should not be set in a ring, where it is likely to get much hard wear. In the same way minerals, which, however beautiful in the fresh condition, lose their beauty on exposure to the atmosphere are unsuitable for use as gems.

We have now shown that only those minerals, which combine beauty of appearance with considerable hardness, and a power of resisting external influences, are suitable for use as ornaments. The mineral substances so distinguished are known as precious stones or gems.

All the essential characters of a gem occur together in but few minerals, so that the number of precious stones is small compared with that of all the mineral species known. Moreover, the minerals distinguished by the possession of the characters of a gem occur for the most part, at least in pieces of good size and quality, in very sparing amount, so that besides their intrinsic beauty they possess the added charm of rarity. This latter character is perhaps the one to which is most largely due the costliness of these objects, for the possession of something rare, something that it is impossible for every other person to possess, has ever exercised a fascination upon human nature.

The minerals which combine the highest degrees of beauty, hardness, durability, and rarity—diamond, ruby, sapphire, and emerald, for example—are by common consent placed in the foremost rank of gems; those in which these characters, especially that of hardness, are less conspicuous, are less highly esteemed. The former may be grouped together as precious stones, while the latter, characterised sometimes by greater beauty, but by lower hardness and more common occurrence, are known as semi-precious stones.

It is impossible to draw a hard and fast line between precious and semi-precious stones; a stone which one person might regard as precious, another would place with semi-precious stones. In deciding the point, not one character but all must be taken into consideration, and the rarity or commonness of the stone set against its other characters. Thus the emerald, though comparatively soft, is one of the costliest of stones owing to its magnificent colour, and the rarity of faultless specimens. Again, precious opal and turquoise, though opaque and comparatively soft, are more valuable than is amethyst, which, though transparent and harder, is yet, on account of its commonness, regarded as only a semi-precious stone.

Just as the essential characters of a gem are developed in different minerals to different degrees, so do these characters differ in degree in different specimens of the same mineral species. The hardness is in all cases the same in the same species, but the transparency and colour may be very different in different specimens, so that while some furnish us with the finest examples of precious stones, others may be entirely unsuitable for ornamental purposes, and the remainder furnish stones of inferior quality. Thus the mineral species beryl includes not only the costly emerald, but also the far less beautiful and less valuable golden beryl and pale greenish-blue aquamarine, and the cloudy and opaque common beryl, which is destitute of the essentials of a gem, and is therefore never used as such. The transparent varieties of minerals used as precious stones are distinguished by the prefix "precious" from the opaque or "common" varieties.

The value of a mineral as a gem does not depend solely upon its natural characters, but is influenced to a very large extent by the fashion of the day. A stone which at one time commands a high price, at another, for no apparent reason, will scarcely find a purchaser; while minerals, at first comparatively unknown to the jeweller, will leap suddenly into popular favour. At one time diamonds are most in favour, at another the so-called fancy stones. At the present time the latter is the case; scarcely more than a dozen years ago the jeweller's stock consisted of diamonds, rubies, sapphires, emeralds, and garnets, with an occasional topaz or aquamarine. Now almost all the stones described in this book, a list of which will be found in the table of contents, and most of which are coloured, are commonly bought and sold in the precious stone market. Many of the minerals now cut as gems are not suitable in every respect for the purpose, and this is specially so in the case of those minerals which are cut and worn more for the association of the wearer with the place of their occurrence than for their intrinsic beauty or suitability.

The minerals which must be reckoned as precious stones are by no means fixed in number, nor is it a fact that a mineral once used as an ornamental stone is ever after used as such. New minerals come into favour and old ones fall out of use, but a certain number, the richest and most beautiful of gems, survive all the changes and chances of fashion, and stand now, where they did ages ago, highest of all in popular esteem.

Of the natural substances used for ornamental purposes other than precious stones, pearls and coral are the most important. These, however, are not members of the mineral kingdom, being products of animal life, and are therefore excluded in the consideration of precious stones. Amber, on the other hand, though not a true mineral substance, finds a place here. It is the fossilised resin of extinct trees, but being a constituent of the earth's crust, as are precious stones, it is customary to regard it and similar substances as within the domain of mineralogy.

Since precious stones are minerals, their study must be considered as a branch of mineralogy. It includes the investigation of their natural characters, such as chemical composition, crystalline form, specific gravity, hardness, cleavage, and their behaviour towards light, as well as an inquiry into their occurrence in the earth's crust, their mode of origin there, and the localities where they are to be found. But since the application of precious stones is a matter of practical importance, a thorough knowledge of the subject must include an acquaintance with the mining and working of precious stones, their use in jewellery and ornaments, and other subjects of a somewhat technical nature.

Another important branch of the same subject is the determination of gems and the recognition of the features which distinguish them from deceptive imitations in glass, or from less valuable minerals of similar appearance. Long familiarity with the appearance of different stones will, in many cases, enable a dealer or amateur, even though destitute of mineralogical knowledge, to identify any given stone at a glance. In other cases, however, a person who depends in this way upon his memory and sense of recognition, is very likely to fall into error, which a scientific mineralogist would avoid by the use of exact methods of determination. It is therefore greatly to the advantage of persons who buy and sell these costly objects to make themselves acquainted with the principles and methods of mineralogy here laid down. Not only does a sufficient practical knowledge of this subject help in avoiding errors of determination, but it also enables one to gather from rough stones valuable indications of the purposes to which they are most suited, and the methods of working most advantageously employed.

The first part of the present work will be devoted to a consideration of the mineral characteristics which are of importance to the specialist in gems, a general consideration of the mode of occurrence of precious stones, and, finally, certain matters relating to the application and working of these stones. The second part will contain a particular and detailed account of every mineral which has been used for ornamental purposes, with special reference to precious stones; while the third part epitomises the characters to be relied on in determining precious stones and for distinguishing them from other precious stones and from imitations.

FIRST PART

GENERAL CHARACTERS OF PRECIOUS STONES

I. NATURAL CHARACTERS AND OCCURRENCE.

A. CHEMICAL COMPOSITION.

PRECIOUS stones in their general chemical relations do not differ essentially from other minerals. They are composed of the same chemical elements, which are combined together according to the same laws. At one time, however, it was believed that, since the characters of precious stones were so remarkable, their chemical composition must also be unique. Hence it was assumed that all precious stones contained a rare and precious earth as a fundamental constituent. More exact chemical investigations have shown, however, that the constituents of the rarest of precious stones are frequently very common substances, such as carbon or alumina. The precious metals—gold, platinum, &c.—never enter into the composition of gems, and the rare elements very exceptionally so. As examples of such occurrence may be mentioned the element zirconium, present in zircon, and the element beryllium, present in emerald, aquamarine, and a few other rarer stones.

The chemical composition of different stones varies considerably in complexity. While it is very simple in some, in others it is complicated by the presence of numerous constituents. In the case of the diamond, the chemical composition is very simple; this, the most important of gems, consists solely of the common and widely distributed element carbon. The carbon of diamond, however, is endowed with special properties, and differs very widely from graphite, the other crystallised modification of carbon, and from coal, which consists largely of carbon. Among gems, the diamond stands alone in the simplicity of its chemical composition.

At least two, and in the majority of cases a number of, elements enter into the composition of all other precious stones. The rarest and most costly of all stones, the red ruby, contains only two elements; and the blue sapphire is identical with the ruby in chemical composition, differing from it only in colour. The two elements of which the ruby and sapphire consist are aluminium and oxygen. The former, an important constituent of clays and other widely distributed minerals, is a metal which in recent years has become of great importance in the arts and manufactures; the latter is an important constituent of atmospheric air. The combination of aluminium and oxygen, known as oxide of aluminium, or alumina, is an essential constituent of many other valuable gems. Rock-crystal, amethyst, agate, opal, and other stones also consist of a simple oxide, the oxide of silicon. This oxide, which is known as silica, is the most important constituent of the earth's crust. Zircon, spinel, and chrysoberyl furnish examples of slightly more complex oxides.

While the group containing the oxides furnishes so many important gems, there are other groups of minerals which are unimportant from this point of view. Such groups are those of the metallic sulphides (compounds of metals with sulphur), the haloid compounds (combinations of metals with chlorine, bromine, iodine, and fluorine), and the sulphates (compounds of sulphuric acid). Although these three groups may include minerals which are occasionally used as ornamental stones, we find none possessing the essentials of a gem to any marked degree.

The group containing the silicates is again an important one, for it embraces the emerald, garnet, chrysolite, topaz, and many other precious stones. Tourmaline may be mentioned as an example of the few gems belonging to this group, the chemical composition of which is specially complex.

Of the other divisions of the mineral kingdom there remains only to be mentioned that in which the phosphates are placed. This division contains only one gem, the turquoise. This important and valuable stone, which is composed of phosphoric acid combined with alumina and water, is remarkable, inasmuch as it is the only costly stone which contains any considerable amount of water as an essential constituent.

The ornamental stone malachite may be mentioned here as being the representative of the carbonates or compounds of carbon dioxide, and at the same time as containing a considerable amount of water as an essential constituent.

To identify any given stone and to determine the mineral species to which it belongs, a chemical analysis is often desirable and, in some cases, essential. Since this method involves the complete destruction of the substance experimented on as such, it is obviously of very limited application in the determination of precious stones of great intrinsic value. In the case of uncut stones a chemical analysis may be made of detached fragments. But with cut and polished stones, not only is a complete chemical analysis impossible, but the mere testing with acid must be avoided.

B. CRYSTALLINE FORM.

Most chemical compounds, including the majority of minerals, frequently occur as solid bodies bounded by plane faces. These shapes have been assumed on the solidification of the substance, and are due to the internal molecular forces exercised by the substance, and not to any external influence. Such definite shapes are known as crystalline forms, and substances occurring in this condition are said to be crystallised. With very few exceptions all precious stones are crystallised. Diamond, ruby, sapphire, emerald, topaz, &c., occur naturally as crystals of the finest development. Only a few, of which the most important is opal, are not bounded by the plane faces characteristic of crystallised substances, but occur only as irregularly-shaped masses. Such substances without definite external form are said to be amorphous.

Crystallised bodies, therefore, differ from amorphous bodies in that on solidification they assume a regular form bounded by plane faces, which is the outward expression of internal molecular forces. Certain peculiarities in the physical characters of crystallised bodies, which are absent in amorphous substances, are also due to these internal molecular forces. Thus it is still possible to distinguish a crystallised from an amorphous body, even though the characteristic regular boundaries of the former should happen to be absent.

The absence of the regular boundaries of a crystallised substance may be due to one or more of a variety of causes. Their free development may have been hindered by external conditions ; as, for instance, when a substance crystallises in a confined space where free development in all directions is impossible. Or, again, as often happens, in extricating a crystal from the matrix, a blow from the hammer may destroy some of the plane faces of the specimen. Moreover, in the process of cutting and polishing precious stones, the natural plane faces are always destroyed. In all these cases, however, the substance still possesses the internal structure characteristic of a crystallised body. The essential difference between a crystallised and an amorphous body lies in their internal structure, on which depends the character of the substance. The presence of plane faces in the crystallised substance is merely the outward expression of its internal structure.

A crystallised body which shows no regular boundaries is said to be *crystalline* or *massive*. When these boundaries are present the body is termed a *crystal*. Portions of crystalline, massive material cannot be distinguished in their external form from an amorphous substance, but their internal structure shows a very essential difference, which will be described later. A crystal, however, on account of its regular boundaries can never be confused with an amorphous body.

The knowledge of crystals and the laws governing the relations between their faces belongs to the special science of *crystallography*. A knowledge of the subject is essential to the correct understanding of the natural relations of minerals, including also precious stones.

It has been established that each crystallised substance, including precious stones, having a definite chemical composition, has also a crystalline form which is characteristic of the substance, or to be more correct, it may exhibit a series of crystallised forms related in such a way that each may be derived from another. Moreover, bodies of different chemical composition will in general be characterised by different crystalline forms, having, as a rule, no mutual relations.

Hence it is possible to distinguish bodies not only by their chemical composition but also by their crystalline form, and this applies equally to precious stones. It is thus obvious that a knowledge of the crystallographic relations of precious stones is not only of theoretical importance, but also of the highest practical importance, for it would enable a buyer of rough stones to distinguish a genuine from a false stone by the form alone, thus avoiding injury to the stone. This method of identification, however, is applicable only when the specimen is crystallised. In the case of massive or crystalline material, the data for its scientific determination can only be obtained from the physical characters of the specimen.

The science of crystallography is not one of which the general principles can be conveyed in a few words. Generally speaking, a complete and thorough study of the subject is necessary to obtain a knowledge of practical value. Since a detailed account of the science of crystallography is quite outside the scope of the present work, the reader must be referred to special works on the subject and to the various text-books of mineralogy, which usually contain a section devoted to crystallography. It will, therefore, be assumed in what follows that the reader possesses a knowledge of at least the elements of the subject, and is further acquainted with the elements of those sciences, such as chemistry, physics, geology, the aid of which is necessary in the study of minerals and precious stones.

It may be stated briefly here that all crystals with few exceptions can be cut by a plane into two equal parts, having the same relation between them as exists between an object and its image in a mirror. Such a plane is known as a plane of symmetry, and crystals of different substances possess different numbers of these planes. The greater the number of planes of symmetry possessed by a crystal the higher its degree of symmetry. Those crystal forms which may be cut in the same manner by the same number of planes possess the same degree of symmetry, and are grouped together into the same *crystal-system*. There are six of these systems, to one or other of which every mineral and every crystallised precious stone must of necessity belong. The names of the different crystal-systems with the number of planes of symmetry characteristic of each are given below:

1. The Cubic System   with 9 planes of symmetry.
2. The Hexagonal System   „   7   „   „
3. The Tetragonal System „   5   „   „
4. The Rhombic System   „   3   „   „
5. The Monoclinic System „   1   „   „
6. The Triclinic System   „   0   „   „

Sometimes the symmetry exhibited by a crystal is such that only half the typical number of faces are developed. These derived forms are known as *hemihedral*, or half-faced forms. These forms must be distinguished from those possessing the full number of faces, which are known as *holohedral*, or full-faced forms. Again, from hemihedral forms may be derived, by a development of only half the faces, another group, the members of which are known as *tetartohedral*, or quarter-faced forms. The hemihedral and tetartohedral classes of the different systems receive special names, which, however, need not be mentioned here. All the holohedral and several of the hemihedral and tetartohedral classes are represented among precious stones.

All precious stones of the same kind, *i.e.*, all diamonds, all emeralds, &c., exhibit forms belonging to the same crystal system; they all possess the same degree of symmetry, and all show the same hemihedral or tetartohedral development if such is present.

It not unfrequently happens that two similarly developed crystals of one and the same mineral are so grown together as to be symmetrical with respect to each other about a certain plane, one crystal being a reflection of the other in this plane, as, for example, is shown for spinel in Fig. 60d. A regular grouping of two crystals in this way is known as a *twin*. Twins may generally be recognised by the presence of re-entrant angles between the faces at the edge of the plane of junction of the two crystals. Simple crystal individuals do not show such re-entrant angles. Sometimes on the second crystal of a twin a third individual may be grown in the same manner, thus giving rise to a triplet. Similarly four crystals grown together in a certain regular manner give rise to a quartet. Such regular growths are often very complex, and it is then no easy matter to discover the mutual relations of the several simple crystals.

The principal crystalline forms are too important to be ignored; they will be described and figured below with the description of the various precious stones. To those who possess even a small acquaintance with the laws and terms of crystallography, the description of the different forms and their mutual relations will be easily intelligible; to others, however, it may present some difficulty. But as all the crystallographic details are collected together in a small space, it is open to such persons to omit them. Though their conception of a precious stone in its natural condition will, in such case, suffer, yet a fairly correct idea of the aspect and crystalline form of uncut crystallised precious stones may be obtained from an inspection of the figures.

Amorphous substances, such as opal, which are incapable of assuming a crystalline form, usually occur in irregular masses of indefinite shape, but rounded, spherical, botryoidal, reniform, or nodular masses are also found.

Crystallised bodies, and, consequently, many precious stones, are frequently not of uniform structure throughout; they do not consist of a single crystal individual, but of several irregularly grown together. The compact mass which results from such a collection of crystalline individuals is known as a crystalline or massive *aggregate*. The constituent particles of such an aggregate may be of various shapes; they may be developed fairly equally in all directions, or they may be considerably elongated or shortened in one or more directions. Thus arise granular, columnar, fibrous, shelly, scaly, or other kinds of aggregates. A granular aggregate is coarsely or finely granular according to the size of the constituent particles.

Sometimes the particles are so fine that they cannot be distinguished with the naked eye, nor even with the help of a simple lens, and the mass then appears to be perfectly homogeneous. The microscope, however, reveals the fact that it is in reality an aggregate of minute grains, fibres, or scales. A truly homogeneous body appears homogeneous even under the highest powers of the microscope. A mass built up of minute particles, but with an external appearance of apparent homogeneity, is known as a *compact* aggregate. It often shows the rounded exterior of an amorphous body, and while its constituent particles may show regular crystal-faces the aggregate as a whole never does.

Specimens of such compact aggregates are frequently opaque, and their microscopic examination necessitates the preparation of a slice sufficiently thin to be transparent. A plate with parallel sides is cut and one side is polished. The plate is then fixed to a slip of glass with Canada-balsam, the unpolished surface being uppermost. The plate is then ground down till it is so thin as to be transparent, when the upper surface is polished. To preserve the section a glass cover-slip is cemented over it with Canada-balsam. Many important and interesting facts respecting the character of minerals and precious stones have been learnt from the microscopic examination of such *thin sections*, as they are called. The method has been specially useful in the examination of turquoise, chalcedony, and agate, where special difficulties lie in the way of other methods.

C. PHYSICAL CHARACTERS.

A. SPECIFIC GRAVITY.

One of the most important characters of a precious stone is its density. On this quality depends the weight of a stone of any given size. Thus of two bodies of equal size but of different material, the one having the greater density will exceed the other in weight. To give a concrete example, a cubic inch of iron weighs rather more than a quarter of a pound, while a cubic inch of oak weighs half an ounce. The cube of iron is, therefore, eight times heavier than the cube of wood.

Instead of measuring the density of a substance it is more convenient to compare the weight of any given volume with the weight of an equal volume of some standard substance. The substance usually selected as the standard is water at a temperature of 4° C. The ratio of the weight of any volume of a substance to the weight of an equal volume of water at the above temperature is known as the *specific gravity* of that substance. The specific gravity of a body is found, therefore, by dividing its weight by the weight of an equal volume of water. To calculate how many times one substance is denser than another the specific gravity of the former must be divided by that of the latter.

Experience has shown that each chemical substance, each mineral, and also each precious stone, has a definite specific gravity, which in most cases differentiates it from all other substances. This character furnishes an important means of identification, which is specially valuable in the case of precious stones, for by this method the most costly cut stone can be identified and suffer no injury in the process. With the exception, perhaps, of the optical characters, no other feature is as important as a means of determination.

Every dealer in jewels should therefore be able to make a rapid determination of the specific gravity of any given gem with sufficient accuracy for practical purposes. The time expended in acquiring the necessary manipulation and the cost of the apparatus will be amply rewarded. It is proposed to give here a detailed account of the methods in use for the determination of specific gravity, not only for those conspicuous for the accuracy of the results they furnish, but also such as would be chosen when rapidity and ease of manipulation rather than extreme accuracy are needed.

It will be noticed that the value of the specific gravity of any given mineral, as quoted in text-books or works of reference, varies between certain narrow limits. This is due, firstly, to small errors in determination ; and, secondly, to the impossibility of obtaining two absolutely identical specimens of the same mineral, since there may be, in certain cases, small or even considerable variations in chemical composition (isomorphous replacement); and, again, crystals frequently contain as enclosures various amounts of different impurities.

METHODS FOR THE DETERMINATION OF SPECIFIC GRAVITY.

1. *Method with the Pycnometer.*—This is perhaps the most accurate of the several methods available for the determination of specific gravity. The pycnometer or specific gravity bottle (Fig. 1) is a small vessel of thin glass with a wide neck, into which fits a ground-glass stopper. The stopper is perforated longitudinally by a very fine canal.

FIG. 1. Pycnometer (actual size).

To find the specific gravity of a stone its weight g is first observed. Next the weight p of the specific gravity bottle, filled with distilled water, is found; this observation can be made once for all (for the same flask), and need not be repeated at each new determination. Care must be taken that the water rises to the top of the perforation in the stopper; this is usually effected by filling the flask quite full and then inserting the stopper. Before weighing, the flask must be well dried on the outside. The stone is now placed in the flask. It displaces an amount of water equal in volume to its own bulk. The stopper is replaced so that water rises to the top of the perforation. The flask must be again dried and weighed. Let this weight be denoted by q. The weight of the flask, full of water, together with the weight of the stone is $g + p$. The weight of water displaced by the stone in the second part of the operation is consequently $g + p - q$, and this represents an amount of water equal in volume to the volume of the stone. Since then the weight of the stone is g, and the weight of an equal volume of water is $g + p - q$, the specific gravity, d, is therefore given by

$$d = \frac{g}{g + p - q}.$$

To take a numerical example; let the weight of a stone be $g = 4\cdot382$ in grams or whatever unit is used; the weight of the bottle filled with water be $p = 15\cdot543$; the weight of the bottle containing both the stone and the water $q = 18\cdot680$. Then the weight of the displaced water is $g + p - q = 4\cdot382 + 15\cdot543 - 18\cdot680 = 1\cdot245$ and

$$d = \frac{g}{g + p - q} = \frac{4\cdot382}{1\cdot245} = 3\cdot52.$$

This is the specific gravity of the stone, in this case a topaz.

To avoid serious error in determinations of specific gravity the presence of bubbles of air must be carefully guarded against. These often cling with great pertinacity to the stone, but may usually be dislodged with the help of a clean platinum wire or by gently warming the flask. Should any collect under the stopper, the flask must be emptied and refilled with distilled water.

When all the precautions mentioned above are carefully attended to, the accuracy of the determination varies with the delicacy of the balance. With a good balance and a little practice the pycnometer method is capable of giving results accurate to the third place of decimals. It has the further advantage of enabling the operator to determine the specific gravity of several small stones or fragments taken together. The application of this method of determination is limited in two directions: it is useless, on the one hand, for determining the specific gravity of stones too large to pass through the neck of the bottle, and, on the other hand, is not sufficiently accurate when only very small quantities of material are available.

2. *Method with the Hydrostatic Balance.*—This method is more frequently used, and with careful manipulation is perhaps quite as accurate as the method just described. It depends on the fact that a body when immersed in water weighs less than when in air. According to the well-known principle of Archimedes, the loss in weight is equal to the weight of the water displaced, that is, of a volume of water equal to the volume of the body.

The stone is first weighed in air; let this weight be g. It is then suspended from the arm of the balance by a hair, fine wire, or thread, and weighed in water; let this weight be f. It is obvious that the difference in weight, $g - f$, is the weight of the water displaced, that is, of a volume of water equal to the volume of the stone. The specific gravity, d, of the stone

is therefore given by $d = \dfrac{g}{g - f}$.

The hydrostatic balance used in the above operation differs in no essential respect from an ordinary balance. It is merely arranged so that the right-hand scale-pan hangs from a much shorter support than the other. Frequently the right-hand scale-pan of an ordinary balance can be replaced by one with shorter supports and a small hook on the under side. When the stone is immersed in water, the thread or wire which carries it is attached to this hook. For the purpose of conveniently holding the stone, the lower end of the thread or wire may carry a small clip, as shown in Fig. 5, or the wire may be simply wound round the stone so that it rests in a stirrup or in a small spiral. A basket of this description is shown in Fig. 2. The water is placed in a glass vessel under the right-hand scale-pan with the short support, and the wire carrying the clip or other arrangement is immersed in water during the whole operation, so that it is weighed in water even before the stone has been fixed in position for the second weighing. It is then unnecessary to specially determine the weight of the wire with its attachment and the loss of weight of this in water, as the effect in one weighing is cancelled by that in the other.

FIG. 2. Basket of platinum wire for holding stone in determination of specific gravity.

The use of a balance with specially arranged scale-pans, as described above, is by no means essential, however, for the determination of specific gravity. Every jeweller has a good balance with scale-pans having supports of equal length, and this can easily be used as a hydrostatic balance, as illustrated in Fig. 3. For this purpose, the vessel containing water is placed on a small table or bench, such as is shown in Figs. 3 and 4, which stands over the scale-pan of the balance, leaving the latter quite free to move. The thread or wire with the attachment for carrying the stone is fastened to the hook on the upper part of the right-hand scale-pan. Obviously the water-containing vessel must not be so large as to interfere with the movement of the balance, and the length of the wire must be such that

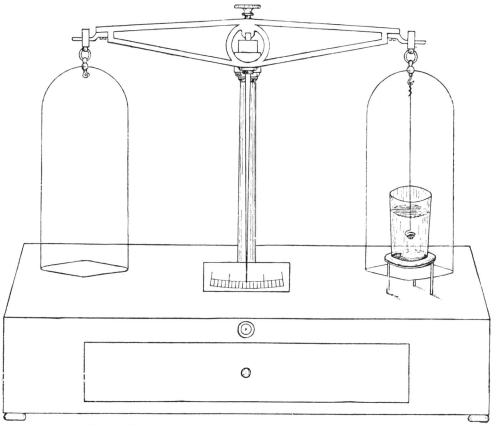

FIG. 3.   Ordinary balance with arrangement for hydrostatic weighing.

the stone it carries will not touch the bottom of the vessel nor rise partly out of the water when the balance is swinging.

In the determination of a specific gravity with such a balance the best mode of procedure is as follows : A fragment of a mineral or metal or any object, the weight of which is greater than that of the stone whose specific gravity is to be determined, is placed in the left-hand scale-pan. This acts as a counterpoise, and must remain throughout the whole operation. It has been pointed out above, that the wire with its carrying attachment must remain immersed in water till the completion of the operation. Weights are then placed in the right-hand scale-pan so as to balance the counterpoise; let the weight required be m. These weights are then replaced by the stone; equilibrium is restored by adding a weight, l, in the right-hand scale-pan. The weight of the stone will therefore be $m - l = g$ say. The stone is then attached to the end of the wire and immersed in water, care being taken that it hangs freely without touching the sides and bottom of the vessel. By adding more weights to the right-hand scale-pan the balance is again brought into equilibrium. If the total weight is now t, then, the loss in weight of the stone, when weighed in water, is $t - l$, and this is also the weight of the water displaced, that is, the weight of a volume of water equal to the volume of the stone. Hence the specific gravity of the stone is, as before,

$$d = \frac{g}{t - l}.$$

To take a numerical example. If the weight first added to balance the counterpoise be $m = 10\cdot784$ grams (or other unit), and the weights which, together with the stone, balance the counterpoise be $l = 4\cdot803$ grams, then the weight of the stone is $g = m - l = 10\cdot784 - 4\cdot803 = 5\cdot981$ grams. Let the weight added when the stone is immersed in the water be $t = 7\cdot060$. Then the loss of weight of the stone will be $t - l = 7\cdot060 - 4\cdot803 = 2\cdot257$ grams, and $d = \frac{g}{t - l} = \frac{5\cdot891}{2\cdot257} = 2\cdot65$. This is the specific gravity of rock-crystal (quartz).

Other conditions being equal, the more delicate and sensitive the balance the more accurate will be the specific gravity determination. Under favourable conditions and with careful weighing the determination should be correct to the third place of decimals.

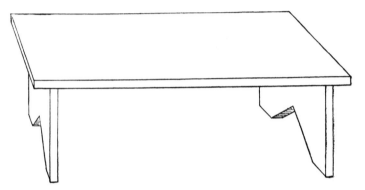

FIG. 4. Bench for use in hydrostatic weighing with an ordinary balance.

Certain precautions, however, must be attended to. In the first place, all parts immersed in water must be quite free from adhering air-bubbles; these may often be dislodged with the help of a clean platinum wire, but frequently it is advisable to bring the water almost to the boiling-point while the stone and wire are immersed in it. For this purpose the wire must be detached from the balance; but before replacing the vessel of water on the balance it should be allowed to cool, which process may be hastened by immersing the vessel, still of course containing the wire and stone, in a bath of cold water. Should the stone and wire be at all greasy through being handled, they will not be properly wetted by the water, and should then be washed in alcohol, ether, benzene, or a solution of soda; in the latter case they must be afterwards rinsed in clean water. Finally it must be borne in mind that the percentage of error in the determination of a very small stone is greater than in that of a larger one, since small errors in weighing influence results more in the former case than in the latter.

When the specific gravity of a number of stones is to be taken, a counterpoise is chosen which exceeds the heaviest of them in weight. This may then remain throughout the whole series of operations and the value of m be determined once for all. Two weighings only are then necessary to find the value of l and t for each stone. From l and t and the constant value m the specific gravity can be calculated in each case.

The specific gravity of several fragments or small stones may be determined by placing them together in the wire basket, shown in Fig. 2, and weighing them as a single stone.

The use of the counterpoise, as described above, has the effect of neutralising any error in the zero point of the balance. Unless special accuracy is required the counterpoise may be dispensed with, especially when a good balance with the zero accurately adjusted is available. The stone is then weighed in the usual way by placing it in one scale-pan and the necessary weights in the other. Let its weight thus determined be p, and its weight when immersed in water be q; then the loss of weight will be $p - q$, and the specific gravity is $d = \dfrac{p}{p - q}$.

In the above determination two weighings only are necessary, whereas, when a counterpoise is used, three must be made. When, however, a series of determinations are made with one counterpoise two weighings suffice, and either method is equally expeditious. For the purpose of determining a stone or distinguishing it from another, the value of its specific gravity, obtained without the use of a counterpoise, is generally sufficiently accurate. The following is a numerical example of this method. A garnet (cinnamon-stone) weighed in air 4·375 grams (p), and in water, 3·168 grams (q); the loss in weight is therefore $p - q = 4·375 - 3·168 = 1·207$ grams. Hence the specific gravity is

$$d = \frac{p}{p - q} = \frac{4·375}{1·207} = 3·63.$$

Since determinations of specific gravity are not, under ordinary conditions, made with water at the temperature of 4° C., it is necessary, when accuracy is required, to reduce the results of calculation to this standard. For the practical purpose of the jeweller, however, the direct observation is quite sufficient.

3. *Method with Westphal's Balance.*—While methods 1 and 2, described above, are susceptible, as has been shown, of extreme accuracy, they have a disadvantage in the amount of time which must be expended on careful weighing. The method now under consideration combines a degree of accuracy sufficient for all practical purposes with a considerable economy in time; it is therefore valuable to the practical jeweller. The balance used in this method is named after its maker, the mechanician Westphal, of Celle, in Hanover. It enables a specific gravity to be readily and quickly determined, correct to the second place of decimals, or under favourable conditions to the third place. It has the advantage of cheapness over the hydrostatic balance, and, moreover, can be used for other purposes, as will be shown later.

Westphal's balance with accessories for determining the specific gravity of solids, and therefore of precious stones, is illustrated in Fig. 5. In principle it is really a simplification of the hydrostatic balance with a counterpoise, the left-hand scale-pan and counterpoise of the latter being replaced in Westphal's balance by a counterpoise fixed to the beam. It consists of a beam, *abc*, to which is fixed a knife-edge of hardened steel at *b*. This knife-edge, which is directed downwards, is supported by, and turns on, a grooved steel plate fixed to the curved brass piece *de*, itself supported by the brass column *f*. The latter slides in the tube *hh*, and can be fixed at any convenient height by means of the screw *g*. Passing through the disc *l*, attached to the foot *k*, of the instrument, is a levelling screw *m*, directly beneath the end of the balance beam; by means of this the column *f* can be adjusted so as to be accurately vertical.

The beam carries at one end (the left in Fig. 5), a heavy weight of brass, which takes the place of the counterpoise and left-hand scale-pan in the ordinary hydrostatic balance. At the same end, *a*, of the beam is a pointer which, when the beam is horizontal, indicates zero on the scale attached to the piece *de*. At the opposite end, *c*, of the beam (on the right in Fig. 5) is fixed a knife-edge with its edge directed upwards. On this rests a hook, from which is suspended, by short platinum wires, the scale-pan n. On the under side of this pan is a hook for attaching the fine platinum wire and clip p, which holds the stone to be tested. This portion hanging from c corresponds to the right-hand scale-pan with short supports of the hydrostatic balance.

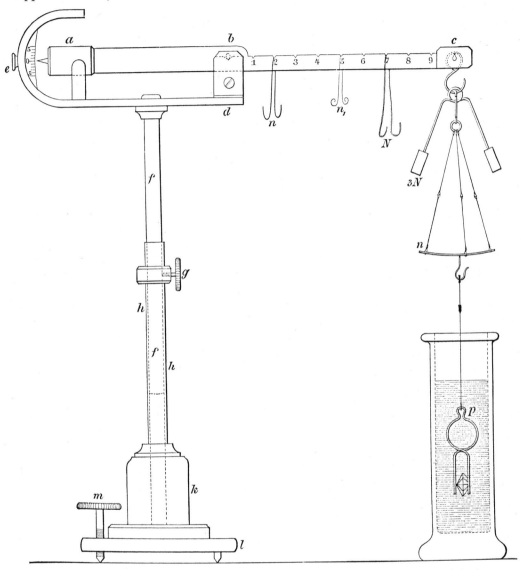

FIG. 5. Westphal's balance for determining the specific gravity of solids. (Half actual size.)

Between the knife-edge b and the end c the beam is divided into ten equal parts, the equally distant lines of division being numbered consecutively from b towards c. The upper side of the beam is notched at these lines of division. The weights are of special construction; some being for the purpose of hanging on the hook under c, and others, known as riders, rest when in use in the notches on the beam itself, as shown in Figs. 5 and 7. These weights are quite arbitrary, and need not necessarily be multiples or sub-multiples of any recognised unit; they are related to each other, however, in a certain definite manner suitable to the purpose of the instrument. The normal weight, N, when placed on the hook at c, corresponds to the unit weight, but when placed in the notches of the beam numbered 1, 2, 3, &c., it has the value $\frac{1}{10}N$, $\frac{2}{10}N$, $\frac{3}{10}N$, &c., that is, $\frac{1}{10}$, $\frac{2}{10}$, $\frac{3}{10}$, &c., of the unit. A second weight n has one-tenth the value of N, or $n = \frac{1}{10}N$. When placed on the hook at c its value is $\frac{1}{10}N$, and when placed in the notches 1, 2, 3, &c., it has the values $\frac{1}{10}n$, $\frac{2}{10}n$, $\frac{3}{10}n$, &c., or $\frac{1}{100}N$, $\frac{2}{100}N$, $\frac{3}{100}N$, &c. Lastly, there is a third weight $n_1 = \frac{1}{10}n = \frac{1}{100}N$, which is its value when suspended from c, but when placed in the notches 1, 2, 3, &c., it has the values $\frac{1}{10}n_1$, $\frac{2}{10}n_1$, $\frac{3}{10}n_1$, &c., or $\frac{1}{100}n$, $\frac{2}{100}n$, $\frac{3}{100}n$, &c., or $\frac{1}{1000}N$, $\frac{2}{1000}N$, $\frac{3}{1000}N$, &c. The weights n and n_1 are used only as riders, and of the normal weights, N, one will be required for use as a rider and the others for suspending from the hook under c. For convenience, larger weights, multiples of the normal weight ($2N$, $3N$, &c.), are also supplied for suspending at c.

The operation of weighing is performed in the following manner: When the beam is horizontal and the pointer indicates zero on the scale at e, let there be a certain number of the normal weights N on the hook c, one of the normal weights in one of the notches on the beam, and weights n and n_1 in certain other notches. The number of N weights on the hook c will give the whole number of the required reading, and the riders N, n and n_1 on the beam give the first, second, and third decimal places of the same unit. For example, there may be at c three of the weights N, and the riders N, n and n_1 at the divisions 7, 2, and 9 respectively; the reading will then be 3·729 of the unit N, or 3·729N. If there is no rider N and riders n, n_1 at divisions 3 and 5 respectively, then the reading is 3·035. The arrangement of the weights shown in Fig. 5, corresponds to the reading 3·725N, and in Fig. 7 to 2·707N.

Throughout the whole series of weighings for the determination of a specific gravity the clip for holding the stone and part of the suspending wire must remain immersed in water. The support f is adjusted in the tube h so that, during the swinging of the beam, the clip shall neither touch the bottom of the vessel nor rise out of the surface of the water, but remain completely immersed in approximately the central part of the vessel. The determination of specific gravity according to this method involves three separate weighings, as described below. One of these may, however, be reduced to a constant and used throughout a series of determinations.

(1) Sufficient weights are placed on the beam to bring the pointer to zero.

The following example illustrates the method of manipulating the weights: The normal weights N, $2N$, $3N$, $4N$, successively hung on the hook c were each found to be insufficient to move the beam, but $5N$ brought it past the horizontal position. One N was therefore removed and $4N$ left on the hook. The rider N was then placed on the beam at the divisions 9, 8, 7, &c., successively; at the third division the beam was still tilted down to the right, but when the rider was at the second division the beam was tilted to the left; the rider was therefore left at the second division. In the same way the rider n finds a place at 5, and n_1 at the same division, in which case it may hang from the rider n, as shown in Fig. 7, where n_1 hangs from N. The counterpoise of the balance therefore corresponds to the weight 4·255N. A fourth decimal place in the reading may be obtained by placing the rider n_1 between the two divisions 5 and 6. If, for instance, it is placed midway between divisions 5 and 6, the reading would be 4·2555N; if nearer to 5 than to 6, then it would read 4·2553N.

(2) The stone of which the specific gravity is to be determined is now placed in the scale-pan and the weights readjusted until the beam is again horizontal. In the case quoted, the weight required was 3·812N. Hence the real weight of the stone was $(4·255 - 3·812)N = 0·443N$.

(3) Finally the stone is fixed in the clip p and immersed in the water ; the weight now required to restore equilibrium was $3.9785N$. The loss of weight of the stone was therefore $(3.9785 - 3.812)N = 0.1665N$, and the specific gravity $d = \dfrac{0.443}{0.1665} = 2.66$. This is again the specific gravity of rock-crystal (quartz), and the stone may therefore be identified as quartz.

This method of determination enables the specific gravity of a stone to be found correctly to two places of decimals with very little trouble, provided that the precautions already mentioned have been observed : namely, that the stone is free from air-bubbles, that it does not come in contact with the sides of the vessel nor rise out of the water, and that it is not too small. The specific gravity of a stone weighing half a carat, that is about one-tenth of a gram, can be determined accurately to the second place of decimals ; though the figure in the second place will be uncertain when the stone only weighs $\frac{1}{4}$ or $\frac{1}{5}$ of a carat, the determination is still useful for practical purposes. With stones smaller than this, however, the results are not sufficiently reliable. If supported in the basket shown in Fig. 2, or in a net made of platinum gauze fixed to the clip, a number of such small stones may be weighed together.

In this method, as previously, the first weighing, giving the constant for the counterpoise of the instrument and the particular wire and clip to be used, may be performed once for all, so that afterwards only two weighings are necessary, and this effects a considerable saving in time. Should the stone, whose specific gravity is to be determined, be so heavy that it raises the counterpoise by its own weight, then suitable additions must be made to the weight of the latter, but in this case the balance will lose in sensitiveness. Usually, however, the weight of the counterpoise is sufficient for most of the purposes for which the instrument is intended.

(4) *Method with Jolly's Spring-balance.*—The spring-balance invented by, and named after, Jolly, formerly a physicist in Munich, possesses considerable advantages, for by its means the specific gravity of stones of fair size can be determined with sufficient accuracy and very simple manipulation, no weights being required. The construction of the instrument is shown in Fig. 6. A vertical rectangular support, *acd*, about a yard and a half in length, stands on a base *b* furnished with levelling screws. The vertical support carries on one face a strip of plane mirror on which a scale is engraved. From a horizontal projection at the upper end, *a*, of the vertical support hangs a spiral of fine steel wire. This carries at its lower end a fine platinum wire, to which are attached, one above the other, two small cups, *m* and *m'* (Fig. 6, *A*), of glass or platinum gauze. The length of wire lying between the two cups also bears two reference marks at *o* and *o'*. The lower cup *m'* is immersed in water contained in the vessel *g* which rests on the stand *h*. This stand, *h*, can be moved up and down the vertical support and fixed in any desired position.

In using the instrument, which for the first reading must remain unloaded, the lower

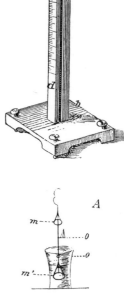

FIG. 6. Jolly's Spring-balance for determining specific gravity.

cup m' is immersed in the water in the vessel g until the reference mark at o' is exactly in the surface of the water ; the position of the reference mark at o on the vertical scale is then read.   To effect this, the eye of the observer is so placed that the reference mark o, which is an acute triangle, exactly covers its reflection in the mirror, when the position of the upper angle on the scale is read ; by this means error due to parallax is avoided.   As an example, let us suppose that o stands at division 45 on the vertical scale.   The stone to be determined is then placed in the upper cup m ; this will stretch the spiral spring, and the stand h bearing the vessel of water must be lowered until o' again stands in the level of the water.   The new position of o in the mirror scale is now read ; let it be at division 75. Then the weight of the stone in air corresponds to $75 - 45 = 30$ scale divisions.   The stone is now placed in the lower cup m', which always remains immersed in water ; since the weight is diminished the spiral will shorten.   The stand h will now require to be raised until o' is again in the surface of the water ; suppose the reading on the scale is now 65. The loss in weight of the stone in water is represented by $75 - 65 = 10$ scale divisions and the specific gravity is, therefore $\frac{30}{10} = 3\cdot0$, corresponding to colourless, transparent tourmaline.

(5) *Method with heavy liquids.*—Within recent years this method for the determination of specific gravity has become of considerable importance.   It depends on the fact that a body placed in a liquid will sink or float according as the density of the liquid is less or greater than that of the body.   A stone placed in a liquid heavier than itself will rise to the surface ; if placed in a liquid lighter than itself it will sink to the bottom ; while if the stone and liquid are of equal density the former will remain stationary at any point within the latter.   The movement upwards or downwards of a stone placed in liquid is quicker or slower according as the difference in density between the stone and the liquid is greater or less.

The liquid for use in the application of this method must fulfil a variety of conditions. First, it must be as heavy as possible, so that its use may be extended not only to the lighter gems, but also to as many as possible of the denser ones, which, if placed in a light liquid, would merely sink to the bottom and render their discrimination impossible.   Secondly, the liquid should be clear, transparent, and colourless, so that there is no difficulty in observing the movement of the immersed stone.   Thirdly, it must not be thick or viscous, otherwise the free movement of the stone would be impeded.   Finally, it must mix readily and perfectly in all proportions with a second lighter liquid, so that its density may be easily varied.

All these conditions are fulfilled by methylene iodide, a compound of carbon, hydrogen, and iodine having the chemical formula CH_2I_2.   It is one of the heaviest liquids known, having at ordinary temperatures a specific gravity of about $3\cdot3$.   Owing to its high coefficient of expansion, its density varies, however, very considerably with the temperature ; at $10°$ C. it is $3\cdot3375$; at $15°$ C. it is $3\cdot3265$; and at $20°$ C. it is $3\cdot3155$.   Methylene iodide is, further, perfectly transparent, very mobile, and of a pale yellow colour.   It is readily miscible in all proportions with benzene, which is a light liquid of specific gravity $0\cdot88$.   Thus by mixing methylene iodide and benzene together a series of liquids is obtained varying in density between $0\cdot88$ and $3\cdot3$, the lower value being less than the density of water, and the higher being three and a third times as great.

To determine the specific gravity of a stone by this method, it is first placed in pure methylene iodide contained in a tall cylindrical vessel, such as is shown in Figs. 5 and 7. If the stone sinks, we know it is heavier than the liquid, that is, it has a specific gravity greater than $3\cdot3$, but how much greater cannot be determined.   If it remains suspended in the liquid, neither rising nor falling, even when moved about with a glass rod, we know that

its specific gravity is identical with that of the liquid, which is about 3·3 at ordinary temperatures. In the third case, if the stone should rise to the surface, even after being pressed
down with a glass rod, we know that its specific gravity is less than that of the liquid.
When this happens, benzene is added drop by drop and the mixture well stirred. The
addition of benzene is cautiously continued until a mixture of such a density is arrived at that

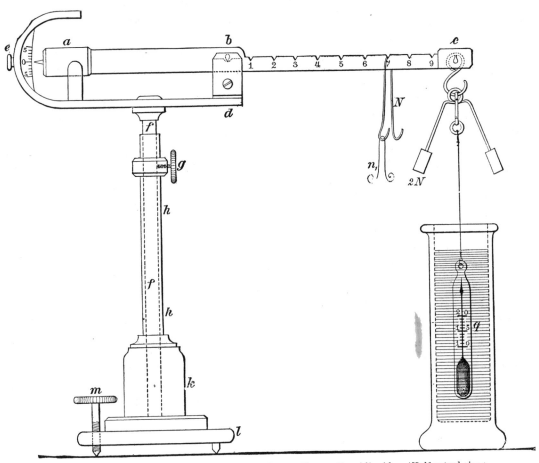

FIG. 7. Westphal's balance for determining the specific gravity of liquids. (Half actual size.)

the stone no longer rises to the surface, but remains suspended in the liquid, moving neither
up nor down. We then know that the mixture has the same specific gravity as the
stone.

The value of the specific gravity of the mixture of methylene iodide and benzene, and
consequently that of the stone, has now to be determined. This may be done by means of
the pycnometer, which is weighed first full of water, and then full of the mixture.
Deducting from each of these weights the weight of the pycnometer itself, the weights of
equal volumes of water and of the mixture are known; and dividing the latter by the former
the specific gravity of the mixture is found.

The specific gravity of a liquid is determined more conveniently, and with sufficient
accuracy for practical purposes, by means of Westphal's balance. This instrument, together
with the accessories necessary for determining the specific gravity of a liquid, is shown in
Fig. 7. The small scale-pan previously used (Fig. 5) is now replaced by a glass float, *q*,

containing a thermometer. This hangs by a fine wire from the hook c, and is sufficiently heavy to balance the counterpoise and bring the pointer to zero. If, however, the pointer should not stand exactly at zero, it may be brought to this position by turning the levelling screw m. When the float is immersed in a vessel containing distilled water, its loss in weight is equal to the weight of the displaced water. The pointer is brought to zero again by placing a unit weight, N, on the hook, c, the sizes of the float and the weights having been so arranged that this shall be the case. The loss of weight in the float is, therefore, represented by $1N$. Any other liquid which requires a unit weight, N, to bring the beam again into the horizontal position will have the same specific gravity as water, that is, a specific gravity of 1. Should twice or thrice the unit weight, $2N$ or $3N$, be required, then the specific gravity of the liquid is 2 or 3, that is, it is two or three times as heavy as water. For intermediate values, the riders must be used in the manner explained previously. Thus, for example, let us suppose the float immersed in some liquid, which to bring the beam into the horizontal position requires $3N$ at c, N at the second division, n ($= \frac{1}{10}N$) at the fifth division, and n_1 ($= \frac{1}{100}N$) at the ninth division. Then the specific gravity of the liquid is given directly by the reading 3·259. The specific gravity of the liquid contained in the vessel in Fig. 7 is, in the same way, 2·707. Hence the specific gravity is given directly by the readings, and there is no necessity for the smallest calculation.

With this instrument it is possible with a little practice to determine the specific gravity of a liquid correct to the second place of decimals, and the whole operation can be performed in a few minutes. All that is necessary is to immerse the float in the narrow glass cylinder containing the liquid, and by the addition of weights to bring the beam into the horizontal position.

The use of **indicators** enables the determination of the specific gravity of a liquid to be performed with still greater rapidity; though the values obtained by this method are only approximate, they are sufficient for all practical purposes connected with the determination of precious stones. There are used as indicators either small, differently weighted glass bulbs, known as specific gravity beads, or small mineral fragments of different specific gravities, ranging by small amounts from the specific gravity of the lightest to that of the heaviest of precious stones. The following minerals, among many others, may be selected for such a series of indicators: chalcedony (sp. gr. = 2·560), microcline (sp. gr. = 2·591), petalite (sp. gr. = 2·648), labradorite (sp. gr. = 2·686), calcite (sp. gr. = 2·728), &c., this being a portion of a series of indicators suitable for the use under discussion.

Such a series would be used in the following manner: When the liquid has been so diluted that its specific gravity is identical with that of the stone to be determined, the lightest of the series of indicators, chalcedony, say, is put into it. Should it float it is taken out (and should be washed with benzene), and each of the series tried in succession until one is found which sinks to the bottom of the vessel. To take a special case, let us suppose that petalite floats while labradorite sinks. We should then know that the specific gravity of the liquid, and therefore of the stone under examination, lies between 2·648 and 2·686. There would then be a probability, or at least a possibility, that the stone is quartz (rock-crystal, amethyst, &c.), which has a specific gravity of 2·65. In practice, a set of mineral fragments, the specific gravity of each of which has been accurately determined, should be kept solely for use as indicators, and it should be possible to readily distinguish one fragment from another.

The method of determining specific gravity by the aid of heavy liquids, and specially by that of methylene iodide, has the advantage of giving results which are quickly and easily arrived at and sufficiently accurate for practical purposes; moreover, it is equally useful in the case of fragments or even splinters of material so small that with other methods the result would be unreliable. Unfortunately, however, the application of this particular liquid is limited to the determination of stones whose specific gravity does not exceed 3·3. It is true that other liquids are known having a greater specific gravity than that of methylene iodide, but each has some disadvantage and fails to fulfil all the necessary conditions mentioned above.

The density of methylene iodide may be increased to 3·6 by dissolving in it iodine and iodoform to the point of saturation. Stones with a specific gravity of 3·6 will then remain suspended at any point in the liquid, while those that float can be made to remain suspended by diluting the solution with benzene or pure methylene iodide. As before, the specific gravity of the liquid can be determined by the help of a series of indicators, or by Westphal's balance. The denser liquid obtained in the way just mentioned has the disadvantage of being deeply coloured and almost opaque; it is therefore difficult to observe the movements of a stone immersed in it, and to determine at a glance its approximate specific gravity. Nevertheless, in the absence of a better substitute it must be made use of, and is valuable in certain cases.

Recently, however, a liquid has been discovered even heavier than methylene iodide saturated with iodine and iodoform, dense enough, in fact, for the determination of the heaviest of precious stones. This is a double nitrate of silver and thallium, with the chemical formula $AgTl(NO_3)_2$, which, although solid at the ordinary temperatures, melts at 75° C. to a perfectly clear and transparent liquid with a mobility equal to that of water. It has a specific gravity of about 4·8, and in it the heaviest of transparent precious stones, namely, zircon, will float. It is miscible in all proportions with water, and hence liquids of any required density can be obtained by simple dilution. When the liquid has been so diluted that its specific gravity is identical with that of the stone under examination, its value can be found by means of Westphal's balance, or by the aid of a series of indicators, the latter being the more convenient with this liquid.

Such a determination presents rather more difficulty than one performed with methylene iodide, inasmuch as the liquid must be kept at a certain temperature. For this purpose the solid silver thallium nitrate is placed in a thin glass beaker of about the size and shape of the vessel shown in Figs. 5 and 7, and heated on a water-bath or over a small spirit or gas flame until it fuses. A little water is then added; this not only lowers the specific gravity but also the temperature at which fusion takes place, the melting-point sinking to 60° or even to 50° C., a fact which adds considerably to the value of the liquid for practical use. In diluting the liquid with water, great care must be taken to avoid adding too much, since a small amount of water will make a considerable difference in the density of the mixture. This mistake can be avoided by adding a little too much water at first, and then driving off the excess by evaporation, constantly stirring and watching the behaviour of the stone, which will show when the density of the liquid becomes identical with its own by remaining suspended at any point. Since the specific gravity of the liquid varies not inconsiderably with the temperature, it is important that it should be determined either by indicators or by Westphal's balance at the temperature the liquid had when the stone was observed to remain suspended in it. By means of this heavy liquid, then, the specific gravity of the heaviest of precious stones may be determined with a sufficient degree of accuracy, the only exceptions being those with metallic lustre, namely, iron-pyrites and hæmatite, which are sometimes used for ornamental purposes.

For the practical worker in precious stones, the determination of specific gravity is simply a means to an end, namely, the discrimination of stones similar in appearance and the identification of others. Hence it is often only necessary to ascertain whether the specific gravity of any particular stone exceeds a certain value. As an example, let us suppose that a doubt exists as to whether a colourless stone is rock-crystal (quartz, sp. gr. = 2·65) or topaz (sp. gr. = 3·5); by simply placing it in methylene iodide (sp. gr. = 3·3) the doubt is settled at once, for if rock-crystal it will float, but if topaz it will sink.

Methods such as this can be very advantageously used for the rapid discrimination of precious stones. It is necessary, however, to be provided with a series of liquids of various known densities in which the stone under examination may be dropped. The approximate value of its specific gravity can be learnt by simply observing its movement upwards or downwards in these liquids. As has been pointed out before, a slow movement up or down indicates that the difference in specific gravity between the stone and the liquid is small; a quick movement indicates a greater difference; while an absence of movement shows that the specific gravity of the stone is identical with that of the liquid.

In practice a good series is furnished by the following four liquids :

No. 1. Methylene iodide saturated with iodine and iodoform. Specific gravity = 3·6.
No. 2. Pure methylene iodide. Specific gravity = 3·3.
No. 3. Methylene iodide diluted with benzene. Specific gravity = 3·0.
No. 4. Methylene iodide further diluted with benzene. Specific gravity = 2·65.

The liquids of this series may be numbered consecutively from the heaviest to the lightest, and will be frequently referred to below as liquids No. 1, No. 2, No. 3, and No. 4.

With such a series of liquids it is possible to make an approximate determination of the specific gravity of almost any precious stone with great ease and rapidity, and this will be of considerable aid in its recognition. The stone under observation should be first placed in liquid No. 1; should it sink, which can be easily seen in spite of the deep colour of the liquid, its specific gravity is greater than 3·6. If, on the other hand, it rises to the surface, it must be removed with a pair of forceps, wiped with a cloth moistened with benzene, and placed in liquid No. 2. Should it sink in this liquid, we then know that its specific gravity lies between 3·6 and 3·3; if it remains suspended then its specific gravity is exactly 3·3. If, on the contrary, it floats to the surface, it must be taken out and placed successively in liquids No. 3 and No. 4, and similar observations made. When a stone slowly sinks or slowly rises in either of the liquids we know that its specific gravity is slightly greater or slightly less than that of the liquid. A stone of specific gravity 3·02, for example, would slowly sink in liquid No. 3.

The series of liquids for such determinations should be kept ready to hand in wide-mouthed glass bottles properly labelled and closed with ground-glass stoppers. The latter precaution is to avoid evaporation of the methylene iodide, which is somewhat expensive (four shillings per ounce), and of the very volatile benzene, and thus prevent alterations in the specific gravity of the liquids. When not in use the bottles should be kept in a dark place, since exposure to light causes methylene iodide to slowly decompose with separation of iodine which darkens the liquid. When after long use, methylene iodide has become dark in colour it may be decolourised by shaking it up with a dilute solution of caustic potash, which must afterwards be poured off or removed by means of a separating funnel.

The specific gravity of the four standard liquids is very liable to change, partly on account of evaporation and partly on account of the small quantities of liquid introduced with the stones if they are not well dried after immersion. Hence the specific gravity of each of the four liquids must be frequently checked by means of Westphal's balance or, better still, by the use of indicators. These indicators may conveniently be kept in the bottles; each should be chosen so that its specific gravity is near that of the liquid in which it is to be kept. When the indicators show that the specific gravity of any one liquid has altered, this may usually be corrected by simply adding more benzene.

A crystal or fragment of quartz (sp. gr. = 2·65) is a good indicator for liquid No. 4, and should always remain suspended in the liquid. Liquid No. 3 may contain as indicators a phenakite (sp. gr. = 2·95) and a rose-red tourmaline (sp. gr. = 3·02); the former will float and the latter slowly sink if the liquid is of the correct specific gravity. In liquid No. 2 dioptase (sp. gr. = 3·29) should float and olivine (sp. gr. = 3·33) should slowly sink. Finally in liquid No. 1 topaz (sp. gr. = 3·55) must float and hessonite (sp. gr. = 3·65) must sink.

These four liquids enable us to classify for purposes of identification all precious stones according to their specific gravity into five groups, namely:

I.	Stones with a specific gravity greater than 3·6.					
II.	„	„	„	„	between	3·3 and 3·6.
III.	„	„	„	„	„	3·0 „ 3·3.
IV.	„	„	„	„	„	2.65 „ 3·0.
V.	„	„	„	„	of	2·65 „ less.

The stones of group I. will sink in each of the four liquids, while those of other groups will float in one or other of the liquids.

As an example of the help such a series of liquids can give in the identification of a precious stone, let us suppose that a doubt exists as to whether a colourless, transparent stone is rock-crystal (sp. gr. = 2·65), phenakite (sp. gr. = 2·95), or colourless tourmaline (sp. gr. = 3·02). If it remains suspended when placed in liquid No. 4 it must be quartz. If it sinks in liquid No. 4 but floats in liquid No. 3 it will be phenakite; if, on the other hand, it sinks in No. 3 it must be tourmaline. Supposing the unknown, colourless stone should be either diamond (sp. gr. = 3·5) or zircon (sp. gr. = 4·65), then in the former case it will float in liquid No. 4, and in the latter case it will sink.

It is important that while observations are being made the liquids should be at the ordinary temperature (15 − 20° C. = 59 − 68° F.), and should not be subjected to any great variations in this condition, since, as was noted above, the specific gravity of methylene iodide is considerably altered by changes of temperature.

In the third section of this book, which deals with the determination of precious stones, full use will be made of these four liquids, and of the convenient classification of precious stones into five groups, based on their differences in specific gravity. At this point it will be useful to give a tabular list of the more important precious stones, arranged according to their specific gravity from the heaviest to the lightest, and divided into the five groups as determined by their behaviour in the four standard liquids. As already mentioned, the specific gravity of any one precious stone shows small variations, which are indicated in the table.

Precious Stones arranged according to Specific Gravity.

GROUP I. (sp. gr = 3·6 or more).

Zircon	4·6—4·7
Almandine	4·11—4·23
Ruby	4·08
Sapphire	4·06
"Cape Ruby"	3·86
Demantoid	3·83
Staurolite	3·73—3·74
Pyrope	3·69—3·78
Chrysoberyl	3·68—3·78
Kyanite	3·60—3·70
Hessonite	3·60—3·65
Spinel	3·60—3·63

GROUP II. (sp. gr. = 3·3—3·6).

Topaz	3·50—3·56
Diamond	3 50—3·52
Epidote	3·35—3·50
Idocrase	3·35—3·45
Sphene	3·35—3·45
Olivine	3·33—3·37

GROUP III. (sp. gr. = 3·0—3·3).

Jadeite	3·3
Axinite	3·29—3·30
Diopside	3·2—3·3
Dioptase	3·29
Andalusite	3·17—3·19
Apatite	3·16—3·22
Spodumene	3·15—3·20
Tourmaline (green)	3·1
,, (blue)	3·1
,, (red)	3·08

Euclase	3·05
Fluor-spar	3·02—3·19
Tourmaline (rose-red)	3·02
,, (colourless)	3·02

GROUP IV. (sp. gr. = 2·65—3·0).

Nephrite	3·0
Phenakite	2·95
Turquoise	2·6—2·8
Labradorite	2·70
Aquamarine	2·68—2·75
Beryl	2·68—2·75
Emerald	2·67

GROUP V. (sp. gr. = 2·65 and less).

Quartz	
Smoky-quartz	
Amethyst	2·65
Citrine	
Jasper	
Hornstone	2·65
Chrysoprase	
Cordierite	2·60—2·65
Chalcedony	
Agate, &c.	2·60
Obsidian	2·5—2·6
Adularia	2·55
Haüynite	2·4—2·5
Lapis-lazuli	2·4
Moldavite	2·36
Opal	2·19—2·2
Jet	—1·35
Amber	1·0—1·1

B. CLEAVAGE.

It has previously been briefly pointed out that crystallised bodies are distinguished rom amorphous bodies by certain peculiarities of internal structure. Whereas the substance of an amorphous body possesses identical properties in every direction through it, the substance of a crystallised body possesses different properties in different directions. An important character of crystallised bodies, and one which shows considerable variation in different directions, is the degree of cohesion existing between the ultimate crystalline particles of which the mass is built up. In many such bodies the cohesion in certain directions is so feeble that a slight blow is sufficient to cause them to break into fragments. On examination, these fragments will be found to possess perfectly plane surfaces, which are the surfaces of minimum cohesion in the substance. This phenomenon is shown to perfection by calcite, a crystal of which, if allowed to fall, will break into fragments bounded by perfectly bright and even surfaces.

The best way to produce this separation or splitting along plane surfaces is to place a chisel or knife edge on the crystal in the proper position, and to drive it in with a single sharp blow from a hammer.

The direction within a crystal, along which there is minimum cohesion, is known as the *direction of cleavage*, and the plane surface of separation is known as the *cleavage face*. The cleavage directions and faces are always identical both in number and direction in all specimens of the same mineral species. The ease with which cleavage takes place, and the perfection of the resulting cleavage faces, are also constant in all specimens of the same species, but different in different species. Some minerals exhibit little or no cleavage, while in others, notably calcite, cleavage is produced very easily, and the surfaces of separation are perfectly bright, smooth, and even.

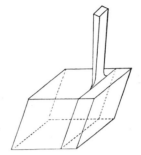

FIG. 8. Cleavage of calcite.

Among precious stones possessing the property of cleavage to a high degree may be mentioned topaz, which cleaves in one direction, and diamond which cleaves in four directions. In others, as, for example, emerald, cleavage takes place with difficulty, and the cleavage faces are uneven and frequently interrupted by irregular areas. Quartz, garnet, tourmaline, &c., are other examples of precious stones possessing no distinct cleavage ; the difference of cohesion in different directions being so small that the stones will not split along plane surfaces.

In amorphous bodies, as, for instance, opal, the degree of cohesion between the constituent particles, like all other physical characters, is identical in every direction, so that here plane cleavage faces are impossible, and as a fact never occur. When a body shows sure indications that it possesses the property of cleavage, we are safe in inferring from that fact alone that the material of which the body is composed is crystallised and not amorphous. Hence it is sometimes possible to distinguish between a genuine crystallised precious stone and a glass imitation, since glass, being amorphous, can have no cleavage.

If in the same crystal there are three or more directions of cleavage, it will then be possible to develop out of it by cleavage a body bounded entirely by cleavage faces ; such a body is known as the *cleavage form* of that particular crystal. Calcite, for example, cleaves with equal facility in three directions, inclined to one another at equal oblique angles. It is therefore possible to obtain from any crystal of calcite a cleavage fragment having the form of a rhombohedron, a solid figure which resembles a cube with two of the opposite corners pressed together. In the same way, the four cleavages of diamond will give a cleavage form identical with the regular octahedron.

Such cleavage forms resemble natural crystals in possessing plane regular faces, but whereas in crystals these faces are the result of natural growth, in cleavage forms they have been produced by artificial means. In connection with the cutting of precious stones and the purposes to which they are to be applied, a knowledge of the cleavage possessed by different stones is most desirable. The property of cleavage considered from this point of view will be treated in detail under the descriptions of individual stones.

Cleavage frequently affords a simple means by which a stone in the rough condition may be identified or distinguished from others of similar appearance. As we have already seen, the cleavage directions and faces are always identical in number, direction, and quality in all specimens of the same mineral species, and in general differ from those of other species. The cleavage of a stone is thus one of its characteristic and distinguishing features. As an example of the use which can be made of this character, let us suppose a case in which it might be very difficult to decide which of two stones is an aquamarine, and which a certain colour-variety of topaz, both being of a sea-green colour and very similar in general appearance. Aquamarine has a very imperfect cleavage in one direction, while topaz has a perfect cleavage also in one direction. Should one of the stones show a distinct cleavage, there can then be no doubt that it is topaz and not aquamarine. If, however, no distinct cleavage can be made out, the evidence must be considered as negative, since a cleavage face need not necessarily be developed or outwardly visible even on a mineral which cleaves with great facility.

The cleavage of a mineral is not always expressed as a cleavage surface forming one of the external boundaries to the stone. Fairly perfect cleavage is often indicated by the presence of plane cracks running in a certain direction inside the crystal itself. Frequently such crevices give rise to the brilliant rainbow colours of thin films; the film here being air or simply a vacuous space. The cleavage of the stone is thus manifested by these iridescent colours in a very beautiful manner. On a surface parallel to which there is a very perfect cleavage there is often to be seen a peculiar lustre resembling that of mother-of-pearl; this is limited to crystals possessing a perfect cleavage, and hence its occurrence may be taken as an indication of the presence of such. Even in faceted stones cleavage may be sometimes recognised by the iridescent colours and pearly lustre due to internal plane fissures.

From the æsthetic and commercial points of view, however, the presence of such cleavage fractures in a cut stone is far from desirable, since they give rise to irregularities in the reflection and refraction of light which seriously diminish the beauty and consequently the value of the stone. The presence of cleavage cracks or "feathers" is a very bad fault in a transparent precious stone, for a small and scarcely noticeable crack may in course of time extend and cause the stone to break into fragments. Rough stones showing any marked cleavage cracks are useless for cutting, since in the process they will probably break.

Stones which cleave with great facility should be treated with special care when mounted as gems, for a fall or blow, or a sudden rise in temperature (arising perhaps from immersion in hot water), may be sufficient to give rise to, or further develop, a cleavage crack, which may result in the complete fragmentation of the stone.

Although the property of cleavage in some cases leads to undesirable results, yet considerable advantage may be derived from it in others. A stone with a distinct cleavage, such as topaz, too large for a single gem, may be easily reduced by cleaving to any desired size with no loss of material; a stone not possessing this property must be sliced to the required size, a process involving the expenditure of much time and trouble. Again, by cleavage, portions of rough stones may be easily and quickly removed which otherwise would have to be got rid of by grinding, a laborious and costly operation. Moreover, the cleavage fragments can be utilised in the fashioning of smaller gems, and waste of material thus avoided.

The facile cleavage of the diamond is utilised very largely in the production of cut stones. As we have already seen, the cleavage form of the diamond is an octahedron, and this approximates to the shape of a brilliant, which is the form of cutting usually adopted for the diamond. The first stage in the transformation of a rough diamond into the cut stone is therefore the development of the octahedral cleavage form, and this is quickly and easily performed owing to the ready cleavage of the mineral. This property of the diamond then obviates both the necessity for the laborious and expensive process of grinding in the production of the cut stone, and also the waste of material consequent on this process.

Fracture.—The fractured surface of a mineral not possessing the property of cleavage is not plane, but uneven and irregular. The particular character of the fractured surface, or *fracture* as it is called for brevity, is different in different minerals, and, as it is more or less characteristic, it must be taken into account in the identification of rough stones.

The fractured surface frequently has the rounded form of a molluscan shell, and the two surfaces, respectively convex and concave, which fit together, both exhibit regular, circular ridges and grooves concentric about the point where the specimen received the blow which caused the fracture. Since these circular markings resemble the lines of growth on a molluscan shell, this type of fracture is known as a conchoidal fracture. Perfect conchoidal fracture is shown by artificial glass and also by the natural volcanic glass, obsidian. The surfaces of the conchoidal fracture may vary in extent, and also in the degree of curvature, being at times almost plane, hence such fractures may be distinguished as flat- or deep-conchoidal, and large- or small-conchoidal. The last, or sub-conchoidal fracture, merges into what is known as uneven fracture. As mentioned above, the fractured surface may approximate to a plane surface, never, however, being truly plane; this is known as even fracture, and is well shown by jasper; it merges into the flat- and large-conchoidal types.

Sometimes the fragment separated from a specimen by a blow from a hammer shows on the fractured surface loosely attached splinters, lighter in colour than the main mass of the stone. This class of fracture is said to be splintery, and is excellently illustrated by chrysoprase. Naturally there may exist every gradation between a typical splintery fracture and a smooth fracture.

Precious stones are frequently penetrated by cracks which are the forerunners of fractures. Such cracks considerably lessen the transparency and beauty, and consequently, the value of a stone; specimens showing such flaws are avoided by gem-dealers. Though of rare occurrence in many stones, in others, e.g., emerald, they are often present in great numbers.

These internal cracks due to fracture resemble the cracks shown by stones possessing a cleavage in that they often exhibit iridescent colours; as, for example, is sometimes seen in rock-crystal. Here, however, the cracks, and the bands of colour to which they give rise, are more or less markedly curved, and are thus quite distinct from the plane surfaces of cleavage cracks.

C. HARDNESS.

For a mineral which is to be used as a gem, an important and, indeed, indispensable property is that of hardness. By the hardness of a mineral is understood the resistance which it offers to being scratched or marked by another body. The greater the resistance, the harder the mineral. Only the harder stones, when used as gems, are capable of preserving unimpaired their transparency, lustre, and play of colours. Softer stones when newly cut may display all these qualities, but in use they soon become scratched on the surface, which detracts considerably from their beauty; a single scratch on the back of a transparent stone, that is on the side away from the observer, is many times reflected, and thus the bad effect is multiplied. The beauty of opaque stones is also greatly marred by scratches, but those on the front side of the stone only will be observable in this case.

The degree of hardness is of considerable importance in identifying and distinguishing precious stones, and is a character of which the dealer in gems should make frequent use. Hence the necessity for acquiring a knowledge of the different degrees of hardness possessed by different stones.

The method of testing the relative hardness of two stones is simplicity itself. A sharp corner of the one is rubbed with a certain pressure across a smooth surface of the other;

the stone which is scratched is the softer of the two, and if neither is scratched the stones are of equal hardness.

In this way it can be shown that all specimens of the same mineral species have the same degree of hardness, and that this quality will differ more or less considerably in different minerals. The hardness of a mineral is, therefore, one of its characteristic features, and it affords a means whereby precious stones may be identified or distinguished.

From observations on the relative hardness of minerals made in the way just described, all minerals can be arranged according to the degrees of hardness they possess in a series ranging from the softest to the hardest. From such a series, the late Viennese mineralogist, Mohs, selected the hardest, the softest, and eight minerals of intermediate hardness, and with them constructed a table for use as a **scale of hardness.** The ten selected minerals were numbered consecutively from 1 to 10, No. 1 being the softest and No. 10 the hardest, The scale is given below :

1. Talc.	6. Felspar.
2. Gypsum.	7. Quartz.
3. Calcite.	8. Topaz.
4. Fluor-spar.	9. Corundum.
5. Apatite.	10. Diamond.

It must be borne in mind that the difference in hardness between any two consecutive members of this series is by no means identical. Thus, for example, the difference in hardness between diamond (10) and corundum (9) is vastly greater than between corundum (9) and topaz (8); greater indeed than the difference which exists between corundum (9) and talc (1). The different minerals in this scale of hardness are chosen solely with a view to practical convenience in mineralogy, namely to afford a means whereby the relative hardness of any mineral may be expressed with clearness and brevity by a number.

To express the hardness of any given stone in this way we must first ascertain to which member of the scale it corresponds in hardness ; the number of this member then expresses the hardness of the stone, which may be written H = 8, for example. By this it is understood that the hardness of the stone corresponds to No. 8 on Mohs' scale, that is, it has the same hardness as topaz. In the same way, if the hardness of the stone lies between that of quartz and of topaz, H = 7—8; should it be nearer quartz, then H = $7\frac{1}{4}$; or nearer topaz, then H = $7\frac{3}{4}$; while if it lies apparently midway between them, H = $7\frac{1}{2}$. In the last case the stone would scratch quartz with the same ease as it is itself scratched by topaz. H = $7\frac{1}{4}$ means that topaz scratches the stone more easily than the stone itself scratches quartz ; while H = $7\frac{3}{4}$ means that the stone easily scratches quartz but is not so easily scratched by topaz. Beyond this these numbers have no exact meaning.

Specimens of the ten minerals which form the scale of hardness should be kept specially for the purpose of determining hardness. They should be crystals with sharp edges and smooth faces, and of a convenient size. In testing any given stone a sharp edge of the scale mineral is rubbed over a smooth face of the stone, the scale minerals being used in consecutive order from the softest to the hardest. It is important to distinguish carefully between a scratch on the surface of the stone undergoing examination and a streak of powder which may arise from abrasion of the corner of the scale mineral. To avoid this mistake the surface should be wiped and then examined with a lens.

To take an example, let us suppose that the stone to be tested is not scratched by any member of the scale until topaz is tried ; its hardness will then lie between 7 and 8. If it is not capable of itself scratching quartz its hardness is exactly that of quartz, namely, 7. Should the quartz, however, be scratched by the stone, its hardness is then H = 7—8, or, as explained above, it may be fixed at $H = 7\frac{1}{4}$, $7\frac{1}{2}$, or $7\frac{3}{4}$ according as its hardness approximates more nearly to that of quartz, lies midway between that of quartz and topaz, or approaches more nearly to that of topaz.

It is sometimes sufficient to determine the hardness of a stone approximately, and, in such cases, when the exact degree of hardness is not required, the scale of hardness need not be used. The softest mineral, talc (No. 1 of the scale), is greasy to the touch. No. 2 on the scale, namely gypsum, can be easily scratched with the finger-nail, but this is impossible in the case of calcite (No. 3). A knife scratches calcite easily, fluor-spar (No. 4) less easily, apatite (No. 5) still less easily, and felspar (No. 6) only with difficulty, while quartz (No. 7) cannot be scratched at all with a knife. Quartz and members higher in the scale will strike fire with steel more or less readily, while felspar (No. 6) only does this with difficulty and to a small extent, and lower members of the scale not at all. Minerals harder than apatite (No. 5) are capable of scratching ordinary window-glass, and this substance may be fixed approximately at No. 5 in the scale of hardness. The more a mineral exceeds apatite in hardness the more easily will it scratch glass.

Minerals used as precious stones have the highest degree of hardness. The hardness of the most valuable corresponds to Nos. 10, 9, and 8 on the scale; those of less value have a hardness denoted by 7, rarely lower than this. Hardness above that of quartz is therefore known as gem-hardness; a mineral below this standard has little application as a gem, since it will be readily scratched even by dust. Among other constituents, dust contains minute mineral particles especially of quartz, and in cleaning a stone of hardness less than 7 by rubbing it with a cloth it will be scratched by these particles of quartz, and in course of time lose its beauty, becoming dull, rough, and lustreless. Stones of gem-hardness are not so scratched and damaged. Moreover, if stones of different hardness are allowed to rub against each other, as may easily happen if several mounted gems are kept together loosely in a box, then the harder stones will scratch and damage the softer ones. Since diamonds are usually represented in collections of jewels, all other stones, including ruby and sapphire, being softer, are liable to suffer if due care in this respect be not taken.

With few exceptions, therefore, precious stones possess a high degree of hardness, and very nearly all are capable of scratching glass, a substance usually conveniently at hand as window-glass or as a watch-glass. Since glass naturally will not scratch glass, a genuine precious stone may be easily distinguished from its imitation in glass by the test of hardness. As an aid to the identification of a stone, its position in the scale of hardness should be determined as described above. In the case of a cut stone, however, the process must be reversed to avoid damage to the stone; that is, the scratching power of the cut stone must be tried upon the scale minerals, commencing with the lower members, until the hardest the stone is capable of scratching is found. In such cases only an approximate value of the hardness can be arrived at, but it will usually be sufficient.

For such purposes there is no need to use the complete scale of hardness; the softest as well as the hardest members may be omitted. As a standard for the fifth degree of hardness a small plate of glass serves excellently, and is more easily obtainable than a good piece of apatite. There will be required in addition pieces of felspar, quartz, and topaz. The quartz should be a colourless transparent crystal (rock-crystal); the topaz should have a smooth, cleavage surface, so that the slightest scratch may be easily and surely recognised whenever the surface is examined with a lens. For the practical determination of gems the use of any other than these four members of the scale of hardness is superfluous. The softer precious stones, with a hardness less than that of apatite, will be recognised by their incapability of scratching glass; combined with other easily observed characters, this will usually be sufficient to determine the identity of the stone. Stones which are harder than topaz are but few in number; they are corundum (including ruby and sapphire), chryso-beryl, and diamond, the hardest of all stones. These stones stand alone in their power of scratching topaz; they may be readily distinguished from each other by the specific gravity or other determinable characters, as in the case of the few stones which do not scratch glass.

Determinations of hardness must be performed on cut stones with the greatest care, for it is possible that corners of the stone may chip off even when being pressed against a softer stone, and especially so when the cut stone possesses a good cleavage as in topaz or diamond. The loss of a corner would not be serious in a rough stone, since, in the process of cutting, broken edges are removed; but it would be fatal to the perfection and beauty of a cut stone. This test of hardness then, though useful in the case of rough stones, must only be used with caution in the case of valuable cut stones.

In place of the scale of hardness, the use of which has been just explained, the dealer in precious stones more frequently uses other instruments, and specially a hard steel file. This easily scratches minerals with a hardness of 5, and only slightly those with a hardness of 6, giving more or less powder according as the hardness of the stone is less or greater. Quartz is of about the same hardness as hardened steel of good quality, of which the file should be made. Stones with a hardness of 7 are therefore only with difficulty marked by the file, while harder stones will rub and polish the file, which will leave a shining, metallic mark on the stone. An approximate idea of the hardness of a stone may be obtained from the pitch of the sound emitted when the file is rubbed on the stone. Provided that stones similar in size are used for testing, then the harder the stone the higher the note emitted.

In the case of cut stones the file is too clumsy an instrument, and the practical jeweller uses in its place a pencil of very hard steel furnished with a sharp point. This pencil scratches felspar easily and glass still more easily; it scarcely touches quartz, however, and has no effect on harder stones. The girdle of a cut stone is a suitable part on which a trial of its hardness may be made; it being by the girdle that the stone is fixed in its setting, a small scratch in this region is unnoticed. The steel pencil is especially useful in distin-guishing genuine precious stones from their softer glass imitations, since the former cannot be marked by it, while the latter are scratched with ease. As before mentioned, however, the greatest care is needed in testing cut stones, especially the transparent kinds, so that even this more refined method has certain limitations.

The hardness of a stone is naturally a question of great importance in the process of cutting; the material of the grinding disc and the grinding powder, to be described later, must be chosen according to the degree of hardness of the stone. When worked under similar conditions, with the same kind of abrasive material, the harder the stone the longer and more difficult will be the process of grinding. As a rule also, the harder the stone the sharper will be its edges and corners when cut, and the more susceptible will be its faces of a brilliant polish. The edges and corners of softer stones are much less sharp, and con-sequently these stones have a less pleasing appearance. A high degree of hardness is thus not only essential for the preservation of the beauty of a stone, but is also one of the properties on which its beauty depends.

From the time required for grinding a facet on a stone, it is possible to form an estimate of the hardness of the stone on this facet. It not infrequently happens that a stone can be more easily and quickly cut in certain directions than in certain others; moreover, not only do the different natural faces of a crystal vary in hardness, but the hardness on any face is not identical in all directions. The hardness of a crystal, therefore, like the other physical characters, varies with the direction.

These differences in hardness, however, are usually very small, and require for their detection an instrument of special construction capable of precise measurement; such an instrument is known as a sclerometer. The somewhat rough method of scratching, described above is useless for the detection of such small differences in hardness; it is applicable, however, in the case of kyanite. The hardness in different parts of a crystal of this mineral varies between that of apatite (5) and that of quartz (7). No other mineral used as a gem shows variation in hardness between such wide limits. Certain differences in hardness, shown by different specimens of the same mineral species, may be attributed in part to the fact that the hardness has been determined in different directions; this difference in crystallised precious stones, however, is so small as to be of little importance. In amorphous stones, such as opal, and in glasses, the hardness, like all other physical characters, is the same in all directions.

Finally, it must be noted that the hardness of a mineral is distinct from its **frangibility**, the quality on which depends the ease or difficulty with which a stone is broken by a blow from a hammer. The frangibility of a stone depends not only on its hardness, but also, and to a great extent, on the quality of cleavage it possesses. Contrary to popular opinion, the diamond, in spite of its enormous hardness, is very brittle and can be easily broken to pieces. Certain peculiarities of structure greatly diminish the frangibility of some minerals; this is especially the case in those of which the structure is that of a matted aggregate of very fine fibres or needle-shaped crystals of microscopic size. An example of such a mineral is furnished by nephrite (jade), which, although its hardness is scarcely equal to that of felspar, offers a very great resistance to the hammer, and can only be broken with considerable difficulty. Such substances are described as being tough, while those which are easily frangible would be described as brittle. A high degree of brittleness is not a desirable quality in a precious stone, since the stone is liable to be broken in use unless special care is taken.

In the following table are given all the more important minerals, which may be used as gems or as ornamental stones, arranged in order of hardness, from the softest to the hardest. The numbers refer to their degrees of hardness on Mohs' scale:

Precious Stones arranged according to Hardness.

Amber	$2\frac{1}{2}$	Demantoid	$6\frac{1}{2}$
Jet	$3\frac{1}{2}$	Idocrase	$6\frac{1}{2}$
Malachite	$3\frac{1}{2}$	Olivine	$6\frac{1}{2}$
Fluor-spar	4	Chalcedony (agate, carnelian, &c.)	$6\frac{1}{2}$
Dioptase	5	Axinite	$6\frac{3}{4}$
Kyanite	5—7	Jadeite	$6\frac{3}{4}$
Haüynite	$5\frac{1}{2}$	Quartz (rock-crystal, amethyst, citrine, jasper, chrysoprase, &c.)	7
Lapis-lazuli	$5\frac{1}{2}$		
Sphene	$5\frac{1}{2}$	Tourmaline	$7\frac{1}{4}$
Hæmatite	$5\frac{1}{2}$	Cordierite	$7\frac{1}{4}$
Obsidian	$5\frac{1}{2}$	Garnet (red)	$7\frac{1}{4}$
Moldavite	$5\frac{1}{2}$	Andalusite	$7\frac{1}{2}$
Opal	$5\frac{1}{2}$—$6\frac{1}{2}$	Staurolite	$7\frac{1}{2}$
Nephrite	$5\frac{3}{4}$	Euclase	$7\frac{1}{2}$
Diopside	6	Zircon	$7\frac{1}{2}$
Turquoise	6	Beryl (emerald, aquamarine)	$7\frac{3}{4}$
Adularia	6	Phenakite	$7\frac{3}{4}$
Amazon-stone	6	Spinel	8
Labradorite	6	Topaz	8
Iron-pyrites	6	Chrysoberyl	$8\frac{1}{2}$
Prehnite	$6\frac{1}{2}$	Corundum (ruby, sapphire, &c.)	9
Epidote	$6\frac{1}{2}$	Diamond	10

D. OPTICAL CHARACTERS.

Those qualities of precious stones which depend on their behaviour towards light are known as optical characters, and are of special interest and importance. The transparency and lustre, the colour and play of colours of a stone, depend largely on its optical characters. Moreover these qualities furnish a means whereby the stone may be easily determined, and with no risk of injury such as accompanies the testing of its hardness. It is important, therefore, to be acquainted, at least to a certain extent, with the laws of optics, and with some of the instruments used in the investigation of optical phenomena; these are dealt with below as fully as space allows.

1. Transparency.

The majority of precious stones are transparent, but in the uncut condition the free passage of light through the stone is often obstructed by rough and uneven faces. When such faces are removed by cutting, and the cut surfaces polished, an apparently cloudy specimen often becomes beautifully clear and transparent. The transparency of such costly stones as diamond, ruby, and sapphire, is often very perfect, while the same property exists in less costly stones, such as rock-crystal and amethyst. The greater the transparency of a specimen of any given precious stone the more highly is it prized. The only jewels of the first rank which are not transparent are the noble opal and the turquoise; in stones of less value, such as agate, chrysoprase, malachite, and others, this is more frequently the case.

Transparent bodies allow the free passage of light through their substance; an object viewed through a perfectly transparent substance will have no blurred edges, but will present a clear and sharp outline. A stone which combines complete absence of colour with perfect transparency, as in diamond and rock-crystal, would be described as water-clear or limpid. A perfectly water-clear stone with the highest degree of transparency, and free from any trace of colour, is known to jewellers as a stone of the first or purest *water*, and stones of this high quality are especially prized. Should the stone show a very slight cloudiness or tinge of colour, scarcely noticeable perhaps to the unpractised eye, it is known as a stone of the second water; similarly a stone which shows a further departure from the standard of perfection in these qualities is known as a stone of the third water. This subject will be again reverted to under the special description of diamond.

A substance which in a mass of some thickness allows a large proportion, but not all, of the light emanating from any source to pass through it, is known as a semi-transparent substance. Any object, for example a flame, viewed through such a substance will not be seen distinctly, but will be blurred in outline. A substance through which some of the light of a flame can pass, but through which it is impossible to see even a blurred outline of the flame, is described as being *translucent*. As an example of a semi-transparent stone chalcedony may be mentioned, while opal is an example of a translucent stone. In some cases light can only pass through a very thin splinter or a sharp edge of a broken stone; such stones are translucent only at their edges, being quite opaque in mass. A chrysoprase held in front of a light will show a dark centre surrounded by a lighter border. Opaque stones, even when thin, completely cut off all light, hence when held before a light they present a uniformly dark outline with no lighter border. Opaque stones then, for example hæmatite, owe their beauty not to their transparency, but to the fineness of their lustre and colour.

Different specimens of the same kind of stone vary greatly in transparency, and consequently in value; while one specimen may be perfectly transparent, another may be so cloudy and opaque as to be useless as a gem. The cloudiness in such a case is due to the presence of numerous cracks and fissures in the stone, or to foreign matter included in its substance, either of which obstructs the free passage of light through the stone, scattering it at the surface.

Cracks and fissures are specially frequent in stones, such as topaz, which possess a good cleavage. They are not confined to such stones however, but are frequently found in those which possess no distinct cleavage, such, for instance, as the green emerald, which is almost always penetrated by numerous cracks. Their presence naturally reduces the transparency of the stone ; perfectly faultless specimens of emerald are of the greatest rarity. Enclosures of foreign matter are of not uncommon occurrence in crystallised minerals. Thus black and other coloured grains are sometimes found in the substance of diamond, and numerous scales of mica in that of emerald. These enclosures may be so small as to be only visible under a high power of the microscope ; when distributed evenly throughout the substance of the stone, as they usually are, their effect is to make the whole stone cloudy. On the other hand a few enclosures of larger size will leave portions of the stone clear.

The substance of some precious stones contains enormous numbers of extremely minute cavities often arranged in strings, and giving rise to a silky or cloudy glimmering or sheen, which greatly impairs the transparency and beauty of the stone in which they occur. This kind of cloudiness, present as a fault in precious stones which would otherwise be transparent, is known to jewellers as " silk."

The transparency of a mineral is largely dependent upon its structure. While crystals, at least as far as precious stones are concerned, are usually transparent, an aggregate of small crystals of the same kind, that is a compact crystalline aggregate, is usually opaque, or at most translucent. The reason for this is clear; at the boundaries of each of the minute constituent grains, fibres or scales of a crystalline aggregate, a certain amount of light will be scattered and lost, and thus never reach the eye. For this reason chalcedony, chrysoprase, &c., are not transparent, although they are built up of minute transparent crystalline grains of quartz, a mineral which in its most perfectly crystallised and transparent condition is known as rock-crystal.

The varying degrees of transparency possessed by different precious stones for Röntgen (X) rays has an important application in their determination; this will be dealt with in the third part of the present work.

2. LUSTRE.

When light falls upon a body a portion of it is thrown back or reflected from the surface, while another portion enters its substance. It is the portion of light reflected from the surface on which depends the lustre of the body.

The lustre of a body varies with the proportion of light reflected at its surface; hence different **degrees of intensity of lustre**, distinguished as splendent, shining, glistening, glimmering, and dull, exist in different stones. The lustre of a perfectly smooth surface, reflecting a sharp image of an object, is splendent ; a surface which reflects a less sharp image is shining ; the image reflected from a surface of glistening lustre is still less sharp ; a surface giving only a feeble reflection has glimmering lustre ; lastly, a dull surface reflects no light.

The lustre of most precious stones, especially the more valuable, is splendent, as is often seen on the natural faces of a crystal, but more frequently when the stone has been cut and polished. A high degree of lustre adds very considerably to the beauty of a stone, and the object of polishing is to render this quality as perfect as possible. What is known as the " fire " of a precious stone is connected with its lustre, and this quality only exists with a specially high degree of lustre ; the term " fire " has, however, sometimes another meaning, as we shall see further on under Optical Dispersion.   Very few of the more valuable precious stones are devoid, in the cut condition, of a brilliant lustre ; of these the most important is turquoise, which, even after being polished to the fullest possible extent, shows a certain dulness of surface.   This is due to a certain extent to the softer character of the stone ; for the harder precious stones, such as diamond and ruby, are susceptible of a higher degree of polish than the softer stones, such as turquoise.

Each kind of stone is capable of receiving a certain degree of polish depending on the physical characters of its substance.   And while there is for every stone a certain maximum lustre, which cannot be exceeded, even with the most persistent polishing, this lustre may often, from a variety of causes, fall below the maximum.

Different precious stones are not only characterised by different degrees of intensity of lustre, but also by different **kinds of lustre** ; and this in many cases enables one to distinguish stones which are otherwise similar in appearance.   Thus it would be possible for the least practised eye to distinguish at a glance a genuine diamond from its imitation in rock-crystal, simply by the difference in lustre.

Degree of lustre and kind of lustre are both loosely referred to as lustre.   Though it has been attempted to give some idea of the different degrees of lustre existing in different stones, yet no adequate conception of the different kinds of lustre can be derived from a mere verbal description.   It is far preferable to acquaint oneself with the different kinds of lustre by actually comparing substances showing the different kinds.   Thus a piece of burnished metal, a sheet of glass, a polished diamond, the mother-of-pearl lining of a shell, a layer of greasy oil, or a piece of satin, may each possess a high degree of lustre, the quality or kind of which is however different in every case.   The different kinds of lustre exhibited by the substances just mentioned are taken as types ; and the different kinds of lustre existing in minerals can be referred to one or other of these types.   Thus we have metallic lustre, glassy or vitreous lustre, adamantine (diamond) lustre, pearly lustre, greasy lustre, and silky or satiny lustre ; while more minutely descriptive terms can be derived from these, as, for example, metallic-adamantine, metallic-pearly, &c.

In the description of a mineral it is important to be able to recognise and name its particular kind of lustre.   As explained above, each kind differs in intensity, so that we may have strong or feeble vitreous lustre, &c.   Both degree and kind of lustre depend on the properties of the particular substance and are therefore, under certain conditions, characteristic of that substance.   It is, however, to be noted that the kind of lustre may be considerably modified by certain peculiarities of structure shown by a mineral, so that it sɪ not an invariable character of a mineral species.   The kind of lustre depends not only on light reflected from the surface of a stone, but also, in part, on light which has penetrated into its substance and suffered some modification before again passing out.   As examples of this influence of structure on lustre may be cited the silky lustre of satin-spar, a finely fibrous variety of calcite, and the greasy lustre of elæolite, a variety of nepheline containing vast numbers of microscopic enclosures ; contrasted with these is the vitreous lustre shown by the more usual varieties of the minerals calcite and nepheline.

Metallic lustre, being exhibited exclusively by perfectly opaque substances, is found in only a few of the less important precious stones, as, for example, hæmatite.

Vitreous lustre, on the other hand, is best shown by perfectly transparent minerals, and is of very frequent occurrence ; it is present to a more or less marked degree in the majority of transparent precious stones, such as rock-crystal, topaz, ruby, sapphire, emerald, and others. It is, however, liable to be modified in substances possessing certain properties; thus, should a substance possess a high refractive index and also a high dispersion, the vitreous lustre will pass into **adamantine lustre**, which, again, may show an approach to metallic lustre. Characteristic adamantine lustre is possessed only by diamond, but an approach to it is shown by zircon, especially when colourless.

Silky or **satiny lustre** is exhibited by minerals possessing a finely fibrous structure, as, for example, the ornamental stone satin-spar, the fine green malachite, and the golden tiger-eye.

Pearly lustre is exhibited exclusively in those faces of crystals parallel to which there is a direction of perfect cleavage, and then only when cleavage cracks have been developed in the interior of the crystal. Topaz, felspar (the moonstone variety), and other stones, sometimes show pearly lustre, but only on faces parallel to the perfect cleavage; all other faces have the usual vitreous lustre.

Greasy lustre appears to be associated with the presence of numerous microscopically small enclosures, which in many minerals are of constant occurrence. Elæolite, which is sometimes cut for ornamental purposes, shows a typical greasy lustre; other minerals, such as olivine, of which the lustre is usually vitreous, may show an approach to greasy lustre.

The lustre of some minerals, as, for example, turquoise, resembles that of wax, and is described as **waxy lustre**. Others, again, have the lustre of resin: **resinous lustre** is shown by many garnets, such, for instance, as hessonite, which, when massive, sometimes closely resembles resin in appearance.

3. Refraction of Light.

The refraction of light, and the phenomena connected with it, have an important bearing on the study of precious stones.

We have already noticed that of the light which falls upon a transparent body, such as a precious stone, a portion is reflected at the surface, while another portion enters its substance and is propagated in straight lines through it. When the incident ray of light strikes the bounding surface of the transparent body perpendicularly, the light which passes into the interior of the body is propagated in the same direction as that of the incident ray. If, however, the incident ray strikes the surface obliquely, the path taken by the light through the substance of the body will not coincide in direction with the incident ray, but will be in a new direction; the ray may then be said to be bent or refracted.

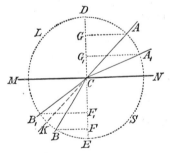

FIG. 9. Refraction of light on passing into a precious stone.

In Fig. 9 let *MN* be the surface of separation between the transparent body (precious stone), *S*, and the air, *L*. A single ray of light travelling in air in the direction *AC*, and striking the separating surface at *C*, will not be propagated in the stone in the same straight line, namely, along *CK*, but will be bent or refracted into the direction *CB*. *CB* is then the refracted ray corresponding to the incident ray *AC*. The directions *AC* and *CB*, and also *DE*, the normal to the surface at *C*, all lie in the same plane, which is perpendicular to *MN*, and in Fig. 9 is the plane of the paper. This plane is known as the plane of incidence. Whenever light passes from air into a stone, the refracted ray *CB* is always nearer the normal *DE* than is the incident ray *AC*; that is, the light is bent *towards* the normal. This may be expressed otherwise by stating that the angle of incidence, *ACD*, is greater than the angle of refraction *BCE*.

When the angle of incidence is greater than *ACD*, the angle of refraction will be greater than *BCE*. In Fig. 9, let A_1C represent another ray of light in the same plane of incidence, such that the angle of incidence A_1CD is greater than *ACD*, then the corresponding refracted ray is represented by CB_1. It will be seen from the figure that the angle of refraction B_1CE is greater than *BCE*, which is the angle of refraction corresponding to the angle of incidence *ACD*. Similarly in every case the angle of refraction varies with the angle of incidence, and this variation is governed by a definite law, namely, the law of refraction.

In the plane of incidence and with *C* as centre (Fig. 9), let a circle of any convenient radius be drawn. Let the circle cut the incident rays *AC* and A_1C at the points *A* and A_1, and the refracted rays *BC* and B_1C at the points *B* and B_1. From these points drop perpendiculars, *AG*, A_1G_1, *BF*, B_1F_1 upon the normal *DE*. Then the ratio of the perpendicular *AG* to the corresponding perpendicular *BF* is the same as the ratio A_1G_1 to B_1F_1, and will always be constant for the same substance whatever may be the angle of incidence. Hence, when light passes from air into any particular stone, the following relation holds for all rays :

$$\frac{AG}{BF} = \frac{A_1G_1}{B_1F_1} = \ldots = n,$$

where *n* is a constant for that particular substance, but is different for different substances. This constant *n* is known as the refractive co-efficient, the refractive index, or the **index of refraction** of the substance. As just pointed out, the refractive index is independent of the angle of incidence ; it has a certain definite value in all specimens of the same kind of precious stone, and will be different in different stones.

Since, in the passage of light from the air into a stone, the angle of incidence is always greater than the angle of refraction, it is easily seen from Fig. 9 that the perpendiculars *AG* and A_1G_1 will always be greater than the perpendiculars *BF* and B_1F_1; the index of refraction of all precious stones is therefore, when compared with that of air, always greater than unity.

The index of refraction of a stone can be determined accurately to several places of decimals by various methods. For the purpose of identifying precious stones, however, such a degree of accuracy is unnecessary, and refractive indices will be given here, as a rule, to only two decimal places. The following values may be given as examples, that of air, of course, being 1 :

Water .	$n = 1\cdot33$
Fluor-spar .	$n = 1\cdot44$
Spinel .	$n = 1\cdot71$
Garnet .	$n = 1\cdot77$
Diamond	$n = 2\cdot43$

In passing from air into any of these substances, the bending of the rays of light is greater the greater the refractive index of the substance, and conversely. The value of the refractive index is in many precious stones very high, but is far higher in diamond than in any other gem. The values for other stones will be given under the special description of each. In comparing two substances with different refractive indices, the one with the higher refractive index is known as the " optically denser " substance, while the other would be described as the " optically rarer " ; thus precious stones are " optically denser " than water or air.

A ray of light in passing from air into a stone immersed in liquid will be twice bent ; once at the surface of separation between the air and the liquid, and again at the surface of separation between the stone and the liquid.   The amount of bending depends in each case upon the difference in the refractive indices of the two media through which the ray passes. Thus, if the refractive index of the liquid is much greater than that of air, the ray of light will be much bent in passing from air into the liquid.   Similarly, if the refractive index of the stone is not much greater than that of the liquid, the ray will experience but little bending when entering the stone ; while if the index of refraction of the stone and that of the liquid are identical, there will be no bending of the ray of light, and it will travel through both in the same straight line.

The use of methylene iodide in determining specific gravities has already been described.   Another of its convenient properties is a very high index of refraction, the value of which, moreover, can be diminished by diluting the liquid with benzene.   If a stone be immersed in methylene iodide so diluted with benzene that the refractive index of the liquid is the same as that of the stone, there will be no bending of the rays of light, and they will pass in straight lines through the liquid and the stone.   Provided that the liquid and the stone are of the same colour, the result will be that the latter becomes invisible and cannot be detected.   If the index of refraction of the liquid be changed by the addition of benzene or of methylene iodide, the boundaries of the stone will become visible ; its outlines will grow sharper and more distinct as the difference between its refractive index and that of the liquid is increased by the further addition of either one or other of the liquids.

The phenomenon just described is sometimes made use of for the purpose of discovering hidden cracks, enclosures, and other flaws in precious stones.   The stone is immersed in a strongly refracting liquid such as methylene iodide ; its external boundaries will then become less distinct or, if the stone has the same refractive index as that of methylene iodide, invisible.   Any flaws in the interior of the stone will thus be rendered prominent and can be easily seen.

Light is refracted not only when passing from an optically rarer into an optically denser medium, as, for instance, from air into precious stone, but also in the reverse case, as, for example, when a ray of light in a stone passes out into the air.   In the passage of light from a denser to a rarer medium, the law of refraction still holds good.   We shall see from Fig. 10, however, that the refracted ray is in this case bent *away* from the normal, or, in other words, the angle of incidence is less than the angle of refraction ; while in the previous case the refracted ray was bent *towards* the normal, and consequently the angle of incidence was greater than the angle of refraction.

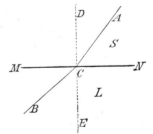

FIG. 10.   Refraction of light on passing out of a precious stone.

In Fig. 10, let MN be the surface of separation between the stone S and the air L.   It will be seen that the angle of incidence ACD of the ray AC in the stone is less than the angle of refraction BCE of the refracted ray; also that the refracted ray BC is bent away from the normal.   In this case also, the bending of the ray is greater the greater the index of refraction of the stone, but the amount of bending is the same whether the light passes from stone to air or *vice versâ*.   In one case the light travels in the direction ACB, and in the other in the direction BCA.

In the case also of the passage of light from a denser to a rarer medium, the angle of refraction increases with the angle of incidence.   In Fig. 11, where MN is the surface of separation between the precious stone S and the air L, the ray AC, incident upon the surface MN at C is bent into the direction CB, A_1C into the direction CB_1, and so on.   As the angle of incidence ACD becomes greater and greater so the angle of refraction BCE also becomes greater and greater. When the angle of incidence reaches a certain value, represented by A_2CD, the corresponding angle of refraction B_2CE will be a right-angle; the refracted ray will then emerge from the stone in a direction parallel to the bounding surface MN.

Obviously at 90° the angle of refraction has reached its maximum value and no further

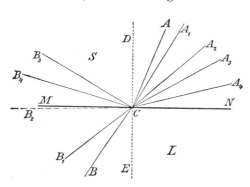

FIG. 11. Total reflection.

increase is possible. Should the angle of incidence now be increased, even by a small amount, it will then be impossible for the ray of light to leave the stone, and it will be refracted no longer, but simply reflected by the bounding surface back into the stone. In Fig. 11, the incident ray A_3C is reflected from the surface MN, along the line CB_3 inside the stone. This takes place according to the usual laws of reflection, the angle of incidence A_3CD being equal to the angle of reflection B_3CD. In the same way, every ray incident upon the surface MN at a greater angle than A_2CD, will be unable to pass out of the stone, and will be reflected back again by the surface MN; A_4CB_4, for example, is the path of such a ray and its reflection.

When light, travelling in one medium, as, for example, air, strikes the surface of a denser medium, such as a precious stone, a portion of it enters the stone and is refracted as described above, while the remaining portion is reflected from the surface. This takes place invariably, whatever may be the angle at which the incident light strikes the surface of the denser medium. In the reverse case, when light travelling in one medium, for example a precious stone, strikes the surface of a rarer medium, for instance air, the same thing may happen, that is, the light may be partly reflected and partly refracted, but this does not happen invariably as in the former case.

It was seen from Fig. 11, that when the angle of incidence exceeds a certain fixed value (A_2CD) the light is not refracted at all, but is reflected from the bounding surface back into the stone. In all other cases, as has been shown, light incident upon the surface of separation of two media is divided into a refracted portion and a reflected portion. Since in this particular case the light is not so divided, but the whole of it is reflected, this kind of reflection is known as internal total reflection, or, briefly, as **total reflection.**

Total reflection takes place at the surface of separation of two media only when the light travelling in the denser medium strikes the surface at an angle exceeding a certain degree of obliquity. Total reflection never takes place when light passes from a rarer to a denser medium. In this case there will always be refraction, for when the incident angle reaches a maximum of 90°, since the refracted ray is bent *towards* the normal, the angle of refraction will be less than 90°, and the light will pass out of the rarer into the denser medium. It is always possible then for light to pass from air into a precious stone, but it cannot pass out again unless it strikes the surface of the stone at an angle not exceeding a certain degree of obliquity.

The limiting angle A_2CD in Fig. 11 is known as the *critical angle* or the *angle of total reflection*. Its value depends upon the refractive indices of the two substances at the boundary of which reflection and refraction takes place. The greater the difference in the refractive indices the smaller will be the angle of total reflection, A_2CD. If the difference is very small the incident ray will make a large angle with the normal before total reflection takes place.

In diamond, which has a very high refractive index relative to air, the angle of total reflection is small, namely 24° 24′, which is represented by the angle A_1CD in Fig. 12. A ray of light inclined to the normal at an angle slightly less than A_1CD will be refracted and pass out into air in the direction CB_1 while one inclined at a slightly greater angle will be totally reflected in the stone in the direction CB'_1. The ray A_3C, making a still larger angle with the normal, will be totally reflected along CB_3; while the ray A_2C will pass out of the stone along CB_2, not undergoing total reflection.

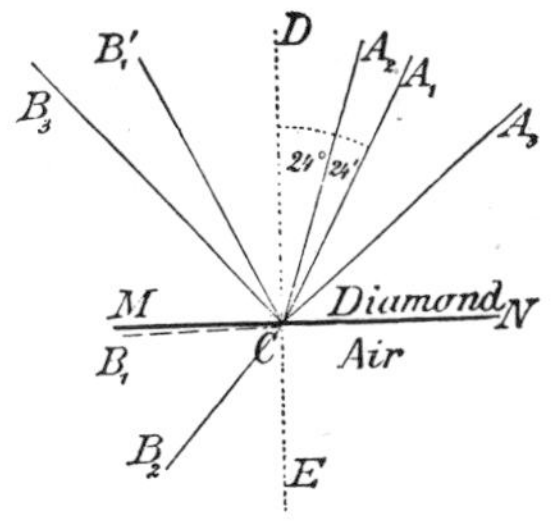

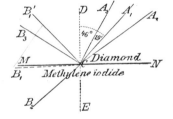

FIG. 12. Total reflection in diamond when surrounded by air.

If the optically denser body is, instead of diamond, glass, having, say, a refractive index of 1·538, then the angle of total reflection will no longer be 24° 24′ but 40° 30′, the body, as before, being surrounded by air. In this case, only those rays which are incident at an angle greater than 40° 30′ will be totally reflected.

Since the angle of total reflection increases when the difference between the refractive indices of the two media decreases, it follows that the angle of total reflection will be greater if the stone is surrounded by water instead of air. The angle of total reflection for a diamond placed in methylene iodide, the refractive index of which is 1·75, will be 46° 19′, the angle A_1CD in Fig. 13. Some of the rays, the obliquity of which causes them to be totally reflected when the diamond is surrounded by air, will be refracted when the surrounding medium is methylene iodide ; thus fewer rays will in this case be totally reflected. The use made of this fact will be mentioned later.

FIG. 13. Total reflection in diamond when surrounded by methylene iodide.

Total reflection has a considerable influence on the path taken by the rays of light in a transparent cut stone. The beauty of transparent cut stones largely depends on the fact that the light which falls on the front of the stone is totally reflected from the facets at the back and passes out again from the front to the eye of the observer. If the light were allowed to pass out at the back of the stone, the latter would lose much of its brilliancy ; only when there is total reflection at the back of the stone does it appear, as it were, to be filled with light. The greater the proportion of light thus reflected from the back of a stone, the more brilliant will be its appearance. But to enable us to trace out the exact path of a ray of light in a cut stone, we must first consider some of the phenomena of refraction rather more closely.

Up to the present we have considered only the behaviour of a ray of light at the boundary of different bodies, namely, in passing from air into a liquid or into a precious stone, and *vice versâ*, in passing from a precious stone into air or liquid. By combining these observations, the complete path of a ray of light passing through a precious stone is easily arrived at.

In Fig. 14, let MN, PQ, be parallel sides of a transparent body, and let AB be a ray of light from a source, such as a small bright flame, falling obliquely upon MN. On passing into the plate, the ray is bent towards the normal, DE, and takes the path BC. This portion of the ray meets the second surface PQ at C, the angle of incidence, BCD_1, being equal to the angle of refraction, since the normals are parallel. On passing out into the air, the ray is again refracted, this time away from the normal, and takes the path CF. From the geometry of Fig. 14, it is easily seen that the second angle of refraction, FCE_1, is

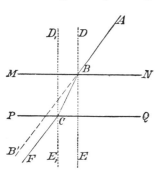

equal to the first angle of incidence, ABD; and that the paths of the ray outside the plate, namely AB and CF, are parallel. The direction of the ray on emerging from the plate is therefore the same as the original direction, but its path has been shifted a small distance, represented in Fig. 14 by $B'F$. On observing a small object A through a transparent body with parallel sides, it will be seen in very nearly the position it really occupies; this will not be the case however when the bounding surfaces, MN, NP (Fig. 15), are not parallel.

Fig. 14. Path of a ray of light through a plate with parallel sides.

Let the bounding surfaces, MN, NP, of the transparent body in Fig. 15 be inclined to each other at an angle MNP. We are then dealing with the path of a ray of light through a prism. As before, let the path of the ray of light incident upon MN be AB; on entering the solid it will be bent towards the normal GH, and will take the path BD. On emerging into air, the ray will be bent away from the normal

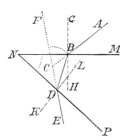

KL and will take the path DE. The angle between the original path of the ray in air and its final path is ACF, and this measures the total amount of bending it has undergone. The source of light A, if observed through the prism, will appear not in the position it actually occupies, but at some point on the line ECF which makes with the direction AB an angle ACF. This angle varies under different conditions. It will be greater the greater the refracting angle MNP of the prism, and the greater the refractive index of the substance of the prism; it depends also upon the angle of incidence, ABG. But it has a certain minimum value which cannot be diminished by either increase or decrease of the angle of incidence; this minimum value of the angle ACF is known as the angle of minimum deviation.

Fig. 15. Path of a ray of light through a prism.

In passing through a prism, the differently coloured constituents of white light are separated, and we have the phenomenon known as **dispersion**. The beautiful appearance

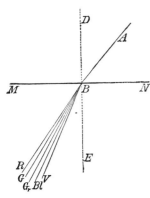

of many precious stones, and specially of diamond, is due to their dispersion of light. The coloured constituents of white light, from a source such as the sun or a lamp, differ not only in colour but also in refrangibility or capacity for being refracted. Thus, the refrangibility of red light is the smallest, and that of violet light the greatest; yellow, green, and blue light occupy in this respect intermediate positions in the order in which they stand.

It follows, then, that though we have hitherto spoken of a substance as having a single refractive index, this is only strictly true for monochromatic light, such as that given out by a Bunsen flame, or a spirit-lamp flame coloured by the vapour of either of the metals lithium, sodium, thallium, and indium. If white light be used, the refractive index of the

Fig. 16. Dispersion of light.

substance will be different for each constituent of the light, that for red light being the least and that for violet light the greatest.

When white light passes through a prism, then, the red rays will be deviated or bent out of their course least, the violet rays most, and the other rays will fall in their proper order between the two extremes. In Fig. 16 the ray of white light *AB* falls upon the surface *MN* of a refracting substance. Owing to the different refrangibilities of the constituents of the ray, these latter are separated and we get the original single ray of white light split up into red (*R*), yellow (*G*), green (*Gr*), blue (*Bl*), and violet (*V*), rays, deviating from each other slightly in direction. Between the rays of the colours just mentioned lie rays of intermediate tints. The decomposition of white light into its coloured constituents, or the dispersion of light, varies according to the *dispersive power* of the refracting substance. It is the more distinct the greater the angle between the extreme red ray and the extreme violet ray.

We have now to consider the dispersion of the light which passes through a precious stone. We will take first the case in which the stone has the form of a plate with parallel sides, as in Fig. 17, and afterwards the case in which these bounding surfaces are inclined to each other and so form a prism.

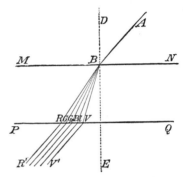

The ray of white light, *AB*, falling obliquely on the surface *MN* of the precious stone, is split up into the differently coloured rays lettered *BR*, *BG*, *BGr*, *BBl*, *BV*. These rays pass out of the precious stone at the surface

FIG. 17. Dispersion of light by a plate with parallel sides.

PQ in the directions *RR'*, *VV'*, &c., all being parallel to the original white ray *AB*, as was explained before in connection with Fig. 14. The eye placed at *R'V'* will receive all these differently coloured rays at the same time and in the same direction; the effect of this will be to produce in the eye the sensation of white light just as if the ray of light from *A* had not passed through the plate. With such a parallel-sided plate, then, a decomposition of white light into its coloured constituents takes place, but is not observable, since the effect produced by the first surface is neutralised by the parallelism imparted to the rays at the second surface.

The dispersion of light produced by a prism, on the other hand, is very noticeable, and is illustrated in Fig. 18. A ray of white light, *AB*, falls upon the surface *MN* of the prism, and is separated into its variously coloured constituents. Between the extreme red ray, *BR*, and the extreme violet ray, *BV*, lie the yellow, green, blue, and rays of intermediate colours. On passing again into air at the second surface, *NP*, of the prism, these rays are again refracted, and emerge still more widely separated.

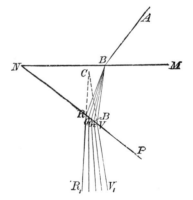

FIG. 18. Dispersion of light by a prism. Formation of the spectrum of white light.

The angle between the extreme red ray *RR₁* and the extreme violet *VV₁* is R_1CV_1; and, as before, this measures the amount of the dispersion, and varies with the substance of which the prism is made. An eye placed at R_1V_1 will receive this bundle of coloured rays, diverging apparently from *C*, the various colours being perfectly distinct and brilliant. The ray of white light thus gives rise to an elongated band of colour which is known as a *spectrum*. The red end of the spectrum lies nearest to the refracting edge, *N*, of the prism, and the violet end furthest away from it; the other colours lying between these two, and following each other with no break or interruption in the same order as the colours of the rainbow, namely, red, orange, yellow, green, blue, indigo, violet. The spectrum may be conveniently shown to a number of persons at once by placing a white screen in the path of the coloured rays.

Fig. 19 gives a perspective view of the path of rays of light from a candle-flame, *A*, through the prism *MNPM'N'P'*. The ray of light *AB* falls on the face *MNM'N'* of the

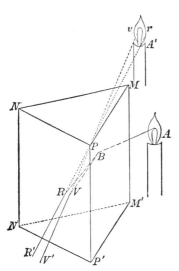

prism, and is resolved into the prismatic colours; the red ray travelling along *BR*, the violet ray along *BV*, and rays of other colours between. These rays inside the prism meet the face *NPN'P'*, and on passing into the air are further refracted and separated, the red ray taking the path *RR'*, the violet *VV'*, and so on. Since rays of light emanate from every luminous part of the candle flame, a complete image of it will be seen at *A'* by an eye placed at *R'V'*. In the direction *V'V* the image will be coloured violet, that is, the side *v* of the image nearer the refracting edge *NN'* of the prism will be violet, while the margin *r* of the image lying on the line *R'R* will be coloured red. To an eye placed at *R'V'* the image will be seen to the left of the actual position of the object, as is shown in Fig. 19; the image is thus nearer the refracting edge of the prism than is the object.

FIG. 19. Path of the rays of light through a prism. (Perspective view.)

The length of the spectrum formed by a prism depends upon a variety of conditions. It is longer the greater the angle between the rays RR^1 and VV^1; this, in its turn, depends upon the dispersive power of the substance of the prism, for the spectra given under similar conditions by two similar prisms, but constructed of different substances, will differ in length. The amount of dispersion produced by a prism will obviously vary with the difference between the degree of refraction of the red rays and of the violet rays; the difference between the refractive indices of a substance for red light and for violet light is indeed frequently regarded as a measure of the dispersive power of the substance.

Amongst precious stones, and indeed the majority of known substances, diamond has by far the greatest dispersive power. The differences in the refractive indices of diamond and of window-glass for red and for violet light, that is the dispersive power of these substances, are given below :

Red light, $n = 2 \cdot 407$
Violet light, $n = 2 \cdot 465$
Dispersive power of diamond $= 2 \cdot 465 - 2 \cdot 407 = 0 \cdot 058$.

For window-glass :

Red light, $n = 1 \cdot 524$
Violet light, $n = 1 \cdot 545$
Dispersive power of glass $= 1 \cdot 545 - 1 \cdot 524 = 0 \cdot 021$.

The dispersion produced by diamond is therefore more than double that produced by window-glass; as a result of this, the spectrum given by a prism of diamond will be more than twice the length of that given by a prism of glass having the same refracting angle. The prismatic colours are transmitted to the eye by diamond widely separated from each other, and the stone owes much of its beauty to this fact; in glass and other substances of less dispersive power, more or less overlapping of the prismatic colours takes place, and this renders them less perceptible to the eye as separate sensations.

The beautiful play of prismatic colours, shown by many precious stones, and especially by diamond, is quite independent of the colour of the stone itself, but is due to the decomposition of white light into its coloured constituents by refraction within the stone. The greater the dispersive power of a stone the more marked will be this play of prismatic colours ; on account of the specially high power of dispersion of diamond, the play of colours exhibited by this gem is far in advance of any other precious stone.

This play of prismatic colours is sometimes, especially by English jewellers, referred to as the "fire" of a stone. The same term, "fire," is, however, also used to denote the brilliancy of lustre of a stone ; it was used in this sense above when dealing with the quality of lustre.

Any two facets of a cut stone which are not parallel may constitute a prism and thus give rise to the decomposition of white light into its coloured constituents. The facets at the back and front of a cut stone should be so related as to give the maximum decomposition of white light. Further, the faces at the back of the stone must be steeply inclined, so that light, entering the stone from the front and being resolved into its component colours, will strike the back faces of the stone at such angles that it is totally reflected by them and passes out again at the front of the stone.

The more perfectly the form of cutting fulfils these conditions, namely, the greatest possible decomposition of white light into its coloured components, and the greatest possible internal reflection of this light from the back facets, the more beautiful will be the cut stone. The form of cutting most suitable for bringing out the beauty of the diamond is that known as the brilliant. This form is shown from different points of view in Figs. 29 and 52 among others, and in section in Fig. 20.

The form of a brilliant will be discussed in detail later ; here it need only be mentioned that its numerous facets give it approximately the shape of a double four-sided pyramid, of which one apex is trunacted by a large plane, the table, and the other by a smaller plane. A brilliant is placed in its setting so that the table *lm* (Fig. 20) is at the front towards the observer, while the small truncating plane *hi* is turned to the back away from the observer.

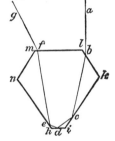

FIG. 20. Path of a ray of light in a brilliant.

The path of a ray of light inside a stone cut as a brilliant is shown in Fig. 20. Let us suppose a ray of light *ab* to fall on the oblique facet *kl*, and to be refracted within the stone in the direction *bc*. The refracted ray *bc* falls very obliquely on the facet *ki*, and forms with the normal to this facet an angle greater than the critical angle of the substance ; it will therefore be totally reflected in the direction *cd*, and *cd* and *cb* will be equally inclined to *ki*. In the same way the ray travelling along *dc* is again totally reflected from the surface *hi* in the direction *de*, and is then reflected from the surface *hn* in the direction *ef*. The ray travelling along *ef* strikes the facet *lm* at a high angle, that is, at an angle less than the critical angle of the substance ; it is therefore possible for it to pass out of the stone into air along the path *fg*. This direction, *fg*, will not, as a rule, coincide with the original direction of the ray *ab*, since in its journey through the stone it has undergone two refractions and three internal reflections. Moreover, as a consequence of the two refractions undergone by the original ray of white light, *ab*, it will be split up into its component colours, and, on emerging from the stone, will present to the observer a beautiful play of prismatic colours. To avoid obscuring the diagram, the different paths of differently coloured rays are not shown in Fig. 20, as they are in Figs. 17 and 18 ; the path, as shown in Fig. 20, may be regarded as the mean path for the several colours, or, more correctly, as the path which would be taken by monochromatic light within the stone. Other rays of light entering the front and side facets of the stone will be refracted and totally reflected in the same manner, and will therefore follow a path very similar in direction to the one shown in Fig. 20. The whole stone will therefore appear to be full of light, and will emit flashes of rainbow colours.

The many beauties of the diamond can be traced back to the optical characters of the stone; its high index of refraction causes a large proportion of the light which enters the front facets of a suitably cut stone to be totally reflected from the back faces, while from its high dispersive power results a wide separation of the rays of differently-coloured light, and, in consequence, a fine play of prismatic colours. These features of a cut diamond are specially noticeable when the stone is contrasted with another colourless stone, cut in the same manner, for example, rock-crystal. The latter appears in comparison dull and dead, owing to the fact that it possesses neither the high index of refraction nor the great dispersive power of the diamond. The highly refractive and dispersive glass called strass, when cut in the form of a brilliant, may, however, closely resemble a diamond in these characters.

From what has been said above, it is easy to see that the cutting of a stone is a very important factor in developing the potential beauty with which its optical characters endow it. A diamond cut in the form of a good brilliant, far exceeds in play of colour and general brilliance a similar stone cut in any other form, such, for instance, as a rosette (rose-cut), which does not fully utilise the optical characters of the stone.

4. Double Refraction of Light.

Hitherto we have considered only those substances in which a single refracted ray corresponds to a single incident ray. There are, however, many bodies, including many precious stones, which have the property of splitting a single incident ray of light into two refracted rays which are propagated in their substance along paths differing slightly in direction.

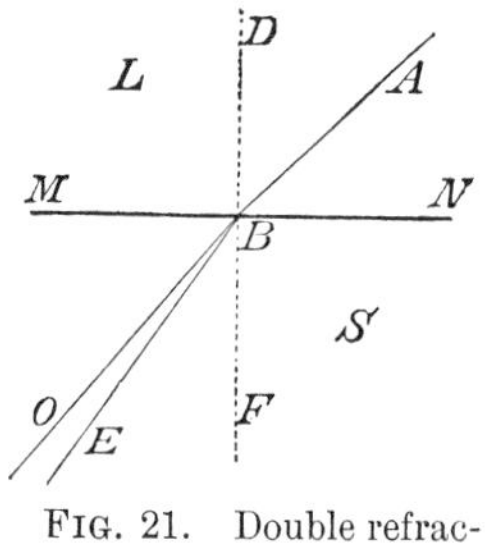

Fig. 21. Double refraction of a ray of light.

In Fig. 21 the ray AB, travelling in air L, is incident upon the surface MN of the stone S at B, where it is split into the two refracted rays BO and BE, inclined to one another at a very small angle OBE, which never exceeds a few degrees.

Bodies which behave towards light in this way are described as being **doubly refracting** or birefringent, in contradistinction to the **singly refracting** bodies hitherto considered. Substances exhibiting the phenomenon of double refraction may also be described as **optically anisotropic,** while those which exhibit single refraction are described as being **optically isotropic.**

As far as regards the transparency, lustre, colour, and play of colour of a stone—those characters in short which affect the beauty of the stone—it is unimportant whether the light within it is singly or doubly refracted.

The phenomenon of double refraction can be easily observed by the aid of special instruments. The detection of its presence or absence is a valuable aid in identifying and discriminating precious stones in the cut condition. Thus by the aid of an appropriate instrument we can decide whether a certain red stone is a doubly refracting ruby or a singly refracting spinel, two stones which, though very similar in appearance, are very dissimilar in rarity and costliness. It is also possible by this means to distinguish glass imitations, which are always singly refracting, from genuine precious stones, which are for the most part doubly refracting.

The kind of refraction, single or double, exhibited by a body is a necessary consequence of the crystalline structure of its substance, and varies in the different crystal systems. All amorphous bodies, together with all those which crystallise in the cubic system, are singly refracting, while all other crystals, without exception, namely, those included in the hexagonal, tetragonal, rhombic, monoclinic, and triclinic systems are doubly refracting. It is thus possible from the behaviour of a stone with respect to the refraction of light to learn whether, on the one hand, it is amorphous or crystallises in the cubic system, or whether, on the other hand, it crystallises in one of the five remaining crystal systems; and this observation can be made on a very small irregular fragment of the mineral. Thus in the example just quoted we know that the singly refracting spinel must crystallise in the cubic system, while the doubly refracting ruby crystallises in one of the remaining five systems, namely, the hexagonal.

Since the observation of the kind of refraction, whether single or double, exhibited by a stone is a step towards determining to which of the crystal systems it belongs, and moreover is frequently a decisive test of its identity, it is important to be acquainted with the method of making this observation. In the third part of this book, dealing specially with the determination of precious stones, considerable use will be made of this method, and it will also be mentioned under the description of each species of precious stone.

In some substances the phenomenon of double refraction is directly observable, for an object, when viewed through a plate of the substance, will appear double instead of single, as is more usually the case, for example with a plate of glass. Each of the two refracted rays *BO* and *BE* (Fig. 21) gives an image of the object; these two images are, as a rule, very close together, but in some few minerals they may be so widely separated as to be both distinctly visible.

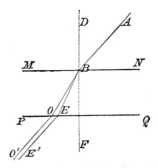

In Fig. 22, let *MNPQ* be a plate of doubly refracting substance with the surface *MN* parallel to the surface *PQ*. The incident ray of light *AB*, striking the surface *MN* at *B*, enters the plate and is split up into the two rays *BO* and *BE*; these emerge from the surface *PQ* in the directions *OO'* and *EE'* both parallel to *AB*. Each of these rays *OO'* and *EE'* gives rise to an image of the source of light, and an eye placed at *O'E'* will see one image along *O'O* and another

FIG. 22. Path of light through a doubly refracting plate.

along *E'E*. Other conditions being equal, these two images will be the more widely separated the thicker the plate is.

A substance which shows the phenomenon of double refraction to a very marked degree is calcite or Iceland-spar, which on this account is also called doubly refracting spar. If a crystal, or, better still, a transparent cleavage rhombohedron of Iceland-spar is placed over an object, such, for instance, as the page of a book, the letters, when viewed through the spar, will appear double, as shown in Fig. 23.

In calcite the two refracted rays are inclined to each other at a comparatively large angle, much greater than in the majority of other minerals. The greater the angle of separation of the two refracted rays (*OBE* in Fig. 21) the greater the double refraction of the mineral, and different substances differ considerably from each other in this respect.

The double refraction of the majority of precious stones is not very strong; and as usually only a small thickness of such substances is available for examination, the two images of an object viewed through the stone will be very close together or partly overlap

FIG. 23.   Double refraction by calcite or doubly refracting spar (German, Doppelspath).

and then tend to appear as a single image.   They would thus, by simply viewing an object through a thin plate, appear to be only singly refracting, whereas in reality they are doubly refracting.

It is possible, however, in such cases to bring about a wider separation of the two images by using a prism instead of a parallel-sided plate of the stone.   This is illustrated in Fig. 24, where, as in the case of single refraction (Fig. 18), the rays of white light are decomposed into rays of differently coloured light.   The ray of light AB, coming from a small flame at A, on entering the prism is split into two rays travelling in the directions BO and BE.   In consequence of dispersion, each of these rays is separated into its coloured components BO_r to BO_v and BE_r to BE_v; and on passing out at the second surface of the prism NP, are again refracted, and thus emerge still more widely separated.   To an eye placed at $O'_r E'_v$, two images of the flame, $O'_r O'_v$ and $E'_r E'_v$, will be visible close together or partly overlapping.   Each image shows the columns of the spectrum of white light as did the image seen through a prism of singly refracting substance; moreover, if thrown on a screen, the red ends, O'_r and E'_r, of both spectra will be nearer the refracting angle of the prism, and the violet ends, O'_v and E'_v, further away.

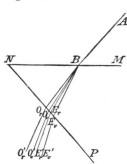

FIG. 24.   Path of light through a doubly refracting prism.

Fig. 25 gives a perspective view of the path of light in a doubly refracting prism, similar to the one given by Fig. 19 in the case of a singly refracting prism.   The two faces of the prism $MNM'N'$ and $NPN'P'$ are inclined together at the refracting angle MNP and intersect in the refracting edge NN'.

A ray, AB, emitted by the centre of the candle flame, A, strikes the face $MNM'N'$ of the prism at B, and is refracted along BO and BE.   These two refracted rays pass out at the second face $NPN'P'$, and take the directions OO' and EE'.   To an eye placed at $O'E'$, two images of the candle flame will be visible in the directions $O'OA^o$ and $E'EA^e$.   Many precious stones show the two images A^o and A^e quite close together, often, indeed, overlapping more or less.   As was the case with the single image given by a singly refracting prism (Fig. 19), each of the double images has a red margin r and a violet margin v.

Now every facet at the front of a cut transparent gem forms with any facet at the back (provided they are not parallel) a prism ; and through every such pair of facets can be seen, when viewed in the proper direction, an image of a small flame. As a matter of fact, a large number of such images will be seen, since for any one facet at the front of the stone there will be several at the back, each of which may form with the front facet a prism and give rise to an image. The images given by singly refracting stones are single, as in Fig. 19, while doubly refracting stones give two images very close together, as shown in Fig. 25. This difference enables us to distinguish a singly refracting from a doubly refracting stone.

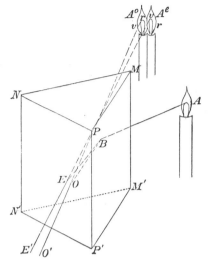

FIG. 25. Path of light through a doubly refracting prism. (Perspective view.)

For this purpose the stone should be held with the largest front facet, namely, the table, close to the eye, and a small flame viewed through it. On turning the stone about, a position will be arrived at when numerous coloured images of the flame become visible, each being single if the stone is singly refracting, or double if it is doubly refracting. Each image, whether double or single, has originated by refraction through a prism formed by one of the facets at the back of the stone and the table at the front. The images seen through a doubly refracting stone are shown in Fig. 26a, while those seen through a singly refracting stone are shown in Fig. 26b.

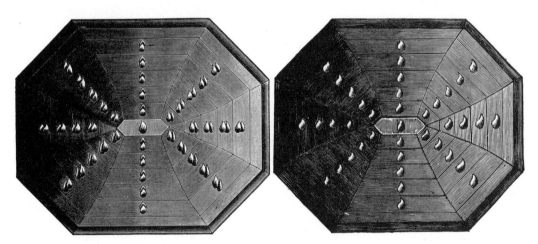

FIG. 26a. Images of a flame observed through a doubly refracting stone.

FIG. 26b. Images of a flame observed through a singly refracting stone.

This experiment is best performed in a dark room so that no light other than that from the small flame passes through the stone.

Instead of using a flame, however, any other convenient object may be observed through the stone, and for this purpose a needle may be used. When the needle is placed in the proper position relative to the stone, there will be seen several coloured single images of it in the case of singly refracting stones, while doubly refracting stones will give coloured double images of the needle. Contrary to the previous case, this experiment must be performed in a lighted room.

When a stone thus examined shows unmistakably double images the fact may be regarded as a decisive proof of the doubly refracting nature of the stone; when, however, single images only are observed the stone cannot be stated to be singly refracting on these grounds alone, for stones which have only feeble double refraction may give double images so close together, or may be overlapping, that to recognise the double character of such images is a matter of considerable difficulty.

The investigation by the direct method of the kind of refraction possessed by a stone thus requires a certain amount of skill, which is only acquired by practice. On this account the re-fraction of stones is often investigated by an indirect method, which has the advantage of being applicable to stones with rounded surfaces, and also to small and irregular fragments of material, neither of which could be used with the method of direct observation. Further, very small cut stones are easily examined by the indirect method, while their examination by the direct method would present difficulties.

The instrument used for the indirect observa-tion of the singly or doubly refracting character of a stone is known as the **polariscope**. A simple form of this instrument, sufficient for the present purpose, is shown, one-third the actual size, in Fig. 27.

This consists of a wooden box, *H*, into the cover, *pp*, of which fits the circular object-carrier, *oo*; the latter consists of a plate of glass in a brass setting, and may be easily rotated. From the box rises the vertical brass rod, *mm*, which carries, on the horizontal arm, *h*, a Nicol's prism,

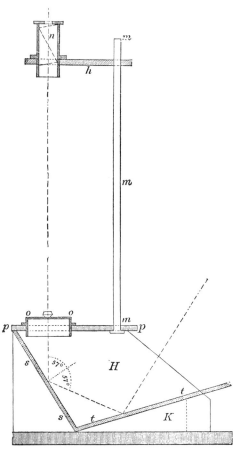

FIG. 27. Polariscope for observation in parallel light. (One third actual size.)

n, constructed of Iceland-spar. This is placed in the same vertical line with the centre of *oo*, and is capable of being rotated in the arm, *h*. In the box, *H*, is fixed, at an angle of 33° with the vertical, a sheet of unsilvered glass, *ss*, or better still, a large number of thin glass plates arranged in a pile. The box also contains an ordinary mirror, *tt*, the inclination of which can be varied by means of the wooden wedge, *K*.

Rays of light from a clear sky enter the open side of the box, as indicated in the figure by the dotted line, and are reflected from the mirror, *tt*, on to the glass plate, *ss*, at an angle of 57° with the normal to the plate, whence they are again reflected in a vertical direction through the object-carrier and the Nicol's prism to the eye of the observer.

Ordinary daylight, after reflection from the glass plate, *ss*, at the particular angle mentioned above, becomes endowed with special properties, and is said to be *polarised*. In other words, the rays of ordinary light which strike the plate, *ss*, are reflected from it as rays of polarised light, and as such reach the Nicol's prism, *n*. On rotating the Nicol's prism, it will be found that in certain positions it does not allow the light reflected from *ss* to pass through, and in these positions the field of view becomes dark, while in other positions it is light. On turning the Nicol's prism through a complete revolution, that is 360°, it will be observed that there are four gradual changes from maximum lightness to maximum darkness or *vice versâ*; the four positions of maximum lightness and maximum darkness being separated by angles of 90°. If the Nicol's prism be turned into one of the two positions in which the field of view has maximum darkness, the polariscope will afford a means whereby singly and doubly refracting stones can be distinguished from each other with ease and certainty.

The different behaviour of singly and doubly refracting substances when examined with the polariscope is as follows : When a singly refracting substance, such as a piece of glass, is placed on the object-carrier, *oo*, and observed through the Nicol's prism, the whole of the field of view will be dark and will remain dark during the rotation of the object-carrier. It should be mentioned here that in this, as well as in all other observations, it is advisable to shade the side light from the object with the hand, or, better still, by means of a tube of black paper placed on the object-carrier and round the object; otherwise light will reach the eye which has been reflected from the surface of the stone without passing through it.

When a doubly refracting body is examined in the same way, it is found that in certain positions the portion of the field which it occupies becomes light. This is due to the fact that the polarised light, which before was unable to pass through the Nicol's prism, becomes so modified by its passage through the doubly refracting substance that it is now capable of passing through the Nicol's prism, when it will reach the eye of the observer. As the object is turned round through 360°, there will be eight changes from maximum lightness to maximum darkness or *vice versâ*; there being four positions of the stone in which the lightness is a maximum, and four in which there is maximum darkness, an interval of 45° lying between each. Through the complete rotation of the object, however, the portion of the field not occupied by it remains dark so long as the Nicol's prism is undisturbed.

There is thus an essential and important difference in the behaviour of singly and doubly refracting stones when examined in polarised light. A singly refracting stone remains dark in the dark field of the polariscope, while a doubly refracting stone changes from light to dark as it is rotated with the object-carrier.

Even in this method, however, there are certain liabilities to error which must be carefully avoided. In all doubly refracting substances the strength of the double refraction is not the same in all directions. Thus the two images of a flame or needle seen through a doubly refracting stone will be further apart when viewed in some directions than in others, while in certain directions a single image only is to be seen. The substance is therefore, along these particular directions, not doubly refracting but singly refracting.

Those directions in a doubly refracting body along which there is only single refraction are known as **optic axes.** All doubly refracting stones can be grouped into two classes: the one containing stones having one optic axis, described as being **optically uniaxial;** and the other containing stones having two optic axes, and described as being **optically biaxial.** The optic axes of any given substance are closely connected both in number and direction with its crystalline form. Thus all hexagonal and tetragonal crystals are uniaxial, and the optic axis of these crystals coincides in direction with the principal crystallographic axis. All rhombic, monoclinic, and triclinic crystals are biaxial, and in the case of rhombic and monoclinic crystals definite relations exist between certain crystallographic and optical directions. Crystals belonging to the remaining system, namely the cubic, are, as mentioned above, optically isotropic, that is, singly refracting.

The fact that doubly refracting crystals are singly refracting along their optic axes must not be forgotten in making observations with the polariscope. A doubly refracting stone, placed in the instrument so that its optic axis coincides with the line of vision, will behave as if it were singly refracting, and will remain dark during a complete rotation of the carrier. A single observation of this kind is therefore not sufficient to prove the singly refracting character of the stone. The probability of a stone being placed in the instrument in this position will, as a rule, be small ; when a stone gives the indications of single refraction, explained above, it should be placed on the carrier in another position and re-examined. A second indication of the same kind may be regarded as conclusive, though in case this second indication should be due to the second optic axis coinciding with the line of vision— a very improbable chance—the stone may be examined in a third position. As a rule, an examination of the stone in two positions will be sufficient to establish its singly refracting character. If, on the other hand, a stone should at the first trial give the indications of a doubly refracting substance, the observation may be regarded as conclusive and further examination is superfluous.

When a stone in the polariscope gives the appearances peculiar to singly refracting substances after examination in two, or even in three, positions, it has been stated above that it may legitimately be concluded that the stone is really singly refracting. We have now to show that, under certain circumstances, such is not the case, and that the stone may be in reality doubly refracting. When a cut stone is examined in the polariscope, the facets on the side turned towards the observer will not be parallel to the facet upon which the stone lies, but they may be very steeply inclined to it. Light travelling vertically upwards from beneath will always be able to enter the stone by the facet on which it lies ; it may, however, strike the upper, steeply inclined facets so obliquely as to be totally reflected and pass out at the sides of the stone, thus never reaching the eye of the observer. The error which this may lead to may be avoided in several ways.

The majority of cut stones have, as shown in Plates II.–IV., a large facet, the table, on one side, and a small facet, the culet, parallel to the table, on the opposite side. If the stone be examined through these two parallel faces, there will be no possibility of internal total reflection. With this object in view, the stone should be placed on the object-carrier so as to rest upon the culet, the table being uppermost ; should the culet be very small the stone may be supported by pieces of wax. With the stone in this position, the light entering it will strike the table perpendicularly and there will thus be no chance of reflection from this facet. Moreover, the position in which the stone rests upon the culet has the further advantage that the whole area of the table is available for the egress of the light which enters the stone by the culet ; whereas, in the reverse position, much of the light which enters by the table will fail to escape by the culet, but will be totally reflected from the side facets.

When a stone, examined in the polariscope in the position just described, gives the indications of a singly refracting substance, this observation, as explained above, cannot be regarded as conclusive, and the stone must be re-examined in another position. In any other position, however, there is a possibility of a doubly refracting stone appearing to be singly refracting owing to total reflection of the light within it. This possibility may be avoided by the following simple device :

The stone is completely immersed in a strongly refracting liquid contained in a small glass vessel placed on the object-carrier. The difference between the index of refraction of the stone and of the surrounding medium will be much less than when the stone was in air, and the result will be, as has already been explained, that a larger proportion of the light will escape total reflection and will pass out of the stone. The amount of light totally reflected will in any case be considerably diminished, but total reflection will not be entirely absent, unless the refractive index of the liquid is exactly the same as that of the stone. In the case of diamond, however, this state of affairs will not exist, since there is no liquid with so high a refractive index.

Liquids used for this purpose should be transparent, not deeply coloured, and of high refractive index. One which fulfils these conditions, and has been already mentioned, is methylene iodide. It is one of the most strongly refracting liquids known, having at the ordinary temperature of 15° to 20° C. an index of refraction of 1·75 for the middle rays of the spectrum; this value for the refractive index is exceeded by only few precious stones, notably the diamond, the index of refraction of which is 2·43. From the upper faces of a feebly refracting stone immersed in methylene iodide there will be no total reflection of light, but this will still take place if a diamond is substituted for the feebly refracting stone. All rays of light, forming with the normal to the surface from which they emerge an angle greater than 46° 19′ (Fig. 13); in other words, all rays travelling vertically upwards will be totally reflected from facets inclined to the horizontal object-carrier of the polariscope at an angle greater than 46° 19′. Total reflection in diamond is thus not eliminated but considerably diminished in amount, the corresponding critical angle for diamond in air being 24° 24′.

A drawback to the use of methylene iodide for this purpose is its high price; monobromonaphthalene is a much cheaper liquid, with a refractive index almost as high as that of methylene iodide; it can therefore be used as a substitute for the latter in optical determinations, but not in determinations of specific gravity, being too light a liquid for this purpose.

It will be well at this point to review the method of using the polariscope for determining the singly or doubly refracting character of a precious stone. The stone is placed on the object-carrier in the dark field of the polariscope and the carrier rotated. If now, all side light being carefully screened off, the field shows alternations of lightness and darkness the stone may be considered to be without doubt doubly refracting. Should the field remain dark during the rotation, the stone must be placed in another position on the object-carrier and again rotated. If this rotation results in alternations of lightness and darkness in the field, the stone is certainly doubly refracting; but should the whole of the field still remain dark we cannot conclude that the stone is singly refracting until it has been proved that the absence of light has not been due to total reflection within the stone. With this object the stone must be examined for the third time, either in the position described above, resting upon the culet and with the table horizontal and uppermost, or immersed in a strongly refracting liquid to diminish or eliminate total reflection. If on rotation the whole of the field still remains dark the stone must be singly refracting. For the examination of stones cut in a spherical form, or those with a rough and irregular surface, it will often be necessary to immerse them in liquid at first. Observations made with the polariscope require no special skill, and with practice and attention to the necessary precautions are very reliable.

Before leaving the subject of refraction certain anomalous cases must be considered. Many singly refracting substances, such, for example, as diamond, occasionally show the appearances peculiar to doubly refracting substances. When this is the case, such substances are said to possess **anomalous double refraction.** The phenomenon is frequently due to internal strains set up on the solidification of the substance or brought about by subsequent causes. These internal strains may be so great in certain crystals, for example those diamonds known as " smoky stones," as to cause such stones to fly to pieces without any apparent reason.

Anomalous double refraction is usually, however, only feeble, and the alternations of lightness and darkness exhibited in the polariscope by minerals exhibiting this character are much less marked than is the case with truly doubly refracting stones. Moreover, the illumination of a doubly refracting body is uniform over the whole of its area ; but in the case of a body showing anomalous double refraction, portions of its area will remain dark during the complete rotation of the carrier, while the portions which become alternately light and dark during the rotation appear as stripes and bands, or in variously shaped sectors. It is thus a comparatively easy matter to distinguish between anomalous and true double refraction.

The phenomenon now under consideration sometimes affords a means whereby a glass imitation may be distinguished from a genuine precious stone. While glass under ordinary conditions is singly refracting, being an isotropic substance, unannealed glass possesses anomalous double refraction. Thus if a fairly thick plate of glass be first strongly heated and then suddenly cooled, internal strains will be set up, and when examined in the polariscope it will show a more or less regular black cross, with the two arms at right angles, sometimes surrounded by coloured circles. Should a supposed precious stone show this or a similar appearance, the observer may regard it as conclusive evidence against the genuineness of the stone.

The refraction of a precious stone is expressed, as explained above, by a number known as its refractive index. In the case of singly refracting substances there is, for monochromatic light, only one refractive index, which is constant for every direction in the stone. The index of refraction of a doubly refracting substance, however, varies according to the direction. It is greatest in one particular direction and least in a direction at right angles to this. These maximum and minimum values vary slightly for differently coloured light, but are constant for monochromatic light. The greater the difference between the greatest and the least values of the refractive indices of a precious stone, the greater will be its double refraction, which is measured by this difference.

The number which thus expresses the strength of the double refraction of a substance is constant for, and characteristic of, that substance, and could be made use of for purposes of identification. Its exact determination is, however, a matter of considerable difficulty and requires special and costly instruments, as well as suitable preparation of the stone to be examined. This method is therefore of no practical value to jewellers.

The refractive indices of the more important precious stones are given in the following table, the values for singly refracting stones being indicated by n, and the greatest and least values for doubly refracting stones by n_g and n_l respectively. In both cases the values apply to the middle rays of the spectrum. The strength of the double refraction of each stone is indicated by $d = n_g - n_l$, that is, by the difference between the greatest and the least refractive indices of the stone.

(a) Singly Refracting Precious Stones.

	n		n
Diamond	2·43	Spinel	1·72
Pyrope	1·79	Opal	1·48
Almandine	1·77	Fluor-spar	1·44
Hessonite	1·74		

(b) Doubly Refracting Precious Stones.

	n_μ	n_l	d
Zircon	1·97	1·92	0·05
Ruby	1·77	1·76	0·01
Sapphire . . .			
Chrysoberyl . . .	1·76	1·75	0·01
Chrysolite . . .	1·70	1·66	0·04
Tourmaline . . .	1·64	1·62	0·02
Topaz	1·63	1·62	0·01
Beryl	1·58	1·57	0·01
Quartz	1·55	1·54	0·01

5. Colour.

An important character of precious stones not yet touched upon is colour. The beauty of opaque and lustreless stones, such as the turquoise, depends wholly upon this character. Every shade of colour is represented among minerals used as precious stones and for ornamental purposes. As has already been mentioned, stones which are perfectly colourless and also perfectly transparent are described as being water-clear, or of the first water.

In the majority of cases colour is a very variable character; there are, however, examples amongst minerals in which the colour is a fixed and essential character, appearing the same whether the mineral is in the largest masses or reduced to the finest powder. Such a stone would be described as being **idiochromatic**, it having a colour of its own, which is essential and characteristic of the mineral. As an example of an idiochromatic stone, malachite, which is always green whether in mass or in powder, may be quoted.

The majority of precious stones are, if perfectly pure, completely colourless. But this purity of composition is, as a rule, not attained, and thus, owing to the admixture of foreign colouring-matter, such stones occur much more frequently coloured than colourless. The colour, being thus due to accidental impurities, may vary in different specimens of the same stone, or even in different portions of the same specimen, and must therefore be regarded as a non-essential character. Stones in which colour is a variable character are distinguished as **allochromatic**, and the foreign matter, to which their colouring is due, may be regarded as pigment. Different pigments give rise to differently coloured specimens of the same mineral species. Such specimens show their colour best in fragments of some thickness; in very thin splinters, or in fine powder, they appear only faintly coloured or even completely colourless.

The variety of colour exhibited by quartz well illustrates the fortuitous nature of this character when due to impurities. Thus, rock-crystal is transparent and water-clear quartz, smoky-quartz is brown, amethyst is violet quartz, citrine is yellow quartz, green quartz is known as plasma, blue quartz as sapphire-quartz, and there are still other coloured varieties, with special names. Again, the mineral corundum, which sometimes occurs colourless, is known as ruby when red and as sapphire when blue; it is also found of many other colours, which will be mentioned in the special description of corundum. Though diamond, in its most valuable condition, is water-clear, yet specimens of every shade of colour are found.

The range of colour shown by any one allochromatic mineral is known as its **suite of colours.** Thus the suite of colours shown by quartz includes brown, violet, yellow, green, blue, &c.; that by corundum includes red and blue and many others. The suite of colours shown by any one mineral will not usually be shown by any other; in nearly every case certain colours will be unrepresented in the suite.

In minerals in which the lustre is other than metallic, a group which comprises nearly all precious stones, eight principal colours may be recognised for the purposes of descriptive mineralogy; these colours are white, grey, black, blue, green, yellow, red, and brown. Intermediate colours may be described by terms compounded of the names of the eight principal colours; as, for instance, reddish-white, greenish-blue, bluish-black, &c. The different shades or tints shown by each of the principal colours are indicated by a descriptive prefix; as, for example, sulphur-yellow, grass-green, indigo-blue, smoke-grey, carmine-red, &c. The colour of a mineral can be judged more correctly by observing it close to the eye, when small differences in colour will be more apparent.

The character of the colour shown by a mineral depends partly on the lustre and transparency of the specimen; it may be described by terms in use in ordinary language, such as lively, warm, fresh, dull, delicate, soft, dirty, dusky, &c. The intensity of the colour shown by a mineral also varies in different specimens; it may be described as deep or dark, when approaching to black; high or full, when pure and intense; light, when approaching to white; finally, as pale, when more nearly approaching to white. In speaking of some precious stones, for example the ruby, it was formerly the custom to describe specimens with a deep or full colour as "masculine," and those with a lighter colour as "feminine." These terms have now, however, fallen into disuse.

Intensity of colour depends on the amount of colouring-matter present; the greater this is, the deeper will be the colour of the stone. When the pigment of a stone is distributed equally throughout its mass, the stone will be uniformly coloured. If, on the contrary, the pigment is present in some parts and absent in others, or present in varying amounts in different parts of the stone, the latter will show corresponding differences in colour.

One and the same stone may be differently coloured in different parts owing to the presence of different pigments; thus sapphire often shows blue spots or patches on a colourless background, and amethyst may show violet areas also on a colourless background. The irregular distribution of colour in such stones detracts considerably from their beauty; specimens of precious stones in which the colour is intense and distributed with perfect uniformity are therefore specially valuable.

The distribution of colour in any one kind of stone is sometimes remarkably constant, appearing repeatedly in a large number of specimens. Thus in the four-sided columns of diopside from the Zillerthal in the Tyrol, which are sometimes used as gems, one end is colourless and the other of a fine, dark, bottle-green colour. In the same way the hexagonal prisms of red, green, or almost colourless tourmaline from Elba frequently have a black termination (so-called negro-heads). A regular arrangement of different colours in the same crystals is sometimes seen in tourmaline, as illustrated in Plate XV., Figs. 8 and 9, where the central portion is red and the external portion green, the two colours being sharply separated from each other. The beauty of agate is due to the arrangement of its various colours in bands. The following terms are used in describing colour distribution: spotted, mottled, clouded, veined, marbled, striated, banded, &c.

Brown or black arborescent, or tree-like, markings are frequently seen in certain specimens of chalcedony, and are described as *dendritic markings*. Stones showing such markings are known as dendrites. They are cut and polished with the object of bringing out the markings as prominently as possible (Fig. 89). Dendrites, among which is moss-agate with its peculiar and moss-like distribution of green colouring-matter, will be further considered in dealing with opal, chalcedony, &c.

The various **pigments** to which the colouring of precious stones is due may be organic or inorganic, and differ much in character. They may exist in considerable amount, but more frequently they are present in such small quantities that very exact chemical analysis is necessary for their detection. In the latter case, the colouring-power of the pigment must be comparable to that of carmine and some other pigments, an extremely small quantity of which is capable of giving a decided colour to an enormous quantity of a colourless substance.

The precise nature of the colouring-matter of many precious stones it has been impossible as yet to determine. Large quantities of the precious stones would be needed to yield an amount of colouring-matter sufficient for a reliable analysis, and here lies the chief obstacle to the investigation. In spite of this difficulty it has been possible in some cases to determine definitely to what substance the colouration is due. Thus, for example, the emerald owes its green colour to the presence, in small quantity, of a compound of the metal chromium, while the apple-green colour of chrysoprase is due to a compound of the metal nickel. Other stones are coloured by compounds of iron or copper; while the brown colour of smoky-quartz is due to an organic substance, which can be distilled off as a dark brown oil, possessing an empyreumatic odour.

The colouring-matter of precious stones is frequently distributed so intimately and uniformly through their substance that it is impossible, with the strongest magnification, to distinguish single particles of the pigment. The relation between the substance of the precious stone and the pigment seems analogous to that which exists between a solvent and a substance dissolved in it. In such cases, it is inferred that the colouring-matter is not an essential constituent of the substance of the stone from the fact that specimens of other colours, or devoid of colour, are known. This intimate association of the pigment with the ground substance of the stone exists, for example, in the green emerald, in the blue opaque turquoise, the colour in the latter case being due to compounds of copper and iron; as also in diopside, the green colour of which is given by a compound of ferrous oxide.

In most of these cases we are dealing with something more intimate than a mere mechanical mixture. The colouring-matter is isomorphous with the ground substance of the precious stone, that is, it has the same type of chemical formula, and when this is the case, the intermixing of the two substances involves not microscopically small particles of each but the ultimate particles or molecules of each substance. Thus to take diopside as an example, we must picture the molecules of the compound of ferrous oxide distributed uniformly between the molecules of the ground substance of the stone and imparting to it its characteristic green colour. The same may perhaps be said of emerald which belongs to the mineral species beryl, specimens of which sometimes occur colourless; also of turquoise and many other precious stones.

In other stones, on the contrary, the colour is due to vast numbers of minute coloured particles, with definite boundaries, mechanically intermixed with the colourless ground-mass of the stone. These particles may be large enough to be just perceptible to the naked eye, or so small as to require a lens or microscope for their detection; they may have the form of grains, scales, fibres, or needles. Small blue grains distributed in large numbers through the colourless ground-mass of lapis-lazuli give to this precious stone its fine blue colour. Green needles and fibres of the mineral actinolite give rise to the green colour of prase, a variety of quartz, which of itself is colourless. Felspar is sometimes coloured red by minute scales of iron-glance (hæmatite), and is then used as an ornamental stone under the name of sun-stone: chalcedony, coloured by a similar red pigment, is the much used carnelian.

Stones coloured in this manner, by the mechanical intermixture of particles of pigment, are more or less cloudy or even opaque; those, on the contrary, in which a more intimate or chemical relation between the colouring-matter and the ground-substance is possible, are clear and transparent.

The **apparent change of colour** shown by many precious stones when exposed to different kinds of illumination is worthy of remark. In most cases the colour seen in clear day-light is the most beautiful, the appearance by artificial light being less pleasing. Thus amethyst by day-light is of a beautiful purple colour, but in candle-light it appears dull grey. Purple corundum or " oriental amethyst," on the contrary, shows its fine colour as well by candle-light as by day-light. Specially peculiar in this respect is the variety of chrysoberyl, known as alexandrite, which, as we shall see later on, is green in day-light and red in candle-light. Yellow diamonds retain their colour in the electric light, but appear colourless in candle-light. Many other stones afford similar examples of a change in colour accompanied by a loss of beauty in artificial light, a property which naturally diminishes the value they might otherwise possess.

The possibility of temporarily masking the colour of yellowish diamonds has, in recent years, frequently led to fraud. Since the discovery of the South African mines, yellowish diamonds are fairly abundant, and therefore comparatively cheap, while perfectly colourless stones command a high price. By giving these yellowish stones a very thin coating of some blue colouring-matter, they can be made to appear colourless, the mixture of blue and yellow light rays producing on the eye the effect of white light. As soon, however, as the blue coating is worn off the fraud becomes apparent.

Not only an apparent, but an **actual change of colour,** may be experienced by some precious stones. As a rule, the colours of precious stones are extremely lasting, only disappearing with the destruction of the stone itself, this being, for example, the case with the yellow diamond, the ruby, emerald, and others. The colour of other stones, however, is less constant, and may be completely destroyed, the substance of the stone undergoing no change in the process. The colouring of such a stone will frequently disappear when the stone is raised to a red heat or even less; this will invariably happen if the colouring-matter is organic in nature, since it will be decomposed at such a temperature. Brown smoky-quartz and reddish-yellow hyacinth behave in this way, becoming completely colourless when heated to redness. Other stones on being heated experience not a loss but a change of colour; thus the violet amethyst becomes yellow, and the dark yellow topaz becomes rose-red in colour. These particular changes in colour are sometimes brought about intentionally in order to obtain yellow quartz (" burnt amethyst ") and rose-red topaz (rose topaz), both of which are used as cut stones, but occur in nature to only a small extent.

Many stones show characteristic changes in colour during the progress of a rise and fall in temperature. Thus the red ruby, at a high temperature, is colourless; on cooling it first becomes green, after which it gradually assumes its original fine red colour. The red spinel behaves somewhat differently under similar conditions; at a high temperature it becomes colourless, and on cooling it regains its original colour, so far resembling the behaviour of the ruby, but at the intermediate temperature it assumes not a green but a violet tint. A high temperature is not invariably necessary to effect a change of colour in precious stones; some stones are so sensitive that their colour fades or disappears merely on exposure to light and air. Certain topazes behave in this way, and after a few months exposure will be recognisably paler in colour; the same phenomenon may be observed in green chrysoprase and in rose-quartz, as well as in some blue turquoises, the colour of the latter of which may gradually change to green. Obviously the value of such stones will be considerably diminished, since it is difficult, if not impossible, to avoid a rapid loss of colour, and therefore of beauty, when they are used under ordinary conditions. Colour lost in this way may sometimes be restored by keeping the stone in darkness, by burying it in moist earth, or by treating it with certain chemicals, all of which devices are made use of by unscrupulous dealers. As a contrast to the behaviour of such stones on exposure to light, it may be mentioned here that amber, instead of being bleached by exposure, is darkened, gradually becoming of a dark, reddish-brown colour.

The **artificial colouring** or recolouring of precious stones, which was known and practised to some extent among the ancients, is of some importance. At the present day agate and similar stones are most frequently subjected to this treatment, the exact methods of which will be dealt with under the special description of these stones. The capacity for absorbing the liquid which imparts its colour to the stone, often even to the central portions, depends on the porous nature of its substance.

Streak.—In speaking above of idiochromatic and allochromatic minerals, we have seen that in the former the fine powder of the mineral is also coloured, the colour being characteristic of the mineral. For the purpose of quickly and easily obtaining a mineral in the state of fine powder, it is rubbed on a plate of rough, unglazed, " biscuit " porcelain. The line of powder left upon the plate by the mineral is known as its streak, the colour of which can be easily observed on the white background. The streak is often characteristic of a mineral, and thus the observation of the streak is a step towards the determination of the mineral. The character is not of much practical value in the determination of precious stones, since on account of their hardness they are much more likely to scratch the porcelain than to leave a streak upon it ; moreover, the streak of most precious stones, as in other allochromatic minerals, is white, and therefore not a distinguishing feature.

6. Dichroism.

An important optical property of many precious stones is that known as dichroism or pleochroism. A stone possessing this property, when observed in different directions will show different colours or shades of colour which may resemble each other more or less closely, or may, on the other hand, differ considerably. A mineral sometimes used as a cut stone, and known as " water-sapphire," exhibits this phenomenon to such a marked degree that it has received the name dichroite, although at the present time it is usually known to mineralogists as cordierite. A crystal of this mineral, when viewed in three particular directions, perpendicular to each other, appears of three distinct colours, namely, a fine dark blue, light blue, and greyish-yellow. In intermediate directions are seen intermediate tints, which approach one or other of the three principal colours according to the direction of the line of view. The three particular directions along which these maximum differences in colour are observable are definitely related to the crystalline form of the mineral ; they are in fact the three crystallographic axes of the rhombic crystal.

The difference in colour shown by cordierite when viewed in different directions is very great, but it is perhaps even greater in some kinds of tourmaline. In this mineral the colour, as seen in different directions through a crystal, varies from yellowish-brown to asparagus-green, or in other crystals (of the same mineral) between dark violet-brown and greenish-blue, or again in others between purple-red and blue, &c. Some dichroic precious stones show only very small differences in colour when viewed in different directions ; the yellowish-green chrysolite is an example. Indeed the majority of pale coloured stones are only feebly dichroic, stronger dichroism being exhibited by minerals having a deeper tone of colour.

Finally there are other minerals, such as garnet and spinel, which show no differences of colour in different directions ; these precious stones behave in this respect like their glass imitations.

Taking refraction as the basis of classification, we have seen that all minerals can be divided into two groups, namely, those which possess single refraction and those which possess double refraction. The former group will include those minerals which are not possessed of dichroism, while all dichroic minerals fall into the latter. Thus amorphous substances and those which crystallise in the cubic system are characterised by single refraction and absence of dichroism, while all coloured minerals included in the remaining five crystal systems are dichroic, and all without exception are doubly refracting.

The phenomenon of dichroism then, furnishes us with additional aid in distinguishing singly from doubly refracting stones. A body showing this character to even the feeblest degree cannot be amorphous nor can it be a cubic mineral. The apparent absence of dichroism however must be considered only as negative evidence in favour of single refraction, since dichroism may be present but so feeble as to be detected only with difficulty. It has been shown above that the phenomena of double and of single refraction enables us to distinguish a ruby from a red spinel, and this is made still more easy from the fact that the hexagonal ruby is distinctly dichroic, while the cubic spinel does not possess this property. In the same way an imitation ruby of red glass could not be confused with the genuine stone, since the former, being amorphous, is not dichroic and shows the same colour in all directions.

The detection of dichroism usually requires the use of a special instrument. The most convenient instrument for the purpose is that devised by the Viennese mineralogist Haidinger, and known as a **dichroscope.** This instrument is inexpensive and easily used, and should be in the hand of every one who buys or sells precious stones, since a single glance through it is sufficient to establish the presence or absence of dichroism in a stone.

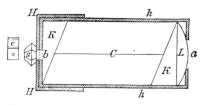

FIG. 28. The dichroscope. (Actual size.)

This instrument is shown in section, and of its actual size, in Fig. 28. It consists essentially of a cleavage rhombohedron, C, of Iceland-spar (calcite), which is longer in one direction than in others. At each of its oblique ends is cemented a glass prism or wedge, K, the outer surfaces of which are perpendicular to the long edge of the calcite rhombohedron. A brass tube, h, encloses these essential portions of the instrument, and has at one end a small square aperture, b, and at the other a circular aperture, a. Between the circular aperture and the glass prism, K, is placed a lens, L, of such a focal length that on looking through the instrument in the direction ab a sharp image of the square aperture, b, will be seen. This image will, however, owing to the intervention of the doubly refracting calcite, not be single, but double. The instrument is so proportioned that these two images, o and e, will appear side by side, in contact but not overlapping. The image o will be only slightly displaced from the axis of the instrument and will be quite colourless ; the image e is rather more displaced, and shows a narrow red border on its inner edge and a narrow blue border on its outer edge, as indicated by striations in the small figure at the side, otherwise the image is colourless. The instrument is so constructed that the distance of the square aperture from the lens can be varied, which enables the images to be sharply focused and adjusted so that their edges are in contact.

In using this instrument, the precious stone to be tested for dichroism is placed over the square aperture, b, and, the instrument being directed towards a clear sky, the observer places his eye close to the round aperture, a. An object-carrier, H, is sometimes provided for the purpose of more conveniently holding the stone. This has the form of a brass tube fitting loosely over the tube, h, and having the closed end perforated by an aperture somewhat larger than the square aperture, b, over which the stone can be fixed with wax, as shown in the figure. This arrangement allows the carrier H, with the stone attached, to be rotated while the calcite rhombohedron remains unmoved. Should this carrier not be provided, the stone may be fixed by wax to a glass-plate, or simply held in the fingers in front of the square aperture, and the instrument rotated in the hand.

If the stone under examination is not dichroic, the two images o and e will be of the same colour and will show no variation while the instrument or the stone is rotated through 360°. If, for example, a red garnet, which crystallises in the cubic system, is examined, the two images o and e will both be of the same red colour as is the garnet itself when viewed without the aid of the instrument.

The images o and e given by a dichroic stone, on the contrary, will be in general differently coloured. In four particular positions, however, at 90° apart, the colours of the two images are identical. On rotating the stone or the instrument a difference between the colours appears, which gradually increases and reaches a maximum at 45° from the original position. Further rotation will again result in a gradual decrease in the colour difference, and at 90° from the original position the colours of the two images once more become identical. The same changes occur during the rotation through the remaining quadrants, and thus a complete rotation of 360° is accompanied by eight changes from identity of colour in the two images to maximum difference in colour between them and vice versâ. The juxtaposition of the two images makes it possible to detect the smallest differences in colour, and consequently the slightest degree of dichroism.

We have previously seen that doubly refracting crystals are singly refracting along the direction of an optic axis; similarly dichroic crystals exhibit no dichroism in these directions. To prove the absence of dichroism in a crystal it is therefore necessary to examine it in two directions, or, as an additional precaution, in a third direction also. After each observation the stone must be fixed on the holder, H, in a new position and again rotated. The absence of dichroism can be conclusively proved only after an examination of the stone in at least three different positions. The dichroism of a stone may be so feeble that it is not possible to detect it even with the aid of a dichroscope; moreover, it must be borne in mind that a coloured doubly refracting stone is not necessarily dichroic, and this feature is naturally absent in colourless doubly refracting stones. The real or apparent absence of dichroism in a stone is therefore no proof of its singly refracting character, but the presence of dichroism is, on the contrary, a conclusive proof of the doubly refracting nature of the stone.

The degree of dichroism in a crystal varies according to the direction through which the crystal is observed. The colours of the two images seen in the dichroscope in the examination of all dichroic stones become the more nearly identical as the optic axis of the stone becomes more nearly coincident with the axis of the instrument. Conversely, the greater the angle between the axis of the dichroscope and the optic axis of the stone the more marked will become the difference in colour between the two images. The two colours between which there is the maximum difference are known as the principal or axial colours; these colours, as seen through the dichroscope, differ in tint from the colours the stone shows when observed with the naked eye in the same direction. Uniaxial dichroic crystals, such as tourmaline, show two principal colours, while biaxial crystals, such as cordierite, show three. The pairs of colours, other than the axial or principal colours, shown by a precious stone in the dichroscope are due to various combinations of the principal colours. The axial colours of each precious stone will be given below along with their special descriptions.

The detection of dichroism in a coloured stone is a simpler matter than the observation of double refraction, and the dichroscope is a less expensive instrument than the polariscope, hence the former is the more often used. The polariscope may also be used to detect the presence or absence of dichroism by removing the Nicol's prism, n (Fig. 27), and placing the stone to be tested on the object-carrier. If the stone is not dichroic, as for instance spinel, there will be no change of colour as it is rotated with the object-carrier. If, on the contrary, a dichroic stone, such as ruby, is examined in this way, the colour will be seen to change as the stone is rotated, varying between two extremes; the change from one extreme to the other will occur four times during a complete rotation of 360°. These two colours are identical with those seen when the stone is examined in the same position in a dichroscope; the advantage of the latter instrument lies in the fact that the two colours can be seen side by side, and thus small differences between them more easily detected. Just as in the use of the dichroscope, several observations must be made before the absence of dichroism can be considered to have been conclusively proved. As explained before, in using the polariscope the portion of the field occupied by the stone may remain dark owing to the total reflection of light within the stone. This can be avoided as before, by placing the stone in a certain position or immersing it in a strongly refracting liquid. Care must also be taken that all side light, which might be reflected from the surface of the stone, is screened off with the hand, or by means of a paper tube placed around the stone.

As we have already seen, dichroism is a character of which important use can be made in identifying precious stones, and in distinguishing them from each other and from glass imitations. Moreover, its observation does not necessitate a mounted stone being removed from its setting, which would often be necessary in the observation of other optical characters.

Dichroism is a character of precious stones which is important also from other points of view, such as that of the lapidary. A stone in which dichroism is strong must be so cut that the rays of light received by the observer have passed through the stone in a direction such that they will appear of the finest colour possible. Such a stone as cordierite, for example, must be so cut that the dark blue colour is prominently brought out, which will give a far more pleasing effect than if the light blue or yellowish-grey were predominant. The beauty and, consequently, the value of two pleochroic stones of the same size and quality will accordingly depend upon the manner in which they are cut, and hence a knowledge of the dichroic properties of stones is of importance to the gem-cutter.

Dichroic stones are sometimes cut and mounted in a manner which will bring out this character as prominently as possible. With this object in view a cube is fashioned out of the stone, the faces of which are perpendicular to the directions in which the greatest differences in colour are exhibited. Such cubes are pivoted at one corner, so that on being turned round the different colours will successively come into view. Cordierite, andalusite, and other stones are cut and mounted in this way, as will be explained in more detail later.

7. Special Optical Appearances and Colour Effects.

In this section we shall consider certain optical peculiarities and colour effects of a special and more or less abnormal kind; these features are not shown by every specimen of a particular mineral species, but only by isolated examples. These appearances are governed by the ordinary laws of reflection and refraction of light, and are due to the peculiar and unusual conditions present in each case. The exact nature of these conditions, and the manner in which they cause the abnormal appearances, is not completely known in every case; as full an explanation as is possible will be given in the description of each particular case.

The **play of prismatic colours** exhibited by the diamond has already been dealt with in detail; we have here the simplest case of the refraction and dispersion of light.

The prismatic colours produced by cracks in the interior of a transparent stone, and best shown in colourless examples, gives rise to the appearance usually known as **iridescence.** The irregular fissures, or more frequently the plane cleavage cracks, inside a crystal represent narrow crevices, which may be vacuous or filled with air; these films give rise to the brilliant prismatic colours known as Newton's rings, or as the colours of thin films or plates. These colours, which are shown to perfection by soap-bubbles, are independent of the colour of the substance itself, or of any colouring-matter contained in it, but are due to purely physical causes connected with the passage of white light through the film. The phenomenon which thus gives rise to the appearance of prismatic colours is known to physicists as the interference of light.

Some iridescent stones, such as rock-crystal, are occasionally cut so as to bring the crack, to which the display of prismatic colours is due, near the surface, and thus render them the more striking. Especially beautiful prismatic colours are shown by some kinds of colourless opal, namely, the so-called noble or precious opal (Plate XVI., Figs. 6–9). These colours are not shown over the whole surface of the stone, but in small discontinuous patches, closely aggregated. This appearance in opal is certainly a kind of iridescence, but as to its exact cause there is still a difference of opinion.

The translucent or semi-transparent variety of potash-felspar or orthoclase, known as adularia, sometimes shows a bluish or milky reflection of light, not from the whole surface but only from certain crystallographic planes. This opalescent appearance is specially prominent when the stone is cut and polished with a rounded convex surface, over which, when the gem is moved, a streak or wave of such reflected light passes. This appearance. being specially pronounced in adularia, is sometimes known as **adularescence.** It has been compared to the soft light of the moon, and specimens showing it to perfection are called moon-stones (Plate XVI., Figs. 4 and 5), and are often used for ornamental purposes. The pearly opalescence of adularia is due to reflection of light from internal platy fractures or planes of separation, and from microscopically small crystal plates embedded in the adularia along these planes.

A similar appearance is shown by some specimens of chrysoberyl, which are also valued as precious stones under the name of cymophane or cat's-eye (Plate XII., Fig. 11), since the sheen of this green, yellowish-green, or brown stone recalls the appearance of the eye of the cat. We shall see later on that there is a variety of quartz having this same appearance; the chrysoberyl variety is therefore distinguished as true or " oriental cat's-eye."

The brilliant colours shown on certain faces of labradorite, a felspar from Labrador (Plate XVI., Fig. 2), as well as by a potash-felspar from Fredriksvärn in southern Norway (Plate XVI., Fig. 3), is also, like adularescence, due to the presence of numerous minute crystal plates enclosed in the felspar and arranged parallel to these planes. The appearance resulting from the peculiar structure of these minerals is known as **change of colours** or **labradorescence.** In most positions these minerals are dull grey and unattractive looking, but certain faces in reflected light, and at a certain inclination to the light, show the most brilliant shades of green, blue, violet, red, yellow, &c. The small plates, which give rise to the reflection of coloured light, may be seen under the microscope embedded in the material; they consist of an unknown substance which is very feebly refracting, but it is possible, however, that some are mere vacuities. The whole of the polished surface of such a mineral may reflect the same colour, or different areas of the surface may show different colours. Except with a particular inclination of the light, however, no colour of any kind is seen. On account of this beautiful exhibition of colour, Labrador felspar is more often used for ornamental purposes than is the felspar of Fredriksvärn, the colour of which is less brilliant and variable.

On certain faces of the minerals hypersthene, bronzite, and diallage, when viewed in a particular direction in reflected light, is to be seen a **metallic sheen**, uniform in character over the whole surface. These minerals consist of non-metallic substances, and the metallic lustre seen on certain faces is due to the presence of numerous minute plates embedded in the substance of the mineral, parallel to certain directions. When cut and polished with a plane or curved surface parallel to these directions, these minerals are sometimes used as ornamental stones. Hypersthene shows a fine, dark, copper-red reflection; while in the other minerals grey, yellow, green, and brown colours are predominant.

A red metallic glittering sheen is also exhibited by avanturine-quartz; here, however, it is not distributed uniformly over the whole surface, but occurs in numerous small isolated points. These can be seen with the naked eye to be due to small scales of mica enclosed in the quartz; in the same way, avanturine-felspar, or sun-stone, encloses small plates or scales of hæmatite.

Beautiful effects due to the modification of light are sometimes seen in minerals which possess a more or less pronounced fibrous structure. Such stones when cut with rounded surfaces in the direction of the fibres exhibit a wave of milky light travelling over the surface of the stone as it is moved about. Ordinary cat's-eye, also known as quartz-cat's-eye (Plate XVIII., Figs. 4a and 4b), consists of quartz enclosing numerous fibres of asbestos all arranged in the same direction; the asbestos may sometimes have been weathered out, in which case the quartz will be penetrated by numerous fine hollow canals. These fibres or canals cause much the same appearance as that seen in adularia and cymophane (oriental cat's-eye), and in this case it also is known as **opalescence** or **chatoyancy**. Quartz-cat's-eye may be green, brown, or yellow, and is similar in appearance to the true or oriental cat's-eye. This similarity does not extend to the structure which is the cause of this appearance, for the sheen of quartz-cat's-eye is in reality of the nature of a fine silky lustre, such as is often shown by minerals possessing a fibrous structure, the character of which is modified, however, in the present case, by the nature of the quartz itself. Another variety of fibrous quartz is tiger-eye which is often used for cheap jewellery; it shows a fine golden reflection, and has a marked tendency to metallic lustre (Plate XVIII., Fig. 5).

The appearance known as **asterism** belongs to the same class of phenomena; it is most frequently seen in ruby and sapphire among precious stones, but is not confined to these. When one of the hexagonal crystals of ruby or sapphire (Fig. 53, e–i) has a plane or curved surface cut at the ends, a six-rayed star may be seen by viewing a flame through the stone, or by observing the milky reflection from the surface of the stone. Such stones are known as star-, or asteriated-sapphires or rubies as the case may be, or simply as star-stones or asterias. The effect is produced by reflection of light from a multitude of extremely fine, hollow and long canals. These canals lie in one plane, and are arranged in three directions inclined to one another at 120°. The planes which contain the canals are perpendicular to the principal crystallographic (vertical) axis of the crystal, that is, they are parallel to the plane in which the stone must be cut. According to another view, the star is due to the reflection from numerous twin-lamellæ arranged in three sets.

Finally, the phenomena of fluorescence and phosphorescence must be briefly described, though they are of little importance in the case of minerals used as precious stones.

Fluorescence is shown to a marked degree by fluor-spar from the lead mines of Cumberland ; the phenomenon, indeed, takes its name from this mineral, which is known to mineralogists as fluor or fluorite. A fluorescent substance appears of one colour in transmitted light and of quite another in reflected light ; thus fluor-spar from Cumberland is green in transmitted light and purple in reflected light. This mineral is, however, very little used as a precious stone ; one which is used more frequently for this purpose is amber, and specimens from certain localities, namely from Sicily and Burma, show a remarkable fluorescence. Amber from these localities varies in colour from yellow to brown in transmitted light, and from green to blue in reflected light. The rounded polished surface of such specimens shows a peculiar sheen, which, according to present tastes, diminishes the beauty of the stone, and consequently its value.

Substances in which the phenomenon of **phosphorescence** is seen emit, when submitted to certain external influences, a soft, white or coloured light which is often only distinctly visible in a dark room. In some cases the emission of light persists for some time, while in others it lasts for a much shorter time, perhaps for only a few moments. Phosphorescence is exhibited by several precious stones, and may therefore aid in their recognition or discrimination. Two pieces of rock-crystal (quartz) phosphoresce when rubbed one against another ; diamond shows a marked phosphorescence when rubbed on cloth ; even when lightly rubbed on a coat-sleeve it will be seen in the dark to phosphoresce brilliantly. Many diamonds also phosphoresce after being exposed to the direct rays of the sun ; they store up the sunlight, as it were, in order to give it out again when placed in darkness. Lapis-lazuli from Chili phosphoresces when warmed to a temperature considerably less than that of red-heat ; white topaz, some diamonds, and other minerals behave in the same way. In many minerals the phosphorescence induced by warming lasts only for a short time, but may be produced again and again on reheating.

E. THERMAL, ELECTRICAL, AND MAGNETIC CHARACTERS.

There is nothing of special importance in the behaviour of precious stones when exposed to the influence of heat, or in their electrical and magnetic characters.

1. THERMAL CHARACTERS.

Different minerals differ very considerably in their **conductivity for heat,** and this character may serve in some cases to distinguish minerals similar in appearance from each other. The majority of precious stones are good conductors of heat, and on this account they are cold to the touch, since the heat of the hand is quickly conducted away. Glass is a somewhat poorer conductor and hence a glass imitation is not so cold to the touch as a genuine stone, since the warmth of the hand is not so quickly conducted away. The difference in the power of conducting heat of genuine stones and their imitations may thus, under certain conditions, afford a means of distinguishing between them ; the specimens tested must not, however, have remained long in the hand nor have been otherwise warmed, neither must they be too small. It is said to be possible for an expert to select, by the sense of touch alone, a diamond out of a bag containing a large number of pieces of glass of similar size and shape.

Amber is one of the feeblest conductors of heat ; its conductivity is much less than that of glass, hence a piece of amber can be easily distinguished from its imitation in yellow glass, since it feels so much warmer to the touch. Another substance having a feeble conductivity for heat is jet, a variety of coal, which is frequently made use of for mourning ornaments. An opaque, black glass is often used for the same purpose, but a single touch of the finger tips is all that is needed to enable an expert to distinguish between the two.

A device for distinguishing a genuine from an imitation stone, depending upon the power of conducting heat, is to breathe upon the stone. The moisture of the breath will condense upon the genuine stone with more difficulty than upon glass, and when condensed will disappear again much more rapidly, since the precious stone is both more rapidly warmed and more rapidly cooled than is glass.

For the purpose of distinguishing rough stones, their **fusibility** before the blowpipe may sometimes be made use of. All glass imitations are easily fusible before the blowpipe, while few of the minerals used as precious stones can be so fused. Red garnet is one such mineral, and can be easily distinguished from other red stones which are infusible before the blowpipe, such as ruby and spinel. The application of this test is naturally limited to rough stones, splinters of which can usually be detached for examination.

2. Electrical Characters.

Many precious stones when exposed to certain external influences acquire a greater or less charge of electricity. They differ from each other in the length of time this charge can be retained, some retaining it for a considerable time, others for a less time, perhaps only a few minutes.

The French abbé, Haüy, the founder of modern scientific mineralogy, attempted to make extensive use of these characters as a means of identifying stones and distinguishing them one from another. In his book, published in 1817, *Traité des caractères physiques des pierres précieuses*, he devoted seventy-two out of a total of two hundred and fifty-three pages to the consideration of electrical characters, while the optical characters are dismissed in thirty-two pages. A comparison with the number of pages devoted to the treatment of these two branches in the present volume, shows how much more important to-day is the consideration of the optical characters of minerals.

The examination of the electrical, as of the optical, characters of a stone, has the advantage that no injury to the stone results therefrom. The observation of electrical characters, however, requires a certain amount of skill and practice; for the detection of the very small electrical charges acquired by most precious stones is difficult; and, further, these observations must be conducted in a perfectly dry atmosphere, a condition not always easy to obtain. Any charge located on the surface of a stone is rapidly lost in a damp atmosphere, and a stone which retains its charge in dry surroundings will rapidly lose it in the presence of moisture. The length of time a stone retains its charge, a test to which Haüy attached great importance, depends largely therefore upon external conditions.

At the time Haüy was engaged on his researches the methods of electrical investigation were, at least for his purposes, fairly well developed, while methods for the optical investigation of minerals had received little or no attention. Observers had indeed noticed that some minerals were singly refracting and others doubly refracting, but there was no polariscope to give precision to their observations and the phenomenon of dichroism had yet to be discovered. We can thus readily understand why Haüy attached so much more importance to the electrical than to the optical characters of minerals and precious stones. With the discovery of the dichroscope and a convenient polariscope the optical characters of minerals assumed their true importance, while their electrical characters became a minor consideration, as may be gathered from their brief mention in this place.

For the purpose of demonstrating the existence of a charge of electricity upon the surface of a stone an instrument known as an electroscope may be used; for very feeble charges an electrometer of complicated construction will be necessary. Haüy employed for this purpose an "electrical needle"; it consisted simply of a brass rod, terminated at either end by a small brass ball, and balanced on a vertical fine steel point, on which it could turn freely like a magnetic needle. An electrically charged body, when presented to either of the balls, would attract it. By giving an electric charge to the balls, they would be attracted or repelled on the approach of a body according as its charge was unlike or like that of the balls. The electric pendulum, consisting of a pith ball suspended by a silk thread, served the same purpose. With the help of such instruments it is easy to demonstrate that minerals, including precious stones, become, under various conditions, charged with electricity; the fact of itself is, however, of little note.

After rubbing on cloth all precious stones, like glass, become positively electrified. Topaz and tourmaline become strongly electrified after such treatment, diamond less strongly, and the majority of precious stones only feebly. Smooth faces are more susceptible of electrification than are rough ones, and hence cut stones furnish the most favourable material for this purpose. In perfectly dry air, some precious stones retain an electrical charge for a comparatively long period; this is especially so in the case of topaz, the electrification of which can be detected after an interval of thirty-two hours; sapphire will retain its charge for from five to six hours, and diamond for half an hour. Colourless topaz, colourless sapphire, and diamond may be distinguished by this difference in their behaviour; after imparting a charge by rubbing with a cloth, the stones should be laid on a metal plate and their electrical state tested from time to time. The majority of precious stones lose their charges with great rapidity, some, indeed, after only a few moments.

Amber, like other resinous substances, becomes negatively electrified on rubbing, and so strongly that it attracts to itself any light bodies, such as pieces of paper. These, after contact with the amber, themselves become charged and are then repelled by it. This particular character of amber is of value as a means whereby it may be distinguished from its imitations, which will be mentioned later under the special descriptions.

The electricity developed on some precious stones when under the influence of changes of temperature is known as **pyroelectricity.** The charge produced in this way on the surface of a stone varies in sign at different areas of the surface, the charge at one point being positive while that at another is negative. Those parts of the surface which become positively electrified on heating become negatively electrified on cooling, and *vice versâ*. Tourmaline and topaz are remarkable for the strength of the pyroelectrical charge they acquire; and this distinguishes them from other precious stones, which when exposed to the same influences acquire but feeble charges, or none at all. Thus, with the help of one of the electrical instruments mentioned above, a red tourmaline can be distinguished from a ruby, and a greenish-blue topaz from an aquamarine of the same colour; for the former in each case will show a strong pyroelectrical charge, and the latter none. During the gradual cooling of tourmaline after being heated, it assumes the power of attracting light bodies to itself, as does amber after being rubbed.

3. Magnetism.

Some minerals, such as magnetite, are magnetic and respond to the influence of a magnet, being attracted by it. Magnetite has a black metallic lustre, and a certain titaniferous variety, namely iserine, takes when polished a very brilliant lustre, and is sometimes used for ornamental purposes. The magnetic character of magnetite distinguishes it from other black stones, all of which are either non-magnetic or very feebly influenced by a magnet.

D. OCCURRENCE OF PRECIOUS STONES.

A complete account of precious stones must include a consideration of the localities at which they are found and the conditions under which they occur in nature. These subjects will be dealt with in a general way here, and again more in detail with the special description of each precious stone.

Precious stones, like other minerals, have two distinct modes of occurrence. They may, on the one hand, be found at that spot in the earth's crust where they had their genesis, or, on the other hand, owing to the weathering and breaking down of the rocks and the action of transporting agencies, we may find them in secondary deposits far from their original home.

Precious stones, in their primary situation, frequently form a constituent of the rocks which make up the earth's crust at that place. They are embedded in the so-called mother-rock, and were formed at the same time as the other constituents of the rock. Under such conditions, stones sometimes show regularly developed crystal-faces, but more frequently their boundaries are irregular and distorted. A perfectly developed crystal of red garnet (almandine) embedded in its mother-rock of gneiss is shown in Plate XIV., Fig. 3, while Fig. 69 shows the completely developed crystal after being isolated from the mother-rock.

Many precious stones and minerals, however, are found not completely embedded in the rock-mass but attached to the walls of cavities in the rock and projecting freely into the interior space. These cavities may be either completely enclosed by the rock, in which case they are of various shapes and sizes, or they may partake more of the nature of cracks and fissures penetrating the rock and varying in width and length between wide limits. The formation of minerals found inside such cavities is always of later date than that of the rock-mass itself. Such later-formed minerals may completely fill a cavity or fissure, or they may form a more or less thick incrustation on its walls.

Such cavities lined with crystals are known as *drusy cavities* or *druses*. Crystals detached from a drusy cavity will show a broken surface at the end by which they were attached to the wall of the cavity, but in other directions they will be perfectly developed in accordance with the type of symmetry peculiar to them. These *attached crystals* differ in this respect from the *embedded crystals*, mentioned above, which latter are equally developed on all sides.

The quartz crystals shown in Figs. 85 *b — d*, are examples of attached crystals broken away from their underlying matrix, while Fig. 85 *a* is a representation of an embedded quartz crystal, equally developed on all sides. In Figs. 85 *b — d*, the irregularly broken point of attachment of each crystal is directed downwards and is fairly large; it is sometimes, however, quite small and may be hardly observable. A group of crystals, of the variety of quartz known as rock-crystal, such as frequently occurs in crevices and fissures in the gneiss of the Alps, is shown in Plate XVII.

More important than the occurrence of precious stones in primary rocks is their presence in loose, secondary deposits, which have been derived from the weathering and breaking down of primary rocks, and are known as **gem-sands** or **gem-gravels**.

The mother-rock, in which the precious stones were originally formed, has been exposed to the action of atmospheric agencies, rain, frost, &c., and has become weathered at the surface. Some of the constituents of the rock are dissolved in water and carried away and thus the cohesion of the mass is destroyed. The more or less loose, clayey, or sandy residue is the weathered product, and this will contain the precious stones which were present in the original rock, since, as a rule, they are unattacked by weathering agencies. The precious stones will be present in the weathered product in relatively greater numbers than in the original mother-rock.

It will be readily understood that it is more profitable to work weathered material than the unaltered primary rocks for precious stones, for not only is the former relatively richer in gem-stones than the latter, but it allows of the stones being easily separated or washed out. The extraction of a gem-stone from solid rock involves much labour and patience, and, even when every care is taken, may result in serious damage to the stone.

The loose, incoherent material which results from the weathering of a rock, when it contains a mineral worth extracting for technical purposes, is known generally as a *sand*, and as a *gem-sand* when it contains precious stones. It is in such sands which, wherever they occur, cover the solid rocks and form the outer portion of the earth's crust, that the most valuable precious stones are found, such, for instance, as diamond, ruby, and sapphire. They are separated from these masses of detritus by the process of *gem-washing*, in which the heavier stones and larger fragments remain behind, while the lighter clayey and sandy constituents are washed away.

When the weathered material has not been carried away by the various transporting agencies, but remains near the parent rock, the precious stones and other minerals it contains will preserve intact the sharp edges and the crystalline form they possessed when embedded in the solid rock. Such cases, however, are rare ; much more frequently the whole of the loose material is transported in streams and rivers, and is finally deposited in a lower part of the valley, far away from its original resting-place. In such river sands and gravels, which are known as alluvial deposits, the mineral fragments, and even the precious stones, in spite of their hardness, become so rubbed by mutual friction during their travels that all angularities are lost, and they present the appearance of smooth, rounded pebbles or grains.

The presence or absence of this smooth water-worn appearance in the mineral fragments of rock detritus is conclusive proof in the one case that water has been the transporting agency, and in the other that it has not. The greater the hardness of the precious stone transported in gravels by water, the less will be the rounding it undergoes ; even diamond, the hardest of materials, may show traces of rounding if the action of other softer stones is only continued long enough.

The precious stones, found in such water-worn materials, are frequently superior to specimens which have not been subjected to the action of running water, and are still to be found in their parent-rock. Such stones are frequently traversed by fissures, often scarcely visible, but enough to make them unfit for use as gems, since, as has been mentioned before, they have a tendency to break along these fissures. Precious stones which have been rolled about and ground together in the bed of a river during long ages have undergone a fairly severe trial ; any which have a tendency to fragment will be reduced to splinters at an early stage of their journey ; those, on the other hand, which survive may be considered to have proved their durability.

As regards the **geographical distribution** of precious stones, it may be mentioned that in former times the most valuable came from India and other parts of the " Orient." It was therefore believed in the Middle Ages that the glowing sun of tropical countries was essential to the development of those qualities in precious stones which are so highly prized, and that specimens from colder countries were deficient in these qualities. Every good stone, of which the locality was not certainly known, was for this reason assumed to have come from the " Orient." A remnant of this belief still lingers in the application of the terms " oriental" to the more valuable, and " occidental " to less valuable stones. It has now long been known that the habitat of the finest of precious stones is by no means confined to the " Orient " and hot countries, such as India, Ceylon, Burma, Siam, Brazil, Colombia, &c., but that equally fine stones may also be found in North America, the Urals, and other Northern Countries. The terms " oriental" and " occidental," as now applied, have no longer a geographical signification, but refer simply to the quality of the stones to which they may be applied. Thus to distinguish cymophane from the more common quartz-cat's-eye it is termed " oriental cat's-eye "; in the same way yellow sapphire is known as " oriental topaz," and yellow quartz as " occidental topaz." The various localities in which precious stones are and have been found will be considered in detail, along with the special description of each precious stone.

II. APPLICATIONS OF PRECIOUS STONES.

The use to which a precious stone is put depends in the first place on its appearance, and in the second on the hardness it possesses. Should it possess beauty of appearance combined with a fair degree of hardness, it may be used as a personal ornament, while if it possesses hardness alone, there are various technical purposes it may serve.

A. TECHNICAL APPLICATIONS.

The technical applications of precious stones are not numerous, and need be but briefly mentioned here.

Since the year 1700 the pivot-bearings of watches and delicate chronometers have been made of some hard precious stone, since this material will best withstand the continual wear of the steel axis. The stones commonly used for this purpose are known as " rubies," but are in reality chrysoberyl, topaz, spinel, or indeed any stone the hardness of which is greater than that of steel. The true ruby would of course answer this purpose, but a stone so valuable for ornamental purposes would naturally not be used when cheaper substitutes are available. Any precious stone which has the required degree of hardness, and which from cloudiness, opacity, or any such blemish, is unsuitable for use as a gem, may be utilised for the purpose.

The pivot-supports of other delicate instruments, such as balances, &c., are made of agate or some other hard stone; by this means the wear is reduced to a minimum, and the delicacy of the instrument preserved unimpaired for long periods. In the manufacture of very fine gold and silver wires, the hole through which the wire is drawn is usually made in some hard precious stone; this will withstand the continued friction, and thus avoid the possibility of gradual increase in the diameter of the hole, and consequently in that of the wire. Tools used in polishing metals and for similar purposes are also made of hard stones, preferably of agate.

Those precious stones which have the greatest technical importance as abrasive agents are naturally those which are at the same time the hardest of stones, namely, diamond and corundum. For such purposes the latter is used in its impurest state, when it is known as emery. The use of these materials in the cutting, grinding, and polishing of precious stones will be dealt with below in the special description of these processes.

The diamond, on account of its extreme hardness, has many other technical applications, which will be noticed in detail further on under the special description of this stone. It is used for engraving and boring precious stones and other hard materials, while its use in rock-drills for mining and other operations is scarcely less extensive than its use as the glazier's diamond.

B. APPLICATION AS JEWELS.

The use of precious stones as gems is much more extensive and varied than for any other purpose. In their rough state they have not, as a rule, a pleasing appearance, and therefore are unsuitable for this purpose ; it is only after cutting and polishing that their beauty appears in all its fulness.

The process of cutting aims at giving each stone such a form as will best display its natural lustre and beauty. Thus the form in one case may be rounded, in another bounded by small faces or facets, the latter being very frequently used. The various modes of cutting in vogue at the present day, each of which is best suited to the idiosyncrasy of the particular stone to which it is applied, are the results of centuries of trial and observation on the part of gem-cutters. Thus the form in which transparent stones are cut differs from that best suited to opaque stones ; and in the same way, the form in which dark-coloured stones are cut differs from that given to lighter or colourless specimens. The appearance of each would suffer if it were given any other than its own appropriate form.

The amount of refraction and dispersion exercised upon light by a transparent stone greatly affects its appearance, as has been shown in the case of diamond. It has also been shown that to obtain a maximum effect, the greater part of the light which enters by the front facets of a cut stone must be reflected from the back facets, and must again pass out by the front facets. Since the path of a ray of light in a stone varies with the refractive index of the stone, and this character is different in different stones, it follows that the form of cutting must be adapted to the requirements of each particular case. It is thus the task of the gem-cutter to give to each stone that form which is calculated to bring out and display its beauties to the greatest possible advantage, and which, at the same time, involves the least possible waste of valuable material.

Gem-cutters, by prolonged experience, have arrived at certain empirical rules which are always applied, and which are modified to suit particular cases. In colourless stones, for example, there must be a fixed proportion between their breadth and their thickness, and there should be also certain relations between the shape of the back and that of the front of the stone.

Too great depth in a cut stone is as inimical to the full effect of its beauty as is too great shallowness. In the one case a stone is said to be *thick* or "lumpy," and in the other *thin* or "spread." Of two similar stones, one of which errs on the side of too great depth, and the other on that of too great shallowness, the latter is to be preferred. The facets at the back of the stone must occupy a certain position relative to the front facets, otherwise the light entering by these will not be totally reflected from the back.

The same rules apply also to coloured stones. In this case the depth the stones are cut is important, and this must vary with their intensity of colour. A deeply coloured stone if too thick will appear dark or almost black, while a pale coloured stone will not exhibit a sufficient depth of colour unless it is cut of some thickness.

So long as the mutual relations of the facets of a cut stone are correct, the direction these take relative to the faces of the natural crystal is in most cases immaterial. In a few special cases, however, the directions of the cut facets must bear a definite relation to certain crystallographic directions in the stone. Thus the special colour effects of labradorite, moon-stone, &c., are only manifest in certain directions; if cut in other directions, the beautiful effects for which these stones are prized would be lost. This is also true in the case of dichroic stones, which, as we have already seen, vary in colour in different directions. Other cases of the same kind will be mentioned with the special description of each precious stone.

In the cutting of any given rough stone, not only must it receive the form best calculated to display its special beauties, but the facets must be cut in such positions as to involve the least possible waste of material, thus obtaining the largest possible size for the cut stone. In considering the positions in which the facets are to be cut relative to the boundaries of the rough stone, there are still other points which may require attention. Thus the rough stone may have a flaw, and in this case the facets should be so placed that the faulty material will be cut away altogether, or, at least, so located in the cut stone that the beauty of the latter is impaired as little as possible.

With rough material containing flaws, a question will often arise as to whether, in the cut stone, size should be sacrificed to beauty, or *vice versâ*. European gem-cutters are generally unanimous in the opinion that such a specimen should be cut so as to attain the highest possible degree of perfection and beauty even if this should involve considerable loss of material. A small stone, all the beautiful features of which are displayed to their full advantage, is more highly prized than a larger stone, the beauty of which is less perfectly developed. In every rough stone, the aim of the gem-cutter is to obtain a cut stone of the largest possible weight combined with the greatest possible beauty, since, the latter condition being fulfilled, the price obtained for the cut stone varies with its weight. The earnings of a cutter of precious stones depend largely upon his skill in treating each stone so as to obtain the greatest effect with the least waste of material.

These principles have not always been followed, for in earlier times the aim in gem-cutting was to reduce the size and weight of the stone as little as possible. This is the case even at the present day in India and the East generally, as well as in various remote parts of the world where precious stones are found. Stones so cut have their facets very irregularly grouped, and consequently much of their beauty is undeveloped. Such stones are unfit for use in European jewellery, and are frequently re-cut according to modern principles; the increased beauty of their appearance so obtained more than compensates for the loss of the material cut away.

We now pass to the consideration of the various shapes and forms in which precious stones are cut with a view to their use in jewellery.

A. FORMS OF CUTTING.

The various forms of cutting which have been found by experience to be most effective for gems and which are at present exclusively used, at least for valuable stones, fall naturally into two groups. The one includes all forms having *facets*, the other embraces forms of a rounded or *cabochon* shape. All faceted forms may be referred to one or other of four types according to the number and arrangement of the facets; forms intermediate between these types may also be met with.

The facets of a cut stone may be more or less uniformly distributed on all sides, or, again, they may be all located on one side, the other side being occupied by a single large facet. In the latter case we have the form of cutting known as the rosette or rose. A cut stone provided with facets on all sides is represented in Fig. 29, *a* and *c* being views from above and below respectively and *b* from the side. When such a stone (Fig. 29) is set as a jewel the side turned towards the observer is known as the upper portion or *crown*, while the opposite side or lower portion is referred to as the *culasse* or pavilion. The facets of the crown and of the culasse meet in the edge *RR* (Fig. 29 *b*), which is known as the *girdle* or edge, and is the portion of the stone which is fixed in the setting. The whole forms, as it were, a double pyramid with truncated summits, each pyramid having a common base in the girdle.

Of the four types of faceted stones the rose or rosette type has been already mentioned ; the remaining three are known as the brilliant-cut, step-cut, and table-cut. The number, arrangement, and grouping of the facets differ in these three types, but each has a crown, a culasse, and a girdle.

These different forms of cutting, which are illustrated in Plates II.–IV., must now be considered more in detail. In these plates, the same figure-number is given to different aspects of the same stone, the addition of the letter *a*, *b*, or *c* to the figure-number indicating that the stone is represented as seen from the side, from above, or from below respectively ; the same letters are also used when only one or two of the three aspects are represented. Plate II. gives a series of forms of the brilliant, and Fig. 1 of Plate III. belongs to the same series. The other figures of Plate III. represents variations of the step-cut, while Plate IV. shows various kinds of rosettes, table-stones, and stones cut *en cabochon*.

The expense involved in a complicated form of cutting with regular facets, grouped in the way experience has shown to be most effective, is very considerable ; such perfection in cutting is never bestowed upon cheap material, but only upon more valuable stones which will repay the outlay. In the cutting of less valuable stones, they receive the correct form, but the facets are reduced in number and less attention is paid to their regular and precise distribution ; by these means the expense of cutting is considerably lessened though the appearance of the stone suffers.

1. **The Brilliant.**—This form of cutting is said to have been originated by Cardinal Mazarin, and was first employed at the time this minister was endeavouring to revive the diamond-cutting industry in Paris. Mazarin caused twelve of the largest diamonds of the French crown to be cut in this form, and these stones have since been known as the twelve "Mazarins." The existence of only one of these stones, however, is now known, and the genuineness even of this is doubted. The superiority of the brilliant over all other forms of cutting for diamond and other colourless, transparent stones, and also for some coloured stones, is now so firmly established that it is at present by far the most generally used. Only in quite exceptional cases is a good diamond cut in a form other than that of the brilliant ; indeed, so generally is this form given to diamonds, that they are often referred to colloquially as " brilliants." Coloured, transparent stones are very frequently brilliant-cut, but not so invariably as is the case with diamonds.

The upper portion or crown, *OO*, of a brilliant (Fig. 29) bears a broad facet, *b*, known as the *table*, while the lower portion or culasse, *UU*, bears a much smaller facet, *B*, known as the *culet* (or collet), both being parallel to the girdle, *RR*. Of other facets, those meeting the table in an edge and lying wholly in the crown of the stone, are known as *star facets* and are lettered *d* in the figure. The *cross facets*, lettered *f*, *g*, *E*, and *D* in the figure, meet the girdle in an edge ; some lie in the crown of the stone and some in the culasse. Between the star and cross facets, which are triangular in shape, lie other larger facets having four or five edges; those which lie above the girdle are lettered *a* and *c* in the figure, while those which are below are lettered *A* and *C*; these facets are not, however, invariably present in the same

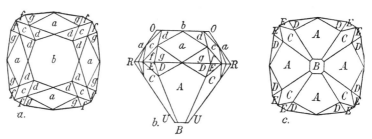

FIG. 29.   Brilliant (triple-cut).   *a*, view from above; *b*, from the side; *c*, from below.

number. The girdle, *RR*, always lies in a plane, and forms the boundary of the stone as seen in Figs. 29 *a* and 29 *c*.

Several varieties of the brilliant-cut are distinguished according to the number of facets present. The *double-cut brilliant*, shown in Plate II., Fig. 1 *a,b,c*, has four triangular star facets arranged so that their four upper edges form the boundaries of the square table, while the four opposite angles of each lie in the girdle. The space between each pair of adjacent star facets is occupied by three cross facets, the central one of each group having the form of an isosceles triangle, and the cross facet on either side having the form of an oblique triangle. On the crown or upper portion of such a stone, therefore, there are sixteen facets besides the table; these facets are arranged in two series, hence the term "double-cut brilliant." The under portion consists of twelve triangular cross facets, which are the same in number and arrangement as the cross facets in the upper portion; between these lie four five-sided facets, intersecting the small culet in short edges.

The *English double-cut brilliant*, differing somewhat from the double-cut brilliant just described, is shown in Plate II., Fig. 2 *a, b, c*. Here the table is the centre of an eight-rayed star, formed of eight triangular star facets, which alternate with eight triangular cross facets. The facets of the lower portion are similar to those of the ordinary double-cut brilliant (Fig. 1 *c*); the corner cross facets having the shape of isosceles triangles are, however, occasionally absent (Fig. 2 *c*).

The number of facets present in the forms of double-cut brilliants does not allow of the perfect development of the brilliancy and the play of prismatic colours of the stone. Such forms are therefore given usually to small and less valuable stones; for large stones the *triple-cut brilliant* is more appropriate. Here three series of facets lie one above the other on the upper part of the stone; the total of thirty-two facets, exclusive of the table, is made up of eight triangular star facets, sixteen triangular cross facets, and eight four-sided facets. The arrangement of these different facets is shown in Fig. 29, and in Plate II. Figs. 3 and 4. The under portion of the stone has also sixteen cross facets, while the small culet is surrounded by eight large, five-sided facets. The form, shown in Fig. 29, and Plate II., Fig. 3 *a, b, c*, in which the girdle has a roughly square outline, is now somewhat out of date; since the eighteenth century the form shown in Plate II., Fig. 4 *a, b, c*, has received more favour. The facets of this form are the same in number and arrangement, but are more nearly equal in size, and the outline of the girdle approximates very close to a circle. The outline of the girdle is not, however, by any means constant, it depends largely upon the natural form of the stone before it is cut. In Fig. 5 *b, c*, it is oval, in Fig. 6 *b, c*, it is pear-shaped, and in Fig. 7 *a, b, c*, it is roughly triangular in outline. The last case is

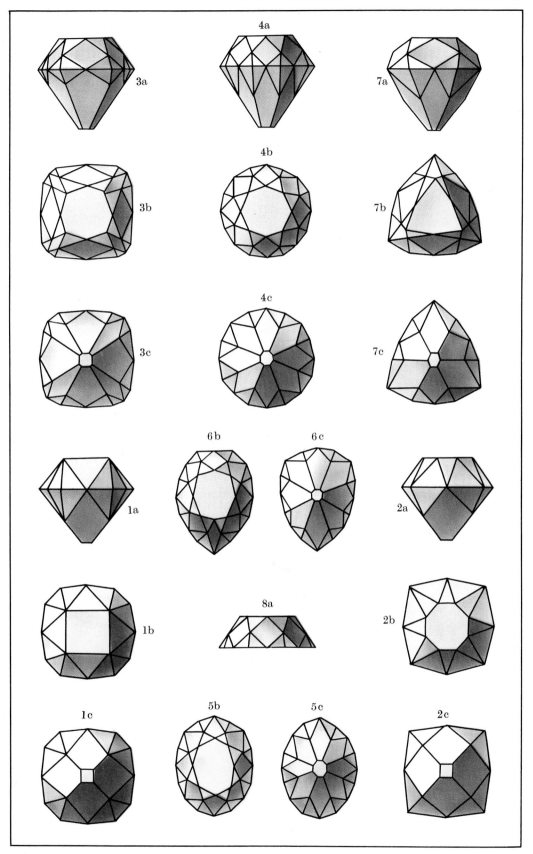

Brilliant Forms.   1a, b, c. Double-cut.   2a, b, c. English double-cut (double-cut brilliant with star).   3a, b, c. Triple-cut, old form.   4a, b, c. Triple-cut, new form, round.   5b, c. The same, oval.   6b, c. The same, pear-shaped.   7a, b, c. The same, triangular.   8a. Half-brilliant.

also noticeable from the fact that the facets, instead of being in multiples of four, are in multiples of three.

The forms just described may be regarded as typical brilliant forms, and are used far more frequently than any other. They are nevertheless subject to certain modifications, not, however, deviating far from the normal types. These modifications usually take the form of variations in the arrangement and number of the facets ; in the latter case further small facets are introduced in groups, which are placed symmetrically relative to the other facets. The majority of the large historical diamonds are cut in the brilliant form, as an examination of Plates X. and XI. will show. On comparing these forms with the normal forms of Plate II. a strong general resemblance, accompanied by differences in minor details, will be noticed.

To bring out all the beauties of a stone, and to display them to the greatest possible advantage, involves infinite care and precision in the cutting. The facets must be regularly and symmetrically grouped, and corresponding facets must be of precisely the same size ; moreover, it is of the greatest importance that all the different parts of the stone should be correctly proportioned. In this connection may be mentioned the following rules which are generally observed, and which are only departed from where there are special reasons for so doing :

The height of the upper portion of the brilliant above the girdle must be one-third, and that of the lower portion must be two-thirds, of the total thickness of the stone from table to culet. The diameters of the table and culet must be respectively five-ninths and one-ninth of the diameter of the girdle ; hence the diameter of the table is five times that of the culet. Few of the best cut and most beautiful brilliants show any essential deviation from these dimensions ; the exceptional cases mentioned above occur when the rough stone is of such a shape that to give it these proportions would involve too great a waste of material ; or, again, in the case of a coloured stone, where the thickness is varied in order to obtain the particular depth of colour desired.

The "Koh-i-noor," the famous diamond now in the English crown jewels (Plate X., Fig. 5), on account of the former reason departs considerably from the typical form. The "Regent," a large brilliant in the French crown jewels, is perhaps the most perfectly beautiful stone of its kind existing at the present day (Plate XI., Fig. 8). It conforms with the greatest precision to the proportions laid down above, and consequently far surpasses the "Koh-i-noor" in brilliancy and play of colours, although the two stones are equal in quality.

It remains to be mentioned that the girdle of a brilliant is sometimes left with sharp edges (Plate X., Fig. 5), as is the custom of English gem-cutters ; or the edges may be ground down (Plate XI., Figs. 8 and 9), as is done in Holland. The former plan improves the appearance and effect of the stone, but the sharp edges are liable to get chipped, which is not the case when they have been rounded off.

Mention may be made here of the *half-brilliant* (or brillonette), which is very occasionally made use of. It is essentially an ordinary brilliant, the under portion of which is replaced by a single large face, which forms a base to the upper portion as in rosettes. This device is occasionally resorted to when the rough stone is very flat, but the appearance of a stone so cut is far inferior to that of a complete brilliant.

The *star-cut*, which is closely related to the brilliant form, was devised by the Parisian jeweller, Caire, at the beginning of the nineteenth century, and is illustrated in Plate III., Fig. 1 *a, b, c.* In this form Caire aimed at combining the advantages of the brilliant with those of the rosette. As may be seen from the diagrams, the facets are arranged in multiples of six, and are distributed with great regularity, which serves to enhance the appearance of the stone. This form of cutting was devised principally for diamonds, to which it gives a very effective star-like or rayed appearance, very little inferior to that of the ordinary brilliant. The cutting of this form from the majority of rough stones is attended with but little loss of material; the form is, however, not in general use.

2. **Step-cut** or **trap-cut.**—The different types of step-cut stones, together with the various modifications of this form, are illustrated in Plate III., Figs. 2 to 8, Figs. 2 to 4 being typical forms. In one of these (Fig. 2 b) the girdle is square; in another hexagonal (Fig. 3 b); in a third it is eight-sided (Fig. 4 b, c); while it may be occasionally twelve-sided. The outline of the girdle may be such that all its diameters are approximately equal, or it may be more elongated in one direction. Above the girdle rises the upper portion of the stone, bearing a large table of the same outline as the girdle (Figs. 2 b, 3 b, 4 b); the lower portion terminates in a small culet (Figs. 2 a, 4 c), or in a point (Figs. 7 a, c). On both portions lie a series of facets arranged in such a way that their edges of intersection are parallel to the corresponding edges of the girdle. In passing from the girdle to the table or to the culet, the facets become successively less and less steeply inclined (Fig. 2 a, &c.). The upper portion has two, or sometimes three, series of facets, each series differing but slightly in their inclination to the table. The facets of different series may be of the same width (Figs. 2 b, 3 b), or the facets of the lower series are wider than those of the uppermost bordering on the table (Fig. 4 b). On the lower portion of step-cut stones, there are usually from four (Figs. 8 a, c) to five series (Figs. 2 a, 4 c, &c.) of facets. None of the facets of these lower series differ in width.

The step-cut is the form employed for less deeply-coloured stones when they are not cut as brilliants. It brings out the colour and lustre of the stone to great advantage; it must, however, be specially proportioned, particularly in the lower portion, to suit the stone to which it is applied. The brilliancy and colour of the stone do not attain their full value with an insufficient number of facets; there are scarcely ever less than four or five series of facets on the lower portion of the stone, and in faintly-coloured stones this number may be increased. In such faintly-coloured stones the lower portion is rather deep, as is shown in the figures, while in stones of a deep colour it is flat, sometimes very flat.

While certain insignificant modifications of the lower portion of step-cut forms are effective in varying the depth of colour of the stone, the upper portion may undergo more marked modifications, a few of which are illustrated in Plate III., Figs. 5 to 8. Here we find the step-like facets of the upper portion replaced by an arrangement of facets similar to that of a brilliant. These forms are therefore, to a certain extent, combinations of the step-cut and the brilliant-cut, and are in general specially suited to stones of a pale colour. The *mixed-cut* (Fig. 5 a, b) is a form in frequent use; it bears on the upper portion a series of triangular star facets and of similarly shaped cross facets, separated by a series of four-sided facets. The mixed-cut brings out in light-coloured stones a stronger brilliancy and lustre than does the typical step-cut. The outline of the girdle in this form need not necessarily be circular, as in Fig. 5, but may be square, hexagonal, &c.

Fig. 6 a, b, shows the *cut with double facets*, a form which differs from the mixed-cut in that several single facets of the latter are replaced by two facets; the arrangement of these facets in two series can be easily made out from the diagrams without further explanation. The cut with double facets is no more effective than is the mixed-cut; it is used simply for the purpose of removing, or rendering inconspicuous, any faults which may exist in the rough stone. In the *cut with elongated brilliant facets* the arrangement of the facets on the upper portion is much the same as in the previous form; the facets, however, are much elongated

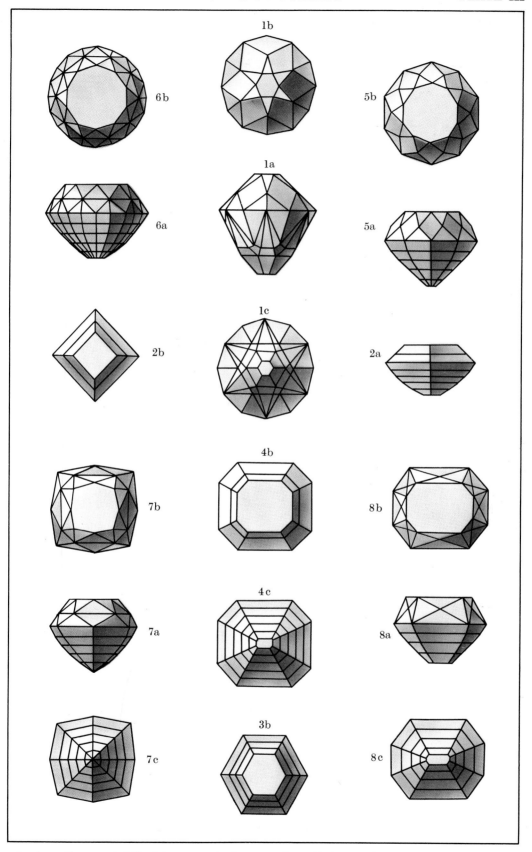

1a, b, c. Star-cut (of M. Caire). 2a, b. Step-cut, four-sided. 3b. Step-cut, six-sided. 4b, c. Step-cut, eight-sided. 5a, b. Mixed-cut. 6a, b. Cut with double facets. 7a, b, c. Cut with elongated brilliant facets. 8a, b, c. Maltese cross.

or shortened (Fig. 7 *a*, *b*, *c*). The outline of the girdle may approach that of a square, as in the figure, or it may be oblong. This form of cutting is peculiarly adapted to stones of an elongated shape, and it brings out their lustre to a marked degree; the elongated brilliant facets seem to compensate for any lack of depth in the lower portion of the stone. Another similar form is that known as the *Maltese cross* (Fig. 8 *a*, *b*, *c*), so called from the cruciform arrangement of its facets. Other similar forms exist, differing but slightly from those already described; a detailed account of these is therefore unnecessary.

3. **Table-cut.**—This term includes a number of forms, all of which are more or less related to, and may be derived from, a four-sided double pyramid or regular octahedron. This octahedral form is the natural crystalline form of many diamonds, and it may sometimes be seen in the stones of jewellery which dates back to the time when no cutting of the rough stones was attempted, but the preparation of the stones for ornamental purposes was confined to the polishing of the natural faces of the crystals. Such stones date back to very ancient times, and are known as *point-stones*. The table-cut, and other forms related to it, are derived from the octahedron by the greater or less truncation of two opposite corners (Plate IV., Figs 11 to 16); a few additional facets may be given to the upper portion of the stone (Figs. 11, 13, 14, 16).

The typical table-stone is derived from an octahedron by cutting two opposite corners to an equal amount. The upper and lower portions of the stone are then exact replicas the one of the other, and the table is of the same size and shape as the culet, the outline of which may be either square or oblong. Fig. 15 *b* shows a view from above of a square table-stone, and Plate XIV., Fig. 2, shows an epidote cut as an elongated table-stone. This form of cutting is not, as a rule, specially effective; it is, however, advantageously used for several coloured stones, including the emerald. The effect of additional facets on the upper portion is to increase the brilliancy and lustre of the stone. With this object in view, the four edges of the table may be replaced by narrow facets (Fig. 11 *a*, *b*), or the four edges between the pyramidal facets may be more or less truncated so that the table becomes eight-sided (Fig. 16 *b*). Again, the upper portion may be of the brilliant form (Fig. 14 *a*, *b*), though the arrangement of the facets in a typical brilliant need not be exactly reproduced.

The two opposite corners of the octahedron may be truncated to a greater or less degree. In the former case the result will be quite a thin table, which is known as a *thin-stone*. This can be modified by the addition of further facets in the manner described for table-stones (Figs. 12 *a*, 13 *b*). A table-stone in which the culet is larger than the table is described as *half-grounded*, while one in which the reverse relation holds is known as a *thick-stone*. Such stones, in which the table is usually double the size of the culet, are described as *Indian-cut*, and many precious stones from the Orient, and especially from India, are of this form; they are usually re-cut in Europe into a more effective form. The thick-stone is, in a way, as already explained, the ground form of the brilliant; all the modifications described for table-stones may be applied equally well to thick-stones.

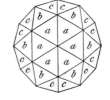

FIG. 30. Rosette
(viewed from above).

4. **Rosette** or **Rose-cut.**—In this form of cutting the stone is bounded on its underside by a single large and broad face, which forms a base to the whole. This form, which consists of an upper portion only, the lower portion being entirely absent, is pyramidal in shape, the uppermost facets meeting above to form a more or less sharp solid angle. A rose of the ordinary type, as seen from above, is shown in Fig. 30, and Plate IV., Fig. 1 *b*. The facets

are in multiples of six, and are arranged in two groups: the upper group, of which the facets are lettered *a*, constitute the *crown* or *star*, while the series lettered *b* and *c* are known as the *teeth* (*dentelle*). The star facets, *a*, and the cross facets, *b* and *c*, are both, as a rule, triangular in shape, as in Fig. 30, but in special cases the cross facets may be four-sided (Plate IV., Fig. 5 *a*).

The appearance due to this arrangement of facets has been compared to that of an opening rose-bud, hence the name applied to this form of cutting. It has been in vogue since about the year 1520, principally for diamonds of small thickness, from which comparatively small brilliants only could be obtained, and these with considerable loss of material. This form of cutting for the diamond is second in importance only to the brilliant, and a diamond cut in this manner is frequently referred to as a rose or rosette. The rose-cut well displays the brilliancy of the stone, but is inferior to the brilliant form in bringing out the play of prismatic colours. It is also applied to coloured stones, for example pyrope or Bohemian garnet, but less frequently than to diamonds.

The number and arrangement of the facets of rosettes may be considerably varied. Some of the modifications which result are distinguished by special names, and are represented in Plate IV., Figs. 1 to 7. The description of Fig. 30 applies to the typical *Dutch rose*, or crowned rose (Plate IV., Figs. 1 *b*, 3 *a*), with six star facets and eighteen cross facets. The character which distinguishes this from other rose-cuts is the height of the pyramid above the base. This height is, as a rule, half the diameter of the whole stone. Further, the distance from the base to the crown should be three-fifths of the total height, while the diameter of the base of the crown should be three-quarters of that of the whole stone. This is the form of rose-cut ordinarily employed; its base is usually round, but it is occasionally oval or pear-shaped (Fig. 2 *b*).

Among the other forms of roses which are much less used is the *Brabant* or *Antwerp rose*. This differs from the Dutch rose in that the star facets form a much lower pyramid, while the cross facets are somewhat more steeply inclined to the base (Fig. 4 *a*); the number and arrangement of the facets is otherwise the same as in the Dutch variety. Two modifications of the Brabant rose with its low crown are shown in Figs. 5 *a* and 6 *a*. Of these the former has six triangular star facets and six four-sided cross facets, while the latter has twelve cross facets in addition to the six star facets. A form with a larger number of facets, the *rose recoupée*, is shown in Fig. 7 *a*, *b*; it has twelve star facets and twenty-four triangular cross facets, the apices of the latter being directed alternately upwards and downwards.

Closely related to the typical roses are a few forms, illustrated in Plate IV., Figs. 8 to 10. Fig. 8 *a*, *b*, shows the very rare form known as the *cross-rosette*, in which the facets are arranged in multiples of eight. A cinnamon-stone, cut in this form more than a hundred years ago, has been recently brought to light, and described by Professor Schrauf. Fig 9 *a* shows a form which may be regarded as two roses joined base to base. This is the *double rosette*; also sometimes known as the briolette or the pendeloque; the latter names are, however, more frequently applied to stones with a pear-shaped outline, to be mentioned presently. This form, which was formerly much used for ear-rings and watch-chain pendants, was given by L. van Berquen, the originator of the modern process of diamond cutting, to the first diamonds cut by him. These included, among others, the " Florentine " and " Sancy " diamonds, both of which are figured in Plate XI. (Figs. 10 and 11).

Next to be mentioned are the *briolettes*, *brillolettes*, or *pendeloques* (Fig. 10), which are bounded by small facets on all sides, and are somewhat elongated in one direction, so that they have a pear-shaped outline. They are often pierced in the direction of their greatest

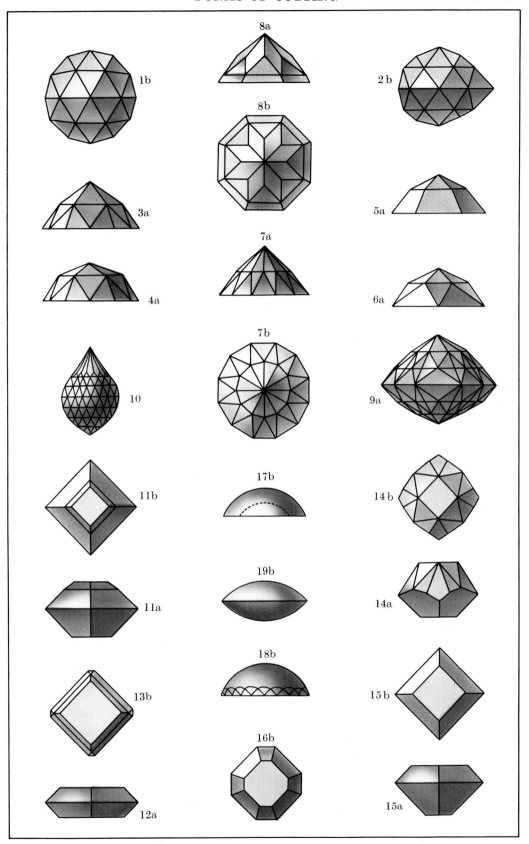

1—8. Rosettes (Rose-cut). 1b. Rose, round. 2b. Rose, pear-shaped. 3a. Dutch Rose.
4a. Brabant Rose. 5a, 6a. Roses of other forms. 7a, b. Rose recoupée. 8a, b. Cross-rose.
9a. Double Rosette (Pendeloque). 10. Briolette. 11a, b. Table-stone. 12a, 13b. Thin-stone.
14a, b. Table-stone, with brilliant form above. 15a, b, 16b. Thick-stone. 17b. Cabochon,
simple (hollowed). 18b. The same with facets. 19b. Double Cabochon.

length so as to enable them to be used as ear-rings or to be strung on a thread with others. The application of the terms briolette and pendeloque is extremely variable ; as mentioned above, they are sometimes applied to the double rosette. Small stones bounded on all sides by more or less regularly distributed facets, not elongated in any one direction more than another, and bored so that they may be strung on a thread, are known as *beads*.

5. **Rounded forms.**—As a general rule, only transparent stones are faceted ; chalcedony and other translucent stones are occasionally cut in this way ; opaque stones, like turquoise, are never faceted, but always cut *en cabochon*. The rounded forms with convex surfaces, characteristic of this style of cutting, are shown in Plate IV., Figs. 17 to 19. Many deeply coloured transparent stones, such as garnet, are often cut *en cabochon*, as are also those stones whose beauty is due to their peculiar optical effects ; such, for instance, as cat's-eye and precious opal. The flat base of these rounded forms is circular or elliptical in outline, and from this rises a more or less convex dome (Fig. 17 *b*). Transparent stones of a deep colour, for example garnet, are sometimes hollowed out at the back, the inner surface having the same curvature as the outer, as is shown by the dotted line in Fig. 17 *b*. Not only is the transparency of the stone increased by this means, but facility is given for removing any faulty portions of the interior of the stone. A stone cut in this manner is known as a *shell*, and, in the case quoted, as a *garnet-shell*. Frequently the flat base just described is replaced by another convex surface of the same or different curvature as the upper portion ; the stone has then the form of a double convex lens, as shown in side view in Fig. 19 *b*. The form with one curved surface is known as the *single cabochon*, while that with two is referred to as a *double cabochon;* a much flattened form having only a slight curvature is described as *tallow-topped* (*goutte de suif*).

The convex dome of transparent or translucent stones cut *en cabochon* sometimes has a border of small facets arranged in one or several series (Fig. 18 *b*). Not infrequently, in the cheaper coloured stones and in glass imitations, the table of the brilliant-, the step-, and the table-cuts is given a slight curvature.

Bastard forms are those which are not pure examples of any of the typical forms described above, but combine in themselves portions of any of these types. Rare and costly gems are never so cut, but bastard forms are common enough in inferior stones and glass imitations. Such stones are often cut also in quite irregular and unorthodox forms, which are not subject to any definite rule, but depend solely upon the caprice of the cutter. Of such forms it is obviously neither possible nor desirable to give detailed descriptions. The facets of these capricious forms are sometimes regularly and symmetrically arranged, but at other times this is not the case, and the stone is then described as *cap-cut*.

The form of cutting specially suited to each individual variety of precious stone will be mentioned with the special description of that stone.

B. PROCESS OF CUTTING.

The method by which a rough stone is transformed into a faceted gem is in principle very simple. That part of the surface of the rough stone at which it is desired to place a facet is rubbed with a harder stone or with some other convenient substance. The harder stone abrades small fragments from the softer, and the surface of the latter is gradually worn away and replaced, if the operation has been suitably performed, by a plane face, the so-called facet. This operation is repeated until all the facets required for the particular form the stone is desired to take are produced. A rounded surface is obtained by a method essentially the same as the one described.

A notice of all the technical details connected with the cutting of precious stones would be entirely out of place here. Only the main principles of the methods which are applicable to all precious stones will here be considered. The special modifications of general methods which are necessary for certain stones, particularly diamond, will be considered when we come to the special description of such stones.

In the process of **grinding**, the harder stone or cutting material, by means of which the rough stone is fashioned into a gem, is almost invariably used in the form of a fine powder. This grinding powder is mixed to a paste with olive-oil (in the case of diamond powder) or with water (in the case of emery, &c.), and placed near the edge of a circular disc or lap about a foot in diameter and an inch in thickness. This disc, which is usually of metal, revolves with great velocity in a horizontal plane about a vertical axis. The precious stone to be ground down is pressed against that part of the disc on which the grinding powder lies. The pressure of the stone against the revolving disc causes the powder to become embedded in the soft metal of the disc. This then acts as a file, the hardness of which is equal to the hardness of the grinding powder. By the gradual abrasion of the material of the stone over the area which is being ground the facet develops, the length of time occupied depending on the hardness of the precious stone and of the grinding material.

At short intervals during the progress of the work the gem-cutter must ascertain the size to which the facet has grown, so as to avoid making it too large. A facet which exceeds the other corresponding facets in size is said to be over-ground. Such an irregularity in a stone greatly diminishes its value. Great care is also necessary to avoid the over-heating of the stone during the operation of grinding. Neglect of this precaution results in the development of small cracks, known as " icy flakes," in the interior of the stone, which cause it to be dull and so diminish its beauty. Before beginning the actual work of grinding, the particular form in which the stone is to be cut, and also its most favourable orientation with respect to the boundaries of the rough stone, must be decided so that the precise position and direction required for each facet may be given to it by the cutter.

One of the most obvious essentials in the grinding of a stone is a means whereby it may be retained constantly in one position. For this purpose a special kind of holder, the so-called *dop* (or dopp) is used. This consists of a small hemispherical cup of copper attached by the convex side to a stout copper rod. The cup is filled with an easily fusible alloy of tin and lead, which is fused and allowed to cool; immediately before solidification sets in, the stone is placed in the cooling alloy in the position desired, and so that about one-half is embedded in the alloy and the other half projects out of it. By this means the stone is fixed in the holder in an unalterable position. In the case of stones of comparatively little value the holder just described may be replaced by a stick of cement, or by a rod of metal or wood, to which the stone may be fixed by a cement consisting of pitch, resin or shellac, and the finest brick-dust.

The rod of the dop or the stick of cement is fixed in a clamp at one end of a small bar, perpendicular to which at the other end are two short legs. This apparatus is placed so that the two legs rest on a fixed table, while the precious stone in its holder rests upon the grinding disc, which is parallel to and a little higher than the table. The stone is pressed against the upper surface of the disc by loading the bar with leaden weights, which are larger or smaller according to the hardness of the stone to be ground. To avoid irregularly loading the grinding disc, two stones are ground at the same time, these being placed at opposite ends of a diameter of the disc. In the case of a stone of little value the rod to which it is fixed is simply held in the hand until the facet is ground down to the required size, but the result is naturally less perfect than when a mechanical clamp is used.

When a facet is completed the dop is fixed in a new position in the clamp in such a way as to ensure the second facet being correctly placed. By repeating this operation the half of the stone not embedded in the alloy is faceted all over, the different positions of the facets being attained by varying the inclination of the dop or holder in the clamp. Formerly the position of the holder in the clamp necessary to produce any given inclination between the facets was judged of by the eye; this rough method was naturally not susceptible of any great degree of accuracy, and, indeed, frequently gave results very far from what was desired. More recently various appliances furnished with graduated arcs have made it possible to turn the holder through any required angle, which thus ensures that the facets are accurately located in the desired position.

When the projecting portion of the stone has been faceted as far as possible, the alloy must be re-fused and the stone embedded in a new position, so that a fresh portion will be exposed for grinding. This will usually require to be done several times before the stone has received its full number of facets, when it is finally freed from the alloy or cement and cleaned.

The completely faceted stone thus obtained is by no means ready for use as a gem. Its facets are dull and rough, and when examined through a lens they will be seen to be beset with scratches and pits marking the places from which the surface material has been abraded by the cutting powder. To render the stone bright and shining, the roughnesses and irregularities in the surface of the facets must be removed by polishing. This process is not commenced until the whole of the grinding is completed.

The process of **polishing** is precisely the same in principle as that of grinding; the same machine and apparatus are employed, but the cutting material, now known as the polishing material, is softer than before. It may be of about the same hardness as that of the stone to be polished or it may be softer. The stone is placed in a holder, and its rough facets brought to bear one by one upon the polishing disc supplied with the polishing material, which have replaced the grinding disc and grinding powder used in the previous operation. The abrasive effect of the polishing disc is much less marked; it gradually obliterates the small striations and pits, which are the cause of the dull appearance of the stone, and the facets become brighter and brighter. Finally, a point is reached when their brilliancy is not increased by continued polishing; this marks the maximum polish of which the particular stone is susceptible and any further efforts are superfluous. It is important that the maximum degree of polish should be imparted to every stone, otherwise its full beauty will not be apparent.

If the softer polishing powder is used for cutting instead of the grinding powder, the facets will not require any final polishing, but will leave the disc in the most perfectly polished condition. This is the case, as we shall see later, in the cutting of diamonds, since no harder cutting material can be found than their own powder; the process of cutting is, under these circumstances, extremely lengthy and proportionately expensive. It is for this reason that stones other than diamond are cut with a grinding material of greater hardness than that of their own substance. The process of cutting is much shortened by this means and the roughness of the facets can be easily removed by a final polishing with softer material.

As a preliminary to the grinding and polishing of a stone an operation known as *rounding* is performed, with the object of obtaining a first rough approximation to the form the stone is finally to assume. The worker holds the stick of cement or other holder in his hand and presses the stone on the grinding disc in the approximate position for each facet. The rough form so obtained is then ground down more exactly as explained above. With diamonds the preliminary shaping of the stone is performed by a process known as *bruting*. This consists in rubbing together two diamonds, each being cemented at the end of a stick or holder, until the desired form is obtained. The operation is performed over a trough, so that the particles detached shall not be lost.

In order to obtain the cabochon-cut or other rounded forms the dop or the stick of cement is held in the hand and constantly turned so that the stone performs a rolling motion on the surface of the rotating disc. The production of such rounded forms requires a special skill. The harder and more quickly abrasive grinding powder will naturally be used in these cases also and the stone afterwards finished with a suitable polishing material.

The material of which the **grinding disc** or lap is made is varied according to the hardness of the stone to be cut, harder metals being used for the harder stones and *vice versâ*. The disc may be made of iron, steel, copper, brass, tin, lead or pewter; wooden discs also are sometimes used. The upper surface must be perfectly plane, but roughened somewhat, at least near the margin where the grinding takes place. The disc is usually driven by water- or steam-power; it rotates at the rate of two or three thousand revolutions per minute, and sometimes at an even greater rate. The harder the stone to be cut the greater is the rate at which the disc is rotated, as the rapid motion greatly intensifies the action of the grinding powder; so much is this the case that powder of the same substance as the stone to be cut can be employed for grinding, provided the velocity of the disc is sufficiently high.

For the grinding of softer stones, especially varieties of quartz, a grindstone or disc of sandstone is employed without grinding material other than the substance of the sandstone itself. Other details of this process will be given later when we deal with the cutting of agates.

The material of the **polishing disc** or lap may be the same as that of the grinding disc used for the same stone, but as a rule a softer material is employed. Polishing discs are frequently made of wood covered with leather, cloth, felt or paper.

The most important **grinding** or **abrading material** is corundum, the hardest of all minerals except diamond. The pure and transparent varieties of this constitute the ruby, sapphire, and other costly precious stones, but it occurs also in nature in an opaque form in large masses; and the finely granular, black variety known as *emery* is specially abundant. This mineral owes its black colour to the inter-mixture of softer minerals which, however, do not seriously affect its hardness. Emery occurs in large masses, especially in Asia Minor and in the Island of Naxos in the Grecian Archipelago; also at Chester in the State of Massachusetts, U.S.A., and at other places. Commercial emery is largely obtained from Naxos and from Asia Minor, and, in accordance with the various uses to which it is put, is ground to various degrees of fineness. Crystallised common corundum is used for similar purposes; it occurs in a few localities in large masses of comparative purity, and not being mixed with softer minerals possesses a hardness greater than that of emery. Other hard minerals, such as topaz and garnet and sometimes even quartz, are occasionally employed as grinding materials.

In recent years an artificial grinding material, called *carborundum*, has been largely used as an abrasive agent, especially in the United States. It was first prepared in large quantities by the firm of Acheson of Pittsburg in Pennsylvania; the method employed being simply the fusing together of quartz-sand and coal at the enormously high temperature of the electric furnace. The substance obtained is a compound of carbon and silicon having the chemical formula SiC, and consisting of 30 per cent. of carbon and 70 per cent. of silicon. It frequently crystallises in very distinct hexagonal plates, which are translucent, greenish-yellow in colour and very brilliant. It is considerably softer than diamond, but scratches corundum with ease; its great brittleness renders it easily reduced to powder in spite of its great hardness. Carborundum can be obtained cheaply and with little difficulty in crystalline blocks weighing a hundredweight, and it will doubtless gradually replace emery for abrasive purposes.

Finally, the hardest and most important grinding material is *diamond*. Diamond often occurs so impure as to be useless as a gem; this impure material is the so-called bort, which when finely powdered becomes an important abrasive agent. The black, opaque, finely granular variety of diamond known as carbonado, when finely powdered also furnishes a useful grinding material. In spite of the fact that even these varieties of diamond are of very high price, their use in grinding precious stones greatly cheapens the process, for, on account of their enormous hardness, a considerable saving in time and labour is effected. Since the discovery of the South African diamond fields, the price of diamond dust has been considerably lowered, and it is frequently advantageous at the present time to use this material, instead of emery-powder, in the cutting of many precious stones; the economy effected in time and labour more than compensating for the higher price of the grinding material. In cutting the diamond no choice of grinding material is at present possible, since diamond-powder is the only substance hard enough for the purpose.

The **polishing material** is varied according to the nature of the precious stone to be operated upon. In the form of the very finest powder, such diverse substances as tripolite, rotten-stone, jeweller's rouge, pumice-stone, putty-powder (tin oxide), and sometimes a variety of clay known as bole, are all employed for this purpose. The polishing material, like the grinding material, is made into a paste before being applied to the lap or polishing disc; water is generally used for this purpose, but with tripolite sulphuric acid is sometimes employed.

It has already been mentioned that different precious stones are worked with different grinding powders and on laps of different material, these two conditions being varied to suit the particular characteristics of the stone, that of hardness receiving special attention. The choice of material for the lap and of grinding and polishing powder lies between certain somewhat arbitrary limits, thus the same method for one and the same kind of precious stone is not always exactly followed. All precious stones may be conveniently grouped in a few classes according to their hardness; those of each group may be worked in the same manner and with the same materials. The following grouping shows such an arrangement.

a. **Very hard stones.** Ruby, sapphire, and other varieties of corundum.

Ground on an iron, brass or copper lap with diamond-powder. Emery works only very slowly.

Polished on a copper disc with tripolite.

b. **Hard stones.** Spinel, chrysoberyl, topaz.

Ground on a brass or copper disc with emery. (With topaz a tin or lead disc even may be used.)

Polished on copper with putty-powder or tripolite.

c. **Stones of medium hardness**. Emerald, beryl, aquamarine, zircon, tourmaline, garnet, rock-crystal, amethyst, agate, jasper, chalcedony, carnelian, chrysoprase, &c.

Ground on copper or tin or lead with emery.

Polished usually on tin with tripolite or on zinc with putty-powder, sometimes also on wood.

Garnets of fairly considerable size for use as larger ornaments are ground with emery or garnet-powder on a leaden disc and polished on a tin disc with tripolite and sulphuric acid.   Smaller garnets, on the contrary, which are strung as beads after being pierced with a fine diamond point, are ground on a disc of fine sandstone with emery and olive-oil, and polished on a wooden disc with tripolite and water or on a tin disc with tripolite and sulphuric acid.   Rock-crystal and amethyst are ground on a copper or lead disc with emery, and polished on a tin disc or on a wooden disc covered with felt, with putty-powder, tripolite or bole.   For grinding agate, jasper, chalcedony, carnelian, and chrysoprase a disc of copper, tin or lead is often used with garnet or topaz-powder instead of emery; while for polishing, pumice-stone, jeweller's rouge or putty-powder on a tin disc, or pumice-stone on a wooden disc is employed.   Agate and other varieties of quartz are, however, often worked in another manner, which will be considered under the special description of agate.

d. **Soft stones.**   Obsidian, chrysolite, opal, adularia, turquoise, lapis-lazuli.

Ground with emery on a disc of lead or tin.

Polished with tripolite on tin or hard wood, or sometimes with pumice-stone on wood.

e. **Glass imitations.**   These are usually ground and polished on wooden discs; emery being used as the grinding material, and tripolite as the polishing material.

Not infrequently, before the process of grinding a precious stone can proceed, a preliminary preparation of the stone is required.   Many precious stones, especially the most valuable, such as diamond and ruby, occur in nature in relatively small but perfectly pure fragments.   In such cases no preliminary preparation is needed, and the stone can be at once cut into any desired form.   It is otherwise, however, with many precious stones, such, for example, as aquamarine; the naturally occurring crystals and fragments of such stones may be too large for a single cut stone, or may include material which is cloudy or faulty and unfit for cutting.   In such cases the specimen must be divided into several pieces of convenient size, and the faulty and undesirable portions removed by a process less lengthy and costly than that of simply grinding them away.

This operation is performed with the aid of a thin metal disc, usually of soft iron, the edge of which is charged with some hard cutting powder, preferably diamond.   This *cutting* or *slitting disc* usually rotates in a vertical plane on a horizontal axis; by pressing the stone against the cutting edge of the rapidly rotating disc it will be slowly cut through by the small splinters of diamond which are embedded in the metal.   The division of the stone can also be effected by means of a wire smeared with cutting powder, stretched in a bow and used as a saw.   This method is, however, very slow, and is now rarely practised.

The superfluous or undesirable material of cheap stones, which occur in large masses, is not cut away, but simply broken off by the blow of a hammer; a mode of procedure which cannot be recommended for valuable stones, unless, as in diamond and topaz, they possess certain known directions of easy cleavage.   Stones which can be cleaved with such facility may, as we have already seen, be readily reduced in certain directions with a chisel and hammer with no fear of losing valuable material, so that by this means the work of cutting and grinding is considerably lessened.   This subject will be again considered, especially with reference to the diamond, under the special description of each stone.   The fragments of valuable material thus broken or cut away are carefully collected and preserved; they may be utilised for the fashioning of smaller gems, or, if of sufficient hardness, pulverised and used as a cutting and grinding material.

As the treatment of precious stones must be varied to suit the different nature of each stone, each requiring different contrivances and methods, so different branches of the gem-cutting industry can be identified, each establishment dealing, as a rule, with but one kind of stone, to the exclusion of others. In diamond-cutting works diamonds only are cut, while the work of other establishments is limited to the treatment of other precious and semi-precious stones to the exclusion of diamonds; such establishments are known as precious-stone or fine-stone-cutting works. Another branch of the industry is concerned exclusively with the large ornamental stones with plane surfaces, or only a small number of facets, such as are suitable for use as stones for signet-rings, crosses, and so forth: here the less valuable stones only are used, such as agate, chalcedony, jasper, &c. In addition to the objects just mentioned, articles such as letter-weights, cups, vases, boxes, etuis, inkstands, stick and umbrella knobs and handles, knife-handles, &c., are fashioned at these large-stone-cutting works, and such materials as granite, marble, serpentine, &c., which do not fall under the head of precious stones, are made use of in the industry beside the minerals mentioned above. The work carried on respectively at the large- and the small-stone-cutting establishments is now to a large extent regarded as different branches of the same trade, and is often directed by the same firm, but the diamond-cutting industry is a distinct and specialised calling, which is never combined with other branches of the trade.

C. BORING.

Not infrequently precious stones, such as garnets, are strung together and worn as beads, which necessitates that they shall be pierced. In the cases in which precious stones have a technical application, such, for instance, as the making of pivot-supports for watches, and the orifices through which very fine gold and silver wires are drawn, it is often necessary to bore a hole through the centre of the stone. The boring is usually effected by the rapid rotation of a fine diamond point, fixed in a metal holder, which acts like a drill. The diamond point of the drill is often replaced by a steel point charged with diamond powder moistened with oil. For convenience in conducting this operation, special machines are constructed by means of which hard stones are bored with ease and rapidity.

D. WORKING ON THE LATHE.

Many stones, especially the softer ones, occurring in large masses, furnish material for the manufacture of balls and other rounded objects. Such articles may be turned on the lathe; this machine is more appropriate for the class of work carried on in the large-stone-cutting works, and is seldom used in the working of precious stones. Nevertheless the hardest stones used for gems may be worked in this way, the steel turning-tool being replaced by a diamond point; as, however, the turning of precious stones is but rarely undertaken, it need not be further considered here.

E. ENGRAVING.

Precious stones are not only cut in various forms, but they are also engraved with devices such as figures, crests, monograms, or with inscriptions. In the cutting of a stone, the lapidary strives to give it such a form as will best display its natural beauty; this beauty depends essentially on the characters of the stone, not on the form given it by the lapidary; this form being simply a means to an end, namely to develop to the uttermost the natural beauties of the stone. The engraver, on the other hand, aims at producing a work of art of value in itself; the material upon which the artist works is a secondary consideration, for he will probably be able to produce just as fine an engraving on some other stone of an entirely different character.

The art of engraving and cutting precious stones is very ancient, much older indeed than that of faceting. It is mentioned by writers of the earliest historical times, and specimens of this art dating back to very early times are preserved in our museums. The art of engraving precious stones is still practised, especially in Italy, but the popularity, at the present day, of engraved gems is not comparable with that of faceted stones. The cutting of precious stones with a view to the production of an engraving is known as the glyptic art, and is thus distinguished from the grinding of facets upon the stone, which can scarcely rank as an art.

Engraved precious stones are generally known as *gems*. The device engraved upon a gem is either sunk in the stone so as to lie below its surface, in which case the gem is known as an *intaglio*; or the device is in relief so as to lie above the surface of the stone, a gem so engraved being known as a *cameo*. Intaglios are frequently used for seals or signets to produce a raised cameo-like impression; for this purpose they are commonly engraved with a crest or monogram. Cameos, on the other hand, have no application of this kind, but are used merely as ornaments. The art of engraving intaglios is known as *sculpture*, while that of producing cameos is known as *tornature*. Of the two arts, the former is the more ancient, but the antiquity of the latter is well established by the number of cameos, in the shape of a beetle—the so-called scarabs—found in Egyptian tombs.

All kinds of stones, whether hard or soft, opaque or transparent, have been and are employed in the production of **intaglios.** The harder the stone the sharper and clearer will be the engraved figure, and the more irksome and lengthy the process of engraving. The engraving of the diamond, in spite of its hardness and the consequent difficulty in working, is occasionally effected; ruby and sapphire have also been sometimes worked in this manner; the harder precious stones are, however, much less frequently engraved than those which are softer and offer less resistance to the process. Specimens of this art, dating from the earliest times, are still in existence; these comprise engravings executed on emerald, aquamarine, topaz, chrysolite, turquoise, rock-crystal, amethyst, plasma, chalcedony, carnelian, agate, heliotrope, opal, lapis-lazuli, nephrite, obsidian, magnetite, and many other stones. At the present day the materials most frequently used are quartz and chalcedony, together with such varieties of these as agate, onyx, &c., also hæmatite and a few others. The material of the intaglio shown in Plate XX., Fig. 6, is carnelian, another example of intaglio is shown in Fig. 92.

Transparent stones cut as **cameos** are very rarely seen; opaque stones of fine colour are usually chosen for the purpose, those constituted of differently coloured bands, as in onyx and sardonyx, being specially suitable. Different portions of the device of a cameo cut in such stones may lie at different levels; thus, supposing for example that the device is a human figure, a white layer may be worked to form the face and hands of the figure, and a black layer for the hair and garments. In the cameo shown in Plate XX., Fig. 7, the white figure and the red background are at different levels in the red and white-banded stone; other specimens of this kind of work are represented in Figs. 93 and 94. Opaque stones of one colour throughout, such as turquoise and malachite, are also used in the cutting of cameos; the material of the Egyptian scarabs is very frequently not a precious stone at all, but serpentine or some similar stone. In Italy, where the industry of cameo-cutting especially flourishes, the shells of certain marine molluscs are employed instead of the stones mentioned above; in these shells, as in many agates, red and white layers occur in regular alternation. The majority of cameos sold, for example, in Naples, are made of such material; they may be readily distinguished, however, from a genuine cameo, cut from onyx, &c., by the fact that a shell-cameo is soft enough to be scratched with a knife, and will effervesce when touched with a drop of acid.

The tool used in cutting or engraving is a very small iron wheel fixed at the end of a rotating axis in a lathe. The small wheel, which may be conical, hemispherical, or disc-shaped, and often not more than a twelfth of an inch in diameter, is charged with moistened diamond-powder. The stone to be engraved, after being cut to the required form and polished, is placed in a holder and its surface pressed against the rotating wheel. The outline of the device to be engraved is obtained by moving the stone about while the cutting is taking place, more or less prolonged working gives a deeper or shallower engraving. The final polish must, as a rule, be given after the cutting process is completed ; this and the last touches to the engraving are given by hand with a graving tool furnished with a diamond point.

Etching.—An alternative to the difficult, lengthy, and costly process of engraving is furnished by the simpler, quicker, and cheaper process of etching. The process is, however, only applicable to certain stones, and the figures produced are less clear and beautiful than those created by the engraver. The method requires that the stone used shall be susceptible to the action of some acid ; hence none of the more valuable precious stones are available as material, since they are unacted upon by acids. Those stones, however, which consist wholly of silica, namely rock-crystal, chalcedony, agate, &c., are acted upon by hydrofluoric acid as easily as is glass, and by its means devices may be etched upon them. The polished surface of the stone to be etched is covered with a thin coating of wax, upon which the outline of the device is drawn with some sharp instrument ; the surface of the stone along this outline is therefore laid bare while other parts are protected by the wax. The stone is then placed in liquid or gaseous hydrofluoric acid, which eats away the surface of the stone where it is not protected by a layer of wax. There soon appears a hollowing out of the material along the outlines of the device, and this will be deeper the longer the acid is allowed to act. After removing the wax and cleaning the stone the device (monogram, crest, &c.) sketched upon the wax will appear as if cut in the stone.

F. COLOURING AND BURNING.

The methods adopted for altering or improving the natural colours of stones may conveniently be considered here. Such a change of colour, which has already been stated to be possible under the general discussion of colour, is effected in various ways. We shall not now discuss the change of colour produced in a stone already set and mounted by a surface coating of colouring-matter, but only those methods by which a change in the colour of the whole mass of the stone is effected.

Those precious stones which have a porous structure can be artificially coloured through their whole mass with great ease. The stone to be coloured is allowed to lie in the liquid in which the colouring-matter is dissolved ; its porous structure causes it to become after a time saturated with the liquid, which penetrates to the innermost parts of its mass. The stone is then taken out and allowed to dry, during which process the solvent evaporates and the colouring-matter in solution is left behind, lodged in the interstices of the stone, and imparts its colour to the stone. This method is not infrequently practised, and many agates are remarkable for the ease with which they can be coloured by its use. In other cases the use of two liquids is necessary to produce an artificial colour, the *rationale* of the method being that by the interaction of the two liquids a chemical precipitate is formed, which is deposited in the pores of the stone, and imparts to it the desired colour. In this method the stone is first placed in one liquid, in which it is allowed to remain until completely saturated : it is then taken out and dried and placed in the second liquid, when precipitation takes place. The coloured precipitate so produced is regularly distributed in the interior of the stone, so far as the stone is uniformly porous and capable of absorbing liquids. This process of colouring will be described in greater detail under the description of agate. The exact methods of producing the artificial colours, which are black, yellow, blue, green, and brown, are in many cases preserved as a trade secret.

The writings of Pliny show that these arts were known even in ancient times, and the methods then employed for colouring agates are apparently identical with those now practised. At that time, however, a process was known by which certain colours, such for instance as the fine green of the emerald, could be imparted to rock-crystal, a process which is unknown at the present day. Rock-crystal, not being porous, cannot be coloured artificially by the methods described above; the only process known at the present day is to plunge the stone when strongly heated into a cold, coloured liquid; the abrupt change in temperature causes the stone to become penetrated by numerous cracks, into which the coloured liquid enters, and on evaporation deposits its colouring-matter. Rock-crystal so coloured is not, however, very suitable for cutting on account of the cracks developed in it by its sudden cooling; the method therefore is of no practical significance as compared with the colouring of agates, which is of great commercial importance.

Some precious stones when subjected to the action of heat become either completely decolourised or changed in colour, the original colouring-matter being in the one case destroyed and in the other altered. This process, which is known as **burning**, is often employed for increasing the natural colour of many stones, for rendering it more permanent, for completely changing the colour, or for removing unsightly patches. The heating and cooling must be very slow and regular and all sudden changes of temperature avoided; otherwise the stone may develop cracks, or the change in the original colour may not take place uniformly throughout the whole mass of the stone. For the purpose of attaining a uniform rate of heating and cooling the stone is embedded in some powdered material in a crucible; the material made use of being coal-dust, fine sand, iron-filings, clay, quick-lime or wood-ashes, &c. In some cases only a comparatively slight heating is necessary, but often the temperature must be raised to a red-heat in order to destroy or change the colour.

The pigment to which the colour of a stone is due is in many cases unstable at high temperatures, becoming changed into some other body, which is either colourless or coloured differently from the original substance. Thus the change or destruction of the colour of a precious stone can only be effected by burning when the pigment to which its colour is due is altered on exposure to heat.

The yellow Brazilian topaz becomes rose-red when heated, and is then known as " burnt topaz." Amethyst when exposed for a short time to a gentle red-heat in a mixture of sand and iron-filings loses any darkly coloured patches it may have had; after strong and pro-longed heating to redness the violet colour is changed to brownish-yellow, the stone being then known as " burnt amethyst." Many of the naturally occurring brown carnelians become, when heated, a bright red; in this case the original brown colouring-matter is a hydrated oxide of iron, which is changed into the bright red anhydrous oxide by the action of heat. Burning causes yellowish-red hyacinth to become colourless, and at the same time appreciably increases the lustre of the stone. The blue sapphire also completely loses its colour on heating. Other similar cases might be cited; they will be mentioned, since the change of colour effected by burning is of some technical importance, each in its proper place with the special description of each kind of precious stone. The majority of precious stones, however, undergo no alteration in colour even at the highest temperatures.

G. MOUNTING AND SETTING.

The majority of precious stones are destined, after being cut, to be devoted to purposes of jewellery. The less valuable stones are occasionally bored with holes and strung together as beads for personal ornaments, such as necklaces and bracelets. It rarely happens that the whole of a personal ornament, such for instance as a finger-ring, is cut wholly in stone ; this may be done, for example, with nephrite, a stone which occurs in sufficiently large masses and is possessed of the necessary toughness and firmness for the purpose. Much more frequently the stone is firmly and permanently fixed in a piece of metal of suitable shape and of more or less artistic workmanship ; this is known to jewellers as the *setting* of the stone.

The setting of precious stones and the manner in which different kinds of stones are associated affords scope for the exercise of much taste and judgment; these matters are naturally, however, regulated to a large extent by the fashion current at the moment. A single stone is sometimes set by itself in an article of jewellery ; when this is the case the stone should be of large size and as perfect a specimen of its kind as possible. Usually, however, the effect of such a stone would be enhanced by a border of small stones of another kind ; thus a large and fine opal is often surrounded by a border of small diamonds, the opacity and opalescent lustre of the one forming a pleasing contrast with the transparency and adamantine lustre of the other. This kind of setting is known as carmoizing. Both for decorative work and for personal ornament different kinds of stones are associated in elegant groups, representing butterflies, flowers, and other objects; here again practice, discrimination and taste are required in order to produce effects of contrast worthy of the beauty of the individual stones.

Gold and silver are the only metals used as the material for the setting of valuable stones. In cheap jewellery some substitute for these metals, such, for example, as gilded brass, is employed. The beauty of some stones is best displayed in a setting of silver, as is the case with diamond ; while gold is a more effective background for rubies and other stones. The girdle, when present, is the portion of a cut stone which is held by the metal setting ; when there is no girdle, as in rosettes, the stone is fixed by the lower margin ; other forms of cut stones are fixed in a variety of ways.

In the kind of setting described as an *open* (*à jour*) *setting*, the metal is in contact with the stone at a few points only along the margin, so that the stone is exposed to view on all sides, it being possible to view an object through it. In another method of setting, the stone is fitted into a metal receptacle of the same size and shape as itself, so that it can be seen only from the front; the back and margin of the stone being concealed by the metal. With this kind of setting, which is described as a *closed setting*, it is impossible to look through the stone, but sometimes the bottom of the metal receptacle is hinged so that it may be opened and closed, and the back of the stone exposed to view, if desired.

In the open setting (*à jour*) the stone is surrounded by a ring of metal from which several small metal pins or claws project. These are slightly cleft at their extremities, so that each somewhat resembles a pair of small pincers, which grasp the stone at the girdle or margin and hold it, as it were, suspended. This kind of setting is specially adapted to transparent, colourless stones and to coloured stones of flawless quality whose natural perfections require no improvement.

The mounter of gems must be guided in the choice of a setting for a given stone by the form in which it is cut. For stones such as brilliants with an upper and a lower portion, the open setting is employed, the broad table of the stone being, of course, placed towards the observer. Faulty stones are sometimes set with the table towards the back, as in the so-called Indian setting. Stones, on the contrary, which have no under portion are rarely, and rosettes never, mounted in an open setting; they are much more effective in a closed setting. A stone is held very firmly and permanently in a closed setting, and this is especially the case when cement is used to fix it to the metal, as is very frequently done. In an open setting, on the contrary, there is much more likelihood of the stone becoming, loosened from the claws which hold it, and therefore of its ultimate loss.

Flawless stones of a good colour, which are destined to be mounted in a closed setting, need only to be simply inserted in the receptacle described above. But those in which the colour, lustre, or other quality leave something to be desired can be improved by certain artifices in mounting and their faults more or less concealed.

The artifice which has been longest practised is designed to conceal any dark patches the stone may have, and is known as " mounting on moor." A black pigment made by mixing burnt ivory and mastic is applied to those parts of the closed setting over which the lighter portions of the stone will rest. The stone, when set, will then appear to be uniformly coloured, the patchiness being effectively concealed.

An artifice more frequently used is designed to improve the lustre and colour of the stone to which it is applied. Thin plates of gold, silver, copper, tin, &c., which are known as *foils*, are laid under the stone; they may be of their own natural colour or they may be artificially coloured in some suitable manner; in any case they show their own strong lustre. Instead of metallic foils, pieces of silk with a coloured sheen or cuttings of peacock's feathers and similar substances are sometimes used. An uncoloured, natural foil shows its lustre and body-colour through the stone beneath which it is placed, and causes it to appear more brilliant and of a finer colour than would otherwise be the case. A golden foil will give a deeper yellow tint to a pale coloured stone, while a dull stone may be made to appear brighter by placing beneath it a bright and shining foil. A peculiar variation of this use of the foil exists in the Orient in the mounting of rubies, the back of the stone being hollowed out and filled in with gold, a device which considerably heightens the effect of the stone as regards brilliancy and colour.

In the employment of foils, it is desirable that the stone and the foil should be of corresponding colours. As the natural colours of the metals employed are often unsuitable the foils are sometimes artificially coloured blue, red, yellow or green, these colours being always placed on a white metal. Carmine, saffron, litmus, &c., are some of the pigments used for this purpose, intermediate tints being obtained by mixtures; the pigment is dissolved with isinglass in water and so applied to the metal.

Instead of using a foil, the pigment may be applied to the inside of the case in which the stone is set, or even to the back of the stone itself. It is actually possible by the judicious application of colour at the back of a colourless stone to give the effect of a coloured stone, or even by applying a coating of various tints, to produce the effect of a play of colours. This latter device is now often applied to rock-crystal or colourless glass with the purpose of imitating the play of prismatic colours characteristic of the diamond. Stones so treated, which have sometimes quite a pretty effect, are often used under the name of " iris " for cheap jewellery, pin-heads, &c. It is especially in the Orient, however, that the artifices under consideration have been developed to great perfection, Eastern jewellers being possessed of marvellous dexterity, which they often make use of for the deception of buyers of gems.

By associating several stones of the same kind and of an exactly identical shade of colour in one piece of jewellery a very fine effect is produced; there is however often considerable difficulty in obtaining naturally coloured stones of exactly the same shade of colour. This difficulty may be overcome by coating the back of a dark stone with a light pigment or a pale stone with a darker pigment, and thus securing a uniform depth of colour.

A very effective artifice is that of placing beneath a stone a second of the same form of cutting. Large rosettes are frequently treated in this way, a smaller stone and a foil being placed under the rosette in the closed metal case in which it is set; by this device the brilliancy and lustre of the rosette are wonderfully increased. Similar manipulations will be further considered when we come to treat of the imitation of precious stones.

The use of these and similar artifices for increasing the beauty of a stone is naturally attended with less difficulty when the stone is mounted in a closed setting and one side of it entirely hidden from view, than when an open setting is used. Even in the latter case, however, such artifices may be made use of to a certain extent; thus, a thin strip of foil, or a coating of pigment is applied to the inner side of the setting just below the girdle of the stone; this often has the effect of increasing the brilliancy and colour of the stone. A ruby of too pale a tint mounted in an open setting may be treated in this way, the inner rim of the setting being coated with carmine-red enamel, which gives the stone a very beautiful depth of colour. Other precious stones are treated in corresponding ways.

H. FAULTS IN PRECIOUS STONES.

The beauty and value of a precious stone naturally depend on the absence of all disfiguring faults within its substance or upon its surface. Thus a perfect specimen of a gem must be free from cracks and fissures in its interior and its lustre and polish must be uniform and uninterrupted over the whole surface. A transparent stone should be perfectly clear, with no cloudy patches, and free from all enclosures, especially of small, opaque, foreign substances. Colourless stones ought to be quite free from any faintly coloured patches; while the colour of coloured stones must be uniform and regularly distributed, so that the stone shows no light or dark patches, or differently coloured portions of its substance. Exception to the latter rule is, of course, made in such a stone as agate, the effect of which depends on a difference of colour in different portions of its substance. Each imperfection of the kinds just noted, each crack, each dark or cloudy or differently coloured patch, is a fault in the stone, and as such detracts from its beauty. It is in transparent stones that faults are especially noticeable, and in a cut form they are reflected again and again from the facets and thus rendered still more obvious.

Small insignificant faults, when they are few in number, do not render a stone entirely unsuitable for decorative purposes, but they do diminish its value, and that sometimes very considerably. When, however, the appearance of a stone is so disfigured by the presence of numerous glaring faults that its use for ornamental purposes is out of the question, it becomes absolutely worthless, unless indeed its hardness enables it to serve some useful technical purpose.

The more obvious faults of precious stones, such for example as the presence of light, or dark, or differently coloured patches, are easily detected; they are indeed often apparent at the first glance. Frequently, however, the detection of faults requires a practised eye, since a clever gem-cutter will so arrange the facets of a stone that any faults it may have become quite inconspicuous and almost unnoticeable to an unskilled observer. When considering the subject of the refraction of light it was mentioned that the faults of transparent stones may be made more conspicuous by immersing the stone in a strongly refracting liquid, such as methylene iodide or monobromonaphthalene. This device is due to Sir

David Brewster, who for the same purpose made use of Canada-balsam, oil of anise or sassafras-oil.

It is not difficult, by one or other of the artifices already described, to conceal or make inconspicuous the various faults to which precious stones are liable. On this account, therefore, it is a rule to be observed that valuable stones of high price should never be purchased in a setting, but in a loose and unmounted condition, which admits of a thorough and complete examination of the stone being made. Such an examination should be made before the purchase not only of cut-stones, but also of uncut, rough stones. Small faults in the latter are often very difficult to detect, since the roughness of the surface interferes more or less considerably with the transparency of the stone. In such cases it is advisable to place the stone in a highly refractive liquid, which will have the apparent effect of lessening the roughness of the surface and increasing the transparency of the stone. Even when placed in water such stones will appear more transparent than in air. In examining a rough stone it is important to determine whether any fault it may have lies quite in the interior of the stone or near the surface. In the latter case it may often be removed in the process of cutting, and a somewhat imperfect rough stone may be transformed into a gem of flawless beauty.

The nature of the faults which are of the most frequent occurrence in precious stones may be gathered from what has already been said. Those of the nature of coloured patches, enclosures of large foreign bodies and such like, need no further description; other faults, however, which occur again and again with the same characteristic appearance are distinguished by jewellers with special names and receive special mention below.

1. **Sand.**—Small grains of any foreign substance, of a white, brown or reddish colour scattered singly through the material of the stone are known as sand.

2. **Dust.**—This is the name by which extremely small particles of foreign matter scattered in great numbers through the substance of a stone are known.

3. **Clouds.**—By this term is meant muddy or cloudy patches of various colours—white, grey, brown, reddish, greenish, &c.—which may occur in the substance of a stone and which when brought to the surface in the process of cutting, give it a dull appearance which no amount of polishing will remove. They are most frequent in diamonds and pale rubies.

The three kinds of faults just described are all due to the inclusion of small mineral grains as impurities in the substance of the precious stone. If not too small, they may sometimes be seen with the naked eye or with a good lens, but more frequently the powerful magnification of a microscope is required. Their presence is best demonstrated, however, when the stone is examined in polarised light; in the dark field of the polariscope such inclusions will sometimes appear bright and vividly coloured.

4. **Silk.**—This term signifies the whitish, shimmering streaks, disposed in certain directions, which sometimes mar the appearance of a stone. Such streaks are in reality strings of microscopically small cavities in the substance of the stone, which may be quite empty or may, on the other hand, contain a liquid. Such cavities are not at all uncommon in precious stones; they are sometimes of quite appreciable size, as in topaz, sapphire, &c., when they may be seen with the naked eye or with a lens. The cavities, to which the fault known as "silk" is due, are however definitely arranged in bands and strings, and only become visible as single objects under strong magnification. By scattering at their surfaces the light which should pass directly through the stone, these minute cavities produce the dull, whitish shimmer. They have the same effect as " clouds " in that, when they occur on the surface of a stone, a perfect polish over that area is impossible.

5. **Feathers.**—Under this name are included cracks and fissures which may be present in all kinds of precious stones, and which exert a disturbing action on the path of the rays of light passing through the stone. They may be of large or of almost microscopic size, and may occur singly or aggregated together in large numbers. They are especially common in stones which possess a very perfect cleavage, such as diamond and topaz; they then have the direction, regularity and flatness peculiar to cleavage cracks. Faults of this nature are, however, also present in stones which possess no marked cleavage, such as quartz and garnet, but here they are irregularly curved and bent. In such cracks, brilliant, iridescent colours are often to be seen, and when this is the case the cracks are more noticeable. The existence of feathers, which do not exhibit such interference colours, is very difficult to detect, even with a lens; they may be best demonstrated by placing the stone in methylene iodide.

Feathers are more to be feared than any other kind of fault, since there is always a tendency for these small cracks to extend, thus adding to the disfigurement of the stone, and perhaps in the end causing its complete fracture. This is especially likely to happen during the grinding, owing to the vibration consequent on the operation, or it may be brought about by subsequent careless handling, and often even with no apparent cause. It is therefore very desirable before going to the labour and expense of cutting a stone, to make certain that it is free from such faults. This may be done as mentioned above, by immersing the stone in a strongly refracting liquid and inspecting it with a lens. Another method is to heat the stone and then quickly cool it by immersing it in cold water; any incipient cracks will be made to develop by this treatment and thus become more distinctly visible, or the stone may even fracture along the cracks; this operation is of course risky and should not be attempted with valuable stones.

6. **Icy flakes.**—These are small cracks which are not of natural occurrence in precious stones, but are developed during the process of grinding if a stone has been allowed to become too hot. Their presence is manifested as dull cloudy areas on the surface of the stone which are incapable of receiving a good polish. Such faults can be avoided by keeping the temperature of the stone down during the process of grinding.

I. ARTIFICIAL PRODUCTION.

As in the case of many minerals, it has been possible to produce the majority of precious stones by artificial means. These artificial products are in every respect identical with naturally occurring precious stones—namely, in their chemical composition, crystalline form, and in all their physical characters. When it is possible to obtain such artificially formed precious stones of sufficient size and of the clearness, transparency, and fine colour of the naturally occuring precious stones, they will be equal in value to the latter, and equally applicable to decorative purposes. To consider artificially formed stones inferior to natural stones is nothing but baseless prejudice. They differ from the latter in no respect save origin, having been produced under artificial instead of natural conditions; they are therefore truly genuine stones, and in no sense must they be regarded as imitations.

Many have been the experiments made with the object of producing minerals by artificial means, and in numerous instances such efforts have been successful. In the case of precious stones the results, although of the greatest scientific interest, have had, up to the present, little or no practical importance, since the stones obtained have been but of very small size, often microscopically minute, and thus useless as gems. Only in the case of two of the more valuable precious stones, the ruby and turquoise, have results of importance been yet obtained. The French chemist, Frémy, has prepared crystals of ruby, which, though not large, are yet of sufficient size to be mounted as gems. It appears also that a method has been discovered for the artificial production of turquoise. The details of this method are, however, kept secret. These subjects will be reconsidered when we come to treat specially of ruby and turquoise.

It may probably be safely asserted that the artificial production of every precious stone in a form suitable for decorative purposes is only a question of time. But the possessor of natural gems need not fear on this account a depreciation in the value of his jewels, since the artificial products hitherto obtained are but just within measurable distance of the required standard. Moreover, research in the direction of the preparation of artificial rubies has shown that the cost of artificial production, owing to the expense of raw material of the necessary purity and the costly nature of the apparatus required, is quite equal to the price commanded by natural stones.

It is probably possible, even at the present day, to so improve on the apparatus and methods of manipulation in the artificial manufacture of rubies that fine crystals may be produced at less cost. Naturally such researches have been frequently undertaken, although possibly often in secret, owing to the value a happy discovery might have. The possession of the secret by which costly precious stones could be prepared at comparatively small cost, in a condition equal to that of natural stones, would indeed be a source of wealth! The artificial production of precious stones in large quantities would, of course, very soon bring their price down to a minimum, and would also depreciate the value of natural stones. Thus it would result that precious stones which had previously been rare and costly objects, and their acquisition possible only to the rich, would come to be within the reach of all classes. This being so, their possession would cease to distinguish the upper and wealthy classes from less-favoured individuals, and hence precious stones would lose the attribute to which at the present time a large part of their value is due.

J. COUNTERFEITING:

In dealing in objects of such value as precious stones, it is not surprising to find that efforts are often made to substitute for a genuine and costly stone one of similar outward appearance, but of less value, in order to deceive an inexperienced buyer. In place of fine stones of high price, attempts are made to pass off stones of less value or glass imitations of the same colour; or, in place of faultless specimens, genuine stones disfigured by the presence of faults, which are hidden by one device or another as completely as possible. Often two small stones are cemented together so that they appear as a single large one; or, again, the upper portion of a cut stone may be genuine while the lower is false.

The inventive genius of dishonest dealers in precious stones is responsible for many other methods by which the unwary purchaser may be deceived. Any person desirous of obtaining a genuine precious stone of any considerable value must be prepared to exercise the greatest caution, unless he is dealing with a well-known and reliable man whose integrity is above suspicion. The more costly the stone the greater is the caution necessary, for the possibility of greater gain is more inducement to fraud. In such cases fraudulent devices are concealed with greater dexterity, and for their detection a sharp eye is necessary as well as expert knowledge, and such experience can only be acquired by familiarity with the trade.

The deceptions practised by Eastern dealers in precious stones are notorious. Many a traveller in India, Burma, Ceylon, &c., with no thought of suspicion in his mind, has bought some apparently beautiful stone, only to learn when too late that he has acquired some utterly worthless object—perhaps a piece of cleverly prepared bottle-glass! There is still more scope for fraud in mounted stones, the setting of which may be used to conceal all kinds of deceptions. In this connection there will be no harm in repeating the rule, that costly and valuable precious stones should never be purchased in a mounted condition.

It is not to be denied that certain artifices, which have been already described, amount to an illusion, inasmuch as they make the stone appear better than it actually is. Such artifices, however, cannot be considered fraudulent, since they are openly practised and are known to all persons concerned. Moreover, a lower price will be asked, at least by a respectable dealer, for a stone that has been so treated than for one which stands in no need of artificial improvement. There are indeed many devices, similar to those which have been described, which are adopted quite openly and in all good faith, and are made use of by every fair-dealing jeweller. Such devices, which fall under the head of recognised and allowable manipulation, are not hidden from an intending purchaser, nor is a higher price set on the stone than its natural qualities justify.

We may contrast with such a transaction one in which a yellowish diamond has received a thin coating of blue colouring-matter, and has then been sold as a colourless, water-clear diamond at a correspondingly high price. There can be no two opinions as to the nature of this latter transaction. There are many cases, however, where it is difficult to draw the line between an artistic device and a fraudulent artifice; the decision in such cases will turn on the behaviour of the dealer, whether he gives a genuine description to the stone and asks a price corresponding to its natural qualities, or whether, on the other hand, he conceals its deficiencies and demands a correspondingly higher price.

The buying and selling of precious stones is then, as we have seen, a trade in which fraudulent practices are particularly easy. It would not be practicable to detail every single possibility of fraud, especially as the oldest tricks appear again and again in new dresses. Such frauds as are most frequently practised will be described below:

1. **Substitution of less valuable stones.**—This can only be effected when the cheaper stone resembles to a certain extent the more valuable one in colour, lustre, and general appearance, and if possible approaches it also in some essential character, such as specific gravity or hardness. In such cases a little special knowledge of the subject is necessary in order to distinguish between the two stones. In this way a colourless topaz may be substituted for a diamond, since both stones are colourless, and both the lustre and the specific gravity of the topaz approach those of the diamond. To give another example, either colourless zircon or colourless sapphire may be substituted for diamond, and according to Mawe, a London jeweller, these stones at the beginning of the nineteenth century commanded a high price since they were especially suitable for selling as diamonds at a still higher price. The variety of the yellow quartz, known as citrine, is substituted for yellow topaz, and red spinel is often offered for ruby; other similar cases might be mentioned.

Some of the stones mentioned above cannot in their natural condition be sold as substitutes for more valuable stones of another kind. Thus hyacinth (zircon) is naturally of a yellowish-red colour, and only becomes colourless and acquires a stronger lustre after it has been heated; similarly, blue sapphire is rendered colourless by heating. For the same purpose, stones are not only decolourised but also artificially coloured. A fine blue colour is imparted to chalcedony, so that, to a certain extent, it resembles lapis-lazuli and may be used instead of that mineral in cheap jewellery and ornaments of various kinds.

An experienced eye will usually be able to detect such fraudulent attempts at the first glance, but there are cases in which this is not possible without a more thorough examination of the stone according to the methods of scientific mineralogy. These methods will be detailed in the third section of this book, and under the description of each kind of precious stone it will be stated how that stone may be distinguished from others which resemble it in general appearance.

2. **Doublets.**—A cut stone, which consists of an upper and a lower portion cemented together so as to present the appearance of a single stone, is known as a doublet. There is less deception here when the two portions consist of genuine material, for example diamond, the two small stones forming together a large and apparently single stone, which, if really single, would be of greater value than the two stones mounted separately. Such a combination of two small, genuine stones may be referred to as a *genuine doublet*.

Very frequently, however, the upper portion only of the doublet is genuine, the lower portion being cut from comparatively worthless material, such as quartz or glass. When skilfully contrived, such a doublet has the appearance of a single stone of the same material as that of the upper portion, and at a first glance shows all the beauty such a stone would have. Such combinations are known, from the material of their upper portion, as diamond-, ruby-, sapphire-doublets, &c. It is said that in Antwerp at the present time diamonds and colourless sapphires are often combined in this way. The advantage to be derived from such a proceeding is very evident; the dealer is able to sell what appears to be a large stone but which in reality consists of comparatively little genuine material. When the lower half of a *semi-genuine doublet* of this kind consists of glass, this may be fused to the upper portion and a more intimate and permanent union effected than if the two portions were fixed together by cement or mastic.

A fraud of this kind is difficult to detect when the stone is mounted in a closed setting. Detection is easier when the stone is unmounted, for with the help of a good lens the line of junction of the two portions may be seen, or sometimes the prismatic colours of thin films may be visible where air has penetrated along the plane of junction. The two portions of a doublet cemented together by mastic will fall apart when the stone is placed in hot water, but this of course will not happen when the two parts are fused together. The compound nature of a doublet made, of glass, and of a doubly refracting stone such as ruby, is easily recognised by the different behaviour of the two parts in polarised light. The difference in the refractive index of the two parts will also serve the same purpose, especially with doublets of colourless stones such as diamond and rock-crystal. For the purpose of demonstrating this difference the stone is immersed in a strongly refracting liquid, such as methylene iodide, and this diluted until one or other part of the stone becomes invisible. As explained in the section on optics, this will happen when the index of refraction of the liquid is the same as that of the stone. In the case of a doublet of quartz and diamond immersed in methylene iodide diluted with benzene the quartz will become invisible, while the more strongly refracting diamond will still preserve its sharp outlines.

Such elaborate devices for the detection of a doublet are, however, only necessary when it is very cleverly made, and when the substances of the two portions are well matched. Indian jewellers are specially expert in the production of good doublets. When less carefully contrived and put together, there will be sufficient contrast between the two portions to make the doublet easily recognisable as such.

Doublets, of which the upper portion consists of rock-crystal or other colourless stone, and the lower part of a coloured glass, are known as *false doublets*. Here the colour of the lower portion is imparted to the upper harder portion. The same effect is obtained when between the upper and lower uncoloured portions is placed a thin layer of coloured material, a plate of metal, or even a piece of coloured gelatine-paper. When the two portions are differently coloured, the stone may be instantly recognised as a doublet by holding it up to the light and viewing it from the side, or observation with a lens will disclose the coloured layer between the two colourless portions. Here, as in all cases, when examining a doublet, the stone must of course be unmounted.

The construction of *hollow doublets* is somewhat peculiar ; these consist of an upper portion of rock-crystal or colourless glass, which is hollowed out below, the walls of the hollow being finely polished. The cavity so hollowed out is filled with a coloured liquid, and closed with a plate of rock-crystal or glass, or by a complete lower portion of the same material. The whole doublet if viewed from above, that is from the table, appears of the same colour as the liquid ; when viewed from the side, however, the boundary of the cavity containing the coloured liquid is plainly visible.

3. **Glass imitations.**—The manufacture of glass imitations of precious stones has reached a high degree of perfection. The varieties of glass suitable for this purpose are known as paste, and this name is also applied to the imitations themselves, which are often substituted for genuine precious stones. This species of fraud, which is common enough at the present day, was known and practised by the ancients, and attention was drawn to it by Pliny, who gave eloquent warnings on the subject.

The manufacturer of such kinds of glass aims at producing a substance which will, as far as possible, exhibit the more beautiful and valuable characters of genuine precious stones, and which, at the same time, will be in price as far removed as possible from the latter. The method at present followed is to produce a mass of glass which shall be as clear, transparent, and colourless as possible. When a material for coloured imitations is required, the colourless glass must be again fused with some metallic oxide capable of producing the desired colour.

The majority of precious stones can be so successfully imitated in glass that only a very practised eye can distinguish without more detailed examination a genuine stone from its paste imitation. Some of these artificial glasses possess not only the same clearness and transparency, but also in a large measure the lustre and high index of refraction and dispersion of a diamond of the purest water. Others again may exhibit a colour comparable with that of the finest ruby, sapphire, emerald, or topaz, &c.

The one point, however, in which all artificial imitations fail is hardness ; they have the hardness of glass (H = 5), and are, as a rule, softer than ordinary window-glass. In spite of this fact they take a high polish, which, however, after use is soon lost ; neither is the sharpness of their corners and edges retained for any length of time. Although when new these glass imitations are very similar in general appearance to genuine stones, and may be substituted for them with, in most cases, but little fear of detection, yet after they have been in use a short time they become dull and anything but beautiful objects. If it were possible to give these artificial glasses the hardness of true precious stones, they would in many cases be almost as suitable for personal ornament as are the latter, since the objection to their use, which has been just mentioned, would not exist. This drawback to the utilisation of the soft artificial glasses as precious stones is frequently overcome by the use of the semi-genuine doublet, the lower and larger portion of the doublet being of glass, and the upper smaller portion of some hard stone, such as quartz.

An artificial glass may, in almost all cases, be distinguished from a genuine stone by its lack of hardness. Glass is, as we have already seen, easily scratched by a hard steel point, which will not touch the great majority of precious stones. In addition to other methods, an aluminium pencil has recently been used for the purpose of distinguishing between genuine stones and glass imitations ; the point of the pencil when drawn over glass leaves a shining, silvery line, which is not the case when the material is a true precious stone. Glass, being an amorphous substance, is singly refracting, while many precious stones are doubly refracting ; this difference may, with the help of the polariscope, prove useful in distinguishing the two. Again, singly refracting glass is never dichroic, hence a stone which, when examined with the dichroscope shows different colours, cannot be glass. Some precious stones, for example diamond, are, however, singly refracting, and not dichroic : these could not be distinguished from ordinary glass by the aid of the polariscope alone, unless, indeed, the black cross shown by unannealed glass, as already mentioned, should happen to be observed. There is usually a difference in the specific gravity of a stone and of its glass imitation ; with very heavy glasses, however, the specific gravity of which may be as high as 3·6 to 3·8, this character may in certain cases approach more or less closely that of the precious stone it imitates. Finally, it is to be noted that the manufacture of a glass absolutely free from small air bubbles and other irregularities, such as streakiness, banding, &c., which never occur in precious stones, is very difficult. Observation with a lens, or when necessary with a microscope, will often result in the detection of such bubbles and streaks, the presence of which will prove the false character of the stone. Moreover, there may often be seen at the edge or girdle of a faceted specimen the marked, conchoidal fracture of glass, which is often present in a characteristic manner, different from anything seen in a genuine precious stone.

The material used for the production of imitations of precious stones is, in most cases, a readily fusible, colourless glass, rich in lead, and known by the names *strass*, paste, or Mainz flux. The qualities which this substance must show before everything else are the most perfect transparency and clearness and freedom from colour ; it is therefore of importance that the raw materials used in its manufacture should be of the greatest possible purity. The constituents of strass are, as a rule, the same as those of ordinary glass with the addition of one or two other substances, especially of red-lead. The most important constituent is quartz, which must be quite free from iron, and is best suited for this particular use in the purest form of rock-crystal. Potash is used in the form of potassium carbonate (potashes), which must also be as chemically pure as possible ; potassium nitrate often replaces the carbonate, since this salt can be more easily obtained in a pure condition ; for the same reason another salt, potassium tartrate, is sometimes used. Potash, as a constituent of strass, is sometimes replaced altogether by thallium, which can be used in the form of any of its salts, the product thus obtained being known as thallium-glass. Lead is employed in the form of red oxide (red-lead), which is prepared from chemically pure metallic lead. A little white arsenic is sometimes added, but this is not an essential constituent, and because of its poisonous nature is often omitted. For the purpose of increasing the fusibility of the mixture, a little borax or pure boracic acid is added as a flux ; this, however, does not enter into the composition of the glass, but is volatilised by the heat of the glass-furnace.

These materials, after being powdered finely and intimately mixed, are fused together in a Hessian crucible, and kept at as constant a temperature as possible, which should not be higher than that just sufficient to produce complete fusion. The fused mass, which should then be homogeneous, and as free from bubbles as possible, is allowed to remain for about twenty-four hours in the furnace, during which time it cools gradually and slowly. Any disturbance of the fused mass must be avoided in order to guard against the introduction of air bubbles, which cannot be again expelled, and which render the product unsuitable for the purpose for which it is intended.

The constituents mentioned above are not used in the same proportions in all cases.

The amount of lead especially varies very considerably, and is sometimes entirely absent, though a glass free from lead cannot be correctly termed a strass. Many recipes are given for the preparation of glasses suitable for the imitation of precious stones. A few of the best containing varying amounts of lead are given below :

3 parts of fine quartz-sand, 2 of saltpetre, 1 of borax, $\frac{1}{2}$ of white-arsenic.

9 parts of quartz, 3 of potassium carbonate, 3 of fused borax, 2 of red-lead, $\frac{1}{2}$ of white-arsenic.

8 parts of white glass free from lead, 3 of rock-crystal, 3 of red-lead, 3 of fused borax, $\frac{2}{3}$ of saltpetre, $\frac{1}{6}$ of white-arsenic.

$7\frac{1}{2}$ parts of quartz, 10 of red-lead, $1\frac{1}{2}$ of saltpetre.

A mixture which is frequently used is 32 per cent. of rock-crystal, 50 of red-lead, 17 of potassium carbonate, 1 of borax, and $\frac{1}{3}$ per cent. of white-arsenic.

The greater or less the amount of red-lead in the mixture, the more or less rich in lead will the resulting glass be, and the other constituents will vary accordingly. The amount of silica in lead-glasses varies between 38 and 59 per cent., potash between 8 and 14 per cent., and lead oxide between 28 and 53 per cent. As an example of the chemical composition of a lead-glass (strass) used to make an imitation of diamond, the following analysis may be given : silica (SiO_2) 41·2, potash (K_2O) 8·4, lead oxide (PbO) 50·4 per cent.

The physical characters of these glasses vary very considerably with the chemical composition, the amount of lead present having a specially marked influence in this direction. When this element is present in smaller amount the hardness of the glass is rather greater, but the specific gravity, as well as the index of refraction and the dispersive power, are lower. These latter properties are increased with an increase in the amount of lead present ; a glass very rich in lead, such as the one of which the percentage chemical composition is given above, has an index of refraction and a dispersive power comparable with those of diamond, and will therefore have the brilliancy and play of prismatic colours characteristic of this stone. This, indeed, is the object of the addition of lead to glasses which are to be used as imitations of precious stones ; the increase in the amount of lead also raises the specific gravity of the resulting glass, this being sometimes as high as 3·6 or 3·8, higher, that is to say, than that of diamond.

The play of prismatic colours is even finer in glasses in which thallium replaces potassium than in those in which lead is the only heavy metal present. The presence of this heavy metal as a constituent of the glass very considerably increases its dispersion and index of refraction ; such thallium-lead-glasses are, as regards their optical characters, much superior to the ordinary strass of the composition mentioned above. The specific gravity is also higher and reaches 4·18 to 5·6, increasing with an increase in the amount of thallium. A glass containing a moderate proportion of thallium, and with a specific gravity of 4·18, has a dispersion of 0·049 ; that of ordinary lead-glass (flint-glass of Fraunhofer) is only 0·037, the dispersion of diamond being 0·057.

Different glasses, varying in their physical characters according to their chemical composition, may therefore be employed for different purposes. A stone which is to imitate the diamond must have a high index of refraction and a high dispersion, and for this purpose a glass rich in lead, or, better still, a lead-glass containing thallium, will be used. A precious stone possessing only a low index of refraction may, on the other hand, be imitated by a strass containing but little lead, or even by one from which lead is altogether absent.

The recipes given above should produce, when the materials are quite pure, a perfectly colourless glass. A coloured glass is obtained by the addition to the strass of a colouring substance. The substances usually employed for this purpose are metallic oxides, which must be in as pure a state as the other constituents of the strass. In the manufacture of a coloured glass, the colourless strass already prepared, and the requisite amount of metallic oxide, are both reduced to a state of fine powder, and are then intimately mixed by being passed through a sieve. The mixture is then fused at a moderate temperature, and allowed to remain in this condition for about thirty hours, after which it is very slowly cooled. Only a very small amount of the metallic oxide is necessary to produce any required colour, the actual amount differing with different oxides. The depth of colour imparted by any given oxide will, of course, depend on the amount of it used ; a light colour will be given by a very small amount, while a larger amount may produce a colour so deep that thick pieces of the glass will appear black and opaque. Between these two extremes every gradation of colour is possible. As an example of the intense colouring power possessed by some metals, it may be stated that one part of gold will impart a vivid ruby-red colour to 10,000 parts of strass, while this same amount will impart an unmistakable rose colour to 20,000 parts of strass.

The substances employed for the production of differently coloured strass are many and varied. Cobalt oxide or smalt produces a blue colour, to which a tinge of violet may be given by the addition of a small quantity of manganese oxide. Yellow is produced by silver oxide or chloride, and by antimony oxide or the so-called red-antimony, which is a mixture of the oxide and sulphide. The addition of a small amount of coal also produces a yellow colour, the intensity of which varies from a light honey-yellow to yellowish-brown according to the amount used ; a beautiful golden-yellow is obtained by adding in addition to the coal a little manganese oxide. The use of coal for the production of a yellow colour is, however, only possible in glasses free from lead. Chromium oxide and copper oxide each produce a green colour, to which a bluish tinge may be imparted by the addition of a little cobalt oxide, while a yellowish-green is obtained by adding red-antimony. A mixture of cobalt oxide and red-antimony produces a green colour, due to the combination of the blue of the cobalt and the yellow of the antimony. Red may be obtained by the addition of various substances, namely, cuprous oxide (Cu_2O), gold oxide, gold chloride, or purple of Cassius, the last named being used for the production of ruby-glass, so called from the resemblance of its colour to the red of the ruby. A red colour inclining to violet is obtained by the use of manganese oxide which should be as free as possible from iron, a pure violet being obtained by the use of a little cobalt oxide in addition to this ; a larger amount of cobalt oxide produces a reddish-brown colour. Black glass, which remains black even in the thinnest layers, is produced among other methods by adding a large amount of tin oxide and afterwards fusing again with a mixture of manganese oxide and hammer-slag from iron-works.

An opaque, white glass, that is an enamel, is obtained by the addition of a small quantity of either tin oxide, calcium phosphate, or bone-ashes. This opaque glass is capable of colouration by metallic oxides, and hence imitations of opaque stones such as turquoise are possible, the blue colour of this stone being imitated by adding a little copper oxide and cobalt oxide. The appearance of opal, chalcedony, and other translucent stones, and even to a certain extent the colour bandings of agate, may be imitated in glass by methods very similar to those above described.

It is not by any means to be supposed that pastes can be produced at a very low cost. The production of a strass suitable for making good imitations of precious stones is a comparatively expensive operation, the price of materials of the necessary purity being high, and the appliances and apparatus used in the manufacture necessitating the outlay of some considerable capital. For this reason, only the more costly precious stones are imitated in this more perfect manner.   Poorer imitations, which can be recognised at a glance even by the most unsophisticated, are made from common materials with no special care ; the cost of their production is low and they are used in the most inferior so-called ornaments.

The material for the imitation of precious stones having been produced by the methods described above, is ground, polished, and mounted, these processes differing in no wise from the grinding, polishing, and mounting of genuine stones, which has already been described.

Attempts appear to have been recently made to produce a glass imitation of a precious stone which, besides the usual constituents of this substance, shall contain those characteristic of the stone imitated.   Thus a rough chemical analysis of this material would be similar to that of the genuine stone.   Imitations of emerald have recently come into the market, which contain seven to eight per cent. of beryllium oxide, an essential constituent of emerald but not ordinarily of glass.   All the physical characters of the material are those of green glass and not of emerald.   Of the place and method of preparation of this material nothing is known.

K. VALUE AND PRICE.

The esteem in which the different kinds of precious stone are held does not by any means depend solely on their beauty, durability, or similar characters, but is influenced by various external conditions.   The price demanded for precious stones is therefore fluctuating, since it is regulated, as in the case of any other objects which are bought and sold, by the laws of supply and demand.   A large supply and a small demand results in a low price, and *vice versâ* ; when the supply and demand both vary in the same direction, that is, when they both rise or both fall equally, the price remains stationary.

The supply of each kind of precious stone depends essentially on the frequency with which it occurs in nature and on the extent to which it is mined.   For reasons which have already been pointed out, precious stones which are of very common occurrence even when possessed of considerable beauty are never held in very high esteem, and consequently never command a high price, the price of the cut stone often only slightly exceeding the cost of cutting.   Stones on the contrary which possess the merit of rarity are much sought after and valued far more highly.

The supply of any one kind of precious stone in the market varies at different times and this causes a corresponding variation in price.   The exhaustion of a locality, which has formerly supplied a large number of stones, will result in a rise in the value of that particular stone, while the discovery of a new source of supply has an opposite effect.   The history of the various discoveries of diamond is an instructive example of this fact.   In the seventeenth century, the price of the diamond rose steadily higher and higher on account of the gradual exhaustion of the Indian mines which were the only ones then known.   The discovery of the rich Brazilian mines in 1728 caused a rapid and marked fall in the price of diamond ; with the gradual exhaustion of the Brazilian deposits, the price again gradually rose until the discovery of diamonds in South Africa in 1867.   So large has been the supply of diamonds from this locality that the price, for average material at least, is lower than it has ever been before.

The amount of production is not, however, the only factor which influences the supply. A large accumulation of stock thrown suddenly upon the market has the effect of lowering the prices.   Of interest in this connection is the statement made by Kluge in 1860 to the effect that a few years before, at the Easter fair of Leipzig, the price of diamonds suddenly fell fifty per cent. owing to the fact that the Brazilian Government had paid the interest of the national debt in diamonds instead of in cash.

The causes which operate to produce fluctuations in demand are more intricate and difficult to trace. The earning capacity of a nation, and consequently the general prosperity of the people, the general trend of events, the wide-spread existence of a taste for ornament or display, fashion, and such like considerations, are all factors which influence the demand for precious stones. Since precious stones are purely articles of luxury for which there is no absolute need, and which it would be possible to dispense with completely, they are only extensively used in times of peace and commercial prosperity when the necessities of life are abundant and easily obtained. At such times, and especially when public events create and foster a taste for display, the price of precious stones will rise. When, however, the purchasing-power is diminished in consequence of war or of industrial crises retrenchment will first be made, naturally not in the necessities of life but in its luxuries; there will be little or no demand for precious stones, and, moreover, the heirlooms or recent acquirements of old families will be thrown on the market and will help to accentuate its downward tendency.

Many examples of this rise and fall in the value of precious stones may be found in French history. Thus, during the period, of lavish display immediately preceding the French Revolution, when the European Courts vied with each other in extravagance and luxury, the price of precious stones, and especially of diamond, rose high. During the Revolution and the series of miserable wars which followed, precious stones fell in value, only to rise again steadily during the long years of peace which followed Napoleon's fall. This steady rise culminated in the year 1848, the events of which caused a sudden but temporary fall of seventy-five per cent. in the value of precious stones.

The tremendous effect of a commercial crisis is shown, for example, by the statement of the traveller J. J. von Tschudi, that during the great depression in trade and exchange of 1857 and 1858 in Brazil diamonds sank to one-half their original value. At such crises the larger and more valuable stones suffer the greatest depreciation, since the demand for the smaller and more moderately priced stones does not fall away to the extent of that for the highly priced stones. The rise in price of precious stones during a period of prosperity is exemplified in a remarkable manner by their value in the sixteenth and seventeenth centuries when treasure from the rich silver mines of South America came pouring into Europe; and again after the discovery of the Californian and Australian goldfields in 1848 and the following years.

The demand for precious stones regardless of their kind, or for one kind in preference to another, is affected very powerfully by the arbitrary and capricious fashion of the moment. At times of national disaster or commercial depression the effect of fashion on the general demand for precious stones must necessarily be small, but at other times, when the demand has revived, this factor makes itself felt in a preference now for one kind of stone now for another. The most beautiful and costly stones, the diamond, ruby, sapphire, and emerald are indeed always sought after, but it is otherwise with those of less prominent beauty. The recent history of "oriental cat's-eye," a variety of chrysoberyl found in Ceylon, forms an instructive example of the way in which a stone may be suddenly brought into favour. For many years there was no demand whatever for this stone, it was stocked by no jewellers, and its value was correspondingly low. When, however, the Duke of Connaught gave a betrothal ring containing chrysoberyl to the Princess Louise Margaret of Prussia the stone became fashionable, first in England and then elsewhere. So extensively was it used that Ceylon could scarcely supply the demand, while the price of course rose very considerably. The freaks and caprices of fashion afford much scope for speculation in precious stones. As an example of this may be mentioned the acquirement by a French

Company of the so-called topaz mines in Spain. Topaz, which was formerly much worn and therefore prized, is now, in common with other yellow stones, regarded with but little favour and its price is therefore low. The mines mentioned above had been acquired in the hope that sooner or later the topaz may regain its former popularity; it may be stated here, however, that the mineral derived from these mines is not true topaz but quartz of a beautiful yellow colour, which is frequently sold for topaz.

It will not now be surprising to learn that those precious stones, which always have been and always will be most highly prized, have in past times varied greatly in their relative value; in other words, different stones have at different periods been held in the highest esteem. According to C. W. King, to whom we are indebted for much important historical work in connection with precious stones, the diamond was the most highly esteemed of precious stones among the Romans, and also in earlier times in India; in the estimation of the Persians, however, it occupied the fifth place, following after pearl, ruby, emerald, and chrysolite. Benvenuto Cellini placed on record that in the middle of the sixteenth century ruby and sapphire were esteemed more highly than diamond, which had only one-eighth the value of ruby, this latter stone being prized above all others. The Portuguese author, Garcias ab Horto, writing at the same time (1565), placed diamond in a series of precious stones, arranged according to their value, in the third place, giving the first place to emerald, and to ruby, when clear, the second. We find a parallel to this at the present time, for diamond is to-day far exceeded in price by ruby, and is often equalled in price by emerald. These comparisons of course refer to stones of the same size and quality and, when cut, with the same perfection of form.

The value attached to a precious stone depends very largely on the size of the specimen, which is estimated from its weight. The special unit of weight almost universally used is the **carat**. This is supposed to have the weight of a seed of an African leguminous tree, known to the natives as "kuara," a species of *Erythrina* (*E. abyssinica*); the fruit of this tree when dry is characterised by its very constant weight, and is said to have been used in Africa for weighing gold. It is supposed that it was afterwards adopted in India as a standard of weight for precious stones. According to another view, the carat is the weight of a seed from the pod of the locust-tree, its name being derived from the Greek word *keration*, signifying the fruit of the locust-tree. The origins claimed for this standard of weight being so diverse, it is not surprising to find that its value, like that of the old pound and ounce, varies not inconsiderably in different countries. On an average the carat does not differ in value much from a fifth of a gram (200 milligrams), or about $3\frac{1}{6}$ English grains. The exact values in milligrams of the carat at different places are tabulated below:

	Milligrams.		Milligrams.
Amboina	197·000	Paris	205·500
Florence	197·200	Amsterdam	205·700
Batavia	205·000	Lisbon	205·750
Borneo	205·000	Frankfurt-on-Main	205·770
Leipzig	205·000	Vienna	206·130
Spain	205·393	Madras	207·353
London	205·409	Livorno	215·990
Berlin	205·440		

The fractions of the carat used in weighing precious stones are $\frac{1}{2}$, $\frac{1}{4}$, $\frac{1}{8}$, &c., down to $\frac{1}{64}$, smaller fractions than these being neglected; these fractional parts of the carat are usually expressed with a denominator of sixty-four. One sixty-fourth of a carat of 205 milligrams is equal to 3·203 milligrams. The fourth part of a carat is known as a grain, being, however, not an ordinary grain but a " diamond-grain," " pearl-grain," or " carat-grain "; it is a unit but rarely used. In France 144 carats equal one ounce.

The practical inconveniences which result from the discrepancies between the weight of a carat in different countries can easily be imagined. So firmly established, however, is the use of this unit in almost all civilised countries, that there seems no prospect of replacing it by the more convenient gram of the metric system. The change to grams could be effected with no great confusion, since the weight of half a carat very nearly corresponds in all cases to 100 milligrams or $\frac{1}{10}$ gram. The gram, however, finds very little favour with dealers in precious stones, although in Germany since 1872, in Austria since 1876, and in Holland for some time, it has been the lawful unit of weight for precious stones. In 1871, and again in 1876, a syndicate of Parisian jewellers proposed that the carat should universally have the value of 205·000 milligrams, a value it has always had in Leipzig and in the Dutch East Indies. This proposal has met with considerable favour, and it is probable that before long this value for the carat will be universally accepted, and that other values will fall into disuse, since the jewel-dealers of London and Amsterdam, which are the centres of the trade, are at one with their Parisian colleagues in this matter. At the same time, it is proposed to subdivide the carat according to the decimal system instead of the present cumbrous and inconvenient division into sixty-fourths.

In England dealers in precious stones, especially the less valuable so-called semi-precious stones, sometimes make use of troy weight, as it is also employed for precious metals. An ounce troy (480 grains) = 31·103 grams = 151·707 carats (of 205 milligrams). This carat then is equal to 3·165 grains, and inversely a grain = 0·316 carat. Further, a grain troy, avoirdupois or apothecaries', is equal to 1·264 " carat-grains," " pearl-grains," or " diamond-grains "; and one " diamond-grain " is equal to 0·791 grain troy. The word grain is therefore ambiguous, and a weight given in grains is likely to lead to confusion and error, unless it is definitely known what system of units is referred to. This confusion, however, is confined to British weights, for in no other country is the grain troy used for precious stones.

Some other units of weight of little importance are in local use at certain places where precious stones are found. The more important of such units will be briefly mentioned here since they are sometimes to be found in books of travel and in old descriptions of precious stones, as well as in more recent reports of the occurrence of precious stones in various countries, and there is often difficulty in obtaining information concerning such units.

In Brazil the weight of gold and precious stones is estimated in oitavas, an oitava being $\frac{1}{8}$ ounce, and 128 oitavas going to the pound. The oitava, which corresponds in weight to $17\frac{1}{2}$ carats (sometimes given at 18), is subdivided into thirty-two vintems. Some-times, however, the carat-grain is used as a subdivision of the oitava. Since four carat-grains are equal to one carat, one oitava is equal to 70 (or 72) grains.

While this Brazilian unit of weight has a direct connection with the carat, the unit used in India, especially in former times, is quite independent and distinct from it. This Indian unit varies in different localities, and has also varied in value at different periods. The Indian unit of weight, used principally in Sambalpur, is the masha; it is subdivided into eight ratis, a rati being the weight of the scarlet and black bead-like seed of the plant *Abrus precatorius*; the rati is itself subdivided into four dhans. The value of a rati varies at different places and times between 1·86 and 2·25 grains troy. On an average, therefore, one rati = 2 grains troy = $2\frac{1}{2}$ carat-grains = about $\frac{2}{3}$ carat. In Nagpur in 1827 one rati was actually equal to 2·014 grains troy; but at the present day it is usually equal to $1\frac{7}{8}$ or 1·88 grains troy, which again corresponds to 2·370 carat-grains or diamond-grains. Tavernier reckoned the value of the rati at $\frac{7}{8}$ carat. The unit of weight at Golconda (Raolconda, Kollur, and Visapur) is the mangelin; this Tavernier valued at $1\frac{3}{8}$ carat.

The miscal is a Persian weight, equivalent to forty ratis; it is usually taken to correspond to $74\frac{1}{2}$ grains troy. Two miscals make one dirhem.

The value of each kind of precious stone varies with the size of the specimen, but in some cases the increase in value is not directly proportional to the increase in size. Some stones, such as topaz, aquamarine, &c., occur frequently in fairly large masses : of these there is therefore no more difficulty in obtaining a large cut specimen than there is in acquiring one of small size. The value of the stone will then vary directly as the weight, so that a specimen of double the size will cost twice as much. It is otherwise, however, with stones such as diamond and ruby, large specimens of which occur much less frequently than do smaller stones. The latter are more abundant, larger stones are comparatively few, while very large specimens are of great rarity, and cannot be produced when demanded, but must be waited for until they happen to be found. The ratio of the increase in price of such stones is higher than that of their increase in weight ; thus, if the weight of a stone is doubled its value will be more than doubled.

A rule was formerly given by which the price of large specimens of costly stones, and especially of diamond, could be arrived at. This rule, having originated in India, is known as the Indian rule ; it is also referred to as Tavernier's rule, because of its introduction into Europe by the French traveller Tavernier, who travelled as a dealer in precious stones in India and the East in the seventeenth century, his famous *Six Voyages* being published in 1676. It has, however, been pointed out by Schrauf that the rule had been made known in Europe almost a hundred years previously (1598) by the English traveller Lincotius, and that its mention in one of the oldest and most famous books on precious stones, the *Gemmarum Historia*, by Anselm Boetius de Boot, published in Hanover in 1609, was derived from this source.

According to this rule the price of a diamond which exceeds one carat in weight is obtained by squaring its weight in carats, and multiplying by the price of a stone of one carat. If, for example, the price of a stone weighing one carat is £10, then the price of one weighing five carats would be $5 \times 5 \times 10 = £250$. In general, if the price of the carat-stone is p, and the weight of the stone to be valued is m carats, then its price is given by $m \times m \times p = m^2 p$.

This rule has, however, never been generally adopted anywhere ; it merely serves to give a rough approximation to the value of large diamonds. In former times the price of smaller diamonds, as given by this rule, was fairly correct and agreed very closely with their actual market value; later, however, it could not be applied even to stones of moderate size, since it gave them a price higher than that for which they could actually be sold. This disproportion is even greater in the case of larger stones; the original rule has therefore, following the Brazilian diamond dealers, been modified, so that instead of taking the price of a carat-stone equal in quality to the one to be valued, the price of a carat-stone of inferior quality is taken as the multiplier p. Even with this modification the calculated value does not completely agree with the actual market value. Later, Schrauf in 1869 suggested another rule for estimating the value of large diamonds ; here half the weight in carats of the stone is multiplied by its whole weight plus two, and this by the price of a carat-stone. According to this rule, the value of a stone of 5 carats, the value of the carat-stone being taken at £10 as before, would be $2\frac{1}{2} \times 7 \times 10 = £175$, or, in a general expression, $\frac{m}{2} \times (m + 2) \times p = \left(\frac{m^2}{2} + m\right) p$. At the time this rule was promulgated, it gave results which closely approximated to market prices; since the discovery of the South African diamond-fields, however, large stones have come into the market in much greater numbers than previously, so that even this rule is no longer applicable for trade purposes. The subject of price will be again referred to when we come to treat specially of diamonds and other precious stones.

We must now consider the relative value of cut and uncut stones. A cut stone will naturally be more expensive than a rough stone of the same quality and size. To the value of the rough stone must be added the cost of cutting; and this, especially in the case of the harder stones, and most of all in the diamond, is very considerable. Furthermore, a considerable portion, often one-half or more, of the material of the rough stone is lost in the process of cutting; a cut stone is, therefore, in its rough condition, often double the weight of the same stone when faceted, and this larger weight is taken into account when the stone is sold.

The particular form in which a stone is cut is also an important factor in determining its price, since the cutting of more complicated forms with numerous facets is more expensive than that of simpler forms with fewer facets. Thus the price of a rose diamond of the best quality is only about four-fifths of that of a brilliant of the same weight and quality.

The value of a precious stone varies to a very great extent according as the features on which its particular beauty depends are strongly marked or insignificant; and in this connection small differences of quality, scarcely noticeable to an unpractised eye, are all taken into account. A diamond of the second water, cut in the form of a brilliant and weighing one carat, is usually considered to be two-thirds the value of a similar stone of the first water. Further information of this kind may be obtained from the table published in 1878 by Vanderheym, which is given below in the section dealing with the value of diamonds. The presence or absence of the various faults to which precious stones are liable, and which have been already considered, of course affects the value of a stone to a very large extent, the presence of a large number of faults sometimes rendering an otherwise costly stone absolutely worthless.

III. CLASSIFICATION OF PRECIOUS STONES.

In the present section we propose to consider the various systems of nomenclature and classification adopted for precious stones.

In scientific mineralogy, precious stones are regarded simply as minerals and are classified accordingly. The classification of precious stones adopted by jewellers, however, is more or less arbitrary in nature and differs somewhat widely from the system used by mineralogists. Both scientific mineralogists and dealers in precious stones nevertheless agree in bringing together as of one kind all those stones which resemble each other in their essential characters, and in distinguishing by a special name the stones of that kind from those of another kind. In arranging precious stones into such kinds, the characters which are considered essential by a specialist in jewels may not be so considered by a mineralogist; and, conversely, what a mineralogist considers an essential feature may not have the same importance in the classification of a precious stone specialist. From the mineralogical point of view, a species is defined by the chemical composition and the crystalline form, together with the several physical characters of the stones it embraces. These characters must be constant for the same species, or at least vary within certain limits in a certain definite manner; characters which are liable to vary in different specimens, such, for instance, as colour, are regarded as non-essential. It is far otherwise, however, in the case of precious stones; here the application of a particular specimen depends largely on its colour, hence this character plays an important part in the grouping of precious stones according to the second method of classification, while characters, such as chemical composition and crystalline form, having but slight influence on the application of a stone for ornamental purposes, are much less relied upon.

Owing to these differences in the principles of classification, it is easy to understand that many stones which may be brought together in a mineralogical classification, on account of their similar chemical composition and crystalline form, under the same species, and may be known by the same name, may, in the artificial system of classification, be divided among several groups and be known by different names on account of differences in colour. On the other hand, stones of the same colour, which a jeweller may consider of the same kind, and to which he may apply but one name, or at least one with a qualifying prefix signifying small differences of colour or hardness, may by a scientific mineralogist be grouped under different species according to their chemical and crystallographic differences and be recognised by different names.

A good example of the first case is afforded by the mineral species corundum. Mineralogists include in this species all those stones which are composed of pure alumina and which crystallise in the hexagonal system. The stones of this species are all of the same hardness (H = 9) and specific gravity (sp. gr. = 4), while other physical characters are equally constant. It is therefore in accordance with the principles of scientific classification that such stones should be grouped in the same species and be known by the same name. Different specimens of this species of mineral, however, may differ widely in colour; red, blue, yellow, green, yellowish-green, greenish-blue, yellowish-red, violet, and colourless specimens having all been found. All the colour-varieties mentioned above are not of equal importance for purposes of ornament, but they are considered by the jeweller, in spite of their mineralogical identity, as distinct and separate stones, and as such are distinguished by special names; these names are given below in the order in which the colour-varieties were mentioned above: ruby, sapphire, "oriental topaz," "oriental emerald," "oriental chrysolite," "oriental aquamarine," "oriental hyacinth," "oriental amethyst," white sapphire (leuco-sapphire). The mineral beryl is another case in point; the mineralogist includes the deep green, bluish-green, greenish-blue, and yellow specimens in the same species, to which he gives the name beryl, since they all agree in chemical composition and crystalline form, and differ only in colour; the jeweller, on the contrary, refers to the deep green variety as emerald, to the greenish-blue and bluish-green varieties as aquamarine and to the yellow varieties as beryl.

Another example of the method of classification adopted by jewellers may be given. All light greenish-yellow to yellowish-green transparent stones, whatever may be their chemical composition and crystalline form, are referred to by jewellers as chrysolite. Thus this name comes to include such essentially dissimilar minerals as olivine, chrysoberyl, idocrase, corundum, and the peculiar moldavite or bottle-stone. To distinguish these one from another, such descriptive terms as olivine-chrysolite, opalescent chrysolite for chrysoberyl, "oriental chrysolite" for yellowish-green corundum, &c., are used. The original signification of the prefix "oriental" has already been explained.

Minerals used as precious stones may be classified into groups according to various systems: thus their position may be decided by the feature on which their beauty depends; by their essential mineralogical characters; by the frequency of their occurrence in nature;

or more often, according to their value. Frequently they are divided into two main groups, the true precious stones or jewels, and the semi-precious stones. K. E. Kluge, in his *Handbuch der Edelsteinkunde*, published in 1860, distinguishes five groups of precious stones, characterised by their value as gems, their hardness, optical characters, and rarity of occurrence. Other methods of grouping are, of course, equally possible. There are no sharp lines of division between such groups, which are to a certain extent arbitrary, and there are many stones which would be placed by one authority in one group, and by another authority in another group. As an example of a possible method of grouping, the following **classification by Kluge,** in which the stones are arranged according to their market value, may be given.

1. TRUE PRECIOUS STONES OR JEWELS.

Distinguishing characters are: great hardness, fine colour, perfect transparency, combined with strong lustre (fire), susceptibility of a fine polish, and rarity of occurrence in specimens suitable for cutting.

A.　*Gems of the First Rank.*

Hardness, between 8 and 10. Consisting of pure carbon, or pure alumina, or with alumina predominating. Fine specimens of very rare occurrence and of the highest value.

1. Diamond.
2. Corundum (ruby, sapphire, &c.).
3. Chrysoberyl.
4. Spinel.

B.　*Gems of the Second Rank.*

Hardness, between 7 and 8 (except precious opal). Specific gravity usually over 3. Silica a prominent constituent. In specimens of large size and of fairly frequent occurrence. Value generally less than stones of group *A*, but perfect specimens are more highly prized than poorer specimens of group *A*.

5. Zircon.
6. Beryl (emerald, &c.).
7. Topaz.
8. Tourmaline.
9. Garnet.
10. Precious Opal.

C.　*Gems of the Third Rank.*

These are intermediate in character, between the true gems and the semi-precious stones. Hardness, between 6 and 7. Specific gravity usually greater than 2·5. With the exception of turquoise, silica is a prominent constituent of all these stones. Value usually not very great; only fine specimens of a few members of the group (cordierite, chrysolite, turquoise) have any considerable value. Specimens worth cutting of comparatively rare occurrence, others fairly frequent.

11. Cordierite.
12. Idocrase.
13. Chrysolite.
14. Axinite.
15. Kyanite.
16. Staurolite.
17. Andalusite.
18. Chiastolite.
19. Epidote.
20. Turquoise.

2.　SEMI-PRECIOUS STONES.

These have some or all of the distinguishing characters of precious stones, but to a less marked degree.

D. Gems of the Fourth Rank.

Hardness 4–7. Specific gravity 2–3 (with the exception of amber). Colour and lustre are frequently prominent features. Not as a rule perfectly transparent; often translucent, or translucent at the edges only. Wide distribution. Value as a rule small.

21. Quartz.
    A. Crystallised quartz.
        a. Rock-crystal.
        b. Amethyst.
        c. Common quartz.
            α. Prase.
            β. Avanturine.
            γ. Cat's-eye.
            δ. Rose-quartz.
    B. Chalcedony.
        a. Chalcedony.
        b. Agate (with onyx).
        c. Carnelian.
        d. Plasma.
        e. Heliotrope.
        f. Jasper.
        g. Chrysoprase.

    C. Opal.
        a. Fire-opal.
        b. Semi-opal.
        c. Hydrophane.
        d. Cacholong.
        e. Jasper-opal.
        f. Common-opal.
22. Felspar.
        a. Adularia.
        b. Amazon-stone.
23. Labradorite.
24. Obsidian.
25. Lapis-lazuli.
26. Haüynite.
27. Hypersthene.
28. Diopside.
29. Fluor-spar.
30. Amber.

E. Gems of the Fifth Rank.

Hardness and specific gravity very variable. Colour almost always dull. Never transparent. Low degree of lustre. Value very insignificant, and usually dependent upon the work bestowed on them. These stones, as well as many of the last group, are not faceted, but worked by the ordinary lapidary in the large-stone-cutting works.

31. Jet.
32. Nephrite.
33. Serpentine.
34. Agalmatolite.
35. Steatite.
36. Pot-stone.
37. Diallage.
38. Bronzite.
39. Bastite.
40. Satin-spar (calcite and aragonite).
41. Marble.
42. Satin-spar (gypsum).

43. Alabaster.
44. Malachite.
45. Iron-pyrites.
46. Rhodochrosite.
47. Hæmatite.
48. Prehnite.
49. Elæolite.
50. Natrolite.
51. Lava.
52. Quartz-breccia.
53. Lepidolite.

Among the stones enumerated above are a few such as marble, alabaster, &c., which are never worked for personal ornaments, but only for other decorative objects; these stones will not be considered in the present book. On the other hand, there are certain stones omitted from Kluge's list which will receive attention here, although they are but rarely applied to the use of personal ornament. In the description which is now to follow, the different precious stones are not arranged in classes, but are dealt with one after another in the order of their relative value, combined to some extent with mineralogical characters. Stones belonging to the larger families of minerals are placed in juxtaposition, although individual members of each group may differ considerably in value. The following is a tabular review of the precious stones here dealt with, and the order in which they are taken.

Arrangement of Precious Stones adopted in the present work.

Diamond.
Corundum.
> Ruby, Sapphire including star-sapphire and white sapphire, "Oriental aquamarine," "Oriental emerald," "Oriental chrysolite," "Oriental topaz," "Oriental hyacinth," "Oriental amethyst," Adamantine-spar.

Spinel.
> "Ruby-spinel," "Balas-ruby," "Almandine-spinel," Rubicelle, Blue spinel, Ceylonite.

Chrysoberyl.
> Cymophane ("Oriental cat's-eye"), Alexandrite.

Beryl.
> Emerald, Aquamarine, "Aquamarine-chrysolite," Golden beryl.

Euclase.
Phenakite.
Topaz.
Zircon.
> Hyacinth.

Garnet Group.
> Hessonite (Cinnamon-stone), Spessartite, Almandine, Pyrope (Bohemian garnet, "Cape ruby," and Rhodolite), Demantoid, Grossularite, Melanite, Topazolite.

Tourmaline.
Opal.
> Precious opal, Fire-opal, Common opal.

Turquoise.
Bone-turquoise.
Lazulite.
Callainite.
Olivine.
> Chrysolite, Peridote.

Cordierite.
Idocrase.
Axinite.
Kyanite.
Staurolite.
Andalusite.
> Chiastolite.

Epidote.
Piedmontite.
Dioptase.
Chrysocolla.
Garnierite.
Sphene.

Prehnite.
> Chlorastolite.
> Zonochlorite.

Thomsonite.
> Lintonite.

Natrolite.
Hemimorphite.
Calamine.
Felspar Group.
> Amazon-stone, Sun-stone, Moon-stone, Labradorescent felspar, Labradorite.

Elæolite.
Cancrinite.
Lapis-lazuli.
Haüynite.
Sodalite.
Obsidian.
Moldavite.
Pyroxene and Hornblende Group.
> Hypersthene (with Bronzite, Bastite, Diallage), Diopside, Spodumene (Hiddenite), Rhodonite (and Lepidolite), Nephrite, Jadeite (Chloromelanite).

Quartz.
> Crystallised quartz: Rock-crystal, Smoky-quartz, Amethyst, Citrine, Rose-quartz, Prase, Sapphire-quartz, Quartz with enclosures, Cat's-eye, Tiger-eye.
> Compact quartz: Hornstone, Chrysoprase, Wood-stone, Jasper, Avanturine.
> Chalcedony: Common Chalcedony, Carnelian, Plasma, Heliotrope, Agate with Onyx, &c.

Malachite.
Chessylite.
Satin-spar (Fibrous Calcite, Aragonite, and Gypsum).
Fluor-spar.
Apatite.
Iron-pyrites.
Hæmatite.
Ilmenite.
Rutile.
Amber.
Jet.

Appendix: Pearls and Coral.

SECOND PART

SYSTEMATIC DESCRIPTION OF PRECIOUS STONES

DIAMOND.

THE diamond, although not the most valuable of precious stones, yet unquestionably exceeds all others in interest, importance and general noteworthiness. It is therefore fitting that this stone should stand at the head of the series now awaiting consideration, and should, moreover, receive at our hands more detailed treatment. In hardness, in the perfection of its clearness and transparency, in its unique constants of optical refraction and dispersion, and finally in the marvellous perfection of its lustre, the diamond surpasses all other minerals. For these reasons, and despite the fact that it is not of very great rarity even in faultless specimens of fair size—nine-tenths of the yearly trade in precious stones being concerned with diamonds alone—it is very greatly valued as a gem; moreover, on account of its extreme hardness, it has several technical applications.

A. CHARACTERS OF DIAMOND.

1. CHEMICAL CHARACTERS.

Diamond is distinguished from all other precious stones no less by its chemical composition than by its unique physical characters, for no other gem consists of a single element. It is pure crystallised carbon, its substance is therefore identical chemically with the material of graphite and charcoal. The extraordinary difference in the appearance of diamond and that of other forms of carbon depends solely on the crystallisation of the material and the physical characters consequent on this.

The fact that the one and only constituent of diamond is pure carbon was already known at the end of the eighteenth century, and was suspected even earlier than this. In the year 1675 Sir Isaac Newton had arrived at the conclusion that diamond must be combustible; this conclusion, though correct in itself, was based on theoretical grounds, now known to be mistaken, connected with the high refractive index of the substance. In 1694–5 researches respecting the **combustibility** of diamond were conducted at the " Accademia del Cimento" of Florence, by the Academicians, Averani and Targioni, at the instigation of the Grand Duke Cosmos III. of Tuscany. Diamonds were exposed to the intense heat of a fierce charcoal fire or were placed in the focus of a large burning-glass. A stone so treated did not fuse but gradually decreased in size and finally disappeared, leaving behind no appreciable amount of residue. These experiments proved that the substance of diamond, as such, is destroyed at a high temperature; whether its disappearance was due simply to volatilisation, as in the case of sal-ammoniac, was of course undecided at that early date. Investigations into the chemical nature of diamond and the meaning of its apparent destruction when exposed to heat were undertaken later by the famous French chemist, Lavoisier, as well as by Tennant, Davy and others.

During the year 1772 and later, Lavoisier, the founder of modern chemistry, demonstrated that the disappearance of diamond only took place when it was heated in air, and that it might be exposed to the highest temperatures without loss of weight, provided that any contact with air was prevented. He further showed that the air occupying the space in which a diamond had been heated, and in which it had finally disappeared, possessed the property of turning lime-water milky, as does carbon dioxide (carbonic acid gas); and, moreover, that the lime-water so clouded effervesced when brought into contact with an acid, just as it does when clouded by the addition of carbon dioxide. The consideration of these facts led him to repeat his experiments, replacing diamond with ordinary carbon; the results were found to be identical, and there was nothing for it but to conclude that the disappearance of diamond was due to combustion. In spite of these apparently conclusive experiments, Lavoisier did not at that time venture to assert that the substance of carbon and of diamond was completely identical.

This was left to be proved by Smithson Tennant, who in 1797 demonstrated that the combustion of a certain weight of diamond resulted in the production of the same amount of carbon dioxide as did the combustion of an equal weight of pure carbon. This observation was confirmed later by other chemists, for example by Sir Humphry Davy, who in 1816 showed in addition that the combustion of diamond was unattended by the formation of even a trace of water. This proved that the conclusions of Arago and Biot, namely, that diamond, on account of its high refractive power, must contain a hydrocarbon, were incorrect. Later, all these results were confirmed by the well-arranged experiments of Dumas and Stas, as well as of Erdmann and Marchand, and others. The combustion of diamond in oxygen gas has now long been an every-day chemical lecture experiment.

These researches have been considered for some time to have finally settled the question as to the constitution of diamond. Recently, however, Krause has suggested that this question should rather be regarded as still an open one, and that the experiments which have been described should be taken to prove simply that the atomic weight of the element of which diamond is composed is identical with that of carbon. He has further suggested that between the two, diamond and ordinary carbon, there might possibly be a relation similar to that existing between the metals nickel and cobalt, which have the same, or very nearly the same, atomic weight and very similar chemical characters. In order to decide this point, Krause allowed the gases produced on the one hand by the combustion of diamond, and on the other by that of pure carbon, to be absorbed by caustic soda. In both cases he obtained crystals: in the one case these were, of course, crystals of sodium carbonate; in the other, the crystals produced agreed so completely with the crystals of sodium carbonate in crystalline form, amount of water of crystallisation, specific gravity, fusibility, solubility, electrical conductivity, &c., that there could be no reasonable doubt of the identity of the two products. This experiment, then, proves definitely and conclusively that the product of combustion of diamond is carbon dioxide, and that the substance of diamond consists, therefore, of pure carbon.

A century previous to the work of Krause, Guyton de Morveau had made experiments with the idea of confirming or overthrowing the results of Lavoisier and Tennant, thinking it inconceivable, as did the majority of his contemporaries, that the rare and costly diamond and a common and widespread substance such as carbon could consist of one and the same chemical element. The method he adopted for the purpose differs from the usual methods of chemical analysis, and is interesting on account of its originality. It depends on the fact that soft bar-iron, when heated with charcoal, takes up a certain amount of carbon and becomes converted into steel. In his experiment, Guyton de Morveau replaced charcoal with diamond, and succeeded in converting the soft iron into steel, the characters of which were identical with those of steel produced by the ordinary process. His experiments thus supplied further proof of the chemical identity of carbon and diamond.

The behaviour of diamond, when raised to a high temperature, varies according to whether it is in contact with air or not. In both cases, however, the stone will be easily cracked or fractured if the rise of temperature is too sudden; such damage to the stone may be avoided by ensuring that both the heating and the subsequent cooling shall be slow and gradual.

In a stream of oxygen gas, a crystal of diamond begins to burn at a low red-heat. It will gradually rise in temperature until it reaches a white-heat, and will then burn uninterruptedly with a pale blue flame, even after the source of heat, such as a gas-flame, applied at first for the purpose of raising the temperature to the point of combustion, has been removed. The crystal gradually decreases in size, and finally disappears, the flame at the last moment often flickering brightly like that of an expiring lamp-flame. The combustion of diamond proceeds gradually from the exterior inwards; it is unattended by fusing, or, indeed, by any great alteration in the general form of the crystal, or in the physical characters of its substance, the material of the inner portion remaining unaltered during the combustion of the exterior.

It has been mentioned above that the combustion of diamond in a current of pure oxygen will proceed even when the source of heat is withdrawn; it is otherwise, however, when the diamond is burning in atmospheric air. Should the source of heat in this case be removed combustion will cease, owing to the fact that the oxygen of atmospheric air is largely diluted with nitrogen, a gas which does not support combustion. In the one case the heat evolved during combustion is sufficient to keep the stone above the temperature of ignition, while in the other it is not.

The temperature to which a diamond crystal must be heated in the air before combustion is started, is higher than the **temperature of ignition** in pure oxygen. According to Lavoisier it is a little lower than the melting-point of silver, this being fixed at 916° C. Moissan has recently determined the temperature of ignition of diamond in oxygen at 690° to 840° C. Small crystals are more easily induced to burn than are larger ones; according to Petzholdt, small diamonds placed on platinum foil, heated from below with a blowpipe flame, disappear in a very short time, the whole experiment occupying but a few minutes. Diamond dust burns with greater ease and rapidity the greater its fineness; thus powder of an extreme degree of fineness, when heated on platinum foil over the flame of an ordinary spirit-lamp, burns almost instantaneously with a brilliant glow. Whether in a finely divided condition or not, diamond burns much more easily than does the other crystallised modification of carbon, namely, graphite.

The oxidation of diamond powder, that is, its chemical union with oxygen, takes place with comparative ease if it is mixed with saltpetre, and the mixture then fused. The necessary oxygen is supplied by the decomposition of the saltpetre, and the diamond powder is very quickly burnt up. Diamond powder is also easily oxidised when heated at 180° to 230° C. with a mixture of potassium chromate and sulphuric acid. Diamond resists the action of such powerful chemical reagents as caustic potash, hydrofluoric acid, concentrated sulphuric acid, aqua regia (a mixture of hydrochloric and nitric acids), a mixture of sodium chlorate and nitric acid, iodic acid, and other energetic solvents. Few other substances resist the action of these reagents in the way diamond does ; it will remain in them unaltered even at high temperatures.

On examining a partially burnt crystal of diamond, it will be seen that its edges and corners are more or less rounded, and that its faces are no longer brilliant but dull, rough, and scarred.   On crystals which are bounded by faces of the octahedron, special markings are seen when such faces are examined with a lens or, better still, with a microscope. These markings are regular triangular depressions like inverted pyramids, the bases being equilateral triangles, of which the edges are in all cases parallel to the octahedral edges of the crystal, as is shown in Fig. 31 r.   The direction of these triangular pits is the reverse of that of the natural depressions of diamond crystals, shown in Fig. 31 q, n, and o.   Such pits may occur singly on the face of the crystal, or they may be close together and in large numbers ; they are of precisely the same character as etched or corrosion figures, such as may be produced on the faces of other crystals by the action of fused alkalis, or of solvents such as water and acid.   These depressions may indeed in the present case be regarded as corrosion figures, since they are produced by heating the diamond crystal in air or with saltpetre, the etching agent being then hot oxygen gas or fused saltpetre. The production of etched figures is due to the unequal action of the oxygen over the surfaces of the crystal, the crystal being attacked first at isolated points on the faces, where the material is slowly consumed.

As has been previously mentioned, a diamond heated away from contact with air undergoes no diminution in weight. The experiment may be performed by packing the diamond in charcoal powder in a closed crucible and heating it in an electric furnace.   The temperature may be as high as the furnace can produce, and may be maintained for any length of time, yet the diamond will still remain unaltered in weight, since in the absence of oxygen there can be no combustion of its substance. A prolonged exposure to great heat does, however, produce other changes ; the surface of the diamond becomes blackened and soft enough to leave a mark behind it when rubbed on paper. This is due to the **transformation to graphite** of the surface material ; this change in state of the substance of diamond to the other crystallised modification of carbon, namely graphite, is however, brought about only when a very high temperature is reached. According to G. Rose, who specially investigated the point, a diamond heated out of contact with air undergoes no change whatever when heated to the temperature at which cast-iron melts, nor even when exposed to the fiercest heat of a porcelain furnace. At higher temperatures, about that at which bar-steel melts, or in the electric furnace, a superficial blackening and conversion into graphite begins ; if the exposure to the temperature is prolonged sufficiently, this conversion proceeds until the whole of the substance of the diamond is changed into graphite, the original external form of the crystal being, however, still retained.

The behaviour of diamond with respect to its alteration into graphite when heated under other conditions, namely, in the presence of air, has not yet been thoroughly investigated. While in some experiments no blackening, even at the highest temperatures, has been observed, in others this phenomenon has been seen ; in these cases, however, the blackening may have been due to a sooty coating derived from the burning material which supplies the source of heat and not to the alteration of diamond into graphite. Many observers, including Lavoisier, have noticed that black spots are formed on the surface of a diamond undergoing combustion. When combustion is again allowed to proceed these spots may disappear, or they may be still apparent at lower depths as the outer parts of the stone slowly burn away.   According to Rose, no alteration into graphite takes place when a diamond is heated or burnt in a muffle or before the blowpipe, or perhaps even before the oxyhydrogen flame. When placed in the focus of a concave mirror, however, or when subjected to electric sparking, such a change is observed, but in neither of these cases can the blackening possibly be due to a sooty coating derived from the vapours of the source of heat. It is stated by Jaquet that a diamond placed in the electric arc given by one hundred Bunsen cells softens and becomes converted into a coke-like mass, the specific gravity of which is 2·678, while that of the diamond experimented upon was 3·336. He observed further, that whereas the material of diamond is a bad conductor of electricity, when converted into coke or graphite it becomes a good conductor.

Similar observations have been made by Gassiot, who has stated that before the alteration of diamond into a coke-like mass it softens and has the appearance of a body about to melt. Other statements respecting the melting of diamond, or of appearances referable to this change of state, are to be found in scientific literature. Berzelius reports that he observed a bubble on the surface of a burning diamond, and Clarke saw bubbles on the surface of a diamond when strongly heated in the oxyhydrogen flame. Other observers, on the other hand, under exactly similar conditions, have failed to notice any appearance of the kind, and in the absence of unanimous testimony it is still doubtful whether diamond does really fuse at high temperatures. Observations of the kind quoted are not altogether free from error; the rounding of the edges and corners of a partly-consumed diamond crystal would give it the appearance of having been fused; the rounding is, however, due to the fact that these prominent portions burn more rapidly than do the faces. The Emperor Francis I. sought to obtain a large diamond by fusing together several small ones; the attempt was, however, a complete failure, and the diamonds were burnt.

Probably the highest temperature to which diamond has been artificially subjected was reached in the experiments of Despretz, who employed for the purpose the electric spark given by five hundred to six hundred Bunsen cells. He reported that in the absence of air the usual change into graphite took place, and that if the heating was sufficiently prolonged beads of fused material were formed. Similar beads were also obtained from other varieties of carbon, but it is possible that these consisted of the mineral residue fused into a hard mass. If, however, this were the case, it would appear that the carbon had been volatilised, since combustion could not have taken place. It is very desirable that the researches of Despretz should be confirmed by further observation.

The whole of the substance of a perfectly colourless and transparent diamond is converted, when exposed to sufficient heat, into carbon dioxide, and no residue whatever remains behind. In the case of a deeply coloured or otherwise impure diamond combustion is not so complete, a small amount of incombustible **ash** remaining behind after the diamond has been converted into carbon dioxide. This residue consists of inorganic impurities differing in chemical composition in different stones; these have been enclosed in the diamond during its growth, and are the cause of the colour or cloudiness of the stone.

This residual ash varies very considerably in amount in different stones. In the purest stones it is almost imperceptible, while in less pure stones it varies from $\frac{1}{2000}$ to $\frac{1}{500}$ of the total weight (0·05 to 0·2 per cent.). The largest amount of ash, amounting to as much as 4·2 per cent., is present in carbonado, a peculiar variety of black, porous diamond found in Brazil. These impurities are often evenly distributed throughout the crystal. Occasionally, however, they are collected together at one or more points, which then appear coloured and cloudy, the surrounding portions being colourless and transparent. Such impurities in the diamond are isolated during combustion, but are more or less altered in character by the heat, sometimes being fused into beads, as mentioned above. The uniform distribution of impurities through the whole mass of the crystal is occasionally shown by the incombustible residue remaining behind as a porous mass, and having the form of the original diamond crystal.

The ash of the diamond is of a brownish colour. It contains some yellow flakes, and sometimes a few black grains which are attracted by a magnet. Its precise character depends, of course, upon the nature of the impurity in the diamond. Occasionally a few small, transparent, crystalline grains are present in the ash which have an action on polarised light; these and kindred impurities require a microscope for their detection. Chemical examinations of the ash of diamonds show that silica and iron oxide are invariable constituents, while lime and magnesia appear also in certain cases. An analysis of the ash of carbonado has given: silica 33·1 per cent., iron oxide 53·3, lime 13·2, and a trace of magnesia.

The constituents of the ash of diamond are, as a rule, very finely divided and distributed throughout the mass of the stone, the individual particles of the impurity not being recognisable even under the strongest magnification. Particles of foreign matter are sometimes, however, large enough to be seen with a lens or even with the naked eye; these bodies, which are referred to as **enclosures**, are isolated grains, splinters, scales, plates, needles, or fibres. They have definite sharp boundaries, and not infrequently are bounded by plane crystal-faces; they may occur in the diamond singly or in groups.

The nature and character of large enclosures is sometimes definitely known, but more frequently this is not the case. A peculiar and rare occurrence is the enclosure of a small diamond within a larger one, the two sometimes differing from each other both in crystalline form and in colour. In some cases the smaller enclosed diamond is quite free from the larger stone, and when the latter is cleaved open, the small enclosed stone falls out uninjured and perfect. The most commonly occurring enclosures in diamond are small black grains of irregular outline; they occur in large numbers in diamonds from all localities, and were formerly considered to consist of some carbonaceous substance. This, however, is not always the case. The black enclosures found in a diamond from South Africa by E. Cohen had the characters of hæmatite or ilmenite, and he is inclined to the opinion that all such enclosures consist of one or other of these two minerals. Many of these black grains are incombustible, and therefore inorganic; but others, according to the observations of Friedel, are consumed with the diamond, and hence must consist of some carbonaceous substance. In a diamond from the Cape a black, viscous, asphalt-like mass has been found, and similar enclosures have been reported in a few Indian crystals. Beside the minerals already named, several others have been determined with more or less certainty to occur as enclosures in diamond; these include, among others, quartz, topaz, rutile, iron-pyrites, which occur in the form of irregular grains or sometimes as well-developed crystals. Scales of gold have been found, though rarely, as enclosures in diamond crystals from Brazil. Vermiform aggregates of green scales are sometimes observed; these, however, are differently interpreted by different observers: Des Cloizeaux considers them to be a kind of chlorite, while Cohen regards the green scales in Cape diamonds as some copper compound. Red enclosures are very occasionally met with in Cape diamonds; they are of unknown nature.

Special mention must be made of enclosures of very fine green needles and fibres interwoven and matted into coil-like masses. In these and in aggregates of a similar kind, the structure of plant cells has sometimes been supposed to have been recognised; the distinguished botanist, Göppert, indeed, held that such enclosures were undoubtedly of a vegetable nature. It has since been proved, however, that they consist of inorganic material. There is no single case in which the vegetable nature of a diamond enclosure has been conclusively proved, although the attention of botanists has been more than once directed to this point.

All the minerals which have yet been mentioned as occurring as enclosures in diamond, must have been formed before the diamond commenced its gradual growth around them. There are other foreign bodies, however, which must have been introduced after the formation of the diamond; thus, water containing iron in solution has sometimes penetrated the cracks and fissures of a diamond, and has left a brown deposit of limonite filling up the crack or fissure.

The enclosures of diamond do not invariably consist of solid matter. Not infrequently there exist cavities in the substance of the diamond which may be vacuous or may contain liquid; these **fluid enclosures** are, however, usually of microscopic size. The liquid they often contain does not, as a rule, completely fill the cavity, part of the space being occupied by a bubble of gas, which is sometimes fixed in position and at other times movable, thus clearly indicating the fluid nature of the contents of the cavity. In some cases it can be safely inferred from the behaviour of the liquid when the diamond is heated that it is liquid carbon dioxide; this point will receive further consideration, however, when we come to consider the origin of diamond. In other cases the properties of the liquid point to its being water or a saline solution.

Other cavities in diamond are quite empty or only filled with gas; like the fluid enclosures these are by no means rare, and, when present at all, occur in large numbers. When observed under the microscope they appear quite black, especially at the visible margins; this is owing to the fact that the rays of light travelling through the stone are almost totally reflected at the surface of separation of the substance of the diamond and the bubble of gas, they therefore fail to reach the eye and the cavity appears dark. This is a fruitful source of error, for such appearances are liable to be mistaken for solid enclosures of a black colour. Such mistakes may be avoided, however, by careful observation, for the outline of cavities is usually rounded, while that of solid enclosures is irregular and angular; moreover, most cavities allow the passage of some light, at least in the centre; they will therefore appear to have a bright centre surrounded by a dark border, which would not be the case with solid enclosures. The presence of these cavities is of practical significance, since to them is due the cloudiness of the diamond, and those faults which have been already considered under the name "silk." From a theoretical point of view, they will no doubt help to throw light on the obscure question of the origin of diamond.

2. CRYSTALLINE FORM OF DIAMOND.

The diamond is one of the most perfectly crystallised of minerals. Almost every single stone is bounded by more or less regularly developed faces. Massive specimens without crystal-faces are scarcely ever found, and when such are met with they are, as a rule, fragments of large crystals or rounded pebbles, of which the original external crystalline form has been destroyed. As is usually the case with embedded crystals, that is, those which have grown embedded in the mother-rock, most diamonds are bounded on all sides by crystal-faces. Sometimes, however, irregular areas, by which the crystal might have been attached, can be made out with more or less certainty.

The faces of diamond crystals differ from those of most other crystallised minerals, in that they are, as a rule, much curved and rounded instead of being perfectly plane, as is usually the case. This curvature is due to the mode of growth of the crystal, and not to subsequent attrition, as might be thought. It renders the exact determination of a crystal, according to the methods of crystallography, very difficult, and for this reason many questions regarding the crystallisation of diamond are still open to debate. In what follows, the most important general crystallographic relations will be dealt with.

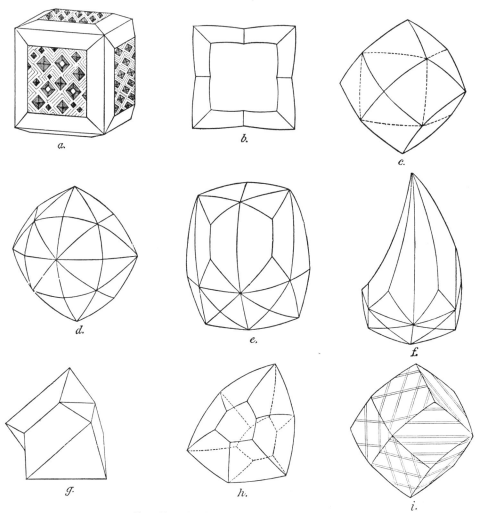

FIG. 31, *a–i.* Crystalline forms of diamond.

while special features peculiar to diamonds from particular localities will be mentioned under the description of these localities.

Observations on the crystalline form of diamond date back to the beginning of the seventeenth century, many diamond crystals having been described by Keppler, Steno, Boyle, and others. Romé de l'Isle and Haüy, the founders of scientific crystallography, were, at the beginning of the nineteenth century, the first to correctly interpret the different forms, and to determine the hemihedral development of the crystals. Great credit is also due to Gustav Rose for his exhaustive study of diamond crystals made at a later date. The results of his investigations were published in 1876 after his death by A. Sadebeck, who added numerous observations of his own.

Crystals of diamond belong to the cubic system, and, according to the views of the majority of mineralogists, to the tetrahedral-hemihedral division of this system. Certain peculiarities, however, render the hemihedrism of the crystals open to question, and some authorities prefer to consider them as holohedral.   All the typical simple forms of the cubic system have been observed in diamond crystals, either alone or in combination with other

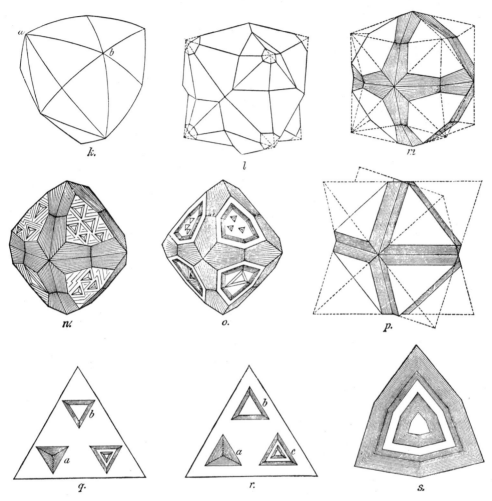

FIG. 31, *k-s.*   Crystalline forms of diamond.

forms.   Some of the more commonly occurring forms, which will be described in some detail, are shown in Fig. 31, *a–p.*

Crystals having the form of a regular cube (Fig. 31 *a*) occur very frequently, but are usually small; this habit is specially characteristic of Brazilian crystals, and is rarely met with in specimens from other localities, especially the Cape.   The faces of the cube are always dull and rough, and show a shallow depression, increasing in depth towards the centre of the face.   The roughness is due to the presence of square-based, pyramidal depressions placed diagonally on the cube face; these are usually small, but may be of fair size.   They occur more or less isolated or closely aggregated together (Fig. 31 *a*).   When observed with a lens or, better still, under the microscope, the pyramidal faces bounding the shallow depressions may be distinctly seen; they are marvellously plane and smooth, but just as frequently rough and irregular, and between these two extremes all gradations have been found. Such a cube of diamond in its matrix is shown in Plate I., Fig. 1.

In most cubes of diamond, however, each edge is replaced by two faces, as shown in Fig. 31 *a*; the twenty-four faces thus derived, would, if produced or enlarged sufficiently, give rise to the form known as the four-faced cube, or tetrakis-hexahedron. These faces are, however, as a rule, small; they are dull and uneven, and are irregularly striated perpendicularly to the cubic edges. Each face is often divided centrally by a narrow furrow, running perpendicularly to the edge and towards the centre of the cube face; this is illustrated in Fig. 31 *b*, which shows one cubic face together with the four adjacent faces of the four-faced cube. A crystal, bounded only by the twenty-four faces of the four-faced cube and with no cube faces, is occasionally met with in diamonds from Brazil and India; the faces of this form are then bright, but always curved.

The cube is also frequently modified in ways other than by the replacement of its edges. Not infrequently, for example, its eight corners are truncated by the eight faces of the octahedron. Moreover, each of the twelve edges of the cube may be replaced by a single plane face; these twelve truncating faces, if extended, would give the form known as the rhombic dodecahedron, which is of frequent occurrence, and is shown in Fig. 31 *c* and *i*. Its faces are sometimes plane and striated parallel to the longer diagonal (Fig. 31 *i*); as a rule, however, they are more or less curved, the lines of intersection of the faces being of course also curved; in this latter case the faces are not striated but are smooth and bright (Fig. 31 *c*). These curved faces frequently have a shallow groove running across them in the direction of the shorter diagonal, as indicated by the dotted line in Fig. 31 *c*; the form is then, strictly speaking, no longer a rhombic dodecahedron, but approaches to that of a tetrakis-hexahedron. The largest Brazilian diamond yet found, and known as the " Star of the South," is an irregularly developed rhombic dodecahedron; it is shown in its rough condition in Fig. 48. This form is frequently to be met with in Brazilian diamonds.

When the faces of the rhombic dodecahedron are grooved in the direction of the longer diagonal as well as in that of the shorter (Fig. 31 *d*), we obtain a form known as a hexakis-octahedron, bounded by forty-eight similar faces, which are always strongly curved, smooth, and bright. The hexakis-octahedron, which is of extremely frequent occurrence in diamond, approaches, as shown in Fig. 31 *d*, the form of the rhombic dodecahedron; at other times the same kind of form may approximate to the octahedron, each of the eight octahedral faces being replaced by six faces. Hexakis-octahedral crystals of the diamond are frequently much distorted by elongation in one direction, as shown in Fig. 31 *e*, a still greater distortion of the same form being represented in Fig. 31 *f*. Such distorted forms, which appear at a first glance to be quite distinct from that of Fig. 31 *d*, on a closer examination will be seen to be easily derived from that form.

Both the rhombic dodecahedron and the hexakis-octahedron are sometimes, on account of the strong curvature of their faces, almost spherical in shape. Formerly, when the principal localities for diamond were Brazil and India, the spherical form was known as the *Brazilian type*, and the octahedral form as the *Indian type*.

Occasionally, only half the faces of the hexakis-octahedron are developed, namely, those occupying alternate octants. The hemihedral form so derived is that of the hexakis-tetrahedron, shown in Fig. 31 *k*. The faces of this form, which is of rare occurrence, are always curved, smooth, and bright. If the symmetry of the diamond is really tetrahedral-hemihedral, the complete hexakis-octahedron may be regarded as a combination of two hexakis-tetrahedral forms, but the faces in adjacent octants would then have different surface characters, and this has not hitherto been observed.

A regular or **twin intergrowth** between two hemihedral crystals frequently takes place and results in the production of a holohedral form. The twin intergrowth of two hexakis-tetrahedra gives rise to the twinned crystal, shown in Fig. 31 *l*, in which for the sake of clearness the edges are represented as straight instead of curved lines. The two crystals interpenetrate at right angles, and the sharp corners, *a* (Fig. 31 *k*), of one individual project from the obtuse corners, *b*, of the other, the faces of the two interpenetrating individuals thus forming re-entrant angles. The sharp projecting corners of such a group are not always present, usually being truncated, as is indicated in the figure ; the truncating faces of each individual belong to the tetrahedron, and are never curved but always perfectly plane. The truncation, shown in Fig. 31 *l*, is only slight, while that of Fig. 31 *m*, is more pronounced. These eight truncating faces together complete the octahedron, the faces of which are plane, as is shown in *m* and *n* of Fig. 31, while its edges are replaced by re-entrant grooves, formed, as explained above, by the interpenetration of two hexakis-tetrahedra. On observing the figures it will be seen that these grooves are striated in the direction of their length. The size of the grooves depends on the degree to which the corners of the hexakis-tetrahedra are truncated by the faces of the tetrahedra. When the truncation is a maximum the grooves will be completely absent; but an octahedron of diamond in which such re-entrant grooves are not to be seen is a rarity. An octahedron of diamond with the sharp edges of the geometrical form must be considered to be the same as shown in Fig. 31, *m* and *n*, in which the truncation has quite obliterated the grooves ; in other words, it is the limiting form of such twinned crystals.

This twin intergrowth is simpler when the two individuals are tetrahedra instead of hexakis-tetrahedra, as in the case considered above. Such a twin-crystal is shown in Fig. 31 *p*, where the projecting portions, removed by truncation, of the two interpenetrating tetrahedra are represented by dotted lines. Here the grooves are quite straight, and of the same width throughout, and they do not show the nick in the middle as in the previous twinned form, in which also the grooves widen out away from this nick.

This simpler twinned form, consisting merely of two interpenetrating tetrahedra, is, however, of very rare occurrence in diamond. On the other hand, the form consisting of two interpenetrating hexakis-tetrahedra, as shown in Fig. 31 *m*, is very characteristic of diamond, and is of frequent occurrence. This figure has therefore been drawn again in Fig. 31 *n*, the dotted lines having been omitted and the characteristic markings on the faces inserted. The small faces of the hexakis-tetrahedra, which form the re-entrant grooves due to the twinning, are always somewhat curved and exhibit a delicate striation in the direction of their length. A slightly different form of such an interpenetrating twin of octahedral habit is shown in Fig. 31 *o ;* this also is a frequently observed form of diamond crystal. Here the edges of the octahedron have, in place of grooves, two small planes meeting at a very obtuse angle in a short edge at the middle of, and perpendicular to, the octahedral edge ; and away from this short edge formed by their mutual intersection they gradually widen out. These small planes are curved and finely striated, as shown in the figure, the octahedral planes being as before perfectly plane.

The twinned forms just described (Figs. 31 *m, n, o, p,*) are very characteristic of diamond, and they constitute the octahedral or Indian type. Crystals of this kind, of which one in its matrix is represented in Plate I., Fig. 2, are sometimes known in the trade as " points."

It has already been pointed out above that while the faces of the rhombic dodecahedron and of the hexakis-octahedron show a convex curvature, those of the octahedron are plane and even. The octahedral faces are, however, characterised by the presence of striations and pits, both of which are repeated on the surface with definite regularity and have a definite orientation. The striations are parallel to the symmetrical six-sided outline of the octahedral faces, as shown in Fig. 31 *o*, for the whole crystal, and in Fig. 31 *s*, for a single face. They may be either coarse or fine in character, and may be present in small or large numbers. The portions of the face of the octahedron between the striations are often very smooth and bright. These striations are due to the fact that the octahedral face is raised by very low steps towards its centre, each step having the same sharp outline as the margin of the octahedral face itself. It is as if numerous very thin plates, all of the same shape but gradually diminishing in size, had been piled, with their centres exactly superposed, on the octahedral face, so that each layer forms a step, and so a line of the striation.

The triangular pits are regular pyramidal depressions, of which the bases are equilateral triangles. They are usually small and often only to be seen distinctly under the microscope. The pyramidal faces inside the pits are finely striated and may terminate in the apex of the pyramid, as shown at *a* in Fig. 31 *q*; or they may not extend to such a depth into the interior of the crystal, the apex of the pyramid being then truncated by a triangular face parallel to the face of the octahedron, as at *b*, Fig. 31 *q*. Sometimes on this inner face there is a smaller pyramidal depression as at *c*, Fig. 31 *q*. These depressions are of the same general character as those produced on the octahedral faces of a diamond during its combustion; but while the corners of the pits of natural origin are adjacent to the octahedral edges (Fig. 31 *n*, *o*, *q*), this position is occupied by the sides of the pits produced by etching (Fig. 31 *r*); thus the two positions are the reverse of each other. The pits occur singly or in large numbers, and the striations may or may not be also present on the same face (Fig. 31 *o*, *n*).

Beside, the twin-crystals formed by the interpenetration of two hemihedral crystals, illustrated in Fig. 31, *l* to *p*, diamond presents still another type of twin-crystal, which is illustrated in Fig. 31, *g* to *i*. Here two octahedral or rhombic dodecahedral crystals are united together along a face of the octahedron. Fig. 31 *g*, shows two octahedra symmetrically united in this manner, the two individuals having one octahedral face in common. This kind of twin-growth is frequent in diamond but still more so in the mineral spinel, so that the law which governs this kind of twinning is referred to as the spinel twin-law. At the line of junction of the two individuals, three re-entrant angles alternate with the same number of salient angles. These spinel twins of diamond, which are known to the diamond-cutters of Amsterdam as " naadsteenen " (suture-stones), are very frequently flattened in a direction perpendicular to the common octahedral plane; they are, indeed, sometimes reduced to mere thin plates, but the faces and edges always have the surface characters described above.

Very frequently two rhombic dodecahedra or two hexakis-octahedra are twinned according to the same law on a face of the octahedron; that is, the two individuals have a face in common which occupies the position of an octahedral face, and about which they are symmetrical. These twin-growths also are much compressed in a direction perpendicular to the twin-plane; this is illustrated in Fig. 31 *h*, which represents a lenticular or heart-shaped crystal with curved faces. In this crystal only six faces of each of the hexakis-octahedra are developed, and these form low six-sided pyramids with a common base parallel to the six-sided octahedral face shown in the figure.

Fig. 31 *i* represents another kind of twin growth of rarer occurrence, in which the crystal has the form of a rhombic dodecahedron (Fig. 31 *c*). Parallel to one or more of the possible faces of the octahedron, which if present would truncate the corners in which three edges meet, are very thin lamellæ in twin positions to the main crystal. Large numbers of these twin-lamellæ may be present, and give rise to striations on the faces of the crystal.

Striations due to the same cause may also be present on the faces of the hexakis-octahedron, where, as before, they are parallel to one or other of the octahedral faces.

All these twin-groupings are quite regular and conform to certain definite crystallographic laws. Other intergrowths of two or more diamond crystals may be met with, in which the grouping is irregular and accidental, and cannot be referred to any general rule, the relative positions of individual crystals being determined by chance. In such intergrowths may be found small crystals growing singly on a larger one, or several crystals of more or less equal size may be united in an irregular group. Such groups are unsuitable for cutting as gems and are usually devoted to technical purposes; the same is true to a certain extent in the case of the twinned crystals above described. Irregular groupings of diamond crystals may, in a crystallographic sense, be referred to as **bort**; in the technical sense, however, the term bort includes all stones which, from some reason or another, are unfit for use as gems; and this term is even applied to simple crystals disfigured by some serious fault, such as imperfect transparency, bad colour, &c.

Bort occurs in a peculiar spherical form, being built up of a large number of small crystals radially arranged, so that the whole group takes the shape of a more or less perfect sphere (Plate I., Fig. 3). Numerous small points project from the surface of the sphere, these being the corners of the individual crystals which form the group. These spheres of bort are found in all diamond mines to the extent of from two to ten per cent. of the total output. Not infrequently only the outer shell of the sphere has the radially fibrous character just described, the central portion being occupied by a large, regularly-formed single crystal, which is usually so loosely attached to the radially crystalline shell that it falls out when the latter is broken.

Massive diamond with a granular crystalline structure and a black colour is known as **carbonado** or "carbonate" (Plate I., Fig. 4). Since it is applied to technical purposes only, it may be regarded in this sense as bort. It is found almost exclusively in the State of Bahia in Brazil; its characters will be further described when the occurrence of diamonds at this locality is under consideration.

Size of diamond crystals.—The size of diamond crystals varies between somewhat wide limits. The smallest which come into the market sometimes measure less than a millimetre in diameter, but still smaller specimens occur in nature. Small stones, measuring not more than one-quarter or one-third of a millimetre along the edge may be separated from a parcel of Brazilian diamonds by sifting with a sieve of fine mesh; the majority of these are octahedra, while cubes and rhombic dodecahedra are but rarely present. The faces of these very small crystals have the same surface characters as those of the larger crystals. By carefully washing for diamonds on the Cape diamond-fields, it is possible to obtain many stones very much smaller than those which usually come into the market, some indeed weighing no more than $\frac{1}{32}$ carat. In the method of washing formerly practised at the Cape and also in Brazil, a large number of the smallest diamonds were lost, their value not being sufficient to justify a special collection of them; the improved washing machinery now in use is, however, capable of saving all the stones however small.

Stones of microscopic dimensions have only recently been observed; previous statements of supposed occurrences, such, for example, as their presence in the xanthophyllite of Zlatoust in the Urals, being based on errors of determination. Microscopic diamonds have now been observed in large numbers in the diamond-bearing rock of the Cape, and there is no reason to doubt that they are present in other diamantiferous deposits.

Smaller diamonds occur in larger number; larger stones are more limited in number; while very large specimens are so extremely rare and valuable that they are known by special and distinctive names, and in most cases form part of the crown jewels of various countries; these famous stones will be described further on in a special section.

The average size of diamonds found in different countries varies very considerably; formerly, when India and Brazil were the only localities at which diamonds were known to exist, stones exceeding twenty carats in weight were of great rarity. During the most productive period of the mines of Brazil, two or three years would elapse before a second stone of this size would be found, while very few stones exceeding one hundred carats in weight were ever found. The largest stone ever found in this locality, that known as the " Star of the South " (Fig. 48), weighed in the rough $254\frac{1}{2}$ carats. The " Braganza," of the Portuguese crown, said to weigh 1680 carats, would rank as the largest diamond ever found

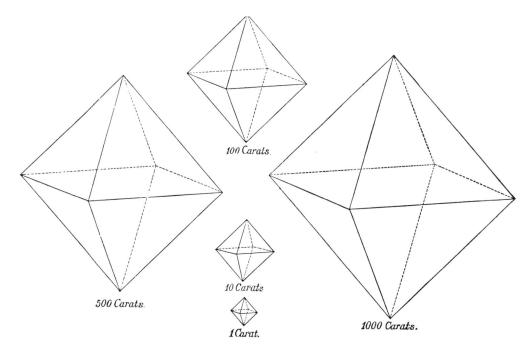

FIG. 32. Actual sizes of octahedral crystals of diamond of 1 to 1000 carats.

in any locality were it indisputably a diamond; the probabilities are, however, that it is a fine piece of colourless topaz.

The chances of obtaining large diamonds in the Indian deposits were more favourable, a considerable number of diamonds exceeding one hundred carats in weight having been found there. Most of the large Indian diamonds are only known in their cut condition so that their original weight can only be estimated. Of large Indian diamonds, known in the rough condition in recent times, the " Regent " in the French crown jewels, is the heaviest; it weighed before cutting 410 carats, and produced a beautiful brilliant of $136\frac{14}{16}$ carats. Other large Indian stones are described below in the section on famous diamonds; they are comparatively few in number. The heaviest of the large diamonds of ancient times is known as the " Great Mogul," which is said to have originally weighed $787\frac{1}{2}$ carats; there is no authentic information, however, either as to its weight or to its present whereabouts. The island of Borneo has produced one or two large stones; the largest reported diamond, weighing 367 carats, is, however, like the " Braganza," almost certainly not diamond, and probably nothing more valuable than a piece of rock-crystal.

Since the discovery of the South African diamond-fields, large diamonds have become less rare; as we shall see later on, stones up to 150 carats in weight have been found there with comparative frequency, while not a few of several hundred carats have been met with. The largest undoubtedly genuine diamond ever discovered, either here or elsewhere, was found at the Cape, in 1893, and weighed $971\frac{3}{4}$ carats; a more detailed description with a figure (Fig. 51) of this stone will be given later. Probably the largest crystal of diamond to be seen in a public collection is the "Colenso" diamond, presented to the British Museum by Professor John Ruskin; this is a symmetrically developed octahedron weighing $129\frac{2}{3}$ carats.

It has been already stated that the size of diamonds, as of all other precious stones, is estimated from their weight expressed in carats. It will be, however, difficult for the general reader to form a correct mental conception of the size of a given stone from its weight in carats alone; hence Fig. 32 is designed to show the actual sizes of diamonds weighing 1, 10, 100, 500, and 1000 carats respectively, each having the form of a regular octahedron, which is the form most frequently presented by crystals of diamond. In the special section devoted to the consideration of the larger and more famous diamonds, figures are given representing the actual sizes of these stones, usually in their cut form (Plates X. and XI.), but in a few cases in their rough form. Plate IX. gives the actual sizes of brilliants varying in weight between one and one hundred carats, and Fig. 44 the actual sizes of rosettes, varying between one and fifty carats.

3. SPECIFIC GRAVITY OF DIAMOND.

The specific gravity of diamond as determined by various observers varies between 3.3 and 3.7. Reliable determinations made on pure stones free from enclosures have, however, in every case yielded values not lower than 3.50 and not much higher than this; the mean value may, therefore, be placed at 3.52. The following are values obtained in particular instances by careful observers using pure material:

3.50 — 3.53	(*Dumas*).
3.524	Brazilian diamond (*Damour*).
3.520 — 3.524	Colourless and yellow diamond from the Cape (*von Baumhauer*).
3.517	Brazilian diamond (*J. N. Fuchs*).
3.529	"Star of the South" from Brazil (*Halphen*).
3.5213	"Florentine" (*Schrauf*).
3.50	Diamond from Burrandong, New South Wales (*Liversidge*).
3.492	Colourless diamond from Borneo (*Grailich*).

The fall of the last value below 3.5, is due to the attachment of a few air bubbles to the stone during the weighing in water.

The small differences in the specific gravity values given in the above table are probably due to the presence of various impurities. Since coloured diamonds always contain a small amount of impurity, the specific gravity will vary with the colour, as is shown in the table below:

		Sp. gr.
Colourless diamond	. . . . .	3.521
Green ,,	. . . .	3.524
Blue ,,	. . . .	3.525
Rose ,,	. . . .	3.531
Orange ,,	. . . .	3.550

Other values sometimes given are: colourless diamond 3.519, light yellow and green

3·521; for colourless Cape diamonds 3·520, and for yellow diamonds from the same locality 3·524.

Determinations which give results much above or much below the mean value of the specific gravity of diamond, namely, 3·52, and specially those which approximate to the extreme values, 3·3 and 3·7, must be regarded either as inaccurate or as having been made on impure material.

Black carbonado has a much lower specific gravity than pure crystals of diamond, values ranging from 3·141 to 3·416 having been determined. This is due to the porous nature of the material, the numerous air spaces enclosed in its substance causing it to be lighter, bulk for bulk, than are crystals of diamond.

4. CLEAVAGE OF DIAMOND.

When a diamond crystal is broken on an anvil by a blow from a hammer, or when it is subjected to sudden changes of temperature, it breaks into a number of fragments which are usually bounded by perfectly plane and bright surfaces. These surfaces of separation, or cleavage, will be found to have always a definite direction in the crystal, being parallel to one or more faces of the octahedron. If a chisel be driven into an octahedron of diamond in a direction parallel to an octahedral face the crystal will be divided into two portions, and the smooth, bright surfaces of separation will be parallel to the same octahedral face. By suitably varying the position of the chisel, the crystal may be divided in the same way into two other portions of which the surfaces of separation will be parallel to any other of the faces of the octahedron. It is not possible, however, to produce a cleavage in a cube of diamond which shall be parallel to the faces of the cube; in these directions there will be irregular fractured surfaces only. If the chisel is so placed that a corner of the cube is removed, a cleavage surface will be produced, this being as before parallel to a face of the octahedron, the faces of which also truncate the corners of the cube in the natural crystals. The cleavage surfaces of all crystals of diamond, whatever be their outward form, are always parallel to the faces of the octahedron, and in no other direction can plane cleavage surfaces be obtained. Diamond thus possesses an octahedral cleavage only, which is perfect and obtained with the greatest ease; this gem may indeed be regarded as one of the most perfectly cleavable of minerals.

This perfect cleavage with plane even surfaces throughout can, however, be obtained only in simple crystals. When we are dealing with an intergrowth of two or more crystals twinned according to the spinel-law (Fig. 31, *g* to *i*) or irregularly grouped together, the cleavage surfaces will have different directions in each individual, and will not pass uninterruptedly from side to side of the stone as in simple crystals; it is thus impossible to divide such a stone by a single cleavage surface.

From every simple diamond crystal, no matter what may be its external crystalline form, there may be obtained by cleaving parallel to all the octahedral faces a cleavage fragment having the form of an octahedron (Fig. 32). The great importance of this property of cleavage in connection with the faceting of diamonds has already been touched upon, and will be again referred to under the special description of the process of diamond cutting. The property of perfect cleavage is not, however, a desirable one from every point of view, for it is often responsible for the appearance of incipient cracks in the stone, which, if they further develop, seriously diminish its value.

5. HARDNESS OF DIAMOND.

In respect to its hardness, diamond stands alone among all other substances, whether natural or artificial. The hardness possessed by some artificial substances, such, for example, as crystallised boron and carborundum, does, however, approach that of diamond. This gem stands at the head of Mohs' scale, and receives the number 10 as a measure of its hardness. Between this and the next hardest natural substance, namely corundum (ruby and sapphire), there is a wide gap, the difference in hardness between diamond and corundum being far greater than that which exists between corundum and talc, the softest of all minerals. The unique degree of hardness thus possessed by diamond renders it easily recognisable, since it scratches all other substances without exception, and is itself scratched by none.

It is a remarkable fact that degrees of hardness exist in diamonds among themselves, this being shown by the fact that diamonds from one locality are capable of scratching those from other localities. Thus the Australian stones are harder than those from South Africa, which are said to be the softest of all diamonds; and the beautiful black diamonds of Borneo are harder than those of other colours. It is also remarkable that many South African diamonds gradually assume their characteristic hardness only after a more or less prolonged exposure to air.

Diamond forms no exception to the general rule that the hardness of a crystal is not everywhere the same. It has been observed that the powder obtained by rubbing the surface of diamond crystals in the operation of bruting, which will be described in the section on diamond cutting, is more efficacious in the process of grinding than is the powder obtained by pounding up large fragments of diamond. It may naturally be inferred from this, that diamond crystals must be harder on the exterior than in the interior. On the surface itself, however, differences in hardness are distinctly perceptible, some faces of the crystal being more easily scratched than others, while on each face there are certain directions along which scratching may be more readily effected than in others. This being so, it follows that the process of grinding will also be more difficult in certain directions and on certain parts of the stone than in others. This subject will, however, be treated more fully in the section devoted to diamond cutting.

The great degree of hardness possessed by diamond renders it exceptionally suitable for use in personal ornament, since the sharpness of the edges and corners of the cut stone and the lustre of the polished facets are retained in spite of long continued wear.

Several important technical applications of diamond depend on the enormous hardness it possesses; these will be fully discussed in a special section, and we need only mention here the use of diamond powder in the cutting of the harder precious stones and of diamond itself. The hard Australian diamonds, however, are unattacked by the powder of other softer diamonds, they can only be worked by the help of their own powder.

In spite of their enormous hardness, the diamond crystals found in river-sands and gravels often show signs of wear and tear, their edges and corners being rounded and their surfaces dull and roughened. This has been effected by long ages of grinding against the pebbles and quartz-grains, and occasionally the precious stones of river-sands and gravels; thus even diamond itself cannot escape the action of time.

The hardness of diamond has often been confused with its **frangibility** or brittleness. It has been supposed, especially in ancient and mediæval times, that hammer and anvil may be shattered but not the diamond which lies between. This statement was made by Pliny, the great naturalist of ancient days, who was killed in 79 A.D. at the first historic eruption of Vesuvius. He proceeded to say further that the **fragmentation of a diamond** may be effected by subjecting it to a preliminary immersion in the warm blood of a goat, but that even under these circumstances the hammer and anvil will also be broken! According to Albertus Magnus (1205–1280), the blood is more efficacious if the goat has previously drunk wine or eaten parsley!

Such being the views then held respecting the unbreakable and indestructible character of the diamond, it is easy to understand why the Greek word *adamas*, signifying unconquerable, should have been applied to this stone, although its application to the diamond is singularly inappropriate and inaccurate when its extreme frangibility is considered. Many a doubtful stone has been submitted to the test of the hammer, with the belief that the blow would be resisted only if the stone were a genuine diamond. Probably many beautiful stones have been sacrificed to this old belief. As a matter of fact, diamond is easily fractured, a very moderate blow from a hammer sufficing for the purpose; its perfect cleavage places it among the most brittle of minerals.

6. OPTICAL CHARACTERS OF DIAMOND.

Transparency.—In its pure condition diamond is most beautifully clear and transparent; the presence of enclosures of foreign matter, however, often diminishes the natural transparency of the stone, in some cases causing almost complete opacity. Dark coloured diamonds, especially brown and black specimens, are frequently transparent only at their edges, and black diamonds are often completely opaque. The transparency of a crystal depends also upon the condition of its surface; if this should be roughened, as will be the case after a prolonged rolling about on the bed of a river, the stone will appear dull and cloudy, although its interior may be perfectly transparent, as is evident when the rough surfaces have been removed by cutting.

On the degree of transparency depends largely the quality known as the *water* of a diamond. A stone which is perfectly transparent, colourless, and free from all faults is described as a diamond of the first or purest water. A small degree of cloudiness in a diamond does not entirely unfit it for use as a gem; when, however, the cloudiness exceeds a certain amount the stone can be applied only to technical purposes.

Lustre.—The lustre on the smooth face of a diamond, beside being extraordinarily strong and brilliant, is very peculiar in character and is intermediate between the lustre of glass and that of metal. Being characteristic of diamond, it is known as adamantine lustre, and is shown by very few minerals and by still fewer precious stones. It is therefore possible after a little practice to readily distinguish diamond from other transparent substances, such as glass, rock-crystal, &c., by the character of the lustre alone. As we have already seen, however, there is an artificial glass known as strass, which possesses an adamantine lustre and which is therefore much used in the manufacture of imitation diamonds.

Adamantine lustre is frequently absent from the natural faces of diamond crystals especially after they have become dulled by friction in a river-bed. In such cases, the stone has a peculiar lead-grey metallic appearance, similar to that which is artificially produced by bruting, an operation in the process of diamond cutting which consists of the rubbing together of two diamonds with the object of obtaining an approximation to the form they are finally to assume. Adamantine lustre is seen to perfection on the polished facets of a cut diamond, since here the incident light is reflected quite regularly. The lustre of diamonds which are dark coloured, and therefore have little transparency, approaches that of metals. The same metallic lustre is seen on the facets of a perfectly transparent stone when light falls upon it at a very small inclination, the light being reflected from the facet in such a way that the latter has the appearance of highly polished steel. This phenomenon can be observed by placing the stone with a perfectly smooth facet close to the eye and inclining it towards the light, until, in a certain position, the metallic reflection becomes evident.

Perfect adamantine lustre, in all bodies which possess it, is combined with perfect transparency, very strong refraction, and marked dispersion of light. All substances including diamond itself, which possess adamantine lustre are thus also characterised by strong refraction and dispersion of light; and, conversely, all substances possessing the two latter qualities will be found to exhibit adamantine lustre. Not only the quality but the intensity of the lustre shown by a stone depends upon the strength of its refraction of light; light rays falling obliquely upon the surface of a stone will be the more completely reflected the higher its index of refraction is. Thus diamond, having a higher index of refraction, will reflect more rays of light from its surface, and will therefore show a stronger lustre than will a substance having a lower index of refraction. The qualities of lustre and brilliancy are known collectively as the " fire " of a stone. It will be evident from what has been said that the " fire " of diamond is specially fine.

Refraction of light.—Diamond, like all other substances which crystallise in the cubic system, is singly refracting. A ray of light incident obliquely upon the plane face of a diamond is propagated in the substance of the stone as a single ray, the direction of which, however, differs from that of its path in the surrounding medium. This difference is, in diamond, very considerable, much more than in the majority of other substances; in other words, the index of refraction of diamond is very high.

The power of breaking up white light into its constituent colours, that is, the **dispersion,** possessed by diamond is likewise very marked. The blue rays of light undergo a much greater refraction when passing into diamond than do the red rays; hence the spectrum produced by a prism of diamond is very long, the red and blue ends being widely separated. The various colours into which white light, in passing through a cut diamond, is broken up are widely separated and distinctly perceptible; hence the beautiful play of brilliant, prismatic colours upon which so much of the beauty of diamond depends, and which differentiates it so markedly from other colourless stones, such as rock-crystal, topaz, colourless sapphire, &c., which have a lower dispersion and consequently a less beautiful play of colours. This subject has, however, been fully dealt with above in the section devoted to the consideration of the passage of light through a cut stone.

The action of every diamond upon light is not absolutely identical. A satisfactory explanation of the small differences which exist cannot, however, at present be given. The fact that one stone has a finer appearance than another is probably due to slight differences between them in the refractive index and in dispersive power. In respect of play of prismatic colours Indian diamonds rank highest. Next to these we may place Brazilian stones from the district of Diamantina in the State of Minas Geraes, and from the Canavieiras mines in the State of Bahia. Relatively inferior to these, but yet with a fine play of prismatic colours, are the majority of Cape diamonds. It is a remarkable fact that in many cases diamonds from the Cape and from Canavieiras exhibit a finer play of prismatic colours in artificial light than in daylight, which is the reverse of what is usually the case.

The refractive power and the dispersion of diamond are both given by the values of the refractive indices for different coloured rays. These values give the strength of refraction directly, and the difference between the refractive index for red and that for violet rays is a measure of the dispersion. A comparison of the following determinations by Walter, with similar constants for other precious stones, will show that the refraction and dispersion of diamond are in all cases the greater :

		n
Red light (B line of the spectrum)	. . . .	2·40735
Yellow „ (D „ „)	. . . .	2·41734
Green „ (E „ „)	. . . .	2·42694
Violet „ (H „ „)	. . . .	2·46476

The dispersion co-efficient is thus—

$$2·46476 - 2·40735 = 0·05741.$$

For comparison, the following values of the refractive indices of a particular glass may be given :

	n
Red light	1·524312
Yellow „	1·527982
Green „	1·531372
Violet „	1·544684

The dispersion co-efficient is here—

$$1·544684 - 1·524312 = 0·020372,$$

less than half as great as that of diamond. The spectrum produced by a prism of this glass will be only about half as long as one produced by a similar prism of diamond under the same conditions.

Anomalous double refraction. — Diamond, being crystallised in the cubic system, should be singly refracting, that is, isotropic. This, however, is only strictly true for such stones as are perfectly colourless, or of a yellowish colour, and are quite free from enclosures of foreign matter, cracks, and other flaws. Such faultless stones when rotated in the dark field of the polariscope remain dark. As previously mentioned, the stone under examination should be immersed in methylene iodide, so as to diminish total reflection as far as possible.

Deeply-coloured stones, and those disfigured by cracks, enclosures, or other faults, when placed in the dark field of the polariscope, allow the passage of light to the eye, but, as a rule, to only a small extent. They have, under these circumstances, a greyish appearance, brilliant polarisation colours being rarely seen. The feeble double refraction possessed by such stones is not an essential character of the substance of the diamond itself, but is due to disturbing influences; hence it is distinguished as anomalous double refraction. During its rotation in the polariscope it rarely happens that such a stone is uniformly dark or uniformly light over its whole surface; as a rule, certain areas are dark while others are light, and *vice versâ*. Frequently certain regularly bounded areas or fields behave in a similar manner during rotation, while adjacent fields behave differently. In most cases, however, the areas showing these differences in behaviour have no definite arrangement relative to each other, and areas showing a feeble double refraction are often enclosed in areas which are perfectly isotropic.

The doubly refracting portions of the stone usually surround enclosures or cracks, and it is in the immediate vicinity of these that double refraction is strongest and the polarisation colours most brilliant. As the distance from a flaw of this kind increases the double refraction becomes feebler, and at a certain distance disappears. Sometimes a black cross, the arms of which consist of two dark brushes, is seen when a stone is examined in the polariscope: the arms of the cross are mutually perpendicular and their point of intersection coincides with an enclosure in the diamond. It is clear that such an appearance is due to a strain in the diamond brought about by the presence of the enclosure, and that the strain will be less in portions further removed from the enclosure.

Although the anomalous double refraction of diamond is, as a rule, but feeble, stones exist in which it is comparatively strong, and which show much brighter polarisation colours. This is the case in the " smoky stones" of South Africa, which, because of the great internal strain in their substance, have a tendency to fall to powder for no apparent reason. A parallel case is that of the drops of glass known as " Prince Rupert's drops," which also show strong double refraction as a consequence of internal strain.

There is never the slightest danger of confusing anomalous with true double refraction, for a mineral with true double refraction, such for example as rock-crystal, colourless sapphire or topaz, will appear much more brilliantly illuminated when examined in the polariscope, and, moreover, will be uniformly light or uniformly dark over its whole surface.

Colour.—Diamond is often regarded as the type of what a perfectly clear, colourless, and transparent stone should be. It can by no means, however, be always so regarded, since cloudy and opaque diamonds are actually more common than those which are clear and transparent, while very great variety in colour is found in this mineral. A great number of diamonds are indeed perfectly colourless, and correspond strictly to the popular conception of the stone; this number is, however, only one-fourth of the total number of diamonds found; another quarter show a very light shade of colour, while the remainder, at least one-half of the total, are more or less deeply coloured.

Perfectly colourless diamonds are, at the same time, most free from impurity. Absolutely pure carbon, crystallised in the form of diamond, shows no trace of colour whatever, and stones of this purity are naturally highly prized. A peculiar steel-blue appearance is sometimes observed in stones which combine absence of colour with perfect transparency. With the exception of a few specially beautifully coloured stones of great rarity, these *blue-white* diamonds are the most highly prized of all; they are not of great rarity in India and Brazil, but occur in South Africa with far less frequency.

Any colouring-matter intermixed with the substance of a diamond imparts its colour to the stone, the tone of which will be faint when the pigment is present in small amount and deeper when it is present in greater amount. In all cases the amount of colouring-matter relative to the mass of the stone is extremely small.

Investigations into the precise nature of the various colouring-matters present in diamonds have seldom been undertaken on account of their difficulty and expense. There can be no doubt, however, that the colouring-matter of many diamonds is of an organic nature, possibly some one or other of the hydrocarbons; in other cases the pigment is probably inorganic material in an extremely fine state of division. We have already seen that coloured diamonds contain a small amount of ferruginous material which remains behind as an incombustible ash after the diamond is burnt away, and that with colourless diamonds this is not the case. There seems sufficient grounds here for the inference that in such cases the colour of the stone is due to the inorganic, incombustible, enclosed material, especially as the colour is neither altered nor destroyed after exposure to high temperature, which would be the case were it organic in nature. In the few recorded cases in which a change of colour has been observed on strongly heating the stone, there can be no doubt as to the organic nature of the colouring-matter.

The colouring of many diamonds is so faint that an unpractised observer, unless he is able to compare such a stone with an absolutely colourless diamond or to place it against a background of pure white, will fail to recognise that the stone is coloured at all. The practised eye of the diamond merchant, however, needs no such assistance in recognising the most faintly coloured stones. Such stones are rather lower in value than absolutely colourless specimens of the same clearness and transparency, but the difference in price is not very considerable. The shades of colour which appear most frequently are light yellow, grey, and green. A faintly yellow diamond is not observable as such in any artificial illumination other than the electric light, and then appears to be a colourless stone. Diamonds of a faint bluish tinge are known, but are much less common.

As mentioned above, diamonds showing a pronounced colouration constitute about one-half of the total output. Almost all the colours of the mineral kingdom may be represented in numerous and varied tints, so that the suite of colours of the diamond is very extensive. A magnificent collection of differently coloured diamonds, the most beautiful and the richest in existence, is preserved in the treasury of the royal palace at Vienna. It was brought together by Helmreichen, who spent many years in Brazil, and was so enabled to make the series very complete. The colour which occurs most frequently in diamonds is yellow, in various shades, such as citron-yellow, wine-yellow, brass-yellow, ochre-yellow, and honey-yellow, but sulphur-yellow has not as yet been observed. Most of the Cape diamonds are coloured with one or other of these tints of yellow. After yellow, green is the most commonly occurring colour, especially in Brazilian diamonds. Oil-green or yellowish-green is seen most frequently, then pale green, leek-green, asparagus-green, pistachio-green, olive-green, siskin-green, emerald-green, bluish-green and greyish-green. Brown diamonds are also common at all localities; the different shades are light-brown, coffee-brown, clove-brown, and reddish-brown. Shades of grey, such as pale grey, ash-grey, smoke-grey, are not rare. Black diamonds in well-formed crystals are unusual. The different shades of red, a colour which is rarely met with in diamonds, are lilac-red, rose-red, peach-blossom-red, cherry-red, hyacinth-red. Blue in its two shades, dark blue and pale sapphire-blue, is the rarest of all colours to be met with in diamonds.

The colouring of diamonds is seldom intense, pale colours being much more usual than deeper shades. Diamonds which combine great depth and beauty of colour, with perfect transparency, are objects of unsurpassable beauty; for, in addition to their fine colour, they possess the wonderful lustre and brilliant play of prismatic colours peculiar to the diamond, so that other finely-coloured stones, such as ruby and sapphire, are not to be compared with them. Only a few stones of this description are in existence; they are among the most highly-prized of costly gems.

Of such deeply coloured and perfectly transparent diamonds, bright or deep **yellow** specimens are, since the discovery of the South African diamond-fields, the least rarely met with. The largest of these yellow Cape diamonds is shown in Fig. 52; it is a beautiful orange-yellow brilliant, weighing 125⅗ carats, and is in the possession of Tiffany and Co., the New York firm of jewellers. A few fine yellow stones dating back to ancient times are preserved in the " Green Vaults " at Dresden.

Diamonds of a fine **green** colour are distinctly rare, only a few examples being known; the same may be said of red diamonds and, even more emphatically, of blue diamonds. The most beautiful green diamond known is a transparent brilliant weighing 48½ carats, preserved in the " Green Vaults " at Dresden; it will be again mentioned in the section devoted to famous diamonds. Another green diamond of the same quality is now in America. Tschudi mentions two beautiful specimens from Brazil, one of an emerald-green and the other of a sea-green colour, while the existence of other Brazilian stones with a colour very similar to that of the yellowish-green of uranium glass, but inclining more to yellow, is mentioned by Boutan.

The ten-carat ruby-red stone, which belonged to Czar Paul I. of Russia, and which is said to be still preserved with the Russian crown jewels, is often mentioned as an example of a **red** diamond; nothing more definite concerning it is, however, known. A better authenticated example is the " Red Halphen " diamond, a ruby-red brilliant weighing one carat; while recently Streeter has reported the discovery of a beautiful red stone in Borneo, and its sale in Paris. Several examples of beautifully transparent rose-red diamonds are known; such, for instance, as that of the fifteen-carat stone belonging to the Prince of Riccia, a few smaller specimens in the treasury at Dresden, and a thirty-two-carat stone, the most beautiful rose-red known, in the treasury of Vienna. A rose-coloured brilliant, called the " Fleur de pêcher," is among the French crown jewels, and Tschudi mentions a peach-blossom-red stone from the Rio do Bagagem, in Minas Geraes, Brazil.

Blue diamonds are the rarest of all. A magnificent blue brilliant of $44\frac{1}{4}$ carats, the " pearl of coloured diamonds," was formerly in the possession of Mr. Hope, a London banker. It is probably a portion of Tavernier's blue diamond of $67\frac{1}{8}$ carats, stolen in 1792 with the French crown jewels. A small diamond of a deep blue colour, and a pale blue one of forty carats, are preserved in the Munich treasury.

Black diamonds perhaps deserve a brief mention. Crystals of a uniform black colour have been found in Borneo, and also very rarely in South Africa. The opacity of such stones, combined with their high degree of lustre, almost metallic in its character, render them, when cut, of peculiar beauty, and well suited for use in mourning jewellery. These crystals of black diamond must not be confused with the black carbonado of Brazil, to be described later. A few **brown** stones of a delicate and beautiful coffee shade are known; these also come from Brazil.

As is almost always the case with precious stones and other minerals, the colour of which is due to enclosed foreign matter in an extremely fine state of division, so also in the diamond the distribution of the colouring-matter is not always perfectly uniform throughout its whole mass. The pigment may be collected or accumulated in isolated patches, while the rest of the stone is either colourless or less deeply coloured. In numerous cases, only the thin surface layer of the crystal is coloured, the interior of the stone being colourless; this occurs often in Brazilian stones, especially those from the Rio Pardo, in the Diamantina district. When the outer layer, which is often pale green in colour, is removed in the process of cutting, a perfectly colourless stone is obtained. Tschudi mentions a fine emerald-green brilliant from Brazil, which before cutting had a sooty black appearance; another specimen of similar appearance retained its black colour almost entirely after cutting, a few facets only appearing white.

Not infrequently the bulk of a rough diamond is colourless, the edges and corners only being coloured; many Brazilian stones are of this description, as well as specimens from South Africa, including some of the " smoky stones " already mentioned. In these the deep smoky-grey colour is sometimes confined to the corners of the stone, the interior being faintly coloured or entirely colourless; a stone so coloured is described as a " glassy stone with smoky corners." Diamonds in which these conditions are reversed also occur, the edges and corners being colourless, and the central portion coloured.

Sometimes, though rarely, a stone shows two differently coloured portions; the two portions of one mentioned by Mawe were coloured respectively yellow and blue. Stones showing a number of differently coloured sectors, sharply separated from each other, and radiating from a central point, are also of rare occurrence. Thus smoke-grey and colourless rays may have a regular star-like arrangement, or may form a figure like the club of playing cards, on the faces of the octahedron.

Of interest is the fact that diamond sometimes shows a play of colours like that of precious opal. Des Cloizeaux mentioned a few such stones which differed from opal in this respect only in that the colours were less brilliant. Pale blue and yellow stones have been reported by Mawe to show a somewhat similar appearance.

The colour of diamonds is by no means in every case unchanging and unalterable. Some stones are bleached by sunlight; thus a red diamond on exposure to sunlight is reported to have gradually lost its colour and become white. A diamond in the possession of the Parisian jeweller, Halphen, undergoes a peculiar change in colour on exposure to heat. This stone, which is of a faint brownish colour and weighs four grams (about twenty carats), assumes in the fire a beautiful rose-red colour. If kept in darkness this colour is retained for about ten days, after which it returns to its original brownish colour; should the stone be exposed to diffuse daylight, or to the direct rays of the sun, the change to the original colour is much more rapid. The change to rose-red can be produced at will by again exposing the stone to the action of heat. Could means be devised for retaining the rose-red colour of the stone, the possessor would benefit to the extent of many thousand francs, since it is valued when brown at 60,000 francs, and when rose-red at from 150,000 to 200,000 francs. Halphen has also seen a diamond which when rubbed assumed a rose-red colour: this colour, however, was lost again almost immediately.

The colour of diamonds is in some cases affected by exposure to a high temperature. According to Des Cloizeaux, pale green diamonds, after being heated in the oxyhydrogen flame, became light yellow; brown crystals under the same conditions become greyish. Baumhauer also witnessed the colour of one diamond change from green to yellow, and of another from dark green to violet, under the influence of a high temperature. Wöhler caused green diamonds to assume a brown colour by heating them, but found that brown stones remained unaltered in colour. Yellow diamonds, especially those from the Cape, retain their colour at the highest temperatures.

It has already been mentioned that very faintly coloured stones command a somewhat lower price than do those which are perfectly colourless. Hence many attempts have been made to transform faintly coloured stones into the more valuable colourless stones. This is readily effected in those Brazilian diamonds, which have a colourless central portion surrounded by a coloured external layer of no great thickness. The outer coloured layer is in these cases simply burnt away by heating the stone in a crucible with a little saltpetre. The operation is very brief, the coloured external layer disappearing in one or two seconds. This device involves no actual change of colour, but is simply a removal of the coloured portions, which could have been effected just as well by the more lengthy process of grinding.

Attempts have been made, however, to decolourise diamonds in which the undesirable pigment is distributed through the substance of the whole stone. Probably the first to make experiments in this direction was the Emperor Rudolph II.; according to the report of his gem-expert, Boetius de Boot, the Emperor was acquainted with a method by which every diamond could be decolourised, and rendered perfectly colourless. This important secret, however, died with its possessor. At a later date the Parisian jeweller, Barbot, claimed to be able, by the employment of chemical means and a high temperature, to decolourise green, red, and yellow stones, while dark yellow, brown, and black stones only slightly lost their colour. Barbot's method was also preserved as a secret, so that it is impossible to put his assertion to the test; it is probable, however, that he did not possess the power to which he laid claim, in spite of the fact that he described himself on the title-page of one of his books as " Inventeur du procédé de décoloration du diamant." Our present knowledge of the constituents of diamond pigments makes us unwilling to believe too readily in the possibility of their complete destruction ; at all events, no method is at present known which is effectual in all cases.

Although it is impossible actually to destroy the colour of yellow diamonds, such as now so often come into the market, it is easy to disguise their yellow tint and make them appear colourless. This device has often been practised for fraudulent purposes, and was successfully carried out in Paris a few years ago. The yellow stone is placed in a violet liquid, such as the dilute solution of potassium permanganate used for disinfecting purposes. On being taken out and allowed to dry the stone becomes coated with a thin film of the violet substance. The combined effect of yellow and violet colours in certain proportions is to produce in the eye the sensation of white light ; hence, when the violet layer is of a certain thickness, the stone will have the appearance of being perfectly colourless. Should it still appear yellow after the first trial, it may be immersed a second or third time, while if the violet colour is too deep, some of it may be washed off. Instead of a solution of potassium permanganate violet ink may be used for this purpose. A stone treated in this way will, of course, remain apparently colourless only so long as the violet coating remains intact ; directly this is rubbed off, which readily happens, the yellow colour of the stone becomes apparent. A more permanent coating is said, however, to have been recently devised for this purpose. The methods by which yellow stones can be made to appear colourless are very old ; ultramarine is supposed to have been used by the ancient inhabitants of India for this purpose.

According to the investigations of Petzholdt, which are confirmed by every diamond-cutter, the colour of diamond powder or dust varies from grey to black, and is darker the finer its state of division.

Phosphorescence.—Many erroneous statements have been made with regard to the phosphorescence of diamond. Thus it has been stated that diamond phosphoresces in darkness after exposure to the direct rays of the sun, the phosphorescence being specially marked after exposure to blue light, and less so after exposure to red light. It is even said that after being screened by a board or paper from the direct rays of the sun, so that the stone is exposed to diffused daylight only, it will be seen to glow brightly when placed in darkness. Exact researches, however, have proved that only very few diamonds phosphoresce after exposure to sunlight, and that neither the direct rays of the sun nor intense artificial light cause phosphorescence in the majority of stones. Streeter reports that a yellow stone of 115 carats, after exposure to lime-light lit up a dark room ; and Edwards describes a water-clear diamond of 92 carats, which after one hour's exposure to electric light emitted in a dark room a light which lasted for twenty minutes, and was so strong that a sheet of white paper placed near the stone could be distinctly seen. Of 150 diamonds of various forms, sizes and qualities examined by Kunz, only three showed the phenomenon of phosphorescence after exposure to the light of the electric arc.

Although exposure to light has in diamond so small an effect in exciting phosphorescence, the phenomenon is easily produced by rubbing the stone. Kunz observed that all the diamonds he examined, without exception, became self-luminous after being rubbed on wood, leather, woollen or other material. Some stones needed only to be drawn once across the substance, especially if it were of wool, to render them self-luminous ; the most marked phosphorescence was, however, developed in stones by rubbing on wood against the grain. According to other statements, rubbing on metals (iron, steel, copper) is effective.

Whether diamonds are capable, as a rule, of giving out light after being raised to a temperature below red heat is doubtful, but some specimens, which are unaffected by sunlight and remain quite dark, are induced to glow by exposure to electric sparks. But here, as in all cases, the phosphorescence can be produced only when the stone has not previously been exposed to a strong heat.

The light given out by a phosphorescing diamond is in almost all cases feeble, and much less intense than that emitted by many other phosphorescent substances. The light, which is usually yellow in colour, but may under certain circumstances be blue, green, or red, is strongest when induced by electric sparking. Remarkable observations have been made on the appearance of different faces of a phosphorescing crystal of diamond. Dessaignes (1809) stated that a diamond after exposure to the sun's rays emitted light from the cube faces, but not from the octahedral faces, which remained quite dark. Maskelyne described a diamond crystal which emitted a beautiful apricot-coloured light from the cube faces, a bright yellow from the faces of the rhombic dodecahedron, and a yellow light of another shade from the octahedral faces.

All these appearances are, as a rule, of brief duration. A case is, however, recorded of a diamond which continued to phosphoresce for an hour after the removal of the exciting cause.

The phosphorescence of diamond is said to have been first observed in 1663 by the famous English physicist Robert Boyle.

7. ELECTRICAL AND THERMAL CHARACTERS.

A diamond, whether rough or cut, becomes positively electrified on rubbing; the charge so acquired is quickly lost, never being retained more than half an hour. In contrast to graphite, the other crystallised modification of carbon, which is a good conductor of electricity, the conductivity of diamond is so inappreciable that the stone ranks as a non-conductor.

Diamond being a good conductor of heat appears cold to the touch, and by this means can be distinguished from other substances, as already explained.

B. OCCURRENCE AND DISTRIBUTION OF DIAMOND.

Diamond has been found in all five continents, but not to the same extent in each. It has been longest known in **Asia**, where the famous old Indian deposits have probably been known and worked from the earliest times; now, however, they are almost completely exhausted. In close geographical connection with these are the deposits in Borneo, but the supply from this island, in comparison with the rich treasure of India, has always been limited. Reported discoveries of diamonds in the Malay Peninsula, where, according to one account, the famous "Regent" of the French crown jewels was found, in Pegu and Siam and the islands of Java, Sumatra and Celebes, are for the most part unauthenticated; and the same may be said of the reported occurrence in China (province Shan-tung), Arabia, &c.

In **America** the famous Brazilian diamond-fields were discovered at the beginning of the eighteenth century, and have compensated for the exhaustion of the Indian mines; the richest yield of stones has been given by the mines in the States of Minas Geraes and Bahia. Recent finds have been made in another part of the South American continent, namely in British Guiana. Well authenticated, but of little commercial importance, is the occurrence of diamond in the United States of North America; a small number of stones having been found in the eastern States of Georgia, North Carolina, South Carolina, Kentucky, Virginia, Wisconsin, and in the western States of California and Oregon. Reported occurrences in other parts of the American continent, namely Sierra Madre in Mexico, and the gold mines of Antioquia in Colombia, South America, require confirmation.

The continent of **Africa** is, at the present time, by far the most important source of diamonds, which have been collected here since the late sixties in ever increasing numbers, far surpassing the yield from any other region. The exact locality of the deposits is on the Vaal River, and in the neighbourhood of the town of Kimberley, both these localities being in the division of Griqualand West, in the north of Cape Colony; also in the adjoining Orange River Colony, which, however, is of far less importance. Compared with the yield of the African fields, all others are insignificant, although in comparatively recent times the markets of the world were supplied from the sources which are now of such minor importance. At the present day the diamond fields of the Cape are the source of 90 per cent. of the stones which come into the market. The reported occurrence of diamonds in the auriferous sands of the river Gumel, in the province of Constantine, in Algeria, is unauthenticated; three stones were said to have been found here in 1833, but nothing more has been heard of this reputed discovery. The statement of Dr. Cuny, an African traveller, that in the fifties a whole camel-load of diamonds was brought from Western Africa to Darfur seems rather incredible.

In **Europe**, diamonds have been found in Russia, in the Urals in the east, and in Lapland in the west; the stones are, however, met with only in small numbers, and their importance lies in their mineralogical rarity. The reported occurrence of a few small diamonds in Spain has some degree of probability; but the supposed discovery of diamonds in a stream in Fermanagh, Ireland, needs authentication. A reputed discovery in Bohemia is certainly false; in 1869 a single small diamond was noticed in a parcel of garnets at some cutting works at Dlaschkowitz; the matter was thoroughly investigated by V. von Zepharovich, who proved beyond doubt that the diamond must have been introduced into the parcel at the works, where such stones are used for boring garnets.

Diamonds have been found in recent times in **Australia**, especially in New South Wales, not altogether in inconsiderable numbers; and Australian stones are at least mentioned in the markets.

Finally we must record the interesting fact that diamond is not only a constituent of the earth's crust, but also of extra-terrestrial bodies, the presence of small stones having been in recent years proved in several **meteorites**.

With regard to the mode of occurrence of diamonds, it is to be noted that in the majority of localities they are found in secondary deposits, such as sands and gravels. These masses of débris produced by the weathering of the original mother-rock of the diamond are usually entirely loose and incoherent; occasionally, however, as in Brazil and India, they are converted by some cementing materials into firm conglomerates, breccias and sandstones. In Brazil these rock masses, like the loose sands and gravels at other places, lie on the surface, and must therefore be reckoned among the most recent deposits of the earth's crust. In India, and to a certain extent also in Brazil and North America, the diamantiferous fragmentary rocks belong to earlier geological periods, being interbedded with some of the oldest rocks, and thus representing the sands and gravels of very remote ages. When these older fragmentary rocks come to the surface, they are themselves in course of time attacked by weathering agents and supply material for new secondary deposits, from which diamonds are won by the ordinary process of washing.

These relations will be further considered with the description of each special diamantiferous deposit.

The nature and character of the original mother-rock, in the débris of which the diamond is now found, has nowhere been determined with the certainty and clearness as to detail that is desired, although many important steps have been made towards the solution of this important problem. In the following pages we will consider in detail the facts connected with each well-established occurrence of diamond, and endeavour to determine the origin of the stone in each case so far as the available observations permit. In any case it is certain that the original mode of occurrence and the mother-rock are not the same at all localities: in some cases the mother-rock is without doubt one of the older crystalline rocks, such as a gneiss or a crystalline schist, or an eruptive rock, such as granite ; in other cases it is highly probable that diamond originated as a secondary mineral in crevices in the rock known as itacolumite, as will be specially considered when we come to treat of the Brazilian deposits. In the South African diamond-fields, the stones are found for the most part embedded in a green serpentine-like rock, instead of in loose sands as is more usually the case. This mode of occurrence, which is peculiar to this locality, and differs from that of all others, will be considered in detail under its appropriate heading.

The different diamantiferous deposits will be dealt with below in the following order :

1. India.
2. Brazil.
3. South Africa.
4. Borneo.
5. Australia.

6. North America.
7. British Guiana.
8. Urals.
9. Lapland.
10. In meteorites.

1. INDIA.

Diamonds have been known longer in this country than in any other, and the most beautiful, famous and many of the largest stones were found here. A diamond river in India is referred to by Ptolemy ; and the fact that diamonds were known to, and highly prized by, the ancient inhabitants of the country is proved by the rich adornment of the oldest temples of religion with this and other precious stones. The sacred shrines and idols show, moreover, that the art of diamond cutting has been long understood. Until the discovery of the Brazilian deposits in 1728, the supply of the whole world was derived almost entirely from the Indian sources, Borneo being at that time the only other known locality.

The occurrences of diamond in India are distributed over an extensive area of the country. C. Ritter in his *Erdkunde von Asien* (vol. iv., part 2, p. 343, 1836) collected together the various scattered reports concerning the diamond localities, and was the first to give a detailed and connected account. More recently (1881), Professor V. Ball has given an exhaustive account, in which he has incorporated all the latest information, in the official *Manual of the Geology of India* (Part III. pp. 1-50).

That the occurrence of diamonds in India is almost entirely confined to the eastern side of the Deccan plateau is to be gathered from the finds of the present day and from the reports of earlier times. The southern boundary of the region in which diamonds have been found is the river Penner in latitude 14° N. ; from this river the diamond localities form a frequently interrupted line running northwards on the east side of the Deccan plateau, crossing the Kistna, Godavari and Mahanadi rivers, and reaching the southern tributaries of the Lower Ganges in Bengal, between the rivers Son and Khan, in latitude 25° N.   Any other diamond localities outside the area just marked out (see map, Fig. 33) are unimportant, and the reports concerning them are often uncertain.   In general, many of the reported localities for diamond are doubtful, there being no exact and reliable information respecting them, or they are simply based on the existence of old mines.

It is often supposed that all Indian diamond mines are of the greatest antiquity.   In many cases the date at which the workings were commenced is not known ; but the working of the most important deposits known at the present day does not date back to very remote periods, probably in all cases subsequent to the year 1000 A.D. and sometimes much later. Of a few mines it is known exactly when work began, as will be mentioned below.

Diamonds are found in India in compact sandstones and conglomerates, in the loose, incoherent weathered products of these rocks at places where they lie on the surface, and in the sands and gravels of those rivers and streams which have flowed over the diamantiferous strata or their weathered débris and have washed out the stones from their former situations.

The diamantiferous sandstone of India is of very wide distribution.   It belongs to the oldest division of the sedimentary formations of the country which usually rest directly upon the still older crystalline rocks, such as granite, gneiss, mica-schist, hornblende-schist, chlorite-schist, talc-schist, and similar rocks.   Fossils have not been found in these sandstones, so that it is not possible to determine exactly to which of the European formations they correspond in age ; they may however be safely stated to belong to the Palæozoic period, and possibly to the Silurian division of this period.

The oldest bedded rocks known to Indian geologists are included in the Vindhyan formation.   Only the lower division of this formation is represented in the Madras Presidency in southern India, and is there known as the Karnul series.   In northern India, for instance in Bundelkhand, these lower beds are overlain by the later beds of the Upper Vindhyan formation.   As far as is yet known, the diamantiferous sandstones of the whole of India belong to this Vindhyan formation ; but while in the southern diamond districts, and probably also in the districts of the Godavari and Mahanadi rivers, they belong to the lower division, namely, the Karnul series, in northern India, for example in Bundelkhand, they belong to the upper part of the Vindhyan formation.

The Lower Vindhyan formation (namely the Karnul series) consists mainly of limestones with interbedded clay-slates, sandstones, conglomerates, and quartzites.   In southern India at the base of this series of beds are beds of sandstone and conglomerates which are known as the Banaganapalli group and here constitute the diamantiferous strata.   The whole of the Banaganapalli sandstones are on an average ten to twenty feet thick ; they are usually coarse grained, sometimes argillaceous, at other times very compact and siliceous, and in places felspathic and ferruginous ; they are dark in colour, being red, grey or brown.   The pebbles of the interbedded conglomerates have been derived from the denudation of older rocks, and consist for the most part of quartzite, variously coloured hornstones and jasper, as well as compact clay-slates.

The diamonds are found in an earthy bed containing abundant pebbles ; this bed is clearly and definitely marked off from other beds and is not repeated at any other horizon. The diamonds, which may themselves be regarded as pebbles since they also show signs of rounding, lie scattered singly among the other pebbles which are of the same materials as those just mentioned.   This earthy bed, in which alone the diamonds are found, is of little thickness ; in exceptional cases its thickness is stated to be two and a half feet, but it often measures less than a foot, and rarely exceeds this amount.

In Bundelkhand the diamond-bearing stratum belongs to the middle division of the Upper Vindhyan formation, namely the Rewah group, and is situated at the base of this group in the Panna beds. It is usually a red, ferruginous conglomerate, the pebbles of which consist, as in southern India, of quartz, variously coloured jasper, quartz-schists, sandstone, nodules of limonite, &c. The diamonds appear to bear a close relation to certain sandstone pebbles in this bed.

It is often stated, although perhaps further confirmation of the fact is needed, that in Bundelkhand diamond is sometimes found in fragments of a compact, greyish, siliceous sandstone with a peculiar glassy appearance, embedded in the stone in the same way as are the sand grains of which it is composed. These sandstone pebbles in the conglomerates of the Rewah group have been most probably derived from beds of the Lower Vindhyan formation, which, by their denudation, supplied material for the deposition of the later beds of the Upper Vindhyan formation. Thus the diamonds now found in the Upper Vindhyan formation originally belonged to the Lower Vindhyan, where, in southern India, they are still found. With the denudation of these older rocks the diamonds were set free and again deposited with the material of the younger beds, some remaining embedded in fragments of the original rock, while others became isolated and are now found among the pebbles of the conglomerate.

The diamantiferous sandstones and conglomerates are now elevated, and crop out at the surface of the ground, or are covered by younger strata. Where these strata are not so protected, as when a valley cuts across them, they will be exposed to the action of denuding agents, and will be reduced to soft incoherent sands in which the diamonds lie loosely, the whole constituting a diamantiferous sand.

The diamond-bearing strata, together with the sands derived from them by weathering, are everywhere exposed to the action of streams and rivers which transport the material to lower levels. The next resting-place of the diamond is therefore the sands and gravels of the river bed or its alluvial deposits. The most recent of these alluvial deposits lies at the present level of the river; others are found at higher levels on the sides of the valley, having been formed before the valley had been cut down to its present depth. These diamond-bearing alluvial deposits have a close connection with the diamond-bearing beds from which they have been derived. In any district where diamonds occur in the strata they will also be found in the beds of the streams and rivers, although not always in numbers sufficiently great to repay work on a large scale.

The mining of diamonds is at the present day, just as in former times, almost entirely in the hands of natives of the lower castes. Attempts on the part of Europeans to work the diamond-bearing deposits on a large scale, and according to modern methods, have never been attended with success. The work in many cases is tedious and difficult, and, moreover, the methods used must be altered to suit the conditions in different localities, which vary considerably. The same methods are for the most part now employed as were in use in the oldest times of which records exist; at any rate, they are identical with those seen and described by Tavernier, the French traveller and dealer in precious stones, in 1665.

The working of the surface layer of sands, that is the loose, weathered product of the sandstone beds, and of the river alluvium, is easy. It consists essentially in removing the larger masses of rock and in washing away the finer earthy material with water. From the sandy residue thus obtained the diamonds are picked out, usually by the women and children of the workers who dig out the gravels.

The working of the sandstone beds is more arduous, and is only attempted where they lie on the surface or at a very small depth beneath it. Where they are overlain by younger beds of any thickness, they are inaccessible to the natives, whose appliances for the sinking of shafts and other mining operations are few and primitive; moreover, in such cases the cost of working would be prohibitive, and the mining of the diamonds can only be effected where the strata crop out on the surface of hill-sides, the workings penetrating to only a very small depth even in these more favourable situations.

Where the diamond-bearing bed lies at a small depth below the surface, a pit or shaft of a few square feet or yards in section is sunk to meet the desired bed, the shaft being usually about 20 feet, rarely 30 feet, and in a few cases 50 feet in depth. The workings at the bottom of the pit extend only to such distances as the stability of the material overhead will permit. The diamantiferous rock so obtained is, when necessary, carefully broken up, and the diamonds obtained from it by washing and sorting in the same manner as from the loose sands and gravels.

The excavation of the hard, solid beds of sandstone which often overlie the diamantiferous stratum is a matter of no small difficulty to the worker whose tools are inadequate for the purpose. In a few districts the difficulty is somewhat lessened by the employment of a device often made use of by the old German miners. A large fire is kindled on the spot at which it is desired to sink a shaft, and when the rock below is strongly heated, it is suddenly cooled by the application of cold water. This causes the rock to crack in many places, and thus the work of excavation is rendered less arduous.

Diamantiferous sandstone, which has been removed from its natural bed, and from which diamonds have been extricated, is often allowed to be exposed to the various atmospheric weathering agencies for some time, and is then again worked over, when a further yield of diamonds may be given, this being sometimes repeated several times. This fact has given rise to a belief among the natives that this second crop of diamonds has originated in the waste rock, or that it is the result of a fusion together of the smaller diamonds originally left behind; similar beliefs are also met with in South Africa. The actual explanation, of course, lies in the fact that during the interval in which the waste rock is exposed to the air, weathering takes place, and any stones which may have been embedded in the larger fragments of rock are thus set free and easily picked out by the searchers. A mass of rock which has once been worked over will naturally be the poorer both in the number and the size of the diamonds it contains. In spite of this, however, the refuse heaps from old diamond mines are in many places at the present time being continually turned over and diamonds as continually found.

C. Ritter arranged the Indian diamond mines known to him in five groups, according to their geographical distribution, and described them in order from south to north. In what follows this grouping will be adopted, the smaller mining districts not mentioned by Ritter being introduced in appropriate places, and information derived from later reports, especially those of V. Ball, incorporated with the matter given by Ritter. A rather different grouping of the mines is given by Ball. The map (Fig. 33) shows the distribution of the diamond-fields in India.

1. The Cuddapah Group on the Penner River.

This group includes the most southerly mines, those furthest to the east are in the neighbourhood of Cuddapah on the river Penner, where numerous mines have been worked for several centuries with varying success. At the present time the majority of the mines in this group—perhaps, at times, the whole of them—are abandoned, but this by no means indicates that the supply of diamonds has been completely exhausted. The spot at which

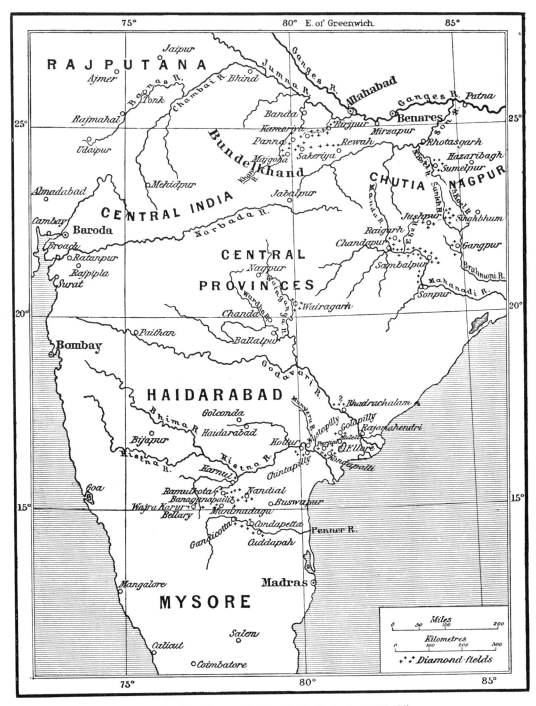

FIG. 33. The Diamond-fields of India (Scale, 1 : 12,000,000).

diamonds have been most abundantly found is Chennur (Chinon), near Cuddapah, on the right or southern bank of the Penner river. Westward of this, that is, up the river and on the same bank, mines are situated at Woblapully (Obalumpally). On the other bank of the river are the mines of Condapetta, referred to by the travellers who formerly visited and described this district, and which probably corresponds to Cunnapurty of the present day. West of Chennur, diamonds have also been found at Lamdur and Pinchetgapadu, and at a few other places, of which Hussanapur (Dupand) may be mentioned as having at the beginning of the nineteenth century yielded many stones. Still higher up the valley of the Penner diamonds were formerly sought at Gandicotta, but with little success.

All these mines are referred to as the **Chennur** mines. At Chennur itself the abandoned mines are in the Banaganapalli sandstone or in the weathered products of this rock. Many stones, some of very fine quality, have been found here. In two particular cases £5000 and £3000 were obtained for single specimens. After a long period of idleness, mining operations were, in 1869, again commenced, but without success. Under the surface soil of this neighbourhood is a stratum $1\frac{1}{2}$ feet thick of sand and gravel with clay, beneath this a tenacious blue or black clay, 4 feet thick, and underlying all, the diamantiferous layer 2 to $2\frac{1}{2}$ feet in thickness, and differing from the clay above only in that it contains many large pebbles and boulders. The pebbles thus included in the diamantiferous clay consist of various minerals; among others there are yellowish transparent quartz, epidote, red, blue and brown jaspery quartz, round nodules of limonite the size of a hazel-nut, and corundum. The boulders are often the size of a man's head, and consist of sandstone, basalt, often of hornstone, as well as fragments of felsite, a rock of which the hills standing 1000 feet above Cuddapetta are constituted.

At Condapetta the mines are from 4 to 12 feet deep. Here there is a bed of earthy sand, 3 to 10 feet thick, resting on a bed of pebbles, which vary in size between that of a nut and that of a cobble, and among which the diamonds are found, usually loose, but sometimes cemented to the pebbles. The latter usually consist of ferruginous sandstone or conglomerate, among these being others of quartz, chert, and jasper, the latter being sometimes blue with red veins; also porphyry containing crystals of felspar. The greater number of these pebbles have been derived from the surrounding mountains, but some—for example, those of porphyry—have been transported by water from greater distances. The mines here, as at Chennur, are only worked in the dry season, since in the rainy season they become filled with water, the removal of which would entail too much labour.

The mines at Woblapully were opened somewhere about the year 1750. The diamonds found here are flat and much worn and rounded, so that they show no definite crystalline form. They are specially hard and have a high lustre. In colour they are clear white or clear honey-yellow, also cream-coloured and greyish-white. They are found in alluvial deposits of varying widths which follow the course of the river, and consist chiefly of much-rounded nodules of limonite of about the size of a nut. This district has not been systematically explored, the mines, of which the average depth is 16 feet, are very irregularly scattered about, and have apparently never been of any great importance.

Following up the Penner valley and then turning to the north we reach Munimadagu and Wajra Karur, two important diamond localities in the Bellary district.

The first of these, **Munimadagu**, is sixteen miles west of Banaganapalli and forty-one miles east of Wajra Karur. Here, in a circular area some twenty miles in circumference, are a number of mines which in former times, especially during the period between the beginning of last century and the year 1833, supplied the important market and cutting-works of Bellary with the bulk of their material. The systematic working of the mines on the particular diamantiferous bed has, however, now been given up, although a few stones are occasionally still found in the neighbourhood. The diamond-bearing stratum is of small thickness, and rests upon granite, gneiss, and similar rocks.

Wajra Karur is another locality from which a more abundant yield of diamonds was obtained in former times than is the case at the present day. To emphasise the fact that diamonds are still to be found here, we may mention the stone of $67\frac{3}{4}$ carats discovered in 1881, from which was cut a beautiful brilliant of $24\frac{5}{8}$ carats, valued at £12,000. Some of the largest and most famous of Indian diamonds are said to have been found here. The occurrence of diamonds at this place is peculiar: they lie loosely scattered about on the surface of the ground, and there is no definite diamond-bearing bed. The rocks at the surface are granite and gneiss, and the diamantiferous Banaganapalli sandstone has not been detected in the district. The diamonds are often washed out of the soil by heavy rains, and are then picked up casually, or an organised search for them may be made by the people of the district.

In order to explain the peculiar mode of occurrence of diamond at this locality, it has been supposed that in earlier geological times a diamantiferous bed covered a large area in the neighbourhood of Wajra Karur, and that this has since been entirely removed by denudation, leaving the diamonds behind as an unalterable residue. Although there is nothing impossible about this view, it is supported by no definite facts.

Later investigators have attempted to explain the mode of occurrence of diamond in this district in other ways. To the west of the town of Wajra Karur a pipe of blue rock, very similar in character to a volcanic tuff, was found in the granite or gneiss. This closely resembles the richly diamantiferous rock of Kimberley, in South Africa, and was therefore supposed to be the original mother-rock of the Wajra Karur diamonds. This bluish-green, tuffaceous rock, with interspersed blocks of granite and gneiss, was worked on a large scale by an English company with absolutely no success, not a single diamond having been found.

More recently another solution of the problem has been offered by the French traveller, M. Chaper, who searched the district for diamonds in 1882. This explorer found that the surface rock lying just beneath the soil, which in the neighbourhood of Wajra Karur is gneiss, is penetrated by numerous veins of various igneous rocks. These veins very frequently consist of a coarse-grained, rose-red or salmon-coloured pegmatite containing epidote (pegmatite being a special variety of granite). In the upper, much-weathered portion of such pegmatite veins M. Chaper himself collected two small diamonds, which were accompanied by irregularly bounded grains of blue and red corundum (sapphire and ruby) as well as by other minerals. The two diamond crystals were octahedral in form with perfectly sharp edges, and showed no signs of having been water-worn. Numerous diamonds are said to have been found under the same conditions by the natives. Chaper was convinced that the diamonds he collected had been originally formed in the pegmatite, and had been loosened from it only by the weathering of the matrix. This theory would of course apply equally well to all the other regularly developed crystals of diamond found at the same place.

The Indian geologist, Mr. R. B. Foote, has raised a doubt as to the correctness of Chaper's observation, and specially of the deduction he drew therefrom, suggesting that the French traveller was deceived by his native attendant. A confirmation of Chaper's statement is much to be desired, since it would be of considerable help in elucidating the general problem connected with the identity of the original mother-rock of Indian diamonds. The original matrix of all Indian diamonds may possibly have been similar in character to the rock in the neighbourhood of Wajra Karur, the weathering and breaking down of which has given rise to the sandstones and conglomerates in which the diamonds are now found, but which cannot under any circumstances be regarded as their place of origin. In support of Chaper's view may be mentioned the fact that diamonds in the lower Penner district are sometimes associated with the minerals which Chaper observed at Wajra Karur —namely, ruby, sapphire, and epidote. Foote meets this argument with the statement that ruby and sapphire have never been found at Wajra Karur except with the two specimens found by Chaper, and these, moreover, he considers show signs of workmanship. Were it further confirmed, the reported occurrence of diamond in pegmatitic rocks, both in Lapland and in Brazil (Serra da Chapada, in the State of Bahia), would afford support to Chaper's views.

2. The Nandial Group between the Penner and Kistna Rivers.

This group lies near the town of Banaganapalli, and only about seventeen miles north of the last group. It is situated on the northern margin of the plain, which extends from the western slopes of the Nallamalais as far as the town of Nandial (lat. 15° 30′ N., long. 78° 30′ E.). The mines of this group, which are sometimes referred to—for example, by V. Ball—as the Karnul diamond mines, lie to the east, south-east, and west of Nandial, and are partly in the diamantiferous bed itself and partly in the sands. This group, of which a few only of the more important workings can here be mentioned, includes some of the most famous mines ever worked in India, the majority of which, however, are now abandoned.

The mines at **Banaganapalli,** the village which gives its name to the group of strata containing the diamantiferous sandstone, lie to the north-west of Condapetta and to the south-west of Nandial. According to the observations of Dr. W. King, the sandstones together with the diamond-bearing bed rest unconformably upon the older sedimentary rocks beneath—that is, the lines of bedding of the two series differ in inclination. These older sedimentary beds comprise shales and limestones with interbedded trap-rocks. The diamond-bearing bed and its associated sandstones are from twenty to thirty feet thick. They are penetrated on the hill slopes by pits never exceeding fifteen feet in depth, at the bottom of which the diamond-bearing bed has been removed as far in all directions as the stability of the overlying rock will permit. This bed, which is only from six to eight inches in thickness, is constituted of a coarse sandy or clayey conglomerate or breccia, consisting largely of variously coloured fragments of shales and hornstone. Large diamonds have apparently never been found here. The crystalline forms of most common occurrence are those of the octahedron and the rhombic dodecahedron. Workers of the present day confine themselves for the most part to turning over the refuse-heaps of abandoned mines in search of small stones, but a few mines in the sandstone are being actively worked at the present time.

The mines of **Ramulkota** are situated to the north-west of Banaganapalli and about nineteen miles south-south-west of Karnul They are in the Banaganapalli sandstone and are worked more deeply and extensively than are those of Chennur, near Cuddapah in the Penner valley. The stones found here are small and not very regular in form ; they may be white (*i.e.*, colourless), grey, yellow or green in colour. The exact output at the present time is not known. The mines in the sandstone are not now worked, but the washing of the neighbouring diamond-bearing sands is carried on to a small extent. Captain Newbold, who visited this district in 1840, saw only twenty men at work here, but in the dry season the number was said to be increased to 500. The rich and famous mines mentioned by Tavernier under the name Raolconda are probably identical with the mines of Ramulkota ; at the time of his visit (1665) these mines had been worked for 200 years and were a source of much wealth. After the working of these mines had ceased, their very situation became completely forgotton; they were at one time supposed to lie five days' journey west of Golconda, near the junction of the Bhima and Kistna rivers, and eight or nine days' journey from Visapur (now Bijapur); the researches of V. Ball have now, however, practically established the identity of these mines with the Ramulkota mines of the present day.

3. The Ellore (or Golconda) Group on the Kistna River.

The mines of this group are situated on the lower portion of the Kistna river and include some of the oldest and most famous of Indian diamond mines, the largest and most beautiful of Indian stones having been derived from these so-called Golconda mines. They derive their name, not from their situation, but from the fact that the diamonds from these mines were sent to the market held near the old fortress of Golconda, not far from Haidarabad, this being also the market for stones from Chennur. At the time of Tavernier's visit to these mines, more than twenty were being worked, most of them being extraordinarily rich. With two or three exceptions, the whole were later deserted, and the situations of many of them, including some which Tavernier described as being most famous, are now forgotten.

The richest of the mines to the east of Golconda were those of **Kollur**, which lies on the right bank of the Kistna, west of Chintapilly and in latitude 16° 42½' N. and longitude 80° 5' E. of Greenwich. This place was referred to by Tavernier under the name Gani Coulour, and now sometimes figures as Gani. This latter is a native word said to signify " mine," while the word Coulour, from which is derived the now common place-name Kollur, is of Persian origin. These mines are not identical, as has often been supposed, with the also far-famed mines of Partial; the latter, which will be described below, are situated somewhat further east and on the left bank of the Kistna.

The discovery of the diamantiferous deposit at Kollur was made about 100 years before Tavernier's visit, namely, about 1560. A 25-carat stone was first accidentally found, and numerous others soon followed, many weighing from 10 to 40 carats, and some still more. The quality of the stones, however, was not always as satisfactory as their size, cloudy and impure specimens being frequent. Such famous diamonds as the " Koh-i-noor," now in the English crown jewels, and the " Great Mogul," the whereabouts of which, unless it is identical with the " Koh-i-noor," is now unknown, were very probably found in these mines, in addition to some beautiful blue stones, including the " Hope Blue " diamond. Tavernier stated that 60,000 people were engaged in these mines at the time of his visit; to-day, however, they are completely deserted, as are also numerous other workings situated in the valley of the Kistna, between Kollur and Chintapilly, and between the latter place and Partial. The diamonds here lie in a loose alluvium, which is thus a diamond-sand.

In following the course of the Kistna river, a little beyond where it is joined by the Munyeru river, to the east of Chintapilly, we reach the **Partial** mines, standing on the left bank of the river. These mines also were formerly very rich and probably yielded the " Pitt " or " Regent " diamond, now in the French crown jewels. The workings, which are here in the loose decomposed mass of the diamantiferous bed and in the river alluvium, have been abandoned for a long period, although the diamantiferous bed is probably not exhausted; in 1850, according to Dr. Walker, only two mines of this group were being worked. Near to Partial, and belonging to the same group, are the old mines of Wustapilly, Codavetty-Kallu, &c.; the latter is said to have been especially rich, there being a legend to the effect that waggon-loads of diamonds had been taken away. Here again the diamonds occur in sands which are now no longer worked.

Still further east, on the left (north) bank of the Kistna, but at some distance from the river, are the **Muleli** or Malavilly mines, situated between the village of the same name and that of Golapilly, to the north-east of Condapilly, and about six or seven hours' journey west of Ellore. Here pits fifteen to twenty feet deep are excavated in a conglomeratic sandstone or in the surface débris derived from its disintegration. These sandstones rest on gneiss and belong to a somewhat later series of beds than does the Karnul series. The diamantiferous stratum, which according to many observers is overlain by a bed of calcareous travertine, consists mainly of pebbles of sandstone, quartz, jasper, chert, granite, &c., as well as of large fragments of a limestone conglomerate, which show no traces of having been water-worn. All the minerals which accompany diamond at Cuddapah are also present here, with chalcedony and carnelian in addition. These mines have been worked at least as recently as the year 1830, but the yield has since fallen off and they are now abandoned.

In the district in which this group is situated, which lies partly in Haidarabad, the " Hyderabad Company " of English capitalists has acquired working rights. The Company's total output of diamonds in the year 1891 was 862¾ carats, valued at 15,530 rupees. The annual output of the whole group of mines is at the present time little greater than this, being perhaps about 1000 carats.

To the north of the district just mentioned, diamonds are said to have been found at Bhadrachalam on the Godavari river. Their occurrence here is, however, doubtful, if not mythical, few if any stones having been found; the whole district is little known, and rendered extremely inaccessible by the thickness of the surrounding forests. Much richer and more important, at least in former times, is the fourth group of diamond mines now to be described.

4. The Sambalpur Group on the Mahanadi River.

This group is situated a good distance to the north-west of the previous group, and lies between latitude 21° and 22° north, in the Central Provinces. The diamonds known to the ancients may have been those of the Mahanadi river, the diamond river mentioned by Ptolemy being supposed to be in this district, and being, in fact, identified by many authors with the Mahanadi river itself. The occurrence of diamond is limited to the neighbourhood of Sambalpur, no other part of the river having given any yield. The mining district extends over a fertile plain, which at the town of Sambalpur stands 451 feet above sea level, and forms the stretch of land between the Mahanadi and Brahmani rivers. The date of the first discovery of stones here is unknown, but Sambalpur has been a familiar diamond locality since very remote times.

The diamonds are found for the most part in the neighbourhood of the confluences of the Mahanadi with some of the tributaries on its left bank. These tributaries, which flow into the river from the north, rise in the Barapahar hills; one of these, which joins the Mahanadi a little above Sambalpur, is the Ebe, and is sometimes considered to be the diamond river of the ancients, but whereas the occurrence of diamonds here has not been proved, there is no doubt as to their occurrence in the Mahanadi valley. In former times the stones were collected in the river-beds after the rainy season. They were found in the Mahanadi river only on the left bank, never on the right, and not higher up than where the Manda tributary enters the main river at Chandapur; according to some accounts, which however are probably incorrect, the mouth of the Ebe is the furthest up-stream limit to the occurrence of diamonds, and this river is therefore often considered to be the one down which the diamonds were transported into the Mahanadi. The whole diamond-bearing stretch of the Mahanadi is about twenty-eight miles long, being limited eastwards by a bend in the river at Sonpur.

One of the most important points on the Mahanadi appears to have been **Hira Khund**, a name which signifies diamond mine; this is an island about four miles long, which lies near the village of Jhunan and divides the river into two branches. Every year about the end of March or later, that is, in the dry season when the river is very low, people flocked in thousands to this place to search for diamonds. The branch of the river on the north side of the island was dammed up, and the diamond-bearing sands and gravels of the river-bed dug out and washed for diamonds by the women. The southern branch of the river was never worked for diamonds, although in the opinion of some experienced persons, they were there to be found, possibly in greater numbers than in the north branch. The damming-up of the south branch would, however, present greater difficulty since the volume of water here is greater and the current stronger than in the north branch.

Diamonds are found near Sambalpur in a tough, reddish mud containing sand and gravel. This material is probably the weathered product of the rocks of the Barapahar hills brought down by the rivers which rise there. The solid rock of this region is not, as far as is known, worked for diamonds, although it is very similar to the rocks which in all parts of southern India yield the precious stone. A certain number of diamonds are found in the small streams which rise in this neighbourhood, near Raigarh, Jushpur, and Gangpur.

Large stones are said to have been found in the Mahanadi with some frequency. The largest was found at the island of Hira Khund in 1809; it weighed 210·6 carats, but ranked only as a stone of the third water, and its subsequent history is unknown. Generally speaking the stones found here were very good in quality, the diamonds of the Mahanadi and of Chutia Nagpur ranking amongst the finest and purest of Indian stones. In the Mahanadi, diamonds are associated with pebbles of beryl, topaz, garnet, carnelian, amethyst, and rock-crystal; these minerals, however, have probably been derived from the granite and gneiss through which the river flows and not from the mother-rock of the diamond. The Mahanadi yields also a fair amount of gold, which is separated from the river sands and gravels by washing at the same time as are the diamonds.

At the present day, diamonds are found in this district only occasionally; systematic work was carried on down to about the year 1850, when, owing to the poorness of the yield, it was discontinued.

The mines of **Wairagarh**, in the Chanda district of the Central Provinces, may be conveniently described with this group. They are about eighty miles south-east of Nagpur, very ancient, and identical with those mentioned by Tavernier under the name Beiragarh; their identity with those of Vena (Wainganga) is uncertain. The remains of these mines are still to be seen on the Sath river, a tributary of the Kophraguri, itself a tributary of the Wainganga. The mines were formerly rich, but have been abandoned since 1827. The stones lie in a red or yellow, sandy, laterite-like earth, but the rock from which this alluvial material was originally derived is unknown. According to Professor V. Ball, this diamond-bearing stratum has a far wider distribution than is generally supposed, and will perhaps at some future time become of importance.

To the north of the Sambalpur district, in the **Chutia Nagpur** (the ancient Kokrah) division of Bengal, diamond mines were formerly worked. These mines are said to have yielded in the sixteenth and seventeenth centuries many large and fine stones, which are stated to have been obtained from one of the rivers of the district. The identity of this river is not exactly known, but it is supposed to be the Sankh, a tributary on the left side of the Brahmani, also a river in which diamonds have been found but at a later date; even such occasional finds are not now, however, to be made.

In Tavernier's time some famous mines, which were described by him, existed at **Sumelpur,** but their exact situation is now not known. According to the account of this traveller, the diamonds were here washed from the sands and gravels of the River Gouel. This river is supposed to be identical with the North Koel river, a tributary of the Son, which in its turn flows into the Ganges, and on the banks of which are the ruins of the ancient town of Semah or Semul, supposed to be identical with Tavernier's Sumelpur (Semelpur). This town must not be confused with Sambalpur, a town on the Mahanadi river which has been mentioned above. The stones found in this district were originally derived from the hills forming the watershed of the rivers North Koel and Sankh. Tavernier states that 8000 people were at work in these mines at the time of his visit, in the dry season at the beginning of February. Many other statements respecting the early finds of diamonds in Chutia Nagpur are now regarded as false, having nothing more substantial than fable as their foundation.

5. The Panna Group in Bundelkhand.

This, the most northerly group of Indian diamond mines, is situated between the Khan and Son rivers in latitude 25° N., and lies on the northern margin of the Bundelkhand plateau where this borders the plain of the Ganges and Jumna. Some of the mines lie in the immediate neighbourhood of Panna (Punnah), to the south-west of Allahabad on the Ganges, others are further away to the west, south and east of this town; all are classed together as the Panna mines. Large stones are not known to occur in this district nor do any appear to have been found in former times, though the number of smaller diamonds of good quality found now as well as formerly is considerable. The form of the crystals is that of the octahedron or of the rhombic dodecahedron. They occur in the special diamantiferous stratum and in the loose surface material derived from the weathering of the same, and have also been transported with river-gravels. The diamond stratum here belongs, as previously remarked, not to the Lower, but to the Upper Vindhyan formation.

In the neighbourhood of Panna, especially to the north and north-east, there are numerous mines; the most important lie close to the town and occupy altogether an area of less than twenty acres. The diamond-bearing stratum is sometimes not more than a span in thickness, and it lies deeper here than at other places where such a stratum is worked, being overlain by a bed of clay of considerable thickness containing pebbles and rock-fragments; these consist usually of sandstone, but at the base of the bed there are numerous fragments of ferruginous laterite. The absence of solid rock above the diamond-bearing stratum makes it impracticable to work the latter for any considerable distance underground; in order to reach this it is therefore necessary to excavate wide and deep pits, measuring about 20 yards across and 10 to 15 yards in depth, a proceeding which involves much labour and time. The diamantiferous stratum consists of a ferruginous clay which contains besides diamonds, fragments of sandstone, quartz, hornstone, red jasper, &c., and deserving of special mention, a green quartz (prase), the abundant occurrence of which is considered a good sign by the diamond seekers. The interior of a diamond mine in this district is illustrated in Plate V. The miners at work in the wide pit are watched by the soldiers of the native ruler. On the left of the drawing are seen the baskets in which the excavated material is hauled up to the surface for subsequent treatment; towards the right is represented a series of earthen bowls, arranged as a chain-pump, for removing water from the pit.

In the mines of Kamariga, north-east of Panna, the diamond-bearing stratum consists of loose, ferruginous earth; it is overlain by a bed 20 feet thick of the firm and coherent Rewah sandstone interbedded with bands of shale. The solidity of the superimposed rock allows the diamond-bearing stratum to be worked underground from the bottom of the pits for some distance, so that the work is here much lighter than at Panna. There are also several mines at Babalpur, all of which are now abandoned.

At Birjpur, to the east of Kamariga and near to Babalpur, there are mines standing on the right bank of the upper course of the river Baghin. The diamond-bearing stratum differs from that at Kamariga, being a firm conglomeratic sandstone, which crops out at the surface and overlies other sandstones; the mining of diamonds is here, therefore, comparatively easy.

At all the mines mentioned above the diamond-bearing stratum itself is worked; the workings in the remaining mines of this group are, however, in the various sands and gravels derived from this stratum.

At Majgoha (Maigama), south-west of Panna and the most westerly point of the district occupied by this group of mines, the mode of occurrence of the diamonds is peculiar. They lie in a green mud, which is penetrated by veins of calcite and is covered by a thick deposit of calcareous travertine or tufa. This mud is found in a conical depression in the sandstone, about two-thirds of which it fills. This depression is 100 feet deep and 100 yards wide and being cone-shaped diminishes in diameter as its depth below the surface increases; it may possibly be an old diamond mine filled up by the green mud. The miners work to a depth of 50 feet and assert that the mud increases in richness as greater depths are reached. The mine is now apparently abandoned; it is not, however, considered to be exhausted but is reserved for future working.

The mines at Udesna and Sakeriya are of some importance; at the latter place, the diamantiferous gravel is overlain by yellow clay and in part also by laterite. These mines have been worked until recent times, and possibly may not be altogether abandoned even now. At Saya Lachmanpur, fourteen miles from Panna, diamonds are found on the top of Bindachul hill.

Finally, we must notice the long stretch of sands in the valley of the Baghin river below Birjpur. The principal mines are at the lower end of the upper part of the valley, where the pebbly diamantiferous stratum is overlain by about 12 feet of dark brown clayey sand. At the upper end of the valley are two waterfalls, each with a fall of 100 feet, and at the foot of each diamonds are collected at levels which are respectively 700 and 900 feet below that at which the diamond-bearing stratum occurs *in situ*.

The Panna mines are at present the most productive diamond mines in India. The profits of the workers are, however, greatly diminished by the heavy tribute exacted by the native princes, to whom the land on which the mines are situated (with the exception of Saya Lachmanpur) belongs. All stones exceeding 6 ratis in weight are appropriated, together with one-fourth of the value of all other stones found. In spite of this exaction, more than three-fourths of the inhabitants of Panna and the surrounding villages obtain their livelihood by searching for diamonds. Owing to the oppressive taxation, dishonesty is rife among the workers, stones being concealed whenever opportunity occurs.

Another place at which diamonds are said to have been found is Simla, on the lower ranges of the Himalayas and to the north of Delhi, this locality being thus quite removed from the districts described above. Here, about 1870, a few diamonds are reported to have been found after a great storm; this occurrence is by no means an established

PLATE V

DIAMOND MINE AT PANNA, INDIA

fact, but it agrees with an old Indian tradition that diamonds have been found in the Himalayas.

From the mines of these various diamantiferous districts have been derived the enormous number of diamonds, often of large size and great beauty, which, in the course of centuries, have slowly accumulated in the treasuries of Indian princes or have been used in the gorgeous adornments of idols, sacred shrines, and temples. Up to the tenth century almost all the diamonds discovered remained in the country, and it was not till the invasion and plunder of India by other nations that any portion of these treasures was carried away, first into other eastern countries and subsequently into Europe. The first of these occasions was the invasion by the Persians under Mahmud of Ghazni, at the end of the tenth and the beginning of the eleventh century. The magnificence and number of the diamonds amassed in India at that time is related by Ferishtah, the Persian historian of the rise of the Mohammedan power in India. We learn from his account, which was published in 1609, that Mohammed the first, of the Ghuridem dynasty in Persia, who in 1186 founded the Mohammedan rule in India, left at his death 500 muns (= 400 lbs.) of diamonds; all this enormous treasure he had amassed during the thirty-two years of his Indian sway.

Europeans became acquainted with the riches of India mainly through the writings of the Italian traveller Marco Polo, who at the end of the thirteenth century spent many years in Central Asia, China, &c. According to C. W. King, the Portuguese writer Garcias ab Horto was the first to publish, in 1565, any authentic account of Indian diamonds. Towards the end of the seventeenth century the French traveller Tavernier made himself intimately acquainted with the occurrence and mining of diamonds in India, and succeeded in actually viewing the wealth of precious stones amassed by the Great Mogul, Aurungzebe. Tavernier, who in the capacity of a merchant in precious stones spent the years between 1665 and 1669 in India, wrote a detailed description of his journeyings about the country, which is at the present time of the greatest value.

As commercial relations between Europe and the Orient gradually arose and developed, an increasing number of Indian stones found their way into Europe. The principal Indian market for diamonds, and indeed for all precious stones, was, and still is, Madras. At the time of the annexation of India by Britain, a considerable number of Indian stones found their way into English hands; this was the fate of the most famous and beautiful of Indian diamonds, the "Koh-i-noor." Originally the property of the ruler of Lahore, this diamond passed on the dethronement of this prince into the possession of the East India Company, by whom it was presented in 1850 to Queen Victoria.

India has now lost all its former fame as a country rich in diamonds; the most productive mines have long ago been exhausted, and only the poorer deposits still remain. During the devastating wars and native struggles for supremacy, many only partially exhausted mines were abandoned and their very sites forgotten, while from the same cause the demand for diamonds fell off. Moreover, the oppressive and unreasonable tribute demanded by native rulers in former times, and to a certain extent at the present day also, so crippled the industry that many diamond seekers forsook the mines for more lucrative employments, to return perhaps under more favourable conditions.

The chief blow, however, to the diamond mining industry of India was the discovery of the precious stone in Brazil, a country from which diamonds have now been sent to the market since 1728. There could be no competition between these rich and unworked deposits and the Indian mines, whose age can be counted in centuries or even tens of centuries. More recently, the rich yields of the South African diamond-fields have made a profitable mining of the Indian deposits still more impossible. Since in India no new and rich deposits have been discovered to take the place of the old, worked-out mines, as has been the case in Brazil, the time cannot be far distant when India must be excluded from the list of diamond-producing countries.

It has been thought that the diamond-mining industry of India might revive were mining operations to be in the hands of Europeans instead of in those of the natives. Several attempts have been made in this direction, but up to the present have been attended with but little success. The mines most suited for experiments of this kind are those situated in districts directly under English control, namely the Chennur mines in the Penner valley, and those of Karnul and Nandial, Sambalpur, and Chutia Nagpur. Though the economic, social, and legislative conditions even here are none too favourable for the under-taking and carrying out of systematic work, they are less adverse than in districts under the sway of native rulers, such, for example, as those in which the Golconda and the Panna groups of mines are situated, and which are very inaccessible to Europeans. As the geological structure of the country is worked out and becomes better known, it is possible that new occurrences of the diamantiferous beds may be discovered, though it must be said that at present there is no immediate prospect of such discoveries.

The insignificance of the annual output of Indian diamond-mines has already been commented upon; the proportion of these stones which reaches the European markets is still more insignificant; indeed, it is doubtful whether any appreciable number leave the country at all. This state of affairs finds its parallel in the times preceding the eleventh century; now, just as then, the stones are kept in the country to satisfy the passion for gems of the great Indian princes and magnates. Another inducement to dealers to keep the stones in the country is the fact that they will frequently make a higher price there than in the European markets, where they must undergo comparison with the treasures of the whole world and where the price is regulated by the inexorable laws of supply and demand. So brisk is the demand for diamonds in the Indian markets that the native supply is barely sufficient, and many foreign stones are imported, especially from the Cape.

There are not many detailed statements of the mineralogical characters of Indian diamonds; a few, however, have been collected and are given below.

It is often stated that the usual crystalline form of Indian diamonds is that of the octahedron, while that of Brazilian crystals is more often the rhombic dodecahedron, the two being often distinguished as the Indian and Brazilian types respectively. This view, however, is not in complete agreement with some recent scientific investigations of stones which are certainly known to have been found in India. It appears on the contrary that the octahedral form is seldom seen in India, the more characteristic forms being the tetrakis-hexahedron and the hexakis-octahedron. Of fourteen crystals of diamond in the Museum of the Geological Survey of India at Calcutta, which were examined by Mr. F. R. Mallet, nine show a tetrakis-hexahedron alone, two show this form with subordinate faces of the octahedron, two are octahedra in combination with a tetrakis-hexahedron, and one is an octahedron in combination with the rhombic dodecahedron. A tetrakis-hexahedral form is thus present in thirteen of these fourteen crystals, and on eleven of them it occurs singly or predominates over other forms; on the other hand, the octahedron is present on five crystals only, and on only three of these does it predominate. Of the fourteen crystals examined, five were from the Karnul district (four tetrakis-hexahedra and one octahedron with tetrakis-hexahedron), one from Sambalpur (tetrakis-hexahedron with octahedron), four from Panna (much distorted tetrakis-hexahedra), the remaining four being said to have come from Simla. Also of thirty-one Indian diamonds in the mineralogical collection at Dresden only six are octahedra, while octahedral faces are present on only two or three more; the majority show the form of a hexakis-octahedron, and a few also that of the rhombic dodecahedron. The crystalline form of the stones found in different districts, when known, has been mentioned above under the special description of each district.

That large diamonds in considerable numbers were formerly found in India has already been stated; a detailed description of the largest and most beautiful will be given in a separate section devoted to the consideration of famous diamonds. The stones found at the present day are usually of small size, so that in this respect also the finds of the present day do not compare favourably with those of earlier times; large stones are, however, occasionally met with even now, as is shown, for example, by the discovery of a stone weighing 67⅜ carats at Wajra Karur in 1881.

With respect to the quality of Indian diamonds not many detailed accounts are available. Though reports dealing with single mines may mention the existence of stones of poor quality, yet, as a general rule, Indian stones rank high in the possession of the most desirable qualities. An Indian stone often shows a combination of lustre, purity of water, strength of fire, and perfect " blue-whiteness " of colour, such as is absent from Brazilian and South African stones. Moreover, India can claim for its own all the finely-coloured stones of blue, green, and red, not however yellow diamonds, which come mainly from South Africa.

2. BRAZIL.

Diamonds were first discovered in Brazil about the year 1725, in the neighbourhood of Tejuco, which is situated in the State of Minas Geraes. According to the usual accounts they were first found during the gold-washing of the auriferous sands of the Rio dos Marinhos, a tributary on the right bank of the Rio Pinheiro. The glittering of the stones attracted the attention of the gold-washers, although they were ignorant of their real nature. The stones were collected and taken occasionally (1728) to Lisbon, where they came under the notice of the Dutch consul, who recognised them to be diamonds of the best quality.

Then began an eager search all over the district, but specially in the water-courses, and it was found that all the streams and rivers there were more or less rich in diamonds. The Portuguese government claimed the stones as crown property, and marked out a definitely bounded diamantiferous district, called the Serro do Frio district, which was to be under its own control, and subject to special laws and regulations preventing the ingress of unlicensed diamond-seekers, while a strict military supervision forbad any dishonesty among the workers.

More extended search showed that diamonds were not confined to the district of Serro do Frio; numerous important discoveries were made in various parts of Minas Geraes and in other States, namely, in São Paulo and Paraná towards the south, in Goyaz and Matto Grosso in the west, and towards the north in Bahia and perhaps also Pernambuco. Discoveries of new and rich deposits have from time to time been made up to a quite recent date, so that it may be safely assumed that further discoveries are in store in the future, such discoveries being the more probable on account of the fact that many of the diamond-fields hitherto worked are situated in districts almost wholly unexplored.

Up to the present time the State of Minas Geraes has maintained its reputation as an important diamond-yielding region in spite of the fact that, owing to long years of mining operations, its present yield is now much reduced, especially when compared with the yield of the years immediately following the first discovery of diamonds. The place of Minas Geraes, as the State from which the richest yields are derived, is now taken by the State of

Bahia, which came into special prominence in the later decades of the nineteenth century. The yield of other States, compared with that of the two above mentioned, is unimportant, but all are as yet too little explored to permit of a final opinion as to their capabilities.

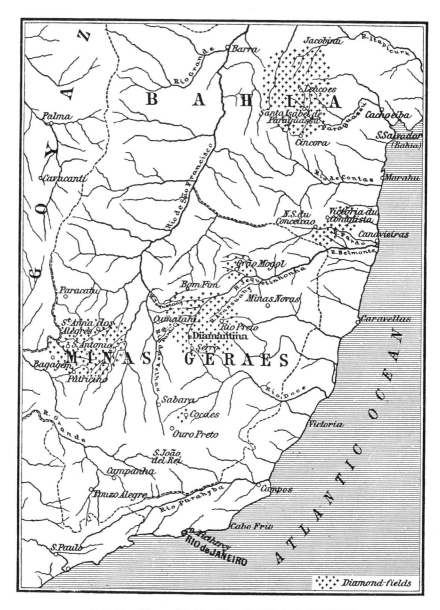

FIG. 34.   Diamond-fields of Brazil.   (Scale, 1 : 10,000,000).

Minas Geraes and Bahia are, however, the only States of commercial importance in respect to the amount and continuity of their production of diamonds, it being doubtful whether stones are found in anything but insignificant numbers in other States.

The important diamond-bearing districts of Minas Geraes and Bahia are shown in the accompanying map (Fig. 34) taken from Boutan. It is proposed now to deal with Brazilian occurrences, taking the different States in the order of their relative importance, and treating

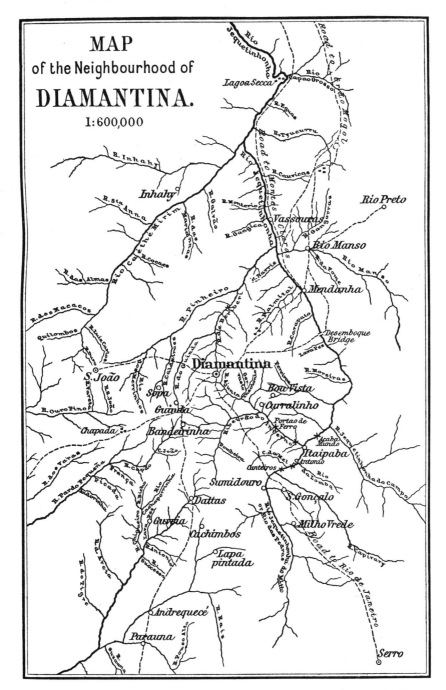

FIG. 35.   Diamond-fields of the Diamantina district, Brazil.   (Scale, 1 : 600,000).

them with more or less fulness according to the greater or less detailed character of published accounts. We will begin with the long famous localities of Minas Geraes, of which the majority have been very fully examined, and which, to a certain extent, serve as a type of those which follow.

It is usual to distinguish four diamond-fields in the State of **Minas Geraes**, namely, those of Serro do Frio or Diamantina, Rio Abaété, Bagagem, and Grão Mogol; of these, the first, that of Serro do Frio or Diamantina is the most important.

A sketch-map, after De Bovet, of the district of Serro do Frio or **Diamantina,** is given in Fig. 35. The area is roughly elliptical in outline, the longer axis, stretching from Serro in the south to the Rio Caéthé Mirim in the north, being about fifty miles in length; while the shorter axis, from the Rio Jequetinhonha in the east to a line drawn parallel to the Rio das Velhas through the villages of Dattas and Parauna, is about twenty-five miles. It is a wild mountain district traversed by the northern end of the Serra do Espinhaço; this mountain range runs parallel to the meridian, and forms the watershed separating the Rio de São Francisco and its tributary the Rio das Velhas from the Rio Jequetinhonha and the Rio Doce. The district forms, roughly speaking, a plateau, the rugged margins of which are cut by deep, steep-sided valleys. The principal town, Tejuco, which since the discovery of diamonds has been known as Diamantina, is situated at a height of 4000 feet above sea level and in latitude 18° 10′ S. and longitude 43° 30′ W. of Greenwich; the district of which it is the capital is now usually known by the same name.

The diamonds occur both on the plateau itself and in the valleys which cut into it; the richest and best known of these river valleys is that of the Rio Jequetinhonha, with its two branches Jequetinhonha do Campo and Jequetinhonha do Matto (Rio das Pedras) rising in the Serro do Itambe. The general direction of this river is south-west to north-east, its mouth is in the Atlantic seaboard, near to Belmonte, the latitude of which is about 16° S., and in the lower part of its course it is known as the Rio Belmonte. It yields diamonds from its source down to Mendanha, the stones being found not only in the main river but also in its tributaries. While the tributaries on the right bank, such for instance as the Rio Capivary and Rio Manso, which do not rise on the plateau of Diamantina, are poor in diamonds, the tributaries of the left bank which have their sources on this plateau are rich in diamonds, the Ribeirão do Inferno, Rio Pinheiro, Rio Caéthé Mirim, and to a less degree the Rio Arassuahy, being worthy of special notice. Other important diamond-bearing streams are a few small water-courses flowing westward from the plateau directly or indirectly into the Rio das Velhas, a tributary of the Rio de São Francisco; of these may be mentioned the Rio das Dattas, Rio do Ouro Fino, Rio do Parauna with its tributary the Ribeirão do Coxoeira, and especially the Rio Pardo Pequena, which has yielded a large number of extremely beautiful stones, and is probably, after the Jequetinhonha, the most important of all.

Next in importance come the deposits of the Rio Jequetahy and the Serra de Cabrol to the north-west of Diamantina; these are separated from the deposits previously mentioned by a zone from which diamonds are absent. With these deposits may be mentioned a small working in the Jequetinhonha valley, about sixty miles below Diamantina. An occurrence which is remarkable in being completely isolated from the other diamond-yielding localities is that at Cocaes, where a few small diamonds have been found; this is situated considerably to the south of Diamantina, and only thirty miles north of Ouro Preto, the capital of the State of Minas Geraes.

Another locality which must be specially noticed is the basin of the Rio Doce, on the east side of the Serra do Espinhaço. The river basin is separated from the rich diamond district of the Rio Jequetinhonha by only a narrow mountain ridge, but in spite of this close proximity, only an insignificant number of stones have been found here, the explanation of which will be given later.

To the west of the Diamantina district is the **Rio Abaété,** a tributary on the left bank of the Rio de São Francisco; this river is fed by the Rio Fulda and Rio Werra, and on the left bank by its tributary the Rio Andrada. Into the Rio de São Francisco flow also the Rio Indaia, the Bambuy, the Barraehudo, as well as the Paricatú, with its tributaries Santo Antonio, d'Almas, de Somno, de Catinga, de Prata, and others. The diamonds of this region were discovered by unlicensed searchers (garimpeiros) in 1785, who worked at first without a concession; in the Rio Abaété they found one of the largest of Brazilian diamonds, which weighed 138½ carats. Although in 1791 there were as many as 1200 licensed workers at the place, the deposits seem to have been very quickly worked out subsequent to the year 1795, and in 1807 work here practically ceased.

This district embraces a stretch of country on the eastern slope of the Serra da Mata da Corda, about 300 miles long, and it is here that the rivers mentioned above have their sources. On the western side of the same range, still in Minas Geraes, but near the border of the State of Goyaz, is the district of **Bagagem**, having about the same length as the district of the Rio Abaété, the two districts having together a width of about 250 miles. The whole area embraced by these districts, though it has been only partially explored, has yielded a large number of diamonds, many of which are of considerable size. These include a stone of 120⅜ carats, and also the famous "Star of the South," the largest of Brazilian diamonds, which was found in 1853, and in its rough condition weighed 254½ carats.

A new diamantiferous deposit, which, however, does not appear to be very rich, has recently been discovered and worked in the district at Agua Suja, about twelve miles south of Bagagem. The diamonds are here associated with blocks of rock, identical with that which occurs *in situ* not far away, together with much magnetite and also ilmenite, decomposed perofskite, pyrope, and rutile. Some of these minerals, more especially the perofskite and pyrope, have not hitherto been found associated with diamond at any other Brazilian locality. This association of minerals recalls the mineral constituents of the " blue ground " of Kimberley in South Africa, which will be described later, as will also the various minerals hitherto found in Brazil associated with diamond.

One other diamantiferous district in the State of Minas Geraes remains to be mentioned, namely, that of **Grão Mogol** (Grão Mogor), which is situated about 180 miles north of Diamantina, in a mountain range to the north-west of, and on the left side of, the Rio Jequetinhonha. Although this district was first searched in 1813 diamonds were not found here until 1827; it is remarkable as being the only locality at which diamonds occur in the solid sandstone, which, at one time, was thought to be their original mother-rock. Though the yield from this district is now small, it was formerly rather considerable, 2000 people being employed in the industry in 1839.

The **geological relations** of the diamantiferous districts of the State of Minas Geraes, especially that of Diamantina, have been frequently investigated, and, at least in the case of the latter, are fairly well understood, though many doubtful points still await elucidation. The investigations which have been made are due, at the beginning of the nineteenth century, to L. von Eschwege; a little later to Spix and Martius; in the fifties, first to Heusser and Claraz and then to Claussen and Helmreichen; and in recent times to various geologists resident in Brazil, namely, Gorceix, De Bovet, Orville A. Derby, and others.

We learn from their observations that the principal rock in the Serra do Espinhaço is usually a thinly laminated sandstone or quartzite, the laminæ bearing numerous scales of pale green mica on their surface. Some of the thin laminæ or slabs are so peculiarly constituted that they can be bent without being broken, such specimens being hence described as flexible sandstone. The increased size of the quartz grains and pebbles renders the rocks in places more coarse-grained in character, so that it resembles a conglomerate rather than a sandstone. This laminated sandstone, which is of great geological antiquity, is usually regarded as a sedimentary rock rather than as belonging to the crystalline schists; it is very abundant in the Serra Itacolumi, in the southern part of Minas Geraes, and has thus come to be known as itacolumite. Interbedded with it are clay-slates, and various schists such as mica-schist, hornblende-schist, hæmatite-schist, &c. The rock is penetrated for short distances by veins which usually contain crystals of quartz. The beds of itacolumite and associated rocks, together with the underlying gneiss, mica-schist, and hornblende-schist, are usually inclined at a steep angle.

On the mountain-tops the itacolumite is overlain unconformably by a younger quartzite, the bedding of which is less steeply inclined than is that of the underlying rock. It is very similar in appearance to the itacolumite, and in places it merges into a conglomerate just as the itacolumite does. From the fact that irregular and angular projections of the lower rock are covered by the younger quartzite, it is evident that the two rocks are perfectly distinct, and probably belong to very different periods.

At some places, and conspicuously so in the basin of the Rio de São Francisco, the beds of itacolumite are associated with slates and limestones, in which fossils of Silurian and Devonian age are found. These slates and limestones have no direct bearing on the occurrence of diamonds, since, as we shall see later, the itacolumite must be regarded as the diamond-bearing rock; they may, however, serve to determine the geological age, at present unknown, of the itacolumite when its relation to these rocks has been made out, which has not yet been accomplished.

We have already seen that the mode of occurrence of the diamond differs in each of these districts. Three kinds of diamantiferous deposits are distinguished according to their situation, whether on the plateau or in the valley, and, in the latter case, whether above or below the present high-water level. These are known respectively as river-deposits, valley-deposits, or plateau-deposits, according as they are found in the existing water-courses within the present limits of high water, on the sides of the valley above high-water level, or covering more or less large areas on the summits of plateaux.

Both the river-deposits and the valley-deposits are without exception constituted of sands, the plateau-deposits also having in part a similar constitution; these sands, or alluvial deposits, consist of débris which has been transported by water, and which contains more or less rounded rock-fragments, among which the diamonds occur singly and isolated. The amount of rounding which the rock-fragments have undergone may be regarded as indicating the distance to which they have been transported from their original situation. In places, however, the rock-fragments of the plateau-deposits show no trace of having been water-worn; when this is the case, such deposits have undoubtedly been formed on the spot they now occupy, and consist usually of much weathered rock-masses, as will be shown in a special description of certain plateau-deposits.

An attentive consideration of the distribution of the three classes of deposits leads to the recognition of a certain connection between them which is of some interest. The various diamond-bearing districts of the plateau are at the same time the collecting grounds of the diamantiferous streams and rivers; it is a natural conclusion then that the stones now found in the sands of the river valleys have been carried there, together with sand, gravel, and other débris, from their original situation on the plateau by these same rivers and streams. This is especially the case in the neighbourhood of the town of Diamantina, which stands on a plateau, the surface beds of which consist of diamond-bearing rock. The rivers which have their sources in these rocks are in their lower courses rich in diamonds, whereas in other rivers, such, for example, as the Rio Doce and its tributaries, which rise among rocks from which diamonds are absent, no diamonds are to be found.

The connection thus existing between the deposits of the plateau and those of the valley leads to the view that the **mineral associations** of diamond, whether they occur on the hills or in the valleys, are essentially the same over the whole of Minas Geraes. The material of these deposits consists mainly of grains and fragments of the surrounding rocks, from the weathering of which they have been derived, and includes besides the diamonds various minerals which may be in a fresh unaltered condition, or more or less weathered and decomposed. The mineral most frequently and abundantly present everywhere is quartz, of which the transparent and colourless varieties occur, as well as the compact varieties such as hornstone, jasper, &c. All three modifications of titanium dioxide, namely, rutile, anatase, and brookite are met with, the last being represented by the variety known as arkansite; crystals of anatase are sometimes completely altered to rutile, while preserving at the same time their own external form; these pseudomorphs are known in Brazil as "captivos." Other minerals found in the deposits are oxides and hydroxides of iron, especially magnetite, ilmenite (titaniferous iron-ore), hæmatite, hæmatite having the external crystalline form of magnetite (the so-called martite), and limonite; also iron-pyrites, either unchanged or altered into brown hydroxide of iron (göthite), tourmaline, various kinds of garnet, fibrolite, lazulite, psilomelane, talc, mica, yttrotantalite, xenotime and monazite, kyanite, various complex hydrated phosphates (goyazite, &c.), diaspore, staurolite, sphene, and topaz, both white and blue but not yellow. In addition to diamonds, gold is frequently washed for, and is associated with platinum, the latter, however, not in sufficient quantity to be of any commercial importance. Some of the minerals mentioned above are distinguished in the district by local names; thus the black rounded pebbles of tourmaline are known as "feijas" (that is, black beans), and the brown pebbles, consisting of a hydrated phosphate, or of titanium or zirconium oxides, are called "favas" (that is, broad beans).

The minerals mentioned above are not of equally frequent occurrence; the most constant associates of diamond, after the different varieties of quartz, are the oxides of titanium (rutile, anatase, and brookite), hæmatite and martite, pebbles of black tourmaline, and specially xenotime and monazite. Even these, however, occur in varying abundance and frequency at different places; thus the same minerals do not occur associated together in the same way in every river, nor indeed in every part of the same river, this depending on the fact that the lighter minerals are transported at a greater rate than the heavier, and that some are more liable to be altered and reduced to powder than are others.

It should be mentioned here that while in the deposits of Salobro, in Bahia, corundum is found associated with diamond, it is entirely absent from the State of Minas Geraes.

Diamond-diggers are guided to a certain extent in their search for the precious stone by the presence or absence of the minerals usually associated with it, which they refer to as the *formation*. While by reason of their more sparing occurrence and small size diamonds may easily be overlooked, the associated minerals occur usually in larger and more conspicuous crystals and fragments, and are therefore more readily seen. Where the "formation" is absent a search for diamonds is useless, and never undertaken, since they are never found apart from their associates. It by no means follows, however, that diamonds are to be found wherever the "formation" exists; they may be altogether absent, or present in numbers insufficient to pay for the labour of working.

The different constituents of the "formation" are not regarded alike by the diamond-diggers. Those to which a special importance is attached, as being certain indicators of the presence of diamonds, are tourmaline pebbles ("feijas"), the oxides of titanium (especially anatase, less so rutile and brookite), iron oxides (magnetite, ilmenite, hæmatite, and limonite), the phosphates ("favas"), &c.; other minerals, such, for instance, as lazulite, are considered unimportant.   Opinions on this matter naturally vary, and are to a certain extent arbitrary, but it may be taken as a safe rule that the presence of those minerals, which are most constantly associated with diamond, is an indication which must not be disregarded.

We now pass to a more detailed consideration of the three classes of diamond-bearing deposits, namely those of the rivers, valleys, and plateaux, as they occur in the district of Diamantina and elsewhere in Minas Geraes.

The **river-deposits** are the richest of the three ; they are found in the valleys below the existing high-water level, and at the present time are the only deposits of importance, not only in this district but also in the whole of Brazil, and this in spite of the fact that the average size of the stones so found is smaller than that of the diamonds of other deposits.   In connection with the question of size, it is remarkable that stones found in the lower courses of a river are smaller than those in the upper part, and that eventually a point is reached in the river course at which the diamonds disappear altogether.   This is strikingly shown in the Rio Jequetinhonha and other rivers, in which, 60 miles below Diamantina, only very small stones are to be found.   In these rivers the material of the diamantiferous deposit is much rounded, more so than in others ; the edges and corners of the diamonds are also considerably worn.   The fact that the stones diminish in size the farther down the river they are found can easily be explained, when it is considered that material transported by water becomes more and more worn as the distance over which it travels increases, and, moreover, that the smaller the stones become, the more easily are they transported by water and the greater will be the distance they are carried from their original situation.

The diamantiferous débris which lies in the beds of the rivers and the bottom of the valleys consists mainly of rounded fragments of rocks and quartz brought down by the streams and rivers from their sources and upper reaches.   This débris is usually mixed with clay to a greater or less extent, the resulting material in the state in which it is worked for diamonds being known to the diamond-diggers as *cascalho*.   This is usually loose and incoherent, showing no signs of bedding ; at times, however, it has a firmer consistency due to the presence of the clay.   The upper portion of the mass is sometimes bound together, to a greater or less depth, by a ferruginous cementing material so as to form a conglomerate. This conglomerate, consisting largely of rounded quartz grains and pebbles, occurs in extensive beds or in isolated blocks known as " tapanhoacanga," or " canga," which may enclose crystals of diamond.   Such a fragment of conglomerate, with a diamond embedded in it, is represented in Plate I., Fig. 1 ; similar specimens are often exhibited in collections as examples of the occurrence of diamond in its mother-rock, a view which, as we have seen, is incorrect.

The " cascalho " of the diamond-diggers thus contains the diamond with its associated minerals as a finer constituent, and rounded rock-fragments as coarser material, the whole being intermixed with clay or with limonite, which may cement the material together into a more or less firm mass.   This material lies in the beds of the water-courses resting immediately on the solid rocks beneath ; in a few instances, however, the rich diamond-bearing " cascalho," the " cascalho virgem " of the Brazilians, extends upwards to the surface through the whole of the fluviatile deposits.   It has a very variable thickness, and is usually covered by a layer of material from which diamonds are absent, the so-called " barren cascalho " ; this upper layer varies in thickness, from a few centimetres to twenty or thirty metres ; in its lower portion it usually consists of an accumulation of larger rock-fragments.   The " barren cascalho " is constituted of materials similar in character to those of the more deeply situated diamond-bearing layer, to reach which it is necessary to divert the water which flows over the barren layer.

Although the diamantiferous "cascalho" is spread fairly uninterruptedly over long stretches of the beds of streams and rivers, yet its distribution over the whole course of the river is by no means regular. Here it may be accumulated in masses of great thickness, there to only a sparing amount, while in a third place it may be altogether absent. Moreover, the number of diamonds present in the material varies in different rivers, and in different parts of the same river; it is recorded of certain rivers in the Diamantina district, however, that the diamonds were so regularly distributed through the "cascalho" that it was possible to estimate with accuracy the weight in carats of the precious stone which a certain amount of this material would yield; this case is, however, very exceptional.

A large accumulation of specially rich "cascalho" at one particular point is the result of the presence of certain conditions which exist only at that point; such an accumulation is sought for with eagerness. In the beds of the rivers cylindrical holes of greater or less depth are sometimes bored in the solid rock by the action of the running water, such pot-holes or "giants' kettles" being formed in the same way in many other parts of the world. In addition to these, long channels, hollowed out of the bed of the water-course, and following its course for a certain distance, or running obliquely across it, are also to be met with, and are sometimes known as "subterranean cañons." Such hollows in the bed of a stream occur where the water has passed over softer beds, these being worn away to a greater depth than are the surrounding harder rocks. The hollows so formed may be small or of considerable size, and are often filled up with a specially rich "cascalho." In a small hollow in the bed of the Ribeirão do Inferno, which joins the Jequetinhonha near Diamantina, 8000 to 10,000 carats of diamonds were found, the neighbouring part of the river-bed being very poor. Again, in a small pot-hole in the bed of the Rio Pardo, diamonds to the weight of 180 carats were obtained by four negroes in the short space of four days. Again, the three mines in the valley of the Jequetinhonha, which recently have been specially prolific, namely, S. Antonio, with Canteiras above, and Acaba Mundo below, the mouth of the Ribeirão do Inferno, were worked in depressions of the nature of channels or "subterranean cañons" in the river-bed.

The **valley-deposits** ("gupiarras" of the Brazilians) are, as a rule, of small extent; they are formed of the same material as are the river-deposits, and the diamonds are associated with the same minerals. This deposit is also known as "cascalho," and sometimes also as "gurgulho"; the latter term, however, is more often applied to the material of the plateau-deposits. The valley-deposits also follow the direction of the present water-courses, being situated at the sides of the valley above the present high-water level; they are, as a matter of fact, river-deposits laid down at a time when the bed of the river had not been excavated to the extent it now is. In many cases the successive levels of the former beds of the river are marked out on the sides of the valley by a series of such deposits or river-terraces.

The material of these terraces is much less worn than is that in the bottom of the valley. As a general rule, it is found that the rounding of the rock-fragments is the more pronounced the lower is the level of the terrace in which they occur, and further that the material of any given terrace becomes more worn the further it is deposited from the source of the river. At the bottom of the same valley in which river-terraces are to be seen is the present bed of the river with its deposits, the material of which is more worn and rounded than that of any of the valley-deposits. It is therefore possible by means of this difference for a person acquainted with the region to distinguish a small sample of river-deposit from one of valley-deposit.

The " cascalho " of the valley-deposits rests, as a rule, not directly upon the solid rock, but upon a variously-coloured layer of fine sand mixed with clay; this is not of any great thickness, and is called " barro." It also contains diamonds, and passes gradually, with no sharp line of demarcation, into the " cascalho " above. The " barro," however, is always distinctly bedded, while the true " cascalho," whether on the sides or the bottom of the valley, shows no signs of bedding. It is often, but not invariably, covered by a layer of red muddy earth.

The " cascalho " of the sides of the valley is usually less rich in diamonds than is that found at the bottom; the stones it does contain, however, are less worn and rounded, and relatively larger than those found in the present river-bed.

Plateau-deposits are found at numerous spots on the hills near Diamantina, and in other diamantiferous districts of Minas Geraes. A rich yield of diamonds was obtained from many of these in former times, but at the present day a few only are worked, and these are of less importance than are the river-deposits.

On the hills near Curralinho (Fig. 35), between the Rio Jequetinhonha and the town of Diamantina, lying about due east of the latter, are the rich mines Bom Successo and Boa Vista. On the plateau south-west of Diamantina, and between the basins of the Rio Pinheiro and the Rio Pardo Pequeña, are the mines La Sopa and Guinda, which are now being worked, there being here two diamond-bearing beds of different ages one above the other.

Further on in the same direction, and about twelve miles west of Diamantina, in the district where the Rio Caéthé Mirim and the Rio Pinheiro take their origin, are the specially noteworthy deposits of São João da Chapada, which will be described below. A little to the south of this place, in the neighbourhood of the source of the Rio Ouro Fino, are the diggings of La Chapada, which were formerly very rich, and are now only partially exhausted.

As regards the character of the plateau-deposits, the material of which they consist is very similar to that of the river-deposits, differing from it, however, in the presence of a larger proportion of the heavier of those minerals usually associated with diamond. This is to be expected, seeing that the lighter materials would be the more easily carried away by running water, and the heavier minerals more liable to be left behind. Thus we find the oxides of titanium and of iron present in great abundance, though even here the amount is exceeded by that of the different varieties of quartz. The material of these plateau-deposits is known as *gurgulho*, it occurs usually in horizontal beds, and is built up of coarse blocks of the surrounding rocks, with a more or less red clayey earth. In this material the diamond and its associated minerals are embedded; so indiscriminately, however, is everything coloured by the red clayey earth that it is impossible to distinguish one mineral from another until the material has been washed. In some deposits the earthy material has been removed by a natural process of washing, and here the diamonds and their associated minerals are from the first distinctly seen. The rock and mineral fragments in the " gurgulho" are very slightly, if at all, rounded, and the diamonds themselves still preserve their perfectly sharp edges and corners, and the original natural characters of their faces.

The proportion of diamonds and their associated minerals present in a given weight of the material is rather smaller in " gurgulho " than in other deposits, but the average size of the stones is greater. The distribution of the diamonds is sometimes very irregular, large numbers, aggregating in weight up to 1700 and 2000 carats, being found in a single small nest, while few, if any, in a considerable area of the surrounding "gurgulho."

Under the diamond-bearing "gurgulho," and resting immediately upon the solid rock, there is usually a layer of clay, in which also a few diamonds are to be found. Above the "gurgulho," just as in the valley deposits, is a layer of red clay of varying thickness, from which diamonds are absent. When this layer is absent, as it sometimes is, the "gurgulho" forms the actual surface of the ground and is covered by vegetation. It is said that the observation of diamonds attached to the roots of plants, scratched up to the surface by fowls, or picked up by children at play, has led to the discovery of rich deposits.

Plateau deposits at other places, such as, for example, **São João da Chapada**, on the plateau of Diamantina and about twenty miles west of this town, differ very widely from those just considered. The mines here are situated on the watershed between the Rio Jequetinhonha and the Rio das Velhas, and on the prolongation of the straight line which connects the important deposits of Boa Vista, on the hills near Curralinho (Fig. 35) with those of La Sopa. These deposits were discovered in 1833. Extensive workings were carried on for a long period, but were finally discontinued owing to the exhaustion of the deposit. In spite of this the place remains extremely important from the scientific point of view, for here may be gathered data which afford material help in solving the problem as to the nature of the original mother-rock of diamond in this region.

The diamond occurs here in variously coloured clays, which lie in a trench 40 metres deep, 60 to 80 metres wide, and 500 metres long, somewhat resembling a deep railway cutting. These clays are distinctly bedded, being inclined 50° to the east, and regularly and conformably interbedded with them are beds of itacolumite inclined at the same angle. All the strata, the clays as well as the itacolumite, are penetrated by numerous small veins filled for the greater part with quartz (rock-crystal), rutile, and hæmatite.

The yield of diamonds from these clays was very variable, but on the whole the deposit was considered poor. Tschudi, who visited the place in 1860, reported that in his presence forty-four carats were obtained in two hours, while on another occasion only ten small stones were found in twelve tons of material. The associated minerals are the same as elsewhere, the three just mentioned being specially abundant. It is a noteworthy fact, that where the associated minerals occurred in abundance there diamonds were plentiful, but where, on the other hand, the minerals were present to only a sparing extent, diamonds also were hard to find.

The minerals associated with the diamond are present at this locality in less proportion than in the ordinary "cascalho" or "gurgulho," and the same is true also of the diamond itself. As has already been mentioned, the minerals which occur most frequently are quartz, hæmatite, and rutile, other oxides of iron and of titanium, tourmaline, &c. All are found, like the diamond itself, in perfectly sharp crystals. Even the softest of the minerals found here have preserved intact the sharpness and angularity of their edges and corners. None show any indication of having been transported by running water.

These circumstances have led those who have personally investigated the deposit, namely, Orville A. Derby and Gorceix, to the conclusion that here, in these beds, the diamond is seen in its original home, and that here, in the quartz-veins by which the rocks are penetrated, it slowly took on the shape and form in which we now know it. Although no diamond has ever been found actually in a quartz-vein, yet the minerals associated with it occur in such situations with great frequency, and their constant association with the diamond, not only here but at all other localities of Minas Geraes, seems to point to a common origin for both. The fact that the diamond itself has never been found in a quartz-vein may perhaps be explained by the extreme rarity of its occurrence as compared with that of other minerals. The clays in which the precious stone lies, are decomposition products of the rocks which were originally penetrated by the quartz-veins, and which, like the surrounding schistose rocks, have been reduced to their present state of disintegration by exposure to the action of weathering agencies.

The deposit at **Cocaes**, near Ouro Preto, appears to be very similar to that at São João which we have been considering. The diamonds here occur at a height of 1100 feet above sea-level, on a plateau of itacolumite overlying mica-schist and beneath this granite-gneiss. The minerals here associated with diamond are quartz, ilmenite, anatase, rutile, magnetite, hæmatite, martite, tourmaline, monazite, kyanite, fibrolite, and gold. Of these minerals the first three in the list predominate, and quartz only occurs in rounded fragments. Since the diamond and its associated minerals occur here in a belt running east and west, it is possible that here also they have been derived from a mineral vein similar to many carrying gold and other minerals, which traverse the district of Minas Geraes in an east to west direction.

The occurrence at **Grão Mogol**, in the district of Minas Novas, is of a different type again. This town is situated in the extreme north of the State of Minas Geraes, on the left or northern bank of the Rio Jequetinhonha and about 190 miles north-east of Diamantina. As well as in the normal "gurgulho," diamonds are here found in a solid, compact, conglomeratic sandstone containing much green mica, especially along the planes of bedding. According to some accounts this is to be regarded as a single, isolated, sandstone block of enormous size; others, however, attribute to the diamond-bearing rock an extension of 300 to 400 metres. This deposit was discovered in 1833 and was worked in the thirties and forties, fragments of the sandstone being detached by means of blasting powder. All the fragments of sandstone with embedded crystals of diamond, which are sometimes, though rarely, to be seen in mineralogical collections, have come from this locality. Such specimens are not, however, in all cases genuine, for the crystals of diamond have sometimes been artificially set in the rock.

This diamond-bearing sandstone has been, and is now by some geologists, considered to be itacolumite. Those who hold this view regard the sandstone or itacolumite as the original mother-rock of the diamonds now found in it, it being considered that they are as truly constituents of the rock as are the quartz-grains. Later and more detailed examination has, however, rendered it probable that this sandstone is not itacolumite but the more recent quartzite, such as we have seen to be superimposed unconformably in the Serra do Espinhaço on the beds of itacolumite. This quartzite, although very similar in general appearance to itacolumite, is yet geologically quite distinct and probably of a much later date, having no doubt been formed of material derived from the weathering of the diamantiferous itacolumite. Which of these two views is the more correct has not yet been definitely decided. If the rock be really itacolumite, the origin of diamond at this place will differ from that at São João; if, on the other hand, it should be the later quartzite, which is more probably the case, then its occurrence here is in complete harmony with that at São João, for the later-formed quartzite must of necessity contain not only the constituents of itacolumite but also the minerals, including the diamond, which filled the veins by which it was penetrated, as is in fact the case.

A comparison of the different diamantiferous deposits leads inevitably to the conclusion that each may be regarded as typical of some one stage in the development of a single process.

Thus at São João da Chapada, and elsewhere on the plateau, we see the diamond still at the place and in the rock in which it was originally formed, though the latter has been, in part at least, altered by weathering to a soft clayey mass. In such a case we may distinguish the deposit as original or primary.

Other plateau-deposits, where the rock-fragments are but slightly, if at all, rounded, must have been laid down at an early period when the plateau had been eroded by water-courses to only a slight extent and before the present valleys came into existence. The diamonds and their associated minerals were indeed carried away by water from the disintegrated mother-rock, in which at São João they still remain, but they were re-deposited at spots not very far distant, as is proved by the fact that they are so little water-worn. The diamonds and other minerals were probably re-deposited on the floors of shallow lakes, a hypothesis which would account for the bedding of the material in which they occur. Such deposits are described as secondary or derived.

The slow but never ceasing erosion of the plateau by streams and rivers resulted in the course of ages in the formation of the valleys of the present day. Here, high up on the sides of the valley, the most ancient deposit marks the level of the original river-bed. The material for this deposit was derived partly from the primary or original deposit and partly from the secondary plateau-deposit. Some of the diamonds of the oldest valley-deposits have therefore changed their situation twice, and the material, having undergone a second transportation, is therefore more appreciably rounded. As the rivers carved out for themselves deeper and ever deeper channels, so fresh deposits were laid down, the material of each successively lower level being more and more water-worn, until the wearing down process culminates in the much rounded material of the present river-bed. The older valley-deposits are now to be found forming the terraces high up on the sides of the present valleys, while those in the present river-bed itself constitute the deposits described above as the river-deposits.

What has been said above with regard to the **original mode of occurrence** of diamond in Minas Geraes may be summarised as follows: The home of the diamond is located in those portions of the plateau-deposits in which the diamantiferous rivers take their origin. The diamonds gradually decrease in size and number and finally disappear further down the valleys. The rock, which is *in situ* in the neighbourhood of the plateau-deposits, is everywhere itacolumite, interbedded with schists and covered by the younger quartzite. This itacolumite is evidently the source from which the diamonds and the material in which they are found have been derived. So much was established by L. von Eschwege as early as the beginning of the nineteenth century; this observer noticed that in the Diamantina district diamonds were found only in those rivers, such, for example, as the Rio Jequetinhonha, which flow down the western slopes of the Serra do Espinhaço which are formed of itacolumite, and that, on the other hand, no diamonds are found in those rivers, such, for example, as the Rio Doce and its tributaries, which rise on the eastern side of this range, these slopes being formed of gneiss, mica-schist, &c. As has been already pointed out, those rivers which flow through strata composed of itacolumite are diamantiferous, while in those flowing through districts from which itacolumite is absent no diamonds are found.

The occurrence of the minerals associated with diamond, especially the most important of them, such as quartz (rock-crystal), oxides of iron and of titanium, tourmaline, &c., is also confined to the itacolumite; they do not, however, occur embedded in the rock but in the veins, consisting mainly of quartz, by which it and the interbedded schists are penetrated. The circumstance that the diamond is invariably associated with these minerals, and with them alone, points to the conclusion that it originated in the mineral-veins, as was first insisted upon by Gorceix. This conclusion receives additional support from the fact that Brazilian diamonds, instead of exhibiting a perfect and complete development on all sides such as is characteristic of embedded crystals, frequently show on one side an area by which they seem to have been attached during their growth and development, impressions of quartz-crystals being sometimes seen on such areas of attachment. Moreover, diamonds have been found enclosed in, or attached to, the surface of crystals of quartz, anatase, and hæmatite, and this could scarcely be explained except on the supposition that these minerals have all grown together at the same time and in the same vein. It has been stated by Gorceix that a few diamonds have in places been met with actually in the mineral-veins themselves, and, though in small numbers, have been extracted ; he compares such occurrences with that of the yellow topaz found near Ouro Preto in quartz-veins penetrating decomposed schists. In these districts, then, the diamond is a vein mineral, while in other localities it is an original constituent of the primitive crystalline rocks.

The precise **method of winning** diamonds adopted in Brazil depends more or less upon the nature of the deposit. A diamond-working is known in Brazil as a *serviço*, those in a river-deposit being distinguished as " serviços do rio," while those in valley- and plateau-deposits are distinguished respectively as " serviços do campo" and " serviços da serra." The methods in each case have changed but little during the whole period the deposits have been worked ; the greater part of the labour is performed by negroes working formerly as slaves, but now as freemen.

In the **serviços do rio**, or workings of a river-deposit, the first step is the diversion of the water in order to lay bare the " cascalho " or diamantiferous material. Only a small portion of the river-bed is laid bare at a time, the operation being effected either by cutting a new channel for the river, or by building a dam in the middle of the stream and parallel to its course, so as to confine the water to a bed one-half its previous width, or by conducting the water away in wooden channels. After removing the barren detritus from the surface of the river-bed so laid bare, the diamond-bearing " cascalho " is dug out. This latter is loose and easily worked, but the " canga," or masses of conglomerate, are often so compact that blasting must be resorted to, and thus the working becomes more lengthy and expensive.

The work of excavating the " cascalho " can only be pursued during the dry season, from May to the end of September, when the volume of water in the rivers is at its smallest. During these months as much as possible of the diamond-bearing " cascalho " is excavated and conveyed to a higher level, being deposited, however, as near the stream or river as safety will permit. In the wet season the level of the river rises rapidly and to a marked extent, thus making the excavation of the " cascalho " a matter of impossibility. At this season the material previously excavated is washed and the diamonds it contains collected ; the place at which the operation of washing is conducted is known in Brazil as a *lavra*.

Before the " cascalho " is washed, the larger fragments are separated from the finer material either by hand or by means of a sieve. This fine material is then placed in a shallow, wooden dish of a special kind, known as a batea, and agitated in running water ; the lighter and finer portion is thus carried away, and from the heavier remaining part the diamonds are picked out by hand, the process of washing being all the while proceeding. The washers exhibit a wonderful skill in distinguishing the smallest diamonds, such as might easily be overlooked by even a practised eye, from other mineral fragments.

Plate VI. is a picture of the actual working of a Brazilian diamond washing. The negroes on the left are standing in the stream and washing the " cascalho " in their bateas.

PLATE VI

DIAMOND-WASHING IN BRAZIL

Another party of workers on the right is engaged in filling up the bateas with fresh material from the " cascalho " heaped up on the banks of the stream, and carrying them down when filled to the workers standing in the water. The negroes are all the time under the strict supervision of overseers armed with whips, whose duty it is to urge on the workers and to guard against thieving; in order to minimise opportunities for stealing, the clothing of the negroes is of the scantiest description. Each time a stone is found the worker, by raising his hand, signs to the overseer, who takes possession of the treasure. This picture in which the overseers are armed with whips dates back to the days of slavery; since the emancipation of the slaves such coercive measures have, of course, been discontinued, but otherwise the system is unaltered.

The **serviços do campo** on the sides of the valleys above the present high-water level can be worked at all seasons of the year. The water from a neighbouring stream is caused to flow over the deposit to be worked; by this means the surface earth and clay are carried away and the diamond-bearing " cascalho " is laid bare. Since sufficient water for this purpose is only to be obtained in the rainy season this part of the work is usually reserved for that period. The " cascalho " when excavated is washed and the diamonds are picked out of the concentrate, in the same way as in the " serviços do rio."

In the **serviços da serra** the removal of the masses of barren sand and earth covering the " gurgulho " of the plateau-deposits is effected in the same manner, namely, by the agency of running water. As, however, on the plateau there are no natural watercourses having a sufficient head of water, it is necessary to construct artificial reservoirs in which the rain-water may be stored. The water is conducted from the reservoir to the places at which it is required in wooden channels and the diamond-bearing bed thus laid bare as far as possible. As in other cases, the " gurgulho " is first washed and the diamonds then picked out by hand.

In the period immediately following the discovery of diamonds in Brazil, it was the practice of the Portuguese Government to demand in return for the concession of mining rights a certain sum for every slave it was proposed to employ, the total number of slaves so employed to be fixed by agreement. This tax was continually being raised, and so irksome became the conditions imposed on prospective miners that no one could be found to undertake the work. Then from the year 1740 concessions were granted on the payment of a fixed sum, but as the mineral wealth of the country still remained undeveloped, the mining was taken over altogether by the Government from the year 1772 until the separation of Brazil from Portugal. The choicest of the stones found in this period therefore found their way to Lisbon, and were preserved with the Portuguese crown jewels, a collection which comprises many unique and matchless gems. The larger proportion of the Brazilian output was bought by merchants and sent to Europe through Rio de Janeiro and Bahia.

In spite of the laws of almost draconic severity levelled against illicit diamond-mining and trading, there was, besides the Government production, a great deal of surreptitious mining by unlicensed persons (" garimpeiros ") of which of course no records were made. It has been estimated, however, that the contraband production was at least equal in amount to that of the Government. Moreover, a large proportion of the most perfect and beautiful stones fell into the hands of illicit traders, since a Government employee would scarcely risk detection for the sake of a stone of average or poor size and quality. According to other accounts the illicit trade was not of such extent and importance; in any case, however, those engaged in it, when relieved from the necessity of meeting the heavy taxes and high cost of production of the legitimate product, must have found their transactions very remunerative.

In 1834, the year in which the independence of Brazil was established, the Government monopoly of diamond-mining ceased.   Since this date the concession of full mining rights has been granted to any petitioner on the payment of a small tax, varying in amount with the area he proposes to work.   The landowner is also entitled to demand 25 per cent. of the rough production, and a duty of $\frac{1}{2}$ per cent. is imposed on exported stones.

The negro slaves, by whom the whole of the actual labour connected with the mines was formerly done, were subjected to the strictest supervision.   To minimise the temptation to conceal valuable stones, the finders of large diamonds received special rewards; thus, at one time, the fortunate finder of a diamond of $17\frac{1}{2}$ carats received his freedom, but later, when the price of slaves rose, this custom was dropped.   Those slaves, on the other hand, who were detected in the act of concealing diamonds, were treated with barbaric severity.

As may be gathered from the scene pictured in Plate VI., the whole of the work was done by hand, the " cascalho " being carried in baskets on the heads of the negroes, and no attempt made to save time and labour by the introduction of machinery or mechanical appliances.   Even at the present day the same primitive methods are still in use, the difficulties in the way of the transport of large and heavy pieces of machinery to such inaccessible regions being almost insuperable.   It is always more practicable therefore to employ hand labour, especially as, in addition to previous considerations, there is the fact that since any one locality is soon exhausted it would be necessary to move the machinery very often.   The occupation of diamond-mining is very lucrative only under exception- ably favourable circumstances ; as a rule, the working expenses are very high and the losses by embezzlement considerable.

Brazilian diamonds, when they first appeared in the market, were not favourably received by the diamond-buying public, and were asserted to be either not diamonds at all or inferior stones from India.   On this account many Brazilian stones were sent first to Goa, a Portuguese possession in India, and from thence entered the market as Indian stones. When this arrangement came to the ears of the Dutch merchants, they at once entered into a contract by which they secured a monopoly of the trade in Brazilian diamonds, which were subsequently sent direct from Rio de Janeiro and Bahia to Amsterdam.   In consequence of a treaty entered into at a later date with the English Government, the whole output was sent to London ; in recent times the majority of Brazilian stones are purchased by French houses and put on the Paris market.

In the preceding pages the production and occurrence of diamonds in the State of Minas Geraes, and especially in the district of Diamantina, have been described in some detail, the total output from this State alone having exceeded that of the rest of Brazil.   Other States in which diamonds occur have been already named ; with the exception of Bahia they are much less known than is the district of Diamantina ; their production is also much below that of either Bahia or Minas Geraes and is now probably everywhere at an end ; this being so, only a short notice of them will be given.

In the State of **São Paulo,** to the south of Minas Geraes, diamonds have been found in the rivers flowing into the Rio Paraná.

In the State of **Paraná** diamonds have been found, more especially in the basin of the Rio Tibagy.   This river runs through the Campos of Guarapuavas and empties itself into the Rio Parapanema, which is a tributary of the Paraná.   Diamonds are found also in the tributaries of the Rio Tibagy, especially the Yapo and the Pitangru, and are everywhere associated with a somewhat considerable amount of gold.   These rivers are remarkable for the presence in their beds of pot-holes and channel-like depressions, very local in their occurrence, and often containing a large quantity of stones.   Just as in the districts previously considered, the diamantiferous deposits may be distinguished as river-, valley- and plateau-deposits. The discovery of diamonds in Paraná was accidental; the stones found were invariably small, rarely exceeding a carat in weight; they were usually, however, of good colour and lustre. Systematic search was undertaken a few years ago, but the yield was small and unremunerative, in spite of the considerable amount of gold present; it was, therefore, soon abandoned. The stones here are supposed to have been washed out of the Devonian sandstone through which the rivers mentioned above flow, and the sandstone itself may have been formed from the weathered débris of itacolumite.

In the State of **Goyaz**, on the western border of Minas Geraes, diamonds have been found in the Rivers Guritas, Quebre-Anzol, S. Marcos, and Paranayba. The upper part of the River Araguaia, bordering on the State of Matto Grosso and its right tributary the Rio Claro (lat. 16° 10′ S., long. 50° 30′ W., of Greenwich), and others in Goyaz are specially rich. The yield from these rivers has been considerable, the diamonds found up to the year 1850 in the Rio Claro alone amounting to an aggregate weight of 252,000 carats valued at £400,000.

In the State of **Matto Grosso** diamonds have been searched for in some of the rivers as far as the Bolivian frontier, and in places a rich yield has been obtained. The majority of the stones have been found in the neighbourhood of Diamantino (not to be confused with Diamantina, formerly Tejuco, in Minas Geraes), in the district of the source of the Paraguay and its tributaries, especially the Rio Cuyabá, a tributary on its right bank (lat. 15° 45′ S., long. 56° W., of Greenwich). The stones from here are usually small and often coloured, some, however, are of the purest water; they are distinguished by the possession of a very brilliant surface, a feature which is usually absent from Brazilian stones. Up to 1850 the State of Matto Grosso had yielded diamonds to the weight of about 1,191,600 carats valued at £1,850,000.

The geology of Goyaz and Matto Grosso is but little known; travellers, however, state that itacolumite is widely distributed; we may therefore assume that the occurrence of diamond in these States agrees in all essential points with that in Minas Geraes.

With respect to productiveness, the State of **Bahia** stands second to Minas Geraes; while the latter, however, is now for the most part exhausted, in the former new and rich deposits have been discovered. Thus the present yearly production of Bahia exceeds that of Minas Geraes, but the reverse is the case when the total production of the two States is compared.

Diamonds had been discovered in Bahia as far back as the year 1755; further search, however, was at that time prohibited by the Government in the fear that the agricultural prosperity of this fertile State might suffer. In spite of this prohibition more and more finds were made, until at the beginning of the nineteenth century the production was quite considerable. It has continued to grow, until now the yearly output exceeds that of Minas Geraes.

The first finds were made on the eastern slopes of the **Serra da Chapada** and, north of this, in the Serra do Assuâria, which forms the continuation northwards of the Serra do Espinhaço, a range of mountains stretching across the greater part of Minas Geraes and passing through the district of Diamantina. The stones are found in sands and gravels in the water-courses, and are accompanied by the minerals which constitute the most important associations of diamond at Diamantina, namely, the oxides of titanium and of iron, tourmaline, and quartz (rock-crystal). In addition to these are a few others, which do not occur in Minas Geraes. In a sample of diamond-sand from the Serra da Chapada, Damour determined the following minerals: pebbles of rock-crystal, crystals of zircon, tourmaline, hydro-phosphates, yttrium phosphates (sometimes containing titanic acid), diaspore, rutile, brookite, anatase, ilmenite, magnetite, cassiterite, red felspar, cinnabar, and gold. Garnet and staurolite have also been observed here and recently euclase, but the last only as a rarity. Of these minerals, cassiterite, felspar, and cinnabar have never been found in Minas Geraes in association with diamond. Schrauf argued from the occurrence of these minerals, and especially from the association together of tourmaline, garnet, zircon, staurolite, rutile, &c., that the rocks, from which have been derived the diamond-sands of the Serra da Chapada, were allied to the gneisses and syenites of southern Norway. It has been stated in descriptions of the geological structure of these mountains that they are built up of these particular rocks, but neither in this nor in other diamond districts in Bahia has any thorough geological investigation been made, and since the minerals associated with diamond are the

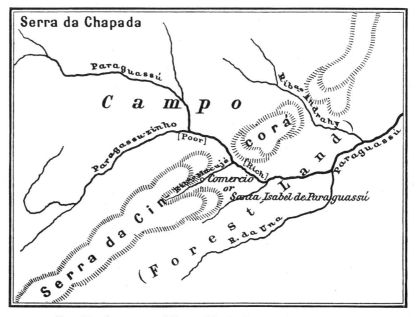

FIG. 36.   Occurrence of diamond in the Serra da Cincorá, Bahia.

same in Bahia and in Minas Geraes, it is probable that the occurrence is also the same, namely, in itacolumite.

Especially rich finds were made in the year 1844 in the **Serra da Cincorá** (Sincorá). This range is situated in longitude about 41° W. of Greenwich, and extends from south-west to north-east between latitudes 13° 15′ and 12° 15′ S. It forms the south-eastern spur of the Serra da Chapada (Fig. 36), with which it is connected at its southern end ; it separates the basin of the Rio de São Francisco from that of the Rio Paraguassú, and constitutes the collecting-ground of these rivers. This range, the Serra da Cincorá, and that of the Serra da Grão Mogol in Minas Geraes, closely resemble each other, both are rugged and inhospitable, and it is highly probable that the Serra da Cincorá consists of itacolumite, although the neighbouring heights are built up of granite and gneiss.

The discovery of diamonds here was due to the observation of a slave, a native of the diamond district of Minas Geraes, who, while engaged in minding cattle, was so struck with the similarity of the soil to that of his home that he began searching for diamonds, and before long collected 700 carats. Scarcely had this find become known, when eager searchers flocked in thousands to the place. According to some accounts, as many as 25,000 people had settled in the neighbourhood in the following year; other estimates, however place the number at from 12,000 to 14,000. Many of these fresh arrivals came from the Serra da Chapada and the Serra do Assuâria, where, in consequence of the stream of emigration, diamond-mining was almost entirely abandoned; the majority, however, were workers from Minas Geraes, where the yield of diamonds had long been gradually diminishing.

The yield of the newly discovered fields was very rich and raised the ever sinking diamond production of Brazil to its former high level. It is said that during the most productive period the daily yield averaged 1450 carats; soon, however, the yield began to decrease and the number of workers fell to 5000 or 6000. Up to the year 1849 the total output of diamonds of this district was 932,400 carats, and this immense production had lowered the prices of the stone fifty per cent. According to the estimates of diamond merchants, Bahia produced in the year 1858 54,000 carats, while from Diamantina came only 36,000 carats.

The occurrence of diamond in the Serra da Cincorá is confined to the alluvial deposits of the rivers. According to J. J. von Tschudi, who quotes the statement of the traveller V. von Helmreichen, the first discovery was made on the banks of the Macujé, a small tributary on the right bank of the Paraguassú. Here, besides a few small villages, there sprang up in consequence of the finds the principal town of the district, Santa Isabel de Paraguassú (also known as Comercio), lying about 190 miles to the west of the town of Bahia. Later, diamonds were discovered at a distance of forty-five miles from Santa Isabel. The principal place to the north of Santa Isabel is Lençoes, in the neighbourhood of which is Monte Vereno, a well-known diamond locality, where the diamond sands consist largely of fragments of itacolumite. Other important localities are Andrahy, Palmeiros, San Antonio, and San Ignacio.

The washings on the west side of the Serra have been poor; a considerable number of diamonds were, however, obtained from the Macujé itself and from those parts of the Paraguassú and Andrahy rivers which cut through the Serra. On the latter river, the principal washings are situated on the small tributary streams of its right bank. In the bed of the Paraguassú river are depressions rich in diamonds similar to those found in the diamond rivers of Diamantina.

Diamonds from the Serra da Cincorá are known as " Cincorá (Sincorá) stones," or as " Bahias," in order to distinguish them from the " Diamantina stones." They are considerably inferior in quality to the latter and command a much lower price. They are usually coloured yellow, green, brown, or red, and almost all have an elongated, irregular form which makes them less suitable for cutting. Diamonds of the purest water are rarer here than elsewhere in Brazil, and in size they are usually small, the large stone of $87\frac{1}{2}$ carats found at the beginning of the fifties being an exception to the general rule.

It is in the diamantiferous district of Cincorá that the peculiar variety of diamond mentioned several times above, namely, the black **carbonado** (" carbonate "), is almost exclusively found. Although found in association with the ordinary diamond, it is so utterly unlike it in appearance that it might be taken for anything rather than diamond.

In contrast to the ordinary diamond, carbonado very rarely exhibits a crystalline form of any regularity, still the octahedron, rhombic dodecahedron, and the cube, with rough faces and rounded edges and corners, have been observed. A crystal of carbonado with the form of a cube is represented in Plate I., Fig. 4. The substance occurs much more frequently, however, in irregular rounded nodules, varying in size from that of a pea to a mass exceeding a pound in weight. The average weight of the nodules is 30 to 40 carats, but specimens weighing from 700 to 800 carats have been occasionally met with. They sometimes have the appearance of being fragments broken from a larger mass, and some show a fine striation similar to that of fibrous coal; this latter feature is believed to be due to friction between several fragments.

The surface lustre of carbonado is dull and sometimes slightly greasy; the interior of the nodule is usually rather brighter and shows numerous brightly shining points. The colour of the exterior always lies between dark grey and black; a fractured surface is a little lighter in colour and shows a tinge of brown, violet, or red.

This substance is but rarely absolutely compact, almost invariably it is more or less markedly porous, so that it is very similar in appearance to coke. When heated in water, numerous air bubbles are expelled from the spaces in the porous material. Its cohesion is usually considerable, but some samples are easily powdered. A microscopic examination of the powdered material shows it to consist of very small octahedra of ordinary diamond, usually semi-transparent, and containing many small opaque inclusions; they are nearly always of a light brown colour and only very rarely water-clear. Carbonado is therefore nothing more than a finely granular, porous to compact aggregate of minute crystals of diamond, and is not, as is sometimes incorrectly stated, amorphous diamond. It differs also from the black diamonds which occur at some localities in regular crystals built up of a uniformly compact substance. Some specimens of carbonado aggregates are penetrated in places by ordinary diamond of a lighter colour, and having the usual strong lustre and non-porous character. Cases are also known of the enclosure in a nodule of carbonado of a small, simple, colourless crystal of diamond, the compact substance of which passes gradually into the porous substance of the carbonado shell, just as do the streaks of paler coloured diamond which sometimes penetrate the dark carbonado. The walls of the cavities in the porous carbonado are sometimes, though rarely, encrusted with minute colourless crystals of diamond.

The largest specimen of carbonado known was found July 15, 1895, in Bahia, in the neighbourhood of the town of Lençoes, between the Rio Rancardor and the stream known as the "Bicas." It is about the size of a man's fist, and when first found weighed 3167 carats; since it was taken from the ground it has gradually lost 19 carats in weight, so that its present weight is 3148 carats, or about 650 grains (nearly $1\frac{1}{2}$ pounds avoirdupois). The heaviest specimen previously known weighed only 1700 carats, and was of inferior quality.

The essential constituent of carbonado, as of ordinary diamond, is carbon; the former, however, contains a much larger amount of impurity than does the latter. After combustion, this impurity remains behind as an incombustible residue, and sometimes forms a skeleton outline of the original fragment or nodule of carbonado. The amount of incombustible ash varies from $\frac{1}{4}$ to over 4 per cent. of the weight of the carbonado burnt. Three specimens examined by Rivot contained 96·84, 99·10, and 99·73 per cent. of carbon, and 2·03, 0·27, and 0·24 per cent. of ash respectively. This ash resembled in appearance a yellow, ferruginous clay, and enclosed microscopic crystals of an undetermined substance. By treating finely-powdered carbonado with aqua regia a portion of the mineral matter constituting the ash may be dissolved out, the solution being found to contain iron and a little calcium, but no aluminium or sulphuric acid. Dana gives as the composition of carbonado: carbon 97, hydrogen 0·5, oxygen 1·5 per cent.; the presence of the last two constituents, however, requires confirmation. The view has been expressed that carbonado is a mixture of crystallised and amorphous carbon, but it is not supported by a microscopical examination of the material.

The hardness of carbonado not only equals that of diamond, but may even exceed it, and its hardness is supposed to be greater the less distinctly it is crystalline. Carbonado cannot therefore be cut by ordinary diamond powder, or at least only with extreme difficulty; it forms a valuable cutting material for ordinary diamonds, and large quantities are used as a grinding material for this and other purposes which require exceptionally hard material. On account of its great hardness, combined with the absence of cleavage (in the mass), carbonado is specially suitable for the rock-drills of boring machinery; moreover, it possesses another advantage over the diamond in that it can be easily shaped into any required form and size, while with ordinary diamond either a natural crystal or a cleavage fragment must be used.

The specific gravity of carbonado is, on account of its porous nature, lower than that of diamond crystals. The values 3·012, 3·141, 3·255, 3·416, &c., have been determined; the last three of these values were determined with the three specimens of which the chemical composition is given above, and in the same order. Carbonado, when reduced to powder, has of course the same specific gravity as ordinary diamond.

That the occurrence of carbonado is almost entirely confined to the district of the Serra da Cincorá has already been mentioned. It was found for the first time in the year 1843 in the "gupiarras" of the river San José, and all the carbonado required for technical purposes is derived from this source. In Minas Geraes carbonado may be said to be completely absent; in South Africa it is present in very small amount; and in India and Australia no trace of it has been met with. In the diamond sands of Borneo it is less rare, and here are to be found nodules of carbonado enclosed by a shell of colourless diamond. In every locality in which it occurs this black, porous variety of diamond is associated with crystals of the usual kind, they are found in the same rocks, and have no doubt a common origin and mode of formation.

The production of carbonado in the Serra da Cincorá, which in former times was considerable, has now appreciably diminished, being scarcely more than 350 grams per month. This, and its ever increasing application for technical purposes, has caused a tremendous rise in price. When first found little use was made of it, and it could be bought for about 2½d. per gram; now, however, for ordinary qualities the same weight costs 32s. and the better qualities 80s., and the price shows a tendency to rise still higher.

Diamonds in considerable numbers have also been found in the southern part of the State of Bahia, near the border of Minas Geraes. This district may be regarded as a continuation in a north-easterly direction through Grão Mogol of the diamond-fields of Diamantina. The stones are found near Salobro (signifying brackish) in the alluvial deposits of the Rio Pardo. This river and the diamantiferous river Jequetinhonha (Rio Belmonte) both empty themselves into the Atlantic Ocean at the foot of the Serra do Mar and near the small haven of **Canavieiras**. The mines are about two days' journey inland from this seaport town, and from it they derive their name of the Canavieiras mines.

The discovery of diamonds here was made in 1881 or 1882 by a forester who had previously searched for diamonds in other districts. Scarcely was the occurrence made known, when the virgin forest, in spite of the unhealthy malarial climate, became peopled by 3000 or more diamond miners. The treasure was obtained at a depth of two feet below a white clay containing decomposing vegetable matter, so that the deposit is a very recent one. The diamantiferous stratum is much more clayey than any in Minas Geraes; it has throughout the character of a plateau-deposit. Diamonds are also found in the rivers Salobro and Salobrinho, tributaries of the Rio Pardo, especially in the "gupiarras" or valley-deposits lying above the present high-water level, just as in the valleys about Diamantina.

The minerals associated with the diamond in these clays are not only less in amount but also differ in kind to a certain extent from those found in Minas Geraes. Monazite in yellowish and reddish broken crystal fragments is present in abundance, also zircon, usually brownish to white in colour, but sometimes violet, and in addition kyanite, staurolite, almandine, hæmatite, ilmenite, magnetite, iron-pyrites, and a somewhat considerable amount of corundum. The occurrence of corundum is remarkable, as hitherto it has been found in no other Brazilian deposit, while all the other minerals mentioned do occur in association with diamond in various parts of Brazil. We may contrast with the occurrence here of corundum the complete absence of certain minerals, which in other parts of Brazil are frequently found with diamond, namely, rutile, anatase, tourmaline, and the hydro-phosphates.

As regards the origin of the diamonds found here, it has been supposed that they are derived from the gneiss, granite, and other ancient crystalline rocks of the neighbouring coast range, the Serra do Mar. In the diamantiferous deposit, however, there is no trace of felspar or mica, two essential constituents of these rocks; moreover, the minerals chrysoberyl, andalusite, tourmaline, beryl, &c., which are frequently present in such rocks in Brazil, are also conspicuous by their absence from these deposits, so that this suggested origin for the diamond seems decidedly doubtful. For a satisfactory determination of the mother-rock of these diamonds, further investigation is required; in any case, it does not seem to be itacolumite, since this rock has not been observed in any part of the surrounding district.

Immediately after their discovery, the yield of these mines was so abundant that other diamond districts became more or less deserted. The stones are distinguished by great purity and freedom from colour, as well as by their very regular octahedral form, which obviates any necessity for preliminary cleaving, and enables them to be cut at once. For a time these mines supplied a large proportion of the total Brazilian output; they may not, however, have been as rich as they appeared, for it has been asserted that many Cape diamonds were sent to Canavieiras in order to be put on the market as Brazilian stones and so command a higher price, just as in former times Brazilian stones were shipped to India to enter the market as Indian stones. At the present time the yield, compared with what it once was, has fallen off considerably, the deposit being now almost exhausted. The same is true to a greater or less extent for all the known diamond-fields of Brazil, and generally speaking it may be said that all are now worked to only a small extent.

Brazilian diamonds, generally considered, show certain characters which are common to all diamonds, but possess other characteristics peculiar to themselves which enable an expert to recognise their Brazilian origin and sometimes even to name the actual district in which they were mined.

In **size** Brazilian diamonds are almost invariably small, being surpassed in this respect by Indian and especially by South African stones, many of which are above the average size. The average weight of Brazilian stones is $\frac{1}{4}$ carat or perhaps less. Large numbers of diamonds smaller in size than the head of an ordinary pin are lost in the process of washing, their size not being sufficient to repay the trouble of collecting. Stones the weight of which lies between $\frac{1}{4}$ and $\frac{1}{2}$ carat are frequent, those varying in weight from 1 to 5 or 6 carats are rare, and the occurrence of still larger stones most unusual. In Diamantina, when the yield was most abundant, only two or three stones of 16 to 20 carats were found yearly, and several years might elapse before the discovery of one of still larger size. Generally speaking, a lot of 10,000 Brazilian stones will contain only one stone of 20 carats, while 8000 of them will weigh but one carat or less each. From 1772 to 1830, the period during which the mines were under Government management, only eighty stones exceeding an oitava (= 17½ carats) were secured by rightful owners; what may have been stolen is, of course, not known.

The largest Brazilian diamond is the "Star of the South," or "Southern Star" (Fig. 48), which was unearthed in the fifties at Bagagem. In its rough condition it weighed 254½ carats, and when cut as a brilliant 125 carats. A stone of 138½ carats was found in the Rio Abaété, and one of 120⅜ carats in the Caxoeira Rica near Bagagem, while one of 107 carats was reported from Tabacos on the Rio das Velhas. No other stones exceeding 100 carats have been heard of. The famous "Braganza" of the Portuguese crown jewels, a reputed diamond as large as a hen's egg and weighing 1680 carats, is probably only a pebble of transparent, colourless topaz; accurate information on the subject cannot, how-ever, for obvious reasons, be obtained from the Portuguese Government.

The **crystalline form** of Brazilian diamonds is by no means constant, varying in stones from different districts. Moreover, stones from different localities are not equally regular in form, those from the Cincorá district, for example, being more distorted and misshapen than stones from Minas Geraes or Salobro.

Generally speaking, the principal forms for all localities are the rhombic dodecahedron and the hexakis-octahedron, both having rounded faces and often deviating considerably from the ideal form (Fig. 31, c to f.) The octahedron, which is rare, is also frequently distorted, sometimes appearing in the form of triangular plates. The predomination of cube faces (Fig. 31 a) is especially characteristic of Brazilian crystals; such forms are very frequent here, but rare in other countries. The tetrahedron and other hemihedral forms, especially the hexakis-tetrahedron (Fig. 31 k), are only rarely found; twinned rhombic dodecahedra (Fig. 31 h) occur frequently; twinned octahedra (Fig. 31 g) are, on the other hand, rare.

Irregular intergrowths of diamond crystals are frequently met with; indeed the famous "Star of the South" formed part of such an intergrowth, since its rough surface showed several impressions of smaller diamonds. Nodules of bort occur not infrequently; often they are almost perfectly spherical in form (Plate I., Fig. 3), the surface, however, being rough owing to the projection of the corners of the small octahedral crystals which build up the radial aggregate. On the whole, about one-fourth of Brazilian stones are useless as gems; these are also described as "bort" and are applied to technical purposes.

The surface of a rough diamond, that is of the natural crystal, is either smooth and shining, or rough, striated, and dull. Rough stones are usually opaque or translucent, but are sometimes completely transparent; in the latter case they exhibit a fine play of prismatic colours, such as is usually only apparent after cutting. The peculiar surface lustre, characteristic of stones from Matto Grosso, has been previously mentioned; it is found on no other Brazilian diamonds. Diamonds penetrated in all directions by cavities, so that their structure comes to resemble that of pumice-stone, are occasionally met with. Regularly formed depressions may sometimes be seen on the surface of a crystal; very frequently these depressions have the shape of crystals of quartz and must have been formed by the diamond resting during its growth on a quartz crystal. Diamond crystals showing evidences of contact with other minerals have been often described; the "Star of the South" (Fig. 48) is undoubtedly such a crystal, the broad under surface being very probably the area by which it was attached to the parent rock.

The **colour** and the qualities depending on this feature vary considerably, differing in different localities. About 40 per cent. of Brazilian diamonds are completely colourless and of these 25 per cent. are of the purest water and the first quality, the beautiful and highly prized " blue-white " being not of very great rarity. About 30 per cent. show a slight tinge of colour, and though the remaining 30 per cent. have a pronounced colour, stones of a deep and beautiful shade are rare. Next to colourless stones, those of a dull whitish or greyish tint occur most frequently. The lighter tones of colour are, as we have already seen, frequently confined to the surface of the crystal, which may be removed by grinding or by the simpler process of burning, and thus the colourless heart of the crystal obtained. Such stones, and also those in which the colour is confined to the edges and corners, have been found in the district of Diamantina and especially in that of the Rio Pardo and the Serra da Cincorá. Deep tints of colour usually permeate the whole substance of the stone. Diamonds which are differently coloured in different parts have also been met with. The enclosure of foreign bodies in diamonds is frequently seen ; these may be dark in colour or black, and sometimes resemble the moss-like markings of a moss-agate. The colours which have been observed in Brazilian stones are yellow, red, brown, green, grey, and various shades of black ; blue is rare, but a few stones showing a beautiful shade of this colour are said to have been found.

Passing now to the consideration of the general quality of Brazilian stones, it may be stated that this on the whole is good, and surpasses that of Cape diamonds, which, as a rule, have a yellowish tinge. The quality of Brazilian stones very nearly approaches that of Indian diamonds, the best " blue-white " Brazilian diamonds being in no way inferior to the choicest of Indian stones.

The various diamond localities of Brazil do not, however, produce stones of uniform quality ; the largest, most beautiful, and those most free from colour, have been found at Bagagem. All the stones mined here do not by any means, however, tally with the above description, many are coloured brown or black, and besides their undesirable colour often exhibit an irregularity of form and numerous other small faults which combine to render them of little value. The stones from the Canavieiras mines stand next in order of quality to those from Bagagem. These, though small, possess a perfect whiteness, few faults, and great regularity of form ; by daylight they exhibit a fine lustre and play of prismatic colours ; by artificial light, however, these qualities are less marked and the stones compare unfavourably with Cape diamonds. Diamantina takes the third place in the quality of the diamonds it produces, and stones from different localities in the district show certain differences among themselves which are well known to the inhabitants ; thus some mines yield white stones exclusively, others yield only coloured stones ; the latter, as a rule, predominate ; the same applies also to the district of Grão Mogol. Diamonds from the Cincorá district rank lowest of all ; three-fourths of these are coloured, almost all are of irregular forms unfavourable for cutting, and about one-half are fit only to be used as bort. The colour of diamonds from Bagagem and Canavieiras is confined to the surface, which is usually bright and only very seldom dull. The surface of stones from Diamantina is not infrequently decidedly rough, it is seldom bright except when the stones have the form of a regularly developed octahedron.

The **production** of Brazilian diamonds has from the time of their discovery, about 1725, been very considerable. For the eighteenth century and the early decades of the nineteenth century exact official returns were given, but for the years immediately following the first discovery, and also for quite recent years, no absolutely reliable records exist, and the various statements which are met with are based on more or less inaccurate estimates. The official returns account only for stones acquired in a legitimate manner and, of course, leave out of the calculation such as have been surreptitiously mined or obtained by dishonest means. W. L. von Eschwege, at one time chief mining inspector in Brazil, estimated the contraband product to have been at least as large as the legitimate output, while other estimates place it at one-fifth or one-third of this.

The same authority, W. L. von Eschwege, estimated the yearly production between 1730 and 1740 at 20,000 carats, but for the first twenty years he gives the annual production as 144,000 carats, probably in this estimate making an allowance for smuggled stones. According to the official returns, the total production between 1740 and 1772 was 1,666,569 carats, corresponding to an average yearly production of about 52,000 carats, while between 1772 and 1806 the total of 910,511½ carats, corresponded to a yearly average of about 26,800 carats. For the latter period, 1772 to 1806, F. dos Santos gives the total production as 1,030,305 carats. The production even thus early had therefore considerably fallen off, and was still further diminished during the period between 1811 and 1822, when it stood at 12,000 carats. The total legitimate production of diamonds in Brazil from 1730 to 1822 is estimated by von Eschwege to be 2,983,691⅓ carats. From the first discovery to the year 1850 the total output is given as 10,169,586 carats, or about two tons, and is valued at £15,825,000. Of this, at least 5,844,000 carats, valued at £9,000,000, that is, more than half, has been contributed by the State of Minas Geraes alone.

In 1850 and 1851, in consequence of the discovery of the Cincorá mines, there was a very heavy production, namely, 300,000 carats per annum, but in 1852 it had sunk to 130,000 carats. From 1851 to 1856 the average yearly yield was 196,200 carats; from 1856 to 1861 it was 184,200 carats; and during the following years remained about the same in amount. In 1858 the leading diamond merchant of the country estimated the average annual output for all previous years at about 90,000 carats, of which 36,000 came from Minas Geraes and 54,000 from Bahia. In 1860 and 1861 the yield appears to have again risen.

For more recent times Boutan gives the following totals compiled from information derived from various sources: Diamantina from 1843 to 1885, 1,500,000 carats; other localities in Minas Geraes, together with Goyaz, Matto Grosso, &c., up to 1885, 1,500,000 (?) carats. Chapada in Bahia from 1840 to 1850, 100,000 carats; from 1850 to 1885, 1,500,000 carats. Since diamond-mining ceased to be a Government monopoly, no official records of the production have been kept; the data given above have therefore been compiled from the records of the amounts paid as export duties on diamonds and may be regarded as coming somewhere near the truth, since the number of diamonds exported does not differ widely from the number mined.

The marked fluctuations in the yearly averages, which will be observed on studying the numbers quoted above, are due to the exhaustion of old deposits and the discovery of new ones. Thus the rise in the yield which has recently taken place is due to the discovery of the Canavieiras mines, and it may be reasonably expected that in the future similar new and rich deposits will be discovered, which will have the effect of again raising the total yield. The enormous and steady production of the South African diamond-fields naturally makes the prospector less eager to start in search for new Brazilian deposits. Such, however, may be at any time accidentally discovered, as has, in former times, frequently happened, especially in Bahia.

3. SOUTH AFRICA.

The diamond mines of South Africa are, at the present day, by far the most important and richest in the whole world; at least nine-tenths of the diamonds now marketed being the so-called Cape stones. The diamond markets of the world are now completely controlled by the owners of the South African mines, the output from Brazilian, and especially from Indian, mines being so insignificant in comparison that their effect on the market is inappreciable.

The first exact scientific account of the Cape diamond-fields is due to Professor Emil Cohen, who visited the region in 1872, and his observations are still of great importance. Numerous other inquirers have continued his investigations and have cleared up many details, but no essentially novel theories have been advanced. Comprehensive accounts of these deposits have been published by Moulle, Chaper, Boutan, Reunert, Stelzner, and others, and the details given below are taken from the original works of these and other investigators. A map of the South African diamond-fields is given in Fig. 37.

Diamonds were first found in this region in the year 1867, reported discoveries at dates preceding this—for example, in the eighteenth century—being, for the most part, unfounded. Many versions of the circumstances under which the first discovery was made are in existence. According to one, a traveller of the name of O'Reilly saw a child playing with a bright and shining stone in the house of a Boer by name Jacobs, whose farm, " De Kalb," was situated a little to the south of the Orange River, and not far from Hopetown. This stone the traveller showed to Dr. W. Guybon Atherstone at Grahamstown, who determined it to be a diamond crystal weighing $21\frac{3}{16}$ carats. After being exhibited at the Paris Exhibition of 1867 it was purchased for £500 by Sir Philip E. Wodehouse, then Governor of Cape Colony. O'Reilly obtained from the same Boer a second stone weighing $8\frac{7}{8}$ carats, which had also been accidentally found on his farm ; this also passed into the possession of the Governor of the Colony at a price of £200.

According to another version, the diamond of $21\frac{3}{16}$ carats, the Boer child's plaything, first passed into the hands of Schalk van Niekerk, a Boer who was otherwise connected with the history of the discovery of diamonds in South Africa, since in 1869 he obtained from a Kaffir a stone of $83\frac{1}{2}$ carats, which came into the market under the name of the " Star of South Africa." Schalk van Niekerk is said to have handed over the stone previously obtained to O'Reilly for determination. In any case, it seems to have been the latter who took the initiative in identifying the stones, and thus firmly establishing the occurrence of the diamond in South Africa, so that to him is due all the credit of the discovery.

Scarcely had these events been made known, when the Boers living in the neighbourhood of Hopetown commenced a vigorous search for diamonds. They were rewarded by the discovery of a few scattered stones, but there was no rich, continued yield such as is characteristic of a regular deposit. The searchers soon extended themselves over a wider area, and in the year 1868 the workings on the Vaal River were commenced, and here the yield was much greater. The first actual diamond deposit was met with in 1869, in the neighbourhood of the places now bearing the names of Pniel and Barkly West.

In the years which followed, news of the finds of diamonds gradually spread in Cape Colony, and soon diamond-diggers from the four corners of the earth congregated on the banks of the Orange and Vaal Rivers. Reported rich discoveries attracted miners to the spot in still larger numbers, in spite of the long and toilsome journey across the arid Karoo region, where, in the dry winter season, the region is more than ordinarily barren and inhospitable, and the route is marked out by the bodies of beasts of burden which have perished by the way. Two years after the first discovery of diamonds, namely, in 1869, this previously uninhabited district became peopled by a white population of 1000 souls. These settled on the Vaal River at Pniel and Klipdrift, the latter now known as Barkly West. Here they washed the surface sands of the river for diamonds, and some time elapsed before any systematic digging operations were undertaken.

It was soon discovered, however, that in this region diamonds were by no means confined to the river sands. In December 1870, a digger from the Vaal observed that the children of a Boer, whose farm, "Vooruitzigt," was situated (Fig. 38) on the plateau

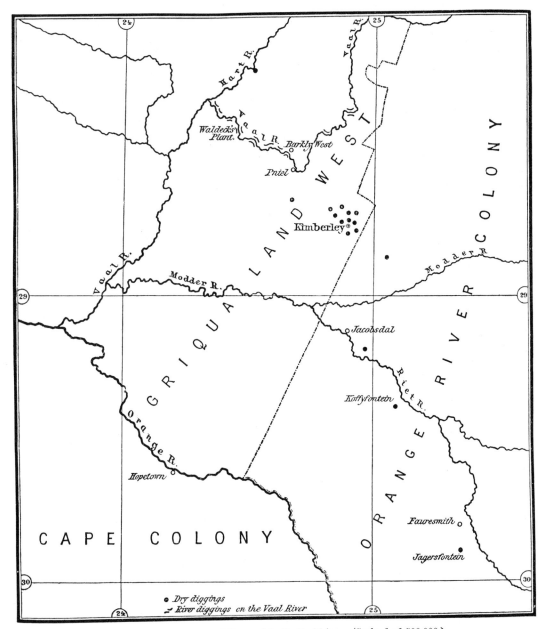

FIG. 37.   Occurrence of diamond in South Africa.   (Scale, 1 : 1,500,000.)

between the Vaal and Modder rivers, and about fifteen miles south of the former, had collected in the neighbourhood a number of small diamonds, of the true nature of which, however, they were ignorant. According to another story, van Wyk, a Boer who lived at "Du Toit's Pan" farm, situated in the same neighbourhood, discovered diamonds in the walls of his dwelling-house which had been built of mud dug out from a neighbouring pond. Both stories end in the same way; these accidental finds stimulated further search, which resulted in the discovery of the mine now known as Du Toit's Pan mine (also written Dutoitspan), the first of the four famous mines of Kimberley, the town which sprang up at this spot and became the centre of the diamond-mining industry.

A great influx of people or "rush" to the newly discovered locality at once took place. These newcomers proved a source of great irritation to the Boers in possession of the land, who, seeing that it was impossible to dislodge their unwelcome visitors, sold their valuable possession to an English Company for £6000, a ridiculously low sum considering the discoveries that had been made and were to be expected. The conditions under which the eager searchers for treasure had to work were indeed harassing; exposed to all the intensity of the hot African sun, tormented by storms of dust and insects, deprived of many of the necessaries of life, obliged to fetch drinking water from a great distance, and, for the lack of more permanent dwellings, forced to camp out in the open, their lot was no enviable one, and numbers perished of want and privation. The survivors had no cause, however, for disheartenment in the yield of the deposit; new finds were constantly made, and the conditions of life gradually improved.

Soon another rich deposit, only about half a mile from Du Toit's Pan, was discovered, and became known as the Bultfontein mine, while still another on the farm, " Vooruitzigt," of a Boer named de Beer, who himself commenced mining operations, became the famous " Old de Beer's mine," or, shortly, De Beer's mine (often written De Beers). Finally, on July 21, 1871, a new discovery was made close to the last mentioned mine; this was at first known as " Old de Beer's New Rush," or as the " Colesberg Kopje." Later, however, it became known as the Kimberley mine, and proved to be the richest of the whole group. These four mines, which still form the nucleus of the diamond-producing area, are all situated close to the town of Kimberley, which was founded by the diamond miners, and which has now a white population of 30,000. Two miles to the south-west of Kimberley is the suburb of Beaconsfield with 10,000 to 11,000 inhabitants. The situation of the mines is shown in Fig. 38; they all lie in a circular area not more than three miles in diameter, and besides the four important deposits there are half a dozen others too insignificant to be worked to any extent.

After the first accidental discovery had drawn attention to the occurrence of diamond here, the four important mines mentioned above were all discovered in the course of six months. Very soon following these discoveries, other but less important deposits were found to the south of Kimberley, namely, the Jagersfontein mine near Fauresmith and the Koffyfontein mine on the Riet River between Jacobsdal and Fauresmith, both in the Orange River Colony. The Jagersfontein mine was discovered almost simultaneously with the Kimberley mine, from which it is situated about eighty miles distant. Practically the whole of the present enormous production of diamonds in South Africa is derived from these six mines and from the washings on the Vaal River.

The method of winning diamonds in these mines furnishes a great contrast to the work of collecting them from the river sands. In the latter case the sands are washed in a manner similar to that employed in Brazil and India. In early days on the arid and waterless plateau of Kimberley, the stones were picked out of the dry fragmented rock, such workings being known as " dry diggings," to distinguish them from the " river diggings " on the Vaal. These terms are still in use, but the former is now somewhat inappropriate, as at the " dry diggings " water is now also used to separate the diamonds from their matrix.

All the diamond mines of South Africa, which are of any importance, lie to the north of the Orange River, and are confined to a comparatively limited area, as may be seen by reference to the map (Fig. 37). They are situated in the stretch of country lying between the line of longitude 26° E. of Greenwich and the fork of the Orange and the Vaal rivers, the two principal water-courses of South Africa. The north or right-hand bank of the Vaal must, however, be also included, and the very first discovery of diamonds in South Africa was made a few miles to the south of the Orange River. All the known mines and washings lie in a quadrangle bounded by parallels of latitude 28° and 30° S., and by meridians of longitude 24° and 26° E. The town of Kimberley lies very near the centre of

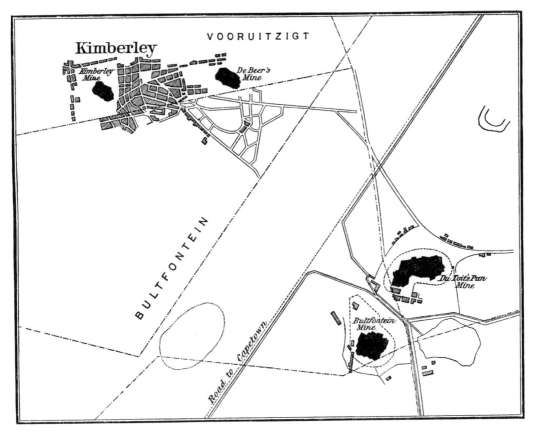

FIG. 38. Diamond mines at Kimberley. (Scale, 1 : 40,000.)

this quadrangle, and the boundary between Cape Colony and the Orange River Colony very nearly coincides with the north-east and south-west diagonal. The Kimberley mines are not only central in position but also in importance, for they supply 90 per cent. of the total output of South African diamonds.

The diamond localities of this district (with the exception of the washings on the Vaal River) are situated on an almost straight line, 125 miles in length, running north-north-west and south-south-east, from the confluence of the Hart River with the Vaal, to beyond Fauresmith in the Orange River Colony. On this line, about fifteen miles from the Vaal, Kimberley is situated in latitude 28° 42′ 54″ S., and longitude 24° 50′ 15″ E., of Greenwich, at a height of 4050 feet (1230 metres) above sea-level. Koffyfontein is about forty miles, and Jagersfontein about double this distance, from Kimberley. A stone of 70 carats was once picked up at Mamusa, on the far side of Jagersfontein, but the find has remained an isolated one.

Outside this district no diamonds have been found; within the district they are confined to a few isolated points, some of which have not yet been properly investigated, since, the yield being poor, they were abandoned almost as soon as they were discovered.

False assertions as to the occurrence of rich deposits in certain localities have sometimes been made with the sole object of attracting diamond miners, thus promoting the sale of food and spirituous liquors, and incidentally enriching the vendors thereof; a flocking together of miners attracted by such assertions is known as a "canteen rush."

The mines mentioned above, from which rich yields are at the present time derived, were all known as far back as 1872. Since that time other districts have been vigorously prospected, but without success; still the region is extensive enough to warrant the belief that fresh discoveries may yet be made, especially as in 1891 a new deposit was found in the Kimberley district, one mile east of Du Toit's Pan, on the farm "Benauwdheidfontein," of J. J. Wessels, senior. This deposit lies under a thick layer of calcareous tufa, and the mine known as the Wesselton or Premier mine promises to become of importance.

Before the discovery of diamonds the whole of this now important stretch of country was almost valueless, and was peopled by only a few hunters and Boers, who derived a meagre living from its scanty vegetation, and whose lot no one was inclined to envy. There were thus in this region no rigidly defined spheres of influence, and when it suddenly acquired an enormous value and importance complications arose in the shape of rival claims, various portions being asserted to be the property of the Orange Free State, the Transvaal, or of native chiefs. In 1870 the diamond-fields near Pniel, on the Vaal River, were proclaimed as British territory, on behalf of a native chief who had ceded his rights to Great Britain, and on November 17, 1871, the British flag was hoisted at Kimberley. The matter was formally settled in July 1876, by the London Convention, according to which the Government of the Orange Free State agreed to give up its claim to the diamond-fields in consideration of a payment of £90,000 from the British Government. Griqualand West, the division in which Kimberley is situated, remained a Crown Colony until October 1880, when it was formally incorporated in Cape Colony. In it are situated all the rich diamond mines of South Africa, with the exception of the Koffyfontein and Jagersfontein mines, which are in the Orange River Colony, but which yield only about 6 to 7 per cent. of the total South African output.

Not only has the discovery of the precious gem enormously increased the importance of South Africa as a country, but it has also so raised the value of the comparatively small plots of land on which the mines stand, as to make a comparison between their present and their former values of interest. Thus the farm "Vooruitzigt," on which now stand the De Beer's and Kimberley mines, was bought from its owner in 1871, the time of the discovery of diamonds there, for £6000, while only four years later £100,000 was paid for it by the Cape Government, the transfer being made with the object of putting an end to the frequent and ever arising disputes between the mine-owners and the miners as to the dues to be paid by the latter to the former.

It is now intended to consider the different deposits in more detail, commencing not with the most important but with those first discovered, namely, the river diggings.

River Diggings.

The richest of these deposits lie on both banks of that portion of the Vaal River flowing between the mission stations, Pniel and Barkly West (formerly Klipdrift), to the east, and Delport's Hope, at the junction of the Vaal with the Hart River, to the west, Barkly West being at the present day the centre of the diamond-washing industry. In addition, diamonds have been found in small numbers further up the river at Hebron, and even as far as Bloemhof and Christiana in the Transvaal ; also in the opposite direction, at the junction of the Vaal with the Orange River. A few diamonds have also been found in the Orange River, between its confluence with the Vaal and Hopetown, as well as in some of the tributaries of the Vaal, notably the Modder and the Vet. The yield in all these places was, however, so poor that the workings were soon all abandoned except the portion of the Vaal River mentioned above, and a stretch of its valley, parallel to the same portion of the river, and measuring fifty miles in a straight line, or seventy-two following the windings of the river. At the present day whole series of mines even in this region are practically deserted, the workers having left the river for the far richer dry diggings of Kimberley. The production of the river diggings up to 1871 was of some importance, but is now quite insignificant ; in spite of the poorness of the yield, and the miserable conditions under which they have to work, a small number of a certain peculiar class of diamond-miners still cling tenaciously to their holdings in the hope no doubt of better days coming. Counting both black and white men, their number for many years probably did not exceed two or three hundred ; they work singly or in twos or threes, not in large companies, and are most frequently to be seen in the neighbourhood of New Gong-Gong, Waldeck's Plant, and Newkerke. The amalgamation of the "dry diggings" to form the De Beers Consolidated Mines, has had the effect of increasing the number of river diggers, it being estimated that there are now 1000 of them, exclusive of native workers. Companies have been formed with the object of working the deeper beds of river sand, but have met with little success. The river-diggings, on account of their poor yield, are known as "poor men's diggings."

The bed of the Vaal is strewn with blocks of basalt, often amygdaloidal in character, and with other rocks which are probably of metamorphic origin. These blocks are usually of considerable size, and have been washed down from the sides of the valley and from the surrounding hills ; between them lies a loose material consisting of gravel, sand, and mud, and it is in this that the diamonds are found. The whole deposit, which varies in thickness up to 40 feet, rests on basalt, this rock being *in situ,* and is here and there scooped out to form deep hollows, known as pot-holes or "giant's-kettles," similar to those found in the beds of the diamond-bearing rivers of Brazil, which have been worn out by the continued whirling of pebbles in the eddies of the stream. The diamond-bearing débris accumulates in these depressions, which often yield a rich harvest to the finder.

The search for diamonds was at first confined to the bed of the river, but it was soon discovered that the sands and gravels of the river-terraces were as rich or richer than the river-bed, so that these also came to be worked. The terraces and their workings are usually only a few yards above the present high-water level, but one or two are 200 feet above this level. The workings in the river-terraces are easier to manage and more secure than those in the river-bed, since the latter are liable to be flooded, and thus considerably damaged ; it has, therefore, been proposed in recent times that the stream should be diverted into another channel, but this scheme has never yet been carried out.

The diamonds found in this sandy clay are, as a rule, distinctly water-worn, though not of course to the extent of the other pebbles and sand grains which accompany them. These accompanying pebbles consist of various minerals, the different varieties of quartz (agate, jasper, silicified wood, &c.), which have all travelled down from the upper courses of the river, being especially abundant. Pebbles of the rocks which occur *in situ* in the neighbourhood are present in large numbers in these alluvial deposits. The minerals which are associated with the diamond in the dry diggings are less abundant, but small fragments of garnet, ilmenite, vaalite, &c., are met with. It is among these pebbles that the diamond is to be found; its distribution is, however, extremely irregular, a miner who hits on a favourable spot may make his fortune in a very short time, while his comrades toil on month after month unrewarded by the smallest success.

The method of work does not differ essentially from that followed in the diamond-washings of other countries or in the gold-washings of the same country. The sand and clay in which the diamonds and other pebbles are embedded, must first be excavated; this, when the diamantiferous material is overlain by blocks of basalt, &c., of considerable size, is no light task. This material is placed in a cradle, and the clay and fine particles washed away by rocking the cradle under a stream of running water; what remains after this process is put through a sieve, and the coarse residue, which contains the diamonds, is spread out on a sorting table and the diamonds picked out by hand. This final operation is easily performed, for the peculiar lustre of diamonds enables a practised sorter at once to distinguish them from other pebbles.

The yield is not very great, only on an average about 15,000 or 20,000 carats a year; in 1890, however, 28,122⅔ carats, valued at £79,231, were obtained; a production of 30,000 carats (about 13 lbs. avoirdupois), is seldom reached, and never exceeded.

The quality of the yield in part compensates for its small quantity, stones from the river diggings being on the average far superior to those from the dry diggings. The average value of the former is in consequence much higher than that of the latter; for example, in the eighties a river-stone weighing one carat was worth 56s., while a carat stone from Kimberley only fetched on an average 22s. 9d.

A few specially large stones have been secured in the river diggings, such, for example, as the "Star of South Africa," a diamond of the purest water, weighing, in its rough condition, 83½ carats; also the slightly yellow "Stewart," weighing 288⅜ carats, which was found at Waldeck's Plant on the Vaal River.

The sands and gravels in which the diamonds are found in the river diggings are secondary deposits. It has been suggested that these sands and gravels have been derived from a deposit similar to that in which diamonds are now found in the dry diggings, and situated somewhere in the neighbourhood of the source of the Vaal River. The denudation of such a deposit would supply the diamantiferous débris carried down by the river. That the diamonds have been transported some distance is shown by their distinctly water-worn character, and in all probability the original deposit was situated somewhere below Bloemhof in the Transvaal, since no diamonds have been found above this town. The fact that very few of the minerals associated with the diamond in the dry diggings occur in the Vaal River is easily explained when we consider that these minerals are not very hard and would be reduced to powder before they had been transported any great distance by the running water; whereas the harder minerals, found in the basin of the upper part of the Vaal, and now associated in the river deposit with diamonds, would resist the action of the water for a longer period and would be transported over greater distances. Furthermore it is possible that the characteristic minerals of the dry diggings now known may have been of sparing occurrence in these original deposits, if not indeed absent altogether. The higher quality of the river stones as compared with those from the dry diggings does not militate against the truth of this theory as to their origin, since the quality of stones found in the Jagersfontein dry diggings is well above the average; it simply leads to the conclusion that the deposit from which the river sands and gravels were derived was also above the average in quality.

Dry Diggings.

The nature of these deposits was not at first known, and they were supposed to be similar to the river deposit and to consist merely of superficial layers of alluvium. It was soon recognised, however, that this was by no means the case, and that the deposits were absolutely unique in character. The geographical position of these deposits has been already described, they are situated on a high plateau, far removed from any watercourses and formed of rocks belonging to the Karoo formation. This formation, which has a total thickness of about 10,000 feet, consists of sandstones and shales with numerous intruded dykes and bosses of igneous rocks, variously referred to, according to the form of the mass and the character of the rock itself, as trap, dolerite, melaphyre, basalt, diabase, &c. The age of the sedimentary rocks is not exactly known as yet, but in any case they are later than the Carboniferous, the lower beds probably corresponding with the Permian, and the upper beds with the Trias of Europe. In this upper and younger part occur the deposits of diamonds in Griqualand West which we have now to consider.

The account which follows deals mainly with the half-dozen mines having the richest yield, and specially with the four best known Kimberley mines, others being passed over as insignificant or not completely examined. The main features of all are identical, and as the individual deposits differ only in unessential points, it is unnecessary to consider each one singly in any great detail.

The diamond-bearing material is contained in pipes or funnel-shaped depressions which penetrate the Upper Karoo beds in a vertical direction to an unknown depth. The outline of a cross-section of one of these depressions may be circular, elliptical, kidney-shaped, or more or less irregular. The rock which fills these pipes differs entirely from the surrounding beds of the Karoo formation, the so-called "reef," and is sharply separated from them. The occurrence of diamonds is confined exclusively to the material filling the pipes; nowhere in the surrounding reef of sandstone and shale, or elsewhere in the Karoo beds, has a single stone been found, although enormous quantities of these rocks have been removed in the course of the mining operations.

The upper extremities of the pipes are elevated above the surface to the height of a few yards each, thus forming a small kopje; in the case of the Wesselton mine, however, there was a slight depression. The pipes vary in diameter from 20 to 750 yards, the usual diameter being from 200 to 300 yards. In 1892 the diamond-bearing material had been excavated in the Kimberley mine, which is the deepest of all, to a depth of 1261 feet, and, as in the other mines, with no sign of exhaustion; the rock is therefore continued to an unknown depth.

The cross-sections of different pipes taken at the earth's surface differ widely both in shape and area, as will be seen from the following data: Du Toit's Pan (Dutoitspan), 192,000 square yards in area, of a flat horse-shoe shape, 750 yards long and 200 yards broad; Bultfontein, 118,000 square yards in area, almost circular in outline with a diameter of 363 yards; De Beer's (De Beers), 66,000 square yards in area, elliptical in shape, measuring 320 yards from east to west and 210 from north to south; Kimberley, 49,000 square yards in area, oval in shape, 290 yards long and 220 yards broad, with a small projection measuring 37 yards towards the east. The size of the pipe of the Jagersfontein mine is not exactly known, its cross-section is between 100,000 and 110,000 square yards; exact details respecting the Koffyfontein mine are also wanting, but in any case it is smaller than the mine last mentioned. A peculiar feature of the Kimberley mine is the gradual contraction of the pipe in sectional area as greater depths are reached; thus at a depth of about 300 feet the two diameters are reduced to 260 and 160 yards respectively, and the contraction is continued as still lower depths are reached. A diagrammatic section of the Kimberley mine is given in Fig. 39, an explanation of which is given below.

The **rocks composing the reef** are, on the whole, much the same everywhere, still, in the various mines, certain differences do exist.

The neighbourhood for a considerable distance round Kimberley is covered with a layer of red clay, 1 to 5 feet thick; underlying this is a bed from 5 to 20 feet thick of calcareous tufa, also of wide distribution. This tufa is of recent origin and has no genetic connection with either the reef or the diamond-bearing pipes, since it covers both indiscriminately, and to a certain extent penetrates cracks and crevices in them. Beneath this tufa lie the rocks of the Karoo formation which constitute the reef.

The uppermost part of the reef in the Kimberley mine consists of a series of bedded shales, 40 to 50 feet thick, greenish-grey in the upper part and yellowish or greyish in the lower; they are of varying hardness, and at different levels in the mine are interbedded with a fine-grained to compact olivine-basalt. Beneath these pale shales are about 270 feet of black bituminous shales, very similar in character to the shales of the English coal-measures; certain of these beds are impregnated with iron-pyrites, and they often contain nodules of clay-iron-stone, small bands of calcite, and thin layers of coal, while interbedded with them near their base is a sheet of basalt one foot thick. Beneath the black shales is a hard grey or green amygdaloidal diabase (melaphyre), the base of which is not exposed in the open workings, but is seen in the underground shafts at a depth of 440 feet below the upper surface of the mass.

Beneath this igneous rock the shafts penetrate a bed of quartzite of about the same thickness, and under this again black shales, both of which are penetrated in places by dykes of eruptive rock (dolerite). The deepest shaft of the mine has not yet penetrated to the base of the black shales, so that the total thickness of these beds is unknown. Probably at still greater depths, as yet untouched by mining operations, there are deep-seated rocks, such as granite, gneiss, or olivine-rocks, but this question will be discussed later.

In the De Beer's mine, a sheet of basalt 47 to 61 feet in thickness is met with in the upper part of the reef, otherwise the beds are the same as in the Kimberley mine. A similar sheet of basalt is present in Du Toit's Pan mine, but is absent from the Bultfontein mine. The walls of the pipe consist here, as far as they have been laid bare, only of shales, which are much displaced, sometimes having an inclination of at least 15° to the horizon; this is also the case to a certain extent in the De Beer's mine, while in other places the beds are horizontal. In the Du Toit's Pan and Bultfontein mines the shales have not yet been penetrated to their base, and their thickness appears to be greater here than in the Kimberley and De Beer's mines, which lie a little further to the north.

The **material filling the pipes**, like that of the surrounding rock, is essentially the same in every mine, and in every part of each mine, but in all mines the upper portions of the pipes to a fairly considerable depth have suffered the effects of weathering. Observable differences do exist, however, and an experienced miner can sometimes recognise not only from which mine, but also from what part of a particular mine, any given specimen of material has been taken. These small differences are usually connected with variations in colour, hardness, and composition, the nature of the enclosed minerals and fragments of foreign rock, &c., and are, as a rule, unimportant.

The different kinds of rocks constituting the material which fills the pipes are separated by no trace of bedding planes, but masses of rock, slightly different in character have been recently observed to be separated from each other in quite another way.

Vertical, or nearly vertical crevices, not more than three-eighths of an inch across and filled with a mineral substance resembling talc in character, penetrate the material down to the lowest depth to which the mines have been worked.   These divide the whole contents of each pipe into a number of vertical or nearly vertical columns, each differing slightly from the others in composition, but showing no difference in its own mass.

These small variations in the material filling the pipes, as well as its character as a whole, do not depend in any way upon the nature of the various rocks of the surrounding reef. It was formerly contended that the character of the reef had a more or less marked influence on the richness in diamonds of the material filling the pipes ; thus it was feared that when the base of the black shale in the Kimberley mine had been reached, the yield of diamonds would cease, since the formation of diamonds was supposed to have been dependent on some way on the presence of carbon in these shales. In consequence of this belief, the value of mining claims for a time fell ; but the yield of diamonds at lower levels, where the pipe is surrounded by melaphyre, turned out to be just as good as at the higher levels in the shale.

Between the material filling the pipes and the enclosing rocks or reef there is always a sharp line of demarcation and never a gradual transition.

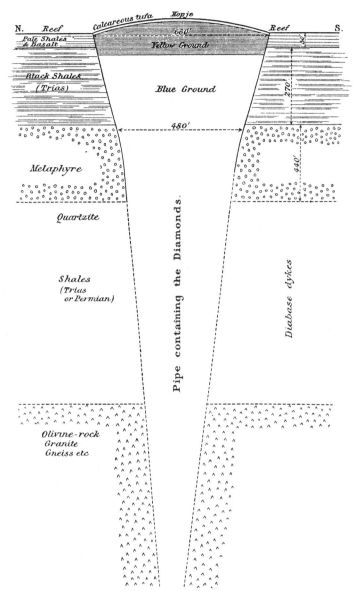

FIG. 30.   Diagrammatic section through the Kimberley mine.
(Scale, 1 : 4,000.)

Usually the two sets of rocks are in immediate contact, but not infrequently they are separated by a space, sometimes of considerable width, into which project beautiful crystals of calcite. Other secondary minerals are also found in the numerous crevices by which, in addition to the vertical cracks, the rock is penetrated.

The actual diamond-bearing rock itself which fills the pipes must now be considered. In the upper portion of the pipes it consists of a light yellow, soft, sandy or friable material known to the diamond miners as " yellow ground " or " yellow stuff." This upper portion, which has a thickness of from 50 to 60 feet, has now, in the Kimberley mine, been completely removed in the course of mining operations; in the other mines, however, a little still remains to be seen. The rock at a greater depth has the character of a volcanic tuff or breccia, it is of a green or bluish-green colour, and is known as the "**blue ground**" or "blue stuff." Throughout the whole depth to which it has been worked it shows no deviation from these characters.

The passage of the "yellow ground" into the "blue ground" is as a rule abrupt, and the line of division is never quite horizontal, but inclined from 5° to 15° to the horizon. Sometimes there is an intermediate reddish layer, known as "rusty ground" which passes upwards into the "yellow ground" and below into the "blue ground." Neither the "yellow ground" nor the "rusty ground" is anything more than the weathered upper portions of the "blue ground;" the latter originally filled the pipes up to the surface, but the portion exposed to atmospheric influences became altered and transformed into what is now known as "yellow ground." Similarly the "rusty ground" is a layer in which the alteration has not proceeded as far as in the "yellow ground"; the uppermost layer, therefore, of "blue ground" marks the level below which the weathering process has not yet commenced. In the early history of the mines, this change in the colour of the diamantiferous material also had the effect of diminishing the value of claims, since it was feared that the "blue ground" might be deficient in yield. Experience of course showed that these apprehensions were groundless, for the rock at greater depths proved as rich, if not richer, than the upper levels.

The "blue ground," which thus fills the pipes, and from which the uppermost "yellow ground" has been derived, has the appearance of dried mud, and consists of a green, or dark bluish-green ground-mass, which gives its colour to the whole rock. It binds together numerous fragments, larger or smaller in size, and with sharp, or in some cases rounded corners, of a green or bluish-black serpentine rock. The actual material of the mud-like ground-mass, and of the blocks which it cements together, is identical, the one being in a finely divided condition, and the other in compact masses. These are the chief constituents of the "blue ground," but it contains also numerous mineral grains as well as fragments of foreign rocks in large numbers. A piece of "blue ground" of its natural colour, and containing a crystal of diamond embedded in it, is depicted in Plate I., Fig. 2.

Although the ground-mass is not very hard, it has a certain amount of toughness which renders it difficult to work with a pick-axe; it readily yields, however, to the chisel. It can be scratched with the finger-nail and is somewhat greasy to the touch. The qualitative chemical composition of the "blue ground" is almost identical throughout the whole mass, but certain differences in the quantitative composition of different portions are detected in analysis. All analyses which have been made of this material record the presence of silica and magnesia in varying amounts, some ferrous oxide, usually only a little lime, some water and carbonic acid, and little or no alumina. The material is thus essentially a mixture of hydrated magnesium silicate and calcium carbonate.

The following is a quantitative analysis of a specimen of "blue ground" from the Kimberley mine given by Professor Maskelyne and Dr. Flight:

	Per cent.
Silica (SiO_2)	39·732
Alumina (Al_2O_3)	2·309
Ferrous oxide (FeO)	9·690
Magnesia (MgO)	24·419
Lime (CaO)	10·162
Carbon dioxide (CO_2)	6·556
Water (H_2O)	7·547
	100·415

The carbon dioxide (carbonic acid) is present in nearly sufficient amount to combine with the whole of the lime to form calcium carbonate; deducting this, the remainder, consisting of hydrated magnesium silicate, with some of the magnesium replaced by ferrous oxide, has approximately the composition of the mineral serpentine. It has thus become customary to speak of the whole rock as a serpentine breccia, and this term, or that of volcanic tuff or agglomerate, will be used in referring to the diamantiferous material.

The blocks of foreign rock embedded in the breccia, which are often known as boulders, have usually perfectly sharp edges and corners, though occasionally these may be rounded. The size of these rock fragments varies from that of a small splinter to that of a block several thousand cubic yards in dimensions. In the pipe of De Beer's mine there is a block of olivine-basalt called "the island," which has a sectional area of 330 square yards, and has been traced to a depth of 237 yards. Large masses of similar rock occur commonly in all the mines, they are referred to as "floating reef," in contradistinction to the "main reef" which surrounds the pipe. This "floating reef" is more frequently met with in the upper than in the lower levels of the pipes. Smaller fragments of the same rock have, however, been met with at the greatest depths to which the mine shafts have been sunk, and here as elsewhere they form a large proportion of the material filling the pipes, through which they are distributed with the greatest irregularity.

Some of the rock fragments agree completely in character with the rocks of the main reef, frequently consisting of amygdaloidal basalt (melaphyre), shales, &c. In some places, the highly bituminous and carbonaceous shales are present in such large amounts that sometimes the presence of the fire-damp characteristic of coal-mines has been observed. It has been asserted that diamonds occur only in those portions of the agglomerate in which bituminous shales are present in large amount, and it has been argued from this that the diamonds were actually formed from the carbonaceous matter present in these shales. There is, however, reason to believe, as will be shown below, that the diamonds were formed not in the pipes themselves, but at far greater depths in the interior of the earth from which they have been brought up by the action of volcanic forces.

Beside the blocks, which have evidently been detached from the reef surrounding the pipes, there are others which have not been found *in situ* in the neighbourhood, and which, therefore, must necessarily have been brought up from below. In the Kimberley mine at depths below 230 feet, there are found large blocks, several cubic yards in extent, of grey or greyish-white sandstone, the grains of which are bound together by a calcareo-argillaceous cement. They are of much the same character as the sandstone which, in other localities, forms part of the Middle Karoo formation, and which from geological considerations must form part of the reef at the Kimberley diamond mines at a great depth below the surface. There also occur, though not so frequently, fragments of quartzite, mica-schist, talc-schist, eclogite, and granite. The last named rock is rarely found, and when met with is so decomposed as to be only doubtfully recognisable as granite. It was found in numerous large blocks, and in smaller fragments in the upper portion of a small mine known as Doyl's Rush about a mile from Kimberley. Such rocks crop out at the surface some distance north of the diamond-fields; it is therefore probable that their southern extension lies at a great depth below Kimberley, and forms the base of the reef. Rock fragments of materials not found in the reef enclosing the pipes, which in all probability have been brought up from below, are called "exotic fragments."

The minerals embedded in the agglomerate are usually distributed through it with some regularity, but very sparingly; they constitute only about $\frac{1}{4000}$ of the total mass of the rock and are therefore rather inconspicuous. A complete collection can only be made from the residue left after the process of diamond-washing.

Among these minerals the most important, but not the most frequently occurring, is the diamond : it is found in crystals developed regularly on all sides, and also in fragments, such as would result from the breakage of larger crystals. It is remarkable, however, that different portions of the same crystal are never found lying close together. The edges and corners of the crystals are always perfectly sharp, not even the faintest trace of rounding can be detected, so the stones of the dry diggings are easily distinguished from those of the river diggings. A more detailed description of the special characteristics of Cape diamonds will be given later, here we are concerned only with their mode of occurrence.

The diamond is a constituent part of the agglomerate in which it is embedded, and its mode of occurrence in no way differs from that of other minerals contained in the rock. Each crystal or fragment of a crystal occurs alone, firmly embedded in the agglomerate, from which it can be extracted only with difficulty ; its surface is usually clean, but in some cases is coated with a layer of limonite (iron hydroxide) or with a calcareous film, both of which are easily removable. Until recently, no diamond had ever been observed attached to another mineral in such a way as to suggest that the two grew side by side at the same time. The discovery, however, of a diamond crystal attached in this way to a garnet shows that such a growth does take place, though rarely.

Diamonds are to be found at the surface, and downwards through the "yellow ground," the " rusty ground," and the " blue ground," as far as the deepest mines have yet penetrated ; they do not occur, however, in equal number in all mines, nor in different portions of the same mine ; numerical details will be given later. In the Kimberley mine, which is unique in this respect, the richness of the yield increases rapidly as lower levels are reached. The different columnar divisions of each pipe vary in the number of diamonds contained, some being so poor that the working of them is unprofitable, others on the contrary being just the reverse. The total number of diamonds contained in a given mass of any particular column is so constant that it is quite possible to calculate beforehand how many carats of stones a certain amount of " blue ground " will yield.

The presence of diamonds in the " blue ground " is of enormous economic importance ; regarded as a rock constituent, however, they are quite insignificant, being present in such small amount that, had they been less highly prized, and of less general interest, they would probably have been scarcely mentioned in a petrographical description of the rock. A striking illustration of their sparing occurrence is furnished by the fact that in the richest part of the richest mine, namely the Kimberley mine, they constitute only one part in two millions, or 0·00005 per cent. of the " blue ground." In other mines the proportion is still lower, namely one part in forty millions, a yield which corresponds to five carats per cubic yard of rock, and which can be profitably worked. When the absolute amount of diamond present is so small, slight variations in this amount in different parts of the rock, though of great economic importance, are of little scientific significance.

In respect to the **associated minerals** of the diamond in the agglomerate, certain differences exist between the various mines and between different parts of the same mine. These minerals occur either in homogeneous grains of the same kind, or in small groups consisting of minerals of various kinds. Those of most frequent occurrence are red garnet, green enstatite, and vaalite (an altered mica), others are less widely distributed, some indeed being regarded as great rarities. The most important of the minerals associated with the diamond in these deposits will be now considered in order.

The garnet is of constant occurrence, and always in relatively considerable amounts.

It is found in the form of rounded or angular grains, crystals, or even indications of crystalline form, being never observed. The grains are usually in a fresh and unaltered state, and therefore appear bright and transparent, some, however, are cloudy and opaque, and of a reddish-brown colour, in consequence of a process of decomposition having commenced. The colour of the unaltered garnets is variable, a deep wine- or hyacinth-red is most frequent, red tinged with violet is less common, while light or dark brownish-yellow, and a beautiful ruby-red are colours which are seen but rarely. Garnets of this ruby-red colour are cut for gems and enter the market under the name of "Cape rubies." In size the garnet grains vary from mere dust up to the size of a walnut. All specimens yet examined contain a little chromium, and have the chemical composition of pyrope, itself well known and much used in jewellery under the name Bohemian garnet.

The members of the pyroxene group most frequently met with are enstatite (and bronzite) and chrome-diopside. The enstatite has the usual composition, but not the usual appearance of this mineral. It occurs generally in fragments about the size of a hazel-nut. It is transparent, with the colour of green bottle-glass, and has a distinct cleavage and a conchoidal fracture. It closely resembles olivine in appearance, and is frequently confused with this mineral. It is often found intergrown with garnet in such a way that single grains of garnet are enclosed by a shell of enstatite. This variety of enstatite is of more common occurrence than is the garnet. Another variety of enstatite (bronzite) also occurs, but more rarely. It is brown in colour and less unlike the ordinary mineral in appearance; moreover, it has a distinct plane of separation in one direction.

Chrome-diopside, sometimes referred to as chromiferous diallage, though less common than garnet, is yet very frequently met with. It occurs in irregular polyhedral grains of about the same size as the garnet grains and with no trace of crystal-faces. It is emerald-green in colour, translucent in mass, but transparent in thin splinters, and is usually distinctly cleavable in one direction. Wollastonite, another mineral of the pyroxene group, is also said to occur in the "blue ground."

The amphibole group of minerals is represented by the green smaragdite, which, however, is of rare occurrence. It has possibly been derived by the alteration of chrome-diopside. The occurrence of tremolite and asbestos has also been reported.

An altered magnesium mica occurs everywhere in small shining scales of a greenish or brownish colour or completely bleached. These thin plates or prisms frequently have a regular six-sided outline, and show the characteristic cleavage of mica; optically they are almost uniaxial. This altered mica, which is distinguished as vaalite, sometimes occurs aggregated into brown balls the size of a hen's egg, and in some places forms the chief constituent of the "blue ground." The glittering scales of mica embedded in the "blue ground" are sometimes mistaken at first sight by the unpractised eye for diamonds.

Ilmenite (titanic iron ore) is another mineral frequently associated here with the diamond. It occurs in shining black rounded grains with no indication of crystal-faces. It contains some magnesia and is not magnetic. Formerly the diamond miners imagined this mineral to be the black variety of diamond known as carbonado, and at present found almost exclusively in Brazil. They were not easily convinced of their error, and the name they gave it, carbonado, still remains. True carbonado occurs only very sparingly at the Cape. Magnetite (magnetic iron ore) in grains and of the usual character is said to be of frequent occurrence. Chromite (chromic iron ore), found in brilliant shining black grains up to the size of a pea, and with a conchoidal fracture, is also fairly common. Zircon, known to the Kimberley miners as "Dutch bort," occurs very rarely in transparent to translucent grains of a very pale flesh colour, and about the size of a lentil or pea. Other minerals associated with diamond in the "blue ground" are iron-pyrites, sapphire, kyanite topaz, and on very rare occasions colourless olivine. Apatite has been detected by chemical tests, and gold was once found enclosed in eclogite at the Jagersfontein mine. Under the microscope, graphite, tourmaline, rutile, and perofskite, among other minerals, have been detected. The common mineral quartz, on the contrary, has never yet been observed.

The majority of the minerals mentioned above occur in all the mines, but some are confined to particular pipes. Thus gold has been met with only in the Jagersfontein mine, and up to the present the occurrence of sapphire also is confined to the same mine.

The parti-coloured residue left by washing the "blue ground" after sorting out the large rock-fragments consists largely of grains of red garnet and zircon, the green minerals of the pyroxene and amphibole groups, and black ilmenite and magnetite mixed with small fragments of diabase. The absence from this residue of the other minerals mentioned above is explained either by their rarity or by their having been lost in the washing process. Diamonds are of course present, and are picked out by hand.

All the minerals mentioned above are original constituents of the "blue ground," and were already formed at the time it first filled the pipes. There are others, however, which are of secondary formation, owing their origin to the weathering processes undergone by the upper layers of the "blue ground." Such a secondary mineral is calcite, a not unimportant constituent of the rock-mass, and occurring also in veins and crevices and as crystals encrusting the walls of cavities in the rock. Other secondary minerals are zeolites, especially mesolite and natrolite, sometimes found in beautiful groups of acicular crystals; also in places rough fragments of a bluish hornstone. Barytes, which is of rare occurrence, is also probably a later-formed mineral. All these minerals of secondary origin, but particularly the zeolites, are found most abundantly in the upper part of the pipes, which is more exposed to the action of atmospheric agencies. At successively lower levels they diminish in amount and finally disappear.

Stanislas Meunier has described a total of eighty different species from the "blue ground," but the existence of some of these as distinct mineral species probably requires confirmation.

One other rock found in the "blue ground" of De Beer's mine remains still to be mentioned, but is of no great importance. It penetrates the "blue ground" as a dyke five to seven feet thick, and on account of its tortuous path is known locally as "the snake." It is a compact greenish-black rock of much the same composition and consisting of essentially the same minerals as the "blue ground," but it contains no diamonds.

The **manner in which the pipes have been filled** with the material we have been considering has been explained in many and various ways. The first investigator to formulate a theory in accordance with all the observed facts was Emil Cohen, and the views he propounded in 1873 have never been seriously controverted by any one of the numbers of observers who have followed him in this field of inquiry.

He regards the pipes as volcanic vents or chimneys comparable with those, also extinct, of the Eifel, and considers that the serpentine breccia now filling the pipes was brought up from below by the action of volcanic forces, but at what period of geological history this took place neither he nor later authorities can say. To quote Cohen's own words:

"I consider," he says, "that the diamantiferous ground is a product of volcanic action, and was probably erupted at a comparatively low temperature in the form of an ash saturated with water and comparable to the material ejected by a mud volcano. Subsequently new minerals were formed in the mass, consequent on alterations induced in the upper part by exposure to atmospheric agencies, and in the lower by the presence of water. Each of the crater-like basins, or perhaps more correctly funnels, in which alone diamonds are now found, was at one time the outlet of an active volcano which became filled up, partly with the products of eruption and partly with ejected material which fell back from the sides of the crater intermingled with various foreign substances, such as small pebbles and organic remains of local origin, all of which became embedded in the volcanic tuff. The substance of the tuff was probably mainly derived from deep-seated crystalline rocks, of which isolated remains are now to be found, and which are similar to those which now crop out at the surface, only at a considerable distance from the diamond-fields. These crystalline rocks, in which the diamonds probably took their origin, were pulverised and forced up into the pipes by the action of volcanic forces, and, embedded in this erupted material, these same diamonds, either in perfect crystals or in broken fragments, are now found. Analogous cases of the simultaneous ejection of broken and of perfect crystals are afforded by some of the active volcanoes of the present day, and moreover, in many other localities, the mother-rock of the diamond is probably to be found in the older crystalline rocks. At any rate, these rocks contain, as a rule, just those minerals which are most frequently associated with diamond. The beds of shale and sandstone interbedded with sheets of diabase were broken through and fractured by the force of the eruption, and so large blocks (floating reefs) and small fragments of these rocks became embedded in the tuff. Since in well-borings in the neighbourhood of the mines bands of coal are often met with interbedded with the shales, the coal, which is occasionally found in the diamond-bearing ground, and which has been incorrectly thought to have some genetic relation with the diamond, must have been derived from the seams of coal interbedded with the shales."

The fact that there is no genetic relation between the coal found in the tuff and the diamonds, or in other words that the diamonds have not been formed in the pipes from fragments of coal, is clearly shown by the frequent occurrence of diamond crystals in broken fragments. Had the diamonds been actually formed in the " blue ground," it would be difficult to find any explanation of the occurrence of so many broken crystals. If, on the other hand, we suppose them to have been formed in a deep-seated crystalline rock, which by the action of powerful volcanic forces was pulverised and forced up into the pipe or funnel, the fragmentation of many of the crystals follows as a matter of course.

That the material filling the pipes was not washed into them by flowing water is proved by the absence of any trace of wear in the minerals and rock-fragments enclosed in the tuff, all of which preserve intact the sharpness of their edges and corners. Had the soft and fragile materials, such as the abundantly occurring shales and mica, been transported by water over even the shortest distance, they would inevitably show some sign of their journeying.

A volcanic origin for the diamantiferous deposit thus appears to be the only possible conclusion which can be drawn from the observed facts ; it should be noted, however, that according to this theory the diamond itself did not originate in the same way, but was formed in a deep-seated rock before the eruption took place. Cohen's theory is so closely in agreement with the observed facts, that it has been very generally accepted, and up to the present has only required modification in a single particular. In this theory it is assumed that each pipe was formed and filled up by a single manifestation of volcanic activity and that, excluding of course the effects of subsequent weathering and alteration, the pipe as we now see it is the product of this single eruption. A consideration of the vertical columns into which the pipes of " blue ground " are divided, and which differ from each other in such characters as colour, composition, contained minerals and richness in diamonds, has led

Chaper to the conclusion that each of these vertical columns is the product of a distinct eruption. Since the columns are similar in general character and differ only in minute details, he considers that they have been formed by a series of eruptions of the same type; in short, that each diamantiferous deposit or pipe is the product of a long-continued period of volcanic activity. Thus, according to Chaper's view, the pipe of the Kimberley mine, in which fifteen columns have been observed, is the result of fifteen successive eruptions. Further observations in this direction are, however, desirable.

From the considerations brought forward above, it seems very probable that the South African diamonds were formed in a deep-seated crystalline rock which became fragmented and erupted to the surface by the action of volcanic forces; and moreover, that the greater part of this ejected, fragmentary material fell back again into, and filled up the vent or crater produced by the eruption. From the nature of the minerals which accompany the diamonds in the volcanic tuff, it is perhaps possible to draw some conclusions as to the character of the rock in which the diamonds were formed. Almost all the minerals, which are constituents of the rocks generally known as olivine-rocks, and which are widely distributed in the earth's crust, are found amongst the minerals associated with the diamond in "blue ground." It is therefore highly probable that the original mother-rock of Cape diamonds was an olivine-rock, situated at a great depth below the earth's surface and containing as constituents biotite (represented by the altered mica, vaalite), enstatite (bronzite), garnet, and all the other minerals already mentioned, including of course the diamond. Such a rock, which would be similar to a lherzolite in composition, has indeed, though in a somewhat different sense, been named *kimberlite*, and from this, the "blue ground" filling the pipes has been referred to as a kimberlite-breccia or a kimberlite-tuff. This kimberlite-breccia or tuff, at least as far down as it has been reached by mining operations, has undergone great alteration, its originally predominant constituent olivine being almost completely altered to serpentine, so that very little of it is now to be seen. This more or less complete alteration of olivine to serpentine in an olivine-rock is not at all unusual, being a matter of common observation in all parts of the world. The other constituents of the original rock have undergone less alteration and are in a more or less fresh condition. At greater depths the decomposition of the olivine has been less complete, and here may be found traces of kimberlite still unaltered, in which the olivine retains more or less completely its original character.

The foregoing pages have been devoted to the consideration of the manner in which the diamantiferous rock-mass actually occurs in the pipes. The question which naturally follows, namely how the diamond itself was formed in its original mother-rock, the kimberlite, will be treated generally below. We must first, however, notice certain other theories as to the formation of the pipes, which are more or less opposed to that of Cohen, as set forth above. According to the theory first promulgated by the late Professor H. Carvill Lewis, and which has some substantial support, the "blue ground" is not fragmentary material or tuff, but was forced up from below into the pipe as a molten mass which consolidated on cooling. According to this view, therefore, the "blue ground" is an ordinary igneous rock, which solidified in the situation in which it is now found, and it was with this supposed origin in his mind that the name kimberlite was proposed for the diamantiferous rock by Carvill Lewis. This rock, which was originally an olivine-rock, is supposed to have subsequently undergone the same alteration processes as described above.

There appears to be a similar, though very sparing occurrence, of diamonds near the village of Carratraca in the province of Malaga in Spain. According to the statement of

A. Wilkens, a mine-owner resident there, a few diamonds were found in the seventies along with pebbles of serpentine in a stream, in the neighbourhood of which serpentine with nickel ores occurs *in situ*. It is therefore not impossible that these diamonds had been derived from the serpentine. Similar relations between diamonds and serpentine rocks have also been reported from Australia and the western part of North America.

Although the association of diamond with serpentine in South Africa renders it very probable that the former has been derived from an olivine-rock, yet it is a noteworthy fact that the only mineral found actually inter-grown with and firmly attached to the diamond is garnet. Professor Bonney has recently (1899 and 1901) described the occurrence of colourless octahedra of diamond as a constituent of rounded boulders of eclogite. These boulders of eclogite, which is an igneous rock composed of garnet and green diopside, came from the "blue ground" of the Newland's Diamond Mine in Griqualand West, about forty-two miles north-west of Kimberley. The same observer describes the occurrence, also in this mine, of rocks rich in olivine, such, for example, as saxonite and lherzolite, in which, however, diamonds have not yet been observed.

At all other known diamond localities, especially those of India, Brazil and Lapland, olivine or serpentine as a mineral associated with diamond is conspicuous by its absence. In such localities, therefore, the mother-rock of the diamond cannot be an olivine-rock. On the other hand, diamonds have occasionally been found in meteoric stones, of which olivine is an invariable constituent, and the association of these two minerals in extra-terrestrial matter is a fact of considerable interest and importance.

The **mining operations** for obtaining the diamonds at the dry diggings were commenced at the end of the year 1870 ; by 1872 the industry was in a flourishing condition, and since this date it has steadily developed. At first the deposits were worked, regardless of future inconvenience, in an irregular and haphazard fashion, the aim of the miners being to amass the greatest possible amount of treasure with the least possible immediate expenditure of labour and money. Thus much valuable ground was covered with débris, which subsequent workers were forced to remove at a great sacrifice of time, labour and capital. In the deposits more recently discovered, the authorities have profited by former mistakes and mining operations have from the first been carried out in a systematic manner, with due regard to future necessities.

Each diamantiferous area was at first divided into square lots or claims, as was the custom in the gold-fields of California and Australia and also at the river diggings of South Africa. These claims in the Kimberley and De Beer's mines were 31 feet, and in the Du Toit's Pan mine 30 feet square ; each claim therefore had an area of 100 square yards or a little more. In the Kimberley mine there were 331 such claims, in the De Beer's mine 591, in the Bultfontein mine 886 and in Du Toit's Pan, 1430. In the three last-named mines the claims were laid out in such a way that there was no means of access to those in the centre except over the surrounding lots; this inconvenient arrangement materially increased the difficulty of mining and transporting material. When the Kimberley mine was opened, the Government Inspector of Mines in what was then the Orange Free State, profiting by past experience, arranged that every claim should be directly accessible by the construction of fourteen or fifteen road-ways, each 15 feet wide and all running in a north and south direction across the narrowest part of the mine. By this regulation every possessor of a claim lost $7\frac{1}{2}$ feet of ground, and until the advantage of the arrangement was realised it was bitterly opposed. In Plate VII. is shown the Kimberley mine as it appeared in 1872, with these road-ways.

Up to 1877, no single individual was permitted to possess more than two claims, the only exception to this rule being that of the discoverer of the mine, who was allowed three. Every intending digger had the choice of any of the claims which happened to be vacant, and each tenant of a claim paid the owner of the land 10s. per month in return for a licence permitting him to work the claim. Until 1873, the penalty enforced for leaving a claim unworked during a period of seven days was forfeiture of the claim, which could then be transferred to another digger.

To keep the whole of a claim constantly worked proved somewhat too heavy a tax on the energy and resources of a single individual, the claims therefore came to be divided up, one man making himself responsible for a half, a quarter or even one-sixteenth of a claim.

More important than the sub-division of the claims was the amalgamation of several under one management, a system which began to be adopted in 1877, after the regulation preventing it had been rescinded. Companies were formed to buy up a number of claims, and these, being under one central control, could be worked more expeditiously and economically; before very long, there were very few claims, or portions of claims, worked by single individuals. Thus in the middle of the eighties, almost all the claims into which the Kimberley mine was divided were in the possession of one or two large companies, while ten years before, these same claims were the separate property of about 1600 persons; the same change also took place in the management of the other mines. The number of claims in the possession of each company, of course, varied considerably, some having as few as four and others as many as seventy. Many of these companies were formed with perfectly legitimate objects, others however were nothing more than swindles, and the claims they had acquired were usually very soon abandoned.

The immediate result of the formation of these companies was a large increase in the production of diamonds; thus while the total output of diamonds in 1879 was about two million carats, in 1880 and 1881 it suddenly rose to over three millions. This large increase was rightly ascribed to the advantages resulting from the partial amalgamation of claims which had taken place, and it was strongly urged that this policy should be pursued to its logical conclusion, and that the whole of each mine should be placed under one management and one system of working. This proposition met at first with great opposition, but was effected in 1887 by the managers of the De Beer's mine, a company which, formed in 1880, gradually acquired claim after claim, until in 1887, with a capital of £2,332,170, it came into possession of the whole of the De Beer's mine. The formation and development of this company, which since 1887 has been known as the "De Beers Consolidated Mines, Limited," had the effect of greatly reducing the working expenses of the enterprise, which from 1882 to 1887 had amounted to 40 per cent. of the value of the output. In 1882 the production of the diamonds cost the company 16s. 6d. per carat, while in 1887 this amount had been reduced to 7s. 2d.; at the same time the deposit had increased in richness as greater depths were reached, an increase in the production of about 40 per cent. having taken place. This increase in the richness of the deposit, combined with a diminished cost of production, naturally affected the dividends of the company, which rose from 12 per cent. in 1886 to 16 per cent. in 1887 and 25 per cent. in 1888.

In spite of the success which has attended this effort in the direction of amalgamation, the management of the other mines has not yet been altogether unified, though they are more or less under the control of the powerful and heavily capitalised De Beers Company. This company now has possession of the whole of the Kimberley mine, and the new Wesselton mine, as well as of parts of the Du Toit's Pan and Bultfontein mines. Neither of these two latter mines, however, is now worked, since the open workings have become

PLATE VII

KIMBERLEY DIAMOND MINE IN 1872

covered by falls of reef and the underground workings are not yet organised. An idea of the importance and influence of the De Beers Company may be gained from an inspection of the returns dealing with the production of diamonds. Thus from April 1, 1890, to March 31, 1891, this company alone produced 2,195,112 carats of diamonds, valued at £3,287,728, this being more than 90 per cent. of the total yield (2,415,655 carats) of the four mines at Kimberley, or indeed of the whole of South Africa. This result is of course due in some measure to the large amount of capital, £3,950,000, at the command of the company.

The inception of this company and its pursuit of a policy of buying up all available claims resulted in a considerable rise in the price of the latter, £10,000 or even £15,000 being asked for single claims, and proportionate prices for portions. The claims thus acquired a definite market value, which depended on the richness of the deposit at that particular place, usually known fairly accurately, and which of course varied at different times. Thus the claims in the Kimberley mine in 1875 were worth from £200 to £2500 each, in 1878 from £50 to £6000, and in 1882 from £150 to £15,000; the value of the whole mine being in these years £525,000, £1,300,000 and £4,150,000 respectively. At one time the value of the shares in the Kimberley mine amounted to £8,000,000.

In the other mines the deposit was poorer and the price of claims correspondingly lower. In the year 1880 the values of the richest claims in the Kimberley, De Beer's, Du Toit's Pan, Bultfontein, Jagersfontein and Koffyfontein mines were in the proportion of $10 : 5 : 2 : 1 : \frac{1}{10} : \frac{1}{15}$. In other words, the richest claim in the Kimberley mine was 150 times more valuable than the richest claim in the Koffyfontein mine; for the former £15,000 would be demanded and paid, while the latter would cost at the highest from £30 to £100.

For a short time after the opening of the mines each owner of a claim worked alone on his own piece of ground. It was found, however, that comparatively cheap labour could be obtained by employing the native Kaffirs, and these were soon engaged in large numbers. It is stated that in the seventies 10,000 to 12,000 Kaffirs were employed in the Kimberley mine alone, and by some authorities this number is doubled. The diamantiferous rock was excavated by the help of pickaxes or blasted with gunpowder, the latter agent being replaced later on by dynamite. The excavated material was then either loaded into carts or simply carried away from the mine. The whole mine was thus honey-combed with square pits which varied in depth in different claims, those which had been vigorously worked being very deep and enclosed by high vertical walls, and others having the appearance of rectangular columns, so high that they sometimes fell over and buried neighbouring claims with débris. The road-ways by which the claims in the Kimberley mine were separated, soon came to be mere walls, the surfaces of which rose high above the floors of surrounding claims and gave the whole mine a peculiarly striking appearance, as may be gathered from Plate VII.

Owing to the ease and rapidity with which the tuff composing these walls became weathered, they formed anything but stable boundaries, and as early as 1872 they had to be removed. After their removal, the mine had the appearance of one gigantic pit; the rock subsequently excavated could not then be removed in the same manner as before, and other means had to be devised. The mine was surrounded by high, wooden stagings provided with ropes and winding machinery, by the aid of which the diamond-bearing material was hauled up in sacks or buckets of hide. The owner of every claim, or part of a claim, had his own hauling rope, so that at this time, about 1874, the total number of these ropes was very large and gave the mine, which is pictured in the upper figure of Plate VIII., the appearance of a huge cobweb. The winding was first effected by hand windlasses, then by horse-power, and finally by steam, the delay in the adoption of the latter being caused by the cost of importing machinery and coal. In spite of this difficulty, there were in 1880 no less than 150 steam-engines employed at the Kimberley mines, and in 1882 this number had been increased to 386 with a total horse-power of 4000, and this was further supplemented by the use of 1500 horses and mules.

The continual increase in depth of the claims was attended by increasing difficulty in excavating the tuff and by frequent accidents, due to falls of loosened material. These difficulties were still further complicated by the fact that falls of reef also began to take place. Often masses of rock would fall sufficient to bury, wholly or in part, many of the surrounding claims; and in such claims no further excavation of "blue ground" was possible until the overlying mass of reef had been removed. In September of 1882, in the

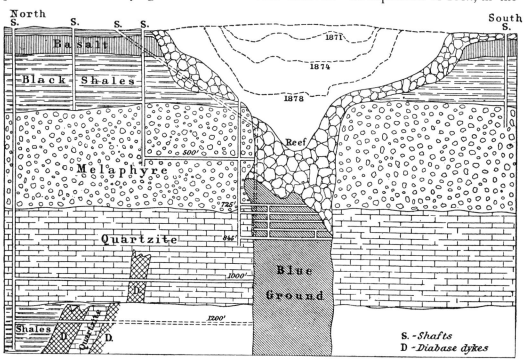

FIG. 40. Section through the Kimberley mine. (Scale, 1 : 4800.)

Kimberley mine, there was a fall of reef, estimated at about 350,000 tons, which buried no less than 64 claims; in 1878 one-quarter of the total area of the mine was strewn with fragments of reef. In 1879 and 1880, £300,000 was expended in removing this fallen material, and in 1882, £500,000 more was spent for the same purpose, and even then this obstacle to progress was not entirely removed. From the Kimberley mine alone a total of about four million cubic yards of reef have been removed, at a cost of £2,000,000. To what an extent the difficulties occasioned by a fall of reef influence the production of stones can be seen from the fact that the yield of the Kimberley mine, during the 18 months which preceded the catastrophe mentioned above, was 1,429,728 carats, but in the following 18 months only 850,396 carats. The frequent falls of masses of reef and the removal of other masses which threatened to fall, resulted in a great increase in the surface area of the mine. Thus in the middle of the eighties, the Kimberley mine, a representation of which is shown in the lower figure of Plate VIII., was a crater-like pit 385 yards long, 330 wide and 400 feet deep.

The appearance of water in the mine still further added to the embarrassment of the workers, and constituted a difficulty which was quite insuperable so long as the owners of the claims worked independently. The necessity for co-operation was met in 1874 by the institution of the Kimberley Mining Board, a body which undertook all work of public benefit, such as the removal of water, of fallen reef, and of reef about to fall, the expense incurred being shared equally by the owners of the claims. It was about this time that the formation of companies began to take place, although at first this form of co-operation was strongly condemned by individual miners, yet as time went on it became more and more apparent that the increasing difficulties and expense of working could only be overcome in this way. The larger capital at the disposal of the companies enabled them to employ the best machinery and to adopt all the improved modern methods of working, and thus to decrease the working expenses, and at the same time to increase the production.

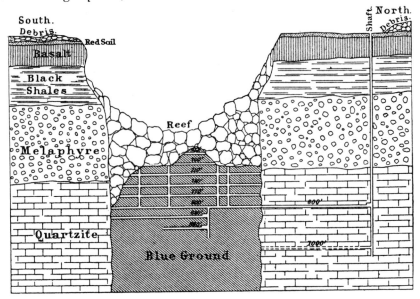

FIG. 41. Section through the De Beer's mine. (Scale, 1 : 4800.)

Although the amalgamation of individuals and capital rendered it possible to prolong for a time the system of open workings, yet, as time went on, it became very evident that this system could not be continued indefinitely, and that the open workings would have to be replaced by systematic underground workings, if the treasure hidden away in the depths of the mine was ever to be reached. A very successful beginning was made at the Kimberley mine in 1885, and in 1891, at this same mine, a shaft was driven into the reef to a depth of 1261 feet, from which horizontal galleries or tunnels were excavated to meet the diamond-bearing rock. In the section of the underground workings of the Kimberley mine shown in Fig. 40 may be seen these tunnels or galleries, situated partly in the diamantiferous pipe itself and partly in the surrounding reef. The lowest depth at which material could be excavated in the open workings was about 400 feet, so that the construction of the under-ground workings made accessible large quantities of fresh material. Moreover, the new system did away with the liability of the workers to injury from falling reef, and many of the earlier regulations dealing with this danger, became then unnecessary. The same system was also introduced in the De Beer's mine, a section through which is given in Fig. 41, although here the falls of reef had been less troublesome.

The earlier methods of **extracting diamonds from the rock** when excavated, were as primitive as were those first adopted for mining the rock. It has been mentioned above that the dry diggings are situated on an arid plateau, and at the time of their first discovery the water required for every purpose had to be fetched from the Vaal River, many miles away. This necessity forbad the washing of the diamantiferous material as was practised at the river diggings. The mass had therefore to be coarsely broken up with wooden pestles and the coarse and fine material separated by sieves ; the material of medium grain was then, as in the river diggings, spread out in a thin layer on a sorting-table, and any diamonds it contained picked out by hand.

By this method all the stones which passed through the fine sieve, the mesh of which was about $\frac{1}{8}$ to $\frac{3}{16}$ inch, were of course lost, these smaller stones being not then considered worth the time and trouble involved in their collection. The larger rock-fragments separated by the use of the coarse sieve with a mesh of $\frac{3}{8}$ to $\frac{5}{8}$ inch were thrown aside, though many would of course contain diamonds. It is estimated that during the period in which these methods were practised, at least as many diamonds were overlooked as were found, and in 1873 the débris was reworked and yielded a rich harvest. The material taken from the richest part of the mine has been worked over even a third time, and thanks to the use of improved methods, the result amply repaid the workers for their trouble. Hundreds of poorer miners, who were not fortunate enough to possess a claim, gained a living by working over the material of old mine heaps, as is still done at some places in India.

The lack of water was not felt for long ; very soon a main 18 miles long, bringing water from the Vaal, was constructed, and this supply was further supplemented by the numerous springs in the district, and by the water pumped out from the mines themselves. Thus it soon became possible to treat the diamantiferous material in the same way as at the river diggings, and so the term dry diggings came to be a misnomer. At first, the " blue ground " was reduced to fragments and then washed by the aid of the same simple appliances as had been in use at the river diggings. Improved methods, however, were gradually introduced ; thus in 1874, a washing machine worked by hand was employed for the first time, and this in 1876 and 1877 was itself replaced by a machine driven by steam. The construction of this was so much improved that it was capable of dealing with almost two thousand times as much material as could formerly be treated by washing, and of collecting stones which, on account of their small size, had formerly been lost. The diamonds are picked out by hand from the heavy residue, and are finally freed from any foreign matter which may adhere to them, by treatment with a mixture of sulphuric and nitric acids, after which they are ready for the market.

The " blue ground " excavated from the deeper parts of the mine is too hard and compact to be washed without previous treatment. It is therefore spread out in thin layers on the hardened ground of large fenced-in spaces, known as depositing floors. Here, exposed to frost, rain and sunshine, it gradually weathers, becoming friable and crumbling, when it is fit to undergo the process of washing. The weathering of the material, which is accompanied by a change from the normal colour of " blue ground " to that of " yellow ground," takes from one to nine months, according to the character of the weather to which it has been exposed, and to the mine from which the material was taken. " Blue ground " from the Kimberley mine weathers in about half the time required for the same process by the material from De Beer's mine ; the latter sometimes requires several years for the completion of the process, while a few months is usually all that is necessary for material from the Kimberley mine.

PLATE VIII

KIMBERLEY DIAMOND MINE IN 1874

KIMBERLEY DIAMOND MINE (WEST SIDE) IN 1885

The longer the period required for the weathering process, the more will the profit derived from the yield be diminished. For during this period there are many expenses and losses incurred, such for example as ground rent, which is very high, wages of labourers and watchmen, losses due to thieving, &c. Any means whereby the slow natural process could be hastened would therefore be welcomed, but up to the present no such means have been devised.

A factor which has largely contributed to the hardships of the South African diamond fields is the high price of the ordinary necessities of everyday life. This scantily-peopled region, in which only the barest necessaries could at one time be obtained, became inhabited with comparative suddenness by a population of at least 30,000 white people. The many and various articles necessary to their existence on these barren arid wastes had all to be conveyed from Capetown, Port Elizabeth, or some other seaport town. The transport was effected in waggons, drawn by horses, mules or oxen, and the long and difficult journey to Kimberley occupied several weeks. The rates for transport from Port Elizabeth to Kimberley, a distance of 500 miles and requiring about four weeks, were from 10s. to 30s. per 100 lbs of goods, and from Capetown to Kimberley, a journey of 650 miles, occupying about six weeks, they were still higher. Other prices were of course correspondingly high: thus, Cohen relates that in the year 1872 a bottle of beer cost 3s. 6d., and good Rhenish wine 18s. a bottle; a cabbage could never be obtained for less than 3s., potatoes were as high as 1s. per lb., and eggs were 6s. a dozen. At some seasons of the year a day's supply of fodder for a horse cost 15s., English coal fetched £16 10s. per ton, and a waggon load of wood of about 4½ tons was worth £30. The same authority states that £8000 was paid for a steam-engine of 100-horse power delivered in Kimberley. It is not surprising then, that with these prices for coal and machinery, steam power was so long in coming into general use, especially as it was not at first known that the diamantiferous deposits were so extensive. The cheapest food available was antelope flesh, a whole animal the size of a deer costing only from 3s. to 8s.; meat, therefore, was the staple article of food, and every drop of water had to be bought.

The wages paid to overseers and miners had of course to correspond with these high prices. The overseers and officials, who were all white men, were paid up to £2000 per annum. White miners, of whom in 1882 and 1883 there were about 1500, received from £4 to £8 per week, while the native workers, about 11,000 in number, were paid 22s. to 30s. per week.

All these details apply to the time when Kimberley was still unconnected by railway with the coast towns. Since 1885, it has been joined to Capetown by a line 647¼ miles long, and to Port Elizabeth by one of 485⅓ miles. The construction of these railways considerably diminished the cost of transport, and, in consequence, the price of many of the necessaries of life fell; moreover, it became possible to make more extensive use of coal, which was brought both from England and also from the South African mines at Stromberg in the Indwe district of Cape Colony, a place which has also been connected by rail with Kimberley.

For comparison with the prices quoted above, a few of more recent date may be given. In 1891 a ton of English coal cost at Kimberley £8 10s., and 100 lbs. of wood fetched 2s. The transport of goods from Port Elizabeth to Kimberley costs from £6 to £8 per ton, and the journey occupies only about thirty hours, instead of four weeks, as was formerly the case. The reduction in the cost of living is of course accompanied by a corresponding fall in wages; from £3 to £6 10s. per week is paid to white men, while Kaffirs earn at most 24s. per week, exclusive of housing, wood, water and medical attendance.

The climate of Kimberley cannot be considered anything but healthy; in winter it is mild and pleasant; in summer, however, from September to March, it is often very hot, in spite of its elevation of 4012 feet above sea level.   There is often no rain for months together, and the whole of the rainfall usually takes place in a few heavy downpours.   Since the erection of suitable dwellings for the miners and the improvement in their mode of living, the deadly camp-fever has been almost unknown, and the district can no longer be considered an unhealthy one, a consideration which has an important bearing on the output of diamonds.

Year.	Weight in carats.	Value per carat.	Total value per year.	Total value for 5 years.
		£ s. d.	£	£
1867 ⎫ 1868 ⎬	200	—	650	
1869	16,550	1 10 0	24,813	
1870	102,500	1 10 0	153,460	
1871	269,000	1 10 0	403,349	
1872	1,080,000	1 10 0	1,618,076	
				2,200,348
1873	1,100,000	1 10 0	1,648,451	
1874	1,313,500	1 0 0	1,313,334	
1875	1,380,000	1 2 6	1,548,634	
1876	1,513,000	1 0 0	1,513,107	
1877	1,765,000	19 6	1,723,145	
				7,746,671
1878	1,920,000	1 2 6	2,159,298	
1879	2,110,000	1 4 6	2,579,859	
1880	3,140,000	1 1 6	3,367,897	
1881	3,090,000	1 7 0	4,176,202	
1882	2,660,000	1 10 0	3,992,502	
				16,275,758
1883	2,410,000	1 2 9	2,742,470	
1884	2,263,734	1 4 9	2,807,329	
1885	2,439,631	1 0 5	2,489,659	
1886	3,135,061	1 2 4	3,504,756	
1887	3,598,930	1 3 7	4,242,470	
				15,786,684
1888	3,841,937	1 1 0	4,022,379	
1889	2,961,978	1 9 3	4,325,137	
1890	2,504,726	1 13 3	4,162,010	
1891	3,255,545	1 5 8	4,174,208	
1892	3,039,062	1 5 8	3,906,992	
				20,590,726
Total	50,910,354	Mean 1 4 8	62,600,187	

In spite of the many and varied difficulties which have been encountered, the development of mining operations at Kimberley has been so extensive that, although the stones are of relatively sparing occurrence in the " blue ground," an enormous number must have been found.   An idea of the extent of the **output** may be derived from an inspection of the above table, which is copied from Reunert.   In this table is given the yearly export of diamonds from South Africa since 1867, the total value of this export, and the mean value per carat, the whole of the information having been derived from the most reliable sources available. The yearly export, though not exactly identical with the production, approaches it very nearly, and is sufficiently close for all practical purposes. The numbers quoted in the table may differ slightly from other returns, but are accurate enough to convey a correct idea of the gigantic scale of the output.

It should be remarked that the numbers given in this table for the years 1867 to 1882 are based only on estimates. Exact statistical records have only been kept since the establishment of the "Board for the Protection of Mining Interests" in 1882. It may be difficult, from the numbers given in the table, to form a correct conception of the enormous quantity of diamonds which have been exported from South Africa; a few concrete examples are therefore appended as an aid to the imagination. The total weight of stones exported amounts to almost 51,000,000 carats, which is equal to 10,500 kilograms, or nearly $10\frac{1}{3}$ tons. These stones would fill a box five feet square and six feet high; they would also form a pyramid having a base nine feet square and a height of six feet.

An exact record of the yield of each of the Kimberley mines has also been kept since September 1, 1882. The unknown, but probably very considerable, number of diamonds stolen by the workers from their legitimate owners, cannot of course be included in these records; the value of the diamonds misappropriated every year is variously estimated at from £500,000 to £1,000,000. During the three years between September 1, 1882, and September 1, 1885, the four Kimberley mines, from which, as has already been mentioned, over ninety per cent. of the total South African output is derived, have yielded, according to official returns, the following amounts in carats:

	Sept. 1, 1882 to March 1, 1884.	March 1, 1884 to Sept. 1, 1885.	Total for the 3 years.
Kimberley mine	$1,429,726\frac{7}{8}$	$850,396\frac{1}{4}$	$2,280,123\frac{1}{8}$ carats
De Beer's mine	656,427	$790,908\frac{3}{4}$	$1,447,335\frac{3}{4}$ "
Du Toit's Pan mine . . .	$709,877\frac{1}{8}$	$773,306\frac{3}{4}$	$1,483,183\frac{7}{8}$ "
Bultfontein mine	$738,230\frac{1}{4}$	$877,647\frac{1}{2}$	$1,615,877\frac{3}{4}$ "

This gives the yearly average for the four mines together at $2,372,809\frac{3}{8}$ carats, valued at £2,628,289 *3s. 7d.*

In the year 1886, the production of these four mines, and of a few others of less importance, as well as of the river diggings, amounted to:

	Carats.	Value. £.	s.	d.
Kimberley mine	889,864	836,767	17	7
De Beer's mine	795,895	739,937	2	8
Du Toit's Pan mine	$700,302\frac{1}{4}$	909,023	11	5
Bultfontein mine	$661,339\frac{1}{4}$	623,339	17	3
St. Augustine's mine	$239\frac{1}{4}$	317	19	4
River diggings	$38,672\frac{7}{8}$	181,156	9	2
Orange River Colony	$73,303\frac{3}{4}$	121,654	15	1
	$3,159,617\frac{3}{8}$	3,412,197	12	6

The figures in the three tables given above are in all probability too low, since there are many sources the supply from which it is difficult or impossible to estimate. Thus the total production of the river diggings, and of the Jagersfontein and Koffyfontein mines in the Orange River Colony, is not exactly known, the numbers in the table referring not to the total production, but to the diamonds sent from these mines and diggings to the central market at Kimberley. The first of the above three tables gives the total yearly production for the whole of South Africa, from the discovery of diamonds in 1867 up to the year 1892. Details connected with the production in certain years of individual mines are collected together in the second and third tables.

Formerly, when the claims were in the possession of single individuals or small companies, the aim of the owners was to obtain and sell as many stones as possible. Now, however, the output is controlled by the " De Beers Consolidated Mines," and only a certain number of stones are placed on the market, in order to keep up the price. Experience has shown that the annual demand for diamonds, both for jewellery and for technical purposes, amounts in value to about £4,000,000. Taking the average value of rough stones at 21s. per carat, this corresponds to a weight of rather over 3,800,000 carats, or about 15⅓ cwts. ; the yearly production of Cape diamonds is rather over 3,000,000 carats, and the difference between these weights represents the amount supplied by Brazil, India, Australia, and Borneo.

Although the total weight of stones collected is so enormous, yet the **relative amount of diamond in the " blue ground "** is extremely small. The proportion which this constituent bears to the whole mass varies both in different mines and in different parts of the same mine. Thus in some mines the " blue ground " excavated from successively lower depths has shown a marked increase in richness. It would be naturally of great importance to those interested, were it possible to foretell whether such an improvement in yield would be maintained or not ; this, however, is not possible, and it is equally impossible to give any explanation of the variation.

The Kimberley mine, since its discovery in July 1871, up to the present day, has been the richest of all the deposits. Many of the original miners made their fortunes in less than a month, and one case is quoted in which diamonds to the value of over £10,000 were found in the short space of a fortnight. A cubic yard of " blue ground " from the Kimberley mine contains more diamonds than a mass of equal size from any other district ; this being so, mining operations were here prosecuted with great vigour, all the other mines being at one time forsaken. Owing to the want of reliable statistical reports dealing with early times, it is not possible to determine with certainty whether the deposit increases in richness as greater depths are reached, or not. Probably it does not, and if this be so, the Kimberley mine differs in this respect from the others.

Boutan has collected statistics dealing with the content of diamonds in the " blue ground " excavated from the Kimberley mine by certain companies. From the year 1881 to 1884, this varied between 3·04 and 7·17 carats per cubic metre (about 1·3 cubic yards), an amount corresponding to two- to five-millionths of a per cent. This yield, however, applies only to the richest parts of the " blue ground," the mean yield for that part of the deposit which is worked, taking rich and poor together, is about 4·55 carats per cubic metre (3·5 carats per cubic yard). If, however, the material of the western side of the mine, which on account of its poverty is not worked, is also included, the mean yield for the whole deposit will be 4·20 carats per cubic metre of " blue ground," or on the average three-millionths of a per cent.

The dimensions of the portion of the deposit which is worked being known, it can be calculated that the excavation of " blue ground " to a depth of one metre would result in the production of 88,000 carats of diamonds, which at £1 per carat would be of the aggregate value of £88,000. From the same part of the deposit, a cubic metre of worked material would contain on an average £4 11s. worth of diamonds.

The De Beer's mine is 1⅕ times the size of the Kimberley mine ; the central point of the former is situated 1771 yards to the east of the central point of the latter. The deposit ranks next to that of the Kimberley mine in richness, although it was at first very poor, only yielding ⅓ carat to the cubic metre of rock. The yield, however, increased rapidly as greater depths were reached ; at a depth of 300 to 400 feet it had increased tenfold, so that 3½ carats of stones were then obtained from a cubic metre of rock. From the year 1882 to 1884 the yield obtained by some companies varied between 1·28 and 3·52 carats ; the mean yield for the whole mine was estimated at 3·15 carats per cubic metre of rock, worth, at the higher price commanded by stones from this mine, £3 9s.

The richness of this mine varies not only with the depth, but also at different places on the same level. The best part of the deposit is not surpassed in richness by any part of the Kimberley mine, while other parts are so poor that they are not worked at all. The central portion is very rich, and extensions of this stretch out especially towards the north and south, forming a great contrast to the western third of the mine, which is extremely poor. A beautiful yellow octahedron, weighing 302 carats, was found in the eastern side of the deposit, on March 27, 1884.

The increased richness of the lower lying parts of the deposit led to an attempt being made, soon after the opening of the mine, to excavate the deeper portions by means of underground workings, leaving the poorer portions standing above. The attempt was very successful as far as yield was concerned, but, owing to the imperfect methods adopted, was attended by so many accidents that it had to be abandoned. Since 1885, however, when, as we have already seen, the construction of underground workings began to be more skilfully engineered, the excavation of the deeper lying material has been resumed.

The Bultfontein mine is situated 4840 yards to the south-east of the Kimberley mine. A cubic metre of the surface material yielded only a small fraction of a carat, but here also a rapid and regular improvement in the deposit as lower depths were reached was manifested, the yield at a depth of 200 feet having increased threefold. The increase in the richness of the deposit took place in this mine with almost mathematical regularity, and was attended both by an improvement in the quality of the stones, and by a diminution in the number of fractured crystals. In 1887 a depth of 460 feet had been reached, a depth which has never been exceeded in open workings. In the period 1881 to 1884 the yield varied between 0·56 and 1·27 carats per cubic metre of " blue ground," the mean yield being about 1·05 carats, so that a cubic metre of rock contained diamonds to the value of about 23s. Underground workings have not yet been established in this mine so that from it may be derived an idea of the appearance presented by the other mines in earlier days.

Du Toit's Pan mine is 1320 yards distant from Bultfontein mine, and 3542 from De Beer's mine. In 1874 the mine was almost deserted, the yield being so small, and it has only been systematically worked since 1880. Here again the surface rock was poor, and yielded at the best of times only ¼ carat per cubic metre of material ; here also the deposit improved at greater depths, but not so rapidly as in the De Beer's mine. At a depth of 175 feet, at which the yield had doubled itself, a peculiarity not hitherto noticed in any other mine was observed : the richness of the deposit was found to be absolutely identical at all points on the same level, so that no variation in the yield was experienced. From this point downwards the yield rapidly increased, approaching that of the Kimberley and De Beer's mines. From 1881 to 1885 the yield varied between 0·31 and 1·11 carats, the mean yield being 0·77 carat per cubic metre of " blue ground," having the average value of 22s. In this mine, as in the Bultfontein mine, the increase in richness of the deeper lying deposit was accompanied by an improvement in the quality of the stones, and by a diminution in the number of broken crystals. The open workings were here excavated to a depth of over 400 feet, and underground workings have been scarcely as yet commenced.

The Jagersfontein mine, near Fauresmith, in Orange River Colony, contains only 0·10 to 0·35 carat of diamond per cubic metre of "blue ground." The poorness of the yield is, however, in some measure compensated for by the singular beauty and size of the stones. For the year ending March 31, 1891, the average value per carat of stones from this mine was 37s., stones from the Kimberley mines being worth only 25s. 6d. per carat. The largest diamond known was found in this mine in 1893; it weighed 971¾ carats and will be figured (Fig. 51) and described later on. A very fine stone of 655 carats was found here also at the end of 1895. The mine was opened in 1880, was abandoned for a time about 1885, but was subsequently re-opened.

The Koffyfontein mine, also in the Orange River Colony, gives a smaller yield still, amounting to only about two-thirds that of the Jagersfontein. The stones, however, are of good quality and are worth about 30s. per carat; from December 1887 to April 1891, 9912 carats of diamonds, valued at £14,640, were mined here.

The relative importance of the different mines is also shown to a certain extent by a comparison of the number of workers employed in each. Thus in the year 1890 the numbers were as follows·

	Whites.	Blacks.
De Beer's mine	682	2780
Kimberley mine	495	1800
Du Toit's Pan mine	67	400
Bultfontein mine	37	300
	1281	5280

The number of persons employed in the mines at Kimberley in the year 1892 is given in the following table. This includes two mines not before specially mentioned, namely Otto's Kopje and St. Augustine's, the former being situated a couple of miles to the west of Kimberley, and the latter in the town itself.

Name of Mine	Above ground.		Below ground.		Total.		Grand Total.
	Whites.	Blacks.	Whites.	Blacks.	Whites.	Blacks.	
Kimberley . .	372	982	133	822	505	1804	2309
De Beer's . .	693	2098	229	1812	922	3910	4832
Du Toit's Pan .	—	—	—	—	96	654	750
Bultfontein . .	—	—	—	—	186	933	1119
St. Augustine's .	9	15	10	13	19	28	47
Otto's Kopje . .	3	54	—	—	3	54	57
	1077	3149	372	2647	1731	7383	9114

We turn now to the consideration of the characters and the quality of Cape diamonds, that is to say, the form and condition of crystallisation, colour, size, &c., peculiar to stones from this region.

These diamonds usually occur as distinct crystals, symmetrically developed in all directions and with perfectly sharp edges and corners; but fragments of larger crystals, bounded by cleavage surfaces, and which are therefore cleavage fragments, also occur with considerable frequency. These cleavage fragments are sometimes of fair size, the original crystals, of which these fragments are part, probably varied in size from 3 to 500 carats; large cleavage fragments are known as "cleavages," while fragments weighing less than a carat are referred to as "splints." It is a remarkable fact that these cleavage fragments are nearly always white, that is colourless, or at least very faintly coloured; fragments of a dark colour, or of a decided yellow, are extremely rare, so that we must conclude that such stones offered greater resistance to fracture than did the colourless diamonds.

The **crystalline form** is on the whole very regular, and the edges and corners never show signs of having been water-worn except of course in stones from the river diggings. Octahedra with curved and grooved edges (Fig. 31, n and o) are very frequent, while rhombic dodecahedra with curved faces (Fig. 31 c), and with singly or doubly nicked faces (Fig. 31 d) are rare. Crystals of this kind, when not unduly distorted, are greatly prized, especially the octahedra, for it is possible to give such stones the desired brilliant form with very little preliminary cleaving and loss of material. Cubes (Fig. 31 a), which are specially characteristic of Brazil, are practically non-existent at the Cape, extremely few diamonds with this form having been found. While hemihedral forms (Fig. 31 k) are of rare occurrence, twinned crystals, on the other hand, are very abundant; the twinning takes place according to the usual law, with a face of the octahedron as the twin-plane, and the individuals of the twin being two octahedra (Fig. 31 g), two rhombic dodecahedra, or two hexakis-octahedra (Fig. 31 h), which are much flattened in the direction of the twin-axis. The external form of twin-crystals varies with the development of the individuals, and may be tabular, lenticular, heart-shaped, &c. On account of their small thickness they are not very suitable for cutting as brilliants, and are generally used for rosettes; they are for this reason less highly prized than are other forms, such as the octahedron, and command a lower price. When the junction of the two individuals in flattened twin-crystals is distinctly to be seen, the stones are known in the trade as "twins," while those in which the junction is less conspicuous are referred to as "macles" (mackel).

Besides the occurrence of twinned crystals consisting of two individuals which have grown together in a symmetrical manner, there occur groups consisting of two or more individuals irregularly intergrown. An example of this irregular intergrowth is furnished by the spheres of bort, which have been already described and which occur very frequently both here and in Brazil. The surface of these spheres is seldom quite smooth, the projecting corners of the numerous small octahedra, of which the sphere is built up (Plate I., Fig. 3), being the cause of the irregularities of its surface. The size of these peculiar crystal aggregates is sometimes quite considerable, spheres weighing as much as 100, or even 200 carats, having been found. Occasionally, the centre of a sphere of bort is occupied by a single large, colourless crystal, which falls out of the rough, grey shell, when the latter is broken.

The **size** of the Cape diamonds is extremely variable, and ranges from that of the largest to that of the smallest stones yet found in any country.

When the operation of washing is performed with sufficient care, it is possible to collect numerous stones weighing no more than $\frac{1}{32}$ carat (about 7 milligrams). The improved washing machinery now in use is capable of collecting stones of this small size just as easily as larger specimens. Formerly these small stones were lost in the process of washing, and this gave rise to the belief that diamonds less than $\frac{1}{4}$ carat either did not occur at all, or only very rarely, at the Cape. The existence, hitherto unsuspected, of large numbers of microscopically small diamonds, together with particles of carbonado and of graphite, in the "blue ground" has been recently demonstrated; the occurrence together of diamond and graphite is worthy of special remark.

The most salient feature of the South African diamond-fields, as compared with those of other countries, is the prevalence of stones of large size. It will be remembered that in Brazil the discovery of a stone of 17 carats was such an event that its finder, if a slave, was rewarded with his freedom. In South Africa stones of this size occur in hundreds and in thousands; and the discovery of a stone of 100 carats causes less excitement than did the finding of a 20-carat stone in Brazil. Stones of 80 to 150 carats are of common occurrence, scarcely a day passes in which a stone between 50 and 100 carats in weight is not brought to light. Since the year 1867, when the South African deposits were discovered, the number of large stones, which have been found there, far exceeds not only the number unearthed in India in the course of a thousand years and in Brazil during a period of 170 years, but also the total production of large stones in these two countries added together. Diamonds which weigh after cutting upwards of 75 carats have occurred at the Cape in greater numbers than in any other known locality. While the mean size of Brazilian diamonds is scarcely one carat, the majority of South African stones are of this or larger size, excepting, of course, those stones which are rejected as being unsuitable for cutting.

We have already mentioned that the largest diamond known, the " Excelsior," was found at the Jagersfontein mine in 1893. It is a stone of the first water, weighing $971\frac{3}{4}$ carats, and will be described and figured (Fig. 51) in the section dealing with large diamonds. The next largest Cape diamond is the one of 655 carats found in the same mine in 1895, which is stated to be of unusually fine quality. Another stone of 600 carats, but of poor quality, is said to have been found in this mine. A stone of $457\frac{1}{2}$ carats was found in one of the mines, but which one is not recorded; one almost as large, weighing $428\frac{1}{2}$ carats, was obtained from the De Beer's mine, while in 1892 the Kimberley mine yielded a diamond of 474 carats, from which was cut a brilliant weighing 200 carats. " The Julius Pam," a stone of $241\frac{1}{2}$ carats, which gave a brilliant of 120 carats, came from the Jagersfontein mine. A few large stones have also been contributed by the river diggings, the largest being the " Stewart " of $288\frac{3}{8}$ carats, which was cut as a brilliant weighing 120 carats.

Although the diamond-fields of South Africa are unique as concerns the number and size of the stones found there, the same can by no means be said of the **quality** of diamonds from this region. Not only are the stones frequently so dark and unpleasing in colour that they can only be applied as bort for technical purposes, but they are also very often disfigured by "clouds" and cracks, the so-called "feathers." Moreover, these cracks, especially in stones from the Du Toit's Pan mine and from the diggings on the Vaal River, are often rendered still more conspicuous by being filled with films of limonite. The presence of enclosures of foreign matter is also common; these are usually black and resemble particles of coal, but are probably hæmatite or ilmenite. There are also green enclosures of a pecular vermiform character, which, according to Cohen, are probably some compound of copper, and red enclosures of unknown nature. It is stated by Streeter that on an average only 20 per cent. of Cape stones are of the first water, 15 per cent. of the second, and 30 per cent. of the third, the remaining 35 per cent. being bort. According to Kunz, however, only 8 per cent. are of the first quality, 25 per cent. of the second, and 20 per cent of the third quality, the remainder being bort.

Cape diamonds show a great range of **colour**. Perfectly colourless or pure white to deep yellow, light to dark brown, green, blue, orange, and red specimens have all been found. At the same time the stones may be transparent and clear or cloudy and opaque.

Pure white, absolutely colourless stones are very rare, still the finest blue-white diamonds, such as are found in India and Brazil, are not altogether absent. Only about 2 per cent. of the total number of stones found reach the standard of absolute perfection, among such the most general form is that of a symmetrically developed octahedron. The " Porter Rhodes," found in the Kimberley mine on February 12, 1880, is one of the finest of Cape diamonds; it is said to weigh 150 or 160 carats, and is a stone of singular beauty. The largest diamond known, that of $971\frac{3}{4}$ carats, as well as those of 655 and $209\frac{1}{4}$ carats respectively, all from the Jagersfontein mine, are also of this high quality. As a rule, large stones are patchy and impure or coloured yellow, often a deep shade of yellow, which greatly diminishes their value. The otherwise poor deposits of Jagersfontein and the river diggings are remarkable for the purity and beauty of the stones found there, especially in the latter.

The majority of what are usually regarded as white Cape diamonds are in reality more or less tinged with yellow ; this, though not apparent to an unpractised eye, is at once remarked by an experienced diamond merchant. Stones of this tint are described as being " Cape white," while others, in which the faint yellow tint is replaced by an equally faint greenish tinge, rank as " first by-water." Although the yellowish and greenish tinge is so slight, yet it manifestly exercises a considerable influence on the lustre and refractive power of the stone. Such a stone scarcely attains to the fire and play of colour of a perfectly colourless Indian or Brazilian stone ; moreover, even though cut in the best brilliant form, it will appear dusky when compared with the latter and will therefore be less highly prized.

Stones of a distinct, though pale, yellow colour are specially common ; they vary in shade from a canary- or straw-yellow to a light coffee-brown. They form the majority of those Cape stones which are suitable for cutting, and are naturally less prized than the Cape whites or others already mentioned. As a rule, these stones, the different shades of which are distinguished by the terms second by-water or off-coloured stones, pale yellow and dark yellow, are less disfigured by faults than are the colourless stones. The abundance of these pale yellow stones is a feature peculiar to the South African diamond-fields ; nowhere else are they found in such numbers. Before the discovery of these deposits, stones of this colour were extremely rare and were sought after as much as are now the stones of a fine red, blue, or green colour, which are still rare. Such diamonds are referred to as " fancy stones," and are perhaps more rare at the Cape than at other localities ; a representative of such " fancy stones " from the Cape is a rose-violet diamond of 16 carats. Diamonds of these beautiful colours, even when found, are invariably small. Transparent stones of a dark brown or black colour are very rare ; though the qualities most highly prized in colourless diamonds are absent in such stones, yet, on account of their rarity and their application in mourning jewellery, they command a high price. Very darkly coloured or impure stones, as well as those which are cloudy and opaque, are unsuitable for cutting and are used as bort.

Another unique feature of the Cape diamond-fields is the occurrence of the peculiar " smoky stones," which have been already mentioned. These occur for the most part at Kimberley and are scarcely known elsewhere ; they are distinguished by their very regular octahedral form and by the possession of a peculiar smoky-grey colour, which is either distributed uniformly or accumulated at the edges and corners of the stone, which, in the latter case, is known as a " glassy stone with smoky corners." In these diamonds there is a liability, as has been already mentioned, to fall to powder with no apparent external cause ; this is certain to happen sooner or later when such a stone is once taken out of the ground, and many and various are the devices adopted by the unfortunate possessor to postpone the catastrophe, at any rate, until he has prevailed on some inexperienced buyer to take the stone. Thus, immediately after it is taken from the rock, the finder will perhaps place it in his mouth, or smear it with grease ; and when it must be sent on a journey it will often be placed inside a potato, this being considered the safest method of packing such stones, probably because they are thereby protected from contact with other diamonds or hard objects, the slightest scratch being sufficient to bring about the bursting of the stone. The singular behaviour of these stones is due to the existence of intense internal strains in their substance ; the same phenomenon being also the cause, as we have seen, of the strong anomalous double refraction possessed by some diamonds.

The collective characters of the stones found in each mine and in each part of a mine are distinctive, but single stones of every quality occur in all mines. Thus, though it may be impossible to state the particular mine in which a single stone was found, yet an experienced Kimberley diamond merchant would have no difficulty in naming the mine, or portion of a mine, from which a parcel of stones had come, provided that the parcel formed a fair sample of the yield of that particular deposit.

The stones found in the rich Kimberley mine are usually poor in quality ; and broken fragments, the latter invariably uncoloured but containing many black enclosures, are present in great abundance. A large percentage of the material yielded by this mine, especially from the north side, is unsuitable for cutting and only applicable as bort, 90 per cent. of South African bort being furnished by this mine. Broken fragments are confined to a certain extent to the middle and south side of the deposit ; while the north-east corner and the west side of the mine have yielded brown octahedra and " smoky stones " in great abundance ; yellow diamonds, so numerous everywhere else, are here almost wholly absent. The stones found in the east and south-east portions of the deposit closely resemble those from Du Toit's Pan mine.

From the De Beer's mine are obtained crystals of every kind and colour, the surface of which is almost invariably finely granular, glimmering, and somewhat greasy, surface characters which are met with in crystals from no other deposit. Bort is rare, but broken fragments containing black specks are abundant. Large yellow rhombic dodecahedra are very frequent, the De Beer's stones being, on the whole, remarkable for their large size, while stones from the Kimberley mine are conspicuous for their whiteness.

The diamonds found in the Du Toit's Pan mine are usually well crystallised and of considerable size, yellow octahedra being often specially large. Bort, very small stones and " smoky stones," are practically absent, and crystals disfigured by black specks are seldom met with. The colour of stones from this mine is often rather dark, but the proportion of Cape white and yellow stones found is greater than elsewhere in this region. On the whole, the diamonds yielded by this mine are more beautiful than those of any other deposit in the neighbourhood of Kimberley.

The Bultfontein mine yields principally small white octahedra, much modified on their edges and usually full of faults and spots. Large stones, broken fragments, bort, and deeply coloured stones are here practically absent.

The average value of stones from the different mines of course varies in correspondence with the variations in quality we have just been noticing. In the first column of the following table, compiled from the estimates given by Moulle, will be found the average price per carat of rough stones from the different mines during the period between September 1, 1882, and the end of March 1884. The corresponding prices for 1887, given in the second column, are somewhat lower, but the proportion existing between them is about the same and has indeed remained practically unaltered up to the present day.

	1882–4.		1887.		
	s.	d.	s.	d.	
River stones	54	11	46	7	per carat
Du Toit's Pan mine . . .	28	1	24	3	,, ,,
Bultfontein mine	21	0	17	11	,, ,,
De Beer's mine	20	11	17	5	,, ,,
Kimberley mine	19	2	17	2	,, ,,

These four mines yield, on an average, respectively, 0·77, 1·05, 3·15, and 4·55 carats of diamonds per cubic metre of "blue ground," so that the stones found in mines of which the yield is poor, surpass in quality those found in richer mines.

In the Jagersfontein mine, as has been already mentioned, are found the whitest, largest, and most transparent of Cape diamonds, some of which approach, or even equal, the beautiful blue-white Brazilian and Indian stones which are so highly prized. The abundance of white stones in this mine is sometimes thought to be connected with the complete absence of iron-pyrites, which is found everywhere else and has been supposed to be the cause of the yellow colour of Cape diamonds. The beauty of these white stones is unfortunately, however, often impaired by the presence of spots and blemishes of various kinds; moreover, in addition to regularly and symmetrically developed crystals, irregular intergrowths are not infrequently met with, so that a considerable proportion of stones from this mine are unsuitable for cutting and have to be discarded. The stones found here which are free from faults are of singular beauty; they are comparable to the diamonds of Bagagem in Brazil and command the very highest price.

It has not hitherto been mentioned that the Kimberley and De Beer's diamonds are supposed to be less hard than stones from Du Toit's Pan and Jagersfontein mines and from the river diggings.

The whole of the South African **diamond trade** centres round Kimberley. The stones usually change hands in large lots and are often placed on the market directly they come from the washing machinery. In other cases they are first sorted into parcels containing various qualities; this process offers great scope to the skill and discretion of the diamond merchant, for the amount obtained for a lot of stones depends largely on the arrangement of the stones of different size, quality, colour, &c., into parcels.

Various trade names for different kinds and qualities of diamonds have been evolved side by side with the development of the traffic in these stones. Only about four such terms were originally in use; a much greater number are at present in existence, and the significance of some of the most important will now be given below.

Crystals or *Glassies* are white, or nearly white, perfect octahedra.

Round stones are crystals with curved faces; these are sub-divided according to colour into Cape white, first by-water, and second by-water.

Yellow clean stones is a term which includes all yellow stones, these being grouped according to their shade of colour into off-coloured (the lightest shade), light yellow, yellow, and dark yellow.

Mêlé is a term applied to crystals varying from white to yellow (by-water) and often also to brown, weighing on an average not more than $1\frac{1}{2}$ to $1\frac{3}{4}$ carats. The term "small mêlé" is applied to similar stones as small as $\frac{1}{20}$ carat. All stones characterised by this term are round or glassies, never broken fragments.

Cleavage is the term applied to crystals containing spots, to twinned crystals, and to others which need to be cleaved before they can be cut; thus the term "black cleavage" is applied to stones which, in the rough condition, appear much speckled, but which, after cleaving, give fine stones. Large blackish diamonds are referred to as " speculative stones"; their value depends on their size and on the probability of obtaining good cleavage fragments from them. For stones of this sort (cleavage) weighing less than $\frac{3}{4}$ carat the trade name is *Chips.*

A collection containing black cleavage, stones of a brown or poor yellow colour and bort, forms a " parcel inferior," the contents of which are unsuitable for cutting and are pulverised for grinding powder or applied to other technical purposes.

The London jeweller, Mr. Edwin W. Streeter, in his book " Precious Stones and Gems," gives the following list of trade names for the various kinds of rough Cape diamonds : this differs somewhat from that given above, but will be easily comprehended by the reader of the foregoing pages :

White Clear Crystals	Bright Brown
Bright Black Cleavage	Deep Brown
Cape White	Bort
Light Bywater	Yellows
Light White Cleavage	Large Yellows and Large Bywaters
Picked Mêlé	Fine Quality River Stones
Common and Ordinary Mêlé	Jagersfontein Stones
Bultfontein Mêlé	Splints
Large White Chips	Emden
Small White Chips	Fine Fancy Stones
Mackel or Macle (flat, for roses).	

These different sorts of stones naturally differ widely in **value**; moreover, prices which were current before the discovery of the Cape diamond-fields have been somewhat modified in consequence of the enormous increase in the production due to this discovery. Thus, stones which were rare elsewhere, but abundant at the Cape, have fallen in value, while those which are rare also at the Cape have retained their former value.

In this way the price of perfectly colourless stones of the first water has not fallen in consequence of the discovery of the Cape diamond-fields, but is as high as ever it was. The price of yellow or yellowish stones of 10 to 150 carats in weight is, on the contrary, much lower. To such stones Tavernier's old rule, according to which the value varied with the square of the weight, is inapplicable, the price of such stones now varies directly with the weight; sometimes, however, it is in a still lower proportion, so that when the weight of a stone is doubled the price is not always necessarily doubled.

Naturally some considerable time must elapse before prices adjust themselves to new and unknown conditions. Thus, for the first large stones found at the Cape a price in consonance with Tavernier's rule was demanded; such prices were seen to be too high and were soon regulated to accord with the changed conditions. As early as 1876 rough Cape white stones of good quality, and up to 6 carats in weight, had fallen in value from 30 to 50 per cent., the largest and smallest stones having suffered the greatest depreciation. It should be borne in mind, however, that these Cape whites were not quite equal in quality to the white Brazilian stones. The discovery of the Cape diamond-fields caused a still greater depreciation in the value of bort, the price of this material having in 1873 fallen 85 per cent.; in 1876, however, the depreciation in the price of bort was only 70 per cent., and it continued to rise in value owing to its increasing application for technical purposes.

The price of diamonds at the Cape, as elsewhere, depends not only on the quality of the stones but also on the conditions of supply and demand, and varies from day to day. According to the statements of E. Cohen, the price of bort varied from 1875 to 1880 between 1s. 9d. and 5s. 8d. per carat ; for Cape whites, of 2 to 6 carats in weight, between £3 15s. and £7 10s. per carat, and for fragments of 1 to 2 carats, between 8s. and 24s. per carat.

According to the estimate of Anton Petersen, as quoted by E. Cohen, the following prices for rough stones were in 1882 paid at the mines :

		£ s.		£ s.	
First water (highest quality) . .	4 carat stones	15 0	to	18 0	per carat.
Best Cape white	1 ,, ,,	1 10	to	1 15	,, ,,
,, ,, . . .	6 ,, ,,	4 0	to	5 0	,, ,,
Light yellow (off-coloured) . .	1 ,, ,,	15	to	1 0	,, ,,
,, ,, ,,	6 ,, ,,	2 0	to	2 10	,, ,,
,, ,, ,, .	20–40 ,, ,,	2 5	to	3 0	,, ,,
,, ,, ,, .	100 ,, ,,	3 15	to	6 0	,, ,,
Bort		6	to	8	,, ,,

These prices which are exceptionally low, were current only on the Cape diamond-fields and not in the European markets, one market being perhaps influenced by circumstances which do not affect the other.

The prices per carat, stated by Boutan to have been current in Kimberley on July 31, 1883, are tabulated below :

Varieties.	Weight of stones in carats.	Price per carat.
Crystals or Glassies ⎫	1 average	55s.
,, ,, ⎬ Cape White or White ⎰	2 ,,	75s. to 80s.
,, ,, ⎪	3 ,,	95s. to 100s.
,, ,, ⎭	4 ,,	120s.
,, ,,	5 to 8 and more	According to size
Cape White Round Stones	1 to 2 ,, ,,	40s. to 45s.
,, ,, . .	3 to 4 ,, ,,	47s. 6d. to 52s. 6d.
,, ,, . .	5 to 8 ,, ,,	55s. to 60s.
First By-water Round Stones . . .	1 to 2 ,, ,,	⎰ 10 per cent. less than
,, ,, ,, . .	3 to 4 ,, ,,	the Cape White
,, ,, ,, . .	5 to 8 ,, ,,	⎱
Second By-water Round Stones . .	1 to 2 ,, ,,	⎰ 5 per cent. less than the
,, ,, ,, . .	3 to 4 ,, ,,	First By-water
,, ,, ,, . .	5 to 8 ,, ,,	⎱
Yellow Clean Stones	1 to 3 ,, ,,	23s. 6d. to 28s. 6d.
,, ,, . .	4 to 10 ,, ,,	30s. to 40s.
,, ,, . .	up to 40	42s. 6d. to 47s. 6d.
Dark Yellow Clean Stones . . .	1 to 3 and more	22s. 6d. to 27s. 6d.
,, ,, . .	4 to 10 ,, ,,	28s. 6d. to 37s. 6d.
,, ,, . .	up to 40	40s. to 45s.
Mêlé	$\frac{1}{4}$ average	27s. 6d.
,, ...	$\frac{1}{3}$,,	31s. 6d.
,, ...	$\frac{1}{2}$,,	35s.
,, ...	$\frac{3}{4}$,,	40s.
,, ...	1 ,,	46s.
Cleavage	$\frac{3}{4}$,,	14s. 6d.
,, ...	1 ,,	17s. 6d.
,, ...	2 ,,	24s.
,, ...	3 ,,	28s. 6d.
,, ...	4 to 5 ,,	32s. 6d.
,, ...	Large Stones	32s. 6d.
,, ...	$\frac{1}{2}$ average	12s. 6d.
Good White Square Chips . . .	$\frac{1}{4}$,,	8s. 6d.
,, ,, . . .	—	6s. 0d.
Small White Square Chips . . .	—	5s. 6d.
Common White Square Chips . .	—	5s. 0d.
Common Cleavage and Chips . .	—	4s. 6d.
Bort		

Boutan also remarks on the lowness of these prices which were consequent on a commercial crisis; they reached their lowest level in 1885, having fallen 20 per cent., and after this date began to rise again.   In the following table is given the average value per carat, calculated from the weight and value of the total export during the years 1883 to 1891:

	s.	d.					s.	d.
1883	23	7			1888		19	11
1884	22	9			1889		29	4
1885	19	3			1890		30	7
1886	21	1			1891		25	2
1887	21	8						

It should be remarked here that during the period in which the Cape deposits have been worked, the average quality of the diamonds has remained practically the same, so that the above numbers represent approximately the mean market value for each year.

It will be readily understood that with objects like diamonds, so costly and, yet at the same time, so easily hidden, there are possibilities for very considerable **illicit trade**. Those engaged in the mining, washing, and sorting of diamonds, especially the Kaffirs, constantly find opportunities for secreting stones, in spite of the strict supervision to which they are subjected.   Although the mining employees each time they leave work have to undergo a rigorous personal search, yet diamonds are continually being smuggled through and placed on the market by illicit diamond buyers (I.D.B.).   It is estimated that 30 per cent. of the total output is thus diverted into illegitimate channels.

The strictest of laws and regulations have from time to time been devised and rigidly enforced with the object of suppressing theft of, and illicit trade in, diamonds.   Thus a man convicted of diamond stealing or illicit diamond buying was sentenced to several years of penal servitude; under no circumstances were natives allowed to sell stones, and white men were obliged to procure a written licence before engaging in the trade of buying and selling diamonds, and to submit for the inspection of the authorities a properly kept register of all transactions.   The difficulty of obtaining witnesses, and therefore of convicting a person of an illicit transaction, made the enforcement of these and similar regulations somewhat of a dead letter; moreover, the profit attending an illicit transaction successfully carried out was so large that the risk of conviction failed to act as a deterrent.   Since March 1, 1883, still more stringent regulations have been in force; a person suspected of, and charged with, the illicit possession of diamonds, must defend himself against the charge by furnishing a satisfactory explanation of the circumstances leading to his arrest.   Moreover, search-warrants are now granted in the case of white men as well as of natives.

These regulations are in force not only in the diamond-fields but in the whole of Cape Colony, and they were also adopted in the Orange Free State.   The illicit trade has, therefore, been checked, but not altogether stamped out.   The cunning and ingenuity shown by Kaffirs in concealing and disposing of stolen stones is unexampled.   As an illustration we may quote the case of a native who, in 1888, was suspected of being in the unlawful possession of diamonds.   On the approach of his pursuers he shot one of his oxen with a rifle loaded with the stolen stones, and after the police had made an unsuccessful search he extracted the diamonds from the dead body of the ox.   In the same year another native, who died in a mysterious manner, was discovered to have swallowed a 60 carat diamond, which proved itself too much for the constitution even of a Kaffir.

The comparatively recent introduction of the compound system has resulted in making the robbery of diamonds by natives almost an impossibility.   The native workers in the

De Beer's and Kimberley mines, among whom representatives of almost every South African tribe are to be found, live in what is known as a compound, and are debarred from all intercourse with the outside world. This compound is a rigidly guarded enclosure, several acres in extent, in which all the necessaries of life can be purchased as well as other objects specially attractive to the native taste. Water, wood, and medical attendance are supplied to the workers gratuitously, and no effort is spared to make their enforced stay as little irksome as possible. On entering the employment of the company the native contracts to stay for at least three months, during which time he sees no one but the officers of the company; at the end of this time he may renew his contract or terminate the engagement. Before leaving the compound, however, an exhaustive search of his person and belongings is made, and he has further to submit to the administering of a strong purgative. In spite of the restrictions by which life in the compound is hedged in, and the absolute prohibition laid on the sale of intoxicating liquors, the workers are by no means averse to the system, and often renew their contracts again and again. It has been found, moreover, that the system reduces the possibility of fraud to a minimum.

4. BORNEO.

The information concerning the diamond-fields of Borneo given below is derived, for the greater part, from the investigations of R. D. M. Verbeek, the director of the

FIG. 42. Diamond-fields of the Island of Borneo. (Scale, 1 : 15,000,000.)

Geological Survey of the Dutch East Indies, as set forth in E. Boutan's book " Le Diamant " (Paris, 1886).

The diamond-fields of Borneo fall into two well-defined groups, one in the west of the island, in the district of the River Kapuas, the mouth of which lies a little below the town of Pontianak, the other in the south-east of the island, not far from the town Bandjarmassin, and nearly opposite the island of Laut (Fig. 42). The three portions into which the western group may be divided are situated on as many different rivers, one being on the river Kapuas, a little below its confluence with the Sikajam, and the other two respectively on the rivers Landak and Sikajam, both tributaries of the Kapuas. The Landak deposits seem to have been known since the time the Malays settled in the island, and were mentioned by the Dutch mariners who first visited the coast ; indeed, from the beginning the Dutch regarded the trade in diamonds in Borneo as their special monopoly.

In the west of the island diamonds occur in beds of alluvium, in masses of débris at the foot of mountains, and in the beds of streams and rivers flowing through diamantiferous districts. The alluvial deposits consist of gravel, sand, and more or less ferruginous clay, more rarely of conglomerate and sandstone. They are distinctly bedded, and vary in thickness from 2 to 12 metres, the diamonds being confined to the lowest bed, which consists of gravel.

These ancient gravels, which themselves show little or no signs of bedding, contain diamonds throughout their whole mass and are formed of more or less rounded rock-fragments. They are essentially river deposits, and occur in isolated patches of small area at the foot of the mountains or in the valleys, but always above the existing high-water level. The rock-fragments of which these gravels are composed differ widely in kind; white, yellow, or rose quartz predominates, but there are also present hard and compact grey and black quartzites, quartz-schists, clay-slates, quartz-sandstones, hornstones, hornblende, blue and violet corundum, and, in sparing amount, fragments of igneous rocks, so decomposed, however, that it is difficult to determine their original nature. In addition to these there are also to be seen scales of white mica, grains of magnetite, a few particles of cinnabar, and usually a little gold.

It is from these gravels that the diamonds now found in the beds of streams and rivers have been washed out. Both sedimentary and igneous rocks are found in situ in the neighbourhood ; among the former are clay-slates and quartz-schists with quartzites of Devonian age, conglomerates and clayey sandstones of much later date, probably belonging to the lowest Tertiary, that is, to the Eocene age. The igneous rocks include granite, diabase, gabbro, andesite, and melaphyre.

Diamonds are only found in places where the beds of Eocene conglomerate and clayey sandstone crop out at the surface, and it has been thought by C. van Schelle, a mining engineer in Borneo, that it is from these beds that the diamond has been derived. In any case the Devonian beds need not be considered, for no diamond has ever been found in alluvial débris derived from, or resting on, Devonian strata, in spite of the fact that such material has been carefully worked over for the gold it contains. The original mother-rock and the mode of origin of the diamond are therefore here as much a mystery as elsewhere, for no single crystal has ever been found in anything but what is obviously a secondary situation.

The working of the diamond-fields is in the hands of Chinese and Malays ; the former work the deposits lying above high-water level, while the latter apply themselves to the alluvium in the present-day water-courses, extracting the diamantiferous gravel by excavating small deep pits reaching down to the solid rock, and washing the gravel in baskets. The methods in use in both cases are very primitive and inadequate, and no thorough investigation of the deposit has yet been made. An improvement in the system might probably be easily made if the diamond-seekers, who are for obvious reasons very uncommunicative, could be persuaded to volunteer the necessary information.

The diamonds of Borneo are, on the average, of poor quality; the proportion of faulty and unpleasingly coloured stones being sometimes stated to be greater here than in Brazil. The diamonds are almost invariably either more or less water-worn or fragmentary and irregular. The predominating crystalline forms are the octahedron and the rhombic dodecahedron; regular octahedra, which are not infrequent, are known to the Malays as "perfect stones," since according to their ideas such stones require little or no cutting. Cubes are rare, but twinned crystals very frequent.

Borneo diamonds exhibit a fair range of colour; the majority though colourless are disfigured by faults or blemishes of some kind or another. A few of the highly prized "blue-white" stones are found, and are of such singular beauty that their equal is nowhere to be found. After the colourless stones, those with a faint blue or yellow tinge are most abundant; more or less darkly coloured stones (bort), as well as those of a grey colour (carbonado), are fairly common. Stones in which a grey or black kernel is enclosed in a colourless and well-crystallised shell are sometimes met with; such a stone is known to the Malays as "soul of the diamond," and is considered to augur a poor deposit. Although the stone itself is regarded as a talisman, and worn round the neck in the belief that it will bring luck to its owner, yet at the spot at which it was found work is immediately abandoned and a fresh place chosen. On the other hand, the presence of the blue corundum is considered to be a good sign by the diamond seekers. Diamond crystals of a deep, black colour, quite distinct from carbonado, are occasionally found; when cut, such stones, though giving no play of prismatic colour, display a magnificent lustre, and are in great request for use in mourning jewellery.

With regard to the size of stones from this locality, it may be asserted that 95 per cent. of the whole output is constituted by stones which weigh less than 1 carat. Next in abundance come stones between 1 and 5 carats in size, while those exceeding this size are very rare. Several diamonds of large size were found in the district belonging to the Malay Prince of Landak, and are now in his possession; owing to their massive silver setting they cannot be weighed, but several have been estimated by C. van Schelle at over 100 carats. In the possession of the Rajah of Mattan is a supposed diamond the size of a pigeon's egg, and weighing 367 carats; this stone, which is probably only rock-crystal, will be again mentioned in the section devoted to large diamonds. The same prince is in possession also of two large and undoubtedly genuine stones, the "Segima" of 70 carats and another of 54 carats, both said to have been found in the island.

While in 1880 the mines on the Sikajam river were worked by about forty Chinese only, those in Landak gave employment to about 350 workers. The alluvial deposits on the Kapuas river are no longer systematically worked; single pits may be sunk here and there, but the production is quite insignificant.

The diamond-bearing deposits in the south of the island, namely, in the districts of Tanah-Laut, Martapura, and Riam are of recent formation, and overlie Eocene strata in the same way as those described above. These Tertiary strata, which in places include thin beds of coal, rest on ancient crystalline rocks, such as mica-schist, chlorite-schist, talc-schist, and hornblende-schist, and like these are inclined and faulted. Interbedded with the Tertiary strata, and specially towards their base, are sheets of recent eruptive rocks (andesites). The diamond-bearing deposits form a broad band round the seaward slopes of the Tertiary hills, while the gold-sands of the region, which contain no diamonds, rest on ancient schists. The actual diamantiferous stratum is constituted of more or less rounded pebbles of various minerals and of sand, either loose or bound together by clay. The mineral most abundantly present is quartz of various colours, after which come fragments of andesite and micaceous sandstone. A blue mineral, formerly thought to be quartz but which has now been proved to be corundum (sapphire), though of no value as a gem has yet a certain importance as an indication of the nature of the deposit. It occurs in the same manner as at Landak, and its presence is regarded by miners as indicating the existence of diamonds in the deposit; it is only after they are satisfied as to the presence of the blue mineral that they apply themselves to an exhaustive search for diamonds.

As a rule, the diamonds are found lying singly and loose in the gravel; sometimes, however, they are cemented by limonite to a pebble or rock-fragment. They are often accompanied by scales of gold and platinum and by grains of chromite and magnetite. The thickness of the diamond-bearing bed varies between 20 centimetres and 2 metres, beds of the greater thickness being usually found filling up depressions in the surface of the ground. The bed rests on a blue clay and is overlain by 1 to 6 metres of gravel and sand, and sometimes, as in the neighbourhood of Bentok, by a layer of nodules of limonite. This diamond-bearing stratum is found mainly in the neighbourhood of rivers and in surface depressions, which in the rainy season become filled with water.

The mining methods adopted here by the Malays appeared to be the same as those practised at Landak; the workings were mainly in the neighbourhood of the village of Tjampaka, in the district of Martapura, where in the year 1868 stones to the value of £1250 had been found; also near Banju-Irang, Bentok, and Liang Angang, all in the district of Tanah-Laut. Thousands of small mines are still to be seen in these districts; the majority of them, however, are now abandoned, for since the great fall in the price of diamonds in 1878, the miners can easily obtain more lucrative employment in the gold mines, tea plantations, &c. A Franco-Dutch Company in 1882 obtained the concession of a stretch of country of 2000 hectares, that is about eight square miles in area, for a period of twenty-five years, with the purpose of diamond mining. On this area, which lies between Tjampaka and Banju-Irang, machinery was set up, but in the very next year, 1883, the work was abandoned, and up to the present has not been recommenced. From the above accounts it is clear that the production of the whole southern group is quite insignificant.

Diamonds are also found in the Kusan district, which lies between the rivers Danau and Wauwan in the State of Pegattan, this latter being a Dutch dependency in East Borneo. The stones are of good quality, but here also the yield is poor.

It is impossible to arrive at anything more than an approximate estimate of the production of diamonds in Borneo. From an early date the Malay princes assumed the right of appropriating at a fixed price all stones exceeding 5 carats in weight found in their own dominions. Thus these stones never leave the country, and no record of their occurrence is kept. In the table given below will be found a few returns published by the Dutch Government in carats and Dutch florins (one florin = 1s. 8d.) of diamonds imported into Java.

Year.	Carats.	Value (in florins).	Year.	Carats.	Value (in florins).
1836	5473	110,601	1843	1315	23,900
1837	5245	97,140	1844	—	46,450
1838	5947	117,750	1845	—	68,825
1839	3884	92,552	1846	—	128,450
1840	1891	62,410	1847	—	96,210
1841	2122	56,520	1848	—	67,200
1842	3980	80,875			

It will be seen from the above table that the practice of recording the weight in carats of the imported diamonds ceased in 1844; moreover, the Customs Register, from which the above table has been compiled, was discontinued after 1848, so that there is no record of succeeding years. The number of stones imported into Java in each year, as set forth in the above table, represents very approximately the yearly production of Borneo, for it was at this period that the old Dutch East India Company was in its most flourishing condition, and the general prosperity created a demand for diamonds which drew almost the whole of the production of Borneo to Batavia; but all this ceased with the abolition of the company. In 1823 and 1831 the Dutch, seeing the demand for diamonds which existed in European markets, sought, unsuccessfully however, to increase the production by organising systematic working of the deposits.

A few estimates of the production of recent times have been made by the merchants at Ngabang, the capital of Landak; they are as follows:

Year.	Carats.		Year.	Carats.
1876	4062		1879	6673
1877	5271		1880	3013
1878	6359			

In the previous century the yield appears to have been much richer; while the deposits have been gradually exhausted, no new ones comparable in richness to the old have been discovered, and the abundance and comparative cheapness of Cape stones has rendered impracticable the exploitation of the poorer deposits. It is stated that in 1738 diamonds to the value of eight to twelve million Dutch florins were mined in Borneo, and even as late as the beginning of last century the value of the annual yield is said to have been as much as a million florins. The estimated annual yield in more recent times has been already given; at the present day it is supposed to be about 5000 carats.

The majority of the stones are roughly cut by the Malays in the island at Ngabang and Pontianak; there are diamond-cutting works also at Martapura, and the natives have been acquainted with the art of gem-cutting for centuries. At the present time scarcely any diamonds are exported, and it has even become customary to import Cape diamonds. The stones which are yielded by the country circulate almost exclusively in Oriental countries, very few finding their way to Europe.

5. AUSTRALIA.

In the year 1851 diamonds were discovered in one or two of the Australian goldfields, and later on in a few of the stanniferous gravels of the same continent. They are present in not altogether insignificant numbers, and up to the year 1890 a total of 50,000 diamonds had been found. New South Wales has up to the present time furnished the greater part of the yield, but a few stones have been found in Victoria and Queensland as well as in South Australia and Western Australia.

Australian diamonds are decidedly small, the largest stone yet found, which came from New South Wales, was an octahedron, and weighed $5\frac{5}{8}$ carats; an octahedral crystal from South Australia weighed $5\frac{5}{16}$ carats. The average weight of diamonds from New South Wales, compared with which the yield from the other States is negligible, is only $\frac{1}{4}$ carat; the great majority of stones vary in weight between $\frac{1}{8}$ and $1\frac{1}{2}$ carats. According to the statements of diamond-cutters, Australian diamonds are harder than the majority of stones from other parts of the world, and can only be cut with their own powder; they have a peculiarly strong surface lustre, and in spite of their extra hardness are usually much water-worn.

In **New South Wales** there are two principal diamond districts (Fig. 43). One is a stretch of country extending to the north-west of Sydney, as far as the Cudgegong river, and to the west of Sydney, as far as the Lachlan river. The other diamond

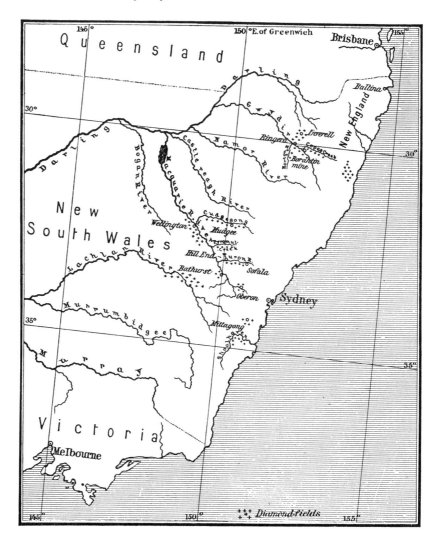

Fig. 43.   Diamond-fields of New South Wales.   (Scale, 1 : 10,000,000.)

district is in the north-east corner of the State, in the district of the Gwydir river, a tributary of the Darling; it embraces the neighbourhood of Inverell and Bingera, and extends to the east of these townships into New England. In these districts the diamond occurs in sands together with gold and tin-stone (cassiterite), and with one possible exception it has never been found in the solid rock; it is therefore impossible to make any suggestion as to the nature of the rock in which the diamond was formed.

In the southern diamond districts the diamond-bearing débris is mainly confined to ancient water-courses of Pliocene (a subdivision of Tertiary) age. When the precious stone is found in the beds of recent rivers and streams, it is always associated with material derived from these older deposits, which has been redeposited by natural agencies or during the process of gold-washing, &c. In this district the diamond is invariably accompanied by gold and it was in the gold-washings that the first discovery of diamonds was made. The diamantiferous gravels and sands of these ancient river deposits, which are always above, and often far above, the present water-courses, are very frequently overlain by a sheet of compact basalt, which must be penetrated before the diamond and gold-bearing stratum can be reached. Re-deposited masses of material, containing both gold and diamonds, often lie on the basalt, having been washed down from the upper part of the valleys.

The first discovery of diamonds in Australia was made in this State in 1851 ; the stones were found in Reedy Creek, a tributary of the Macquarie river, sixteen miles from Bathurst ; a few were found in the same district in 1852, in Calabash Creek. In 1859 a few stones, having the form of triakis-octahedra, were found in the Macquarie river, near Suttor's Bar, and at Burrandong ; in the same year a hexakis-octahedron, weighing $5\frac{1}{8}$ carats, was found in Pyramul Creek. These places are all situated in the same district, and at none of them were more than a few stones found.

In 1867, however, diamonds in greater number were met with near Warburton, or Two Mile Flat, on the Cudgegong river, nineteen miles north-west of Mudgee ; and in 1869 the systematic working of an area of about 500 acres in this district was commenced. The working, which was not very profitable, was carried on at Rocky Ridge, Jordan's Hill, Horse Shoe Bend, and Hassalt Hill, as well as at the places already mentioned. The ancient river-deposits in which the diamonds are found lie under a capping of columnar basalt, and occur at isolated spots along the course of the Cudgegong river, more or less distant from the present river course, and at heights up to 40 feet above the present high-water level. They rest on the eroded edges of perpendicular sedimentary strata, which are interbedded with compact greenstones, and probably belong to the period of Upper Silurian deposits. The diamond-bearing débris consists of coarse sand and mud intermingled with pebbles of quartzite, sandstone, clay-slates, and quartz-slates, accompanied by waterworn grains and crystals of quartz, jasper, agate, silicified wood (this in large amount), and other siliceous minerals, also cassiterite (the " wood-tin " variety), topaz, common corundum (sometimes of a lavender-blue colour), sapphire, ruby, a peculiar variety of corundum called barklyite, zircon, garnet, ruby-spinel, brookite, magnetite, ilmenite, tourmaline, magnesite, nodules of limonite, grains of iridosmine, and, of special importance, gold. The quartz pebbles are frequently encrusted with oxides of iron and manganese. The whole mass of diamantiferous débris is in some places loose and incoherent, and in others bound together to form a solid conglomerate, the cementing material being a green, white, or grey siliceous substance, or a brown or black ferruginous or manganiferous substance. The deposit in places attains a thickness of 70 feet ; the diamonds, which are of small size, are scattered through it so sparingly and irregularly that the working of it cannot be profitably prolonged for any length of time.

In spite of the poor character of the deposit, 2500 stones were found during the first five months of work. All were small, the largest being the octahedron of $5\frac{5}{8}$ carats mentioned above, which, when cut, formed a beautiful colourless brilliant, weighing $3\frac{5}{16}$ carats. The stones average in weight about $\frac{1}{4}$ carat, and vary considerably in colour, passing from perfectly water-clear through various shades of yellow, pale green, and brown to almost black ; a twinned octahedron of a beautiful dark-green colour was once found. The commonest crystalline forms are the octahedron, which occurs both as simple and twinned crystals, the rhombic dodecahedron, triakis-octahedron, and hexakis-octahedron ; one crystal with the form of a deltoid dodecahedron has been found. The crystals are, as a rule, much water-worn ; when this is the case their surfaces are sometimes smooth and bright, at other times rough and dull. No spheres of bort, such as are found in Brazil and South Africa, appear to occur in Australia.

Solitary specimens of diamond have been found at many other places in this district. At Bald Hill, near Hill End, on the Turon river, a stone of $5\frac{1}{8}$ carats was found, and a number of diamonds, which though of small size were of excellent quality, were met with in the old gold-mines of Mittagong. Again, near Bathurst, a black diamond, the size of a pea, and having the form of an almost spherical hexakis-octahedron, was found. Diamonds have also been collected from the gravels underlying the basalt at Monkey Hill and Sally's Flat, in Co. Wellington, just as they occur at Mudgee. Uralla, Oberon, and Turnkey are other localities at which more than solitary specimens of diamonds have been found.

The occurrences mentioned above were all in ancient river gravels; among existing water-courses in which diamonds have been found may be mentioned the Abercrombie, Cudgegong, Macquarie, Brook's Creek, Shoalhaven, and Lachlan rivers. The stones found in existing streams are much worn, and many are broken; from this, and also from the fact that the minerals forming the gravels of these water-courses are identical with those of the ancient river deposits found underlying the basalt, we may conclude that the gravel of the present rivers is redeposited material derived from the ancient river-beds.

The mode of occurrence of the diamond in the north of New South Wales, especially in the district of the Gwydir river, in the neighbourhood of Bingera and Inverell, is of some importance. As pointed out by Professor A. Liversidge, diamonds are found in the valley of the Horton or Big river, seven or eight miles from Bingera, under just the same conditions as at Mudgee. The diamond-bearing deposit is 2 to 3 feet thick, and occurs in isolated patches, the material which originally lay between having been denuded away. These patches of diamantiferous material are scattered over an area measuring four by three miles, in a valley which is opened towards the north, but enclosed otherwise by the Drummond Range. The deposit consists of sandy and clayey material, and has probably been deposited in former times by the Horton river. The rocks of the locality are clay-slates of Devonian or Carboniferous age, and the sheet of basalt which occurs in the neighbourhood appears to overlie deposits similar to those now being considered. Here also the diamantiferous material is in places cemented together to form a solid conglomerate; it includes boulders and fragments of the underlying clay-slates, and, when clayey, contains crystals of gypsum. The associated minerals are practically the same as at Mudgee, barklyite is, however, here absent. Black tourmaline is regarded as a specially characteristic associate of the diamond, and its appearance is hailed with joy by the miners.

Diamonds occur here rather more plentifully; they are colourless or straw-yellow and small, the largest weighing only $2\frac{6}{8}$ carats. On an average only twenty stones are found in each ton of material, and a stock of 1680 stones weighed no more than about 140 carats.

More recently diamonds have been discovered in the tin-gravels of the neighbourhood of Inverell, and their occurrence here appears to be sufficiently abundant to justify systematic working. Cassiterite (tin-stone), rock-crystal, sapphire, topaz, tourmaline, monazite, &c., are here associated with diamond; gold, however, is apparently absent. Several companies have been formed, and many thousands of stones, averaging $\frac{1}{4}$ to $\frac{1}{3}$ carat in weight, have been obtained from the different mines; the largest of these stones weighed $3\frac{5}{8}$ carats. From the Borah tin-washings, situated at the junction of Cope's Creek with the Gwydir river, 200 stones were obtained in a few months, the largest of which weighed almost $1\frac{1}{2}$ carats; while in the Bengonover tin-washings, only a few miles away, a stone weighing nearly 2 carats was found. Diamonds have also been found in most of the alluvial tin-workings on Cope's, Newstead, Vegetable, and Middle Creeks, in the Stanifer, Ruby, and Britannia tin-washings, and elsewhere in the same district.

All the occurrences of diamond in New South Wales, described above, are in secondary deposits of alluvial origin; recently (1901), however, Mr. E. F. Pittman, the Government Geologist of New South Wales, has described its occurrence in what may perhaps be the mother-rock. At Ruby Hill on Bingera Creek, twelve miles to the south of Bingera, diamond has been found in the breccia filling a volcanic pipe. This breccia consists of angular fragments of clay-stone, felsite, basalt, eclogite, &c., with calcite, garnet, zircon, chrome-diopside, and other minerals; it bears a very striking resemblance to the diamantiferous material which fills the Kimberley pipes, the principal difference being that it shows no sign of serpentinisation.

Finally, we must mention the peculiar occurrence of diamond at Ballina, in New England, where solitary specimens have been found in the sands of the sea-shore. The diamond-bearing deposit is here exposed to the action of the waves of the sea, and the solitary specimens found in the shore sands have probably been washed out of the deposit by the waves.

The output of diamonds in New South Wales, as published in the official returns of the Department of Mines, amounted in 1899 to 25,874 carats, valued at £10,349 12s.; in 1900, owing to lack of water, and the reconstruction of the mining company, there was a smaller output of 9828½ carats, valued at £5663 1s. Although a fairly considerable number of diamonds have been met with in New South Wales, yet the other Australian States are very poor in this respect; it is probable, however, that there will be important finds in the future.

In **Queensland,** conglomerates have been observed at Wallerawang and on the Mary river, which are remarkably like the diamond-bearing deposits of Mudgee and Bingera; no diamonds have, however, as yet been discovered in them. At other places in Queensland, namely, on the Palmer river and the Gilbert river, the precious stone has been found.

In **South Australia** about 100 stones have been found in the alluvial gold-washings of Echunga, twenty miles to the south-east of Adelaide; it was here that the octahedron of $5\frac{5}{16}$ carats, previously mentioned, was found. In **Victoria** a few diamonds were met with in 1862 in the Owens and in the Arena goldfields; a larger number of stones were found in the Beechworth district of the same State, upwards of sixty crystals, none however exceeding 1 carat in weight, having been collected. Diamonds have also been stated to occur in the neighbourhood of Melbourne, in association with ruby, sapphire, zircon, and topaz.

Finally, from **Western Australia** also, a certain number of diamonds have come, small crystals rich in faces having been found near Freemantle, in a sand containing zircon, ilmenite, rock-crystal, red, yellow, and white topaz, and apatite. More recently, in 1895, it was reported that diamonds had been found in the north-west of the State, at Nullagine, in the Pilbarra gold-field; many leases have been taken up, but so far no important finds have been made. From 230 tons of auriferous ore treated in 1900 only twenty-five small diamonds were obtained.

Tasmania has recently been added to the list of diamond-producing countries. According to newspaper reports, a large number of stones were found at the end of the year 1894 in Corinna, one of the richest goldfields of the island. The reported occurrence caused a rush of thousands of diamond-seekers into Tasmania from the Australian mainland; many companies for the exploitation of the deposits sprung up, but apparently with no marked results.

6. NORTH AMERICA.

The occurrence of the diamond in the United States of North America is so sparing that it has no effect whatever upon the diamond markets of the world. American stones are, however, greatly prized in the States, both for patriotic reasons and also on account of their scientific interest.

There are two principal diamond-producing regions, one in the extreme east and the other in the extreme west of the country; the former occupies the eastern slope of the southern part of the Appalachians, while the latter lies at the western foot of the Sierra Nevada and the Cascade Range. Though the two regions are so widely severed, yet in each the stones occur under very similar conditions, being found in loose detrital materials, in gravel and sand, and everywhere in association with the same minerals, namely, garnet, zircon, magnetite, anatase, monazite, and specially with gold, in the search for which diamonds are frequently found. This agreement in the mode of occurrence of the diamond in the two regions, must be attributed to the fact that in both the detrital material has been derived by the weathering and denudation of the crystalline silicate rocks of which the surrounding mountains are built, and that these rocks are essentially identical in character in both regions, although those of the east are older than those in the west.

A third diamantiferous district has been recently discovered, namely, the region of the Great Lakes; here the stones have been found in glacial deposits mainly in the State of Wisconsin, but also in Michigan and Ohio.

According to Mr. George F. Kunz, the well-known American expert in precious stones, a considerable number of diamonds have hitherto been found in the eastern region, in the States of Georgia and North Carolina, very few in South Carolina, and still fewer in Kentucky and the southern part of Virginia. From Virginia came the "Dewey" diamond, the largest ever met with in the United States. It was found by a labourer in 1855 in an excavation in the village of Manchester, and had the form of an octahedron with rounded edges, weighing in the rough $23\frac{3}{4}$ carats and when cut $11\frac{11}{16}$ carats. This stone is not of the purest water and its beauty is impaired by other flaws, so that it would not be actually worth more than 300 to 400 dollars (about £62 to £83); in spite of this, however, it has been sold for about ten times this amount. It was the only specimen found at this spot.

In North Carolina diamonds have been found, usually associated with gold, in the district about the east foot of the Blue Ridge. The mountains of the district are built up of crystalline schists; itacolumite, the flexible sandstone which occupies so important a position in the Brazilian deposits, is also found here, though at present no diamonds have been discovered in it. The stones hitherto met with are for the most part octahedra; the largest yet found, weighing $4\frac{1}{2}$ carats, was discovered in 1886. A stone valued at 400 dollars is said to have been found in South Carolina; in this State, as in North Carolina, diamonds are found associated with gold and in the vicinity of itacolumite; the largest, an octahedron of $4\frac{1}{12}$ carats, was found in 1887. About the year 1886 a single small stone was found in a river sand in Kentucky.

During a search for gold in Wisconsin, at the end of the eighties, a few small diamonds were found associated with grains of quartz, magnetite, ilmenite, and with grains and crystals of the varieties of garnet known as almandine and hessonite (or perhaps spessartite). A few large diamonds have been found in this State; thus in 1893 an almost colourless stone, weighing $3\frac{14}{16}$ carats, and having the form of a rhombic dodecahedron, was found in clay at the town of Oregon, Dane County. Previous to this, in 1876, a yellow diamond of the same form and weighing 16 carats was found with several others near Eagle in Waukesha

County; this stone was not recognised as a diamond until 1883. It had been bought by a Milwaukee clockmaker, who did not know what it was, for a dollar. A second still larger stone, stated to have been found about the same time in the same district, was mislaid before its real nature was known. In the year 1886 a pale yellow diamond, with the form of an irregular rhombic dodecahedron, measuring 20 by 13 by 10 millimetres and weighing $21\frac{1}{4}$ carats, was found at Kohlsville in Washington County. Another stone of $6\frac{13}{32}$ carats, found at Saukville in Ozaukee County in 1880, was not determined to be diamond until 1896. Altogether, since 1883, seventeen diamonds, varying in weight from $\frac{1}{2}$ to $21\frac{1}{4}$ carats, have been found in glacial moraines in the region of the Great Lakes of North America, principally in the State of Wisconsin, but also in Michigan and Ohio. The predominating crystalline forms are the rhombic dodecahedron and a hexakis-octahedron; the stones are colourless, or tinted with green or yellow. By plotting the diamond localities and the directions of the glacial striæ on a map, Professor W. H. Hobbs has recently (1899) shown that the diamond probably came from somewhere near James Bay on Hudson Bay; a more detailed study of the glacial geology of the region will, however, be needed before the home of the diamond can be exactly located.

In the western region a certain number of diamonds have been met with in the States of California and Oregon; in the former the stones occur in gold-bearing detritus belonging to two different periods of formation. Here, in Tertiary and even earlier times, the Sierra Nevada and Cascade Range were drained by immense rivers, whose beds, which have been traced for great distances, became filled with auriferous débris derived from these mountains. Later on mighty volcanic eruptions took place, and the surface of northern California and of Oregon was flooded with thick sheets of lava partly filling up the river valleys. The streams and rivers of the present day, rising in the same mountains, cut out for themselves new courses in these volcanic rocks, and have deposited in their beds auriferous débris derived from the same mountains, and therefore of the same nature as the débris laid down in the ancient river-beds. It was from these latter masses of débris that the enormous amount of gold yielded by the Californian goldfields in the early days of their discovery, namely, about the year 1848, was mainly derived. These later gold-sands are now exhausted, and mining is at the present day confined to the earlier deposits of Tertiary and Pre-Tertiary alluvium, which are overlain by lavas and which contain diamonds as well as gold. The pebbles and diamonds of this alluvium are often cemented together by limonite to form a solid conglomerate, which is very similar in appearance to the " tapanhoacanga " of the Brazilian diamond-fields.

The first find of diamonds took place in 1850; since then single stones, usually only of small size, have been met with every year, the largest weighing $7\frac{1}{4}$ carats. The diamonds actually present probably far exceed those actually found in number, for, during the process of winning the precious metal, the solid, auriferous conglomerate is stamped to a fine powder, and thus any diamonds present in it are also crushed and destroyed. As a matter of fact, the presence of splinters of diamond in this crushed material has been frequently observed. Moreover, it is possible that many stones have been lost on account of the practice of ignorant miners, prevalent both here and in other countries, of testing the genuineness of a supposed diamond by means of the hammer and anvil; should such a stone be genuine the test, owing to the brittleness and perfect cleavage of the diamond, results in its complete fragmentation.

The possible occurrence of diamonds in those parts of North America, for example Indiana, which are geologically very similar to other diamond-bearing districts, has often been suggested. In many such places, however, the search has been unsuccessful, and stones reported to have been found in other places have in many cases been placed there with the object of swindling a credulous public.

As an example of the almost incredible extent to which the public have been swindled by false reports as to the occurrence of diamonds, an account of a supposed discovery in the State of Arizona may be given. In the year 1870, a fabulously rich occurrence of various precious stones, including the diamond, was reported to have been discovered somewhere in the West. 80,000 carats of rubies and a single diamond weighing 108 carats, said to form part of the find, were exhibited in a San Francisco bank. Shortly after this a smaller lot of stones, said to be the result of a second search, were on view in this city, and the attention of capitalists was soon enlisted. On May 10, 1872, a Bill in the interests of the diamond-miners was passed by Congress, and an expedition for investigating the locality was fitted out. After some trouble the locality was found, and in the course of a week the members of the expedition had collected 1000 carats of diamonds and 6000 to 7000 carats of rubies, and returned well pleased with their success. Another expedition failed to find the place, and an investigation by the officers of the United States Geological Survey proved the supposed discovery to be a gigantic swindle, the locality having been " salted." The supposed rubies were in reality ordinary garnets, and although the smaller diamonds were genuine the 108-carat stone was nothing but rock-crystal. It was ascertained that a speculative American had imported a large number of rough Cape diamonds, and had scattered them about the neighbourhood so plentifully that stray stones were found there for some years afterwards. The initial outlay of the speculative American was amply repaid by the three-quarters of a million dollars subscribed by Californian and other capitalists.

Diamonds are sought for very diligently in America; it is not unusual for gold miners and labourers engaged in the work of excavation to wear rings set with small, rough diamonds for the purpose of familiarising themselves with the appearance of this stone in its rough condition. In spite, however, of the alertness of persons engaged in such occupations, only a small number of stones continue to be found, though it is always possible that future discoveries of importance may be made.

7. BRITISH GUIANA.

In recent years diamonds have been found in another part of South America, about 2000 miles north-west of the famous Brazilian localities, namely, in the gold-washings on the upper course of the River Mazaruni in British Guiana. The discovery was made accidentally in 1890 by Edward Gilkes, who, while prospecting for gold along the Putareng creek, a tributary of the Mazaruni, found a few diamonds in the batea he was accustomed to use for gold-washing. The locality is situated in latitude 6° 14′ N. and longitude 60° 18′ W., about 150 miles above the town of Bartica on the confluence of the Mazaruni and Essequibo rivers. It is reached after a twelve to twenty days' journey, according to the state of the river, which has many falls and rapids, from Georgetown. The exact spot is situated about four miles from the Mazaruni, and is reached by a narrow trail across swampy land and through tropical jungle, everything having to be carried on the heads of Indians.

The rocks of the Mazaruni valley are largely gneisses and granite traversed by dykes of diabase and other similar rocks. The diamond-workings at present under consideration are situated on the side of a hill, and penetrate (1) 18 inches of pure, white quartz-sand, (2) 18 inches of yellowish sandy clay, with fragments of quartz and portions of sand and gravel cemented together by iron oxide, in which small diamonds are occasionally found, (3) 7 feet—

the present limit of working—of clay, which becomes more and more gravelly and the constituent fragments larger and more frequently cemented together with iron oxide, as greater depths are reached. Some of the pebbles are much rounded, and have sand and smaller pebbles attached to them by a felspathic cement, while others are sharp and angular. Some consist of felsite and concretionary iron-stone, but most are of quartz. Associated with these pebbles are grains of ilmenite and small rounded pebbles of black tourmaline and pleonaste, and occasionally of topaz and corundum. When dug out, the gravel is carried in wooden dishes to a little creek hard by, where it is washed in sieves of one-sixteenth inch mesh, the residue being picked over while wet. The diamonds, originally found by Mr. Gilkes in 1890, were obtained at the foot of the hill in the bottom of the valley. The diamantiferous gravel here contains many crystals of quartz, and rests upon a bed-rock of kaolin, differing in both these respects from that which lies on the hill-side.

Up to 1900 diamonds had been found only over an area of country measuring 200 yards in length by about 100 in breadth, but it is probable that the diamantiferous gravels are much more widely distributed. The mode of occurrence of the diamond in these gravels and the minerals with which it is associated are very much the same as in Brazil. The diamond has not yet been found here in its mother-rock; if this should at any time be discovered, British Guiana may become an important diamond-producing country.

As yet there have been found only some few thousands of small diamonds, which have the form of octahedra, and are exceptionally white and brilliant. The smallest are of very small size and the largest about $1\frac{1}{2}$ carats, but there are very few exceeding a carat in weight. During the ten years between 1890 and 1900 between 2000 and 3000 diamonds were found, while, according to custom-house returns, the total export of diamonds up to January 28, 1902, amounted to £10,000. A parcel of 282 stones sent to London during the year 1900 was valued at £2 8s. per carat. During a period of six weeks in the following year, a New York company obtained 8227 small diamonds with an aggregate weight of 767 carats, which were valued at £1920 or £2 10s. per carat. A dozen companies have since been organised and are now at work, and fresh ground is constantly being opened up, so that the diamond-mining industry of British Guiana is likely to develop rapidly.

We are indebted for the above account of the occurrence of diamonds on the upper Mazaruni river to Mr. G. F. Kunz's Annual Reports on Precious Stones, in which is brought together much information from various sources.

Another occurrence of diamond in British Guiana is reported by Professor J. B. Harrison, the Government Geologist of that colony. This is in the gold-washing claims of the Omai creek, this stream being a small tributary of the Essequibo river, which it joins at a spot about 130 miles above the mouth of the latter. From a part of the bed of Gilt creek, one of the tributaries of this stream, measuring about 500 feet in length and 50 in breadth, some 60,000 ounces of gold and some hundreds of small diamonds have been recovered by the somewhat crude methods hitherto in use. The auriferous gravels of this stream consist of fragments of more or less decomposed diabase, pebbles of concretionary iron-stone and angular quartz. They yielded at one time hundreds of very small diamonds, the majority of which were perfectly clear and colourless octahedra, the remainder being of various shades of pink, green, and clear yellow.

It is stated by Mr. G. F. Kunz that in **Dutch Guiana** also diamonds have been found for years past in the tailings of the gold-washings. They have been for the most part small and have attracted but little attention, the gold being the chief object sought for. One fine stone, however, is reported to have been found about the year 1890 and to have been cut in the United States.

8. URAL MOUNTAINS.

The discovery of diamonds in the Urals resulted from the famous expedition made in 1829 to this region by Alexander von Humboldt, with Gustav Rose and Ehrenberg, at the desire of Czar Nicholas. In 1823, in his *Essai géognostique sur le gisement des roches*, Humboldt had expressed an opinion, based on the similarity between the Brazilian and Uralian gold- and platinum-bearing deposits, that diamonds very probably existed in the Uralian deposits just as they were known to do in Brazil. This conclusion, which was supported by the fact that the minerals associated with gold and platinum in the Urals and in Brazil were practically identical, had been previously and independently expressed by Professor Moritz von Engelhardt of Dorpat, who later investigated and reported on the first diamond occurrence in the Urals. Humboldt was so convinced of the truth of his opinion, that on his departure he assured the Czarina that he would not again appear before her Majesty unless he had some Russian diamonds to show.

Throughout their whole journey the explorers spared no pains in their search for the precious stones; every gold-bearing sand they met with was subjected to microscopical examination in order to detect the presence of diamond; their efforts, however, were not crowned with the success they deserved.

Better fortune fell to the lot of Count Polier, who accompanied the expedition part of the way and to whom Humboldt had communicated some of his own enthusiasm on the subject. On leaving Humboldt's party, therefore, the Count set himself seriously to work in the mining district of Bissersk (about latitude $58\frac{1}{2}°$ N.), in the gold-washings on the estates of his wife, the Princess Shachovskoi. Here the first Uralian diamond, indeed the first European diamond, was found on July 5, 1829. The exact locality was the small gold-washing of Adolphskoi, near the larger washing of Krestovosvidshenskoi, twenty-five versts (seventeen miles) to the north-east of Bissersk, and four versts (about three miles) from the mountain ridge on the western or European slope of the Urals. It is situated in a side stream of the Paludenka, one of the head-streams of the Koiva, which flows into the Chussovaya, itself a tributary of the Kama river.

The muddy-looking gold-sand of the Adolphskoi washings contains, besides diamonds and gold, a few grains of platinum, also quartz, limonite, magnetite, much iron-pyrites (either bright yellow and unaltered or altered on the surface to limonite), chalcedony, anatase, &c., and fragments of the neighbouring rocks. All these minerals and rock-fragments have been derived from the mountain ridge which overhangs the stream, and which is principally composed of a quartzose chloritic talc-schist, which has been suggested to be identical with the Brazilian itacolumite, but which, according to the investigation of G. Rose, in no way agrees with this. This chlorite-talc-schist contains subordinate beds of hæmatite, grey limestone, and especially dolomite, coloured black by carbonaceous matter. This dolomite immediately underlies the gold-sands of the Adolphskoi washings, and was considered by von Engelhardt to be the original mother-rock of the diamond. Other observers regard the chlorite-talc-schist as the mother-rock; since diamonds have as yet only been found loose in the sands and never embedded in rock, the point remains a disputed one.

Only about 150 diamonds have hitherto been found in the Adolphskoi gold-washings, so that the discovery of this locality has not in any way affected the diamond market. The stones are colourless to yellowish, perfectly transparent and very brilliant; a few crystals, however, show dark brown or black enclosures; their crystalline form is almost invariably the rhombic dodecahedron, the faces of which are curved and nicked along the short diagonal (Fig. 31 c). The largest weighed $2\frac{17}{32}$ carats, the five coming next in order of size weighed respectively $1\frac{1}{4}$, $1\frac{1}{8}$, $1\frac{1}{16}$, $1\frac{1}{32}$, and 1 carat, while the remainder were small, the smallest weighing only $\frac{1}{8}$ carat; the twenty-eight stones first found had an aggregate weight of $17\frac{9}{16}$ carats. A recent discovery of five stones at this locality led to the institution of a systematic search, which, however, has been unattended with any marked success.

The occurrence of diamonds in the Urals is not confined to the Adolphskoi washings, for in 1831 two small diamonds, one weighing $\frac{5}{8}$ carat, were found in the Medsher gold-washings, fourteen versts (nine miles) east of Ekaterinburg. Again in 1838, a small stone weighing $\frac{7}{16}$ carat was found in the Kushaisk mine, which lies in the sands of the Goroblagodatsk mining district, twenty-five versts (seventeen miles) from the smelting furnaces of Kushvinsk and east of Bissersk. In the next year a crystal weighing $\frac{7}{8}$ carat was found in the Uspenskoi mine in the sands of the district of Verchne-Uralsk in the government of Orenburg. Solitary stones have been found also at other places, for example, recently in the Charitono-Companeiski sands on the Serebrianaya river in the district of Kungur, government of Perm; among these was a twin-crystal showing several hexakis-tetrahedra in combination, and having a thickness of 5 millimetres. Among these finds were a small colourless stone from the Kamenka mine, in the Troitzk district, government of Orenburg, and also the first diamond discovered in the southern Urals; this latter is a perfectly transparent, yellow hexakis-octahedron of $\frac{3}{5}$ carat, and was found in 1893 in the gold-washings of Katshkar. This latter discovery is of interest, for it shows that the diamond is more widely distributed in the Urals than was formerly thought to be the case; moreover, the minerals with which it is associated in the southern Urals are the same as in Brazil, from which we may conclude that the diamond originated in a similar manner in the two countries.

The occurrence of diamonds in the Urals is so rare and the stones themselves are so small that there are persons who doubt the genuineness of the occurrence, and express the opinion that the stones which have been met with found their way to this locality in order to fulfil Humboldt's prophecy. No definite proof of fraud has, however, been brought forward, and Russian mineralogists, who have closely studied the question, are satisfied that the occurrence is genuine, their opinion being supported by recent discoveries of stones having been made. A number of rough diamonds acquired from other countries, have been distributed by the Russian Government among the managers of mines, in order that the miners shall become familiar with the appearance of rough stones, and the possibility of diamonds being overlooked avoided.

9. LAPLAND.

In a far western corner of the Russian empire, namely, in Russian Lapland, a few small diamonds have been recently found. At the time of the expedition of C. Rabot in the second half of the eighties, a few stones were found in the valley of the Pasevig river which flows into the Varanger Fjord, an arm of the Arctic Ocean, and forms the Russo-Norwegian frontier in longitude 30° E of Greenwich. This river flows over gneiss which is penetrated by numerous veins of granite and pegmatite, by the weathering of which the diamond-bearing sand has originated.

According to the investigations of C. Vélain, these sands contain the following minerals, named in the order of their frequency of occurrence: Garnet (almandine) in rose-red rounded grains, forming half the total bulk of the sand, zircon, brown and green hornblende, glaucophane, kyanite, green augite, quartz, corundum, rutile, magnetite, staurolite, andalusite, tourmaline, epidote, felspar (oligoclase), and, lastly, the rarest constituent, diamond. The diamonds occur as small, angular, rarely water-worn, water-clear grains or broken fragments. These rarely exceed 0·25 mm. in diameter, though one crystal has been found measuring 1·5 mm. across. The transparency of the stones is greatly impaired by the presence of numerous enclosures, some being cavities containing gas, while others are microscopic crystals of an unknown substance. That these small grains are indubitable diamonds is demonstrated both by their hardness and by the fact that they are combustible in oxygen, the products of combustion being pure carbon dioxide.

The minerals associated with the diamond in Lapland are practically the same as in India and Brazil; epidote, however, while present in India is absent in Brazil, and the hydrous chloro-phosphates, so abundant in Brazil, are here absent. Vélain has expressed the opinion that the diamond here originated in the pegmatite; the mother-rock and the precious stone having been formed concurrently, as is also supposed by Chaper to be the case with the pegmatite at Wajra Karur, near Bellary in southern India, described above. In any case the Lapland diamonds must have been derived from one of the ancient crystalline rocks mentioned above, since no other type of rock is present in the whole of this region. No recent accounts of this locality have been published, and further investigation is much to be desired, since it would probably shed fresh light on the problem as to the nature of the original mother-rock of the diamond, and on the doubtful occurrence of diamond in pegmatite at Wajra Karur. Though of no commercial or economic importance, the discovery of Rabot and Vélain is of great scientific interest and should be assiduously followed up.

10. DIAMONDS IN METEORITES.

In recent years our knowledge of the distribution of diamonds has been extended in an interesting direction by the observation that this mineral occurs in a number of meteorites in the form of small, usually microscopic, grains of a grey or black colour, closely resembling carbonado. Diamond is thus a substance which is not confined to the earth, but is present in extra-terrestrial bodies, fragments of which, from time to time, fall upon the earth's surface. From an æsthetic point of view, meteoric diamonds are, of course, valueless; their interest and importance in connection with the natural history of the mineral is, on the contrary, very considerable, and it is fitting that this particular occurrence of the diamond should receive appropriate mention, especially as on it various theories as to the mode of origin of the diamond in the earth's crust have been based.

The meteorite which fell in Russia on the morning of September 22, 1886, in a field three miles from the village of Novo-Urei, on the right bank of the Alatyr, a river in the Krasnoslobodsk district of the government of Penza, was the first in which diamonds were observed. It was examined by Messrs. Jerofejeff and Latshinoff, and was found to consist of the minerals olivine and augite, with interspersed carbonaceous matter and metallic nickeliferous iron. The carbonaceous substance contained small greyish grains, the hardness, specific gravity, chemical composition, and appearance under the microscope of which, proved them to be undoubtedly diamond (carbonado). The results arrived at by these investigators have been fully confirmed by others. In this stone diamond was present in the proportion of 1 per cent., so that, since the whole meteorite weighed 1762·3 grams (rather less than 4 lbs.), the total amount of diamond present was 17·62 grams or 85·43 carats.

Black grains of diamond have also been observed in the meteoric stone of Carcote, in the desert of Atacama, in Chile. Diamonds have subsequently been found, usually in meteoric irons, for example, in that which fell at Arva in Hungary, and at Cañon Diablo in Arizona.

Many meteoric irons contain small cubes of graphite, having the same crystalline form as cubes of diamond ; this cubic form of graphitic carbon, to which the name cliftonite has been given, is present in the meteoric irons which fell at Arva in Hungary, at Toluca in Mexico, at Youndegin in Western Australia, in Cocke County and at Smithville in Tennessee, and perhaps also in a few others. It is, however, highly probable that these cubes were originally diamond, and were changed into graphite by the agency of heat, the possibility of such a change being effected artificially by heating diamonds away from contact with air, having been previously mentioned above. If this be so, the occurrence of diamond in meteorites is much more general than has been supposed, and now that attention has been drawn to the matter, it is probable that closer examination will demonstrate the presence of diamond in many other meteorites in which its absence has not been definitely proved.

C. ORIGIN AND ARTIFICIAL PRODUCTION OF THE DIAMOND.

The problem as to the origin of the diamond in nature is one which has received no small amount of attention. Many and various are the suggestions which have been from time to time put forward, but few are based on scientific considerations, the majority being purely imaginative, and therefore valueless as working hypotheses.

Before formulating any useful hypothesis as to the mode of origin of the diamond in nature, it is necessary to learn as much as possible of the conditions under which diamonds occur in all parts of the globe and in extra-terrestrial matter, and of the manner in which they may be artificially produced. Of neither of these subjects is our knowledge much in advance of that of former years. The artificial production of diamonds is an art yet in its infancy, and for the elucidation of the problem as to their natural origin, experiments in the artificial production under conditions corresponding as closely as possible to natural conditions, are required. A close study of the conditions under which diamonds occur in nature is desirable therefore, not only as an aid in making such experiments, but also with a view to the collection of detailed information respecting the minerals associated with the diamond, a knowledge of the mode of origin of which would be a substantial help in the solution of the problem.

Almost every mode of origin, possible and impossible, for the diamond has, at one time or another, been brought forward : thus some have conceived the formation of diamond to have been brought about by the vital processes of plants ; others have derived the precious stone from organic remains : and yet others from inorganic substances. Some assume a high temperature to have been an essential of the process ; while others, on the ground that diamond subjected to high temperatures is converted into graphite, consider such a condition an impossibility. A few of the many theories which have been brought forward are set forth below :

The earliest is that of the celebrated physicist, Sir David Brewster, who unreservedly expressed the opinion that the formation of diamonds was due to the vital processes of plants, the process of formation having been similar to that of the formation of resin, and that the diamond at one time was viscous like a resin. The view that the diamond had been separated out from the sap of some plant in much the same way as a form of silica, the so-called tabasheer, is separated out and deposited in the knotty stems of the bamboo, was accepted also by the Scotch mineralogist, Jameson, and similar views were held by Petzholdt.

D'Orbigny regarded the diamond as a decomposition product of extinct plants; the same view was held by Wöhler, who assumed the alteration to have taken place at a low temperature, and vigorously disputed the theory which demanded a high temperature for the formation of the diamond. J. D. Dana, on the other hand, regarded a high temperature if not as an essential, at least as a probable condition, and considered that the diamond might have been derived from organic substances by the same processes which effect the metamorphism of rocks. Göppert entertained similar views, owing to his belief that in the course of his detailed investigation of the enclosures of diamond he had detected plant remains. By theorists of this school it was supposed that the decomposition products of decaying vegetable gradually escaped, leaving behind a substance which contained an ever-increasing proportion of carbon; this substance, having been at length transformed into pure, amorphous carbon, was supposed to be capable of taking on the crystalline form of diamond. Very similar views were held by G. Wilson, who supposed that hydrogen and oxygen gradually escaped from woody matter and left behind a substance resembling anthracite, which, by further alteration, he conceived might be transformed into diamond. These processes were assumed to take place at a low temperature, since at higher temperatures graphite, and not diamond, would be formed.

The opposite opinion was held by Parrot, namely, that the alteration of woody matter took place at high temperatures; he suggested that the transformation into diamond of small particles of carbonaceous matter, strongly heated by volcanic agencies, was effected by a sudden cooling. Carvill Lewis has expressed similar views with special reference to the origin of South African diamonds. He considered the diamond to be formed in the kimberlite at the time this was erupted into the pipes as a molten igneous rock. Numerous fragments of the carbonaceous and bituminous shales, through which the igneous rock forced a passage, were caught up by the igneous mass, and Carvill Lewis supposed the heat of this mass to have converted the carbon contained in the fragments of shale into diamond. According to the views of other investigators the igneous rock itself contained carbon, which crystallised out of the molten mass as diamond, before it was erupted into the volcanic pipes.

C. C. von Leonhard also invoked the aid of volcanic heat, but supposed the carbon to be volatilised, and diamonds to be formed by the crystallisation of the sublimed carbon. G. Bischof, while he does not combat the view that the diamond has been formed from vegetable matter, makes no definite statement with regard to its mode of origin other than the opinion that a high temperature is an impossible condition.

Liebig supposed that by some kind of decomposition a product growing ever richer in carbon was separated out from a fluid hydrocarbon, and that this product, when it finally became pure carbon, crystallised in the form of diamond; he pointed out that such a mode of origin could only conceivably take place at low temperatures, the combustibility of the substance rendering the process impossible under the conditions of a high temperature and the presence of oxygen. Berthelot, though not referring specially to diamond, has asserted that a separation of carbon from such a liquid could take place only under the influence of heat, a statement directly opposed to the assumption made by Liebig. Chancourtois brought forward a theory to the effect that diamond has been formed by the slow oxidation of emanations of a gaseous hydrocarbon, the hydrogen forming water, part of the carbon forming carbon dioxide, and the remainder crystallising as diamond, the whole process being analogous to the formation of sulphur from hydrogen sulphide, the oxidation of the hydrogen being accompanied by the separation of crystals of sulphur.

A few authorities, including the mineralogist, J. N. Fuchs, suppose that large amounts of carbon dioxide are present in many places in the interior of the earth, and that this has played an essential part in the formation of the diamond.

Göbel suggested that at high temperatures carbon dioxide might be reduced by certain metals, such as aluminium, magnesium, calcium, iron, or by silicon, &c., the carbon crystallising out during the reduction as diamond. In connection with the existence of drops of liquid carbon dioxide enclosed in cavities in certain diamonds, Simmler stated the opinion that liquid carbon dioxide at a high temperature and pressure is capable of dissolving carbon, and that from this solution carbon may crystallise out as diamond. These assumptions were not, however, supported by the investigations of Gore and of Dölter, who failed to establish the solubility of carbon either in liquid carbon dioxide or in gaseous carbon dioxide above the critical temperature and under great pressure.

The compounds of carbon with chlorine are sometimes assumed to be the original source of the carbon of the diamond. A. Favre, and later H. St. Claire Deville, admitted the possibility of the formation of diamond from such compounds, the former having been induced to entertain this idea from the fact that certain minerals associated with the diamond in Brazil can be artificially produced from chlorine compounds. Gorceix, who was well acquainted with Brazilian deposits, considered such an origin for diamonds from this region to be quite within the range of possibility, the carbon being supplied by chlorine or fluorine compounds. Without committing himself to any details of the process, Damour also considers it possible that Brazilian diamonds may have originated by the interaction of a variety of suitable compounds. Finally, we may mention the hypothesis for which Gannal is responsible, namely, that the diamond may have been formed by the decomposition of carbon bisulphide. Other possible modes of formation will be mentioned when the methods employed in the artificial production of diamonds are under consideration.

A consideration of the character of the various diamantiferous deposits, which are scattered over the face of the globe, and often widely separated, leads inevitably to the conclusion that there is no single mode of origin common to all diamonds, but that in different deposits the diamond has originated in different ways. If the diamond really occurs in India and Lapland embedded as an original constituent in granite-veins penetrating gneiss, and in South Africa in an olivine-rock associated with gneiss, it almost certainly follows that in these localities the diamond has been formed in the same way as the igneous rock in which it occurs.

Unfortunately, however, this brings us no nearer the truth, for the exact mode of formation of such rocks is still one of the obscure questions of geology. It is probable that such granite-veins (pegmatite) are due to the solidification, presumably at not very high temperatures, of masses of fused silicates saturated with water. Such a mode of origin is, however, not likely in the case of the gneisses and rocks interfoliated with them, such as the olivine-rock in which the diamonds of the Cape were originally contained, and in the alteration product of which, namely, the serpentine-breccia, they are now found. If, on the other hand, this original olivine-rock is not interfoliated with gneiss at some depth below the earth's surface, but is an eruptive rock which has penetrated the gneiss, as Carvill Lewis has urged, then its mode of origin may not differ essentially from that of pegmatite, and the South African diamonds may have been formed in the same way as those of India and Lapland. If, then, in these countries the diamond is, or has been, a constituent of an igneous rock, we must conclude that it was during the cooling and solidifying of the fused mass of rock that the diamond crystallised out, the carbon of its substance, if not present as a normal constituent of the rock, being derived from bituminous foreign matter. The existence of enclosures of liquid carbon dioxide in the minerals of such rocks, especially in the quartz of granite and gneiss, but also in olivine and even in diamond itself, has a special significance in this connection. Luzi has demonstrated that in the presence of water and of compounds of fluorine, carbon is soluble in a fused silicate. Though in the experiments of this investigator the dissolved carbon separated out in the form not of diamond but of graphite, it is not inconceivable that under other conditions, such as the high pressure and temperature of the earth's interior and the presence of other substances, diamond itself might be formed. The more recent experiments of I. Friedländer (1898) have demonstrated that graphite is soluble in fused olivine, and that on cooling diamond separates out, facts which have an important bearing on the origin of South African diamonds.

The diamonds which, together with crystals of quartz and other minerals, are found in crevices in the itacolumite of Brazil must have originated in quite a different way. There is not the slightest doubt that the crystals of quartz and of the accompanying minerals have been deposited from aqueous solution, perhaps even at ordinary temperatures. If this mode of occurrence of the diamond is really a fact, we can only assume that the diamond originated in the same way as the minerals with which it is associated, but as to the nature of a solution capable of depositing diamonds only negative statements can be made. Gorceix, who first expressed the opinion that Brazilian diamonds originated in the same way as the minerals with which they are associated, considered that this common origin must be sought not in the direction of deposition by solution, but rather in the interaction of gases, such as compounds of chlorine and fluorine and water-vapour rising up from the interior of the earth.

The diamonds of the Adolphskoi gold-washings in the Urals have been supposed to have been originally embedded in a bituminous dolomite. Engelhardt, who first suggested the probable identity of the bituminous dolomite with the mother-rock of the diamonds of this district, supposed the diamonds to have originated by the transformation of the bituminous material, but made no suggestion as to the means whereby such a transformation might be effected.

The occurrence of diamond in the meteoric stone of Novo-Urei, on account of its association with olivine and augite, is comparable with its occurrence in South Africa, and the mode of origin of the diamond in South Africa and in extra-terrestrial matter of this type is probably one and the same. The origin of diamond in meteoric iron is, however, of a different kind. Under ordinary conditions the excess of carbon taken up by molten iron crystallises out on cooling in the form of graphite, and crystals of this modification of carbon are frequently to be seen both in ordinary cast-iron and in most meteoric irons. Moissan, however, has recently demonstrated that when a mass of molten iron solidifies under great pressure, the carbon separates out as diamond. The existence of diamond in meteoric iron may conceivably be due to causes other than high pressure during its solidification, such, for example, as the presence of nickel, phosphorus, and other chemical elements.

It is obvious from what has been said that the origin of the diamond in nature is still to a great extent shrouded in mystery. For the complete elucidation of the problem further study of the various modes of occurrence of the precious stone, and of the minerals associated with it, together with more extended experiments in its artificial production, are desirable and necessary.

Very few facts shedding light on the problem as to the origin of diamond have hitherto been gleaned from experiments in the **artificial production** of the precious stone, the observation and study of diamantiferous deposits having been a much more fruitful method of attacking the problem. Although various experimenters have from time to time asserted their success in producing artificial diamonds, it is only in quite recent years that absolutely unquestionable results have been attained.   The methods employed by various workers have, as a rule, differed from each other ; thus in one case it has been sought to obtain diamonds by fusing or volatilising carbon in the intense heat of the electric furnace ; in another by the separation of carbon from one of its liquid compounds at ordinary temperatures, or at a high temperature combined with great pressure.   Some of the most important investigations have been made by Despretz and Hannay, and of the more recent experimenters Moissan has been most successful.   Even the crystals obtained by Moissan scarcely exceed microscropic size, so that though their scientific interest is great, they are inapplicable as gems.

In the experiments of Despretz (1853), electric sparks were continually passed through a vacuum for a period exceeding a month ; the terminals made use of were respectively a carbon cylinder and a platinum wire.   At the conclusion of the experiment it was found that the latter had received a coating of particles of carbon, which, under a magnification of 30 diameters, appeared as small octahedra, and were said to scratch corundum.   In other experiments in which the terminals were a carbon point and a platinum wire, the electric current was passed through acidulated water, and similar, though less marked, results were stated to have been obtained.   In neither case, however, were the particles of carbon proved beyond question to be diamond.

In 1880 it was demonstrated by J. B. Hannay, a Scotch chemist, that metallic sodium, and still more metallic lithium, is capable at a high temperature of separating carbon from a hydrocarbon ; the same worker also claimed to have established the fact that, at a high temperature and pressure, carbon could be separated in the same way from nitrogenous organic substances.   The investigation was carried out by placing lithium and paraffin (the latter to play the part of a hydrocarbon) and a little sperm-oil in a very strong, sealed, wrought-iron cylinder, which was then exposed to a very high temperature ; the interaction of these substances thus took place under great pressure.   It was hoped that the carbon separated from the paraffin by the lithium would, at the moment of its separation, dissolve in the sperm-oil, and that on cooling diamond would crystallise out from this solution.   A crystalline mass, containing 97 per cent. of carbon was indeed obtained, but its identity with diamond is, as before, doubtful.

Since 1893 more successful experiments having the same object in view have been devised and performed by Moissan, the celebrated French chemist.   He adopted the method of causing carbon to dissolve in iron at the very high temperature of the electric furnace, and then subjecting the molten mass to rapid cooling by immersing the crucible in which it was contained in cold water, or by pouring the molten substance into a mould of iron filings, or by other means.   The object of the rapid cooling was to produce an exterior shell of solid metal enclosing liquid material under tremendous pressure ; it was hoped that the carbon crystallising out from the liquid under this great pressure would assume the form of diamond, instead of graphite as under ordinary conditions.   At the close of the experiment, the mass of iron was dissolved in acid, and some black grains and small, water-clear crystals were obtained, which possessed all the properties of diamond and were completely combustible in oxygen, yielding carbon dioxide as the sole product of combustion.   The largest crystals obtained by this method are about $\frac{1}{2}$ millimetre ($\frac{1}{50}$ inch) in diameter ; identical results are obtained when the experiment is performed with molten silver instead of iron.   There can no longer be any doubt that by this method it is possible to produce genuine diamonds.

Another successful method of producing artificial diamonds has been recently (1898) discovered by I. Friedländer. A small piece of olivine was fused in the gas-blowpipe and the molten mass stirred with a rod of graphite. After cooling, those parts of the silicate which had been in contact with the carbon were found to contain vast numbers of brown crystals of microscopic size (0·001 mm. in diameter). These crystals were found to be octahedral or tetrahedral in form, to be unattacked by hydrofluoric and sulphuric acids, to have a high refractive index, to sink slowly in methylene iodide, to burn away when heated in a current of oxygen, and to be unaltered by heating in a current of carbon dioxide. All these characters point to one conclusion, namely, that the crystals so produced are diamond, and still further proof is furnished by the fact that the stony mass containing them is capable of scratching corundum.

When we essay to draw conclusions as to the origin of diamonds in nature from experiments in their artificial production, we should be careful that the conditions of the artificial production and of the natural occurrence are parallel. For example, the experiments of Moissan are most helpful in explaining the origin of diamond in meteoric iron, while those of Friedländer suggest that the diamonds of South Africa and of meteoric stones have been formed by the action of a molten silicate magma upon graphite or some carbonaceous material. Friedländer himself suggests that, in the case of the South African deposits, the carbon may have been derived from the carbonaceous shales which are penetrated by the pipe of diamond-bearing " blue ground "; there are, however, objections to this view, as has been shown already.

Further experiments in the artificial production of diamonds are desirable, especially with a view to the discovery of a liquid capable of depositing carbon in the crystalline form of diamond; when more knowledge on this point has been obtained, it will, perhaps, be possible to explain the origin of diamond in pegmatite veins and in itacolumite, as well as in olivine-rock and in eclogite (p. 197).

D. APPLICATIONS OF DIAMOND.

The natural beauty of the diamond renders it primarily an object of æsthetic value; only faulty, opaque, or unpleasingly coloured specimens are applied to technical purposes for which a material of great hardness is essential.

1. APPLICATION IN JEWELLERY.

The beauty of a diamond depends but rarely upon the tint of the pigment it may contain, but is rather associated with the marvellous lustre and play of prismatic colours so characteristic of this stone. This play of colour differs in degree in different stones, and depends to a large extent on the method of cutting which has been adopted; uncut stones, with their rough, and often somewhat irregular faces, either do not show any play of colours, or display it to only a very limited extent.

How far the ancients were acquainted with the art of diamond-cutting, or even with the polishing of the natural crystal-faces of the stone, is not certainly known, but that they were not entirely ignorant of the process is apparent from their writings.

In India, the ancient home of the diamond, the art of polishing the faces of natural crystals was practised in the remotest times; when or how the device of faceting stones was discovered or introduced in this country is not known, but it was practised in the seventeenth century, at the time of Tavernier's visit (1665). According to native ideas in

India, the only object of cutting a stone is the removal of faulty portions, and a natural octahedron of which the faces have been polished is preferred. In spite of this, various forms of cutting are more or less in vogue ; the most general forms are the thick-stones (Plate IV., Fig. 15, *a, b*), table-stones, and thin-stones ; the first named form, on account of its generality in India, is often referred to as the "Indian cut." Such forms of cutting, together with others in which the facets are more numerous, are admired and met with, not only in India, but elsewhere in the Orient, namely in Persia, Arabia, Bagdad, &c. The Oriental diamond-cutter follows the outlines of the rough stone as closely as may be, striving to reduce the loss of material to a minimum. The European diamond-cutter, on the contrary, aims at developing to their fullest extent the optical properties of the stone, and makes economy of material only a secondary consideration. In many cases an irregular gem, "lumpy stone," or "pebble," cut by an Oriental, has passed into the hands of a European, and has been re-cut, the greatly enhanced beauty of the European cut stone compensating for the loss of material involved in a second cutting process. Such was the fate of the famous "Koh-i-noor," among other stones ; Plate X., Fig. 4, *a, b*, shows the form of the Indian cut of this stone, and Fig. 5, *a, b, c*, its form after being re-cut.

Diamond-cutting in India was not, however, entirely in the hands of native lapidaries, for Tavernier states that the "Great Mogul," the large diamond named after the ruler of Delhi, its possessor, was cut rather unsuccessfully by Hortensio Borgis, a Venetian cutter. The diamond-cutting industry has flourished in Europe since the end of mediæval times, and European ideas have had a certain influence upon the development of the art in India.

In all Western countries in the middle ages, diamonds were used in the rough condition, with the natural faces polished, or in the form of point-stones, thick-stones, table-stones, &c., which were the forms of cutting usual in India at that time. At this period gems were used not so much as personal ornaments by women, but more often for enriching robes of state, such, for example, as the coronation mantle of Charles the Great, and for ornamenting reliquary shrines, sceptres, crowns, scabbards, &c. Practically nothing is known of the diamond-cutting industry in Europe until the beginning of the fifteenth century, when a skilled artisan named Hermann appeared in Paris, and did much to develop the art. As early as 1373 the existence of diamond-polishers at Nürnberg is mentioned, but nothing is known as to the methods practised by these workers.

The gradual development of the art of gem-cutting and the spread of the knowledge of this art was accompanied by the gradual growth of the custom of wearing diamonds as personal ornaments by women. The custom was introduced subsequently to the year 1431, in the time of Charles VII., in the French court by Agnes Sorel. The taste for this form of personal ornament had grown amongst the ladies of the court of Francis I. to such an extent, that edicts, levelled against the excessive use of gems as personal ornaments, were issued both by Charles IX. and Henry IV., without, however, having any effect. From the French court the custom gradually spread over the whole of Europe.

The large demand for diamonds thus caused gave a new impulse to the diamond-cutting industry, and during the course of the fifteenth century the art made its greatest strides. The advancement was due, to a certain extent, to the influence of the Dutch lapidary of Bruges, Ludwig van Berquen, who invented his particular process in the year 1476. Although some credence has been given to the statement of Robert van Berquen, that his grandfather was the originator of the modern method of diamond-cutting, namely, the use of diamond powder, yet the device had probably long before been known in Europe. What L. van Berquen probably did was so to improve the technique of the art that greater precision in the arrangement of the facets could be attained. Owing to irregularity in cutting, the play of prismatic colours in table- and point-stones was often scarcely observable at all, and the stones cut after Berquen's method offered a great contrast in this particular.

Among the first and most famous diamonds cut by L. van Berquen are said to have been those in the possession of Charles the Bold, Duke of Burgundy, some of which were lost at the time of his defeat by the Swiss. Certain of these stones are probably still at the present day in the form in which they left Berquen's hands, and they bear witness to the high degree of perfection to which this artist had attained. According to Schrauf, the cutting of the "Florentine" (Plate XI., Fig. 10, *a*, *b*), and of the "Sancy" diamonds (Fig. 11, *a*, *b*), was the work of van Berquen; they are cut in the briolette or pendeloque form, a form which van Berquen was the first to adopt.

This particular form of cutting was not often copied, at the present time it is quite unused and is never shown by recently cut stones. The different varieties of the rose or rosette form of cutting (Plate IV., Figs. 1–7), which were introduced in the sixteenth century (about 1520), on the contrary grew quickly into favour, and at the present day are in general use and frequently seen. This form of cutting is most advantageous for thin and flat stones, since it involves but little waste of material and at the same time permits the full display of the lustre of the stone. It is, however, inferior to certain other forms of cutting in that it fails to develop to the fullest extent possible the beautiful play of colours so characteristic of a cleverly cut diamond.

The rose form was in vogue for about a century, and was then largely superseded by the most perfect form of cutting yet devised, namely by the brilliant form. This form was invented in the middle of the seventeenth century, and the idea is said to have originated with Cardinal Mazarin. The stones first cut in this form were double-cut brilliants (Plate II., Fig. 1, *a*, *b*, *c*), and had on the upper part sixteen facets besides the table. At the end of the seventeenth century the triple-cut brilliant (Fig. 3, *a*, *b*, *c*,), with thirty-two facets on the upper part, was introduced by Vincent Peruzzi of Venice. This form of cutting, which is still more favourable for the display of the optical properties of the stone, is in use at the present day, with no alteration except that the size of the facets is more equalised, as shown in Fig. 4, *a*, *b*, *c*, of the same plate. The various forms of cutting which have subsequently come into use do not differ in any essential respect from those already described. The star-cut, for example, of M. Caire (Plate III., Fig. 1, *a*, *b*, *c*), by means of a slight modification, combines an economy in the rough material, with no inferiority in the display of the optical qualities of the stone.

The loss of material involved in the cutting of a stone in the brilliant form is very considerable, sometimes amounting to one-third, one-half, or to an even greater proportion of the rough stone. The "Regent," for example, which is the most perfect brilliant known, weighed in the rough 410 carats, while its weight after cutting was only $136\frac{7}{8}$ carats, or only one-third as much. The "Koh-i-noor," as cut in India, weighed $186\frac{1}{16}$ carats, and after re-cutting in England, $106\frac{1}{16}$ carats; again, the "Star of the South" weighed in the rough $254\frac{1}{2}$ carats, and as a brilliant 125 carats. The beautiful play of colours obtained by the use of this form of cutting more than compensates for the waste of rough material; in no other form is this character brought out so prominently, and a good brilliant with a fine play of colours, though small, is more highly prized than a larger stone cut in an inferior form, and consequently with a less fine play of colours.

The brilliant is always so mounted in its setting that the broad facet or table is turned towards the observer. Only rarely, in cases in which the stone has faults to be concealed,

PLATE IX

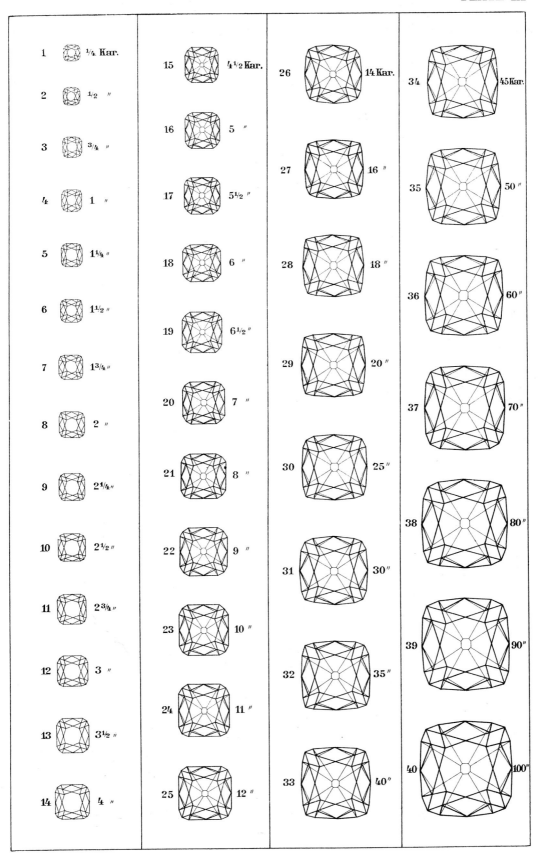

ACTUAL SIZES OF BRILLIANTS (DIAMONDS) OF 1/4 TO 100 CARATS

is the position reversed and the so-called Indian setting adopted. The dazzling appearance of the brilliant is due to the way in which the rays of light entering the stone are reflected from the facets at the back, pass out by the front facets and reach the eye of the observer in the manner already described. As compared with a brilliant, other diamonds appear dull and lifeless, for the arrangement of their facets does not admit of the passage of light rays in such a way as to produce the most favourable effect, either as to brilliancy or play of colours. It is essential, however, in order to produce the greatest effect, that even the brilliant form should conform rigidly to the rules of proportion which have been already laid down. The "Regent," for example, the proportions of which are strictly accurate, is a far more dazzling and brilliant stone than is the "Koh-i-noor," which is cut with too small a depth.

The brilliancy and fire of a cut diamond is enhanced by suitable illumination; the source of light should not be too large, otherwise the separation of the differently coloured refracted rays is masked, and the light reflected appears to be white; neither should the source of light be surrounded by an opal shade. A brilliant appears at its best when illuminated by a number of small flames; and the effect can be still further increased by attaching the stone in its setting to a thin metal rod or wire, when the quivering motion imparted to the stone by every movement produces rapidly changing flashes of colour.

Although each of the different forms of cutting which have been described may under various circumstances be made use of for the diamond, yet there are but two forms in general use, the first and most important being the brilliant, the other, the rose or rosette. The diamond is the only gem which is so invariably cut in these forms, and hence is often loosely referred to as a brilliant or a rosette.

Whenever the form of a rough stone permits, it is always cut as a brilliant, no matter what its size may be. Plate IX. shows in actual size a series of diamonds cut in the brilliant form, viewed from above, and ranging in weight from $\frac{1}{4}$ to 100 carats; from a study of this series some idea of the actual sizes of stones of different weights may be gained. As a rule only small diamonds of little thickness, fragments cleaved off in the fashioning of a brilliant from a large stone, and large diamonds which have not sufficient depth to be cut as brilliants, are cut as rosettes. Sometimes, by preference, a large thin stone is made into several small brilliants and not into a single large rosette.

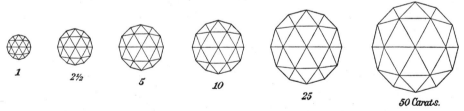

FIG. 44.   Actual sizes of rose diamonds of 1 to 50 carats.

As in Plate IX., a series of brilliants in actual size is shown, so Fig. 44 shows the actual sizes of a series of rose diamonds ranging in weight from 1 to 50 carats. Stones of surprisingly small size are often to be met with cut as roses, with regularly arranged facets; they may be so small that 1500 or even more weigh no more than a carat. Stones of very small size are not generally cut as brilliants. Small roses, of which 100 or 160 are required to make up the weight of a carat, are known as piece-roses; the Dutch lapidaries are specially skilled in the art of cutting extremely small stones. Very minute splinters of diamond are often furnished with a few irregular facets, when they are known as senaille, and, like the smallest roses, are used to form a setting round a large gem (carmoizing). Very thin laminæ of diamond are ground down, polished on both sides, and the edges furnished with small facets ; they are then used to cover small miniatures set in rings, &c., producing a very striking effect, and are now known as portrait-stones or brilliant-glass.

A few trade expressions made use of by jewellers may be explained here. Very small diamonds are referred to as salt-grains, very large ones as solitaires, nonpareils or paragons. All cut diamonds exceeding 50 carats in weight were formerly known as solitaires, while those exceeding 100 carats have been referred to as majestic diamonds. Stones weighing less than a carat are known as carat-goods, those of 1, 2, &c., carats as carat-stones, two-carat-stones, &c.

2. DIAMOND-CUTTING.

The general principles of the art of gem-cutting have been already considered ; the cutting of the diamond, however, on account of the perfect cleavage and enormous hardness of the stone, requires special methods, which must be separately considered.

As we have seen, diamonds are most frequently cut in the brilliant form, which form is comparable to that of an octahedron of which two opposite corners have been truncated. A truncated octahedron, therefore, can be transformed into a brilliant by simply adding the necessary facets, hence the form of crystal which can be most conveniently cut as a brilliant is the octahedron. Crystals of the form shown in Fig. 31, n and o, are therefore specially suited for the fashioning of brilliants. The rhombic dodecahedron and the hexakis-octahedron (Fig. 31, c and d) are also suitable ; but stones, whose form differs widely from that of the regular octahedron, for example Fig. 31, e and f, cannot be so easily transformed into brilliants. Before such a stone is faceted it is reduced by cleavage to the octahedral form, in order to avoid the tedious process of grinding away portions which need to be removed. The property of cleavage then is very useful to the diamond-cutter, for not only is he spared much labour in grinding, but the fragments removed by cleavage can be utilised in the fashioning of smaller gems ; moreover, the property can be made use of for the purpose of removing the faulty portions of a stone or of dividing a large stone of unsuitable form into several smaller ones. The operation is, however, one which demands the greatest care ; the worker should be capable not only of detecting the direction of cleavage from the outward form of the rough diamond, but also of recognising the existence of twinning in a crystal. Any attempt either to cleave a twinned crystal or to cleave an ordinary stone in a wrong direction, will probably be attended with more or less complete fracture of the stone.

The operation of **cleaving** a diamond, which is entrusted to trained workmen, is performed in a manner now to be described. The stone to be cleaved is fixed to the end of a rod with some kind of cement, such as a mixture of shellac, turpentine, and the finest brick-dust, and in such a position that the direction of cleavage is parallel to the length of the rod. A second diamond with a projecting edge is fixed to a similar rod with the edge uppermost. By grinding the sharp edge of the second diamond against the first, a nick in the direction in which the stone is to be cleaved is cut to a sufficient depth. The rod supporting this diamond is set on a firm elastic base, a sharp, strong chisel is placed in the proper direction in the nick, and the cleavage effected by dealing the chisel a single sharp blow with a hammer. The cement may be loosened by heating, and the stone placed in another position if it is desired to cleave it in another direction. The powder produced when the nick is made is caught in a small box provided with a sieve, and is utilised in the process of grinding.

It has been stated by Tavernier that the custom of cleaving diamonds has been practised in India since very early times ; in Europe, however, the art was acquired much more recently, and is said to have originated with the English chemist and physicist Wollaston (1766–1828), of whom it is related that by cleaving away the faulty exterior portions of a large diamond he was enabled to dispose of the stone at a considerable profit.

Stones which, either by nature or by the hand of man, have been given the shape of an octahedron, have already the ground-form of the brilliant and can be at once faceted. The work of grinding the facets is facilitated by a preliminary operation, which is entrusted to special workers and is not performed in the process of cutting any other gem. This operation, by which the shape and position of the facets are roughly marked out, is known as **bruting**, rubbing, or greying the stone. The stone to be bruted is fixed to a handle, and, with the exception of the area on which the facet is to be made, is embedded in cement or in a fusible alloy of lead and tin. This projecting portion is rubbed with a strong pressure upon the projecting portion of another stone similarly mounted and prepared, and thus a facet, in approximately the correct position and with a fairly even but rough surface, is developed upon each of the stones. The powder abraded from the two stones during the operation is carefully preserved for use in grinding. During the operation of greying, which, by the way, derives its name from the grey metallic appearance of the facets so made, any over-heating of the stone by friction must be carefully avoided, since it leads to the development of " icy flakes " in the interior of the diamond. The operation is attended by a peculiar grating sound, which is said to be so characteristic that by this alone the possessor of a practised ear can determine whether the two stones which are rubbed together are diamonds or some less hard gems.

At the completion of the first stage of the operation the stone is removed by warming the cement or alloy, placed in another position, and the remaining larger facets successively marked out in the same way. The smaller facets are not so marked out by a preliminary operation, but by the subsequent process of grinding. When ready for the grinding process the stones are bounded by a number of fairly even, rough faces, with a grey, somewhat metallic lustre ; they have no longer the appearance of diamonds, but resemble dull grey metallic bodies with the general contours of the form of cutting the stone is finally to take.

In the combined process of **grinding and polishing**, the preliminary disposition of the facets, which may be slightly incorrect, is rendered strictly accurate by the completion of the grinding, their rough surfaces are rendered smooth and shining, and the smaller facets are added. The grinding process is the same as in the case of other gems as already described, the diamond being imbedded in the fusible alloy of a dop and placed on the grinding disc. Since in the grinding of diamonds the disc must be charged with diamond powder, which of course has the same hardness as the stone itself, the operations of grinding and polishing take place simultaneously, and any separate polishing process is superfluous. Any dirt or foreign matter which may adhere to the stone after the process of grinding is removed by treatment with fine bone-ash or tripolite.

In the process of grinding it is by no means immaterial in which direction the grinding disc moves across the facet which is being worked. Owing to the fact that the diamond, as well as other precious stones, has a different degree of hardness in different directions, the grinding of its facets can be accomplished with comparative ease in some directions, while in others the process is extremely tedious. To avoid injury both to the stone and to the grinding disc, the diamond must be ground " with the grain " ; and the operator ought to make himself familiar with these directions of least resistance, otherwise his work will be unnecessarily prolonged. When, for example, the table of a brilliant is to be developed upon an octahedron, the grinding disc should move from centre to centre of two opposite octahedral faces; if allowed to move from edge to edge, the facet can only be developed with the greatest difficulty, for in this direction the hardness of the diamond is much greater

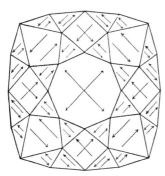

than in the other. The directions of least resistance to grinding on each of the facets of a brilliant are indicated in Fig. 45 by arrows. The large four-sided facets above and below and to the right and left of the table, are the faces of the octahedron.

We have thus seen that the three operations in the process of diamond-cutting are entrusted to as many classes of skilled workmen, namely cleavers, bruters, and grinders or polishers.

The order in which the facets of a brilliant are ground has also a certain importance. Starting from the octahedral ground-form, the table and culet are in every case first developed. The correct proportions of a brilliant are

FIG. 45. Directions of least hardness on the facets of a brilliant.

attained by grinding away five-ninths of the upper half for the table, and one-ninth of the lower half of the stone for the culet, the upper portion of a perfect brilliant being one-third, and the lower being two-thirds of the whole thickness of the stone from table to culet.

Some rough stones are of such a shape that they cannot be cut into the usual brilliant form, but are given an oval or triangular outline; in this case, the method of procedure

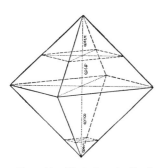

described above requires a slight modification, as also when the stone is to be cut as a rose or in some form other than the brilliant. In the latter cases the cleavage of the stone does not play so important a part, but otherwise the mode of procedure is much the same.

In past times the diamond-cutting industry has centred now round this town, now round that. The important invention ascribed to Ludwig van Berquen was made in 1476 at Bruges; in the fifteenth and sixteenth centuries, however, most of the work was done in Antwerp, where the workers of L. van Berquen had settled. Later on Amsterdam became the centre of the industry, and through many vicissitudes this city has retained its supremacy up to the present day. In Amsterdam there are now seventy diamond-cutting establish-

FIG. 46. First stage in the development of a brilliant from an octahedron, showing the position of the table and culet.

ments, large and small, fitted up with all the modern technical appliances, and using steam as the motive-power. The industry gives employment to more than 12,000 people, all of whom are Jews; in one establishment alone there are 450 grinding machines and 1000 employees, and in the whole of Amsterdam there are said to be a total of about 7000 grinding machines (skaifs) at work. Amsterdam, however, no longer monopolises the industry, for skilful cutters are now to be found in Antwerp, Ghent, Paris, St. Claude in the French Jura, London, and specially in Germany, more particularly at Hanau; diamond-cutting works are also to be found at Berlin and at Oberstein on the Nahe, a town which has long been well known as the centre for the working of agate and other varieties of quartz. In America the diamond-cutting industry has been introduced at Boston. But Amsterdam still holds the lead, and the largest and most valuable stones are always entrusted to the cutters there, who are held to be the most skilful and who best understand how to provide quite small stones with regularly arranged facets.

While the softer precious stones are often submitted to the operation of **engraving,** the diamond is very rarely so treated. Whether diamonds were engraved at all by the ancients is a matter open to grave doubt; only a few engraved diamonds belonging to more recent times are known; one of these bears the portrait of Don Carlos, and another was engraved with the Spanish arms for Charles V. The engraving of the diamond is never attempted at the present day, since the result of such attempts is in no way commensurate with the labour expended. That the art was not entirely unknown in the Orient is evidenced by the existence of a beautiful Indian octahedron of 30 carats, described by Boutan, one face of which was engraved with a devotional motto. According to G. Rose's account, some of the faces of the irregularly-formed diamond known as the "Shah," now in the Russian crown jewels, were engraved in Persian characters with the names of Persian kings. Two of the faces of the "Akbar Shah," another large diamond, were engraved with Arabic inscriptions, but these, like the engravings on the "Shah," had to be sacrificed when the stone was re-cut.

Only rarely have diamonds been bored and threaded as beads; the art is said to be practised at the present day at Ghent and Venice, in the latter city being the last remains of an old diamond-cutting industry which once flourished there. The boring is effected by the use of diamond powder, the perforation being started with a diamond point and continued with a steel point charged with diamond dust.

3. TECHNICAL APPLICATIONS.

The value of the diamond in its technical applications depends, as a rule, upon its exceptional hardness, and only in a few cases on its high refractive index.

The high index of refraction of the diamond led to an attempt to utilise this substance for the construction of microscope objectives. A diamond lens having only a slight curvature will give the same magnification as a lens of much greater curvature constructed of some less strongly refracting substance, such as glass. The disadvantages connected with the use of strongly curved lenses would be thus avoided, and, moreover, diamond lenses on account of their hardness would not be liable to be scratched by particles of dust and other matter. Experiments in this direction were made mainly by Pritchard, under the direction of Dr. Goring, between 1824 and 1826; although Pritchard was successful in preparing a few suitable lenses their use has never been adopted, probably on account of the difficulties connected with their construction and the prohibitive cost of the material.

Very extensive use is made of the diamond for the purpose of cutting glass, every glazier being in the possession of a tool known as a **glazier's diamond.** The stone set in this tool must be bounded by two rounded crystal-faces meeting in the curved cutting edge, which should not be too obtuse. This cutting edge is drawn with a slight pressure over the surface of the glass to be cut, and produces a fine scratch, not more than $\frac{1}{200}$ inch in depth, but which is sufficient to cause the glass to be easily broken in the direction of the scratch. The cutting edge, when properly used, cuts into the surface layer of glass like a wedge; when drawn across the glass by an unpractised hand, it simply tears instead of cutting the surface, and this also happens when a sharp pointed splinter of diamond is used instead of the curved cutting edge. In the direction of the jagged furrow produced by such means glass will not break as it does along a clean cut. Wollaston investigated this matter in detail, and found that the edge formed by the intersection of two curved natural faces of the diamond is specially adapted for cutting glass, and that artificially prepared edges of similar construction, made of softer stones, were almost equally efficacious. He constructed such edges of ruby, sapphire, quartz, &c., and while these were well adapted for cutting glass, the straight edge formed by the intersection of two plane faces of a diamond was found to be quite unsuitable for the purpose.

For a glazier's diamond, a small natural crystal of suitable form, such, for example, as the curved rhombic dodecahedron, or other crystal with curved faces (Fig. 31, c, d, &c.), is used. This is fixed in a metal setting by a fusible alloy, with the cutting edge projecting, and the whole furnished with a wooden handle. The use of the tool requires a little practice, which needs to be acquired for each particular diamond; a slight deviation from the correct method of handling the tool militates against its effectiveness. The majority of the stones used in the construction of glazier's diamonds are said to come from Borneo and Bahia.

Sharp splinters of diamond, such as are often obtained in cleaving diamonds preparatory to the process of grinding, are often mounted in a similar manner and used for the purpose of drawing and writing on glass and other hard substances. Such diamond-points are also useful in boring holes in glass, porcelain, precious stones, &c., and are employed now, as in ancient times, in the engraving of precious stones, such as the ruby and sapphire. In recent times, however, the diamond-point for engraving has been replaced by a small, rapidly rotating metal disc or point charged with diamond powder and olive-oil.

There are many purposes for which the extreme hardness of the diamond renders it specially valuable. Thus it is used as a cutting tool in the lathe for turning the edges of watch-glasses and pivots of specially hard steel, such as are used in instruments of precision of all kinds; for the boring of cannon, as, for example, in the works of Krupp at Essen; in the manufacture of the finer mechanical tools; for boring small holes in large stones through which fine gold and silver wire is drawn; in the turning and working of hard stones, such as granite, gneiss, porphyry, &c.; for the pivot supports of the most accurate chronometers and other delicate instruments, and for many other purposes.

The diamond, however, at the present time, has a wider application in a direction which has not hitherto been indicated, namely, in the construction of **rock-drills.** Since its introduction in 1860, the diamond rock-drill has grown steadily in importance, and is now widely used in the many boring operations connected with mining, tunnelling, and the sinking of artesian wells, prospecting bores, &c. The rotating, boring crown of the drill is studded with carbonado, and, compared with other boring appliances, penetrates the rock with extraordinary rapidity. The fashioning of sharp-edged furrows on the grinding surfaces of millstones, for which in recent years special machines have been devised, is also effected by means of the diamond; for these, and all other technical purposes, small diamonds of poor quality, bort, and carbonado are used.

Diamond powder is now used very largely, not only in the grinding of the diamond itself, but also in the grinding and cutting of other precious stones, even such as are soft enough to be cut with emery. The economy in time and labour, and the superiority of the results attending its use, more than compensate for the increased cost of the material. The same substance is also used for the purpose of slicing through hard stones, the cutting being effected by a rotating disc of soft iron, in the edge of which are embedded fine splinters of diamond.

4. LARGE AND FAMOUS DIAMONDS.

There are a comparatively small number of diamonds in existence which, either on account of their size, beauty, or historic and ancient associations, possess a special interest. While the origin and early history of many stones in existence at the present day is a complete blank, there are others, of which reliable accounts and drawings are given in ancient writings, whose present whereabouts is entirely unknown; the latter may have been destroyed or lost, or, on the other hand, they may lie hidden in the treasure-houses of some Oriental princes, whose predecessors possessed a taste for the collection of gems.

All the older famous diamonds of large size and enormous value, which are known by special names, come from India; only in comparatively recent times, namely, about the middle of the eighteenth century, have stones of remarkable size been found in Brazil, while the discovery of the South African diamonds was still later. The South African deposits have already yielded more large stones than are comprised in the aggregate yield of India and Brazil during hundreds of years; these stones are usually, however, of a yellowish tinge, and are, in consequence, less highly valued than are the blue-white diamonds of India and Brazil. Only a few of the many large stones which have been found in South Africa have, in consequence, received distinctive names. The value of these rare stones is naturally enormous, and they usually find a place amongst the crown jewels of different countries, rarely entering the possession of private individuals except in the case of wealthy collectors, especially in eastern countries.

The subject of famous diamonds is specially dealt with in a book entitled, *The Great Diamonds of the World* (London, 1882), by Mr. E. W. Streeter; also in *Le Diamant* (Paris, 1886), by Mons. E. Boutan, who has made a careful study of the tangled history of each stone. Much of the information given in the account which follows has been derived from these sources, as well as from older works. Most of the well-known famous diamonds are figured in their cut condition and actual size in Plates X. and XI.; the form of cutting most general is that of the brilliant, but examples of other forms will be found.

A few of the large stones, of which accounts have been given, are very probably not diamond at all, but some one of the minerals with which diamond is often confused. Among these is, in all probability, the "Braganza," which, if genuine, would rank as the largest of known diamonds. This stone, which is the size of a hen's egg, and weighs 1680 carats, came from Brazil, but the exact locality is unknown. It is preserved with the Portuguese crown jewels, and is not available for detailed examination; should it be proved to be topaz, which is very probably what it is, its value, formerly placed at £224,000,000, would at once sink to a comparatively insignificant amount.

Another large diamond, the genuineness of which is open to question, is a stone belonging to the Rajah of Mattan, in Borneo; it is known there as the "Danau Rajah," but is generally referred to as the "Mattan." It weighs 367 carats, and, if a genuine diamond, is by far the largest ever found in Borneo. It is pear-shaped, and about the size of a pigeon's egg, and is said to have been found in 1787, in the district of Landak, in western Borneo; the name "Danau Rajah," however, suggests the neighbourhood of the River Danau, in the south-east of the island, as a more probable locality. The stone is said to have been examined at Pontianak, in Borneo, in 1868, when it was declared to be rock-crystal; this decision is generally accepted, although it has been stated that an imitation, and not the real stone, was submitted for examination.

The genuineness of the diamonds now to be described is unquestionable; of these the Indian stones will be first considered, and afterwards the Brazilian and the South African.

The large Indian diamonds are often supposed to be of very ancient discovery, the majority, however, probably do not date back to very early times. No definite information can be gleaned from ancient writings, but it is a well-established fact that the diamonds in the possession of the Romans were all of small size.

Probably the largest of Indian diamonds is the **Great Mogul,** the history of which is very obscure. This was seen in the treasury of the Great Mogul, Aurungzebe, in 1665, by Tavernier, who both drew and described the stone in detail. This diamond had then the form of a very high and round rosette (Plate X., Fig. 2), and was of good water. It weighed $319\frac{1}{2}$ ratis, which Tavernier calculated to be equivalent to 280 carats, assuming 1 rati = $\frac{7}{8}$ carat. By authorities, who consider this value of the rati too high, the equivalent is given as 188 carats. The rough stone is supposed to have been found between 1630 and 1650, in the mines at Kollur, and to have originally weighed $787\frac{1}{2}$ carats, a weight which would make it unquestionably the largest of Indian diamonds.

The considerable disparity between the weight of the rough stone and its weight when cut, has been attributed to the unskilful manner in which it was cut by Hortensio Borgis, the Venetian diamond-cutter, who at that time was domiciled in India. The subsequent history of the " Great Mogul " is a complete blank ; it has been variously supposed to have been lost or destroyed, to be in existence under another name, such as the " Orloff" diamond, or the " Koh-i-noor," to be in the possession of the Shah of Persia, or to be lying forgotten among the jewels of some Indian prince.

Another large diamond of the same weight, namely, 320 ratis, is described in the memoirs of Baber, the founder of the Mogul dynasty. According to this account the stone had long been famous in India, and had formed part of the spoils of war of many an Indian prince, finally passing into the possession of Baber in 1556. This stone is regarded by Professor Story-Maskelyne as being identical with the diamond seen at Delhi, and described as the " Great Mogul " by Tavernier, and identical with the stone at present known as the " Koh-i-noor "; this view is very generally accepted.

The **Koh-i-noor** was appropriated in 1739 by Nadir Shah, the Persian conqueror of the Mogul Empire ; in 1813 it passed into the possession of the Rajah of Lahore, and after the British annexation of the Punjab, became the property of the East India Company, which in 1850 presented it to Queen Victoria. The stone had then the form of an irregular rosette (Plate X., Figs. 4a, 4b), with numerous facets above, below a broad cleavage surface, and on the side a second smaller cleavage surface. The weight of the Indian-cut stone was $186\frac{1}{16}$ carats, which agrees closely with the weight of 320 ratis, recorded long before as the weight of the stone described by Baber. In order to improve its form, which was very far from perfect, it was re-cut in England in 1852 by the diamond-cutter, Voorsanger, of the Amsterdam firm of Coster ; the work of re-cutting occupying thirty-eight days, of twelve hours each.

The " Koh-i-noor " is now a stone of considerable beauty, weighing $106\frac{1}{16}$ carats ; its new form (Plate X., Figs. 5a, 5b, 5c,) is, however, too thin for a perfect brilliant ; moreover, it is not of the purest water, and the colour is slightly greyish. In spite of these blemishes it is valued at £100,000. The question as to the identity of the " Great Mogul " with the " Koh-i-noor " can scarcely now be decided. Tennant regarded them as identical, and suggested that the " Koh-i-noor " and the " Orloff" are both parts of the rough stone of $787\frac{1}{2}$ carats, mentioned by Tavernier, and that the third and remaining portion of it is the plate of diamond weighing 132 carats, often mentioned as having been taken by Abbas Mirza with other jewels from Reeza Kuli Khan at the capture of Coocha, in Khorassan. Tennant constructed models of these separate portions in fluor-spar, a mineral which has the

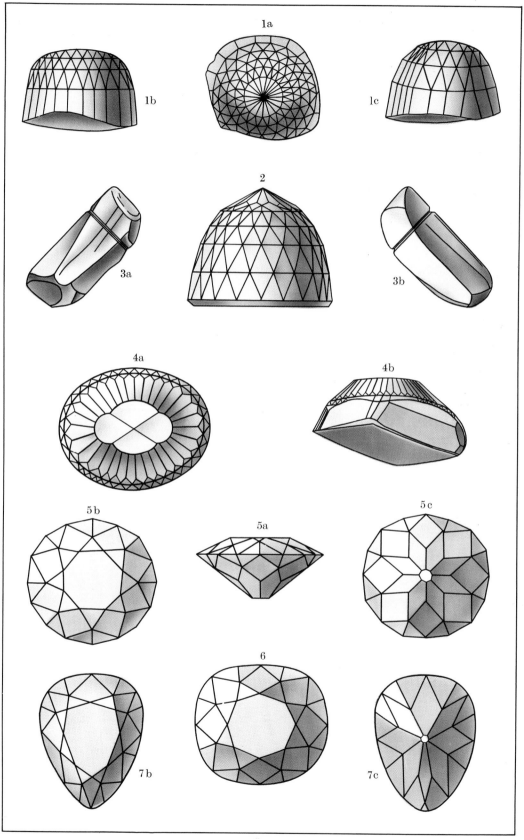

1a, b, c. Orloff.   2. Great Mogul.   3a, b. Shah.   4a, b.   Koh-i-noor, Indian cut.   5a, b, c. Koh-i-noor, new form.   6. Stewart (from South Africa).   7b, c. Mr. Dresden's (from Brazil).

same octahedral cleavage as diamond, and by piecing the portions together arrived at the conclusion that the rough stone had the size of a hen's egg, the form of a rhombic dodecahedron, and a weight of about $793\frac{5}{8}$ carats, which agrees closely with Tavernier's account.

Opinions differ also as to the derivation of the name "Koh-i-noor," which is sometimes said to signify "Mountain of Light," and is supposed to have been given to the stone by Nadir Shah. It has also been supposed to be a corruption of Kollur, the locality at which it was found, and the name by which it is said to have been formerly known in India.

The **Orloff** is the largest of the diamonds comprised in the Russian crown jewels, and usually forms the termination of the imperial sceptre; it is a stone of the finest water, perfectly pure and with a brilliant lustre. In form (Plate X., Figs. 1a, 1b, 1c,) it is very similar to that of Tavernier's drawing of the "Great Mogul," being an almost hemispherical rosette bounded on the lower side by a cleavage surface, as was the case with the Indian-cut "Koh-i-noor." Its height is 10 lines, its greatest diameter $15\frac{1}{2}$ lines, and its weight $194\frac{3}{4}$ carats. This stone has had a chequered career; it is said at one time to have formed one of the eyes of an idol in the Brahmin temple on the island of Sheringham, in the Cauvery river near Trichinopoly. It was stolen from here, at the beginning of the eighteenth century, by a French soldier, passed into the hands of an English ship's captain, and so found its way into Europe, and in 1791 was bought in Amsterdam (being on this account sometimes known as the "Amsterdam" diamond) by Prince Orloff for the Empress Catharine II. of Russia for the sum of 1,400,000 Dutch florins.

There is a story to the effect that this stone came into the possession of the Russian crown through an Armenian, named Schafras; this story probably, however, applies not to the "Orloff" but to another large diamond in the Russian crown jewels, namely, the **Moon of the Mountains.** This diamond, which weighs 120 carats, became the booty of Nadir Shah, who used it for the adornment of his throne. At his assassination, it was stolen with other jewels by an Afghan soldier, from whom it passed into the possession of the Armenian Schafras. The latter sold it in 1775 to Catharine II. for 450,000 roubles, an annuity of 4000 roubles, and letters of nobility.

The **Polar Star,** a beautiful brilliant of 40 carats (Plate XI., Fig. 15), also belongs to the Russian crown, as does the peculiarly shaped stone known as the **Shah.** This latter stone was presented in 1829 to the Czar Nicholas by the Persian prince, Chosroes, the younger son of Abbas Mirza. It is of the purest water and in form a very irregular prism (Plate X., Figs. 3a, 3b), 1 inch $5\frac{1}{2}$ lines long and 8 lines wide in the thickest part. The boundaries of the stone are partly cleavage faces and partly artificially cut facets; on three of the latter the names of three Persian kings are engraved, so that the "Shah" is one of the few examples of engraved diamonds. Professor Gustav Rose, who saw the stone soon after it was brought to St. Petersburg, gave the weight as 88 carats, but this does not agree with a subsequent statement to the effect that the stone has been re-cut and its weight reduced from 95 to 86 carats, the interesting inscriptions being lost in the process.

Another engraved diamond is the **Akbar Shah,** so called from its first possessor, the Great Mogul, Akbar; when in the possession of Jehan, Akbar's successor, Arabic inscriptions were engraved on two of its faces. It subsequently disappeared for a long period, reappearing again in Turkey, under the name of the "Shepherd's Stone," comparatively recently, and still recognisable as the "Akbar Shah" by its Arabic inscriptions. It at first weighed 116 carats, but after re-cutting in 1866 its weight was reduced to 71 or 72 carats and the inscriptions were lost in the process. In 1867 the stone was sold to the Gaikwar of Baroda for £35,000.

One of the largest of Indian diamonds is the **Nizam,** a stone of 277 carats, which has been known only since 1835, and which is supposed to have been picked up by a child on the ground in the neighbourhood of Golconda. This, however, is not the only version of the discovery of this stone, and its original weight has been placed at 440 carats; it is supposed to be at present in the possession of the Nizam of Haidarabad.

The **Great Table,** of Tavernier, was seen in 1642 at Golconda by this traveller, who states that it weighed $242\frac{3}{16}$ carats, and that it was the largest diamond he had seen in India in the hands of dealers. His offer of 400,000 rupees for the stone was rejected and, as in the case of the "Great Mogul," its subsequent history is obscure.

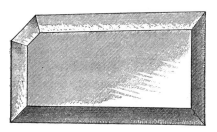

FIG. 47.   The "Great Table," a large Indian diamond mentioned by Tavernier.

The Shah of Persia is in the possession of two large diamonds of which also very little is known. One of these, the **Darya-i-noor** (Sea of Light), weighs 186 carats, and the other, **Taj-e-mah** (Crown of the Moon), weighs 146 carats. Both are of the purest water and cut as rosettes; they were formerly set in a pair of armlets which were valued at one million sterling.

A large diamond of singular beauty, perhaps the most perfect of all, is the **Regent** or **Pitt,** at present preserved with the French crown jewels. In its rough condition it was the largest of all Indian diamonds, the genuineness of which is unquestionable. It was found in 1701 in the Partial mines on the river Kistna in southern India (or according to another account in the Malay Peninsula), and was bought for £20,400 by Governor Pitt of Fort St. George, Madras. In 1717 it was acquired in its rough state by the Duke of Orleans, then Regent of France, for 2,000,000 francs (£80,000). The operation of cutting was performed in London; it occupied two years and cost £5000; the weight of the stone was reduced from 410 to $136\frac{14}{16}$ carats, and the portions detached in the cuttings remained the property of the former owner. The stone when cut (Plate XI., Figs. 8a, 8b, 8c), was a brilliant of the most perfect form; its colour, however, does not reach the same high standard of perfection. In the valuation of the French crown jewels, made in 1791, this diamond was stated to be worth 12,000,000 francs (£480,000). In 1792 it was stolen in company with many other crown jewels, but was subsequently recovered, and after being pledged at the time of the Revolution was redeemed by Napoleon. Being an object of general interest, it was not disposed of with the other crown jewels, but has remained up to the present time one of the most beautiful and valuable of the jewels belonging to the French nation.

The **Florentine,** "Grand Duke of Tuscany" or the "Austrian," is a large diamond now in the treasury of the imperial palace at Vienna. It has the form of a briolette (Plate XI., Figs. 10a, 10b), with the facets arranged in nine groups radiating from the centre. Its weight is $133\frac{1}{5}$ Vienna carats (27·454 grams), the weight of $139\frac{1}{2}$ carats, which is sometimes given, being in the smaller Florentine carats. The stone though distinctly yellow in colour, is beautifully clear and shows a fine fire. According to the usual but disputed account, this stone was cut by L. van Berquen for Charles the Bold, who lost it on the battlefield of Granson, where it was found by a Swiss soldier. After frequently changing hands, it passed into the possession of the Grand Duke Francis Stephen of Tuscany, who brought it to Vienna, its present resting-place.

The **Sancy** diamond, a stone of $53\frac{1}{16}$ carats, though much smaller is very similar in form to the "Florentine," and is also stated to have been cut by L. van Berquen for Charles the Bold. At the death of the latter, at the battle of Nancy in 1477, the stone is supposed to have been taken by a soldier to Portugal, where it was acquired by the French nobleman de Sancy, who about 1600 sold it to Queen Elizabeth of England.   It was carried back to France by Henrietta Maria, the Queen of Charles I., and passed into the possession of Cardinal Mazarin as a pledge.   Together with seventeen other large diamonds it was left by the latter to Louis XIV., and in the inventory, made in 1791, of the French crown jewels was valued at 1,000,000 francs.   At the time of the Revolution it was stolen in company with the "Regent" ("Pitt"), but unlike the latter was not recovered.   It reappeared ten years later as the property of the Spanish crown; from 1828 to 1865 it was in the possession of Prince Demidoff, by whom it was sold for £20,000.   It is now said to be the property of the Maharaja of Patiala, and so, after many vicissitudes, to have returned to the land of its origin.   So many stories are related of this stone that it seems not improbable that the history of other large diamonds has been confused with that of the "Sancy."   It was exhibited at the Paris Exhibition of 1867, and is figured in Plate XI., Figs. 11a, 11b.

The **Nassak** diamond derives its name from its long sojourn in the temple to Siva at Nassak on the upper Godavari river.   From the possession of the last independent Prince of Peshawar, it passed in 1818 into the hands of the East India Company.   At that time it was of an unsymmetrical cut-form and weighed 89½ carats; the form in which it was re-cut, namely, that of a triangular brilliant, is shown in Plate XI., Figs. 13a, 13b, 13c.   In 1831 it was bought for £7200 by Emanuel, a London jeweller, who soon afterwards disposed of it to the Duke of Westminister, in whose family it still remains.

The **Empress Eugénie** diamond is a beautiful brilliant of unknown origin, weighing 51 carats.   It was given by Catharine II. of Russia to her favourite, Potemkin, in whose family it remained until it was acquired by Napoleon III. for a wedding-gift to his bride Eugénie.   After the dethronement of the latter it came into the possession of the Gaikwar of Baroda in India.

The **Pigott** is a brilliant brought by Lord Pigott from India to England about the year 1775, and afterwards disposed of to Ali Pasha, the Viceroy of Egypt.   All trace of this stone has since been lost, and, according to report, it has been destroyed. Its weight is given by Mawe, who saw the stone shortly before it was sold to Ali Pasha, as 49 carats, but other values up to 81½ carats have been given at various times.

The **White Saxon Brilliant** is one of the most beautiful of known diamonds; it is square in outline with an edge measuring $1\frac{1}{12}$ inches in length, and weighs 48¾ carats. For this stone August the Strong is said to have paid 1,000,000 thalers.

The **Pasha of Egypt** is a fine eight-sided brilliant of 40 carats, purchased by the Viceroy Ibrahim of Egypt for £28,000.

The comparatively small diamond known as the **Star of Este** surpasses in beauty many of those already mentioned.   Its intrinsic beauty is absolutely flawless, and the brilliant form in which it is cut is as perfect.   Its weight is $25\frac{13}{32}$ Vienna carats (5232 milligrams), only about half the weight, that is to say, of the "Empress Eugénie" or the "Sancy" diamond.   Compared with these stones, however, it does not appear sensibly smaller, so perfect are its proportions and so regular the cutting   It is at present in the possession of the Archduke Franz Ferdinand of Austrian-Este, eldest son of the Archduke Karl Ludwig.   In 1876 it was valued at 64,000 Austrian florins, a former valuation having been 200,000 to 250,000 francs.

Excluding the yellow South African diamonds, stones which combine large size with beauty of colour are rare and are all of Indian origin.   Of these the following are most famous:

The **Hope Blue** diamond is characterised not only by the possession of a beautiful sapphire-blue colour—an extremely rare tint in diamonds—but also by a brilliant lustre and fine play of colours. Its existence has been known of since 1830, and it at one time formed part of the famous collection of precious stones of Henry Philip Hope, who bought it for £18,000. It is a perfect brilliant weighing $44\frac{1}{4}$ carats.

A beautiful blue, triangular brilliant of $67\frac{2}{16}$ carats, and valued in 1791 at 3,000,000 francs, was preserved among the French crown jewels up to the year 1792, when it was stolen, together with the "Regent" and others. It had been cut from a rough stone, weighing $112\frac{3}{16}$ carats, brought from India by Tavernier for Louis XIV. There are substantial grounds for the suggestion that when this brilliant was stolen it was divided, and the portions re-cut and placed on the market about 1830 in a new form. It is very possible that the "Hope Blue" diamond is one of these portions; another being a stone of $13\frac{3}{4}$ carats of the same blue colour, and formerly in the possession of Duke Karl of Brunswick, who sold it in 1874 in Geneva for 17,000 francs; the third portion may be identical with a stone of $1\frac{1}{4}$ carats of the same colour, once bought for £300 and now in the possession of an English family.

The **Dresden Green** diamond, preserved in the "Green Vaults" of Dresden, is the most famous representative of stones of this colour. It is of a very fine clear apple-green, intermediate between the colour of emerald and chrysoprase, perfectly transparent and faultless in every way. It is almond-shaped in form, being $1\frac{1}{12}$ inches long and $\frac{5}{6}$ inch thick, and weighs 40 carats, not, as is sometimes stated, $31\frac{1}{4}$ or 48 carats. Since 1743 it has been the property of the Saxon crown, and 60,000 thalers is said to have been paid for it by August the Strong.

Very few diamonds famous for their size have come from Brazil, the only important exceptions being two stones found, in the 'fifties of the nineteenth century, in the district of Bagagem, in the western part of Minas Geraes, both of which were acquired by the Gaikwar of Baroda, a purchase which would seem to indicate that India can no longer satisfy the taste of her native princes for gorgeous jewels.

The **Star of the South**, found at the end of July 1853, is one of these two famous Brazilian diamonds. The rough stone, which was examined by the French mineralogist,

FIG. 48. "Star of the South." Two views of the rough stone. (Natural size.)

Dufrénoy, was described as being an irregular rhombic dodecahedron with convex faces (Fig. 48), and as weighing $254\frac{1}{2}$ carats. The stone showed in a few places small octahedral impressions of other diamonds, as if the larger diamond had once formed one of a group of crystals; in other places the octahedral cleavage was discernible. A few small black plates enclosed in the stone have been considered to be ilmenite (titaniferous iron ore), since this mineral has been shown to occur as an enclosure in diamond. The rough stone fetched 430 contos de reis, about £40,000. It was cut in Amsterdam, and produced a beautiful pure brilliant of 125 carats (Plate XI., Figs. 9a, 9b, 9c), which was bought by the Gaikwar of Baroda for £80,000.

Mr. E. Dresden's diamond was found at the same place as the last-mentioned

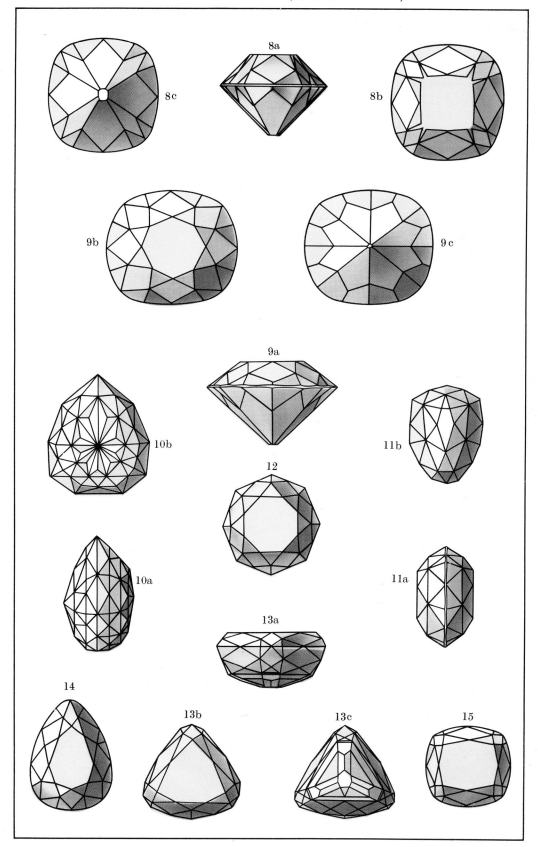

8a, b, c. Regent. 9a, b, c. Star of the South (from Brazil). 10a, b. Florentine. 11a, b, c. Sancy. 12. Pasha of Egypt. 13a, b, c. Nassak. 14. Star of South Africa. 15. Polar Star.

stone, and almost at the same time. It weighed, in the rough, 119½ carats, and was therefore smaller than the "Star of the South," and its appearance suggested that it might be a fragment of a larger crystal. It was transformed into an egg-shaped brilliant (Plate X., Figs. 7*b*, 7*c*) of 76½ carats, the process of cutting not involving in this case a very large loss of material.

It has already been mentioned that the supposed large diamond, the "Braganza," came from Brazil. Some other large Brazilian diamonds have been mentioned above under the description of Brazilian deposits, one of these being the large stone found at the beginning of the nineteenth century on the Rio Abaété, in Minas Geraes, as to the history of which nothing is known.

Only a few of the large diamonds which have been found in South Africa are distinguished by special names. Some of these were discovered and named before the comparative abundance of large stones in these deposits was known; others, however, so far surpass other large diamonds in size and beauty that it is only fitting that they should receive distinctive names. Some of these diamonds have already been mentioned under the description of the South African deposits.

The first large diamond found in this country was discovered in 1869 in the river diggings, and is known as the **Star of South Africa.** It weighed, in the rough, 83½ carats, and formed, when cut, an oval, three-sided brilliant (Plate XI., Fig. 14) of 46½ carats of the purest water, comparable with the best Indian and Brazilian stones. It was sold to the Countess of Dudley for nearly £25,000, and is therefore sometimes referred to as the "Dudley" diamond.

The **Stewart,** a much larger stone, was found in 1872 in the river diggings, known as Waldeck's Plant, on the Vaal. It weighed, in the rough, 288⅜ carats, and for many years remained the largest of Cape diamonds. The rough stone was first disposed of for £6000, but on again changing hands made £9000; it gave a slightly yellowish brilliant of 120 carats (Plate X., Fig. 6).

The **Porter Rhodes** diamond was found at Kimberley on February 12, 1880. Its weight in the rough has been variously given at 150 and 160 carats. It is a perfectly colourless blue-white stone, and, on the whole, may be considered to surpass all other South African diamonds in beauty. It was valued by its owner at £200,000.

FIG. 49. "Victoria" diamond of 457½ carats from South Africa. (Actual size.)

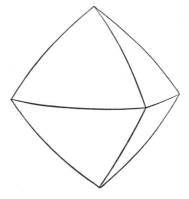

FIG. 50. Outline of a diamond of 428½ carats from South Africa. (Actual size.)

A stone of 457½ carats, from the South African deposits, reached Europe in 1884, of which nothing as to its exact origin is known. The rough stone, which had the form of an irregular octahedron, is shown in its actual size in Fig. 49. A very beautiful colourless brilliant of 180 carats was cut from it, which is variously known as the **Victoria,** "Imperial," or "Great White," and is valued at £200,000.

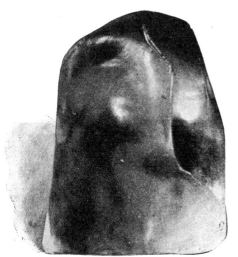

The largest brilliant, the genuineness of which is unquestionable, is one of 288½ carats, which was cut from a stone of 428½ carats found on March 28, 1880, in the De Beers mine. This was yellowish in colour and had the form of a fairly regular octahedron, the outline of which is shown in Fig. 50 in its actual size. In the direction of its longest axis it measured 1⅞ inches. Another large diamond, which weighed in the rough 655 carats, was found in the Jagersfontein mine at the end of the year 1895.

The largest of all known diamonds is the **Excelsior,** afterwards called the "Jubilee," in honour of the celebration of the sixtieth anniversary of the accession of Queen Victoria. The rough stone is represented in

FIG. 51. Largest known diamond, the "Excelsior," weight 971¾ carats. From the Jagersfontein mine in South Africa. (Actual size.)

its actual size and form in Fig. 51. It came from the Jagersfontein mine in Orange River Colony, and weighed 971¾ carats, measuring 2½ inches in length, 2 inches in breadth, and 1 inch in thickness, thus surpassing in size even the "Great Mogul," which in its rough condition is supposed to have weighed 787½ carats. It was found on June 30, 1893, by a Kaffir, who received as a reward £500 in money and a horse equipped with saddle and bridle. It is said that an agreement existed between the mine-owners and certain diamond merchants by which the latter were to purchase every stone found in the mine during a certain period at a uniform price per carat. This period ended on June 30, and the "Excelsior" was one of the last stones to be found on that day, so that the mine-owners instead of the merchants came very near to profiting by this lucky find. The stone is of a beautiful blue-white colour and of the purest water, and has been valued by different experts at amounts which vary between £50,000 and £1,000,000; the latter value, however, seems somewhat prohibitive. The rough stone, though of such perfection of colour, lustre, and water, had a black spot near the centre of its mass which had to be removed by cleaving the stone in two. From the larger portion was cut an absolutely perfect brilliant weighing 239 international carats of 205 milligrams, and measuring 1⅝ inches in length, 1⅜ in breadth, and 1 inch in depth.

FIG. 52. The "Tiffany Brilliant," 125½ carats. (Actual size.)

The orange-yellow **Tiffany Brilliant,** now in the possession of the Tiffany Company of New York, is also a Cape diamond. It is one of the finest of yellow diamonds, and at the present time is the largest brilliant in America, weighing 125½ carats. The form of the stone can be seen in Fig. 52 in its actual size.

5. VALUE OF DIAMONDS.

The valuation of a diamond, involving as it does a nice appreciation of the defects and of the good points of the stone, and the striking of a just balance between the two, is a matter of no little difficulty, and can only be performed with accuracy and rapidity by an expert. In this section we shall confine ourselves to a consideration of the value of diamonds which are to be used as gems, neglecting those to be applied to technical purposes, the value of which depends on the weight and the current market price.

Of all the characters which help to determine the value of a diamond there is perhaps none more potent than that of size. Other things being equal, the larger the diamond the greater its value, and, moreover, the ratio of progression in price is greater than that of progression in weight, owing to the comparative rarity of large stones. Since the discovery of the South African deposits, however, this disparity has been less marked, and the value of stones not exceeding a certain size and which are of frequent occurrence, is influenced to a large extent by the exigencies of the trade. Exceptionally large and beautiful stones, the so-called solitaires, paragons, or nonpareils, have, corresponding to the rarity of their occurrence, an exceptional value, which is subject to no rules and is governed solely by the special circumstances of the case.

The value of a diamond depends very largely upon the form in which it is cut. Although during the process of cutting the weight of a rough stone is reduced by one half or even more, yet its intrinsic value is greater than before, on account of the almost immeasurable improvement in its appearance effected by the faceting. The brilliant is by far the most effective form of cutting, and at the same time is the form which involves the greatest expenditure of skill in the cutting, hence a brilliant-cut diamond commands a higher price than a rose or indeed any other form. Among brilliants themselves different degrees are recognisable, a stone which is correctly proportioned and which bears a large number of facets having a greater value than one less admirable in these respects. A brilliant which possesses no cross facets, the large facets being produced until they meet in the girdle, is described as being " once formed "; while the terms " twice formed " and " thrice formed " are applied respectively to stones which bear cross facets only below the girdle, and to those which possess these facets both above and below the girdle. The value of a brilliant, therefore, is the greater the more complex is its form of cutting, and in the same way the value of stones cut in any of the other forms varies with the symmetry and completeness of that form. A perfect brilliant of one carat has at least four times the value of a rough stone of the same weight and quality, and five-fourths the value of a rose of this size and quality.

The value of a rough stone also is influenced to a certain extent by its form, for, as we have seen, stones whose form in the rough approximates most nearly to that of the cut stone are most favourable for cutting. Thus octahedral and rhombic dodecahedral crystals can be fashioned into brilliants with less labour and loss of material than is the case with irregularly shaped stones, which often need considerable preliminary shaping, if not actual division into portions suitable for cutting. Among such stones must be included flat specimens, like the twinned crystals shown in Fig. 31, g and h, which cannot be cut as brilliants and are suitable only for cutting as roses. Another property which greatly facilitates the process of cutting is that of cleavage; a simple crystal, from which the cleavage octahedron can be readily developed, is therefore far more desirable than a twinned crystal, such as is shown in Fig. 31 i, or an irregular crystal group which, as often as not, can be utilised only as bort.

The value of a diamond depends most of all, however, on the degree of its transparency, clearness, and purity, the colour it possesses, and its freedom from flaws.   Of these qualities transparency and clearness stand first in importance, and the possession of these qualities in perfection renders a diamond extremely valuable.

Those faults which impair the transparency and lustre of a stone diminish its value very considerably.   Large enclosures of black, brown, or of some other colour are frequently seen, as are also enclosures of " sand " and " ash," and yellow spots technically known as " straw."   A fine surface polish over certain areas of a stone is often made impossible by the presence of white, grey, or brown " clouds " or by " icy flakes " of no definite colour, which are developed when the stone is allowed to become over-heated during the process of grinding.   The existence of internal cracks following the direction of cleavage, and known as " feathers," not only impairs the transparency of the stone, but also renders it liable to fracture during the process of grinding or when in use as an ornament.   All these faults, even if insignificant in extent, become very obvious in the cut stone, numerous images of them being reflected into the eye of the observer from the various facets of the stone.   Should they be present in large numbers the stone is not worth cutting, but is regarded as bort.

With regard to the colour of diamonds, stones which are perfectly colourless and water-clear are, as a rule, most highly prized, the so-called blue-white quality, which is more rare in stones from the Cape than in those from India or Brazil, being specially admired. Even a trace of colour, so small as to be indistinguishable to an unpractised eye, lowers the value of a stone very considerably, the diminution in value being still greater when the colour is more perceptible.   Of coloured diamonds, those displaying tones of blue, grey, red, and yellow are preferred to those which are coloured brown or black.   A coloured diamond which is lacking in transparency is of very much less value than one of the same colour which is clear and transparent.

Those diamonds which, in addition to perfect transparency and clearness, possess a pronounced and beautiful colour, are on account both of their rarity and beauty very highly esteemed, and always command a much higher price than the most perfect of colourless specimens.   Among these so-called " fancy stones," red, blue, green, and yellow specimens are included, the last-named, however, since the discovery of the Cape deposits, are by far the most common.   Compared with colourless diamonds, coloured specimens exist in quite insignificant numbers.

Diamonds showing different degrees of transparency and clearness and freedom from faults are usually classified as stones of the first, second, and third water, and are valued accordingly.   Stones of the *first water* (1st quality) are perfectly colourless, transparent, and water-clear; they are free from any fault or blemish or tinge of colour and stand first in point of value.   Colourless stones showing insignificant faults, or stones which are free from faults, but tinged with colour, are placed in the second division and referred to as stones of the *second water ;* while stones of the *third water* display very obvious faults or a colour of undesirable depth.   A further division of the stones of the latter description is sometimes made, and in this class are placed the smallest diamonds which can be used as gems.   It is by no means easy, however, in every case to place any given stone without hesitation in one or other of these three or four classes, and it may often be observed that a stone referred to as being of the second water by one jeweller will be placed in the first class by another.   Generally speaking, it may be said that a brilliant of the second water has only about two-thirds of the value of a similar gem of the first water ; while the values of two roses of the first and second qualities are in the ratio of four to three.

Taking the value of a brilliant of the first water as unity, that of a similar brilliant of the second water will be $\frac{2}{3}$, while the values of roses of the first and second water will be expressed by the fractions $\frac{4}{5}$ and $\frac{3}{5}$. It may be remarked here that it is almost impossible to classify rough stones in this way, since the qualities on which the classification depends are not sufficiently obvious until the stone has been cut.

It appears from the writings of Pliny, that among the ancients the diamond was regarded as the most costly of precious stones, and indeed of all personal possessions. Such, however, is not the case at the present time, for the price of a colourless diamond of good size is always exceeded by that of a ruby of the same size, and generally also by that of an emerald, or even of a blue sapphire if of special beauty. This, of course, does not apply to the few diamonds which possess a fine colour in addition to their other beautiful qualities, the price of such stones being more or less prohibitive.

While the relative value of diamonds of different qualities changes but little, the absolute prices paid depend on a variety of conditions and are subject to considerable fluctuation.

The earliest record in existence of the price of a diamond is that made by the Arabian Teifaschius, who, in the twelfth century, valued a 1 carat diamond at 2 dinar (about £6). In the year 1550, Benvenuto Cellini placed the value of a beautiful stone of the same weight at 100 golden scudi, a sum which is stated by Schrauf to be equivalent to 200 Austrian florins (£20), and by Boutan to 1100 francs (£44). This latter value is abnormally high, and is probably based on an incorrect estimate of the value of the scudi. In 1609 Boetius de Boot gave the value of the carat-stone at 130 ducats (about £22), while the price mentioned in the anonymous work, *The History of Jewels*, published in London in 1672, is from 40 to 60 crowns (£8 to £12). This large fall in the value of the diamond is probably to be attributed to the effects of the Thirty Years War. According to Tavernier, the price of a carat-stone in 1676 was £8, and this statement is confirmed by contemporary writers both in Holland and at Hamburg. The price of rough diamonds had sunk in 1733 to £1 per carat, but this fall was due to the panic which followed the discovery of diamonds in Brazil. In the next year the price of the carat-stone had risen to £1 10s., at which it stood for several years subsequently. In 1750 the famous London jeweller, David Jeffries, the author of a *Treatise on Diamonds and Pearls*, records the value of a fine one-carat cut stone at £8, which is the same as the value given by Tavernier in 1676. In a work on precious stones, entitled *Der aufrichtige Jubelier*, published at Frankfurt-on-the-Main in 1772, the high price of 120 thalers (£18) is mentioned for a stone of the same description.

At the time of the French Revolution prices fell very considerably, and as far as can be ascertained from the valuation of the French crown jewels and from the prices fetched by the many less valuable stones which changed hands at this time, it would seem that in 1791 a one-carat cut stone would fetch no more on an average than £6. When more settled times came, however, and Napoleon's luxurious court was established, the price again rose, and in 1832 £9 could be obtained for a one-carat brilliant, and rough stones of a quality suitable for cutting fetched 42s. to 48s. or even £3 per carat. Later on still, in the year 1859, rough stones of the same description were worth from £4 to £5 5s. per carat, while in 1860 and 1865 £13 to £18 was paid for a one-carat cut stone.

In the year 1869, shortly before the Cape diamonds came on the market, the following prices, according to Schrauf, were current: rough stones suitable for cutting, and similar to those which come in large parcels from the countries in which they are mined, cost £5 per carat; parcels of stones, the larger proportion of which could be used only as bort, made £1 to £2 per carat; while parcels containing nothing but bort were sold for 4s. to 6s. per carat. The prices recorded for cut stones show the importance which was attached not only to the quality of a stone but also to the form and manner in which it had been cut.

A one-carat brilliant of the first water was worth £20 to £25, one of the second water £15, while one-carat roses of the first water were worth only £15 to £18; a brilliant of $\frac{1}{2}$ carat would fetch £6, one of $\frac{3}{4}$ carat £12, and one of $\frac{1}{10}$ carat £1; for small roses, of which 50 go to the carat, £15 per carat was paid; very small roses of about 1000 to the carat cost about 6d. each. Only at most prosperous times, in the sixteenth and at the beginning of the seventeenth centuries, were such high prices paid as were current for diamonds in 1869. In the following table, compiled by L. Dieulafait, may be seen the prices in francs (25 francs = £1) which were paid for brilliants of 1 to 5 carats in the years 1606, 1750, 1865, and 1867. The prices current in the year 1878, which are given further on, are incorporated in this table in order to show the fall which took place in consequence of the discovery of the South African diamond-fields, and which followed a steady rise in the years 1867 to 1869.

Brilliant of	1606.	1750.	1865.	1867.	1878.
1 carat	545	202	453	529	110
2 ,,	2182	807	1639	2017	350
3 ,,	4916	1815	3151	3529	625
4 ,,	6554	2470	—	—	975
5 ,,	8753	5042	8067	8823	1375

The prices current for brilliants of ordinary size at the end of the 'seventies is best seen from the following table, which was compiled by Vanderheym, on behalf of the syndicate of Parisian jewellers, for the Paris Exhibition of 1878. Two brilliants of weights from $\frac{1}{2}$ to 12 carats and of four qualities were exhibited, and the prices in francs given in the table are for the pair of stones:

Weight in carats.	1st quality.	2nd quality.	3rd quality.	4th quality.
1	220	180	150	120
$1\frac{1}{2}$	400	300	250	200
2	700	600	480	400
$2\frac{1}{2}$	950	800	625	525
3	1250	1020	780	660
$3\frac{1}{2}$	1600	1225	945	720
4	1950	1440	1120	960
$4\frac{1}{2}$	2350	1642	1305	1080
5	2750	1900	1500	1250
$5\frac{1}{2}$	3250	2117	1705	1430
6	3700	2340	1920	1620
$6\frac{1}{2}$	4250	2567	2112	1820
7	5000	2765	2310	1995
$7\frac{1}{2}$	5800	3000	2550	2175
8	6700	3240	2800	2360
$8\frac{1}{2}$	7600	3485	3060	2550
9	8500	3735	3330	2700
$9\frac{1}{2}$	9400	3990	3562	2897
10	10300	4250	3800	3050
$10\frac{1}{2}$	11400	4515	4042	3255
11	12500	4840	4290	3465
$11\frac{1}{2}$	13700	5175	4600	3737
12	15000	5400	4800	3900

The prices given in the above table of course apply only to the time at which it was compiled. A striking feature of the table is the difference which exists between the prices of stones of the same weight but of different qualities, especially in the case of stones of the first and second waters. The difference between the value of a 1-carat stone of the first water and one of the second water is much greater than between stones of the second and third waters, and in larger stones the difference is still greater. Thus a 12-carat stone of the first water is worth almost three times as much as a stone of equal weight of the second water, the values of stones of this size of the second and third quality being in the ratio of nine to eight. The explanation of the apparent anomaly lies in the fact that in the Cape deposits large diamonds of the first water are rare, while stones of large size but inferior quality are abundant.

A consideration of the table will also show to what a small extent the values of diamonds at the present day are in agreement with the so-called Tavernier's rule, according to which the value of a stone is proportional to the square of its weight. While the value of a 12-carat stone of the first quality would be, according to Tavernier's rule, $110 \times 12 \times 12 = 15,840$ francs, its actual value in 1878, according to the table, was 7500 francs, or not quite half. The application of the rule to smaller stones results in a calculated value which is still further removed from the actual value; thus the value of a 6-carat diamond of the first water calculated by this rule would be $110 \times 6 \times 6 = 3960$ francs, while it is actually worth but 1850 francs. At the present time, this tendency is even more marked than it was in 1878; the value of stones up to 15 carats is approximately proportional to their weight, so that a 2-carat stone is worth about double, and a 3-carat stone about three times as much as a 1-carat diamond. This holds good, at any rate, for the three inferior qualities of stones, but in the case of diamonds of the first water the increase in value is not proportional to the increase of weight.

The price of a 12-carat stone of the first water calculated by Schrauf's rule, according to which the value of a 1-carat stone is multiplied by the product of half the weight of the stone into its weight plus 2, would be $110 \times 6 \times 14 = 9240$ francs, the tabulated value being 7500 francs; the value thus calculated, although nearer the mark than in the former case, is still considerably too much. As in the case with Tavernier's rule, the values calculated by Schrauf's rule for smaller stones are still further from their actual value, the calculated worth of a 6-carat stone being $110 \times 3 \times 8 = 2640$ francs while it is actually worth but 1850 francs. At the present time the market price of a fine 1-carat brilliant is £15; in exceptional cases, however, £20 to £25 may be given for such a stone.

The price of stones of exceptional size, that is of those weighing anything over 12 carats, is not governed by rule, and depends very much on what a rich person or State is disposed to give for them. Diamonds of exceptional size and of unusual colours are not common articles of commerce, and their price, while always, of course, very high, depends on the number of would-be purchasers which can be found for them.

With regard to the prices current for smaller diamonds, it is impossible to say much more than has been already said, for, after all, the value of stones of ordinary size depends to a very large extent on their quality. The price of cut gems and of rough stones always differs very widely; the latter are not, as a rule, bought and sold singly but come into the markets in large parcels, those from the Cape being carefully sorted and arranged according to quality, while parcels from Brazil consist of unsorted stones of all qualities.

6. IMITATION AND COUNTERFEITING.

Attempts have often been made by unprincipled dealers to pass off stones of little value or worthless imitations as genuine diamonds. The gems of inferior value most frequently used for this purpose are colourless topaz, zircon rendered colourless by heating, white sapphire, spinel, beryl, tourmaline, phenakite, and even rock-crystal and other minerals. In all these stones, however, the beautiful play of prismatic colours so characteristic of the diamond is far less marked, as is also, except, perhaps, in the case of colourless zircon, the peculiarly high lustre of the diamond. No one in the least degree familiar with the appearance of the diamond would for a moment confuse it with any of the stones just mentioned. Among the physical characters by which the diamond may be distinguished from other colourless gems are hardness, specific gravity, and refraction of light, the spinel alone of the minerals mentioned above being singly refracting like the diamond. The diamond is much less frequently confused with coloured than with colourless gems.

In absence of colour, in transparency, lustre, and play of prismatic colours, some kinds of glass, especially strass, resemble the diamond with astonishing closeness. This material is, therefore, largely used in the manufacture of imitation diamonds, and so closely does the appearance of a piece of freshly-cut strass simulate that of a genuine diamond that it is possible even for an expert to be deceived. The genuineness, or otherwise, of such a stone can, however, be easily and conclusively proved by a simple test of the hardness with a steel point or file.

The construction of so-called doublets for the purpose of deception is by no means infrequent. In such cases the upper portion of the brilliant is of diamond, while the lower is of glass or of some colourless stone such as white sapphire. The device by which the yellow tinge of a diamond is temporarily concealed, namely, by applying a thin coating of some blue substance, has been already referred to. The play of prismatic colours, characteristic of the diamond, is imitated with a certain amount of success by painting the under side of the counterfeit stone. Articles of this description, known as irises, have found a ready sale, without any attempt at passing them off for anything other than what they are.

CORUNDUM.

Some of the most beautiful and valuable of precious stones, including the red ruby and the blue sapphire, belong to the mineral species corundum. All such stones are alike in the possession of those physical characters which essentially define a mineral species. Their appearance, however, owing to the great variety of colour displayed, may be very diverse, and thus the species furnishes a large number of gems, each with a distinct and characteristic colour, but having the same chemical composition and crystalline form.

Chemically considered, corundum is pure alumina, the oxide of the now much used metal aluminium. The chemical formula Al_2O_3, by which this oxide is represented, corresponds to 53·2 per cent. of metal and 46·8 per cent. of oxygen. Chemical analyses of naturally occurring corundum, however, always show the presence of some impurity, the amount of which is smaller the clearer and more transparent is the material used in the analysis. Foreign impurities are sometimes present in large amount, up to 10 per cent. or even more, and when this is the case the stone is rendered cloudy and loses its æsthetic value. The analysis of natural corundum has demonstrated the presence of iron oxide, silica, and occasionally traces of chromium oxide. The chemical composition of a beautiful transparent red corundum, the so-called " oriental ruby," and of a blue corundum or " oriental sapphire " of equally fine quality, is given below :

	Ruby.	Sapphire.
Alumina (Al_2O_3) . . .	97·32	97·51
Iron oxide (Fe_2O_3) . . .	1·09	1·89
Silica (SiO_2) . . .	1·21	0·80
	99·62	100·20

It is on the presence of such foreign substances as iron oxide and in part probably on chromium oxide that the variety of colour found in this species depends.

Corundum occurs not infrequently in well-developed crystals belonging to the rhombohedral division of the hexagonal system. A series of the more frequently occurring forms, which are of two different habits, is shown in Fig. 53, a—i. In some a hexagonal prism is more or less largely developed and terminated at the two ends by basal planes perpendicular to the prism planes, faces of the primitive rhombohedron occupying alternate corners. Most of the crystal-faces are smooth ; the basal planes, however, bear regular, triangular striations, as in the crystal shown in Plate I., Fig. 5. Crystals with these three forms are shown in Figs. 53, a, b, c ; in a and b the prism predominates, the only difference between the two being the greater size of the rhombohedron faces in b ; in c the prism faces are narrow, while the rhombohedron faces and the basal planes are all about equal in size. Fig. 53 d shows a combination of the same forms with a double hexagonal pyramid in addition, the twelve faces of which replace the edges between the prism faces and the basal planes. This hexagonal bipyramid is present in all the remaining figures, e to i. In Fig. 53 e it occurs alone, and in the remaining forms it is predominant ; in f it is in combination with the basal planes, and in g with the basal plane and a rhombohedron, the faces of which replace alternate corners above and below. In h there are three such hexagonal bipyramids with different inclinations, each successive pyramid being less steeply inclined the nearer it is to the end of the crystal; in combination with these three pyramids are the basal planes and a narrow hexagonal prism. The frequent repetition or oscillation between pyramids of this kind gives rise to horizontal striations on the faces, such as is shown in *f*. In Fig. 53, *i*, a combination of two hexagonal bipyramids with the hexagonal prism and an acute rhombohedron is shown. As mentioned above, crystals of corundum occur in one of two habits, that is with either the prism or the hexagonal pyramids predominating. The former is the more characteristic for red corundum or ruby, and the latter for blue corundum or sapphire. A crystal of ruby is shown in Plate I., Fig. 5, and a sapphire crystal in Fig. 7 of the same plate, both stones being represented in their natural colours.

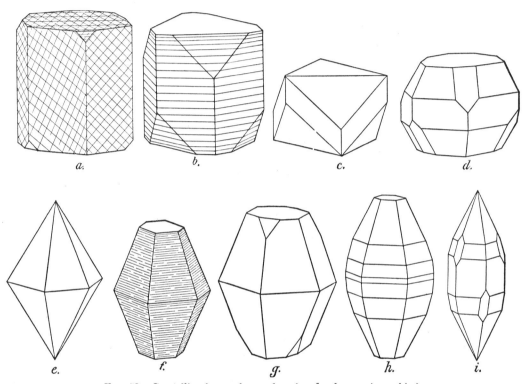

FIG. 53.　Crystalline forms of corundum (*a—d*, ruby ; *e—i*, sapphire).

Twin intergrowths are often met with in cloudy corundum, but less frequently in transparent material suitable for use as gems. These are of two kinds : in the one, large numbers of thin plane lamellæ, parallel to a face of the primitive rhombohedron, occupy twin positions in the crystal, as indicated in Fig. 53, *a* ; in the other, illustrated by *b* of the same figure, the lamellæ are parallel to the basal planes. Owing to this cause the faces of crystals often bear fine striations, which differ in direction in the two kinds of twin intergrowth. In the first, the striations are present on the basal plane in three sets of parallel lines intersecting at 120° or 60°, and on the prism and rhombohedron faces in two sets intersecting at an oblique angle. In the other kind of twin intergrowth, the basal planes are smooth, while the faces of the prism and rhombohedron are horizontally striated, the striations on the prism faces being perpendicular to the prism edges.

This twin lamination of corundum crystals makes the mineral appear to have two cleavages, one parallel to one or more faces of the primitive rhombohedron and the other parallel to the basal plane. Such a crystal when dropped or struck with a chisel will separate along plane surfaces in these directions. This splitting up, which is known as a platy separation, is not a true cleavage but is due to want of cohesion between the individual lamellæ. If the division were due to cleavage the lamellæ after separation could be split up again in the same direction, which is not the case. Moreover, the property of splitting along surfaces parallel to the faces of the rhombohedron and to the basal plane is possessed only by those crystals which are penetrated by twin-lamellæ parallel to these faces. In crystals in which twin-lamellæ are absent all trace of platy separation is also absent, the fracture being conchoidal as is the case with many other non-cleavable minerals.

Corundum is brittle, and among other physical characters it possesses that of hardness to a high degree. After diamond, it is the hardest of all minerals, having the number 9 assigned to it in Mohs' scale of hardness. It is, however, much more nearly approached in hardness by certain other minerals than it itself approaches diamond in this respect. Its hardness renders this mineral very valuable as a grinding and polishing material, the cloudy and opaque varieties, especially the compact black emery, being much used for this purpose, while rather superior qualities are utilised for the pivot supports of watches and various delicate instruments. There are degrees of hardness among the different varieties of corundum, the blue sapphire standing first in this respect.

The specific gravity of corundum is very high ; that of pure material is very near to 4, values varying between 3·94 and 4·08 having from time to time been determined on pure material. Greater variations on either side of the mean value of 4·0 are due either to errors of observation or to the determinations having been made on impure material. No difference has been observed in the specific gravity of differently coloured varieties. Corundum is thus one of the densest of precious stones, and this character renders it easily distinguishable from other minerals which may resemble it in general appearance. It sinks rapidly, not only in methylene iodide but also in the heavier liquid (sp. gr. = 3·6) obtained by dissolving iodoform and iodine in methylene iodide.

It is not attacked by acids either in the cold or when warmed, and is completely infusible before the blowpipe. Many specimens of corundum when heated in a dark room display a beautiful phosphorescence. When rubbed with cloth or leather the mineral acquires a charge of positive electricity, which it retains for a considerable time.

Corundum varies greatly in appearance. Most frequently it is cloudy and opaque, and only a small proportion is clear and transparent and valuable from an æsthetic point of view. The common cloudy and opaque varieties of corundum will not be here considered in detail, but our attention will be directed to the transparent varieties known as noble or precious corundum.

The lustre of precious corundum is very fine, and is displayed to great advantage by the polished facets of a cut stone. It approaches that of diamond in brilliancy, but differs from it in character, being not adamantine but vitreous, like that of many other precious stones and glass. So brilliant and perfect a lustre and so marked a fire is displayed by no other precious stone with the exception of diamond, and perhaps also of colourless hyacinth (zircon), so that by these characters alone the stone may be distinguished from other gems of the same colour. Even when a specimen of corundum is of a poor colour it will still be cut as a gem, since the fine lustre of the mineral will redeem the stone from insignificance. Moreover, owing to the great hardness of this stone, the lustre is retained even after rough usage and hard wear.

Corundum is optically uniaxial and doubly refracting. Its refraction, though strong, is considerably less than that of diamond ; its double refraction is small, the refractive indices for the ordinary and extraordinary rays differing but slightly. In a crystal from Ceylon they have been determined for yellow sodium light to be: $\omega = 1\cdot7690$; $\varepsilon = 1\cdot7598$. The dispersion produced by corundum is also small, the refractive indices for different colours of the spectrum differing but slightly ; hence the mineral shows no marked flashes of prismatic colours as does the diamond.

The high index of refraction, small dispersion, and considerable hardness of corundum render the colourless or pale-coloured varieties very suitable for the preparation of microscopic lenses. Pritchard who, as we have already seen, made use of diamond for this purpose, in 1827 constructed lenses of very pale blue sapphire ; they have never, however, come into general use. Transparent corundum finds its most extensive application in jewellery, the fine appearance of the stone being due to the combination of transparency and high lustre with fine colour. The mineral corundum includes some of the most beautifully coloured precious stones known, and we will now consider the different colour-varieties of the mineral.

Absolutely pure crystallised alumina has no colour and is perfectly water-clear. It is then known as leuco-sapphire ; it is, however, but rarely found in this condition, more usually showing a more or less pronounced colour. In many cases the colouring-matter is irregularly distributed, sometimes being aggregated in patches surrounded by colourless portions of material ; not infrequently also different portions of one and the same crystal are differently coloured. As has been already stated, the various colours shown by corundum are due to the intermixture with the ground substance of various foreign substances, the nature of which in particular cases has never been determined. The colours vary in tone from light and pale to dark and intense ; stones showing pale tones of colour have been described as " feminine," and those coloured more deeply as " masculine."

The phenomenon of dichroism is always observable in deeply coloured specimens of corundum, it is not seen in very pale coloured varieties, and is the more noticeable the deeper the colour of the specimen.

Several varieties of precious corundum are recognised ; these are distinguished from each other by their colour, and from the jeweller's point of view differ much in importance and value. The two varieties which occur with the greatest frequency are red corundum, or ruby, and blue corundum, or sapphire, the latter being more abundant than the former. All other coloured varieties are in comparison almost rare. They are known by the same names as certain other stones of the same colour, being distinguished from these by the prefix " oriental," which is meant to signify the possession of specially noble qualities, such as great hardness and fine lustre. The same prefix is often applied to ruby and sapphire themselves with the object of distinguishing them from other precious stones of the same colour. Moreover, in the case of sapphire, it serves to distinguish stones of the true sapphire-blue from other colour-varieties of the species, to which, with the exception of ruby, the term sapphire is sometimes extended. It should be remembered that the only character which the different colour-varieties of corundum have in common with the stones after which they are named is their colour ; thus, by the term " oriental emerald," must be understood transparent corundum of a green colour.

The different colour-varieties of corundum are tabulated below :

Variety.	Colour.
Ruby (" oriental ruby ")	red.
Sapphire (" oriental sapphire ")	blue.
Leuco-sapphire	colourless.
" Oriental aquamarine "	light bluish-green.

Variety.						Colour.
" Oriental emerald "	.	.	.	.	.	green.
" Oriental chrysolite "		.	.	.	.	yellowish-green.
" Oriental topaz "		.	.	.	.	yellow.
" Oriental hyacinth "	.	.	.	.	.	aurora-red.
" Oriental amethyst "	.		.	.	.	violet.

The different colours of these varieties of corundum usually appear just as beautiful when viewed by artificial light as by daylight, which is not always the case with the stones, after which they are named. The colour of certain varieties of corundum can be in some cases destroyed, and in others changed by the application of heat ; this point, however, will be considered later on.

The different colour-varieties of corundum occur as irregular grains and as well-developed crystals embedded in the mother-rock, which, as a rule, is an old crystalline rock, such as granite or gneiss. The gem-varieties are found with especial frequency as secondary contact minerals, which have been developed in limestone by contact with a molten igneous rock. By the weathering and denudation of such rocks, the embedded crystals are set free, and are subsequently found with other water-worn débris in the beds of streams and rivers. It is in these derived deposits that the most beautiful specimens of the varieties mentioned above are found in all countries in which the original mother-rocks occur.

Having briefly considered the characters common to all corundum, we pass now to the consideration of the varieties suitable for use as gems, and begin with the most costly of all stones, namely, the ruby.

RUBY.

CHARACTERS.—Of all the colour-varieties of precious corundum the red, or ruby (" oriental ruby "), is the most highly prized. It is probably identical with the anthrax of Theophrastus, and is one of the stones referred to in mediæval times as carbuncle. It has all the general characters of corundum, and is only distinguished from other varieties by its red colour. A natural crystal of ruby is shown in Plate I., Fig. 5, and a faceted stone in Fig. 6 of the same plate.

The tone of colour differs in different specimens, being sometimes deep and intense (" masculine " ruby), sometimes pale and light (" feminine " ruby). The lighter shades vary from pale rose-red to reddish-white, some specimens being so faintly tinged with red as to appear almost colourless. The darker colours are either pure red, carmine-red, or blood-red ; the red of the majority of rubies, however, has a more or less distinct tinge of blue or violet, this being specially noticeable in transmitted light. The shade of colour which is most admired is the deep, pure carmine-red, or carmine-red with a slight bluish tinge. This colour has been compared by the Burmese to that of the blood of a freshly-killed pigeon, hence the references to such stones as being of " pigeon's-blood " red. The various shades of red of the ruby are remarkable in that they lose none of their beauty in artificial light, a statement which cannot be made respecting any other precious stone of the same colour.

The colouring of rubies is not always perfectly uniform, colourless layers being sometimes interposed between portions coloured red. In such cases, the stone will often become uniformly coloured throughout after heating. Provided the stone is gradually heated it may be raised to the highest temperatures with no fear of fracture. The interesting changes in colour exhibited by certain gems when gradually heated and then allowed to cool have been already described.   During cooling the ruby becomes first white and then green, finally regaining its original red colour, so that in this stone the colouring-matter is neither permanently changed nor destroyed by exposure to high temperatures.   It is otherwise, however, with the sapphire, for this gem at a high temperature loses its beautiful blue and takes on a dull grey colour.

The red colouring-matter of the ruby is therefore certainly not organic in nature, as seems to be the case with those gems which lose their colour on heating.   It is more likely to be some compound of chromium, an element whose presence has been detected in the analysis of some rubies.   That the colouring of the ruby is due to chromium is also suggested by the fact that the colour of the so-called " ruby " glass is obtained by adding a small amount of chromium oxide to the other constituents of the glass.   The same substance is also used by M. Frémy for the production of the red colour of his artificially prepared rubies.   Some of the crystals produced by this investigator were partly red and partly blue, resembling in this respect certain natural rubies which occur rarely in Burma.

The dichroism of deeply coloured rubies is very noticeable ; with the exception of stones of very pale colour, a difference in the colour of every ruby can be observed when viewed in different directions.   On looking through a dark-coloured crystal of ruby, such as is illustrated in Fig. 53, a—d, in a direction perpendicular to the basal planes, it will appear of an intense red colour, either pure red or with a slight tinge of violet.   If, however, the light received by the eye has passed through the crystal in any direction perpendicular to a prism face or edge, the stone will appear much lighter in colour.   On allowing the light which has passed through the crystal in this direction to enter the dichroscope, the two images, in that position of the instrument in which the greatest difference in colour is shown, will be one light, and the other dark red usually tinged with violet.   In all other directions in which the light may travel, with one exception, the two images will be more or less differently coloured.   This exceptional direction is perpendicular to the basal planes and coincides with the direction of the optic axis.   Along this direction the crystal is singly refracting, and the two images seen in the dichroscope are of the same deep red colour as the crystal appears when viewed in this direction without the intervention of the dichroscope. The dichroism of the ruby affords a means whereby it may be distinguished with certainty from other red stones, such as spinel and the different varieties of garnet, which crystallise in the cubic system, and thus being singly refracting can show no dichroism.

The fact that the colour of the ruby varies with the direction in which it is viewed, makes it necessary that the form of the cut gem should have a certain definite relation to that of the crystal in order to obtain the finest colour-effect.   The plane of the largest facet of the cut stone, namely, the table, must coincide as closely as possible in direction with the basal planes of the crystal in order to obtain the greatest depth in colour of which the stone is capable.   The greater the angle at which the table is inclined to the basal plane of the crystal the poorer will be the colour-effect produced, and when the table is perpendicular to the basal plane, and therefore parallel to the prism faces of the crystal, the minimum colour-effect is the result.

Some rubies show on the basal plane, or still more plainly on a cut and polished curved surface approximating to the basal plane in direction, a six-rayed star of glimmering reflected light.   Such stones are known as *star-rubies*, or asteriated rubies, sometimes also as ruby cat's-eye.   The appearance is similar to that seen in the star-sapphire, but, as a rule, less marked ; it will be therefore considered in greater detail under sapphire.

VALUE.—A clear, transparent, and faultless ruby of a uniform deep red colour is at the present time the most valuable precious stone known.   Except in ancient times, it is probable that the ruby has always held a foremost place in the estimation of connoisseurs. This, however, is not true of stones of a pale red colour, which are always less highly prized, on account both of their light shade of colour and of the fact that they occur more abundantly and in larger size than do stones of a true pigeon's-blood red.

The value of the finest ruby, therefore, far exceeds that of a diamond of corresponding size and quality. One-carat diamonds of the first water are of far more frequent occurrence than rubies of the same size and quality, while large rubies are still rarer than large diamonds. A fine deeply-coloured ruby of 3 carats is a great rarity, whereas it is by no means unusual to come across fine diamonds of this size. Again, while 10-carat diamonds are of moderately frequent occurrence, rubies of the same weight scarcely ever occur, while only very few specimens of still larger stones are known. It is therefore to be expected that larger rubies should command exceptionally high prices; indeed, the prices of stones of ordinary sizes may be arrived at very closely by the application of Tavernier's rule. The relation between the ratio of the weight and the value of a large and a small stone is very different when, on the one hand, the two stones are diamonds, and when, on the other, they are rubies. Thus, while a 1-carat ruby is worth twice as much as a 1-carat diamond, a 3-carat ruby of the first quality is worth ten times as much as a diamond of the same description, that is to say, that while a 3-carat brilliant of the first water would be valued at about £150, a ruby of the same description would be worth about £1500. The value of a 5-carat diamond of the first quality would be about £300, while that of a similar ruby would be £3000. These values, of course, apply to stones in the cut condition, the weight of which uncut would be about doubled. For rubies of still larger size there is no fixed market price; almost fabulous sums have been paid for very fine stones of large size required for some special purpose. A fine ruby of $9\frac{5}{16}$ carats has been recently valued by Mr. G. F. Kunz, the American gem expert, at 33,000 dollars (£6776). Again, £10,000 is stated by Mr E. W. Streeter, the London jeweller, to have been paid for a cut ruby of $32\frac{5}{16}$ carats, and double this amount for another weighing $38\frac{9}{16}$ carats; both of these stones were faultless specimens of magnificent colour.

It is recorded by Benvenuto Cellini in the middle of the sixteenth century that a carat ruby was eight times the value of a carat diamond, the price of the former being 800 golden scudi (£160) and that of the latter 100 scudi (£20). The ratio at the present time is only about two to one, the market price of a fine 1-carat ruby being about £25, and that of a brilliant of the same weight about £15, only in very exceptional cases £20 or £25 being paid. The particular shade of colour shown by a ruby exercises an enormous influence on its value, thus a carat stone of a pale rose colour is worth at the most but £1, which contrasts strangely with the value of a stone of equal size, but of a deep red colour.

The value of any particular ruby does not reach the high figures mentioned above unless it is an absolutely faultless specimen. The faults most commonly met with are lack of clearness; existence of cloudy portions (so-called "clouds"), specially frequent in light coloured stones; milk-like, semi-transparent patches ("chalcedony patches"); small internal cracks and fissures ("feathers"); unequal distribution of colour, and so on.

Just as some few diamonds, on account of their singular beauty, large size, or unique colour, have become famous and well known all the world over, so certain rubies on account of their exceptional size have acquired more or less fame and renown. Tavernier states that he saw two rubies, in the possession of the King of Bijapur, in India, which weighed $50\frac{3}{4}$ and $17\frac{1}{2}$ carats, and which he valued at 600,000 and 74,550 francs respectively. Other large rubies have been occasionally met with in India and specially in Burma. The King of Ava was reported to be in the possession of a ruby mounted as an ear-pendant which is the size of a small hen's egg. A few specimens of similar exceptional size are known in Europe. Kaiser Rudolph II. of Germany possessed a ruby of flawless beauty and of the size of a hen's egg, which was valued by the gem expert Boetius de Boot at 60,000 ducats (about £28,000). It is related that in 1777 Gustavus III. of Sweden presented to Catharine II. of Russia a beautiful ruby of the size of a pigeon's egg; the present whereabouts of this stone is, however, unknown. The largest of the fine rubies set in the French crown, according to the inventory made in 1791, weighed 7 carats, and was then valued at 8000 francs (£320). Another weighed $25\frac{11}{16}$ carats, but on account of its pale colour was valued at no more than 25,000 francs. Other rubies of large size will be mentioned under the description of localities. The largest ruby known is said to be from Tibet; it weighs 2000 carats, but is not perfectly transparent. The largest ruby yet found in Burma is also a little cloudy; its weight is given by Streeter at 1184 carats. A tabular crystal of ruby of a rich red colour, and in part perfectly transparent, was presented to the British Museum by Professor John Ruskin; it has a weight of $162\frac{2}{3}$ carats.

RUBY AS A GEM.—The facets of a cut ruby are ground on a rotating iron disc precisely as in the diamond. The use of diamond-powder as a grinding material is now very general in Europe since it considerably expedites the process. The operation of grinding is followed by that of polishing, which is effected on a copper disc charged with tripolite moistened with water.

The forms of cutting adopted for the ruby are those generally used for the diamond. The brilliant form (Plate I., Fig. 6) is frequently chosen, since this displays the beauties of the stone to the best possible advantage. In order to increase the transparency of the ruby, however, the brilliant is cut thinner and flatter than is allowable in the case of the diamond. Owing to the strong refraction of the ruby, the rays of light which enter the stone by its front facets are totally reflected by the back facets and pass out by the front of the stone, the fine red colour of the ruby having been imparted to them during their passage through it. It is this colouring of the rays of light, together with the brilliant lustre of the stone, which gives the ruby its effectiveness. Owing to the small dispersion of corundum, the magnificent play of prismatic colours characteristic of the diamond is almost absent in the ruby. This being so, the step-cut or trap-cut form of cutting (Plate III., Figs. 2—4) is just as effective as the brilliant for the ruby, or indeed for any coloured stone which shows no play of prismatic colours. The mixed-cut, of which the upper portion consists of brilliant facets and the lower those of the step-cut, is also an effective form (Plate III., Fig. 5). Table-stones, point-stones, and similar forms are scarcely ever cut now; the few examples met with are the work of former times. Flat and thin rubies are usually cut as roses (rosettes), since this form involves little loss of material and, at the same time, produces a good effect. Very small stones are irregularly faceted; they are used to form a contrasting border round some larger precious stone.

In Burma, the chief home of the ruby, the stones are cut *en cabochon*, that is to say with a rounded surface, before they come on the market. When this form of cutting does not display the beauties of a stone to the best advantage it is re-cut in Europe. It is obviously to the purchaser's advantage to buy a ruby cut *en cabochon* rather than an uncut stone, since in the former case it will be possible to detect any faults in the interior. With the exception of the asterias or star-rubies, this gem is seldom in Europe cut *en cabochon*; in the exceptional case mentioned, the rounded form of cutting is obviously the most suitable for displaying the six-rayed chatoyant star for which the stone is peculiar.

Clear and transparent stones of a full deep colour are usually mounted in open settings (*à jour*); those of poorer quality are often backed by a foil of gold or copper or red glass, which materially improves their appearance. In Burma it is customary, instead of setting such a stone on a foil, to hollow out the underside and fill it in with gold.

Besides being faceted and cut *en cabochon*, rubies are sometimes engraved with inscriptions or figures, this being most frequently done in the East. Such antique gems of ruby engraved with the head of Jupiter Serapis and a figure of Minerva are known.

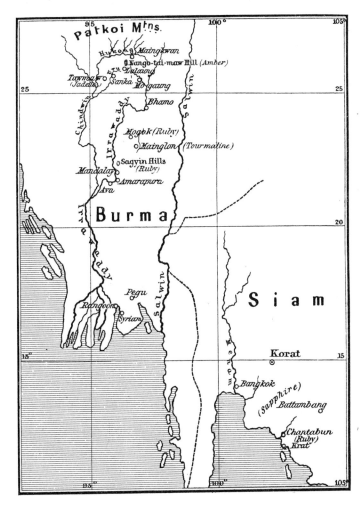

FIG. 54. Occurrence of ruby and sapphire in Burma and Siam. (Scale, 1 : 15,000,000.)

FIG. 55. Ruby-fields of Burma. (Scale, 1 : 10,088,500.)

OCCURRENCE.—While the poorer qualities of ruby are widely distributed, clear, transparent material suitable for cutting is found in but few countries, of which Burma, Siam, and Ceylon are alone of commercial importance at the present time.

Now, just as in former times, **Upper Burma** furnishes us not only with the finest but also with the largest supply of rubies. The distribution of precious stones (ruby, red tourmaline, jadeite, and amber) in this country is shown on the map in Fig. 54, the ruby localities being given in special detail in Fig. 55. The ruby mines of Upper Burma were worked at least as early as the fifteenth century and have ever since supplied the greater part of the material used in jewellery, including the finest stones known. The majority of the rubies which are now put on the market come from Burma. It is probable, however, that part of this supply is the gradually accumulated stock of former times, and that the yield of the mines is now smaller than formerly.

The Burmese ruby mines were mentioned long ago by Tavernier. According to his account, which, however, was not based on personal observation but on second-hand information, they were situated in the "Capelan Mountains," in Pegu, twelve days journey in a north-east direction from the town of Syriam, now a small village close to Rangoon. The yield at that time (second half of the seventeenth century) was apparently not very great, and was estimated at 100,000 écus (£22,500) per annum by Tavernier, who adds that he found the importation of rubies from Europe into India a lucrative business.

Tavernier's error in describing the locality of the ruby mines has been repeated again and again, and is even now current in the text-books of the present day. There is not the least doubt that the mines referred to are those which are still being worked in Upper Burma, and which are very much further removed from Syriam than Tavernier stated them to be. The distance from here to Mandalay is at least thirty-six days journey, and from Mandalay to the principal ruby district of Mogok is another eight days journey, the less important district of the Sagyin Hills lying, however, a little nearer. Until recently the exact location of these mines was a secret jealously guarded by the Burmese, who thus rendered them practically inaccessible to Europeans. Since the annexation of the country in 1886 by Britain, more detailed information has been obtainable, and a part of the workings has been taken over by Europeans. The district was officially visited and reported upon in 1888 by Mr. C. Barrington Brown. The rocks and minerals collected there were examined by Professor J. W. Judd, the result of their joint examination being published in 1896 in the *Philosophical Transactions* of the Royal Society of London.

The district of Mogok is the most important "ruby tract," or "stone tract," and embraces an area of forty-five square miles, or, if some abandoned mines are included, sixty-six square miles. The ruby-bearing area is, in all probability, much greater than this, extending to the south and east into the independent Shan States, and has been estimated by Lockhart, who for two years was resident engineer to the Burma Ruby Mining Company, at 400 square miles. This opinion is supported by the recent discovery of an old ruby mine in the river gravels of the Nampai valley, near Namseka village, in the Mainglon State. The district, which is mountainous, and scored by deep valleys, lies to the east of the Irrawaddy, from which it is separated by a plain thirty miles in width, in which a few unimportant ruby mines are worked by the natives.

This district has formed a part of the kingdom of Burma since 1637 ; its chief town and centre of the trade in precious stones is Mogok, latitude 22° 55' N., longitude 96° 30' E. of Greenwich, thirty-four miles in a straight line (but fifty-eight by road) from the river, and ninety miles north-north-east of Mandalay. A little below Mandalay is Ava, formerly known as Ratanapura (= city of gems), the old capital of Burma, round which the trade in precious stones of the whole country centres. Mogok stands at an elevation of 4100 feet above sea-level, while the highest point of the district has an elevation of 7775 feet. In spite of this the country is covered with thick forests, and is unhealthy both for Europeans and natives. The principal mines are situated in the valleys in which stand the towns of Kathay and Kyatpyen (= Kapyun). The mountains surrounding the latter town have been conclusively proved by Prinsep to be identical with the "Capelan Mountains" of Tavernier.

The mother-rock of the ruby and of the minerals, such as spinel, with which it is associated, is a white, dolomitic, granular limestone or marble, which forms whole mountain ranges in this district, and which, according to the investigations of Dr. F. Noetling, of the Indian Geological Survey, is of Upper Carboniferous age. These rocks were originally compact limestones of the ordinary kind, which have been altered by contact with intrusive masses of molten igneous rock ; this caused the calcium carbonate to re-crystallise out as pure calcite, while the impurities contained in the original limestone crystallised out separately as ruby and its associated minerals. The alteration of rocks by contact with a mass of molten igneous material is known to geologists as contact- or thermo-metamorphism ; the results of the process are frequently to be observed in all parts of the world, but, although corundum is often to be found in such altered rocks, fine ruby of gem-quality is only rarely met with. Such were the conclusions as to the geology of the district and the mode of origin of the ruby arrived at by Professor Max Bauer, from information and specimens supplied to him by Dr. F. Noetling, and published in a scientific journal in 1896, and in the German edition of the present work. The point of view adopted by Mr. C. Barrington Brown and Professor J. W. Judd, explained in the paper published shortly before, and which has already been mentioned, must not, however, be passed over without notice.

These authors describe the white crystalline limestone, which alone contains the ruby and spinel, as occurring in thick bands interfoliated with gneisses. These gneisses are usually of intermediate chemical composition, but sometimes of more acid, and at other times of more basic character ; the crystalline limestones are more intimately associated with the basic gneisses (pyroxene-gneisses and pyroxene-granulites, with pyroxenites and amphibolites). These contain crystals of calcite, and as the proportion of calcite present increases, they merge gradually in the limestones. It is concluded, on these grounds, that the limestones have been derived by the alteration of the lime-felspar in these basic rocks. This felspar (anorthite), being a silicate of calcium and aluminium, would, on alteration, give rise to calcium carbonate and hydrated aluminium silicates, the former being deposited as calcite, and the latter as silica (opal), and various aluminium hydroxides (diaspore, gibbsite, bauxite, &c.). Under other conditions of temperature and pressure these may have been afterwards converted into crystallised anhydrous alumina, that is ruby.

In the masses of crystallised limestone occurring *in situ* precious stones are only sparingly present, being found in much greater abundance in the clayey and sandy weathered products of the mother-rock, which lie on the sides of the hills, fill up the bottom of the valleys, and are often overlain by similar detrital material containing no precious stones. This secondary gem-bearing bed consists of brown or yellow, more or less firm, clayey, and at times sandy, material, known to the Burmese as " byon," which may be regarded as the residue after the solution of the limestones by weathering processes. It contains beside ruby, sapphire, and other colour-varieties of corundum, spinel (Tavernier's " mother of ruby "), tourmaline, large fragments of quartz, grains of variously coloured felspars, nodules of weathered iron-pyrites, and other minerals of more or less value, together with fragments of the rocks which occur *in situ* in the neighbourhood. Sometimes in the river alluvium, instead of clayey and sandy material, there are pure gem-sands consisting mainly of minute sparkling grains of ruby.

The gem-bearing layer lies on a soft decomposed rock of characteristic appearance. When the natives reach this level in their excavations they know that the " byon " extends no further down, and that work at that spot must be abandoned. The " byon " lies about 15 to 20 feet below the surface of the floor of the valleys, and is from 4 to 5 feet in thickness, though occasionally it may thin off to a few inches. On the sides of the hills the bed of " byon " may be 15 to 20 feet thick, and sometimes as much as 50 feet.

A peculiar feature connected with " byon " is its occurrence in caves in the limestones. These can be traced for miles underground, now as wide and high chambers or vaults, now as small crevices and narrow cracks. These caves are either wholly or in part filled with the " byon," which is usually covered over with a thick deposit of calcareous tufa in stalactites and stalagmites of the most fantastic shapes.

Previous to 1886 the deposits were mined exclusively by the natives, who adopt methods differing according to the conditions. In alluvial deposits in the valleys the " byon " layer is reached by excavating pits (" twinlones "), 2 to 9 feet square. When the excavation is made in loose, crumbling material the sides of the pit are supported by bamboo. From the bottom of the pits are driven horizontal galleries from one pit to another, so that as much as possible of the gem-bearing earth may be excavated. The light, earthy part of this material is removed by washing, and the remaining sand then searched for precious stones. The actual work of excavating can only be undertaken in the dry season of the year.

The ruby-bearing layer on the sides of the hills is reached by means of open cuttings or trenches (" hmyaudwins "). Their excavation is usually effected by means of running water, which is led in bamboo pipes often over considerable distances to the spot where it is required. The flow of water thus obtained washes away the superimposed débris and all the lighter part of the gem-bearing layer, leaving the heavy precious stones behind. This kind of work is naturally carried on in the rainy season, since large volumes of water are required.

Finally, we come to the " loodwins," or workings in the gem-bearing material, filling the limestone caves. This material is excavated and washed for precious stones in the ordinary way. The workers in cuttings on the hillside occasionally come upon limestone caves ; a specially large one was found and worked about the year 1870 on the Pingudaung Mountain near Kyatpyen.

The mines situated in the alluvial deposits of the river valleys are the most important, and the greater part of the yield is derived from the mines in the valleys in which stand the towns of Kyatpyen, Kathay, and Mogok, the latter valley being especially rich. The cave deposits are probably rich enough to pay for the introduction of European mining methods ; the primitive efforts of the natives are attended by great danger and loss of life, and by very meagre returns.

In former times intending miners were obliged to procure a licence before undertaking any work ; they were also required to pay a tax and to hand over to the king all stones exceeding 1000 rupees in value. Whether the finder of such a stone received anything in return for it depended entirely upon the caprice of his sovereign. It was natural that attempts should be made to evade this obligation ; many large and valuable stones were broken up into pieces small enough to be legitimately retained by the finder, while others found their way into the hands of illicit dealers.

Persons desirous of trading in rubies were required to obtain the permission of the Government of Burma, and were subject to a special tax. The monthly yield of stones was about 50,000 to 100,000 rupees worth, and before being put on the market they had to be taken to the Ruby Hall in Mandalay. Side by side with the legitimate trade there flourished a trade in smuggled stones, the finest of which found their way through Lower Burma into India, being in many cases sold in Calcutta. In the time of the last king of Upper Burma (deposed in 1886) it is said that the illegitimate trade in rubies in Lower Burma amounted to between two and three lacs of rupees per annum.

Thousands of small rubies with rounded surfaces, rudely fashioned, are set in a great variety of articles belonging to the Burmese regalia. These were taken from the palace of

King Theebaw at Mandalay at the time of the British conquest of Upper Burma, and are now preserved in the Indian section of the Victoria and Albert Museum at South Kensington.

In 1886, when Burma became part of the British Empire, the monopoly of the ruby mines by the natives came to an end. In the neighbourhood of Mogok work on a large scale was carried on first by an Anglo-Italian and then by an English company. In return for the concession of mining rights the Indian Government demanded from the company a yearly payment of four lacs of rupees (about £25,000), and from each native miner at first twenty, and afterwards thirty, rupees. It would appear from the fact that attempts have been recently made to get the payment reduced, that the operations of the company have not been altogether successful. Not content with working the alluvial deposits of the valleys in which rubies have been searched for for centuries, the company has also tapped the ruby-bearing deposits on the Pingudaung Mountain, near Mogok, and on the Kyuktung Mountain.

The " byon " yields not only ruby but also other colour-varieties of precious corundum, namely, sapphire, " oriental topaz," &c., common corundum, and frequently precious spinel. Beside being the most valuable and beautiful of the different varieties of corundum the ruby is here also the most abundant, about 500 rubies being found to one sapphire, and other colour-varieties of precious corundum are still rarer. The unequal proportions in which ruby and sapphire exist in these deposits is partly counterbalanced by the much greater size of the crystals of sapphire. The majority of the rubies found here do not exceed $\frac{1}{8}$ carat in weight, and large stones, when found, are often full of all kinds of faults. Flawless stones of 6 to 9 carats are rare, and very few reaching a weight of 30 carats have ever been found.

In the year 1887 a stone of 49 carats was found, and in 1890 one of 304 carats. The discovery in earlier times of two stones of 172 and 400 carats has been reported. The two most beautiful rubies found here were sold in Europe by the King of Burma in 1875. Both were of a magnificent colour, and before they were re-cut weighed 37 and 47 carats. After being re-cut in Europe they sold for £10,000 and £20,000 respectively. Cloudy corundum unsuitable for cutting as gems because of its lack of transparency, occurs in much larger pieces, some of which have weighed over 1000 carats. A stone of this description weighing 1184 carats is figured by Streeter. This, together with other stones of exceptional size, was found since the English occupation of the country. On the whole, the proportion of large rubies found recently in the mines of Burma seems to have increased, but in almost every case these large stones are unfit for cutting as gems.

The colour of the rubies of Upper Burma is, as a rule, some shade of deep red. In that country the shade most admired is pigeon's-blood red. Stones of this colour, transparent and free from faults, command high prices even at the mines. Rubies of a poorer tone of colour are also found, but not as frequently as in Ceylon, where they predominate over the stones of deeper shades.

When found embedded in its original matrix, namely, the white crystalline marble, the ruby has always a regular and well-developed crystalline form, diagrams of which are shown in Fig. 53, *a* to *d*. When found in the gem-earths this symmetrical form is not always missing, though, as a rule, rubies from this deposit are irregular in outline, while those picked out of the alluvial sands of the river valleys are usually much rounded. It is the custom among the natives not to sell a ruby in its natural form, but to give it some artificial shape or another, usually quite irregular and not calculated to enhance the natural beauties of the stone. Such specimens have to be re-cut in Europe. The two large rubies, for example, which came to Europe in 1875 were roughly cut *en cabochon*. By re-cutting the weight of the one was reduced from 37 to $32\frac{5}{16}$ carats and of the other from 47 to $38\frac{9}{16}$ carats. The native lapidaries are for the most part settled at Amarapura near Mandalay.

Almost all the Burmese rubies which now come into the market are found in the district around Mogok. Valuable stones, however, are reported to have been found in the river gravels of the Nampai valley near the village of Namseka, which lies fifteen miles south-west of Mainglon (Fig. 54), in latitude 22° 46′ N. and longitude 96° 44′ E. Assuming this occurrence to be a fact, Dr. F. Noetling explains it by supposing that the gravels in this outlying district have been washed down from the ruby-bearing area by the Mogok stream when in flood. At the time of Dr. Noetling's visit a large excavation had been made in these gravels; in them he found spinel, tourmaline, &c., but his search for rubies was unsuccessful.

A second ruby district in Upper Burma, less important, however, than Mogok, exists in the neighbourhood of Sagyin, twenty-one miles north of Mandalay. Here a range of low hills built of crystalline limestone rises up out of the alluvial plain of the Irrawaddy, itself two miles distant. This white marble is for the most part overlain by red clay; it is much creviced and penetrated by caves, and indeed in all respects closely resembles the marble of Mogok. The ruby has here two modes of occurrence. In places in which the marble contains few or no embedded rubies, its crevices are often filled up by fragments of the same rock, rich in rubies and firmly cemented together. In other cases the crevices and caves in the limestone are filled, just as at Mogok, with brown clayey material produced by the weathering of the limestone. In this are found the precious stones together with other minerals, namely, ruby, sapphire, red and black spinel, amethyst, brown chondrodite, very pale blue apatite in small grains and crystals, reddish-brown mica, &c. The precious stones are separated from this weathered material by washing. A more systematic working of the deposits would be likely to yield better results. The rubies found here are sometimes said to be paler and inferior in quality to those from the Mogok district, but this statement is disputed by many observers.

It is asserted that rubies have been found, associated with spinel and as usual embedded in granular limestone, at a place further north, near the village of Nanyetseik, between Mogaung and the jadeite mines of Sanka; also at still another locality on the Upper Irrawaddy. The position of these two localities may be seen from the map (Fig. 55); the occurrence of ruby here is, however, decidedly doubtful. According to native reports, rubies and spinels occur in the limestone of two hills lying a little to the north of the Sagyin Hills. It may be mentioned finally that during the construction of the railway from Rangoon to Mandalay, abandoned ruby mines were met with near the town of Kyoukse, about thirty miles south of Mandalay.

The occurrence of rubies in **Siam** has been long known, but it is only recently that the deposits have been carefully investigated and systematically worked. Prospecting for precious stones in this country was for long rendered impossible or, at least, extremely difficult by the exercise of royal and official privileges. Now, however, an English company, known as "The Sapphires and Rubies of Siam, Limited," has obtained a concession of mining rights in this country. Details of the work are given by Mr. E. W. Streeter in his book, *Precious Stones and Gems*.

Though some of the Siamese rubies equal those of Burma in beauty, the majority are very dark in colour and generally inferior. The mines are situated in the provinces of Chantabun and Krat; a few rubies are found also in the sapphire mines of Battambang, south-east of Bangkok (Fig. 54).

The mines of Chantabun are about twenty hours journey by steamer from Bangkok. They lie not far from the coast of the Gulf of Siam (Fig. 56), and near Chantabun, the capital of the province of the same name. The lofty mountains of this region consist of greyish granite, and the lowlands of limestone. The latter may possibly be, as in Burma, the mother-rock of the ruby, but this point has not as yet been determined. At present the precious stone is only known to occur in sands, which have hitherto been worked according to the most primitive methods by the natives. The workers are for the most part Burmese, and their usual method of working the deposits is to excavate a small shaft which never exceeds 24 feet in depth. Precious stones were at one time very abundant in this region; according to a missionary report of the year 1859, it was possible in half an hour to collect a handful of rubies from the "Hill of Gems," an eminence standing to the east of the town of Chantabun. This particular accumulation is now dispersed, but the town of Chantabun remains the centre of the trade in precious stones of this region.

More detailed information respecting the mines in the province of Krat has been given by Demetri and others. Krat, the capital of the province, lies not far from Chantabun, in a south-south-easterly direction, and is on the sea-coast. The mines of this region are scattered over a wide area, and are divided into two groups thirty miles apart. Those of one group are known as the mines of Bo Nawang, and of the other as the mines of Bo Channa. At the time of Demetri's visit the men employed in the two groups of mines numbered about 1250.

The mines of Bo Nawang, situated in the neighbourhood of the village of Nawang, near the eastern margin of the map (Fig. 56), cover an area of about two square miles. They are small pits, 2 to 4 feet deep, sunk in a coarse yellow or brown sand, which extends over a wide stretch of country and overlies a bed of clay. The rubies are found at the base of the sand in a layer of material 6 to 10 inches thick. As elsewhere in Siam they are accompanied by sapphires, and, though small, are said to be superior to rubies from other Siamese localities. The mines have only been systematically worked since the year 1875.

The mines of Bo Channa lie about thirty miles to the north-east of the other group, and are scattered over an area about a mile square. The ruby-bearing sand is 6 to 24 inches thick, and a few of the mines reach a depth of 24 feet. The natives are of opinion that the stones have been washed down by the river from the Kao Sam Nam, and many fine stones are reported to have been found in the rivers rising in this mountain. The mines have been worked since 1885, always under unfavourable conditions due to the unhealthiness of the climate.

Between the provinces of Chantabun and Krat lies the ruby district of the sub-province of Muang Klung (or shortly Klung), shown in the map (Fig. 56). It is situated to the north-east of the town of Chantabun, and is reached after traversing twelve miles of rough road. The centre of the district, which extends for a distance of seven miles, is the small Burmese village of Ban Yat. The valleys of this district are from 600 to 800 feet above sea-level, while the hills dividing them have an elevation of 500 feet more. The gem mines are situated in the valleys and on the sides of the hills. All the valleys are traversed by small mountain streams, affluents of the river Ven, upon the banks of which narrow patches of alluvium are laid down. It is these alluvial deposits which are worked for gems. No alluvium is laid down in the upper part of the valleys, since here the streams are too rapid; it is only in the lower and wider parts that the streams are sufficiently slow to lay down a deposit. These small patches of alluvium are worked only in the dry season; in the wet season the miners confine their attention to the deposits on the sides of the hills, which lie above the present high-water level of the streams. These deposits overlie a trap-rock of the nature of basalt, which is the principal, if not the sole, constituent of the hill ranges. The gem-gravels are made up of fragments of this rock, and the separating layer of tenacious grey, brown, or yellow clay is also, in all probability, a decomposition product of

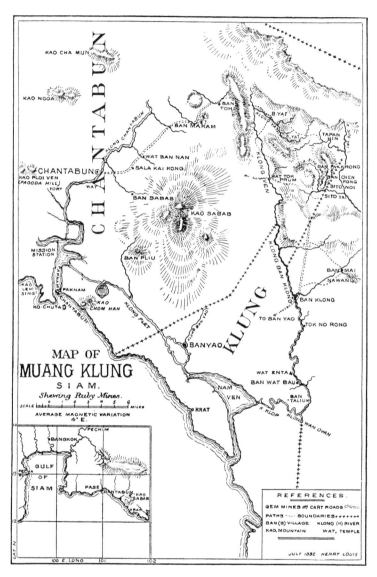

FIG. 56.   Ruby and sapphire mines of Muang Klung in Siam.

the same rock.   On these grounds it is concluded that the basaltic trap-rock is here the mother-rock of the ruby ; this conclusion, however, requires the support of further evidence.

The gem-bearing layer varies in thickness from 10 inches to 5 feet, and is overlain by a sandy and clayey deposit from $2\frac{1}{2}$ to 12 feet thick, containing no precious stones.   In the clayey gravel are found ruby and sapphire, as well as common corundum ; quartz, in good transparent crystals, and crystals of zircon and ilmenite are abundant, while topaz is very rare.   Of these minerals, the first two only are commercially valuable and sought after by the miners.   Rubies are much more frequently met with than are sapphires, the occurrence being in the proportion of about two to one. Good specimens of both are rare, the rubies being pale in colour and lacking in lustre, while the sapphires are opaque and dull.

The Burmese method of working the deposits is very simple. Small parties of three or four men working together sink a pit, usually about 4 feet in diameter, through the surface of the gem-bearing gravel. This they remove in baskets, leaving undisturbed all boulders too heavy to lift. The mines give employment to about 200 men, whose work consists of excavating the gem-bearing gravel, washing away, in the usual manner, the lighter earthy portions, and picking out from the residue any gems it may contain. Stones to the weight of about 500,000 carats are produced annually; their aggregate value is, however, no more than from £2000 to £3000, so much of this weight being of inferior quality.

In the gem-sands of the island of **Ceylon** (Fig. 59) a few rubies, together with a far larger number of sapphires and other gems are found. Many stones preserve distinctly the outlines of their original crystalline form, which agrees completely with that of the rubies of Burma (Fig. 53, *a—d*); others occur as rounded grains. The gem-bearing sands lie on the hill-sides above the present high-water level of the streams, and also on the floors of the river valleys. The neighbourhood of Ratnapura and Rakwana and the district about the foot of Adam's Peak are specially rich. Though it is said that fine rubies of good colour, equal to or better than those of Burma, are sometimes found in Ceylon, yet, as a general rule, Cingalese rubies are pale in colour and not of very great value. The occurrence of sapphire in Ceylon is of far more importance; it will be treated in detail in its appropriate place. According to Tennant, the mother-rock of the ruby in Ceylon, as in Burma, is a crystalline dolomite limestone or marble, which occurs *in situ* near Bullatotte and Budulla. The mother-rock of the sapphire is probably different, as we shall see later; this is thought to be gneiss.

The mainland of **India**, though so rich in common corundum, is very poor in the precious variety. A few stones suitable for cutting have been found with common corundum in Mysore and in the Salem district of Madras; also in the alluvium of the Cauvery river, which flows into the Bay of Bengal some distance south of Pondicherry. The occurrence of the precious stone in the sands and gravels of this river bears a striking similarity to its occurrence in the river alluvia of Ceylon. The ruby has been stated to occur in the gravels of other Indian rivers; in many of these cases, however, it is probable that the supposed ruby is in reality garnet, a stone which is widely distributed in India. Many of the rubies preserved in the treasuries of Indian princes have probably been brought from Burma or from Badakshan, a locality for ruby which has yet to be mentioned.

In **Afghanistan** permission to work the ruby mines near Jagdalak, thirty-two miles east of Kabul, has been obtainable from the Amir since the 'seventies. The rubies found here lie in a micaceous crystalline limestone; many show a distinct crystalline form, which is identical with that of rubies from Burma. These stones were originally described as being spinel, but specimens which have come to Europe have been proved to be indubitable rubies. The occurrence of ruby in this locality is strikingly similar to its occurrence in Burma; as in Burma and Ceylon, so probably in Afghanistan also, spinel occurs associated with the ruby.

A ruby of 10½ carats was brought to Europe by a traveller from Gandamak, a place about twenty miles from Jagdalak, and in latitude about 34⅓° N. and longitude 70° E. Nothing further as to this occurrence is known, and it is possible that both place-names refer to the same occurrence.

The ruby mines of Badakshan were famous in olden times, and they supplied some of the vast store of treasure amassed by the Great Mogul. They are situated (Fig. 57) in Shignan, on the bend of the Oxus river, which is directed to the south-west, in latitude about 37° N. and longitude 71½° E. They lie between the upper course of the Oxus and its right tributary the Turt, near Gharan, a place the name of which is said to signify "mine," sixteen miles below the town of Barshar, in the lower, not the higher, mountain ranges. This locality is by no means a familiar one, and reports as to the mode of occurrence of the ruby here are very conflicting. According to one they are found in a white earth; according to another in a red sandstone; while yet a third states them to be found in a magnesian limestone. From analogy with the Burmese occurrence, the last-named mode of occurrence seems the most probable.

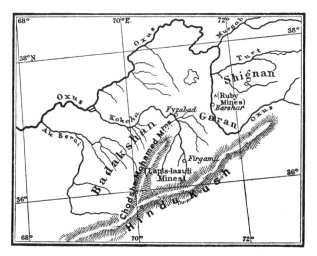

FIG. 57. Ruby mines in Badakshan on the Upper Oxus. (Scale, 1 : 6,000,000.)

Rubies are said to have been found formerly in these mines in large numbers, and associated with the variety of spinel known as "balas-ruby." Marco Polo, who visited the mines in the thirteenth century, states that the output from them was strictly limited by the ruler of the country in order to keep up the value. Part of the output was paid away as tribute to the Mongol Emperor, another part to other rulers, while the remainder was put into the market. The yield appears to have fallen off in later times, till in the end work was altogether discontinued. It is stated that the mines were reopened in the year 1866; whether they are being worked at the present day or not is unknown, but, according to a recent report, they are practically exhausted, and give employment to only about thirty persons, the few stones that are found being the property of the Amir of Afghanistan. A stone the size of a pigeon's egg is said to have been found here in 1873.

It is possible that the rubies and spinels which have recently come into the market through Tashkent, and which, according to the merchants, were mined in the Tian-Shan Mountains, are in reality from these same mines. There is no reliable information as to the existence of ruby mines in the Tian-Shan Mountains or in Tibet, so that the 2000-carat ruby recently received by Streeter, and said to be from Tibet, may also have been found in these mines on the Oxus.

Compared with the importance of the occurrence of ruby in Asia, that in all other parts of the world is insignificant.

In **Australia** rubies of small size have been found in the gold-sands sometimes associated with the diamond, never, however, in large numbers. Such occurrences have been noted in the sands of the Cudgegong river (Fig. 43), in a few of its tributaries near Mudgee, and at a few other places in New South Wales. In Victoria the gold-sands of Beechworth and Pakenham have yielded rubies. In all Australian ruby localities, however, this stone is very much less common than the sapphire. Moreover, red garnets have been mistaken for rubies time after time. Thus, many years ago, an abundant occurrence of rubies in the Macdonnell Ranges of the Northern Territory of South Australia was reported. No less than twenty-four companies were very shortly formed for the working of the deposits. A more thorough examination of the stones, however, showed them to be red garnets, of fine quality, but compared with the true ruby almost valueless. These same garnets are now sometimes sold as " Adelaide rubies."

The **United States** of North America yield a few rubies, occurring rarely associated with common corundum, which is very abundant in this country. In the Lucas mine on Corundum Hill in Macon County, North Carolina, small amounts of transparent red corundum, sometimes suitable for cutting, have been found. The boss of serpentine which forms the main mass of Corundum Hill is traversed by large veins of common corundum. Rubies of much better quality have been found more recently in Cowee Creek, also in Macon County, about five miles from Franklin, and have been described (1899) by Professor J. W. Judd and Mr. W. E. Hidden. These authors point out that there are three distinct modes of occurrence of corundum in North Carolina and the adjoining States :

(1) In the ordinary crystalline schists and gneisses of the district, as long prismatic crystals usually of a purplish tint and not of gem quality.

(2) In the olivine-rocks, and the serpentine derived from them, which are intrusive in the crystalline schists, as crystals often of large size and showing great variety of colour, but seldom or never clear and translucent.

(3) In certain garnet-bearing basic rocks at Cowee Creek, as small tabular and short prismatic crystals, which frequently exhibit the transparency and colour of the " oriental ruby."

These garnet-bearing basic rocks include eclogite, amphibolite, and other similar rocks of igneous origin. They have been much weathered, however, and are represented solely by a soft decomposition product known to American petrologists as " saprolite." In this material the rubies occur in " nests " and " bands," and also in what appear to have once been cavities in the original rock. These cavities, when the corundum is pale coloured, appear to have been filled with felspathic material; but when the corundum is of a ruby-red colour, the surrounding space is filled up with chloritic material. The associated minerals are garnet, in great abundance, sillimanite, kyanite, staurolite (often very clear and gem-like in character), cordierite, zircon, monazite, and others, together with minute quantities of gold.

The corundum found here varies in colour from ruby-red through different shades of pink to white. Many of the red crystals exhibit the beautiful so-called pigeon's-blood tint, and are in no way inferior to the finest Burmese rubies. Enclosures of various kinds are, however, frequent; these may be extremely minute (" silk " of jewellers), giving rise to a cloudiness (" sheen ") in the faceted gems, or they may be larger reniform masses of clear red rutile or black ilmenite. Some crystals of ruby have been found to enclose crystals of the newly discovered variety of garnet known as rhodolite, to be described in its appropriate place. Enclosures of this kind, however, in no way impair the transparency and beauty of the ruby. Some few specimens of ruby have been found perfectly free from enclosures and large enough to give a cut gem of very fair size.

Although the Cowee Creek rubies are very like Burmese stones, yet their mode of occurrence is totally different, for in the former locality the white crystalline limestone of Burma is absent, as are also the fine red spinels so characteristic an associate of the rubies of Burma.

In the State of Montana a few rubies have been found in association with sapphire; they are usually of a pale rose-red colour like those of Ceylon, stones of a fine deep colour being only occasionally met with. It is hoped that a more systematic working of these deposits, especially at Ruby Bar, will result in more frequent discoveries of stones of good colour. In America, as in Australia, garnets have been frequently mistaken for the more costly ruby, and have been collected and sold as such.

In Europe red corundum, suitable for cutting as gems, is practically absent, and the same is the case in the continent of Africa, the so-called " Cape rubies," occurring in South Africa in association with diamond, being not ruby but garnet.

ARTIFICIAL PRODUCTION.—Ruby is the only valuable precious stone which hitherto has been produced by artificial means in crystals of fair size showing all the characters of the

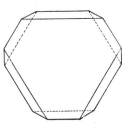

FIG. 58. Crystal of artificially prepared ruby. Magnified. (After Frémy.)

natural minerals. The honour of this achievement belongs to the French chemist Frémy, whose efforts in this direction have, after many trials, at last been crowned with success. His object was attained by fusing together in an earthen crucible at a high temperature (1500° C.), a mixture of perfectly pure alumina (Al_2O_3), potassium carbonate, barium (or calcium) fluoride, and a small amount of potassium chromate, the whole mass being kept in a molten state for a week. The series of reactions which take place under these conditions probably begins with the formation of aluminium fluoride. This compound, as a result of contact with the moisture of the atmosphere and furnace gases—a contact rendered possible by the porous nature of the crucible—yields aluminium oxide (alumina). This, by taking up chromic oxide from the potassium chromate, assumes a red colour and crystallises out as ruby. When isolated, after cooling, from the fused mass, in which the crystals are embedded, they are found to differ in nowise from naturally occurring crystals of ruby.

The artificial crystals so formed have always the form shown in Fig. 58, which represents a rhombohedron in combination with extensively developed basal planes, faces which bound natural crystals of ruby also, as shown in Fig. 53, a—d. The thin tabular crystals produced by this method are always of small size, never exceeding ⅓ carat in weight. Their size is increased when larger amounts of material are allowed to interact in the crucible. The colour of the artificial product varies from pale to dark red, according to the conditions of the experiment. The most beautiful and characteristic ruby-red colour was produced by the addition of 3 to 4 per cent. of potassium chromate. The colour-results seem, however, somewhat difficult to control, for the crystals often more or less incline to a violet colour, sometimes, indeed, being quite blue, while crystals coloured red at one end and blue at the other have been occasionally produced. From these observations Frémy concludes that the colour of naturally occurring sapphires, as well as of rubies, may be due to chromium. More than 3 to 4 per cent. of the chromium salt is taken up only with difficulty, and the crystals receive a violet tint, differing very markedly from the colour of naturally occurring rubies.

Artificially formed rubies which, of course, differ in no way from naturally occurring stones, except in their mode of formation, have been mounted as gems, both in a cut and in an uncut condition. Having the same hardness as natural corundum, they have also been utilised as the pivot-supports of watches.

The cost of production of artificially made rubies is so high that they are no cheaper than stones formed by nature; moreover, their small size strictly limits their general application. Before his death Frémy expressed a hope that crystals of much greater size would result from experiments conducted in a crucible of 50 litres capacity. However this may be, there is no immediate prospect of the artificial ousting the natural product.

Other investigators, experimenting in the same direction, have been successful in producing crystals of corundum, notably J. Morozewicz. His fused silicates yielded crystals of spinel as well as of corundum. The corundum crystals were tabular in habit and reached a diameter of 1·5 millimetres. The various colours—red, blue, yellow, and greenish-yellow —of these crystals must have been due to the presence of iron, for in the experiments of this investigator chromium was not an ingredient of the fused mass.

The peculiar, fine carmine-red rubies of considerable size and unknown origin, which appeared in the market in 1885 at Geneva, may be mentioned here. They have the hardness and specific gravity of the natural mineral, but are less brilliant, and in all probability are artificial products. The colour as seen in the spectroscope is more like that of the artificial crystals prepared by Frémy than of natural crystals, and, moreover, certain appearances under the microscope point in the same direction. The origin of these stones is mysterious, and, if artificial, nothing as to their mode of preparation is known. According to one report they have been formed by fusing together several small rubies; this, however, is scarcely credible, since at the extremely high temperature of the melting-point of corundum the ruby assumes a dull grey colour. Some authorities again have supposed them to be formed by a method analogous to Frémy's, while yet others have supposed each stone to consist of several small rubies held together in a matrix of glass of the same colour and refractive index. The success which has been attained so far in the artificial production of rubies is encouraging, and affords grounds for the hope that still greater achievements will be possible to future investigators.

DISTINCTION FROM OTHER RED STONES.—It is only natural that attempts should be made to substitute for the costly ruby some less valuable stone of similar colour. The two stones most frequently passed off as, and mistaken for, rubies are spinel and garnet. The so-called rubies of cheap jewellery are in reality either the variety of spinel, known as "ruby-spinel," or red tourmaline (rubellite), while topaz may be substituted for pale red ruby. Red quartz will scarcely pass as a substitute for ruby, but red glass (paste) is frequently so passed off.

The crystalline form of the above-mentioned substitutes will, if exhibited, serve to distinguish each from the ruby. In either the rough or cut condition, spinel, garnet, and glass may be readily distinguished from ruby by their single refraction and the absence in them of dichroism. Red tourmaline and quartz have a much lower specific gravity than ruby; the latter sinks heavily in methylene iodide, while the two former float easily. Rose-red topaz can only be substituted for pale rose-red ruby; since there is little difference between them in value it is not so important from a pecuniary point of view to be able to distinguish the one from the other. The specific gravity, however, affords a distinguishing characteristic, since topaz (sp. gr. = 3·5) floats in the heaviest liquid, while ruby (sp. gr. = 4·0) sinks. One can scarcely fail to distinguish the ruby, from any stone which may be substituted for it, by its great hardness. After the diamond corundum is the hardest of all known minerals, and will scratch any of the stones mentioned above with ease.

The word ruby is often used in the designation of stones belonging to mineral species other than corundum. Rose-quartz, for instance, is known as "Bohemian ruby," rose-red topaz as "Brazilian ruby," red garnet as "Cape ruby," and also as "Adelaide ruby"; "Siberian ruby" is the name given to red tourmaline (rubellite), and "false ruby" to red fluor-spar; while certain varieties of spinel are referred to as "ruby-spinel" and "balas-ruby."

In the manufacture of the so-called ruby-glass various pigments have been used for the purpose of reproducing the colour of the ruby. Manganese salts give a fairly close imitation, but the colour which results from their use is too strongly violet. The best results are obtained with gold salts, purple of Cassius, &c., which are fused with the glass or strass. The use of gold salts necessitates the greatest care, otherwise the glass will be cloudy. A glass coloured with gold salts after first being cooled is yellowish-green, the fine red colour only appearing after the glass has been annealed, an operation which is known as " tinting." By the use of gold salts, glass of the finest ruby-red colour can be obtained, and by varying the percentage of gold in the strass different shades of colour are produced. It is an interesting fact that fine ruby-glass has been found in ancient Celtic graves.

SAPPHIRE.

CHARACTERS.—Sapphire (" oriental sapphire ") is the name given to blue corundum. Sapphire differs from ruby most essentially in colour, it is in addition, however, slightly harder, being the hardest of all the varieties of corundum ; and, moreover, is stated to have a slightly higher specific gravity, the specific gravity of ruby being given as 3·99 to 4·06, and that of sapphire as 4·08. The form of a crystal of sapphire agrees completely in its general symmetry with that of a crystal of ruby ; the two crystals differ somewhat in habit however. The prism and rhombohedron, usually well developed in the ruby, are subordinate in the sapphire, and here the hexagonal bipyramid predominates, as is shown in Fig. 53, *e–i*, and for a natural crystal in Plate I., Fig. 7.

While the ruby is usually coloured uniformly throughout its substance, the distribution of colour in the sapphire is often very irregular. A single stone may show an alternation of colourless, pale yellowish, and blue portions, or in the colourless ground-mass of a stone there may be patches of a blue colour. Such stones, compared with a sapphire of a uniform blue colour, are almost worthless as gems.

It would be quite possible to collect a series of sapphires showing small gradations in colour from deep blue to yellowish or colourless stones. These latter are known as *white sapphire* (leuco-sapphire) ; they are only rarely perfectly colourless and transparent, usually showing a bluish or yellowish tinge. Sapphires of a definite yellow colour are described as " oriental topaz."

The blue colour of the sapphire disappears on heating, hence it is possible to transform a patchy or pale-coloured stone into a leuco-sapphire, and at the same time greatly enhance its value.

The distribution of the blue patches in the colourless or yellowish ground-mass of a sapphire is usually quite irregular, only occasionally is there any definite arrangement to be observed. In such cases, the crystal may be blue at one end and colourless at the other, or the middle portion may be colourless and the two ends blue, or colourless and blue bands may alternate. Moreover, different portions of the same specimen may exhibit different shades of blue, such as pure blue and the greenish-blue peculiar to the sapphires of Siam, or even colours which are altogether different. Thus, crystals of sapphire are known which are blue at one end and red at the other, and others of which the two ends are blue and the middle part yellow. A crystal answering to this latter description and weighing 19⅓ carats is exhibited in the mineralogical collection in the museum of the Jardin des Plantes in Paris.

The peculiar distribution of colour in such sapphires has been sometimes ingeniously utilised ; for example, the figure of Confucius, preserved in the museum at Gotha, is carved out of a parti-coloured sapphire in such a way that the head of the figure is colourless, the legs yellow, and the body pale blue.

Every shade of blue, from the palest to the darkest, is represented amongst sapphires. The very dark shade of blue, closely approaching black, is described as inky; very pale " feminine" sapphires are sometimes described as "water-sapphires," while stones of the darkest shade are variously known as "indigo-sapphire," "lynx-sapphire" or "cat-sapphire." So long as the depth of its colour does not interfere with the transparency of a sapphire, the darker it is in colour the more highly is it prized. The colour of sapphires shows as great a variety of tone as of shade. Thus, we have stones of indigo-blue, Berlin-blue, smalt-blue, cornflower-blue, greyish-blue, and greenish-blue, the last being specially common. The most admired tone of colour for a sapphire is an intense cornflower-blue. A really fine sapphire will combine with this colour a beautiful velvety lustre; the latter character, though occasionally seen, is by no means common. A fine blue crystal of sapphire is shown in Plate I., Fig. 7, and a faceted stone in Fig. 8 of the same plate.

The blue of the sapphire is always more or less tinged with green, this being very noticeable when one looks through the stone in certain directions. Like the ruby the sapphire is distinctly dichroic, the phenomenon being very marked in dark coloured stones but scarcely noticeable in stones of a light shade of colour. Looked at in the direction of the optic axis, that is to say, along the line joining the apices of the hexagonal bipyramid or perpendicular to the terminal basal planes, a crystal of sapphire appears of a pure blue colour, more or less intense or inclined to violet, according to the particular character of the stone. In a direction perpendicular to this the stone appears paler, and its blue colour is distinctly tinged with green; observed in intermediate directions the sapphire will appear of intermediate tints. The dichroism of the sapphires of Siam, which have lately come into the market in large numbers, as well as of those from Le Puy, in Auvergne, and from some other localities, is especially well marked.

If the light passing through a crystal of sapphire in the direction of its optic axis be received in a dichroscope, the two images formed by the instrument will be identical in colour—either pure blue or blue tinged with violet—and the colour will remain unchanged when the stone or the instrument is rotated. If examined in the direction perpendicular to this, the two images will, as a rule, be coloured differently. In the position in which the greatest difference in colour exists, the one will be of a pure dark blue and the other usually of a paler greenish-blue, but sometimes of a yellowish-green.

It follows from these facts that the pure blue colour of a sapphire crystal is best displayed in the cut stone when the table of the latter is perpendicular to the optic axis, and parallel to the basal planes, of the crystal. It will be remembered that it is advantageous for the same reason to cut crystals of ruby also in this manner.

The appearance of sapphire in artificial illumination varies in different specimens. In some no difference in colour can be detected, in others the colour becomes darker, or it may change to reddish, purple, or violet. The latter change in colour is rare, and stones which show it are valuable on this account.

While the colour of the ruby remains unaltered after the stone has been exposed to a strong red-heat, that of the sapphire under similar conditions disappears, although in other respects the stone remains unchanged. When exposed to very high temperatures, however, the sapphire, like the ruby, becomes grey and cloudy. The decolorisation of the sapphire does not take place with equal facility in all stones. Indian sapphires lose their colour most easily; and there are stones the colour of which it is impossible to completely destroy. From the fact that sapphires can be decolorised by heat, it has been argued that their colour is due to some organic compound. Some authorities have referred it to the presence of a small amount of iron, which has been detected in analysis, while others, relying on Frémy's experiments in the artificial production of rubies, consider it to be due to small quantities of some compound of chromium.

Asterias (Star-sapphires). There is often to be seen on the basal planes of sapphire crystals a six-rayed star of chatoyant light. This appearance, which is known as asterism, and is often very beautiful, is best displayed by cutting the crystal in which it exists *en cabochon*, the centre of the curved surface lying in the axis of the crystal. The rays of the star spread out to the margin of the stone, and the movements of the latter are followed to a certain extent by the star, the centre of which is always directed towards the light. A perfect six-rayed star is, however, seen less frequently than a patch of chatoyant light, which may be more or less rounded or elongated in outline, in the latter case being regarded as a single ray of the star. This patch or star of milky, shimmering, and opalescent light is sometimes tinged with a red or blue colour. The rays of the star may be narrow and sharply defined, showing up against the dark surface of the stone like silver threads, or they may be broad and ill-defined, merging imperceptibly into the darker portions of the stone. A sapphire in which the star is sharply defined, is much prized, and is known variously as a *star-sapphire*, an asteria or star-stone, an asteriated sapphire, or as a sapphire-star-stone. A stone which shows only an irregular patch of opalescent light is known as *sapphire-cat's-eye*, " *oriental girasol*," or opalescent sapphire. To rubies showing the same appearance corresponding names are applied, namely, *star-ruby*, asteriated ruby, ruby-star-stone, ruby-cat's-eye, and opalescent ruby. The phenomenon of asterism is not confined entirely to red and blue corundum, but is also occasionally seen in yellow corundum or " oriental topaz." A stone of this kind is, like ruby-cat's-eye, included in the term " oriental girasol " when it shows an elongated or round patch of opalescent light ; it is then called a " *topaz-cat's-eye*," and when it shows a regular star it is called a " *star-topaz*."

No exceptional value is attached to asteriated stones ; a fine star-sapphire is about equal in value to an equally fine stone of the ordinary kind, though large star-rubies fetch rather higher prices than ordinary stones ; small ones can be obtained for comparatively little. None of the asteriated varieties of corundum are confined to any special locality, being found wherever precious corundum is found.

The phenomenon of asterism has been variously explained. Some consider it to be due to the reflection of light from the surface of the twin-lamellæ, which are present in such crystals in large numbers, and are arranged so that their planes are parallel to the faces of the primitive rhombohedron (Fig. 53 *a*). The existence of these lamellæ is indicated by the striations on the basal planes. These striations are grouped in three sets inclined to each other at angles of 60°, and were considered by Babinet to be the cause of the star of opalescent light. Another and more probable explanation is that it is due to the reflection of light from the surface of a multitude of microscopically small tubular cavities or rifts enclosed in the crystal, and grouped into three sets, each of which is parallel to a face of the hexagonal prism ; corundum crystals also enclose minute tabular crystals, consisting of alteration products of the corundum, and arranged, like the rifts, in three sets inclined at 60° to each other. The six rays of the star are produced by the total reflection of light from the surfaces of these tubular cavities, and perhaps also from the surfaces of the tabular crystals. The phenomenon is only to be observed in stones in which there are large numbers of these enclosures, such stones being usually cloudy and having a metallic sheen. Star-stones are never in fact quite clear and transparent throughout their whole mass ;

frequently also they are built of alternate blue and colourless layers. The same phenomenon may be observed in many opaque specimens of common corundum, especially in the brown adamantine-spar, which is sometimes cut so as to show the asterism. Enclosures of the kind described above are more frequent in blue sapphire than in corundum of any other colour, and, as a consequence, star-sapphires are commoner than other varieties of asteriated corundum.

In Europe star-sapphires only, as a rule, are cut *en cabochon*; in India this form of cutting is much more frequently employed, not only for star-stones but also for others. Such stones, however, on their arrival in Europe are always re-cut with facets. Both the form and methods of cutting employed for the sapphire are identical with those used for the ruby, as is also the mounting of the stone. The colour of the sapphire is frequently intensified by placing a piece of blue silver-foil beneath the stone in its setting.

VALUE.—Sapphires of large size and fine quality are far more common than rubies of the same description, hence the latter always command higher prices than the former. Thus a flawless carat sapphire of perfect transparency, velvety lustre, and of a uniform deep cornflower-blue colour, will seldom fetch more than £10, while £25 will be easily obtained for a ruby of corresponding size and quality. Sapphires of this description, weighing between 2 and 3 carats, are about equal in value to diamonds of good quality and of the same weight. Faulty stones, the colour of which is pale or of irregular distribution, do not fetch more than a few shillings per carat. Since large sapphires are far more common than large rubies, there is a much smaller disproportion between the prices of large and of small sapphires than between those of large and small rubies. In the case of sapphires, indeed, the prices are almost proportional to the weight, a stone of double the weight being not much more than double the value, and so on. The flaws seen most commonly in sapphire are in general the same as in ruby, namely, clouds, milky and semi-transparent patches, white glassy streaks, alternation of differently coloured layers, areas showing silky lustre, &c.

Some few sapphires of exceptional beauty and size have acquired wide renown. The most magnificent of these is one of 951 carats seen in 1827 in the treasury of the King of Ava, as described by the English Ambassador at the Court of that monarch. It is reported to have been found in Burma, and to be not absolutely flawless. In the collection of the Jardin des Plantes in Paris is a rough stone of $132\frac{1}{16}$ carats; this is the "wooden-spoon-seller's" stone, and is said to have been found in Bengal by a man who followed that particular trade. It is known also as the "Rospoli" sapphire, after the family in whose possession it formerly was, and is one of the most magnificent of blue sapphires, free from all patches and faults. In the same collection is preserved another fine sapphire, 2 inches long and $1\frac{1}{2}$ inches deep. A beautiful sapphire, weighing over 100 carats, is the property of the Duke of Devonshire; the lower portion of this stone is step-cut while the upper is cut as a brilliant. Among other noted sapphires may be mentioned a dark, inky, faultless stone weighing 252 carats, which was exhibited in London in 1862, and a fine blue stone, with a yellow patch on one side, which weighed 225 carats, and was exhibited in Paris in 1867.

OCCURRENCE.—The mode of occurrence of sapphire is practically the same as that of ruby. It is found in sands and in solid rock, frequently together with ruby, in the manner already described. There is probably no single locality where one stone is found without the other; they are invariably associated together, here one and there the other predominating, and with them are usually found other varieties of precious and common corundum. Ruby predominates at the localities specially described above for this gem.

Sapphire is the more abundant of the two in Siam (the two, however, coming from different mines), in Ceylon, at Zanskar in Kashmir, in the gold and diamond sands of Australia, especially of New South Wales, and in Montana in the United States. Other localities, such, for example, as the European, are unimportant. By far the largest number of sapphires which come into the market are from Siam, the production of other countries being in comparison with this quite insignificant.

Not only the largest number of sapphires, but also the finest quality of stones, come from **Siam** (see Map, Figs. 54 and 56). The most important of the long-known mines of this country, the systematic working of which has recently been undertaken by Europeans, are those of Battambang, in which a few rubies are found with the sapphires. A certain number of good stones are found in the ruby mines of Chantabun and Krat, mentioned above. It is estimated that the mines of Bo Pie Rin in Battambang alone yield five-eighths of the total sapphire production of the world. Many of the stones found here surpass those from all other localities in their intense blue colour and velvety lustre. Many, however, of the so-called inky stones, are so deep in colour that in reflected light they appear almost black. It is a remarkable fact that the larger stones exceeding one carat in weight are almost invariably of finer colour and quality than smaller stones. Although the occurrence of sapphire in Siam was known at least as early as the beginning of the nineteenth century, the mines have been regularly worked only since about the year 1875. It is possible, however, that stones from these mines came into the market through Burma and were sold as Burmese stones. The mines of Siam have, therefore, grown into importance with great rapidity. According to Streeter, to whom the present account is due, the sale of Siamese sapphires by a single firm of London gem merchants amounted, in 1889, to £75,000.

The sapphire in this locality is found in a slightly sandy clay, usually about 2 feet below the surface of the ground. The most important mines are situated in the sides and floor of the Phelin valley. Each is a rough pit almost 4 feet square and 5 to 12 feet deep. As usual in occurrences of this type, the clay is washed away from the excavated mass and the stones picked out of the sandy residue.

So far as is known at present, the sapphire-bearing deposit extends over an area of about 100 square miles. The centre of the trade both for rubies and sapphires is the town of Chantabun, on the Gulf of Siam, in latitude about $12\frac{1}{2}°$ N. In the neighbourhood of this town, besides the ruby mines already mentioned, there are deposits in which sapphire is the predominating gem, and these appear to have been known and worked longer than those of Battambang. The sapphire has not yet been observed to occur in Siam in deposits of any type other than gem-sands, so that little is known of the minerals associated with it in the mother-rock.

As to the occurrence of sapphire in **Burma,** there is little to be added to what has been already said respecting the occurrence of ruby in this country. Sapphires are found at the same localities and under the same conditions, but where one sapphire is found there will be 500 rubies. While, however, rubies of good quality and exceeding 10 carats in weight are of extremely rare occurrence, large sapphires are found with considerable frequency. The discovery of sapphires weighing 1988, 951, 820, and 253 carats respectively, has been reported. Stones weighing 6 to 9 carats, though common, are often faulty. The largest faultless stone yet found in Burma weighs $79\frac{1}{2}$ carats; all others show considerable faults. The colour of Burmese sapphires is usually so dark that they appear almost black, they are seldom comparable in quality with those from Siam, and do not command a high price.

The sapphire occurs in **Ceylon** associated with many other precious stones. The yield of gems of this island is not large, the total value of the annual production being said to be no more than £10,000. The locality is, however, remarkable for its variety of gem-stones, namely, sapphire, ruby, topaz, amethyst, cat's-eye and other varieties of quartz, garnet (almandine and cinnamon-stone), zircon (hyacinth), chrysoberyl in its different varieties, spinel, tourmaline, moon-stone, and others which are rarer and of less importance. In association with the precious stones, there are found fragments of common corundum, magnetite, felspar, calcite, &c. Of the above-mentioned precious stones the sapphire is by far the most frequent.

The precious stones and the minerals with which they are associated were originally, for the most part, constituents of certain granite and gneissic rocks, by the weathering and disintegration of which they have been set free. While the sapphire and garnet were originally embedded in gneiss, other precious stones, such as the ruby and spinel, have been derived from the crystalline limestones (marbles) which are associated with the gneiss. The gems occur in their mother-rocks only sparingly, and are never obtained directly from them, but from the sands, gravels, and clays formed by weathering. These secondary deposits, in which the gems weathered out of the solid rock have been accumulating for long periods of time, are found in the beds of the streams of the present day, and on the sides of the hills above the present high-water level.

FIG. 59. Occurrence of sapphire in Ceylon.

The richest locality for gems is in the south of the island, on the southern slopes of the mountains in the Saffragam district. On this account the principal town of the district has received the name of Ratnapura (or Anarhadnapura), which signifies the " City of Rubies." The occurrence of gems is, however, by no means confined to this one locality, stones being found in the western plain between Adam's Peak and the sea, near Neuraellia, Kandy, Matella, and Ruanwelli, and in the river-bed of the Kalany Ganga near Sittawake, six miles east of Colombo. Also near Matura, on the south coast of the island, and in the rivers on the east in the neighbourhood of the Mohagam river. The localities specially rich in sapphires are the Saffragam district and the neighbourhood of Matura, where a considerable number of stones of large size and fine quality are found.

The gem mines near Ratnapura were visited and described by Ferdinand Hochstetter, during the voyage of the Austrian frigate *Novara*. They are situated on the Kalu Sella, a small tributary of the Kalu Ganga, partly in the bed and partly on the right bank of the river. The mines, which reach a depth of 30 feet, were not being worked at the time of Hochstetter's visit, and were filled with water. The uppermost layer is a thick yellow clay with nodules of limonite resembling our boulder clay in appearance. Below lies unctuous black clay and clayey sand; then bituminous clay enclosing abundant plant remains, the teeth and bones of elephants, &c.; then sand, and finally a bed of pebbles with red, yellow, or sometimes blue clay. This constitutes the gem layer, and is known as the stone-gravel or " malave." The gems are found mainly between the large pebbles; they are specially abundant when the layer contains a greenish, talcose, partly decomposed mica.

In the Kalu Ganga, between Ratnapura and Caltura, most of the gems are washed from the sands above small rapids in the river.

The gem mines of Ukkette Demy, near Ratnapura, were visited in 1889 by J. Walther, of Jena, who was kind enough to furnish the following unpublished details : The mines lie in a valley basin about 3 kilometres wide, in which several side streams deposit the débris weathered from the surrounding ancient crystalline rocks, such as gneisses, &c. The strata in which the mines are sunk include an upper layer of 80 centimetres of mud, then 50 centimetres of white sand, with a few bands of black vegetable matter; beneath this a metre of dark yellow clay, and then the gem layer consisting of a tough clay, which may be white, yellow, red, or green, and encloses much-decomposed boulders of the surrounding crystalline rocks. The gem-bearing clay, which rests on a bed of gravel 3 metres thick, is richest when white and poorest when green. The precious stones have doubtless been derived from the gneisses, &c., of the neighbourhood, since grains of sapphire have frequently been found in decomposed boulders of these rocks contained in the deposit.

The sapphires of Ceylon are not of very good quality; though a few stones of a rich colour are found, the majority are too pale to be of any great value. Star-sapphires are not of unusual occurrence, and yellow ("oriental topaz") and white (leuco-sapphire) stones are abundant, while parti-coloured sapphires are not infrequently met with. The original crystalline form of some stones is distinctly recognisable, although the edges are usually not quite sharp; others are much worn and rounded. Large stones are rarely found here, and the ruby is far less abundant than the sapphire.

Another important locality at which, since 1881 or 1882, sapphires in large numbers have been found, is the Zanskar range of **Kashmir**, in the north-west Himalayas. The exact locality of these finds was for a long time a secret, which was jealously guarded, especially from Europeans, first by the original discoverers and then by the Government of Kashmir. The first geologist who succeeded in visiting the locality was Mr. T. H. D. LaTouche, of the Indian Geological Survey.

According to his report these deposits are situated in a small upland valley in the upper part of the district of Pádar, about thirteen days' journey south-east of Srinagar, the capital of Kashmir, a few miles to the east of the village of Machél, and a little west-north-west of the village of Soomjam. Soomjam is higher than any other village on the south-western slopes of the lofty Zanskar range. It is about half a day's journey down from the Umasi Pass, and has an altitude of 11,000 feet. It lies in latitude 33° 25′ 30″ N., and longitude 76° 28′ 10″ E., on the Bhutna river, a tributary of the Chináb.

The valley in which the sapphires are found is 1000 yards long and 400 yards wide at its lower end; it has an elevation of 13,200 feet above sea-level, and its floor rises towards the north-west, the average angle of slope being about 20°. The first find is said to have been made in the sapphire-bearing rock which forms a precipice at the head of the valley. This rock, which was laid bare by a landslip, is at an altitude of 14,800 feet, and lies very near the limit of perpetual snow. A large number of gems were at first won from the solid rock; very soon, however, it was discovered that they existed in equal abundance in the loose detrital material weathered from these rocks and deposited on the floor of the valley.

The rocks of the district, mainly mica-schists and garnetiferous gneiss with interfoliated crystalline limestone, are penetrated by veins of granite, and it is in these veins that the sapphire, associated with an abundance of dark-brown tourmaline, is found. The material formed by the weathering of the granite is laid down in the valley as a white bed of little thickness, and is described as being overlain by a reddish-brown earth. The gems can be picked out by hand from this deposit " like potatoes," though they are, of course, also won by washing. The dark-brown tourmaline, mentioned above as being present in the granite veins, is also found in these secondary deposits.

The fine blue colour of the sapphires of this locality first attracted the attention of the inhabitants, who, not knowing the value of the stones often used them for striking fire. They were so abundant at first that large numbers were collected by the natives and sold to the gem merchants of Simla and Delhi, who, supposing them to be blue quartz or amethyst, purchased them very cheaply. When their true nature became known many expeditions were sent out to the Zanskar range with the object of collecting as many of these valuable stones as possible. The prices, of course, rose, and very quickly reached the figure at which sapphire is usually sold, namely, about £20 per ounce. Later on the stones fell again in value owing to the large number which were put on the market. Soon the Maharajah of Kashmir, in whose dominions the deposit is situated, began to interest himself in the matter. Those persons who had already found stones were allowed to retain them, but any further search could only be made by duly licensed individuals, who had to pay for the privilege. This arrangement still holds good.

The sapphires found in the Zanskar range are frequently in well-developed crystals, of the forms shown in Fig. 53, e to i. Numerous dark-brown or green tourmalines of small size are often observed enclosed in, or growing on the surface of, the crystals of sapphire. The crystals are sometimes very large, specimens suitable for cutting having been found measuring 5 inches in length and 3 inches in thickness, while a few are said to have attained a length of a foot. Irregular grains and fragments of the gem are frequently met with, but many of these are probably due to the fracture of crystals during their extraction from the mother-rock. The stones found in the loose weathered material on the floor of the valley are more or less rounded, showing that they have been transported some distance by running water. Some are of considerable size, weighing 100 or even 300 carats.

The crystals of sapphire are often bluish-white or bluish-grey, but specimens of a finer and richer colour are also frequently found. Single crystals often show a difference of colour in different portions; thus the centre of a crystal may be of a fine blue colour, and the two ends colourless. The majority of the stones found here possess, wholly or in part, a milky cloudiness; silkiness of lustre is also a common fault. Only transparent and finely-coloured stones are valuable as gems. Large cloudy crystals often have a small portion clear and transparent, which is carefully cut away by the lapidary and transformed into a gem. The yellow, brown, and red varieties of corundum are rare at this locality.

These mines are not the only places in this remote region where sapphires worth cutting have been found. At some distance away, but still in the same neighbourhood, are several places at which sapphire occurs under exactly similar conditions as far as is known. Thus, stones, which were not at first recognised as sapphires, were brought down from the Sacha Pass to the gem-market at Delhi, and others have been found in the gneiss and mica-schist of the upper Raini valley, below the Hamta Pass in Kulu, Punjab, as well as at other places.

All varieties of precious corundum—ruby, sapphire, " oriental topaz," " oriental emerald," &c.—are found in the **United States** of North America, being specially abundant in two particular regions. The first of these regions includes the western portions of North Carolina and of South Carolina and extends into Georgia and Alabama. Almost all the precious corundum found in this region comes from Macon County in North Carolina, where the crystals, which are usually well developed, are enclosed in an olivine-rock (dunite). The occurrence of corundum in rocks other than dunite in North Carolina, and specially at Cowee Creek in Macon County, has already been dealt with under ruby. In these localities the pure mineral often forms the nucleus of large masses of common corundum. In the Culsagee mine on Corundum Hill, near Franklin in Macon County, a crystal weighing 311 pounds was once found. This, however, was not of gem quality and was coloured partly red and partly blue. At the same mine rubies, sapphire, "oriental topaz," and a few "oriental emeralds," &c., suitable for cutting as gems, have been found. Fine star-stones occur here also, as well as in Delaware County, Pennsylvania.

The other region which is specially rich in precious corundum is situated in the west. Sapphire and other colour-varieties of corundum have been known since 1865 to occur in the neighbourhood of Helena on the upper reaches of the Missouri river, in the State of Montana, being first discovered during the process of gold-washing. Again the true nature of the stones was not at first recognised, and they were sold at much below their actual value. Since 1891 these deposits have been systematically worked for gold, and at the same time large numbers of the precious stones have been collected. They are found in masses of glacial débris known as "bars," which are laid down on the sides of the valleys parallel to the river-courses and at a height of 300 feet above the present high-water level of the upper Missouri. These glacial sands and gravels containing gold overlie black shales, probably of Lower Silurian age, which are associated with limestones, quartzite, and rocks of igneous origin. It is in the lowest layer of these sands and gravels, with a thickness of only a few inches, that the sapphire is principally found. The sapphires are most abundant at Eldorado Bar, Spokane Bar, French Bar, and Ruby Bar, and these deposits are still being worked. Spokane Bar near Stubb's Ferry, twelve miles to the east of Helena, is approximately the central point of this district, which extends along the Missouri for at least fifteen miles and embraces an area of certainly no less than eleven and a half square miles.

The sapphires frequently occur as well-developed crystals, having the form of a short hexagonal prism with basal planes, an unusual type for this gem. Irregular grains are also found which, like the crystals, are more or less rounded. Neither crystals nor grains attain to any considerable size, measuring at the most from $\frac{1}{4}$ to $\frac{1}{2}$ inch in diameter and rarely exceeding 9 carats in weight. Though small in size the stones are abundant in number, as evidenced by the fact that an acre of the deposit at Eldorado Bar yielded no less than 2000 ounces of sapphire. Many of these stones, however, would be unsuitable for cutting, since the predominant tints of the sapphires of this locality are all pale.

The colours, though almost always pale in shade, show great variety of tint, red, violet, yellow, blue, green, bluish-green, and all possible intermediate colours being met with. Bluish-green and green corundum is specially abundant, while the pure blue and the red varieties are absent. Occasionally a stone with a red nucleus and a border of another colour is met with. Some green and blue stones appear red by artificial light. Almost all the colour-varieties of corundum from this region, which are suitable for cutting, have a peculiar metallic sheen, which is very characteristic and is not seen in stones from any other locality. They are remarkable also for the brilliancy of their lustre, and, according to the statements of lapidaries, are specially hard.

Corundum is associated in these glacial sands with many other minerals, among which are crystals of white topaz not exceeding $\frac{1}{4}$ inch in length, fine ruby-red garnets the size of a pea (which have often been mistaken for true rubies), kyanite, cassiterite in small, rounded grains (stream-tin), iron-pyrites altered to limonite, chalcedony, and small rounded fragments of calcite.

As already mentioned, the rocks occurring *in situ* in the district and underlying the gemmiferous sands are penetrated by dykes of igneous material. In one of these dykes, consisting of mica-augite-andesite, crystals of sapphire, garnet (pyrope), and sanidine have been found ; and it has been argued from this that in every case the sapphires originated in similar situations and have been set free by the weathering of the igneous rock. This origin for the sapphire is not universally accepted, although parallel cases may be found in the occurrence of fine blue sapphire in the volcanic rocks of other regions, such, for example, as the basalts of Unkel on the Rhine, Niedermendig on the Laacher See, Calvarienberg near Fulda, and Expailly near Le Puy-en-Velay in France, &c.

More recently sapphires have been found at Yogo Gulch in Fergus County, also in the State of Montana, and seventy-five to one hundred miles east of the Missouri bars. According to G. F. Kunz and others they occur here in a yellow earthy material, which also may owe its origin to the weathering of an igneous rock. The blue stones vary in shade from light to dark, some being of the true sapphire or cornflower-blue, while there are others which incline to an amethyst or almost ruby shade of red. The crystals are rhombohedral in habit, and in this respect differ from the sapphires found near Helena.

The amount of corundum of a quality suitable for cutting which comes into the market from **Australia** is not altogether insignificant. The mineral is found in gold-sands with diamond and in stanniferous and other similar sands and gravels in Victoria, South Australia, Queensland, and especially in New South Wales. In the last named State, sapphires are found in the north-east corner in the New England district, especially in the neighbourhood of Bingera and Inverell, and indeed at all the localities which have been already mentioned for diamond (Map, Fig. 43). Sapphire occurs here under exactly the same conditions as does the diamond, and it is even more widely distributed. An occurrence of the stone in Tasmania has also been recently reported.

Australian sapphires, as a rule, are too dark to be of much value as gems ; they vary from perfect transparency and absence of colour through various shades of blue and grey to almost absolute opacity and dark blue colour. Crystals showing a fine sapphire-blue colour are met with occasionally, and fine star-sapphires are not uncommon. A few rubies are found, but corundum of a fine green colour, that is " oriental emerald," is more abundant, every hundred stones always including two or three specimens of " oriental emerald." The original crystalline form of the stones, a hexagonal bipyramid (Fig. 53, e, &c.,) is frequently well preserved, but more often they are in the form of irregular grains or rolled pebbles, like the other constituents of the sands. From a commercial point of view the Australian output of sapphires is unimportant.

In **Europe** a well-known and often mentioned locality for sapphires is the Iserwiese, the district in which is the source of the Iser river, which drains the Iser mountains in northern Bohemia. Sapphire, together with ceylonite, zircon, garnet, and iserine, is found here in loose, alluvial material derived from the weathering of granite. The sapphires sometimes occur as small hexagonal prisms, but more often as water-worn grains of various shades of blue and with various degrees of transparency. While pale blue stones are usually cloudy and opaque the darker ones are, as a rule, transparent. Single sapphires of the finest quality are said to have been found here, all, however, of small size ; stones over 4 carats in weight are extremely rare. The deposit, never very extensive, has been systematically worked for many years and is now practically exhausted.

Single stones suitable for cutting have also been found in the garnetiferous sands of Meronitz in Bohemia, in the auriferous sands of Ohlapian in Transylvania, of the Urals, of Madagascar, of Borneo, and of some other regions. It is, however, unnecessary to give a detailed account of the occurrence at these localities since in each case the stones are present in such small numbers.

Counterfeiting.—The blue stones which may be mistaken for, or passed off as, sapphire are cordierite ("water-sapphire"), kyanite (sapparé), blue tourmaline ("indicolite"), blue topaz, and blue spinel. Amongst such stones may perhaps be included also haüynite, blue diamond, and aquamarine, which in some cases may resemble the sapphire. All, however, without exception, differ from the sapphire in density, most of them being considerably lighter and floating in the heaviest liquid, while corundum sinks heavily; spinel and kyanite alone have a density near that of this liquid (sp. gr. = 3·6). With the exception of diamond these stones, too, are all considerably softer than corundum, by which they can easily be scratched; many of them, indeed, may be scratched even by topaz.

Blue tourmaline, moreover, may be distinguished from sapphire by the difference in the tone of its colour, which is an indigo-blue. Kyanite again is characterised by the existence of a system of fine rectangular cracks, which are absent in the sapphire, and are due to the presence of perfect cleavages and twinning. The blue of kyanite, however, is very similar to that of sapphire, hence the name sapparé, but its transparency is less perfect. Cordierite is charactērised by its very strong dichroism, far stronger than that of sapphire. The specific gravity of topaz is its most salient distinguishing feature. Diamond, spinel, and haüynite are singly refracting, and show no dichroism; the same is true also for blue glass, but this substance may be recognised also by its softness.

The colour of sapphire is easily imitated in glass by adding to the strass a little cobalt oxide, one part of cobalt oxide to seventy or eighty parts of strass giving a very fine sapphire-blue colour. The same effect may be produced under certain conditions by the use of iron. Thus, chemical analysis has shown that the beautiful blue colour of an antique vase, ornamented with bas-relief in white, now preserved in the British Museum, is due not to cobalt but to iron. The blue colour of the slag from iron furnaces is also due to the same metal. It is not, however, customary at the present day to use iron for the purpose of colouring glass.

White sapphire, diamond, colourless spinel, zircon, topaz, rock-crystal, and phenakite, as well as colourless strass, may each be mistaken the one for the other by the uninitiated. Of these, sapphire, zircon, and spinel sink slowly in the heaviest liquid (sp. gr. = 3·6), while all the rest float. Diamond only is capable of scratching leuco-sapphire, while this itself scratches all the others. Glass, diamond, and spinel are singly refracting, and can thus be distinguished from the other stones mentioned. Taking into account all these differences, it should not be a matter of great difficulty to distinguish a colourless sapphire from the colourless stones it somewhat resembles.

OTHER COLOUR-VARIETIES OF PRECIOUS CORUNDUM.

In addition to the true or oriental ruby and the oriental sapphire there are other varieties of transparent corundum, which are distinguished from these and from each other solely by their colours. We have already seen that these varieties are known by the name of some precious stone which they resemble in colour with the qualifying prefix "oriental." Thus certain of these colour-varieties of corundum are referred to as "oriental aquamarine," "oriental emerald," "oriental chrysolite," "oriental topaz," "oriental hyacinth," and "oriental amethyst." The precious stones from which these varieties take their names are sometimes given the prefix "occidental"; all are softer than corundum and are easily scratched by it. With the exception of zircon (hyacinth), the specific gravity of which is greater than that of corundum, all the "occidental" are lighter than the "oriental" precious stones; while the latter sink heavily in the heaviest liquid (sp. gr. = 3·6) the former float in this, some indeed floating in pure methylene iodide. Very little familiarity with the appearance of "oriental" and "occidental" precious stones enables one to distinguish the former from the latter solely by the difference in lustre; and this difference has led to the term "oriental," conveying by its use an impression of great hardness and brilliant lustre in the stone to which the term is applied.

None of the colour-varieties of precious corundum now under consideration are abundant in nature. They occur as more or less isolated examples, together with ruby and sapphire, at the localities where these precious stones are found, namely, in Burma, Siam, Ceylon, Montana, North Carolina, &c. Together with the ruby and sapphire they are collected from the various deposits, and are cut and mounted in the same manner as are these stones, so that further comment on this subject is superfluous.

"**Oriental aquamarine**" is pale bluish-green or greenish-blue in colour, and resembles in this respect, and also in transparency, the variety of beryl known as aquamarine. "Oriental aquamarine" sometimes inclines most to green and other times to blue; specimens are also met with of a dark greenish-blue colour, a transition shade between the colour of the sapphire and that of the aquamarine. Such stones are remarkable for their specially strong dichroism.

"**Oriental emerald**" is corundum of a more or less intense green colour resembling that of the emerald, another colour-variety of beryl. While the "oriental emerald" always shows a tinge of yellow, and is thus inferior to the true emerald in purity and depth of colour, it surpasses the latter in transparency and lustre. So rare is this variety of corundum that its very existence has been doubted, and it has been suggested that the supposed specimens of "oriental emerald" are in reality true emerald or beryl. This idea, however, is negatived by the well-established occurrences of the stone not only in Burma, Siam, and Ceylon, but also in New South Wales, Montana, and at the Culsagee mine in Macon County, North Carolina, where a crystal measuring 100 by 50 by 35 millimetres was once found. On account of its great rarity the "oriental emerald" far surpasses in value the finest sapphires, but falls short of the value attached to the ruby. It is distinguished from the true emerald by its greater hardness and specific gravity, and by the fact that it is much more markedly dichroic; the two colours shown by the dichroscope are blue and green. This variety of corundum sometimes varies in colour according as it is viewed in reflected or transmitted light. Thus a stone from Chantabun, in Siam, appeared in reflected light of a deep bottle-green and in transmitted light of a bluish-violet colour.

"**Oriental chrysolite**" is of a pale yellowish-green colour; its tint is more yellow than that of the last variety of corundum considered, and corresponds very closely to that of chrysolite (olivine) or to pale coloured chrysoberyl. It is much commoner than "oriental emerald." Clear and transparent greenish-yellow chrysoberyl, with no chatoyant lustre, is sometimes referred to as "oriental chrysolite"; it is distinguished from chrysolite proper by its much greater hardness.

"**Oriental topaz**" ("topaz-sapphire," yellow sapphire) is of a pure yellow colour. The value of this stone depends upon the particular shade of its colour; specimens of a saffron-yellow tinged with red or of a pure citron-yellow are most highly prized. In the majority of stones the colour is a pale straw-yellow, or it may incline to green or brown; in the former case it approaches the colour of "oriental chrysolite." Precious corundum with a more or less pronounced yellow colour is fairly common; the finely coloured "oriental topaz," however, is much rarer, and being both rarer and more beautiful in colour than "oriental chrysolite" is more highly prized. The price of stones showing great depth and intensity of colour is as high as that of the finest sapphires. A not uncommon fault in these stones is the existence of a peculiar, avanturine-like, glittering appearance, probably due to the presence of small enclosures. The appearance which gives their names to star-ruby and star-sapphire is sometimes seen in "oriental topaz," which is then referred to as "asteriated topaz" or "topaz-cat's-eye." Tavernier states that he saw among the jewels of the Great Mogul an "oriental topaz" of 157¾ carats, which he valued at 271,600 francs (£10,777). Another stone of this kind weighing 29 carats was in the possession of the Parisian jeweller, Caire. It was remarkable for the Arabic inscriptions it bore, not engraved merely on the surface but penetrating the whole thickness of the stone, and was probably an Eastern amulet.

"**Oriental hyacinth**" ("vermeille orientale") varies in colour from pale aurora-red to reddish-brown. The presence of a pronounced tinge of yellow or brown makes its colour very different from that of the ruby. This colour-variety of corundum is not an important one; it sometimes shows the sheen already mentioned as being present in "oriental topaz." Its specific gravity of 4·0 distinguishes it from true hyacinth (zircon), the specific gravity of which is 4·6 to 4·7.

"**Oriental amethyst**" (violet ruby, "amethyst-sapphire" or purple sapphire) is violet in colour and is of more importance than the last-named variety of corundum. Its tint is often of a bright violet-blue, closely resembling the various shades of colour of the true amethyst (a variety of quartz). Sometimes, however, its colour inclines to rose-red or purple, and when this is the case the stone appears either like certain almandine-garnets or like certain spinels. This stone, therefore, may be of almost any shade of colour between the red of the ruby and the blue of the sapphire. It is distinguished from the true amethyst by its strong dichroism, which is apparent even to the naked eye. The light which reaches the eye along the axis of the crystal and out by one of the basal planes is of a warm violet colour, while that which travels through the crystal in a direction perpendicular to this is pale and almost colourless. This is a point which must be remembered when the stone is cut as a gem, the lapidary arranging that the table is parallel to the basal planes of the crystal, otherwise the stone will appear pale and insignificant.

The "violet ruby," which by daylight always appears more or less red, has a still more pronounced colour, and is even more beautiful by candle-light. Caire has described such a stone, which was blue like the sapphire by day and of a fine purple-red by artificial light. We may contrast with this the dull grey appearance of the true amethyst in candle-light. The Maltese Cross, shown in Plate III., Fig. 8, is the form of cutting best suited to the "oriental amethyst"; it is cut, however, in all the forms employed for other coloured stones including ruby and sapphire. An "oriental amethyst" of a full deep colour is worth approximately as much as a good sapphire.

All the varieties of corundum hitherto considered are clear and transparent. Cloudy and opaque corundum, when it possesses some beautiful feature, such as a fine colour, may be cut as a gem. A case in point is that of **adamantine-spar**, a semi-transparent, hair-brown corundum, the basal planes of some crystals of which show, like star-stones, a beautiful bluish-white sheen. When such a stone is cut *en cabochon* in this direction it presents an appearance very similar to that of asteriated ruby. China is considered to be the principal locality for adamantine-spar; it is also found at other places together with precious and common corundum.

SPINEL.

The precious stones which are most appropriately considered after corundum are those belonging to the spinel group of minerals. Their colour often resembles that of the ruby, but in all other characters the two minerals are perfectly distinct, so that the names "ruby-spinel" and "balas-ruby," which are sometimes given to certain colour-varieties of spinel, are misleading and incorrect. Spinels of a sapphire-blue colour are also known, but, like black spinels, they are of little importance.

In scientific mineralogy the spinel group includes a very large number of minerals of varied composition but of identical crystalline form and chemical constitution. Of all these minerals of the spinel group, differing widely from each other in chemical composition, hardness, colour, transparency, &c., there is but one which is generally used as a gem, and this particular stone is therefore distinguished as *precious spinel*, or noble spinel.

Precious spinel is a compound of alumina (the sole constituent of ruby) with magnesia, its composition being represented by the formula $MgO.Al_2O_3$ or $MgAl_2O_4$. This compound is in itself colourless, so that the various colour-varieties of spinel owe their tints to the presence of small quantities of foreign substances. The colour both of the ruby and of the red spinel is thought to be due to the presence of chromic oxide (Cr_2O_3), but, according to Doelter, the presence of the small amount of iron, as shown in the following analysis, is sufficient to account for the colour of these stones. The analysis referred to was made by Abich on a red spinel from Ceylon.

Alumina (Al_2O_3)	70·43 per cent.
Chromic oxide (Cr_2O_3)	1·12 ,,
Magnesia (MgO)	26·75 ,,
Ferrous oxide (FeO)	0·73 ,,

Spinel crystallises in the cubic system, and the form of the crystals can often easily be made out, even when they are very much rounded and water-worn. This form is most

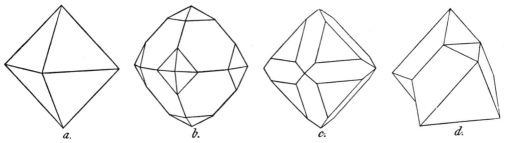

a.   b.   c.   d.

FIG. 60. Crystalline forms of spinel.

frequently an octahedron (Fig. 60 *a*), uncombined with other forms and usually with faces developed on all sides. Fig. 60 *c* illustrates the truncation of the edges of the octahedron by faces of the rhombic dodecahedron, the result of which is a not uncommon form. A less frequent form, except in the case of black spinel, is shown in Fig. 60 *b*, in which each of the corners of the octahedron are replaced by four faces of an icositetrahedron.

Twin-crystals of spinel are common. In Fig. 60 *d*, the two individuals are united in such a manner that one face of the octahedron is common to both, and the two individuals are symmetrical about this face. The other octahedral faces form alternate salient and re-entrant angles at the plane of junction. The twinning together of two octahedra in this manner is of such frequent occurrence in spinel that such compound forms, which occur in several other minerals, including the diamond, are said to be twinned according to the spinel-law. The two individuals of a spinel-twin have often very little thickness in the direction perpendicular to the common octahedral face. The crystal, then, has the form of a triangular plate with alternate salient and re-entrant angles at the edges. One of the individuals of the twin may be twinned in the same way with a third octahedron, and this again with a fourth, and so on. This may give rise to very complicated groups.

Spinel has no cleavage, or, if any, a very imperfect one, and its fracture is irregular to conchoidal. The mineral is brittle and hard, being the fourth hardest precious stone known ; it immediately follows chrysoberyl, and is very little harder than topaz, the number of which, on Mohs' scale of hardness, is 8. The specific gravity is fairly high (sp. gr. = 3.60 to 3·63), not far removed from that of diamond. Spinel becomes positively electrified when rubbed, but acquires no pyroelectrical charge when heated or cooled. It is unattacked by acids, and infusible before the blowpipe.

The lustre of spinel, though of the common vitreous type, is very brilliant, especially on polished facets. It is suceptible of a very high degree of polish, not, however, equalling the ruby in this respect. It is stated to be possible for an expert to distinguish a ruby from a spinel by the difference in brilliancy of lustre alone. Some spinels are beautifully clear and transparent, while others are cloudy and opaque, the latter being, of course, valueless as gems. All varieties of spinel, since they crystallise in the cubic system, are singly refracting, that is to say, optically isotropic. Thus the polariscope offers a simple and ready means for distinguishing a spinel from a ruby. The refractive power of spinel is fairly high, being about the same as that of corundum. The refractive indices for different colours of the spectrum do not differ widely ; they were determined for a pale red spinel as follows :

$$n = 1\cdot71 \text{ for red light.}$$
$$n = 1\cdot72 \text{ for yellow light.}$$
$$n = 1\cdot73 \text{ for blue light.}$$

The dispersion, as in the ruby, is therefore small, and the cut gem produces no marked display of prismatic colours, such as one is accustomed to see in the diamond.

When absolutely pure the substance of spinel is perfectly free from colour, and colourless octohedra of the mineral have been found in nature, though rarely. Except in the matter of lustre, such crystals will resemble octahedra of diamond very closely, both minerals, moreover, being optically isotropic and of nearly the same specific gravity. They are very easily distinguished, however, by the great difference in hardness which exists between them. Dufrénoy stated the weight of a perfectly colourless spinel, which came from India in a cut condition, to be 12·641 grams (61½ carats).

Precious spinel is commonly, however, red in colour, of shades which incline to violet and blue on the one hand and yellow on the other. It is stated that in all red spinels, whatever be their shade of colour, a tinge of yellow reflected from the interior of the stone, especially if it be cut, can be detected, by which they can be distinguished from the ruby. Spinel being optically isotropic is not dichroic, so that, in contradistinction to the ruby, it appears of the same colour in whatever direction it is viewed. Specimens of spinel showing every possible gradation of colour, from deep red to white or colourless, are in existence; stones of the deepest tone of colour sometimes appear almost opaque. In contrast to the ruby the colour of spinel is very uniform, and spots are rarely seen, so that far fewer stones need to be thrown out from a parcel of spinels than would be the case with a similar parcel of rubies. Faults of other descriptions are also less frequent in spinel than in ruby. Like the ruby, the colour of the spinel remains unaltered by heat; at very high temperatures, however, the stone loses its colour, regaining it as it cools, but not passing through an intermediate condition, in which the colour is green, as does the ruby. Experiments in this direction made on valuable stones must be performed with care as the spinel is easily cracked.

The more deeply coloured a spinel is the more highly is it prized, provided, of course, that the depth of its colour does not interfere with the transparency of the stone. The colour of deep red stones is sometimes almost indistinguishable from that of the ruby. Such stones are known as "*ruby-spinels*" ("spinel-rubies") (Plate I., Fig. 10), and are not infrequently sold as rubies. Carmine-red, blood-red, and poppy-red are the shades of colour most admired in the "ruby-spinel." Very fine stones of cochineal-red or blood-red are known to jewellers as "gouttes de sang."

Spinels of a rose-red or light shade of colour inclined to blue or violet are referred to as "*balas-rubies*" (rubis balais) (Plate I., Fig. 9). They not infrequently combine with this character a peculiarly milky sheen which considerably detracts from their value. Stones the colour of which is more decidedly blue or violet resemble, although much paler, some almandines, and are known as "*almandine-spinels*." Violet spinels, which are not too pale in colour, often resemble both the true amethyst and the "oriental amethyst," and indeed have sometimes been put on the market under the latter name. There should, however, be no danger of mistaking the one for the other, since the spinel is optically isotropic and is not dichroic. To distinguish spinel from almandine and other red garnets is more difficult, since both agree in being optically isotropic and in the absence of dichroism. The colour of the garnet, however, is usually much deeper than that of spinel, while, in the case of almandine, the specific gravity (sp. gr. = 4), which is greater, and the hardness (H = $7\frac{1}{2}$), which is less than that of spinel, may be relied upon. Rose-coloured topaz may closely resemble "balas-ruby," but then topaz is doubly refracting and strongly dichroic. Generally speaking, it cannot be said that "ruby-spinel," "balas-ruby," and "almandine-spinel" are very sharply marked off one from another, since stones showing intermediate characters are usually to be found.

The variety of spinel of a more or less pronounced yellow shade of colour is known as *rubicelle*. This variety, which may be hyacinth-red, orange-yellow, or even straw-yellow, is not esteemed very highly. The rubicelle which accompanies topaz and other precious stones in Minas Novas, in Brazil, has received the name of "vinegar-spinel," on account of its yellowish-red colour. At the particular locality at which it is found it is also known as "hyacinth," also on account of its colour. The name "vermeille," though more commonly applied to certain garnets, is also bestowed upon rubicelle of a decided orange-red shade.

Practically the same forms of cutting are used for the spinel as for the ruby. Finely coloured, transparent stones are cut as brilliants, but the step-cut or a mixed-cut is frequently employed, especially for darker stones. Foils of burnished gold or copper are sometimes used for the purpose of improving the colour and lustre of cut stones.

Spinels of good quality and up to 1 carat in weight are of ordinary occurrence; stones, the weight of which lies between 1 and 4 carats, are not infrequent, but large stones exceeding 8 or 10 carats in weight are rare. As we have already seen, spinels are far more free from faults than are rubies, so that it is not surprising to find that spinels of fine quality are much more abundant than rubies of the same description.

The value of a spinel varies with its colour and transparency, but is always less than that of the ruby. A perfectly transparent "ruby-spinel," up to and not exceeding 4 carats in weight, is worth, at the most, about half as much as a ruby of equal weight; thus a 1-carat "ruby-spinel" will fetch from £5 to £7 10s. The value of larger stones is considerably greater. "Balas-rubies" and other varieties of spinel of the best quality are about half the value of "ruby-spinels"; when exhibiting the milky sheen, described above, they are worth still less.

Although small specimens of precious spinel are much more abundant than large stones, yet a certain number of the latter are in existence. A "ruby-spinel" of $56\frac{1}{16}$ carats, valued at 50,000 francs (£2000), is mentioned in the inventory of the French crown jewels drawn up in 1791; also a "balas-ruby" of $20\frac{6}{16}$ carats, valued at 10,000 francs, and two smaller stones of $12\frac{6}{16}$ and 12 carats, valued respectively at 3000 and 800 francs. Another famous spinel of large size, the "Black Prince's Ruby," is set in the English crown; it is often, though erroneously, referred to as a true ruby. Probably the two largest spinels known are those which were shown at the Exhibition of 1862 in London; both were flawless stones of perfect colour and were cut en cabochon. The one weighed 197 carats, and on re-cutting gave a gem of 81 carats; the other weighed $102\frac{1}{4}$ carats before and $72\frac{1}{2}$ carats after re-cutting.

With respect to mode of occurrence spinel is closely related to corundum, since it is found under the same conditions and chiefly at the same localities as are ruby, sapphire, and the other varieties of corundum. Like corundum, spinel is essentially a mineral of the primitive rocks, being found in gneisses and schists, and especially in crystalline limestones interfoliated with gneisses; it also occurs in limestones formed as the result of contact-metamorphism. The most important localities for spinel are briefly mentioned below, the reader being referred for descriptive details to the account of these same localities given under ruby and sapphire.

In Upper Burma the different varieties of precious spinel are, in association with the ruby, of common occurrence both in the white crystalline limestone or marble and in the gem-sands derived from this. Three-fourths also of the precious stones which are brought for sale by the natives from the neighbouring Shan States are spinels.

Next in importance to Burma come the gem-gravels of Ceylon, especially of the interior of the island in the neighbourhood of Kandy. Fine crystals are not common, but a beautiful, transparent blue spinel, which will be referred to again below, is peculiar to the locality. Here also the mother-rock of the spinel is a granular limestone.

Spinels are abundant in the ruby mines of Badakshan. As early as the thirteenth century, spinels, together probably with rubies, were collected by the famous Venetian traveller, Marco Polo, in the province of Balascia on the Upper Oxus. This province is identical with the Badakshan of the present day, and the term "balas-ruby" is said to be derived from the place-name Balascia. Spinels are found in association with the rubies, which are sold in Tashkent, and which are said to come from the Tian-Shan Mountains; also with those found at Jagdalak in Afghanistan, and with the rubies and sapphires of Siam.

Spinels occur in the gem-gravels of Australia, usually as rounded grains. Here again they are specially abundant in the New England district and the Cudgegong and Macquarie rivers of New South Wales; also in Victoria, for example in Owen's river, and in other States. Single stones have been found also in Tasmania.

The so-called "vinegar-spinel" has already been stated to occur in the gem-gravels of Minas Novas, in Brazil. In the United States of North America, a few spinels suitable for cutting, although rather dark in colour, have been found at Hamburgh in New Jersey. The sapphires of Montana are remarkable in that they are not accompanied by spinels. Other localities for spinel are of even less importance and need not detain us.

Blue Spinel.—Among the colours of spinel, blue is not very prominent; stones of this colour exist, however, and may be referred to as "sapphire-spinels" in correspondence with the term "ruby-spinel" applied to stones of a ruby-red colour. The colour of these stones is due to a small amount of ferrous oxide in combination with alumina, which is present in addition to magnesia. Blue spinel occurs, often in large crystals, at Åker in Södermanland, Sweden; at this locality, however, the mineral is often opaque and scarcely of gem-quality. Transparent stones occur as isolated specimens, together with red spinel, at the localities mentioned above, that is to say, in Burma and especially in Ceylon. In the latter island are found very beautiful, dark blue octahedra. The lustre of these stones when cut as gems, although inferior to that of sapphire, is still very brilliant. In beauty of appearance they do not fall far short of sapphires, and they command a good price.

Black Spinel (ceylonite or pleonaste).—In this variety of spinel a part of the alumina is replaced by ferric oxide and the greater part of the magnesia by ferrous oxide, so that instead of a magnesia-alumina spinel, we get an iron-alumina spinel, the chemical composition of which may be represented by the formula $(Mg,Fe)O.(Al,Fe)_2O_3$. Being only another variety of spinel, its crystalline form is the same as that already described for precious spinel; the combination shown in Fig. 60 *b* is, however, commoner in this variety than in others. Ceylonite is greenish-black in mass and dark green in thin layers; like all spinels it takes a good polish and may be used in mourning jewellery. It is found in loose grains, sometimes exceeding an inch in diameter, in the gem-gravels of Ceylon, especially near Kandy; also as small brilliant crystals in some of the ejected blocks of Monte Somma, the ancient portion of Vesuvius. At many other localities it occurs as a contact-mineral in limestones, which have been subjected to the action of masses of molten granite and other igneous rocks. Large octahedra of black spinel, measuring 3 to 4 inches along the axes of the crystals, are found at Amity in the State of New York; small crystals occur in great numbers in the Fassathal in the Tyrol, and at many other places; few, however, are suitable for cutting. Green spinels, some of which are transparent and have been used as gems, have been found in Mitchell County, North Carolina, and in a lead mine in New Mexico.

CHRYSOBERYL.

In contrast to the variety in colour presented by corundum, a species which has furnished the jeweller with an extensive range of precious stones of identical composition, but dissimilar appearance, the mineral we have now to consider, namely, chrysoberyl, is characterised by the absence of any great range of colour, and displays only a few tints of green and its closely-related colour, yellow.   As the consideration of the mineral spinel was appropriately made immediately to follow that of corundum, on account of the similarity in the colours of the two minerals, so now the next place is given to chrysoberyl on account of its hardness approximating to that of corundum.

The hardness of chrysoberyl is exceeded only by that of corundum and, of course, of diamond.   In Mohs' scale of hardness it is placed between corundum (9) and topaz (8), and has a hardness of $8\frac{1}{2}$ assigned to it, being, therefore, the third hardest mineral known.

Like the other extremely hard minerals, corundum and spinel, chrysoberyl is composed very largely of alumina, containing 80·2 per cent. of this oxide and 19·8 per cent. of beryllia, a compound of oxygen with the metal beryllium, in the same way as alumina is a compound of oxygen with the metal aluminium.   This percentage chemical composition corresponds to the chemical formula $BeO.Al_2O_3$.   Chrysoberyl is, however, never found in nature in this ideally pure condition; most of the material which has been analysed contains iron in small amounts, while in alexandrite, a variety of chrysoberyl found in the Urals, a little chromic oxide is also present.   The following are typical analyses of ordinary chrysoberyl from Brazil and of alexandrite from the Urals:

	Chrysoberyl (Brazil).	Alexandrite (Urals).
Alumina (Al_2O_3)	78·10	78·92
Beryllia (BeO)	17·94	18·02
Ferric oxide (Fe_2O_3) . . .	4·88	3·48
Chromic oxide (Cr_2O_3) . . .	—	0·36
	100·92	100·78

Chrysoberyl crystallises in the rhombic system.   Simple crystals are rare, more or less complicated twin-crystals being most frequently met with; the former have the form of short, rhombic prisms in combination with other forms (Fig. 61 *a*).   Both simple and twinned crystals are tabular in the direction of a pair of parallel faces, which are striated as indicated in the figure.   Two crystals are frequently twinned together in such a way that the resulting form is symmetrical about a plane perpendicular to the striated face, that is to say, each individual of the twin is a reflection of the other in this plane, which is called the twin-plane.   In the compound crystal the striated faces of the two individuals are co-planar, and the two sets of striations meet at the twin junction at an angle of very nearly 60° (Fig. 61 *b*, and Plate XII., Fig. 10).   It frequently happens that three crystals are twinned together according to this same law, and when they also interpenetrate a very complicated group results (Fig. 61 *c*, and Plate XII., Fig. 8).   In such compound forms the boundaries of the individual crystals may be easily traced by the intersection of the three sets of striations at angles of approximately 60°.

Chrysoberyl has no distinct cleavage but a conchoidal fracture. It is brittle and very hard (H = 8½), and has a specific gravity of 3·68 to 3·78. It is unattacked by acids and infusible before the blowpipe. When rubbed it becomes positively electrified and retains its charge for several hours.

The lustre of chrysoberyl is vitreous or slightly inclined to greasy in character; the mineral takes, and on account of its great hardness retains unaltered, a very brilliant polish. With regard to transparency the mineral is very variable, some specimens being beautifully

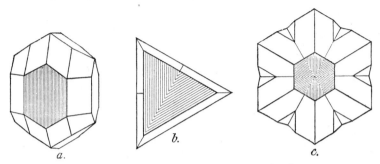

FIG. 61.   Crystalline forms of chrysoberyl.

clear while others are cloudy and opaque. The transparency, even of the clearest specimens, is, however, usually only apparent when the stones have been cut and polished, since the mineral is found most frequently in nature as water-worn and apparently opaque pebbles.

It is easy by means of the polariscope to demonstrate the doubly refracting character of transparent fragments of chrysoberyl. The double refraction of this mineral is not, however, very strong, the two indices of refraction having been determined as 1·756 and 1·747 respectively. The strength of refraction possessed by chrysoberyl is thus also rather small, and about the same as that of corundum. The refractive indices of chrysoberyl for the various colours of the spectrum differ from each other but little, so that the dispersion produced is slight and no prominent play of prismatic colours is seen.

Chrysoberyl shows only a limited range of colour; in Brazil, which is the most important locality of the mineral, it varies from pale yellowish-green to golden yellow and brownish-yellow. The Uralian crystals are of an intense green colour, varying in shade from grass-green to emerald-green. There are thus two varieties of chrysoberyl to be recognised, the one of a pale yellowish-green colour, considered as chrysoberyl proper, and the darker emerald-green variety, which is distinguished by the name of alexandrite. The first named is the more abundant and typical variety, the second being comparatively rare and of less importance.

CHRYSOBERYL PROPER AND CYMOPHANE.

The common variety of chrysoberyl is typically pale in colour. Green strongly tinged with yellow (Plate XII., Figs. 10 and 11), more or less bright olive-green, asparagus-green, grass-green, and green inclining to grey or white, are all shades of colour of which examples may be found among chrysoberyls. The more usual green colour sometimes merges into golden-yellow, pale yellow, or brownish-yellow, occasionally even into brown or black. Chrysoberyl is only feebly dichroic, the difference in the two colours of a crystal is not very distinct even when it is examined with the dichroscope, and is barely perceptible to the naked eye. The colour of chrysoberyl is unaffected by heat. Its yellowish-green tints are very similar to those of chrysolite, and for this reason the mineral is often referred to by jewellers as chrysolite. After the greenish-yellow, brownish-yellow tints are most frequently seen in chrysoberyl.

The transparency of the mineral is very variable. Perfectly clear and transparent stones are free from the chatoyant sheen mentioned below and which is of such frequent occurrence in this precious stone. When of a yellowish-green colour it is sometimes referred to in the trade as " oriental chrysolite," as is also corundum of the same colour. Cloudy and opaque specimens of chrysoberyl often exhibit in certain directions a peculiar chatoyant or opalescent sheen similar to that of cat's-eye (quartz-cat's-eye), only usually much finer. This chatoyant variety of chrysoberyl is illustrated in Plate XII., Fig. 11 ; it is known to mineralogists as **cymophane,** and to jewellers as *chrysoberyl-cat's-eye, oriental cat's-eye, Ceylonese cat's-eye,* more briefly as opalescent or chatoyant chrysoberyl, or simply as cat's-eye.

The chatoyancy characteristic of cymophane and distinguishing it from ordinary chrysoberyl appears as a milky, white, bluish, or greenish-white, or more rarely golden-yellow, sheen which follows every movement of the stone, and is seen to best advantage when the stone is cut *en cabochon.* Extending across the curved surface of such stones is a silvery line or streak of light, especially obvious when the stone is viewed in a strong light. This streak of silvery light may be more or less sharply defined ; its boundaries are usually sharp and clear in small stones, while in large specimens they are often blurred and indistinct, merging gradually into the dark background. These latter are less highly prized than the former, while specimens which show only an irregular patch of light with no sharp borders are still less esteemed. The term cat's-eye should, strictly speaking, be limited to stones which show a sharply defined streak of light, others being referred to as cymophane.

The form taken by the chatoyant reflection depends partly upon the character of the stone, but partly also upon the form in which it is cut ; hence the effectiveness of any particular stone will be increased or diminished by judicious or injudicious cutting. Generally speaking, the greater the curvature of the cut surface the greater is the effect produced. With a slight curvature, the patch of opalescent light broadens out and becomes less well defined, while if the stone be cut with a perfectly plane surface nothing will be seen but a perfectly uniform sheen over the whole surface.

The appearance known as chatoyancy is strictly limited to cloudy chrysoberyl, never being seen in the transparent mineral, and, as a rule, the more cloudy the chrysoberyl the more marked is the chatoyancy. The cloudiness of this mineral is due to the existence in immense numbers of microscopically small cavities in the substance of the stone. Some idea of their abundance may be obtained from the fact that in an area of $\frac{1}{7}$ inch square Sir David Brewster estimated 30,000 of them to be present. Just as in star-sapphires, the optical effect is due to a certain definite arrangement of these cavities, and the stone must be cut with due regard to this arrangement, otherwise the chatoyancy will be enfeebled if not altogether lost.

Chrysoberyl is esteemed for the brilliancy of its lustre and the brightness of its colour. It shows no play of prismatic colours, but in place of this we get the chatoyant effect described above. Of transparent varieties, those which are bright in colour are most sought after, but chatoyant chrysoberyl, that is, oriental cat's-eye, is still more highly esteemed, its value, however, varying with the body-colour of the stone. In this, as in all other cases, the relative value of the different varieties of chrysoberyl is, of course, subject to the caprice of fashion, now the transparent varieties, then the chatoyant cat's-eye being most favoured.

The sudden popularity of chrysoberyl-cat's-eye caused by the use of this stone in the ring given by the Duke of Connaught to his *fiancée*, has been already mentioned. It resulted in a great rise in its price, the stone being now about equal in value to a "balas-ruby."

The finest and largest chrysoberyl-cat's-eye known was included in the famous Hope collection, and is figured by B. Hertz in his *Catalogue of the Collection of Pearls and Precious Stones formed by Henry Philip Hope*, published in 1839. This stone is nearly hemispherical in shape, the diameter in the direction of the splendid chatoyant band measuring 2 inches and slightly exceeding the other diameter. It is dark in colour and the band of light which crosses it is not absolutely perfect, being nicked slightly in the middle. Among other fine stones now known is a magnificent jewel, sold in America, measuring 23 millimetres (nearly 1 inch) in length and breadth and 17 millimetres in thickness, and weighing $80\frac{3}{4}$ carats. It is yellowish-brown in colour, and the band of light which crosses it is wonderfully sharp, narrow, and straight for so large a stone.

The transparent varieties of chrysoberyl, especially those of a fine golden-yellow colour, are cut usually as brilliants, the step-cut and mixed-cut, however, being sometimes employed. Unless the colour is very intense this gem is seldom mounted *à jour*, more usually a closed setting with a foil of burnished gold to deepen the colour of the stone is employed. The opaque varieties, or cat's-eye, are of course cut *en cabochon*. Such stones are usually cut with an oval outline so that the band of light coincides in direction with the major axis of the oval.

The most important locality for chrysoberyl is **Brazil,** the district of Minas Novas, in the north of the State of Minas Geraes, being specially rich. It is found associated with rock-crystal, amethyst, red quartz, green tourmaline, yellowish-red spinel (so-called "vinegar-spinel"), garnet, euclase, and especially with white and blue (but not yellow) topaz.

Chrysoberyl is one of the finest coloured precious stones found in Brazil. It is known to Brazilians and in the trade generally as "chrysolite." It exhibits considerable variety of colour within certain limits, greyish-white, pale ochre-yellow, citron-yellow, olive-green, grass-green, and pale green being shades of colour ordinarily seen, while pure wine-yellow, greyish-yellow, and colourless stones sometimes occur. The last named variety closely approaches the diamond in brilliancy and transparency. Stones of perfect transparency are rare, the chatoyancy of cat's-eye being, as a rule, more or less prominent even in the transparent varieties. Chrysoberyl, especially the variety of a pure green colour, is very highly esteemed in Brazil, and consequently commands a high price, being more expensive in that country than in Europe.

The mineral occurs as pebbles, not, as a rule, larger than a bean. A block of supposed chrysoberyl weighing 16 pounds is reported to have been once found, but it is more likely to have been aquamarine (beryl). In spite of the fact that the pebbles are rounded and water-worn, the broad, striated face, which is shown in Fig. 61, and parallel to which the crystals are usually tabular, is often easily recognisable. They are found in an auriferous mud or clay derived from the weathering of granite and gneiss, rocks which are always to be found in the vicinity of deposits containing chrysoberyl. It would appear from this fact that chrysoberyl was originally formed in such rocks, but so far the mineral has been met with only in secondary deposits. Among the principal localities for the mineral may be mentioned the upper course of the Piauhy, and the neighbourhood about the source of the Calhão stream. These deposits, however, are less rich than in former times, and it is said that at the present day material suitable only for the pivot-supports of watches is found there. Chrysoberyl also occurs associated with diamond in small amount in Minas Geraes.

The occurrence of chrysoberyl in the gold-washings of the Sanarka river, in the country of the Orenburg Cossacks in the Southern **Urals** is very similar to that in Minas Novas, but is quite insignificant commercially. The mineral here is, as a rule, of a fine sulphur-yellow colour, rarely greyish or greenish, and is associated with euclase, rose-red topaz, and other minerals. It occurs almost invariably in very small pebbles, and is accompanied by a small amount of alexandrite, another variety of chrysoberyl.

Most of the chrysoberyl now cut for gems comes from **Ceylon,** and is of the chatoyant variety. As these stones are frequently referred to in descriptions of the precious stones of Ceylon simply as cat's-eye, it is often impossible to decide whether chrysoberyl or the variety of quartz, also known as cat's-eye, is meant. It seems that both the chatoyant and the transparent varieties of chrysoberyl are more abundantly found now than formerly, probably as a consequence of an increased demand and a more exhaustive search. Among the finest specimens of chrysoberyl, deep golden-yellow, pale yellow, yellowish-green, greyish-green, dark green, greenish-brown, and other colours, may be seen, with or without the chatoyant effect. Dark green stones show many of the characters, and specially the marked dichroism of alexandrite, a variety of chrysoberyl which will be described in detail below. The largest chrysoberyl-cat's-eye hitherto known came from Ceylon, and until the year 1815 adorned the crown of the King of Kandy; the other of the two large stones mentioned above was probably also found in this island.

The stones found in Ceylon vary in weight between 1 and 100 carats, and are found accompanying sapphire in the gem-gravels; the principal localities are in the district of Saffragam and the neighbourhood of Matura in the south of the island.

Burma (Pegu) has also been given as a locality for chrysoberyl, but its occurrence here is not a well-established fact. Although the mineral undoubtedly occurs both in India and rather more abundantly in the diamond-washings of Borneo, yet in neither country is the occurrence of any commercial value.

The tendency amongst jewellers to confuse chrysoberyl with chrysolite (olivine) has been already remarked. This confusion is only possible, however, in the case of specimens of chrysoberyl from which chatoyancy, which is never seen in chrysolite, is absent. The two minerals differ too in their physical characters; thus chrysolite, with a hardness between $6\frac{1}{2}$ and 7, is much softer than chrysoberyl. Again, the specific gravity of chrysolite varies from 3·34 to 3·37, while that of chrysoberyl lies between 3·65 and 3·75, so that although both minerals sink in methylene iodide, in the heaviest liquid (No. 1), the former will float and the latter sink. Unless examined in some detail the optical characters give little help in distinguishing these two minerals.

Chrysoberyl-cat's-eye may also be mistaken for quartz-cat's-eye, and *vice versâ*, in spite of the fact that the former is usually more brilliant and finer in every way than the latter. Here, again, a difference in the hardness and specific gravity comes to our aid, the hardness of quartz being only 7 and its specific gravity 2·65. Thus, while quartz-cat's-eye floats in methylene iodide chrysoberyl-cat's-eye quickly sinks.

ALEXANDRITE.

Alexandrite (Plate XII., Figs. 8 and 9) is the name given to that variety of chryso-beryl the colour of which varies between dark grass-green and emerald-green. The colour is probably due to the presence of a small amount of chromic oxide. Alexandrite differs from ordinary chrysoberyl also in the fact that it is very strongly dichroic, a crystal or cut stone appearing, when viewed in a direction perpendicular to the broad striated face, not green but a fine columbine-red inclined to violet. In ordinary diffused daylight, however, this colour is not perceptible, and the stone appears always of a green colour (Plate XII., Figs. 8 and 9, *a*). When suitably cut, then, the same stone which by daylight is green appears in artificial light of a red to violet colour; the alexandrite has therefore been described as an emerald by day and an amethyst by night. To accentuate this peculiar character the stone must be cut of a certain thickness, the difference in colour being much less marked in a stone cut with little depth. A crystal of alexandrite when viewed through the dichroscope in a direction perpendicular to the broad striated face gives an emerald-green and a yellow image; when the direction is parallel to this face one of the images is red.

Until comparatively recent times alexandrite was found only in Russia, in the emerald mines on the right bank of the Takovaya, a small stream eighty-five versts (about fifty-seven miles) east of Ekaterinburg in the **Urals,** a locality which will be considered in more detail under the description of emerald. The stone is found, together with emerald and many other minerals, embedded in mica-schist, close to the line of contact of this rock with granite. It occurs usually in star-shaped triplets, identical or very similar in form to that shown in Fig. 61 *c*, and Plate XII., Fig. 8, and consisting of three crystals twinned together. Simple or twin-crystals (Fig. 61, *a* and *b*,) are very rare. The triplets often measure as much as 9 centimetres across, and sometimes even more; they have a tendency to grow together in groups, one such group being found to contain twenty-two large crystals and many small ones of the same kind. The occurrence was accidentally discovered in 1830, on the very day on which the coming of age of the Czarevitch Alexander Nicolajevitch, afterwards Czar Alexander II., was celebrated, and the mineral received its name in honour of this personage. The, at first, exclusively Russian occurrence of the stone and the fact that it combines the national military colours, green and red, gives it a peculiar value in the eyes of Russians, by whom it is worn with great pride. Crystals of alexandrite are, as a rule, cloudy and full of fissures, and are therefore unfit for cutting as gem-stones; they may, however, contain pure and transparent portions free from cracks and markedly dichroic, and it is from such portions that gems are cut. It follows, then, that in Russia, at least, if not elsewhere, where the stone is used but little, much higher prices are demanded for alexandrite than for ordinary chrysoberyl, and the more so as the mines at the present day are almost completely exhausted.

For a long time alexandrite was known only at the locality mentioned, then it was found with pebbles of ordinary chrysoberyl and other precious stones in the auriferous sands of the Sanarka river in the southern Urals.

Still more recently alexandrites have been found in comparative abundance in the gem-gravels of **Ceylon.** These show the characteristic dichroism of the Uralian stones, while some display, in addition, the chatoyancy of cymophane, a feature never seen in specimens from the Urals. The Ceylonese alexandrites are, on the whole, finer than the Uralian, the columbine-red colour seen in artificial light being especially beautiful; the chatoyant stones, moreover, which may be called alexandrite-cat's-eye, are peculiar to this locality. The largest alexandrite yet found in Ceylon weighed $63\frac{3}{8}$ carats, and those ordinarily found never weigh less than 4 carats. The large stone just mentioned was cut with double facets (Plate III., Fig. 6), and gave a gem measuring 33 by 32 millimetres at the girdle and with a thickness of 17 millimetres. Its colour by day is grass-green tinged with yellow, and by artificial light a fine raspberry-red. Another beautiful stone from Ceylon weighed $28\frac{23}{32}$ carats and measured 32 by 16 by 9 millimetres. Its colour by daylight was a fine sap-green with a trace of red, while in candle-light it appeared of a full columbine-red, scarcely distinguishable from a purplish-red Siamese spinel. Localities for alexandrite, other than Ceylon and the Urals, are not at present known.

BERYL.

The mineral species beryl includes, besides the emerald and the aquamarine, other precious stones of less importance, which are referred to generally by jewellers as beryl. The different varieties of beryl differ only in colour; their other characters are identical, just as ruby and sapphire are mere colour-varieties of the mineral species corundum. It will be convenient to consider the specific characters before passing to a more detailed description of each colour-variety.

The oxide alumina, which enters so largely into the composition of corundum, spinel, and chrysoberyl, is also present in beryl, but in smaller amount and in combination with silica and beryllia. The oxide beryllia, so called on account of its presence in beryl, is also, as we have seen, a constituent of chrysoberyl. Beryl is thus a silicate of the metals aluminium and beryllium, the chemical composition of which is expressed by the formula $3BeO.Al_2O_3.6SiO_2$, and the percentage composition by, silica $(SiO_2) = 66.84$, alumina $(Al_2O_3) = 19.05$, beryllia $(BeO) = 14.11$.

In several analyses of this mineral the presence, in small amounts, of water, iron, alkalies, chromic oxide, and other substances have been determined, while in some beryls, as, for example, the beautiful emerald from Muzo in Colombia, South America, traces of organic matter have been found. The result of the analysis of this stone made by Lewy, together with an analysis by Penfield of aquamarine from Adun-Chalon, in Siberia, is given below. Chromic oxide, which is absent from this specimen of aquamarine and exists as a trace in the emerald, is sometimes present to the extent of 3 per cent.

	Emerald (Colombia).	Aquamarine (Siberia).
Silica (SiO_2)	67.85	66.17 per cent.
Alumina (Al_2O_3)	17.95	20.39
Beryllia (BeO)	12.4	11.50
Chromic oxide (Cr_2O_3) . . .	trace	—
Ferrous oxide (FeO)	—	0.69
Magnesia (MgO)	0.9	—
Soda (Na_2O)	0.7	0.24
Lithia (Li_2O)	—	trace
Water (H_2O)	1.66	1.14
Organic matter	0.12	—

Beryl crystallises in the hexagonal system. The crystals (Fig. 62, a to c) are usually rather long, six-sided prisms with smooth faces, terminated in many cases, and nearly always in emerald, by a single plane at right angles to the faces of the prism (Fig. 62 a), this being known as the basal plane. Not infrequently the edges of the hexagonal prism are truncated by the faces of a second hexagonal prism, and these again by a twelve-sided prism; the resulting form, though in reality a prism, bounded by many small faces (Fig. 62 d), has the appearance of a longitudinally-striated cylinder. For this reason the prism faces of beryl are usually striated in the direction of their length, that is, parallel to their mutual intersections. Moreover, in many cases, the crystals are terminated not only by the basal plane but also by six-sided and twelve-sided pyramids in combination with the prism. Fig. b shows a hexagonal pyramid of the second order, and Fig. c a hexagonal pyramid of the first order, while in Fig. *e* there are two hexagonal pyramids of the first order, one of the second order, and a dihexagonal pyramid in combination with a hexagonal prism and the basal plane. These more complicated crystals are more characteristic of aquamarine.

The crystals are either attached to the matrix by one end, in which case they often form beautiful druses, or they are embedded in it, and are then developed regularly in all directions. In the former case, the free end alone bears regular crystal-faces, while in the latter both ends are developed; these terminal faces are, however, sometimes small and irregular.

The cleavage of beryl is not an important character, crystals of this mineral cleaving only indistinctly in certain directions. The mineral is brittle, and its fracture conchoidal.

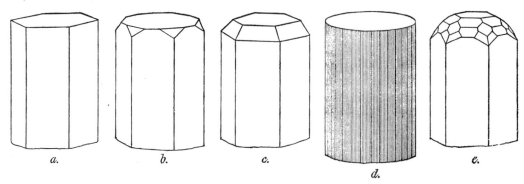

FIG. 62. Crystalline forms of beryl (emerald and aquamarine).

With respect to its hardness it stands a little above quartz, but below topaz, the degree of its hardness being represented on the scale by $H = 7\frac{1}{2}$; this is rather low for a precious stone, and beryl is, in fact, one of the softer of the more valuable gems. The different varieties of the mineral show small differences in hardness among themselves, the Colombian emerald being, for example, a little softer than the Siberian aquamarine. Although the hardness of this stone is not great, it is sufficient to render it susceptible of a fine polish, which, however, is not retained for as long as is the case with harder stones.

The specific gravity of beryl, like its hardness, is rather low, its mean value being 2·7. That of precious beryl varies between 2·67 and 2·75, being always slightly higher than the specific gravity of quartz (2·65). The specific gravity of certain specimens of emerald from Muzo has been found to be 2·67, while for Siberian aquamarine the values 2·68 to 2·75 are given. Beryl will thus always float in methylene iodide, and when pushed beneath the surface quickly rises again; in liquid No. 4 with the specific gravity of quartz it slowly sinks. This character affords a ready means by which it may be distinguished from certain stones of similar appearance.

With the exception of hydrofluoric acid, beryl is unattacked by acids. When a fragment is heated before the blowpipe it becomes white and cloudy, and fuses, only with difficulty, at the edges to a white, blebby glass.

Different beryls differ greatly in appearance, especially in respect to colour and transparency, some being cloudy and opaque, others beautifully clear and transparent; all possible gradations between these two extremes are known. The opaque variety, known as common beryl, usually occurs as crystals in coarse-grained granite. Such crystals have been known to measure 6 feet in length, and to weigh $2\frac{1}{2}$ tons; they are useless, however, for gems, since, besides being opaque, they are usually of an unpleasing yellowish- or greenish-white colour. Only the transparent or semi-transparent precious beryl is used for cutting as gems; this is usually of a beautiful colour, often green or blue, but sometimes yellow. All varieties of beryl have the common vitreous lustre.

In correspondence with its crystalline form, all hexagonal crystals being birefringent, beryl is doubly refracting, only, however, to a small extent, for the greater and lesser indices of refraction for the same colour differ but slightly. Its refraction is also small. In the case of emerald from Muzo the greater and lesser refractive indices have been determined to be 1·584 and 1·578, and in the case of Siberian aquamarine 1·582 and 1·576. The dispersion is also small, the refractive coefficients given by the same crystal for differently coloured rays of light differing but slightly. This may be seen by comparing the refractive indices of a crystal of beryl for red, yellow, and green light which are given below:

				Red.	Yellow.	Green.
Greater refractive index	.	.	.	1·566	1·570	1·574
Lesser " "	.	.	.	1·562	1·566	1·570

It follows, then, that scarcely any play of prismatic colours, such as is characteristic of the diamond, is seen in beryl; its beauty depends mainly on its strong lustre, and on its fine body-colour. There is a certain amount of variety in this latter character, but very much less than in corundum. Green and bluish-green beryl is most common, yellow rather less so, pale red and water-clear stones rare. Different varieties of beryl are distinguished by their colour; bright grass-green beryl being known as *emerald*. Other varieties, which are always of a pale colour, are referred to as *precious* or *noble beryl*. Of these light-coloured varieties, the pale blue, bluish-green, or yellowish-blue, is distinguished as *aquamarine*, the yellowish-green as "*aquamarine-chrysolite*," while the yellow variety is known to jewellers as *beryl*, and when of a pure golden-yellow as *golden beryl*. Of all these varieties the emerald is by far the most important as a precious stone, ranking, indeed, with the costliest of gems; aquamarine is also much used, while the other varieties are of less importance.

All transparent beryls, whatever their colour if not too pale, are distinctly dichroic; differences in colour can often be observed with the naked eye, and with the dichroscope are, as a rule, unmistakable. On account of this property, it is possible, therefore, to distinguish genuine beryl from coloured glass imitations, or from other gem-stones which it may resemble in appearance.

The characters by which the different varieties of beryl are distinguished must now be considered. These varieties, which differ from each other principally in colour, are by no means equally valuable as gems, the emerald being by far the most costly.

EMERALD.

Emerald is the name given to beryl of a pure and intense green colour; the particular shade of colour seen in this variety of beryl is often alluded to in ordinary language as emerald-green, but emeralds may be also grass-green, green tinged with yellow, or celadon-green tinged with grey. Beryls of a bluish-green colour are not included in this variety. Many specimens of emerald are very pale in colour, varying in intensity down to greenish-white; these are, however, not cut as gems; only those of a beautiful and deep emerald-green to grass-green are highly prized. The particular shade of green characteristic of the emerald is shown in Plate XII., Figs. 1—3; it is almost unrivalled in depth and brilliancy, and is often compared to the fresh green of a meadow in spring. The finest stones possess a peculiar velvety lustre, like that shown by some dark blue sapphires.

According to F. Wöhler, the colour of emerald from Muzo in Colombia withstood subjection for an hour to a temperature at which copper readily melts. Although emerald from this locality has been shown by Lewy to contain a small amount of organic matter, its colour cannot, therefore, be due to this, but probably depends upon the presence of chromic oxide, 0·186 per cent. of this substance having been found in the specimen examined by Wöhler. That the deep green of the emerald can be produced by so small an amount of chromic oxide has been proved by fusing white glass with the same percentage of this metallic oxide, a glass having the intense green of the finest emeralds being produced. More recently it has been shown that the colouring-matter of Uralian and Egyptian emeralds also is very probably due to chromic oxide.

Emeralds of good, full colour are distinctly dichroic; the images shown by the dichroscope are respectively emerald- or yellowish-green and bluish-green.

The colour of the emerald is not always distributed uniformly through its substance. The differently coloured portions may occur irregularly or in layers; in the latter case the layers are, as a rule, parallel to the basal plane of the crystal, that is to say, perpendicular to the prism faces.

The transparency of the emerald is perfect only in rare cases. The majority of crystals are rendered cloudy and dull, not only by fissures and cracks, but also by the presence of microscopic enclosures, which in places are accumulated in large numbers. These enclosures may be fluid or solid, scales of mica being specially common. Cloudy and opaque crystals of emerald are usually dull in colour, approaching the characters of common beryl and being useless for cutting as gems. Perfectly clear and transparent stones are naturally the most valuable, but fissured and cloudy specimens, provided they possess the fine emerald-green colour, have a certain value.

Compared with other precious stones, the rarity of perfect specimens of emerald is unique. The most common faults are those which have been just mentioned, fissures being almost invariably present. Stones which are clouded by fissures are described as "mossy." Irregularities in the distribution of colour, and dull and cloudy patches, are also frequently to be seen.

The disparity between the value of a perfect and of an imperfect emerald is enormous. A faultless emerald is worth as much, or nearly as much, as a ruby, and certainly more than a diamond. A one-carat stone, perfect in colour and transparency, is worth at least £20, and large stones, on account of their rarity, have a value out of all proportion to their size. As a matter of fact, a perfect emerald weighing but a few carats is so rare that almost any price will be given for it by collectors. Fissured stones, which are cloudy but of good colour, are much cheaper; when the colour is pale they are worth no more than £5 or even £2 10s. per carat. The value of such stones is more or less proportional to their size, large stones of this description being by no means uncommon.

Flawless emeralds of large size are extremely rare, so that only small stones are available for cutting as gems. Emeralds of considerable size have been known, but their quality leaves much to be desired; moreover, in the case of large stones found and described in early times, it must be remembered that the name emerald was applied to other stones of a green colour. The ancient Peruvians are said to have numbered among their deities an emerald the size of an ostrich's egg. Again, there is reported to be in the treasury at Vienna an emerald which weighs 2205 carats, while Schrauf states that in the same place is preserved an ink-well cut out of a single stone, besides other large emeralds cut as table-stones. One of the largest and finest emeralds known belongs to the Duke of Devonshire. It is a natural crystal of the form characteristic of emerald, namely, a hexagonal prism with a basal plane. This stone (Fig. 63) measures 2 inches across the basal plane, and weighs $8\frac{9}{10}$ ounces or

1350 carats; it is of the finest colour, clear and transparent, and almost faultless. This stone came from the emerald mines at Muzo in Colombia, where crystals of the length and thickness of a finger are by no means rare. Crystals of equal size are found in the Urals and are not specially rare; one measuring 8 inches in length and 5 inches in diameter is preserved in the collection of the Imperial Institute of Mines in St. Petersburg, and still larger crystals have been reported. Probably the largest is in the possession of the Czar of Russia; it is said to measure 25 centimetres (nearly 10 inches) in length and 12 centimetres in diameter. One or two very large stones, formerly thought to be emeralds, have on closer examination proved to be green glass; such, for example, is one weighing 28¾ pounds in the Reichenau monastery above Chur, in the Rhine Valley, Switzerland.

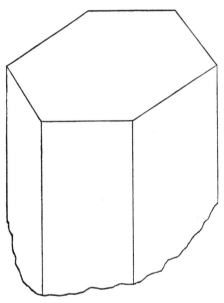

FIG. 63.   Crystal of emerald belonging to the Duke of Devonshire.   (Actual size.)

The form in which an emerald is cut depends upon the character of the rough stone. Perfectly faultless, transparent fragments, when not too dark, are cut as brilliants or as rosettes. Most frequently, however, the step-cut (Plate XII., Fig. 3) with brilliant facets on the upper portion is adopted. The emerald, though not infrequently cut as a simple table-stone, is probably never, at least in Europe, cut en cabochon. Cut gems, perfect in colour and transparency, are mounted à jour; paler stones are provided with a green foil placed beneath them, while fissured or otherwise faulty stones are mounted in a closed setting blackened inside.

Natural crystals of emerald are, as a rule, too large and too much flawed to be cut as single gems; they are, therefore, sawn into portions of suitable size and purity, great care being taken to avoid unnecessary loss of material. In many crystals, clear and transparent portions suitable for gems have to be cut out of the main mass of the crystal, and in this operation special care is required. Each portion so cut out of a crystal is faceted in the form best suited to its particular shape.

Compared with the precious stones hitherto considered, the emerald, in its mode of occurrence, is unique, for it is found exclusively in its primary situation, that is to say, in the rock in which it was formed. It is one of the minerals characteristic of crystalline schists, and in many places is found embedded in mica-schists and similar rocks. The famous occurrence at Muzo in Colombia is the only exception to this rule, the emerald being here embedded in calcite veins in limestone. This occurrence has called forth the perfectly groundless supposition that the emeralds here were originally formed in crystalline schists and were afterwards deposited in the calcite veins. The emerald practically never occurs in gem-gravels, in the way in which diamonds, rubies, &c., occur.

The earliest known emerald locality is doubtless that in **Upper Egypt**, not far from the coast of the Red Sea and south of Kosseir. Though the occurrence of emerald in Ethiopia was known to the ancients, the locality, in course of time, became completely forgotten, and ancient accounts of the occurrence were regarded as erroneous. It has been supposed that true emeralds were first introduced into Europe at the end of the sixteenth century from South America; they had been found previously, however, both with Egyptian mummies and also among the ruins of the two Roman cities, Herculaneum and Pompeii. These latter, which were discovered long before the end of the sixteenth century (1566), could not have been brought from South America, the most important locality at the present day, but probably came from Egypt or, as also mentioned in ancient writings, from Scythian lands, and thus perhaps from the Urals, where they are still found.

The ancient Egyptian mines were re-discovered in the second decade of the nineteenth century by Cailliaud, a member of the expedition organised by Mehemet Ali Pasha; they have been frequently visited since by European travellers. The workings were partly surface and partly underground, the timbering of the latter being frequently found in a well preserved state. The deposit was worked to a considerable extent, some of the mines being large enough to admit of 400 men working together at the same time. The facts which led these ancient miners to suspect the existence of emeralds in these deposits, and the date at which the workings were commenced, are alike unknown. The appliances and tools which have been found in the mines date back to the time of Sesostris (1650 B.C.). It is recorded in ancient inscriptions that, in the time of Alexander the Great, Greek miners were employed in these mines; and it is evident that they were worked during the reign of Cleopatra, for emeralds bearing an engraving of herself were used for presentation by this queen.

There is no subsequent record of the mines until their re-discovery by Cailliaud, who, with the permission of Mehemet Ali, re-opened them in 1819, the actual work being performed by Albanian miners. Perhaps on account of the poorness of quality of the stones the work was soon abandoned, and apparently with great suddenness, for a number of baskets filled with material ready to be drawn up to the surface have been discovered in the mine just as they were left by the Albanian miners.

These ancient mines are situated in a depression of the long range of mountains which borders the west coast of the Red Sea; in the same range are to be found gold and topaz mines. The emerald mines are in two groups, one being known as the Jebel (= Mount) Sikait (also called Sakketto), and the other, about ten miles to the north, as the Jebel Sabara (Zabara, Zubara, &c.), both being a little south of latitude 25° N. The most important and extensive of the two groups of mines is that of the Jebel Sikait; it is connected with the Red Sea fifteen miles to the east by the Wadi Chamal, and judging from the ruins of houses, temples, and other buildings which are still to be found there, must have been the site of a town of no inconsiderable size. Hundreds of shafts of various depths have been driven into the hill, which is 600 to 700 feet in height. These so-called Cleopatra's emerald mines have recently (1899) been again visited by Mr. D. A. MacAlister with the view of re-working the old mines. The ancient workings on the Jebel Sabara are similar, but less extensive.

The emeralds found here are of a fine, though not very deep, colour; at both places the mother-rock is a dark mica-schist interfoliated with talc-schist, and containing in the Jebel Sikait district augite and hornblende in addition. The mother-rock of the emeralds found in the Urals and in the Salzburg Alps, to be described later, is precisely similar in character.

It has occasionally happened that fine emeralds of a good colour, some cut and some rough, together with other precious stones, have been thrown up by the sea on the beach near Alexandria. These stones are apparently part of a sunken treasure, and probably came originally from the ancient mines in Upper Egypt, being similar both in quality and in the character of the minerals with which they are associated to stones known to have come from these mines.

Emeralds from **South America** were first introduced into Europe at the end of the sixteenth century, and from this period up to the year 1830 all the emeralds which came into the market were brought from this country.

At the time of the Spanish conquest of South America many large and beautiful emeralds were found in the possession of the Peruvians. The mines from which these stones had been derived were probably at the time of the invasion deserted and filled in by the natives, for the search made for them by the Spanish conquerors was altogether unavailing. They are supposed to have been situated in the Manta valley near Puerto Viejo, from whence is said to have come the emerald the size of an ostrich's egg, which was worshipped by the ancient Peruvians as a deity. However that may be, it is certain that at the present day no emeralds are found in Peru.

The number of stones which the Spaniards took from the natives and shipped to Europe must have been enormous. José d'Acosta relates that the ship by which he voyaged from Peru to Spain in 1587 carried two cases, each of which contained no less than a hundredweight of emeralds. This large importation of emeralds from Peru, together with the abundant yield from the mines soon afterwards discovered in Colombia, had the effect of very considerably lowering the price of these stones, which up to then had been so rare in Europe. The South American emeralds were far finer than any previously introduced into Europe whether from Egypt or elsewhere, and hence emeralds of good quality came to be distinguished as " Peruvian," or " Spanish," just as the finest specimens of other precious stones were given the prefix " oriental," whether they came from the Orient or not. Many of the emeralds now in use as gems are the same stones as those brought over to Europe by the Spaniards from Peru. In most cases, however, their shape has been altered from time to time in order to conform to the passing fashion of the day. It is said that the Spaniards were possessed of the idea that a genuine emerald would withstand a blow from a hammer, and that many Peruvian stones were in consequence reduced to splinters by being subjected to this test.

The Spaniards found the natives of Mexico also in possession of very beautiful emeralds, in many cases cut with great skill into peculiar and characteristic forms which are not seen elsewhere. Five stones cut into the shapes of fantastic flowers, fishes, and other natural objects were brought to Europe by Cortez. Since nothing is known as to the natural occurrence of emeralds in this country, it is inferred that the ancient Mexicans obtained the rough stones either from Peru or from the mines in Colombia.

Though the Spaniards were unsuccessful in searching for naturally occurring emeralds in Peru and Mexico, and could obtain the beautiful green stones only from the treasure stored up in the graves and temples of the ancient Peruvians and Mexicans, they were more fortunate in the country now known as **Colombia** or New Granada. Here the deposits from which the natives obtained their stones were easily found, and it is from this same source that the emeralds which now find their way into the markets of the world are for the most part derived.

Besides the Colombian deposits there is no other well-authenticated occurrence of emerald in South America, the existence of the supposed Peruvian deposits being by no means unquestionable. This being so, it has been suggested that the emeralds found by the Spaniards in the possession of the natives of Venezuela and Ecuador, and specially of Peru, were all derived from the Colombian deposits. The term " Peruvian emerald," except when used to describe the quality of a stone, is therefore misleading, South American emeralds

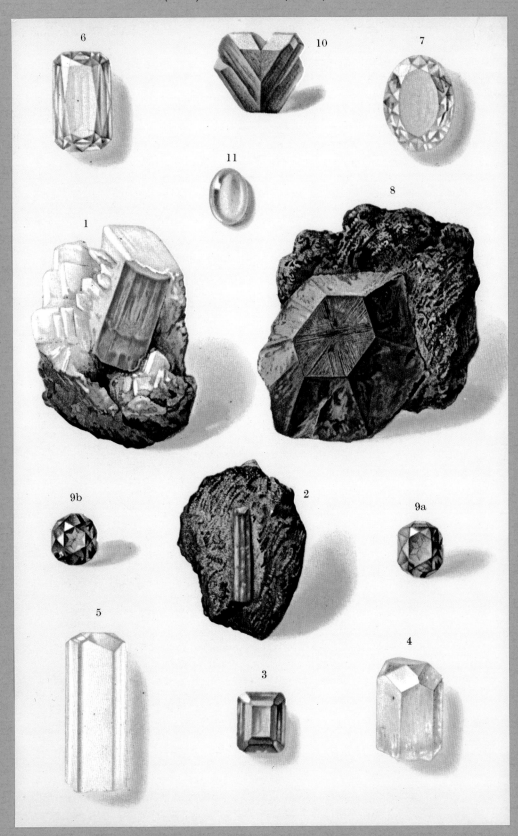

1. Emerald, crystal in calcite (Colombia).   2. Emerald, crystal in mica-schist (Salzburg).
3. Emerald, cut.   4. Beryl (golden beryl), crystal.   5. Aquamarine, crystal (Siberia).   6, 7.
Aquamarine, cut.   8. Chrysoberyl (Alexandrite), crystal (Urals).   9a The same, cut-stone by
day-light.   9b. The same, cut-stone by candle-light.   10. Chrysoberyl, crystal (Brazil).
11. Chrysoberyl (Cymophane), cut.

being more strictly described as Colombian   Whether emerald mines ever existed in Peru and other parts of South America or not, it is certain that at present the Colombian are the only deposits known.

The Spaniards first learnt of the existence of Colombian emeralds on March 3, 1537. A gift of emeralds was offered to the Spanish conquerors by the Indians, who, at the same time, pointed out the source from which the stones were derived. This spot, known as Somondoco, a name still in use, lies nine leguas (about twenty-three miles) distant from Guatequé, close to the waterfall of Nagar, over which the Garagoa flows before joining the Guario, a tributary of the Upia, which in its turn feeds the Rio Meta. The place is situated on the eastern slopes of the Cordillera of Bogotá, in latitude about 5° N. and about half a degree east of Bogotá (formerly Santa Fé de Bogotá) the capital of Colombia. The wild and inaccessible nature of the region soon drove the Spaniards to abandon the workings in spite of the richness of the deposit. No exact records of this occurrence and of the situation of the old mines are in existence, and doubt has sometimes been thrown on the authenticity of the occurrence. It is probable, however, that the majority of emeralds mined in Colombia in former times came from this spot. The deposit at Somondoco is now (1901) being worked by an English company, but as yet only second quality stones have been found.

A short time after the discovery by Europeans of Somondoco as a locality for emeralds, another, about 100 miles distant, richer and of greater importance than any now known, was discovered. This locality is the only one in Colombia at which fine emeralds are now met with. The stones occasionally found in ancient graves or mountain lakes, which latter were the sites of votive offerings, are all of poor quality, while the naturally occurring stones are frequently of admirable colour and transparency.

The mines now under consideration are situated in the country of the wild Muzo Indians, who for a long while successfully resisted the Spanish attempts at conquest. They were partially subdued in 1555 by the Spanish under Luiz Lanchero, who, in the same year, founded the town of Santissima Trinidad de los Muzos, the present village of Muzo, in the Itoco Mountains. This latter name was at that time applied to the town itself as well as to the mountains.

In spite of the continued hostility of the Indians, the mining of emeralds was commenced in 1558, an old mine in the mountains, of which all trace is at present lost, being first worked. Later, the centre of the workings was situated about a legua (about two and a half miles) from Muzo, work being commenced here in the year 1594. Numerous other mines were opened in the same district in this year, but were afterwards abandoned for various reasons. Some have been reopened and are being worked at the present day.

The district is situated in the Tunka valley in the eastern Cordilleras of the Andes, which branch away near Popayan from the main chain and stretch along the right or east bank of the Rio Magdalena in its northward course. It is a wild, mountainous region, and its inhospitable character, combined with the hot, damp, and unhealthy climate, renders the search for emeralds anything but an easy task. Crystals of emerald, not, however, of very good quality, have been found at not a few places in this region, so that it is probable that many other emerald localities are still to be discovered.

During the period which has elapsed since the discovery of these deposits they have been worked with varying success in many different spots ; at one time under Government direction, at another by private enterprise. At one time service in the mines was made compulsory for the neighbouring Indians, and this short-sighted policy resulted in so serious a depopulation of the country that mining operations were appreciably hindered by lack of workers. The deposit was at first worked in underground levels ; later, open workings were adopted, partly in order to render possible a stricter supervision of the workers and to avoid the loss through thieving of a large proportion of the output. The yield of these mines was on the whole small and extremely variable, the labour of several months being sometimes unrewarded by a single find, while on the other hand emeralds to the weight of 100,000 carats would be found in one day. The places at which workings are commenced are chosen entirely at random, for there is nothing to indicate the probability of one spot being more favourable than another. No really reliable statements as to the total yield of the mines are obtainable, but as far as is known it is very variable; thus, for example, in the year 1849 it averaged 12,400 carats per month, and in the 'fifties 22,386 carats per annum.

The most important mine at the present day is situated one and a half leguas to the west of Muzo, in latitude 5° 39′ 50″ N., and longitude 74° 25′ W., of Greenwich; it is about 150 kilometres (ninety-four miles) NNW. of Bogotá, and lies 878 metres (2897 feet) above sea-level. It has been worked for a long period, but not uninterruptedly; it ceased, for example, in the middle of the eighteenth century in consequence of a serious fire, and was only recommenced in 1844. The mine has been at one time worked by the Colombian Government, at another leased to natives or to European companies. In the interest of the whole locality much secrecy is observed in the granting of such leases, so that there are many points on which it is impossible to get information. From 1849 to 1861 the mine was worked by an English company, who paid the Government for this privilege 14,200 dollars and 5 per cent. of the net profits. From 1864 to 1875 a French company, under the direction of Gustav Lehmann, paid the Government 14,700 dollars per annum for permission to work all the mines. The number of workers employed in the mines has varied at different times from 100 to 300. The stones were at first sent to London, but later were placed on the market at Paris.

There are several detailed descriptions of the most important of these mines, which agree among themselves very completely. From them we learn that it is situated on the left side of a small mountain valley called Minero, or at the present time Carare, which joins the valley of the Magdalena river towards the north-east. It is 60 metres above the bottom of the valley, and has the form of a funnel, the upper diameter of which measures 200 metres, and the lower 50 metres. On the side towards the mountain it reaches a depth of about 120 metres, but on the opposite side only 20 or 30 metres; its walls are very steeply inclined. The rock in which the mine is excavated is a dark bituminous limestone; this rests on red sandstone and clay-slates, and contains ammonites, which show it to be of Lower Cretaceous (Neocomian) age.

The emeralds are found in this rock in " horizontal veins," or, more correctly speaking, in single nests embedded in calcite, which is either dark and bituminous or water-clear like Iceland-spar. A crystal of emerald in such a matrix is represented in Plate XII., Fig. 1. Associated with it are very fine crystals of quartz, some water-clear and others green; also brilliant, well-developed crystals of iron-pyrites, having the form of pentagonal dodecahedra, green gypsum, rhombohedra of black dolomite, and finally crystals of parisite, a fluo-carbonate of cerium and other rare metals, named after Paris, by whom the mine was re-discovered, and who held a lease of it for many years.

The emeralds are usually of the finest dark green colour, but paler or almost colourless stones are also found, as well as crystals which are quite black, the latter being specially remarkable for their velvety lustre. Occasionally crystals are found which are green on the exterior but colourless inside. The crystals are classified for trade purposes according to transparency and depth of colour. Almost all have the simple form of a six-sided prism with basal plane (Figs. 62 *a*, and 63). They rarely exceed the size of a man's thumb, and are usually smaller. Frequently they are broken across in one or more places, the cracks being filled up with thin layers of calcite, so that as long as the crystal remains in its matrix it appears whole and unbroken, the fracture only becoming evident when the crystal is detached from the matrix. Together with the well-formed crystals are found rounded fragments of emerald, a fact which affords a certain support to the theory that the calcite veins are not the primary situation of the emeralds, but that they have been washed into these veins from gneissic or granitic rocks.

Some crystals have the peculiarity of falling to pieces, with no apparent cause, after being taken from the mine. It has been sought to avoid this by placing the emeralds when first unearthed in a closed box, thus protecting them for a few days from the action of light and allowing them to dry slowly. This device is not, however, as a rule, successful. Moreover, most of the emeralds which come from the mine clear, transparent, and free from fissures, in course of time lose their transparency and assume the usual turbidity of this stone owing to the development of fissures within them. In this connection we may recall the statement that emeralds, both from this and from other localities, only acquire their own particular hardness after they have been taken from the mine for some time. Fine emeralds suitable for use as gems are known in Colombia as "canutillos," and poorer stones as "morallion."

Since there is nothing to indicate in what part of the mine emeralds are likely to occur, the workers simply loosen blocks of rock from any part of the walls until a nest of emeralds, the presence of which is indicated by green quartz crystals, is met with. This is then carefully broken out and taken away. The material loosened from the walls of the mine is allowed to fall to the bottom, and when it has accumulated to a certain extent it is washed out into a canal constructed for this purpose, by the sudden fall of a head of water stored on the heights above the mine. The canal empties itself into the Minero, which carries the mine débris still further away. This is the method adopted at the present day, but in former times when the Spaniards were in possession the workings were all underground.

The only other locality of importance for emeralds beside Colombia is the **Ural Mountains.** There is here only one mine from which emeralds are obtained, the same in which Uralian chrysoberyl, that is to say, alexandrite, is found. It is situated on the right bank of the Takovaya, a tributary stream of the Bolshoi Reft (that is to say, Great Reft) which flows into the Pyshma, eighty-five versts (about fifty-seven miles) east of Ekaterinburg.

The finest of the Uralian emeralds are quite equal in transparency and beauty of colour to South American stones. In this, as in other localities, perfect crystals are rare, the majority being fissured and opaque, and the colour, in many cases, being irregularly distributed or too pale. The crystals commonly have the form of a hexagonal prism, often terminated irregularly, but sometimes with a basal plane like Colombian crystals; other forms scarcely ever occur. In size Uralian emeralds often exceed those from other localities, especially South America. Some of exceptional size have already been mentioned; the largest have a length of 40 centimetres (15¾ inches), and a thickness of 25 centimetres, but they are not, as a rule, of good quality.

The mode of occurrence of the emerald in the Urals is similar to that in Egypt, but differs from that in Colombia. The stones are found embedded in a mica-schist, which is interfoliated with chlorite-schist; this is also the mode of occurrence at Habachthal in the Salzburg Alps. A crystal of emerald in a matrix of mica-schist from the latter locality is represented in Plate XII., Fig. 2. Scales of mica are found on the surface of, or inclosed in, emerald crystals from all these localities. Uralian crystals occur singly or in groups; they are often grown together in parallel position, but occasionally radial aggregates of columnar crystals are met with.

The emerald locality on the Takovaya was discovered accidentally in 1830, a peasant noticing a few small green stones among the roots of a tree torn up by the wind. These stones were picked up and taken to Ekaterinburg, where the gem-cutting works of the Czarina, Catharine II., had been established as far back as 1755, and where the many beautiful stones found in the Urals were and are still worked. After this the locality was carefully examined, and a mine opened in the mica-schist. With the emeralds found in this rock are associated alexandrite, phenakite, apatite, rutile, fluor-spar, and other minerals, besides another variety of beryl, the pale-coloured aquamarine. Emerald was at first comparatively abundant at this locality, the yield, however, has gradually fallen both in quality and quantity, and the mines are by no means in full work. They have recently (1900) been rented by a British company ; the venture, owing mainly to theft of stones, has not, however, been successful.

This is the only spot in the Urals at which emeralds occur in large numbers. Only once has a finely coloured and transparent stone been found elsewhere, namely, in the gold-sands in the valley of the stream Shemeika, in the Ekaterinburg mining district. The emeralds reported by the ancients to come from Scythian lands may actually have been found in the Urals, but nothing is exactly known as to their origin.

The occurrence of emerald in the **Salzburg** Alps is similar to that at Takovaya ; the crystals found at the former locality are, however, smaller, and their lustre less brilliant, so that from a trade point of view they are unimportant. The spot at which they are found lies above the Sedlalp (or Söllalp) on a steep wall of rock, the " Smaragd-Palfen," on the east slopes of the Legbach ravine, a side branch of the Habachthal. It is 7500 feet above sea-level and very inaccessible. The deposit is not rich enough to justify any extensive workings ; the stones have been mined by irregular methods and at the risk of the workers' lives for a long period, it is said since the time of the Romans.

Here also the form taken by the emerald crystals is that of a hexagonal prism, and on the surface of the crystals scales of mica and needles of black tourmaline are often to be seen. In colour the crystals are sometimes of a fine, dark emerald-green, but more often of a pale grass-green or greenish-white ; moreover, the colour is frequently irregularly distributed. Perfectly transparent crystals are rare, the majority are turbid, semi-transparent, or translucent to opaque, only a small proportion being fit for use as gems. The white or pale-coloured crystals are usually larger and purer than the green ones. The crystals vary from a line to an inch in length and from $\frac{1}{8}$ to 3 lines in thickness ; stones exceeding these dimensions are exceptional. The mother-rock in which the crystals are embedded is a finely granular mica-schist, dark-brown or greenish in colour and resembling clay-slate ; it is interfoliated with a green mica-schist, which is rich, in some places, in chlorite, and in others in hornblende. A crystal from this locality is shown in its matrix in Plate XII., Fig. 2. Iron-pyrites occurs in association with the emeralds. The finest and largest stones are said to be found in comparatively thin veins of mica with a thickness of about 1 to 3 inches.

Besides the locality described above, there are a few other places in the neighbourhood at which emeralds are found ; none, however, are of any importance.

Among other European emerald localities we may briefly mention Eidsvold, on the southern end of Mjösen lake in Norway. The crystals, which are here embedded in granite, are nearly all turbid and pale in colour, and are therefore not, as a rule, cut as gems.

All emerald localities other than those which have been mentioned are unimportant, and it would seem that in some supposed localities the occurrence of emerald is doubtful. Thus, for example, it appears that there has been no well-authenticated occurrence of emerald in India or Burma, although both countries are often described as emerald localities. The green stones, the occurrence of which in Rajputana, in north-west India, is fairly authentic, may very possibly be chrysoberyl.   The emerald is a stone which is highly prized in India, but the emeralds now in the country were probably brought either from South America or perhaps from the Urals.   This is probably the history of the emeralds which are now exhibited in the collection of jewellery in the Indian Section of the Victoria and Albert Museum, South Kensington.   Among the Burmese regalia there exhibited is a fine slice, about 2 inches across, of a large hexagonal crystal of emerald.   At the present day a large number of emeralds are sent from London to India, and it is also stated that South American stones are sent direct to India to be cut after the manner customary in that country, after which they are placed on the market as stones of Indian origin.

Emerald is said to occur as pebbles in Algeria, namely, in the Harrach and Bouman rivers, and also *in situ* in the neighbourhood, but according to other statements the mineral in question is green tourmaline.

The emerald localities in **Australia** are not important.   Mount Remarkable in South Australia is one, and there are a few in New South Wales.   At one of these, nine miles north-east of the township of Emmaville in the County of Gough, N.S.W., mining operations, first for tin-stone and then for emerald, have been carried on, not apparently, however, with very successful results.   The emeralds are found here in a pegmatite vein, which is an offshoot from a mass of granite penetrating clay-slates, probably of Carboniferous age.   The associated minerals are topaz, fluor-spar, cassiterite, and mispickel.   The colour of these emeralds ranges from a pale shade of green to a moderately bright grass- or emerald-green; the crystals never have any great depth of colour, and they resemble beryl almost more closely than typical emerald.   The largest crystal which had been found previous to 1891 measured $1\frac{1}{4}$ inches in length, and the largest faceted stone weighed $2\frac{1}{8}$ carats.

A number of fine emeralds have been found in North America.   Small crystals have been met with at numerous places in the eastern parts of the **United States**.   In the State of North Carolina they occur in druses in gneiss at many places in Alexander County, and especially at Stony Point.   Here also are to be found other varieties of precious beryl, together with hiddenite, the so-called " lithia-emerald."   During the course of a few years stones to the value of 15,000 dollars (about £3000) were obtained at this spot by the Emerald and Hiddenite Mining Company; at the present time, however, the mine appears to be exhausted.   Only a few of the emeralds found here were suitable for cutting as gems; the largest and finest stone found yielded a faceted gem weighing 6 carats.   Russell Gap Road in the same county is also mentioned as a place where emeralds have been found.   A few good crystals have been met with near Haddam in Connecticut, and near Topsham in Maine, but the occurrence of emerald as a whole in North America has only local significance.

In former times Brazil was considered to be a country in which fine emeralds abounded, and after the Portuguese conquest strenuous efforts were made to discover naturally occurring stones.   Not a single emerald, however, has been found in this country, and it seems probable that green tourmaline, which abounds in Brazil, was mistaken for emerald.

It is certain that in ancient times the name emerald was applied loosely to a large number of green stones, such, for example, as green jasper, chrysocolla, malachite, and others.   Even at the present day the name with a distinguishing prefix is applied to several green stones; thus "oriental emerald" is green corundum; "lithia-emerald" is hiddenite, a green mineral belonging to the pyroxene group and found with the true emerald in North Carolina; "emerald-copper" is dioptase, a beautiful green silicate of copper. The two latter are both used as precious stones.

The green minerals which are sometimes substituted for the emerald, and which may be mistaken for it, include green corundum, known as "oriental emerald," green garnet, known as demantoid, hiddenite, diopside, alexandrite, green tourmaline, and perhaps also chrysolite and dioptase. Each of these minerals has a higher specific gravity than the emerald; each sinks in liquid No. 3, and some even in the heaviest liquid, while the emerald floats in both. Moreover, the "oriental emerald" is much harder; the demantoid, the colour of which has usually a yellowish tinge though sometimes very similar to that of the emerald, is singly refracting. Hiddenite is very rare, and is considered to be more valuable than the emerald; it is used as a gem practically in America only. Diopside is much more of a bottle-green colour than is the emerald. Alexandrite is distinguished from emerald by its hardness and its remarkable dichroism. The colour of green tourmaline, though often not dissimilar to that of pale emeralds, is frequently distinctly bluish in character; this mineral is easily distinguished from emerald, however, by its specific gravity, which is 3·07, slightly greater than that of liquid No. 3, in which, therefore, it sinks. Chrysolite is yellowish-green, and can be distinguished from emerald by its colour and its faint dichroism. Finally dioptase is always of a very dark emerald-green colour; it is only semi-transparent and far softer than the emerald. A more detailed account of the characters by which the emerald may be distinguished from other green stones which resemble it more or less in appearance is given in Table 14, Part III. of this book.

A glass of a fine emerald-green colour may be obtained by fusing together 4608 parts of strass, 42 parts of pure copper oxide (CuO), and 2 parts of chromic oxide. It differs from emerald in being optically isotropic, in the absence of any trace of dichroism, and in being much softer. An imitation of emerald which contains from 7 to 8 per cent. of beryllia is sometimes put on the market at the present time. It has a fine emerald-green colour, but is not perfectly transparent; it encloses numerous small air-bubbles and is not dichroic; its specific gravity is 3·19. It is obvious that we have here a glass to which beryllia has been added in order to give it a chemical composition similar to that of true emerald.

PRECIOUS BERYL.

AQUAMARINE, "AQUAMARINE-CHRYSOLITE," AND GOLDEN BERYL.

There are several colour-varieties of transparent, precious beryl. The most typical colours are the light blue, greenish-blue, or bluish-green of aquamarine, the yellowish-green of "aquamarine-chrysolite," and the yellow of yellow beryl, or golden beryl as the finest specimens are called. Rose-red and colourless beryl is less common, and is not, as a rule, faceted. These varieties differ from the emerald in colour; they are also, as a rule, richer in faces, as shown in Fig. 62, *b* to *e*, and in Plate XII., Figs. 4 and 5, the emerald, as already noticed, seldom showing forms other than the simple combination of a hexagonal prism and basal plane (Fig. 62 *a*). In the following pages aquamarine will be fully dealt with and other varieties somewhat briefly, since they do not differ essentially from aquamarine in character or mode and place of occurrence.

Aquamarine is characterised by a pure sky-blue, bluish-green, or greenish-blue colour, very similar to the tint of sea-water; hence its name, and the old saying that this stone when placed in the sea becomes invisible. Aquamarine of a deep shade of colour is very rare; it is found, in small amount and of a fine deep, sapphire-blue, at Royalston in Massachusetts, U.S.A. A distinction is sometimes made between sky-blue beryl and beryl of a greenish-blue or bluish-green colour, the former being considered as aquamarine proper, (Plate XII., Fig. 7), and the latter referred to as Siberian aquamarine. All pale bluish and greenish beryls are, as a rule, however, included in the term aquamarine.

The colours shown by precious beryl, and especially by aquamarine, are fine and brilliant, and their beauty is still more noticeable in artificial light. The colour in every case is supposed to be due not to chromium, as in the emerald, but to iron, which is always present to the extent of $\frac{1}{2}$ to 2 per cent. Experiments have been made to test the stability of the colour of common greenish and yellow beryl from granite in the neighbourhood of Dublin. After an hour's exposure to a temperature of $357°$ the crystals were observed to be still translucent, but to have lost all their colour. When the crystals were fused a colourless, cloudy mass was obtained.

The dichroism of aquamarine of a sufficiently deep colour is appreciable; of the two images seen in the dichroscope, one is a pure but pale blue and the other very pale yellowish-green, almost colourless. The dichroism of specimens of a still deeper colour can be observed with the naked eye.

Aquamarine, and indeed all precious beryl, is, as a rule, very uniformly coloured, irregularities in the distribution or character of the colouring being rare. Flawless and perfectly transparent stones are also very much less rare than are emeralds of the same description; fissures and turbid or cloudy patches are sometimes to be seen, however. These latter are caused by the enclosure of numerous microscopically small cavities closely aggregated and either empty or containing a liquid. When these cloudy patches are present it is impossible to produce a good polish, although beryl, free from such faults, is susceptible of a very brilliant polish. In some crystals transparent and cloudy portions alternate, in which case the latter must be removed by cutting before the former can be utilised.

Precious beryl, including aquamarine, is, as a rule, cut in the brilliant form or in some modification of the step-cut (Plate XII., Figs. 6 and 7). On account of the paleness of its colour the cut stone must have a certain depth or it will show too faint a colour. The lustre and colour of beryls is often improved by the use of foils; thus aquamarine is placed upon a silver foil or is mounted in a closed setting with a black lining. Very beautiful stones with not too pale a colour are mounted in an open setting (à jour). A magnificent faceted aquamarine, weighing $179\frac{1}{2}$ grams ($875\frac{1}{2}$ carats), is to be seen in the mineral collection of the British Museum.

Crystals of beryl often have the form of long and relatively thin prisms, and in correlation with this the girdle of the faceted stone has often an elongated outline. Large prisms of beryl are often cut in the East into dagger-handles and other articles of considerable size. In gems of such an elongated form the direction of greatest length coincides with the direction of the principal axis of the crystal, and the stone is set in such a position that its dichroism is most apparent. Aquamarine has been, and is, much used as a vehicle for the expression of the engraver's art; its comparative softness renders the work less arduous than is the case with many other precious stones. It is said that in ancient times beryl was the material of which the lenses for spectacles were constructed, and that from this originated the German word " Brille " (spectacles).

Transparent, finely coloured and flawless crystals of precious beryl, specially of aquamarine of considerable size, are by no means uncommon. Prisms of beryl of gem quality, and of the length and thickness of a man's thumb, are frequently met with, and the discovery of still larger specimens is not unusual. In his work on precious stones, Barbot, the late Parisian jeweller, mentions a rough aquamarine of rare beauty of which the weight was about 10 kilograms (22 pounds), and for which 15,000 francs (£600) was asked. Again, a beautiful grass-green beryl, weighing 15 pounds, was found, in 1811, in Minas Novas, Brazil, and similar finds are often reported. It is not surprising, then, to find aquamarine and the precious beryls generally among the lowest priced gems, a carat stone of medium quality being obtainable for a few shillings. Only those stones which are exceptionally beautiful in colour and perfect in every other respect command higher prices, and even these fall far short of the value of a fair emerald. In this connection it may be mentioned that the value of beryl, unlike that of emerald, is proportional to the size of the stone.

Precious beryl, and especially aquamarine, is a mineral of somewhat wide distribution, occurring in gem-quality at many localities. Like the emerald it is met with, for the most part, in its primary situation in druses in coarse-grained granite and similar rocks. Its occurrence in secondary deposits, such as gem-gravels, is less usual, but not so rare as is the case with emerald.

Brazil is a country in which fine beryl is abundant. The stones are often cut before they are exported, but as the form they are given leaves much to be desired they are usually re-cut when they reach Europe. The mineral is found in great abundance, associated with chrysoberyl, white and blue topaz, &c., as pebbles in the sands of the Minas Novas district in the north-east corner of the State of Minas Geraes; also, though sparingly, associated with diamond in the diamond-sands of the same State. These localities, which have been already mentioned under chrysoberyl, will be described in greater detail when Brazilian topaz is under consideration. Among the pebbles of aquamarine are sometimes some of considerable size; one weighing 15 pounds, which was found in the year 1811 near the source of the Rio S. Matheus, in Minas Novas, has been already mentioned. Another fine pebble weighing 4 pounds was found soon after at the same place; but, as a rule, the pebbles are much smaller, their greatest diameter being no more than from 2 to 5 lines. The character of the rock in which the pebbles were originally formed is not certainly known; it is probably, however, a coarse-grained granite, since aquamarine is often found in a similar situation, and other precious stones found in Minas Novas are known to have been formed in a rock of this description.

In the neighbourhood of Rio de Janeiro aquamarine occurs in coarse-grained granite veins penetrating gneiss. At Vallongo in the year 1825 a fine crystal, weighing 4 pounds and valued at £600, was found. Previous to this had been found at the same place a transparent, faultless stone, which measured 7 inches in length and 9 lines in thickness.

Beryl is abundant also in the Ural Mountains and elsewhere in Siberia. At many places crystals of gem-quality, associated, as in Brazil, with topaz, are to be found, so that the importance of Siberia as a locality for beryl is comparable to that of Brazil.

In the **Urals** it is found at various places in the neighbourhood of Ekaterinburg in the Government of Perm, also on the Ilmen Lake near the Ilmen Mountains, as well as in gold-washings on the Sanarka river in the Southern Urals, the two latter localities being in the Government of Orenburg.

In the Ekaterinburg district it is found principally in the neighbourhood of the villages of Mursinka (Mursinsk) and Shaitanka (Shaitansk), occurring in drusy cavities in coarse-grained granite, which is penetrated by veins of fine-grained granite.

The finest beryl to be found in the Urals occurs in the neighbourhood of Mursinka. It is usually in transparent, well-developed hexagonal prisms, which may be wine-yellow, greenish-yellow, yellowish-green, bluish-green, or pale blue in colour, and which range in length from a few millimetres to three decimetres (1 foot). The crystals are, as a rule, single, but intergrowths are occasionally met with in which the crystals are arranged irregularly or in parallel position. A group of fine yellowish-green or asparagus-green crystals, perfectly transparent and grown together in parallel position, was found in 1828. The group, which measures 27 centimetres in length and 31·2 centimetres in circumference,

is now in the collection of the Imperial Institute of Mines at St. Petersburg, and has been valued at 43,000 roubles (£6800). The cavities in the rock, to the walls of which the crystals are attached, are usually filled with brown clay, and the presence of this substance is considered to indicate that beryl is to be found not far away. Associated with the beryl are quartz, felspar, mica, and black tourmaline, also topaz and amethyst, of which more will be said later. There are numerous pits or mines from which these variously coloured stones are won. For the most part the stones are worked in the gem-cutting establishments of Ekaterinburg. Formerly all the mines clustered round the village of Mursinka, but later other mines were opened in the neighbourhood of the villages of Alabashka, Sisikova, Yushakova, Sarapulskaya, and others, the population of which consists almost exclusively of gem-seekers. The beryls of Shaitanka were known as far back as the year 1815; they are all colourless or of a pale rose shade, and therefore of less importance as gem-stones.

FIG. 63a.   Occurrence of beryl near Mursinka, Urals.
(Scale, 1 : 125,000.)

Magnificent specimens from this and other localities are to be seen and admired in all mineral collections. The position of the mines in the neighbourhood of Mursinka is shown in the accompanying map (Fig. 63a), of which more will be said when amethyst is dealt with.

The pale apple-green beryls which accompany the emerald at Takovaya are of less value. Those found on the Ilmen Lake also are only in part of gem-quality. They occur on the eastern shores of this lake, six versts (four miles) north-east of the smelting works of Miask in the Ilmen Mountains, and to the south of Ekaterinburg, in the Zlatoust mining district, latitude about 55° N. Crystals of beryl from this locality sometimes reach a length of 25 centimetres; they are bluish-green inclining to leek-green in colour, much fissured, and, as a rule, only translucent. They occur, together with topaz crystals, also fissured, and green felspar (amazon-stone), in pegmatite veins penetrating the rock known as miascite.

The occurrence of beryl in the gold-washings of the Sanarka river in the Southern Urals is also of small importance; here the mineral is found as pebbles associated with topaz, chrysoberyl, &c.

The beryl of the **Altai Mountains** is distinguished less for the beauty of its crystals than for their size, prisms with a length of 1 metre (39⅓ inches) and a thickness of 15 centimetres being met with. These crystals, which have the usual form, namely, a hexagonal prism terminated by a basal plane perpendicular to the prism planes (Figs. 62a, and 63), range from sky-blue to greenish-blue in colour, and occur in brown, much fissured quartz, the exact locality being a spot in the Tigirezh Mountains. The mineral is here at the best only translucent, and therefore rarely of use as a gem.

Of greater importance is the occurrence of beryl in the Nerchinsk district of the province of **Transbaikalia** in south-east Siberia, Nerchinsk itself being in longitude 116° E. of Greenwich on the upper course of the Shilka river, a tributary of the Amur. There are here two stretches of country in which beryl, and especially aquamarine, abounds, the one being the mountain range Adun-Chalon and its southern continuation, the mountains of Kuchuserken, and the other the neighbourhood of the Urulga river on the northern side of the Borshchovochnoi Mountains.

The variously coloured precious stones which occur at Adun-Chalon (Adun-Tschilon) have been known since the year 1723. The output of gems from these deposits was formerly very considerable; it reached its highest in the year 1796, when no less than 5 poods (180 pounds) of pure aquamarine, suitable for cutting as gems, was obtained. The crystals of beryl are found here attached to the walls of cavities in a topaz-rock, which consists mainly of finely granular quartz and small topaz crystals, and occurs as veins penetrating the granite. The aquamarine in these cavities is accompanied by topaz and smoky-quartz, frequently also by other minerals. The highest mountain of the Adun-Chalon range has two peaks, separated by a narrow valley. The western peak is known as Hoppevskaya Gora, that is to say, Schörl Mountain; it consists almost entirely of topaz-rock, and is scarred from foot to summit with the workings of gem-seekers. The mineral is by no means, however, confined to this mountain, numerous mines being scattered about an area of two square versts in the neighbourhood. These mines are nothing but open pits or trenches of the most primitive kind, without timbering, and never more than three fathoms in depth; from these, short tunnels are worked in the rock in all directions. Immediately beneath the turf covering the southern slopes of the Hoppevskaya Gora is a layer of loose material, containing much iron-ochre, derived from the weathering of the topaz-rock. In this layer fine specimens of aquamarine, and its customary associate topaz, are to be found. A hexagonal prism of transparent beryl, 31 centimetres (over 1 foot) in length and 5 centimetres in diameter, from Adun-Chalon, is preserved in the British Museum collection of minerals.

The beryls of Adun-Chalon differ from the smooth-faced prisms of the Urals and of the Borshchovochnoi Mountains (or Urulga river) in that the prism-faces are deeply striated (Fig. 62 d). The crystals are, as a rule, greenish-blue in colour, but sky-blue, yellowish-green, wine-yellow, and colourless specimens are met with; and every degree of transparency is represented. The crystals are often united in groups, which are frequently invested with a thin surface layer of iron-ochre, the substance with which the drusy cavities are, as a rule, filled.

The country between the rivers Shilka and Unda in the Borshchovochnoi Mountains abounds with fine beryl. A large amount of the mineral was obtained about the middle of the nineteenth century, for the most part from the granite mountains which border the Urulga river, a tributary of the Shilka on its right bank. Beryls from the neighbourhood of the Urulga are remarkable for their size, transparency, and beautiful colour. The majority are yellowish-green, the remainder being variously tinted or colourless. The crystals may reach a length of 10 centimetres and a thickness half as great; they are frequently developed with great regularity. Beryl from the Urulga river is in general very similar to that from Mursinka in the Urals.

In other parts of Asia precious beryl occurs but sparingly. Aquamarine has been found at some places in **India,** and various objects worked in this mineral have not infrequently been found in ancient tombs, temples, &c. Most of it appears to have been obtained in the Coimbatore district of the Madras Presidency, as at Paddur or Patialey, where, at the beginning of the nineteenth century, the mineral was obtained from cavities in a coarse-grained granite. When all the more easily obtained stones had been taken, work was abandoned. Later on, aquamarine was discovered at Kangayam in the same district; specimens from this locality were shown at the Vienna Exhibition of 1873, and others are preserved in the British Museum. Here was once found a stone of the most perfect transparency, which weighed 184 grains (900 carats) and sold for £500.

Pale blue crystals of fair size, sometimes measuring as much as $3\frac{1}{4}$ inches in length, are found at many places in the Punjab in granite veins penetrating gneiss. They are, however, almost invariably much fissured and unsuitable for gems. In the Jaipur State in Rajputana aquamarine is mined in the neighbourhood of Toda Rai Sing in the Ajmer district, in the Tonk Hills, and at various places lying within a radius of 38 miles from Rajmahal on the Banas river. Most of these crystals are quite small and therefore, in spite of their fine colour, of little value. They are found buried in marshy ground, and have probably been derived from the granite veins which penetrate the sedimentary rocks of Rajputana in large numbers. Small crystals of yellow beryl occur embedded in a thick vein in the Hazaribagh district in Bengal. Other reputed Indian localities require authenticating.

In Burma, pebbles of aquamarine are reported to have been found in the Irrawaddy. Whether this is so or not, it is certain that beryl is of only sparing occurrence in Burma; while in Ceylon, a locality so rich in other precious stones, it is practically non-existent.

Although in **Europe** many localities for common beryl are known, precious beryl of gem quality occurs but sparingly. In the Mourne Mountains, in County Down, Ireland, crystals of aquamarine of a beautiful and comparatively deep blue colour occur, together with topaz, in cavities in granite; these, however, are rarely perfectly transparent.

In the **United States** of North America numerous localities are known, from which fine stones of various colours, and of a quality suitable for cutting, have been obtained. The mineral is found, for example, with the emerald in Alexander County, North Carolina, while at Russell Gap Road, in the same county, more aquamarine of gem quality was found than anywhere else in the United States. Fine blue aquamarine is found also in Mitchell County, North Carolina, and green beryl at Stoneham, in Oxford County, Maine; a fine bluish-green fragment, found recently at the latter place, gave an almost faultless brilliant, weighing $133\frac{3}{4}$ carats, and measuring 35 millimetres in length and breadth and 20 millimetres in thickness. Golden-yellow beryl of good quality is found at Albany in Maine, in Coosa County in Alabama, and at a few other places. At Royalston in Massachusetts there occur, with other varieties of precious beryl, some of a fine blue colour comparable to the blue of the sapphire; it is by far the most beautiful blue beryl known, but, unfortunately, occurs only in quite small crystals. Beryl is also found in Colorado, namely, on Mount Antero, ten miles north of Salida, at a height of 12,000 to 14,000 feet above sea-level. The crystals, which range in colour from a pale to a dark shade of blue, are found, together with phenakite and other minerals, attached to the walls of drusy cavities in granite. They vary in length from 1 to 4 inches, and in thickness from $\frac{1}{10}$ inch to an inch; from the largest a faceted stone of about 5 carats can be cut. There are many other localities in America at which beryl is found, but none of any commercial importance.

A small amount of beryl occurs also in Australia; at several places in New South Wales for example. Here, again, the occurrence has no economic significance.

Precious beryl of a yellow colour, and also the yellowish-green "**aquamarine-chrysolite**," come principally from Brazil, although it is to be found in good quality at some of the localities already mentioned, for example, in Siberia associated with aquamarine. Beryl of a deep, pure yellow, such as is represented in Plate XII., Fig. 4, is known as **golden beryl**. It occurs at many beryl localities in North America, especially at Albany in Maine; it has been collected also in the vicinity of New York City, and in Litchfield County, Connecticut. It is always of sparing occurrence in the States, and, though highly prized there, does not in general command high prices, only exceptionally fine stones costing more than a few shillings per carat.

Certain of the several varieties of precious beryl are liable to be mistaken for other precious stones which they resemble in appearance; the exceptionally low specific gravity of beryl, however, prevents any serious confusion. Aquamarine resembles in colour " oriental aquamarine," euclase, some tourmalines, and blue topaz; its resemblance to blue topaz is so close that the latter is often known in the trade as aquamarine. Each of the four stones mentioned above, however, sinks in liquid No. 3 (sp. gr. = 3·0), while beryl floats. In the same way yellow beryl, that is to say, " aquamarine-chrysolite " and golden beryl, may be distinguished from other yellow and greenish-yellow stones of similar appearance, namely, from yellow topaz, " oriental topaz," " oriental chrysolite," chrysolite, and chrysoberyl, all of which sink in liquid No. 3. To distinguish between yellow beryl and yellow quartz (citrine) is less easy, for there is no great difference between the hardness and specific gravity of these two minerals. In liquid No. 4 (sp. gr. = 2·65) citrine remains suspended while beryl slowly sinks; moreover, a smooth surface of quartz will be untouched by citrine, but will be distinctly, though not deeply, scratched by beryl. The stronger dichroism of beryl may also serve sometimes to distinguish it from citrine.

A glass resembling aquamarine in colour may be obtained by fusing together 3456 parts of strass, 24 parts of glass of antimony, and $1\frac{1}{2}$ parts of cobalt oxide. The single refraction, entire absence of dichroism, and low degree of hardness of this imitation, are the characters whereby it is distinguished from genuine aquamarine.

EUCLASE.

Euclase is one of the rarest of minerals and is only occasionally cut as a gem, when it commands fancy prices. It resembles beryl, and specially aquamarine, in many ways; its chemical composition, for example, differs from that of beryl only in the presence of a little water and in the proportions of the constituents, its chemical formula being $H_2O.2BeO.Al_2O_3.2SiO_2$.

The mineral crystallises in the monoclinic system. The crystals are prismatic in habit and the prism faces are deeply striated parallel to their mutual intersections; they are terminated at the two ends by obliquely placed faces, as shown in Fig. 64. The crystals have a perfect cleavage parallel to their one plane of symmetry; this cleavage plane truncates the two acute edges of the rhombic prism. Owing to the perfect cleavage, crystals of euclase are liable to become fissured and then broken, and when being cut, unless exceptional care is taken, they chip at the edges.

The mineral has a hardness (H = $7\frac{1}{2}$) slightly exceeding that of beryl; it is somewhat heavy, having a specific gravity of 3·05 to 3·10; when rubbed it acquires a not inconsiderable charge of electricity. Its lustre is vitreous, but in the direction of cleavage is sometimes pearly; the mineral is susceptible of a high polish and is frequently perfectly clear and transparent. Its refraction, double refraction, and dispersion are all small. Its colour resembles in many respects that of precious beryl, being either green with a tinge of blue (Plate XIII., Fig. 5), or green with a yellowish tinge; it is almost invariably pale in shade, deeply coloured stones being rare and perfectly colourless ones quite unusual. Stones of a rather deep blue-green colour, as represented in the plate just quoted, are most admired; they resemble some aquamarines and blue topaz very closely, but may be easily distinguished from either of these by the difference in the specific gravity and by the existence of a distinct dichroism in euclase.

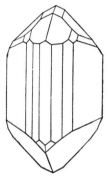

FIG. 64. Crystalline form of euclase.

Very few localities for euclase are known, and nowhere is it found in abundance. It was first met with in Brazil, in the neighbourhood of Ouro Preto (formerly known as Villa Rica), in Minas Geraes. It occurs here, associated with yellow topaz, in nests in the quartz veins by which the clay-slates, which accompany itacolumite, are traversed. It would appear, however, that topaz and euclase are never found actually side by side in the same nest or druse. The principal locality is Boa Vista, near Ouro Preto (Fig. 67). A euclase weighing over $1\frac{1}{2}$ pounds was reported by L. von Eschwege from this district, but the majority of the stones found there are much smaller, and, moreover, they are often broken into fragments along the cleavage plane.

Euclase is also found in the gold-washings of the Sanarka river in the Ural Mountains, situated in the Government of Orenburg. It occurs here in loose crystals, many of which, as in Brazil, are merely cleavage fragments; they may reach a length of $1\frac{1}{2}$ inches, but, as a rule, are much smaller. They vary in colour from grass-green to greenish-blue, and are associated with topaz, chrysoberyl, and other minerals.

Small crystals of euclase, of a pale yellowish colour, have been found in recent years in mica-schist in the Grossglockner district of the Austrian Alps; this occurrence, however, is solely of mineralogical interest.

PHENAKITE.

Like euclase, phenakite has but little importance as a gem. It contains beryllia but no alumina, being a silicate of beryllia with the chemical formula $2BeO.SiO_2$. It crystallises in the rhombohedral system, and the crystals, which are hemihedral with parallel faces, usually have the form of hexagonal prisms terminated by the faces of a rhombohedron or of a hexagonal pyramid, sometimes also by small faces of other forms, as shown in Fig. 65, a to c.

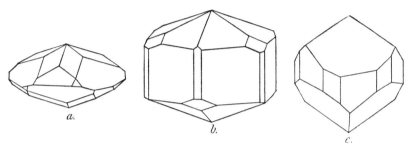

a. *b.* *c.*

FIG. 65. Crystalline forms of phenakite.

The cleavage of phenakite is very imperfect and its fracture is conchoidal. Its hardness $(H = 7\frac{1}{2} - 8)$ is slightly greater than that of either beryl or euclase; while its specific gravity (sp. gr. = 2·95 to 3·0) is rather less than that of euclase, and the mineral just floats in liquid No. 3.

The lustre of a fractured surface of phenakite is brilliant and vitreous; that of the natural crystal faces is usually, however, much duller. It is susceptible of a very brilliant polish, and has then a lustre comparable to that of the sapphire. The mineral is frequently water-clear, but may be cloudy or only translucent. Usually it is colourless, but yellow, brown, and rose-red phenakite have been found. Except for its brilliant lustre, colourless, water-clear phenakite resembles rock-crystal in appearance; the refraction and double refraction of the two stones are very much the same, the former being a little greater and the latter a little less in phenakite. Water-clear phenakites, and indeed all stones of this description, are cut in the brilliant form, a form which displays the lustre and brilliancy of the stone to the best advantage. A phenakite brilliant has certain resemblances to the diamond, but never shows the brilliant play of prismatic colours characteristic of this gem. Two very fine faceted phenakites, weighing 43 and 34 carats respectively, are exhibited in the British Museum of Natural History.

Phenakite is a less rare mineral than is euclase, but the number of localities at which it is found is almost as limited as for euclase. The white phenakite, which occurs with emerald and alexandrite embedded in mica-schist at Takovaya in the Ekaterinburg district of the Urals was the first to be met with. At this locality crystals with a thickness of 10 centimetres and a weight of $1\frac{1}{2}$ pounds are found. Phenakite also occurs with topaz and green felspar (amazon-stone) at Miask, on Lake Ilmen, in the Urals, but this locality is of less importance. The Takovaya stones, those at least which are sufficiently transparent, are usually cut in Ekaterinburg, and are placed on the market at the fairs of Nizhniy Novgorod. Not many of these gems leave Russia, but some find their way to the Orient (Persia, India, &c.), through the dealers who frequent the Nizhniy Novgorod fairs.

Phenakite has been found comparatively recently in North America, chiefly in Colorado. One of the localities in this State is Topaz Butte, near Florissant, sixteen miles from Pike's Peak, where it occurs as flat rhombohedral crystals, and, as at Miask, associated with topaz and amazon-stone in veins penetrating granite. The other locality is Mount Antero, in Chaffee County, ten miles north of Salida, where it occurs as prismatic crystals, sometimes an inch in length, on quartz and beryl. These American phenakites are cut as gems, and are valued on account of their national origin. Other American localities, like the European, have no trade importance. In Europe small brown crystals, scarcely suitable for cutting, were formerly found in the iron mines of Framont, in the Vosges Mountains. The small crystals of phenakite, which have been found in recent years in mica-schist in the Canton Valais in Switzerland, are of mineralogical interest only.

TOPAZ.

Topaz is the most familiar of yellow stones, and for this reason its name is often applied to other minerals of the same colour. Thus, yellow corundum, as we have seen, is known as "oriental topaz," yellow quartz (citrine) is referred to variously as "occidental topaz," "Bohemian topaz," and "Spanish topaz," while yellow fluor-spar is sometimes known as "false topaz." The mineral species to which mineralogists apply the name topaz includes not only the stones known as precious topaz, or as Brazilian, Saxon, Siberian, or Tauridan topaz, but also blue, red, and colourless stones, which are known to dealers in precious stones by other names.

Topaz is a fluo-silicate of aluminium with the formula $(AlF)_2SiO_4$ and the percentage composition of, silica 33·3, alumina 56·5, and fluorine 17·6 ; from this it will be seen that alumina forms a large part of the mineral, as it does also of most of the precious stones hitherto considered. Besides the constituents already mentioned, other substances, such as ferrous oxide, lime, alkalies, water, &c., are sometimes present in small amount. Until recently the water, which is often present, was considered to be an impurity due in part to the alteration of the material by hydration. Penfield and Minor, however, have shown (1894) by a series of carefully conducted analyses combined with detailed determinations of the optical and other physical constants of the mineral, that water is one of its essential constituents and not a mere impurity. The amount of water present in the specimens which they analysed varied from 0·18 to 2·50 per cent. The specimen which contains only 0·18 per cent of water is almost pure fluor-topaz, and its composition is expressed by the formula already given, $(AlF)_2SiO_4$. Specimens containing more water may be regarded as hydro-fluor-topaz, in which the water is present as hydroxyl (OH), which replaces fluorine isomorphously, so that the formula becomes $[Al(F,OH)]_2SiO_4$. A mineral in which the whole of the fluorine is replaced by hydroxyl, and which would have the formula $(Al.OH)_2SiO_4$, has not yet been met with. The isomorphous replacement of fluorine by hydroxyl in this mineral is accompanied by small variations in its physical characters, such as specific gravity, refraction, double refraction, &c. ; these variations are very slight and of purely scientific interest.

Topaz crystallises in the rhombic system ; all crystals have certain features in common, but show differences in habit. A combination of two rhombic prisms forming elongated, eight-sided columns, often deeply striated parallel to their length, is almost invariably to be seen. The terminal faces differ according to the locality from which the crystal comes. As a rule, they are developed regularly at one end only of the crystal, the other end having been attached to the matrix in the drusy cavity in which the crystal grew. A few forms taken by topaz crystals are shown in Fig. 66, *a* to *d.*

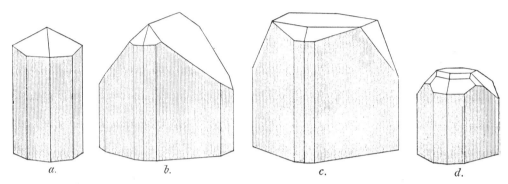

FIG. 66.   Crystalline forms of topaz.

Fig. 66 *a*, and Plate XIII., Figs. 2 and 4, show a simple form of crystal especially characteristic of topaz from Brazil and Asia Minor ; here the only terminal faces are those of a rhombic octahedron or pyramid. In Fig. 66 *b*, the faces of this rhombic octahedron are small, and two large dome faces, give a roof-like termination to the crystal ; this habit is characteristic of topaz crystals from the Adun-Chalon Mountains, near Nerchinsk, in Siberia. Crystals from Mursinka, in the Urals (Fig. 66 *c*, and Plate XIII., Fig. 1), have, in addition to these faces, a largely developed basal plane at right angles to the prism faces. The crystal shown in Fig. 66 *d*, is a combination of two prisms, three rhombic octahedra, a dome, and the basal plane ; this habit is characteristic of crystals from Schneckenstein in Saxony (Plate XIII., Fig. 3). More complicated crystals, with a much larger number of faces, are to be found at other localities ; the examples cited are sufficient, however, to give a general idea of the crystalline forms of topaz.

Crystals of topaz as small as a pin's head have been found, but very large ones weighing several pounds are not at all unusual. Thus, for example, a beautiful transparent crystal of topaz, weighing more than 25 pounds, was found in the neighbourhood of the Urulga river in Siberia. A crystal of topaz, 2 feet in length and 137 pounds in weight, has been found quite recently (1901) in Sætersdalen, Norway, and is now exhibited in the British Museum.

Topaz differs from the majority of precious stones in the possession of a very perfect cleavage. There is only one direction of cleavage, and this is parallel to the basal plane— that is to say, at right angles to the length of the striated prism. In consequence of this cleavage, topaz crystals, when removed from the matrix, almost invariably break away with a smooth, shining, plane face ; the lower ends of the crystals in Fig. 66 are terminated by such cleavage planes. A crystal of topaz, which is too long to be cut as a single stone, may be readily cleaved with a chisel into fragments of suitable size, and thus much laborious work avoided. The drawback connected with this perfect cleavage is that it is the cause of a tendency in the stone to develop plane, even fissures. The presence of such fissures, which is often indicated by brilliant iridescent colours, detracts considerably from the beauty and value of the stone. To avoid the development of these fissures, the stone must

1. Topaz, blue crystal (Urals). 1a. The same, cut. 2. Topaz, dark yellow crystal (Brazil).
2a. The same, cut. 3. Topaz, pale yellow crystal (Saxony). 3a. The same, cut. 4. Topaz,
rose-red crystal (Brazil). 4a. The same, cut. 5. Euclase, crystal (Brazil).

not be allowed to fall or to be jarred in any way; and when undergoing the process of cutting great care is necessary, since the perfect cleavage renders the stone liable to chip at the edges and to become fissured or broken by the jarring of the grinding disc.

The hardness of topaz is represented by 8 on Mohs' scale. It scratches quartz with ease, but is itself readily scratched by corundum. Of the minerals hitherto considered, it is surpassed in hardness only by diamond, corundum, and chrysoberyl. On account of its hardness it takes a good polish and exhibits a brilliant lustre, which is also to be seen on the natural crystal-faces.

Topaz is a comparatively heavy mineral; its specific gravity, determined on different varieties, ranges from 3·50 to 3·57. Colourless topaz is often rather heavier than the coloured varieties; its specific gravity has been determined at from 3·53 to 3·56. This value is almost exactly the same as that of diamond, so that it is impossible by the density alone to distinguish between a diamond and a colourless topaz, which, when cut, have a certain resemblance. The specific gravity of the reddish-yellow topaz of Brazil (Plate XIII., Figs. 2 and 2a) and Asia Minor has been determined to be 3·50 to 3·55, while that of the greenish-blue from Nerchinsk is 3·53. Such small variations in the specific gravity are due to differences in the chemical composition depending upon the replacement of fluorine by hydroxyl. According to some determinations the specific gravity may vary between 3·4 and 3·6; this greater departure from the mean value, 3·5, is probably due either to impurity of material or to inaccuracy of determination.

When rubbed, topaz becomes strongly electrified and capable of attracting to itself any light bodies such as shreds of paper. Some topazes possess this property in a more marked degree than do others; thus, for example, those from Schneckenstein in Saxony acquire a charge of electricity when merely rubbed between the fingers, while in the case of certain Brazilian topazes a pressure of the fingers, exercised in the direction of length of the prismatic crystal, is sufficient; also, when heated and allowed to slowly cool, topaz becomes electrified and acquires a greater charge than would any other precious stone under similar circumstances, with the exception of tourmaline; on this account it is said to be pyroelectric. The charge may be retained for thirty hours or more after the stone has cooled down to its original temperature. This phenomenon, under certain circumstances, affords a means by which topaz may be distinguished from other stones which it may resemble in general appearance.

In the blowpipe flame topaz does not fuse, but becomes cloudy and opaque owing to the loss of water and of fluorine; coloured stones lose their colour. Acids, whether hot or cold, have no action on topaz.

More important than any other feature, however, are the optical characters of topaz, that is to say, its behaviour towards light. In this connection we may begin by distinguishing between cloudy and opaque topaz, the so-called "common" topaz, and that which is clear and transparent, "precious" topaz. The former, besides being opaque, is usually nondescript in colour, so that it is unsuitable for gems. A variety of common topaz, known as pyrophysalite, occurs as large crystals in granite near Fahlun in Sweden; another variety, known as pycnite, is found as columnar aggregates in the tin mines of the Erzgebirge between Bohemia and Saxony. Our attention must be devoted, however, not to these varieties of common topaz but to precious topaz, the transparency, colour, and lustre of which combine to make it a very beautiful gem.

Its lustre is of the ordinary glassy or vitreous type; on the cleavage face, however, it is pearly. The brilliant lustre of the natural crystal-faces has been already mentioned, and is specially noticeable on the prism faces. The lustre of a cut topaz which has been well polished is almost comparable with that of the diamond.

Topaz is not a highly refractive substance, its indices of refraction only slightly exceeding 1·6. Being a rhombic mineral it is doubly refracting, but here again the two indices of refraction differ from each other only slightly, so that the double refraction is not strong. The refractive indices for variously coloured light also differ but slightly, so that the dispersion is likewise small. Very little play of prismatic colours is shown, therefore, by a faceted topaz, which in other respects somewhat resembles the diamond. The greatest, mean, and least value of the refractive index of one and the same crystal for red and for violet light is given in the table below :

Red light	.	·	.	1·618	1·610	1·608
Violet light	.	.	.	1·635	1·627	1·625

These values will differ slightly for other crystals, especially when the latter differ in colour or in place of origin, owing to variations in chemical composition.

The range of colour exhibited by topaz is considerable. The purest variety is perfectly **colourless** and pellucid, and is of frequent occurrence. It is found as crystals at Miask, in the Urals, among other places, and in still greater abundance, in the form of rounded, water-worn pebbles, in the streams and rivers of Diamantina and specially of Minas Novas, in the State of Minas Geraes, Brazil. These pebbles, which are met with also in Australia, especially in New South Wales, are often perfectly colourless and transparent, and are then known to the Brazilians as "*pingos d'agoa*" (drops of water). Colourless topaz is sometimes known to the trade as "*goutte d'eau*," the French equivalent of the term.

The "Braganza," a supposed diamond belonging to the Portuguese crown jewels and weighing 1680 carats, is probably nothing more than one of these topaz pebbles of unusual transparency and beauty. These stones are often called "slave's diamonds" on account of their resemblance to the diamond. When cut they are not infrequently passed off as diamonds, and as the specific gravity is almost exactly the same as that of diamond, resort to some other means by which they may be distinguished is necessary. This is a matter of no great difficulty, for topaz, beside being much less hard than diamond, is also doubly refracting, while diamond, like other cubic minerals, is singly refracting. Topaz may, however, be distinguished from other colourless stones, such as rock-crystal, phenakite, and colourless sapphire, by the difference in specific gravity. Thus, in methylene iodide rock-crystal (sp. gr. = 2·65) and phenakite (sp. gr. = 2·98−3·0) both float, while topaz quickly sinks. In the heaviest liquid, on the other hand, colourless sapphire sinks while topaz floats. Moreover, topaz differs from the minerals just mentioned in its capacity for acquiring charges of electricity.

The colour of topaz, though usually pale, is sometimes deep and intense, and in this case the dichroism of the mineral, though scarcely apparent to the naked eye, can be easily observed in the dichroscope.

Topaz is very frequently **blue** in colour, either a pure blue or a blue tinged with green, but scarcely ever a pure green. A blue crystal of topaz is represented in Plate XIII., Fig. 1, and the gem cut from it in Fig. 1a of the same plate. Dark blue topaz is very unusual; the mineral is almost invariably pale in shade, sometimes so pale that it may be more correctly described as blue-white. Such stones are common among the "pingos d'agoa" of Brazil as well as amongst crystals from Mursinka, near Ekaterinburg, in the Urals; these latter are known as *Siberian* or *Tauridan topaz*. Stones of a darker shade of pale blue are referred to as "*Brazilian sapphire*," a term which is applied also to the blue tourmaline, which occurs in Brazil in association with white and blue topaz. Bluish-green and greenish-blue topaz is so very similar in appearance to aquamarine, that a careful examination is sometimes necessary in order to distinguish between them. The difference in specific gravity is here a valuable aid; in pure methylene iodide topaz sinks, while aquamarine floats. Topaz bearing this resemblance to aquamarine occurs at various localities, but specially in the district about Nerchinsk in Siberia, and when cut is always passed off as aquamarine. True aquamarine is more abundant and more widely distributed than is topaz, especially topaz of this particular colour, so that here we have the very unusual case of a rarer mineral substituted for one less rare. The dichroism of blue topaz is most apparent when its colour possesses a tinge of green, and the greatest contrast between the two images of the aperture of the dichroscope exists when one is practically colourless and the other almost pure green. In the case of aquamarine, the two images are coloured yellowish-white and clear sky-blue respectively. Topaz of a yellowish-green colour like chrysolite is rare; the typical colour of the mineral is the one we are now about to consider, namely, yellow.

Yellow topaz exists in a great variety of shades, ranging from the palest possible shade of pure yellow up to dark brownish yellow, usually tinged more or less with red. Yellow topaz is the only variety which is recognised by jewellers as topaz; it is by no means always of the same tint, and stones showing different shades of yellow differ in value and are distinguished by special names.

A fine saffron-yellow topaz, the so-called *Indian topaz*, occurs in Ceylon, not, however, in abundance, and as a great rarity in Brazil. Very beautiful topaz of a dark yellow colour, tinged with red or brown, occurs in great abundance at the Brazilian localities. A crystal of this description is represented in Plate XIII., Fig. 2, while Fig. 2a illustrates a faceted stone of a somewhat different tint. Topaz of gold-yellow, honey-yellow, wine-yellow, and other shades is also found in Brazil though in less abundance; the gold-yellow variety is distinguished as *Brazilian topaz*.

Saxon topaz is of a pale wine-yellow colour; a crystal of this variety is illustrated in Plate XIII., Fig. 3, and a faceted stone in Fig. 3a. It occurs at Schneckenstein, near Auerbach, in Saxon Voigtland. Occasionally it is tinged with green, and is then known as "*Saxon chrysolite.*"

The dichroism of dark yellow topaz is fairly well marked; the two images of the dichroscope aperture being coloured respectively light and dark yellow, or yellow and red. The paler the stone the less marked is the contrast in colour of the two images, and with quite pale yellow stones the difference is scarcely apparent at all.

The stones which are most likely to be mistaken for yellow topaz are yellow sapphire, the so-called "oriental topaz," and yellow quartz, the so-called citrine or "occidental topaz." The latter exhibits the same fine tints and is often substituted for topaz. The fraud may be easily detected by the difference in the specific gravity of the two minerals, just as rock-crystal is distinguished from water-clear topaz. The difference in specific gravity enables us also to distinguish "oriental topaz" from true topaz in the same way that colourless sapphire is distinguished from colourless topaz.

Topaz of a pronounced **red** colour occurs in nature but rarely. It is met with occasionally in Brazil associated with crystals of a yellow colour, and is usually of a light rose-red inclining to a lilac shade of colour, very similar to the colour of "balas-ruby." In spite of this resemblance the two gems need never be mistaken the one for the other, since the "balas-ruby" (spinel) is singly refracting and not dichroic, while topaz is dichroic and doubly refracting. This variety of topaz, a crystal and faceted stone of which is represented in Plate XIII., Figs. 4 and 4a, is known to jewellers as *rose-topaz*.   When of a deep red colour it is sometimes referred to as " *Brazilian ruby.*"

Rose-topaz, which is so rare in nature, may be produced artificially by subjecting yellow topaz, especially the Brazilian, to a gradual rise of temperature, when it assumes the red colour of rose-topaz.   Most of the rose-topaz sold by jewellers as " burnt " topaz is the yellow variety altered by heating.   The rise and fall of temperature to which the stone is subjected must be very gradual, otherwise the crystal will be fissured.   The darker the original colour of the stone the darker will be its colour after heating.   There are various methods in use for the artificial production of the red colour of rose-topaz ; in one, for example, the stone is packed in a crucible with powdered charcoal, sand, ashes, or any other powder, slowly heated and then slowly cooled ; in another, it is enclosed in many wrappings of tinder ; this material is then fired and the change in colour thereby effected.   When the latter method is adopted too great a rise of temperature must be avoided, otherwise the stone will be completely decolorised, besides being rendered fissured and cloudy.

" Burnt " topaz is much more strongly dichroic than is naturally occurring rose-topaz, or, indeed, than topaz of any other colour; the two images seen in the dichroscope, when showing the greatest possible contrast in colour, are respectively dark cherry-red and honey-yellow.   It has been supposed that naturally occurring rose-topaz has been derived from yellow-topaz by the action of heat, but L. von Eschwege, and others familiar with the mode of occurrence of the mineral in Brazil, have shown that crystals of the rare rose topaz occur together with the common yellow variety ; this view, therefore, cannot be correct.

A change of colour is induced in some topazes simply by exposure to sunlight.   Such a change has been observed in crystals from the Urulga river, Siberia, the original dark wine-yellow colour changing after a few months' exposure to dirty white.   It may be mentioned here that the finest topaz crystals in the British Museum collection came from this locality, and for this reason are protected from the action of light.   Some pale blue stones have been observed to become pale yellow after exposure to sunlight.   These and similar instances indicate that the colour in such cases is due to an organic substance ; those stones, on the other hand, which are unaffected by light, but become red on exposure to heat, probably owe their colour to a metallic oxide, since exposure to high temperatures would destroy any organic pigment.

All these varieties of precious topaz are made use of as gems ; that is to say, all specimens which are sufficiently transparent, finely coloured, and free from faults.   Inferior stones, the so-called " fallow topaz," are crushed and powdered, and in this form utilised as a hard, grinding material.   The form of cutting best suited for coloured topaz is seen in the faceted stones represented in Plate XIII., Figs. 1a, 2a, 3a, 4a ; these are step-cut, the table being somewhat small and the steps narrow and equidistant from each other.   The brilliant form is sometimes adopted for coloured stones, but is more often seen in colourless topaz, " pingos d'agoa," &c.   Yellow topazes are not infrequently table-cut.   In the case of light-coloured stones, like the Saxon topazes, for example, an added brilliancy and depth of colour is given by the use of a burnished gold, or in some cases of a red, foil.   Blue topaz is always backed with a pale blue shining foil ; on a dark foil it presents a peculiar and not altogether attractive appearance.   Only the finest and most transparent of stones, whatever be their colour, are mounted *à jour*.

Topaz varies in value according to its quality ; large crystals are found quite as frequently as small, consequently the value of cut stones is proportionate to their size. Topaz of any colour is not at the present time a gem favoured by the votaries of fashion, and hence can be purchased at very moderate prices. This applies more particularly to the common yellow topaz; the red, dark brownish-yellow, colourless, and fine blue varieties command somewhat higher prices. The finest topaz is, at the present time, not worth more than 10s. per carat, while much less will be paid for inferior qualities. About thirty-five years ago topaz had quite three times its present value; thus, for a water-clear or rose-topaz weighing 1 carat about 30s. would be paid, for a burnt topaz about 18s., and for ordinary yellow 12s. The wholesale price of uncut yellow topaz is now from 1s. to 20s. per pound.

The faults, the presence of which reduces the value of a stone, are principally impure colour, fissures in the direction of cleavage ("feathers"), and turbidity. Cavities, either vacuous or filled with liquids of various kinds, are also frequently present.

The artificial production of topaz has not at present been achieved with certainty. Good imitations of topaz can be made by fusing strass with a certain amount of glass of antimony (antimony oxide) and with a trace of purple of Cassius (a compound containing gold), or with a little iron oxide. Purple of Cassius gives a darker, more reddish-yellow, and iron oxide a paler yellow. Such imitations may be distinguished from genuine stones by their single refraction, lower specific gravity, much lower degree of hardness, and by the entire absence of dichroism.

Topaz occurs commonly in the old crystalline silicate rocks, namely, in gneiss and crystalline schists as well as in granite. The crystals are attached to the walls of cavities or crevices in these rocks and are often accompanied by tin-stone (cassiterite), aquamarine (beryl), &c. The general conditions of the occurrence are such that topaz must be regarded as the product of fumarole action, the mineral having probably been formed by the interaction of vapours containing fluorine, which were liberated in crevices at the time of the intrusion of the igneous rock. By the weathering and breaking down of the mother-rock the topaz crystals are set free, carried away with the débris, and, as rounded pebbles, find a final resting-place in the alluvial deposits of rivers and streams. In recent years topaz crystals have been met with in the drusy cavities of later volcanic rocks, such as rhyolite; this is a much less common mode of occurrence and has no commercial significance.

Topaz of gem-quality occurs at several localities, many of which have already been briefly mentioned, but must now receive more detailed consideration.

The most important European locality is the Schneckenstein, near Gottesberg, in the neighbourhood of Auerbach, in Voigtland, Kingdom of **Saxony**. The Schneckenstein, which is situated four kilometres south-east of the railway station of Hammerbrück, is a steep wall of rock projecting from the surrounding mica-schists, and in appearance resembling an old ruin. It consists of comparatively small fragments of schists rich in tourmaline, cemented into a firm and hard mass by quartz and topaz; the whole rock-mass is known as a topaz-rock. Crystals of topaz, together with quartz, tourmaline, &c., are attached to the walls of cavities in this rock, and the cavities are often partly filled up with white or yellow kaolin. A portion of the wall of such a drusy cavity is represented in Plate XIII., Fig. 3. The free ends of the topaz crystals have a moderately complex termination, the terminal faces including a large basal plane (Fig. 66 *d*). The crystals vary in size, the smallest having a length and thickness of a few lines, while the largest measure 4 inches in length and 2 inches in thickness. The majority have a length and thickness of about $\frac{3}{8}$ inch; larger crystals are rare.

In colour these topazes are mostly pale wine-yellow, rarely a dark wine-yellow, colourless or white; the darker the colour the more valuable is the stone. Crystals of a greenish tint, known as "Saxon chrysolite," are sometimes met with; those of a pure yellow are distinguished from them by the name Saxon topaz. This so-called "Schnecken topaz" was at one time much admired and sought after ; the specimens of decorative art, now to be seen in the "Green Vaults" at Dresden, bear witness both to the exceeding beauty of some of these stones and to the favour in which they were at one time held.

During the eighteenth century, certainly as far back as the year 1737, Schneckenstein topaz was systematically mined and placed on the market. The stones were sorted into three groups ; the largest and purest were referred to as ring-stones (*Ringsteine*), the next quality as buckle or clasp-stones (*Schnallensteine*), and inferior stones as *Karmusirgut*. No mining has been carried on here for a long period, and the terms just mentioned have long since been forgotten in the locality.

Brazil, where, as we have seen, are to be found diamond, beryl, and chrysoberyl, is no less rich in topaz. All the colour-varieties of this mineral are found there in abundance, especially in the State of Minas Geraes, other Brazilian localities being of small importance compared with this.

Brazilian topaz is either blue, yellow, or colourless. The colourless and blue varieties always occur together as water-worn pebbles in secondary deposits ; yellow topaz, on the other hand, is met with only in its primary situation. Moreover, the localities for the colourless and blue and for the yellow varieties are widely separated.

White and blue topaz has already been mentioned as occurring in the district of Diamantina in association with diamond, and with beryl and chrysoberyl in the district of Minas Novas. This latter, which is known also as the district of Arrassuahy, is the most important locality for the blue and white varieties of topaz. It is situated in the north-east of the State of Minas Geraes, to the north-east of Diamantina, in the middle reaches of the diamond-bearing river Rio Jequetinhonha, known in its lower course as the Rio Belmonte, and to the south of this river. The gem-bearing deposits of this region extend over the plateau between the Rio Jequetinhonha and the Rio Arrassuahy towards the south and east as far as the Serra das Esmeraldas, a part of the Serra do Espinhaço. The precious stones which occur here are, or at least were at one time, of great commercial importance. The colourless topaz pebbles found here are known as "pingos d'agoa," or as "minas novas," after the district, while the blue stones are known in Brazil as "safiras" (that is to say, sapphires). In association with these two varieties of topaz are found garnet, chrysoberyl, aquamarine, rock-crystal, red quartz, amethyst, transparent spodumene, andalusite, and green tourmaline. The latter mineral, on account of its colour, was supposed to be emerald, hence the name Serra das Esmeraldas given to a mountain range in the neighbourhood. The principal localities are in the wooded and inaccessible wilds between the Rio Jequetinhonha and the three source-streams of the Rio S. Matheus, usually known as the Rio Americanas. Topaz pebbles are found loose in the débris of these streams, as well as in others which flow into the Jequetinhonha ; one of these, the Ribeirão Calhão, is well known and has been already mentioned as a locality for chrysoberyl. Workings for precious stones are reported to be in existence also on the upper Rio Piauhy.

Topaz is extremely abundant here, much more so than any of the other precious stones mentioned. It occurs as broken fragments, or more frequently as rounded, water-worn pebbles, the size of which varies between that of a pea and that of a chestnut. Larger fragments or pebbles the size of a man's fist or head, and weighing several pounds, have been met with, but are rare. The best quality of white topaz is said to be found in the Rio Utinga, but the "pingos d'agoa" are by no means confined to the bed of this river. The blue topaz is sometimes dark in shade, and sometimes pale or almost colourless ;

it is found as pebbles ranging in weight up to several ounces. Those of a dark shade are the most valuable.

The original situation of the blue and colourless topaz pebbles has not yet been ascertained. The commonest rocks in the neighbourhood are granite and gneiss, and it is probably from such that the stones have been derived. In many parts hereabouts there is a surface layer, sometimes as much as 14 feet thick, of weathered material, consisting mainly of quartz fragments, containing the same precious stones as are to be found in the river beds. This weathered material has been derived from the underlying granite and gneiss; it seems very probable, therefore, that the precious stones contained in it had a

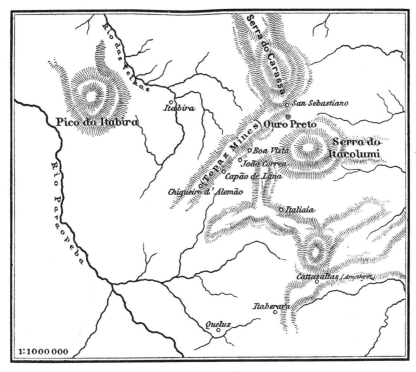

FIG. 67. Occurrence of yellow topaz near Ouro Preto in Brazil. (Scale, 1 : 1,000,000)

similar origin, having been formed, perhaps, in the quartz veins by which the underlying rocks are penetrated. Small isolated grains of topaz and other precious minerals are to be found actually embedded as constituents in these rocks. The thick mantle of weathered material, together with the precious stones it contains, is gradually carried away by the action of running water, and during the transportation the stones assume the rounded form characteristic of the pebbles of a river bed. The mode of occurrence of topaz in these secondary deposits has a great general resemblance to that of diamond at Diamantina, though at present diamond has not been met with in Minas Novas.

The distribution and mode of occurrence of yellow topaz is quite different. Fig. 67 is a map of the district in which it occurs. The precious stone was here discovered about the year 1760 in the neighbourhood of Ouro Preto, then known as Villa Rica, in the south-west of Minas Geraes, of which State it is the capital. At that time yellow topaz was in great demand, and the search for it was prosecuted with great vigour. It is most abundant in a chain of hills extending for one and a half legoas (about six miles) in a south-west to north-east direction from Capão de Lana through João Correa and Boa Vista to Ouro Preto. The deposit has been traced as far south as Chiqueiro d'Alemão.

The topaz is here confined to a band, a few hundred yards wide, which extends with little interruption throughout the range of hills in the direction mentioned. This is the primary situation of the stone, that is to say, the place where it was formed. Water-worn pebbles of yellow topaz are rare, but have been met with in the "tapanhoacanga" of the neighbouring streams, a term which was explained in connection with the occurrence of diamond in Brazil. Although the topaz now lies unchanged at the place where it was originally formed, yet the rock in which it occurs has undergone considerable decomposition and alteration. These rocks consist of clay-slates associated with itacolumite. They are penetrated by quartz veins, and it is probable that the topaz, like the diamonds of Diamantina, was formed in cavities in these quartz veins. The clay-slates are altered in places by weathering into a soft clayey mass, and at isolated spots in this mass are found druses or nests, containing detached topaz crystals embedded in a clay or scaly kaolin, which ranges in colour from white to dark brown. These nests are probably isolated portions of the quartz veins by which the rock was penetrated and in which the topaz crystals were formed; crystals are also found, however, in the clayey mass itself.

The minerals associated with topaz are practically the same as have been frequently observed to occur with diamond in the quartz veins which intersect the itacolumite and accompanying rocks. Besides quartz (rock-crystal and smoky-quartz) they include ilmenite, hæmatite, rutile, black tourmaline, and the rare euclase; all occur in broken fragments embedded in the clay. It should, however, be noted that euclase is never found actually with topaz, but always in a druse by itself.

A different opinion as to the origin of yellow topaz in Brazil has been recently (1901) expressed by Orville A. Derby. He states that it occurs near Ouro Preto, usually in nodules in a clayey matrix which has resulted from the decomposition of a mica-schist. This latter, he considers, has been formed by the metamorphism of an igneous rock of the augite- or nepheline-syenite group, in the drusy cavities of which topaz had crystallised out.

The mode of occurrence of topaz at Saramenha, half an hour's journey from Ouro Preto, is somewhat different. Here the crystals are embedded in a deposit of brown iron-stone (limonite) intermixed with micaceous iron-ore (hæmatite), in which, after removal, they leave sharp, bright impressions. The mineral is here pale yellow in colour and abundant in quantity.

The topaz which occurs in the neighbourhood of Ouro Preto varies in shade from a pale yellow to a dark wine-yellow. As a general rule, the darker the kaolin in which the topaz crystals are embedded the darker are these crystals. A finely coloured crystal from this district is represented in Plate XIII., Fig. 2, and a faceted stone in Fig. 2a, of the same plate. The most beautiful of the stones found in this district are those having the rich colour of old Malaga wine. Red crystals (Plate XIII., Fig. 4,) also occur; they are usually of a pale rose shade, but may be a dark ruby-red, when they are known as "Brazilian ruby," a term which is also applied to stones the red colour of which has been produced by artificial means. A faceted "Brazilian ruby" is represented in Plate XIII., Fig. 4a; the stone is highly prized by connoisseurs.

The degree of transparency varies in different specimens, and the crystals are not all of gem-quality; thus among a thousand stones there may perhaps be but one perfect example, all the rest being faulty in some way or another.

With regard to size, crystals with a length of 6, or even of 10 inches, and a thickness of 2 or 4 inches, have been described by L. von Eschwege. Such large stones, however, are almost always more or less faulty, and are rarely suitable for cutting. The majority are much smaller, about the length and thickness of a little finger. The form of the crystals is usually quite simple, like that shown in Fig. 66a.

In this locality excavations are made in the clayey mass in which the topaz occurs, and the larger nests, when met with, are carefully removed and opened. The crystals which lie loose in the clay are obtained by allowing a stream of water to play upon the loosened masses of clay in the mine. By this means the lighter material is washed away, and the heavier topaz crystals caught in the meshes of a net spread out for that purpose.

The annual output of topaz at one time amounted to as much as 18 hundredweight, but on an average was not more than 7 or 8 hundredweight, a large proportion being yielded by the estates of Capão de Lana and Boa Vista, which are specially rich in topaz. It is said that the mining of topaz at one time afforded employment to as many as fifty persons. The stones find their way into the market by way of Rio Janeiro, some being cut on the spot. The valley of Ouro Preto is studded with innumerable abandoned mines, mute witnesses of former activity in this district. As the demand for these stones gradually fell off the mines were one by one abandoned, and systematic work has now ceased for a long time. Many are of opinion that the locality is practically exhausted; others aver, however, that there are still rich treasures to be found.

The occurrence of topaz in **Mexico** is of little commercial importance. It is found at La Paz in the State of Guanaxuato, at San Luis Potosi, and at Durango, in stanniferous deposits. The crystals are pale in colour or colourless and water-clear.

The mineral is widely distributed in the **United States** of North America, but crystals of gem-quality are somewhat rare, the best material coming from the Western States. Transparent and water-clear, bluish, and greenish crystals are found, together with beryl and other minerals, in granite, at Harndon Hill, near Stoneham, in Maine; also at other places in the neighbourhood, and at North Chatham in New Hampshire. Topaz crystals, very similar to those from Saxony, are found in the granite of Trumbull, Connecticut, but they are usually cloudy and rarely of gem-quality.

In Colorado fine crystals of a pale blue colour, or colourless and water-clear, and occasionally of considerable size, are met with. They occur with phenakite and other minerals in drusy cavities in granite at various points in the Pike's Peak region, in El Paso County. Thus, for example, at Florissant, twelve miles north of Pike's Peak, they are found embedded in green felspar (amazon-stone); and in the neighbourhood of Devil's Head Mountain, about thirty miles from Pike's Peak, colourless, reddish, wine-yellow, and pale blue crystals, similar to those of Mursinka in the Urals, are found in the solid rock or loose on the ground. Another, not altogether unimportant, locality is Mount Antero, about ten miles north of Salida, in Chaffee County, Colorado. The Colorado localities have yielded the best specimens of North American topaz of gem-quality; two of the largest after cutting weighed respectively 125 and 193 carats. At several places topaz has been found also in younger volcanic rocks, namely, in rhyolites; for example, at Nathrop in Chaffee County, and on Chalk Mountain in Colorado.

Very fine colourless crystals are met with embedded in solid rock, or loose in its weathered product in the Thomas Range, forty miles north of Sevier Lake in Utah, and at the same distance north-west of the town of Deseret on the Sevier river. The topaz found at these localities in the State of Utah is perhaps the finest in the United States.

A few stones of gem-quality have been met with at all the localities mentioned, and at some others. They are prized by the American as a production of his native country, but North America as a source of topaz has no commercial significance.

Crystals of **Russian** topaz are remarkable both for size and beauty, stones of fine quality and as much as 31 pounds in weight having been found. They are often cut at Ekaterinburg, together with the variously coloured precious stones with which they are found ; they find their way into the markets, in the rough or the cut condition, by way of the fairs of Nizhniy Novgorod.

As in Minas Novas, so also at most of the Russian localities, topaz and beryl occur together ; the one mineral is never found without the other, except in the Altai Mountains where beryl occurs, but no topaz has at present been found. The distribution of Russian topaz is practically the same as that of Russian beryl, which has been already dealt with. It will be unnecessary, therefore, to give here anything more than a few facts relating specially to the occurrence of topaz.

Topaz is specially abundant in the neighbourhood of the village of Alabashka, near Mursinka (Fig. 63a), in the Ekaterinburg district of the **Urals**. It is found in druses in granite, together with smoky-quartz, beryl, large yellow crystals of felspar, small crystals of white albite arranged in spherical groups, and red plates of lepidolite ; these minerals all occur in well-developed crystals, and the combination of different colours renders the druse a very beautiful object. The smallest crystals of topaz are about the size of a pin's head, while the largest are several centimetres in length. They are usually bluish in colour, as represented in Plate XIII., Figs. 1 and 1a, sometimes light bluish-grey or greyish-white, rarely colourless. As a rule, they occur singly in the druses, but sometimes grouped together in parallel position. The usual crystalline form is the simple one represented in Fig. 66c, and in the coloured figure just cited. With regard to transparency, some crystals are perfectly clear, while others are only translucent ; the transparent ones are cut at the works in Ekaterinburg and fetch a moderately high price. The gem-mines near Mursinka will be again considered when we come to treat of amethyst.

Another Uralian locality for topaz is the neighbourhood of the smelting works of Miask, on the east side of Lake Ilmen. Its mode of occurrence here is the same, namely, in drusy cavities in pegmatite ; these cavities are sometimes filled with a white clay, embedded in which are topaz crystals which have been detached from the walls of the cavity. The pegmatite-veins are here found at four places, traversing a rock known as miascite. Associated with the topaz is green felspar (amazon-stone), in which it is frequently embedded, also phenakite, mica, and other minerals. Two varieties of topaz occur here. One is colourless and perfectly transparent, like the " pingos d'agoa " of Brazil, and occurs as symmetrically developed crystals rich in faces. The other variety is of a dirty yellowish-white colour, translucent only at the edges, and so fissured and decomposed or, as it is described at the place, rotten, that the crystals, which are bounded by only few faces, may be easily crushed between the fingers. Both these varieties occur in crystals of about the same size as those found at Alabashka.

Topaz is also found in the gold-washings, belonging to a merchant named Bakakin, in the valley of the Sanarka (a tributary of the Ui, which itself feeds the Tobol), as well as in a few tributary streams in the Southern Urals (Government Orenburg). The crystals found here are so very similar to Brazilian topaz that their Uralian origin was at first doubted. They usually retain their crystalline form, which is simple, like that shown in Fig. 66a. Their colour is generally some shade of yellow ; some, however, are red and a few quite colourless. Many are beautifully transparent. The largest crystals have a length of $2\frac{1}{2}$, and a thickness of $\frac{3}{4}$ centimetres. The topaz in these river-sands is associated with a great variety of precious stones, some of which have been already mentioned. They include quartz (amethyst), corundum (ruby), chrysoberyl (alexandrite and cymophane), spinel, chalcedony (carnelian, agate, &c.), staurolite, kyanite, euclase, tourmaline, garnet, beryl, &c. In the case of rose-topaz its place of origin is known ; it occurs with green chromiferous tourmaline and green chromiferous mica (fuchsite) in quartz veins or nests in carboniferous limestone, which in this district forms a deposit extending over a wide area.

The topaz found in the Adun-Chalon Mountains, in the Nerchinsk district of **Transbaikalia**, is much fissured and far from being perfectly transparent. It forms with quartz the so-called topaz-rock, veins of which penetrate the granite. It has been already mentioned, in the description of beryl, that cavities in this topaz-rock are lined with crystals of beryl, smoky-quartz, and topaz, and that owing to the weathering of the rock these minerals lie loosely scattered in the surface soil.

In the mountain range, Kuchuserken, topaz was first met with at the beginning of the fifties of the nineteenth century. Although this range may be considered as a continuation of the Adun-Chalon Mountains, yet the topaz found here is more like that which occurs with beryl in granite near the Urulga river, in the Borshchovochnoi range.

The topaz of the last-named locality is distinguished by its exceptional beauty of colour and transparency and by the size of its crystals. In respect to the large size of the crystals it exceeds all other Russian topaz. Thus a perfectly transparent, dark honey-yellow crystal found here weighed 3 pounds, another fine transparent crystal of a pleasing dark wine-yellow colour weighed over 25 pounds, while a third measured 19 by 21 centimetres, and weighed 31 pounds ; this, however, which has been already mentioned, was only translucent and of a dirty yellow colour. Several very fine crystals from this district are preserved in the British Museum collection of minerals. In the majority of crystals the colour is something between the brown of smoky-quartz and the yellow of Brazilian topaz ; unfortunately this colour is speedily bleached on exposure to light. Sometimes it is dark honey-yellow ; stones showing light tints of this and other shades of yellow are also seen, as well as pale-blue, bluish-white, and perfectly colourless examples. The crystals occur singly or in groups, the individuals of a group having grown together in parallel position.

The Daurien district in the southern part of Transbaikalia is another locality for topaz ; fine water-clear and well-developed crystals are found in the Shilka river, the upper course (or main supply stream) of the Amur.

Fine topazes also occur elsewhere in Asia. Those found in the neighbourhood of Mukla, or Mugla, in **Asia Minor**, resemble the yellow Brazilian topaz so closely both in form and colour that they can scarcely be distinguished from them. No details are known as to the locality or mode of occurrence. The stones vary in shade from a dark honey-yellow to pale wine-yellow ; sometimes they are rose-red, rarely blue. Their form is the same as that of the Brazilian crystals, Fig. 66a, and Plate XII., Figs. 2 and 4.

The occurrence of topaz in India is not well authenticated. In those instances in which it is supposed to have been found, it is probable that quartz or some other mineral has been mistaken for it. The occurrence of topaz in **Ceylon** is, on the other hand, well established. It occurs in abundance as colourless and pale or dark yellow pebbles in the gem-gravels, together with sapphire and other precious stones, which are all collected and sent to market together. The fine saffron-yellow variety of topaz, mentioned above, occurs as a great rarity in Ceylon ; it is distinguished as " Indian topaz." A large pebble, weighing 12 pounds 13 ounces, of perfectly colourless and transparent topaz, probably from Ceylon, is to be seen in the British Museum collection of minerals.

In recent times the mineral has been found in **Japan** as water-clear, pale-yellow, or greenish-blue crystals of moderate size. They occur in river gravels at various places, and have been derived from pegmatite veins intersecting granite and gneiss. Many of the crystals are well suited for cutting as gems, and Japanese topaz will probably become of importance commercially. Blue, green, and yellow topaz has been found also in Kamchatka.

In **Africa** topaz was found in former times in the same district of Egypt in which emerald occurs, namely, on Jebel Sabara, near the Red Sea. Numerous ancient topaz mines have been rediscovered here, but have been scarcely worked at all in modern times owing to the low price of topaz. Risk Allah is the only place in this region where topaz is mined at the present time. The mineral occurs also in German South-West Africa, sometimes turbid and cloudy, but mostly transparent and water-clear, though not of a quality suitable for cutting. It varies in colour from wine-yellow to brownish-yellow and is rarely distributed.

Finally, **Australia** as a topaz locality must be mentioned. The mineral is distributed widely in this continent, and occurs especially in gravels. Colourless, bluish, greenish, and yellow pebbles, the latter very like Brazilian stones, are found associated with cassiterite and diamond in the stanniferous gravels of the granitic region of New England in the north-east corner of New South Wales. The cassiterite (tin-stone) and topaz have both been derived from the granite. Topaz occurs, in a similar manner, in the rivers further south as an associate of diamond, the distribution of which is shown in the map, Fig. 43. The topaz pebbles found here are often beautiful and of considerable size, the largest weighing several ounces. They are colourless or blue, sometimes yellow. Yellow topaz pebbles have been found also in Owen's river in Victoria and at other places. At all these Australian localities topaz is sought for and cut as gems; this is probably scarcely the case with the topaz accompanying cassiterite in Tasmania, which is of poor quality.

ZIRCON.

Although zircon is of less importance and is less frequently cut as a gem than the precious stones hitherto considered, yet it has a certain vogue, the transparent yellowish-red variety, distinguished by the name hyacinth (jacinth), being most used.

Zircon is a compound of the oxides of silicon and zirconium; that is to say, a compound of silica and zirconia. It contains 23·77 per cent. of silica (SiO_2) and 76·23 per cent. of zirconia (ZrO_2), a composition corresponding to the chemical formula $ZrO_2.SiO_2$.

The forms taken by the crystals of this mineral belong to the tetragonal system and are usually very simple; four of the commonest forms are represented in Figs. 68a to d. The crystals are usually short, comparatively thick, and with faces symmetrically developed on all sides; they are bounded by square prisms and tetragonal octahedra of two orders. Hyacinth, which is practically the only variety used as a gem, scarcely ever occurs in any form other than that shown in Figs. 68b and c, and in Plate I., Figs. 11 and 12. We have here a square prism of the second order, with its edges sometimes truncated by narrow faces of a square prism of the first order (Fig. 68c), and terminated by a tetragonal octahedron, or pyramid, of the first order, so that at each end there is a four-faced pyramidal termination. The other forms shown in the figures are those assumed by common zircon.

Zircon has a very imperfect cleavage, scarcely observable in fact; its fracture is distinctly conchoidal. The mineral is harder than quartz but softer than topaz, its hardness being represented on the scale by $7\frac{1}{2}$; this is not very great, but is sufficient to

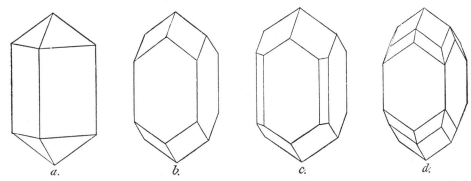

a.   b.   c.   d.

FIG. 68.   Crystalline forms of zircon.

admit of a brilliant polish, so that an artificially polished facet, like a natural crystal-face, shines with a brilliant, adamantine-like, vitreous lustre. The specific gravity is very high ; it varies between 4·610 and 4·825, the mean value for the hyacinth variety being 4·681. Zircon is thus denser than any other precious stone, heavier, indeed, than any mineral not containing the heavy metals (lead, silver, copper, &c.) in large amount, and when placed in the heaviest liquid it quickly sinks.

Zircon may be cloudy and opaque, or clear and transparent. The opaque, common zircon is usually brown or grey in colour, sometimes between green and black, and is little used as a gem. A fire-red, cloudy zircon, called after its place of origin " Ceylonese zircon," is sometimes cut as a gem. Precious zircon is not always perfectly transparent; in such cases the stone, though markedly translucent, is still pleasing in appearance by virtue of its brilliancy and lustre, which is comparable to that of the diamond. Zircon is only rarely perfectly colourless and water-clear; crystals answering this description occur implanted on chlorite-schist at Wildkreuzjoch, in the Tyrol, and also in Ceylon. More frequently it is green, brownish-red or brown, and sometimes violet ; but by far the commonest tint is a brownish shade of orange resulting from a mixture of red and yellow in about equal proportions. The latter colour inclines in some stones more to red, and in others to yellow, and some are dark and others lighter in shade. Zircon of this colour, which is known as *hyacinth*, and is practically the only variety commonly cut as a gem, is represented in Plate I., Figs. 11 and 12. Transparent green zircons, like the one illustrated by Fig. 13 of the same plate, are sometimes cut as gems, as are also the reddish-brown, brown, and violet varieties. It is only exceptionally, however, that these latter are sufficiently transparent for this purpose, and when they are, they are sometimes mistaken by dealers for tourmaline.

The reddish-yellow colour characteristic of hyacinth is known as hyacinth-red. The same colour is seen in cinnamon-stone or hessonite (Plate XIV., Figs. 7 and 8), a variety of garnet which occurs in association with hyacinth in Ceylon. So much alike are these two gems that hessonite is often sold by jewellers for hyacinth ; indeed, it has been stated that practically the whole of the so-called hyacinth bought and sold in European markets is in reality hessonite, although this stone is far inferior both in brilliance and lustre to the true hyacinth-red zircon. The means by which the two stones may be distinguished will be given under hessonite ; it may be stated here, however, that the distinction is based on the fact that hessonite is singly refracting and hyacinth doubly refracting.

The very pale straw-yellow or colourless zircons from Ceylon are also cut as gems, and are called by jewellers "cerkonier" or *jargon* (jargoon). Though this variety of zircon occurs but rarely in nature, it can be produced artificially to any amount by heating hyacinth of the ordinary colour, this being very easily decolorised by heat. Thus, a stone on being brought near to the tip of a blowpipe flame suddenly loses its red colour, and becomes colourless or tinged with grey, sometimes with rose-red or straw-yellow. The same change of colour takes place when hyacinth is heated in a glass-tube. If the experiment is made in a dark room it will be observed that the stone, although at a temperature below red-heat, suddenly emits a phosphorescent light and becomes decolorised. Other important changes take place at the same time ; the specific gravity of the stone is increased by 0·1, or even more, while the lustre, always brilliant, becomes still more so. So brilliant indeed are these ignited, colourless or pale-coloured hyacinths, that when cut as rosettes it is impossible for any one other than an expert to distinguish them on mere inspection from diamonds, and there is no doubt that they are occasionally passed off as such. The stones found at Matura, in Ceylon, in the eighteenth century, were, in fact, regarded as diamonds of inferior quality, and were known as " Matura diamonds." The diamond, like hessonite, differs from hyacinth in that it is singly refracting ; its hardness, moreover, is, of course, enormously greater, and its specific gravity is less ; in the heaviest liquid (sp. gr. = 3·6) diamond floats and hyacinth rapidly sinks.

The phenomena attending the decolorisation of hyacinth have been somewhat closely investigated with a view to learning the nature of the colouring substance. It is found that crystals when heated in the presence of oxygen—for example, in the oxidising flame—do not lose their colour completely, but become paler. When, on the other hand, they are heated out of contact with oxygen—for example, in the reducing flame—they are completely decolorised ; and if these decolorised stones are again heated in the presence of oxygen they assume a pale red colour. Moreover, it has been observed that a very strongly ignited hyacinth becomes dark brown in colour. From these observations it is inferred that the colour of zircon is due to the presence of iron ; as a matter of fact, every specimen of zircon hitherto analysed has been found to contain small amounts, ranging up to 2 per cent., of iron oxide.

The colour and lustre of some hyacinths is liable to change even at ordinary temperatures if the stones are exposed to light, especially to the direct rays of the sun. In some cases the colour becomes pale, while in a few stones it changes to a brownish-red which gradually becomes more decidedly brown. At the same time the adamantine lustre becomes gradually more vitreous in character. Such altered stones, if kept in darkness, will recover their original colour and lustre to a large extent, but not altogether. Although these changes are not undergone by all hyacinths, it is advisable not to expose the gem to sunlight unnecessarily.

Zircon is more strongly refracting than any other precious stone with the exception of diamond. Being a tetragonal mineral it is doubly refracting ; the values for the greatest and least refractive indices of a crystal of a hyacinth from Ceylon were determined to be 1·97 and 1·92 respectively. The difference between the two, 0·05, is a measure of the double refraction, which is thus specially strong. On the other hand, the refractive indices for different colours do not differ much, hence the dispersion of zircon is small and its play of prismatic colours correspondingly insignificant, so that, although in brilliancy and lustre it may compare with the diamond, yet in the former respect no comparison is possible.

The dichroism of hyacinth, as of all varieties of zircon, is very feeble; it is almost impossible to detect any difference between the two images seen in the dichroscope. This instrument, which is frequently so useful in discriminating gems, is therefore of no assistance whatever in distinguishing the feebly dichroic hyacinth from hessonite, which has no dichroism at all. The dichroism of zircon of other colours, though stronger than that of hyacinth, is feebler than that of any other coloured doubly refracting precious stone.

A characteristic feature of many zircons, discovered by Prof. A. H. Church, is the presence of black absorption bands in the spectrum of white light which has traversed the stone. These absorption bands are attributed to the presence of small quantities of uranium compounds.

Some few characters of zircon still remain to be mentioned. It is infusible before the blowpipe, and is not attacked by acids, not even by hydrofluoric acid. When rubbed it becomes slightly electrified, but the charge is not sufficient to render this character of use for purposes of determination.

Zircon occurs in the older crystalline silicate-rocks, such as granite, gneiss, and other similar rocks of mountainous districts. Opaque zircon is a common constituent of such rocks, and precious zircon, including hyacinth, is found under similar conditions. The crystals are, as a rule, embedded in the rock, and are only rarely found attached to the walls of drusy cavities. Some few of these rocks contain such an amount of common zircon that the name of the mineral is used as a distinguishing prefix, as in the zircon-syenite of the neighbourhood of Fredriksvärn and Laurvik in the south of Norway; while some other localities, notably in North America, yield common zircon by the hundredweight. Isolated crystals of zircon of the hyacinth variety are sometimes found embedded in the younger volcanic rocks; for example, in the basalt at Expailly near Le-Puy-en-Velay (Department Haute-Loire) in France; in Germany in the so-called mill-stone lava of Niedermendig on the Laacher See, in the basalt of Unkel on the Rhine, and in some basalts in the Siebengebirge. A crystal of hyacinth, partly freed from the black basalt in which it is embedded, is shown in Plate I., Fig. 12. It is improbable that such zircon crystals were actually formed in the basaltic rock; their presence there may be explained by supposing that fragments of granite, or rock of similar nature containing these crystals, were caught up by the glowing, fluid basalt magma and all their constituents melted down except the resisting hyacinth, which remained unaltered, thus becoming an apparently normal constituent of the basalt.

Crystals of zircon are set free by the weathering of the mother-rock, carried away with the rock débris by running streams, and thus eventually become a constituent of sands and gravels. Owing to the unalterable nature of their substance, such crystals remain perfectly fresh and unweathered. The zircon used for cutting as gems is derived exclusively from such sands and gravels, never from the solid rock.

Various localities in the island of Ceylon send to the markets of the world almost the whole of the supply of hyacinth and other gem varieties of zircon. They are quite abundant, and are collected from the gem-gravels, together with spinel, sapphire, cat's-eye, and other Cingalese gems. The principal sources are the deposits in the neighbourhood of the town of Ratnapura in the Saffragam district, and those of Matura in the south of the island (Fig. 59); from the latter place come the colourless and pale-coloured, ignited hyacinths known as "Matura diamonds."

The crystalline form of the zircons found in these sands is still recognisable, although the crystals, like those of the other precious stones with which they are found, are much rounded. The crystals of hyacinth found in Ceylon are, as a rule, rather small, at most no larger than a lentil; specimens the size of a pea are rare, and still larger stones quite exceptional. The dimensions of two exceptionally large stones have been given as $5\frac{1}{2}$ and 6 lines in length and $4\frac{1}{2}$ and 7 lines respectively in thickness. Other colour varieties of precious zircon, which accompany hyacinth in Ceylon, occur in crystals of larger size, fine stones a centimetre in length being by no means unusual. There is no doubt that the different varieties of zircon found in the gem-gravels of Ceylon have been derived from the same rocks in which the sapphires, for example, with which they are associated, also took their origin. In a few rare cases crystals of hyacinth have been found actually in the matrix, which is a granite or gneissic rock, like the mother-rock of sapphire already described.

Compared with Ceylon, other localities for zircon are unimportant. Many supposed occurrences in India are by no means well authenticated; such as, for example, in the alluvial gravel at Ellore in the Madras Presidency, and in granite at Kedarnath on the Upper Ganges. The occurrence of hyacinth with ruby in Upper Burma has been reported.

The occurrence of zircon in Europe is well established, but unimportant. It is found with sapphire in sands, very similar to those of Ceylon, in the Iserwiese in the north of Bohemia; the crystals from this place are, however, smaller in size and fewer in number than in the sands in Ceylon. These zircons, sapphires, and other precious stones with which they are found have been derived from gneiss. The hyacinths which occur in the streams near Expailly, in France, have been weathered out of basalt; here again the mineral occurs under the same conditions as in Ceylon, but in small crystals few in number.

The occurrence of zircon in Australia, though of little importance in the trade, must not be forgotten. It is found in auriferous, and also in diamantiferous, sands, more especially at various places in New South Wales; fine specimens have been met with at Mudgee in this State.

Fine, richly coloured zircons are found in the gold-sands of North Carolina in the United States; the crystals are unfortunately, however, too small for cutting.

In conclusion we must consider the manner in which zircons are used in jewellery. The coloured stones are most frequently cut as table-stones or thick-stones, or sometimes they are given step-cut or brilliant-cut forms, according to their transparency and depth of colour. Fine stones of a pure colour require no special devices to improve their appearance, but inferior specimens are mounted on a gold foil or in a closed setting lined with black. Colourless stones, especially those which have been burnt, are usually cut as rosettes, a form which, on account of the brilliant lustre and absence of any play of prismatic colours, is more suitable than the brilliant, though the latter is sometimes employed. These burnt hyacinths were at one time, on account of their peculiar dusky lustre, used in mourning jewellery in preference to diamonds.

Hyacinth is not worth much at the present time; the demand for the gem has fallen off very considerably, and the genuine stone is rarely met with in the trade. Quite small stones are, of course, cheap, on account of the supply being large; it is only larger stones that are of any appreciable value. A good, faceted 1 carat stone of fine colour is valued at from 50s. to 75s., while a number of small stones of similar quality and weighing 1 carat together would not fetch at the most more than 10s. or 12s. Corresponding values also hold good for zircons of other colours.

The similarity in general appearance between hessonite, or cinnamon-stone, and hyacinth, and between diamond and burnt hyacinth, together with the methods by which they may be distinguished, have been already mentioned. Another stone which may resemble hyacinth, more or less, is yellowish-red corundum, known on this account as " oriental hyacinth." Its lustre is as brilliant and strong as that of true hyacinth, from which it is distinguished by its greater hardness (H = 9) and lower specific gravity (sp. gr. = 4·0). The two stones differ also in another respect; for "oriental hyacinth" is distinctly, though feebly, dichroic, while the dichroism of true hyacinth is so feeble as to be scarcely observable.

The name hyacinth is sometimes also applied to red crystals of ferruginous quartz of the variety known as "Eisenkiesel," which occurs, for example, embedded in gypsum at Santiago de Compostela in the north of Spain, and is known as "Compostela hyacinth." It is much inferior to true hyacinth both in lustre and transparency; moreover, being quartz, its specific gravity is only 2·65 and it floats in methylene iodide. Some of the colour-varieties of tourmaline are somewhat similar in appearance to certain zircons, less often, however, to hyacinth. They may be readily distinguished, however, for tourmaline is strongly dichroic, and being much lighter than zircon floats in methylene iodide. Rose-topaz is also sometimes substituted for hyacinth; here again the former is of quite a different shade of colour and is strongly dichroic.

Imitations of hyacinth in coloured glass may be easily distinguished from genuine stones by the fact that they are singly refracting and much less hard.

THE GARNET GROUP.

Garnet is extensively used as a gem, and is to be found adorning some of the costliest as well as the simplest articles of jewellery. If the ordinary display in a jeweller's window is observed, it will often be found that at least one half of the gems exposed for sale are garnets of various kinds.

Garnet differs from diamond, corundum, and many other precious stones hitherto considered in that its chemical composition is not fixed and unchangeable, but is subject to considerable variation. The minerals grouped together as garnet have some physical characters in common; they all have the same crystalline form and the same type of chemical constitution. The several members of the group differ from each other, however, in the chemical elements of which they are composed; the garnets, in fact, form what is called an isomorphous series, such as is often met with in the mineral kingdom.

The point of agreement in the chemical composition of all garnets is the association of three molecules of silica (SiO_2) with one molecule of a sesquioxide, represented generally by R_2O_3, and with three molecules of a monoxide, represented by MO. The chemical formula which expresses the composition of the whole garnet group in general terms is therefore $3MO.R_2O_3.3SiO_2$. The various members of the group differ from each other, however, in the nature of the monoxide and sesquioxide which take part in their constitution; thus the monoxide may be lime (CaO), ferrous oxide (FeO), or magnesia (MgO), occasionally also manganous oxide (MnO), or chromous oxide (CrO), while the sesquioxide may be alumina (Al_2O_3), or ferric oxide (Fe_2O_3), or sometimes chromic oxide (Cr_2O_3).

These different monoxides and sesquioxides are associated together in the most varied proportions, always, however, conforming to the general formula given above. All the varieties of garnet, which it is theoretically possible to construct by different combinations of the oxides mentioned above, are not actually known to exist in nature; the small number, which are known, are distinguished according to the particular oxides present. Omitting those of less importance, these are:

1. Calcium-aluminium garnet . . . . $3CaO.Al_2O_3.3SiO_2$.
2. Iron-aluminium garnet . . . . . $3FeO.Al_2O_3.3SiO_2$.
3. Magnesium-aluminium garnet . . . $3MgO.Al_2O_3.3SiO_2$.
4. Calcium-iron garnet . . . . . $3CaO.Fe_2O_3.3SiO_2$.
5. Calcium-chromium garnet . . . . $3CaO.Cr_2O_3.3SiO_2$.

The results of chemical analyses show that each of these garnets may occur in nature in a moderately pure condition. In most garnets, however, the part of the monoxide or of the sesquioxide is not played exclusively by calcium oxide, ferrous oxide, &c., or by aluminium oxide, ferric oxide, &c., but by mixtures of two or more oxides. Thus, there are garnets which contain, beside silica and alumina, two monoxides—lime and ferrous oxide—of which now the first, and now the second, predominates. Thus in one case the mineral approaches in character to a calcium-aluminium garnet, and in the other to an iron-aluminium garnet, and it may be considered to be a mixture in varying proportions of the two molecules $3CaO.Al_2O_3.3SiO_2$ and $3FeO.Al_2O_3.3SiO_2$. The members of the garnet group are thus isomorphous mixtures of certain fundamental compounds, five of the most important of which have been given above; a few others will also be mentioned later when each kind of garnet receives special consideration. The garnet group is divided into a number of species known by particular names, the division being based upon differences in chemical composition. The following table of the analyses of a few gem-varieties of garnet gives an idea of the diversity in their chemical composition, a composition which can, however, be reduced to one common type by applying the principle of isomorphous mixtures:

	Hessonite, Ceylon.	Almandine.	Demantoid (emerald-green), Urals.	Pyrope, Bohemia.	Pyrope (hyacinth-red), Cape.	Pyrope (dark-red), "Cape ruby."
Silica (SiO_2) . . .	40·01	40·56	35·50	41·35	40·90	39·06
Alumina (Al_2O_3) . .	23·00	20·61	—	22·35	22·81	21·02
Chromic oxide (Cr_2O_3) .	—	—	0·70	4·45	1·48	—
Ferric oxide (Fe_2O_3) . .	—	5·00	31·51	—	—	2.69
Ferrous oxide (FeO) . .	3·31	32·70	—	9·94	13·34	18·70
Manganous oxide (MnO) .	0·59	1·47	—	2·59	0·38	0·58
Lime (CaO) . . .	30·57	—	32·90	5·29	4·70	5·02
Magnesia (MgO) . .	0·33	—	0·21	15·00	16·43	12·09
Total . .	97·81	100·34	100·82	100·97	100·04	99·16

The different varieties of garnet, though so diverse in chemical composition, nearly all occur in well-developed crystals of the same kind. The crystals are met with embedded in rock, with faces fully developed on all sides, like the crystal represented in Plate XIV., Fig. 3, from which the surrounding matrix has been partly removed; also attached to the walls of drusy cavities or crevices in rocks, such a druse being shown in Fig. 7 of the same plate. The crystalline forms are those of the cubic system; the most important are represented in Figs. 69a to d. The rhombic dodecahedron (Fig. 69a) is so common and characteristic of garnet that it is sometimes known as the garnetohedron. The twenty-four edges of this form are often more or less widely truncated by planes, which, as shown in

Fig. 29*b*, are usually delicately striated in the direction of their length. Sometimes the faces of the rhombic dodecahedron are more largely developed than are the truncating faces (Fig. 29*b*); at other times the reverse is the case, and the rhomb-shaped faces are small. These truncating faces belong to the icositetrahedron (Fig. 69*c*), a simple form, uncombined with others, frequently taken by garnet. The edges of the rhombic dodecahedron are in many cases not only truncated by the icositetrahedron, as in Fig. 69*b*, but the edges of

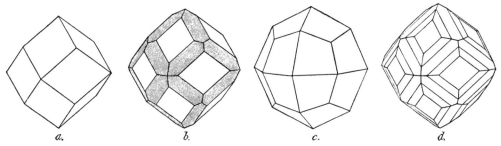

FIG. 69.   Crystalline forms of garnet.

intersection of these two forms are further truncated by delicately striated faces, the result being a form like Fig. 69*d*. This second series of faces are those of a hexakis-octahedron, a solid bounded by forty-eight faces, which is the greatest number possible on any single uncombined form. The simple hexakis-octahedron uncombined with other forms has not been observed in garnet. The mineral rarely takes a form other than those mentioned; those forms having a lesser number of faces, such as the octahedron and the cube, which, as a rule, are commonest in other minerals, are rarely seen in garnet.

The cleavage of garnet is more imperfect than in most other minerals; the fracture is sub-conchoidal to uneven. It is fairly hard, but this character varies in different varieties. All red garnets, which are the varieties chiefly used as gems, are harder than quartz but less hard than topaz, that is to say, for red garnets H = 7−8. The hardness of some green garnet is rather less; the demantoid, for example, which is sometimes used as a gem, has a hardness of $6\frac{1}{2}$ only, and is scratched by quartz; it is sufficiently hard, however, to scratch glass, so that it may be distinguished by this means from glass imitations. The pure emerald-green calcium-chromium garnet known to mineralogists as uvarovite is rarely cut as a gem, but is very nearly as hard as topaz. Garnet in the form of powder is a valuable grinding agent for precious stones and other hard substances, and is also used in the manufacture of the so-called emery-paper. It is the most widely distributed of any mineral with a hardness greater than that of quartz, and can be sold in large quantity at a low price. Good stones free from fissures serve for the construction of the pivot supports of watches, &c.

The specific gravity of garnet is another feature which varies to a large extent in different varieties. The variation is due to the diversity in chemical composition, the greater the proportion of heavy metal, such as iron, present in any one variety, the heavier will be that variety. The calcium-aluminium garnet, with a specific gravity of 3·4, is the lightest, while iron-aluminium garnet, with a specific gravity of 4·3, is the heaviest. The specific gravities of other varieties lie between these two extremes, and will be mentioned with the description of each. The specific gravity is a feature which enables us to distinguish garnet easily from other stones of similar appearance and from glass imitations.

The colour of garnet is not due to any intermixed pigment, but depends on the chemical composition of the mineral itself. This being the case, the colour, whatever it may be, is distributed throughout the substance of the stone with perfect uniformity and without patchiness. When heated the mineral retains its colour, or if this be altered, it returns to the original shade when cool again. Pure calcium-aluminium garnet is perfectly colourless; this white, so-called leuco-garnet is, however, never cut as a gem. The commonest colour for garnet is red. Every shade between the palest and one dark enough to be almost black is represented; while the most diverse tones of red are met with, the most usual being tinged with brown, yellow, or violet. Red garnet, the colour-variety which is almost exclusively used for gems, was formerly one of the stones to which the name carbuncle was applied. It is probable that the term carbuncle formerly included all red stones, and not only the ruby, to which the application of the term is preferably limited at the present time. The name of the mineral is said to have been derived from the colour of the gem-varieties, red garnets having been compared to the flowers and seeds of the pomegranate-tree.

Green garnet, the colour of which is comparable to a certain extent to that of the emerald, though usually more yellowish or brownish, is also cut as a gem, but much less frequently. The finest emerald-green variety, the calcium-chromium garnet, or uvarovite, unfortunately occurs in such small and imperfectly transparent crystals that it is useless as a gem.

The colour of garnet is due to iron, and to a lesser extent to manganese and chromium. Iron is responsible for the reds, yellowish-greens, and the commonly occurring yellows and browns, while the colour of the emerald-green garnet, uvarovite, is due to chromium.

Black garnets also occur, their colour being also due to the presence of iron; they are occasionally used in mourning jewellery. Blue is a colour conspicuous by its complete absence in the garnet group. The subject of colour will be further considered when the different varieties of garnet are dealt with.

As usual, in all minerals, different specimens of garnet show different degrees of transparency; most crystals are turbid and opaque; but amongst all varieties, numerous specimens of perfect clearness and transparency, sometimes combined with the deepest and darkest shade of colour, are to be found, and it is these alone which are cut as gems.

The natural faces of crystals vary in brilliancy, the lustre being sometimes very strong, at other times more feeble, owing to the roughness of the surface and to other causes. The freshly fractured surface of a transparent stone is, however, always brilliant, and by grinding and polishing the lustre is still further increased, cut stones being very brilliant. The lustre of garnet is the ordinary vitreous kind, so strongly inclined, however, to resinous lustre that some garnets closely resemble a piece of resin in external appearance.

Garnet, being a cubic mineral, is optically isotropic, that is to say, it is singly refracting; anomalous double refraction is to be observed in a few rare cases, but scarcely ever in perfectly clear and transparent stones such as are cut as gems. The mineral has a somewhat high index of refraction; this, however, like the other physical characters, varies with the chemical composition. The index of refraction for red light ranges from 1·74 to 1·79 in the different varieties. The dispersion is almost always small; indeed, the only variety which shows any very appreciable play of prismatic colours is the green calcium-iron garnet known as demantoid. The value of the garnet as a precious stone depends upon its strong lustre and the depth and fulness of its colour.

In some cases when a candle-flame is observed through a stone, a four- or six-rayed star of light, similar to that shown by a star-sapphire, is seen. This appearance, however, is rare and does not add to the beauty of the stone as a gem, nor to its value as a precious stone.

The fact that garnet is singly refracting, prevents its being mistaken for other stones which it may resemble in appearance, such, for example, as ruby or emerald, although this character does not distinguish it from a glass imitation. The absence of dichroism in a cubic mineral like garnet is, moreover, a further aid in its discrimination. The colour is the same in whatever direction light passes through the crystal, and the two images seen in the dichroscope are absolutely identical in shade. The absence of dichroism is most useful in distinguishing garnet from ruby. So similar in colour may the two stones be that even the practised eye of an expert fails to discriminate between them. As we have already seen, the garnet is frequently mistaken for ruby; for example, on account of the similarity in colour the fine red garnet associated with the diamond in South Africa is known as "Cape ruby."

As a rule, garnet fuses before the blowpipe with moderate ease; a few varieties fuse with more difficulty, and some are quite infusible. Crystallised garnet is unattacked by acids, except hydrofluoric acid; after fusion, however, the material does not resist their action. The specific gravity of the mineral is also considerably less after fusion; thus the specific gravity of a yellowish-red calcium-aluminium garnet fell from 3·63 to 2·95. The varieties richest in iron are the most easily fusible; these, moreover, have a slight action on the magnetic needle, and the mass which remains after fusion is attracted by a magnet. All garnets when rubbed on cloth acquire a feeble charge of positive electricity.

The forms of cutting employed for garnet are those best suited to more or less darkly coloured stones. Most varieties are cut *en cabochon*, with a circular or oval outline, and with a very considerable curvature, so that the stone is high and hemispherical in shape. In the case of very dark specimens, the underside is hollowed out so as to render the stone thinner and more transparent, a device adopted for scarcely any other precious stones. These so-called garnet-shells (Plate IV., Fig. 17*b*) have been found in numbers in Roman ruins, so that the device was evidently known in ancient times. The table-cut and the step-cut are the most usual forms, while the mixed-cut is not infrequently seen. With dark-coloured stones each of these forms must be cut as thinly as possible. The table or large facet at the front of the stone, instead of being plane frequently has a convex curvature. The rosette or brilliant is used for some kinds of garnets and irregular, fanciful forms are also met with. A few cut garnets are represented in Plate XIV., Figs. 4, 6, 8, and 10, and in Plate XVIII., Fig. 7. Grains of garnet are often provided all round with small facets, arranged regularly and systematically or in no particular order; these are bored and strung together for bracelets and necklaces. Stones of the lighter shades of colour are mounted *à jour*, while the darker specimens are often mounted upon a burnished foil of silver or copper.

The different varieties of garnet differ very considerably in value. The worth of a stone depends for the most part on the beauty of its colour and the rarity of its occurrence. Particulars as to prices will be given later on under the description of different varieties.

The commonest fault in garnet is the presence of fissures along which the stone is apt to fracture. Garnets are often, however, almost ideally pure; they are transparent and faultless much more frequently than are many other precious stones.

Garnet is one of the most important of minerals, the common, imperfectly transparent varieties being widely distributed throughout the earth's crust. Transparent precious garnet is less abundant, but occurs under exactly the same conditions. Garnet is for the most part a mineral characteristic of the ancient crystalline-silicate rocks, especially crystalline schists, such as gneisses and mica-schist; it is found also in eclogite, serpentine, and other rocks. As already stated, the crystals are either attached to the walls of drusy cavities in the rock or embedded in it. Garnet is much less common in intrusive rocks, such as granite, and all varieties, with the exception of black garnet, or melanite, are of sparing occurrence in volcanic rocks. Garnets are also found in some limestones at places where the rock has been baked by contact with a molten igneous rock, the garnets being a so-called contact product in the limestone. The occurrence of precious garnet in its original situation is, however. of little importance from the gem-seeker's point of view. But few garnets are extracted from the solid rock; for the most part they are picked up in the sands and gravels of rivers and streams, having been set free by the weathering of the mother-rock and carried away with the rest of the débris.

We have already seen that there are many varieties of garnet differing from each other in chemical composition. Garnets which agree in chemical composition are further classified according to their external characters and are distinguished by particular names. Many of these varieties are solely of mineralogical interest, but a few are sufficiently transparent to be used for gems, and these we must now consider in some detail. They include the light yellowish-red hessonite or cinnamon-stone, the dark violet-red almandine, the blood-red pyrope from Bohemia, the magnificent "Cape ruby," the fine green demantoid from the Urals, and, as rarities to the ordinary jeweller, the yellowish-red spessartite, the brownish-green grossularite, and the black melanite.

HESSONITE.

Hessonite, or *cinnamon-stone*, as may be seen from the table of analyses above, is essentially a calcium-aluminium garnet containing small quantities of ferrous and manganous oxide, or, in other words, mixed with smlla amounts of iron-aluminium garnet and manganese-aluminium garnet. The rich, warm yellowish-red colour of the stone is due to these two constituents, calcium-aluminium garnet being of itself colourless. The colour of this garnet is hyacinth-red, sometimes inclined to orange or to honey-yellow. The colour varies somewhat according to the distance at which the stone is held from the eye. It appears distinctly red only when held at some distance away; close to the eye it often appears nearly pure yellow, the red being almost completely invisible. Hessonite is also remarkable in that its colour by lamp-light is considerably more brilliant and fiery than by day. The colour is well seen in Figs. 7 and 8 of Plate XIV.; the former is a representation of a druse of crystals having the form of Fig. 66d, which is not unusual in hessonite; and the latter of a faceted gem.

The appearance of hessonite has been compared to sugar-candy, but more often to the bark of the cinnamon-tree. It is from the latter resemblance that it has derived its name, which is very appropriate, since most of the hessonite of gem-quality comes from the cinnamon island of Ceylon. The colour of hessonite is, however, most strikingly similar to that of hyacinth. So much alike are the two stones that they were only discovered to belong to distinct species at the end of the eighteenth century. Previous to this, hessonite had always been regarded as hyacinth (zircon), a mistake easily made, seeing that the stones are found together in the same gem-gravels in Ceylon. Even now the stones are never distinguished in the trade, and a large quantity of hessonite is sold as hyacinth. This is especially so in the case of large specimens, for hyacinth scarcely ever occurs in crystals of large size, while fragments of hessonite of good quality and considerable size are by no means rare. When any difference is made by dealers in the application of the two terms, the darker specimens of hessonite are referred to as hyacinth and the lighter as cinnamon-stone. The substitution of hessonite for hyacinth is not done with the object of deception, but arises solely from confusion of names: although the lustre of hyacinth is far superior to that of hessonite, yet the colour of the latter is quite equal to that of hyacinth. A perfectly transparent, finely coloured, and faultless cinnamon-stone cannot, therefore, be any more inferior to hyacinth in value than it is in beauty of appearance.

Although hyacinth and hessonite are frequently mistaken the one for the other in the trade, yet their discrimination is really a simple matter. Hyacinth is much heavier than hessonite, for while the specific gravity of the latter lies between 3·6 and 3·7, that of hyacinth ranges from 4·6 to 4·7. Hessonite again is singly refracting, while hyacinth has strong double refraction. The lustre of the two stones differs also, that of hyacinth being stronger and more adamantine in character, while that of hessonite is strongly vitreous inclining to resinous, grains of hessonite being particularly resinous in appearance. Moreover, hyacinth is somewhat harder than hessonite; for the former $H = 7\frac{1}{2}$, while for the latter $H = 7\frac{1}{4}$, so that hessonite is only slightly harder than quartz. To distinguish between hessonite and yellowish-red spinel (rubicelle), on the other hand, is less easy, for the colour of the latter often closely resembles that of hessonite; moreover, the two stones both crystallise in the cubic system and are therefore singly refracting; they are of about equal hardness and very nearly the same density, the specific gravity of spinel being slightly less, namely, 3·60 to 3·63, and its hardness rather greater, namely, $H = 8$. Under these circumstances it is sometimes impossible to say whether a faceted stone or an irregular fragment is hessonite or spinel. When the crystalline form is observable it is easy, however, for spinel always crystallises in octahedra, while hessonite rarely takes this form, but more often that of Fig. 69d. The refractive indices of the two stones are also almost the same. The only certain means of distinguishing between stones similar or identical in so many respects is to make a chemical analysis, and this in the case of faceted stones is not always feasible. A glass imitation can, of course, be easily distinguished by its hardness and specific gravity.

A few other characters of cinnamon-stone remain to be mentioned. The index of refraction is slightly less than that of other garnets; for red light $n = 1·74$; anomalous double refraction is sometimes to be observed. Hessonite fuses to a greenish glass somewhat readily when heated before the blowpipe. Although it contains only a small amount of iron, the mineral has a slight action on the magnetic needle.

It has been mentioned already that hessonite occurs in **Ceylon**; this island (Fig. 59) is almost the only locality for hessonite of gem-quality, and it is probable that all the stones on the market come from thence. It is found in smaller or larger fragments, some lying loose, some still in the solid rock, which is gneiss containing actinolite, magnetite, and other minerals. Blocks of considerable size containing portions of gem-quality are found, amongst other localities, at Belligam, a few miles from the Point de Galle. It is the rounded pebbles found in the gem-gravels, especially in the district of Matura, which are most used for cutting as gems. These pebbles, the largest of which are several pounds in weight, are finer and purer and less fissured than are the angular fragments which have not been water-worn. These also, however, are traversed by cracks and fissures, the presence of which is the commonest, and almost the only fault usually present in cinnamon-stone.

The hessonite which occurs at other localities is less suitable for cutting, the specimens being small or imperfectly transparent. Still, there are a few localities in **Europe**, especially in the Alps, which yield, or have yielded, a small amount of hessonite of gem-quality. In early times fine " hyacinth-garnets from Dissentis " or " from St. Gotthard " were sometimes cut as gems. They occur with epidote in quartz in a small crevice in mica-schist in the Alp-Lolen in the Maigels-thal on the boundary between Cantons Uri and Graubündten (Grisons). The crystals vary in size, but none are much bigger than a pea ; each usually encloses a grain of quartz. At the present time they are scarcely sought for at all. Beautiful druses of hessonite occur in crevices in serpentine (Plate XIV., Fig. 7), on the Mussa-Alp, in the Ala valley in Piedmont. The crystals of hessonite are here associated with crystals of dark green chlorite and of pale green diopside : a number of the latter are represented among the garnets in the figure just quoted. These, as well as very similar specimens from Achmatovsk, in the Urals, are beautiful objects, to be seen in all mineral collections, and illustrate the natural occurrence of this stone in a very striking manner.

Hessonite is rarely cut *en cabochon*; more usually it is cut with facets (Plate XIV., Fig. 8) in one or other of the forms mentioned above. The colour of this stone being pale it is unnecessary to hollow it out at the back or to make it specially thin. Cut hessonites are usually mounted upon a burnished foil, they are rarely set *à jour*.

SPESSARTITE.

The spessartite from Amelia Court House, Virginia, U.S.A., is very similar in colour to hessonite. It is a manganese-aluminium garnet, containing manganous oxide in place of lime. At the locality mentioned it is found in the mica mines in the granite as beautiful, clear crystals, which have yielded stones of very good quality weighing from 1 to 100 carats. Spessartite from other localities is scarcely suitable for cutting as a gem.

ALMANDINE.

Almandine is the deep red variety of garnet to which the name carbuncle used to be given. The name was applied to other red stones, but most frequently to garnet. It is generally believed that the word almandine is derived from Pliny's name for the stone, which was carbunculus alabandicus, since, according to his statement, it was found near the town of Alabanda, in Caria (Asia Minor), where also it was cut. At the present time transparent specimens of this kind of stone are commonly referred to simply as precious garnet.

Almandine, as shown in the analysis quoted above, is an iron-aluminium garnet containing, beside the predominating ferrous oxide and alumina, small quantities of ferric oxide, manganous oxide, &c.

The red of almandine is always dark in tint, but varies somewhat in different specimens. The colour is no doubt due to the large amount of iron which enters into the composition of the mineral. It is often distinctly tinged with violet, and is then described as columbine-red (Plate XIV., Figs. 3 and 4; Plate XVIII., Fig. 7). Shades of colour between brownish-red and reddish-brown are also not infrequently seen. The brownish-red stones are sometimes known to jewellers as vermeille garnet (vermilion garnet), or simply as "vermeille"; but the term is somewhat loosely applied, and often includes the Bohemian garnet or pyrope, which is deep red with a tinge of yellow. In artificial light almandine loses but little of its beauty; the colour, however, is then more inclined to orange or hyacinth-red and approaches that of hessonite. When heated, almandine becomes black, but returns to the original red colour when cooled, though the fine appearance of the stone is somewhat impaired by this treatment.

A remarkable phenomenon connected with almandine and with only one other precious stone, namely zircon, is the presence of dark absorption bands in the spectrum of light which has passed through the stone. In the case of almandine the characteristic black bands occur in the green part of the spectrum, and can be seen with the aid of an ordinary pocket spectroscope. These absorption bands are perfectly characteristic of almandine and distinguish it from all other precious stones. The phenomenon affords an easy means of discriminating between almandine and red spinel, both of which are singly refracting and therefore devoid of dichroism.

Almandine in colour often approaches very closely to ruby, but may be readily distinguished from the latter by its single refraction and absence of dichroism. The two minerals differ also in specific gravity, that of ruby scarcely exceeding 4·0 while that of almandine varies between 4·1 and 4·3, a value which is higher than for any other garnet. Again, almandine is only slightly harder than quartz, its hardness being $7\frac{1}{4}$, so that it is scratched by topaz and still more easily by corundum or ruby.

Not only is almandine heavier than hessonite, but its optical refraction is greater also, the refractive index of the former for red light being $n = 1\cdot77$. Before the blowpipe almandine fuses to a magnetic mass with moderate ease. Even before fusion almandine has a slight action on the magnetic needle like hessonite, the action of which is feebler, however, since it contains less iron.

Though not as brilliant as ruby, almandine, when cut and polished, has a fine lustre. It is cut usually in the forms adopted for other garnets. Fig. 4 of Plate XIV. represents a rosette of almandine. This stone is frequently also cut *en cabochon* (Plate XVIII., Fig. 7), more often than is hessonite, for example. Stones treated in this way are usually hollowed out, and are then known as garnet-shells; their colour is then not too deep and the lustre is advantageously displayed by the curved surface. Foils of burnished metal placed beneath the stone produce a fine effect.

The value of a stone depends on its size and purity, on the absence of faults, especially fissures, and in particular on its colour, which must show up brightly even if the stone be of considerable thickness. The nearer it approaches the fine, lustrous, velvety-purple of the ruby the greater will be the value, and the price of such stones may reach that of sapphires of medium quality. Stones of a brownish tinge, like the vermeille garnets, are little prized and are very cheap, as are also those of small size, impure colour, or with fissures or other faults.

Cloudy and opaque almandine of a quality not suitable for gems is the most widely distributed of all garnets. It is the common garnet of mineralogists, and is found in very well-developed crystals, sometimes many pounds in weight, in gneiss and mica-schist, sometimes also in granite and other rocks. This mode of occurrence is illustrated in Plate XIV., Fig. 3. Transparent precious garnet, such as is used for cutting as gems, occurs together with, and in the same manner as, the cloudy and opaque garnet, though the former is of more sparing occurrence than the latter. As is the case with so many other precious stones, almandine does not always remain in its original mother-rock, but is often set free by the weathering of the rock, and ultimately becomes a constituent of the sands and gravels of running streams, from which it is obtained in the form of rounded pebbles. Almandine of gem-quality is not only more abundant than hessonite, but is also more widely distributed. The more important localities are detailed below.

The locality standing first in importance, at which both hessonite and almandine occur, is **Ceylon**. Pebbles of almandine suitable for cutting are here, however, smaller and far less abundant than are those of hessonite. Near Trincomalee, on the eastern side of the island, almandine is said to occur embedded in a hornblende-schist. It is also found in gem-gravels in the southern and south-western parts of the island. On account of its similarity to ruby it is no doubt sometimes mistaken and substituted for that stone. It is consequently occasionally referred to as " Ceylonese ruby," a somewhat misleading term since the true ruby also occurs in Ceylon.

It is frequently stated that the most important of all localities for the finest almandine is **Syriam,** the ancient capital of the former kingdom of Pegu, which was conquered by the Burmese and now forms part of the British province of Lower Burma. Syriam is now only a small village near the important trade centre of Rangoon (see Map, Fig. 54). Both are situated on the alluvial deposits which form the delta of the Irrawaddy. According to Dr. F. Noetling, of the Indian Geological Survey, garnet does not occur here at all; it is probable, therefore, that almandine was brought from some other place to Syriam when the latter was the capital of the kingdom. But no precious almandine has as yet been observed to occur in any part of Burma. Nowhere in Pegu, that is to say, in the region of the lower Irrawaddy, are any precious stones met with, while in Upper Burma the only red stones found are ruby, spinel, and red tourmaline. It is said that the inhabitants of the neighbouring Shan States on the east bring almandine into Burma, where it is sold as ruby. However that may be, it is certain that the supposed occurrence of almandine at Syriam is by no means well authenticated.

In consequence of the supposed occurrence of almandine at Syriam (Syrian), this stone has sometimes been distinguished as " Syrian garnet " (not to be confused with Syria). In course of time, however, this term has come to signify a colour distinction, and is now applied to almandine, the colour of which inclines to violet and approaches that of the ruby or of the " oriental amethyst." " Syrian garnet," then, is a term which includes some of the finest and costliest stones, while " vermeille garnet " is the term given to the cheapest and least prized brownish varieties.

Garnet is of wide distribution in **India.** The precious almandine occurs there in such large amounts that it forms a not unimportant product of the country. It is collected and cut at many places, especially at Delhi and Jaipur. Whether all the garnets collected in India belong to the variety almandine is, however, doubtful, since chemical analyses have not been made; we shall therefore here treat of the occurrence of garnet generally, at such places in India where it is obtained in any amount. The stones suitable for cutting as gems appear to be all obtained by excavating and washing the weathered products of gneiss and similar rocks. There are workings of this kind at Kondapalli in the Godavari district (lat. 16° 38′ N., long. 80° 36′ E. See Map, Fig. 33). The garnets found here have been derived from a hornblende-gneiss, and have long been famous: those at present obtained are, however, of little value. At Bhadrachalam, on the Godavari river in the Central Provinces, as well as at Mahanadibett, in Orissa, garnets of the same kind are obtained. Stones of better quality than those of the last-named locality come from Gharibpeth, eight miles south of Paloncha in Haidarabad. They occur, with much kyanite, at a depth of 8 feet below the surface in weathered material, derived probably from granite or gneiss. The stones obtained are tested as to durability by a smart blow with a hammer; those which resist the blow are fit for cutting, and are sent for this purpose to Madras.

The garnet mines in Rajputana are a more important source of supply. The mines of Sarwar (lat. 26° 4′ N., long. 75° 4½′ E.), in the Kishengurh State, are often mentioned. The privilege of working in these mines is granted by the Rajah on a payment of one rupee per man per day. This source of revenue alone brings in 50,000 rupees per annum, so that there must be a daily average of 130 to 140 persons at work in these mines. According to

Tellery, the manager of the garnet works at Jaipur, which are mentioned below, stones from Sarwar are smaller than those from the garnet quarries of Kakoria, but in colour and lustre are surpassed by no others. Taste in Europe and America at the present day, however, inclines to stones of a more decided violet tint.

The garnet quarries of Kakoria have just been mentioned. Kakoria is situated in the State of Jaipur, and is probably identical with the place marked Kakor in the official Indian atlas, in lat. 26° 1′ N. and long. 75° 59′ E. of Greenwich. The quarries of Rajmahal (lat. 25° 23½′ N., long. 75° 21½′ E.) are also situated in this State, but their yield is less abundant. Garnets are obtained at Meja (lat. 25° 25′ N., long. 74° 37′ E.), in Udaipur, and also at several places in Meywar, but the yield is not as abundant as at Sarwar or at Kakoria, and the stones are of quite ordinary quality. Garnet of gem-quality is found at many other localities, none of sufficient importance, however, to warrant special mention. From the quality and size of the stones Tellery concludes that the Indian garnets described in ancient writings came from Rajputana.

Of **American** localities those in Brazil must be first mentioned. Almandine occurs here in rounded grains, which, though small, are finely coloured and transparent. They accompany the topaz found in the Minas Novas district of Minas Geraes. Stones of gem-quality are also said to occur in Uruguay. Numerous localities are known in the United States of North America, at some of which transparent stones suitable for cutting are found, though never in abundance. Among such may be mentioned the purple-red pebbles found in the Columbia river in the States of Washington and Oregon, some of which are of good quality and considerable size, with a weight between half a carat and half an ounce. The occurrence of almandine in Greenland is more important; the stones, which are of a fine colour and very transparent, although much fissured, occur, as a rule, embedded in chlorite- or mica-schist.

In **Australia** almandine, together probably with other varieties of garnet, is widely distributed. It is very abundant in the rivers of the Northern Territory of South Australia, the larger stones being of a bright cherry-red or yellowish-red colour, and the smaller light red inclined to violet. These stones, which were at first supposed to be rubies, were found in large numbers in the gravels of the Maude, Florence, and Hale rivers. They fetched a high price, and no less than twenty-four ruby companies, working some hundreds of claims, were floated. When it became known that the supposed rubies were in reality garnet, the companies instantly collapsed and work was suspended. At the present time very few garnets are collected in Australia for cutting as gems. The mistake made in the identification of these stones has led to their being sometimes known as "Adelaide rubies."

Garnet of gem-quality has recently been met with in German East **Africa**, where it is found in the Namaputa stream, a tributary of the Rovuma. It has here been weathered out of hornblende-gneiss, in which it is irregularly distributed as rounded enclosures up to the size of a man's fist. Most of the stones are clear and transparent and of a columbine-red colour with a tinge of brownish-red. Many fine gems, said to surpass the Indian in quality, have been obtained, but whether the deposit could be worked on a large scale is as yet doubtful. A chemical analysis of this garnet proves it to be almandine, with much of the ferrous oxide replaced by magnesia; the specific gravity is 3·875.

Almandine suitable for cutting is also found in **Europe**, but not in large amount nor of specially good quality. A certain number of these stones are collected every year in the Alps, which is the most important European locality. Specially remarkable are the rhombic dodecahedral crystals, measuring as much as an inch across, which occur in the dark mica-schist and the chlorite-schist of the upper Zillerthal in the Tyrol, the exact locality being on the Rossrucken opposite the Berlin Hut in the Zemmgrund. They are first quarried and then freed from the mother-rock by grinding against each other in a rotating barrel. The majority are sent to Bohemia, where, as we shall see presently, an important garnet-cutting industry has been developed. To this country are sent garnets from all parts of the world, and these, together with the stones which actually occur in the country, are cut and used in the fashioning of various articles of jewellery. Most of the garnets found in Bohemia, however, belong not to the variety known as almandine but to that known as pyrope. Almandine of gem-quality is nevertheless found in Bohemia, especially in the alluvial ground in the neighbourhood of Kuttenberg and Kollin, such stones being known as "Kollin garnets." The occurrence of almandine here, as elsewhere in Europe, is unimportant. Other European localities for almandine which may be mentioned are Mittelwald, in the Rohoznabach of Hungary, where crystals of considerable size are sometimes found, and Alicante in Spain.

PYROPE.

Pyrope, or *Bohemian garnet*, is distinguished by its deep, rich, blood-red colour, which has always an unmistakable tinge of yellow (Plate XIV., Figs. 5 and 6), sometimes even verging upon hyacinth-red. Violet tints are never present in pyrope, and a garnet which shows a tinge of this colour is almost certain to be almandine: in the case of other tints, however, it is not possible to judge by colour alone. On account of the yellowish tint of its colour, pyrope is included in the term vermeille garnet, while some practical jewellers limit the application of the term to pyrope. It is highly probable that this stone was one of those to which the name carbuncle was formerly given. Pyrope is very similar in colour to some rubies, but, like almandine, it can be distinguished from this gem by the fact that it is refracting and devoid of dichroism, as also by the fact that its specific gravity is less than that of ruby, being only 3·7 to 3·8. The specific gravity of pyrope affords a sure means whereby it may be distinguished from almandine when this cannot be done by colour alone, since almandine is considerably denser, having a specific gravity between 4·1 and 4·3.

Pyrope is essentially a magnesium-aluminium garnet, but of more complex composition than the garnets hitherto considered. Besides magnesia it contains a not inconsiderable amount of lime, ferrous oxide, manganous oxide, and chromous oxide, the latter of which figures in analyses as chromic oxide. The magnesium-aluminium garnet is thus mixed with calcium-, iron-, manganese-, and chromium-aluminium garnet. The colour, which is almost invariably deep and rich, depends on the presence of small quantities of iron and manganese, perhaps also of chromium.

In contrast to almost all other garnets, pyrope scarcely ever occurs in distinct crystals. The few which have as yet been found have the form of a cube with curved faces, a form which is unique as far as other garnets are concerned. Pyrope occurs usually in irregular grains, with a dull, rough surface, although that of a fresh conchoidal fracture is bright and shining. The hardness (H = $7\frac{1}{4}$) is slightly greater than that of quartz. The refraction is greater than that of any other red garnet, the index of refraction for red light being 1·79; the substance is perfectly isotropic and shows no anomalous double refraction. Pyrope differs also from other red garnets in its behaviour before the blowpipe, since it fuses with great difficulty; it is possible to fuse only the thinnest splinters to a black, magnetic glass.

Pyrope is usually perfectly clear and transparent so far as its dark colour allows. That from Bohemia is all, without exception, of ideal purity. This absolute purity and freedom from enclosures of every individual stone is unparalleled among other precious stones. Moreover, the transparency is rarely impaired by fissures, as is the case with other garnets. When heated, pyrope behaves like almandine and becomes black and opaque; on cooling again it recovers to the full its original transparency and colour, which is not the case with almandine.

As to its mode of occurrence, pyrope is always found in olivine-rocks or in serpentine, an alteration product of the former. It occurs embedded in these rocks as irregular grains, among many other places at Petschau, in Bohemia, and Zöblitz, in Saxony, from which locality come the specimens represented in Plate XIV., Fig. 5. In collecting pyrope places are sought where the serpentine is completely weathered to a loose earthy material. The grains of garnet, being little affected by the weathering process, lie scattered loosely through this material, from which they can be separated with little trouble. Such are the conditions under which pyrope occurs in the north of **Bohemia**, where it is specially abundant, and from whence it is almost exclusively obtained. This variety of garnet, at the present time so much admired, occurs nowhere else in just the same manner, and is hence described as Bohemian garnet. The occurrence has given rise to an important industry in northern Bohemia, where now are cut not only garnets found in Bohemia itself, nor only pyrope, but garnet of all kinds from all parts of the world, from the Zillerthal, from India, Ceylon, Asia Minor, Australia, the United States, Greenland, &c., and in addition all other precious stones with the single exception of diamond.

The garnet-cutting works of Bohemia are very old-established and have seen many vicissitudes. After a period of decay, the industry received a fresh impetus through the establishment of baths at Carlsbad, Teplitz, and other places. Thousands of persons from all parts of the world were attracted there to benefit by the waters, and many carried away with them as souvenirs of their visit pretty articles of jewellery set with Bohemian garnets. The increased demand so created led to their becoming an important article of export. The importance of this particular industry may be judged from the fact that at the present time in Bohemia there are 3000 men engaged in garnet-cutting, some hundreds of garnet-drillers, about 500 goldsmiths and silversmiths, and some 3500 working jewellers. The collecting of garnets employs some 350 or 400 persons, so that, including the many persons whose work is indirectly connected with the industry, there must be between 9000 and 10,000 persons gaining their livelihood by labour connected with the working of this precious stone.

There are a few cutting works at Prague, but many more in the neighbourhood between Reichenberg and Gitschin, of which those at Rovensko, Semil, Sobotka, and Lomnitz may be mentioned. The centre of the industry, however, is at Turnau on the Iser, and here a Government school, at which the working of precious stones is taught, has been established. There are a few cutting-works on the German side of the border, at Warmbrunn, in Silesia, for example, and other places.

In the district where cutting is carried on, garnets, though known to occur, are not abundant; they have been found, for example, at Neu-Paka, a little to the east of Gitschin, where the few crystals of pyrope hitherto found in Bohemia were met with. The material for the cutting-works is obtained almost exclusively, however, from the neighbourhood of Teplitz, Aussig, and Bilin, in the Bohemian Mittelgebirge, some distance to the west. The garnet-bearing deposit covers an area of over seventy square kilometres and the mineral is abundant over an area of about one-tenth of this. The principal localities are, among others, Stiefelberg, near Meronitz, also the neighbourhood of Chodolitz, Dlaschkowitz, Podsedlitz, Chrastian, Tremschitz, Starrey, Schöppenthal, Leskai, Triblitz, Jetschan,

Semtsch, Solan, and Schelkowitz; at all these places garnets are now systematically collected. In the year 1890 there were in this district 142 owners of garnet-fields, and stones to the value of 80,000 gulden (£8000) were obtained by the labour of 362 persons The trade in garnets was kept in the hands of about seventeen merchants.

The stones are found in a clayey or sandy gravel belonging to the glacial drift and resting on beds of Cretaceous age. In this gravel grains of garnet completely freed from their mother-rock occur in large numbers. Some, however, are found embedded in a brown semi-opal occurring in masses, the largest of which is about the size of a man's head. These masses of opal are to be regarded as the remains of the serpentine in which the pyrope was originally embedded, most of which, as serpentine, is now completely destroyed. The garnets embedded in the masses of opal are not utilised, only those lying free in the gravelly material being collected and cut.

The deposit of gravel in which the pyrope occurs differs somewhat in different places. At Chrastian, beneath a layer of soil, one metre in thickness, is a layer, two metres thick, of garnetiferous gravel with a light grey loamy base; below this is another layer of garnetiferous gravel 4 metres thick bound together with a yellowish-brown clayey material. The whole rests upon a bed of fuller's earth belonging to the Senonian division of the Upper Cretaceous formation. At Meronitz the garnet-bearing layer is a peculiar clayey calcareous conglomerate.

Garnets are sometimes washed out of the loose gravel by rain-storms, and, owing to this, good specimens are occasionally found lying loose on the surface of the ground. For the most part, however, the stones are obtained in excavations. The surface-soil is removed and the garnet-bearing layer penetrated by pits of greater or less depth, which are refilled when the valuable material has been excavated. Only at specially rich spots are large excavations undertaken, where also underground mining operations are carried on to a small extent. The garnet-bearing earth is washed in suitable vessels to remove the lighter clayey particles, after which the stones are picked out by hand and sorted according to size by means of sieves. The stones are classified according to the number required to make up a loth ($= 16\frac{2}{3}$ grams, or rather less than $\frac{1}{2}$ oz. avoirdupois), and are referred to as "sixteens," "thirty-twos," "hundreds," and so on, according as 16, 32, or 100 stones make up a loth. Most of the stones are very small, 500 or more in the aggregate weighing a loth. Those of which 400 make up the weight of a loth are very numerous and of little value. Stones the size of rice grains are worth more, as also are those the size of a pea, which, however, are not found every day, while several years may elapse between the finding of pyropes of the size of a hazel-nut. It is estimated that in every 100 kilograms (220 lbs.) of garnets there are only two to three "thirties," and in 2000 kilograms only one "sixteen."

It will be seen from this that a moderate number of stones of fair size are met with, but that really large stones are rare. In the *Gemmarum et Lapidum Historia* of Boetius de Boot, published in 1609, is mentioned a pyrope, the size of a pigeon's egg, in the possession of Kaiser Rudolph II., which was valued at 45,000 thalers (£6750). A very fine stone, the size of a hen's egg, is now preserved in the Imperial Treasury at Vienna. In the "Green Vaults" at Dresden is one measuring 35 millimetres in length, 18 millimetres in breadth, and 27 millimetres in thickness, that is, about the size of a pigeon's egg; it weighs $468\frac{1}{2}$ carats, and is set in an Order of the Golden Fleece.

Since all Bohemian pyropes are of the same quality and purity, their value varies only with their weight. Small stones are very cheap, but the price of larger ones is by no means inconsiderable; no rough stone found in recent years has realised more than 500 florins

(£25). Boetius de Boot states that large stones were worth as much as a ruby of equal size; this is not now the case, in spite of the estimation in which pyrope is held, and of the fact that its colour is equal in beauty to that of some rubies.

The very smallest grains of pyrope are not cut as gems, but are utilised in a variety of ways, for example, as counterpoises for delicate balances, for the preparation of grinding powder, and even as ornamental gravels for garden walks, which gives a good idea of the abundance in which they are found. There is nothing attractive about the appearance of the stones in the rough; the process of cutting, however, brings out the brilliancy of their colour, which is displayed by smaller stones just as advantageously as by larger. In spite of this, only stones exceeding a certain minimum size are cut as gems. Almost all the usual forms of cutting are utilised for pyrope. As in the case of almandine, it is frequently cut with a curved surface, *en cabochon*, when it is usually hollowed out at the back, but may or may not be provided with small marginal facets. The light reflected from the curved surface blazes with a wonderful fiery red colour. Still more frequently pyrope is cut in a faceted form, either as a table-stone or a low step-cut, often with a curved table. Brilliants and rosettes are also to be seen as well as fanciful forms in which the facets have no recognised arrangement. Pyrope is more frequently used for the manufacture of beads than are other garnets; only the smaller stones are used for this purpose, each has a hole drilled through it and is faceted regularly all over. The cut stones are either mounted upon a burnished copper or silver foil in a closed setting blackened inside, or *en pavé*. In the latter case the stones are fixed by means of small claws or pins over close-set perforations in a metal plate, the whole forming a kind of garnet mosaic.

There are only a few other localities where pyrope of gem-quality is found. Other than Bohemia the only European locality is Elie in Fifeshire; the so-called "Elie rubies" are of purely local interest, however.

The occurrence of pyrope in the western part of the **United States** is more important. The mineral is specially abundant in Arizona, New Mexico, and southern Colorado, and, as frequently happens, was at first mistaken for ruby, a mistake out of which arose the local trade names "Arizona ruby" and "Colorado ruby." In New Mexico pyrope occurs as angular or rounded grains in sands at Santa Fé, but most abundantly in the Reservation of the Navajo Indians, together with olivine and chrome-diopside. Pyrope is here collected by the Indians from the sands of ant-hills and scorpion-hills, as well as from the mother-rock. In Arizona pyrope occurs loose in sands, and, in the north-east of the State, embedded in the mother-rock. Here also it is collected by the Indians and occasionally by soldiers stationed there. The angular or rounded fragments measure $\frac{1}{8}$ to $\frac{1}{4}$ inch across; larger grains, ranging up to $\frac{1}{2}$ inch in diameter, are rare. The quality of these stones is good, about half being fit for cutting; of these about one quarter are of ordinary quality, exceptionally fine stones, especially those exceeding 3 carats in weight, being rare. Many enclose a network of fine needles, probably of rutile.

American pyropes on an average are smaller than the so-called "Cape rubies," to be described presently. They have an equally fine appearance by daylight, but in artificial light the American stones are superior to the African, the latter appearing somewhat dull. The so-called "Arizona rubies" and "Colorado rubies" are rather extensively used, more so than is the case with the pyrope found, for example, in the gold washings of the Counties of Burke, MacDowell, and Alexander in North Carolina, and from other districts in the United States.

The occurrence of pyrope in Mexico is of no more importance; it is known to occur in the State of Sonora and in that of Chihuahua, especially on the Jaco Lake, where its mode of occurrence is the same as in Arizona, and where it is collected by the Comanche Indians.

Of all varieties of garnet one of the finest is the dark, blood-red pyrope, which occurs in association with diamond in **South Africa.** This also was at first supposed to be ruby, and was collected and sold as such for some time, hence the term " *Cape ruby.*" Several different kinds of garnet are found in association with diamond at the Cape. Some are of a deep wine-red colour, some of a hyacinth-red, almost the colour of hessonite, while others, fewer in number, are brownish-yellow and deep blood-red.

The last named is the much prized " Cape ruby " and is the only one cut as a gem. It is a magnesium-aluminium garnet containing some manganese oxide and ferrous oxide, and differing but slightly in chemical composition from the Bohemian pyrope, as may be seen from the analysis quoted above. The " Cape ruby " must therefore be classed with pyrope and not with almandine, as is sometimes incorrectly done. Not only on account of its chemical composition, but also on account of its specific gravity, which is 3·86 (that of Bohemian pyrope being 3·7 to 3·8, and that of almandine 4·1 to 4·3) and of its colour, should this classification be adopted. The colour approaches indeed much more closely to that of pyrope, being an almost pure carmine-red more or less tinged with yellow and not very deep in shade (Plate XIV., Fig. 6), thus differing distinctly from the columbine-red of a good almandine. The hardness is $7\frac{1}{4}$, the same as that of Bohemian pyrope and of almandine. The " Cape ruby " fetches larger prices than any other garnet, stones of moderate size being worth £10 to £12 10s. per carat.

It has already been stated that the " Cape ruby " occurs in association with diamond in South Africa. It is found in the form of irregular angular grains with an uneven surface in the diamond-bearing rock known as the " blue ground " and the " yellow-ground." The mother-rock is thus an olivine-rock, or, more commonly, the weathered equivalent of this, namely, serpentine, just as is the case with the pyrope of Bohemia, North America, and all other localities. The " Cape ruby " is far less abundant than is the paler red pyrope by which it is accompanied. The grains are larger on the whole than are the grains of pyrope found in Bohemia and America ; they never exceed a certain maximum size, however, which is much less than that of the largest diamonds found at the same place. The residue of heavy minerals obtained by washing the diamantiferous material contains, besides diamonds, red garnets and green grains of an augitic mineral ; and from this residue the diamonds and " Cape rubies " are picked out. In the diamond-bearing rock of the " dry diggings " the " Cape ruby " is somewhat of a rarity, being far more abundant, though still uncommon, in the " river-diggings," that is to say, in the sands and gravels of the Vaal river, where it sometimes occurs in pebbles so smooth and rounded that they appear to have been polished. Here, as in the " dry-diggings," the stone is collected as a secondary product.

There still remains to be described a new variety of red garnet, recently (1898) described by Messrs. W. E. Hidden and J. H. Pratt, for which the name **RHODOLITE** is proposed. In many respects it is intermediate between almandine and pyrope, but more closely related to the latter, though differing from both in colour. Its occurrence in association with ruby at Cowee Creek and Mason's Branch in Macon County, North Carolina, has been mentioned already in the description of corundum. It is found as water-worn pebbles in the gravels of these streams, and also, together with ruby, in a decomposed, basic igneous rock, known as " saprolite," and, in the form of small crystals, enclosed in crystals of ruby. The colour is pale rose-red inclining to purple like that of certain roses and rhododendrons, hence the name rhodolite. It lacks the depth and intensity of colour which makes garnets, as a rule, such dark-looking stones especially by artificial light. The peculiarly beautiful rose tint of

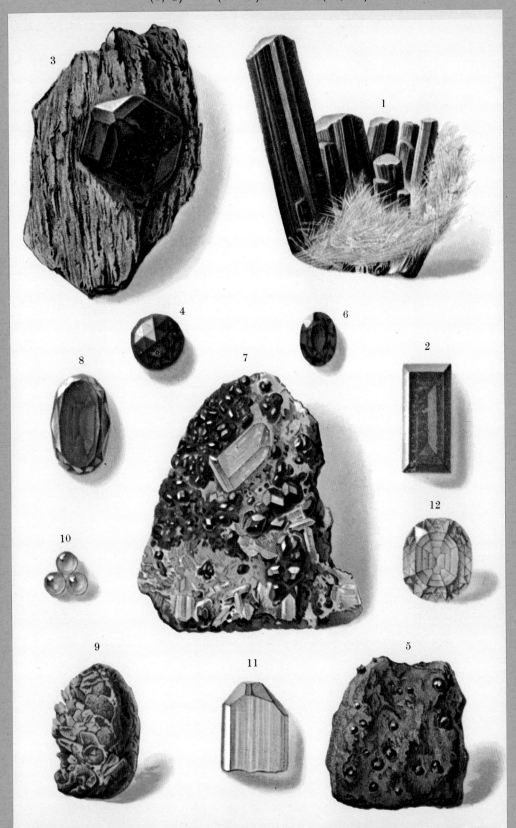

1. Epidote, crystals (Salzburg). 2. Epidote, cut. 3. Almandine, crystal in mica-schist.
4. Almandine, cut [see also Pl. XVIII, Fig. 7]. 5. Pyrope (Bohemian Garnet) in matrix.
6. Pyrope ("Cape-ruby"), cut. 7. Hessonite, crystals with diopside (Piedmont). 8. Hessonite,
cut (Ceylon). 9. Demantoid, rough (Urals). 10. The same, cut. 11. Olivine (Chrysolite),
crystal. 12. The same, cut.

rhodolite combined with its transparency and brilliancy renders it an even more striking object by candlelight than by daylight. The lustre of rhodolite is comparable with that of demantoid, a green garnet from the Urals; this, together with its freedom from internal flaws and inclusions, makes it when cut a very striking and beautiful gem. The chemical composition of this new variety of garnet is shown by the following analysis:

SiO_2.	Al_2O_3.	Fe_2O_3.	FeO.	MgO.	CaO.	
41·59	23·13	1·90	15·55	17·23	0·92	= 100·32

The chemical formula which represents this composition is:

$$2(3MgO.Al_2O_3.3SiO_2) + 3FeO.Al_2O_3.3SiO_2;$$

in other words, rhodolite is a combination of two pyrope molecules with one almandine molecule. The specific gravity, 3·837, is more in agreement with that of pyrope than with that of almandine; on the other hand, in spite of the preponderance of the pyrope molecules, an examination by Professor Church of the absorption spectrum of rhodolite shows the existence of the bands which are characteristic of almandine.

Mr. G. F. Kunz reports, on the authority of Mr. W. E. Hidden, that several crystals of rhodolite were found, during the summer of 1901, embedded in a decomposed saprolitic rock; these crystals are of considerable size, one weighing $3\frac{1}{2}$ pounds and yielding 300 carats of fine red material, free from flaws and suitable for cutting. The yield of rhodolite in that year was about 200,000 carats, valued at about £4000.

DEMANTOID.

Demantoid is a beautiful green precious stone belonging to the group of calcium-iron garnets, as is shown by the analysis quoted above. The stone ranges in colour from a fine emerald-green to a brownish- or yellowish-green, and is sometimes indeed almost colourless. Demantoids of two shades of colour are represented in Plate XIV.; Fig. 9 illustrates the mineral in its rough condition, and Fig. 10 shows three cut stones. The colour most commonly seen is a light yellowish-green. The emerald-green variety, as shown by the above analysis, contains a small amount of chromium, and the beauty of its colour is no doubt due to the presence of this element. The paler green and yellowish-green stones contain no chromium; their colour, therefore, must be due to the iron which is present.

The lustre, the brilliancy of which is heightened by polishing, is strongly vitreous inclining to greasy, while the transparency and purity of the mineral is usually perfect. The index of refraction and the dispersion are both high, and by artificial illumination a faceted stone often shows a fine play of prismatic colours.

Demantoid is softer than any other garnet, its hardness being only $6\frac{1}{2}$, which is less even than quartz. The specific gravity ranges from 3·83 to 3·85. It fuses before the blowpipe to a black magnetic glass, but only when in the thinnest of splinters. Demantoid differs from all other garnets in being easily and completely decomposed, even in its natural condition before being fused, by acids.

The mineral has hitherto been found only in the Ural Mountains. It was discovered in the 'sixties in the form of greenish-white or almost colourless pebbles in the gold-washings of Nizhni-Tagilsk. It was met with subsequently in the Sissersk (Syssertsk) district on the western slopes of the Urals in the stream Bobrovka, which flows into the Chussavaya, at a spot about ten versts south-west of the village of Poldnevaya, and twenty versts to the south of the smelting works of Polevskoi, first as pebbles in the gold-washings and afterwards *in situ* in the underlying mother-rock. It is distinguished as Bobrovka garnet from the locality at which it is found.

The demantoid occurs here, with dolomite, a little clayey material, and magnetite, in veins of chrysolite, which penetrate a peculiar grey to greenish-grey serpentine rock; it is found sometimes also in the serpentine itself. The garnet is embedded in this fibrous chrysolite and coated with a layer of the same; it occurs either as isolated irregular grains or more commonly in nodules, the surface of which is irregularly grooved and furrowed (Plate XIV., Fig. 9). These nodules measure from ¼ to 2 inches across and are greasy and cloudy in appearance. Each is built up of a large number of irregular grains of demantoid packed closely together, but separated from each other by a coating of serpentine. Each grain has a brilliant lustre and a perfectly conchoidal fracture. As a rule, each nodule is divided by deep, prominent grooves into a small number of portions, and the grains which build up these several portions are separated by finer grooves. Distinct crystals are rarely found; the rhombic dodecahedron and icositetrahedron, and also combinations of these two forms, have nevertheless been observed. The rounded outline of the grains sometimes appears to be due to the combination of numerous imperfectly developed crystal-faces.

Demantoid is frequently cut and worn as a precious stone at the place of its origin, that is to say, in the Urals and elsewhere in Russia; outside that country it is little used. It is cut *en cabochon* (Plate XIV., Fig. 10), and frequently also in various faceted forms. On account of its yellowish-green colour, the shade which is most frequently seen, demantoid was at first thought to be chrysolite, and is even now known by this name in the Urals. It may be distinguished from chrysolite, however, by its single refraction and high specific gravity, demantoid sinking in the heaviest liquid (sp. gr. = 3·6) while chrysolite (olivine) floats.

The chromiferous emerald-green variety of demantoid is very similar in appearance to the emerald, and is therefore sometimes called "Uralian emerald"; this term, however, is somewhat misleading, since true emeralds are also found in the Urals. The characters mentioned above as serving to distinguish demantoid from chrysolite also serve to distinguish it from emerald. The manner in which demantoid occurs precludes its extensive use as a precious stone, the grains which build up the nodules described above being always very small. Were it not for this fact the lustre, colour, and play of prismatic colours of demantoid would no doubt render it one of the most highly prized of precious stones, its lack of hardness not being sufficient to seriously affect its application in this direction.

Other Gem-Varieties of Garnet.

There are still to be mentioned a few other varieties of garnet which are used for ornamental purposes. The brownish-green calcium-aluminium garnet known as *grossularite*, fine crystals of which occur in the Vilui river, Siberia, is sometimes cut under the name of "gooseberry-stone." A beautiful rose-pink, though rarely perfectly clear and transparent, calcium-aluminium garnet occurs in large, well-developed rhombic dodecahedral crystals in a finely granular limestone at Xalostoc, in the State of Morelos in Mexico, and is sometimes employed as a gem.

The black calcium-iron garnet, *melanite*, is used to a limited extent in mourning jewellery; it differs from all other garnets in occurring exclusively in volcanic rocks, such, for example, as those of the Kaiserstuhl, near Freiburg in Breisgau, and at Frascati, in the Albanian Hills, not far from Rome.

Another calcium-iron garnet, known as *topazolite* on account of its similarity in transparency and colour to yellow Brazilian topaz, occurs in well-developed crystals in the Ala valley in Piedmont.

TOURMALINE.

The name tourmaline, like garnet, is given to a group of isomorphous substances, the chemical composition of which is constant and definite in its general type but variable with regard to the elements which enter into it. These substances agree very closely in their crystalline form, but, owing to differences in chemical composition, differ somewhat in other physical characters, and it is these differences which serve to distinguish one tourmaline from another. To several varieties, distinguished from each other by differences in specific gravity, colour, transparency, and so on, mineralogists have given special names; and of these varieties, those which are sufficiently transparent and pleasing in colour find an extensive application as gems. To the ordinary jeweller the name tourmaline and the several variety names recognised by mineralogists are alike practically unknown. The gem-varieties of tourmaline are distinguished by jewellers solely by their colour, and are referred to by the names of better-known gems to which a qualifying prefix is added.

The physical characters of tourmaline depend more or less directly on the chemical composition; it is therefore advisable to consider this first. In order to give an idea of the chemical composition of different tourmalines a table of analyses of differently coloured specimens is given below. These analyses refer to: I., colourless tourmaline from De Kalb, St. Lawrence Co., New York; II., pale green tourmaline from Haddam Neck on the Connecticut River, U.S.A.; III., red tourmaline from Shaitanka in the Urals; IV., brown tourmaline from Dobrowa, near Unterdrauburg on the Drau in Carinthia; V., dark blue tourmaline from Goshen, Massachusetts, U.S.A.; VI., black tourmaline from Unity, New Hampshire, U.S.A.

	I. Colourless. De Kalb.	II. Pale green. Haddam Neck.	Red. Shaitanka.	IV. Brown. Dobrowa.	V. Dark blue Goshen.	VI. Black. Unity.
Silica (SiO_2) . . .	36·72	36·96	38·26	38·09	36·22	36·29
Titanium dioxide (TiO_2) .	0·05	0·03	—	—	—	—
Boron trioxide (B_2O) .	10·81	11·00	9·29	11·15	10·65	9·04
Alumina (Al_2O_3) . .	29·68	39·56	43·97	32·90	33·35	30·44
Ferrous oxide (FeO) . .	0·22	2·14	—	0·66	11·95	13·23
Manganous oxide (MnO) .	—	2·00	1·53	—	1·25	—
Magnesia (MgO) . .	14·92	0·15	1·62	11·79	0·63	6·32
Lime (CaO) . . .	3·49	1·28	0·62	1·25	—	1·02
Soda (Na_2O) . . .	1·26	2·10	1·53	2·37	1·75	} 1·94
Potash (K_2O) . . .	0·05	—	0·21	0·47	0·40	
Lithia (Li_2O) . . .	—	1·64	0·48	—	0·84	—
Water (H_2O) . . .	2·98	3·10	2·49	2·05	2·21	172
Fluorine (F) . . .	0·93	1·13	0·70	0·64	0·82	—
Total .	101·11	101·09	100·70	101·37	100·07	100·00
Specific gravity . . .	3·049	3·089	3·082	3·035	3·203	3·192

It will be seen from these analyses that tourmaline is a silicate of very complicated composition; in fact, no other precious stone is so complex in character; in this respect, therefore, there is a marked contrast between tourmaline and diamond, the composition of the latter being the simplest possible. No tourmaline has all the fourteen elements indicated, and those which do occur are always present in variable amounts; this tends to make the constitution still more complex. Besides silica, there is always present boron, aluminium, magnesium, sodium, potassium, and water, the last of which is expelled only at a red-heat. Fluorine is very rarely absent, but lithium and manganese enter into the composition of only a few tourmalines; iron, as ferrous oxide, is an important, but variable, constituent, which may be absent, present in small amount or in considerable amount, as much as 20 per cent. Tourmalines containing a large amount of iron are always dark in colour and imperfectly transparent, frequently quite black and opaque, and are therefore unfit for use as gems.

The number of the constituents of tourmaline, together with the difficulty of accurately determining the proportions in which they are present, and the fact that these proportions vary in every specimen that is analysed, make it impossible to arrive at a chemical formula which satisfies every condition and is unexceptionable in every way. Every formula hitherto proposed is based to a certain extent on supposition, and no single one has been generally accepted as final. The first two analyses quoted above have been recently made (1899) by Professor S. L. Penfield and Mr. H. W. Foote, with the object of establishing a formula for the mineral. Every care and precaution was adopted, and their results have given rise to much discussion. The general formula they propose is $H_9Al_3(B.OH)_2Si_4O_{19}$, the nine atoms of hydrogen being supposed to be replaceable by variable amounts of aluminium, alkalies, magnesium, and iron. The special formulæ constructed to suit particular cases are necessarily very complex. According to another view, all varieties of tourmaline are, like the garnets, isomorphous mixtures of a small number of fundamental molecules of perfectly fixed and definite composition, the differences in the chemical composition of the different varieties of the mineral being due to the relatively varying amounts in which these fundamental molecules are present, as are also the differences in physical characters. Even if this theory be correct, the determination of the exact constitution of the fundamental molecules is still one of the problems of mineralogical chemistry.

In contrast to the chemical composition, the crystalline forms of all varieties of tourmaline are in close agreement. The crystals belong to the hexagonal system with hemimorphic-rhombohedral symmetry. A prism of greater or less length is nearly always developed, and is terminated by rhombohedra, scalenohedra, or by the basal plane, singly or in combination. Corresponding faces of these forms are inclined to each other and to the prism faces at angles which vary in different crystals irrespective of the chemical composition, only, however, to a small extent, at most only about a degree of arc. Such close crystallographic agreement in substances of different chemical composition is explained on the principle of isomorphism, the different varieties of tourmaline being regarded as an isomorphous series of minerals.

There is a peculiar and characteristic feature connected with crystals of tourmaline which may be seen in the accompanying figures (Figs. 70a to e), the arrangement of the faces at one end of the prismatic crystals differs from that of the faces at the other end; such crystals are said to be hemimorphic. The hemimorphism of tourmaline is rarely very distinct, for the crystals are, as a rule, attached at one end to the matrix and terminal faces developed only at the free end. Doubly terminated crystals of tourmaline may be readily distinguished by this hemimorphic development from any other mineral which they may resemble in appearance. In Fig. 70, this hemimorphic development is shown most conspicuously by the crystals lettered *b*, *c*, and *d*, there being many more faces present on the upper than on the lower ends. Further, the hemimorphic development is shown not only by the number and arrangement of the terminal faces, but also by that of the prism faces. For example, in Fig. 70*a*, the prism has only three faces instead of six, the number usually present on crystals belonging to the hexagonal system ; again, in Figs. *b* to *e*, instead of a prism of twelve faces there are only nine, this being a combination of a hexagonal with a trigonal prism. This feature is so characteristic of crystals of tourmaline that they may be recognised with certainty by it alone, even when no terminal faces are present.

The faces of the prism are usually more or less deeply striated in the direction of their length ; that is to say, parallel to the principal trigonal axis of the crystal, as is represented in the figures. This striation is specially prominent when more than nine prism faces are

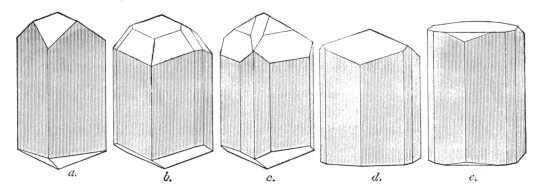

FIG. 70.   Crystalline forms of tourmaline.

developed, the crystals then having the appearance of cylinders, in which, however, a triangular arrangement can still be detected (Plate XV., Figs. 8 and 9). The terminal faces are usually smooth and not striated ; some, however, are rough and dull. The form of crystals of tourmaline varies somewhat according to the locality at which they occur, but there is no essential difference between them. Of the diagrams of Fig. 70, *a* represents a brown crystal from Ceylon, *b* and *c* two green crystals from Brazil, *d* a red crystal from Shaitanka in the Urals, and *e* a rose-red crystal from the island of Elba. These are all forms taken by precious, transparent varieties of tourmaline suitable for cutting as gems ; such crystals are usually small in size, rarely exceeding the length and thickness of a little finger.

Tourmaline possesses no distinct cleavage. The fracture is uneven to imperfectly conchoidal ; and, the mineral being very brittle, most crystals are penetrated by numerous irregular cracks and fissures which tends to make them useless as gems. Tourmaline is just sufficiently hard to scratch quartz, but is itself easily scratched by topaz ; its hardness is thus between 7 and $7\frac{1}{2}$, and may, as a rule, be taken as $7\frac{1}{4}$.

The specific gravity of tourmaline is not constant for all varieties, but ranges from slightly over 3·0 to 3·2. All tourmalines sink in liquid No. 3 (sp. gr. = 3·0), though some only slowly, and all float in pure methylene iodide. The density of the mineral varies with its chemical composition, increasing with the amount of iron present, as may be seen from the table of analyses with the corresponding values of the specific gravity, quoted above. Only in a few exceptional cases is the specific gravity slightly less than 3·0 or slightly over 3·2. It has already been pointed out that the greater the amount of iron present in any given tourmaline the darker will be its colour and the more imperfect its transparency.

These darker and more dense tourmalines are not cut, the paler and lighter varieties only being suitable for gems; the specific gravity of the latter lies between 3·0 and a value slightly in excess of 3·1.

The common vitreous lustre of tourmaline is much heightened by polishing; indeed, all tourmalines are susceptible of a good polish. In respect of brilliancy of lustre tourmaline surpasses beryl, especially by artificial light; the latter mineral, however, is superior to tourmaline in the richness of its colours.

Tourmaline varies in transparency and colour to a considerable extent. Most of it is black, or, at least, very deeply coloured, and quite opaque in mass, but in sufficiently thin splinters it is transparent. Tourmaline which is transparent in mass is comparatively rare, and is distinguished as "precious tourmaline" in contrast to the darkly coloured and opaque "common tourmaline." Precious tourmaline is much lighter in colour, and is the only variety suitable for cutting as a gem; perfectly clear and faultless specimens are rare and command a moderately high price. Tourmaline is very variable in colour, more so than most other minerals used as gems; the colour variations will be dealt with in some detail below.

In striking contrast to black tourmaline, the so-called "schörl," is the colourless variety, which, however, even when transparent, is not perfectly water-clear, being usually faintly tinged with red or green. Colourless tourmaline is known to mineralogists as achroite; it is rarely cut as a precious stone and is not of frequent occurrence. Red tourmaline is of greater importance: this variety is of a pale rose-red shade, lighter in some specimens, darker in others. It may even be of a fine ruby-red colour, and is then known as rubellite or, on account of its occurrence in Siberia, as siberite. A violet tint is sometimes seen owing to the admixture of blue with the typical red colour. The darker red tourmaline only is important as a gem, rose-red specimens not being used at all. Precious tourmaline of various tints of green, ranging in shade from pale to dark, is of much more frequent occurrence. A pure emerald-green is rarely seen, bluish-green and especially yellowish-green being much more common. Blue tourmaline, at least in transparent specimens, is rare; it is known to mineralogists as indicolite, and is usually somewhat deeply coloured, being sometimes a pure indigo-blue, at other times showing a pronounced tinge of green. Brown tourmaline, to which the name dravite is applied, is also widely distributed; it is either pure brown, greenish-brown, or reddish-brown, and ranges in shade from a colour of considerable depth to somewhat pale brownish-yellow and straw-yellow.

Crystals of tourmaline may be of one uniform colour throughout or differently coloured in different portions. Thus, for example, the terminal portions of prisms of colourless tourmaline from the island of Elba are frequently black; such crystals are known as "negro-heads." The change from colourless to black material is abrupt, but there is no absolutely sharp boundary; these conditions are sometimes reversed, a black crystal having white ends. Prismatic crystals coloured rose-red at one end and green at the other, as represented in Plate XV., Fig. 5, are not rare; the transition from one colour to another in the middle of the crystal is gradual. Also of interest are the crystals from Chesterfield, in Massachusetts, and from other localities, in which there is a red central portion enclosed by a green shell, the transition between the differently coloured portions being sharp, as represented in Plate XV., Figs. 8 and 9.

The colour of tourmaline is not due to the mechanical intermixture of pigment, but is a property of the substance of the mineral itself, and even in the darkest crystals is distributed with perfect regularity. It may be supposed that the fundamental molecules mentioned above have each their own characteristic colour, and that the different colours of the isomorphous series of minerals, known collectively as tourmaline, are due to the association of these molecules in different relative proportions.

When a tourmaline contains, beside its constant constituents, small amounts of manganese and lithium with little or no iron, it is usually colourless, rose-red, darker red, or light green according, apparently, to the proportions in which iron and manganese are present. The darker red shade probably appears when a relatively considerable amount of manganese is present, while with a rather larger amount of ferrous oxide the colour is dark green, as is so often the case in silicates. Some green tourmalines, however contain chromic oxide, the substance to which the emerald owes its magnificent green colour.

In brown tourmaline there is practically no iron, manganese, or lithium, but a much larger amount of magnesium than is present in other varieties. The presence of a large amount of ferrous oxide is probably the cause of a blue colour, but apparently no transparent blue tourmaline has as yet been chemically analysed. The tourmaline richest in iron is, as has been stated, black and opaque in mass, but in thin sections is transparent and brown, green, or blue, in colour. The colours of tourmaline withstand the action of heat very markedly, in many cases remaining essentially unaltered after exposure to a red-heat. For example, dark-green stones after this treatment are still green, but of a pale or greyish shade, a change which renders them unsuitable as gems.

The dichroism of tourmaline is a very prominent feature; it is apparent in quite pale-coloured stones, but is more marked in the darker varieties. Tourmaline is, in fact, more strongly dichroic than any other precious stone, with the exception perhaps of cordierite (dichroite), but this is seldom cut as a gem-stone. In all cases the colour of the light which travels through a crystal of tourmaline in a direction parallel to the prism edges—that is to say, along the principal or optic axis—is darker than that which travels in a direction perpendicular to this. Again, a moderately thick slice of a dark-coloured crystal cut perpendicular to the optic axis may be quite opaque, while a plate of the same thickness, but cut parallel to the optic axis, may be transparent. The colours visible in these two directions are also usually different, as has been explained in the general account of dichroism given in the first part of this book. Very frequently it is possible to observe this difference in colour with the naked eye, unaided by the dichroscope. The maximum difference in colour of the two images of the dichroscope aperture will be seen when the crystal is viewed through in a direction perpendicular to the prism edges; one image will, as a rule, be darker than the other, and the particular colours shown will depend on the colour of the crystal. Thus with brown crystals the two images will be dark brown and pale brown to yellow; with red crystals they are darker and lighter red, and so forth. If the crystal is deeply coloured, one of the images will be almost or quite black and the other a light shade of the colour shown by the crystal.

In consequence of the strong dichroism of tourmaline, it is necessary that a crystal with a considerable depth of colour should be cut in a certain direction, namely, with the plane of the table or large central facet parallel to the prism edges. By this means the light which reaches the eye of the observer from the stone has travelled through it mainly in a direction perpendicular to the principal or optic axis of the crystal, thereby ensuring for the stone the best possible appearance. If, on the other hand, the stone is cut so that the table is perpendicular to the prism faces, that is to say, parallel to the basal plane, then the light will travel through the stone mainly in a direction approximating to that of the principal axis of the crystal, and the gem will have a dull, cloudy, and unpleasing appearance. Some of the Brazilian tourmalines, when cut in the manner first described, display a fine green colour, but in the other appear quite dark and only imperfectly transparent. The same phenomenon may be observed in crystals from Paris, in Maine, U.S.A., which give gems of a fine dark-green or of an unpleasing yellowish-green according to the direction in which they are cut. Only in the cases where the crystal is pale in colour is it advantageous to cut it so that the table facet is perpendicular to the prism edges, the resulting gem-stone being thus rendered darker in colour than it would otherwise appear. With the requisite knowledge it is thus open to the lapidary to very materially improve the appearance of a stone by cutting it in a judicious manner.

The optical refraction of tourmaline is somewhat feeble, but its birefringence is fairly strong. There is a slight difference in the refraction of stones of different colours; that is to say, this character varies with the chemical composition. An increase in the amount of iron present in the mineral is accompanied not only by an increase in the depth of its colour, but also by an increase in the refractive index. The following are values for the greatest and least refractive indices which have been determined for tourmaline of different colours:

	Greatest refractive index.	Least refractive index.
Red tourmaline	1·6277	1·6111
Colourless tourmaline . . .	1·6366	1·6193
Green tourmaline	1·6408	1·6203
Blue tourmaline	1·6530	1·6343

A very characteristic feature of tourmaline is the readiness with which it becomes electrified. When rubbed it acquires in a very short time a comparatively large charge of electricity, which it retains for some time; and when subjected to changes in temperature it becomes electrified still more readily. The behaviour of tourmaline in this respect is closely connected with the hemimorphic development of its crystals. When a crystal is heated, one end becomes positively and the other negatively electrified, but on cooling its polarity is reversed. A faceted stone will, of course, behave in the same way, the portions corresponding to the poles of the crystal being positively or negatively electrified. The largest electric charges are acquired by light-coloured crystals of transparent, precious tourmaline, which are free from fissures. Under favourable conditions the charge may be so strong that shreds of paper and similar light objects are energetically attracted. This pyroelectrical property of tourmaline was observed in Holland at the beginning of the eighteenth century, when the mineral first became known. Because it was observed to have the power, when cooling, of attracting ashes to itself, the name *aschtrekker*, meaning in Dutch ash-drawer, was bestowed upon it. No other precious stone resembling tourmaline in the smallest degree, with the exception, perhaps, of topaz, is as strongly pyroelectric, so that this feature serves to distinguish red tourmaline, for example, from ruby and other precious stones. The electrical properties of the mineral may be demonstrated in a convenient manner by dusting a mixture of red-lead and sulphur through a muslin sieve on to a cooling-stone, when the sulphur will be attracted to the positively electrified portion of the stone and the red-lead to the negatively electrified portion.

Another of the characters of tourmaline is that it is unattacked by acids. The colourless, pale green, and red varieties are infusible before the blowpipe, while the darker varieties melt or run together and form a white to dark brown slag.

As regards the mode of occurrence, tourmaline is confined almost entirely to older crystalline rocks such as granite and gneiss. Other modes of occurrence, for example, in granular dolomite at Campo-longo and in the Binnenthal, in Switzerland, are rare, and,

1. Idocrase, crystals (Piedmont).   2. The same, cut.   3. Idocrase, cut (Vesuvius).   4. Dioptase, crystals (Siberia).   5. Tourmaline, rose-red and green crystal (Elba).   6. Tourmaline, red crystal (Siberia).   7. Tourmaline, green crystal (Brazil).   8, 9. Tourmaline, red and green crystal (Massachusetts).   10. Tourmaline, brown cut-stone (Ceylon).   11. Tourmaline, blue cut-stone (Brazil).

as far as precious tourmaline is concerned, unimportant. The precious varieties are found almost exclusively in the rocks first mentioned, mainly in granite, and especially in its more coarsely crystallised variety known as pegmatite. The light-coloured crystals are attached to the walls of drusy cavities in such rocks, while in other druses of the same rock-mass there may be crystals of different colours, including black. Typical examples of this mode of occurrence may be seen in the granite of San Piero, in the island of Elba, of Penig, in Saxony, and specially at Paris, in Maine, U.S.A. Other localities, in particular those at which stones suitable for cutting are found, will be mentioned later. Darker crystals, brown, blue, or black in colour, are often found embedded in the rock itself, black crystals being met with very frequently. Crystals of tourmaline are often weathered out of their granitic mother-rock and are then to be found in sands and gravels. It is from such deposits that the finest gems are derived, these being collected along with other precious stones at various localities, especially in Brazil and Ceylon.

All varieties of tourmaline, so long as they are transparent and finely coloured, are suitable for cutting as gems, and, as a matter of fact, material of the most varied character is applied to this purpose. The colourless achroite is little used, and pale-coloured stones generally are not much prized. Stones of a full red, green, blue, or brown-colour are most admired, red stones being the most valuable, green the most abundant, and blue and brown the least important.

Tourmaline is rarely cut as a brilliant, the table-cut and a low step-cut being more generally adopted. The colour of cut stones is sometimes improved by the use of a suitable foil. Other than the frequently occurring fissures, already mentioned, tourmaline exhibits but few faults, enclosures of foreign substances, for example, being quite exceptional.

Each of the colour-varieties of precious tourmaline will be now treated of in some detail.

COLOURLESS TOURMALINE or **ACHROITE** occurs as crystals, which are perfectly, or almost, water-clear, but, as a rule, these are too small to give gems of much value. The acicular crystals are found, together with tourmaline of other colours, in the island of Elba, also as fine crystals associated with green tourmaline in the dolomite of Campo-longo, in Switzerland, and at some other localities, but everywhere as a rarity. Crystals of colourless tourmaline in some quantity and of moderate size have been found perhaps only in the neighbourhood of Richville, near De Kalb, St. Lawrence County, in the State of New York, where they occur, as in Elba, attached to the walls of drusy cavities in granite.

Achroite is readily distinguished from all other colourless and transparent stones by its specific gravity, which is 3·022, so that it just sinks in liquid No. 3 (sp. gr. = 3·0) and floats in liquid No. 2, which is pure methylene iodide (sp. gr. = 3·3). Phenakite, colourless beryl, and rock-crystal float in the former liquid, while diamond, colourless topaz, spinel, sapphire, and zircon all sink in the latter. In beauty of appearance, however, achroite has nothing to distinguish it from many other colourless and transparent stones, except in some cases its fine lustre. In common with all other varieties of tourmaline it may be distinguished from glass imitations by its double refraction and its hardness, as well as under certain conditions by its electrical properties.

RED TOURMALINE or **RUBELLITE** (siberite) may be of various shades of colour, from pale rose to dark carmine-red, sometimes tinged with violet. The colour may be so like that of certain rubies that it is difficult, even for an expert, to discriminate between these stones on mere inspection. The same similarity in colour may also exist between this variety of tourmaline and certain specimens of balas-ruby (spinel) and rose topaz. From all these stones tourmaline is distinguished by its specific gravity, which in the present variety is 3·08; it therefore floats in pure methylene iodide, while the stones mentioned above all sink. The dichroism of red tourmaline is not very pronounced; the two images seen in the dichroscope vary in colour between pale rose and dark red, the former having sometimes a tinge of yellow and the latter usually a tinge of violet. Other precious stones of a red shade show different pairs of colours in the dichroscope, so that tourmaline may be distinguished from them by means of this instrument.

The principal locality for this beautiful red stone is in the Ekaterinburg district of the **Ural Mountains**, namely, in the immediate and further vicinity of the village of Mursinka. (Map, Fig. 63a.) It is mined here with amethyst, topaz, beryl, and other variously coloured stones, and sent to be cut to the works at Ekaterinburg. It is on account of its occurrence on the east side of the Urals that this variety of tourmaline has received the mineralogical name of siberite, while on account of its resemblance to the ruby it is known to jewellers as "Siberian ruby." The village of Shaitanka, thirty miles south of Mursinka and forty-five miles north of Ekaterinburg, deserves special mention as a locality for red tourmaline. The mineral occurs here with albite, quartz, green mica, and red lithia-mica (lepidolite), in druses in a very coarse-grained granite, and is usually implanted upon the albite and the lithia-mica; the crystals are also found lying in a yellow clay which is probably a disintegration product of the granite. They are prismatic in habit and deeply striated in the direction of their length. In colour they vary in shade between a paler or darker cherry- or carmine-red and violet-blue; tourmaline crystals of a pale olive-green or of some shade of colour between pale liver-brown and dark brown or black are also found at the same place. In nearly every case there is a slight difference in colour between the two ends of a crystal. At Sarapulskaya, seven and a half miles from Mursinka, groups of dark cherry-red crystals, usually of small size and radiating from a common centre or arranged in parallel, are found associated with tourmaline of other colours in a black earth, which occurs, mixed with granite débris, at the foot of a hill of granite.

There is also a sparing occurrence of red tourmaline in the district of Nerchinsk, in Transbaikalia.

The "Siberian ruby" is specially prized in Russia on account of its national origin, and is frequently worn as a gem; the nearer its colour approaches the red of the ruby the more valuable does the stone become. These "Siberian rubies" find less favour outside Russia, at any rate in Europe. A finely coloured specimen of the stone is represented in Plate XV., Fig. 6.

The places mentioned above are the principal sources from whence red tourmaline is derived; it occurs, however, at some other localities, but, as far as material of gem-quality is concerned, only in small amount. It is found with ruby, sapphire, spinel, zircon, &c., in the gem-gravels of Ceylon and especially of Burma.

Its distribution in **Burma** differs from that of the ruby, it being found near Mainglon, twenty miles south-east of the town of Mogok, the centre of the ruby district. (See maps, Figs. 54 and 55.) Tourmalines, both red and black, are found as water-worn pebbles in the sands of the Nampai valley, near Namseka village. The Chinese work the deposits by excavating numerous small and shallow pits, and in the rainy season the stone is obtained by washing. The whole of the material obtained in these ways is sent to China, where it is used in the making of buttons for the adornment of mandarins' caps, and is probably held there in as high esteem as the ruby itself. Lower down the valley are numerous mines which are now quite abandoned. The Nampai stream drains a district of gneissose rocks, and it is, therefore, not improbable that the rubellite found in its sands and gravels is derived from granite-veins penetrating the gneiss. Two very fine specimens of crystallised rubellite from Burma are exhibited in the Mineralogical Gallery of the British Museum, one of these, remarkable for its size and shape, being seven inches high and six inches across, was given by the King of Ava to Colonel Symes when on an embassy to that country in 1795; the other, not so large, but of a fine deep colour, was presented to the Museum in 1869 by Mr. C. S. J. L. Guthrie.

There is an important occurrence of beautiful rose-red tourmaline in the State of Maine in the **United States** of North America. The tourmaline of Maine is probably the finest in the world; rose-red, blue, green, and other varieties are obtained in great abundance. Amongst other important localities may be mentioned Mount Mica, about a mile east of Paris, where, as at Shaitanka in the Urals, the crystals occur with red lithia-mica attached to the walls of drusy cavities in a coarse-grained granite. Since the discovery of this locality in 1820, tourmaline of various colours has been constantly derived from this source, the value of the total production up to the year 1890 being estimated at 50,000 dollars. In the United States these stones are much prized on account of their national origin, just as in the case of Russian tourmaline. After Mount Mica, the most important locality in Maine is Mount Apatite at Auburn, discovered in 1882. Since that time, some 1500 crystals, colourless and of various shades of colour such as rose, lilac, pale blue, dark blue, green, and yellow, have been found. These when cut gave gems ranging in weight from 6 to 8 carats, but never more. Some of the tourmalines found here are peculiar in appearing of a darker shade of colour when cut than when in the rough condition. The red crystals from Paris are sometimes surrounded by an external layer of green tourmaline; the best examples of parti-coloured crystals, however, are the large prisms from Chesterfield in the State of Massachusetts (Plate XV., Figs. 8 and 9), and certain Brazilian stones. Sometimes in cutting such parti-coloured crystals, the central red portion only is utilised, the colour of which in American stones is generally very similar to that of the ruby. At other times, however, the crystal is cut so as to exhibit its parti-coloured character, and the contrast between the differently coloured portions of the gem has a peculiar effect.

Beautiful crystals of red and green tourmaline have been recently found at Mesa Grande in San Diego County, California. They occur in coarse-grained granite and are often well terminated. Many are of considerable size and transparency, and of great beauty. Rubellite is the commonest variety, but the characteristic zonal arrangement of colour, both concentric and in horizontal bands, is to be seen in many specimens.

A few fine red tourmalines are associated with the green tourmaline so abundant in Brazil, but they are of little importance.

The red tourmaline of the island of Elba and of Penig in Saxony is generally too pale in colour, and usually also occurs in crystals which are too small for cutting as gems.

GREEN TOURMALINE is the most widely distributed of the precious varieties of this mineral, and consequently is lower in price. It is rarely emerald-green, but when this is the case its colour lacks none of the depth of that of the true emerald. More commonly it is yellowish-green, but grass green, greenish-yellow, and, indeed, all possible shades, light and dark, are to be met with (Plate XV., Figs. 7, 8, and 9). The dichroism of this variety is very pronounced; the two images seen in the dichroscope are yellowish-green and bluish-green, which are usually very deep, to almost black, in shade; yellow, brown, and violet are also sometimes to be seen.

The principal locality for green tourmaline is **Brazil**, where it occurs, together with other colour-varieties, as prismatic crystals, the largest of which measure $1\frac{1}{2}$ inches in length and $\frac{1}{2}$ inch in thickness. It is specially abundant in the small Ribeirão da Tolha, ten leguas from Chapada, and also in the district of Minas Novas in the State of Minas Geraes, where it occurs with white and blue topaz. It is sometimes of a fine emerald-green colour, and was indeed formerly thought to be emerald; and until its identity with the far less costly tourmaline was established, it was sought for with great eagerness. On account of this similarity the stone is known to jewellers as " Brazilian emerald"; it is emblematic of the priesthood in Brazil, and is much worn by priests as a ring-stone.

Another important source is the gem-gravels of **Ceylon**, where tourmaline of a yellowish-green colour, similar to that of chrysolite (peridot) occurs in abundance. Some of these stones are yellowish-green only on one side, the other being white with a milky opalescence. From the locality at which it occurs and its resemblance to chrysolite, this stone is known to jewellers as " Ceylonese chrysolite," and also as " Ceylonese peridot." In Ceylon, as in Brazil, it is accompanied by tourmaline of other colours, but the Ceylonese stones are less deeply coloured than the Brazilian. The name tourmaline originated in Ceylon, where turamali is the name used by Cingalese jewellers for hyacinth (zircon).

The occurrence of tourmaline of a fine green colour in the **United States** has been already mentioned. At Paris in Maine, and Chesterfield in Massachusetts, it is found not only as the external shell of red crystals, but also as crystals which are green throughout, and which, like the red stones, are often used as gems. The finest faceted stone cut from the green tourmaline of Paris measures 25 millimetres across and is 18 millimetres thick.

It is possible for green tourmaline to be mistaken for other precious stones of the same colour; for example, for emerald, chrysolite, hiddenite, and demantoid. From all these green tourmaline is distinguished by its specific gravity of 3·107, and by its strong dichroism, a feature which is completely absent in demantoid and insignificant in the other stones.

BLUE TOURMALINE or **INDICOLITE** (indigolite) is rare. It may be light or dark in shade, and of a pure indigo-blue, a smalt-blue, or a blue more or less markedly tinged with green. A faceted blue tourmaline is represented in Plate XV., Fig. 11. The colour is sometimes not to be distinguished from that of sapphire, while other specimens may closely resemble aquamarine in this respect. Indicolite may be distinguished from either of these stones by its specific gravity, which is 3·16, and by its dichroism, this feature being specially prominent in blue tourmaline. This variety occurs with green tourmaline, though in less abundance, in Brazil, and because of this circumstance is known to jewellers as " Brazilian sapphire." A few crystals suitable for cutting are found at Paris and other places in Maine, at Goshen in Massachusetts, and elsewhere in North America; also at Mursinka in the Urals. Fine specimens of indicolite occur with green tourmaline, lepidolite, and quartz in the granite south of Pahira, near Hazaribagh in Bengal. The largest crystals found here measure an inch in length; the central portion of the crystals is sometimes indigo-blue and the outer layers green. Blue tourmaline in association with the yellow and brown varieties occurs also with the sapphire of the Zanskar range in Kashmir. Everywhere, however, good transparent tourmaline of a fine blue colour is rare and much more valuable than the green variety.

BROWN TOURMALINE (dravite) still remains to be mentioned. This variety is sometimes clear and transparent enough to be cut as a gem and is then a very pretty stone. The colour varies from dark brown of different shades, through light brown to yellowish- or reddish-brown. Beautiful transparent stones, both brown and yellow, accompany the green tourmaline of Ceylon; from this island comes the brown faceted stone represented in Plate XV., Fig. 10. Among the brown crystals found embedded in mica-schist at Dobrowa, near Unterdrauburg on the Drau in Carinthia, are some which are clear enough for cutting;

the majority, however, are cloudy and unsuitable for this purpose. There is a similar occurrence at Crawford, in the State of New York, and some of the brown tourmaline found in the limestone of Gouverneur and Newcomb, in New York, is sufficiently clear and free from fissures to give good cut stones; but, as a rule, North American tourmaline of brown colour is rarely cut for gems.

OPAL.

The widely distributed mineral opal, like the still more frequently occurring quartz, consists mainly of oxide of silicon, that is to say, of silica, but differs from quartz in being not crystalline but amorphous. Besides silica, opal always contains water, the amount varying in different specimens. Various impurities are frequently present, and when in any amount render the stone cloudy and often of a deep colour, so that it is unfit for use as a gem. The variety almost exclusively used for this purpose is that known as the "precious" or "noble" opal; it is conspicuous amongst all others for the magnificent play of colours produced by the refraction and reflection of light in its colourless substance. This is the variety to which attention in what follows will be mainly directed; a few of the varieties, which show no play of colour and which are grouped together under the term "common opal," will receive brief mention later on.

The chemical composition of various kinds of opal used as gems may be seen from the table of analyses given below. The variableness in the amount of water present, and the diversity in the substances present as impurities, should be noticed:

—	Precious opal. Hungary.	Fire-opal. Mexico.	Milk-opal. Silesia.	Cacholong. Faroe.	Menilite. Paris.	Hydro-phane. Saxony.
Silica (SiO_2) . . .	90·0	92·0	98·75	95·32	85·50	93·13
Alumina (Al_2O_3) . .	—	—	0·10	0·20	1·00	1·62
Iron oxide (Fe_2O_3) . .	—	0·25	—	—	0·50	—
Lime (CaO) . . .	—	—	—	0·06	0·50	—
Magnesia (MgO) . .	—	—	—	0·40	—	—
Soda (Na_2O) . . .	—	—	—	} 0·13	—	—
Potash (K_2O) . . .	—	—	—		—	—
Water (H_2O) . . .	10·0	7·75	0·10	3·47	11·00	5·25
Organic matter . . .	—	—	—	—	0·33	—
Total . .	100·0	100·00	98·95	99·58	98·83	100·00

Since opal is an amorphous substance, it never possesses regular plane-faced boundaries, but occurs usually in rounded nodules, as botryoidal encrustations, as stalactites, and in other forms. There is, of course, a complete absence of cleavage; the fracture is conchoidal, often typically so. The mineral is moderately brittle, sometimes, indeed, very brittle, when it is easily fractured and broken. It is not very hard; $H = 5\frac{1}{2} - 6\frac{1}{2}$; that is to say, it is softer than quartz, so that though opal will scratch glass it is itself scratched by quartz. Because of its brittleness and low degree of hardness it is advisable to protect a gem of opal from a blow or fall of any kind, and from contact with harder substances, such as dust.

The specific gravity also is less than that of quartz; it lies between 1·9 and 2·3, the exact value depending upon the chemical composition, that is to say, upon the amount of water and impurities present.

The lustre is usually of the common vitreous type, though in some opals it may be greasy, resinous, or waxy. The lustre of natural specimens is only moderately strong; it is increased by cutting and polishing, but even then is in no way remarkable. One variety only, hyalite or glassy opal, is perfectly transparent; this is clear and colourless like glass, but is rarely used as a gem. Both the common and the precious varieties of opal are, as a rule, cloudy, being at the best only translucent or semi-transparent. In a pure condition the mineral is perfectly colourless, the tint of the coloured varieties being due to the presence of impurities. In colour these varieties are usually brown, yellow, or red, of various shades; green opal is rare, black is known, and the cloudy varieties of milk-opal are white. The optical refraction of the mineral is low, the index of refraction for precious opal having been determined to be 1·44. Being amorphous, opal is, of course, singly refracting.

When heated the mineral is easily fractured, so that it is desirable that cut stones should be protected from sudden changes of temperature. The constituent water is expelled below a red-heat, when the specimen, if not so already, becomes cloudy and opaque. Opal fuses in the oxyhydrogen flame, but is infusible in the ordinary blowpipe flame. It is attacked by only one acid, namely, hydrofluoric, but differs from quartz in being soluble in caustic alkalies.

Opal is found almost exclusively in the cavities and crevices of basaltic, trachytic, and other volcanic rocks; it is occasionally met with in serpentine, but never in rocks which contain no silica. All the different varieties of opal may occur in association with each other and with other minerals composed of silica, such as chalcedony and quartz, with which opal often forms a more or less intimate mixture. Both opal and these other minerals are in all cases alteration products of the rocks in which they occur. The silica dissolved out by water circulating through the rocks, which is sometimes, as in volcanic regions, very hot, is redeposited in the cavities and crevices of the rock when the solution cools or evaporates. The silica thus deposited is at first gelatinous, but on drying it takes on the characters of opal. The rounded form of the masses in which the mineral occurs is a natural consequence of its mode of formation, and is similar to that of the stalactites which originate by the deposition of calcium carbonate from water. Moreover, in some rocks silica has been found in the soft and wet, gelatinous condition in which it was deposited, and on exposure to the atmosphere has been observed to harden and dry up and eventually to become indistinguishable from opal.

Hitherto we have considered only the characters common to all opal; those varieties which are used for ornamental purposes will now be considered individually in more or less detail.

PRECIOUS OPAL.

The most important and valuable variety is the precious or noble opal, also known as the oriental opal and as the celestial opal. The features on which depend the value and beauty of other precious stones are in the opal insignificant or absent. Thus it is not transparent, has no pronounced body-colour, and compared with other stones has no very strong lustre and only a low degree of hardness. Its beauty depends solely upon the magnificent play of delicate colours seen on its surface, a feature which is to be found in no other stone, so that in this respect opal is unique.

Precious opal, as a general rule, is translucent or at most semi-transparent, a greater degree of transparency being exceptional. When seen by transmitted light the stone appears reddish-yellow in colour, but in reflected light it is colourless with a milky cloudiness, or milk-white with a faint shade of blue or pearl-grey. A pronounced body-colour, such as yellow, red, blue, green, or black, is very rarely seen. Of these, yellow, ranging from wine-yellow to sulphur-yellow, and red, especially a yellowish-red shade, are less infrequent than others. Rose-red opal, of which a magnificent example is preserved in the "Green Vaults" of Dresden, is very rare. Black opal is also rare and is sometimes of very great beauty, the play of colours showing up with striking effect against the dark background of the stone.

The play of colours characteristic of all precious opal is only shown when the stone is seen by reflected light; in transmitted light it is completely absent. The display of colour may be visible over the whole surface of the stone, or may be limited to isolated spots which merge imperceptibly into the surrounding uncoloured portions. Again, the whole surface may show a play of one uniform colour, yellow and green being in such cases much admired. In other stones there may be areas over each of which there is a play of a single colour, the play of colour over any one area differing from that over any other, and the different areas merging gradually into each other. Moreover, in some opals minute spangles of various colours are distributed in large numbers over the surface of the stone, giving a variegated kaleidoscopic effect, which has been compared to the iridescence of the neck-plumage of some pigeons or of a peacock's feather. The opals of which the general colour effect is more uniform resemble mother-of-pearl more closely. The colour of precious opal of good quality is always, however, more fiery than that of any of the objects to which it has been compared. An attempt at the reproduction of the colour effect of a few precious opals is given in Figs. 6 to 9 of Plate XVI.

In attempting a word-picture of the appearance of precious opal one cannot do better than quote Pliny, who described this stone as combining in itself the fiery red of the ruby, the magnificent green of the emerald, the golden yellow of the topaz, the deep blue of the sapphire, and the rich violet of the amethyst. All these colours may, as a matter of fact, be detected in one and the same stone; it often happens, however, that a few only are present, while some stones display but one. The play of colours is indeed very variable and never identical in any two stones, especially those from different localities. Thus, for example, in the Hungarian opal the colour is distributed irregularly in small patches and spangles giving a variegated effect (Plate XVI., Figs. 8 and 9), while in the Australian opal large areas of the surface display one uniform colour (Plate XVI., Figs. 6 and 7).

A number of varieties of precious opal are recognised, the distinction between them being based on differences displayed in the play of colours. Those stones in which close-set, angular patches of colour form a minute variegated mosaic, as it were, are known as *harlequin-opal*, a term which is also applied sometimes to stones in which the ordinary play of colours has a yellowish-red instead of a white background. In a *flame-opal* the colours are distributed more or less regularly in bands and streaks, while the whole surface of a *gold-opal* glows with golden light. The name *girasol* is sometimes applied to an almost transparent opal, over the surface of which there travels, as the stone is moved about, a wave of blue light; the same term is, however, also applied to other precious stones. *Opal-onyx* is built up of alternate layers of precious and of common opal. Other varieties also are distinguished, some of which will be mentioned under the various localities at which they are found.

The value of an opal depends in the first place upon the brilliancy and beauty of the colours it displays, and in the second place upon the uniformity with which the play of colours is distributed over the surface of the stone. The stones which show a brilliant play of colours over the whole surface are most valuable, while in inferior stones the colours are dull and there are portions of the surface which show no play of colour.

When precious opal is exposed to the action of heat it loses its constituent water; the play of colours then disappears and the stone becomes cloudy. Some stones indeed slowly lose water at ordinary temperatures, thus suffering a gradual diminution in beauty and value. It is stated that in such cases the play of colours may be restored by immersing the stones in oil, but that, as the oil gradually decomposes, the stone becomes poorer and poorer in appearance until at last the play of colours completely disappears, and the stone itself assumes a dirty brown tinge. Hungarian precious opal is least subject to such changes, and for this reason is worth more than that from other localities.

The substance of the precious opal is in itself colourless, and the brilliant play of colours so characteristic of this gem is due purely to changes effected in the incident rays of light during their passage through the substance of the opal, probably in a way which does not differ essentially from that whereby the iridescence of certain specimens of quartz and of other minerals arises. The drying up and solidification of the gelatinous silica would be attended by the development of a network of cracks and fissures; these cracks, by their action on the rays of light at their surfaces, give rise to a display of the rainbow colours characteristic of thin plates. Microscopical examination has demonstrated that these cracks are sometimes lined with a film of opal, the refractive index of which differs from that of the main mass. It has therefore been conjectured that the play of colours of the opal may be due in part to this or to some other circumstance, seeing that it is so much more brilliant and magnificent in this stone than in any other iridescent mineral. It is indeed possible that the phenomenon in opal has not as yet been completely explained by any of the various theories which from time to time have been promulgated. There can be absolute certainty only on one point, namely, that the colours of the precious opal are effects of the interference of light and not of an admixture of pigment, since they are pale or completely absent when the stone is viewed by transmitted light.

On account of its much fissured condition, precious opal, although perhaps slightly harder, requires more care in handling than does common opal. Sudden and extreme changes in temperature must in particular be guarded against, in order to avoid the fragmentation of the stone. For the same reason, special care is necessary during the processes of cutting and grinding.

Precious opal is in almost all cases cut in a rounded form, for, not only does the existence of facets if anything detract from the colour effect of the stone, but owing to its softness the edges between the facets would very soon lose their sharpness. Opal is, therefore, but rarely cut in faceted forms, though the table-cut and the step-cut are sometimes to be met with. According to the form of the rough stone, a cut opal may be circular or oval in outline and more or less convex, so that it may resemble the half of a pea, a bean, or an almond. It is ever the aim of the lapidary to perform the operation of cutting with as little waste of the valuable material as possible, while at the same time he must contrive so that the play of colours is displayed to the best advantage. This not infrequently requires great skill and much thought and consideration; the removal of the matrix and of those portions of the stone which show no play of colours with the least possible waste of precious material, and in such a manner as to ensure an uninterrupted

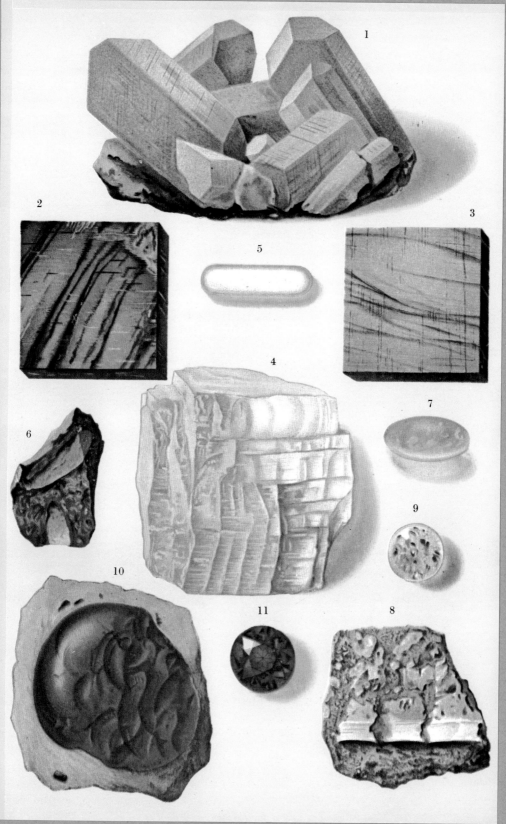

1. Amazon-stone, crystals. 2. Labradorite, polished. 3. Labradorescent Felspar, polished.
4. Moon-stone, rough. 5. The same, cut. 6. Precious Opal, rough (Australia). 7. The same,
cut. 8. Precious Opal, rough (Hungary). 9. The same, cut. 10. Fire Opal, rough. 11. The
same, cut.

play of colours over the whole surface of the cut stone, often presents a problem of considerable intricacy.

By the employment of various devices the play of colours of precious opal can be increased to a certain extent; thus, for example, a cut stone, which is not too thick and opaque, may be placed upon a variegated foil, a piece of a peacock's feather, or a bright, polished plate of mother-of-pearl. The stone is rarely mounted *à jour*, but is best set in a black case and surrounded by a border of small diamonds or of coloured transparent stones of some sort. In the same way, the effect of a large diamond, ruby, or sapphire is greatly increased when set with a border of small opals.

Opal is a precious stone for which there is a considerable demand, and it consequently commands high prices. The value, as we have seen, depends in part upon the character of the play of colours, those in which red and green are predominating colours having been specially favoured, though this may be but a fleeting preference. A perfect stone should be neither too transparent nor too opaque, since in both cases the play of colours will be less brilliant; neither should it be cut too thick or too thin. Until recently the price of the larger and better specimens of opal was governed in the trade by their special qualities and size, and not according to their weight. Now, however, the weight of a stone expressed in carats is one of the factors which determines its price. Fine Hungarian stones are almost equal in value to brilliants of the same weight. Large opals, especially those with a considerable thickness, on account of the relative rarity of their occurrence, are dear, and the price of still larger stones is more than proportionate to the increase in size. A carat stone showing a brilliant play of colours is worth at least 50s.; stones which are inferior in this respect, as is the case with many of the so-called "Mexican" opals from Central America, are worth very much less. In the middle ages precious opal of fine quality was probably valued still more highly than it is now, and the stone was held in high esteem by the Romans.

No successful imitation of precious opal in glass has hitherto been achieved; any imitation can be instantly distinguished from the genuine stone by the appearance of the counterfeit play of colours. More successful attempts are sometimes made by mounting common opal upon a variegated foil in a blackened case, a fairly good imitation of the play of colours of precious opal being thereby produced. Black opals with a brilliant play of colours sometimes appear on the market; it is probable, however, that such stones have been treated in some way unknown.

The occurrence and mode of origin of precious opal differ in no wise from those of common opal. Everywhere the various kinds of common and precious opal occur in association with each other and with other minerals consisting of silica, such as quartz and chalcedony. It occurs as small patches in larger masses of common opal, and there is a gradual passage from one variety to the other; in the winning of opal those portions showing a play of colours are sought for and extracted from the main mass of valueless material.

By far the most important opal locality, and the one which yields the most valuable material, is the neighbourhood of the village of Czerwenitza (Hungarian Vörösvágás) in the Tokaj-Eperies Mountains, near Kaschan and Eperies, and in the Saros Comitat in northern **Hungary**. The mines are located on the Simonka mountain (Dubnik Hill), and especially on the Libanka mountain. The opals found here in former times were sent to Constantinople, and from thence found their way to the cities of the west, especially Amsterdam. This circumstance gave rise to the belief current till the end of the eighteenth century that the opal was found in the East, and accounted for the stone being known as " oriental opal."

The expression is still in use even now, especially in the case of exceptionally fine stones, although it has long been known with certainty that the supposed oriental opal localities in Egypt, Arabia, Cyprus, Ceylon, &c., do not in fact exist.   As early, indeed, as the end of the seventeenth century Tavernier, the French traveller and dealer in precious stones, stated his belief that precious opal was to be found only in Hungary, but this statement appears to have been overlooked.

The Hungarian opal mines are situated fifteen miles to the south-east of Eperies.   At the foot of Simonka, the highest mountain of a wild, forest region, is the small settlement of Dubnik, which owes its existence to the occurrence of opal in that region.   Here are found the many beautiful Hungarian stones so much prized as gems all the world over. There is little doubt but that the Romans obtained their opals from this identical spot, while records of the working of the deposit in the fourteenth century are actually in existence.

The mother-rock of the opal is here a brownish or greyish volcanic rock, technically described as a mica-hornblende-andesite.   The portions of the mother-rock which contain opal are much weathered and bleached, the felspar being altered to kaolin and in part to opal.   The precious opal occurs in nests in certain bands of the andesite, which are separated off from the barren rock by sharp lines of division or by open crevices.   In these nests precious opal is accompanied by hyalite, milk-opal, and other varieties of common opal, into which it gradually passes.   The precious opal occurs in much smaller proportion than the common opal, so that from a large mass of material after the removal of the common opal, only a small amount of opal of gem-quality will be left.   Here, as elsewhere, the opal frequently occurs in rounded masses, indicating that it has been deposited from solution.   The water, by the agency of which the opal was formed, was probably supplied by hot springs; although now dry in the immediate neighbourhood where the opals are found, such hot springs are met with at no great distance away.   Moreover, it is said that specimens of opal, showing no play of colour, are found saturated with moisture underground in the mines, and that on exposure to the air they dry and the play of colours gradually appears.

In former times the mining of opal was carried on entirely by private enterprise.   The deposits of this locality were worked principally by the inhabitants of the village of Czerwenitza, which is situated about an hour's journey to the south.   They obtained the gem out of surface workings, traces of which remain at the present day in the form of heaps of débris. A certain proportion of stones have been set free by the weathering of the andesitic rock, and such are said to have been brought to the surface from time to time in the operation of ploughing or by the agency of rain-storms.   The exclusive right of mining opal in this region was first claimed by the Government in 1788, and in place of surface workings, the method exclusively adopted till then, systematic underground mining operations were commenced, but in a very short time were entirely abandoned.   For several decades after this all work ceased, when the present system of leasing the mines to private individuals began to be adopted.   It was reported in 1877 by Professor Gerhard vom Rath that the rent per annum was 15,000 florins, while the working expenses for the same period amounted to 60,000 florins, so that to leave a margin of profit the yield could not have been very small.   By improved methods of mining it was still further increased, so that the mines became very lucrative.

At the present time the workings are confined to the Libanka mountain, situated about half a mile west of Dubnik.   On the east side of the mountain, opal mines and old débris-heaps extend for four and a half miles from north to south.   The galleries, which lie at four or five different levels one above the other, have a total length of four and a half miles, and the hill is penetrated by an adit. The workings are excavated by preference in a conglomerate of andesite blocks, possessing great hardness and solidity. The miners, of which in 1877 there were 150, loosen the opal-bearing rock with great caution, and carefully free the precious material contained in the detached fragments from the mother-rock. On the same spot there are also cutting works, which find employment for six men ; the stones are worked with emery on a leaden disc. There is a tradition that in the year 1400 no less than 300 persons were employed here in the mining of opal ; even if this number be not exaggerated the yield would probably be less than it is at present with fewer workers but better tools and methods.

The yield is very variable, and depends to a great extent upon a fortuitous combination of circumstances. Not infrequently precious opal may be searched for in vain for a distance of 10 or 12 yards. Large specimens are now very rare, and several years may elapse between the finding of specimens of the size of a hazel-nut. Some of the large specimens met with in former times are exhibited in the collection of minerals preserved in the Imperial Natural History Museum at Vienna. In this collection is to be seen the largest known specimen of Hungarian opal ; it is uncut, but quite free from the mother-rock, and exhibits a most beautiful play of colours. It is wedge-shaped in form and about the size of a man's fist, being $4\frac{3}{4}$ inches long, $2\frac{1}{2}$ inches thick, and $\frac{1}{2}$ to 3 inches high ; it weighs 34 loths or nearly 600 grams (about 3000 carats). An Amsterdam dealer in precious stones is said to have offered for this fine opal half a million florins (£25,000) ; it has been valued at 700,000 florins, but Partsch in his guide to this collection (1855) values it at 70,000 florins only, and this has been copied into other works. The specimen was found in the seventies of the eighteenth century near Czerwenitza. A smaller stone, also remarkable for its purity and magnificent colour, of the form and size of a hen's egg, is perhaps a portion of the above-mentioned specimen ; it is preserved in the Imperial Treasury at Vienna.

Another extensive find has more recently been made, namely, at the end of the eighties of the nineteenth century ; in this case the opal occurred as a large mass, not as small nests as it usually does, in the andesitic mother-rock. The mass measured 15 metres in length and 20 centimetres in thickness ; it consisted for the most part of milk-opal, but in two places was intersected by precious opal of fine quality and bordered here and there with the so-called oculus, that is to say, opal with a less brilliant play of colours. This particular occurrence was also remarkable in that the play of colours instead of being disposed in very small patches and spangles, as is characteristic of Hungarian opal, occupied large patches of the surface as in Australian opals. The difference in the appearance of opal from these two localities will be understood on comparing Figs. 6 and 7 with Figs. 8 and 9 of Plate XVI.

Besides pure opal, *mother-of-opal* is also mined in Hungary. This term is applied to a rock containing specks of precious opal of greater or less size, but always too small to be worth isolating from the rock in which they are embedded. The dark mother-rock flecked with the bright prismatic colours of the opal forms a material which can be applied very effectively to many decorative purposes, and when the flecks of opal are numerous and close-set, mother-of-opal may even be used in jewellery. The effectiveness of the stone is sometimes further enhanced by soaking the always more or less porous mass in oil, and afterwards exposing it to a gentle heat. The matrix is much darkened by this treatment and consequently forms a better background for the flecks of precious opal, which are unaffected by the process. It is possible that the black opal mentioned above is produced by similar treatment ; nevertheless, there is no doubt that black opal does occur in nature, though very rarely.

Precious opal just as fine as that of Czerwenitza is found under the same conditions at other places in the north of Hungary. It occurs, for example, in a quartz-trachyte at Nagy-Mihály, east of Kaschau on the Laborcza in the Ujhely Comitat. The mineral, however, is not abundant and the occurrence has no commercial importance. The same is also true of other localities in Europe, such as, for example, in the neighbourhood of Frankfurt-on-the-Main in Germany, and at Neudeck in Bohemia; also in the basalts of the north of Ireland and the Faroe Islands, where precious opal has, on rare occasions, been found with the abundantly occurring common variety.

There are a few localities outside Europe at which precious opal has been found in considerable amount, but inferior in quality to that found in Hungary, which, in fact, at present is the finest known. These localities, all of which are situated in America and Australia, must now be enumerated.

The Central American State of **Honduras** may be first mentioned. The occurrence of opal here is already of some commercial importance, and the resources of the district are apparently not fully exploited. The stones resemble Hungarian opals in some respects, but are usually more transparent and less fiery. Their one undesirable feature is the tendency of the colours gradually to fade when exposed to the air. This, however, is not the case with all stones, and some have been found comparable, both in beauty and in the permanence of their play of colours, to the finest Hungarian opals. The precious opal found in Honduras occurs for the most part in the department of Gracias, in the west of the State, under the same conditions as in Hungary, namely, in a weathered volcanic rock. Here also all the varieties of opal occur in association together, in some districts in masses of gigantic size. The dark-coloured trachyte of the central districts, especially of the department named above, is penetrated by veins and bands of different varieties of opal, some being of large size and extent. Precious opal is found embedded in these veins and bands at numerous places, and here mines are worked. These mines are usually very inaccessible and far distant from lines of communication, and on this account the deposit is less extensively worked than is the Hungarian.

The best known mines are in the neighbourhood of the town of Gracias (Gracias a Dios), others are situated near Intibukat and a few others of importance at Erandique. Here also the mineral resources are undeveloped, and a largely increased yield would probably follow the employment of systematic methods of working. The different varieties of opal occur here in small irregular veins in the trachyte; these, which are almost vertical, stretch from north-east to south-west, and often divide, or string out, only to reunite further on. The precious opal occurs in isolated plates in the common opal, sometimes interlaminated with this so as to produce an onyx-like stone of peculiar but pretty appearance; at other times it is met with in larger masses. Mining operations are carried on principally in a hill of red trachyte three miles long and 250 feet high. For a distance of half-a-mile along this hill precious opal has been found at every point where search has been made. Mines have also been sunk in the neighbourhood of Erandique, but the deposits have nowhere been systematically worked.

At the places hitherto mentioned, opal is actually known to occur and has indeed been mined there. There are other places, however, in this country where opal has not been actually found, but where all the conditions point to its probable existence. There are some such promising localities between Intibukat and Las Pedras, also in the neighbourhood of Le Pasale and Yukusapa, and on the slopes of the large mountain of Santa Rosa. The opal mines in the valley between Tamba and the Pass of Guayoca also give promise of an abundant yield, large masses of opal of all kinds having been found. Among these different varieties is a pearl-grey opal with a play of red light; this has no market value, but its occurrence is taken as an indication of the existence of better stones.

It is evident that there are occurrences of opal in Honduras which are unknown to white men from the fact that fine stones are constantly brought into the towns for sale by Indians. These localities may extend over the border of Honduras into Guatemala, since precious opal from this State is to be seen in various collections. Neither the exact localities nor details connected with the mining of opal in this country are known. It is said that a belt of opal-bearing trachytic rock extends from Honduras northward through Guatemala, perhaps as far as Mexico, where opal is of frequent occurrence and is mined.

The occurrences in **Mexico** are of some importance, especially in the mines of Esperanza, where precious opal is so common that specks of it are often to be seen in the stones of buildings. These mines are situated ten leagues north-east of San Juan del Rio in the State of Queretaro and extend over an area measuring thirty leagues in length and twenty leagues in breadth. The occurrence was accidentally discovered in 1835 by an agricultural labourer, but systematic operations have been in progress only since 1870. The precious stone is found here as elsewhere in a trachytic rock of reddish-grey colour and porphyritic structure, of which Ceja de Leon and Peineta among other hills are built. In these hills are sunk many mines remarkable for the amount and variety of the material they yield. Thus a single block of rock from the Simpatica mine usually contains precious opal, harlequin-opal, lechosos-opal (a variety presently to be mentioned), milk-opal, and fire-opal. One of the largest mines is the Jurado; it is an excavation in the trachyte 150 feet deep, 100 feet wide, and some hundred feet long. Many other smaller workings are to be seen, though at present but few are in active operation.

The opal-bearing rock is sent to Queretaro, twenty-five leagues off, where almost the whole of the product of the mines is cut, but in so rough a fashion that the precious material is shown to very little advantage. The work is done by twenty native lapidaries in three cutting works. Very little uncut material is exported. In the mines themselves about a hundred Indians are employed; 50,000 cut stones are sold yearly, and with improved methods the production could be easily doubled. Large numbers are sent to the United States, where, in some districts, they are sold to travellers at the railway stations as home products. Others are exported to Europe, especially to Germany, where they are used in cheap jewellery. Central American and Mexican opals are very variable in price, but are always worth far less than Hungarian stones. The cheapest stones are worth no more than a few cents apiece, while the best will fetch a hundred dollars; parcels containing a hundred or more pieces of opal are often sold at less than ten cents apiece. Higher prices are paid for exceptionally fine stones, but they do not equal the sums paid for Hungarian opals.

Mexican precious opal often occurs in common opal in layers which are too thin for cutting. Cavities in the mother-rock are filled completely, or sometimes to only one-half or two-thirds of their extent, with these masses of opal. The different varieties are disposed in horizontal layers, and the uppermost is often a botryoidal layer of glassy hyalite. Such a mode of occurrence clearly indicates that the opal has been deposited from water containing silica in solution.

Precious opal occurs here in a considerable number of varieties: all are remarkable for the intensity of the colours reflected from their surfaces, and in this respect are comparable to Hungarian stones. Mexican opals frequently show extensive patches of one uniform colour, while over the whole surface of some stones there is a play of only a single colour, red, green, or yellow, which either remains unchanged as the stone is moved about or passes into other colours.

The Mexican harlequin-opal is often remarkable for the variegated colours of its surface markings. The variety known in that country as *lechosos-opal* is a beautiful fire-red opal with a magnificent emerald-green play of colour showing flashes of carmine-red and dark violet-blue. Some stones show a reflection of emerald-green light combined with a very fine dark ultramarine-blue. An opal with a magnificent rose-red play of colour was exhibited in Paris in 1887. These varieties vary in quality according to the place from which they come, the stones from certain localities having quite a distinctive character.

It would appear from what has been said as to the beauty of Mexican and Central American opal and the abundance in which it exists, that the introduction of improved methods of mining and of cutting the rough material would result in such an extension of the opal-industry as to seriously reduce the trade in Hungarian opal. This, however, is not the case, for all opal from this region has a tendency gradually to become either opaque or transparent, the play of colours in either case being more or less completely lost. This feature, it is true, can be restored by soaking the stone in oil, but the restoration is not permanent. Moreover, some of these stones have also a tendency to crack and fall into pieces in course of time with no apparent reason. When these considerations are taken into account, it is not surprising that Hungarian stones are preferred and that they fetch higher prices; also it is obviously advisable to exercise great care in the purchase of freshly broken Mexican opals.

In the **United States** there is an unimportant occurrence of opal in the neighbourhood of the John Davis river, in Crook County, Oregon. The stones found here are greyish-white and reflect red, green, and yellow light; they are very similar to some Mexican stones, but do not appear to exist in great abundance. In the American continent it would seem that the abundance of precious opal decreases from south to north, Honduras being richest in this stone, Mexico considerably less rich, and the United States very poor. It was stated above that a great deal of the opal sold in the United States as a home product is in reality Mexican in origin.

Australia, especially New South Wales and Queensland, is an important source of precious opal. The stones, which are cloudy or milk-white, reflect light of the finest blue, green, and red colours; these colours are respectively disposed over larger areas than is the case with Hungarian stones (compare Figs. 6–9, Plate XVI.). While in some opals different areas of the surface glow with different colours, merging into each other, however, at their margins, in other stones the whole area reflects light of one uniform colour. The difference between Hungarian and Australian opals has just been pointed out; jewellers sometimes distinguish between them by referring to the latter as *opaline*. There occur also in Australia many stones with the same distribution of colour as in Hungarian opals and equal in beauty to the latter, but with a more decided tinge of yellow in the ground-colour. Many fine gems have been cut from Australian opal which, at the present time, is more abundant in the market than is the Hungarian mineral.

In New South Wales the finest opal is found on Rocky Bridge Creek, Abercrombie river, County Georgina, in a fine-grained, bluish-grey amygdaloidal basalt or trachyte, which has a thickness of 30 feet and is so altered that it may be scratched with the finger-nail. The precious opal, which occurs only in small amount, is deposited in amygdaloidal cavities or in crevices in the rock, and, as elsewhere, is accompanied by common opal and by hyalite. The precious opal, which forms in every case only a small part of the opal masses, is milk-white and reflects principally green, red, and rose-coloured light.

The most important occurrence in New South Wales of opal of fine quality, and the one exclusively mined, is at White Cliffs, on the farm Moomba in County Yungnulgra, about sixty-five miles north-north-west of Wilcannia. The following account of this occurrence is taken from a recent (1901) description by Mr. E. F. Pittman, Government Geologist of New South Wales:

The discovery of opals at White Cliffs was accidentally made by a hunter in 1889. Since that time mining operations have been carried on continuously, though sometimes under great difficulties, as in time of drought the locality is very badly provided with water; opal-mining has, however, now become a settled industry, and a thriving township has been established at White Cliffs. The area within which the mineral has been found in the district is about fifteen miles long and about two miles wide. Prospecting for precious opal is a decidedly speculative business because, as a rule, there are no indications whatever on the surface of the occurrence of the mineral below. It is only in very rare instances that an outcrop of the precious stone can be seen, and the usual procedure is to dig a trench or pit in such a position as fancy may dictate, and trust to luck. Fortunately sinking is easy, as the rock is of a soft nature, and in a fair number of instances the opal has been met with at a very short distance from the surface, though a large majority of attempts are unsuccessful. For several years the belief existed among the miners that it was useless to prospect for precious opal at a greater depth than 12 feet from the surface, but of late the incorrectness of this view has been proved, and the stones have been discovered at a depth of nearly 50 feet.

The precious opal occurs in a white siliceous rock, varying from a sandstone to a fine conglomerate in character, of Upper Cretaceous age. It is sometimes met with in thin flat veins between the bedding-planes of the rock; at other times it forms irregular-shaped nodules, or deposits occupying joints; occasionally fragments of wood are found converted into common opal, while where cracks have occurred in the wood they are filled by precious opal. Fossil bivalve shells and belemnites, entirely converted into precious opal, are not uncommon, and a fair number of opalised bones of saurians have also been found. Although these opalised fossils are of no intrinsic value as gems, they have acquired very high prices through the competition of dealers in curiosities, and are now extremely difficult to obtain. Another curiosity which is not uncommon is a pseudomorph of opal after groups of gypsum crystals; bunches of these, several inches in length, are sometimes found composed of precious opal, though the quality is usually poor. The really valuable opal, however, which is cut and polished as a gem, is found in the irregular nodules and seams in the joints and fissures of the soft siliceous rock. When the miner finds the first indication of such a deposit, he proceeds with great care to excavate the soft rock from all round it, and occasionally masses worth several thousand pounds have been found in this way. The output of the White Cliffs deposit in 1900 was valued at about £80,000.

The deposits of opal in Queensland are far richer than those in New South Wales. The occurrence here differs from that of other regions and is similar to that at White Cliffs described above. The opal occurs in thin strings and veins, and also in larger irregular nodules in a highly ferruginous sandstone or siliceous iron-stone known as the Desert Sandstone. The strings of opal are sometimes so thin that it is impossible to cut stones *en cabochon* out of this material; instead, it is cut in the form of flat plates. The body-colour of the opal found here is milk-white and the light reflected from the stone is dark blue, green, or red. As is the case at other localities, there is a considerable amount of common opal, which has to be cut away from the precious variety. It is difficult to obtain detailed accounts of the occurrence of opal at the different localities in Queensland. In recent years Queensland opal has come mainly from Bulla Creek, where it generally occurs as the nucleus of large nodules of iron-stone. Good specimens are also found on the Barcoo river. The first find is said to have been made on Cooper's Creek. Other localities are the northern part of Mount Tyre near Mount Marlow Station, Opal Range, Winton, Mayne river, Canaway Range, Bulgroo, Micaville, and Listowel Downs. The mineral is thus widely distributed, and, though inferior to Hungarian opal, is extensively used.

FIRE-OPAL.

Next in importance to precious opal comes fire-opal, so named from its fire-red colour. It is likewise known as sun-opal, also on account of its colour; while the term girasol is sometimes applied to this, as well as to other precious stones.

In colour fire-opal ranges from an almost colourless or light brownish-yellow shade to deep brownish-red. The finest tints are like those of some topazes or of hyacinth. The stone is much paler in thin splinters than in thicker pieces; also it is paler by transmitted than by reflected light. Not infrequently several shades of colour are displayed by one and the same specimen, the different tints passing gradually into each other or into perfectly colourless opal. The colour depends, no doubt, upon the presence of a small amount of iron oxide, the presence of which in fire-opal is shown by the analysis quoted above.

The stone is translucent to almost perfectly transparent. The fracture is always markedly conchoidal; the lustre of a fractured surface is always high and can be enhanced by polishing. When cut en cabochon or with facets, fire-opal, if not too light in colour, gives a pretty gem. Fig. 10 of Plate XVI. represents a fire-opal in the rough condition and Fig. 11 a cut stone.

Many specimens of fire-opal exhibit a play of colours similar to that of precious opal, when the two can be distinguished only by the body-colour of the fire-opal. The play of colours of the fire-opal has a pronounced yellow or red for background, but between this and yellow or red precious opal there are all possible gradations. The light reflected by those fire-opals which show a play of colours is often less varied in colour than in the precious opal. The most usual tints are red and green, which in the paler-coloured stones are often fine carmine-red and deep emerald-green; a combination of yellow and blue is also met with, but is much rarer. As a general rule the colours reflected by fire-opal are less brilliant, and the play of colours taken as a whole is less striking than in the precious opal.

Fire-opal while one of the most beautiful of all varieties of opal is, at the same time, the least durable. Thus it may be influenced by contact with water, by sudden changes of temperature, or by the action of light or atmospheric conditions. Some changes in the stone are ascribed to the weather, and a fire-opal is stated to be more brilliant in summer than in winter. If this is really the case, the difference is probably due to the brighter light of the warmer season of the year. While some stones are more durable, others are easily fractured and often lose their lustre and colour for no apparent reason, even when they have been protected from external influences. Very transparent stones exhibiting a play of colours are specially liable to become affected in these ways, and for this reason are unsuitable for use as gems.

The disadvantages of fire-opal as a gem are, however, of little consequence, since the stone, in spite of its fine appearance, is rarely met with in the trade. The price is not as low as might be expected, probably because durable stones of any size are somewhat rare. For a fire-opal measuring $4\frac{1}{2}$ lines in length and $3\frac{1}{2}$ in width, 1200 francs is said to have been paid.

The fire-opal is mainly a product of Mexico, and was first brought to Europe by Alexander von Humboldt at the beginning of the nineteenth century. It is found in any amount here, only in a porphyritic trachyte at Villa Seca, near Zimapan, in the State of Hidalgo, a little to the east of Queretaro and north of the city of Mexico, in latitude 20° 44½′ N. and longitude 81° 41¾′ W. of Greenwich. Together with common opal it fills the cracks and crevices of the mother-rock, and occurs also as isolated masses of larger size, the colour of which varies in the way described above. Many of these opal masses are invested with a layer of snow-white, greyish, or brownish porous material of greater or less thickness, due to the weathering of the stone (Plate XVI., Fig. 10). Besides the locality near Zimapan, the fire-opal is found near Tolima in Mexico, in Honduras, at a few places in North America, in the Faroe Islands, and elsewhere, always, however, together with other kinds of opal and under essentially the same conditions as at Zimapan. All these occurrences compared with that of Zimapan are of little importance, and to the trader in precious stones of none whatever, so that they require no further consideration.

OTHER VARIETIES OF OPAL (COMMON OPAL, SEMI-OPAL, &c.).

The other varieties of opal are not comparable in beauty of appearance either with precious opal or with fire-opal. They are used occasionally in cheap jewellery, but find a more extensive application in the manufacture of fancy goods, such, for example, as the knobs of umbrellas and sticks, for snuff-boxes, seals, knife-handles, &c.; they will therefore receive here only a brief consideration.

One of the varieties of opal which show no play of colours is sometimes perfectly transparent, and when this is the case is either perfectly colourless and water-clear, or tinged slightly with red or brown. It occurs as a secondary formation in the crevices of basalt and other rocks containing silica, in the form of thinner or thicker crusts with a botryoidal surface. From its glassy aspect it is known as *hyalite*, glass-opal, or Müller's glass; it is the purest and clearest variety of opal, but is rarely cut as a gem. Opal intermediate in character between hyalite and common or semi-opal also occurs; it is neither as clear nor as colourless as hyalite, having a faint bluish or yellowish tinge and a slight milky cloudiness.

Opal in its purest condition is water-clear; the presence of impurities of various kinds causes it to lose its transparency, colourlessness, and some of its lustre. Different specimens of opal may thus exhibit great diversity in appearance, while preserving unaltered the characters typical of the species. It is on such differences in transparency, colour, and lustre that the distinction between the varieties recognised by mineralogists is based. There is no sharp separation between these varieties, and, specimens intermediate in character are always to be met with. *Common opal* is translucent, and, as a rule, only slightly coloured. *Semi-opal* is less translucent, and ranges from colourless to deeply coloured. *Opal-jasper* or *jasper-opal* is very slightly translucent, and by reason of the large amount of impurities, especially of ferruginous material, which is present, is deeply coloured—reddish-brown, yellow, and different shades between green and black being met with. The usual vitreous lustre of opals is sometimes replaced by a greasy lustre which may incline to the waxy, the pitchy, or the resinous type. Yellow opal with a waxy lustre is known as *wax-opal*, brown opal with a pitchy lustre as *pitch-opal*, and opal with a resinous lustre as *resin-opal*. Wood, when silicified, furnishes another variety of opal known as *wood-opal*, and there are others which need not now be enumerated.

These different kinds of opal occur for the most part in the manner described above, and are associated together in large masses. The different kinds often occur in layers, or are otherwise regularly arranged with respect to each other and to other siliceous minerals, especially quartz and chalcedony, with which they may be associated. Common opal is so widely distributed that it is scarcely possible to mention every locality. The mineral occurs very abundantly in the basalts of Iceland, the Faroe Islands, the north of Ireland, the neighbourhood of Steinheim, near Hanau, and many other places. It is found in trachyte at a few places in the Siebengebirge on the Rhine, in the volcanic region of the north of Hungary and Transylvania, in Honduras, and throughout the whole of Central America and Mexico to the United States, and in many other places. It is found in serpentine in the neighbourhood of Frankenstein, Silesia, in great abundance. Other modes of occurrence will be incidentally mentioned below.

Opal of all the kinds mentioned above, when cut and polished, usually acquires a good lustre, and, as it is often pleasing in colour, the rounded gem-stones into which it is cut are by no means unattractive in appearance. As, however, the rough material occurs in nature in such abundance, and as, moreover, the finished product is so soft and brittle and lacking in durability, these stones are always low in price and are used only in the cheapest varieties of jewellery. In connection with the abundance of the mineral, it may be mentioned that in former times a uniformly coloured, pale grey, translucent opal of very pleasing appearance was obtained in large quantity at Steinheim, near Hanau, and was cut at Oberstein; when this deposit was exhausted, a supply of similar material was at once forthcoming from the Siebengebirge on the Rhine, so that there was no opportunity for a rise in the price of this variety.

The following different kinds of common or semi-opal are sometimes used for decorative and ornamental purposes:

Milk-opal is a cloudy but highly translucent opal of a milk-white, bluish- or greenish-white colour. It occurs in large amount in decomposed serpentine at Kosemütz in the neighbourhood of Frankenstein in Lower Silesia, and at other localities. Milk-opal sometimes exhibits black arborescent markings, or dendrites so-called, similar to those in certain varieties of chalcedony (compare Fig. 89). Opal of this kind is known as *moss-opal;* it is cut so as to bring the markings as near the surface as possible. Specially fine specimens measuring 3 or 4 inches across are found in Trego County, Kansas.

Opal-agate shows a banded structure, the bands being alternately light and dark in colour, or opal and agate may be banded together in the same way. The arrangement of the layers is the same as in onyx, so that, like this stone, opal-agate may be used for making cameos, &c. It is found at the Giant's Causeway, County Antrim, sometimes at Steinheim, also in the Siebengebirge, and, of specially fine quality, at Guayoca in Honduras.

Prase-opal is a highly translucent opal, the beautiful apple-green colour of which is due to the presence of a small amount of nickel. It occurs at Kosemütz, near Frankenstein, Silesia.

Rose-opal is a semi-opal of a beautiful rose-red colour, probably due to the presence of organic matter. It occurs interbedded with fresh-water limestone at Quincy, near Mehun (dep. Cher), in France. An opal of the same character, which is cut at Oberstein, is said to come from Mokün in Upper Egypt. A variegated rose-red, yellow, and green opal of the greatest beauty is found in large masses in the State of Jalisco in Mexico.

Wax-opal is yellow in colour and is characterised by its wax-like lustre. It is specially abundant in trachytic tuffs in the neighbourhood of Tokaj and Telkibanya in Hungary, hence its name Telkibanya-stone. At the same place occurs also the **pitch-opal**, a dark-brown opal with veins of a lighter colour, and with a brilliant, pitch-like lustre.

Wood-opal of a paler or darker colour arises from the opalisation of fossil wood. The structure of the wood down to the minutest detail is often to be seen in the polished surface of the opal, giving it a curious appearance. This variety occurs in large amount at the Hungarian locality just named, in Tasmania, in the Siebengebirge, and at many other places.

Menilite occurs as greyish-brown, rounded nodules in clayey shale at Menilmontant and St. Ouen, near Paris. When polished it acquires a brilliant lustre, and those stones which exhibit alternate bands of grey and brown are decidedly pretty objects.

Hydrophane is an opal which may be dirty white, yellowish, brownish, reddish, or greenish in colour, and which in its natural condition has little lustre and translucency. In mass it is almost opaque, and very little light passes through even the thinnest of splinters. Hydrophane possesses, however, one very remarkable property on which depends its occasional application as a gem. By the absorption of water it becomes almost perfectly transparent; some specimens even acquire the play of colours characteristic of precious opal, and are then known as *oculus mundi*. The capacity of hydrophane for absorbing large quantities of water is due to the great porosity of the substance; so eagerly does it suck up water that it will adhere to the tongue; moreover, its immersion in water is often accompanied by a hissing sound due to the rapid expulsion of bubbles of air. The transparency of hydrophane, acquired in the way described, is not permanent, however, and on drying the stone gradually becomes again cloudy and opaque, any play of colours it may have acquired being lost. So long as the water in which the stone is immersed is pure the phenomenon may be repeatedly observed. Hydrophane is sometimes used as a gem, and when this is the case it is cut with a rounded surface in the form of a lenticle and set *à jour* in rings or as a pin, so that there is nothing to prevent the stone being immersed in water at will and its peculiar property exhibited. It is not surprising that the behaviour of hydrophane, under the circumstances described, inspires considerable awe and wonder in the minds of Eastern people, and especially of the natives of Java and other East Indian islands, by whom the stone is much worn as an amulet. It is said that a large number of stones are every year exported from Europe, and especially from Oberstein, to these islands and there sold to the natives.

The transparency acquired by hydrophane after immersion in water is very fleeting; a more permanent effect, lasting perhaps as long as a year, is obtained by placing the stone in hot oil. A somewhat different effect again is obtained by allowing the porous mass to become impregnated with pure wax or spermaceti; the stone is then cloudy when cold, but when slightly warmed and the wax melted it assumes a brown or grey colour and becomes highly translucent or almost transparent. For this reason the mineral is sometimes known as pyrophane. It can be coloured by immersion in coloured liquids, and it is said that in former times it was brought into the market dyed red or purple.

Hydrophane is not particularly abundant, and as there is a certain appreciable demand for it it commands a fair price, the value of any given stone depending upon the size of the stone and the degree of transparency or play of colours it acquires when placed in water. The most important locality is probably Hubertusburg in Saxony; the mineral occurs here in a porphyry, either as thin strings or in nodules of chalcedony, with amethyst, rock-crystal, and common opal. When found in the mother-rock the siliceous masses are often still soft and gelatinous, the material gradually assuming the characters of hydrophane as it dries up on exposure to the air. It also occurs with the precious opal of Hungary, with the fire-opal of Mexico, with the various kinds of opal found in the Faroe Islands and Iceland, and at some other localities where opal is found, but always sparingly and in small masses. The majority of the stones which come into the market do not much exceed lentils in size.

Cacholong (*Kascholong* (German), mother-of-pearl-opal, or mother-of-pearl-agate) is an opal with very little translucency, a feeble lustre of the mother-of-pearl type, and a milk-white, reddish, or yellowish colour. It breaks with a large conchoidal fracture with very smooth surfaces. Like hydrophane, it is very porous and adheres to the tongue; but, unlike this, does not become transparent on immersion in water. It is fashioned into all kinds of small articles and fancy goods, and is sometimes cut *en cabochon* for gems, some specimens when polished having quite a pretty appearance. In some cases the stone is built up of alternate light and dark bands of material, as in onyx, or it may be interbanded with thin layers of bluish or greenish chalcedony, specimens of this description being sometimes used for cameos.

Fine specimens of good size are not very frequently met with, and consequently command rather high prices. Cacholong is found in small amount at various localities, usually in thin layers 1 to 4 lines thick, these layers alternating with chalcedony. The name is said to be derived from the Cach river in Bucharia, Central Asia, in which it occurs in the form of loose pebbles; it has been also derived from the Tartar word *kaschtschilon*, meaning beautiful stone. The above-named river has long been mentioned in connection with the occurrence of cacholong, but nothing further about the locality is known. The stone was formerly known to the inhabitants of the region as kalmuck-opal, or, as it was thought to be a kind of agate, as kalmuck-agate. It is also found in the basalts of the Faroe Islands and of Iceland, and as reniform and botryoidal incrustations on the limonite of Hüttenberg in Carinthia; also on the shores of the Bay of Fundy in Nova Scotia. The mineral, which at no time has had any great importance, occurs at all these places in association with opal and chalcedony.

TURQUOISE.

This stone is referred to as oriental turquoise, true or mineral turquoise, and *turquoise de la vieille roche*; its little-used mineralogical name, calaite, is derived from a name used by Pliny for a green stone supposed to be identical with the precious stone now under consideration. Turquoise is always opaque and is usually of a green colour, the best qualities only being blue. It never occurs in distinct crystals, in this respect differing from all the valuable precious stones hitherto considered, with the exception of opal. It is unique also in its chemical composition, since it belongs to the phosphates, a group of minerals which includes no other precious stone of the first rank.

Turquoise is a hydrous phosphate of aluminium, having the formula $2Al_2O_3.P_2O_5.5H_2O$, which corresponds to a percentage composition of: alumina (Al_2O_3), 47·0; phosphorus pentoxide (P_2O_5), 32·5; water (H_2O), 20·5 = 100·0. In the analysis of actual specimens it is found that these proportions are not invariable, a circumstance often observed in the case of substances which do not occur as crystals. Besides these constituents turquoise always contains small quantities of other substances. There is always from 1 to 4 per cent. of iron oxide and from 2 to 8 per cent. of copper oxide, the presence of which is important, since it is to this that the fine colour of the mineral is due. A blue oriental turquoise, probably from Persia, was found on analysis by Hermann to contain:

	Per cent.
Alumina (Al_2O_3)	47·45
Ferric oxide (Fe_2O_3)	1·10
Cupric oxide (CuO)	2·02
Lime (CaO)	1·85
Manganous oxide (MnO)	0·50
Phosphorus pentoxide (P_2O_5)	28·90
Water (H_2O)	18·18
	100·00

Professor S. L. Penfield has recently (1900) investigated the chemical composition of turquoise, and has arrived at the conclusion that the copper and iron, which are always present, are not accidental impurities but are essential constituents of the mineral. The new formula he proposes, namely $[Al(OH)_2, Fe(OH)_2, Cu(OH), H]_3 PO_4$, represents turquoise as a derivative of ortho-phosphoric acid, in which the hydrogen atoms of the acid are largely replaced by the univalent radicals, $Al(OH)_2$, $Fe(OH)_2$, and $Cu(OH)$ in variable amounts.

When a fragment of turquoise is heated over a flame in a narrow tube closed at one end, it decrepitates, that is to say, it flies into small fragments with a loud crackling noise; at the same time water is expelled and condenses on the cool parts of the tube. When heated more strongly, for example, when ignited in a platinum crucible, a brownish-black mass results, usually so incoherent that it falls to powder at the slightest touch; in some cases the fragment of mineral is directly converted by the intense heat into such a brown powder.

Turquoise by itself is infusible in the blowpipe flame; by virtue of the phosphoric acid and copper oxide the mineral contains, it colours this, or any other colourless flame, green. It is usually soluble both in hydrochloric acid and in nitric· acid, but specimens from different localities behave somewhat differently in this respect, some being unattacked by either of these acids.

It has already been stated, that turquoise has not hitherto been found in crystals. It occurs as irregular masses, completely or partly filling cracks and crevices and other cavities in the mother-rock. When a rock cavity is completely filled up, the turquoise usually takes the form of a plate, the thickness of which is rarely more than a few millimetres, while its area may be considerable. When, on the other hand, the cavity is only partially filled, the turquoise forms a lining of greater or less thickness to its walls, the surface of the lining layer of turquoise being frequently mammillated, botryoidal, or stalactitic.

In accordance with the absence of any definite crystalline form, there is a complete absence of cleavage in the mass. The fracture is sub-conchoidal to uneven : a clean, fractured surface shows but little brilliancy of lustre, and has usually a wax-like aspect, though at times the lustre may incline to the glassy or vitreous type. The lustre is greater when the stone is cut and polished, but is never very brilliant, the beauty of the turquoise depending for the most part upon its colour alone. The mineral is opaque, except in the thinnest of splinters through which a certain amount of light only is transmitted.

The naked-eye appearance of a freshly fractured, or cut and polished, surface of turquoise suggests a perfect continuity of structure. If, however, a thin section of the mineral be examined under the microscope, it is found to be built up of innumerable grains of irregular form arranged in an irregular manner. An examination of these grains in polarised light proves them to be doubly refracting, which demonstrates the fact that turquoise, in spite of the absence of any external crystalline form, is not amorphous, but is a compact aggregate of microscopically small crystalline individuals. In examining thin sections of turquoise under the microscope, less transparent portions with circular outlines are sometimes observed ; such appearances are probably due to the beginning of weathering n the turquoise substance. Small foreign bodies, which may possibly be chalcedony, are also visible sometimes under the microscope.

Turquoise is either green or blue, the former colour being much more frequently seen than the latter. The colour in both cases is due to the presence of copper phosphate, and probably also of iron phosphate, in small amount, intermixed with the colourless aluminium phosphate, which constitutes the greater proportion of the substance of the stone. In examining sections under the microscope it is only rarely, especially in blue Persian turquoise, that the pigment is seen to be located in definite strings or in cloudy patches with ill-defined boundaries. In most cases the colouring matter is in an extremely fine state of division, and is uniformly distributed throughout the turquoise substance. Thin sections of the mineral are almost colourless, perhaps faintly yellow ; the blue or green colour appears only in slices of some thickness. It is not at all unusual, however, for very thin sections of a deeply-coloured and almost opaque mineral to appear colourless and transparent.

The colour of turquoise ranges from sky-blue to mountain-green, the latter being not a pure green, but a green containing both grey and blue tones. Turquoise of a very intense and deep colour rarely occurs, but pale shades in great variety and forming a complete series from blue to green are to be met with. Of all these shades, the pure sky-blue of the deepest possible shade is most prized, and it is only turquoises of this colour which in Europe and the East are valued. The more the colour of a turquoise inclines towards green the less valuable does it become, and specimens of a distinct green colour are used as gems nowhere in the Old World, except in some parts of Arabia. It appears, however, that in former times turquoise of a green colour was in certain cases, for example by the ancient Mexicans, thought as much of as the blue variety, and we shall see later on that at the present day the natives of these regions frequently wear green turquoise in preference to blue.

As a rule, the turquoise is of one uniform shade of colour over its whole surface. In the case, however, of stones from certain localities, especially the Sinai Peninsula, there is sometimes visible a network of fine streaks of a paler shade of colour, which in cut stones shows up sharply against the deeper-coloured background. It is characteristic of true turquoise that its blue colour is just as beautiful by candlelight as by daylight, whereas other blue substances resembling turquoise appear of a dingy grey colour.

The colour of some turquoise is very unstable. Many stones, for example, from the Meghara valley in the Sinai Peninsula and from New Mexico begin to grow dull and pale directly they are taken out of the mine, and after a short time their colour completely disappears. It is stated as a general rule that the blue colour of turquoise is unstable and is gradually bleached by sunlight, the blue at the same time assuming a greenish hue. This is not always the case, however, and many turquoises retain their colour unaltered for a very long period. Sir Richard Burton testifies to having seen set in the musket of a Bedouin a very fine blue stone which, in spite of its exposure to sun, wind and weather for at least fifty years, had retained all its beauty of colour. The colour of turquoise is also said to be easily affected by perspiration from the body.

The original fine colour of a stone which has been bleached by wear or by prolonged exposure to sunlight can sometimes be restored by immersing it in ammonia, or by the application of grease; even, it is said, by wearing it in such a way that it comes in contact with the natural grease of the hand. The restoration is not permanent, however, the blue soon disappearing, so that it is advisable to guard against the possibility of fraud in this direction. Since the alteration in colour usually proceeds gradually from without inwards, it is possible to improve the appearance of a stone by repolishing; the operation would, of course, need repeating from time to time.

By the weathering of the mother-rock turquoise completely loses its colour and lustre. Thus rough specimens are often met with, the centre portion of which is of a fine blue colour, but is enclosed by an outer layer of dull white weathered material, which must be removed before the stone is cut. Sometimes the weathering process has proceeded so far that the whole mass is altered into a loose, crumbly material in which there may be found here and there grains of blue turquoise still unchanged.

Since the beauty and value of the turquoise depends almost entirely on its colour, attempts have been made to improve stones which are lacking in this respect by artificial means. A certain amount of success has attended these efforts, the method usually adopted being to impregnate the stone with Berlin-blue after the manner described in detail below under agate. The artificial colouring matter does not penetrate the stone deeply and the coloured layer can be scratched off with a knife. Moreover, stones so treated appear of a dingy grey colour by candlelight, and when immersed in ammonia either become green or lose their colour altogether, which is not the case with stones of a natural colour.

The specific gravity of turquoise is rather variable, values ranging from 2·6 to 2·8 having been observed. It is the least hard of any of the valuable precious stones; its hardness, which is the same as that of felspar, being represented by 6 on the scale. Turquoise is therefore easily scratched by quartz or by a file, but is just hard enough to scratch ordinary window-glass. On account of its softness it requires special care when worn as a gem, although, being opaque, small scratches are less noticeable than in transparent stones.

Whether the ancients were acquainted with turquoise is doubtful, but the stone was certainly known in the Middle Ages. Its use as a gem is very general at the present time, the stone being as much prized in Eastern as in Western countries. Especially in the East, in Turkey, Egypt, Arabia, and Persia, it is much worn, being regarded by Orientals as a lucky stone. Thus it is to be met with everywhere in these countries, if only as a fragment of poor quality set in tin. It is much used in the decoration of the handles and scabbards of daggers and swords and of the trappings of horses and for other similar purposes. The name turquoise is said to signify Turkish gem. In Western countries large turquoises are frequently mounted with a border of small diamonds, while small stones form an effective frame for certain other precious stones of large size.

As is usually the case with opaque stones, turquoise is nearly always cut *en cabochon* with a plane undersurface of circular or oval outline (Plate XX., Fig. 2). Exceptionally large and fine specimens are said to be sometimes cut as table-stones or as thick-stones; but since the existence of facets does nothing, on account of the opacity of the stone, towards enhancing its beauty these forms of cutting are but rarely adopted. The turquoise is often engraved with various devices; in the Orient, for example, with quotations from the Koran, the letters being filled in with gold. Stones which are intended to be engraved are often cut with a flat instead of a rounded surface.

This precious stone, which is so generally prized, has a very considerable value, and in the Middle Ages was worth even more than now. The price of single stones varies with their size and their colour, the most valuable being of a pure sky-blue colour uniformly distributed and free from patches. As the colour inclines more and more to green the stone becomes less and less valuable; while with regard to size, small turquoises are abundant and consequently cheap. Pieces of turquoise the size of a pea are rare, and when of a good colour command a high price. Small stones are bought and sold in thousands, rather larger specimens in dozens, while those above a certain size are sold singly. A carat stone of the best quality may be worth about fifty shillings, but the price of larger stones, owing to their rarity, is not in the same proportion to their weight. In the case of rough specimens it is very essential that they have a certain thickness, so that when cut *en cabochon* they shall not be too thin and flat, as is the case when the turquoise forms only a thin layer on the matrix.

Large turquoises of fine quality are few in number. Among such may be mentioned a heart-shaped stone 2 inches in length, which some time ago was in the possession of a Moscow jeweller, and which had been formerly worn as an amulet by Nadir Shah: an inscription from the Koran is engraved on it in gold, and it is valued at 5000 roubles. A turquoise in the collection of the Imperial Academy at Moscow measures more than 3 inches in length and 1 inch in breadth. The largest and finest stone in existence is said to be one in the treasury of the Shah of Persia. The most important turquoise mines known are situated in the dominions of this monarch, by whom the finest stones were formerly appropriated.

With regard to the occurrence of turquoise in nature it has been stated already that the mineral is found in veins of greater or less extent (Plate XX., Fig. 3) in certain rocks, having been deposited from aqueous solution in the cracks and crevices of these rocks. When the cavity is incompletely filled the turquoise forms a thin crust on its walls, and the surface of the incrustation may be mammillated, botryoidal, stalactitic, &c. The mother-rock of turquoise differs at different localities; thus at one place the matrix may be quartzose slate, at another sandstone, and at a third trachytic rocks, the latter being remarkable as the bearer of the finest qualities of turquoise. The mineral appears never to have been found in limestone; statements as to its occurrence in this rock have been shown to be based on error.

The occurrence of turquoise in **Europe** is only sparing, and what has been found hitherto is almost entirely of the green variety, which is unsuitable for cutting as gems. The colour of European stones may in some few cases incline to blue, but is never of a pure sky-blue. At most localities the turquoise veins appear to be in a matrix of quartzose slate, as, for example, at Oelsnitz in Saxon Voigtland, and at Steine and Domsdorf near Jordansmühl in Silesia.

By far the most important localities for fine blue turquoise are in Asia. Of these the most famous are in **Persia**; hence the finest stones are referred to as " Persian turquoise." The name given to this their favourite stone by the inhabitants of the country is *piruzeh* (Arabic, *firuzeh*); and in the opinion of C. Ritter the word turquoise is a corruption of this.

The most important Persian turquoise mines, and those which yield precious material almost exclusively, are situated in the district of Nishapur, fifteen geographical miles west of Meshed in the province of Khorassan. In recent times details concerning this locality have been given by Tietze, Bogdanovitch, and the Persian General C. Houtum Schindler, who, at the beginning of the eighties, was for some time governor of the mining district and acting manager of the mines.

The mountains in the neighbourhood consist of nummulitic limestone and sandstone associated with clay-slates and interbedded with large masses of gypsum and rock-salt. All these beds have been broken through by younger volcanic rocks belonging to the Tertiary period, and consisting of porphyritic trachytes, or, according to some observers, of porphyry (felsite-porphyry). They form a chain of mountains extending from west to east between Kotshan and Nishapur. The occurrence of turquoise in this district is confined to the southern slopes of Ali-Mirsai, a peak in the chain with a height of 6655 feet. In this limited area are situated all the turquoise mines, not only those at present open, but also many now abandoned which were formerly worked, some being of great antiquity. The mountain is penetrated at a height of 4540 feet by a valley in which is situated the village of Maaden, 5100 feet above sea-level, and in latitude 36° 28′ 15″ N. and longitude 58° 20′ E. of Greenwich. This village is the centre of the area in which turquoise mining is carried on; the mines lie in the immediate vicinity of this to the north-west, and range in altitude from 4800 to 5800 feet above sea-level. All the inhabitants of Maaden earn their livelihood by work connected with the mining, cutting, and selling of this precious stone.

The original mother-rock here consists exclusively of porphyritic trachyte, which occurs in a weathered condition, and in brecciated masses consisting of blocks of the same rock cemented together by brown iron-ore (limonite). The turquoise fills up cracks and crevices in the trachyte and between the blocks forming the breccia; and being the latest formed mineral is deposited in and on the limonite. The latter frequently fills the rock cavities to only a partial extent, and the remaining spaces are filled by turquoise. This is found in layers of greater or less extent and only moderately thick, usually from 2 to 6 and never more than 13 millimetres in thickness. As a rule, it is found between layers of limonite of greater or less thickness, but this is not invariably the case. At other times the turquoise occurs in small masses of irregular shape and ranging in size from that of a pea to that of a bean. These small masses are either distributed irregularly through the rock or collected together so as to form plate-like masses within the limonite. The occurrence of turquoise in small veins running obliquely through larger veins of limonite, and sometimes extending into the surrounding blocks of trachyte, is also to be mentioned. Only in rare cases is turquoise found filling up cavities in the interior of blocks of trachyte forming the breccia. This mode of occurrence is of interest to mineralogists, since it shows that the formation of turquoise follows on the decomposition of felspar crystals of which it often takes the external form; in other words, we have a pseudomorph of turquoise after felspar.

Turquoise is found, moreover, not only in the compact trachyte and in the trachyte-breccia, but also in the masses of débris formed by the weathering of these rocks and slowly accumulated at the foot of the mountain. The precious stone lies loose in the detritus, and is frequently coated with a white crust of weathered material, which must be removed before the fine blue colour of the stone can be seen. Sometimes the whole mass of turquoise is weathered to a white, crumbly material, which is, of course, useless as a gem. The turquoise-bearing deposits of alluvial débris have a thickness of from 2 to 20 metres: close to the foot of the mountain these deposits are less thick, while at some little distance away low hills have been carved out of the originally continuous mass by the action of the weather. Turquoise of good quality is to be found only in the uppermost portion of these secondary deposits to a depth of about 2 metres; at a depth of 6 metres greenish and whitish stones of poor quality only are found, while below this turquoise is completely absent.

There are several hundreds of mines in this neighbourhood; in the year 1876 there were 266 being worked, but the majority of them have since been abandoned. Some of these mines have been worked for centuries and are mentioned in the treatise on mineralogy written by the Arab Mohamed-ibn-Mansur in the year 1300. According to this work there was a legend to the effect that the richest of these mines were opened by Isaac the son of Abraham, and they are consequently known as the Isaac mines. For a long period they have been worked according to the best methods; shafts to the depth of 150 feet were sunk, and levels and galleries driven to a length of 100 feet or more, though of small height and width. Pillars were left to give the necessary support to the roof, and, where necessary, ventilation shafts were sunk, so that the whole working was designed and carried out in a systematic manner.

According to the opinion of General Schindler, mining operations were probably carried on up to 1725 by the Persian Government; and it is to this authority that the adoption of the methods described above was due. The management of the mines was subsequently transferred to the inhabitants of Maaden, and from this time the industry began to decline. Systematic methods were gradually given up; the supporting pillars were removed in order to obtain the turquoise they enclosed, all precautions were neglected, the deposits were worked only with a view to rapid gain, and there was no thought for the future. Consequently the work became very dangerous and the yield decreased; many of the workings became inaccessible, and at some places, where formerly existed properly constructed mines, there are now funnel-shaped depressions 60 to 80 feet across and as much as 250 feet deep, which have been formed by the falling in of the shafts and galleries.

These old mines are not in all cases completely abandoned; the excavation of turquoise-bearing rock is sometimes still carried on, and both the loose rock lying in the workings and the refuse-heaps outside are worked over for turquoise, usually by women and children. New mines are always being sunk, and these are in almost all cases successful, since the deposit of turquoise extends throughout the whole mountainside.

The alluvial deposit also is worked for turquoise; the detrital material is excavated, and after the larger blocks have been sorted out the remainder is washed in order to render the turquoise distinguishable. These washings at one time were of little importance, but came more and more into prominence as mining in the mother-rock became more and more neglected, until now they are by no means insignificant.

About 200 persons were engaged in the 'eighties in the mining of turquoise; of these about 130 were employed in mining operations in the mother-rock and the remainder in the alluvial deposits.

The stones collected here in these various ways are usually roughly cut *en cabochon* on the spot and then taken by the elders of the village, fifteen to twenty in number, into Meshed for sale. Owing to this fact, Meshed is sometimes incorrectly supposed to be a locality for Persian turquoise. From this place the stone travels, usually through the hands of Bucharian merchants, to Russia, especially to Moscow and to Nizhniy-Novgorod, and is sold at the fairs held at the latter place to dealers, by whom it is carried to all parts of the world. Nishapur has likewise been supposed to be a locality for the fine Persian turquoise, but because the stone is rarely to be seen or bought at that place its actual occurrence in the near neighbourhood has frequently been doubted by travellers.

The yield of the turquoise mines at the end of the 'seventies was about 25,000 tomans, or £8300, per annum, one-third of this sum being paid into the State treasury. According to other reports the value of the annual yield is much higher. General Schindler was informed by the turquoise merchants at Meshed that turquoises to the value of £12,000 were exported to Russia annually, while the smaller sales in Meshed itself amounted to £4000. This latter item is made up, for the most part, of turquoises mounted in tin or silver, but never in gold, and sold to pilgrims as lucky stones. Many stones are also exported through Yezd on the Persian Gulf to Constantinople.

In the year 1882 a determined effort was made by the Persian Minister of Mines to reorganise the management of the turquoise mines and thus to increase their yield. For four years but little improvement was noted, then General Schindler was placed at the head of affairs, and it was hoped that as much as 800,000 francs' worth of turquoise might be exported to Paris every year. These expectations were not entirely realised, as in the first year of the new régime turquoises to the value of 300,000 francs only were obtained; the employment of European methods, however, soon led to a substantial improvement in the yield, and the future of the mines became more and more hopeful.

A short time ago Mr. Streeter, a London jeweller, offered to rent and work the mines. As, after a thorough examination of the property, it was found that an outlay of from £50,000 to £60,000 would be necessary to set the mines in good working order, the idea was abandoned. It is said that the work is now likely to be undertaken by an American company.

Persian turquoises from this locality are often of a beautiful dark blue colour, but pale blue and green stones are also frequently met with. Stones found in the alluvial detritus and having a white external crust of weathered material are said to be of a specially fine colour. The colour, as a rule, is permanent, but in some of the newly opened mines turquoises have been found which, in a very short time after being taken out of the mine, lose their colour and become perfectly white. These stones are preserved in damp earth until they are sold to some unsuspecting person, who, in a short time, receives an unpleasant surprise. It is natural that such occurrences should have given rise to a certain distrust and suspicion of Persian turquoise in the minds of dealers in this stone.

Stones from different mines differ in quality, and they are classified on the spot according to size and shape, and especially according to colour, into three groups. Those of a uniform deep sky-blue colour and of a shape suitable for cutting *en cabochon* are classified as ring-stones; these are of the best quality and are not very abundant; they are found most frequently in the alluvial detritus. Stones of medium quality are divided into four sub-classes; the best of these are sent to Europe, the remainder being used in Persia and elsewhere in the Orient. Stones of the poorest quality, that is to say, of a pale blue or green colour, are sent only to Arabia, since in this country size and not colour or quality is the chief consideration. A pound's weight of stones of the first quality is worth at the mines about £90, while the same weight of stones of the third quality is worth only about £5. In Europe the price is far higher: it has been calculated that 25s. would be paid in Europe for a stone which could be got at the mines for 10s. A carat-stone is worth at the mines from 5s. to 10s. according to quality, the higher price being paid only for stones of the best quality.

There are other localities for turquoise in Persia besides Maaden, but all are little known and apparently much poorer. Turquoise has been found recently at Tabbas in the province Khorassan, but not of good quality. Bogdanovitch mentions a deposit of turquoise discovered not long ago, somewhere to the south of Meshed, about eighteen days' journey from this town. Another locality which has been known, though imperfectly, for a longer period is the province of Kerman in the interior of Persia. The mineral occurs at several places north-east of the town of Kerman, in the great range of mountains composed of volcanic rocks which stretches from north-west to south-east. At Chemen-i-Mô-Aspan, four fersakhs (eighteen miles) from Pâriz and opposite Gôd-i-Ahmer there are turquoise mines, which were worked until quite recently; the stones found here have a greenish tinge. At Kârîk, north-east of Shehr-i-Bâbek, there is an old mine with two shafts, one of which was destroyed by an earthquake only a few years ago, while the other has not been worked for many years. A few veins of pale-coloured turquoise were found some years ago near Mashîz, on the slopes of the Cheheltan mountains, the highest peak of which has an altitude of over 12,000 feet. Turquoise is said to occur, and formerly to have been mined, in the neighbourhood of Taft, near Yezd, on the Persian Gulf.

It is stated that there are turquoise mines, yielding mostly green stones, further to the north-west, beyond the Persian frontier between Herat and Western Turkestan. According to the statements of ancient Arabian writers, the precious stone was found at Chodshent, from whence came also the green *callais* (*callaina*) of Pliny, now considered to be identical with turquoise. Other localities in the same region have also been recorded; for example, in 1887 in the mountain range Kara-Tube, fifty kilometres from Samarkand. The turquoise occurs here in limonite and quartzose slate, and the place was, at some unknown time, the scene of mining operations. Finds of turquoise have been made in the same region in our own time; for example, in the Syr Daria country in the Kuraminsk district (in the Kara Mazar mountains), and also in the Karkaralinsk district in the Kirghiz Steppes (Semipalatinsk territory of Siberia). These and other occurrences in the same region have no commercial importance and need no further consideration.

The next most important locality for turquoise in the old world is the **Sinai Peninsula**: the mineral is found for the most part in the neighbourhood of Serbâl, near the west coast. The best known mines are situated in the Wadi Meghâra or Maghâra (meaning hollow valley); these are very ancient and were worked on a large scale in ancient Egyptian times, according to H. Brugsch, as early as the period of the Third Dynasty in the reign of King Snefru, 4000 B.C. The discovery of numerous inscriptions and implements of various kinds proves that a garrison was maintained here by the Egyptians for the protection of the turquoise mines and of an important copper-mining industry. The existence of these turquoise mines was for a long period completely forgotten; they were at length rediscovered by Major C. K. Macdonald. Work was at once recommenced, and some of the finest and largest stones found were shown in London at the Exhibition of 1851. One in the possession of Major Macdonald was as large as a pigeon's egg, but in a very short time lost its colour and became greenish-white and, compared with its original value, quite worthless. The same fate overtook many of the stones exhibited in 1851; one which had been sold for a high price became, in the course of a year, perfectly colourless. Specimens presented by Major Macdonald to the British Museum in 1862 still retain their fine blue colour although they have been exposed to a strong light for many years.

These ancient mines are situated on the northern slope of the Meghâra valley, 150 feet above its floor. This side of the valley is of red sandstone, while in the porphyry, of which the opposite side is formed, no turquoise is found. The precious stone fills up crevices and fissures in the rock, and is found in tabular pieces of about the same dimensions as in Persia; the mode of occurrence is therefore similar to that of the stone in the latter country.

The turquoise of the Sinai Peninsula is not, however, confined to the sandstone of the Wadi Meghâra, but is found in porphyry outside the valley. In the form of thin plates it penetrates the porphyry, which forms part of the Serbâl, and differs from the turquoise found in the sandstone in that its beautiful blue colour is permanent. These stones are collected and sent to market by the Bedouins; moreover, some of the stones sent to Europe by Major Macdonald are said to have come not from the mines in the Meghâra valley but from the porphyry of Serbâl. The exact situation of the mines in this region is carefully hidden by the natives, and no details concerning the occurrence are known. A locality apparently of special importance is Moses' Well; also Neseb or Nasaiph Well between Suez and Sinai. The occurrence of turquoise at this locality is probably distinct and definite in character, since the stones show under the microscope a peculiar structure different from that of turquoise from other localities. It is impossible to definitely locate the place, since every well which supplies drinking water is called Moses' Well by the Bedouins; according to H. Fischer, however, it is situated in latitude 29° N., about five miles from the Serbâl. Adhering to the stones which come from this place is a brownish-red, ferruginous powder formed of friable, granular quartz; it is probable, therefore, that the stones occur in sandstone as at Wadi Meghâra.

The best turquoises from the Sinai Peninsula are quite equal to Persian stones, and some even surpass these in beauty and depth of colouring. As a rule, however, the colour of these stones is of a more whitish-blue, the lustre is more glassy, and the material rather more brittle. Fine stones from this locality appear on the markets as Egyptian or Alexandrian turquoises; they were formerly regarded as artificial products, but detailed examination has shown them to be the natural mineral.

Arabia proper is another turquoise locality; at least three mines are stated to be situated in the " Midianite country "; two of these are supposed to be still worked, but the stones found there very soon lose their colour.

Despite certain statements to the contrary, turquoise has not hitherto been found in any of those Asiatic countries which are remarkable for their wealth of precious stones; that is to say, neither in India, nor in Burma, nor in the Island of Ceylon.

In the new world the principal turquoise deposits are situated in the south-western states of the North American Union. These are not unimportant even now, but in former centuries they were of much more prominent interest. The most important mines are in the State of **New Mexico**, which formed a portion of the ancient kingdom of the Aztecs. The precious stone was much admired by the ancient Mexicans; they prized it more highly than gold, and used it in the decoration of all kinds of objects as well as for a gem. It appears, however, that it was green and not blue turquoise which was held in such peculiar esteem. The green precious stone *chalchihuitl*, so much esteemed by this ancient people, is considered by some authorities to be identical with green turquoise ; others, however, suppose it to have been emerald, jade, green jasper, or some other green mineral.

After the fall of the Kingdom of Mexico the turquoise still continued to be the favourite stone of the inhabitants of the region, that is to say, of the Pueblo and Navajo Indians. W. P. Blake states that the stone is known to these people as *chal-che-we-te*, which is supposed to be a corruption of the old name *chalchihuitl*. So greatly was the stone prized by these Indians that only with the greatest difficulty could they be induced to part with their turquoise-decorated tools and implements to white men. Such objects, moreover, were almost always buried with the dead, as recent excavations in the Indian burial-grounds of that region have shown.

The best known of the ancient turquoise mines is situated on the mountain named after this stone, Mount Chalchihuitl (or Mount Chalchuitl) ; this mine was the first to be rediscovered and was found by William P. Blake in the 'fifties. Mount Chalchihuitl forms part of the conical mountain group Los Cerillos, about twenty-two miles south of Santa Fé, the capital of the State of New Mexico ; it is situated on the northern bank of the Galisteo river, which flows westward into the Rio Grande and separates the Los Cerillos district from the important mining district of the Placer or Gold Mountains.

This mountain group, and in particular the turquoise-bearing Mount Chalchihuitl, consists of sandstone, probably of Carboniferous age, intersected by dykes of augite-andesites. These andesites, and the volcanic tuffs with which they are associated, contain in various parts of the mountains ores of lead, copper, silver, and gold in no inconsiderable amount. They are usually much decomposed and completely bleached by the action of volcanic gases and vapours. The alteration and weathering of the rocks of this range has resulted in the formation of new minerals of various kinds. Thus by the alteration of the felspar in the volcanic rocks kaolin is formed ; from this mineral the turquoise, subsequently formed, derives its alumina, the phosphoric acid being derived from the apatite in the same rocks, and the copper, to which the colour of the stone is due, from the copper ores also embedded in these rocks. All the turquoise appears to have originated in this way, the formation of turquoise always following that of kaolin. The mineral is found here as elsewhere in small nodules and thin veins, with a mammillated or botryoidal surface, in the andesite or andesitic tuff, which is altered to a whitish or yellowish clayey mass. The turquoise is so generally distributed through the rock that patches of it may be seen almost everywhere on the walls of the mine.

One of the ancient Mexican mines, which was without doubt worked before the discovery of America by Europeans, has been described by W. P. Blake as an enormous funnel-shaped pit, the sides of which are steep and precipitous. At one place there are even overhanging rocks forming a kind of cave, while at another the slopes are more gentle, owing to the falling in of waste material from above. An idea of the great age of this artificial excavation may be derived from the fact that on its sides are growing pines, cedars, and other trees hundreds of years old. It is about 200 feet deep and 300 feet wide, and out of it many thousands of tons of solid rock must have been excavated. In its neighbourhood are to be seen similar but smaller pits, and it would seem that the whole surface of the turquoise-bearing mountain was turned over in the search for the precious stone. Beside these surface-workings there exist also underground mines excavated at the same time, some of which are of no inconsiderable extent. These were discovered when attempts were made to rework this old deposit ; and in the old mines were found relics of this long-past age in the shape of miners' tools of various kinds. Everything points to the fact that these ancient mines had been carefully covered up before being left, in order, no doubt, to conceal their exact whereabouts from strangers and unauthorised persons. How extensive must have been these ancient workings is shown by the one fact, among many others, that the heaps of barren rock thrown out from the mines cover an area of no less than twenty acres. Here again are to be found numbers of large growing trees, proving the great age of the heaps.

The abandonment of the mines was due to a great national disaster which befell the Indians in the year 1680. Owing to the undermining of the ground by the Indian miners a large section of the mountainside suddenly fell in, killing a number of workers on the spot. This accident was the immediate cause of the uprising of the Pueblos, which resulted in the expulsion of the Spaniards from the country.

At the beginning of the eighties of last century, after the opening up of the valley of the Rio Grande by the construction of a railway, a company was formed to undertake again the mining of turquoise, and at the same time the metallic ores of the region. It was soon found that though turquoise of a fine blue colour does exist, yet the greater part of the material is green or bluish-green in colour, and that to obtain a single stone suitable for a gem, however small, it was necessary to work through many tons of rock. Throughout the whole deposit the stone is poor in quality, and the company was soon obliged to give up work ; nevertheless, between 1883 and 1886 stones to the value of 3000 dollars were found. At the present time work on a small scale is carried on by a few poor white men and Indians, who, by lighting fires on the rock, make it friable, thus rendering the work of excavation less difficult. As a result of the adoption of this method the greater part of the turquoise is destroyed. What little is saved is roughly worked into rounded or heart-shaped ornaments pierced with a hole. These are sold at Santa Fé or to travellers at the railway stations as objects of local interest. The price at present is very low, only 25 cents (about 1s.) being asked by Indian dealers for a mouthful of such stones. But few of these stones find their way into the hands of the jewellers, for it is only seldom that the Indian dealers have really good stones to offer, and, moreover, because of a fraud attempted some time ago, confidence in them has been greatly shaken. These men placed on the market turquoises of a specially fine dark-blue colour, which was found by Mr. G. F. Kunz to be due to a surface application of Berlin-blue.

Another occurrence of turquoise in the same neighbourhood, from which the ancient Mexicans obtained a rich yield, was rediscovered at the beginning of 1890, and is now known as the " Castilian Turquoise Mine." It is situated seven miles from Los Cerillos, on the road to Santa Fé, and one and a half miles from Bonanza. The mother-rock is the same as at Mount Chalchihuitl, but the turquoise is of a better colour than that found at the latter locality. Several thousand stones with an aggregate value of 100,000 dollars have already been found, some being of a very fine blue colour, though not equal to Persian turquoise.

Also in New Mexico, in the south-west corner of the State, are situated the newly-discovered deposits of turquoise in the Burro Mountains, fifteen miles south of Silver City in Grant County. They are now being worked by a company, and some good stones have already been found. The existence of ancient mine barrows shows that this deposit, like others in the region, had been worked at some period now long past. Here also the turquoise occurs in the rock in the form of strings and veins. There was once found here a plate of turquoise 8 inches across and $\frac{1}{8}$ to $\frac{1}{4}$ inch in thickness ; and it is said that the mines have yielded as much as 10 kilograms of fine turquoise in a month. It occurs for the most part in kidney-shaped masses encrusted with a thin layer of siliceous material. Turquoise occurs in trachyte in the Cow Springs district of this region, and there is yet another occurrence at Hachita in the same county.

Another recently discovered locality for turquoise is situated in the Jarilla Mountains (Doña Anna County, New Mexico), 150 miles east of the Burro Mountains and 200 miles south of Los Cerillos. Here, again, ancient surface-workings reaching down to the solid rock are met with; these, judging from the character of the vessels and tools found there, must be centuries old. The turquoise is found in thin almost vertical cracks and crevices in trachyte, and is sometimes accompanied by copper-pyrites; the mode of occurrence is, therefore, the same as elsewhere in this region. In the Shoo-ar-mé mine in the Jarillas, which has a shaft 70 feet deep, turquoise has been found in abundance. It occurs usually in hemispherical or kidney-shaped masses, but also in irregular masses, completely filling up the cavities in the rock: a slab of turquoise was once found here which was 3 square feet in area and $\frac{3}{4}$ inch thick. Stones found at some depth are usually blue in colour; those which lie nearer the surface are frequently green, probably owing to weathering. Stones which when first taken from the ground are of a fine blue colour, sometimes almost indigo-blue, on drying or exposure to air lose their colour and will then adhere to the tongue. Nevertheless good specimens of permanent colour are frequently found, more than 50 kilograms of good marketable turquoise having been obtained in six months from one of the newly reopened mines.

Turquoise has been discovered at many other places in New Mexico. Many of these deposits were worked by the ancient Mexicans until the solid rock was reached, when, owing to the inadequacy of their primitive methods, the work had to be abandoned.

Other places in the United States have also yielded turquoise, and these will be briefly mentioned.

A large amount of turquoise was obtained by the ancients from a deposit about twenty miles from Tombstone in Cochise County, **Arizona**; it is situated in a spur of the Dragoon Mountains, not far from the former Apachan capital, Cochise, and south-east of the present capital, Tucson. The mountain is now known as Turquois Mountain, and as silver ores also occur in the neighbourhood there has sprung up quite a mining industry, the district in which it is carried on being known as the Turquois District. Several large excavations have been made in the mountain, but for some time now the work has everywhere been given up. The deposit is not as rich as in Mount Chalchihuitl, nor are the ancient workings as extensive. The colour of the precious stone is for the most part some shade of green.

In Mohave County, also in Arizona, is situated the turquoise locality known as Mineral Park. Here finely coloured turquoise has been found in three veins, 1 to 4 inches in thickness and about 100 yards apart; these have been followed up for almost half a mile. Large quantities of turquoise were obtained from this deposit first by the ancient Mexicans and subsequently by the Spaniards.

In the Columbus district of southern **Nevada,** about five miles north of Columbus and half a mile south of the Northern Bell mine, turquoise occurs in a brown sandstone in the form of veins and small grains. The single stones found here, though small, are finer in quality than any occurring elsewhere in North America, some few being of unsurpassed beauty and great value. Most of the turquoises found here are sent to San Francisco; besides these isolated stones the sandstone containing small pieces of turquoise embedded in it is also mined and affords an effectively coloured ornamental stone.

There are two other American localities of which mention must be made, namely, Holy Cross Mountain in Colorado, and Taylor's Ranch, Chowchillas river, Fresno County, California. Though neither are important commercially, yet the latter has a certain interest from a mineralogical point of view, since here turquoise occurs in hexagonal prisms some inches in length as a pseudomorph after apatite.

In Australia turquoise has recently been discovered in the State of Victoria; no details as to the occurrence are known, but turquoise has been obtained from a mine called the " New Discovery."

ARTIFICIAL PRODUCTION.—As in the case of all valuable precious stones, attempts have been made to produce artificially a substance resembling the naturally occurring stone, but saleable at a lower price. A certain measure of success has attended these efforts, since there has been produced a mass of which the chemical composition does not differ essentially from that of naturally occurring turquoise, and of which the colour, lustre, hardness, specific gravity, fracture, and general appearance are the same as in that stone. The manufacture is said to be carried on chiefly in Vienna, France, and England: the method adopted is to submit to great pressure a chemical precipitate of the same composition and colour as turquoise. The details of the method are not exactly known, but it would seem that hitherto it has been impossible to produce stones of any considerable size.

These artificially made turquoises are put on the market together with natural stones; they are of very good colour, and it is impossible by mere inspection to distinguish them from the turquoise of nature. This being so, the appearance on the market of an unusually large supply of good stones naturally creates suspicion in the minds of possible buyers; this was the case with a large supply of Persian stones and of the Egyptian or Alexandrian turquoises mentioned above, all of which, however, proved to be genuine.

Owing to a difference in their behaviour when heated, it is possible to distinguish artificially produced turquoise from the natural stone. The latter, when heated, decrepitates violently and is reduced by ignition to a brownish-black powder, or to a loose mass which easily falls to a powder and does not fuse. The artificial product, on the other hand, does not decrepitate, and on ignition is not reduced to powder, but fuses or runs together into a hard mass, which at least in the interior retains its blue or bluish-green colour; some of the artificial stones even fuse with moderate ease to a black bead. It is obvious that this method of detection can be adopted only when the complete destruction of the turquoise is of no consequence, as in buying a large parcel of stones, or when it is possible to detach a small splinter from the back of a large stone. It is said to be possible to recognise an artificially produced turquoise from the fact that after lying in water it assumes a darker shade of blue, and on the wet surface can be made out a network of cracks; moreover, it is said that such stones become softer after immersion in alcohol. There are always to be found adhering to genuine stones particles of the mother-rock, and especially of brown limonite, which is so frequently associated with turquoise; the presence of such particles was for a long time a sure indication of the genuineness of a stone; this is not now the case, however, for artificial stones are at present furnished with brown specks of hydrated iron oxide in order to imitate natural stones still more closely.

In the manufacture of artificial turquoise the reproduction of all the essential characters of the natural mineral is attempted, and so similar is the artificial product to the natural stone that it is frequently impossible to distinguish between them except by the employment of special tests. Besides these artificial stones other substances are substituted for turquoise, especially a glass paste, which is made by adding to a mass of glass 3 per cent. of copper oxide, $1\frac{1}{2}$ per cent. of manganese oxide, and a trace of cobalt oxide. These paste imitations are easily distinguished from genuine stones; their lustre is of the ordinary vitreous type, which is not difficult to recognise, especially along the margin of the stone, which is almost invariably splintered during the process of grinding, and where also the conchoidal fracture characteristic of glass may be detected. Moreover, unless the paste is made with the greatest possible care, it is almost certain to contain air-bubbles, which are never present in genuine stones. A few other substances, sometimes substituted for turquoise, will now be considered below.

BONE-TURQUOISE.

Bone-turquoise is also known by various other names, such as tooth-turquoise, occidental turquoise, *turquoise de la nouvelle roche*, odontolite, and fossil turquoise. The name is applied to the bones, and especially to the teeth, of certain extinct vertebrates, such as the *Mastodon* and *Dinotherium*, which during the process of fossilisation have taken up phosphate of iron, the so-called blue iron-earth, and so acquired a fine sky-blue colour, or by taking up copper salts have assumed a green colour. The latter case is rarely met with, and as bone turquoise of a green colour is not prized it need not be considered further.

These blue-coloured fossil teeth and bones are found at various localities, and are especially abundant in the Miocene beds of Simorre, Auch, and other places in the department Gers (province Gascogne) in France, where they are in most cases the remains of *Mastodon angustidens*. At Simorre the deposit was for a short time even systematically mined. When first taken out of the ground the teeth are of a dingy greyish-blue colour, which changes when they are heated to a fine sky-blue. The teeth of the mammoth, so often found in Siberia, are also sometimes of a fine blue colour.

Bone-turquoise, like true turquoise, is frequently cut *en cabochon*, and, though much less valuable than the latter, commands a fair price, especially in fine pieces of considerable size. Its colour by daylight is scarcely distinguishable from that of true turquoise, but in candlelight it assumes a dull grey hue, and when immersed in alcohol or water gradually fades. On cut and polished surfaces paler stripes on a darker background may frequently be detected, an appearance which is due to the structure of the tooth. This structure can be clearly made out by examining thin sections of the material under the microscope; and at the same time it will be seen that the colouring matter is collected in small tubular cavities. Specimens showing dendritic markings, that is to say, moss-like patches of a brown or black colour, are met with not infrequently; they are much less valuable than material which is not so marked.

Bone-turquoise may be easily distinguished from the true mineral turquoise. In the first place the former contains up to 11 per cent. of calcium carbonate, hence when a small fragment of bone-turquoise is placed in hydrochloric acid, or a drop of acid placed on a large piece of the same substance, there is a brisk effervescence. Moreover, when heated, a distinct smell of burning becomes perceptible, owing to the presence of organic matter in the substance. When rubbed it becomes electrified and retains its charge for a long time. It is less hard than true turquoise, and is not, therefore, susceptible of as high a degree of polish. The specific gravity, on the other hand, is greater, ranging from 3 to $3\frac{1}{2}$, so that a piece of bone-turquoise sinks in liquid No. 3 (sp. gr. = 3·0), while mineral turquoise floats. The dull grey colour assumed by bone-turquoise in artificial light also serves to distinguish it from mineral turquoise.

An imitation of bone-turquoise may be produced by allowing calcined ivory to remain for a week immersed in a warm solution of copper sulphate, to which excess of ammonia has been added. After this treatment the ivory acquires the same fine blue colour as naturally occurring bone-turquoise.

LAZULITE.

There is, perhaps, but one mineral which, by any possibility, could be mistaken for turquoise, and which may sometimes be substituted for this stone. The mineral lazulite (not to be confused with lapis-lazuli, which will be considered below) probably never finds application as a gem under this name. It occurs in nature as monoclinic crystals of a sky-blue colour, and also in compact finely granular masses known as blue-spar. In chemical composition it is very similar to turquoise, being a hydrous aluminium phosphate, but containing in addition some magnesium and iron. Its hardness is rather less than that of turquoise, being $5\frac{1}{2}$; the specific gravity, $3\cdot1$, is considerably higher, so that lazulite sinks in liquid No. 3 (sp. gr. $=3\cdot0$). The lustre is of the common vitreous type, showing no inclination to waxiness, so that in this respect also lazulite differs from turquoise. Fine crystals of lazulite are found in a friable sandstone at Graves Mountain, Lincoln County, Georgia, U.S.A.; also on quartz which, in the form of thin veins, penetrates clay-slates at Werfen in Salzburg, where the massive blue-spar occurs. Massive material of a fine deep blue colour is also found in Brazil. Lazulite as a precious stone is met with extremely rarely in the trade.

CALLAINITE.

Callainite, or callais, is a mineral which was used as a precious stone in prehistoric times. It is found exclusively in an ancient Celtic grave at Mané-er-H'rock, near Lockmariaquer, in Brittany, as rounded fragments ranging in size from that of a flax-seed to that of a pigeon's egg. In many respects it resembles turquoise, but differs from this stone in being beautifully translucent. It is almost always green in colour, the shades ranging from apple-green to emerald-green; it is sometimes veined and spotted with white, blue, black, or brown. In chemical composition callainite is very similar to turquoise, being a hydrous phosphate of alumina; the constituents, however, are present in rather different proportions in the two stones. Like turquoise, this mineral is not distinctly crystallised, being an aggregate of microscopically small grains. The hardness ranges from $3\frac{1}{2}$ to 4, and the specific gravity from $2\cdot50$ to $2\cdot52$. Callainite was obviously used by the ancient Celts as an ornamental stone, but where the specimens found in these ancient graves were originally brought from has not yet been discovered. The mineral is probably a variety of variscite, but is more transparent and of a finer colour than typical specimens of this mineral.

OLIVINE.

The olivine group embraces a large number of minerals, of which, however, only the one from which the group takes its name has any application as a gem. Precious olivine is known as *chrysolite* and to French jewellers as *peridot*. The name chrysolite is given to this stone on account of its fine yellowish-green colour, but the term in its original meaning is more correctly applied to stones of a pronounced golden-yellow, such, for example, as yellow topaz, which is referred to by Pliny and other ancient writers under this name. The name olivine is also descriptive of the colour of the stone, which is always a green showing shades of yellow and brown like that of the fruit of the olive-tree. No other colour is ever shown by chrysolite of gem-quality, so that this stone differs from many of those hitherto considered, such as diamond, corundum, topaz, in which the range of colours is very large, and in this respect it is more like turquoise.

The chemical composition of chrysolite, and indeed of all the minerals of the olivine group, is comparatively simple. Common olivine, and the gem-variety chrysolite, is a silicate of magnesium having the formula $2MgO.SiO_2$; a portion of the magnesia is, however, always replaced by a corresponding amount of ferrous oxide. The following is the result of an analysis made by Stromeyer of fine, transparent, yellowish-green chrysolite of gem-quality from the Orient.

	Per cent.
Silica (SiO_2)	39·73
Magnesia (MgO)	50·15
Ferrous oxide (FeO)	9·19

Manganous oxide, nickelous oxide, and alumina were also present in minute amounts, but the presence of these constituents need not be further considered here. The amount of iron present varies to a certain extent, and it is on this variation that the differences between the shade of different specimens depend. The colour of chrysolite, as of green bottle-glass, is due solely to the presence of a small amount of ferrous oxide; when this is present in larger amount the stone is darker in colour, and *vice versâ*. In connection with this subject may be mentioned the fact that a silicate of magnesium known as forsterite, a mineral of the olivine group, contains no iron and is perfectly colourless.

Olivine sometimes occurs as distinct crystals, which belong to the rhombic system. A form not infrequently taken by transparent chrysolite of gem-quality is that shown in Fig. 71. Here the faces of the rhombic prism are inclined to each other at an angle of 130° 3′, the side edges are truncated by a pair of small faces of the brachy-pinacoid, and the front and back edges by a pair of large faces of the macro-pinacoid. The combination of these three sets of faces gives an eight-sided prism flattened in the direction of the large pair of faces of the micro-pinacoid. The faces of the micro-pinacoid and of the prism are striated in the direction of their length, that is to say, parallel to the edges of the prism. Above and below the prism faces are triangular faces of a rhombic octahedron or pyramid, and above and below the pinacoid faces there are rectangular faces of a macro-dome and a brachy-dome, the former being represented in the figure as the larger. Finally, the crystal is bounded above and below by a pair of narrow rectangular faces or basal planes, which truncate the two sets of dome-faces and the pyramid. Other forms are sometimes present, as, for example, in Fig. 11 of Plate XIV., but they are very similar to those just described. Crystals of olivine are found not attached to the walls of drusy cavities but embedded in the mother-rock; they are therefore usually developed on all sides.

Olivine has no very distinct cleavage; the best is in the direction of the large macro-pinacoid, and there is a very poor one parallel to the basal plane. The fracture is always conchoidal. The hardness is slightly less than that of quartz, and is usually given as $H = 6\frac{3}{4}$; olivine is thus scratched by quartz, but easily scratches felspar and still more easily ordinary window-glass. Though the hardness of chrysolite compared with other precious stones is low, yet it is sufficient to admit of the stone receiving a good polish; the process of polishing is, however, not easy. On account of its comparative softness and its liability to become scratched and dull this stone is not very highly esteemed and is worn but rarely, especially as a ring-stone.

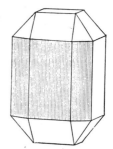

FIG. 71. Crystalline form of olivine (chrysolite).

The specific gravity of pure, transparent olivine ranges from 3·329 to 3·375. The greater the amount of iron present the higher is the specific gravity; hence the darker the colour the heavier the stone. Heavy, dark-coloured olivine, therefore, sinks in pure methylene iodide, but floats in liquid No. 4 (sp. gr. = 3·6). Stones of a light shade of colour and low specific gravity are often of about the same weight, bulk for bulk, as methylene iodide; they will therefore remain suspended at any point in the liquid. A stone having exactly this specific gravity will slowly sink to the bottom when the liquid is warmed, even when the vessel containing it is held in the hand, and will rise to the surface again when the liquid cools. Chrysolite may be readily distinguished from many other green stones by its specific gravity.

A certain amount of olivine is perfectly pure, clear, and transparent, and absolutely free from faults of any kind. Material of this description is termed " noble chrysolite," and this alone is cut for gems. The more abundant and more widely distributed " common olivine " is cloudy and translucent to opaque, and is unsuitable for this purpose. The lustre of olivine is of the ordinary vitreous kind, always, however, inclining to the greasy type; its brilliancy can be increased by polishing, as mentioned above. Being a rhombic mineral, olivine is doubly refracting; the index of refraction is not very high, but the strength of its double refraction is very great, the double refraction of this stone being stronger than that of any other precious stone except zircon. The least index of refraction for yellow light is 1·661 and the greatest 1·697; the difference between these two numbers, 0·036, is a measure of the double refraction; the mean index of refraction is 1·678. The refractive indices for light of other colours have not been determined; they would not vary much, however, from the values given above, since the dispersion is small and no brilliant play of prismatic colours is shown by cut stones.

We have already seen that the shade of colour shown by olivine depends upon the amount of ferrous oxide present. The colour inclines now to yellow, now to brown, and sometimes to green, but there is no marked difference between these shades, and they are never very deep or intense. The usual colouring of chrysolite is shown in Figs. 11 and 12 of Plate XIV., the one representing a crystal and the other a cut stone. Common olivine is not infrequently of a pronounced yellow colour. Specially named colour-varieties of this stone are sometimes, but not universally, recognised. Thus chrysolite proper is pale yellowish-green, peridot is deep olive-green, and olivine yellowish or light olive-green.

The dichroism of olivine is always feeble ; the two images seen in the dichroscope vary in colour between yellowish oil-green and pure grass-green with no appreciable yellow shade.

The other characters of this mineral, not affecting the appearance of the gem, but of use in the recognition of uncut stones, may be mentioned, namely, the fusibility before the blowpipe and the behaviour of the stone towards acids. Only olivine very rich in iron is fusible before the blowpipe ; this particular variety, which is never used as a gem, can be fused, but always with difficulty. All varieties of olivine when reduced to a fine powder are quickly decomposed, especially when warmed, by hydrochloric or by sulphuric acid, with separation of gelatinous silica. This character is utilised, probably unintentionally, in the process of polishing chrysolite, the final polish being given by the use of sulphuric acid instead of water.

The table-stone and the step-cut in their various modifications are the forms usually employed in the cutting of chrysolite ; one such form is shown in Fig. 12 of Plate XIV. Brilliant and rose forms are also sometimes employed. The table facet of table-stones and step-cuts is not infrequently cut with a curved surface, the result being a transition form between a faceted stone and the ordinary curved (cabochon) form which is sometimes used for chrysolite. The colour and lustre of olivine are often improved by the use of a gold foil, or in the case of very pale stones of a green foil.

Olivine is widely distributed throughout the rocks of the earth's crust. It is a constituent of basalt, and occurs most frequently in irregular grains or in large granular aggregates the size of a man's fist or head, or even larger, and consisting of small irregular grains of olivine intermixed with a few fragments of other minerals ; it is only rarely found in sharply defined crystals. Olivine occurs also in other igneous rocks, such as diabases and gabbros ; and rock-masses of large size are to be met with which consist wholly or largely of pure olivine. The mineral again is sometimes found interlaminated in gneiss or crystalline schists. Grains of olivine are sometimes to be found in the weathered débris of such rocks, but the mineral is usually the first to become altered by exposure to weather. Finally, it should be mentioned that olivine is an essential constituent of many meteorites.

The olivine found under the conditions mentioned above is scarcely ever suitable cutting as gems. That which occurs in diabase and gabbro is impure and opaque ; the material found in basalt and similar rocks, as, for example, that from Vesuvius, is frequently pure and transparent, but is almost always in grains of quite small size. The component grains of the larger aggregates also are nearly always of small size ; only rarely, as in the basalt of Mount Kosakow, near Semil on the Iser, in northern Bohemia, are they found of any considerable size. At this locality there sometimes occur transparent pieces the size of a hazel-nut and of a fine green colour from which gems can be cut. The olivine found in meteorites is also sometimes transparent and of a fine colour, but the grains or crystals in which it occurs are always of small size ; in only one or two extra-terrestrial bodies have fragments of transparent olivine been found sufficiently large to yield one-carat stones, and these are in very truth celestial gems.

The source of the chrysolite which is used in the trade for cutting as gems is somewhat obscure. It is probably identical with that of the transparent, finely coloured pebbles not infrequently seen in mineral collections. These pebbles are similar in all respects to cut chrysolites ; the largest are about the size of a walnut and they have obviously been collected in a river sand or gravel, the exact locality of which is, however, unknown.

Both "Pegu" and the "country of the Burmese" are mentioned as localities for chrysolite, but the occurrence of the stone in gem-quality here or in India is by no means well authenticated. The same is true for Ceylon, where chrysoberyl, so often confused with chrysolite, occurs; also for Brazil, the occurrence of chrysolite among the variously coloured stones of Minas Novas having been reported. In this case also it is highly probable that the stone referred to is chrysoberyl, since this stone is usually known to Brazilians as chrysolite.

Chrysolite of gem-quality is said, moreover, to come "from the Orient," "from Natolia" and "from the Levant," finding its way into Western markets by way of Constantinople and Austria. "Egypt" is also mentioned as a locality, especially for the transparent, green crystals, such as are represented in Fig. 11, Plate XIV., and often to be seen in mineral collections. More detailed statements mention Upper Egypt, and a locality east of Esneh between the Nile and the Red Sea, the mother-rock being supposed to be granite or syenite.

None of the occurrences mentioned above are well authenticated, and in the opinion of Mr. G. F. Kunz, the well-known American expert, an opinion based on a large experience of the precious-stone trade, no chrysolite suitable for cutting is at the present time found anywhere in nature. He considers that the material which now comes into the market is derived from old ornaments of various kinds, some dating back a couple of centuries. It is possible that the deposit, from which this old material was obtained, was exhausted or abandoned and that its exact position came to be forgotten. At the same time, however, Kunz records the occurrence of pebbles of chrysolite, suitable for cutting, with garnets in the sands of New Mexico and Arizona. Most of these, however, are small and not of very good colour, so that they are practically useless as gems.

True chrysolite, that is to say, noble olivine, and other precious stones similar in colour, are sometimes liable to be mistaken the one for the other. Thus chrysolite has occasionally been taken for emerald, though the two stones may be easily distinguished by means of the specific gravity, emerald being much lighter than chrysolite, which just sinks in pure methylene iodide, while emerald floats. The supposed emerald which ornaments the shrine of the Three Holy Kings in the cathedral of Cologne is in reality not emerald but chrysolite. The stone with which chrysolite is most frequently confused, however, is chrysoberyl. It has been stated above that this stone is known to the Brazilians as chrysolite; the chrysolite of French jewellers and the "oriental chrysolite" of the trade is also in many cases chrysoberyl. The two can be easily distinguished from the fact that chrysoberyl is both harder and heavier than chrysolite, the former sinking and the latter floating in the heaviest liquid (sp. gr. = 3·6).

Other pale green gems are occasionally referred to by the name chrysolite qualified by some prefix. Thus "Ceylonese chrysolite" is tourmaline of an olive-green colour; "oriental chrysolite" sometimes signifies yellowish-green corundum; the term "Saxon chrysolite" is applied to greenish-yellow topaz from Schneckenstein in Saxony; "false chrysolite" to green bottle-stone or moldavite, which will be considered later on; green specimens of the mineral prehnite are termed "chrysolite from the Cape." In Table 13, in the third part of this book, are given the methods by which these stones may be distinguished.

A yellowish-green glass recently much used for the commoner kinds of ornaments is also sometimes referred to as chrysolite or obsidian. It is very similar in appearance to true chrysolite, but, being singly refracting, is easily distinguished from this in the polariscope.

A good price can be obtained for large, pure chrysolites of a good deep colour, but large stones of average quality are not worth more than from 4s. to 7s. per carat. The mineral was more highly prized formerly than at present; it is now about equal in value to topaz.

CORDIERITE.

Cordierite is also known mineralogically as dichroite and as iolite, while jewellers refer to it as lynx-stone or as lynx-sapphire or water-sapphire (*sapphir d'eau*). The two latter terms are given to this stone on account of its blue colour, and specimens of cordierite have sometimes been mistaken for, or sold as, inferior sapphires. This feature, however, is the only one the two minerals have in common; in all other respects they differ very essentially.

The chemical composition of cordierite is expressed by the formula·

$$H_2O.4(Mg,Fe)O.4Al_2O_3.10SiO_2;$$

it is thus a hydrous silicate of aluminium and magnesium with part of the magnesium replaced by ferrous iron. An analysis of a specimen from the "Orient," probably from Ceylon, gave the following results:

	Per cent.
Silica (SiO_2)	43·6
Alumina (Al_2O_3)	37·6
Ferric oxide (Fe_2O_3)	5·2
Magnesia (MgO)	9·7
Lime (CaO)	3·1
Water (H_2O)	1·0
	100·2

Later investigations have shown that the iron in cordierite is present, not as ferric oxide, as shown in the above analysis, but as ferrous oxide: it is doubtless to this constituent that the colour of the mineral is due.

Well-developed crystals of cordierite are not very commonly met with; the mineral crystallises in the rhombic system, and the crystals, as a rule, have the form of short prisms with basal planes, and with or without small pyramidal faces (Fig. 72). The faces of the crystals are usually rough and the edges somewhat rounded. There is no definite cleavage and the fracture is perfectly conchoidal. The hardness of cordierite is $7\frac{1}{4}$ on Mohs' scale; the mineral is thus slightly harder than quartz. Cordierite is brittle; it fuses before the blowpipe only with difficulty, and is not attacked by acids to any appreciable extent. Its specific gravity is rather variable, probably in correlation with the presence of a varying amount of iron; it ranges from 2·60 to 2·66, but both higher and lower values have been given. As a rule, the specific gravity does not differ widely from that of quartz, being in general a little lower.

FIG. 72. Crystalline form of cordierite.

Only perfectly transparent specimens of cordierite are suitable for use as gems, and these are less common than imperfectly transparent stones. The lustre is vitreous, but on fractured surfaces is inclined to greasy. After polishing, the stone becomes appreciably more lustrous, but is always far inferior to sapphire in this respect. The refraction is low, and the double refraction is feebler than in any other precious stone.

The range of colour shown by cordierite is rather extensive. Colourless, yellow, green, and brown stones are met with, but the most commonly occurring are of a moderately dark blue colour sometimes tinged with violet; only these latter are cut as gems. The most transparent and the most finely coloured stones are cut from pebbles found in Ceylon, the chemical composition of which has been given above. The bulk of the material used for cutting is derived from this source, that from other localities being, as a rule, cloudy and poor in colour. The colour of these pebbles varies between sky-blue and indigo-blue, the paler being sometimes distinguished as water-sapphire and the darker as lynx-sapphire.

The most salient feature of cordierite is its dichroism, that is to say, the difference in colour shown by the same stone when viewed in different directions. The phenomenon is more marked in this than in most other minerals, hence its name of dichroite. The maximum differences in colour are apparent in light which has travelled in directions parallel to the crystallographic axes of the stone, that is to say, in three directions perpendicular to each other, one of these being parallel to the edge of the prism shown in Fig. 72. The light transmitted in one direction is a fine dark blue, in another, perpendicular to this, a pale blue, while that travelling in the third direction is pale yellowish-grey or almost colourless. The light which travels in intermediate directions is intermediate in shade. When cordierite is examined with the dichroscope the images seen have very nearly the colours just mentioned, and this feature is of importance in distinguishing cordierite from other blue stones.

In cutting cordierite the dichroism of the stone must be taken into account. According to the orientation of the cut stone with respect to the crystal, there is produced a darker-coloured lynx-sapphire or a lighter-coloured water-sapphire. The step-cut and the table-cut are the forms most frequently adopted for cordierite; but on account of the depth of colour of this mineral the cut stone must not be too thick. The large front facet or table should be perpendicular to the direction along which light of the darkest blue colour travels, so that the stone will appear of the finest colour possible. As the plane of the table becomes more nearly parallel to this direction, the stone becomes of a more and more dingy pale blue or yellowish-grey colour. Cordierite is also cut *en cabochon*, and when this is the case the same care in the orientation of the cut stone with respect to the crystal is necessary. Cordierites cut *en cabochon* sometimes show a star of opalescent light similar to that exhibited by star-sapphires. The stone may also be cut in such a manner as to exhibit its dichroism to the fullest possible extent. This object is attained by cutting a cube, the faces of which are perpendicular to the three axes of the crystal. The cube mounted by one corner on a pivot, so as to show the three differently coloured faces, forms an interesting and remarkable object.

Cordierite is readily distinguished from sapphire, for the differences between the two stones are many and well marked. The dichroism of sapphire is much less pronounced than that of cordierite, while the hardness and specific gravity are much greater. Thus while sapphire sinks in the four heavy liquids, cordierite, as a rule, floats in all, though it may, in some cases, sink in liquid No. 1. The same features distinguish it from other blue stones, such as blue diamond, blue tourmaline, and kyanite, to be considered later, all of which are appreciably denser.

The occurrence of cordierite in nature is confined almost exclusively to granite and gneiss; it is found in some volcanic rocks, but only in small amount. Crystals regularly developed on all sides, but too dark in colour for gems, occur embedded in granite at

Bodenmais in Bavaria. Irregular masses of material, which, in part, is of a fine blue colour and is sometimes transparent, occur in gneiss at Arendal, Kragerö, Tvedestrand, and other places in Norway, at Orijärfvi, near Åbo, in Finland, and elsewhere. Fine stones are found in granite veins in gneiss at Haddam in Connecticut, U.S.A. The pebbles found in Ceylon are sometimes as large as a nut; they occur with other precious stones in the gem-gravels of the island. Cordierite is also said to occur, together with blue and white topaz, in the district of Minas Novas in Brazil.

IDOCRASE.

Because of its occurrence on Mount Vesuvius idocrase is frequently referred to as vesuvian or vesuvianite. It occurs at this locality in remarkably fine transparent brown crystals, which are sometimes cut at Naples as gems, and, on this account, are known in the trade as "Vesuvian gems." The use of this stone as a gem is not extensive, and is mainly confined to Italy. Crystals of gem-quality and of a green colour are found also in the Ala valley in the Piedmontese Alps; a small number find their way into the gem markets through the neighbouring town of Turin. Idocrase from other sources is scarcely ever cut as a gem, so that it may be regarded as an Italian precious stone.

Chemically, idocrase is a calcium-aluminium silicate containing small amounts of water, iron oxides, and other constituents. The chemical composition was formerly considered to be the same as that of calcium-aluminium garnet; this, however, has been shown to be incorrect, and the composition is now expressed by the complex formula $2H_2O.12CaO.3(Al,Fe)_2O_3.10SiO_2$. Analyses of crystals from the two Italian localities mentioned above have given the following results:

	Brown, Vesuvius.	Green, Ala.
Silica (SiO_2)	36·98	37·36
Titanium oxide (TiO_2)	—	0·18
Alumina (Al_2O_3)	16·70	16·30
Ferric oxide (Fe_2O_3)	2·99	4·02
Ferrous oxide (FeO)	2·01	0·39
Manganous oxide (MnO)	0·57	—
Lime (CaO)	35·67	36·65
Magnesia (MgO)	2·62	3·02
Potash (K_2O)	0·08	—
Soda (Na_2O)	0·43	trace
Water (H_2O)	1·32	2·89
Fluorine (F)	1·08	—
	100·45	100·81

Idocrase crystallises in the tetragonal system; well-developed crystals are of frequent occurrence. They occur usually attached to the walls of cavities and crevices in rocks, and form beautiful druses. The forms taken by two crystals of idocrase are represented in Figs. 73a and b; the former represents a crystal from the Ala valley, and the latter one from Vesuvius.

The crystals in almost all cases take the form of prisms of greater or less length, with four, eight, or more prism-faces, which are distinctly striated parallel to the edges of the prism. The prism-faces are sometimes very numerous, and when this is the case the faces are narrow and the crystal almost cylindrical. The basal planes perpendicular to the prism-faces are usually moderately large ; between the basal plane and the prism-faces there are faces of a square pyramid (Fig. 73a), or of a square pyramid in combination with an eight-sided pyramid (Fig. 73b). These faces are usually very small in size, but sometimes extremely numerous ; indeed, crystals of idocrase have been met with which are richer in faces than crystals of any other mineral.

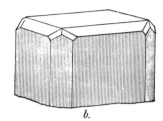

FIG. 73.   Crystalline forms of idocrase.

Idocrase shows only a suggestion of cleavage ; the fracture is imperfectly conchoidal to uneven. The mineral is brittle and the hardness ($H = 6\frac{1}{2}$) is rather less than that of quartz. It can be fused before the blowpipe with moderate ease, and, after being fused, is decomposed by acids ; before fusion it is unattacked by acids. The specific gravity varies between 3·3 and 3·5 according to the chemical composition. The brown crystals are rather heavier than the green ; thus the specific gravity of brown crystals from Vesuvius has been determined to be 3·45, and that of green crystals from the Ala valley to vary between 3·39 and 3·43. The mineral, therefore, sinks in pure methylene iodide, but floats in the heaviest liquid (sp. gr. = 3·6).

In the matter of transparency different specimens of idocrase may differ widely. The majority of crystals are only translucent to semi-transparent, the free end of an attached crystal being frequently more transparent than the other. Only transparent or very translucent crystals are cut as gems : by polishing they acquire a very good lustre, which is vitreous in character, though on fractured surfaces it inclines to be greasy. The refraction is moderately strong, but the double refraction is feeble. The mineral presents a great range of colour, this being due to the iron and manganese which enter into its composition. Yellow, blue, and red, as well as almost colourless crystals, are met with ; but the colours most commonly seen are various shades of brown and green, and it is crystals of these shades which are used almost exclusively for cutting as gems. The dichroism of idocrase is moderately strong ; in the case of green idocrase from the Ala valley the two images seen in the dichroscope have the maximum colour difference when one is pure green and the other yellowish-green.

Idocrase occurs at numerous localities as a contact-mineral embedded in limestone, also in crystalline schists, gneiss, and serpentine. These modes of occurrence are well illustrated at the two localities in Italy already mentioned. The occurrence of the mineral under other conditions is rare, and for the present purpose need not be considered.

The green idocrase of the Ala valley is found on the Testa Ciarva, a bare, precipitous rock on the Mussa-Alp, in a band of serpentine more than a metre in thickness : the crystals are here associated with chlorite, and are attached to pale-green massive idocrase. It is at this same place that hessonite, the yellowish-brown variety of garnet, occurs ; the two minerals are not, however, found side by side. Fig. 1 of Plate XV. represents a specimen from this locality, having one large and several small crystals attached to the matrix. Fig. 2 of the same plate shows a stone cut from one of these crystals, the colour of which is a fine grass-green tinged with yellow. This has, therefore, a certain similarity in appearance to chrysolite, and is even sometimes known by this name. The yellowish tinge of the latter stone is, however, more pronounced, and its dichroism is scarcely comparable with that of idocrase. There is also a certain similarity between idocrase and other green stones, such as diopside, epidote, demantoid, &c.: the methods by which these may be distinguished are given in the third part of this book (Tables 13 and 14).

The idocrase of Vesuvius is found, together with other beautifully crystallised minerals, in the limestone blocks ejected from the old crater of Vesuvius, now represented by Monte Somma. The crystals are attached to the walls of cavities in this metamorphosed limestone, and range in colour from darkest brown to honey-yellow. A cut stone of brown idocrase from Vesuvius is represented in Plate XV., Fig. 3. Some of the pale brown stones found here are much admired; they are not unlike hyacinth (zircon) in colour, and, indeed, are sometimes mistaken for that stone. There is no difficulty, however, in distinguishing between the two minerals, owing to the density of zircon being so much greater than that of idocrase. The methods by which idocrase may be distinguished from other brown stones, such as smoky-quartz, brown tourmaline, axinite, &c., are given later (Tables 9 and 11).

The mineral known as xanthite and found at Amity, in Orange County, New York, is nothing more than dark yellowish-brown idocrase; it is sometimes cut as a gem, but is worn only in the United States.

For both green and brown idocrase the step-cut or the table-cut is employed; other forms are scarcely ever adopted. In correlation with the limited demand for idocrase as a gem, we find that both for brown and for green stones quite low prices are asked.

AXINITE.

In just a few cases transparent crystals of axinite are cut as gems, usually *en cabochon*; but, as a general rule, crystals of this mineral are only translucent, and therefore unsuitable

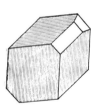

for this purpose. Axinite has a considerable range of colour; it may be of a warm clove-brown, sometimes with a noticeable tinge of violet, or, on the other hand, of less pleasing colours containing a large proportion of grey. The dichroism is moderately strong; the images seen in the dichroscope vary in colour between violet-blue, cinnamon-brown, and olive-green. This feature distinguishes axinite from smoky-quartz, the commonest of brown gems, the dichroism of which is very slight; also from brown tourmaline, which, though strongly dichroic, shows different colours in the dichroscope.

Fig. 74. Crystalline form of axinite.

Chemically, axinite is a silicate of aluminium and calcium, with water and boric acid, and with small quantities of iron and manganese, to the presence of which the colour of the mineral is due. Its composition is represented by the formula:

$$H_2O.6CaO.B_2O_3.2Al_2O_3.8SiO_2.$$

Axinite occurs not infrequently in fine crystals, but most usually in compact masses not suitable for cutting. The crystals belong to the triclinic system, and a frequently occurring form with striated faces is represented in Fig. 74. The crystals are peculiar in that the faces intersect in very acute angles; owing to this they often take an axe-like form, hence the name of the mineral. There is no distinct cleavage. The mineral is brittle. The hardness ($H = 6\frac{1}{2} - 7$) is approximately that of quartz, and the specific gravity varies between 3·29 and 3·30. The lustre on natural crystal-faces is vitreous and frequently very brilliant, and is still further increased by polishing.

Axinite is found attached to the walls of cavities in ancient silicate rocks of various kinds. The best crystals known occur in the gneiss of Le Bourg d'Oisans in Dauphiné (Department Isère). The mineral is found at other places in the Western Alps, less frequently in the eastern (Tyrolese) Alps, at Botallack in Cornwall, and at other localities. The crystals are nearly always small in size, and have very little thickness, so that cut stones have only an insignificant appearance and a correspondingly low value.

KYANITE.

Kyanite, as its name implies, is usually of a blue colour, but may be white, pale yellow, grey, or black. Crystals of a deep cornflower-blue are rare, the commonest are a pale sky-blue. When sufficiently transparent, which is not often the case, this mineral forms very pretty gems.

Kyanite is comparable to a certain extent with sapphire. It has, indeed, been occasionally mistaken and sold for this stone; and the name sapparé, by which it is known to jewellers, recalls the same stone. This latter name arose out of an error made by the Geneva mineralogist, Saussure, junior, who read the label attached to a supposed specimen of sapphire as sapparé; the mistake has long been recognised, but the name remains, having become firmly established, especially among French jewellers.

Kyanite, like topaz, is a silicate of aluminium, but its composition differs from that of topaz in the absence of fluorine. Its composition is represented by the formula $Al_2O_3.SiO_2$; a small part of the alumina is replaced by ferric oxide, and it is probably to this constituent that the colour of the mineral is due. An analysis of fine blue kyanite from St. Gotthard gave:

	Per cent.
Silica (SiO_2)	36·67
Alumina (Al_2O_3)	63·11
Ferric oxide (F_2O_3)	1·19
	100·97

The mineral frequently occurs in definite crystals, which belong to the triclinic system; the form most commonly met with is represented in Fig. 75. The crystals are flat, elongated prisms, usually with a flattened six-sided cross-section, and not infrequently they are slightly bent. They occur usually embedded in gneiss, crystalline schists, and other similar rocks. There is a very perfect cleavage parallel to the broad face, which in the figure is turned towards the front, and there is another less distinct cleavage parallel to one of the two narrower prism-faces next to the broad face. These two narrower prism-faces are striated vertically, that is to say, parallel to the edges, while the broad cleavage-face is striated horizontally. Terminal faces are usually absent, and when present are irregularly developed. At each end of the prism there is usually a plane face oblique to the length of the prism, along which the crystal has broken (Fig. 75); this plane of perfect parting (not true cleavage) gives rise to numerous fine horizontal cracks, which can be seen on the faces of the prism, especially on the large broad face, and are represented in the figure.   Kyanite occurs in lamellar cleavage masses of considerable size, more frequently than in definite crystals. These masses are sometimes of a fine blue colour; they show the perfect cleavage surfaces, and are found in the same rocks as the well-developed crystals.

Kyanite is neither very hard nor very brittle.   A curious feature of this mineral is the fact that its hardness is not the same on all faces of the same crystal, nor is it the same in different directions on the same face.   Thus in certain directions it is easily scratched by

FIG. 75. Crystalline form of kyanite.

felspar, while in others it is scarcely scratched by quartz; the hardness, therefore, varies between 5 and 7.   In no other mineral has there been observed such a marked discrepancy between the hardness of different faces of the same crystal.   In consequence of the comparative softness of kyanite in certain directions, special care should be taken in the wearing of cut stones.

The specific gravity varies between 3·56 and 3·60, the latter value being that of dark blue specimens of kyanite, which alone are used as gems.   The density of the mineral does not thus differ very much from that of the heaviest liquid (sp. gr. = 3·6).   Kyanite is infusible before the blowpipe, and is unattacked by acids.

As a general rule kyanite can only be described as being very translucent; perfectly transparent stones are not at all common; and those which combine transparency with a fine dark-blue colour are still more uncommon. In cutting, portions which are pale coloured or not perfectly transparent are removed as completely as possible, and only material of a fine colour is utilised.

The dichroism of the mineral is distinctly observable, but not strong; it is best shown by stones of a dark colour.   The images seen in the dichroscope vary in colour between pale and dark blue.   The refraction of kyanite is considerable.   The lustre of the crystal-faces is of the vitreous type, while that of the cleavage faces is pearly.   The natural crystal-faces are not specially brilliant, but their lustre is increased to a certain extent by polishing.

Both the table-stone and the step-cut are employed for kyanite; but it is cut perhaps most frequently *en cabochon*, when its fine blue colour is almost comparable to that of the sapphire.   The two stones may be easily distinguished, however, for sapphire is both harder, heavier, and more lustrous than is kyanite.   Moreover, on most cut kyanites there are to be seen fine, close-set lines, corresponding to the cracks mentioned above, running parallel to each other across the surface.   These lines, especially in stones cut *en cabochon*, sometimes give rise to a band of feebly reflected light, similar to the appearance shown by cymophane. Small cleavage cracks in the direction of the perfect cleavage are also not infrequently observed.   The most valuable stones are those which are pure and transparent and of a deep colour, but they are never worth very much, and their use, at any rate in Europe, is very limited.

Kyanite is moderately abundant and is distributed somewhat widely, but material of gem-quality is found at only a few localities, and then in small amount.   Among others may be mentioned Monte Campione, near Faido, on the southern slopes of St. Gotthard, in Canton Tessin.   Definite crystals, though only pale blue in colour, are found here in abundance; they have the chemical composition quoted above.   Associated with them is reddish-brown staurolite, to be considered presently; both are found in a matrix of white, finely scaled mica-schist.

Massive kyanite, sometimes containing portions of gem-quality, occurs also in mica-schist in the Zillerthal and the Pfitschthal in the Tyrol.   At the summit of Yellow Mountain, near Bakersville, in North Carolina, U.S.A., fine dark blue crystals occur in a white quartz-

vein in granite ; a few of these are of gem-quality. Stones suitable for cutting are sometimes to be found also in the river sands of Brazil ; and the mineral is found in association
with the diamond and with other minerals at Diamantina. The best crystals are said,
however, to come from some unknown localities in India, a country in which kyanite is
more extensively used than in Europe. There is no doubt but that kyanite occurs at many
places in India, but it has been suggested that the stones worn in that country have all
come from Europe.

STAUROLITE.

Staurolite consists essentially of silicate of magnesium and aluminium with a small
amount of iron ; it occurs always in well-developed crystals belonging to the rhombic system.
These are elongated prisms usually with six sides ; frequently two crystals are twinned
together, the angle between the prism-edges being approximately 60° or 90°. Staurolite is
usually of a dark reddish-brown colour very similar to that of some garnets ; some specimens,
however, are more like dark yellowish-brown topaz. It is usually cut in the same form as
is garnet, but may be distinguished from this stone by the fact that it is doubly refracting.
It is rarely transparent enough for cutting as a gem. Its hardness is $7\frac{1}{2}$ and the specific
gravity 3·7 to 3·8. The crystals usually occur embedded in mica-schist, argillaceous schist,
or other similar rocks. They are found in large numbers together with kyanite in the
white mica-schist of Monte Campione, near Faido, in Canton Tessin, Switzerland ; a few are
sufficiently pure and transparent for cutting as gems. The mineral occurs also with
euclase and other precious stones in the gold-washings on the Sanarka river in the district
of the Orenburg Cossacks ; and a few grains of it are met with among the diamond-bearing
sands of Salobro in Brazil. Staurolite of a rich garnet-red colour, perfectly transparent and
fit for cutting as gems, has been found recently (1898) with ruby and rhodolite in Mason's
Branch, Macon County, North Carolina, U.S.A. The stone is used to a very limited extent
and is worth very little.

ANDALUSITE.

Andalusite is identical in chemical composition with kyanite, having the formula
$Al_2O_3.SiO_2$. It differs, however, in crystalline form, the crystals belonging, not to the triclinic but to the rhombic system. They take
the form of elongated, almost rectangular columns, which are usually
terminated by basal planes perpendicular to the prism-edges. They are
rarely modified by other faces, and are therefore very simple in form
(Fig. 76). There is a distinct cleavage parallel to the faces of the prism.

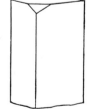

FIG. 76. Crystal-
line form of anda-
lusite.

Such crystals are found in large numbers at many localities, especially
in gneiss and other crystalline schistose rocks. Though often of considerable
size they are useless as gems, for they are nearly always opaque and of a
dingy grey, green, or red colour. For cutting as gem-stones the transparent
pebbles found with white and blue topaz in the gem-gravels of the Minas
Novas district in Brazil are exclusively used. These are usually green, but specimens of a

yellowish-brown colour are sometimes met with. In reflected light the green pebbles usually appear of a dark shade of colour, but some are pale grass-green tinged with yellow. They are strongly dichroic, and this feature is distinctly observable even with the naked eye. When viewed in the direction of the two horizontal axes, indicated in the pebbles by the cleavage cracks, two shades of green are seen, one being rather more inclined to yellow than the other; when, on the other hand, the pebble is viewed through in a direction parallel to the prism-edge it appears of a pretty brownish-red colour. The pairs of images seen in the

dichroscope vary in colour between these principal shades. The two colours characteristic of andalusite are therefore the same as those shown by another dichroic precious stone, namely, alexandrite. Although the green of the alexandrite is more of an emerald-green and the brownish-red is deeper and more intense, yet the similarity between the two stones is close enough to admit of andalusite being passed off as the more costly alexandrite. The latter may readily be distinguished from andalusite by its greater hardness and higher specific gravity, the density of alexandrite being 3·64 while that of andalusite varies between 3·17 and 3·19.

In cutting andalusite, as in the case of other dichroic precious stones, the orientation of the cut stone relative to the crystal must be considered. It may be cut in such a way as to show one of the principal colours, or, on the other hand, so that both colours may be displayed. Cut stones are but little used and their price is low. The lustre of the mineral is of the vitreous type, and is but little increased by polishing. The hardness, $H = 7\frac{1}{4}$, is slightly greater than that of quartz. Like kyanite, andalusite is infusible before the blowpipe, and is unattacked by acids.

The peculiar variety of andalusite distinguished as **chiastolite** (cross-stone) should not be forgotten. It has all the essential characters of andalusite, but occurs in elongated, irregular prisms up to an inch in thickness, which are always embedded in dark clay-slates. The peculiarity of the stone depends on the fact that the prisms are not only surrounded but also penetrated to a greater or lesser depth by the clay-slate. Thus, a rod of the clay-slate varying in thickness in different parts runs centrally throughout the whole length of the crystal. This is connected with the four portions which penetrate the crystal at its corners, so that a cross-section of the prism shows a dark cross on a white background (Fig. 77). The figure shows a number of cross-sections of a single prism arranged serially. From these it is apparent that the enclosed clay-slate increases in amount from below upwards,

FIG. 77.
Chiastolite

the white andalusite substance predominating in the lower, and the dark clay-slate in the upper portion of the prism.

It is on the appearance presented by cross-sections of the prism that the value, such as it is, of chiastolite is due, for, in certain places, especially in the Pyrenees, such sections are worn as amulets and charms. Suitable crystals of sufficient size are to be met with at several localities in this neighbourhood; also at Salles de Rohan, near Brieux, in Brittany, and at many other places. Recently considerable numbers of fine, large crystals of chiastolite have been found in clay-slate at Mount Howden, ten miles north of Bimbowrie, in South Australia; these are of large size, reaching a length of 6 inches and a diameter of 2 inches; the cross-sections take a good polish and show cross-figures of various forms.

Chiastolite is a contact-mineral which occurs in abundance in clay-slates near their contact with granite. It is found, for example, at Hof, in the Fichtelgebirge, and in the slates round the Skiddaw granite in Cumberland, but it usually takes the form of thin needle-like prisms, which are not thick enough for the purpose mentioned above. Crystals as large as those found in the Pyrenees are rare.

EPIDOTE.

Epidote is another mineral which is used as a gem only occasionally when of specially fine quality. Almost the only locality at which transparent, finely-coloured crystals of gem-quality are to be found is the Knappenwand in the uppermost part of the Untersulzbachthal, in Pinzgau, Salzburg. There are many other localities, but they seldom yield stones which are sufficiently transparent and finely coloured for use as gems.

The chemical composition of epidote is expressed by the formula:

$$H_2O.4CaO.3(Al,Fe)_2O_3.6SiO_2.$$

The mineral is thus a hydrous silicate of calcium and aluminium, in which a variable proportion of the aluminium is replaced by ferric iron. An analysis of epidote from the Knappenwand is given below:

	Per cent.
Silica (SiO_2)	37·83
Alumina (Al_2O_3)	22·63
Ferric oxide (Fe_2O_3)	14·02
Ferrous oxide (FeO)	0·93
Lime (CaO)	23·27
Water	2·05
	100·73

Crystals of epidote are of very frequent occurrence. They belong to the monoclinic system and are usually prismatic in habit, the direction of elongation being parallel to the

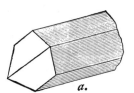 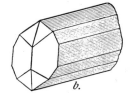 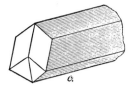

FIG. 78.   Crystalline form of epidote.

axis of symmetry, that is to say, perpendicular to the single plane of symmetry. Owing to the predominance of one pair of parallel faces of the prism the crystals usually present a flattened appearance. The elongated prism-faces are very often distinctly striated parallel to their length, that is to say, parallel to their mutual intersections, while the small terminal faces of the crystals are usually smooth. It frequently happens that two such prismatic crystals grow together in twin position, and when this is the case some of the terminal faces then form re-entrant angles with each other. As a rule, terminal faces are developed at only one end of the crystal, the other being attached to the matrix. A few of the forms most commonly taken by epidote are represented in Figs. 78a to c; the first two of these, a and b, are simple crystals, the third, c, is a twin-crystal.

There is a definite cleavage parallel to one of the prism-faces, and one, rather less definite, parallel to another prism-face. The hardness is $6\frac{1}{2}$, being thus rather less than that of quartz. The specific gravity ranges from 3·25 to 3·5 according to the amount of iron present. The specific gravity of crystals from the Knappenwand, which are comparatively rich in iron, ranges from 3·47 to 3·5 ; these therefore sink in pure methylene iodide, but float in the heaviest liquid (sp. gr. = 3·6). Epidote is fusible before the blowpipe, and the fused mass is decomposed by acids ; fresh, unfused material, however, is not attacked by acids.

Epidote of almost all degrees of transparency is to be met with, but perfectly transparent crystals of a dark colour are rare, except at the Knappenwand. Both the refraction and the double refraction are strong. The range of colour is somewhat extensive ; it depends upon the presence of iron, and the larger the amount of iron present the deeper the colour of the stone. Almost colourless crystals are rarely met with, pale yellow and red stones are more frequent, but the colours most commonly seen are more or less dark shades of pistachio-green. This colour, which may be described as a dark green with tones of yellow and brown, is so characteristic of epidote that this mineral is sometimes referred to as pistacite. This dark pistachio-green colour may be seen in Fig. 1 of Plate XIV., which represents a druse of crystals from the Knappenwand, while Fig. 2 of the same plate represents a cut stone. In reflected light the Knappenwand epidote appears dark green or, in thick crystals, almost black in colour. The light which is transmitted through the prism in a certain direction is, however, of a bright green colour, while that which travels in a direction perpendicular to this is yellowish-brown, sometimes tinged with red. Epidote is one of the most prominently dichroic of minerals ; the images seen in the dichroscope vary between green, yellow, and very dark brown.

The stone is cut in the forms usually employed for other darkly coloured stones, namely, in low step-cuts and table-cuts (Plate XIV., Fig. 2). Cut stones must not be too thick, otherwise the colour will be dark and unpleasing ; it is sometimes improved, however, by placing a burnished foil beneath the stone. According to the orientation of the large front facet or table with respect to the crystal the stone will appear more green or more brown in colour. The lustre of cut stones is vitreous in character and very brilliant.

Epidote is easily distinguished from other green and brown stones by its strong dichroism and high specific gravity. Green and brown tourmaline, which is also strongly dichroic, is much less dense (sp. gr. = 3·0 − 3·1) ; it therefore floats in pure methylene iodide. Diopside, chrysolite, and other green stones which might possibly be confused with epidote are all much more feebly dichroic, and the same is true of smoky-quartz. The confusion of epidote with brown stones, however, is not very likely to occur, since the former is usually cut in such a manner as to display its green and not its brown colour.

This mineral is generally found in ancient silicate-rocks ; the crystals occur either completely embedded or attached to the walls of cavities. At the Knappenwand, in the Untersulzbachthal, Salzburg, crystals occur attached to the walls of crevices in massive epidote, the so-called epidote-schist ; the exact spot is below the Poberg ridge, and was discovered in 1866. Here are found by far the most magnificent crystals of epidote known, and the locality affords one of the most beautiful examples of the occurrence of minerals. Thousands of crystals have been found there, many of which are distributed throughout the mineral collections of the world, while others have been cut as gems. Some are of considerable size, as much as 45 centimetres in length and 3 to 4 centimetres in thickness, but most are much smaller. In association with the epidote are to be found crystals of calcite, apatite, felspar, and certain rare minerals ; also fibres of asbestos, which sometimes form a thick felted mass round the point of attachment of the epidote prisms, as may be distinctly seen in Plate XIV., Fig. 1.

Epidote is found at many other places in Europe, but nowhere in crystals of such size and beauty as at the locality just mentioned. In America stones similar to those from the Knappenwand have been found at Rabun Gap, in Rabun County, Georgia; and fine dark green crystals have come from Roseville, in Sussex County, New Jersey, and from Haddam, in Connecticut; they are only occasionally, however, cut as gems. Again, a few crystals of green epidote are found with green tourmaline in Brazil. There must be many stones suitable for cutting to be found at the numerous localities for epidote, but since the use of this mineral as a gem is so limited and its value is so small, search for them is scarcely likely to be made.

PIEDMONTITE.

Piedmontite is a variety of epidote, in the composition of which alumina is replaced by manganese sesquioxide. This manganese-epidote is found principally in the manganese mines of San Marcello in the Piedmontese Alps, from whence the name piedmontite is derived. It sometimes occurs in magnificent cherry-red crystals, which, when they are of sufficient transparency, are cut as gems.

DIOPTASE.

Dioptase is a mineral of a deep green colour approaching, but always darker than, that of emerald. The two stones differ widely in chemical composition, however, for dioptase is a hydrous silicate of copper with the formula $H_2O.CuO.SiO_2$. The results of an analysis of a crystal from the best and longest known locality, namely, that in Siberia, are given below:

	Per cent.
Silica (SiO_2)	36·60
Cupric oxide (CuO)	48·89
Ferrous oxide (FeO)	2·00
Water (H_2O)	12·29
	99·78

The green colour of dioptase is due to the large amount of copper which is present, and for the same reason the mineral is sometimes referred to as emerald-copper.

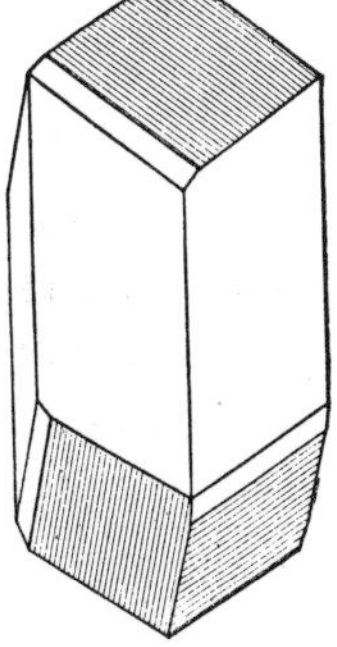

Dioptase occurs usually in well-developed but small crystals. These are rarely larger than a pea, and belong, like crystals of emerald, to the hexagonal system. The six-sided prisms of dioptase, however, are terminated by the faces of a rhombohedron, and in rare cases the alternate edges between the striated rhombohedron-faces and the smooth prism-faces are replaced by narrow faces indicating a tetratohedral development of the crystal. This is shown in Fig. 79, which represents a Siberian crystal. There is a distinct cleavage parallel to the faces of a rhombohedron which truncate the polar edges of the primitive rhombohedron represented in the figure. On these edges there is therefore sometimes to be seen a pearly lustre, but otherwise the lustre of the crystals is of the common vitreous type. Dioptase is not very hard; it is scratched even by felspar and is itself scarcely capable of scratching glass, so that its hardness is approximately

FIG. 79. Crystalline form of dioptase.

represented on the scale by 5.   While the hardness of dioptase is much less than that of emerald, the specific gravity is higher, being 3·28.   The two minerals are therefore readily distinguished by means of these characters, but usually dioptase can be recognised at a glance on account of its dark colour, imperfect transparency, and the presence of numerous small cracks.

The principal locality for dioptase is the hill of Altyn-Tübe on the western slopes of the Altai Mountains in the Kirghiz Steppes in Siberia.   This is a limestone hill, and is traversed by numerous crevices which are filled up for the most part by calcite; it is on this calcite that the dioptase in sparing amount is found: the mode of occurrence is illustrated in Plate XV., Fig. 4.   A few comparatively large crystals of dioptase have also been found in some of the gold-washings in the Yeniseisk Government, where they occurred loose and in a more or less rounded condition.   For a long time the occurrence of large crystals of dioptase was thought to be confined exclusively to Siberia, and the use of this mineral as a gem was limited to Russia, Persia, and countries in the near neighbourhood. This is still the case at the present day, although latterly fine crystals have been found in other parts of the world, especially in the French Congo.

In spite of the fine colour of dioptase, its deficient hardness and transparency prevent its extensive use as a gem ; for the same reasons the price of the stone is always low.

CHRYSOCOLLA.

The amorphous mineral chrysocolla is closely allied to dioptase in chemical composition, being a hydrous silicate of copper, but containing more water than dioptase.   Its hardness, $H = 2 - 4$, is low, sometimes less even than that of calcite; the mineral is lacking also in transparency, but in spite of these drawbacks it is sometimes cut as an ornamental stone on account of its fine green or blue colour.   This is especially the case with stones from the copper mines of Nizhni-Tagilsk in the Urals.   In the Allouez mine, near Houghton, in the copper region of Lake Superior, North America, the mineral occurs mixed with quartz ; this affords a much harder material more suitable for cutting, and from it are obtained magnificent bluish-green stones half a square inch in area.

GARNIERITE.

Garnierite or noumeaite has certain characters in common with chrysocolla, and may therefore be mentioned here.   Like chrysocolla it is opaque, amorphous, of a fine green colour, and softer than calcite.   Chemically it is a hydrous silicate of nickel.   It occurs as large masses in the island of New Caledonia, Australasia, where it is extensively worked as an ore of nickel, and where some few stones are cut for ornamental purposes.

SPHENE.

Sphene or titanite is a combined silicate and titanate of calcium having the formula $CaO.SiO_2.TiO_2$. The crystals belong to the monoclinic system, and are frequently finely developed. Sphene of a brown or yellow colour, opaque and unsuitable for cutting as a gem, occurs embedded in many silicate-rocks; while attached to the walls of crevices in the same rocks are found crystals of the same mineral, which are frequently very clear and transparent. These two varieties are sometimes respectively distinguished as titanite and as sphene: the latter alone is cut as a gem, and that only when perfectly transparent and of fine colour. Sphene is usually green, but may be yellow, brown, or even red: it is always distinctly dichroic. There are many stones which sphene of a green colour may resemble in appearance, such, for example, as chrysolite, idocrase, demantoid, and chrysoberyl. It never resembles emerald, however, since the colour has always a tinge of yellow and is never very deep and intense. Yellow sphene often resembles light yellow topaz in colour. The hardness of the mineral is low: $H = 5\frac{1}{2}$. Its specific gravity is somewhat high, ranging from 3·35 to 3·45; in pure methylene iodide, therefore, the mineral sinks.

Fine crystals, suitable for cutting, are found in crevices in gneisses and schists at various places in the Alps, especially in the Pfitschthal and the Zillerthal in the Tyrol, and also in the Swiss Alps. In America specially large and fine crystals occur at Bridgewater in Bucks County, Pennsylvania; these are often over an inch in length, and from those which are perfectly transparent fine stones, varying from 10 to 20 carats in weight, can be cut. Sphene is used as a gem to only a limited extent, and the price is always low.

PREHNITE.

This mineral has a fine green colour similar to that of chrysolite, and is therefore sometimes cut as a gem; but it is used for this purpose only to a very limited extent. Prehnite is a silicate of calcium and aluminium containing a small amount of water. It sometimes crystallises in tabular forms belonging to the rhombic system, but occurs most frequently as crystal aggregates which take the form of nodular, botryoidal masses with a radially fibrous structure. The mineral occurs, sometimes in masses of considerable size, in the amygdaloidal cavities of older volcanic rocks, such as basalt. It is met with at several places in the Alps, for example, at the Seisser-Alp in the Fassathal, Tyrol, at St. Gotthard, and elsewhere. Prehnite was first discovered at the Cape of Good Hope by Colonel Prehn, the Governor of the Colony, in the latter part of the eighteenth century; hence the names prehnite and "Cape chrysolite." The mineral is also found in the Lake Superior copper region and at many other places in North America, specially fine specimens being met with at Bergen Hill and Paterson in New Jersey.

The hardness of prehnite is rather over 6; the specific gravity ranges from 2·8 to 3·0. The mineral is usually translucent, rarely transparent; it has a vitreous lustre, and may be colourless, yellow, or green. The green variety is the only one suitable for use as a gem;

this is of a rich oil-green shade, and, when cut, may closely resemble chrysoprase in colour and lustre. The two stones may be distinguished, however, by the fact that chrysoprase is harder and much less dense than prehnite.

Chlorastrolite is a mineral which is sometimes referred to the species prehnite. It occurs as small rounded masses with a finely radiate or stellate internal structure, and of a bluish-green colour in the amygdaloidal trap rocks of the Isle Royale, Lake Superior, in the State of Michigan. These rounded masses, in many cases, have been weathered from the rock and are now collected as water-worn pebbles on the shores of the island. Owing to their fibrous structure they exhibit a chatoyant appearance similar to, but less perfect than, that of cat's-eye. When suitably cut they give gems of considerable beauty, which, however, are worn solely in North America. The largest nodule hitherto found has a diameter of $1\frac{1}{2}$ inches, but the majority of specimens are much smaller.

Zonochlorite is a mineral of very similar character; it occurs in the amygdaloidal volcanic rocks of Neepigon Bay on Lake Superior in Canada. The rounded masses, which fill the amygdaloidal cavities, attain a diameter of 2 inches; they are built up of alternate layers of light green and of dark green material, and form rather pretty cut stones. The mineral, however, is rarely cut except in America, and even there is but little used.

THOMSONITE.

The essential characters of a precious stone are not, as a rule, present in thomsonite, but there is one variety of the mineral which is sometimes used for this purpose. This occurs filling amygdaloidal cavities in volcanic rocks at Good Harbour Bay on Lake Superior; these rounded masses are sometimes weathered out of the rock and found lying loose on the shore. Their internal structure shows a central mass of radially arranged fibres enclosed by a few concentric bands which follow the outer boundaries of the mass. In these concentric bands delicate shades of milk-white, yellow, and green alternate with each other, so that a section of the mass has an appearance which resembles that of agate. These water-worn pebbles, the largest of which are an inch in diameter, are collected on the shore and polished; no attempt is made to reach those still enclosed in the solid rock, and stones which are worked are only worn in the place of their origin.

Lintonite is a variety of thomsonite with alternate bands of green and of flesh-red; it is found in the above-mentioned locality.

NATROLITE.

Natrolite is another mineral belonging to the zeolite group; like thomsonite, it is a hydrated silicate of sodium and aluminium. It occurs sometimes as beautiful water-clear crystals of elongated, prismatic habit; these, however, have never been cut as gems. The mineral is also found in masses built up of radially arranged fibres marked by concentric bands of varied colours. Fine specimens of this variety of natrolite occur at Hohentwiel in Würtemberg; in these the concentric bands are coloured alternately isabel-yellow and pale yellow or white. The mineral is susceptible of a good polish, and is sometimes cut in such a way as to display the coloured bands to the best advantage. Even this variety of natrolite can scarcely, however, be regarded as a precious stone, as it is of but little value, and is used only for inlaying and in the manufacture of small ornamental objects of various kinds.

HEMIMORPHITE.

Hemimorphite, otherwise known as electric calamine, is a hydrous silicate of zinc. It sometimes occurs as colourless, transparent, rhombic crystals, but more frequently in spherical or reniform shelly aggregates built up of radially arranged fibres and concentric layers. These rounded masses are frequently of a beautiful bright green or blue colour, which somewhat resembles that of turquoise, and, as in the latter mineral, is due to the presence of a small amount of copper. They are often cut with convex surfaces and used in ornamental work of various kinds. The mineral is not very durable, however, having a hardness of only from 4 to 5. Its specific gravity varies from 3·35 to 3·5, so that by means of these two characters hemimorphite may be readily distinguished from turquoise. Beautifully coloured specimens are found in the zinc mines at Laurion in Attica, at Santander in the north of Spain, at Nerchinsk in Siberia, and at other places; the application of the stone, however, is very limited.

CALAMINE.

Calamine, or zinc-spar, is carbonate of zinc, $ZnCO_3$, and is an important ore of this metal. It is found at the same localities as hemimorphite, and often occurs in the same kind of aggregates, which may be bright green, blue, or even violet in colour. It is used to a certain extent for ornamental purposes, the material from Laurion, in Greece, like the hemimorphite from the same locality, being worked for brooches, ring-stones, and as plates, &c.

THE FELSPAR GROUP.

The felspar group includes a number of minerals which are important constituents of the earth's crust, through which they are widely distributed. Felspars in general are cloudy, opaque, and dull in colour, so that they possess none of the characters which would lead to their application as gems, or even as ornamental stones. There are some few exceptions to the rule, however, and of these a detailed account, preceded by a general description of the characters of felspars, so far as they are of interest for our present purpose, is given below.

All the members of the group are silicates, that is to say, compounds of silicic acid and bases, and in all of them alumina is present. Beside these constituents there is present also either potash, soda, or lime, or soda and lime together. We may, therefore, distinguish potash-felspar, soda-felspar, lime-felspar, and lime-soda-felspar; in the latter, either the lime or the soda may predominate in different varieties. These felspars of different chemical composition have received special names, some of which are mentioned below.

The felspars very frequently occur in well-developed crystals, often of considerable size. Potash-felspar crystallises in the monoclinic, and the other kinds in the triclinic system. All are very similar, however, in general form, and differ essentially only in the

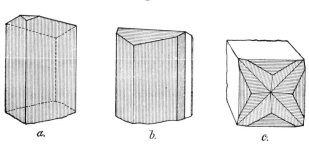

a.   b.   c.

Fig. 80.   Crystalline forms of felspar.

size of the angles between the faces, and this difference at most amounts to but a few degrees of arc. Some of the forms taken by felspar are represented in Figs. 80a to c. In each case there is a rhombic prism, which in the simplest crystal (Fig. 80a) is terminated by two obliquely inclined faces. Other faces are frequently developed, and there is nearly always a pair of parallel faces truncating the acute prism edges (Fig. 80b). Very frequently two or more individuals grow together in accordance with various twin-laws, and give rise to complex groups (Fig. 80c).

Felspars frequently occur as constituents of rocks, such as granite, gneiss, trachyte, &c., when they usually take the form of irregular grains, which are embedded in the rock-mass. They also occur, however, as regularly developed crystals, which are attached to the walls of crevices or cavities in rocks of the same character, often giving rise to druses of great beauty.

There are certain physical characters which all the felspars possess in common. All have two good and easily developable cleavages; one, which is very perfect, is parallel to the obliquely disposed terminal face represented in Figs. 80a and b. On other parts of the crystal the lustre is vitreous, but on this particular face, usually known as the basal plane, the lustre is pearly; and from the cleavage cracks parallel to this face brilliant iridescent colours are sometimes reflected. The second cleavage, which, though good, is rather less perfect than the first, is parallel to the pair of faces which truncate the acute side edges of the prism (Fig. 80b); these faces together form what is known in crystallography as the clino-pinacoid.

The cleavages of monoclinic and of triclinic felspar are essentially the same, the differences between them being unimportant. In monoclinic crystals the two cleavage planes are exactly perpendicular to each other, and for this reason monoclinic felspar has received the name orthoclase, that is to say, cleaving at right angles. In triclinic felspar the two cleavage directions are not quite at right angles, and so this variety is distinguished as plagioclase, that is to say, obliquely cleaving. The two directions are not, however, very oblique; in one variety, for example, the angle is barely 93°. The cleavage of felspar is a feature which, taken in conjunction with its hardness, readily distinguishes it, even when in massive fragments, from other minerals. The hardness of felspar is 6; in fact, this mineral is the one which is chosen to stand sixth on Mohs' scale of hardness. The fracture of felspar in directions other than the cleavage planes is sub-conchoidal to uneven.

The specific gravity varies with the chemical composition between 2·5 and 2·7. The greater the amount of lime present the heavier is the felspar, pure lime-felspar or anorthite having the highest specific gravity of any. All felspars are fusible before the blowpipe, but only with difficulty. Neither pure potash- nor soda-felspar is attacked by hydrochloric acid, but anorthite and other varieties containing much lime are readily decomposed. The greater the amount of lime present the more easily is the felspar attacked by hydrochloric acid, and the more easily and completely is it decomposed.

As already mentioned, common felspar is in most cases dull in colour, cloudy, and imperfectly transparent. The colours most commonly seen are very pale shades of yellow, brown, and red, but more intense shades are also met with. The variety of potash-felspar, known as amazon-stone, has a fine green colour and is sometimes cut as an ornamental stone, but the yellow, brown, and red felspars are never used for this purpose. Quite colourless felspars, more or less perfectly transparent, are by no means rare; the only variety used for ornamental stones is that from the surface of which there is reflected a beautiful milky light.

The precious stones which are included in the felspar group are not much used nor are they of any great value. Nevertheless they have a certain importance. They will be dealt with below in some detail: first, amazon-stone, the use of which, for ornamental purposes, depends solely upon its colour; and secondly, those felspars which display a reflection of milky light or a play of colour, namely, moon-stone, sun-stone, labradorescent felspar, and labradorite. Other members of the felspar group are never used for this purpose.

AMAZON-STONE.

In colour amazon-stone is verdigris-green, sometimes tinged with blue. All shades of this particular colour, from the palest to the darkest, are met with, but only those stones which exhibit perfectly pure dark shades of colour are cut and polished. Stones showing white, yellow, or red patches and streaks are frequently met with, but are useless for ornamental purposes. Amazon-stone is opaque or only slightly translucent, and it acquires no specially fine lustre after polishing; its application as an ornamental stone depends, therefore, solely upon its colour, and the deeper and purer this colour is the more highly is the stone prized. This feature of amazon-stone is supposed by some to be due to the presence of a small amount of copper, but according to other authorities it depends on the presence of organic matter.

Amazon-stone is a potash-felspar. It is found in irregular masses as a constituent of granitic, syenitic, and similar rocks; also as regularly developed crystals, which may reach a length of 25 centimetres, in magnificent druses, in the crevices and fissures of rocks of the same kind. Fig. 1 of Plate XVI. illustrates the latter mode of occurrence, and a single crystal is represented in Fig. 81. The physical characters of amazon-stone are the same as those of other felspars. Its specific gravity, in correlation with the chemical composition, is somewhat low, varying between 2·55 and 2·66.

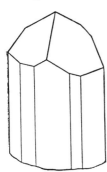

FIG. 81. Crystalline form of amazon-stone.

The name amazon-stone was first given in the middle of the eighteenth century to a green stone from the Amazon river in South America. It appears to be doubtful whether this was the same substance as that to which the name now refers; more probably it was nephrite, jadeite, or some other green mineral, for nothing is known at the present day of the occurrence of verdigris-green felspar in this region. It is known to occur in the Ural Mountains; here it is found in compact masses near Miask on the eastern side of Lake Ilmen as beautiful crystals associated with topaz and other minerals in granitic rocks. It was met with later at a few places in North America; of these occurrences the most beautiful is that of Pike's Peak in Colorado. Here it often takes the form of fine crystals, such as are represented in Plate XVI., Fig. 1; they are enclosed with grey quartz and flesh-red felspar in a coarse-grained granite. Amazon-stone of a fine colour also occurs in the coarse-grained granite of Allen's mica mine, near Amelia Court House in the State of Virginia, from whence have been obtained hundreds of tons of cleavage fragments, ranging up to 6 and 8 inches in length and of a magnificent green colour.

Amazon-stone is usually cut in the form of an oval or circular plate, the upper surface of which may be either plane or convex. These stones do not figure very largely in the precious stone trade, and are used most extensively in the countries in which they are found, namely, in Russia and North America. Several pounds may be paid for specially pure and fine stones of very intense colour or extraordinary size. The mineral is used not only as a gem but also in the manufacture of small objects of various kinds, such as bowls, vases, the stocks of seals, &c.

SUN-STONE.

The term sun-stone is applied to felspar of various kinds which have one feature in common, namely, the reflection of a brilliant red metallic glitter from a background which has little transparency and which is pale or almost white in colour. This metallic reflection is specially intense in direct sunlight or in a strong artificial light. The points which reflect the glittering light may be distributed singly and sparingly over the surface of the stone, or they may be numerous and closely aggregated; in the latter case there is over the whole surface a brilliant and glittering sheen. It is obvious that the name sun-stone is descriptive of this peculiar feature.

The explanation of the phenomenon is comparatively simple. Enclosed in the substance of the felspar are numerous minute and very thin scales of the mineral hæmatite (micaceous iron) arranged parallel to the direction of perfect cleavage in the felspar. The glittering reflection is therefore confined to the cleavage surfaces; other faces, parallel to which there are no inclusions, do not show it. The enclosed scales of hæmatite have a regular six-sided or rhomb-shaped outline, or they may be quite irregular. These scales, in consequence of their excessive tenuity, are transparent; they have a red colour, which may be distinctly seen when thin sections of the stone, cut parallel to the plane of reflection, are examined under the microscope. It is to the reflection of brilliant red metallic light from the surface of these scales that the glittering sheen of the stone is due. The more numerous and regularly distributed are these scales the more brilliant and uninterrupted is the reflection from the surface of the stone. If they are altogether absent there is no trace of the peculiar appearance characteristic of sun-stone; moreover, when the stone is turned about so that the reflecting surface is inclined towards the light at different angles the metallic sheen will be observed to appear and disappear. The metallic reflection is, of course, dull or absent in those portions of the stone in which the enclosures of hæmatite are few in number or altogether lacking, and in working the stone such parts are cut away and discarded. Sun-stone is very similar in appearance to that variety of quartz which is known as avanturine, and for this reason is sometimes referred to as avanturine-felspar.

At the beginning of the nineteenth century sun-stone was a great rarity and very costly. There were only a few small pieces known to be in existence, and the single locality given for it was Sattel Island (Setlovatoi Ostrov) in the White Sea near **Archangel**. The fragments of sun-stone found here were described as masses of cloudy, white, translucent felspar, in which were portions here and there showing a golden sheen. Subsequently the East Indies and Ceylon were mentioned as localities for sun-stone, but the occurrence of the stone there is probably not authentic.

In the year 1831 an occurrence of sun-stone was discovered at Verchne Udinsk on the Selenga, a river flowing into Lake Baikal in **Siberia**. The sun-stone is found here in a narrow vein of felspar, which runs vertically through a black rock. It is of a clove-brown colour, and in this case also the sheen is due to the enclosure of scales of hæmatite, which are arranged parallel to the plane of easier cleavage. The scales are present in large numbers, and when the cleavage face is inclined towards the light at a suitable angle a multitude of shining golden scales become visible. In all other positions the stone appears lustreless and of a uniform brown colour, but when turned in this one direction it appears as if suddenly gilded, producing a surprisingly beautiful effect. Even from broken fragments lying on the surface of the ground, and exposed to the action of weathering agencies, material was obtained superior to any which had been previously found. From a vein of considerable thickness below the surface were found bigger and more compact masses large enough to be worked into objects of some size, such as bowls and vases. Sun-stone also occurs as rounded pebbles in the Selenga river; these had been occasionally collected by passing merchants some time before the mineral was discovered in its original situation.

The most typical and beautiful sun-stone was discovered in the 'fifties at Tvedestrand in the south of **Norway**, where it occurs *in situ*. It is also found under similar conditions at Hitterö on the Christiania fjord. The sun-stone from the same region, for which Fredriksvärn was previously given as the locality, probably came in reality from Tvedestrand. The mineral never occurs in this region in regularly developed crystals, but always in masses embedded in white quartz, which forms a vein penetrating gneiss. This vein has on an average a thickness of a yard and has been worked for a length of at least six yards.

It follows the vertical banding of the gneiss, which in the immediate neighbourhood passes into a mica-schist very rich in mica, or possibly into pure mica. Accompanying the sun-stone in this vein are a variety of minerals, including hæmatite, cordierite, hornblende, zircon, and probably also apatite. The felspar found near the margins of the vein is almost colourless, and does not show the metallic sheen characteristic of sun-stone. That found nearer the centre of the vein encloses more scales of hæmatite, and at the same time exhibits a marked metallic sheen. The finest material is usually obtained from the centre of the vein ; it occurs in irregular masses embedded in stuff of inferior quality which has to be cut away, the better portions only being kept for use.

Sun-stone occurs also in **North America,** for example, at Statesville in North Carolina. Some of the material found there is equal to Norwegian sun-stone, although the enclosed scales of hæmatite are much smaller than those enclosed in material from the latter locality. It is found at Fairfield in Pennsylvania and at other places in the same State. At Middletown, in Delaware County, Pennsylvania, very fine material, little inferior to Norwegian sun-stone, is found, with moon-stone, loose on the surface of the ground. At Media in the same county there is found, besides the brilliant red sun-stone, a variety of felspar which shows the same kind of sheen as sun-stone, but which is green instead of red in colour.

The sun-stone found at all the above-mentioned localities may be described as a triclinic lime-soda-felspar, in which the soda preponderates over the lime ; it is known mineralogically as oligoclase. The avanturine-felspar, so far considered, is thus a variety of the mineral species oligoclase, which is distinguished from ordinary oligoclase by the possession of a metallic sheen due to the enclosure of scales of hæmatite. Like all triclinic felspars, the sun-stone variety of oligoclase, or *oligoclase-sun-stone*, shows a series of fine striations on the principal cleavage face, that is to say, on the face which exhibits the metallic sheen. These striations have the appearance of straight lines running parallel to the plane of the less perfect cleavage, that is to say, parallel to the intersection of the two cleavage surfaces. They are a result of the peculiar repeated twinning of the crystal, and are not present in the avanturine-felspar to be presently considered. This difference, therefore, serves to distinguish the two kinds of avanturine-felspar when in the rough, but on cut and polished stones the striations are not seen.

The appearances characteristic of sun-stone are not limited entirely to oligoclase, but are exhibited also by other kinds of felspar, especially by certain specimens of potash-felspar or orthoclase. In these stones are enclosed thin scales of hæmatite, arranged parallel to the plane of perfect cleavage, which produce a glittering metallic sheen precisely similar to that of sun-stone already described. This *orthoclase-sun-stone* is found principally in North America, for example, at Glen Riddle, in Delaware County, Pennsylvania, where the felspar is salmon-coloured and partly transparent. Beautiful varieties of orthoclase-sun-stone have been discovered near Crown Point, in the State of New York. On the Horace Greeley farm at Chappaqua, New York, have been found small pieces of the same stone, almost equal to that found at Tvedestrand, Norway ; while in Virginia specimens have been met with at Amelia Court House in Amelia County.

Sun-stone is in every case cut with a quite flat or slightly convex surface parallel to the face showing the sheen. The stone is by no means extensively used, and moderately high prices are paid only for the finest specimens.

Avanturine-felspar can be readily distinguished even with the naked eye from avanturine proper, that is avanturine-quartz, so that these stones are seldom mistaken one for another. In doubtful cases the hardness forms a distinguishing feature ; for while the

hardness of quartz is 7, that of avanturine-felspar is only 6, so that the latter is readily
scratched by quartz. Artificial avanturine-glass made in imitation of sun-stone will be
considered under avanturine-quartz.

MOON-STONE.

The name moon-stone is applied to colourless, very translucent, or almost perfectly
transparent felspar, which in a certain direction reflects a bluish, milky light, that has been
compared to the light of the moon. This peculiar feature, like the metallic sheen,
characteristic of sun-stone, is not confined to one member of the felspar group, but is
exhibited by isolated examples of all the different varieties. It is shown to perfection in
orthoclase, and for this reason moon-stone is frequently referred to as a variety of adularia,
and the appearance characteristic of this stone as adularescence. It is by no means correct,
however, to suppose that this feature is peculiar to adularia, for the same reflection of milky
light is to be seen, though rarely, in the colourless and transparent soda-felspar, which is
known to mineralogists as albite; moreover, the same is true of felspars having the chemical
composition of oligoclase, which have been dealt with already under sun-stone. These
adularescent felspars showing a reflection of soft, milky light, are variously referred to as
girasol, fish-eye, wolf's-eye, "Ceylonese opal" or "water-opal."

Adularia is the felspar which most frequently shows the characteristics of moon-stone.
It is a colourless and translucent to transparent variety of pure potash-felspar, for which
the mineralogical term is orthoclase, and its chemical composition is represented by the
formula $K_2O.Al_2O_3.6SiO_2$. It frequently occurs as fine crystals of large size and very simple
form, such as are represented in Figs. 80a and b; it also takes the form of complex twin-
crystals, as in Fig. 80c, which represents four individuals united together in twin position.

The specific gravity is 2·55, the same as for all orthoclase. The milky sheen
characteristic of adularia is not exhibited over the whole surface of the stone, but only over
a certain portion near a face which truncates the front and back edges of the prism (Figs. 80a
and b), and in massive specimens over a corresponding part. The milky sheen is only
visible when this part of the stone is in a certain position relative to the source of light and
the eye of the observer. If the stone be turned out of this position the reflection of milky
light ceases, but the sheen reappears when the stone is replaced in its original position. In
Fig. 4 of Plate XVI. an attempt is made to reproduce the appearance characteristic of an
irregular cleavage fragment of moon-stone.

Only specimens which show this sheen in a typical manner are cut as gems. To display the
beauty of this stone to the best possible advantage, it is cut with a convex, polished surface
of moderately strong curvature about the face which exhibits the sheen. The stone is very
effective in cut and polished spheres, which may be strung together and worn as beads or for
other ornamental purposes, when they have a certain resemblance to white pearls. Moon-stone
is always cut either *en cabochon* or with a plane surface, never with facets. If the plane face
be cut so that it is suitably orientated with respect to the crystal, there will be a milky sheen
uniformly distributed over its surface; but if, on the other hand, the stone be cut with a
convex surface, there will appear a band of bluish, milky light, crossing a colourless and
almost transparent background (Plate XVI., Fig. 5). The area occupied by the band of
light appears almost wholly lacking in transparency, while the area surrounding the band
exhibits no milky sheen. There is no very sharp line of demarcation between the chatoyant
band of light and the surrounding portions of the stone, but it is sufficiently abrupt to form
an effective contrast. The more convex the polished surface of the stone the narrower and

better defined is the band of light; this, however, is true only up to a certain point, for if the band is too narrow it will appear dull. It is at no time very intense or strongly marked, but has always more of the nature of a soft, pearly lustre comparable to the chatoyancy of cymophane or cat's-eye, though the lustre of the band of light in the latter stone is more silky than pearly in character. The effect of a cut moon-stone is heightened by mounting it in a closed, black setting.

The chatoyancy characteristic of moon-stone is exhibited to a variable extent in different specimens of adularia, but in the majority it is completely absent. Moreover, this feature is often more prominent in one portion than in another of the same specimen, and in such cases the inferior portions are cut away and the best used for cutting as gems. The more pronounced the chatoyancy of a stone the greater its value; one the size of a bean with a fine milky sheen is worth from 25 to 40 shillings, and the value increases considerably with the size.

The milky sheen is probably due to the presence of microscopically small, colourless, and brilliant crystal plates embedded in great numbers in the felspar, and arranged parallel to the surface from which the reflection of milky light takes place. The presence of such plates can be observed in all specimens of adularia which show a milky sheen, and the more numerous are the plates the greater will be the prominence of this feature, which, however, is completely absent when there are no enclosures to be seen. Chatoyant specimens of adularia are never perfectly clear and transparent but always cloudy, though possibly only slightly so, and this fact is also due to the same cause, namely, to the enclosure of small foreign bodies.

Splendid specimens of adularia are found at various places in the Tyrolese and Swiss **Alps.** The mineral occurs here in fine crystals, of the forms shown in Fig. 80; these, together with quartz and other minerals, are attached to the walls of crevices in gneiss and other crystalline rocks. This is the most important locality for the mineral, but it is rare for Alpine specimens to exhibit any chatoyancy at all, and still more rare to find the feature sufficiently well marked to make the stone useful for ornamental purposes.

The strongly chatoyant and beautiful moon-stone used for cutting is obtained almost exclusively from the island of **Ceylon.** Its mode of occurrence there differs from that which obtains in the Alps. Massive fragments of irregular shape, and as large, or larger than, a man's fist, are here embedded in a white kaolin-like clay, which has probably been derived from the weathering of a porphyritic igneous rock. In all probability the moon-stone was one of the original constituents of this rock and the only one to resist the action of weathering. It is found under these conditions among other places at Neura Ellia, near which is a spot, to the south-east of Adam's Peak, which is marked on some maps as " Moonstone Plain." It is also of frequent occurrence nearer the centre of the island, and, indeed, is a constituent of many of the rocks of that neighbourhood. It has also been observed to occur in close association with spinel, and in this case probably originated, together with this mineral and possibly also with the ruby, in the same mother-rock, namely, in a crystalline limestone. Ruby and spinel are found under the same conditions at Mogok in Upper Burma, but here moon-stone is present in only small amount. By the weathering of the mother-rock the moon-stone is set free, carried down the rivers and streams, and, as rounded pebbles, finally collected, together with other precious stones, out of the gem-gravels of the island. It is said to be most abundant in gem-gravels at Bellingham, between the Point de Galle and Matura on the south coast of the island, but the greater part of the material imported into Europe from Ceylon for cutting is in the form of irregular masses, not in rounded pebbles, and has therefore been obtained from the original deposits. The stone is frequently cut in Ceylon in rounded forms, but so unskilfully that it usually has to be re-cut in Europe.

A small amount of material is derived from other sources, all of which are less important than that last mentioned. In Brazil fine crystals occur in gneiss in the neighbourhood of Rio de Janeiro, many of which are suitable for cutting as gems.

In **North America** moon-stone is found at various places, but the finest specimens come from Allen's Mica Mine at Amelia Court House in Virginia. These colourless and almost transparent fragments, the largest of which are half an inch across, occur embedded in a coarse-grained granite, from which they are won in the course of mining for mica. Moon-stone from this locality is quite comparable in quality to that from Ceylon.

Here in North America are to be found, besides adularia, other felspars which exhibit the chatoyancy characteristic of moon-stone, though only to a small extent. The external appearance of some of these differs in no wise from that of the *adularia-moon-stone* hitherto considered, but this is not true in all cases. The colourless and transparent soda-felspar, known as albite, sometimes exhibits the chatoyant appearance in question, and may then be distinguished as *albite-moon-stone*. A very beautiful example of this is afforded by the albite of Mineral Hill, near Media, in Delaware County, Pennsylvania, which is sometimes cut as a gem; also by that from Macomb in St. Lawrence County, New York, which is distinguished by the name of peristerite. It occurs with ordinary felspar and is sometimes cut as a gem. Many of the crystals of peristerite are chatoyant, and some of these are as fine as moon-stone from Ceylon; others are coloured with pale shades of green or yellow, and some specimens show different colours at the same time. Adularescent albite, which, as mentioned above, is distinguished by the name of peristerite, is found in crystals and in large massive pieces in veins of coarse-grained granite penetrating gneiss at Bathurst, near Perth, and at various other places in Canada.

Much rarer than moon-stones are transparent felspars with a reddish adularescence and a yellowish colour. They are sometimes referred to as sun-stone, but are quite distinct from the stone of this name described above. They occur at the same localities as moon-stone.

Very good imitations of moon-stone, which are frequently used in cheap jewellery, have recently been made in glass, and it is by no means easy to distinguish them by mere inspection from genuine stones. Glass imitations are, however, always denser and less hard than real stones; moreover, moon-stone is distinctly doubly refracting, while the glass imitations are singly refracting, so that these characters serve to distinguish the two.

LABRADORESCENT FELSPAR.

A beautiful coloured sheen is a noticeable feature of the potash-felspar or orthoclase found in the south of Norway between the Christiania and Langesund fjords. It occurs in masses in an augite-syenite, a rock which has sometimes been referred to as zircon-syenite, and is especially abundant in the veins of coarser-grained material by which the rock is penetrated. As more definite localities, Laurvik and Fredriksvärn, especially the latter, are often mentioned. The surface which shows the coloured sheen has a rather greasy lustre, and has the same orientation in the crystal as that of the chatoyant surface of a crystal of moon-stone. Contrasted with moon-stone, however, this felspar is grey and opaque, and its sheen, instead of being of a milky blue tinge, is of a very fine blue colour, or in rare cases green, yellow, or red. The sheen is also much more intense and brilliant than in moon-stone, and thus approaches more nearly to that of labradorite without ever quite equalling this stone in beauty. A polished plate of labradorescent felspar is represented in Plate XVI., Fig. 3 ; it is rarely used for gem purposes, since it is surpassed in this direction by the abundantly occurring labradorite, but the whole rock mass is frequently worked and utilised for such objects as gravestones and the ornamental facings of shops and public buildings.

LABRADORITE.

Labradorite, labrador-spar, or labrador-felspar, so named because of its occurrence on the coast of Labrador, is the most magnificent of all the felspars. It has an extraordinarily brilliant play of colours combined with an intense metallic lustre ; it thus forms an extremely effective material for many decorative purposes, although the stone in itself is of a dingy grey colour.

Labradorite from the locality mentioned, like oligoclase from Tvedestrand in Norway, the so-called sun-stone, is a lime-soda-felspar, in which, however, there is more lime than soda. The result of an analysis is given below :

	Per cent.
Silica (SiO_2)	55·59
Alumina (Al_2O_3)	25·41
Ferric oxide (Fe_2O_3)	2·73
Lime (CaO)	11·40
Soda (Na_2O)	4·83
Potash (K_2O)	0·30
	100·26

All lime-soda-felspars having a composition approaching that represented in the above analysis are referred to the mineralogical species labradorite, whether they come from Labrador or elsewhere.

The mineral is found but rarely in regular, well-developed crystals belonging to the triclinic system. More usually it occurs in irregular masses, and this is especially the case with that found on the coast of Labrador. As in all other felspars there are two well-defined cleavages, which in this species make an angle of 94 degrees, one of which is less perfect than the other. The more perfect cleavage surfaces have a distinctly pearly lustre, and moreover exhibit the same striations due to twinning as were described in connection with the sun-stone from Tvedestrand, only in labradorite the striations are usually wider apart and less regular and numerous. A very similar series of straight lines or striations, also due to twinning, is to be seen in labradorite on the less perfect cleavage surface.

The other characters of labradorite are essentially the same as in other felspars. Thus the hardness is 6 ; the mineral is fusible before the blowpipe, but with some difficulty ; the specific gravity is low, though rather higher than that of potash-felspar, being 2·70. Other features which distinguish labradorite from potash-felspar, or orthoclase, are the presence of the twin striations, and the fact that it is moderately easily decomposed by hydrochloric acid with the separation of gelatinous silica.

Labradorite is perfectly opaque, and of a rather dark smoke- or ash-grey colour. Naturally occurring specimens have little lustre, but take a good polish. When a fragment of this mineral is turned about in the hand, so that the angle at which light strikes it is varied, in one particular position the dull smoke-grey surface of the stone will be suddenly lit up with a magnificent display of colours. This happens when rays of light are reflected from the less perfect cleavage face, or from a certain other face, but in the latter case the play of colour is less striking. To get the best possible effect the direct rays of the sun or of a powerful artificial light must fall upon the second cleavage surface at a certain definite angle, and the eye of the observer placed in a suitable position to receive the reflected rays. The stone is cut, not with facets, which destroy its effect, but either perfectly plane, or with a very slightly convex surface, which must be parallel to the reflecting surface. If the cut and polished surface deviates far from this position no play of colour will be seen. It is evident, moreover, from what has been said, that the play of colour is only exhibited by a cut-stone when in a certain position relative to the incident light and the eye of the observer, and that it suddenly disappears with the smallest deviation from this position.

This sudden disappearance and reappearance of brilliant chatoyant colours is specially characteristic of labradorite, and constitutes one of its most striking features. On this account the stone is known to jewellers also as *changeant ;* and the play of colour as change of colour or labradorescence.

The sheen of labradorite is metallic, and at the same time brilliantly and intensely coloured. There is no art by which a reproduction or an imitation of it in any way comparable to the original may be produced. The colours recall those of iridescent objects and of precious opal, but in the latter case each surface shows a number of sharply defined and differently coloured patches, while in labradorite there are large areas presenting one uniform colour. The sheen of this stone may perhaps be best likened to certain other natural objects, such as the wings of tropical butterflies, which display the same kind of metallic colours, though even more lustrous and brilliant. As examples may be cited *Morpho cypris* and *Morpho achilles* of a beautiful blue colour, and *Apatura seraphina* which is green in colour, all being from South America.

The range of colour exhibited by labradorite is wonderfully extensive. There are blues of all tints from pure smalt-blue to violet; greens ranging from the purest emerald tint to blue and yellow; the most brilliant golden yellow, a bright lemon-yellow, a deep and intense orange, which shades off gradually in a strong copper-red or a warm tombac-brown. In some stones the metallic sheen varies in colour as the stone is turned about; thus in one position it appears of a green colour and in another yellow; such a change is not, however, frequently met with. In Plate XVI., Fig. 2, an attempt has been made to reproduce the magnificent colour effects of labradorite.

Labradorite of different colours differs also in the frequency with which it is found; thus blue and green are most commonly, and yellow and red most rarely, seen. It is not unusual for the reflecting surface of a specimen to show a sheen of one uniform colour over the whole area of that surface, as in labradorite with a blue sheen from Brisbane in Australia, the variety represented in Plate XVI., Fig. 2. More commonly, however, the same surface displays elongated streaks and irregular patches, which differ in colour and in intensity of colour, and are not very sharply defined. An interesting specimen of labradorite, not from Labrador but from Russia, has been described by the Parisian jeweller Caire. According to his description it displays a perfectly recognisable image of Louis XVI.: the head of the finest azure-blue colour stands out from a golden-green background, and is surmounted by a beautiful garnet-red crown with a border of rainbow colours, and a small, silvery, shining plume. The sum of a quarter of a million francs (£10,000) was demanded in 1799 by the owner of this remarkable object.

The metallic sheen of labradorite is not always displayed uninterruptedly over the whole reflecting surface, for there are often areas which show nothing but the dull body-colour of the stone. These areas often take the form of long, narrow strips with straight, parallel margins, and these may alternate with similar strips showing the most beautiful sheen. These uncoloured patches, especially those in the shape of strips, sometimes display a coloured sheen when the stone is moved into another position relative to the incident light and the eye of the observer, while at the same time the portions, which before were coloured, now assume the dull grey body-colour of labradorite. On replacing the stone in its original position these relations are reversed. Stones in which the sheen is interrupted in this way are much less valuable than those which display a uniform sheen over the whole reflecting surface: these latter are rare and always of small size.

The value of labradorite increases with the depth and brilliancy of its coloured sheen. Stones with a dusky sheen are referred to as "bull's-eyes" (*œil-de-bœuf*), and do not fetch very high prices. The value also depends to a certain extent upon the colour of the stone, since some colour-varieties are less common than others. The price of perfectly faultless stones is rather high, but is much less for less perfect examples. The best material is cut for use as gems; larger pieces of inferior quality are utilised in the manufacture of small objects of various kinds, such as boxes, stick-handles, &c. It is customary, also, to make use of labradorite in the representation of objects with a metallic colour, such as the wings of butterflies in mosaics, and it is used for many other ornamental purposes. At the beginning of the nineteenth century small reliefs representing a mandrill baboon were much in vogue, and these were fashioned out of this stone in such a manner that only the snout and the other parts of the body, which are coloured in the living animal, showed the coloured sheen of the stone.

The chatoyant colours of labradorite have been explained in various ways, and it is possible that the yellows and greens and the blues are due to different causes. In the case of yellow and of green, the chatoyant colours are caused by the inclusion of minute, brownish translucent plates, of what appears to be hæmatite, magnetite, and ilmenite, in the substance of the labradorite. These plates are rhombic, hexagonal, or quite irregular in outline, and under the microscope are seen to be embedded in the felspar in great numbers and all parallel to the surface from which the coloured sheen is reflected. The blue colour, on the other hand, is not connected with the presence of enclosures, for it is sometimes very prominent when enclosures are completely absent. We are probably dealing here with a complicated optical phenomenon connected with the interference of light, for which a complete explanation remains still to be sought.

Labradorite was first discovered by Moravian missionaries among the Esquimaux of the **Labrador** coast towards the end of the eighteenth century. The first stones were brought to Europe in 1775, and specimens from Labrador were presented to the British Museum in 1777 by the Rev. Mr. Latrobe; the largest is a slab measuring 2 feet by 1 foot. The mineral forms one of the constituents of an igneous rock, pebbles and boulders of which are widely distributed in this region. The other constituent is hypersthene, a mineral of the augite group, with a fine copper-red, metallic reflection. The rock is very coarse-grained, and in consequence it is unusual to find pebbles which contain the two constituents side by side; nearly always they are small and consist wholly of labradorite or of hypersthene. As to the conditions under which the rock occurs *in situ* but little is known. The bay of Nunaengoak, on the northern border of the mainland of Labrador, near Nain, is said to abound in the so-called "labrador-rock." East of the mainland is the small Isle of Paul (Tunnularsoak), which, especially in former times, was often referred to as a locality for labrador-spar, while the principal locality has been stated to be an inland lake west of Nain. Near this place the labradorite-hypersthene rock, which is known to petrologists as norite, is said to occur in a very coarse-grained hornblende-granite, portions of which may be seen attached to specimens preserved in collections. According, however, to other views, this supposed granite is in reality a coarse-grained gneiss, that is to say, a member of the crystalline schists. It is stated by Mr. G. F. Kunz that labradorite has not been systematically sought for in this region for over a hundred years.

Hitherto we have considered only the characters of labradorite from the coast of Labrador. The mineral has a very wide distribution as the constituent of many different kinds of rocks, but in by far the greater number of cases the coloured metallic sheen is absent, and the mineral appears of a dull grey or white, not in the least suitable for decorative purposes. Nevertheless, chatoyant labradorite has from time to time been found at other localities, sometimes in such abundance and fine quality as to appreciably lower the price usually asked for good stones. At other places the rock containing the labradorite is worked and used for the decoration of buildings or even as a building stone.

In 1781, soon after the first discovery of chatoyant labradorite in Labrador, specimens of similar character were discovered in **Russia**; and this country has proved to be specially rich in this mineral. It was found first in the form of boulders at Peterhof near St. Petersburg. These boulders usually reflect a blue colour, but their play of colour is not equal to that of specimens from Labrador. Boulders of uncommonly large size, measuring more than 4 feet by 2, were found on the banks of the Paulovka. Numbers of labradorite boulders occur also at Miolö in Finland. The mineral was first discovered in Finland in the twenties of the nineteenth century during the recommencement of work at a very old iron mine at Ojamo, in the parish of Lojo, in the neighbourhood of Abo. It differs somewhat from that found in Labrador, being very markedly translucent and almost colourless instead of grey. Moreover, there are more colour reflections, and these are sometimes arranged with more or less regularity; for example, there may be concentric chatoyant zones around a dark nucleus, the zones differing in colour, but each being uniformly coloured over the whole of its area.

The most important occurrence of chatoyant labradorite in Russia, or probably in any country, is, however, in Volhynia and the country extending to the neighbourhood of Kiev. Together with other minerals, especially diallage, it forms a rock known to petrologists as gabbro. In places where this rock is very coarse-grained, single individuals of labradorite reach a length of 5 inches, but in other places they measure no more than a few lines. The colour of the mineral is variable, it may be dark grey or green, and the same fragment sometimes displays several shades between pale and dark green. There is a very fine play of colour over the face on which this phenomenon is usually observed: green, blue, yellow, and red are all to be seen, but the two first predominate; the yellow usually occurs between stripes of green.

This gabbro with chatoyant labradorite is one of the features of the great south Russian granitic area. It is not found in loose pebbles or boulders, but forms a great part of the solid rock of this region and is excavated in quarries at various spots. It is worked, for example, on the banks of the Bystrievka stream, near Kamennoi Brod in the district of Radomysl, and it is this locality which furnished the material for the coloured columns which ornament the Church of the Saviour at Moscow. Later on discoveries were made west of Kamennoi Brod, at Goroshki, and at many other points in the district of Zitomir, and now the rock has been traced into Government Kherson, where it was discovered in 1867 at Novo-Pavlovsk.

Very fine labradorite with a uniform blue sheen has recently come into the market ostensibly from Brisbane in Queensland.

The mineral is widely distributed throughout the **United States** of North America, and is found in great abundance in Lewis and Essex Counties in the State of New York, both *in situ* and also as boulders in glacial deposits. These boulders in the drift can be traced all the way down to Long Island and New Jersey, and they are so numerous in one of the rivers of Lewis County that it has been named Opalescent River. Large quantities of this labradorite are quarried at Keeseville, Essex County, New York, for monumental and building purposes. The mineral is also to be met with at various places in Pennsylvania, Arkansas, and North Carolina, but in no case is the material obtained from these localities cut as a gem, since labradorite from Labrador is not only more easily obtained but exhibits a finer play of colour, and is susceptible of a higher polish than is the case with material from the United States.

ELÆOLITE.

Elæolite is a variety of the mineral species nepheline. It is a silicate of sodium and aluminium, and crystallises in the hexagonal system. Its hardness lies between 5½ and 6, and its specific gravity varies between 2·58 and 2·64. A characteristic feature is the ease with which it is decomposed by hydrochloric acid. Nepheline is found in nature in two forms, which differ widely in external appearance, but possess in common all the features characteristic of the species. Ordinary or " glassy " nepheline takes the form of colourless, or faintly coloured, crystals or irregular grains ; it occurs as a constituent of many of the younger volcanic rocks, drusy cavities in which are often lined with crystals of glassy nepheline. The best crystals are perfectly colourless and transparent, and take the form of hexagonal prisms, which are usually terminated by the basal plane : they are found in the blocks ejected from the old crater of Vesuvius, now represented by Monte Somma. This " glassy " nepheline has none of the characters essential for a gem, and is, therefore, never cut as such.

The other variety of nepheline occurs as a constituent of ancient plutonic rocks, especially in the elæolite-syenites of certain districts ; in this case it nearly always takes the form of irregular grains, and seldom occurs in definite crystals. This older nepheline differs essentially from the younger, glassy variety in the character of its lustre, which is distinctly greasy, hence the name elæolite (German, *Fettstein*). Moreover, instead of being transparent and colourless, it is cloudy, or, at most, only translucent, and of a colour ranging from bright bluish-green or brown to tile-red. On mere inspection we would assume elæolite to be a mineral perfectly distinct from nepheline ; since, however, the two minerals are in complete agreement in such characters as crystalline form, chemical composition, specific gravity, &c., they must be included in the same mineral species.

The contrast between the external appearance of elæolite and that of glassy nepheline depends upon the presence in the former of numerous enclosures of microscopically small crystals, some of which may be augite or hornblende, while others belong to other mineral species. Both the colour and the greasy lustre of elæolite is due to these enclosures, the presence of which also gives rise to a wave of soft, milky light reflected with special distinctness from stones cut with a convex, polished surface. The broad band of light crossing the curved surface is very similar to that seen in cymophane and in cat's-eye, and travels over the surface as the stone is moved about before the observer. Stones which combine this appearance with an intense and pure body-colour are often very effective and comparatively valuable, since, though the mineral itself is abundant, specimens of this description are rare and seldom appear in the market. Usually it is stones of a green colour which are cut as gems, red stones being scarcely ever used for this purpose.

In external appearance the peculiar specimens of elæolite just described are apt to be confused with cymophane and cat's-eye. Both, however, are harder than elæolite, which can be scratched by quartz, while these cannot. Moreover, they are both heavier and sink in liquid No. 4 (sp. gr. = 2·65), in which nepheline floats.

Elæolite has been longest known from the south of Norway. It occurs in elæolite-syenite in pieces ranging in size up to that of a man's fist at several places in this region, among which may be mentioned Laurvik and Fredriksvärn, the material found at the former place being for the most part brown and green and that at the latter being red. Large fragments of red and of green elæolite are also found in a similar rock on the eastern shore of Lake Ilmen, near the smelting-works at Miask in the Ural Mountains. Greenland is another locality for this mineral; while the principal locality in the United States is Magnet Cove in Arkansas, where fine flesh-red, cinnamon-brown, and yellowish-brown elæolite of gem-quality occurs in abundance. At Gardiner and Litchfield, in Maine, elæolite of a fine green colour is found; and Salem, in Massachusetts, may be mentioned as another locality. In all cases the mineral occurs as a constituent of a rock similar to the one in which it is found in Norway and the Urals.

CANCRINITE.

The yellow cancrinite, which occurs in association with the elæolite of Litchfield, Maine, is sometimes cut and worn as a gem on account of its pretty colour. It is composed of the same chemical elements as elæolite, but contains in addition carbonic acid and water. It crystallises in the same hexagonal forms as nepheline. It is never perfectly transparent, and at best is only strongly translucent; its colour ranges from pale yellow to dark orange-yellow. The same mineral is also found at other localities; and further is not always of a yellow colour, but may be rose-red, green, &c. It is used as a gem only in the United States, and even there but rarely.

LAPIS-LAZULI.

Lapis-lazuli, or azure stone, also known as oriental lapis-lazuli, is an opaque mineral, usually of a magnificent blue colour. It occurs in nature in extremely fine-grained to compact masses with an uneven fracture. The crystals never exceed the size of a pea or bean, and are extremely rare; they have the form of the rhombic dodecahedron, and belong to the cubic system.

The beauty of this stone depends entirely upon its colour. In the finest and best specimens it is a dark azure-blue shading off to blackish-blue. Plate XX., Fig. 1, represents a stone of a fine azure-blue with a slight tinge of black. Deep blue specimens only are used as gems, and their colour is far more intense and beautiful than is that of any other opaque blue stone; it is always deeper than that of turquoise, and on this account the two stones may be readily distinguished. Very pale blue or almost colourless lapis-lazuli is also met with not infrequently; such specimens might possibly be confused with turquoise were it not that they are so seldom used as gems. As in similar cases stones of a pale colour are described as being "feminine," and those of a deep blue as "masculine." The colour may be distributed with such perfect regularity that the stone is of one uniform tint throughout, but more frequently there are bands and patches which are white or some shade of blue differing from that of the mass of the stone. Moreover, the blue colour is often flecked with yellow, shining, metallic specks of iron-pyrites, which are often supposed to be gold by the uninformed. On the decomposition of the iron-pyrites the yellow specks are replaced by patches of rusty brown, which much disfigure the stone. The precious stone known to the ancients as sapphire was probably the blue lapis-lazuli, and not the blue variety of corundum which now bears that name.

Lapis-lazuli, showing shades of colour other than the pure blue, is by no means uncommon. At certain localities there frequently occurs a blue variety slightly tinged with green, but stones of a pure green are very rare, and the same is true for violet and reddish-violet stones, which also appear to be confined to certain localities. It is unusual for a stone to exhibit more than one colour, but blue, green, and red or violet are occasionally seen in the same specimen. When reduced to powder the mineral is always of the same tone of colour, but lighter in shade than it was before.

The colour of lapis-lazuli is not perfectly stable under all conditions; it is altered, for example, by the action of heat. If a pale blue stone be raised to a dull red-heat it frequently assumes a fine dark blue colour, the specimen which was comparatively worthless before is now fit for use as a gem, and has a considerable value. In other cases the pure pale blue or dark green is transformed into a greenish-blue, which is not much admired; and if the temperature is raised too high the stone is completely decolourised. When green and violet stones are raised to a dull red-heat they frequently behave like the pale blue stones, and assume a deep blue colour, which in this case also greatly enhances their value. A greenish-blue lapis-lazuli from Chile loses its colour on heating, but regains it during the process of cooling.

The finely granular structure of lapis-lazuli is apparent even to the naked eye. In the mass the mineral shows no trace of cleavage, and the fracture is sub-conchoidal to uneven. The lustre on a freshly fractured surface is of the vitreous type; it is usually feeble, and though stronger in the material from certain localities, in other cases is quite dull. Even when cut and polished there is nothing approaching a brilliant lustre in this stone, and the more impure and patchy the specimen the more feeble will be its lustre. The lustre acquired by polishing is soon lost when the stone is in use, owing to its low degree of hardness, and it then becomes dull and less pleasing to the eye. Lapis-lazuli may practically be described as a perfectly opaque mineral ; only in the thinnest of splinters is it somewhat translucent.

The hardness of lapis-lazuli is rather low, being about $5\frac{1}{2}$ on the scale ; the mineral is thus readily scratched by quartz and is even scratched by felspar, though it is itself still capable of scratching window-glass. According to various determinations, the specific gravity of the mineral lies between 2·38 and 2·42 ; it will, therefore, float in the lightest of the test liquids, the specific gravity of which is 2·65, the same as that of quartz. It is perhaps the lightest of any of the minerals used as gems.

The mineral is decomposed by hydrochloric acid, and the white material, with which the blue is frequently intermixed, dissolves in the acid with effervescence, thus proving it to be calcite. At the same time the blue colour gradually disappears, and the whole process is accompanied by the evolution of a strong smell of hydrogen sulphide, a smell like that of rotten eggs. When heated before the blowpipe the mineral fuses with difficulty to a colourless and rather clear, bubbly glass.

When examined with a lens, or even with the naked eye, it is quite obvious that lapis-lazuli is not a homogeneous mineral, like diamond, ruby, and other precious stones, but a mixture of several substances ; and this is demonstrated still more conclusively by chemical investigation, and by the examination of thin sections under the microscope.

Analyses show that though all specimens of lapis-lazuli contain the same chemical elements, yet these are not always present in the same proportion, and their relative amounts may vary between wide limits. Thus the percentage of silica, an important constituent and one which is always present, varies between 43 and 67, and there is just as much variation in the case of other constituents. The following analysis is that of a stone from the " Orient," 28·2 per cent. of calcium carbonate and 4·5 per cent. of magnesium carbonate having been deducted :

		Per cent.
Silica (SiO_2)	. . . . . .	43·26
Alumina (Al_2O_3)	. . . . .	22·22
Ferric oxide (Fe_2O_3)	. . . .	4·20
Lime (CaO)	. . . . . .	14·73
Soda (Na_2O)	. . . . . .	8·76
Sulphuric anhydride (SO_3)	. . . .	5·67
Sulphur (S)	. . . . . .	3·16
		100·00

A small amount of chlorine, up to about a half per cent., is also present in some specimens.

The existence of such wide variations in the chemical composition of lapis-lazuli leads one to suppose that the mineral is a mixture of different substances. The appearance of thin sections under the microscope confirms this assumption, for the single mineral constituents and their relation to each other are then distinctly observable. The ground-mass is usually white calcite or limestone of finely granular structure, and in this all the other minerals are embedded. The presence of calcite is the cause of the white patches and streaks in the mineral, and also of its effervescence, when placed in hydrochloric acid. It may be present in large or in small amount and is sometimes dolomitic; that is to say, it contains magnesia, as is shown by the above analysis.

Embedded in the calcite are to be seen numerous grains of minerals of various kinds. A considerable number of these are quite or almost colourless, and consist of augite and of hornblende. The remaining grains are constituted of the true lapis-lazuli substance; they impart to the mineral its colour, and to a certain extent other of its characteristic features. At times they replace all other constituents, so that the whole mass is made up of them almost entirely, while at other times they are distributed singly through the calcite. If these grains are present in large numbers the colour of the stone is deep and full, and according as they are distributed regularly or irregularly through the mass the latter is uniformly coloured, patchy, or streaky. The colour of the stone as a whole depends upon the colour of these grains, and these may be blue, green, or violet, while the blue grains vary in shade from a deep, intense blue to one which is almost colourless. In outline these coloured inclusions are nearly always rounded, angular, or ragged with numerous indentations and projections. Sometimes, however, they take a regular crystalline form identical with that of the larger crystals mentioned above, that is to say, the form of a rhombic dodecahedron; such crystals, therefore, also belong to the cubic system. Their reference to the cubic system is supported by the fact that the majority of the grains are singly refracting; a few indeed are doubly refracting, but these are no doubt cases of anomalous double refraction such as is often observed in cubic minerals. Indications of cleavage parallel to the faces of the rhombic dodecahedron are also sometimes to be observed. Not infrequently a certain number of the small blue grains are aggregated together in circular groups.

These constituents of lapis-lazuli, to which the colour of the mineral is due, do not appear to be all of the same character. The two Swedish mineralogists, Bäckström and Brögger, during the course of an important investigation into the composition of lapis-lazuli, succeeded in isolating those pigment granules which differ in character. It was found that one kind of these granules has the composition of the blue mineral haüynite, which will be considered later, since it is sometimes used as a gem. A second kind has the composition of an artificial substance much used as a pigment and known as ultramarine. Lapis-lazuli may, therefore, be considered to contain natural ultramarine, and, indeed, before the introduction of artificial ultramarine this pigment was derived exclusively from lapis-lazuli, and was naturally very expensive. There are also, sometimes, a few granules of still another kind, differing again in chemical composition, but the two mentioned above are the most important. Their composition is given by the following formulæ:

$$\text{Ha\ddot{u}ynite, } 3(Na_2,Ca)O.3Al_2O_3.6SiO_2.2(Na_2,Ca)SO_4.$$
$$\text{Ultramarine, } 3Na_2O.3Al_2O_3.6SiO_2.2Na_2S_3.$$

Each thus contains a molecule of sodium and aluminium silicate, $Na_2O.Al_2O_3 2SiO_2$, which in haüynite has some of the sodium replaced by an equivalent amount of calcium; in addition to this a certain amount of sodium sulphate enters into the composition of haüynite, and in ultramarine some sodium sulphide.

From the analysis given above it can be calculated that in that particular specimen there was present 76·9 per cent. of haüynite, 15·7 per cent. of ultramarine, and 7·4 per cent. of other blue grains with the chemical composition of the mineral sodalite. This mineral, like haüynite and ultramarine, contains sodium and aluminium silicate, but the sodium sulphate of the former mineral and the sodium sulphide of the latter is replaced in sodalite by sodium chloride. The proportions in which these three pigments are present are very variable;

haüynite is always present in the largest amount, ultramarine in small amount, or sometimes completely absent, while sodalite is present in still smaller proportion. The colouring properties of all three substances appear to be equal, so that the appearance of the stone as a whole is not affected by the proportions in which they chance to be present.

Each of these three silicates is decomposed by hydrochloric acid with the separation of gelatinous silica. The sodium sulphide contained in ultramarine is decomposed by hydrochloric acid with the evolution of hydrogen sulphide, a gas which has the smell characteristic of rotten eggs. When, therefore, lapis-lazuli is treated with hydrochloric acid the presence or absence of this smell indicates the presence or absence of ultramarine. The fact that these three silicates are all decomposed by hydrochloric acid accounts for the decolourisation of lapis-lazuli when subjected to the action of this acid.

It should be clear from the foregoing that lapis-lazuli, as it is brought into the market and applied to various ornamental purposes, is a limestone more or less richly impregnated with the pigments mentioned above. It is probable that these, as well as the other mineral enclosures (augite, hornblende, &c.) contained in lapis-lazuli, have been formed by the action of an igneous magma, such, for example, as granite, on lime-stone. Lapis-lazuli is thus what is spoken of as a contact-product, as is the case with certain other minerals already described.

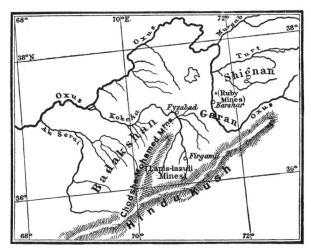

FIG. 82.   Occurrence of lapis-lazuli in Badakshan.
(Scale, 1 : 6,000,000.)

We must now consider the distribution of lapis-lazuli. The occurrence at many of the places stated to be localities for this mineral is by no means well authenticated. In some cases the regions mentioned as localities have never been thoroughly explored owing to their remoteness and inaccessibility, and in others they are merely places where the stone is marketed. Nevertheless, there are localities at which the occurrence of lapis-lazuli is well authenticated, and of which details concerning the conditions under which it occurs and the manner in which it is collected are known. The richest and most important localities are situated in Asia, and it is from this source that stones of the finest quality are derived. There is an occurrence of less importance in Chile, South America, and another, still less important, in the neighbourhood of Rome and Naples.

The longest known lapis-lazuli mines are situated in **Badakshan** in the north-east corner of Afghanistan on the upper reaches of the Amu Darja (river Oxus). The Central Asian occurrence of ruby and spinel already mentioned is in the same neighbourhood, and both localities were visited and described as far back as 1271 by the celebrated Venetian traveller, Marco Polo. The mode of occurrence of the mineral and the conditions under which it is collected have been described later by other investigators.

These ancient mines, which are still being worked, are situated in the upper part of the valley of the Kokcha (Fig. 82), a tributary on the left bank of the Oxus. The place lies to the north of the Hindu Kush, between these mountains and the Chodsha-Mohamed range, in latitude about $36\frac{1}{2}°$ N. and longitude $70\frac{1}{2}°$ E. of Greenwich. There are probably other deposits of lapis-lazuli in this inaccessible region, especially in the Hindu Kush, but that in the upper Kokcha valley is the only one definitely known.

At the part where the mines are situated the valley is only about 200 yards wide and is shut in on both sides by precipitous walls of bare rock. The mines lie about 1500 feet above the bed of the river in a white and black limestone, the mother-rock of the lapis-lazuli. Three varieties of the mineral are distinguished: one of an indigo-blue colour, a second of light blue, and a third which is green in colour. The annual production amounts at the present time to about 36 poods, that is to say, about 5000 kilograms.

The greater part of the lapis-lazuli mined here, and specially the stones of finest quality, is sent to Bukhara, from thence they are sent to Russia, and being brought into the market at the fairs of Nizhniy Novgorod are distributed by the merchants assembled there to all parts of the world. By the time the mineral has reached the market of Nizhniy Novgorod its value has risen considerably. The material which is not sent to Bukhara goes, together with rubies from the same region, to China and to Persia, and it is probable that the lapis-lazuli said to occur in these countries, and in Little Bucharia and Tibet, has been imported from Badakshan. Descriptions of such occurrences to be found in the literature of the subject are always vague, and definite statements as to localities, &c., are sought for in vain. Moreover, the material sold in other parts of Asia, for example, in Afghanistan, Beluchistan, and India, and stated by travellers to occur in those regions, in all probability is imported from the locality in the neighbourhood of the Upper Oxus. The lapis-lazuli from which the ancient Egyptian scarabs were cut, probably came from Badakshan, as did also the material much used elsewhere in ancient times.

The mining methods used hundreds or, it may be said, thousands of years ago are still adopted. At the spot where mining operations are to be undertaken large fires are kindled and the heated rocks soaked with water. In winter the rocks are more easily cracked and fissured by this process, and this season, therefore, is considered most favourable for mining operations. The rock thus loosened and cracked is broken up with large hammers and the barren portions removed until the nests of lapis-lazuli are met with. Around each nest a deep groove is excavated, and the whole mass is then prized out with a crowbar. There are sometimes split off these masses, in a direction parallel to the bedding planes of the rock, large slabs equal to several Taurian maunds in weight, a maund being 30 or 40 pounds or more. It has been suggested that the deep blue colour characteristic of lapis-lazuli from Badakshan is due to heating by the fires employed for breaking up the mother-rock. This, however, is probably not the case, since it appears that in former times pale blue lapis-lazuli, which, it will be remembered, is sometimes changed into dark blue by the action of heat, was found side by side with the dark blue variety. Not infrequently the material from this locality is flecked with yellow iron-pyrites, while at other times this mineral is aggregated in large nests and bands.

Another group of lapis-lazuli mines is situated at the western end of **Lake Baikal** in Siberia (Fig. 83). Deposits are known on each of the streams Talaya, Malaya Bistraya, and Sludianka. According to Laxmann, the lapis-lazuli occurs here in a white granular limestone along the line of contact of this rock with granite. These details have been confirmed by later observers, and the mode of occurrence of lapis-lazuli at this locality is thus quite in accordance with what has been said above regarding the origin of this mineral. The material found in the neighbourhood of Lake Baikal is, in many cases, inferior in quality to most of that which comes from Badakshan, and it also contains much less iron-pyrites. Besides dark blue stones, violet, dark green, and pale red specimens are met with, and occasionally one which shows a bright red centre surrounded by a dull, dark blue border. The latter case would suggest that dark blue lapis-lazuli is derived by the weathering of red or violet material, and if this be so, the dark blue stone of Badakshan must be regarded as having undergone more alteration than has the violet and red material of Lake Baikal.

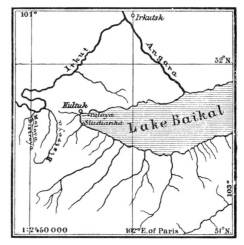

The output of these mines is very uncertain, and the working of the deposit is never a very profitable undertaking. Moreover, in new ground there is nothing to indicate the presence or absence of the mineral, and the choice of a favourable spot for fresh excavations is entirely fortuitous.

In the narrow valley of the small stream Talaya, which has a length of thirty versts (twenty miles) and flows into Lake Baikal two versts to the south of Kultuk, there are on the left side steep cliffs of white dolomitic lime-stone which in places are overlain by granitic rocks. In the limestone are veins filled with a

FIG. 83.   Occurrence of lapis-lazuli in the neigh-bourhood of Lake Baikal.   (Scale, 1 : 2,450,000.)

marly limestone containing scales of mica, blocks of compact limestone, and nodules and fragments of lapis-lazuli (Fig. 84). Up to the year 1853 three mines were being worked in this deposit. The material obtained was poor in quality, however, and after the discovery of the richer deposits on the Malaya Bistraya the mines were abandoned.

The mines on the Sludianka stream are situated twelve versts south of the village of Kultuk; they were worked for a very long period, were abandoned for a time on account of the poor quality of the lapis-lazuli and the hardness of the rock in which it was enclosed, but later were reopened. Here also the mineral is found embedded in white marble at the junction of that rock with granite and gneiss, the latter of which is frequently associated here with marble. Pebbles of lapis-lazuli are also found in the bed of the stream throughout its entire course of thirty-

FIG. 84.   Occurrence of lapis-lazuli on the Talaya River, Lake Baikal.   (a, Granite ; b, Veins in limestone ; c, Nodules of lapis-lazuli.)

five versts. The material found in this region has a great range both of colour and quality; the best is of the deepest and most beautiful ultramarine-blue; the least valuable is pale and cloudy; while the medium qualities sometimes show beautiful transition tints between blue and violet or celadon-green.

The richest deposits are those discovered in 1854 on the Malaya Bistraya (*i.e.* Little Bistraya) stream. All the best stones from this region have come from this particular spot, and the material found there as a whole is wonderfully uniform in quality. The mines are situated on the left bank of the stream, ten versts above its mouth, and no others in the neighbourhood have been worked for a long period. In this region granitic rocks predominate, and in the mountain ridge, which forms the right side of the valley, there are almost vertical beds of white, granular, dolomitic limestone, which has been altered by the granite on which it rests; the lapis-lazuli occurs in the loose material which fills up the crevices and veins in this limestone. The greater the depth of the excavation in this deposit the more abundant and finer in quality does the lapis-lazuli appear to be. The workings cover an area of 7000 square feet, and, as nodules of lapis-lazuli, weighing as much as 3 poods (108 pounds) are found in the Malaya Bistraya, and pebbles of the same kind in the Turluntay, a tributary stream, it is probable that the deposit is still more extensive. Here and there a little sulphur is found in association with the mineral, and on the Malaya Bistraya stones of various shades of dark green are found in addition to the blue variety.

Lastly, lapis-lazuli is found in abundance in the **Chilian Andes.** According to Philippi, the locality is in the Cordillera of Ovalle, only a few cuadras away from the main road leading to the Argentine provinces; it lies at the sources of the Cazadores and Vias, two small tributary streams of the Rio Grande, at only a little distance from the watershed, but still on Chilian soil. The mineral, which is associated with iron-pyrites, occurs in blocks of various sizes in a thick bed of white and grey limestone, which rests on clay-slates and is itself overlain by another bedded rock rich in iron-ore and garnet. This latter bed underlies granite, which forms the upper part of the mountain. The weathering of these rocks has given rise to a small plain of secondary deposits consisting of pebbles of granite, slate, and iron-ore, and among these are found a few loose fragments of lapis-lazuli. The Chilian lapis-lazuli is mined in some quantity; but it is pale blue in colour, often tinged with green and disfigured by white patches, so that it is much less valuable than material from the Asiatic deposits.

Small quantities of earthy lapis-lazuli are found in the ejected blocks of crystalline limestone of Monte Somma, the old crater of Vesuvius; also in the blocks of limestone included in the volcanic tuff of the Albanian Hills, near Rome. Since the material is unsuitable for use as a gem these occurrences require no further comment beyond stating that here also, as in all other cases, the mineral is a product of the contact-metamorphism of limestone.

Among the interesting minerals brought from the ruby-earths of Burma are great blocks of lapis-lazuli. These are of two varieties: in one the quantity of the blue mineral is so great that the rock-masses have a deep indigo tint, while in the other there is a white ground-mass speckled with blue.

Lapis-lazuli was highly esteemed by the ancients and was often engraved and cut in bas-relief. It is still held in esteem and is used for ring-stones, brooches, and for similar purposes, not only in Western countries but also in the Orient and China. Since the beauty of the stone depends upon its blue colour, portions for cutting are chosen with a view to obtaining stones as uniformly coloured as possible. The stone is cut with a plane or slightly curved surface, facets being quite ineffective on account of the complete opacity of the mineral.

Lapis-lazuli is not now as valuable as it once was. The price of a stone depends on its size, and on the purity, uniformity, and depth of its colour; a stone with none of these qualities is almost worthless. Pure, azure-blue lapis-lazuli is the most valuable; the presence of white specks and patches detracts considerably from its value, but less so if they are distributed quite uniformly and regularly. Pale blue and greenish-blue lapis-lazuli is worth but very little.

The rough material used for cutting is usually in small fragments, which are sold by the kilogram. Pieces of the size of a nut are common; if of the best quality they are worth £15 per kilogram. Larger pieces of equally fine quality will fetch in the European markets as much as £25 or £30 per kilogram.

Lapis-lazuli is used much more frequently for small articles, such as letter-weights, candlesticks, bowls, vases, and fancy articles of various kinds, than it is as a gem. Such articles were formerly very expensive, since each was cut out of a single piece of material, and rough blocks of good quality and sufficient size for the purpose are rare. Now such objects are made of metal and veneered with thin plates of lapis-lazuli. The mineral is used also as a decorative material in very ornate buildings, such as the Winter Palace at St. Petersburg and the Castle of Tsarkoe-Selo, in which there are rooms which are wainscotted with lapis-lazuli. The stone is also utilised in mosaics and for inlaying, the yellow, shining specks of iron-pyrites being made to represent stars in a blue sky. Pliny compared the stone to the star-bedecked firmament; and the shining metallic flecks of iron-pyrites do contrast in fact very effectively with the dark blue background of the stone itself.

Formerly lapis-lazuli had a very important technical application as a pigment. Dark-coloured fragments of the mineral were powdered up, the blue constituent separated as far as possible from the colourless portions, and the blue powder thus obtained worked up into a paint known to artists as ultramarine. This was the only fine blue pigment known, and was comparatively costly. It is now replaced by an artificial substance which very closely resembles the ultramarine of nature in colour, chemical composition, and other characters, and which is much lower in price.

There are certain opaque blue stones and artificial substances which it is possible to mistake for lapis-lazuli, and which are occasionally passed off as such. Very close imitations of lapis-lazuli can be made in glass, but the colour is less intense; the specific gravity is higher, and on the smallest broken surface the bright conchoidal fracture of glass can always be seen, as distinct from the dull uneven fracture of true lapis-lazuli. Again, agate is sometimes artificially coloured and sold in the trade as lapis-lazuli; the colour imparted to such stones is always a dark Berlin-blue and not the deep azure-blue of the genuine stone. Moreover, both the hardness and the specific gravity of agate are greater than those of lapis-lazuli. The blue mineral chessylite or azurite, a hydrated basic copper carbonate, is sometimes substituted for lapis-lazuli; this is softer and much heavier (sp. gr. = 3·8) than the latter, and is readily and completely dissolved with effervescence in hydrochloric acid. Turquoise is too light in colour to be mistaken for lapis-lazuli, and the blue mineral lazulite does not resemble it closely enough to admit of the one being substituted for the other.

HAÜYNITE.

This mineral has already been mentioned as one of the coloured constituents of lapis-lazuli. It occurs also in small irregular grains in certain volcanic rocks, and, far more rarely, as regular crystals which have the form of the rhombic dodecahedron. The principal localities are: the neighbourhood of the Laacher See, near Andernach on the Rhine (Niedermendig, &c.); the Albanian Hills, near Rome (San Marino, &c.); and the French Auvergne. Pure haüynite is sometimes of a beautiful blue colour, and almost perfectly transparent; when this is the case it may be cut as a gem, and then commands a fair price. It is said to be worn to a certain extent in France, but it has no importance whatever in the trade.

Haüynite, whether in crystals or in grains, has a definite cleavage parallel to the faces of the rhombic dodecahedron. It is translucent to transparent and singly refracting; its hardness is $5\frac{1}{2}$ and its specific gravity 2·4. These characters serve to distinguish it from all other blue stones.

SODALITE.

This is another blue mineral belonging to the same group.   Like haüynite, it occurs as grains enclosed in lapis-lazuli, and has a limited use as a gem.   It occurs also as larger grains and as crystals belonging to the cubic system.   It is usually dull or quite colourless, but specimens are sometimes met with of a pronounced blue colour and closely resembling lapis-lazuli in appearance.   The material most frequently cut for gems is that found in a syenitic rock, loose blocks of which lie about on the surface of the ground at Litchfield, Maine, in the United States, where the stone is worn on account of its national origin. Similar material is yielded by rocks of the same kind at Ditro, in Transylvania, and at Miask, on Lake Ilmen, in the Ural Mountains.   Fine large masses also occur on the Ice river, in British Columbia, and at Dungannon, in Hastings County, Ontario.   Sodalite was used as an ornamental stone by the ancient inhabitants of the Bolivian tableland, beads of blue sodalite and of fluor-spar, together with arrow-heads of quartz and obsidian, having been found by the traveller, Alfons Stübel, in the ruins of Tiahuanaco, on Lake Titicaca, one of the most ancient cities of South American civilisation.   Sodalite is not known to occur in the region, so that the material for these objects must have been brought from some locality unknown.

OBSIDIAN.

Obsidian is not a simple mineral, but a glassy lava or volcanic glass, belonging to the rhyolite group of rocks.   It is sometimes worked for ornamental purposes, and is known to lapidaries by several names, among which are lava, black lava-glass, volcanic glass, and " glass-agate."

Obsidian, like artificial glass, is perfectly amorphous, and, therefore, optically singly refracting.   It has a perfect conchoidal fracture, such as is seen in glass, and exhibits the vitreous lustre characteristic of that substance, though the lustre may sometimes incline to the greasy type.   Typical obsidian is thus wonderfully similar to ordinary glass, and differs from it markedly only in colour and transparency.   Obsidian may be black, grey, brown, yellow, red, green, and sometimes blue, but is always deeply coloured, and, because of this, almost perfectly opaque.   Very thin splinters alone are transparent and at the same time colourless, or nearly so.   Obsidian may be of one uniform colour, or it may be patchy and streaked with various colours.   Thus a variety from North America, known as " mountain mahogany," is streaked with brown and grey, and when cut shows a grain like that of mahogany.   Obsidian of a uniform black colour is more important and more widely distributed; this variety, when perfectly homogeneous and uniformly coloured, is admired for the silkiness of its appearance, and is cut for ornamental purposes.

Very frequently obsidian is not uniformly coloured, nor even apparently homogeneous in structure, but contains embedded in it crystals, sometimes of appreciable size; such specimens are useless for cutting.   Those which appear to be homogeneous are not so in reality.   When examined under the microscope they are seen to contain large numbers of minute, spherical, or elongated cavities (so-called vapour pores), minute crystals of all kinds, and other enclosures.   These are too small to affect the beauty of the stone in the mass, but they sometimes give rise to the greasy lustre already mentioned, and in a few cases to a peculiarly beautiful, reddish, silver-white, greenish-yellow or golden-green sheen, which shows up very effectively against the dark body-colour of the stone. Obsidian showing a well-marked sheen is much valued, and is worth much more than the ordinary kind.

In the remaining characters, obsidian preserves its resemblance to artificial glass. Thus its specific gravity is low; it varies between 2·3 and 2·5, rarely reaching or exceeding 2·6. In correlation with the fact that the mineral is of the nature of a lava we find the chemical composition different for each occurrence. In every case, however, it contains silicates of the alkalies and of aluminium, and of these alkalies a small amount of potash is never absent. The amount of silica present varies between 60 and 80 per cent., and the same wide variation in amount is shown by the other constituents. These are the same as in ordinary glass, but are present in obsidian in different proportions. The following is an analysis by Abich of a fine black obsidian from the island of Lipari:

	Per cent.
Silica (SiO_2)	74·05
Alumina (Al_2O_3)	12·97
Ferric oxide (Fe_2O_3)	2·73
Lime (CaO)	0·12
Magnesia (MgO)	0·28
Potash (K_2O)	5·11
Soda (Na_2O)	3·88
Chlorine (Cl)	0·31
Loss on ignition (water)	0·22
	99·67

Again, obsidian is very brittle and breaks easily into sharp, angular pieces. On this account care should be exercised both in the wearing of obsidian ornaments and also in the cutting of the mineral. Its hardness is 5 to $5\frac{1}{2}$, the same as that of window-glass; obsidian is therefore scratched by felspar, and still more easily by quartz, while it is itself scarcely capable of scratching window-glass. Acids, with the exception of hydrofluoric, have no action on this substance. It fuses before the blowpipe with intumescence, and then solidifies to a grey, porous mass.

Obsidian takes a high polish, and is worked as an ornamental stone in a variety of ways. The kind which shows a coloured sheen is cut *en cabochon*, the sheen being displayed to best advantage by this form of cutting. The ordinary black variety is used for mourning jewellery of all kinds, brooches, sleeve-links, necklaces, bracelets, &c., but it is not often used for ring-stones. It is usually cut with a plane or slightly convex surface, rarely with a pronounced convexity. Faceted stones in the form of rosettes are frequently seen, as are also faceted or spherical beads of obsidian.

Obsidian was at one time much more extensively used than it is now; at the present time it is replaced by artificial glasses, which in depth and uniformity of colour and silkiness of lustre are more than comparable with the naturally occurring glass. In the case of cut stones it is impossible to decide at once whether the material of which they consist is an artificial or a natural product. There is no difficulty, however, in distinguishing between these natural or artificial glasses and jet, another black mineral often used in mourning jewellery. As we shall see later, jet is a variety of coal, and, like all organic substances, is a bad conductor of heat. It therefore feels warm to the touch, while obsidian and glass, being better conductors, feel cold. Other black stones which may come into the market, black tourmaline and black spinel, for example, are heavier than obsidian, and sink in liquid No. 4 (sp. gr. = 2·65), in which obsidian floats.   Black hæmatite is not infrequently used as a ring-stone, but its lustre is more distinctly metallic, and on unglazed porcelain it gives a red streak, while that of obsidian is colourless.

Obsidian of various kinds is widely distributed.   It is found in some districts in extensive rock-masses built up of irregular, angular, or rounded blocks.   A comparatively large proportion of these rock-masses is sufficiently pure and homogeneous to be cut for ornamental purposes.   The rough material being thus very abundant, it is not surprising to find that the price of a cut stone is very little in excess of the sum paid for the labour of cutting.

The distribution of obsidian is so general that it would be impossible to mention all the localities for this rock by name ; a few only of the most important will now be dealt with.

In Europe the island of Lipari is a locality at which fine obsidian occurs in abundance. A lava stream of obsidian, ranging in thickness up to 100 feet and having a breadth of an eighth of a mile, stretches from Monte Campo Bianco to the sea at Capo Castagno. The material also occurs in great abundance in the neighbouring island of Vulcano.   On the island of Ponza there are dykes of black obsidian penetrating the volcanic tuffs.   It is abundant in Hungary ; and in Iceland there is so much fine material suitable for cutting that obsidian is often referred to by lapidaries as " Icelandic agate."

The country in which in former times obsidian was most extensively used for all purposes is Mexico.   Arrow-heads, spear-heads, knives, and other tools and weapons were fashioned out of obsidian by the ancient Mexicans, and, indeed, by some of the native Indians at the present day.   They had learned the art of striking off a long, thin splinter of obsidian, with an edge so fine and sharp that it could be used as a knife, or even as a razor.   Discoveries in the dwelling- and burial-places of these ancient people have shown that obsidian was fashioned into mirrors, masks, and all kinds of personal ornaments.   The distribution of the mineral is general throughout Mexico, and extends northwards and southwards beyond the borders of that country.   The ancient Mexicans appear to have derived most of their rough material from one particular spot, the so-called Cerro de las Navajas (Hill of Knives), first exactly described by Alexander von Humboldt.   It is situated near Real del Monte, in the State of Hidalgo, north of the city of Mexico and near the town of Atotonilco.   The ancient mines, which were worked long before the conquest of Mexico by the Spaniards, are still to be seen here, the marks of an ancient civilisation. The material found here shows a variety of colours, and specimens with a very fine sheen are met with, but the greater part of it is the ordinary black variety.

Among the localities in the United States at which fine obsidian occurs, may be mentioned Silver Peak, in the State of Nevada, and Obsidian Cliff, in the Yellowstone National Park.   The brown and grey streaked " mountain mahogany " is found, together with other kinds of obsidian, along the Pitt river in California, and there are many other localities in this country which yield material suitable for cutting.

A locality of some importance in Asia is the Caucasus.   Among the obsidian which is mined here is some of the variety which exhibits a coloured sheen.   The material found at Mount Ararat has a very rich sheen, and is worked at Tiflis into personal ornaments, vases, bowls, and other large objects.   The balls of obsidian found in the Marekanka river at Okhotsk in eastern Siberia are known to petrologists as marekanite, and are sometimes utilised for various ornamental purposes.   Each ball may be uniformly coloured brown, grey, yellow, or red, or it may exhibit a number of colours.   Similar material is found at other places, for example, in Mexico.

MOLDAVITE.

Moldavite is a glassy substance, the origin of which has not yet been definitely determined. It is known as bottle-stone, or as pseudo-chrysolite, on account of its resemblance to green bottle-glass and to green olivine (chrysolite), the resemblance being so close that faceted specimens of moldavite can only be distinguished from the substances mentioned by careful examination. To lapidaries the mineral is usually known as water-chrysolite.

Moldavite, like obsidian, has the chemical composition and physical characters of a glass. It can only be distinguished from obsidian with the naked eye by its perfect transparency and its green colour. The colour is never very deep, varying between leek-green and olive-green; specimens of a light brown colour are sometimes met with, but are rarely cut as gems. The mineral is amorphous and therefore optically singly refracting and not dichroic; it is brittle, breaks into sharp angular fragments, possesses a perfect conchoidal fracture and a strong vitreous lustre, all of which features it has in common with obsidian. Its hardness is about $5\frac{1}{2}$ and its specific gravity is 2·36, rather less than is usually the case with obsidian.

Although, externally, moldavite so closely resembles a piece of green bottle-glass or of transparent green obsidian, internally there are well-defined differences. Under the microscope moldavite is seen to contain vast numbers of minute air bubbles such as are seen neither in glass nor in obsidian, and the microscopic crystals always present in obsidian are absent in moldavite. Moreover, chemical analysis shows that the composition of moldavite is variable like obsidian, but that the substance contains more silica than is present either in artificial glass or in obsidian. Furthermore, moldavite contains no potash and very much less lime than is present in glass. The following is an analysis by C. von John of a specimen of moldavite from Trebitsch in Moravia:

	Per cent.
Silica (SiO_2)	81·21
Alumina (Al_2O_3)	10·23
Ferrous oxide (FeO)	2·45
Lime (CaO)	2·10
Magnesia (MgO)	1·08
Soda (Na_2O)	2·43
Loss on ignition	0·04
	99·54

The percentage of silica present may be as low as 76 and as high as 83. Moldavite fuses before the blowpipe only with great difficulty, and the fused mass after cooling is perfectly clear, so that in this respect also the mineral differs from obsidian and from glass.

It will be seen from the foregoing that though moldavite has many characters in common with green glass and obsidian, yet that there are important differences between moldavite and the two latter substances. It is, therefore, still uncertain whether moldavite is to be regarded as a natural glassy lava or as an artificial product. At the localities in Bohemia and Moravia, where the substance is found, there has flourished since ancient times a glass-making industry, and it is thus possible and even probable that moldavite is an artificial glass. Professor Suess has recently advanced the suggestion that moldavites are of cosmic origin and that they represent a hitherto unrecognised type of meteoric stone. He maintains that the peculiar surface markings cannot have been produced by attrition in water, and points to the resemblance these bear to the pittings of meteorites produced by the enormous resistance the latter encounter in their passage through the air.

The mode of occurrence of moldavite throws no light on the origin of the stone, for its presence *in situ* in any solid rock has never been unquestionably established. It is found loose in the ground in pieces which never reach the size of a man's fist, and which are more or less elliptical or flat and disc-like in form. The surface is wrinkled and scarred as if the material had been corroded, and so dark, dull, and rough that the transparency, delicate colour, and strong vitreous lustre of the substance would never be suspected.

The Bohemian localities for moldavite have been known for a long period. One of these is the district between Moldauthein and Budweis, in the south of the country, on the Moldau river (hence the name moldavite). Pebbles of the substance are found in the alluvial deposits of the river or are turned up with the soil in tilling the fields. The district between Prabsch, Klein-Horozek, and Zahoritsch is specially rich, but more so formerly than now. The stones found here are collected and sold to the lapidaries. Radomilitz, west of Budweis, is another locality, but the stones found there are lighter in colour than those met with elsewhere in Bohemia, and, moreover, are stated to occur in the ground-moraine of an ancient glacier of the glacial period. This mode of occurrence is by no means an unquestionable fact; but if it were, it would negative the theory that moldavite is an artificial product. The substance is found under the same conditions as in Bohemia at Kotschichowitz, near Trebitsch, in the Iglawa valley, and at other places in Moravia.

Rounded pebbles, measuring as much as an inch across and quite similar to the Bohemian bottle-stone, but less finely coloured, are found at Santa Fé in New Mexico, U.S.A. In this case the pebbles are, without doubt, a natural obsidian.

Moldavite is not extensively employed for ornamental purposes, and in former years was still less used. Cut stones are not worth more than sixpence a gram. The forms of cutting are those employed for olivine, namely, the table-stone and step-cut; the large front facet is often cut with a slightly convex instead of a plane surface.

In spite of the abundance and cheapness of moldavite, the substance is frequently imitated in an artificially prepared glass, which, when cut, can scarcely be distinguished from the true stone. It is easy, however, to distinguish moldavite itself from the green gem-stones it may resemble, namely, green tourmaline, chrysolite, idocrase, and demantoid, or even emerald. The specific gravity of each of these stones is appreciably higher than that of moldavite, and they all sink in liquid No. 4 (sp. gr. = 2·65), in which moldavite floats. Moreover, they are all harder than moldavite and, with the single exception of demantoid, are doubly refracting and dichroic, so that it is a simple matter to avoid mistaking bottle-stone for any of these precious stones.

THE PYROXENE AND AMPHIBOLE GROUPS.

HYPERSTHENE (with Bronzite, Bastite, and Diallage).

In this class are included those members of the pyroxene or augite group of minerals, which exhibit on one particular face a peculiar metallic sheen, and which depend on this feature for their application as ornamental stones.

HYPERSTHENE.

Hypersthene is remarkable for the display of a magnificent copper-red, metallic sheen, which shows up very effectively against the dark body-colour of the mineral. It is much esteemed as an ornamental stone, especially in France, but when the sheen is absent, as is sometimes the case, the mineral has no other feature of beauty, and is useless for decorative purposes.

The finest material comes from the coast of Labrador, and this is used, probably exclusively, for cutting as gems. The small island of St. Paul is often mentioned as a locality, and for this reason the mineral is also referred to as paulite, while lapidaries know it as " Labrador hornblende." It is associated here with labradorite, famous for its coloured sheen, and, as described above, the two together form rock-masses of considerable size. What has been said respecting the occurrence and distribution of labradorite in this region holds good also for hypersthene. The amount of material found here is considerable, and good specimens free from fissures can be easily cut out of the best portions of the larger rock-masses. Being, therefore, comparatively abundant, hypersthene is not a mineral of very great value.

Chemically the mineral consists essentially of a silicate of magnesium with the formula $MgO.SiO_2$, but a considerable portion of the magnesia is replaced by an equivalent amount of ferrous oxide. The following is an analysis of hypersthene from Labrador :

	Per cent.
Silica (SiO_2)	49·86
Alumina (Al_2O_3)	6·47
Ferric oxide (Fe_2O_3)	2·25
Ferrous oxide (FeO)	14·11
Manganese oxide (MnO)	0·67
Magnesia (MgO)	24·27
Lime (CaO)	2·37
	100·00

The mineral is one of the pyroxenes which crystallise in the rhombic system, but distinct crystals are not found in Labrador. The water-worn masses in which hypersthene occurs here are about the size of a man's fist, and exhibit more or less distinct cleavages and planes of separation. One of these separation planes is specially prominent by reason of the presence of innumerable crystalline plates embedded in the hypersthene. These plates or scales are all arranged parallel to the separation plane ; they have a bright metallic lustre, and possibly consist of brookite, a crystallised modification of titanium dioxide. The tendency of the mineral to separate along this plane often gives rise to fissures in the stone, and special care must be taken during the operation of cutting to avoid the development of such fissures and cracks.

The coppery sheen of hypersthene is exhibited only on that face parallel to which the crystalline enclosures are arranged, that is to say, only on the plane of separation ; no trace of it is to be seen on other faces, and, moreover, when there are no enclosures the sheen is completely absent.   It follows, therefore, that the minute enclosures embedded in the substance of hypersthene are not only the cause of the separation plane, but also of the coppery sheen characteristic of the stone.   The beauty of hypersthene is best displayed by cutting a stone with a slightly convex surface and with the circular or oval base parallel to the plane of separation of the mineral.   On polishing this surface it acquires a fine lustre and its sheen is also thereby intensified.   If the polished surface is flat the metallic sheen is exhibited uniformly over the whole area, but when convex, the sheen is confined to that portion of the surface which is directed towards the source of light, and is then stronger and more intense.   The effect of the sheen is diminished or entirely destroyed if the stone is not cut exactly in the manner described ; and the effect of facets is rather to detract from the appearance of a cut stone.

The body-colour of hypersthene is of a dingy brownish-black, but it forms an effective background for the strong coppery sheen.   The mineral is perfectly opaque in mass but in very thin sections is transparent ; the tabular inclusions described above are to be distinctly seen when such sections are examined under the microscope.

The specific gravity of hypersthene is 3·4.   Its hardness is 6, so that the mineral is scratched by quartz, but is itself capable of scratching glass.   It is brittle and fuses without difficu ty before the blowpipe, giving a black magnetic glass.   It is not attacked by acids.

A few other minerals belonging to the pyroxene group, and more or less closely related to hypersthene, sometimes contain enclosures arranged parallel to a certain face, which also give rise to a metallic, or, in some cases, to a pearly, sheen.   This is in all cases less beautiful than the coppery sheen of hypersthene, but the stones are sometimes cut and polished nevertheless.   Their body-colour is not dark brown as in hypersthene, but some pale shade of brown, grey, or green.   These minerals, which are known by the names of bronzite, bastite, and diallage, will be now briefly described and the features in which they differ from hypersthene indicated.

BRONZITE.

Bronzite is in reality a hypersthene which contains rather less iron than ordinarily. Owing to this difference in the chemical composition of the mineral, the specific gravity is lower, being only about 3·2, the colour is less dark, and the sheen paler and more bronze-yellow in character, though still very strong and with a brilliant metallic lustre. Bronzite sometimes shows indications of a fibrous structure, and when this is the case its sheen has a certain resemblance to that of cat's-eye.   It occurs in association with felspar, and in masses sufficiently large for cutting, at Kupferberg in the Fichtelgebirge ; in serpentine at Gulsen, near Kraubat, in Styria ; on the Seefeld-Alp in the Ultenthal, Tyrol, and at other places.   Bronzite is employed even less extensively than hypersthene.

BASTITE.

Bastite or schiller-spar is mineralogically identical with bronzite and differs from this latter only in external appearance. In colour it is of a pale greyish-green, and the sheen, which varies between the metallic and the pearly type, is also green. The principal locality is Baste in the Radauthal, near Harzburg, in the Harz. Single grains of the mineral, not infrequently rather large in size, occur here embedded in a serpentine, which varies in colour between dark green and black. The paler-coloured bastite with its metallic to pearly sheen contrasts very well with the dark serpentine in which it is embedded. The latter, flecked here and there with patches of sheeny bastite, forms a more decorative material than bastite or hypersthene alone, for when a fragment of serpentine containing bastite is moved about, the sheen does not disappear simultaneously from every patch of bastite but disappears from some only to reappear on others. The mineral is usually cut with a slightly convex or scutiform surface; its application as an ornamental stone is very limited, however, and it is used for the most part in the manufacture of small articles, such as snuff-boxes, letter-weights, &c.

DIALLAGE.

Diallage is rather less closely related mineralogically to hypersthene than either bronzite or bastite. In addition to the constituents of hypersthene it contains a large amount of calcium, and it crystallises, not in the rhombic, but in the monoclinic system. It resembles the other members of the pyroxene group so far considered in that it occurs most frequently in irregular masses and possesses a definite plane of separation, which displays a shining metallic sheen. In colour diallage may be dark brown, various shades of green including a very pale greenish tint and a pale greyish shade; it therefore shows more range of colour than other members of the group. The sheen is usually of the same colour as the stone itself; on the darker stones it is more metallic in character, and on the lighter it is more pearly. The rock known to petrologists as gabbro consists of diallage and felspar, and at many localities it occurs so coarsely grained that the diallage individuals are large enough for cutting; the application of the mineral as an ornamental stone is, however, extremely limited. Such coarse-grained gabbros are found, among other places, at Volpersdorf, near Neurode, in Silesia, at Le Prese in Veltlin, and at many other places in the Western Alps; at Prato, near Florence, and elsewhere in the Apennines; and in the island of Skye.

DIOPSIDE.

Among the minerals of the pyroxene group diopside is remarkable for its transparency and for the beauty of its colour, and on this account it is sometimes cut as a gem. It is a silicate of calcium and magnesium, the composition of which is represented by the chemical formula $CaMg(SiO_3)_2$, and in which a portion of the magnesia is replaced by ferrous oxide.

Diopside crystallises in the monoclinic system, and the crystals usually have the form of rather long prisms with an oblong cross section and with the edges replaced by narrow faces of a rhombic prism. They always occur attached at one end, and may be terminated quite irregularly at the free end, or there may be a greater or less number of obliquely placed terminal faces. Twin-crystals are not infrequent, and irregular, columnar aggregates of crystals are often met with.

There is a moderately perfect cleavage parallel to the faces of the rhombic prism. The crystals are brittle, and have a hardness of 6, almost the same as that of felspar; they are thus easily scratched by quartz but are themselves capable of scratching ordinary window-glass. The specific gravity varies between 3·2 and nearly 3·3, and is higher the greater the amount of iron present. The higher specific gravity is that possessed by the transparent, bottle-green crystals rich in iron from the Tyrol, which furnish most of the material cut as gems.

The lustre is strongly vitreous and is increased appreciably by polishing. The transparency varies much in degree; in some crystals it is very nearly perfect, and those which are less perfectly transparent are not cut as gems. Diopside is green in colour, but the depth of shade depends upon the amount of iron present. Crystals which contain practically no iron are almost colourless; as the amount of ferrous oxide present increases the colour becomes deeper and deeper, and the crystals which are richest in iron are of a fine, deep bottle-green colour. A characteristic feature noticeable even in the most deeply coloured stones is the existence of only a very slight dichroism.

There are but few localities from which material fit for cutting is obtained. The pale greyish-green crystals which occur in association with hessonite in the Ala valley in Piedmont (Plate XIV., Fig. 7) are worked at Turin, and to a certain extent also at Chamounix, and are worn in rings and other pieces of jewellery, more especially in Italy. Similar crystals of a pale oil-green colour occur at De Kalb, in St. Lawrence County, New York, and are worn to a limited extent in North America. The dark bottle-green crystals from the Schwarzenstein Alp in the Zillerthal, Tyrol, are still finer; they attain a diameter of 1 inch and a length of 5 inches, and occur attached at one end to chlorite-schist. Some, especially the smaller crystals, are very transparent and of a fine colour, which, however, is frequently not uniform throughout the whole crystal. Very often the attached end of the crystal is green while the free end is almost colourless, but the reverse is never the case. Such crystals were found formerly in some abundance; the green ends were used for cutting, and the cut stones, like those from Ala, were rather admired, especially in Italy. At the present time they are less frequently found and are worth less than formerly.

The forms of cutting employed for diopside are those generally used for coloured, transparent stones, namely, the step-cut and the various modifications of the table-stone. In the case of dark-coloured stones the step-cut must not be too deep.

Diopside may be confused with other green stones or with green glass. It can be distinguished from the latter by the fact that the glass is singly refracting. It differs from emerald in colour and in specific gravity, being much heavier. Chrysolite (olivine) is often very similar to diopside in colour, shows the same feeble dichroism, and has much the same specific gravity; it is appreciably harder, however, than diopside, which is easily scratched by this stone. Green tourmaline, epidote, and alexandrite are readily distinguished from diopside by their strong dichroism; moreover, the last named is appreciably heavier, and the same is also true of idocrase. Diopside and dioptase can scarcely be mistaken the one for the other, since the difference between them is very marked.

SPODUMENE.

Spodumene is a member of the pyroxene group which usually occurs as opaque, ash-grey crystals; only rarely is it transparent and suitable for gem purposes. A beautiful green, transparent variety is known as hiddenite. Chemically, spodumene is a silicate of lithium and aluminium with the formula $Li_2O.Al_2O_3.4SiO_2$; other elements, including iron, are also present, but only in small amount. From the fact that lithia is an essential constituent of hiddenite, this emerald-green variety of spodumene is sometimes referred to as "lithia-emerald." It resembles the emerald, however, only in the green colour, which is probably due to the presence of a small amount of iron or chromium.

Spodumene occurs in monoclinic crystals of prismatic habit and vitreous lustre. These crystals possess a very perfect cleavage parallel to the faces of the prism. In the transparent varieties the colour is usually pale yellow or yellowish-green, but some crystals (of the hiddenite variety) have an emerald-green tint which, however, is never as deep and pure as that of the finest emeralds. The two stones differ in that while spodumene is rather strongly dichroic, emerald is only feebly so.

Spodumene has a specific gravity of 3·17, and this is another feature which distinguishes the stone from emerald, for the specific gravity of the latter does not exceed 2·7. Moreover, the hardness of spodumene varies between $6\frac{1}{2}$ and 7, while in the case of emerald $H = 7\frac{1}{2}$ to 8. Hence the former mineral is, and the latter is not, scratched by quartz, and, conversely, while emerald is capable of scratching quartz spodumene is not.

Spodumene of gem-quality is exclusively an American product, having been found only at one locality in the United States, namely, at Stony Point, Alexandra County, North Carolina, and in Brazil.

In **North Carolina** the hiddenite variety is found at Stony Point, the name of which place has been altered to Hiddenite, associated with emerald, beryl, quartz, garnet, rutile, and other minerals, in drusy cavities in a gneissose granite. The first specimens of hiddenite were discovered in 1879 by Mr. W. E. Hidden; they had been weathered out of the mother-rock and were lying loosely in the ground. They were transparent and greenish-yellow in colour and were at first thought to be diopside, since at that time spodumene had never been found in fine, transparent crystals. A closer examination revealed their true nature, and later on, during systematic mining operations for emerald in the same locality, crystals of hiddenite were found in the original mother-rock. The size of the crystals varies considerably, the largest prisms having a length of 7 centimetres. Some crystals are remarkable for the possession of a peculiar corroded surface. Some, again, were of an emerald-green colour; these and the more ordinary yellowish-green crystals were all cut as gems. Very few of these cut stones have found their way into Europe, the majority having been kept in the country as objects of local interest; a fine cut stone is, however, to be seen in the Mineral Collection of the British Museum (Natural History). Fine, green, transparent hiddenite is worth from 50 to 100 dollars £10 to £20) per carat, and the mineral is more likely to rise than to fall in value, since the deposit at Stony Point appears to be completely exhausted and no other has as yet been discovered. Altogether about 7000 dollars' worth of rough material has been obtained from this one deposit.

More recently fine, transparent specimens of spodumene of a pale yellow, rather than a green colour, have found their way from **Brazil** into the European markets under the name of chrysoberyl. This yellow, transparent spodumene occurs in Brazil in association with true chrysoberyl and was formerly mistaken for this stone, and it is probable that many supposed chrysoberyls from Brazil would turn out on closer examination to be spodumene. A few transparent pebbles of a beautiful blue colour were found formerly in the Rio de S. Francisco in the neighbourhood of Diamantina in Minas Geraes, and these for a long time were mistaken for blue lazulite.

Hiddenite can be distinguished from other green precious stones without much difficulty. The differences between this stone and emerald have been already pointed out. It is distinguished from chrysoberyl by the fact that it is much softer and much lighter, hiddenite floating in methylene iodide and chrysoberyl sinking heavily. Diopside differs from hiddenite in its specific gravity, which is higher, and its feeble dichroism; and the same is true also of chrysolite. Demantoid, the green variety of garnet, is often very similar in colour, but it is singly refracting, and therefore cannot be mistaken for the doubly refracting and dichroic hiddenite.

RHODONITE.

Rhodonite is a member of the pyroxene group, remarkable for its rose- or raspberry-red colour, which, however, in some cases may incline to a light chestnut-brown. The mineral is used as a gem and also is fashioned into all kinds of ornamental objects; the sarcophagus of Czar Alexander II., for example, is constructed entirely of rhodonite. The material used for such purposes is found at Ssedelnikova, in the neighbourhood of Ekaterinburg, in the Urals; it is finely granular to compact, and has a somewhat splintery fracture. It is worked for the most part at Ekaterinburg. The locality is situated on the eastern side of the Urals, south-west of Ekaterinburg and on the right bank of the Amarilka, a tributary on the right of the Isset; it is distant only a few versts from the gold-washings of Shabrovskoi. The rhodonite is here obtained from the quarries, which lie close together, in what appears to be a black clay-slate. The upper portion of the deposit contains a large admixture of quartz, and is therefore unfit for use. The rhodonite in places is very coarse-grained; such material, though unsuitable for cutting, is of interest mineralogically, since its nature can be easily made out. The whole deposit is penetrated by numerous cracks and fissures, the course of which is indicated by a black discolouration, due to weathering of the material along these cracks.

Rhodonite of the same description is also found, though less abundantly, in the manganese deposits of Wermland, Sweden; the material from this locality is not used for cutting. The American occurrence at Cummington, in Massachusetts, is more important. Here are found blocks of rhodonite, of a fine, rose-red colour and several hundred pounds in weight. The material is equal in quality to that from Russia, and is used for similar purposes.

Chemically, rhodonite is a silicate of manganese, which, when pure, has the formula $MnO.SiO_2$ Usually other constituents are present, especially calcium and iron, in greater or less amount. Crystals belonging to the triclinic system are met with not infrequently, but at localities other than the Urals. Very good ones are found, for example, in the manganese mines in Wermland. These are transparent and of a beautiful colour, but on account of their small size are scarcely ever cut as gems, the massive material already mentioned being the variety worked almost exclusively for decorative purposes. Massive rhodonite has a hardness which lies between 5 and 6, and a specific gravity which varies between 3·5 and 3·6. It is only slightly translucent, and its lustre is feeble, but it is susceptible of a moderately good polish.

Rhodonite is sometimes erroneously referred to as manganese-spar. This is a carbonate of manganese, of which the mineralogical name is rhodochrosite; it is of a pretty rose-red colour, but is too soft to be worked for ornamental purposes.

On account of its colour, which is somewhat similar to that of rhodonite, we may here, in passing, briefly describe a mineral which belongs not to the pyroxene but to the mica group.

LEPIDOLITE.

The colour of this mineral is not a pure rose-red, but shows a tinge of blue or violet, and therefore inclines more to lilac. Lepidolite is a lithia-mica, a finely granular to compact variety of which is found in some quantity at Rozena, in Moravia. It is sometimes fashioned into small ornamental articles of various kinds for the sake of displaying its pretty lilac-red colour, but since the hardness is only 2, and it can be scratched with the finger-nail, it is useless for other purposes.

NEPHRITE. JADEITE. CHLOROMELANITE.

These three minerals are sometimes collectively referred to as nephritoids. They were used as precious stones in prehistoric times, and objects of various kinds fashioned out of them have been found in Europe among the remains of the Stone Age. At the present time their use for ornamental purposes is limited and mainly confined to a few countries outside Europe.

The first mentioned of these minerals, nephrite, belongs to the amphibole or hornblende group, and the other two, jadeite and chloromelanite, which only differ in unessential characters, belong to the pyroxene or augite group. In spite of the fact that these three minerals are classified mineralogically into two different, though closely related groups, they resemble each other very closely in external appearance, in certain other of their characters, and in the purposes to which they are applied. Structurally they may be described as being very finely fibrous to compact aggregates, the individual constituents of which are only recognisable when thin sections of the mineral are examined under the microscope. The substance, especially when polished, appears in each case, as far as can be made out with the naked eye, perfectly homogeneous, and the appearance is rather such as one associates with fused material. When thin sections are observed under a high magnification, however, it is seen that the substance in every case is built up of very numerous fibres matted together. Although the hardness of these minerals is not very considerable, being between 6 and 7 on the scale, yet, on account of their fibrous structure, they are exceptionally tough and more difficult to fracture than any other substances in the mineral world; this character being specially conspicuous in nephrite. Because of their toughness, and also because of their pretty appearance, the nephritoids, even in prehistoric times, were used in the fashioning of idols, ornamental objects, and tools, such as axes and chisels. Such objects are now found in Europe and other countries, in ancient lake-dwellings, graves, &c., and also lying loosely in the surface soil.

Until comparatively recently, the three minerals under consideration were found both in Europe and America only in the worked condition, and the occurrence of rough material *in situ* was known only in Central Asia and in New Zealand. In accordance with these facts, a theory has been elaborated, mainly by Heinrich Fischer, of Freiburg (Baden), that the material, either in its worked or its rough condition, was carried probably from Central Asia to the places where it is now found.

Recently, however, nephritoids in the rough condition have been found in several districts where formerly only worked specimens had been known. Moreover, it has been observed that the microscopic structure of all such specimens is identical, and that it differs from that of the material which occurs in Central Asia. On these grounds, it is argued by F. Berwerth, of Vienna, and especially by A. B. Meyer, of Dresden, that the view held by Fischer is unsupported by fact, and that the objects found in any one region were worked out of rough material found in the same neighbourhood. This view is now very generally accepted, although, in some places where such remains are to be found, the source whence the rough material was derived has not yet been discovered. In these cases it is probable that, unless the deposit was exhausted by prehistoric man, a closer investigation of the district would reveal its location.

The nephritoids are opaque, or at most translucent; they are sometimes brightly coloured, but, as a rule, are an inconspicuous green or grey colour, or almost colourless. Their external appearance is thus widely different from that of gems proper, and their application in Europe is extremely limited. They are highly esteemed, however, by people in a primitive state of civilisation in other parts of the world. Thus the nephrite which occurs in New Zealand is worked by the Maoris, and the jadeite which occurs in Burma by the Burmese in the same way as these substances were worked by the ancient inhabitants of Europe in prehistoric times. The nephritoids are, however, most highly esteemed in China. Together with certain other minerals of similar appearance, they are there referred to as " yu," and are certainly more favoured by the Chinese as a nation than any other stone. There are several varieties of " yu," and they are worked in China not only for personal ornaments but also for plates, bowls, vases, sword-handles, idols, and such like objects, some of the work being executed with amazing skill and taste. Objects fashioned out of nephrite and jadeite are much valued elsewhere in the Orient, in Central Asia, Turkey, &c., but it is in China that the industry is most flourishing, and from this country that a considerable number of worked articles are exported.

NEPHRITE.

Nephrite is known as axe-stone, because it is frequently found fashioned into axe-heads; and also as kidney-stone, because it is often worn as a charm to prevent kidney diseases. Both in English and in French it is often referred to as jade. It belongs to the amphibole or hornblende group of minerals, and its chemical composition is represented by the formula $CaO.3MgO.4SiO_2$, in which a variable amount of magnesia is replaced by an equivalent proportion of ferrous oxide. The following is an analysis of nephrite from Eastern Turkestan:

	Per cent.
Silica (SiO_2)	58·00
Alumina (Al_2O_3)	1·30
Ferrous oxide (FeO)	2·07
Magnesia (MgO)	24·18
Lime (CaO)	13·24
Soda (Na_2O)	1·28
	100·07

The composition of nephrite is exactly the same as that of another member of the amphibole group, namely, actinolite. This mineral is found not infrequently in the form of long, thin rhombic prisms, belonging to the monoclinic system, which occur embedded singly in talc-schist, for example, in the Zillerthal in the Tyrol ; more often it occurs as radial aggregates of acicular crystals at many localities. All the essential characters of nephrite, namely, the specific gravity, hardness, and cleavage, agree completely with those of actinolite, and in both minerals the colour is of a more or less intense green. Nephrite is thus nothing more than a very finely fibrous to compact actinolite, the prismatic crystals of which are reduced to microscopically fine fibres. Observation of thin sections of nephrite under the microscope shows that the fibres have the same characters as the larger prismatic crystals of actinolite, but that these fibres are woven and matted together in an altogether irregular fashion. The disposition of the fibres with respect to each other is to a certain extent characteristic of each occurrence, specimens from different localities differing somewhat in their microscopic structure.

From what has been said regarding the structure of nephrite, it will be readily understood that the mineral never shows any external crystalline form. It occurs always as irregular masses of larger or smaller size or in water-worn blocks. There is never a cleavage through the whole mass of a specimen, but there is sometimes a distinct separation in one direction, which is due to the material having become schistose in character. In this direction the mass can be broken up with comparative ease, but in others, owing to the toughness of the material, this can be accomplished only with great difficulty. It is almost impossible to break up large blocks of nephrite with a hammer, especially when they are in the form of rounded boulders. The method adopted in such cases is to develop cracks in the mass by subjecting it to sudden changes of temperature, for example, by heating it strongly and then plunging it into cold water. The breaking up of the mass into its characteristic splintery fragments can then be completed by the help of a hammer.

Compared with the extraordinary toughness of nephrite its hardness is rather low, being not quite 6 on the scale ($H = 5\frac{1}{2} - 6$). The mineral is therefore harder than glass but softer than quartz. It is brittle, but with suitable tools can be worked on the lathe, the process requiring, however, special precautions and care.

The specific gravity is very nearly 3, but is slightly variable, probably because of the variable amount of iron present. The usual limits are 2·91 and 3·01, but values up to 3·1 and even 3·2 have been given. These high values are probably the results either of the presence of foreign matter (magnetite, &c.) or of inaccurate determination. Hence most specimens of nephrite float in liquid No. 3 (sp. gr. = 3·0), but some specimens slowly sink. The specific gravity is of importance, since it affords a means whereby nephrite may be distinguished from the very similar but much heavier jadeite (sp. gr. = 3·3), which always sinks rapidly in liquid No. 3, and scarcely floats even in pure methylene iodide.

Nephrite is not attacked by acids. Heated before the blowpipe it becomes white and cloudy and fuses with difficulty to a grey slag. In contrast to this behaviour jadeite fuses easily, even in an ordinary flame, and, moreover, it colours the flame bright yellow, which is not the case with nephrite.

This mineral is never transparent, and is strongly translucent only in the thinnest of sections or along the sharp edges of splintered fragments. In mass it is either perfectly opaque or feebly translucent. Fractured surfaces are dull, but smooth polished surfaces have a good lustre of a somewhat greasy character.

The colour of nephrite depends upon the amount of iron present. Like actinolite it is usually of some shade of green, brighter or paler according as there is much or little iron present.   In rare cases iron is completely absent and the mineral practically colourless. Various tints of green are met with, including grey-green, sea-green, leek-green, grass-green, &c. ; moreover, yellow and brown nephrite is known, as well as grey nephrite showing a bluish, reddish, or greenish tinge.   Nephrite of a colour which is compared with that of whey is often much esteemed.   The mineral is usually coloured quite uniformly, but occasionally a specimen is met with which is streaked, spotted, veined, or marbled with several colours or shades of colour.   Nephrite from different localities usually differs in colour; thus at one locality nephrite of a certain colour predominates, while at another that of another colour is more abundant.   This feature, therefore, taken in conjunction with the microscopic structure and the chemical composition serves to determine the locality from whence any particular specimen has come.

With regard to the occurrence of nephrite in nature it may be stated that the mother-rock is in all cases a crystalline schist, the mineral being found with especial frequency in hornblende-schist.   It forms also more or less extensive bands in pyroxene-rock, serpentine, and other rocks of this class.   Nephrite occurs *in situ* principally in Eastern Turkestan and the regions east of this in China, in Transbaikalia, and in New Zealand.   A few years ago a small amount was found in Silesia, but elsewhere the occurrence of nephrite *in situ* is very sparing.   In regions where the mineral occurs in its primary situation, loose boulders are often found in alluvial deposits ; boulders are also met with, among other places, in the lowlands of north Germany.

We will now consider the occurrence and distribution of nephrite, both in the worked and the unworked condition, in some detail.   Most of the nephrite found in **Europe** is in the form of axes, chisels, and other objects, dating back to prehistoric times, and the most famous and best known localities for these interesting remains are the ancient lake-dwellings in Lakes Constance, Zurich, Bienne, and Neuchâtel in Switzerland.   Similar objects are found in the neighbouring districts of southern Baden (on the Ueberlinger See) and Bavaria. The microscopic structure of the stones found at these places differs from that of all other known nephrites.   It is very probable, therefore, that the rough material was obtained from some deposit in the neighbourhood, perhaps from the Swiss Alps.   A few rounded pebbles of nephrite have been found on the shores of Lake Neuchâtel, and these are probably from some primary deposit in the neighbourhood, but in spite of systematic search no nephrite *in situ* has yet been discovered.

A few nephrite pebbles have also been found further to the east in the Sannthal above Cilli, and in the Murthal in Styria, the original deposit being doubtless somewhere in the neighbourhood, but at present undiscovered.   It is certain that nephrite has a wide distribution in the Alps, and as the geological investigation of these mountains proceeds, occurrences of nephrite *in situ* will no doubt be met with.   A few worked specimens of nephrite have been found between Switzerland and Styria, but no rough material.

Outside Switzerland and the neighbouring countries mentioned above, only a few prehistoric articles of nephrite have been met with in Europe.   Tools of jadeite, on the other hand, are comparatively common in Europe, and these also accompany the nephrite objects in Switzerland.   Many prehistoric axes have been found in France ; all, however, are of jadeite, and not a single specimen has been conclusively proved to be nephrite.   In Italy worked articles of nephrite seem to be confined to Calabria and Sicily, but jadeite objects are distributed over the whole country.   A few discoveries have been made also in Greece, but in none of these countries has the rough material yet been found.

In Germany, leaving southern Baden and Bavaria out of consideration, only a few small nephrite axes have been found, most of them in the neighbourhood of Weimar, and in Silesia, for example, at Gnichwitz in the Breslau district. Here in Germany, however, rough nephrite is more common, and is known to occur in several different ways. A few erratic blocks and pebbles have been found in the glacial deposits left by the northern ice-sheet, among other places at Stubbenkammer, in the island of Rügen, at Potsdam, at Suckow near Prenzlau, and at Schwemmsal, north of Düben, in the Bitterfeld district. The blocks of nephrite do not differ in their mode of occurrence from other boulders in the glacial deposits of the North German lowlands, and, like them, come doubtless from Scandinavia, having originated in the crystalline schists so widely distributed throughout that peninsula.

The occurrence of nephrite *in situ* in Germany is limited to Silesia. This locality for nephrite was mentioned by Linnæus (1707–1778), but in course of time the occurrence was forgotten and only rediscovered in the eighties of the nineteenth century. The places at which nephrite is found are the same as those described by Linnæus. One of these is Jordansmühl in the Zobten mountains; here nephrite, usually of a dark green colour, forms a layer of considerable extent, and in places over a foot in thickness between granulite and serpentine. The mineral occurs at the same place as rounded nodules, the largest of which measure 5 centimetres across, and in veins in the serpentine; the nephrite in the latter situation being white or of a pale green colour. The nephrite of which the axes found at Gnichwitz, two hours' journey from Jordansmühl, are made, is very similar in character to the rough material found at this locality. The other locality in Silesia, at which nephrite is found, is Reichenstein, a famous mining centre. The material found here is compact and of a light greyish-green colour, sometimes tinged with red, and is indistinctly schistose; it occurs in layers, the thickest of which are 7 centimetres across, intercalated in a diopside-rock in the Prince adit.

The most important localities for nephrite, from whence alone the mineral is exported, are in Asia. Chief among these is Eastern Turkestan (Little Bucharia) in the **Chinese Empire**; here, in the region south of Yarkand and Khotan, the Konakán and Karalá nephrite quarries are specially well known, but are not now systematically worked. These quarries are situated on the right side of the valley of the Karakash, an upper tributary of the Khotan Daria, 500 feet above and one and a half miles from the stream, in the neighbourhood of Gulbashén and nine miles east of Shahidulla. The latter place is situated on the above-mentioned river at a spot where there is a sharp bend towards the west; it lies in latitude about $36\frac{1}{2}°$ N. and longitude $78\frac{1}{2}°$ E. of Greenwich, in the region of the western termination of the Kuen-Lun mountains, and on the southern slopes of this range. In these quarries there is a layer of nephrite 20 to 40 feet thick between gneiss and hornblende-schist. The mineral occurs *in situ* at many spots on the northern as well as the southern slopes of the Kuen-Lun range, for example, at places further down the Khotan Daria, and on the Sirikia; and as pebbles in all the watercourses draining the northern and southern slopes of these mountains. The nephrite of Eastern Turkestan is generally paler than that found elsewhere.

Another locality at which nephrite occurs *in situ* lies further to the west in the Pamir region and on the Raskem Daria. This river flows eastward, and after being joined by the Tash Kurgan from the south is known as the Yarkand Daria. The nephrite mines lie on the right bank of the Raskem, a little north of the place where it bends suddenly from north-west to north-north-east, in about latitude 37° 4′ N. and longitude 76° E. of Greenwich. The existence of this deposit was long suspected, on account of the presence of pebbles of nephrite in the lower reaches of the Yarkand Daria. It was actually discovered in the year 1880, and the characters of the nephrite pebbles and of the material from this deposit were found to be in complete agreement.

The deposits of nephrite in this portion of the Chinese Empire are not, however, limited to the few spots mentioned above, but extend over an area which stretches from the Rasken Daria eastward over more than 5° of longitude as far as Kiria, in longitude about 82° E. of Greenwich, and probably still further.

Bogdanovitch has recently given a detailed account of the occurrence of nephrite in this region. According to this authority, between Mount Mustagat (longitude about 76° E. of Greenwich) and the meridian of Lob-Nor (longitude about 89° E.) there are no less than seven districts where primary deposits of nephrite are known to occur on the northern slopes of the Kuen-Lun and in the immediate neighbourhood of this range. The mineral is for the most part interbedded in pyroxene-rocks. Pebbles of nephrite are to be found in almost all the water-courses of Kashgar, and mining operations are systematically carried on in the valleys of the Jurunkash, Karakash, and the Tisnab. The workings on the first-named river at Kumat below Rhodan are specially well known. They are situated partly in the latest formed deposits of the river, the course of which is often altered to suit the exigences of mining operations, but more especially in the ancient terraces above the river, the detrital material of which belongs to the glacial period. Above Kumat the floor of the valley mentioned above is riddled with pits measuring from 1 to $1\frac{1}{2}$ metres in depth. The Karangu-Tag hills on the Khotan Daria above Khotan, in longitude about $79\frac{1}{2}$° E. of Greenwich, have been famed since ancient times for their richness in nephrite. The mineral is found here only in secondary deposits and not in its original situation, as at Balyktshi and the places mentioned above. The deposits recently discovered by the above-mentioned traveller at Shanut in the basin of the Tisnab, and at Lishei in the district of the Kiria Daria, are of the same character, as are also those in the famous Mount Mirdshai, or Midai, on the upper reaches of the Asgensal, a tributary of the Yarkand Daria. The primary deposits of nephrite have not been worked since the revolt of the Mahometans and the expulsion of the Chinese; they are assumed to be exhausted so far as concerns material lying near the surface, and the assumption is probably true. All the primary deposits of nephrite are in high mountain regions, many, indeed, above the limit of perpetual snow. From this situation much has been carried down to the valleys below by the agency of running water and glaciers.

According to the mode of occurrence and the manner in which it is obtained three classes of rough material are here distinguished: (1) material quarried out of primary deposits; (2) masses carried down from inaccessible heights by the ice of glaciers and still preserving their sharp edges and corners; (3) water-worn boulders and pebbles from the ancient glacial deposits or the later alluvial deposits of the rivers. These boulders and pebbles, having withstood successfully the jolting and grinding and blows of their journey down from the heights, are more likely to be free from internal cracks and fissures than are the other kinds; and for this reason boulders and pebbles of nephrite, apart from considerations of colour and such like, are more valuable than sharp-edged fragments. The work of quarrying the primary deposits of nephrite is made less arduous by lighting fires on the surface. This practice not only spoils the quality of the mineral, but also causes the mass to break up into fragments of comparatively small size, so that really large blocks are rarely seen. One such rarity is the gigantic monolith of the tomb of Tamerlane in the Gur-Emir mosque at Samarkand. Another was found by Bogdanovitch at the village of Ushaktal, between Karash and Toksun, having been left there in the middle of the eighteenth century on its way to Pekin. This is an irregular block, measuring 133·1 centimetres in length, 111·2 in breadth, and 94·6 in thickness. It probably came originally from the mines at Shanut; and though it has been exposed for a long period to both accidental and wilful damage, is still only one-third smaller than the monolith mentioned above.

Another occurrence of nephrite *in situ* has recently (1891) been discovered still further to the east. The locality lies to the north of the Kuen-Lun range, on the way from Kuku-Nor to the Nan-Shan mountains in the Chinese province of Kan-su. It is stated that the nephrite forms a vein in a soft rock, but the nature of this is not mentioned. It is probable that this deposit is the source of the numerous nephrite pebbles found in the streams and rivers of the district by former travellers. There is a brisk trade in nephrite carried on by the inhabitants of the northern slopes of the Nan-Shan range, round the villages of Kan-chu and In-chu, for example; and in almost all the villages in this region the stone is worked by the natives for the Chinese, while in the town of Su-chu-fu (a little south of latitude 40° N.) there are several workshops. The nephrite found in the Nan-Shan mountains is usually cloudy to translucent and of a light-green, milk-white, or sulphur-yellow colour.

It is not improbable that in the long ranges of the Kuen-Lun and the Nan-Shan there are other places where nephrite occurs *in situ*, since pebbles have been found by natives in the region; and the same is true for other parts of China, for example, in Yun-nan. The deposits actually known, however, have furnished not only a large proportion of the stone known as " yu," which is worked in China into the various objects already described, but also that which is applied to other purposes, and which is described as Central Asian nephrite.

A great many objects fashioned out of nephrite have been found in various parts of Asia, but it is doubtful whether the rough material came in every case from Eastern Turkestan and the other parts of the Chinese Empire mentioned above. Among other places discoveries have been made in Amur, Japan, East Cape, and the Chukchis peninsula; while in Syria and Asia Minor articles made of nephrite have been brought to light during the course of Schliemann's excavations. It is probable that the rough material was obtained in every case from some place in the neighbourhood of the spots where these articles are now found.

Of the occurrences of nephrite in other parts of Asia the first to be mentioned is that in **Siberia,** in the neighbourhood of Lake Baikal, and near the celebrated Alibert graphite mines worked by Faber, the Bavarian lead-pencil manufacturer. Nephrite and graphite are here very closely associated, and numerous scales of graphite are found embedded in the nephrite. Nothing is known regarding the origin of the latter, though here, as elsewhere, it occurs in a crystalline schist which constitutes the predominating rock of the region. Hitherto the mineral has been found only in blocks together with boulders of other material in the alluvial deposits of the water-courses of the region. These boulders, though not very numerous, are of considerable size, weighing as much as 1000 pounds or more. An immense polished block from this locality, weighing 1156 pounds, is exhibited in the Mineral Gallery of the British Museum of Natural History at South Kensington. The primary deposit is probably situated in the rocky mountainous district of Batugol, in the Sayan range to the west of Lake Baikal. The Soyots, or inhabitants of this district, wear the nephrite as ornaments, the women making necklaces and the men tobacco-boxes of it. Among the water-courses in which boulders of nephrite are found, may be mentioned the Byelaya and Kitoy rivers, both rising in the Sayan mountains and both tributaries on the left bank of the Angara, but the former emptying itself into the Angara further from Lake Baikal than does the latter. Also the Bistraya, a tributary on the right bank of the Irkut river which rises in the Chamar-Daban mountain, the Sludianka flowing northward into Lake Baikal (Fig. 83) and the Onot river.

Axe-heads of nephrite are also found not infrequently in eastern Siberia, both in the soil and in the ancient Tchudic graves at Tomsk and in the Altai Mountains.   Rough nephrite is also said to occur in Amur.

The following details respecting the recent discovery of nephrite in Siberia are taken from Mr. G. F. Kunz.   The search for nephrite in Siberia was greatly stimulated in the year 1897 by a command from the Imperial House of Russia that material be obtained for a sarcophagus to contain the remains of Czar Alexander III.   Three expeditions were made by L. von Jascevski, the officer in charge of the Siberian division of the Geological Survey of Russia, to the eastern Urals for the purpose of discovering larger masses of nephrite than had been found before, and, if possible, of finding nephrite *in situ*.   After thoroughly investigating the deposits and obtaining masses of the mineral in the region of the Onot, a region which had been visited by Alibert in 1850, and by Permikin in 1865, he visited the district of the Chara Jalga.   In the bed of this river some masses of nephrite measuring 12 feet in length and 3 feet in width were discovered, but an even more important discovery was that of a ledge of nephrite of a magnificent green colour in its primary situation, this being the first observed occurrence *in situ* of nephrite in Siberia.   The boulders in the stream furnished sufficient material for the purpose of the expedition, and for the past three years the Imperial Lapidary Works at St. Petersburg have been engaged upon the working of a small canopy to be placed over the the tombs of the Czar and Czarina.   The canopy measures 13 feet in height and is constructed wholly of nephrite and rhodonite, of which latter material the entire sarcophagus for Czar Alexander II. had been made.

In **India** nephrite, or material similar to nephrite, has been found, but not in large amount.   The occurrence is not important. and is confined to the southern part of the Mirzapur district in Bengal.   The important occurrence of jadeite in Burma will be dealt with further on.

In **America**, as in Europe, jadeite is more common than nephrite.   Objects fashioned out of nephrite are known to have been found in Central America, Venezuela, and Alaska, and primary deposits of nephrite, or at any rate rough nephrite, is said to occur on the Amazon river.   Some of the material to which the name amazon-stone is applied has been supposed to be nephrite, but whether this is actually so is very uncertain.   The occurrence of nephrite *in situ* at various places in Alaska and in the neighbouring parts of British Columbia is, however, well established.   It is possible that both the Tchudis and the natives of the regions on either side of Behring Strait obtained their rough material from the deposits in Alaska.   It is improbable, however, that the rough material for the nephrite objects found in South America, in Venezuela, Colombia, and Brazil, came also from Alaska. The nephrite out of which these objects are fashioned has definite characters of its own, and is more likely to have been found nearer at hand : where, however, is unknown.

The somewhat remarkable occurrence of nephrite in **New Zealand** was first discovered by Forster, who accompanied Captain Cook.   The nephrite, which is usually of a fine green colour, occurs here partly *in situ* and partly as loose erratic boulders.   From the earliest times this beautiful stone has been fashioned by the Maoris into weapons (battle-axes and clubs), chisels, axes, ear-pendants, idols, and other objects, and is still highly esteemed by them and known under the name " punamu."   They recognise several varieties which are distinguished by special names.   The conditions of the occurrence are not yet known in detail, but there appear to be three localities, all of which are on the west side of South Island.   Fifteen miles from the mouth of the Arahaura (Spring) river occurs a band of " green schists " several feet in thickness ; this is one locality.   Another lies to the south of Mount Cook, in the vicinity of Jackson Bay or on Milford Sound ; the occurrence here is probably in serpentine. The third locality is on Lake Punamu, in the province of Otago. New Zealand nephrite is exported to Europe and there fashioned into objects of all kinds. In these islands there are found two other green stones similar in appearance to nephrite but differing in chemical composition. These stones are known to the natives by the names "kawakawa" and "tangiwai"; they are often mistaken for nephrite and used instead of this stone.

Nephrite, both in the worked and in the rough condition, is found at many other localities in this part of the world. It occurs, for example, *in situ* in New Caledonia, New Guinea, the Marquesas Islands, the New Hebrides, the Society Islands, and Tasmania; but the occurrence in New Zealand is by far the most important.

An extraordinary number of minerals exhibited in collections are incorrectly labelled as nephrite. Almost every mineral which is compact, slightly translucent, and of a colour more or less resembling some shade of nephrite, has at one time or another been set down as nephrite, among other minerals so misnamed being different varieties of quartz, agate, serpentine, and zoisite. The hardness and specific gravity of true nephrite afford a means whereby it may be distinguished from other minerals with little difficulty. Nephrite is, or was, imitated in China by a glass paste called "pâte de riz," which is very similar to true nephrite, but appreciably harder. For a long time jadeite, chloromelanite, and nephrite were included under the common term jade; the differences between these minerals will be explained later.

It will be gathered from what has been said above that in remote bygone ages nephrite had a very extensive application, both for ornamental and utilitarian purposes. This is still the case in the Orient generally, and in China particularly, also among semi-civilised peoples; but in Europe the stone is but little used for any purpose. The fine green varieties, especially those from New Zealand, are occasionally cut *en cabochon* for ring-stones and pins, and whole rings are sometimes carved out of nephrite; but more frequently it is fashioned into small articles such as paper-knives and letter-weights. Nephrite ornaments are, generally, of little value, but very high prices are often paid in Europe for beautiful examples of Chinese art, the value of such articles lying not in the nephrite of which they are made, but in the marvellous workmanship they display.

In China the reverse is the case, and nephrite has an intrinsic value apart from the work expended upon it. "Yu" is an article of considerable commercial importance, and each colour and shade has a particular name and price. The most highly esteemed variety is of a pure milk-white colour and has the greasy lustre of hog's-lard. According to Bogdanovitch pebbles of this quality fetch as much as 200 roubles. The task of working such tough material is arduous indeed; for rough cutting double the weight of material removed is paid in silver; for finishing the expense depends upon the fineness of the work. It is not surprising, therefore, that articles carved out of nephrite are not cheap, even in China, and that they are still less so in Europe.

JADEITE. CHLOROMELANITE.

Jadeite and chloromelanite are very similar to nephrite in external appearance and in hardness, toughness, &c. By French mineralogists all three are included under the name jade, and this significance for the term has been often accepted elsewhere. Since the differences between the three minerals are now recognised the term jade has been given to nephrite, and is accepted as a synonym for nephrite. The word is derived from the Spanish *piedra de la hijada*, meaning kidney-stone; its use is always attended with confusion, and it would be an advantage to dispense with it altogether.

Although jadeite and chloromelanite are apparently so similar to nephrite, chemical analysis and microscopic examination show that they are really dissimilar, and that while nephrite belongs to the amphibole group of minerals, jadeite and chloromelanite must be included in the pyroxene group. All the essential characters of these two minerals are identical; they contain the same constituents, but whereas chloromelanite contains a considerable amount of iron, in jadeite there is very little of this element present. Chloromelanite may, therefore, be considered as a jadeite rich in iron and of a correspondingly dark colour.

Chemically, jadeite is very similar to spodumene, and the variety of that mineral known as hiddenite, the only chemical difference being that the lithium of spodumene is replaced in jadeite by sodium. It is essentially a silicate of sodium and aluminium with the formula $Na_2O.Al_2O_3.4SiO_2$; it always contains small amounts of other substances, however, and on this account no two analyses are ever identical. It must, however, be observed that the simple formula given above cannot be deduced directly from analyses of chloromelanite, and this is a point which requires further chemical investigation. A comparison of the two analyses quoted below, one of jadeite from Burma and the other of an axe-head of chloromelanite from Department Morbihan (Brittany), reveals a close correspondence in the chemical composition of the two substances. If, on the other hand, these two analyses are compared with that of nephrite, it will be observed that in nephrite aluminium and sodium are almost absent, that there is very little calcium either in jadeite or in chloromelanite, and that jadeite contains scarcely any magnesium.

	Jadeite. (Per cent.)	Chloromelanite. (Per cent.)
Silica (SiO_2)	58·24	56·12
Titanium dioxide (TiO_2) . . .	—	0·19
Alumina (Al_2O_3)	24·47	14·96
Ferric oxide (Fe_2O_3) . . .	1·01	3·34
Ferrous oxide (FeO) . . .	—	6·54
Manganese oxide (MnO) . . .	—	0·47
Lime (CaO)	0·69	5·17
Magnesia (MgO)	0·45	2·79
Soda (Na_2O)	14·70	10·99
Potash (K_2O)	1·55	trace
	101·11	100·57

Like nephrite, jadeite and chloromelanite may be described as very finely fibrous to compact aggregates. The minerals have no regular external form; a microscopic examination of thin sections shows them to consist of an irregularly interwoven mass of fine fibres. It is on this structure that the extreme toughness and compactness of the minerals, as well as their uneven splintery fracture, depends.

Transparent specimens of these minerals are never seen; very thin splinters are at most only translucent or feebly transparent. The lustre on fractured surfaces is slight, but is much heightened by polishing, being then somewhat inclined to be greasy; the same lustre may be seen on many rounded, water-worn pebbles. The substance of jadeite in itself is colourless, and many natural specimens are quite or almost white. More frequently the mineral shows a tinge of rose-red or some light shade of colour, such as pale grey, greenish-white, bluish-green, leek-green, or apple-green. Some varieties are white, with more or less sharply defined spots of a fine emerald-green colour. These latter are due to the presence of a small amount of chromium distributed through the stone in this irregular manner. The colour of the varieties which show a uniform shade of pale green is due to the presence of a small amount of iron. Chloromelanite, since it always contains a considerable amount of iron, is never colourless or pale in shade, but always dark green or almost black.

Having considered the features in which jadeite and chloromelanite are in agreement with nephrite, we must now pass to the consideration of their distinguishing characters.

The most important of these is the specific gravity. Jadeite is denser than nephrite, the specific gravity of the former varying between 3·30 and 3·35, while that of the chloromelanite variety, owing to the larger amount of iron present, reaches 3·4. Although in the majority of cases this is a valuable aid in discriminating between these minerals, it does occasionally happen that a specimen of jadeite, owing to the presence of inclusions of foreign matter, has a specific gravity as low as that of nephrite, and cannot be distinguished in this way. It is generally safe to assume, however, that a stone with a specific gravity of 3·3 is not nephrite. There is a slight difference between the hardness of the minerals, that of jadeite ($H = 6\frac{1}{2} - 7$) being rather higher than that of nephrite.

Another important difference between these minerals is the ease with which they can be fused. While nephrite fuses only with great difficulty, jadeite and chloromelanite are very easily fusible; indeed, splinters of typical chloromelanite or jadeite will fuse to a transparent, blebby glass even in the flame of a spirit-lamp without using a blowpipe at all. This is not invariably the case, however, for some specimens of jadeite and of chloromelanite are rather difficultly fusible, though never as much so as nephrite. In performing these blowpipe experiments it will be noticed that jadeite and chloromelanite, since they contain sodium, colour the flame an intense yellow, while nephrite does not do so.

Setting aside chemical analysis, the surest means whereby these minerals may be distinguished is by the examination of thin sections under the microscope. It is always possible to find some fibres which show the cleavage or optical features characteristic of augite or of hornblende, the mineral in the former case being jadeite or chloromelanite and in the latter nephrite. Although only a very small splinter of material is necessary for the investigation of the fusibility, chemical composition, and microscopic structure of any given stone, it may be inadmissible to remove even this from a worked object, and in such cases the only test applicable is the determination of the specific gravity.

Objects worked in jadeite of prehistoric age have been found frequently in Europe, Asia, America, and Africa, but the localities from whence the rough material was obtained are in most cases practically unknown. The only locality which has been thoroughly examined from a scientific point of view, and where large masses of jadeite are known to occur *in situ*, is in northern Burma. The material from this deposit, like nephrite from its Asiatic localities, is distributed over the whole of the Orient, where it is highly esteemed and used for the same purposes as nephrite; from which, indeed, it is often not distinguished, being included with this stone under the term " yu." Like nephrite, jadeite is not much esteemed in Europe, and is seldom applied to purposes of ornament.

Objects made of chloromelanite accompany jadeite articles in France, Switzerland, Mexico, and Colombia, while a large axe of the same material has been found at Humboldt Bay in New Guinea. Chloromelanite in the rough condition has never yet been met with; the articles which are found fashioned out of it all date back to remote antiquity, and are rarer than either nephrite or jadeite objects. Its existence as a distinct mineral was first recognised in an axe-head found in France.

Prehistoric objects of jadeite have a wide distribution in **Europe**. They usually have the form of axes, the so-called flat axes, in contradistinction to nephrite axes, which are generally thicker. In Switzerland, jadeite and chloromelanite objects are found together with articles of nephrite in the ancient lake-dwellings. In France, only jadeite and chloromelanite objects have hitherto been found. In Germany, articles made of jadeite are found all along the course of the Rhine and over the whole of the western portion of the country, namely, in Alsace, Baden, Würtemberg, Hesse, Nassau, Rhenish Prussia, and Westphalia (and in Belgium), and as far northward as Hanover and Oldenburg, and eastward as far as Brunswick and Thuringia. These objects are absent in the eastern part of Germany, but reappear in the Austrian Empire, namely, in Upper Austria, Carinthia, Carniola, southern Tyrol, and Dalmatia. Axes and other objects of jadeite are distributed throughout the whole of Italy. In Greece, and in the neighbouring portions of Asia Minor, numerous specimens have been found, Schliemann having found nephrite objects in excavations at Troy. In Egypt, jadeite often served as the material from which scarabs were cut.

Hitherto jadeite in the rough condition has been found only in small amount in the Swiss and Piedmontese Alps. Among the pebbles derived from the Alps, and which are met with on Lake Neuchâtel and at Ouchy, near Lausanne, on Lake Geneva, are some both of nephrite and of jadeite. Jadeite *in situ* undoubtedly exists at a few places in the crystalline schists of the Alps themselves, for example, at Monte Viso in the Aosta valley, and at San Marcel, both in Piedmont. These occurrences are only important inasmuch as they show that jadeite does actually occur *in situ* in Europe.

In **America**, articles fashioned out of jadeite and chloromelanite by the ancient inhabitants are found in large numbers in Mexico, in Central America, especially Costa Rica, and in the northern part of South America, especially in Venezuela. Jadeite is supposed by some to be the stone known to the ancient Mexicans as " chalchihuitl," but other authorities consider this term to signify turquoise. It is probable that the rough material for these objects was obtained near where they are now found, but no trace of a deposit has hitherto been met with. It has been suggested that jadeite is one of the green stones from the Amazon river to which the name amazon-stone was originally given, but this is very uncertain. Rough jadeite, as well as nephrite, is said to occur in Alaska.

The most important deposits of jadeite are in Asia. Those in **Eastern Turkestan** are of minor importance. The mineral here accompanies or occurs in the vicinity of nephrite, and, like this, is interfoliated with amphibole- and pyroxene-schists, but in less abundance. In the nephrite mines at Gulbashén, in the Karakash valley, jadeite has been found intergrown with nephrite. In the Pamir region jadeite occurs *in situ* in the valley of the Tunga, a tributary on the left bank of the Raskem Daria. The quarries in this deposit are situated about thirty or forty versts from the nephrite quarries in the Kaskem valley, and in latitude about 37° 40′ N. and longitude 76° E. of Greenwich. The deposit was at one time quarried by the Chinese, but since the latter were driven from Yarkand the quarries have been abandoned.

The occurrence of jadeite in **Upper Burma** is much more important. The deposit occupies a limited area on the upper course of the Uru river, and was first thoroughly investigated in 1892 by Dr. F. Noetling of the Geological Survey of India, from whom most of the following particulars are obtained :

The jadeite mines are situated in the sub-division of Mogoung, about 120 miles from this town, and near the river Uru, a tributary of the Chindwin (Maps, Figs. 54 and 55). The mineral is quarried out of the solid rock ; and is also obtained in the form of rounded boulders, which lie in the débris of the Uru river and are probably derived from some unknown deposit *in situ* in the neighbourhood of the river.

The mineral has been obtained from the débris of the Uru river for a much longer period than the primary deposit has been quarried. The boulders occur on the banks of a portion of the river stretching for fifteen or twenty miles down stream from the village and fort of Sanka. Above Sanka pebbles of jadeite are entirely absent, while below the stretch of river just mentioned they are met with so rarely that searchers are scarcely repaid for their trouble. The banks on each side of this stretch of the river have been worked probably for hundreds of years, and the stone is not even yet exhausted. Pits to the depth of 20 feet are sunk in the river alluvium at the foot of the hills which form the sides of the valley. The material excavated out of these pits contains pebbles of jadeite, quartzite, and other rocks. That in the bed of the river is brought up by divers. The pebbles of jadeite are all much rounded, but vary very much in size: three men are said to have been needed to remove one particular block, but boulders of such a size are found only exceptionally.

Good specimens of jadeite are also found, though rarely, in the red, clayey weathered product called laterite, which occurs in the Uru valley. These stones have a colourless nucleus enclosed in a red crust of a certain thickness. This red crust produces the effect of a fine sheen, and is due to the penetration of iron oxide from the clay in which the pebbles are embedded. Such stones, the colouring of which is quite permanent, are distinguished as " red jadeite," and are much esteemed, especially by the Chinese, who pay high prices for them.

The occurrence *in situ* of jadeite in this region has been known since the end of the 'seventies, having been discovered, probably by accident, about fifteen years before Dr. Noetling's visit. A quarry in the deposit at Tawmaw measures now about 100 yards across, and gives employment to between 500 and 600 people of the Katshin race.

The village of Tawmaw is habitable only during the dry season of the year; it is situated in latitude 25° 44′ N. and longitude 96° 14′ E. of Greenwich, six miles west of Sanka and 1600 feet above the Uru river. The jadeite forms a moderately thick bed in a little hill of dark green, or almost black, serpentine, which projects above the surrounding Miocene sandstones.

The labour of quarrying the jadeite is lightened by the practice of lighting fires on the surface. The jadeite, heated to a high temperature, rapidly cools during the night, and becomes cracked and fissured in all directions. The mass is thus broken up into blocks of manageable size, which can be dealt with by the quarryman's hammer. In consequence of this practice the jadeite obtained from the quarry is much inferior in quality to that collected out of pits in the river-banks; in spite of this fact, however, 90 per cent. of the total yield is derived from the quarry, and only 10 per cent. from the river pebbles.

The best of the material is sent on mules by the shortest overland route direct to China, the country in which jadeite is in most request. Another portion of the yield is sent to Mogoung, and from thence in boats to Bhamo, on the Irrawaddy, in consequence of which Bhamo is often incorrectly given as a locality for Burmese jadeite. From Bhamo the mineral is sent down the river to Mandalay, where it is carved in the large lapidary works or only roughly cut and sorted according to quality. What is not used up in Burma is exported through Rangoon by the sea route to China or to Europe.

The mineral found here is known both to the natives and to the Chinese by the Burmese name " kyauk-tsein." It is white, often with a marbled appearance, and contrasts sharply in the quarry with the dark green or black serpentine, by which it is surrounded.

Here and there in the white, translucent jadeite are sometimes patches of a fine emerald-green colour, the material of which differs in nowise from the ordinary white kind. Jadeite of this description is much valued and is carved for ring-stones, or the whole of a ring or bracelet may be fashioned out of it in such a way as to display the bright green spots in the most effective manner.

Fine white jadeite, as well as that spotted with green, is very valuable, even at the quarry. For a block measuring a cubic yard and containing a good deal of green material, £10,000 was demanded, and £8000 was actually offered by a Chinese merchant. A small green stone, large enough for a seal-stone, will fetch between 400 and 500 rupees there, but in Europe will be worth very much less. The value of the whole deposit, which seems inexhaustible, is thus enormous, although of course it must not be supposed that material like that described above is found every day, especially with the primitive methods of quarrying at present employed.

It may be remarked that though isolated specimens of "jadeite from Bhamo" may have the exceptionally low specific gravity mentioned above, yet, as a general rule, jadeite from Upper Burma has the normal specific gravity of 3·3.

This locality in Burma is the only one known to Europeans at which jadeite indisputably occurs *in situ*. It is very probable that there are several others in the same country, and in the region extending far into the Chinese province of Yun-nan, some of which may be worked by natives in the manner employed at Tawmaw. Moreover, in many of the rivers of these regions it probably exists as pebbles, and is sought for just as in the valley of the Uru river, but at present this is not indisputable. It is certain, however, that dark green and white pebbles, said to have been found in "Tibet in the northern Himalayas," are at present cut at Oberstein on the Rhine. They do not agree in character with those from the valley of the Uru, but more detailed statements as to the locality from whence they are brought are not forthcoming. There are often to be seen in mineral collections specimens labelled jadeite from Tay-hy-fu, or Talifu, in Yun-nan (latitude 26° N. and longitude 100° E. of Greenwich). This, however, is not in reality a locality for the mineral, but merely a stage on the journey from the Burmese deposits, described above, to Pekin; and on examination such specimens are found to agree in every particular with the jadeite known to have been found in Upper Burma.

QUARTZ.

No other mineral exists in such abundance, and at the same time affords so many different ornamental stones as does quartz in its several varieties. From one point of view quartz is one of the most important of precious stones, not on account of its value but because of its very wide distribution, and also because of the occurrence of even the most beautiful varieties in large masses. For these and other reasons all the ornamental varieties of quartz are classed with the so-called semi-precious stones.

In order to avoid repetition the characters common to all the varieties of this mineral will be first described, and afterwards the features which distinguish the varieties used as gems and for ornamental purposes.

Quartz is pure silica, that is to say, it is oxide of silicon with the chemical formula SiO_2, and consists, in the purest condition, of 46·7 per cent. of silicon and 53·3 per cent. of oxygen.

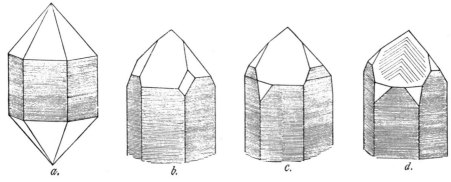

FIG. 85. Crystalline forms of quartz.

More frequently than not it contains impurities of various kinds, a fact to which the variety in colour of the mineral is due. Quartz differs from opal, another mineral which consists largely of silica, in that it is completely free from water.

Quartz differs also from opal in another important respect, namely, in that it is not amorphous but crystallised. Very finely developed crystals of quartz, usually with brilliant faces, are extremely common. They belong to the hexagonal system (Figs. 85a – d), and almost without exception take the form of regular six-sided prisms, the faces of which are characterised by the presence of very distinct striations perpendicular to the edges of the prism. The latter is terminated at one end (Figs. 85b – d), and in completely developed crystals (Fig. 85a) at both ends, by a six-sided pyramid, the faces of which intersect the prism-faces in horizontal edges. In addition to these common faces there are often others of small size (Figs. 53b – d), the arrangement of which indicates that the symmetry of quartz is that of the trapezohedral-tetartohedral division of the hexagonal system. The habit of quartz crystals is rather variable. In many cases the prism-faces are elongated, as in the forms represented in the figures; but sometimes they are short or even completely absent, and in the latter case the crystal becomes a double six-sided pyramid. The faces of this pyramid may be all of the same size, but more frequently large faces alternate with small ones, so that there are three large and three small faces (Figs. 85b – d). Owing to irregular growth it may happen that the faces of the pyramid all differ in size and are arranged in no particular order as to size. The small faces represented in Figs. 85b and c, between the prism- and the pyramid-faces are very often absent; when present they occur in regularly developed crystals on the alternate upper and lower corners (see Figs. 85b and c), but this arrangement is often disturbed by the twinning of the crystals (Fig. 85d).

Quartz crystals occur either embedded in the mother-rock, when they are developed on all sides, as in Fig. 85a, or attached to a rock surface, in which case only the free end is developed (Figs. 85b—d). The attached crystals sometimes form fine druses, as represented in Plate XVII. In this illustration the crystals are of an elongated prismatic habit, but sometimes, when only the terminal pyramid-faces are developed, the surface of the rock appears covered with close-set crystals.

Quartz occurs very commonly also in compact masses. As isolated irregular grains it forms an important constituent of many widely distributed rocks, such as granite, gneiss, &c., and, in more rounded grains, of sand, sandstone, grit, &c. Frequently, also, aggregations of microscopically small quartz grains are met with; these aggregations constitute the different varieties of compact quartz, such as hornstone (which includes the green chrysoprase), jasper, and others. Columnar aggregates are not uncommon, and when the columns or fibres are very slender the mass has a fibrous structure, as, for example, in tiger-eye. Altogether these compact varieties of quartz furnish quite a large number of ornamental stones, each of which will be described in its proper place.

The mineral has no distinct cleavage. The fracture of crystals and crystalline masses is conchoidal, almost as perfectly conchoidal as that of glass; in compact aggregates it is uneven to even, sometimes splintery. Quartz stands seventh on Mohs' scale of hardness; though not as hard as precious stones properly so-called, it is harder than any other widely distributed mineral, and scratches the majority with ease, as it does also window-glass. Steel or iron when struck against quartz gives rise to bright sparks, hence the German name " Feuerstein " (fire-stone) for flint, a compact variety of this mineral. On the other hand, quartz is scratched by most of the more valuable precious stones, being surpassed in hardness by topaz, corundum, and diamond, &c. The mineral is very brittle, and splinters may be broken off, at any rate, from large crystals, with little difficulty; some of the fine grained and compact varieties, however, are much less easily broken.

The specific gravity of pure quartz is 2·65, so that in this respect also quartz differs from opal, which is appreciably lighter. It should be observed that the value given above applies only to pure material, and that the specific gravity of impure varieties may be rather less or rather greater.

Quartz is infusible before the ordinary blowpipe, but can be fused in the oxyhydrogen flame. It is completely dissolved by hydrofluoric acid, but is unattacked by other acids; and is scarcely affected at all by a solution of caustic potash, in which, however, opal readily dissolves. On being rubbed it becomes electrified and retains its charge for nearly an hour.

The many varieties of quartz which occur in nature differ widely in external appearance, these differences depending on variations in structure, lustre, transparency, or colour.

Generally speaking, the lustre of quartz is of the vitreous type; some specimens exhibit a greasy lustre (greasy quartz), while finely fibrous aggregates sometimes possess a very good silky lustre. All varieties of quartz are susceptible of a high polish; the lustre of natural faces and fractured surfaces is often not particularly strong, but is much heightened by cutting and polishing.

In its purest condition quartz is perfectly transparent and colourless, and in many

PLATE XVII

GROUP OF QUARTZ CRYSTALS (ROCK-CRYSTAL): FROM DAUPHINÉ, FRANCE

cases the coloured varieties also freely allow the passage of light. These transparent varieties of quartz are distinguished as precious quartz; between precious quartz and cloudy or opaque common quartz every degree of transparency is to be found.

Chemical examination of the coloured varieties of quartz shows that their colour is due to the presence of impurities intermixed with the colourless quartz substance. In some cases the pigment, the nature of which is unknown, is in the finest state of sub-division, and is distributed uniformly throughout the mass of the stone, so that it is impossible to distinguish individual particles even with the aid of the highest powers of the microscope. In other cases the colouring matter is seen under the microscope to be located in needles, fibres, grains, scales, &c., of other mineral substances, which are embedded in the quartz substance in such numbers as to impart to it their own colour. To the former class belong brown smoky-quartz, violet amethyst, yellow citrine, and rose-red rose-quartz, and to the latter green prase, blue sapphire-quartz, and others. The range of colour shown by quartz is very extensive; no colour is entirely unrepresented, and the majority exist in a number of different tints and shades. There is very often a marked contrast between the colour, or the shade of colour, of different portions of the same specimen; this is shown most typically in agate, that variety of quartz so much used for ornamental purposes. The most important of the coloured varieties of quartz have been enumerated above.

Optically, quartz, being a hexagonal mineral, is doubly efracting, but neither the refraction nor the double refraction is very strong. An inspection of the table given below will show how small is the difference between the ordinary and the extraordinary refractive indices for light of different colours :

	$o.$	$e.$
Red light .	1·5409	1·5499
Yellow light .	1·5442	1·5533
Green light .	1·5471	1·5563
Blue light .	1·5497	1·5589
Violet light .	1·5582	1·5677

Although the double refraction of quartz is not very great, it is strong enough to make the images of any small object, such as a candle-flame, appear double when viewed through a transparent faceted stone (Fig. 26a). By this means quartz may be distinguished from glass of similar colour, since this will show only single images (Fig. 26b). A comparison of the numbers in the table given above shows further that there is little difference between the refractive indices of quartz for light of different colours, and consequently that the dispersion of this mineral is feeble, so that it exhibits no play of prismatic colours comparable to that of the diamond.

A peculiar optical feature possessed by quartz, and by only one other mineral, is the power of rotating the plane of polarisation of polarised light, but this being of purely physical interest need not be dwelt upon here.

The characters common to all varieties of quartz having been described, we must now direct our attention to the features which distinguish the ornamental from each other and from the common varieties. Of the ornamental varieties of quartz there are first those which occur in regular crystals, or in aggregates of crystals, the individuals of which are recognisable as such by the naked eye, though they may sometimes have irregular boundaries. Next we have the compact varieties, consisting of an aggregate of numbers of quartz crystals of microscopic size. The crystallised varieties may be further sub-divided according to colour, and the compact aggregates according to structure and other characters. Thirdly, there is the division which includes chalcedony, the special characters of which will be described later.

The different varieties of quartz which are used for ornamental purposes may, therefore, be classified in the following manner, and will be dealt with below in the same order :

A. CRYSTALLISED QUARTZ.

Rock-crystal.	Prase.
Smoky-quartz.	Sapphire-quartz.
Amethyst.	Quartz with enclosures.
Citrine.	Cat's-eye.
Rose-quartz.	Tiger-eye.

B. COMPACT QUARTZ.

Hornstone (including wood-stone and chrysoprase).	Jasper.
	Avanturine.

C. CHALCEDONY.

Common chalcedony.	Plasma (including heliotrope).
Carnelian.	Agate (including onyx).

A. CRYSTALLISED QUARTZ.

ROCK-CRYSTAL.

Perfectly limpid, colourless, and transparent quartz is known as rock-crystal. It stands out prominently among all other minerals by reason of its clearness and transparency, in which respects it often surpasses even the diamond, although it is not comparable with the latter in lustre or play of colours. An irregular mass of rock-crystal at first sight looks very like colourless glass or pure ice, and for this reason it is sometimes called glass-quartz. In ancient times, and indeed even in the Middle Ages, it was thought to be actually ice, which had been frozen so hard on the highest peaks of the Alps, where rock-crystal is very abundant, that it could not be thawed again. From this belief arose the use of the word crystal, a term first applied to rock-crystal.

This variety of quartz occurs very commonly in fine crystals, the prism-faces of which are almost without exception largely developed, so that the habit of the crystals is columnar (Figs. 85a – d). The small faces on the corners, between the prism- and pyramid-faces, sometimes present in this variety, are represented in Figs. 85b and c. Such crystals are, as a rule, attached at one end to the matrix, from which those represented in Figs. 85b – d are broken off, but crystals developed at both ends (Fig. 85a) are by no means uncommon. Crystals of this variety of quartz differ, therefore, in their development from those of common quartz, in which the prism-planes are short, or even altogether absent, and the pyramid-planes only present, while the small faces at the corners are of very rare occurrence. Rock-crystal often occurs in magnificent groups, like the one represented in Plate XVII. from the neighbourhood of Bourg d'Oisans, in the Dauphiné Alps in France.

There is considerable variation in the size of the crystals. The smallest measure a few millimetres in length and weigh no more than a few milligrams, while the largest, which are least common, measure some metres in length and weigh several hundredweights. The commonest are those of medium size, having the length and thickness of a finger or rather more.

Like all varieties of quartz, rock-crystal often contains enclosures of the most varied kinds, which, on account of the extreme clearness of the substance in which they are embedded, can be seen very distinctly. Beside enclosures of foreign matter, rock-crystal not infrequently contains cavities which are either vacuous or filled partially or completely with liquid. In the former case the remaining space is usually occupied by a bubble of gas, which moves about in the cavity as the crystal is moved. Sometimes such cavities containing liquid and an air-bubble are distinctly visible to the naked eye, but more often they are of microscopic size. In the latter case they are often crowded together in such vast numbers, especially at the attached end of the crystal, that it appears quite cloudy, while the free end is perfectly transparent. In many cases the liquid, which fills these cavities, may be easily proved to be carbon dioxide, but in other cases it is either water or a solution of common salt.

The enclosures of solid bodies, especially of crystals belonging to other mineral species, are more important. They may be extremely small in size but present in very large numbers, so that they impart to the whole crystal a uniform colour, as in the case of green prase and blue sapphire-quartz. On the other hand, these enclosures may be few in number and large enough to be seen with the naked eye, especially when they are conspicuously coloured. Scales of green chlorite, for example, are often seen either embedded in rock-crystals or attached to the surface in such numbers that but little of the colourless quartz substance can be seen, and the crystals appear of a green colour. Blades of white tremolite, needles of green actinolite (Plate XVIII., Fig. 2), and of red or yellowish rutile, are often enclosed in rock-crystal, and in many cases it is on the presence of these and other enclosures, both fluid and solid, that the application of some varieties of quartz depends.

Formerly rock-crystal was much used as a gem, and was cut as a brilliant, table-stone, or rosette. A bright vitreous lustre is imparted to it by polishing, and this can be slightly increased by igniting the stone. Under favourable conditions cut stones show a certain play of prismatic colours, and for this reason it was fashionable at one time to decorate chandeliers, hanging lamps, candlesticks, &c., with prisms and pendants of rock-crystal.

The mineral was at one time much used also for the fashioning of small articles of more or less utility, such as crystal-balls, letter-weights, seal-stocks, &c. In the Middle Ages all kinds of vessels, bowls, vases, and drinking cups, frequently so beautifully engraved with pictured figures as to be transformed into veritable works of art, were carved out of this substance. The art flourished most at the time when the manufacture of perfectly clear and colourless glass was still in its infancy, and rock-crystal was the source from whence material of this description could be most easily obtained. As the glass-making industry developed and reached perfection, the art of working rock-crystal became forgotten, for it was soon found that vessels equally transparent and finely finished could be made in glass with much less labour than in rock-crystal. Articles carved out of rock-crystal are of course more durable and not so readily scratched. Many art collections bear eloquent testimony to the perfection which the art of working rock-crystal had reached among the ancients, while in ancient writings there are to be found many records of historic vessels of this substance.

At the present day rock-crystal is little used for gems or for the purposes described above. On account of its comparatively great hardness and its resistance to chemical reagents it is devoted rather to utilitarian purposes, such as the construction of lenses for spectacles, telescopes, and other optical instruments, lenses of this material being less likely to be scratched than are those of glass.   Its perfect transparency renders it useful for other optical purposes, while it is used also for the manufacture of very exact weights to be employed when extreme accuracy is required, for the pivot supports of various delicate instruments, and for other similar purposes.

The value of rock-crystal, like its use, has much diminished during recent times.   It depends upon the purity, transparency, colourlessness, and freedom from faults of the material, such as enclosures of foreign matter, fissures, cloudy and coloured patches, and anything, in short, which detracts from the uniformity of quality of the stone.   The value of any given stone depends also, of course, upon its size ; small pieces of perfect quality are not uncommon, and for this reason the price of a cut ring-stone, even of the best quality, scarcely ever exceeds ten shillings.   Masses of considerable size and of good quality, on the other hand, are not so easy to obtain, and the larger the size the higher relatively is the price.

Rock-crystal is very widely distributed, and is usually found, together with other minerals, in the cracks and crevices of various ancient rocks, in which it forms druses, often of enormous size.   This mode of occurrence, taken in conjunction with the scarcely ever failing presence of fluid enclosures, indicates very clearly that the mineral for the most part has crystallised from an aqueous solution of silica.   It would be impossible to mention severally all the localities at which rock-crystal occurs ; a few typical occurrences only will be here enumerated.

Such in **Europe** are the high mountain peaks of the Tyrolese, Swiss, Italian, and French Alps.   The crystals, which are attached to the walls of crevices in granite, gneiss, and other similar rocks, are collected and brought into the market by persons known in Switzerland as " Strahlern."   Their task is anything but easy, since the crystals almost invariably occur in the highest and most inaccessible parts of these ranges.   In the search for crystal-bearing druses a " Strahler " is guided by the quartz-veins, which extend like white bands across the faces of the rocks, and in which the druses are usually found.   The character of the sound given out when the vein is struck with a hammer indicates whether there is likely to be a cavity, and therefore possibly a druse, at that particular spot.   If there is, the rock is broken open with a pickaxe or by blasting with powder or dynamite and the crystals obtained.

These cavities and the crystals contained in them are not usually of very large size. Drusy cavities of enormous dimensions are, however, met with occasionally, and are known as crystal-caves or vaults.   Several hundredweight of crystals have been found in one such cavity, and single crystals sometimes weigh a hundredweight or more.

A celebrated find of this kind was made in the year 1719 in a crystal-cave on the Zinkenstock, near Grimsel, in the Bernese Oberland.   One crystal found here weighed eight hundredweight, many weighed a hundredweight or more, and altogether 1000 hundredweight of crystals were taken from this gigantic druse.   From a cave in the Vieschthal, between Münster and Laax, in Upper Valais, 1757 crystals, ranging in weight from 50 to 1400 pounds, were obtained.   An occurrence of rock-crystal, only in comparatively small druses, but often mentioned, is in the slightly auriferous quartz-veins of La Gardette, near Bourg d'Oisans, in Dauphiné (Department Isère), in the French Alps.   From this locality comes the group of crystals represented in Plate XVII. ; they always possess peculiar oblique and unsymmetric terminations, which is characteristic, and distinguishes them from crystals from other localities.   At the beginning of the nineteenth century material from here and elsewhere was cut in the lapidary works of Briançon on the Durance, Department Hautes

Alpes, and the water-clear stones cut here were called "Briançon diamonds." The working of rock-crystal at this place has long been abandoned; and, indeed, the Alpine material has now very little industrial significance, being replaced by Brazilian crystals, which are not only purer but also cheaper.

The weathered débris from the higher Alps, which contains rock-crystal detached from the parent rock, is transported to lower levels by glaciers and streams. The crystals are rolled along the beds of streams and rivers, becoming as they travel further down the valleys more and more water-worn, until at last they take the form of perfectly rounded pebbles, which, on account of surface scratches, appear to be cloudy, but which in reality are perfectly transparent inside. Such pebbles, the biggest of which are the size of a nut, are found in the Rhine, having reached this river through the Aar. At many places in Baden they were at one time cut under the name Rhine-quartz (Germ. *Rheinkiesel*) and constituted a by-product of the gold-washing industry. This *Rheinkiesel* was formerly, though incorrectly, considered to be finer and purer than the rock-crystal which had been brought down the Alps by other means. Similar pebbles were found and occasionally utilised in the same way at other places, for example, at Médoc and at Alençon ("Alençon diamonds") in Normandy, at Fleurus in Belgium, and at Cayenne.

There are many extra-Alpine occurrences of rock-crystal, but only a few will be mentioned here. Magnificently clear, though not very large, crystals occur in the cavities of the world-famous statuary marble of Carrara in Italy. Very fine water-clear crystals, developed on all sides and often showing no distinct point of attachment, occur in the cavities of the dark Carpathian sandstone, or in the clay-slates with which it is interbedded, in the Marmaros Comitat, in north-east Hungary, bordering on Galicia. The crystals range in size from that of a pin's head to that of a nut; they are collected at the surface of the ground usually after heavy storms of rain. They have a wide distribution in the district, but Veretzke, in the valley of the Nagyag river, and Bocsko may be mentioned as typical localties. In reference to the region in which they occur these crystals are known as "Marmorosch diamonds." Small rock-crystals are found in crevices in Triassic (Lettenkohle) marl, in the Hessian county of Schaumburg, on the lower Weser. These were known as "Schaumburg diamonds," and were formerly used as gems, only a small proportion, however, being perfectly clear and fit for cutting.

In England fine, transparent rock-crystal is found in quartz-veins in slate at Tintagel and Delabole, in Cornwall, and elsewhere; they are known variously as "Cornish diamonds," "Bristol diamonds," &c.

Although the occurrence of fine rock-crystal in Europe is very abundant, it is far surpassed by that of other parts of the world. A large amount was being obtained from **Madagascar** at the end of the eighteenth century, and a considerable amount still comes from that island. The material found here is specially pure and clear, and often occurs in blocks of some size, the largest measuring as much as 8 metres in circumference. It occurs in special abundance in the form of isolated, partially water-worn blocks on the slopes of the Befoure mountains, where it is collected for the market. Large blocks of perfect quality, and weighing from 50 to 100 pounds, are not at all uncommon, and it is the abundance of excellent material in Madagascar which has caused the depreciation in prices.

Rock-crystal is common in **India** also. It was, and is still, worked there in various ways, but the objects now carved and worked in this material do not bear comparison with those of by-gone times. The industry is still in operation at Vellum, in the Tanjore district of the Madras Presidency, where brilliants, rosettes, spectacle-lenses, &c., are produced.

The material is obtained in the neighbourhood from a conglomerate of Tertiary age, in which it occurs in the form of pebbles. A once famous centre of this industry is Delhi, the bowls, vases, drinking-cups, and other objects carved there being renowned for beauty of design and skill in workmanship. The art is now forgotten, but the old mines at Aurangpur, fifteen miles south of Delhi, whence rough material was obtained, are still to be seen. There are many other localities for rock-crystal in India, but none appear to have any industrial importance.

Rock-crystal is very abundant in America, and specially so in **Brazil**. Not only are large amounts of very fine and clear rock-crystal obtained in this country, but also many of the coloured varieties of quartz (amethyst, citrine, &c.). The rock-crystal is much used for spectacle-lenses and other optical instruments, and for various other purposes. Brazilian rock-crystal ("Brazilian pebble") is easy to obtain, and is very cheap, and has therefore ousted other material from the market. A finished spectacle-lens cut in Brazil from Brazilian material, according to Mr. G. F. Kunz, of New York, fetches less than the cost of cutting a lens in that city. The States in which the mineral is most abundant are Minas Geraes, São Paulo, and Goyaz, especially in the last named in the Serra dos Cristaes, sixty-five miles from Santa Lucia and 200 miles from the town of Goyaz. The crystals here lie about loose on the ground, and some weighing sixty-four pounds have been found in the surface soil. Beside the rock-crystal there is quartz of every colour and quality. For a long time the occurrence gave employment to 200 persons, who in the space of two years collected 7000 tons of material. Later, however, the demand fell off, and finally almost ceased, mining operations becoming at the same time less active.

There are also many localities for rock-crystal in the **United States** of North America. At Chestnut Hill, in the State of North Carolina, are found pure crystals weighing a hundredweight or more; the largest American crystal known was met with there and weighed 131 kilograms (288 pounds). The next largest American crystal weighing 86 kilograms came from Alaska. On Lake George, in New York, and over a wide area in Herkimer County, in the same State, rock-crystals of small size but developed on all sides occur in cavities in the Calciferous sandstone. In lustre, transparency, and purity these crystals rival even those of Carrara, in Italy. They have been collected in large numbers for upwards of half a century, and both cut and rough stones are sold in the neighbourhood, mostly to tourists, under the name "Lake George diamonds" or some similar term. Some specimens enclose large drops of water and others black grains, often of considerable size, of a bituminous substance; in the former case the stones are of greater, and in the latter of less, value than ordinary specimens. Water-clear rock-crystal occurs in abundance in Crystal Mountain and elsewhere within a forty miles radius from Hot Springs, in Arkansas. Waggon-loads of these so-called "Arkansas diamonds," which are found in crevices in red sandstone, are brought by the farmers to Hot Springs and Little Rock, where thousands of dollars' worth are sold to the visitors at the baths. In the Washita river at Hot Springs there are quartz pebbles like those found in the Rhine, and so eagerly are these sought for by tourists that the supply has been artificially increased by grinding together fragments of rock-crystal in rotating barrels. Rock-crystal occurs abundantly also in Canada.

Rock-crystal of fine quality has recently been found at Mokelumne Hill, Calaveras County, California; an account of this occurrence has been given by Mr. G. F. Kunz in his report on precious stones for 1898. The large crystals are found embedded in the gravels and sands of an ancient river channel; they are only slightly water-worn, but are usually much stained on the exterior. One crystal measures 19 by 15 by 14 inches, and another

14 by 14 by 9 inches. From one crystal a perfectly flawless sphere measuring 5½ inches in diameter has been cut; larger balls, with a diameter of 7⅕ inches, are not entirely free from flaws. The rock-crystal of this locality thus rivals in size and transparency that of Japan, Brazil, Madagascar, and the Alps, which have hitherto been almost the only sources of such material.

Under some circumstances rock-crystal may be mistaken for other water-clear precious stones, and being cheaper is sometimes successfully substituted for one or other of these colourless gems. The resemblance to diamond in some of its features is indicated by the number of names given in different parts of the world to this stone in which the word diamond figures as an affix. Thus it is known as "false diamond" or "pseudo-diamond," and, according to the locality in which the crystals occurs, as "Marmorosch diamonds," "Schaumburg diamonds," "Arkansas diamonds," "Bohemian diamonds," "Irish diamonds," "Paphos or Baffa diamonds," "Fleurus diamonds," "Bristol diamonds," "Isle of Wight diamonds," "Quebec diamonds," and so on, and generally as "occidental diamonds." All these terms signify one and the same stone, namely, rock-crystal, and since even the finest specimens are not for a moment comparable either in brilliancy, lustre, or play of colours with diamond, any real confusion seems impossible.

In case of necessity rock-crystal and diamond can be distinguished by the help of the facts that the former is doubly and the latter singly refracting, that the diamond quickly sinks while rock-crystal floats in pure methylene-iodide, and also by the enormous difference in hardness between the two. The specific gravity of rock-crystal serves to distinguish it from all other colourless stones. These, arranged in order of density commencing with the heaviest, are: zircon, sapphire, topaz, spinel, tourmaline, and phenakite. Phenakite, the lightest of these, has a specific gravity of 2·99, so that it is considerably heavier than quartz, which has a density of 2·65 and remains suspended in the lightest test liquid, in which all the other stones sink.

Although rock-crystal is so cheap and abundant glass imitations are often substituted for it, and many of the so-called false diamonds are in reality nothing but glass. Genuine rock-crystal is always considerably harder, and often also lighter, than the glass imitations; the two can be readily distinguished by the help of the polariscope, rock-crystal being doubly, and glass singly refracting.

SMOKY-QUARTZ.

This is a transparent variety of quartz which is brown to almost black in colour. It is often called "smoky topaz," but has no connection whatever with topaz. Smoky-quartz when perfectly transparent is not infrequently cut, and with its deep, rich colour makes a rather effective gem.

The colour ranges from clove-brown to smoke-grey, passing by imperceptible stages to the perfect colourness of rock-crystal, and, on the other hand, through darker and darker shades till we reach specimens which, at any rate, in thick pieces, are almost perfectly black. Such dark smoky-quartz is distinguished as *morion*. Specimens of this stone are not always uniformly coloured, some portions being lighter and others darker. All darkly coloured smoky-quartz is distinctly, though feebly, dichroic, the two dichroscope images being coloured respectively yellowish-brown and clove-brown tinged with violet. The paler the colour of the stone the less the difference in colour between the two images, and the dichroism of very pale stones is scarcely observable at all. A crystal of smoky-quartz is represented in Plate XVIII., Fig. 3a, and a cut-stone of paler colour in Figs. 3b and c, of the same plate.

The colouring of smoky-quartz is due to the presence of a volatile organic substance containing carbon and nitrogen, which can be distilled off as a turbid liquid. The distillation is accompanied by a smell of burning, which is noticeable even when a dark coloured specimen, that is to say, one containing much colouring matter is broken, or when two fragments of the same are vigorously rubbed together. On igniting smoky-quartz, or on merely raising its temperature to 200° C., the organic colouring matter is completely destroyed, and the mineral becomes indistinguishable from rock-crystal. At a low temperature the brown colour becomes yellow like that of citrine, another variety of quartz. Probably not a little of the yellow quartz which comes into the market is none other than " burnt " smoky-quartz.

With the exception of colour, all the characters of smoky-quartz are identical with those of rock-crystal. The similarity in the habit of the crystals, and their mode of occurrence, is specially striking, and we are, therefore, justified in stating that smoky-quartz is simply rock-crystal of a brown colour. This is not always the case, for we shall see later that amethyst, a violet-coloured variety of precious quartz, differs from rock-crystal not only in colour but also in structure.

All that has been said with regard to the crystalline form (Fig. 85) of quartz, and its occurrence in crevices in the gneissic and granitic rocks of the Alps and at other localities, together with the existence of very large drusy cavities containing hundredweights of the finest crystals, applies equally well to smoky-quartz, and need not be repeated.

The most remarkable occurrence of smoky-quartz in large crystals of deep black morion was discovered in August 1868, in a crystal cave near the Tiefen glacier in Canton Uri, **Switzerland.** The cave was in weathered granite, and out of it was collected in a very short time 300 hundredweights of crystals, 200 hundredweights of which were beautifully transparent and suitable for cutting, and the remainder for museum specimens. Among the latter are some of remarkable size, the largest of which are now exhibited in the Berne Museum. Several of these crystals are distinguished by special names: the " Grandfather " is 69 centimetres long, 122 in circumference, and weighs 133½ kilograms. The " King " is rather thinner and less heavy, but longer and better preserved than any ; it is 87 centimetres long, 100 centimetres in circumference, and weighs 127½ kilograms. The two smallest of the half-dozen crystals preserved at Berne are named " Castor " and " Pollux "; they are 72 and 71 centimetres in length and 65 and 62½ kilograms in weight. Each of these crystals was attached to the matrix at one end, but in the case of one large crystal, which has perfectly developed faces at both ends and on all sides, it is impossible to see the point of attachment, although it must originally have grown attached to the matrix just like the others ; this is 82 centimetres long, 71 in circumference, and weighs 67 kilograms. Another crystal found at the same time and place is preserved in the Mineral Department of the British Museum (Natural History) ; it weighs 299 pounds and is just over a yard long.

Compared with this Alpine occurrence of smoky-quartz all others are unimportant. It is met with accompanying topaz, beryl, and specially amethyst, at Mursinka, in the Urals, and with beryl and topaz in the neighbourhood of Nerchinsk, in Transbaikalia. In the form of pebbles it is found with pebbles of rock-crystal in the Rhine ; and in the same way at Alençon, in Normandy, and again in the gem-crystals of Ceylon.

In **Scotland** it is found on Cairngorm, a mountain on the borders of Banffshire and Inverness-shire, and on this account a brown transparent quartz is often referred to in

1a. Amethyst, crystals.   1b. The same, cut.   2. Rock-crystal with enclosures ("Needle-stone").
3a. Smoky-quartz, crystals. 3b, c. The same, cut.   4a, b. Cat's-eye, green and brown cut-
stones. 5. Tiger-eye, polished. 6. Heliotrope, polished. 7. Almandine, cut [compare Pl.
XIV, Fig. 4].

England as *cairngorm*. The search for crystals of smoky-quartz was formerly a very profitable industry in the districts contiguous to the great granite masses in this part of Scotland, but it has now been practically abandoned. The cairngorms were obtained by digging shallow pits and trenches in the decomposed granite and débris which covers most of the flat hill-tops, and also appears in many of the corries. The mineral occurs, together with large crystals of orthoclase and plates of muscovite-mica and sometimes beryl, lining cavities in veins of fine-grained granite which penetrate the coarse granite.

Material suitable for cutting is met with at several localities in the **United States.** Large quantities, associated with amazon-stone, are found in the coarse-grained granite of Pike's Peak, in Colorado, where several thousand dollars' worth of stones are collected and cut every year. The largest crystal found at this locality is over 4 feet long. At Mount Antero, in Colorado, at Magnet Cove, in Arkansas, and in Burke and Alexander Counties, North Carolina, smoky-quartz is obtained in not inconsiderable amount. Pebbles of smoky-quartz, and also of rock-crystal, are not uncommon on the coast at Long Branch, near Cape May, New Jersey, and are cut and bought by visitors as souvenirs. It would be superfluous, even if it were possible, to enumerate all the many localities for smoky-quartz in the United States. It may be mentioned, however, that here also occur crystals of very large size, weighing upwards of a hundredweight, of the most perfect transparency, and constituting some of the finest of gems.

Smoky-quartz is usually cut as a brilliant or table-stone, sometimes also in the step-cut, the form with elongated brilliant facets, or the Maltese cross (Plate XVIII., Figs. 3*b*, *c*). Under the name of cairngorm it is specially admired as a gem in Scotland. Besides being cut as a gem, smoky-quartz, like rock-crystal, is fashioned into a variety of semi-ornamental objects, its strong lustre and rich colour being displayed by such articles with good effect.

There are but few precious stones of a brown colour, and of these smoky-quartz is the most transparent, and also the most abundant. The brown precious stones for which it might conceivably be mistaken are axinite, idocrase, and brown tourmaline; others are of a more yellowish-brown colour, and therefore distinguishable at a glance from smoky-quartz. Each of the three minerals mentioned above is heavier than smoky-quartz, and the specific gravity of each being greater than 3·0 they all sink in liquid No. 3, in which smoky-quartz floats. Moreover, smoky-quartz is only feebly dichroic, while the other three are strongly so. Brown diamond, which may resemble smoky-quartz in colour, is readily distinguished by its strong and characteristic lustre, its single refraction, complete absence of dichroism and high specific gravity, the last named character causing it to sink heavily even in pure methylene iodide.

AMETHYST.

Amethyst, or occidental amethyst as it is called in order to distinguish it from "oriental amethyst," is quartz of a violet colour. The range of colour includes reddish-violet tints of pale or almost colourless shades, and deep, rich tones of pure violet. It is not uncommon for this stone to show patches of different shades of colour or colourless portions side by side with those of a violet colour, these differently coloured portions being sometimes arranged in regularly alternating bands or sectors. In a few rare cases crystals showing a second colour—yellow or green—have been met with.

Generally speaking, amethyst is cloudy: perfectly clear and transparent material is distinguished as precious amethyst; the latter alone is cut as gems, which are estimated according to their transparency and their depth and uniformity of colouring. Pale-coloured and patchy specimens are almost worthless as gems, but may be utilised in the manufacture of small semi-ornamental objects.

The colour of amethyst is very like that of violet corundum, the "oriental amethyst." It compares unfavourably with the latter in one respect, however, since in artificial light it appears of a dingy grey, while under the same conditions the "oriental amethyst" retains its beauty of colour unimpaired.

Amethyst is dichroic, but this feature is not equally prominent in all crystals, being well marked in some and scarcely appreciable in others. Of the two images seen in the dichroscope one is more reddish and the other more bluish in colour, the difference being more or less well marked according to the character of the crystal under examination.

The colour of this stone does not resist high temperatures. When subjected to the action of heat it changes first to a more or less pronounced yellow, gradually assumes a greenish shade, and finally disappears. The latter change takes place at 250° C., and the whole process of decolourisation takes place very rapidly. The change of colour from violet to yellow has a certain practical significance, since thereby the more abundant violet amethyst can be transformed into the rarer yellow citrine. As a matter of fact, many citrines, which are much prized as precious stones, are nothing other than "burnt" amethysts.

The colour of amethyst has been ascribed to the presence of various substances. The pigment is present in an extremely finely divided state and is mechanically intermixed with the colourless quartz substance, but the individual granules are not recognisable even under the highest powers of the microscope. In patchy specimens the colouring matter is irregularly distributed through the substance of the stone. The pigment has been variously supposed to be potassium ferrocyanide, ferric thiocyanide, or some organic substance, but is most commonly considered to be manganese, which is shown by analysis often to be present, though only in extremely small amount. For example, in a deeply coloured Brazilian amethyst only one-hundredth of a per cent. of manganese was present, while in a stone of a paler colour it was completely absent, so that this evidence cannot be taken as conclusive.

The form taken by crystals of amethyst agrees in all essentials with that of rock-crystal. Amethyst crystals, too, very often have the prismatic habit of rock-crystal, especially when they occur in the drusy crevices of gneiss and such like rocks. They usually differ, on the other hand, from rock-crystal in the absence of faces other than those of the prism and the terminal faces of the hexagonal pyramid, being in this respect more like common quartz. Crystals of amethyst with the pyramidal termination often occur so closely crowded together on the matrix as to form a columnar aggregate, the individuals of which have irregularly developed faces owing to overcrowding. Of the six terminal pyramid-faces it frequently happens that only three alternate ones are developed, the other three being very small, or even completely absent, so that the crystals sometimes have the appearance of cubes. Such cube-like amethysts are often met with amongst the material sent in large amount from South America for cutting.

Amethyst crystals are often built of numerous superimposed laminæ, of greater or less thickness, in twin position with respect to each other. This peculiar structure is indicated by a fine banding of alternately lighter and darker colouring, and also by the existence of two sets of delicate striations meeting at an angle on the terminal pyramid-faces (Fig. 85d). Delicate striations corresponding to this lamellar structure are also to be seen on fractured surfaces of amethyst, giving them a kind of rippled (thumb-marked) appearance. In this connection may be mentioned the so-called sceptre-quartz (Fig. 86), a peculiar form sometimes taken by rock-crystal, but much more frequently by amethyst. In sceptre-quartz then, there is a long, slender, usually colourless, transparent, or cloudy prism of quartz, attached to the end of which in parallel position is a thicker quartz crystal, which is usually transparent and of a violet colour.

Crystals of amethyst sometimes attain a considerable size, the largest known being over a foot in length. These very large crystals are rarely quite transparent or uniformly coloured, and are therefore unsuitable for gems; but there is an abundance of crystals which fulfil these conditions, and which are large enough to supply the market with any amount of rough material.

With respect to the mode of occurrence of amethyst, we have already seen that crystals of elongated prismatic habit usually occur, like rock-crystal, on the walls of crevices and joints in granite, gneiss, and other rocks. Crystals in which only the hexagonal pyramid or three-faced cube-like termination is developed, have a different mode of occurrence. These usually line amygdaloidal, that is to say, almond-shaped, cavities in a black igneous rock, to which the name melaphyre is applied. The cavities were formed, in their efforts to escape, by the steam and gases imprisoned in the molten igneous rock, and have remained after the solidification of the rock. As long as the rock preserved its fresh, unaltered condition, these cavities remained empty, but with the weathering and alteration of the rock the

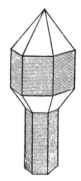

FIG. 86.
Sceptre-quartz.

cavities become wholly or partially filled with secondary minerals. The alteration process is set up by the percolation through the rock of water, which, becoming charged with carbon dioxide and other acids, is enabled to dissolve out many of the constituents of the rock, which are then redeposited in a new form in the cavities. Many and diverse are the secondary minerals formed in this way according to the conditions which prevail in different cases. Amethyst is an important member of this class, and together with it, in the same cavity, agate is frequently found. The secondary minerals thus formed, of course, take the shape of the cavity in which they are deposited, and are therefore referred to as amygdales, the different kinds being distinguished as amethyst amygdales, agate amygdales, &c. The largest may weigh a hundredweight, and the smallest are about the size of a pea. Rocks containing such amygdales are known as amygdaloids.

When the mother-rock becomes completely decomposed these nests of crystals are to be found among the weathered débris, and are often carried away by running water; the crystals they contain are finally deposited in the form of rounded grains and pebbles together with other pebbles in the alluvium of streams and rivers.

At one time the best known amethyst was that which occurs in the cavities of amygdaloidal rocks in the neighbourhood of **Oberstein** on the Nahe, a tributary of the Rhine. A large amount of it used to be cut in the famous lapidary works of Oberstein, but now the local supplies are for all practical purposes completely exhausted. The cutting of amethyst is still carried on at Oberstein on a large scale, but the rough material has now to be imported. A plentiful supply of fine material at low prices can be easily obtained from other parts of the world, so that the exhaustion of the localities in the Nahe valley has not affected the prosperity of the Oberstein lapidary works.

Most of the amethyst used for cutting is obtained from **Brazil** and the neighbouring country of **Uruguay**. The stones, packed in barrels or in skin sacks, reach Europe, and especially Oberstein, in hundreds of tons, and with them are sent other varieties of quartz, such as citrine, colourless rock-crystal, &c.

In the State of Rio Grande do Sul, in southern Brazil, and in Uruguay, amethyst occurs, together with citrine and a large amount of agate, in the amygdaloidal cavities of melaphyre.

Quite recently (about 1900) there has been found in this region an enormous amethyst geode, a portion of which was shown by Herr C. W. Kessler, an agate merchant of Idar, at the Düsseldorf Exhibition of 1902.   It was found by the agate-seekers at an elevation of 600 metres above sea-level in the Serra do Mar, in the State of Rio Grande do Sul, and about ninety miles north of the German settlement of Santa Cruz.   The cavity was only about a metre below the surface in a reddish clay, the weathered product of melaphyre, while the lower portion of it still remains embedded in the solid rock.   It measured 10 metres (33 feet) in length, $5\frac{1}{2}$ in breadth, and 3 in height, and was estimated to weigh thirty-five tons ; about fifteen tons was shipped in ten pieces to Idar.   The whole of the cavity is lined with brilliant crystals of amethyst of a deep bluish-violet colour and averaging about 4 centimetres across.

At a few localities in the State of Minas Geraes, in the northern portion of Brazil, where it is not associated with agate, the mineral has another mode of occurrence as groups of beautiful crystals.   These are found on the Campos dos Cristaes in the neighbourhood of Diamantina, but the finest specimens come from the Ribeirão da Paciencia at Itaberava, near Cattas Altas, south of the town of Ouro Preto (Fig. 67), where they occur under the same conditions as the yellow topaz already described.   In the gem-gravels of the district of Minas Novas are many pebbles of amethyst accompanying the pebbles of white and blue topaz, chrysoberyl, &c., already described, and which, like these, are probably derived from granite and gneiss.

In the **United States** of North America a certain amount of amethyst suitable for cutting is found, none of which, probably, leaves the country.   It is most abundant at Deer Hill, near Staw, in Maine, but comparatively little of this is suitable for cutting.   Good crystals of large size, transparent and finely coloured, are met with in the State of Pennsylvania, namely, in Chester County and other districts, but specially in Providence Township, Delaware County.   Fine specimens have been found in Haywood County, North Carolina.   The amethysts of Rabun County, Georgia, are remarkable in that they frequently contain large fluid enclosures, those in other amethysts being of microscopic size.   The stone is widely distributed in the region of Lake Superior, especially on the Canadian side, Amethyst Harbour being a typical locality ; but most of the material found in this district is unsuitable for cutting.   The amethyst of Nova Scotia is not infrequently used as an ornamental stone, that from the Bay of Fundy and other places being often worked into objects of considerable size.

Another American locality still to be mentioned is Guanaxuato in **Mexico**.   The crystals found here measure as much as a foot in length ; the prism is usually pale in colour, the pyramidal termination alone being of a deep shade, and, moreover, the crystal as a whole is seldom transparent enough for cutting.   Far finer stones than those found at Guanaxuato are frequently found in the ancient Aztec graves, so that there must be other localities in Mexico now unknown.

The amethyst pebbles found in the gem-gravels of **Ceylon**, being the finest known, superior even to Brazilian stones, are much in demand.   They have been derived from the granitic and gneissic rocks of the neighbourhood, and occur with the other precious stones mentioned under ruby, with which they are collected in the manner already described. Amethyst occurs in the same way in a few of the rivers of Burma, also in small amount in India, but in neither country has the occurrence any importance.

The amethyst localities in the **Urals**, on the other hand, are extremely important, especially the neighbourhood of Mursinka in the Alapayev and Reshev mining districts, in the Ekaterinburg division of Government Perm, the village of Mursinka being in latitude

57° 40′ N. and longtitude 30° 37′ E. of Pulkova (the Russian observatory). Here amethyst is found, often just beneath the turf, in the drusy cavities of quartz-veins of no great size running through weathered granite. As already mentioned it accompanies beryl and topaz, which also occur in nests and veins in the granite, though never in the same cavity with amethyst, being always at a much greater depth, so that the collection of these stones is attended with more difficulty. In this district at the present time about 140 pounds of amethyst, 15 pounds of beryl and topaz, and more than 200 pounds of gold-quartz is annually collected.

FIG. 87.   Occurrence of amethyst near Mursinka in the Urals.

The industry is carried on preferably in winter, when it affords employment to 150 or 200 persons, the number of persons employed in the summer not exceeding twenty-five. The mines are the property of the Crown ; there are about seventy-five of them, but only nine are at present worked. According to their position, which is shown in the accompanying map (Fig. 87), they fall into three groups, namely : (1) mines about Mursinka ; (2) the Alabashka mines on the stream of this name ; (3) the mines on the Ambirka stream, also known as the Sarapulskaya mines. The mines east of the rivers Alabashka and Shilovka, especially those near Sisikova and Mursinka, yield amethyst principally, while from those which lie between the villages of Upper and of Lower Alabashka and near Yushakova and Sarapulskaya topaz and beryl are more exclusively obtained, the two last mentioned being localities for red tourmaline (rubellite) also. The precious stones found in this region are for the most part cut in Ekaterinburg, and many remain in the country. A certain proportion, however, find their way into western Europe by way of Nizhniy Novgorod, where great cosmopolitan fairs are held. Generally speaking, Uralian amethysts are pale in colour and patchy, but among them one sometimes meets with specimens of a deep violet colour comparable with the finest of stones from Brazil and Ceylon.

The chief sources for the supply of amethyst are the Urals, Brazil, Uruguay, and Ceylon. Other localities are of but little interest or importance ; the mineral is found, for example, usually in crevices in gneiss, at several places in the Alps, among others in the Zillerthal, Tyrol, a locality which formerly yielded material fit for cutting. Also in veins of metallic ores at Schemnitz in Hungary ; while material suitable for cutting often occurs in Spain with quartz of other colours, Carthagena in province Murcia, and Vich in Catalonia, being mentioned as localities. At the former locality amethyst occurs in water-worn pebbles as it does in Ceylon. Fine crystals have been found in Cornwall, also near Cork and on Achill island, Co. Mayo, translucent crystals up to 8 or 10 inches in length having been found at the last named locality. In the Auvergne, at a spot 40 kilometres from Clermont, amethyst was mined by the Spaniards about 150 years ago, and the mines here have recently been opened up again owing to the increased demand for amethyst: the best material, of a rich purple colour, now obtained at this place fetches 120 to 800 francs per kilogram, according to the size of the rough pieces. Nowhere, however, except in the countries mentioned above, is amethyst mined to any appreciable extent.

Amethyst is cut most frequently as a table-stone or in the step-cut (Plate XVIII., Fig. 1 *b*), the brilliant form being rarely adopted. Stones of a deep, uniform colour are mounted *à jour* without foils, but pale or patchy stones are mounted with a foil of the same colour. Fine large amethysts of a uniform colour now fetch from 10s. to 12s. per carat; they were formerly worth very much more, as can be gathered from the fact that at the beginning of the nineteenth century the celebrated amethyst necklace of Queen Charlotte of England was valued at £2000, while at the present day it would scarcely find a purchaser at £100. The large amount of fine material, discovered during the course of the nineteenth century in South America, is partly responsible for the depreciation in the value of amethyst. Previous to this it was a costly material for superior jewellery, now it is used principally for simpler and cheaper ornaments. Pale coloured or patchy stones are almost valueless, the rough material fetching only a few shillings a pound.

In ancient times amethyst was often used for seal-stones and engraved with various devices, beside being fashioned into larger objects, such, for example, as the bust of Trajan, carried off by Napoleon from Berlin. At the present day amethyst is but little used for such purposes.

On account of the similarity in colour between true amethyst and the far more valuable " oriental amethyst," it is possible to mistake the one for the other, unless it be remembered that the latter is far harder and heavier, and sinks in methylene iodide, while the former floats. True amethyst is distinguished from violet fluor-spar, the so-called " false amethyst," by its double refraction, greater hardness, and lower specific gravity. The double refraction of true amethyst also distinguishes it from violet coloured glass, which from its appearance alone is often not to be distinguished from the genuine stone. Artificially coloured violet quartz is obtained by strongly heating rock-crystal and then immersing it in a solution of some violet coloured substance. The colouring matter penetrates the cracks in the rock-crystal caused by the sudden change of temperature, and, on drying, imparts its colour to the stone. Stones which have been subjected to this treatment are easily recognisable on account of the cracks, and for the same reason they are seldom cut.

CITRINE.

The name citrine is applied to yellow quartz. The crystals of this variety are developed in the same way, exhibit the same two sets of striations meeting at an angle on the pyramid face, and in many specimens the fractured surface has the same rippled, striated character as in amethyst. It is obvious, therefore, that citrine differs from amethyst solely in colour, and even this can scarcely be regarded as a fundamental difference, seeing that amethyst assumes the colour of citrine when exposed to the action of heat. Some, indeed, have gone so far as to assert that yellow quartz seldom or never occurs in nature, and that the greater part of the yellow quartz now in existence is in reality " burnt " amethyst, or possibly " burnt " smoky-quartz, the brown colour of which is, as we have seen, changed to yellow under the action of heat. This assertion, however, is certainly incorrect, for citrine does undoubtedly occur in nature at the localities to be presently mentioned, sometimes in considerable amount.

Citrine is sometimes very pale or almost colourless. Among deeper coloured stones may be seen wine-yellow, honey-yellow, and saffron-yellow specimens, while others have quite a pronounced brown tinge. Stones of a deep brownish-yellow colour are very like topaz (Plate XIII., Fig. 2a), and those of a fine golden-yellow are quite equal in beauty to yellow topaz, and can scarcely be distinguished on mere inspection from the latter stone except by an expert.

This variety of quartz is, in fact, constantly passed off as topaz, with which stone it has nothing in common save colour. It is probably not going too far to state that this stone is never either bought or sold in the trade under its correct mineralogical name, but always under the name of topaz, perhaps with a qualifying prefix such as occidental, Indian, Bohemian, Spanish. Used in this sense then, "Indian topaz" signifies not the saffron-yellow topaz from Ceylon, already mentioned, but saffron-yellow citrine. By "Spanish topaz" is understood citrine of a deep brownish-yellow shade, while the term "golden topaz" is sometimes applied to golden-yellow citrine. The term "false topaz" is also used, but is usually applied to yellow fluor-spar.

It is not difficult to discriminate between citrine and true topaz, for topaz, with a hardness of 8, will scratch citrine. Topaz, moreover, is much heavier than citrine and sinks heavily in pure methylene iodide, in which citrine floats. Finally, while topaz is always rather strongly dichroic, citrine is scarcely dichroic at all.

Citrine is of course only cut as a gem-stone when perfectly clear and transparent, and its value as such depends upon the degree of its transparency, and the richness and purity of its colour. The finest specimens are at least as valuable as correspondingly fine amethysts; and medium material, like amethyst, is sold for a few shillings a pound. The step-cut and the various modifications of the table-stone are the forms usually adopted for citrine, as also for amethyst, topaz, and coloured stones in general.

It was usual formerly to regard citrine as a rare mineral only to be found at a few scattered localities. Goatfell, in the island of Arran, where it occurs attached to the walls of crevices in granite, was one, Bourg d'Oisans, in Dauphiné, here associated with rock-crystal, was a second, while others were mentioned in Hungary and Croatia. It first reached the European markets in quantity in the thirties of the nineteenth century, having been discovered in Brazil and Uruguay, whence it was sent with amethyst to the lapidary works of Oberstein on the Nahe. The mineral occurs most abundantly in Brazil in the States of Minas Geraes and Goyaz, but a large amount of material is also yielded by Rio Grande do Sul, the most southern of the Brazilian States. The principal locality in Uruguay is the neighbourhood of Salto Grande on the Uruguay river. In both of these South American countries citrine is found, together with amethyst and agate, in amygdaloidal cavities in melaphyre. In the neighbourhood of Mursinka, in the Ural Mountains, it is met with in the gem mines together with amethyst, but in much less abundance. A variety of quartz, which when strongly heated assumes a fine yellow colour and which can then be sold as topaz, occurs in Spain at Hinojosa, in the province of Cordova, on the northern slopes of the Sierra Morena. Several hundredweights of this stone is mined annually, but the average quality is poor and it does not sell for more than four or five francs per kilogram. When cut it is bought and sold under the name of "Spanish topaz," but is not very much in favour. A few fine specimens of citrine suitable for cutting have been found in North Carolina, but here, as elsewhere in North America, the mineral occurs in very insignificant quantities.

ROSE-QUARTZ.

Rose-quartz ("Bohemian ruby") is a translucent or semi-transparent, massive quartz with a somewhat greasy lustre and a fine rose-red colour. This colour is not permanent, but quickly disappears on exposure to light or a high temperature. It is probably due to the presence of some organic matter, but has also been ascribed to titanium dioxide, small amounts of which have been found in rose-quartz. Specimens showing paler shades of the same colour merging imperceptibly into milk-white are not uncommon, and contrast well with those of the typical rose-red colour. Stones of a deep shade of this colour are cut with a rounded surface, but are not in much favour and are very low in price. In spite of this, rose-quartz is imitated in glass, so cleverly indeed that it is sometimes only possible to distinguish between the two by the lower specific gravity, greater hardness, and double refraction of the quartz. The mineral is found in large irregular masses in granite in the neighbourhood of Bodenmais in Bavaria, and of Ekaterinburg in the Urals, and in Ceylon, India, Brazil, &c., but must always be classed with the less widely distributed varieties of quartz.

PRASE.

Prase is sometimes referred to by jewellers as "mother-of-emerald" in reference to the fact that it was formerly supposed to be the mother-rock of the emerald. It is a translucent variety of quartz with a somewhat greasy lustre and a leek-green colour. This last named character is due to the presence of innumerable minute fibres and needles of actinolite enclosed in the otherwise colourless and pure mass of quartz. Prase was known to the ancients, and was used in the fashioning of ornamental stones and to represent foliage in mosaics, while as a gem it was frequently engraved. In the latter form it is not uncommon among Roman remains, but the source from whence the Romans obtained their rough material is not now known. There are many more recently discovered localities however; thus crystals and crystalline masses, of the same quality as the material used by the ancients, occur in metalliferous veins with iron-pyrites and zinc-blende at Breitenbrunn between Schwarzenberg and Johanngeorgenstadt in the Saxon Erzgebirge. Also in the Habachthal, in the Salzburg Alps, and at several places in Scotland, Finland, &c. Prase is applied now to the same purposes as in ancient times, but to a very limited extent, and this, combined with its abundance in nature, makes it one of the lowest priced of ornamental stones.

SAPPHIRE-QUARTZ.

Sapphire-quartz (azure-quartz or siderite) is a blue, crystalline quartz, the colour of which is due to the enclosure of a large amount of a blue, fibrous to earthy substance belonging probably to the mineral species crocidolite. It is only faintly translucent, has a slightly greasy lustre, and is not very suitable for cutting, hence it is used to a very small extent and is correspondingly low in price. It occurs in moderately large amount in veins penetrating the gypsum of the Gypsberg at Mooseck, near Golling, in Salzburg.

QUARTZ WITH ENCLOSURES.

We have already seen that quartz frequently encloses other minerals and foreign substances of various kinds. These enclosures may be present singly in comparatively small numbers or in such multitudes as to impart an apparently uniform colour to the quartz substance, as is the case with prase and with sapphire-quartz just described. It is proposed to consider here those cases in which there are present single enclosures of a nature to contrast very markedly with the quartz in which they are embedded. It is obvious that enclosures in translucent or opaque quartz will be seen very indistinctly or not at all, so that it is only the enclosures in very transparent quartz which will engage our attention. On the other hand, the clearness with which enclosures in quartz are seen is not at all affected by the colour of the mineral, objects embedded in amethyst being quite as distinctly seen as those in rock-crystal. These two varieties of quartz are those which most commonly contain enclosures, the different kinds of which will be described below in some detail.

Hair-stone and **Needle-stone.**—These names are given to quartz with enclosures of isolated, needle-like or hair-like crystals of various substances, like that represented in Plate XVIII., Fig. 2, which encloses green needles of actinolite. In other cases the enclosures may be white fibres of asbestos, long, thin crystals of rutile ranging in colour from yellow to red and somewhat resembling straw in appearance, and so on. Quartz containing enclosures of this description is distinguished as needle-stone or as hair-stone according as the enclosed crystals approach more to the thickness and straightness of a needle, or to the fineness and sinuosity of a hair. Enclosures of rutile of a reddish-brown to yellow colour, are referred to as "Venus's hair," and the stone as a whole as "Venus's hair-stone." Enclosures of green hornblende, actinolite, or asbestos are often called "Thetis's hair." The fibres may be straight, bent, crumpled, or wound into a ball. The appearance of green fibres, probably of asbestos, embedded in quartz often resembles that of a piece of moss, and the quartz containing such an enclosure is known as *moss-stone;* such moss-like enclosures are also frequent in agate (moss-agate), to be considered further on.

Enclosures of various kinds are not at all uncommon in the rock-crystal from the Alps and other localities. Some specimens of rock-crystal from Madagascar enclose long grey crystals of manganite with a bright metallic lustre. From the Calumet Hill quarry, near Cumberland, in Rhode Island, U.S.A., is obtained a translucent, milk-white quartz containing numerous needles of black hornblende; a large amount of this material was formerly exported for cutting to Idar and Oberstein on the Nahe, but since 1883 the supplies have ceased. Similar material is obtained in Japan and Madagascar.

FIG. 88. Flèches d'amour from Wolf's Island, Lake Onega, Russia.

In the pale amethyst found in the amygdaloidal cavities of rocks or loose in the soil of Wolf's Island, in Lake Onega, north-east of St. Petersburg, there are long brown crystals of the mineral göthite ("needle-iron-ore") (Fig. 88); and there are many other similar occurrences. These stones are cut in St. Petersburg and Moscow under the name of "Cupid's darts" (*flèches d'amour*). The same name is used for other stones of similar appearance, such, for example, as the beautiful specimens which occur in North Carolina, U.S.A. Like all mineral objects of the kind they are provided with a slightly convex polished surface, and often cut with a heart-shaped outline. Whether such objects are cut and polished or not, depends upon whether they possess a sufficiently pretty or bizarre appearance, and they are sold more as curiosities than as ordinary precious or ornamental stones with a definite market value. Fine examples of the kind have sold for 50s. or more, but much depends upon the purchaser.

Quartz containing Fluid Enclosures.—As already mentioned, rock-crystal frequently encloses cavities which contain fluid of some kind and a bubble of gas, the movement of which follows every movement of the stone. Large inclusions of this kind are not common, but rock-crystal containing specially fine ones is met with in Madagascar, in the Alps, and elsewhere. The rock-crystal of Herkimer County, New York, and of Hot Springs, Arkansas, deserves special mention on this account, while the amethyst of Rabun County, Georgia, is frequently cut for the purpose of displaying its large fluid enclosures. Generally speaking, however, quartz which has nothing to recommend it but its fluid enclosures is cut even more rarely than is hair-stone or needle-stone, and is regarded more definitely as a curious natural object.

Gold-quartz.—This is transparent or highly translucent quartz enclosing veins or grains of native gold. In San Francisco and a few other large towns of western America it is often cut in the form of plates for brooches, or utilised for stick-handles, cuff-links, paper-weights, and other small objects of more or less utility. Some of the gold-mines of California, Oregon, Idaho, and Montana have furnished very beautiful specimens. The value of a stone depends upon the amount of gold it contains, which is estimated by the help of the specific gravity, and also upon the beauty of the specimen. A ring-stone is worth from two to upwards of ten dollars, according to its quality.

Gold-quartz is now much in favour as an ornament, as is testified by the fact that in some years from 40,000 to 50,000 dollars' worth of rough material suitable for cutting has been sold in this region; a single cutting works at Oakland, California, has used annually 10,000 dollars' worth of rough material, and a large firm of jewellers in San Francisco has sold cut stones to the value of 15,000 dollars in the same period. The stones need careful sorting out, and as they are very fragile and difficult to work, only about half of the material destined to be cut actually reaches the market.

White and cloudy gold-quartz is more common than the transparent variety, and recently perfectly black material has been met with. White gold-quartz is artificially coloured rose-red by immersing it in a solution of carmine. Attempts have been made to manufacture the substance by fusing together gold and quartz in an electric furnace, not, however, with very favourable results.

The gold-quartz of Australia, South Africa, and most of the auriferous regions, is just as suitable for cutting as is the Californian, but in none of these lands is it worn to the extent that it is in America. The auriferous quartz of La Gardette, near Bourg d'Oisans, in Dauphiné, which forms the matrix of the beautiful rock-crystals represented in Plate XVII., used to be cut as an ornamental stone. About 200 pounds of gold-quartz is obtained every year from mines in the neighbourhood of Mursinka in the Urals.

Rainbow-quartz (Iris).—This is the name given to specimens of rock-crystal which show brilliant iridescent or rainbow-colours over more or less large surfaces. The colour has no connection with the quartz substance, but is due to purely physical causes connected with the interference of light. The phenomenon is only shown by specimens of rock-crystal which are penetrated by numbers of fine irregular cracks. These cracks contain films of air, and to their presence is due the colours of rainbow-quartz, colours which are of exactly the same nature and arise in the same way as the brilliant rainbow tints of soap-bubbles. Specimens of iris are cut with a slightly convex surface, which should be as closely parallel as possible to the surface which displays the rainbow colours, this being not plane but more or less irregular and curved, corresponding to the conchoidal fracture of quartz. Rainbow-quartz is worth more than rock-crystal, and specimens which show a central portion with a play of colours surrounded by a colourless border have a considerable value. In most cases the iridescence is confined to certain portions of the mass of rock-crystal, and these must be carefully sawn out in order to be cut for ornamental stones. Large crystals are occasionally iridescent throughout their whole mass and can be used in the fashioning of articles of large size, such, for example, as the candelabra in the Vatican collection, which, however, may possibly be made up of several portions.

More or less fine specimens of rainbow-quartz are found occasionally at all the localities at which ordinary rock-crystal occurs. Iridescence can be produced in the latter by striking it with a hammer or by immersing it in cold water after it has been strongly heated, the object in both cases being to develop cracks in its substance. Specimens are, of course, often broken by subjection to this treatment, but this is of little consequence considering the abundance of the mineral. Many other transparent minerals display iridescent colours, and are cut for ornamental stones, all of which are known by the same name of "iris." This term is also applied to cut rock-crystal and also to paste, made to imitate an iridescent stone by the use of vari-coloured foils, and much used in the cheapest of jewellery.

CAT'S-EYE.

The term cat's-eye (quartz-cat's-eye, occidental cat's-eye, schiller quartz) is applied to massive quartz from the surface of which, especially when cut in a rounded form, there is reflected a wave of milky light. The appearance is exactly the same as that of cymophane, a variety of chrysoberyl, also known as cat's-eye, but distinguished from quartz-cat's-eye by the prefix oriental. Unfortunately the distinction between occidental and oriental cat's-eye is not always made, an omission which leads to much confusion, especially in statements respecting the occurrences of these stones. They differ very markedly in almost every character; thus cymophane or oriental cat's-eye is far more brilliant and beautiful and much less common than is quartz-cat's-eye; and the band of chatoyant light is more clearly defined in the former than in the latter. In correspondence with these differences is the fact that cymophane is a much more valuable stone than is occidental cat's eye. The two stones may be easily distinguished by their difference in hardness, chrysoberyl being harder than topaz, and therefore much harder than quartz, and in specific gravity. Chrysoberyl has a specific gravity of 3·7 and therefore sinks heavily in methylene iodide, while quartz with a specific gravity of 2·65 floats in that liquid.

Quartz showing the optical effect known as chatoyancy occurs in compact masses, which are not, however, aggregates of single grains, but of uniform crystalline structure throughout. It has a somewhat greasy lustre, is never transparent, but always more or less translucent. The colour is sometimes white, but more frequently olive-green to dark leek-green, these paler or darker shades of green always containing grey tones. The mineral also occurs of a pronounced brown or yellow colour and red tinged with various shades of brown and yellow. Blue stones occur as rarities. Green and yellowish-brown stones cut *en cabochon* are represented in Plate XVIII., Figs. 4a and b.

The chatoyancy of quartz-cat's-eye is due to the presence of large numbers of fibres of asbestos, which are embedded in perfectly parallel directions in its substance and which in some specimens can be distinctly seen with the aid of a simple lens. Specimens of quartz are frequently met with in which these fibres have been destroyed by weathering, their place being taken by fine, hollow canals, each canal corresponding to a single fibre of asbestos. The whole mass of quartz has in this case therefore a tubular structure, but the optical effect is the same as if the fibres were present.

The chatoyancy of quartz-cat's-eye is displayed to the best advantage when the stone is cut *en cabochon*, with a decidedly convex upper surface, and with the flat base parallel to the direction of the enclosed fibres. The rounded surface is then covered by a band of light of greater or less breadth in a direction perpendicular to that of the fibres, the other portions of the surface showing no chatoyancy. As the stone is turned about the band of light travels across its surface, finally disappearing at the edge of the stone as the light reaches a certain incidence.

The chatoyant band has a lustrous, silky sheen of a yellowish- or bluish-white colour, which has been compared with the shining eye of a cat. The stone is usually cut with a rather elongated oval outline, like that of a coffee-bean (Plate XVIII., Figs. 4a and b), in such a way that the band of light is coincident with its greatest diameter, thus producing the most favourable effect. The cats'-eyes of finest quality are those in which the chatoyant band is of uniform width, not too broad and very sharply defined. Inferior stones are those in which the band is interrupted, too wide, or possessed of ill-defined margins, so that it does not stand out in sharp contrast with the surrounding portions. Specimens in which the band is replaced by a patch of light are also considered to be of inferior quality. The stones most highly esteemed in Europe at the present time are those of a reddish-brown colour and with a delicate bluish-white sheen. They are worth as much as 50s., though at that price they must be very perfect and of some size. Generally speaking, quartz-cat's-eye, especially inferior material, is worth very little, while oriental cat's-eye, even the poorer qualities, always fetches a high price.

The finest quartz-cat's-eye is found in **India** and Ceylon. In this quarter of the world the stone is much admired, especially by the Malays, much more so than in Europe, where its popularity depends upon the vagaries of fashion. The reddish-brown stones are usually stated to come from the mainland of India, and the green and grey specimens from Ceylon, but this distribution may not always be quite constant.

Cat's-eye from India is supposed to come mainly from the Malabar coast, in the south-east, and Quilon and Cochin are mentioned as localities, but these statements are not indisputable, and the mode of occurrence is altogether unknown. Since most of the material reaches Europe in the cut condition it is impossible to decide whether the rough material is found *in situ* or in loose pebbles. At Ratanpur, in the district of Rajpipla, N.N.E. of Bombay, the stone occurs, together with agate, in the form of pebbles, which are undoubtedly derived from the basaltic rocks—the Deccan traps—of the region. Other localities are given in the vicinity of Madras, and in the valley of the Lower Kistna in the neighbourhood of the Palanatha mountains, north-east of Guntur; also in Burma a few stones are met with. Generally speaking the occurrence of cat's-eye in the mainland of India is insignificant, and individual stones never exceed two ounces in weight.

While on the mainland of India quartz-cat's-eye is scarce and oriental cat's-eye, as far as is known at present, is absent, in the island of **Ceylon** both occur in considerable amount. Quartz-cat's-eye occurs here in grains or pebbles, rarely larger than a hazel-nut, in the gem-gravels of Saffragam and Matura, which have been derived from the weathering of granitic rocks.   Most of the stones are green in colour, but there are also brownish-red and yellow cat's-eyes.   Like those found in India, they are cut *en cabochon* before being placed on the market.   A large number are sent to Europe, but many also are kept in the country, as cat's-eye is a favourite ring-stone both in India and Ceylon.   The pure olive-green cat's-eye with a narrow, sharply defined band of light is most highly esteemed by the Cingalese, who are extremely proud of the occurrence of cat's-eye in their island and firmly believe that it is found nowhere else.   This is of course an unfounded belief, for beside localities already mentioned there are several places in Europe where it occurs, though only in inferior quality.

In **Europe** cat's-eye of a pale green colour, but scarcely suitable for cutting, is found with asbestos in small brecciated veins in serpentine at Treseburg in the Harz mountains. Stones of rather better quality occur in the diabase of Hof and other places in the Fichtelgebirge in Bavaria; they are often cut but are much inferior to Indian stones. Cat's-eye of a quality suitable for cutting is not found in Hungary, in spite of the fact that this gem is sometimes referred to by jewellers as " Hungarian cat's-eye."

In Europe cat's-eye is worn principally in rings, pins, brooches, &c., the small size of the finest Indian and Ceylonese stones, indeed, precluding the possibility of any other application.   Larger objects cut from this mineral are rare; as an example may be mentioned a bowl of yellowish-brown cat's-eye in the Vienna treasury measuring 5 inches in length; the block of rough material from which this was cut must have been of considerable size.

A stone very similar in appearance to cat's-eye can be obtained by treating tiger-eye with hydrochloric acid.   The colouring matter is dissolved out by this treatment, and the greyish material which remains shows when cut the chatoyancy of cat's-eye.   Together with the brown cats'-eyes of Ceylon there are sometimes found specimens of satin-spar, a variety of calcite, which show a reflection of milky light very like that of true cat's-eye. This is much softer, however, and in contact with hydrochloric acid it effervesces, while true cat's-eye does not.

TIGER-EYE.

Tiger-eye is a variety of quartz with a finely fibrous structure.   It ranges in colour from yellow to brown, and when cut and polished in the direction of the fibres exhibits a magnificent golden lustre.   A polished piece of tiger-eye is represented in Plate XVIII., Fig. 5.

The mineral occurs in the form of thin plates or slabs, which are bounded by parallel surfaces, and are rarely more than a few centimetres in thickness.   The fibres are arranged parallel with respect to each other and perpendicular to the surface of the plate; they are not always perfectly straight; they may be curved, or each may have a sharp bend at a certain place.

Even on an ordinary fractured surface the silky lustre of the stone is very apparent, and this may be considerably increased by cutting and polishing.   A polished surface turned towards the light usually exhibits a series of magnificently lustrous yellow bands, arranged parallel to the surfaces of the original plate.   These lustrous yellow bands alternate with dull brown bands, which show little or no silky lustre.   A slight change in the position of the stone results in a reversal of these conditions, the dark bands becoming lustrous and the silky yellow bands dark.   Every movement of the stone, therefore, is attended by alternations of brightness and dulness in the bands.   This constant alternation in the appearance of the bands is due to the bends in the constituent fibres of the stone, and is one of its most characteristic features. The chief beauty of ornaments of tiger-eye, in point of fact, depends upon the aspect of the stone changing with every movement of the wearer.

In association with tiger-eye there often occurs another stone, which agrees with the former in every respect save that of colour. Thus, it has a finely fibrous structure, a silky lustre, and the same banded appearance of polished surfaces. The physical characters including the hardness are all the same, but the colour instead of being yellow is dark indigo-blue. This blue mineral is also cut as a gem and is known by the name of **hawk's-eye**. A detailed mineralogical examination demonstrates the fact that it is a colourless transparent quartz, embedded in which are innumerable fine blue fibres, all arranged parallel to each other and perpendicular to the surface of the plate. These fibres consist of the blue asbestos-like mineral crocidolite, a member of the amphibole group, and chemically a silicate of iron and sodium. The colour of sapphire-quartz is due to inclusions of the same mineral, but in this case the fibres are not parallel but arranged quite irregularly.

In their structure and mode of origin tiger-eye and hawk's-eye are very closely connected as will presently be seen. An examination of a piece of hawk's-eye often results in the observation that the stone is not of one uniform blue colour, but that portions of it are yellow. These blue and yellow portions may be present in equal proportions, or the blue may be present in larger proportion than the yellow, or the opposite conditions may prevail. Now these facts clearly indicate that the yellow substance, which in every respect is identical with tiger-eye, has been formed by the alteration of the blue hawk's-eye. Moreover, it appears that it is the crocidolite which has undergone this alteration, its constituents, with the exception of silica and iron, having been dissolved and carried away. The silica which remains behind retains the fibrous form of the original mineral, but assumes a yellow colour owing to the deposition between the fibres of a small amount of hydrated oxide of iron, this also being an alteration product of crocidolite. When in any specimen of hawk's-eye the alteration process has just begun, there will be little yellow patches scattered here and there, which will increase in extent as the alteration proceeds, until finally the blue hawk's-eye becomes wholly converted into yellow tiger-eye, the fibrous structure of the original stone remaining, however, unchanged.

Beside stones which show every stage of transition between hawk's-eye and tiger-eye, there are others which are intermediate in character between hawk's-eye and crocidolite, and tiger-eye and crocidolite. Like hawk's-eye and tiger-eye, crocidolite occurs in parallel-sided plates or slabs, with its asbestos-like fibres perpendicular to the surfaces of the plate. In the fresh condition this asbestiform mineral is of a blue colour, but when altered it is yellow, owing to the oxidation and hydration of the ferrous iron it contains to hydrated ferric oxide. This yellow alteration product of crocidolite, consisting of a mechanical mixture of silica and hydrated iron oxide, has been given the name of "griqualandite." By the infiltration of silica between the fibres of crocidolite tiger-eye and hawk's-eye are formed, so that it is possible to regard these minerals as silicified crocidolite or as pseudomorphs of quartz after crocidolite. The quartz assumes the structure of the original mineral, the fibres of which remain embedded in it. If these remaining fibres are fresh and unaltered, the resulting mineral is blue hawk's-eye; if, on the other hand, they consist of the yellow alteration product, it is yellow tiger-eye. It is also possible, however, that the alteration of the crocidolite, which is accompanied by the change in colour from blue to yellow, takes place in part at least after, instead of before, the silicification of the asbestiform mineral. Because of the relation which exists between crocidolite and tiger-eye the latter is frequently referred to in the trade as crocidolite.

Like the Cape diamond, the minerals now under consideration are found in Griqualand West, not at the same localities but in the neighbourhood of Griquatown, to the west of Kimberley, the centre of the diamond mining area. In former times asbestiform crocidolite and limonite (brown iron-ore) were stated to occur in association with tiger-eye at Lakatoo on the Orange River, and at Tulbagh, the material from the latter locality, according to earlier accounts, being famed for its beauty.

According to Professor E. Cohen, those occurrences of the minerals which are important from an industrial point of view are situated in the mountain range north of the Orange River which, a little west of Griquatown, extends first in a north to south, and then in a north-east to south-west, direction. The continuation of this range on the other side of the Orange River is formed by the Doorn Bergen. On the large official map of Cape Colony of 1876 this range is marked as the Asbestos mountains; but in ordinary maps the name is applied to a much shorter range, lying a little further to the east, and on these the former range is marked as the Lange Bergen.

Tiger-eye occurs at many places in this range, among others in the neighbourhood of Griquatown. The plates are embedded in a finely grained quartz-rock of a reddish-brown, coffee-brown, or ochre-yellow colour. The mountains, which do not stand very high above the plateau, are composed mainly of this rock, which is often very thinly bedded, and may be best described as a jasper-schist. The mineral is quarried here and sent in large quantities to Europe, especially to Oberstein on the Nahe and the neighbouring town of Idar, to be cut.

Tiger-eye was once a great rarity in Europe; not more than a quarter of a century ago it cost upwards of 25s. per carat. Now, owing to the underselling of two rival traders, the stone has been placed on the market in such large quantities that the price has fallen to little more than 1s. a pound.

All the tiger-eye and hawk's-eye which comes into the market is obtained from the Asbestos mountains, but the mineral is not by any means confined wholly to this district, and appears to have a wide distribution in South Africa. The traveller Mauch has found it, for example, much further to the east, on the upper Marico, a tributary of the Orange River. Outside South Africa, however, neither tiger-eye nor hawk's eye has hitherto been found.

While these stones were rare and costly they were cut with a flat or convex polished surface, and were used as gems for rings, brooches, and such like. Later on, when the price had fallen considerably, they began to be used for the manufacture of small articles of utility or ornament, such as the handles of umbrellas, and at the present time figures in bas relief, and intaglios are sometimes cut from fine specimens. Tiger-eye, indeed, has now a considerable application in the manufacture of ornamental and semi-ornamental objects, but hawk's eye, being less abundant, is much less extensively used. In cutting either of these stones care must be taken that the cut and polished surface is as nearly as possible parallel to the fibres; a slight deviation from this rule has a very prejudicial effect on the appearance of the stone.

It has been mentioned above that tiger-eye, after treatment with hydrochloric acid, assumes an appearance similar to that of grey cat's-eye; this is due to the fact that the hydrated iron oxide is extracted, and the fibrous silica left behind. The names tiger-eye and hawk's-eye have reference to the fact that these stones differ from cat's-eye in colour, but when cut *en cabochon* possess exactly the same chatoyant appearance.

B. COMPACT QUARTZ.

HORNSTONE.

Hornstone is a very fine-grained to perfectly compact quartz, consisting of an aggregate of microscopically small grains of the mineral.   The sharp edges of broken fragments are slightly translucent, and the stone is further characterised by its splintery fracture.   These two characters serve to distinguish hornstone from jasper, the latter having a smooth fracture, and being perfectly opaque, even in the thinnest of splinters.   Hornstone is usually of a dingy grey, brown, or yellow colour, so that it resembles horn in colour as well as in being slightly translucent, hence its name, which is an old mining term and not used by lapidaries at all.   As used by mineralogists, the term includes silicified wood and chrysoprase, the two varieties of hornstone which are cut as ornamental stones, as well as several other stones which are not used for this purpose, and which, therefore, need not be mentioned here.

Most hornstones, such as occur abundantly in many metalliferous veins and as nodules in limestone, clay, &c., do not possess the characters necessary for gems, but there are one or two varieties which are more attractive in colour, and which are therefore sometimes cut. One of these, known as chrysoprase, is green in colour ; and another, wood-stone, shows the structure of wood, and is in fact petrified wood.   The surface of wood-stone is sometimes prettily marked, and the substance is often fashioned into small ornamental objects of various kinds.   It is similar in many respects to wood-opal, already described, but differs from it in the fact that the petrifying material is quartz instead of opal.

Wood-stone (fossilised or silicified wood).—This stone has been formed by the impregnation with quartz of the woody substance of plants of former geological ages, and its gradual replacement by the same mineral.   The quartz, thus deposited, possesses characters which, on the whole, resemble most nearly those of hornstone.   Not only is the structure of the wood well preserved, but the identity of the original object can be easily recognised by reason of the perfect preservation of the characteristic external form of its trunk and branches.   When the material is cut, either longitudinally or transversely, and polished, the woody structure becomes still more apparent.   A longitudinal section along the axis of the trunk or branch displays the cells and vessels, alternating bundles of which are frequently coloured.   Transverse sections show these cells and vessels in section, and so perfectly are details of structure preserved that when thin sections are examined under the microscope it is often possible even to determine the nature of the original plant ; many species of fossil palms, pines, &c. have, indeed, been so determined.

In wood-stone the walls of the vessels are usually of a dusky brown colour, while the material which fills up the cavities of the vessels and the spaces between neighbouring bundles is usually much paler in colour.   This only serves to show up still more clearly the woody structure, which, with the high lustre acquired after polishing, renders wood-stone very effective for ornamental purposes.   The markings of a cross-section often recall the speckled plumage of the starling, and such specimens have been referred to as starling-stone. The material is occasionally cut for mounting as a gem, but more frequently, though now less than formerly, it is fashioned into small semi-ornamental objects.   Wood-stone is the material which the ancient Babylonians used for some of their cylinder-seals.

The rough material is widely distributed, and the value of worked articles is little higher than the cost of the labour employed in their manufacture.   In Germany wood-stone is found principally in the Kyffhäuser mountains, the petrified trees being enclosed in sandstones and conglomerates of Permian (Rothliegende) age. Other localities for petrified wood are extremely numerous, but need not be enumerated here; it may, however, be mentioned that silicified wood, often in the form of gigantic trees, occurs in great abundance in the Western States of North America, for example, in Colorado, California, and Arizona, the petrified forest known as Chalcedony Park being situated in the last named State. The material is often cut in these States, more frequently as an ornamental stone for table-tops, pedestals, &c., than as a gem.

Under the mineralogical term beekite are included silicified corals, the petrifying material of which is quartz of much the same character as hornstone. Material in which the white coral is thrown up against a fine flesh-red background is at present cut under the name of "coral-agate"; according to the Oberstein lapidaries the rough material is obtained from the neighbourhood of Aden, Arabia, but similar material is also to be obtained elsewhere.

Chrysoprase.—Chrysoprase is a very fine-grained, moderately translucent hornstone of a beautiful apple-green colour. It possesses all the usual characters of hornstone, including the rough splintery fracture. The colour, which retains all its beauty in artificial illumination, is never very deep, and the palest shades are almost colourless.

The colour of chrysoprase, which can be seen on turning to the representation of a cut stone in Fig. 8 of Plate XX., is due to the presence of about 1 per cent. of nickel. This element is probably present in the form of a hydrated silicate, which, when heated, loses water and becomes decolourised, since the stone itself, when exposed to the action of heat becomes paler and paler, and finally quite white. The temperature necessary to produce this change is not very high, and a seal of chrysoprase, if frequently used, will gradually lose its colour. The same thing happens, moreover, when the stone is exposed to the direct rays of the sun, the decolourisation in the latter case being due not to the action of heat but to that of light.

That the decolourisation of chrysoprase is due to loss of water is demonstrated by the fact that the colour is restored by burying the stone in moist earth or cotton-wool. The colour of a bleached chrysoprase can be restored, or that of a pale stone improved, by immersion in a solution of nickel sulphate. It is even possible to produce chrysoprase artificially by immersing chalcedony for some time in a green solution of a nickel salt. This is sucked up into the pores of the chalcedony, and imparts to it the fine apple-green colour of true chrysoprase. It is sometimes almost impossible to distinguish these artificially coloured stones from true chrysoprase, and a great many are sold as genuine stones. The deception in such cases is not very serious, since artificially coloured chalcedony agrees in almost all its characters with natural chrysoprase, and, indeed, possesses some advantages over the latter, for its colour is usually finer and more uniform, and it is unaffected by exposure to light and heat.

Natural chrysoprase is rather difficult to work, being very liable, on account of its brittleness, to crack and splinter at the edges. Moreover, it must not be allowed to become over-heated during grinding since this has a prejudicial effect on the colour. A stone which has been over-heated not only loses its bright apple-green colour but also, to a great extent, its translucency. If reasonable care be taken in the process of grinding, the colour is retained unaltered, and after polishing the stone acquires a very fine lustre. Chrysoprase is usually cut with a convex or plane surface, which is frequently bordered with one or two series of facets (Plate XX., Fig. 8). It is suitable for ring-stones, pin-stones, &c., but not for seals and signet-rings, because of its tendency to be decolourised by heat. It was at one time much more highly esteemed than it is now; a fine stone of a bright green colour and considerable translucency was once worth upwards of £5, while now it would fetch scarcely half that sum, and stones of inferior quality are of course worth still less. Chrysoprase, however, is the most valuable of those compact varieties of quartz which are used as gems, and generally speaking is one of the most highly esteemed of the so-called semi-precious stones.

This beautiful mineral is used also as a decorative and ornamental material for furniture, mosaics, &c. For example, two tables inlaid with chrysoprase were ordered by Frederick the Great for the Sans Souci palace at Potsdam, and the same substance figures in the beautiful mosaic of the walls of the fourteenth-century Wenzel Chapel in the Hradschin at Prague.

Chrysoprase occurs in thin plates and veins, sometimes of considerable size, which are usually embedded in serpentine, of which it is a weathered product, and from which it derives its nickelous colouring constituent. Large pieces are seldom uniformly coloured; portions of darker and finer colour merge gradually into others which are pale or almost white, or into the yellow or brown common hornstone, which must be removed before the better portions are cut. Masses are frequently met with in which the hornstone passes in places into other varieties of compact quartz, such as chalcedony, and into opal. The latter mineral has been formed at the same time and in the same manner as chrysoprase, and is sometimes coloured green like the prase-opal already mentioned.

The most important localities for chrysoprase are in Silesia, where it occurs at various places in the neighbourhood of Frankenstein, to the south of Breslau. At Kosemütz chrysoprase of a deep, and sometimes also of a pale, colour occurs with chalcedony, opal, asbestos, and other minerals in veins in serpentine. Similar occurrences exist at Baumgarten and Grochau, while at Gläsendorf, Protzan, and Schrebsdorf the mineral lies in a yellowish-brown clayey earth, which overlies the serpentine and is a product of its decomposition. The chrysoprase frequently occurs so close to the surface that it is washed out by heavy rains and collected by peasants. Specimens of moderately large size can be obtained at Frankenstein, but they contain a good deal of impure and light-coloured material. The stones of a bright green colour are usually rare; the finest come from Gläsendorf.

According to an early account (1805) there exists in this district a vein of chrysoprase, three (German) miles in length, traversing the serpentine and associated rocks. This was accidentally discovered in 1740 by a Prussian officer at the northern end of the vein by the windmill of Kosemütz. Frederick the Great interested himself in this Silesian stone, and utilised it in the decoration of the Sans Souci palace. The occurrence was probably only rediscovered by the Prussian officer, for the chrysoprase in the Wenzel Chapel at Prague no doubt came from Silesia, and therefore must have been known in the fourteenth century. At the time of the rediscovery of this fine green stone the name chrysoprase was bestowed on it, although the name had been given by the ancients to an entirely different mineral.

There are no other European localities of any importance. Dark apple-green stones come from Wintergasse, in the Stubachthal, in Salzburg; and Ruda, in Transylvania, is perhaps another locality, but at both the mineral occurs only sparingly.

A certain amount of chrysoprase also occurs at a few places outside Europe. Very fine stones come from India, but exactly where they are found does not seem to be known. The mineral is also found in the nickel-ochre mine at Revdinsk, east of Ekaterinburg in the Urals, and at various places in North America. The most important of the latter is the nickel mine on Nickel Mount, near Riddle, in Douglas County, Oregon, where the mineral is found in veins of an inch in thickness in the nickel ores which occur there in serpentine. It is of a dark apple-green colour, and fine plates measuring some square inches in area can easily be obtained.

JASPER.

Jasper is a very impure variety of massive quartz, which is distinguished from hornstone by its large even conchoidal fracture, the dull lustre of the fractured surface, and by its perfect opacity and deep colour. There is no sharp distinction, however, between jasper and hornstone, nor is jasper definitely marked off from other impure varieties of massive quartz, such, for example, as ferruginous quartz (*Eisenkiesel*). Each of the compact varieties of quartz consists of an aggregate of microscopically small quartz grains; the superficial characters of each depend upon the precise nature and amount of the impurities present. There are thus no hard and fast distinctions between these varieties; one specimen will approach more nearly to the character of typical jasper perhaps, and another to typical hornstone, while one end of a third specimen will show the characters of one variety and the other end of another variety, the middle portion being intermediate between the two. In the same way, there is no sharp line of demarcation between jasper and chalcedony, the next variety of quartz to be considered, and there is every possible gradation between typical jasper and typical chalcedony, so that it is sometimes difficult to decide whether a particular specimen should be classed as one or the other. By lapidaries a stone which is perfectly opaque in the sharpest of splinters is referred to as jasper, and one which is slightly translucent as chalcedony. Mineralogically there is no essential difference between chalcedony on the one hand and jasper and hornstone on the other, as we shall see later.

It has been stated already that jasper is a very impure variety of quartz, containing as much as 20 per cent. of foreign matter or even more. This consists for the most part of clay and iron oxide, these substances in a more or less finely divided condition being disseminated throughout the quartz substance. Organic matter of various kinds has also been observed. It is the presence of such impurities in large amount which conditions the characters of typical jasper, namely, opacity, a large-conchoidal smooth fracture, a dull fractured surface, and a deep colour. A reduction in the amount of impurity present is attended by a lighter colour, a more uneven and splintery fracture, and some degree of translucency in the stone, which thus becomes more akin to hornstone.

The uses to which jasper is applied depend mainly upon its colour, which, in its turn, depends upon the amount of iron present. A stone which contains but little iron is practically colourless, but shows the other characters of jasper owing to the presence of clay. A white jasper of this description having the appearance of ivory is stated to occur as a great rarity in the Levant and to furnish beautiful gems. The colouring of coloured stones is seldom quite uniform, the different colours or shades of colour exhibited by the same specimen may be in irregular streaks and patches or arranged regularly in parallel or concentric alternating bands. Some stones are traversed by straight crevices and fissures filled with quartz of another colour and sometimes of quite different character.

The colours most commonly seen in jasper are brown, yellow, and red, green is fairly common, but blue and black more rare. Several colour-varieties of jasper are recognised some of which are distinguished by special names and will be dealt with in detail later on.

There is considerable variety in the manner in which jasper occurs in nature. It may occur in beds interstratified with other rocks, or in irregular nodules in various ore deposits, especially of iron. Sometimes it is found in the joints and crevices of siliceous rocks, and at other times at spots where certain igneous rocks of the greenstone (diabase) family have intruded into clay-slates, jasper being an alteration or contact product of the latter. Irregular masses of jasper are referred to, independently of their colour, which is usually yellow, brown, or red, as common or German jasper, in contradistinction to the red or chestnut-brown ball-jasper, which occurs as regular nodules or balls in brown iron-ore, or loose on the surface of the ground. All kinds of jasper are of course very common as pebbles in the sands and gravels of rivers and streams and other alluvial deposits.

The different varieties of jasper have been much used as ornamental stones, especially in ancient times, when the stone was engraved, set in mosaics, and fashioned into objects of some size. Its application in the Middle Ages, and in comparatively recent times, was also extensive, but it has now fallen almost into disuse. Specially fine stones of uniform colour are sometimes cut up for gems, and in spite of the dulness of the fractured surface they take a fair polish, although the lustre is never very strong. The stone is principally used, however, for boxes, bowls, vases, table-tops, and small ornamental edifices. The construction of such objects may be accomplished with one large block, or it may be necessary to use several pieces, in which case they must be chosen with due regard to colour. Jasper is too abundant to be worth very much, and the value of all but exceptionally fine and uniformly coloured specimens is small.

Some of the colour-varieties of jasper occur singly and only at certain places, while at other places jaspers of several different colours are found. Owing to the wide distribution of this stone only the most important localities will be here enumerated.

Typical **red jasper** is represented by the ball-jasper of Auggen and Liel, near Mühlheim, in Breisgau. It occurs there as rounded nodules, ranging in size from that of a nut to that of a man's head, in brown iron-ore, with which it is mixed, The nodules are coated with white marl; in the interior they are of a dark, tile-red colour with white, yellow, or greenish stripes or markings.

Fine red jasper (or ferruginous quartz) sometimes traversed by veins of white quartz, occurs not infrequently to the west of Marburg, in Hesse, also in Nassau and other places in Germany, being there a contact product of clay-slate near the junction of this with diabase. The dark blood-red colour is very effective when the stone is cut. This red jasper occurs usually in rather small pieces, but blocks the size of a man's head, or larger, are sometimes found. Löhlbach, near Frankenberg, was formerly noted for beautiful jasper occurring in blocks of considerable size, which was known as " Löhlbach agate." It was once used to a considerable extent, and many artistic objects, worked in this material, are still preserved in the collection at Cassel.

Fine red jasper, as well as that of other colours, is found in the veins of iron-ore in many places in the Saxon Erzgebirge. Fine specimens of all colours are of frequent occurrence in the British Isles, particularly in Scotland.

Brown jasper is represented by the Egyptian jasper, sometimes called Nile jasper, although it does not come from the Nile. It is found in rather rough rounded nodules, on the smooth fracture of which there are concentric brownish-yellow bands alternating with the dark chestnut-brown colour of the rest of the stone. These nodules have been derived from the beds of the Nummulitic formation; they occur in large numbers on the sserir or stony areas of the Egyptian desert. There is a sserir to the east of Cairo, on the slopes of Jebel Mokattam, and over large areas of the Lybian desert there is nothing to be seen but rounded fragments of jasper. The rounding of these fragments has been effected not by water but by the action of wind-blown grains of sand.

A large amount of brown jasper associated with red and yellow jasper is found at Sioux Falls, in Dakota, North America. About 30,000 dollars' worth is cut every year in large works on the spot, the material being used specially for the ornamentation of buildings. It is known in America as "Sioux Falls jasper," and occurs in inexhaustible beds, which are excavated in quarries.

Yellow jasper is much employed in Florentine mosaics, but is otherwise unimportant. It has brownish and white streaks on an ochre-yellow ground, and is obtained from the island of Sicily, from Dauphiné, and elsewhere.

Green jasper is found principally in the Urals, where also it is worked. It occurs, among other places, at Orsk on the Ural river above Orenburg, where it forms a thick bed in gneiss. This bed has furnished blocks of sufficient size to be worked into vases and other large objects, all the cutting being done in the great works at Ekaterinburg. The colour is dark leek-green, and the stone is therefore known by the name of plasma, a variety of chalcedony, which it resembles in appearance. Green jasper is much esteemed in China, and is one of the stones to which the term "yu" is applied.

Blue jasper is always rather dull in colour, frequently showing a lavender or grey tinge, and is seldom used. We may mention here the so-called *porcelain-jasper*, which is not really jasper at all, but is clay baked and hardened by the burning of lignite (brown coal). It is usually lavender-blue in colour, but may be tile-red or yellow; it is widely distributed, especially in northern Bohemia, and a specimen is now and again used as an ornamental stone.

Riband-jasper has differently coloured riband-like bands which alternate regularly with each other. It is very impure and can scarcely be properly regarded as jasper, its chemical composition approximating more closely to that of felspar than to that of quartz. It closely resembles typical jasper in appearance, and, indeed, differs from it only in its fusibility before the blowpipe, and in the large amount of foreign matter it contains. Riband-jasper, in which the contrast between bands of colour is not sufficiently marked to be effective, is common enough; it is found in beds at Lautenthal, in the Harz, at Gnandstein, near Kohren, in Saxony, and other places. The Siberian riband-jasper, on the other hand, in which dark blood-red and leek-green bands alternate with great regularity, is most beautiful. It is said to occur near Verchne-Uralsk, at the junction of the Uralsda with the Ural river, but only in small loose pieces, so that only comparatively small articles can be made of it: larger objects, however, are often veneered with thin plates of riband-jasper. Jasper of exactly the same description is said to occur at Okhotsk, in Eastern Siberia, and good specimens are stated to be found also in Chutia Nagpur, in India. Fine riband-jasper with yellow and red, alternating with white stripes, is found in large amount at Collyer, in Trego County, Kansas. It is an excellent material for cameos, for which purpose onyx, or riband-agate, is also very well suited, owing to its regular banded structure.

The stones which are intermediate in character between jasper and chalcedony, and which may be termed **agate-jasper** or jasp-agate, usually show opaque, dark coloured portions intermixed in various ways with translucent, lighter coloured portions. Such stones are the once much talked of "jaspe fleuré" of jewellers, and they were at one time worked like jasper. The material occurred in large amount principally in Sicily, where a hundred varieties, distinguished by differences in colour and markings, were recognised. A fine agate-jasper occurs at various places in Texas, and is often called in America "Texas agate." In some of these stones the translucent agate predominates, and in others the opaque jasper, the former being sometimes distinguished on this account as agate-jasper and the latter as jasp-agate; they are scarcely ever used as gems, and none are of any importance.

AVANTURINE.

Avanturine or avanturine-quartz is a feebly translucent, fine-grained to compact quartz, with a conchoidal or usually splintery fracture; the surface of which has a speckled, metallic sheen, usually of a reddish-brown colour, but occasionally yellow, white, blue, or green. This appearance is caused by the presence, in the colourless quartz substance, of numbers of enclosures, which can always be seen with the aid of the microscope, and sometimes with a simple lens, or with the naked eye. In some cases these enclosures consist of small silvery, reddish-brown, or sometimes white, scales of mica; in others of minute plates of the green chrome-mica fuchsite, or of similar plates of a blue colour of some unknown mineral, while in other stones the sheen is caused by the existence of numbers of small cracks filled with hydrated oxide of iron. Each crack filled with this substance and every single scale of mica gives its own metallic reflection; the sheen of the mass is the sum total of these reflections, and is the more uninterrupted the more uniformly and closely set in the quartz are these enclosures. As a rule, reddish-brown avanturine closely resembles sun-stone, which for this reason is called avanturine-felspar, avanturine itself being often called avanturine-quartz. The two can be distinguished by the fact that the quartz is the harder and will scratch the felspar.

Avanturine is often set in rings, pins, brooches, cuff-links, &c. It is cut with a flat or slightly convex surface without facets, and acquires by polishing a fine, strong lustre. The more uniform and uninterrupted is the sheen of a specimen of avanturine the more valuable it becomes, and portions with a sheen of this discription are cut out of the large irregular masses of poorer quality which occur in nature. Avanturine was at one time much prized as a gem; now, however, it is more frequently used as a material for bowls, vases, and ornamental objects of various kinds, the sheen being of course less perfect and uniform over objects of this size than over the surface of a small gem. Reddish-brown avanturine with a coppery reflection is the most highly esteemed variety; other avanturine, such as the brown, reddish-yellow, white with a silvery white sheen, black with white spots, green and blue, though rarer, are less prized. The special beauty of avanturines is associated with the isolation of the glancing metallic scales, and the consequent appearance of so many starry, glittering points.

Avanturine is rather widely distributed, and specimens of considerable size are not by any means rare, although those possessing the most desirable characters and of a quality suitable for gems are not to be found at every locality.

The mineral occurs both in primary deposits and also as loose pebbles. The richest localities are in the Urals, where it is found, forming thick beds in mica-schist, at several places in the Taganai range, to the north of Zlatoust on the Ui, a tributary of the Ufa. Also at Kossulina, twenty-eight versts west-south-west of Ekaterinburg, the material found here being superior in colour and sheen, but traversed by cracks and therefore not to be obtained in large pieces. All the material found in this region is cut at Ekaterinburg. White and reddish-white avanturine is found in the Altai mountains at Beloretzkaya, thirty versts from the long-famous lapidary works at Kolivan (latitude about 51° N.) It is worked at Kolivan; and, together with the Uralian avanturine, has furnished material for the bowls, vases, and ornaments which have been from time to time presented by the Czar of Russia to European princes. A vase of this description was presented in 1843 by the Czar to Sir Roderick I. Murchison in recognition of his services in exploring the geology of part of the Russian Empire; it is 4 feet high and measures 6 feet in circumference at its largest part; it is preserved in the Museum of Practical Geology, London. Large blocks of avanturine of faultless quality are worth hundreds of pounds.

Fine specimens of this mineral are occasionally met with in India, but nothing definite is known as to their mode of occurrence or the exact locality. A very pretty green glistening variety from the Bellary district in Madras deserves mention; the scales of mica enclosed in it are of the green chromiferous variety known as fuchsite, and the mineral itself occurs in blocks from which slabs of considerable size can be cut.

Green avanturine of this description is very highly esteemed in China; it is one of the stones referred to as " yu " and is distinguished from the others as the imperial yu-stone. The imperial seal is said to be made of this material, which is esteemed far more highly than is nephrite. The locality from whence the Chinese obtain the stone is not known.

Avanturine is said to have been found at several localities in Europe; for example, in the neighbourhood of Aschaffenburg in Bavaria, at Mariazell in Styria, and at Veillane between Susa and Turin in Piedmont, where it is found as pebbles. Also at Nantes in France, Glen Fernate in Scotland, and in the neighbourhood of Madrid, where it is associated with pebbles of granite.

Avanturine-glass is an artificial product which resembles natural avanturine but possesses an even finer appearance. It is a colourless glass in which are embedded numerous small red octahedra, the faces of which are equilateral triangles. The chemical composition of the material, the well-defined crystalline form, together with the red colour and strong metallic lustre of the enclosures, points to the fact that the latter consist of metallic copper. The much lower hardness of avanturine-glass, together with the form of the enclosures, which can be readily made out with a lens, definitely distinguishes it in all cases from natural avanturine (avanturine-quartz) and from sun-stone (avanturine-felspar).

There is a rather improbable story to the effect that a glass-maker of Murano, near Venice, discovered the art of making this glass by accident (*par aventure*), by dropping some copper filings into molten glass, and that the name avanturine (or aventurine) originated thus, and was afterwards applied to the natural mineral. It is very likely that the fable was invented in order to preserve the secret of the art of manufacturing this magnificent glass by putting curious inquirers off the scent. The art came subsequently to be forgotten or lost, even in Murano, until the year 1827, when it was rediscovered by the glass-maker, Bibaglia, after many unsuccessful trials. The chief difficulty is to prevent the copper from separating out into clusters of crystals, and to obtain these crystals distributed regularly throughout the whole mass of glass as is necessary in order to obtain the most favourable appearance. The product of this art, which is still a trade secret, is a most beautiful glass, much finer than natural avanturine, and is much used in the manufacture of small ornamental objects. It is possible to obtain large blocks of the material so that it can be used for objects of considerable size. Avanturine-glass fetches from 40s. to 50s. per kilogram; it contains about $2\frac{1}{2}$ per cent. of copper and is made of a very easily fusible glass, which melts at a much lower temperature than does the copper.

C. CHALCEDONY.

The chalcedony group includes a number of siliceous minerals of compact structure and fine splintery fracture, which are characterised by the possession of a finely fibrous structure. The fibres are always recognisable under the microscope, and sometimes with a simple lens or with the naked eye; they are always very short and their optical characters differ somewhat from those of quartz. Moreover, the specific gravity and the hardness are both less than those of quartz, the former being 2·59–2·60, and the latter $H = 6\frac{1}{2}$; and in addition the mineral is considerably more soluble in a caustic potash solution than quartz.

Although chemically chalcedony is, like quartz, pure silica, yet since its physical properties differ it must be regarded as another crystallised modification of this substance. Chalcedony was at one time supposed to consist of a mixture of quartz and opal, which would account for its greater solubility in caustic potash. Microscopic investigation, however, has shown this hypothesis to be untenable.

Chalcedony being a fibrous aggregate never assumes a regular external form, but it may, and often does, occur as a pseudomorph after some other mineral. That is to say, it assumes the crystalline form characteristic of that mineral by mere replacement of the substance of the crystal, and not in response to an inherent tendency in the molecules of chalcedony to arrange themselves in that particular form. Chalcedony does, however, occur very frequently in rounded, reniform, botryoidal, cylindrical, and stalactitic forms, in which the fibres are arranged perpendicular to the surface. Such masses of chalcedony are built up of very thin concentric layers arranged parallel to the rounded surface. This banding is never wholly absent, but may be indistinct; it is shown more or less prominently on all surfaces, whether cut or fractured, but is displayed to greatest advantage by a polished surface cut perpendicular to the layers. According as the bands are more or less prominent, the mineral is distinguished as striped or unstriped chalcedony, the former being usually referred to as agate. No very sharp line of demarcation can be drawn, however, between agate and unstriped chalcedony, the one passing insensibly into the other.

A blow from a hammer will sometimes cause a piece of chalcedony to separate along a surface corresponding to the superimposed layers, the surface of separation being frequently smooth and bright and of course parallel to the original surface. As a rule, however, the layers are so firmly bound together that this separation does not take place, although it is very easy to fracture the mineral by a blow perpendicular to the rounded surface, that is to say, in the direction of the fibres. When crushed, chalcedony always breaks in the direction of the fibres; this fracture is uneven and finely splintery, and with a feeble lustre inclined to the waxy type. After cutting and polishing the stone acquires a brilliant lustre of the vitreous type. Chalcedony is translucent to semi-transparent, never perfectly transparent. Light passes through it more readily in a direction parallel to the fibres than in one perpendicular to them; a slab of the mineral cut in a direction perpendicular to the fibres will therefore be more translucent than one of equal thickness cut parallel to the fibres. The different layers of which a specimen of chalcedony is built up vary in translucency, some being almost transparent and others almost opaque. It frequently happens that clear and cloudy layers alternate with each other.

As a rule, chalcedony is colourless, milk-white, or some faint shade of grey, yellow, or blue, but black and pronounced shades of yellow, brown, red, and green are met with occasionally, and blue as a rarity. Some specimens are of one uniform colour throughout, but more frequently the different layers of the stone are differently coloured, the colour, however, being uniform throughout the same layer. This contrast in the colouring of the layers has the effect of bringing much into prominence the banded structure of the stone.

Chalcedony being somewhat porous it can be artificially coloured with ease simply by immersion in a fluid containing colouring matter in solution. The liquid is sucked up into the pores of the stone, and as the stone dries and the liquid evaporates the colouring matter is deposited in these pores and imparts its colour to the whole mass. So porous are some specimens of chalcedony that they will adhere to the tongue owing to the rapidity with which the moisture of that organ is absorbed, and when placed in water the expulsion of the air-bubbles from the pores is so rapid as to cause a hissing noise. Not infrequently the pores, in the form of round cavities or elongated canals, can be recognised under the microscope, or even with a simple lens. Different layers of the same specimen are not equally porous, some will absorb the colouring matter with great rapidity, while others will be scarcely coloured at all.

The intense colours shown by certain specimens of natural chalcedony have in many cases been assumed after the formation of the mineral, by a natural process analagous to the artificial method.

The artificial colouring of chalcedony has become quite a prominent feature of the agate-cutting industry. It is carried on to such an extent that there is actually more of the artificially coloured material sold than of the natural stone. The subject will be treated in more detail, however, when the working of the stone is described.

Chalcedony occurs in layers with a mammillated surface coating the surfaces of rocks in cracks and crevices, and in favourable positions in the form of stalactites. It is found usually in volcanic rocks, which, when chalcedony is present in any amount, are always in an advanced stage of decomposition. Like opal and amethyst, chalcedony is thus an alteration product of the rock in which it occurs, and when the last stages of decomposition have been reached the chalcedony is set free and lies loose in the soil in isolated fragments, which are often carried away by running water and finally deposited as pebbles in the beds of rivers and in other alluvial deposits.

Several varieties of chalcedony are recognised by lapidaries, the distinctions between them being based on differences in colour and the mode of its distribution, differences which are not, however, very sharply defined. It is, moreover, sometimes difficult to decide whether a given specimen should be referred to chalcedony, jasper, or hornstone. Mineralogically chalcedony is determined mainly by the finely fibrous structure, but lapidaries classify the compact quartz minerals according to translucency alone, all the perfectly opaque varieties being referred to as jasper, and all those which are more or less translucent as chalcedony.

The varieties of chalcedony here distinguished are as follows:

> *Common chalcedony* of a faint uniform colour.
> *Carnelian* of a uniform red colour, with which is included brown *Sard*.
> *Plasma* of a uniform dark green colour. This, when spotted with red, is known as
> *heliotrope*, or blood-stone.
> *Agate* with a prominent banded structure. The well-known *onyx* is included under this
> "striped chalcedony."

The sub-classification of these varieties will be given below.

COMMON CHALCEDONY.

This is chalcedony in the more restricted sense, and is known simply as chalcedony. In colour it is white or some very pale shade of grey, yellow, brown, blue, or green ; though, as a rule, it is uniformly coloured, specimens are sometimes met with which show cloudy patches (cloud-chalcedony) and an indistinct banding.   Common chalcedony is built up of layers just as agate is, but being all of the same colour the banded structure is inconspicuous ; specimens in which it is at all prominent are referred not to common chalcedony but to agate.   As examples of chalcedony with a pronounced colour may be mentioned the rare *sapphirine* of lapidaries found at Nerchinsk in Siberia, in Transylvania, and in India, which approaches in colour the blue of the sapphire, and the yellow *ceragate* (wax-agate or semi-carnelian), which has a waxy lustre.   Cloudy milk-white chalcedony is referred to as *white carnelian.*

The fibrous structure of common chalcedony is fairly apparent : the fracture is typically uneven and finely splintery, and the lustre of the fractured and of a cut and polished surface agrees with the description already given.   Though never perfectly clear the mineral is often very translucent, even in thick pieces, but in other cases, especially in milk-white stones, it is almost opaque.   Very translucent stones are termed " oriental chalcedony " to distinguish them from more opaque specimens, which are described as "occidental chalcedony."   The finest " oriental " specimens are not always perfectly translucent throughout, but show delicate cloudy patches, which are by no means prejudicial to their beauty, but rather the reverse.

Common chalcedony occurs as reniform, botryoidal, and stalactitic incrustations on the surface of rocks, and also as a filling in of the cracks and crevices of these same rocks.   It is of moderately wide distribution, but usually occurs only in small amount, the incrustations being too thin to admit of the material being cut.   Thicker masses of greater purity and beauty come from Iceland and the Faroe Islands, and a considerable amount also from India.   The Indian localities will be enumerated below under agate.

Chalcedony was more extensively used both formerly and in ancient times than now, its place having been taken by other stones.   It is cut for ring-stones and seal-stones, and it also furnishes a material for seal-stocks, cups, plates, bowls, vases, &c.   It is worked in Europe, principally at Oberstein and Idar on the Nahe, and at Waldkirch in Baden.   A considerable amount is done also in India, but the industry is of less importance there than in Germany.

It is only exceptionally large and fine specimens of chalcedony which have any considerable value.   The value of a stone depends principally on its translucency and on the uniformity of its colouring; it is important also that there should be no cracks or faults of other kinds.   Cloudy, patchy, or fractured stones are practically worthless.   In spite of the fact that chalcedony is so abundant and so low in price, it has been closely imitated in glass ; such imitations, however, can be distinguished from the genuine stone by the fact that they are less hard, and that their specific gravity is higher.   A few varieties of common chalcedony are sometimes distinguished by special names, for example :

Spotted agate (spotted chalcedony, St. Stephen's stone) is a white or greyish chalcedony with small red spots.   In the finest specimens the spots are no bigger than dots, and these are distributed uniformly over the whole surface so closely that when viewed at some distance the stone appears to be of a uniform rose-red colour.

Mocha-stone (tree-stone or dendritic agate) is a white or grey chalcedony showing brown, red or black dendritic markings resembling trees and plants. These have been formed by the percolation of a solution containing iron or manganese through the fine cracks of the stone, and the subsequent deposition of the colouring matter originally held in solution. The brown and red marking are caused by oxides of iron, and the black by oxide of manganese. The fact that such tree-like markings are formed when a liquid travels in such a confined space can be easily shown experimentally by means of a coloured solution between two plates of glass. The dentritic markings of mocha-stone lie to a large extent in the same plane, and in cutting this stone the lapidary aims at displaying the marking with a coating of chalcedony of only just sufficient thickness to preserve it from injury. The surface of cut stones is either plane or slightly convex, and their outline may be round or oval. A mocha-stone suitable for mounting as a brooch is represented in its actual size in Fig. 89. Certain rare mocha-stones in which the white or grey chalcedony shows, besides dendritic markings, the red dots characteristic of St. Stephen's stone are specially beautiful.

FIG. 89. Mocha-stone.

Dendritic agates of this description are said to have come originally from the neighbourhood of Mocha in Arabia, a seaport at the entrance of the Red Sea; hence the name "mocha-stone." In later times it has been obtained principally from India, where it occurs in the Deccan traps (see under *agate*). Fine stones are met with as pebbles in the Jumna river, and the mineral also occurs in large amount north of Rajkot and the Kathiawar peninsula, and in the bed of the Majam river in the same district. Here are found blocks of spherical, botryoidal, or amygdaloidal form, weighing as much as 40 pounds, as well as rounded pebbles. Fine material suitable for cutting occurs also at various places in North America; for example, at Central City in the Rocky Mountains.

The most valuable mocha-stones are those in which the dendritic markings closely resemble the outlines of trees and plants; stones in which the markings take the form of irregular black and brown patches are worth but little. Very good imitations of mocha-stone are now produced, an Oberstein agate-dealer having succeeded in producing permanent markings of a kind similar to those of mocha-stone on the surface of cut chalcedony. These artificial productions are far more beautiful than the naturally occurring mocha-stone, but otherwise are difficult to distinguish from these. Both the natural and the artificial stones were at one time much used, and commanded a high price, but this is not the case at the present time.

Moss-agate is characterised by the presence of green enclosures, such as are found in many specimens of rock-crystal. These enclosures usually take the form of long hairs and fibres much intertwined, and have the general effect of a piece of moss; hence the term moss-agate. The stone is common in the volcanic rocks (trap) of western India, occurring in places with mocha-stone. It fills irregular veins in the decomposed trap at Rajkot, among other places, where blocks ranging in weight from ½ to 30 pounds are obtained. It occurs also as pebbles in many Indian rivers, for example, in the Narbada, Jumna, and Godavari. A supply of natural green and of artificial yellow and red moss-agates has been obtained for some time from China, and these stones have largely replaced others on the market. Fine moss-agates occur in considerable numbers in the States of Utah, Wyoming, Colorado, and Montana, in North America.

Enhydros are stones which are more curious than beautiful, and are used but little as gems. They are flat, oval, and hollow nodules of strongly translucent, almost colourless chalcedony, partly filled with water. The water thus imprisoned can be distinctly seen through the thin wall of translucent chalcedony, and can be heard when the stone is shaken. These nodules are now found in masses of clay, but they were originally formed in solid rocks of volcanic origin, which in course of time have been decomposed and weathered to clay. The mode of occurrence of these enhydros is the same as that of ordinary chalcedony, and they must be regarded as chalcedony amygdales which have been only partially filled with mineral matter. Throughout the weathering of the rock they retain the form of the original rock-cavity, and when the process is complete can be extracted from the soft clay without injury, which would be impossible while they are embedded in solid rock. Such nodules of chalcedony containing water, and no bigger than a nut, were first obtained from Monte Tondo in the Colli Berici, near Vicenza, in northern Italy, where they occurred at rare intervals in weathered basalt. They were known to the ancients, and are mentioned by Pliny. At the present time they are obtained in considerable numbers from Uruguay, where they occur with agate in weathered amygdaloid, the largest being half the size of a man's fist.

When such enhydros are exposed to dry air, it sometimes happens that the water contained in them slowly evaporates, but is re-absorbed when the stones are immersed in water. This furnishes still another instance of the porous nature of chalcedony, and also throws much light on the origin of agate amygdales to be discussed below.

Enhydros are sometimes polished, although they are used so little as gem-stones. Stones of sizes less than a nut are chosen for this purpose; their surfaces are smoothed and polished very carefully in order to avoid breaking the nodule, and the movement of the enclosed liquid can then be clearly seen. The stones thus prepared are mounted in rings, pins, &c., and are worn more as curiosities than for the sake of any intrinsic beauty they possess.

CARNELIAN.

Carnelian is red chalcedony. It may have every appearance of being uniformly coloured or, on the other hand, the different layers of which it is built up may differ slightly, though appreciably, in colour. Typical carnelian is of a deep flesh-red colour, hence its name, but every shade of colour between this and pure white and yellow is represented. It was mentioned above that white chalcedony is often termed white carnelian; this term is most correctly applied to chalcedony with a faintly reddish or yellowish tinge, every possible shade between this and the deep flesh-red of typical carnelian being represented in natural stones. In some cases portions of the stone are paler than others, and specimens with a pale central portion passing gradually into a dark coloured exterior are not at all uncommon. Fine dark stones of uniform colour and free from faults are described as "carnelian de la vieille roche," or as "masculine carnelian." By transmitted light they appear of a deep blood-red colour, and in reflected light of a blackish-red shade. They are found in India, but are very rare, and on account of their great beauty are highly esteemed. Stones of a pale red, or of a yellowish-red colour, are described as "feminine carnelian," or simply as carnelian. Among several thousand stones there will be probably only a few to which the term "masculine" may be be applied; the rest will be yellowish, brownish, greyish, or too pale in colour, patchy or disfigured by cracks and fissures. Compared with opaque red jasper, which is often of a carnelian colour, all carnelians, whatever be their colour, are strongly translucent.

The colour of carnelian is not due to the presence of organic compounds, as was once supposed, but to that of compounds of iron, the red colour being due to ferric oxide, and the yellow and brown to hydrated ferric oxide. Yellow or brown stones, when exposed to the action of heat, gradually assume the red colour characteristic of carnelian, owing to the hydrated ferric oxide losing water and becoming anhydrous. Many stones, which in the natural condition are of a dirty yellow colour and unsuitable for gems, on being heated acquire the fine carnelian colour, and with it a considerable increase in value.

Stones which contain too small a quantity of iron are always pale in colour and cannot be made to assume the deep flesh-red tint when heated. It is, therefore, desirable in some cases to introduce a little more iron. This is done by immersing the stones in a solution of iron nitrate, made by dissolving some iron needles in nitric acid, or in a solution of iron vitriol, which may be more easily obtained and is just as effectual. On heating, the stones assume the fine carnelian red colour; care must be taken in all these operations, however, that the temperature does not rise too high, for on strongly igniting carnelian it becomes white and dull, and can then be easily crushed to powder.

The mode of occurrence of carnelian in nature is the same as that of common chalcedony and of agate, namely, as incrustations with nodular surfaces, and in the cracks and crevices, and especially in the amygdaloidal cavities, of volcanic rocks. On the disintegration of these rocks the rounded nodules or irregular fragments of carnelian remain loose in the ground, or are transported by running water, and finally deposited as rounded pebbles in the sands and gravels of rivers and streams. In this form carnelian is of moderately common occurrence. The material, which is cut and polished in the lapidary works, comes almost exclusively, however, from India, Brazil, and Uruguay, where it occurs and is collected with chalcedony of other kinds, especially agate, the occurrence being described below under agate. The localities at which chalcedony of finer quality occurs will now be enumerated.

In **India** blocks of carnelian, weighing as much as 3 pounds, are found in the Rajpipla Hills, at Ratanpur, on the lower Narbada river (Fig. 33). The material as it is found in the mines may be blackish, olive-green, milk-white, or, in fact, almost any colour except red. This tint is only acquired after the stone has been heated, the heating being effected partly by a long exposure to the sun's rays and partly by fire. Stones, of which the original colour was olive-green, assume an especially fine tint on heating; they are much prized, and are largely cut in the neighbourhood of Cambay, near Baroda.

Deposits of carnelian are worked also on the Mahi river, north of Baroda, and the mineral is found at many other places in the volcanic district of western India, but is not everywhere collected and worked. Moreover, pebbles of carnelian are found together with jasper and other varieties of chalcedony in almost all the rivers. A very similar occurrence to those in western India is that in the volcanic rocks of the Rajmahal Hills on the Ganges, in Bengal, but this appears to be of little commercial importance.

In **South America** the best known locality for carnelian is Campo de Maia, fifty miles south of the Rio Pardo, which joins the sea at Porto Alegre, Brazil. The stones found in this district are remarkable for their regular spherical form. Wherever agate occurs in this region it is accompanied by carnelian, so that the latter is somewhat widely distributed.

Other places occasionally given as localities for fine specimens of carnelian are situated in Dutch Guiana and Siberia; also at Warwick, in Queensland. Compared with Indian and Brazilian localities, however, all are unimportant. Numbers of carnelians were formerly found in Japan, where they were pierced and strung together as beads, and disposed of to the Dutch, who at one time traded extensively with this country.

For use as a gem carnelian is cut, like chalcedony, without facets, with a plane or convex surface and with a round, oval, or other outline. The other purposes to which it is applied are the same as already described under chalcedony. Carnelian, as a rule, is less brittle than chalcedony and is therefore a more suitable material to engrave upon. Gems of carnelian are often mounted upon a gold or silver foil, which considerably increases their colour and lustre; they are used rather extensively in cheap jewellery, more so than ordinary chalcedony.

It has been stated already that carnelian of a more or less pronounced brown colour is frequently met with. Brown carnelian, whether of a bright chestnut-brown or more of an orange shade, is distinguished as **sard**. This variety is not very sharply marked off from ordinary red carnelian, and it is often difficult to decide which name to apply to a given stone. The finest sard is considered to be that of an orange-brown colour, which in transmitted light appears of a fine red colour. The colour of sard has been compared to that of salted sardines, and from this the name is said to be derived. Some specimens of sard only acquire their characteristic colour after exposure to heat. Many are dotted with numerous opaque spots of darker colour; such stones are described as "sandy sard." Fine sard is uncommon and very valuable. It is found at the localities mentioned for carnelian, and is collected with this stone and with agate. A method is now known by which a fine deep and uniform brown colour can be imparted to chalcedony. This artificially coloured material is known as sarduine, and is in no respect inferior to natural sard in place of which it is often used.

PLASMA.

This is the name applied to green chalcedony, the colour of which ranges from dark leek-green, the commonest shade, through pale apple-green to almost white. The colouring substance is the so-called green-earth (a chloritic or micaceous substance), or possibly sometimes asbestos, like that enclosed in moss-agate. While, however, in the latter stone these enclosures are aggregated in patches conspicuously marked off from the quartz substance in which they are embedded, in plasma they occur in small grains and scales distributed throughout the whole stone and to which they impart a uniform green colour. Owing to its numerous enclosures plasma is much less translucent than the other varieties of chalcedony, and is more like jasper, resembling this stone also in the fact that its fracture is smooth rather than splintery. Microscopical examination shows that the stone possesses the fibrous structure of chalcedony; it is therefore essentially different from the fine-grained green jasper, from which, however, in particular cases it is almost impossible by mere inspection to distinguish it.

Plasma was at one time known only as the material of which objects found among the ruins of ancient Rome and in other Roman remains were made. The place whence the Romans obtained their rough material is still unknown, but at the present time a considerable amount of the mineral is obtained from India. It is especially fine in quality here, and occurs like carnelian in the volcanic rocks of the Deccan, especially in the district south of the Bhima river (Fig. 33) in Haidarabad, and as pebbles in the rivers Kistna and Godavari among others. Plasma of fine quality is said to have been found also at the first cataract of the Nile in Upper Egypt. Oil- or leek-green plasma, sometimes of rare beauty, is found also in the porphyry of the Hauskopf and Eckefels, near Oppenau, in the Black Forest. It occurs here in nodular masses built up of concentric shells of plasma, chalcedony, quartz, and other minerals, alternating with each other. Another locality for plasma in the same part of Germany is the Sauersberg in Baden-Baden, where also it occurs in nodules enclosed in porphyry. For gem purposes, however, plasma from the Black Forest is unimportant.

Heliotrope ("oriental jasper," "blood-jasper," or blood-stone) is a green chalcedony differing from plasma only in that its green colour is spotted, patched, or streaked with a fine blood-red. These markings have been compared with drops of blood, hence the names "blood-jasper" and blood-stone. A famous sculpture executed in heliotrope is preserved in the national library at Paris. It represents the scourging of Christ, and the red marks of the heliotrope are skilfully utilised to represent drops of blood on the raiment. The most valuable heliotrope is that in which the spots are of a full red colour, uniform in size and distributed regularly over the surface of the stone. Material in which the red marking is in streaks or large patches is considered to be inferior. The ground-mass, moreover, which is always appreciably less translucent than the red portions, should be of a uniform deep green shade. Stones in which the red markings are replaced by yellow spots and patches are sometimes met with; they are far less beautiful than ordinary heliotrope, and are scarcely ever used as gems. Red spotted heliotrope is worn, like plasma, in rings, pins, brooches, and similar ornaments, and also is fashioned into small objects of various kinds. The rough material is obtained almost exclusively from India, where it occurs with agate, carnelian, plasma, &c. As localities are mentioned the district north of Rajkot in the Kathiawar peninsula, west of Cambay, where masses weighing as much as 40 pounds are found, and Puna, south-east of Bombay. Heliotrope and other similar stones are often stated to be exported to Europe from Calcutta; it is scarcely probable, however, that material found in the west of India should be exported from an eastern port. The material sent from Calcutta may possibly be obtained somewhere in the east, in the Rajmahal Hills on the Ganges, but nothing is definitely known with regard to this. Compared with the Indian occurrence of heliotrope that of Europe is quite unimportant; fine specimens are found at several places in Scotland, especially in the basalt of the Isle of Rum. Fine heliotrope has been found recently in Australia, and numerous specimens of the same stone come from Brazil where they occur with carnelian, agate, &c.

AGATE.

Agate is the most important variety of chalcedony, and is used far more extensively than any other. It is built up of layers which differ conspicuously from each other in colour and translucency, and on this account has a banded or striped appearance. At times these different layers are very similar in colour and transparency, the banded appearance being then less prominent, but typical agate always shows these sharply contrasting bands.

The width of the bands is usually the same throughout their whole course, and is often, though not always, extremely small. The small size of some may be realised from the fact that in a stone examined under the microscope by Sir David Brewster there were no less than 17,000 definitely marked bands in the space of an inch. A thin plate cut perpendicular to the layers of a very finely banded agate, when held up to the light, shows rainbow colours; in other words, the plate forms a grating which gives a diffraction spectrum. Stones which are finely banded enough to show this phenomenon are known as *rainbow-agates*; they have no importance as gems.

Different layers vary very much in translucency, some being almost transparent, and others practically opaque. The colours of the different layers are, generally speaking, the same as those of common chalcedony. Thus some layers are almost colourless, or show pale shades of grey, blue, yellow, or brown, while the colours of others may be pronounced shades of yellow, red, brown, or grey, green and blue being always rare. Each single layer is usually uniformly coloured throughout its whole extent, and can be identified with one or other of the colour-varieties of chalcedony already considered. Thus the pale-coloured layers agree in character with common chalcedony, the red with carnelian, the brown with sard, and so on. According to the predominant colour of a stone it may be distinguished as chalcedony-agate, carnelian-agate, &c.; and here also may be mentioned agate-jasper (jasp-agate) already described, in which layers of translucent chalcedony alternate with bands of opaque jasper.

The beauty of agate and its application to ornamental purposes depend upon the contrast in colour and translucency between the bands of which it is built up. Finely marked and very translucent agates are sometimes distinguished by the prefix " oriental," stones less perfect in these respects being referred to as " occidental " agates. The majority of agates as they occur in nature are light coloured, and but few show strongly marked colour contrasts, such as deep shades of red, yellow, or brown. These stones, however, like ordinary chalcedony, can be artificially coloured, as we shall see later on when the methods of working agate are under consideration.

The two figures of Plate XIX. illustrate the varied courses taken by the bands shown on a cut and polished surface of agate. According to the direction and arrangement of the bands, different kinds of agate are distinguished.

In *riband-agate* the different layers are parallel to each other, their surfaces being plane or uniformly curved, without indentations or prominences. A surface cut perpendicular to the layers will show straight or curved bandings. A riband-agate in which milk-white cloudy bands alternate with bands of another colour, the two sets being sharply marked off from each other, is known by the general term *onyx*. According to the shade of the coloured bands several sub-varieties are recognised. Thus, the term onyx in its more restricted sense is applied to agate in which the second set of bands are black; when these coloured bands are one of the pale shades characteristic of common chalcedony, the stone is described as *chalcedony-onyx*, when they are red as *carnelian-onyx*, and when brown as *sard-onyx*. From the point of view of the working of agate, the different varieties of onyx have a definite importance, and will be referred to again. In a modification of riband-agate, known as *ring-agate*, the differently coloured bands are disposed in concentric circles. A stone with a dark coloured central spot surrounded by a series of concentric rings has a certain resemblance to an eye, and is therefore referred to as an *eye-agate*. A kind of ring-agate can be artificially produced from ordinary agate or chalcedony: the point of a steel rod is placed on a cut surface of agate and is then smartly struck with a hammer. There is then formed around the point a system of concentric rings, which give the stone a very pretty appearance.

When the banding is disposed so as to form re-entrant and salient angles, its outline being the same as that of the plan of a bastion or fortress, the agate is called *fortification-agate*. The markings of *landscape-agate* suggest the outlines of a landscape picture, and when the banding recalls the outlines of a ruin, as is the case in brecciated-agate, to be described below, the stone is described as *ruin-agate*. In *cloud-agate* cloudy patches contrast with a more translucent background; *star-agate* shows star-shaped figures; *shell-agate* or *coral-agate* resembles in appearance fossilised shells and corals, the petrification of these objects in agate actually at times taking place. A number of other names, most of which are descriptive of the sub-variety to which they are applied, are recognised, but need not be enumerated here.

PLATE XIX

FORTIFICATION-AGATE: FROM OBERSTEIN, RHINE

ONYX-AGATE: FROM BRAZIL

Agate occurs only rarely as veins filling the fissures of rocks. There are typical examples of this mode of occurrence at Halsbach, near Freiberg, in Saxony, where the veins consist for the most part of coral-agate, and at Schlottwitz, near Wesenstein, in the Müglitz valley, in Saxony. The excellent riband-agate found at the latter locality has narrow, brightly-coloured bands arranged parallel to the surfaces of the vein; the latter contains, besides agate, common chalcedony, jasper, quartz, and amethyst. At a certain spot the material of one-half of the vein has been completely broken up by earth movements. The angular fragments of agate thus produced were afterwards cemented together by amethyst, the contrast in colour between these two minerals rendering the resulting stone, the well-known *brecciated-agate*, very effective for decorative purposes. The fragments of agate in brecciated-agate sometimes suggest a representation of ruined buildings, this variety being on that account referred to as ruin-agate. This brecciated-agate was discovered in 1750 and mined in some quantity. Like other Saxony agates, for example those found in porphyry at Altendorf and Rochlitz, it was fashioned into all kinds of articles. A beautiful rose-red ornamental sand was at one time prepared from the coral-agate of Halsbach, but at the present time the mines are almost always filled with water and therefore inaccessible.

Agate occurs much more commonly, however, in the vesicles of certain volcanic rocks, such as porphyries and basalts, and specially in amygdaloidal melaphyres. These almond-shaped or amygdaloidal cavities have already been mentioned under amethyst; besides this mineral most of them contain agate, and this, to distinguish it from the agate which occurs in veins, is sometimes termed amygdaloidal agate. Almost the whole of the material used for cutting is amygdaloidal agate. The cavities which are filled principally with agate are called agate-amygdales; their external surface is usually very rough and pitted.

The layers of agate of which these amygdales are built up usually follow more or less closely the surface of the amygdale. When exactly parallel to the external surface we get riband-agate, and when not exactly parallel we get one or other of the sub-varieties already described. Many South American amygdales are remarkable in that the bands follow the outline of the cavity for part of their course, and then, leaving the wall of the cavity, take a short cut across it (Plate XIX, Fig. *b*). Usually in agates from all other localities, and indeed in many South American amygdales also, the layers of chalcedony closely line the walls of the cavity, as represented in Fig. *a* of Plate XIX.

The agate of the amygdale is only rarely in immediate contact with the rock in which it is embedded; more frequently a thin layer of a green, earthy, chloritic, or micaceous mineral intervenes, the same substance as the so-called green-earth, which occurs enclosed in moss-agate and which imparts to plasma and heliotrope their green colour. The layers of agate which succeed the layer of green-earth do not, as a rule, completely fill up the cavity of the amygdale, and such amygdales containing a central space are known as geodes. The innermost layer of agate enclosing this central space may have a reniform or botryoidal surface, as is common in all varieties of chalcedony, or it may hang in stalactites from the roof of the cavity. Sometimes such a cavity is completely filled up by a later deposition of agate, which encloses the stalactites of the former stage of growth and gives rise to the so-called *pipe-agate*.

Amygdales consisting entirely of agate are, however, very rare; the innermost layer surrounding the central space usually consists of crystallised quartz—often of amethyst—the pyramidal terminations of the crystals projecting into the space. On the other hand, the whole of the central cavity may be filled with crystalline quartz showing no crystal faces (Plate XIX, Fig. *b*). In amygdales of this description there may be only a small central nucleus of amethyst, the bulk of the structure being of agate, or, again, the agate may form only a thin layer enclosing a nodule of amethyst, as already described under amethyst. One accordingly distinguishes agate-amygdales and amethyst-amygdales, though the difference is only one of proportion. In many cases the innermost layer of an amygdale is constituted by crystals of calcite or other minerals, especially the hydrated silicates belonging to the zeolite group, which rest upon the crystals of amethyst.

Sections of agate-amygdales often disclose other peculiarities which are important, inasmuch as they throw light upon the mode of formation of the amygdale. Thus it has been observed that the central cavity of the amygdale is placed in communication with the exterior by a narrow canal, formed by the layers of agate bending sharply outwards at this particular point. At least one such canal, and very frequently several, exist in every amygdale.

The external opening of the channel is frequently to be seen on the surface of the amygdale as a funnel-shaped depression, but is sometimes obscured and only to be made out in sections. These canals may be empty or, on the other hand, completely filled up with agate of the same description as that of the innermost layer of the amygdale, being indeed continuous with this.

An explanation of the origin of agate-amygdales, sufficient to account for all their details of structure, can be deduced without much difficulty from the general character and the mode of occurrence of these structures. First, however, must be noted that the amygdaloidal cavities, in which the agate occurs, are found in the rocks already mentioned only when these have been much weathered and their constituents partly removed. The more advanced the decomposition of the rock—which may indeed proceed as far as almost complete disintegration—the more likely is it that the amygdaloidal cavities will be filled with mineral. On the other hand, the less decomposed is the rock the less likely is agate to be found in its cavities, these cavities in fresh unaltered rock being always quite empty.

It follows from this, therefore, that the material which fills the cavities, namely, the silica, has been derived from the rock in which they are enclosed. During the process of weathering, the silica and other constituents of the rock have been dissolved out by water and subsequently redeposited in the cavities. The banded structure of the amygdale, however, indicates that the deposition did not proceed continuously and uninterruptedly, but that between the formation of two successive layers there was an interval of greater or less duration.

To explain this phenomenon the existence is assumed of hot intermittent springs, such as are now seen to perfection in the geysers of Iceland and in the United States National Park on the Yellowstone river. The essential condition for the formation of amygdales is that the hot or warm water rising up from the depths shall saturate the rocks, and that it shall sink again, leaving the rocks dry for a period. The hot water dissolves out the silica and other constituents of the rock, and the solution fills up the amygdaloidal cavities. When the waters sink these cavities are emptied, only a film of water covering their walls being left behind. On the evaporation of this film, which readily takes place at such a high temperature, a thin layer of silica is deposited on the walls of the cavity. When the hot spring again rises the same thing takes place and a second layer of silica is deposited, and so on, until the cavity is more or less completely filled up. Each time the fluid passes into and out of the cavity by the canals mentioned above, which are for this reason often referred to as tubes of entry or escape, the fluid also perhaps passes to a certain extent through the porous agate itself. Crevices, fissures, and other cavities in the rock are, of course, filled with agate in the same way.

The size of the agate amygdales of course depends upon that of the amygdaloidal cavities of the rock. The smallest of these are about the size of a pea or a hazel-nut, while the largest are of considerable dimensions. The weight of an amygdale depends not only on its size but also on the size of the central cavity. The heaviest known is from Brazil and weighs about 40 hundredweights.

The localities at which amygdale-agate is found are very numerous, but at only a few does it occur in sufficient quantity and suitable quality for ornamental purposes.

At one time the most important occurrence was in the district of the Nahe, a tributary of the Rhine, in what is now the Oldenburg principality of **Birkenfeld,** and in the neighbouring portions of Prussia. A portion of this district was formerly included in the Rhenish Palatinate, and for this reason the Palatinate or Zweibrücken are sometimes given as the localities for these agates even now. Melaphyre and amygdaloidal rocks are distributed very widely in this region, and almost everywhere these contain agate, though not always of the best quality. Very fine material is obtained from the Galgenberg, near Idar, and from the Struth, near Oberstein, both localities being situated in Birkenfeld, the latter on the Nahe and the former close to it in the small side valley of the Idarbach; also from the Rosengarten on the Weisselstein, near St. Wendel, in Prussian territory. The agate of this region has been systematically collected for centuries, and is cut and polished in the numerous lapidary works established there, especially at Oberstein and Idar, which even now turn out a supply sufficient for the whole world.

Other European localities though numerous are unimportant. The mineral occurs in amygdaloidal rock at several places in northern **Bohemia**; for example, on the Jeschkenberg near Friedstein, in the Kosakow mountains near Semil, in the Tabor and Morzinow mountains near Lomnitz, and in the Lewin mountains near Neu-Paka. At these localities many of the amygdales have been weathered out of the rock and lie loose in the ground, or are found as pebbles in the rivers, for example, in the Iser and Elbe. Besides agate, carnelian and other varieties of chalcedony, as well as jasper, are found here and cut at the lapidary works at Turnau, Liebenau, and Gablonz.

Mention should also be made of the so-called Scotch pebbles, very pretty agates, which occur in considerable abundance at Montrose in Forfarshire, in Perthshire, and at many other localities in **Scotland**.

The occurrence of agate in countries other than Europe, especially in South America and to a certain extent also in India, is far more important. From the former country since the exhaustion of the German localities the lapidary works at Idar and Oberstein have obtained an abundant supply of excellent material.

In **South America** the principal localities for agate are situated in the Brazilian State of Rio Grande do Sul and the neighbouring country of Uruguay, the material from this region being termed, irrespective of locality, Brazilian agate. In association with it are found the crystallised varieties of quartz already mentioned, namely, amethyst and citrine, and several varieties of chalcedony other than agate, especially carnelian. In this region, just as on the Nahe, melaphyres and amygdaloidal rocks extend over a wide area, and here also agates and other quartz minerals have been formed in their cavities. Very frequently the amygdales have been weathered out of their mother-rock, which is usually completely decomposed and altered to a red or brown, highly ferruginous clay. When this clay has been washed away by rains the agate amygdales are left behind loose on the ground, and they are often found, too, as rounded pebbles in the alluvial deposits of streams and rivers. The amygdales are usually shaped like a cake, flat on one side and rounded on the other, and are sometimes of considerable size, the one weighing 40 hundredweights, mentioned above, having been found in Brazil.

The principal locality for agate, carnelian, and other varieties of chalcedony is a mountain chain consisting mainly of decomposed melaphyre, which is about 400 miles in length and extends from Porto Alegre, in Rio Grande do Sul, in the east to the district of Salto on the Uruguay river, in Uruguay, in the west. Cutting through this chain in the north are the Rio Pardo and Taquaire, flowing into the Gulf of Alegre, and in the valleys and beds of these rivers carnelian is found, while in the heights above striped agate is more common. From the Campo de Maia, fifty miles south of the Rio Pardo, come sardonyxes weighing as much as a hundredweight and often of magnificent colour. In the tributaries of the Uruguay, in the districts of Tres Cruces and Meta Perro, bluish agate as well as the striped variety is found.

For a long time this locality was the only place from whence bluish-grey agate was obtained. Though dingy and unattractive in themselves they possess two distinct advantages over the coloured agates of Oberstein. In the first place, they are easily coloured artificially; and in the second place, the layers of which they are built up are perfectly straight, which is a great assistance to the lapidary in the cutting of onyxes. Natural stones of a black colour are very rare; among several thousand hundredweights of material there will perhaps be scarcely a single black specimen. Layers of a fine emerald-green colour are also very rare; when they do occur, they are always situated immediately under the amethyst which rests on the agate. Rose-red agate is uncommon, but the deep flesh-red colour of carnelian is rather frequent in Brazilian agates.

The occurrence of agate and the quartz minerals with which it is associated in Brazil was discovered in 1827 by a native of Oberstein. These stores of mineral wealth, which up till that time had been lying idle, were then collected from the surface and from the loose clayey ground and were sent in great amount to Oberstein, these minerals soon becoming important articles of export. In spite of the abundance of material its collection is not very easy, for the localities are situated for the most part in inaccessible regions, and the task of transporting the stones to the coast is extremely arduous. In spite of these difficulties, however, large quantities are sent every year to Oberstein, where but little agate from other localities is now cut.

In order to give an idea of the importance of this export, and incidentally of the agate-cutting industry, the following figures representing the weight of agate, including carnelian and other varieties of chalcedony, obtained from Rio Grande do Sul alone are given:

	Cwts.		Cwts.
1872–3 . . .	3100	1877–8 . . .	1825
1873–4 . . .	3850	1878–9 . . .	1530
1874–5 . . .	1200	1879–80 . . .	1950
1875–6 . . .	1900	1880–1 . . .	380
1876–7 . . .	1720	1881–2 . . .	700

It will be seen that the output varies a good deal; the price of rough material is also subject to fluctuation, varying between 5000 and 10,000 reis per arroba (£2 to £4 per hundredweight). For exceptional material as much as 100,000 to 200,000 reis per arroba may be paid. There are no cutting works in Brazil itself; an attempt to establish such was once made by a few emigrants from Oberstein, but was unsuccessful; articles of cut agate, therefore, have to be imported from Oberstein.

In **India** the mother-rocks of agate and the other varieties of chalcedony, already mentioned, are the amygdaloidal rocks or so called traps of the Deccan plateau. These Deccan traps cover an area of thousands of square miles and extend into the surrounding districts, namely, the ancient kingdom of Gujarat, with its capital of Surat, the district to the west of the Gulf of Cambay, now known as the Kathiawar peninsular, and a portion of Rajputana. Another occurrence which should be mentioned is much further to the east in the Rajmahal Hills, which are situated in latitude 25° N., at the point where the Ganges bends to the west. These hills, as well as the neighbouring portions of Bengal, consist of a volcanic rock similiar to those of the Deccan plateau.

The crevices and amygdaloidal cavities in these rocks are everywhere filled with agate, carnelian, &c., which are set free by the weathering of the mother-rock and are found loose in the ground or as pebbles in the Godavari, Wanda, Kistna, Bhima, and several other rivers rising in or flowing through the Deccan. In some places the angular or rounded blocks of chalcedony are more or less firmly bound together by a ferruginous cementing material, thus forming extensive and sometimes thick beds of conglomerate. These beds of conglomerate or secondary deposits of agate constitute the main source of the material used for cutting.

Although the several varieties of chalcedony are widely distributed throughout India, they are not everywhere of a quality suitable for cutting. Among the numerous localities at which material of good quality is obtained there are two of special importance, which have been mentioned before as localities for moss-agate, mocha-stone, heliotrope, carnelian, &c. These are the neighbourhood of Ratanpur, on the lower Narbada river, in the State of Rajpipla, and the country north of Rajkot, in the Kathiawar peninsula, where the varieties of chalcedony just mentioned are everywhere accompanied by agate.

The best known deposits are at Ratanpur, whence for more than 2000 years the lapidaries at Broach have obtained their supplies of rough carnelian, agate, &c. The best specimens all come from a thin bed of conglomerate, the fine colour of the stones being doubtless due to the ferruginous cement by which they are bound together. This bed is made accessible by the excavation of pits, which measure 4 feet across and about 30 feet in depth, the deepest measuring not more than 50 feet. From these pits extend, in all directions along the agate-bearing bed, horizontal galleries, for distances up to 100 yards. The stones found in this bed are usually under a pound in weight, and among them are a few cat's-eyes. Some need to have their fine colour developed by exposure to heat while others already possess it. Part of the material collected is sent in boats to Broach and Cambay, the sites of the principal native lapidary works, part to Europe — principally to Oberstein which it reaches through London—and the rest to China, a considerable amount of Indian chalcedony, especially carnelian, being cut in that country.

Native lapidaries practice their trade at many places, where suitable rough material is obtained, for example, at Jabalpur, in the Central Provinces (Fig. 33), and at Banda on the Khan, a tributary of the Jumna, in which a large number of pebbles of chalcedony are found. Very important at one time were the lapidary works at Broach, near Baroda, and not far from the mouth of the Narbada river, and at Almadabad a little further to the north. The only lapidary works which are of importance at the present day are those at Cambay, on the gulf of the same name, north of Bombay. Articles worked here are designed and finished in accordance with European, Indian, and Arabian tastes, and together with rough material are exported to these countries.

The murrhine vases, famous in ancient times, are said to have come from Ulein (or Ouzein), in latitude 23° 10′ N. and longitude 74° 14′ E. of Greenwich, in this same part of

India. These, therefore, must have been fashioned out of agate or some variety of chalcedony and not as has been assumed of fluor-spar, which is not known to occur in this region, and, moreover, is rare throughout the whole country.

Applications of Agate.—Agate and other varieties of chalcedony not only furnish a material for ornamental objects of the most varied kinds, but are also applied to many other uses ; in fact, no other stone is applied to purposes so diverse. The character and design of the ornaments manufactured of these stones change with the fashion of the hour, and certain articles which one year are made and sold in their thousands, in the next year will be unsaleable. The favour with which the different varieties of agate and chalcedony are regarded also depends on the caprice of fashion ; at one time red carnelian is most in demand, at another green heliotrope or plasma, and at a third black agate or onyx. Agate ornaments of all kinds were specially popular from 1848 to the middle of the fifties, and this period was the harvest time of the agate industry. It is only specially large objects or articles of great artistic merit for which high prices are demanded ; as a rule, agate ornaments are extraordinarily cheap, but in spite of this the material is imitated very closely in glass. This so-called agate-glass can be easily distinguished from genuine agate by the much greater hardness of the latter.

The objects most freqently fashioned out of agate are small articles of personal ornament. These, which are of the most varied description and are manufactured in enormous numbers, include sleeve-links, breast-pins, hair-pins, ear-rings, pendants for watch-chains, necklaces, bracelets, buckles, rings, ring-stones—often worked as seal-stones, sometimes with raised figures—seals, and signets. The mineral is also largely used as a material for articles of more or less utility, such as stick- and umbrella-handles, children's toys (marbles), match-boxes, toilet-cases, snuff-boxes, seal-stocks, pen-holders, knife-handles, chessmen, counters, bowls and vases of every size and form, holy-water founts, cups, dessert plates, sauce-bowls, candlesticks, &c. The variously coloured chalcedonies are utilised in mosaic work, which is applied to all kinds of decorative purposes. The objects of technical importance for which agate is used include mortars, burnishing tools for gold-workers and bookbinders, smooth stones for paper and card manufacturers, rollers for the use of ribbon manufacturers, and pivot supports for balances and other delicate mechanical instruments.

Since the year 1850 there has sprung up with Central Africa a peculiar trade in charms of brown and black agate, the so-called olives. These objects have the form of cylinders from $\frac{1}{2}$ to 3 inches long, they are pierced in the direction of their length, and must display a white central band. In the middle of the sixties several hundred thousand thalers' worth of these charms were manufactured at Oberstein and exported to the Soudan ; some firms exported these goods to the value of 40,000 thalers (£6000). The demand reached its height in 1866 ; after that date it began to fall off and is now very small. Red carnelian charms having the form of a perforated triangle are exported to Senegal.

During the manufacture of the articles named above and of others the agate undergoes many and varied processes, which include cutting, grinding, polishing, boring, engraving, and artificially colouring. It is essentially a German industry, and is carried on mainly at Oberstein, on the Nahe, and at Idar and other places in the neighbourhood ; also in Waldkirch in the Black Forest, where, however, fewer agates than other precious and semi-precious stones are cut. At Oberstein and Idar, on the other hand, it is agate and the other varieties of chalcedony and quartz minerals which are principally worked ; other stones including malachite, lapis-lazuli, and in recent times even the diamond, are cut there, but in quite insignificant numbers. The whole world is supplied with agate goods from these works, and although the agate sold at watering-places, tourist resorts, and such like places is described to be of local origin this is not actually the case. The agate-cutting industry has been monopolised by Oberstein for centuries, and in no part of the world, not even in India, has it anything approaching a rival. Wherever a cut agate is seen it may be pretty safely stated that it was worked at Oberstein. The mineral is not only cut, bored, engraved, and coloured in these works, but frequently also mounted, usually in gilded brass. Specialisation in these works has been carried out to such an extent that each workman executes his part with perfect skill and the greatest possible rapidity. The consequence is

Fig. 90. Agate-grinding and polishing workshop at Oberstein.

that the agate goods produced here are more perfect in workmanship and lower in price than those manufactured anywhere else. We will now consider the methods employed in rather more detail.

Agate-cutting.—The primary cause of the establishment of agate-cutting works at Oberstein was the presence of abundance of rough material in the neighbourhood. The earliest authentic record of the existence of the works dates back to 1497, but they were doubtless in existence before that date. After flourishing for some centuries, the industry gradually declined owing to the exhaustion of the native stores of rough material. The discovery of the Brazilian deposits about the year 1830 gave a fresh impetus to the trade, all the greater because the fresh material was specially suitable for the application of artificial colouring methods, which had been discovered a short time previously. At the present time scarcely any agate of local origin is cut at Oberstein, the rough material being obtained principally from Brazil, though some Indian chalcedony, especially certain varieties such as carnelian, moss-agate, mocha-stone, &c., is also worked. Material from other parts of the world, not only agate and other varieties of chalcedony, but amethyst, citrine, rock-crystal, and indeed almost all precious stones, including diamond, are also cut there to a certain extent. The rough material is imported from its place of origin by merchants who, following an old custom, dispose of it to the lapidaries by public auction, which is held from time to time in Oberstein or Idar.

The workshops in which the agate-cutting is performed are now fitted with every modern convenience, including grinding discs rotating in a horizontal plane, and steam-power is used throughout. The arrangement of, and the methods adopted in, one establishment do not differ essentially from those of any other.

Besides the workshops fitted with modern appliances, there are still retained the mills driven by water-power, which, with various modifications and improvements, have been in use since early times. There are altogether about 200 of these mills; a series of them are situated on the Idar stream, which flows into the Nahe close to Oberstein, and on which the village of Idar is situated, and others on neighbouring streams. These are reserved mainly for grinding work proper, boring and engraving being performed in special shops. A grinding mill of this description is represented in Fig. 90. In these mills three or five (in the figure three) grindstones of sandstone, which measure up to 5 feet in diameter, are sunk in a pit and are made to revolve three times a second by means of a water-wheel. The front surfaces of the grindstones are provided at either side with ridges and furrows so that the agates can be ground to any desired form.

The rough agate is first broken up with hammer and chisel; the more valuable pieces are roughly cut into the shape they are to assume by a metal disc charged with emery powder or, in recent times, with diamond powder. After this it is ground by being pressed with considerable force against the cylindrical surface or in the groove of the rotating grindstone, which is kept constantly wet by a stream of water. The workman, who performs the operation, lies with his body in a hollowed-out, trough-like bench, the cuirass, which stands close to the grindstone. He is enabled to apply the requisite pressure to the stone by pushing with his feet against two posts firmly fixed at the end of the bench. The stone is held in the hands and turned about on the grindstone until it has assumed the desired form. At each of the grindstones, which are about a foot in width, two workmen can work when necessary, one on either side. During the process of grinding the agate becomes phosphorescent and emits a brilliant reddish-white light.

Fig. 90 is a diagrammatic representation of a grinding-mill, while Fig. 91 is a picture of an actual workshop, namely, that of Herr August Wintermantel, at Waldkirch, in the Black Forest.

Vases, bowls, and such like objects are hollowed out by other workmen on a small grindstone; each process, in fact, is carried out by special workmen with the help of special appliances.

The polishing machine imparts a high polish to cut stones, and leaves them completely finished and ready for sale. It consists of a cylinder of hard wood on a disc of lead or tin, and the polishing material is tripolite applied in a moist condition. This work is so simple that it can be left in charge of children. The man and the two women represented to the left in Fig. 90 are engaged in polishing.

For some purposes stones require to be pierced, and the operation is performed by rapidly rotating steel points charged with emery or diamond powder, or provided with a fine diamond splinter.

Engraved Agates were regarded with great favour by the ancient Romans, and although they are not esteemed as highly at the present day, yet the number of stones treated in this way is not inconsiderable.

The varieties best suited for engraving upon, but not devoted exclusively to this purpose, are the onxyes, including onyx proper, chalcedony-onyx, carnelian-onyx, and sard-onyx. These can be so cut as to display a white or light figure against a darker-coloured background. The flatter an onyx is, and the more regular are its layers (Plate XX., Figs. 5a, b), the better suited it is for this purpose; hence Brazilian agates with their plane layers (Plate XIX., Fig. b) are specially suited for onyx stones, and on that account

FIG. 91. Agate-grinding workshop of Herr August Wintermantel, at Waldkirch (Baden).

more valuable. Stones which are to be engraved have the form of plates, and are cut out of even-layered agates, so that the plane of the plate is parallel to the banding of the stone and is of one uniform colour. The uppermost layer is then partly cut away, so that the portion allowed to remain has the outlines of some figure, usually a portrait. It is generally arranged that the figure cut out of the uppermost layer shall be white or light coloured, this being well thrown up by the background afforded by the coloured lower layer. A *cameo* cut in carnelian-onyx is represented in Plate XX., Fig. 7, and others in Figs. 93 and 94. Sometimes the uppermost black layer is cut through and the figure worked in the underlying white layer, as in the *intaglio* of Fig. 92; in this case also one gets a white figure on a dark background. A seal-stone of carnelian with a letter engraved upon it is represented in Plate XX., Fig. 6. A kind of stone much sought after for cameos is one in which a white layer is partly covered by a red layer. It is then possible to produce a figure showing two colours, the red layer being utilised to represent hair, clothing, or such like. The work is performed, as we have already seen, by a tool known as the style. The actual work of agate-engraving is performed principally in Paris and Italy, but the plates of onyx used by the engravers are prepared at Oberstein. In Italy onyx is largely replaced by plates cut from the thick shells of certain marine molluscs, these shells, like carnelian-onyx, being built up of red and white layers. They are very much softer than agate, and can be cut with much less labour.

It is not only stones with plane surfaces, however, which are cut as cameos, for there are a few onyx vessels in existence decorated in this way, the body of the vessel being formed by a layer of one colour and the raised figures cut in a layer of another colour. The famous onyx vase preserved in the collection at Brunswick is a monument to the skill of ancient artists in this direction.

The **artificial colouring** of stones is an important branch of the agate industry at Oberstein, especially since the supplies of rough material have been obtained principally from Brazil. Most of the agate found in nature is of a dingy grey colour, and, until the discovery of the methods by which it may be coloured, was totally unfit for cutting. The first step was to colour the stones black, this art being stated to have been imparted to an agate merchant at Idar by a customer at Rome, who paid an annual visit to Idar for the purpose of buying onyx. The art, which had been long known in Rome, was afterwards extensively practised at Oberstein, and in course of time was developed and improved. Not only was a black colour imparted to stones but also brown, yellow, blue, green, and red.

The artificial colouring of agate is possible because of the porous nature, not only of this stone but also of all other varieties of chalcedony, by virtue of which they absorb any coloured liquid in which they are immersed. All specimens of agate are not equally porous, neither are all layers of the same piece; some are very porous, readily absorbing a large quantity of coloured liquid and thus acquiring an intense colour, while others are quite or almost non-porous, absorbing colouring matter very slowly and with great difficulty, so that they are only faintly coloured. Specimens answering the former description are described by lapidaries as " soft " and the latter as " hard." In this sense the agate found at Oberstein is " harder " than that occurring in Brazil, which is specially suitable for artificial colouring. In Brazilian agates, however, the outer portion of the amygdale, the so-called skin, is difficult to colour, and the milk-white layers are practically non-porous and cannot be coloured at all. If the stone is allowed to remain long enough in the colouring liquid, this will penetrate to the innermost parts of the stone, so that the whole mass, and not merely a superficial layer, is coloured. It has been observed that the absorption of liquid takes place much more rapidly radially, that is to say, perpendicular to the layers, than along the layers, this being due to the radial extension and arrangement of the pores already described.

The principle of the colouring process is thus quite simple, although in practice there are several points which require attention if a good result is to be obtained, and the work is entrusted only to experienced workmen. The most essential qualification for the work is a familiarity with the appearance and character of different types of stones, but even with this qualification it is not always possible to foretell the result of immersing a given stone in a given liquid. It may happen, for example, that after the immersion in the colouring liquid of a number of stones apparently equally suitable for the purpose, some will be green and others blue. The complete process is still in many cases jealously preserved as a trade secret, as was the case at first with the process of staining the stones black.

The latter process has been known in Oberstein since 1819. The stone to be coloured black is first washed clean and dried without the application of heat, and then immersed

PLATE XX

LAPIS-LAZULI, TURQUOISE, MALACHITE, CHALCEDONY, AND AMBER
(1)   (2, 3)   (4)   (5—8)   (9)

1. Lapis-lazuli, polished. 2. Turquoise, blue cut-stone. 3. Turquoise, green, in matrix.
4a. Malachite, rough. 4b. The same, polished. 5a, b. Onyx, cut. 6. Carnelian (intaglio).
7. Carnelian-onyx (cameo). 8. Chrysoprase, cut. 9. Amber, polished in part.

in an aqueous solution of honey or sugar in a perfectly clean and new pot. The whole is kept at a temperature below boiling-point for two or three weeks, during which time the loss of water by evaporation must be made good in order to keep the stones covered with liquid. The stones are then taken out, washed, and placed in another pot with commercial sulphuric acid (oil of vitriol) and again warmed. The honey or sugar absorbed by the stone during its immersion in the first liquid is decomposed by the sulphuric acid with

FIG. 92.   Antique intaglio.

FIG. 94.   Antique cameo.
(*See* page 521.)

FIG. 93.   Antique cameo.

separation of carbon, which imparts its black colour to the stone. The " softer " stones, even after a few hours immersion in the acid, acquire a deep black colour, others require an immersion lasting for a day or several days, and some pieces only assume the black colour after being immersed for a considerable time. When the stone is as black as it is possible for it to be, it is taken out of the liquid and quickly dried in an oven. It is then cut and polished, and finally rubbed with oil or allowed to soak in this liquid for a day, the oil not absorbed being wiped off with bran. This final treatment hides small cracks and improves the lustre of the stone.

The fine black agates now bought and sold in the markets have been artificially coloured in this way, as have also the onyxes (Plate XX., Figs. 5a, b), in which the black layers, now alternating with the white, were originally greyish or bluish in colour. Not only do highly porous layers become a deep velvety black, but less porous bands acquire a more or less dark shade of brown. The shade of colour imparted artificially to a stone depends, to some extent, on its original colour ; a red layer, for example, after being artificially coloured will have a reddish tinge, and so on. It is a significant fact that, according to the way in which the stone will acquire the black colour, a hundredweight of agate may be worth £5 or £250. When offering such stones for sale, it is therefore customary to submit small fragments as samples for the purpose of testing whether they will acquire a good colour.

The tinting of agates with colours other than black is comparatively unimportant, but a few details of the methods adopted are given below.

A fine lemon-yellow, such as agate in its natural state never possesses, may be imparted by placing well dried agates in a pot of hydrochloric acid and gently warming in an oven. The colouring will be completed in a fortnight.

Blue, ranging in shade from the finest and deepest indigo and azure to a delicate sky-blue, can also be imparted to agate; natural stones of this colour are, however, never found in nature. The agate is first impregnated with yellow prussiate of potash (potassium ferrocyanide), and afterwards warmed in a solution of iron vitriol (ferrous sulphate). By the interaction and oxidation of these salts, a Berlin-blue compound is deposited in the pores of the stone, to which it gives its colour. This method, however, is only one out of several. Artificially coloured blue agates sometimes closely resemble lapis-lazuli, and for this reason are known as "false lapis-lazuli." They may be distinguished from genuine material by a difference in the shade of colour, and by the fact that the latter is softer than is agate.

A green colour is imparted by impregnating the stone with chromic acid, and afterwards exposing it to a high temperature. An apple-green shade like that of chrysoprase can be imparted with a solution of a nickel salt.

Agate is coloured red in the same way as is carnelian, namely, by impregnating it with a solution of iron vitriol and then exposing it to heat. Agate is also frequently coloured brown, as was mentioned above under sard.

Some agates undergo an advantageous colour change by being simply heated or "burned"; the bluish or greyish tints, for example, may thereby be changed to milk-white, and the yellow and brown to a fine red.

MALACHITE.

Malachite is a mineral sometimes used as an ornamental stone, although it has nothing to recommend it for this purpose save a fine green colour. Chemically it is a hydrated carbonate of copper, having the formula $H_2O.2CuO.CO_2$. The percentage composition of the purest specimens is:

Cupric oxide (CuO)	71·95
Carbon dioxide (CO$_2$)	19·90
Water (H$_2$O)	8·15

The water entering into the composition of malachite is easily driven off by heat, the mineral, at the same time, losing its green colour and becoming black. When a fragment of malachite is placed in hydrochloric acid, or a little acid dropped on the surface of the stone, there is a brisk effervescence owing to the evolution of carbon dioxide. This reaction serves to distinguish malachite in its rough condition from other green minerals of similar appearance. When completely dissolved in hydrochloric acid a green solution of copper chloride is obtained, and drops of this impart a magnificent blue colour to a colourless flame.

Malachite sometimes occurs distinctly crystallised, usually taking the form of small needles belonging to the monoclinic system. The mineral occurs much more commonly, however, in the form of compact masses of greater or less size, the crystalline nature of which is indicated by the radially fibrous structure. Compact masses, which are apparently not crystalline, and often even quite earthy in character, are also met with.

Malachite of the finest quality suitable for ornamental purposes occurs as nodular masses often of considerable size, the surface of which may be rounded, reniform, botryoidal, or stalactitic. These nodules have a radially fibrous structure, and are built up of concentric shells. The external rounded surface is often blackish and dull, but fractured surfaces are always green in colour, and show a slight silkiness of lustre owing to the fibrous structure of the mineral. The green colour of such a fractured surface is not quite uniform, and narrow bands, alternately lighter and darker, are often to be seen following the external outlines of the stone, in the same manner as in agate. The presence of these bands together with the fibrous structure gives the stone a kind of grained appearance, which is often very effective for decorative purposes. A nodule of malachite in its natural condition is represented in Plate XX., Fig. 4a, while Fig. 4b, of the same plate, shows a polished slab of the same material.

The physical characters of malachite must now receive our attention. Owing to the large amount of copper present the specific gravity is high; values ranging from 3·5 to 4·0 have been given for different specimens, but the mean value is usually between 3·7 and 3·8. The hardness is only about $3\frac{1}{2}$, so that malachite is scratched even by fluor-spar. Being opaque the liability to become scratched is not as serious a disadvantage as it would be in the case of a transparent stone, but nevertheless it is advisable to protect malachite ornaments as far as possible from injury in this direction. Because of the softness of this mineral it is impossible to obtain a very strong lustre on a cut surface, although the polish is decidedly good. Malachite is not brittle, and can therefore be worked on the lathe.

Malachite is a widely distributed mineral, but generally occurs in small masses only, intergrown with other copper minerals. These impure masses are not suitable for cutting, but they form at many localities not unimportant ores of copper. The wide distribution of malachite is explained by the fact that other cupriferous minerals and ores—copper-pyrites, cuprite, &c.—are readily altered to malachite; in fact, the mineral always originates in this way. Although malachite of inferior quality is abundant at many localities, large masses of pure material suitable for ornamental purposes are by no means common.

The largest amount of malachite suitable for cutting has been found in the **Ural Mountains**, where also the largest and purest masses of material hitherto found have been met with. In a sense, therefore, malachite is a Russian mineral, for in no other country is it found in such abundance. The Urals are very rich in copper, but only a few of the deposits are of importance from our present point of view, the majority yielding only material fit for smelting. Malachite suitable for cutting has been obtained from the copper mines at Nizhni-Tagilsk, at Bogoslovsk in the northern part of the mountains, and at Gumeshevsk further to the south. At the beginning of the nineteenth century there was a considerable yield of material suitable for cutting; this has gradually fallen off, until at the present day stones of this description are obtained only from the Medno-Rudiansk mine, near Nizhni-Tagilsk, the other mines being exhausted or yielding impure material only. The malachite usually occurs in nest-like masses in veins in limestone, from which it must be extracted by the ordinary operations of mining. The material, which is not sold in the market in the rough condition, is cut in the lapidary works at Ekaterinburg.

The mines which formerly yielded the finest material in the greatest abundance were those of Gumeshevsk, situated fifty-six versts south-east of Ekaterinburg and very near the 58th meridian of longitude east of Paris, in the district of the Chussovaya. Reniform, stalactitic, and tube-shaped masses of malachite, of various sizes and of a quality never seen elsewhere, were found in these mines embedded in red clay. The larger of these masses reached a weight of 10 poods (360 pounds), but the majority were smaller than this. The largest single mass of malachite found in these mines is preserved in the collection of the Institute of Mines in St. Petersburg. It is a smooth reniform mass having a height of 3 feet 6 inches, almost the same breadth, and a weight of about 90 poods (3240 pounds); it is valued at 525,000 roubles.

At Nizhni-Tagilsk, in the northern Urals, a little south of latitude 58° N. and in longitude about $57\frac{1}{2}$° E. of Paris, copper ores of a similar nature occur in the same manner as at Gumeshevsk, but fibrous malachite in reniform masses suitable for cutting is much rarer and less fine than at the latter place. In the year 1835 there was found here, however, a mass of malachite of such a size as had never been seen before nor has been since, and which far exceeded the large mass from Gumeshevsk, mentioned above. It was $17\frac{1}{2}$ feet long, 8 feet broad, and $3\frac{1}{4}$ feet high; it was quite solid in the interior, and was estimated to weigh not less than 25 to 30 tons. The whole mass was of a fine emerald-green colour and was thus quite suitable for cutting. The Medno-Rudiansk mine, which alone yields any considerable amount of fine malachite, is situated in the Nizhni-Tagilsk district; the other mines, as stated above, are now exhausted.

This is true also of the mines of Bogoslovsk, situated further to the north, in latitude about $59\frac{2}{3}$° N. and longitude $57\frac{2}{3}$° E. of Paris, on the upper Turya river. From the fact that they stand on this river, fifteen to eighteen versts further to the east, these workings are also known as the Turyinsk mines. Here also malachite occurs in reniform masses, which, however, are poorer in quality than those found at Gumeshevsk, and never of specially large size.

The locality for malachite suitable for decorative purposes next in importance to the Urals is **Australia**. The mineral occurs in this continent most frequently in small masses, valuable only for the copper they contain. The larger masses of malachite of superior quality, which are occasionally met with, are in no way inferior to Uralian material, and resemble this in every particular. The mineral is specially abundant in Queensland, and magnificent specimens have been obtained from the Peak Downs copper mine in that State. Fine malachite occurs also in New South Wales, and at Wallaroo and Burra-Burra in South Australia.

Malachite is worn more frequently set in brooches and ear-rings than as a ring or pin stone. It is usually cut with a plane or slightly convex surface and no facets, these in an opaque stone being quite ineffective. Table-stones and step-cuts, however, are sometimes seen, while the stones to be used as ear-rings are given a club-shaped form.

This mineral is far more extensively used as a material for letter-weights, inkstands, candlesticks, ornamental bowls and vases, and even for objects of considerable size, such as mantel-pieces and table-tops. These larger objects, however, are usually made of copper or some other material and only veneered with thin plates of malachite. The art of veneering lies principally in so piecing these plates together that the joins shall be as inconspicuous as possible, this end being attained by a skilful utilisation of the grained structure of the mineral. The industry flourishes most in Russia, where it is common to meet with large and beautiful objects made of malachite; and those displayed in the palaces of European princes have been in many cases presented by the Czar of Russia. The Isaac Church of St. Petersburg is famous for the beauty of its massive columns of malachite. A number of columns of the same material were found in the temple of Diana at Ephesus, and now adorn the Sophia Church at Constantinople.

The uses to which malachite is applied are thus very similar to those of lapis-lazuli, but malachite in large masses is less rare, and has not more than a tenth of the value of lapis-lazuli. The supply of malachite in small pieces is always more than equal to the demand; the price of such material is therefore low, but large compact masses of fine colour are rare and command much higher prices.

The general appearance of malachite is so characteristic and peculiar to itself that the mineral can scarcely be mistaken for any other stone. Green chrysocolla, the so-called "siliceous malachite," sometimes resembles malachite, but can be distinguished from it by the fact that it does not effervesce when a drop of hydrochloric acid is placed upon it, while malachite, being a carbonate, does do so. This test may be applied to a cut stone with no serious damage, provided the drop of acid is placed on an inconspicuous part and quickly wiped off.

CHESSYLITE.

The chemical composition of this mineral is very similar to that of malachite, but the constituents are present in different proportions, the chemical formula being $H_2O.3CuO.2CO_2$. It has a fine dark blue colour like that of lapis-lazuli, a character to which its other name, azurite, has reference. Its specific gravity is 3·8, and its hardness $3\frac{3}{4}$, so that it is both denser and softer than lapis-lazuli, from which it may also be distinguished from the fact that it effervesces with acid like malachite. In mass, chessylite is scarcely ever perfectly transparent, being at best only translucent. Its lustre is vitreous and the mineral takes a good polish. It is used to only a very limited extent.

SATIN-SPAR.

The term satin-spar embraces certain finely fibrous varieties of three distinct mineral species, which are usually white in colour and possess in common a satiny or silky lustre.

Calcite.—This mineral sometimes occurs as veins with a finely fibrous structure, the fibres being arranged perpendicularly to the two parallel walls of the vein. When the plate-like masses from such a vein are broken across, the fractured surface shows a fine silky lustre which can be increased by polishing. This variety of satin-spar is, therefore, sometimes cut for beads, or ear-rings, or similar ornaments. A cut and polished convex surface shows a band of chatoyant light, as in cat's-eye, which is due to the same cause, namely, the finely fibrous structure of the mineral. Polished objects very soon become scratched and disfigured, for the mineral has a hardness represented by 3 only. Some of the best material is obtained from near Alston in Cumberland, where it occurs in straight regular veins measuring 2 or 3 inches across in a black shale of Carboniferous age. It has a snow-white colour with sometimes a delicate rosy tinge, and the satiny lustre is very conspicuous on polished surfaces cut parallel to the fibres.

Marble is a granular, crystalline aggregate of calcite, but as this variety has no application as a precious stone it need not be considered further. Onyx-marble from Tecati in Mexico and onyx-alabaster from Egypt are varieties of stalactitic marble, which in the majority of cases also consist of calcite.

Aragonite.—This mineral, like calcite, consists of calcium carbonate ($CaCO_3$), but differs from the latter in crystalline form and in physical characters. It also occurs sometimes in finely fibrous aggregates, when it cannot be distinguished on mere inspection from finely fibrous calcite, for which in its varied uses it may be substituted. The calcareous deposits (Sprudelstein) of the hot springs of Carlsbad in Bohemia also consist of aragonite; this material is often banded in red, white, and brown, and is fashioned into all kinds of small articles, which are sold as souvenirs to visitors at the baths.

Gypsum.—This mineral also occurs like calcite, but more frequently, in fibrous veins, the fibres of which are perpendicular to the walls of the veins. When the mineral has a very finely fibrous structure it exhibits a fine satiny lustre, and may be cut for ornaments of various kinds just as calcite is. The hardness is still less, however (H = 2), and the stone can be scratched even with the finger-nail. Material of this character is abundant in the extensive deposits of gypsum, largely quarried for the manufacture of plaster of Paris, in the Triassic rocks of Derbyshire and Nottinghamshire. Massive gypsum with a granular structure is known as *alabaster*, but, like marble, is never used as a gem.

FLUOR-SPAR.

Fluor-spar or fluorite is much too soft for use as a precious stone, but notwithstanding this is sometimes worn as a ring-stone or other ornament for the sake of its fine colour. It is often substituted for more valuable precious stones which it happens to resemble in colour, but its chief use is as a material for ornamental objects of various kinds. When perfectly clear and colourless fluor-spar has an important application in the construction of apochromatic lenses, and the mineral has several other technical applications.

Fluor-spar is an abundant and widely distributed mineral. It occurs in a massive and compact condition, filling veins and crevices in rocks, and is associated with barytes and metallic ores, especially of lead. Magnificent groups of regularly developed crystals resting on the matrix are sometimes found in cavities in these veins, the crystals being finely coloured and transparent enough for use as gems. The finest specimens are found in England, in the counties of Derbyshire, Cumberland, Cornwall, and Devonshire, the two first named being most famed for these crystals. Good specimens occur also in the metalliferous veins of the Harz, in the Erzgebirge, and in the Black Forest. The mineral is so widely distributed that it is only possible here to enumerate the most important localities.

In its purest condition fluor-spar contains 48·72 per cent. of calcium and 51·28 per cent. of fluorine, and is thus fluoride of calcium with the formula CaF_2. The mineral frequently occurs in fine crystals belonging to the cubic system. The cube is the form most commonly assumed, but the octahedron and other simple forms occur alone or in combination with each other. Twin crystals are not uncommon, two cubes interpenetrating in such a way that they are symmetrical with respect to each other about a face of the octahedron. Massive crystalline aggregates of granular or columnar structure, and compact masses of use only for technical purposes, are also common.

Fluor-spar has a perfect cleavage in four directions parallel to the faces of the octahedron, which truncates the corners of the cube. It is brittle, and is the mineral which stands fourth on Mohs' scale of hardness; it is scratched, therefore, by ordinary window-glass. The specific gravity varies between 3·1 and 3·2, so that the mineral sinks in test liquid No. 3 but floats in No. 2. When heated before the blowpipe, fluor-spar generally decrepitates violently and falls into small splinters, which are scattered about with some violence. This is explained by the fact that it usually contains a number of small cavities which are either vacuous or filled with liquid, and this on being exposed to heat expands and reduces the stone to splinters. Fluor-spar alone is not very fusible, but heated with other minerals it melts readily, and for this reason is used as a flux in the reduction of metallic ores, hence its name. Some specimens are remarkable in that when raised to a temperature below red-heat they phosphoresce, that is to say, they emit a beautiful bluish or greenish light. Fluor-spar is completely decomposed by sulphuric acid with the formation of hydrofluoric acid, a gas much used for etching glass and certain precious stones.

The behaviour of fluor-spar with respect to light has an important connection with the uses of the mineral as an ornamental stone. It has a characteristic moist-looking vitreous lustre, and ranges from perfect transparency through all degrees of translucency, to complete opacity. The most important character of the mineral is its colour, which is extremely variable; no other mineral, in fact, displays such a wide range of beautiful colours, and no colour represented in the mineral kingdom is absent. Perfectly pure fluor-spar, which is rare, is limpid and colourless. By the mechanical intermixture of very small amounts of foreign substances, for the most part of organic matter, colour is produced, and this is either destroyed or altered when the fluor-spar is heated. The colour of fluor-spar may be very pale and delicate in shade, or, on the other hand, it may be so deep and intense as to be only recognisable in thin sections of the stone, thick pieces appearing almost black. The powder or, in other words, the streak of the mineral is always white, or at least very pale. Owing to the irregular distribution of the colouring matter fluor-spar often has a patchy appearance. Specimens showing several colours alternating with each other in regular bands are common, this being especially the case in massive, crystalline aggregates. Crystals may have a nucleus which differs in colour from the external portions, for example, the central portion may be yellow and the outer violet.

The fluor-spar used for ornamental purposes must be transparent and of a fine uniform colour. Material of this description is known in the trade by the name of the precious stone it most resembles in colour with the prefix false, " false topaz," " false ruby," " false emerald," " false sapphire," " false amethyst," &c., being some of the terms used for stones of different colour. Coloured fluor-spar may be passed off for stones other than those just mentioned: thus yellow fluor-spar may resemble yellow quartz (citrine) as well as yellow topaz, and red fluor-spar either red tourmaline (rubellite) or red corundum (ruby). It is to be noted that the inaccurate term " false topaz" is applied to yellow quartz as well as to yellow fluor-spar.

Yellow fluor-spar is very common; it is found at Freiberg, Gersdorf, and other places in the Saxon Erzgebirge, in various shades of yellow, including wine-yellow, honey-yellow, and brownish-yellow.

Red octahedra, usually more or less corroded on the surface, occur in crevices in gneiss in the Swiss Alps, but are not abundant. They are found, for example, on the St. Gotthard, where Göschenen is often named as a locality; on the Zinkenstock, near the Grimsel; in the Tavetsch valley in Graubünden; in Wallis; Tessin, &c. The crystals are usually of a light rose-red colour, darker shades being rare.

The colour of green fluor-spar or "false emerald" is sometimes very fine and approaches to that of the true emerald. Crystals from certain English localities, from the porphyry of Petersburg near Halle, and from the metalliferous veins of Badenweiler, are remarkable in this respect. A recently discovered occurrence is that at Macomb, in St. Lawrence County, New York, where thousands of beautiful green crystals, with a total weight of fifteen tons, were found in a single large cavity.

Blue fluor-spar, or "false sapphire," of a very dark colour, is found in the tin mines of the Erzgebirge, and also in salt mines at Hall in the Tyrol. The cubes of fluor-spar from Alston Moor in Cumberland have the peculiar property of appearing by transmitted light of a fine green, and by reflected light of a dark blue colour. The phenomenon from its occurrence in fluor-spar is known as fluorescence. Stones of this description are sometimes mounted à jour in pins, rings, &c., in order to display their fluorescence. Other blue crystals, especially when of a dark shade of colour, have a perceptible violet tinge, while others are lighter in shade and of as pronounced a violet colour as amethyst itself. Magnificent crystals of violet fluor-spar, or "false amethyst," are found in the lead mines of Weardale, in Durham.

These various colour-varieties of fluor-spar are cut in the forms adopted for the precious stones they respectively resemble. They acquire a good polish, but require great care both in cutting and in wear, since the lack of hardness and the perfect cleavage renders them liable to be scratched or cracked and splintered. They are never worth very much, and can always be distinguished from the valuable precious stones they may resemble in colour by their lack of hardness, their specific gravity, single refraction, and by the fact that, in correspondence with their crystalline form, they are not dichroic.

Though little worn as a gem, fluor-spar is somewhat extensively used as a material for ornamental objects such as bowls, vases, candlesticks, letter-weights, or even for columns, mantel-pieces, &c. The so-called spar-ornaments of this description are manufactured chiefly in England of the variety of fluor-spar known as "blue john," which is found in large amount and of fine quality at Tray Cliff, near Castleton, in Derbyshire. This is massive, coarsely-grained material of a dark blue colour tinged with violet, frequently intersected with white and yellow bands. The stones are ground into the desired form and can be worked on the lathe; the process, however, needs great care, for, owing to the brittleness and easy cleavage of the mineral, it is very liable to splinter. Since the commencement of the industry in 1765 many matters of technique have been learnt by experience. The fluor-spar is now, for example, impregnated with resin in order to make it tougher and less liable to splinter. Material so treated can be fashioned into vessels the walls of which are not more than 1 or $1\frac{1}{2}$ lines in thickness, this excessive tenuity being necessary because of the depth of colour of the mineral. When "blue john" is exposed to a temperature just below a red-heat the dark violet-blue colour changes to a beautiful amethystine violet, which is not shown by stones in their natural condition. The operation needs to be performed with great care, for not only is the stone liable to crack, but if the temperature is too high it will be completely decolourised. Owing to the comparative abundance of the mineral and the ease with which rough material is obtained, articles fashioned of fluor-spar do not cost much more than the value of the labour expended upon their production; this is not inconsiderable, owing to the difficulty of the work.

It has been suggested that the murrhine vases of the ancient Romans were made of fluor-spar, but there is no conclusive evidence to support this, and it is more probable, as suggested under agate, that the material was some mineral other than fluor-spar. Pale yellow and rose-red beads cut out of fluor-spar have been found, together with beads of sodalite, in the ancient ruins of Tiahuanaco, near Lake Titicaca, on the high Bolivian plateau.

APATITE.

Apatite is another mineral which occurs of various colours closely resembling those of certain precious stones, and for this reason transparent stones are sometimes cut. Apatite is better suited than fluor-spar for this purpose, since it has a hardness of 5 and it possesses no distinct cleavage. Chemically it is a phosphate of calcium containing chlorine and fluorine ; it crystallises in the hexagonal system, the crystals, which are often very beautiful, usually taking the form of a six-sided prism with a basal plane perpendicular to the prism-faces, or with other terminal faces.

In a pure condition apatite is perfectly colourless and limpid, but by the intermixture of foreign substances it becomes variously coloured. Lilac, violet, or pale green crystals of apatite are found with the tin ores of the Erzgebirge, for example, at Ehrenfriedersdorf in Saxony, and in the old copper mine of Kiräbinsk, near Miask, in the Urals. Pale yellow apatite, the so-called asparagus-stone, occurs in talc-schist in the Tyrolese Alps. The deep green variety, known as moroxite, occurs embedded in crystalline silicate-rocks and in marble at many places ; for example, in North America, especially in Canada ; on the Sludianka, a river flowing into Lake Baikal, in Siberia ; at Arendal, in Norway. Sky-blue crystals are found at certain localities in Australia and Ceylon. Certain green, rose-red, and violet apatites, remarkable for their transparency and the beauty of their colouring, occur with tourmaline in the crevices of the granite of Mount Apatite, near Auburn, in Androscoggin County, in the State of Maine, U.S.A., and were formerly mistaken for tourmaline.

The variously coloured apatites just described, when sufficiently transparent, which is not usually the case, may be cut as gems. The variety most frequently cut, perhaps, is the green moroxite from Canada, but even this is used to only a very limited extent and is very low in price.

The mineral may be distinguished from other similarly coloured stones by its hardness and its specific gravity, the latter feature approaching very closely to the specific gravity of fluor-spar, which is 3·2. Apatite is doubly refracting and slightly dichroic, characters which serve to distinguish it from fluor-spar. From beryl and emerald, to which some cut apatites are very similar in appearance, the mineral may be distinguished, as pointed out above, by its hardness and its specific gravity, apatite sinking in test liquid No. 3 (sp. gr. = 3·0), in which beryl and emerald float.

IRON-PYRITES.

Iron-pyrites, or simply pyrites, is often known to jewellers as marcasite, though by this term mineralogists refer to another species. It is disulphide of iron, its composition being represented by the formula FeS_2, and is the only mineral sulphide with a metallic lustre which is used for ornamental purposes. It crystallises in the cubic system, has a specific gravity of 5·0, and a hardness ($H = 6\frac{1}{2}$) a little less than that of quartz. The mineral is brittle, and when heated before the blowpipe it burns with a blue flame and gives off sulphur dioxide, easily recognised by its penetrating odour. When struck with a steel, iron-pyrites gives out brilliant sparks and a smell of sulphur dioxide, due to the ignition of the particles struck off. It is unattacked by hydrochloric acid, but completely decomposed by nitric acid.

This mineral is of a pale brass-yellow colour and possesses a brilliant metallic lustre, well shown in cut stones, which are usually given the form of a flat rosette. On account of the comparative hardness of the stone the lustre is retained for a long time, and the edges of a cut stone do not very soon lose their sharpness.

Up to the eighteenth century iron-pyrites was much esteemed, especially in France, as an ornamental stone on account of its brilliant lustre and pretty colour; it was used for the decoration of shoe-buckles, garters, snuff-boxes, &c., besides being set in brooches, bracelets, and other articles of personal ornament. Afterwards the mineral grew more and more out of favour until its use was practically given up. Attempts have been made to reinstate it in its former position; thus in the year 1846 a large amount of iron-pyrites, from Geneva and the Jura Mountains, set in an old-world and once admired fashion, was sent to Paris. The articles were readily bought up at first, but being dear and the setting not in accordance with the taste of the period there was no sustained demand for them. There is sometimes used in cheap jewellery at the present time a material, occurring in the neighbourhood of Dublin, which consists of a thin incrustation of small and brilliant crystals of iron-pyrites on the surface of black shales of Carboniferous age. Large polished plates of iron-pyrites, which were probably used as mirrors, have been found in the ancient graves of the Incas. These discoveries first drew attention to the mineral, which was known for a time as Inca-stone. In reference to its supposed health-giving properties it was also known as health-stone, and was much worn in the shape of amulets, as well as set in necklaces, pins, ear-rings, &c., and was possessed of considerable value. Iron-pyrites exists in nature in very great abundance, and is one of the most widely distributed constituents of the earth's crust.

HÆMATITE.

Hæmatite is an opaque mineral with a metallic lustre and dark steel-grey to iron-black colour. Chemically it consists of ferrous oxide, Fe_2O_3, and in its purest form contains 70·0 per cent. of iron and 30·0 per cent. of oxygen. Specially fine rhombohedral crystals occur not infrequently in the extensive and important deposits of iron-ore in the island of Elba, and in veins and crevices in the gneiss of the Alps, and at other places. Only those of some thickness are black and opaque, and exhibit a brilliant metallic lustre; minute crystals of extreme thinness appear by transmitted light transparent and of a fine blood-red colour, hence the Greek name hæmatite (blood-stone). The streak of this mineral on unglazed porcelain is dull and of a dark cherry-red colour, a feature which distinguishes it from all other black stones possessing a metallic lustre.

Hæmatite occurs more abundantly than in crystals as compact irregular masses of a black colour, with a shining metallic lustre, and with the same specific gravity (sp. gr. = 4·7) and the same hardness, namely, that of felspar (H = 6), as the crystals possess. The latter are scarcely ever cut, but the massive material is worked in the lapidary works at Oberstein and elsewhere for the manufacture of ornamental objects. The material used for this purpose, which is obtained in masses of considerable size, is said to come from India, and similar material occurs also in Brazil, in the States of São Paulo and Minas Geraes.

Finely fibrous hæmatite, the application of which is perhaps still more extensive, does not, as a rule, possess the brilliant metallic lustre of the crystals and of the compact crystalline masses just mentioned, and its colour is reddish and more like that of the streak. Specimens are sometimes met with, however, which, while retaining their fibrous structure possess a brilliant metallic lustre and a steel-grey to black colour. Material of this description is as suitable for cutting as the crystalline masses described above, but fibrous hæmatite when distinctly red in colour is useful only as an ore of iron. The latter variety usually occurs in rounded, botryoidal, or reniform masses and is then known as kidney-iron-ore; this occurs lining cavities in massive hæmatite of a pronounced red colour. Hæmatite of this character suitable for cutting was at one time obtained in the veins of iron-ore at Kamsdorf, near Saalfeld, in Thuringia, but these deposits are now practically exhausted; also in the famous old iron-mines in the island of Elba, where magnificent druses of beautiful crystals are often found. Material suitable for cutting is found also in the deposits of iron-ore in Scotland, and in the iron-mines of west Cumberland, but the most important occurrence is in the iron-mines of the north of Spain, near Bilbao, in the Basque Provinces, and at Santiago de Compostela in Coruña. Rough material of suitable quality for cutting is found also at many other localities beside those enumerated above.

The deeper the black colour and the more perfect the metallic lustre of hæmatite the more effective is it for the various ornamental purposes to which it is applied. For ring-stones it is cut with a flat surface, on which is engraved a figure or a letter, so that it may serve as a seal-stone, and this is one of its most general uses. Stones cut *en cabochon* for rings and other articles of personal ornament sometimes display a band of chatoyant light, which, though cloudy and dull, is similar to the characteristic feature of star-sapphire, and is due to the fibrous structure of the mineral. Stones of this description are cut with a slightly convex surface, and are set in brooches, bracelets, medallions, &c., as well as in rings. The material is sometimes used for beads, which are strung together and worn as necklaces or bracelets. Not infrequently such beads are chatoyant, and when this is the case they resemble black pearls in colour and lustre. Small cubes of hæmatite are mounted as pins. Generally speaking, however, the mineral has a very limited application as an ornamental material, for example, in mourning jewellery, and is very low in price.

Hæmatite has been used as an ornamental stone from the very earliest times. Numerous cylinder-seals, some of them engraved, have been found in the ruins of Babylon, and ornamental objects of the same material are found in the ancient Egyptian tombs. In classical times hæmatite was extensively used for intaglios and for other similar purposes, being a stone of fine appearance and easy to work.

The fine powder of hæmatite is much used as a polishing material in the working of precious stones, especially some of the softer kinds, although another material is available and is also used for this purpose, namely, the artificially prepared oxide of iron known as jewellers' rouge. The massive fibrous variety of hæmatite, which is cut as an ornamental stone, constitutes the material of which polishing tools for burnishing gold and silver jewellery are made. The city of Santiago de Compostela is stated to supply almost the whole of the world with these tools.

ILMENITE.

Ilmenite is very similar to hæmatite in appearance and is sometimes used for ornamental purposes. The chief difference between the two minerals lies in the fact that ilmenite contains titanium dioxide as well as iron oxide. A variety of ilmenite known as iserine occurs as black, rounded grains in association with sapphire in the sands of the Iserwiese in Bohemia. Except for the absence of a fibrous structure, ilmenite possesses essentially the same characters as hæmatite, but is susceptible of a higher degree of polish; it is distinguished from hæmatite by the fact that its streak is black instead of red, and that it is occasionally magnetic, which is never the case with hæmatite. The application of the mineral as an ornamental stone is so limited that further consideration is for the present purpose unnecessary, but it may be mentioned in conclusion that an effective ornamental stone occurs at Cumberland, in Rhode Island, U.S.A., which is composed of grains of white quartz embedded in black ilmenite.

RUTILE.

Rutile is a mineral which consists of titanium dioxide (TiO_2), and is frequently found as crystals belonging to the tetragonal system. It ranges in colour from red through brown to black, and possesses a strong metallic to adamantine lustre. Some specimens are sufficiently beautiful to be cut as gems, and may then be mistaken at a first glance for black diamond, from which the stone is distinguished, however, by its lower degree of hardness ($H = 7\frac{1}{2}$), its greater density (sp. gr. = $4 \cdot 2 - 4 \cdot 3$), and, in transparent specimens, by the strong double refraction and marked dichroism. Rutile is of common occurrence, but does not, as a rule, possess the characters essential for a gem; it is, therefore, only rarely cut.

AMBER.

This material, so much used for personal ornaments, is not strictly speaking a mineral at all, being of vegetable origin, and consisting of the more or less considerably altered resin of extinct trees. It resembles minerals in its occurrence in the beds of the earth's crust, and for that reason may be considered, like other varieties of fossil resin, of which it is the most important, as an appendix to minerals.

NATURE AND CHARACTERS.—It is proposed to deal first with true amber or amber proper, the succinite of mineralogists, the principal locality for which is the district of Samland, in the province of East Prussia, and to conclude with a consideration of other resins, which are similar to amber and used for the same purposes, but which are of much rarer occurrence.

In respect to its **chemical composition**, amber, like other resins, consists essentially of carbon, hydrogen, and oxygen. These elements are combined together in somewhat variable proportions, but on an average the material contains 79 per cent. of carbon, 10·5 per cent. of oxygen, and 10·5 per cent. of hydrogen, a composition which is represented by the chemical formula $C_{10}H_{16}O$. A small amount of sulphur is sometimes present, and a little inorganic material, which remains behind as ash when the amber is burnt. Pure amber contains only about $\frac{1}{5}$ of a per cent. of ash, but when enclosures of foreign substances are present this percentage rises considerably.

Amber is not homogeneous nor of simple constitution. Apart from the inorganic ash it contains several substances which can be separated by chemical means. By distillation is obtained a small quantity of oil of amber (an ethereal oil) and some succinic acid; the latter is an especially characteristic constituent of true Prussian amber, in which it is always present, though in variable amount. Perfectly clear and transparent specimens contain 3 to 4 per cent. of succinic acid, cloudy specimens contain more, and in frothy amber there may be as much as 8 per cent. By treating the fine powder with alcohol, ether, and other solvents, four resinous substances, differing from each other in chemical composition and in melting-point, may be separated. The insoluble residue, amounting to from 44 to 60 per cent. of the whole, is a bituminous substance, the so-called amber-bitumen.

Amber is perfectly insoluble in water, and is only slightly attacked after a contact of some duration with alcohol, sulphuric ether, acetic ether, and other solvents. This affords an important distinction between true amber and the many similar resins, which are so often substituted for it, the latter being quickly attacked by alcohol and the other solvents mentioned above. In concentrated sulphuric acid finely powdered amber is perfectly soluble even in the cold, and it is completely decomposed by boiling nitric acid.

When amber is heated it softens, swells, and gives off a characteristic and pleasant odour. Between 280° and 290° C., that is to say at a higher temperature than is the case with other resins, it melts, and is at the same time decomposed with the evolution of the two volatile constituents, oil of amber and succinic acid. These substances are given off in the form of white fumes and are sometimes accompanied by a small amount of water vapour. The fumes have the same peculiar aromatic odour, and owing to the presence of succinic acid in them act as an irritant when inhaled into the respiratory passages, causing violent coughing. The non-volatile residue, amounting to about 70 per cent. of the weight of the original material, is a shining black substance known as colophony of amber. It is soluble in oil of turpentine and in linseed-oil, and its solution in either of these substances is known as amber-lac or amber-varnish, and is much used for varnishing. This lac is characterised by its great hardness on drying and only its dark colour stands in the way of a more extensive application. When heated in linseed-oil amber becomes soft and pliable, a property of which practical use is made, as we shall see later.

When heated in the air amber ignites and burns with a bright sooty flame, hence the German name *Bernstein* for amber. During combustion the same aromatic odour becomes apparent, this being so characteristic of amber as to be sufficient to distinguish it from other resins of similar appearance. It also leads to the use of a limited amount of amber as frankincense.

The **physical characters** of amber are in every respect those of a resin. It is perfectly amorphous and shows no indication of crystalline structure. It occurs in irregular rounded nodules having the form of rods, drops, plates, &c., and never in masses bounded by plane surfaces. There is no cleavage and the fracture is conchoidal, but masses of amber are often penetrated by irregular cracks. Sometimes a shelly, concentric separation is observable, the mass being built up of thin layers one within another, and only loosely held together. Specimens of this kind are known as *shelly amber*, while those which are as compact as if they had been cast are known as *massive amber*. In extreme cases these two kinds differ from each other very widely, but there are specimens to represent every possible gradation between the two. The structure is closely connected with the mode of formation of the amber, and has an important bearing on the practical application of the stone.

The specific gravity of amber ranges from 1·05 to 1·10; the substance is thus only slightly heavier than water, and approximates still more closely to the density of sea-water. Its hardness, $H = 2\frac{1}{2}$, is a little greater than that of gypsum, and it can therefore be scarcely scratched with the finger-nail. It is harder than most other resins, a difference which affords another useful distinguishing feature. It is not very brittle and can therefore be carved, worked on the lathe, or bored with little difficulty—important practical considerations. When amber is cut with a knife parings are not obtained but only powder.

When rubbed on cloth amber becomes strongly charged with negative electricity, and attracts to itself scraps of paper and other light objects; it is, indeed, from the ancient name for amber, electron, that the word electricity is derived. When rubbed very vigorously the characteristic odour becomes perceptible, but the amber does not become sticky as do other resins under similar circumstances, since the temperature of its melting-point is far higher than that induced by the vigorous rubbing. Amber is a bad conductor of heat, and in consequence feels warm when in contact with the hand. This character alone serves to distinguish it from minerals and from glass of similar appearance, since these feel cold to the touch.

In most cases amber possesses a fine resinous lustre, which is considerably heightened by polishing, but some specimens are dull and are not improved by polishing, these being therefore unsuitable for ornamental purposes.

Amber ranges from perfect transparency to complete opacity. In the same specimen there may be clear and cloudy portions side by side, these merging gradually into each other and never sharply defined. This is a characteristic feature of genuine amber, and one which distinguishes it from certain similar substances, to be mentioned below. In transparent specimens it may be observed that amber is singly refracting, this being in accordance with its amorphous character. A feeble double refraction is sometimes observed, especially in the neighbourhood of enclosures of foreign bodies, these no doubt setting up internal strains.

The colouring of amber is very uniform in character, no colour but yellow having been met with in the large quantity of Baltic amber hitherto collected. It varies in shade, however, from the palest yellow to dark yellow and brown. Material which has undergone a surface alteration is often red in colour, but fresh specimens never show this colour. Green and blue amber is very rare and will be considered below.

In spite of the uniformity of its colour several **varieties** of amber are recognised, the distinctions between them being based principally on the association of different shades of colour with different degrees of transparency. These different varieties differ in the capacity for acquiring a polish, and some by reason of their general appearance are more suitable for ornamental purposes than others, and are therefore of greater commercial importance.

Transparent amber is described in the trade as *clear*. Shelly amber is nearly always clear; it is never cloudy throughout and rarely so in alternate layers. Massive amber, on the other hand, is nearly always more or less cloudy; perfectly transparent specimens of massive amber are rare, though more frequent than cloudy specimens of shelly amber. The clear massive variety occurs in masses ranging in colour from almost perfect colourlessness to dark reddish-yellow. Water-clear amber is very rare, and is described as " yellow clear "; the reddish-yellow, or " red clear," is more frequent.

Several varieties of *cloudy* amber are recognised in the trade, namely, ·"flohmig," " bastard," " semi-bastard," " osseous," and " frothy amber." Material which possesses characters intermediate between those of these varieties is distinguished by compound terms of a descriptive kind, such as, " clear-flohmig," " flohmig-clear," " flohmig-bastard," osseous-bastard," &c.

Flohmig amber is slightly turbid, with the appearance of having been clouded by a fine dust; like the clear variety it is susceptible of a fine polish. The term " flohmig " is derived from the East Prussian word " Flohmfett," which signifies the semi-transparent, yellowish fat of the goose or duck, which this variety of amber is supposed to resemble in appearance.

Bastard amber is more turbid, but is still susceptible of a good polish. Various terms are used to signify the extent of the turbidity: thus, material which is cloudy throughout is termed *bastard proper*, while that in which cloudy portions are dotted about in a clear ground-mass is known as *clouded bastard*. Colour distinctions are also recognised: pure white to greyish-yellow shades of bastard-amber are described as *pearl-coloured*, the material with paler tones being known in the trade as " blue amber," not to be confused with the rare amber which is actually blue in colour. Yellow and brownish-yellow bastard amber is described as *kumst-coloured*, from the East Prussian name " Kumst " for cabbage (Sauerkraut), the former being described as pale and the latter as dark " kumst "-coloured. The specimen of amber represented in Plate XX., Fig. 9, is " kumst "-coloured; part of its surface is polished and the rest in its natural condition.

Semi-bastard amber is intermediate in character between bastard and osseous amber, combining the appearance of the latter with the capacity for receiving a polish of the former.

Osseous amber, or more briefly *bone*, is opaque, softer than the varieties described above and inferior to them in its susceptibility of polish. In colour it ranges from white to brown, and, as the name implies, it has the general appearance of bone or ivory.

By the combination of the characters of the different varieties enumerated above, there arises a number of different colour-varieties of amber, which are classified into two groups under the descriptions " variegated osseous clear " and " variegated osseous bastard."

Frothy amber is opaque, very soft, and incapable of receiving a polish ; it often encloses crystals of iron-pyrites in large numbers.

Leaving out of consideration those colour-varieties of amber which are rare or unusual, the pearl-coloured, and next to this the " kumst "-coloured, is the rarest of the varieties of every-day occurrence.   These two kinds of amber are in more general favour in Europe than is the clear amber, and for this reason command the higher prices, but we shall see later on that the fashion and taste prevailing in different countries is not uniform.

The different degrees of turbidity in amber, with which are connected the differences between the numerous varieties of this substance, were at one time thought to be due to the presence of varying amounts of water.   It is now known, however, that the turbidity is due to the enclosure of vast numbers of bubbles of various sizes, but always too small to be seen with the naked eye, or with a simple lens, their identification requiring the examination of thin sections under a high power of the microscope.   These cavities are distributed throughout the ground-mass of the amber, which always consists of a pure clear resin, almost water-clear to reddish-yellow in colour.   The differences in the appearance of the various kinds of amber depend upon the number and the size of these cavities, the smallest of which have a diameter of 0·0008 and the largest 0·02 millimetre.   The cavities are the smallest and the most numerous in osseous amber, having a diameter of from 0·0008 to 0·004 millimetre and a distribution of 900,000 per square millimeter.   " Flohmig " amber contains the smallest number of bubbles, 600 per square millimetre, but these, with a diameter of 0·02 millimetre, have the maximum size.   Between these two extremes lie all the other varieties, the study of which has shown that the more numerous and the smaller are the bubbles the amber contains the more turbid it becomes.   When the cavities are less numerous and larger in size the amber in which they are embedded is clearer, and when it contains no bubbles is perfectly transparent.

The small bubbles of air hinder the passage of light through the amber and thus produce the appearance of turbidity.   A large portion of the light which enters a mass of amber is reflected from the surface of the air bubbles and thus fails to reach the eye. Could these air-spaces be filled with a transparent substance of the same, or nearly the same, refractive index as amber, which varies between 1·530 and 1·547, the turbidity would disappear and the substance would become perfectly transparent.

This, in fact, can be accomplished without any great difficulty by an operation which is known as **clarifying** the amber, one which is frequently performed in the trade for the purpose of making cloudy amber transparent and thereby increasing its value.   The rough material is completely immersed in rape-seed oil in an iron vessel, and then very slowly heated to about the temperature at which the oil boils and begins to decompose.   It is then allowed to cool and this must take place just as slowly and gradually as the preliminary heating, otherwise the clarified amber will become cracked and possibly fractured.   The smaller the fragments of amber operated upon the quicker is the process completed ; the heating of large pieces must be continued for a considerable period, and not infrequently needs to be several times repeated.   The time required for the operation depends also upon the character of the material, for different pieces of amber of the same size will not require the same length of time to complete the operation.   The clarifying process begins on the surface and spreads gradually inwards.

The rationale of the method is the penetration of the fine cracks in the amber and the filling up of the cavities with rape-seed oil, the index of refraction of which is 1·475, only slightly different from that of amber itself. Light is thus enabled to pass through the mass of amber without hindrance and the substance appears in consequence clear and transparent. If the oil is mixed with some colouring matter, this also penetrates the amber and imparts its colour to it.

Unless the greatest care be taken the operation of clarifying amber results in the development of peculiar cracks, which in some aspects resemble fishes' scales. These are at first so small as to be scarcely noticeable, but gradually become more and more conspicuous and begin to show iridescent colours, until towards the end of the operation they become quite obvious as shining, golden cracks. These are known to the amber workers as " sun-spangles," and their presence often serves to distinguish a clarified from a naturally transparent specimen of amber.

Having dealt with the yellow varieties of amber in some detail, we may now briefly consider the rarer kinds of a blue or green colour. *Green amber* ranges in colour from a pale to a blackish-green and from olive-green to the apple-green of chrysoprase, sometimes exhibiting white clouds. The colour of *blue amber* may be azure-, sky-, or steel-blue. Both blue and green amber is turbid, and, in fact, the turbidity has a close connection with the colouring of the stone, for this is due not to the presence of pigment, but to a peculiar modification of the rays of light caused by the presence of the numerous air-bubbles, which, as we have seen above, is the cause also of the turbidity of amber. These minute air-bubbles, to which both the colour and the turbidity of blue amber is due, are arranged in it in layers of some thinness, just as in bastard or osseous amber ; and the colour phenomenon for which they are responsible is of the same nature as that observed in other turbid media. When subjected to the clarifying process blue amber loses both its turbidity and its colour, assuming the yellow colour of ordinary amber.

The phenomenon of *fluorescence* is very conspicuous in some specimens of amber, these appearing of a yellow to brown colour in transmitted light, but of a dark bluish or greenish colour in reflected light. Fluorescent specimens of Prussian amber are rarely seen, but are less uncommon among the amber-like resins of Sicily, Burma, and other localities. Not being suitable for ornamental purposes they are scarcely ever worked, and are worth less than specimens of ordinary amber.

One serious drawback to the use of amber as an ornamental material is its tendency **to change in colour** with the lapse of time. This change in colour is due to a chemical alteration which takes place gradually from without inwards. Pale-coloured specimens become darker, and those which were yellow become red or brownish-red. The change is noticeable after the lapse of only a few years, but differs in character in different varieties of amber. Clear amber becomes slightly darker and redder in colour and numerous cracks develop in its substance. In bastard amber an external layer becomes brown in colour and assumes a waxy lustre. Osseous amber acquires a porcelain-like lustre, and in frothy amber an external layer, sharply marked off from the remainder, becomes quite clear but brittle.

These alteration processes proceed gradually, especially along cracks in the material, until the whole mass has undergone the change. They were at one time attributed to the action of light, but have since been observed to take place in the dark. When a piece of amber is kept in water or otherwise excluded from contact with air, the change which takes place in it is much less in extent, so that the process is simply a case of atmospheric weathering.

Under natural conditions the weathering process has sometimes proceeded so far that only a small nucleus of the mass remains fresh and unaltered, the outer shell being much cracked and fissured, and its surface honeycombed with a shallow sculpturing, such as is represented in Plate XX., Fig. 9. The external weathered layer is easily detachable from the nucleus of fresh, unaltered material, which is often pitted with close-set, shallow, conical depressions. These effects of weathering are only to be seen in specimens which have lain in dry earth, those which have been embedded in perfectly dry sand being often changed and altered throughout their whole mass, and the surface deeply honeycombed. Material, on the other hand, which has lain in water or in moist earth, thus being preserved from contact with air, is often scarcely altered at all and does not show even the surface sculpturing described above.

Beside air-bubbles, the importance of which has been explained already, other **enclosures** of various kinds are found in amber, some of which are of special significance. Drops of water occur not infrequently, but enclosures of solid matter, either organic or inorganic, are more frequent.

The inorganic substance most commonly enclosed in amber is iron-pyrites, which, in the form of quite thin lamellæ, fills up cracks and crevices in many specimens, especially of shelly amber. It is also frequently enclosed in frothy amber as already stated. The presence of iron-pyrites in a specimen of amber naturally interferes with the working of it, and such material is of little value to the turner.

The enclosures of organic material, partly of vegetable and partly of animal origin are of great importance. The vegetable enclosures consist mostly of finely divided particles of carbonised wood, which are black in colour and are present in many specimens in greater or less abundance. The amber retains its usual yellow colour, and does not appear black in consequence of these black enclosures. Black amber does not actually exist, what is known as such being in reality quite another substance, namely, jet, which will be considered later on. The black resins which sometimes occur in company with amber are quite distinct from this and, further, are not suitable for ornamental purposes. The particles of carbonised wood now found enclosed in amber are the remains of the pine-trees from which the amber-resin was exuded, the so-called amber-pine (*Pinites succinifer* of Göppert). Larger fragments of wood, needles, and other parts of the tree, are also found as enclosures, but more rarely. Recognisable remains of other plants also occur though still less commonly, these often consist of flowers and leaves, the structure and form of which are perfectly preserved by the amber in which they are embedded.

This is also the case with animal remains, which are found in amber in great number and variety. These include insects of various kinds, such as ants, moths, and especially flies; also spiders, and as great rarities snails and other small animals. Inclusions are confined almost entirely to the clear shelly amber and are scarcely ever found in turbid massive amber. The animal and plant remains found embedded in amber belong to extinct species, but these do not differ widely from present-day organisms. They lived and flourished at the time known to geologists as the Tertiary period, and were imprisoned in the resin exuded from the pine-trees living at the same time. So perfectly has their form and structure been retained, that these fossil plants and animals are almost as suitable for biological investigation as are living forms, often throwing light on the character of the fauna and flora of the period. A piece of amber containing some organism is often cut for ornamental purposes in such a way as to bring the enclosure into prominence.

WINNING OF AMBER.—The first amber to be collected would naturally be that which had been washed up on to the beach from amber-bearing strata beneath the sea. A certain amount is still obtained in this way, and is known as *sea-amber* or as *sea-stone*. It is distinguished from ordinary amber by the absence of a crust of weathered material. This was, no doubt, present while the substance remained in its original situation, but by the action of the sea was subsequently entirely removed, the only trace of its existence being the presence of a few surface pittings on portions protected from the action of the waves. Being exposed to all the disintegrating forces of littoral waters, masses of amber containing incipient cracks and fissures would be very unlikely to escape fracture, and for this reason sea-amber is usually free from such flaws.

The collection of sea-amber is an easy matter, for it is simply picked up on the flat sea-beaches. During landward wind-storms large quantities of amber are loosened from the floor of the sea and thrown up upon the beach, often entangled with masses of sea-weed. This is sorted over, and the larger pieces of amber are collected, but the smaller fragments, which do not repay the trouble of collecting, are left, and often accumulate at spots high up on the shore. Besides collecting the masses of amber thrown up on the shore the searchers also wade as far as possible into the sea, and by means of long-handled nets drag ashore the floating masses of sea-weed in order to secure the amber entangled in it. The amber thus drawn from the sea is known as *drawn-amber* (German, Schöpfstein), while that which is thrown up upon the beach is referred to as *strand-amber*.

Amber is collected in these ways all along the coast of Samland, but specially on the west coast, north of Pillau; also along the whole of the east coast of the Russian Baltic Provinces, Livonia and Courland; through East and West Prussia; in Pomerania and Mecklenburg; and along the whole coast of the Jutland peninsula in Schleswig-Holstein and Jutland; at some places in greater, at others in smaller amounts. After Samland, the Jutland peninsula with Schleswig-Holstein is the most important locality for amber. It occurs in greater abundance on the west coast, which is washed by the North Sea, than on the east. Stavning peninsula and Fanö Island are stated to be specially rich localities. The substance appears to be less abundant on the North Friesian Islands, Ramö, Sylt, Föhr, &c., but to be very plentiful on the shore of the Eiderstedt peninsula, where at ebb-tide large quantities of amber are exposed on the fore-shore and collected. The richest locality in this neighbourhood is the Hitzbank, a sand-bank which extends from the last-named peninsula far out to sea. The amber-seekers are therefore known here as the Hitz runners. The mouth of the Eider is another prolific spot, but amber is collected along a strip of coast stretching as far south as Büsum, although the yield is small in South Dithmarschen, at the mouth of the Elbe, and on the coasts of Hanover, Oldenburg, and Holland. The search for amber on the fore-shore is attended with great danger owing to the risk of being caught by the returning tide. In North Dithmarschen the seekers, who are known as amber-riders, follow the outflowing tide, often on horses and after collecting as much amber as possible hurry back to the shore as soon as the tide turns. Amber is also often collected from boats in this district. It is said that the yield here has considerably fallen off.

The islands on the coast of Holland and East and North Friesland were referred to by Pliny as " insulæ glessaridæ," that is to say the amber islands, and they have been called also the Electrides. Later on the much richer district of Samland became known to the Romans, who, at the beginning of the time of the Frankish emperors had entered into commercial relations with East Prussia for the supply of the highly esteemed amber, most of the material so supplied being probably strand-amber, with perhaps a little drawn-amber.

Other methods are now adopted in Prussia for the obtaining of sea-amber besides the primitive ones already described, the material being collected from the floor of the sea by the help of appliances of various kinds.

The amber lying at the bottom of shallow waters is scooped and raked up by persons in boats, with the aid of small hoop-nets provided with long handles. The boulders which are strewn over the sea-floor and hinder this operation are sometimes hauled up, and utilised as building stone, a desideratum in this part of the country.   The amount of amber wedged in between such boulders makes their removal quite worth while.   A large amount of amber has been obtained in this way among other places in the neighbourhood of Brüsterort, on the north-west corner of Samland, where, after the removal of the boulders, the amber was raked up with drag-nets.   Amber is obtained in this way on the coast of Samland only; the method has been tried, but unsuccessfully, on the coasts of West Prussia; the amber obtained here consists exclusively of that picked up on the shore or drawn from the sea.

The methods for the winning of amber hitherto described are all somewhat primitive, but the more rational method of **diving** has been adopted more recently and has yielded a rich harvest.   The pioneers of this method were Stantien and Becker, a large firm of amber merchants at Königsberg, and since 1869 the amber lying loose on or embedded in the sea-floor has been collected by divers furnished with every modern appliance.   The sea-floor in the neighbourhood of Brüsterort and the village of Gross-Dirschkeim to the east was first explored, and after the exhaustion of these supplies, a spot further south near Palmnicken was worked.   At the present day, however, even this method is given up by reason of the vastly richer yield afforded by mining operations, but before passing to the consideration of the latter, the operations of dredging and of surface digging for amber must be described.

Dredging for amber is performed not in the open sea, but solely in the Kurisches Haff, and is undertaken only by the firm just mentioned.   The floor of this lagoon near the village of Schwarzort, a little to the south of Memel on the Kurische Nehrung consists of a bed of alluvium very rich in amber.   Towards the east the same bed rises above sea-level and near Prökuls is extensively worked in diggings.   Dredging for amber was commenced in 1860, and this year marked a turning-point in the amber-winning industry, for whereas, up to that date the amber markets were supplied mainly with sea-amber, the supplies subsequently consisted almost entirely of dredged amber.   The latter also is free from cracks and fissures and from the weathered crust, and, indeed, differs in no essential respect from sea-amber.   The work was commenced with three small hand-dredgers and was not at first very successful; when the right spot was found, the undertaking developed to quite an unexpected extent, and so large steam-dredgers provided with powerful machinery were brought into requisition.   The floor of the lagoon was excavated to a depth of from 7 to 11 metres, and about half the annual production of East Prussian amber was obtained in this way.   The industry gave employment to about 1000 workpeople, and incidentally led to a great development of the small fishing village of Schwarzort.   The deposits in the lagoon are now exhausted and no dredging has been done since the end of November 1890.

Besides being picked up on the shore, drawn from the sea, and raked or dredged up from the sea-floor, amber has been obtained since ancient times in **diggings** both on the shore and inland.   The amber thus obtained, the so-called *pit-amber*, differs from sea-amber in that it is enveloped in a thick weathered crust and is much cracked and fissured, though these flaws are not visible on the exterior owing to the crust.   Not only in East Prussia but also in all parts of the district where it occurs, digging for amber in the glacial and alluvial deposits and in the Tertiary strata is carried on.   Formerly the amount of material obtained in this way was small compared with that collected from the sea, but now these conditions are reversed.   Since the year 1873 specially large supplies of amber have been obtained from a greyish-green sandy clay, the so-called " blue earth," an amber-bearing stratum of Lower Tertiary age, which at the present day is the most important source of the material.

The surface **alluvial deposits** were first worked for amber in the south-east of East Prussia, south of the railway line between Ortelsburg and Johannesburg (on the Allenstein and Lyk railway), in a district bordered on the east by the Pissek and on the west by the Omulew river, and extending into Poland as far as the neighbourhood of Ostrolenka on the Narew. A large amount of amber has been found in former centuries in the surface diggings here and elsewhere in Poland, and in West Prussia, especially at Steegen on the Danzig Nehrung. At the last named place and at Prökuls, where are situated the most important of these alluvial deposits, the firm of Stantien and Becker commenced their digging operations; these workings were at first on quite a small scale, but have, although at other places, now developed to an enormous extent, the whole world being supplied with amber from the diggings of this firm. Prökuls is situated on the mainland and on the railway line between Memel and Tilsit, to the south of Memel and opposite Schwarzort. The deposit is identical with that which lies beneath the Kurisches Haff, which was formerly dredged for amber in the neighbourhood of Schwarzort. The diggings at this spot did not, however, yield nearly the amount of amber obtained by dredging, and have therefore long been abandoned.

In **glacial deposits** amber is present everywhere in the North German lowlands, but usually in small amount. At places where the glacial deposits overlie "blue earth" *in situ* amber occurs in greater abundance, but since the discovery of these richer deposits depends upon chance or accident the occurrence has no economic importance. Such deposits may be met with in the excavations necessitated by alterations and improvements, in the digging of sand and gravel pits, or in peat cutting. Small deposits and pockets of amber occur and are worked at many places in East and West Prussia, Pomerania, Mecklenburg, Schleswig-Holstein, Denmark, and further to the west, also in the province and kingdom of Saxony, in Silesia, and further eastward in Russia. A few examples of the richness of the deposits in East and West Prussia and Pomerania are given below. From a small pocket at Krebswalde, near Elbing, 700 pounds of amber was obtained. As rent for the diggings at Schillehnen, near Braunsberg, 400 ducats was formerly paid. The deposits at Gluckau, near Danzig, have been worked for at least 170 years, and as late as 1858 a fine piece of amber weighing 11 pounds 13 ounces was found there. At Karthaus, a large amount of amber was met with in pockets in loam, and at Berent, Konitz, Czersk, Tuchel, and Polnisch-Crone in West Prussia, and Treten and Rohr, north of Rummelsburg in Pomerania, amber has been obtained for more than 100 years from loamy veins, which penetrate the glacial sand to a depth of 23 metres.

The total amount of amber obtained from alluvial and glacial deposits is as nothing compared with that derived from **Tertiary strata,** namely, the banded sands of the lignite formation, and especially the "blue earth." Practically the whole of the genuine amber which now comes into the market is obtained from these deposits. The workings of the latter, both surface and underground, are confined to the coast east and south of Brüsterort on the north-west corner of Samland, and are entirely absent from the interior of the country, from the remaining portion of the Baltic coast, and from the coast of the North Sea.

Wherever the amber-bearing Tertiary beds are accessible, whether above or below sea-level, they have been worked for many centuries in **open workings.** Important workings are situated at Kraxtepellen, Gross-Kuhren, Klein-Kuhren, Georgswalde, Rauschen, Sassen, Wannenkrug, &c. A great wealth of material was found in the "blue earth" at Loppehnen, four-horsed waggons being required for its removal.

When the working of the "blue earth" in open diggings was commenced is not definitely known, but the diggings were probably in full operation as early as 1836. To reach the amber bed, which is only about one and a half spades in thickness, it is necessary to remove a great weight of superimposed material, consisting of later Tertiary strata (the lignite formation), and glacial deposits, often several metres thick, besides banking up the pits to prevent the inrush of the sea. The cost of working is thus considerable, and the fact that the deposit can be worked at a profit bears witness to its richness. In the "banded sands" of the lignite formation which overlie the "blue earth" are irregularly distributed pockets of amber. Though a considerable amount of material has been obtained in open workings, the sands are not now systematically worked because of the expense attending the process, and the bulk of the material is obtained from underground mines in the "blue earth."

Mining operations in the "banded sands" were undertaken by the Government as far back as the end of the eighteenth century (1781), but after working for twenty-four years these were abandoned. To the firm of Stantien and Becker belongs the credit of having successfully initiated the system of underground mining in the "blue earth," a system which has been followed with increasing profit up to the present day.

At the beginning of the seventies two attempts were simultaneously made in this direction. The Royal Prussian Mining Administration opened workings at Nortycken, near Rauschen, some distance inland from the north coast of Samland, but these had to be abandoned because of the impossibility of preventing the entry of water into the pit from the water-bearing blown sands lying above the "blue earth." The workings opened by Stantien and Becker at Palmnicken, between Pillau and Brüsterort, on the west coast of Samland, were a brilliant success. The success of this attempt led, in 1870, to the construction of a large open working on the shore itself, the output of which for a period of five years showed a steady increase. The amber-bearing stratum lies here 6 to 8 metres below sea-level, and dams of massive wood-work were required to protect the open diggings from the sea. The underground workings are free from this objection, as also from the interruption of work in the cold season of the year, and, moreover, they do not necessitate the lying fallow of a large area of fruitful land. At this place the whole of the amber-bearing "blue earth" is excavated from shafts, levels, and galleries, the amber so obtained being freed from the earth which adheres to it by washing in specially constructed appliances.

The amber thus obtained and cleaned, the so-called *dam-stone*, is enclosed in a thick crust of weathered material, which is removed in the cask-washers. In this operation the amber is placed with water and sharp sand in rotating barrels, which are kept in motion until the last trace of the opaque crust is removed. Another operation, the so-called Klebs' washing, completes the preparation of the rough material, which cannot then be distinguished from sea-amber. It is next examined with regard to colour, transparency, and the presence or absence of cracks, with the object of deciding its value and the class of work for which it is best suited, an impossibility in the case of material still enclosed in its opaque crust. The stones thus prepared are then sorted, the different qualities being placed on the market separately.

The increased yield of the mines has more than compensated for the exhaustion of the deposits in the Kurisches Haff, which at one time was dredged for amber. In the year 1893 the mines yielded 6000 hundredweights of amber, half of which was suitable only for the manufacture of varnish, while the other half consisted of pieces of medium size suitable for ornamental purposes. Beside the 600 men engaged in the mines, 400 more find employment in the sorting-rooms at Königsberg, so that the production of amber by the firm of Stantien and Becker alone provides a livelihood for upwards of 1000 men and their families.   In 1884 the total production of amber in East Prussia was 3000 hundred-weights, of which 1000 hundredweights was obtained by dredging at Schwarzort, where 1000 workpeople were employed ; 1700 hundredweights from the mine at Palmnicken, employing 700 workers; 200 hundredweights were obtained by divers out of the sea at Palmnicken ; and the remaining 100 hundredweights were picked up on the shore, drawn from the water, raked up from the sea-bottom, or dug up at various spots.   In 1874, ten years before, the total production was only 1100 hundredweights, from which the rapid increase in yield can be seen.

The winning of amber has occupied the inhabitants of the Baltic since very early times.   Articles of amber have been found in graves of the Stone age in East Prussia, showing that the material was highly esteemed even at that time.   It is not surprising to find that from the earliest times efforts have been made by the ruling powers to obtain control of the amber deposits.   Thus, amber was once declared to be the property of the German Crown, the existence of some ancient right being possibly the basis of the declaration.   The material has remained Crown property up to the present day in all the districts which were not taken by the Poles, that is to say, in East Prussia.   In West Prussia and other districts, though the amber-winning industry is subject to certain imposts, the material itself was not, nor is it now, the absolute property of the Crown.

Up to the year 1811 the rights of the State were strictly enforced, and the privilege of collecting and selling amber from the sea-shore was granted only to persons who paid for it.   The impossibility of preventing unlicensed persons from collecting amber, and the demoralisation of the villages on the coast in consequence of the continued evasion of the law, led the Government in 1811 to lease their rights, first to a company and afterwards to a contractor.   Under these conditions, which lasted until 1837, unlicensed persons were strictly forbidden to pick up even the smallest fragments of amber, and any infringement of these regulations was visited with the severest punishment.

These restrictions did not entirely achieve their object, for at certain favourable spots along the coast the inhabitants of the villages still succeeded in smuggling a certain amount of amber.   In 1837 the irksome restrictions were wholly removed, and the shore from Nimmersatt on the Russian border as far as Polsk, east of Danzig, was leased to the shore communities themselves, who then had the right to pick up amber on the shore, draw it out of the sea, rake it up from the sea-bottom, dig for it in the land bordering on the sea, and sell it to whomsoever they would.   Further to the west, as far as the mouth of the Weichsel, the town of Danzig had long before that time rights to work in the same manner. In 1868, however, when it had been found that a profitable working of the littoral deposits of amber required the expenditure of a considerable amount of capital and skill, not in the power of the villagers to give, the mining rights were withdrawn from the inhabitants of the shore villages in favour of persons better fitted to exercise them.   The subsequent increase in the total production of amber, consequent on the introduction by Stantien and Becker of dredging in 1860 and mining in 1873, has been already pointed out.   Dues are paid by this firm and by others engaged in similar operations to the owners of the rights.

An interesting light is thrown on the development of the amber-producing industry by a comparison of the yearly revenues derived by the State from this source.   Up to the year 1811, when the industry was State-managed, the yearly income was £1100.   From 1811 to 1837, when the rights were leased to a company and then to a contractor, the yearly income amounted to £1500 ; the taxation of the village communities brought in £1700 ;

and in later times the amber revenues have amounted to about £35,000, the exact sum received by the Prussian treasury in the year 1894–5 being £35,500. Of this, £33,850 was contributed by the firm of Stantien and Becker alone for the mining rights of the Palmnicken mine and other places. The remaining £1650 was paid for the right to collect amber along certain stretches of shore, which for some years had been knocked down to the highest bidder, and many of these workers also were under the control of the firm just mentioned.

A more or less systematic winning of amber also exists in the interior of the country, but it is impossible to single out localities for special mention. Pieces of amber picked up casually must be yielded up to the State officials, who are authorised to pay the finder a reward fixed by law. The material accumulated in this manner is sold periodically by the State.

WORKING OF AMBER.—Every piece of amber of a suitable size and quality is worked for ornaments or for articles used by smokers, the latter application being far more extensive than any other. The material suitable for this purpose is known as *work-stone*. Pieces which are impure or too small, together with the fragments detached in the working of larger stones, are melted down and used for the manufacture of lac and varnish, material of this kind being known as " varnish." The same kind of material has been used to a certain extent in recent years for the preparation of pressed amber, of which more will be said below. About half of the total production of amber must be placed in the " varnish " category, its value being about one-tenth that of the annual yield.

The application of the so-called work-stone must now be considered more in detail. The material is mostly turned on the lathe, but it may be fashioned into the desired form also by cutting and grinding, and a certain amount is cut up into thin plates. By immersion in hot linseed-oil, amber is not only clarified, as stated above, but is also softened and made flexible, a fact of great importance in the amber-working industry.

Nearly one-half of the total production of amber is devoted to the manufacture of articles for the use of smokers, namely, cigar- and cigarette-holders, mouthpieces for the same, and for pipes, &c. This manufacture is one of the staple industries of Vienna, the articles made there being famous all the world over for their excellence. A quantity of material worth 40 per cent. of the value of the annual yield of rough material goes to Vienna, and this includes only the best qualities of amber. The German towns in competition with Vienna for this trade are Nürnberg, Königsberg, Ruhla near Eisenach, and Erbach in the Oldenwald. Nürnberg and Erbach are engaged exclusively in the manufacture of articles for the use of smokers, which are all exported, while Ruhla manufactures the same class of goods, but for home use. In France, Paris and St. Claude in the Jura, are engaged in the same manufacture, the articles being for home use, and the value of the rough material employed being about 10 per cent. of that of the total yield. In England there is no important manufacture of amber goods; in Holland and Belgium ornamental articles of amber are manufactured, but not for export. In Russia both smokers' requisites and ornamental articles are manufactured at Polangen and Krottingen to the north of Memel on the Prussian border, the industry affording a livelihood to the whole of the population of the district. At Zhitomir, in Volhynia, are made only articles used by smokers, including the cigar-holders mounted with Tula silver, supplies of which are sent to Warsaw, St. Petersburg, Riga, Ostrolenka, and Odessa. In North America amber is worked for the same class of goods, but only for home use. After a period of depression, due to the pressure of Viennese competition, the industry in Turkey, especially at Constantinople, is now in a flourishing condition, and is still growing.

Thin plates of amber for use in inlaid work, mosaics, &c., were once much in request, but are manufactured now only in small numbers.

Ornamental objects of amber are manufactured in great variety, and in accordance with the taste of different peoples. Perhaps the commonest of such articles are beads, rounded or faceted, and perforated so that they can be strung together and worn as necklaces and bracelets, or used as rosaries by Roman Catholics and Mohammedans. Also pieces of special form for necklaces and bracelets, brooches, and other articles, these being often delicately carved.

A certain number of amber ornaments are manufactured, as we have seen, in Russia (at Polangen and Krottingen), at Constantinople, and in England. The industry flourishes also in China and Korea, where round beads for mandarins' chains are made in great numbers. China now uses annually for this purpose from £7500 to £10,000 worth of rough amber, while formerly the beads were imported ready-made from Germany.

The total production of amber ornaments in each of the countries enumerated is, however, small, and Germany in this respect comes before all, while for smokers' requisites Austria stands first. Danzig, Berlin, Stolp in Pomerania, and Worms manufacture almost exclusively ornamental articles, with which they supply the whole world, with the exception of the countries mentioned above. Some of these articles remain in Europe, but the remainder are exported from Hamburg, London, Marseilles, Bordeaux, Livorno, Trieste, and Genoa, some passing through Moscow and the fairs of Odessa and Nizhniy Novgorod to Turkey, Persia, Armenia, the Caucasus, Siberia, various parts of Africa far into the interior, China, India, Arabia (where numerous rosaries are disposed of to pilgrims going to Mecca), the West Indies, North and South America, &c. The articles must be made to suit the special requirements of each country, and certain classes of goods, which are more in request than any others, are manufactured in large quantities. This is the case, for instance, with beads, and in the wholesale trade six varieties are distinguished, namely:

1. *Olives*, elongated, elliptical beads.
2. *Zotten* (German), cylindrical, slightly rounded, almost plane, at the two ends.
3. *Grecken* (German), like "Zotten" but shorter.
4. *Beads proper*, spherical.
5. *Corals*, beads with facets.
6. *Horse-corals*, flat, clear beads faceted at the two ends.

These different beads are made of various sizes and in different qualities of amber, those of bastard being the most valuable. "Bastard olives" and "bastard beads" constitute at the present time the most valuable article of export of the German amber-industry. According to the size and colour of the beads, the price varies in

"Bastard olives" from £2 10s. to £25 per kilogram.
"Bastard beads" „ £3 12s. „ £15 „ „

Another article manufactured in large numbers is the *manelle*. This is a flat, polished disc of amber, in the middle of which is cemented an amber bead, the latter being of clear amber and the disc of bastard, or *vice versâ*. The bead is not infrequently set upon a piece of tin foil to increase the lustre, and the underside engraved with flowers or other devices. These "manelles" serve as the centre-pieces of necklaces and bracelets, and are much appreciated in Persia, Armenia, and Turkey.

Cylinders of amber were for a long time much sought after by certain races in Central Africa and South America to be used as ornaments for the ears. To meet this demand, now to a large extent fallen off, these " cylinders" were manufactured in large quantities, and of various sizes, the largest being about 5 centimetres in length and 2 in diameter, but with a rather broader base.

Other amber ornaments need not be described in detail since there are none of a particular type which remain long enough in favour to justify their manufacture in large numbers. New designs and devices must be constantly brought out to meet the ever-changing demands of popular taste. In the same way the taste of the people of different countries must also be studied by the manufacturer of amber goods, not only with regard to the design of these goods, but also with respect to the variety of amber in which they are executed. Thus for articles exported to Russia, fine bastard amber only must be used; while in Holland the most admired variety is clear amber; in Germany, both clear and bastard amber is favoured; in France, bastard amber; in China, clear amber; in West Africa, the semi-osseous varieties with a brownish tinge; and so forth.

The value of the whole of the rough amber annually used up lies between £100,000 and £150,000. Of this, 40 per cent. is taken by Austria, 20 per cent. by Germany, 10 per cent. by Russia, 10 per cent. by France, 10 per cent. is used in the manufacture of varnishes, and the remaining 10 per cent. is used in the home manufactures of North America, China, Turkey, and other countries already mentioned.

The Amber Trade.—We have already seen that the amber trade is almost completely controlled by the firm of Stantien and Becker, since they are responsible for the production and marketing of almost the whole of the yield. The initiation of mining operations by this firm effected a complete revolution in the trade, for whereas in former times almost the whole of the annual yield consisted of sea-amber, and only a very small proportion of dug-amber, these conditions are now reversed. The supposed superiority of sea-amber over dug-amber lay in the fact that the former was free from the enveloping crust of weathered material, so that its colour and quality could be seen at a glance, and, moreover, was, as a rule, sound and free from cracks. In the case of dug-amber, with each piece enclosed in a thick opaque crust, it was impossible to judge of the quality, and the purchase of a parcel of such material was a risky speculation. This objection to purchasing rough amber was overcome by removing the opaque external crust by the method already described. The dug-stone had then no disadvantages compared with sea-amber, and even possessed a certain advantage over the latter, seeing that after the treatment to which it was subjected for the removal of the crust, every piece could not fail to be absolutely sound and free from cracks.

Another new and important departure, with which the same firm is to be credited, was the system of sorting the rough amber into **trade varieties** before placing it on the wholesale market. The rough amber is sorted out with regard to colour and quality, the size of the pieces, the number that go to make up a pound, and the suitability of their form to different purposes; merchants are thus enabled to buy rough material, the whole of which is exactly suited to their requirements. Previous to this, the rough amber had been classified to a certain extent, but not in accordance with the requirements of a more extended trade, and it is unnecessary to enumerate here the names by which these original trade varieties were known. The classification introduced by Stantien and Becker has been gradually coming into general use since 1868. The brief review of it, which now follows, is taken from R. Klebs, who has made a thorough study of the amber-producing industry, and to whom we are indebted also for much of the information already given.

One of the chief aims of the amber-worker is to produce any required article with the least possible waste of rough material. Thus, for the fashioning of a long, thin cigar-holder a piece of amber, approximating as closely as possible to the form of this object, should be chosen. The form of the pieces of rough amber is thus of the utmost importance, and the preliminary classification of the rough material is based on this character. The material thus sorted is then again classified according to size and quality, and irrespective of clearness or turbidity, these features being of little importance from this point of view. Amber of an unusual colour is not recognised in the trade classification, being too rare to possess any commercial significance. The classification given below applies specially to massive amber, but shelly, osseous, and other varieties of amber are sorted for trade purposes in the same way.

1. *Tiles* (German, *Fliessen*).—Tabular pieces, about three times as long as they are broad, and with a thickness of at least 75 millimetres and a length of 25 centimetres. The most valuable are those in which the two surfaces are approximately parallel. They are known as "work-stone-tiles" (German, *Arbeitssteinfliessen*), and are sorted into five classes:

"Work-stone-tiles," No. 1, with 10 to 12 pieces to the kilogram.

,,	,,	,,	2,	,,	30	,,	,,
,,	,,	,,	3,	,,	60	,,	,,
,,	,,	,,	4,	,,	100	,,	,,
,,	,,	,,	5,	,,	170	,,	,,

Pieces which lack the regular, rectangular form of "work-stone-tiles" are known as "ordinary tiles." Of these, ten trade varieties are distinguished: No. 0 is the first variety, and consists of material of which 2 or 3 pieces are required to make up the kilogram, while in variety No. 7, 360 pieces go to the kilogram. "Tiles" are used for the manufacture of smokers requisites, such as cigar-holders, mouthpieces for the same, and so forth.

The No. 1 variety of "ordinary tiles" fetches £7 2s. per kilogram, while the price of the No. 7 variety (the smallest pieces) is 9s. per kilogram. Variety No. 0 is so rarely met with that it can scarcely be considered as an ordinary trade variety. The specially selected "work-stone-tiles" are worth more than the "ordinary tiles." The price of varieties Nos. 1 and 2 is $33\frac{1}{3}$ per cent. higher, that of No. 3, 50 per cent., that of No. 4, 25 per cent., and that of No. 5, 10 per cent. higher.

2. *Plates* (German, *Platten*).—Pieces of amber of the same tabular form, but thinner than "tiles." Seven trade varieties are distinguished:

No. 0 "plates." With an area of from 40 to 60 square centimetres.

,, 1	,,	,,	,,	13 to 26	,,	,,	(about 50 pieces to the
,, 2	,,	80 pieces to the kilogram.					kilogram).
,, 3	,,	170	,,	,,			
,, $3\frac{1}{2}$	,,	260	,,	,,			
,, 4	,,	350	,,	,,			

"Polangen plates." Still smaller than No. 4.

"Plates" also are used mainly in the manufacture of smokers' requisites, especially for cigarette-holders, but also for ornamental articles; for example, "manelles," "horse-corals," crosses, and bells on the tesbih (rosaries) of Mohammedans.

3. *Ground-stone* (German, *Bodenstein*).—Large, rounded pieces of amber of good colour.

1. "Fine ground-stone" . . . 10 pieces to the kilogram.
2. "Ordinary ground-stone" . 14 to 16 ,, ,,

"Fine ground-stone" costs £2, and "ordinary ground-stone" 25s. per kilogram.

This variety of amber is often carved and used for ornamental objects of minor importance, also for the mouthpieces of Turkish hookahs, which are often decorated with gold and turquoise.

"Bockelstein" is a "flohmig" variety of "ground-stone," which is worked to form the centre pieces of necklaces, destined for export to Central Africa and South America. Large "Bockelsteine" are 10 per cent. dearer than "ground-stones."

4. *Round amber* (German, *Runder Bernstein*).—Round pieces of amber are divided according to colour into clear and turbid ("bastard"). According to size fourteen trade varieties are distinguished:

"Bastard round" and "clear round"	.	.	.	No. 1,	50 pieces to the kilogram.	
,,	,,	,,	. . .	,, 2,	100	,, ,,
,,	,,	,,	. . .	,, 3,	170	,, ,,
"Bastard ground-stone" and "clear ground-stone"	.	.	320		,, ,,	
"Bastard Knibbel" and "clear Knibbel"		.	,, 1,	600	,, ,,	
,,	,,	,,	.	,, 2,	820	,, ,,
,,	,,	,,	.	,, 3,	1600	,, ,,

"Clear round" and "bastard round," No. 1, costs 32s. per kilogram; No. 3, 17s. to 18s. per kilogram; and "clear Knibbel" and "bastard Knibbel," No. 3, 1s. 7d. per kilogram.

Osseous amber, especially in "Fliessen," has a particular classification. "Osseous Fliessen" is sorted according to size and colour into four lots. It is used for the manufacture of smaller mouthpieces, and its price is 25 per cent. lower than the corresponding material in "bastard amber." "Round osseous" is classified according to the size of the pieces into three sorts.

According to its structure *shelly amber* is sorted into two lots, one being described as "large, fine shelly amber" and the other as "unsorted shelly amber." The best qualities of "large, fine shelly amber" are worth 42s. per kilogram, while the price of "unsorted shelly amber" is only 3s. per kilogram. As a general rule, however, "shelly amber" is broken up, the best pieces, according to purity and suitability of size and form, being used for mouthpieces or beads, and the remainder included with the better and smaller pieces of "varnish amber." The latter is sorted according to quality and purity into ten trade varieties. "Shelly amber" is worked to only a small extent; specimens remarkable for their enclosures are usually placed in collections for scientific study, or are used as ornaments, this being especially the case when the specimen encloses an insect, for at one time bracelets, each bead of which contained such an enclosure, were much esteemed.

There remains now to be mentioned only the class of material known in Germany as *Brack*. This includes pieces of amber of large size, but so cracked and blebby or so impure that they are useless for ordinary purposes. This kind of material is sometimes bought as a speculation, or it may furnish the amber-worker with a cheap material for the bases of large objects. It is classed into "large Brack," including the purer pieces, and "ordinary Brack."

The trade varieties of amber and the prices quoted above were current in 1883. A comparison of these prices with those of earlier times shows that rough amber has fallen in value, this being especially true of the larger and more valuable sorts, the single exception being afforded by the small, clear amber. This fall in price is conditioned partly by the increase in production, an increase with which the manufacture and export has not quite kept pace; partly by the manufacture of imitation amber, especially by the development of the celluloid industry in North America, and, finally, partly by the use of artificially pressed amber in place of large pieces of natural occurrence. It may be mentioned here that the largest piece of amber yet found weighed 9·7 kilograms (21⅓ pounds). It is of a very beautiful bastard colour and is valued at £1500. It was found in 1860 at Cammin, in Pomerania, and is now preserved in the Museum für Naturkunde at Berlin.

IMITATION AND COUNTERFEIT AMBER.—The legitimate trade in amber suffers to a considerable extent by the substitution of cheap imitations for genuine amber. These imitations are sometimes more, sometimes less, clever, but can always be detected by the application of a few simple tests.

The difference between genuine amber and an imitation substance is usually apparent to a practised eye at a glance. This is specially the case with bastard amber, the colour of the turbid portions being so soft and pure, and passing so gradually and imperceptibly into the clear amber interlaminated with it, that the general appearance of the stone can never be reproduced in an imitation.

If, however, mere inspection is not sufficient to determine the nature of a doubtful specimen, it must be subjected to some or all of the tests described below under the different imitation substances.

The clumsiest imitation of amber is that made of yellow **glass.** This, which is usually made in imitation of clear amber, is now scarcely ever used for smokers' requisites, but is manufactured into beads, large numbers of which are sold, for the most part in China, as amber beads. This glass imitation of amber can be distinguished by the fact that it feels cold to the touch, by its greater hardness and greater specific gravity, and by the glassy conchoidal fracture which is distinctly visible at places where splinters have broken off the edge.

Celluloid, which latterly has found such an extensive and varied application, can be manufactured to resemble very closely many kinds of amber. Imitation amber of celluloid has been called "ambre antique." The use of this substance for articles, such as the mouthpieces of cigar-holders, can usually be detected by the fact that they have been moulded, not turned or ground, to the desired form. Moreover, in the imitation substance the alternating stripes of clear and cloudy material are sharply defined, this sharpness never being seen in cloudy varieties of genuine amber. When the imitation substance is rubbed a smell of camphor becomes perceptible, but very little electricity is developed. Again, with a knife, parings may be cut off celluloid, but genuine amber gives a powder when cut. The parings adhere to a hot platinum wire and take fire, flaring up with a bright flame and with the evolution of an acid smell. Amber, owing to its higher melting-point, does not adhere to a hot platinum wire, and it burns slowly, giving off a characteristic aromatic odour. Celluloid is quickly attacked by sulphuric ether, in which it dissolves, while amber may lie in this liquid for a quarter of an hour without sustaining any serious damage.

The extremely inflammable nature of celluloid cannot be too often insisted upon, and its use for smokers' requisites must be strongly deprecated. Although the inflammability of celluloid is often denied by the manufacturers, yet the fact remains, and all attempts to render it uninflammable have been as yet unsuccessful.

Amber differs from the other **resins,** which are frequently substituted for it, in possessing a higher melting-point, greater hardness, slighter solubility in alcohol, ether, and similar liquids, as well as in the presence of succinic acid as a constituent, and the evolution of a characteristic odour when rubbed or burnt.

Of these resins the most important is **copal,** which is often dug out of the earth, and is exported in large quantity from East and West Africa, South America, and Australia. In colour and general appearance it resembles some kinds of amber, and, like this substance, often encloses insects, but articles made of copal always have a dirty appearance. Owing to its lower melting-point copal, when rubbed with the hand or on cloth, becomes sticky; it is soft enough to take an impression even of the finger-nail, and when immersed in acetic ether it loses its lustre and swells up. All these characters serve to distinguish it from amber, and, if more were needed, it becomes less strongly electrified on rubbing, and, when burnt, does not give off the smell characteristic of amber. In order to produce the latter feature copal is sometimes melted up with pieces of amber, but owing to the difference in the melting-points of the two substances they do not mix, and after the mass has solidified the pieces of amber are easily recognisable lying in the copal. This substance is unsuitable for certain of the uses to which amber is put; for example, it is too brittle to allow of the worm of a screw being cut on it.

Dammar-resin mixed with powdered amber, and clear copal-colophony mixed with Venetian turpentine, furnish materials for the manufacture of imitation amber articles, such as cigar-holders. These imitations of amber show a turbid, " kumst "-coloured ground-mass, in which lie sharply defined masses of clear material, and in which insects—often ants—are embedded. The artificiality of this substance is very apparent, for clear and bastard material is rarely seen in combination in genuine amber, and, moreover, when the mass is broken it becomes obvious that the insects are made of metal. If made of copal the substance quickly swells up when placed in acetic ether, and if it consists of dammar-resin it loses its lustre when immersed in sulphuric ether for a period of from ten to fifteen minutes. Genuine amber is only affected after a much longer subjection to this treatment. Like copal dammar-resin also becomes sticky when rubbed.

Amber containing enclosures is sometimes manufactured by boring a hole into a suitable piece of genuine amber, placing some animal, such as a lizard or a tree-frog, in the hole, and filling it up with melted dammar-resin. It is not uncommon to find objects so treated mounted in gold and highly prized by the unsuspecting owner. When treated with alcohol or ether the melted resin is, of course, easily dissolved out.

The use of the imitations of amber described above is now almost superseded by that of **pressed amber** or **ambroid**, a substance produced from genuine amber, and first brought into the market at Vienna. Attempts had been made from time to time to devise some means of utilising small pieces of amber other than by converting them into varnish. This was at last accomplished, and the smaller pieces of amber are now welded together, as it were, by the application of a great pressure and an elevated temperature.

The method employed depends upon the fact that at a temperature between 170° and 200° C. amber softens. Pieces of rough amber after being freed from all impurities are placed in a flat mould of steel, the steel cover of which is then hermetically sealed. The mould is then placed in an oven, of which the temperature can be regulated to a nicety, or in a bath of glycerine or paraffin. By means of the hydraulic press, a pressure of from 8000 to 10,000 atmospheres is applied to the cover of the mould, and this pressure welds the pieces of amber, which are softened by heat, together to form a flat cake. These flat cakes of pressed amber are known in the trade as Spiller imitations. A much finer product is obtained when the amber, softened by heat, is driven under high pressure through a metal sieve, the resulting mass being by this method more thoroughly intermixed.

The pressed amber so produced can be obtained in all the varieties in which amber occurs, the " flohmig " and clear material being remarkably similar to natural amber. There is a difference apparent under the microscope however, for the rounded cavities of natural amber are flattened, elongated, and pressed out in a dendritic fashion in pressed amber. " Flohmig " pressed amber is more like " flohmig-clear," in which turbid and clear portions occur in parallel stripes. At the junction of the turbid and clear portions there is to be observed in transmitted light a yellowish-red colour, which in reflected light and against a dark background changes to blue. This appearance is very rare in natural amber, and never seen at all in bastard or in clear natural amber. Moreover, in pressed amber the clear and turbid portions are always sharply defined instead of merging imperceptibly the one into the other, as in natural amber. In clear portions of pressed amber, too, there are almost always to be seen small brownish patches and veins, and even if these are absent the material is never glassy clear, but always exhibits clouds and streaks, such as are seen when different liquids mix or when sugar dissolves in water. Many of the characters of pressed amber are, of course, identical with those of natural amber, such, for example, as hardness, high melting-point, marked tendency to develop frictional electricity, the giving out of an aromatic odour when rubbed or burnt, and the difficult solubility in the liquids mentioned above.

Between 600 and 700 hundredweights of pressed amber is now produced annually, and the material fetches from 25s. to 30s. per pound. It is used chiefly in the manufacture of cheap articles for the use of of smokers, and recently in the manufacture of beads for exportation to Africa. It can be worked in precisely the same way as natural amber.

In the foregoing account the chief consideration has been given to the true Baltic amber, known to mineralogists as succinite. Being an almost exclusively German product it has been dealt with in considerable detail ; it may also be stated here that owing to the amber-working industry being essentially a German trade, many of the trade terms quoted above have no equivalent in the English language. On the south-east coast of England a few pieces of amber are occasionally picked up. Besides the Baltic amber there are numerous other resins of a similar nature and applied to similar purposes, which may be included in the term amber used in its widest sense. They differ from amber proper in many of their characters, especially in the absence of succinic acid, and for this reason they have latterly been distinguished by mineralogists from succinite by special names. From a commercial point of view they are quite unimportant, but as they are of local interest in the places at which they occur the most important will be briefly described below.

GEDANITE.

Several other resins accompany succinite, but only one, gedanite, is suitable for ornamental purposes. It is known to amber-workers as " brittle," " friable " or " unripe " amber, and is usually transparent, or, at any rate, strongly translucent, and of a clear wine-yellow colour, rarely dirty yellow and opaque. Most of the pieces have the appearance of having been rounded and rubbed, and are dusted over with a snow-white powder, which can be wiped off. There is no succinic acid in gedanite, and hence the fumes given off when the substance is burnt are not irritating, although the smell is very like that of burning amber. The melting-point is about $140°$ C., being thus lower than that of amber, but higher than that of copal. Its hardness, $H = 1\frac{1}{2} - 2$, is less than that of amber. Its solubility is much the same, but gedanite is more easily attacked by oil of turpentine than is amber. When rubbed it acquires a strong charge of negative electricity, when it attracts to itself scraps of paper and other light bodies.

Owing to its great brittleness gedanite does not compare favourably with amber as a workable material. It is true that it can be turned on the lathe to any desired form, but, owing to its brittleness, it cannot well be bored, nor a screw cut on it. For the same reason articles made of gedanite must be handled withgreat care. In consequence of these disadvantages the different kinds of gedanite are not worth more than a third of the value of corresponding qualities of amber. No distinction is made in the trade between articles made of succinite and those made of gedanite, and the services of an expert are required when it is necessary to determine whether a given article is made of gedanite or of true amber.

The occurrence of gedanite is confined to the amber-diggings of the Prussian coast. The material is found in small amount with dug-amber, but never with sea-amber, probably because it is too brittle to resist the battering of the waves and the pebbles of the beach.

ROUMANIAN AMBER. (ROUMANITE.)

Roumanite, or Roumanian amber, is rarely yellow, but is usually brownish-yellow to brown. It is transparent to translucent, and scarcely ever opaque. Fluorescent specimens are sometimes met with, finer even than Sicilian amber, which is regarded as fluorescent amber *par excellence*. A characteristic feature of Roumanian amber is the presence of numerous cracks, which, however, do not seriously affect the cohesion of the material. Notwithstanding the fact that many of these stones are quite full of cracks, they can be turned, cut, polished, and otherwise worked without being broken. The substance is brittle, and has a conchoidal fracture. When rubbed it acquires a charge of negative electricity. The hardness slightly exceeds that of true amber. Succinic acid is present in variable amount (up to 3·2 per cent.), but on an average in less amount than in Prussian amber. The presence of a comparatively large amount of sulphur amounting to 1·15 per cent. in roumanite is a characteristic feature. The substance offers a still greater resistance to solvents than amber. When heated it gives off a peculiar aromatic odour, and at the same time a smell of hydrogen sulphide (like the smell of rotten eggs), which is due to the presence of sulphur. It fuses at 300° C. without swelling up, and gives off fumes, which act as an irritant on the respiratory passages.

This resin occurs enveloped in a closely-adhering, weathered crust, which is always very thin, and of a dark yellowish-grey to reddish-brown colour. It is found as nodules in carbonaceous, laminated shales, or as interrupted layers in sandstone beds in the district of Buseo. At Buscou, on the railway line from Bucharest to Braila, it is found within a radius of about a mile in the earth on common-land; while at Valeny di Muntye rounded fragments are found among the pebbles of a brook. The strata in which roumanite occurs, or in which it originated, belong to the later Tertiary period (the Congeria beds). Most of it is sent to Vienna, where, under the name of "Roumanian amber," it is manufactured into cigarette-holders and other useful or ornamental articles. To a certain extent it enters into competition with Prussian amber, but, owing to its comparative rarity and higher price, this competition is not serious.

The substance known in Roumania as "black amber" is not amber at all, but jet, a variety of coal which will be considered presently.

SILICIAN AMBER. (SIMETITE.)

Sicilian amber differs somewhat conspicuously from Baltic amber in appearance. It is usually transparent, and, as a rule, darker in colour than the latter. Reddish-yellow shading off to clear wine-red is not uncommonly seen, clear and dark brown, yellowish-white, and garnet-red colours also occur, while some specimens are of such a deep red colour that in reflected light they appear black. Among the more abundant transparent specimens are some which are only translucent or opaque. A blue or green fluorescence is a striking feature of this amber, and one which is frequently present. Another characteristic feature is the presence of a thin crust of yellowish-red or dark-red to black weathered material, which passes gradually into the fresh and unaltered paler coloured material in the interior.

Sicilian amber has the same hardness, the same fracture, and nearly the same specific gravity as Baltic amber, and like this acquires, on being rubbed, an electrical charge. When heated it fuses without previously swelling up, and gives off dense white fumes, which contain no succinic acid and do not, therefore, irritate the respiratory passages.

Among other places, Sicilian amber occurs in rounded pebbles in the neighbourhood of the mouth of the river Simeto, south of Catania, having been washed out of Tertiary strata, in which it was originally embedded, by that river, hence the name simetite. The material, together with Baltic amber, is manufactured into ornamental articles at the town of Catania. With Sicilian amber are sometimes found pieces of a black resin with a brilliant fracture, which is less hard than the transparent simetite; when heated it gives off a different smell, and is probably an entirely different substance.

BURMESE AMBER. (BURMITE.)

In Burma, also, is found an amber-like resin which is worked for ornamental purposes. The colouring is fairly uniform, and is sometimes of a clear, pale yellow, the colour of light sherry. In darker specimens this colour passes into a reddish shade, and this, in its turn, into a dirty brown colour; this is the most usual tint, and material of this colour has the appearance of colophony or solid petroleum. A few pieces are clear and almost colourless, or of a pale straw-yellow, but the majority are somewhat turbid, and exhibit a marked bluish or greenish fluorescence, which greatly diminishes their value.

Burmite is slightly harder than succinite; it is brittle but easy to work, and is often penetrated by cracks which are filled with calcite. It is difficult to obtain large pieces free from cracks, and this again makes the material less valuable.

The district in which Burmese amber is found is in the north of the country (see Maps, Figs. 54 and 55). The long-famous mines are situated not far distant from the jadeite mines, in a hill three miles south-west of Maingkwan in the basin of the Hukong, the upper course of the Chindwin river, in latitude 26° 15′ N. and longitude 96° 30′ E. of Greenwich. The pieces are distributed sporadically throughout a bluish-grey clay belonging to the Lower Miocene division of the Tertiary formation. They are smooth and flat, and the largest are of the size of a man's head. The material is highly esteemed both by the inhabitants and by the Chinese, and is worked to represent animals and idols and also for ear ornaments. The yield was always scanty, and, on this ground alone, it seems scarcely probable that Burmese amber should reach the European markets. On the other hand, a large quantity of Baltic amber is exported through India to Burma, where it is sold as Indian amber more cheaply than the native product. It has been stated that the Burmese mines are not now being worked, and if this is the case, the material which still comes into the native markets must be part of an old stock. A large piece of amber, 11½ inches long, carved to represent a duck, was taken from King Theebaw's palace at Mandalay, and is now preserved with the Burmese regalia in the Indian Section of the Victoria and Albert Museum at South Kensington. One of the presents given by the King of Ava to Colonel Symes, when on an embassy to that country in 1795, was a box containing " amber in large pieces, uncommonly pure."

Amber-like resins are obtained in other countries also, one which appears to be very rich in this respect being southern Mexico. The material is brought to the coast by natives from some unknown locality in the interior, and is shipped as " Mexican amber." It is of a rich golden-yellow colour, strongly fluorescent, and so abundant as to be used by the natives as fuel. Details of the occurrence are quite unknown, and an examination of the material itself is needed before it can be decided whether it consists of succinite or of another similar resin.

JET.

Jet (" black amber "; German, *Gagat, Agstein;* French, *jais*) is a variety of fossil coal often worked for mourning ornaments and other articles. Material to be suitable for this purpose must combine a number of characters, which are not, as a rule, associated in ordinary coal. Thus it must be compact, dense, and homogeneous, characters which are expressed by a perfect conchoidal fracture. It must contain no foreign matter, and specially no iron-pyrites, a common impurity in coals. Moreover, the original internal woody structure must not be retained, the preservation of the external form of the original stem or branch from which the coal was formed does not, however, make the material unsuitable for the purpose, but only emphasises its derivation from extinct trees.

Material which is to be used for ornamental purposes must be free from patchiness, and must be of a deep, pure black colour. Jet of a fine velvety black is most esteemed, that showing a brownish shade being considered inferior. The lustre, which is of a somewhat pronounced greasy kind, should not be too feeble and should be considerably enhanced by polishing; material with only a dull, glimmering lustre is quite worthless. Finally, the substance must be tough enough to be cut with a knife, worked on the lathe, filed or ground in the usual manner, and sufficiently hard to stand a reasonable amount of wear without being damaged. The hardness of genuine jet varies between 3 and 4.

Like all varieties of coal jet is perfectly opaque; the specific gravity is 1·35; the specimens which are said to float on water are, therefore, probably porous. When heated before the blowpipe the material easily ignites, being strongly impregnated with bituminous matter. It burns for a time with a very smoky and sooty flame, giving off an unpleasant odour, and leaving behind a shining, porous, coke-like residue. Like all substances of organic origin jet is a very poor conductor of heat, and hence feels warm to the touch, this feature being especially noticeable in comparison with black minerals or with glass, and serving to distinguish jet from these substances.

A coal having the properties enumerated above is described as a pitch-coal. From ordinary pitch-coal of frequent occurrence, which is usually very brittle, jet is distinguished by its greater toughness and firmness, and by the fact that it can be worked for ornamental articles. Coals which possess the characters detailed above in a more or less perfect degree are found at various localities, and at these places the principal jet-working establishments are situated.

The principal and, indeed, the only jet-cutting works in England are situated at **Whitby,** on the Yorkshire coast. There are but few establishments of the kind on the continent, and compared with the importance of the Whitby industry they are quite insignificant. Whitby has, therefore, the same importance in England, as the centre of the jet-cutting industry, as Oberstein has in Germany as the centre of the agate-cutting industry.

The hard jet of Whitby appears to have been used in Britain in pre-Roman days; it is alluded to by Caedmon, and mentioned in 1350 in the records of St. Hilda's Abbey. It was formerly extensively mined in the cliffs of the Yorkshire coast, near Whitby, and elsewhere; in Eskdale, Danby Dale, and in several of the dales that intersect the East Yorkshire moorlands. The hard jet occurs in the black shales of the *Ammonites serpentinus* zone of the Upper Lias, frequently in the form of flattened masses or layers, which in rare cases have been found to reach a length of 6 feet. So rich are these black shales in jet that they are often referred to as the jet-rock. The richest deposit is at Robin Hood's Bay, four miles south-east of Whitby.

A considerable amount of material is annually obtained, the yield in the year 1880, for example, being 6720 pounds. Two qualities of jet are worked at Whitby, a harder and better quality ranging in price from 4s. to 21s. a pound, obtained for the most part in the neighbourhood, and a softer, poorer, and cheaper quality, which is imported in large quantities from Aragon in Spain. The value of the jet-goods turned out by the Whitby works yearly amounts to about £100,000; in the year 1855 it amounted to £20,000. Between 1200 and 1500 persons are engaged in England at the present time in this industry.

At Whitby is also worked another substance which is of English origin and similar to jet, namely *cannel-coal.* This is of a greyish or brownish-black colour, less brilliant, less susceptible of a good polish, and more brittle than jet. It is found in large masses in the Coal Measures at Newcastle, and other places in England and in Scotland. Owing to its occurrence in large masses, this substance can be used as a veneer for surfaces of considerable size, this being impossible in the case of true jet.

Jet occurs and is worked in certain parts of the Continent. The rough material obtained in **Spain** is exported to England, the jet-working industry which once flourished there having now almost died out. The jet localities are situated in Aragon, Galicia, and Asturia, and what is done in the way of working the material is performed at several places in Asturia.

In **France** the material occurs in the greensand of the Cretaceous formation in the department Aude, province of Languedoc, where also an ancient jet-working industry once flourished. As in Yorkshire the jet occurs as thin plates, which rarely reach a weight of 15 pounds. The chief localities are Monjardin, near Chalabre, on Mount Commo-Escuro, and Bugarach, on Mount Cerbeiron, where mining was carried on, though not systematically. An additional supply of rough material was obtained from Spain, and it has been stated that some of the Spanish jet is superior in quality to the French.

The jet-working industry flourished in France in the eighteenth century, and in the year 1786 there were 1200 people employed in it, principally in the communities of

Sainte-Colombe, Dourban, Segure, Payrat, Bastide, and others. At that time about 1000 hundredweights of jet of local and foreign origin was annually worked up. The finished articles were exported in large quantities to Spain, 180,000 francs' worth of goods being received by that country annually, also to Italy, Germany, Turkey, and other parts of the Orient. With the fall of jet ornaments into disfavour came the decay of the industry, and in 1821 the net gain from the rough material and finished articles amounted only to 35,000 francs, while at the present day the industry is practically dead.

In **Würtemberg** jet is found, under the same conditions as at Whitby, in the *Posidonia* beds of the Upper Lias; for example, at Schömberg, Balingen, Boll, and many other places in the Swabian Alps. Abundance of jet is here easily obtained, and efforts have been made to establish an industry to rival that of Whitby. These attempts have received liberal Government support, but in spite of this, the workshops established at Gmünd, Balingen, and other places have been obliged to close, being unable to compete successfully with Whitby.

In **North America** material equal in quality to Whitby jet is found in the southern part of Colorado, in Wet Mountain Valley, and especially in El Paso County. It is very little used, however, for the manufacture of ornaments, and this is also the case with the fine material found at Pictou, in Pictou County, Nova Scotia. On the other hand, a black coal with a somewhat metallic lustre, known as anthracite, is sometimes used in the same way as is jet, especially that from Pennsylvania. In America the use of jet for mourning ornaments is largely replaced by " black onyx," that is to say, by an artificially coloured onyx or agate, which is of a deeper black, brighter, harder, and more durable than jet, and which can be obtained from Oberstein very cheaply. At present there has been no attempt to establish a jet industry in the United States, in spite of the occurrence of abundance of rough material of suitable quality.

Jet furnishes a material for the manufacture of mourning ornaments of all kinds, including brooches, bracelets, necklaces, cross-shaped pendants, &c. It is also used for such articles as rosaries, snuff-boxes, ink-stands, candlesticks, and stick-handles. These objects are usually first roughly fashioned with a knife or file, and then finished on the lathe or grinding lap. They may be more or less artistically carved; and, finally, are polished, this operation being performed with the palm of the hand.

Jet articles, even of the best quality, are worth but little, the only exceptions being in the case of objects of special artistic design and workmanship. Notwithstanding the cheapness of the genuine material, it is not uncommon to see mourning ornaments and other articles, purporting to be of jet, made in reality of some other black substance. A material which frequently replaces the use of jet is glass, either natural (obsidian) or artificial. It is never difficult, however, to decide whether one is dealing with jet or glass, for the latter is harder, heavier, and much more brilliant than the former, and, moreover, feels cold to the touch, while jet feels warm. Other substances used in place of jet are black onyx, black tourmaline, and black garnet (melanite), each of which differs from jet in the same ways as glass. An artificial product of much the same chemical composition as jet is vulcanite. These substances are very similar in appearance, and both feel warm to the touch; but vulcanite, even when lightly rubbed with a cloth, becomes strongly electrified, and readily attracts bits of paper, while jet does not. Vulcanite in a plastic condition can be pressed into a mould, and articles made of it are therefore often decorated in bas-relief. The blunt contours of such figures, however, make it at once clear to the expert that he is dealing not with figures carved in jet, which are remarkable for sharpness of outline, but with the impression of a mould.

THIRD PART

THE DETERMINATION AND DISTINGUISHING
OF PRECIOUS STONES

THE DETERMINATION AND DISTINGUISHING
OF PRECIOUS STONES

UNDER the description of each precious stone mentioned in this work there will be found a method of distinguishing it from precious stones of similar appearance or from imitations. By the application of the tests there laid down it is possible to determine whether a supposed diamond, for example, is really such, or whether it is another precious stone of similar appearance, or merely a glass imitation.

There are many cases in which the colour of a precious stone—always the first and most important feature to strike the eye—offers no obvious clue to its identity. We may, for example, meet with a red stone which might equally well be ruby, spinel, garnet, topaz, tourmaline, fluor-spar, or even red glass.

An experienced jeweller or mineralogist would seldom be in doubt in such a case, for he would be guided by external characters such as transparency, lustre, shade of colour, &c., all observable with the naked eye or with a lens. And in the case of a rough, uncut stone the identification is made more easily by the evidence afforded by the crystalline form of the stone, the character of its fractured surface, and the presence or absence of cleavage, evidence which in skilful hands usually points to a correct conclusion.

Glass can frequently be distinguished from genuine precious stones by the fact that it is warmer to the touch, and that, when breathed upon, it receives a film of moisture more easily, and retains it for a longer period, than do precious stones.

In cases where the more obvious characters of a stone are insufficient to establish its identity one has to fall back on its less conspicuous features, the observation of which may require the aid of some specially designed instruments and appliances.

These instruments and appliances to be of any practical value must be simple and substantial, as cheap as possible, and such that determinations made with their aid can be as well performed by the working jeweller as by a trained mineralogist. The methods adopted for the determination should be such as can be employed without injury to the stone, especially when the latter is cut, the avoidance of small surface injuries in uncut stones being of less importance. If the method of determination can be applied to mounted stones so much the better, but in many cases this is impossible, and gems for which large sums are asked should always be purchased unmounted.

The features which best fulfil the requirements outlined above are the optical characters and the specific gravity. The observation of these features is therefore a matter of considerable importance, and has been dealt with in detail in Part I. of this work. It is proposed here to recapitulate briefly the main facts of the subject, and for details to refer the reader to Part I., or to the special description of each precious stone given in Part II.

The **specific gravity** is best and most conveniently determined by the aid of certain heavy liquids, especially methylene iodide, which can be diluted to any extent with benzene until the stone under observation remains suspended in the liquid. The specific gravity of the liquid, and therefore of the stone, can then be determined by Westphal's balance (Fig. 7), or more conveniently by means of indicators, such as fragments of various minerals, of known specific gravity. In the case of stones which sink in pure methylene iodide, the specific gravity of which at ordinary temperature is 3·3, a heavier liquid, obtained by saturating methylene iodide with iodine and iodoform, may be used; or their specific gravity may be determined by the use of the pycnometer, the hydrostatic balance, or Westphal's balance (Fig. 5). Stones with a specific gravity exceeding 3·6 will sink even in this heavier liquid, and for them a still heavier liquid, molten silver-thallium nitrate, must be used. For ordinary purposes an exact determination of the specific gravity is unnecessary, and the four standard liquids recommended above will be found quite sufficient. These being so frequently referred to may be repeated here:

No. 1. Methylene iodide saturated with iodine and iodoform. (Sp. gr. = 3·6.)
„ 2. Pure methylene iodide. (Sp. gr. = 3·3.)
„ 3. Methylene-iodide diluted with benzene. (Sp. gr. = 3·0.)
„ 4. Methylene iodide further diluted with benzene. (Sp. gr. = 2·65.)

The data furnished by the use of these liquids enable us to classify precious stones into five groups, a classification which, taken in conjunction with the other characters of a stone, is a valuable aid in determining its identity.

The specific gravity method of determination is just as applicable to rough as to cut stones; the former when under determination should be free from all adhering foreign matter, and the latter should of course be unmounted. The merest fragment of a stone, with a density less than 3·3 or 3·6, will float in one or other of the heavy liquids, and thus indicate approximately what its specific gravity is; but for the exact determination of heavier stones, unless silver-thallium nitrate (sp. gr. = 4·8) is used, a rather larger fragment will be needed.

In establishing the identity of a stone next in importance to the specific gravity come the **optical characters.** The chief of these for our present purpose is the character of the refraction, whether double or single. This may be determined sometimes by direct observation, for, with cut stones, each facet forms with the one next the eye a prism, and the image of a small flame given by this prism will be single in the case of singly refracting stones (Fig. 26b) and double with doubly refracting stones (Fig. 26a). In the case of feebly doubly refracting stones the two images overlap so much that they appear to be one, so that it is not possible by these means to distinguish such stones from stones which are singly refracting. Moreover, observations of this nature can only be made on stones which are perfectly transparent and bounded by smooth crystal-faces or plane polished facets; irregular broken fragments, or stones cut *en cabochon*, will not give sharp images of the flame.

For these reasons, therefore, it is necessary in some cases to resort to the **polariscope** (Fig. 27) for aid in the determination of the nature of the refraction of a stone. The stone is placed on the object-carrier of the instrument with the planes of polarisation crossed, that is to say, in the dark field. If during the course of a complete revolution of 360° the stone changes from light to dark four times it is indisputably doubly refracting. If, on the other hand, the stone remains during a complete rotation of the carrier uniformly dark, like the rest of the field of view, it may be singly refracting. This, however, is not sufficient proof of the fact, for doubly refracting crystals when viewed in the direction of an optic axis present the same appearances. The stone must, therefore, be placed upon the object-carrier in another position, and if on rotation it appears alternately light and dark it must be doubly refracting, while if, on the contrary, it remains dark, we may conclude that it is singly refracting. Absolutely conclusive evidence as to the refraction of a stone is only obtained, however, when the appearance of an alternately light and dark field shows that it is doubly refracting. Cut stones should be examined in two positions, but the two facets on which they successively lie should not be parallel. It should always be borne in mind that the rays of light which pass into a strongly refracting stone may undergo total internal reflection and not emerge from the stone in the desired direction. When this is the case the stone will remain dark during the rotation of the carrier, even though it be strongly doubly refracting. In order to avoid this ambiguity, the gem may be attached to the carrier with wax in such a position that the largest facet, for example, the table in brilliants or the base in rosettes, shall be directed towards the observer and parallel to the object-carrier. Another device which serves the same purpose is to immerse the stone in methylene iodide or monobromonaphthalene or other strongly refracting liquid contained in a vessel with a plane transparent bottom. This device makes it possible to examine in the polariscope not only gems with plane facets but also stones cut *en cabochon* and quite irregular fragments. For the examination of a stone in the polariscope perfect transparency is by no means a *sine quâ non*; a considerable degree of transparency is quite sufficient to admit of the different degrees of illumination at different stages of the rotation being distinctly observed.

The existence of anomalous double refraction in certain stones must be borne in mind, but is not likely to lead to error. In all these observations with the polariscope it is necessary to cut off all light incident upon the stone from the sides by placing upon it an opaque tube of paper or by using the hand in a similar manner.

An absolute proof of the double refraction of a stone is obtained when it is shown to be dichroic. When any transparent and not too faintly coloured stone is placed in front of the **dichroscope**, Fig. 28, and held towards the light, two coloured images of the aperture of the instrument are seen. If these images be differently coloured the stone is indisputably dichroic, and consequently doubly refracting. If, on the other hand, both images appear of the same colour and remain so during a complete rotation of the stone relative to the dichroscope, then the stone may be characterised by the absence of dichroism, and it may be singly refracting. It is possible, however, in such a case that the stone is really dichroic, though so feebly so that the difference in colour of the images is not noticeable. Moreover, the light may have passed through the stone along an optic axis, which also would account for the images being of the same colour. It is necessary, therefore, to make a second observation with the stone in a different position ; and if now the two images differ in colour the stone is indisputably dichroic and doubly refracting. If, however, they are still of the same colour the stone may be devoid of dichroism and singly refracting ; but the evidence cannot be regarded as conclusive. In making observations with the dichroscope it is necessary to avoid the possibility of internal total reflection by placing the stone with its largest facet over the opening of the instrument.

The dichroism of some precious stones is strong enough to be apparent to the naked eye. The use of the dichroscope in such cases is superfluous, except to confirm one's direct observation or to determine the precise shades of colour shown by the two images. These shades are in a measure characteristic of each stone, and are therefore given a place in the tables which follow. As a means of establishing the identity of a stone, the observation of dichroism has the advantage of being applicable to stones which are mounted *à jour* as well as to cut and uncut unmounted stones.

In the possession of every person having to do with precious stones there should be a dichroscope, a polariscope of the kind described and figured above, and a series of heavy liquids with indicators, or, in place of these, a Westphal's balance. No special skill or theoretical knowledge is required in the use of these instruments, and their judicious employment constitutes a safeguard against the many cases of loss which arise through errors of determination.

It is desirable or necessary at times to take into consideration other characters of the stone, the determination of which may possibly result in a slight injury. Thus it is permissible to determine the hardness of a single cut stone, but tests for the fusibility or the behaviour towards acids can only be applied when a parcel of rough stones is at the disposal of the experimenter. In buying a parcel of gems it often pays the merchant to sacrifice one stone in order that an exhaustive determination, including perhaps a chemical analysis, may be made of it. In the case of rough stones it is often possible to detach a small splinter for detailed examination, and a slight scratch, or spot marked by acids, is of no consequence, since it will be removed when the stone is cut.

Minute differences in **hardness** cannot be relied upon for the purpose of discriminating stones, since differences of the same degree often exist between different faces of a crystal, or in different directions on the same face. The determination of the hardness of a stone is best performed by drawing a projecting edge or corner across the smooth surfaces of the different minerals which constitute the scale of hardness. We have already seen, in the earlier part of this work, that for the determination of the hardness of all ordinary precious stones pieces of only three minerals are necessary, namely, felspar (H = 6), quartz (H = 7), and topaz (H = 8), the pieces of which should have smooth faces and preferably should be artificially polished. No. 5 of the scale may be replaced by a piece of glass, lower members, as also Nos. 9 and 10, are not often needed. In the case of cut stones the edge with which the scratch is made should be chosen at the girdle, which will be enclosed and hidden within the setting. But even with this precaution the operation must be performed with great care, for the pressure may cause the stone to splinter at the edge, especially when it possesses a perfect cleavage.

It is necessary sometimes to reverse the operation and to attempt to scratch the stone itself. The instrument employed by preference in such cases is a pencil of specially hardened steel, provided with a sharp point, which will scratch quartz slightly and glass easily. It is easy in this way to distinguish glass imitations from genuine precious stones, such as the diamond, ruby, sapphire, &c., which are not scratched by the steel point, and the damage caused to the worthless imitation is not of very great consequence. Extra care is only necessary when dealing with the softer precious stones, such as chrysolite, &c.; but it is advisable in all cases to choose a spot on which to apply the test, which will be hidden when the stone is mounted. A scratch on almost any part of a transparent stone detracts considerably from its beauty, but a scratch on the back of an opaque stone is of little consequence. A rough stone may be scratched anywhere without fear, and the hardness of different faces and in different directions of the same face determined.

Instead of the steel pencil a file of hard steel is frequently employed; this readily marks the softer stones, and emits at the same time a lower note than with harder stones. Cut stones should be tested with the file only on the girdle, and even then with the greatest care. Owing to all these difficulties only a limited use can be made of the character of hardness. Recently, however, a very good method, depending upon hardness, has been discovered by which glass imitations can be distinguished from genuine precious stones. An aluminium pencil drawn across a clean, dry surface of glass leaves a metallic silvery streak, but on the surface of a precious stone the aluminium leaves no mark.

The behaviour of a precious stone towards acids is another character of which only a limited use can be made. It is useful, for example, when carbonates, such as malachite, are in question, for a drop of acid placed on a rough stone, or on the back of a polished one, causes a brisk effervescence, and does no particular damage. The fusibility can only be determined upon fragments of rough stones, and, for our present purpose, is of little importance.

The magnetic and **electrical characters** of a stone are often useful in determining its identity. The phenomenon of pyroelectricity exhibited by tourmaline to such a marked degree often serves to identify this stone, and the existence of this property can be demonstrated without the slightest risk of injury to the stone. The supposed tourmaline is warmed in an air-bath or on a sheet of paper held over a flame ; and while cooling it is dusted over with a mixture of red-lead and sulphur shaken through a sieve. Mutual friction causes the red-lead to become positively, and the sulphur negatively electrified, and if the crystal during cooling has acquired statical charges of pyroelectricity, the red-lead will be attracted to the negative pole of the crystal and the sulphur to the positive pole.

Quite recently it has been discovered that the **Röntgen (X) rays** afford another means whereby certain precious stones may be distinguished from their imitations. The most important case is that of the diamond. This is perfectly transparent to the rays, but glass, topaz, rock-crystal, &c., are opaque, and will appear in a photograph taken by X rays with sharp outlines. Corundum (ruby and sapphire, &c.) is semi-transparent, while spinel and blue tourmaline, like glass, are opaque, so that here again the former may be distinguished from the latter. Amber and other similar resins, as well as jet, are transparent to a marked degree, and can, therefore, be distinguished from glass imitations, which are opaque to the rays. The whole method is as yet in its infancy, but will no doubt become important as a ready means of establishing the identity of a diamond, whether mounted or unmounted, without injury to the stone. Moreover, a large parcel of diamonds may be photographed, and the presence of any stone not diamond readily detected.

In what follows, the characters described above will be utilised to distinguish precious stones of similar appearance one from another. The first step is to classify all stones into three main groups :

    (a) Transparent stones.
    (b) Translucent and opaque stones.
    (c) Stones with special optical effects.

A classification based upon transparency or translucency is difficult to. follow in practice, for large specimens of ordinarily transparent stones are sometimes only translucent, and one specimen of the same mineral species may be perfectly transparent while another is perfectly opaque. In the scheme which follows, therefore, stones which may be either transparent or translucent will be placed in both classes. The stones included in classes a and b are arranged in sub-groups according to colour, and those in the third class according to the nature of the optical phenomenon to which their characteristic appearance is due.

A. TRANSPARENT STONES.

These are classified into fourteen groups according to colour :

1. Colourless	8. Reddish-brown
2. Greenish-blue (sea-green)	9. Smoke-grey and clove-brown
3. Pale blue	10. Reddish-yellow
4. Blue	11. Yellowish-brown
5. Violet	12. Yellow
6. Lilac and rose	13. Yellowish-green
7. Red	14. Green

In the tables which follow, each markedly transparent precious stone will be found in one of these fourteen groups, and in cases where the same stone shows two or more colours, or a shade more or less in harmony with the colours characteristic of several groups, it will be included in each, so that there will be no difficulty in finding it. The stones included in each colour-group are further classified according to specific gravity, as determined by the four standard heavy liquids. They are placed in the tables in order of decreasing specific gravity, and in three other columns are tabulated the values of the specific gravity and hardness, and the character of the refraction of each ; while in a fourth column the presence or absence of dichroism, its strength, and, in some cases, the colours of the dichroscope images are indicated.

It should be possible from these tables to establish the identity of almost any precious stone one may happen to meet with. The remarks appended to each table are intended as a help, mainly in cases where the specific gravity places several stones in one or other of the five sub-divisions.

The names of the more important precious stones, and those most commonly met with, are printed in the tables in heavier type, and special attention is paid to such in the remarks.

1. COLOURLESS STONES.

Division.	Name.	Specific gravity.	Hardness.	Refraction.
I. (Sp. gr. over 3·6)	Zircon Corundum Spinel	4·6—4·7 3·9—4·1 3·60—3·63	$7\frac{1}{2}$ 9	Double Double Single
II. (Sp. gr. = 3·3—3·6)	**Topaz** **Diamond**	3·50—3·56 3·50—3·52	8 10	Double Single
III. (Sp. gr. = 3·0—3·3)	Tourmaline	3·022	$7\frac{1}{4}$	Double
IV. (Sp. gr. = 2·65—3·0)	Phenakite Beryl	2·95 2·68—2·75	$7\frac{3}{4}$ $7\frac{3}{4}$	Double Double
V. (Sp. gr. under 2·65)	**Rock-crystal** Opal	2·65 2·0	7 6	Double Single
	Glass	Variable	5	Single

The stones included in Division I. sink in liquid No. 1, and this high specific gravity is a feature which marks them off from all the others. They are distinguished *inter se* by differences in their optical characters, zircon and corundum (" white sapphire ") being doubly refracting and spinel singly refracting. Colourless spinel is very rare and is scarcely ever met with cut as a gem. Zircon and corundum are commoner, and not infrequently are substituted for the diamond; the latter, however, is distinguished by the fact that it floats in liquid No. 1. Zircons and "white sapphires" of some size may be distinguished by an exact determination of their specific gravities; and another difference between the two stones lies in the hardness, for the latter readily scratches a smooth surface of topaz while zircon does not. Moreover, colourless zircon has a brilliant adamantine lustre, while the lustre of corundum is of the vitreous type. Finally, cut colourless zircons are nearly always small, at the most no larger than a pea, and there is often a perceptible reddish tinge about them, left after heating the yellowish-red hyacinth, which is never exhibited by colourless corundum.

Division II. embraces topaz and diamond; the specific gravity is practically identical, but topaz is doubly refracting and diamond singly refracting; and there is also an enormous difference in hardness, diamond scratching topaz very easily and deeply. Moreover, the strong adamantine lustre of diamond is very characteristic, and the magnificent play of prismatic colours, shown by cut stones, still more so, so that it is scarcely possible to mistake diamond for topaz or for strass. The last-named is readily scratched by a steel point or marked by an aluminium pencil, and also feels warmer to the touch than does diamond.

Colourless tourmaline is the only stone embraced by the third division, and is of very rare occurrence as a gem.

Phenakite and beryl, the two stones which constitute division IV., can be distinguished only by an exact determination of their specific gravity: if performed with the aid of methylene iodide the smallest fragments of material will suffice. Characteristic of phenakite is its specially strong lustre, by which it is distinguished from colourless beryl, which is rarely cut as a gem.

Rock-crystal falls into division V. and cannot, therefore, be mistaken for other and heavier stones.

From many of the stones in this group glass can be distinguished by the fact that it is singly refracting. So, indeed, also is opal, but the transparent, glassy variety of opal known as hyalite is practically never used as a gem. It may be recognised by the fact that it is capable of scratching glass, though it itself is easily scratched by a steel point. The feeble anomalous double refraction always shown by water-clear opal also serves to distinguish it from glass.

2. GREENISH-BLUE (SEA-GREEN) STONES.

Division.	Name.	Specific gravity.	Hardness	Refraction.	Dichroism.
I.	"Oriental Aquamarine"	3·9—4·1	9	Double	Not very strong
II.	Topaz	3·50—3·56	8	Double	Distinct (colourless and greenish-blue)
	Diamond	3·50—3·52	10	Single	Absent
III.	Fluor-spar	3·1—3·2	4	Single	Absent
	Euclase	3·05—3·1	7½	Double	Observable
IV.	Aquamarine	2·68—2·75	7¾	Double	Distinct (bluish and yellowish)
	Glass	Variable	5	Single	Absent

The two members of this group most likely to be confused are aquamarine and topaz, since they are often identical in colour. There need be no confusion, however, since they differ very widely in specific gravity, the latter falling into Division II. and the former into Division IV. Euclase, a rare mineral of much the same colour, is distinguished by the same feature, namely, the specific gravity.

The distinctions between corundum (" oriental aquamarine "), diamond, and topaz have been dealt with in the first table.

The specific gravity, low degree of hardness, and single refraction unite to distinguish fluor-spar from other stones of the same group; it is always rather darker in colour than are aquamarine, topaz, or euclase. Glass is singly refracting and much softer than any of the stones included in this group except fluor-spar.

3. PALE BLUE STONES.

Division.	Name.	Specific gravity.	Hardness.	Refraction.	Dichroism.
I.	Sapphire	3·9—4·1	9	Double	Feeble
II.	Topaz	3·50—3·56	8	Double	Observable (colourless and bluish)
	Diamond	3·50—3·52	10	Single	Absent
III.	Tourmaline	3·1	7¼	Double	Distinct
IV.	Aquamarine	2·68—2·75	7¾	Double	Feeble
	Glass	Variable	5	Single	Absent

The remarks given under the first and second tables will enable the stones brought together here to be distinguished; those of more frequent occurrence are readily recognised by the specific gravity alone.

4. BLUE STONES.

Division.	Name.	Specific gravity.	Hardness.	Refraction.	Dichroism.
I.	Sapphire	3·9—4·1	9	Double	Distinct (dark blue and pale greenish-blue)
	Spinel	3·7	8	Single	Absent
II.	Kyanite	3·60	5—7	Double	Observable
	Diamond	3·50—3·52	10	Single	Absent
III.	Fluor-spar	3·1—3·2	4	Single	Absent
	Tourmaline	3·1	7¼	Double	Strong (pale blue to dark blue)
V.	Cordierite	2·60—2·66	7¼	Double	Strong (pale blue, dark blue, and yellowish-grey)
	Haüynite	2·4	5½	Single	Absent
	Glass	Variable	5	Single	Absent

By far the most important of these is sapphire; the only other blue stones of consequence as gems are spinel and tourmaline. The former is distinguished by the fact that it is singly refracting, while sapphire and tourmaline differ widely in density. The colour of tourmaline is usually very dark and inclined somewhat to green, while that of sapphire is usually a pure blue; moreover, tourmaline is very much more strongly dichroic than is sapphire.

Kyanite almost invariably exhibits a series of fine straight cracks running in one direction; it is not perfectly transparent as a rule, and, compared with sapphire, has little lustre. It remains suspended in or sinks slowly to the bottom of liquid No. 1, in which sapphire readily sinks. Diamond of a deep blue colour is extremely rare; it is recognisable by its specific gravity, hardness, and single refraction.

Cordierite is not a gem ordinarily met with in the trade; it is distinguished by its low specific gravity and strong dichroism, with the characteristic shades of colour.

Glass and haüynite are both singly refracting and not dichroic, but the specific gravity of the former is considerably higher than that of the latter.

5. VIOLET STONES.

Division.	Name.	Specific gravity.	Hardness.	Refraction.	Dichroism.
I.	**Almandine**	4·1—4·2	7¼	Single	Absent
	" Oriental Amethyst "	3·9—4·1	9	Double	Distinct
	Spinel	3·60—3·63	8	Single	Absent
III.	Axinite	3·29—3·3	6¾	Double	Strong (violet, brown, green)
	Apatite	3·2	5	Double	Feeble
	Fluor-spar	3·1—3·2	4	Single	Absent
V.	**Amethyst**	2·65	7	Double	Feeble
	Glass	Vari ble	5	Single	Absent

Apatite and fluor-spar are scarcely ever used as gems: their specific gravity and lack of hardness distinguish them from other violet stones, and the difference in optical refraction distinguishes the one from the other. Axinite is included in the same division; it is characterised by specially strong dichroism, and its colour is not pure violet, but markedly brownish in shade.

Of the stones included in this group, the one met with most commonly is the true amethyst, which constitutes Division V., and is readily distinguished from the members of the first division by its low specific gravity and feeble dichroism.

Almandine is distinguished from the other stones included in Division I. by its colour, which is better described as red inclined to blue than as pure violet. It differs both from " oriental amethyst " and from true amethyst in that it is singly refracting, and from the former in its hardness. " Oriental amethyst," amethyst, and spinel are, perhaps, most conveniently distinguished by the presence or absence of dichroism, which is strongest in the first, feeble in the second, and absent from the last. " Oriental amethyst " and spinel are capable of scratching quartz, but amethyst, of course, is not, and spinel differs from the other two in being singly refracting. The only well-marked difference between spinel and almandine is one of density; the former remains suspended or slowly sinks in liquid No. 1, while the latter quickly sinks. The slight difference in hardness may enable one to discriminate between these stones, but in certain cases it is difficult to distinguish one from another.

Glass differs in hardness from all the violet stones ordinarily used, being readily scratched by a steel point; it is distinguished both from "oriental amethyst" and from true amethyst by its single refraction.

6. LILAC AND ROSE-COLOURED STONES.

Division.	Name.	Specific gravity.	Hardness.	Refraction.	Dichroism.
I.	**Ruby**	3·9—4·1	9	Double	Feeble
	Spinel ("Balas-ruby")	3·60—3·63	8	Single	Absent
II.	**Topaz**	3·50—3·56	8	Double	Strong (red and yellow)
	Diamond	3·50—3·52	10	Single	Absent
III.	Fluor-spar	3·61	4	Single	Absent
	ourmaline	3·02	7¼	Double	Distinct (pale red and dark red)
V.	Rose-quartz	2·65	7	Double	Very feeble
	Glass	Variable	5	Single	Absent

Of the stones of this group, the first three are commonly met with, tourmaline is less common, and the others make only rare appearances in the precious stone market. "Balas ruby" exhibits not infrequently a milky cloudiness. Topaz and tourmaline both show differently coloured images in the dichroscope. Topaz is distinguishable also from ruby and spinel by the difference in specific gravity, and the two last named differ from each other both in the character of their optical refraction and in the fact that dichroism is feeble in the one and absent in the other. Glass is easily recognisable by its lack of hardness and by its single refraction.

7. RED STONES.

Division.	Name.	Specific gravity.	Hardness.	Refraction.	Dichroism.
I.	**Almandine**	4·1—4·2	7¼	Single	Absent
	Ruby	3·9—4·1	9	Double	Distinct (pale red and dark red)
	Pyrope				
	("Cape ruby")	3·86	7¼	Single	Absent
	(Bohemian garnet)	3·7—3·8	7¼	Single	Absent
	Hessonite	3·65	7¼	Single	Absent
	Spinel	3·60—3·63	8	Single	Absent
II.	**Topaz**	3·50—3·56	8	Double	Strong (red and yellow)
	Diamond	3·50—3·52	10	Single	Absent
III.	Fluor-spar	3·1	4	Single	Absent
	Tourmaline	3·08	7¼	Double	Strong (rose and dark red)
V.	Fire-opal	2·2	6	Single	Absent
	Glass	Variable	5	Single	Absent

Of these, red fluor-spar, red diamond, and fine opal are all rare.

Division I. embraces the garnets—almandine, hessonite or cinnamon-stone, " Cape ruby," and Bohemian garnet; the last two do not differ essentially and both belong to the sub-species pyrope. These, together with spinel, are distinguished from ruby by their single refraction, and from each other by differences in colour. Almandine is purplish-red (inclined to blue), "Cape-ruby" and Bohemian garnet are both dark blood-red with a yellowish tinge, and hessonite is pale yellowish-red. The different varieties of garnet are characterised also by not unimportant differences in density. The variety of spinel known as "ruby-spinel" is very similar in colour to ruby, but is easily distinguishable by the means indicated already. On the other hand it is often difficult to distinguish spinel from garnet, especially in the case of the reddish-yellow spinel (rubicelle) and hessonite, which agree in the character of their refraction, in the absence of dichroism, in colour, and very closely in specific gravity; it is sometimes possible, though difficult, to distinguish cut stones by their difference in hardness. There is less difficulty in distinguishing rough stones, since spinel always occurs in octahedra, while hessonite scarcely ever takes this form, and spinel is infusible and hessonite easily fusible before the blowpipe. The fusibility of hessonite and almandine distinguishes them also from the infusible pyrope.

Red tourmaline and topaz in colour are very similar to each other, and also sometimes to ruby, but each of the three differs very definitely from the others in specific gravity, and a further distinction is afforded by the fact that one of the two images shown by topaz in the dichroscope is distinctly yellow, this not being the case with red tourmaline or ruby.

In the second division diamond is distinguished from topaz by its single refraction and lack of dichroism, and these same features serve to distinguish fluor-spar from tourmaline, both of which are included in Division III.

The specific gravity of fire-opal is always much lower than that of any other stone in this group. It is singly refracting, always rather cloudy, and sometimes shows a play of colours like that of precious opal. Glass is distinguished from the stones of this group in the usual way; the most convenient distinction between glass and opal is that of the difference in specific gravity, the density of glass being scarcely ever less than 2·6.

8. REDDISH-BROWN STONES.

Division.	Name.	Specific gravity.	Hardness.	Refraction.	Dichroism.
I.	Zircon	4·6—4·7	7½	Double	Very feeble
	Almandine	4·1—4·2	7¼	Single	Absent
	Staurolite	3·73	7½	Double	Feeble
	Hessonite	3·65	7¼	Single	Absent
II.	**Topaz**	3·50—3·56	8	Double	Strong (yellow and red)
III.	Tourmaline	3·1	7¼	Double	Strong (pale brown and dark brown)
V.	Citrine	2·65	7	Double	Feeble
	Fire-opal	2·2	6	Single	Absent
	Amber	1·08	2—3	Single	Absent
	Glass	Variable	5	Single	Absent

Staurolite is rarely met with, it is seldom perfectly transparent and always very darkly coloured. Tourmaline and almandine of a reddish-brown colour are rarely cut as gems.

Zircon, hessonite, topaz, and citrine can be readily distinguished by the help of the character tabulated above and by the remarks appended to previous tables.

Amber differs from all the other members of this group in feeling warm to the touch, and in the fact that it acquires a strong charge of electricity on being rubbed.

Glass and opal are distinguished in the way indicated under the preceding table.

9. SMOKE-GREY AND CLOVE-BROWN STONES.

Division.	Name.	Specific gravity.	Hardness.	Refraction.	Dichroism.
II.	Diamond	3·50—3·52	10	Single	Absent
	Epidote	3·47—3·50	$6\frac{1}{4}$	Double	Strong (green, yellow, brown)
	Idocrase	3·4	$6\frac{1}{2}$	Double	Distinct
III.	Axinite	3·29—3·30	$6\frac{3}{4}$	Double	Strong (violet, brown, green)
	Andalusite	3·17—3·19	$7\frac{1}{2}$	Double	Strong (yellow and red)
V.	Smoky-quartz	2·65	7	Double	Feeble
	Glass	Variable	5	Single	Absent

Of the stones of this group, practically the only one which is widely distributed is smoky-quartz. Andalusite and epidote are rare, and axinite still more so, but brown diamond is less uncommon. The characters given in the table are sufficient to distinguish any one of these stones from any other, and from glass without much difficulty.

It is sometimes a little difficult, however, to discriminate between epidote and idocrase, and one has to rely on the fact that the former is more strongly dichroic than the latter.

Andalusite is distinguishable from axinite by the greenish tint of its colour, and by the fact that the dichroscope images are differently coloured.

10. REDDISH-YELLOW STONES.

Division.	Name.	Specific gravity.	Hardness.	Refraction.	Dichroism.
I.	Hyacinth	4·6—4·7	$7\frac{1}{2}$	Double	Very feeble
	" Oriental hyacinth "	3·9—4·1	9	Double	Distinct
	Pyrope	3·7—3·8	$7\frac{1}{4}$	Single	Absent
	Hessonite	3·65	$7\frac{1}{4}$	Single	Absent
	Spinel (Rubicelle)	3·60—3·63	8	Single	Absent
II.	Topaz	3·50—3·56	8	Double	Strong (red and yellow)
V.	Fire-opal	2·2	6	Single	Absent
	Glass	Variable	5	Single	Absent

The characters which distinguish pyrope, hessonite, and spinel one from another have been given already under Table 7. Hessonite and hyacinth are sometimes very similar in colour, and are often mistaken the one for the other, in spite of the fact that hyacinth has a much stronger adamantine lustre than has hessonite ; there is also a fundamental difference between them in the character of their refraction, hessonite being singly and hyacinth doubly refracting. "Oriental hyacinth" is distinctly dichroic, but the hyacinth variety of zircon is only very feebly so.

The density of topaz places it in a division apart from all the other stones of this group, and it is further characterised by strong dichroism.

11. YELLOWISH-BROWN STONES.

Division.	Name.	Specific gravity.	Hardness.	Refraction.	Dichroism.
II.	**Topaz**	3·50—3·56	8	Double	Distinct (yellow and brownish-red)
	Diamond	3·50—3·52	10	Single	Absent
	Epidote	3·47—3·50	$6\frac{1}{2}$	Double	Strong (green, yellow, brown)
	Idocrase	3·35—3·45	$6\frac{1}{2}$	Double	Distinct (green and yellow)
	Sphene	3·35—3·45	$5\frac{1}{2}$	Double	Distinct
III.	Axinite	3·29—3·30	$6\frac{3}{4}$	Double	Strong (violet, brown, green)
V.	**Citrine**	2·65	7	Double	Feeble
	Fire-opal	2·2	6	Single	Absent
	Amber	1·08	2—3	Single	Absent
	Glass	Variable	5	Single	Absent

Of the stones of this group, topaz, amber, and the yellow variety of quartz known as citrine are of common occurrence. Amber feels warm to the touch, is very light and soft, and when rubbed becomes strongly electrified, attracting to itself any light objects, so that it can scarcely be mistaken for any of the stones with which it is here grouped. The means whereby amber may be distinguished from resinous and glass imitations have been fully described under amber and need not be repeated.

Topaz and quartz may be distinguished by the difference in specific gravity alone, but the greater hardness and stronger dichroism of the former furnishes additional aid in this direction.

Sphene is less hard than is idocrase or epidote; these may be distinguished from each other by an accurate determination of their specific gravity. Epidote is characterised also by very strong dichroism.

12. YELLOW STONES.

Division.	Name.	Specific gravity.	Hardness.	Refraction.	Dichroism.
I.	**Hyacinth**	4·6—4·7	$7\frac{1}{2}$	Do ble	Very feeble
	" Oriental topaz " }	3·9—4·1	9	Double	Feeble
	Chrysoberyl	3·68—3·78	$8\frac{1}{2}$	Double	Feeble
II.	**Topaz**	3·50—3·56	8	Double	Distinct (pale yellow and dark yellow)
	Diamond	3·50—3·52	10	Single	Absent
	Chrysolite	3·33—3·37	$6\frac{1}{2}$	Double	Feeble (green and yellowish-green)
III.	Fluor-spar	3·1	4	Single	Absent
IV.	Beryl	2·67—2·76	$7\frac{3}{4}$	Double	Feeble
V.	**Citrine**	2·65	7	Double	Feeble
	Fire-opal	2·2	6	Single	Absent
	Amber	1·08	2—3	Single	Absent
	Glass	Variable	5	Single	Absent

The commonest stones of a yellow colour are citrine, topaz, and the yellow variety of corundum known as "oriental topaz," they are easily distinguished from each other by the differences in their specific gravity. Several other stones of this group are not altogether uncommon in the precious stone market.

The colour of hyacinth is never pure yellow, but is always definitely inclined to red, while the yellow of chrysoberyl and chrysolite has always a greenish tinge. In stones of not too small size, "oriental topaz" may be recognised by an exact determination of the specific gravity. Hyacinth is not capable of scratching topaz, but this latter is scratched both by "oriental topaz" and by chrysoberyl: and "oriental topaz" will scratch chrysoberyl, a specimen of which may be conveniently kept for this test.

Topaz, diamond, and chrysolite are distinguished from each other by differences in hardness and in their behaviour in the polariscope, while the specific gravity is in each case sufficient to distinguish them from the stones included in other divisions. Topaz and citrine differ both in specific gravity and in hardness; the former sinks in pure methylene iodide, and, moreover, is capable of scratching quartz.

Although beryl and citrine fall into different divisions of this group, there is very little difference in their specific gravities, and in some cases there may be uncertainty as to the identity of these stones. Beryl, nevertheless, is always rather heavier than citrine (quartz), and sinks in liquid No. 4, in which citrine remains suspended. It is also characterised by its capability of scratching quartz, which, of course, is not possessed by citrine. Beryl is both lighter and harder than chrysolite.

Amber, fire-opal, and glass are distinguished in the manner already explained in the remarks appended to preceding tables.

13. YELLOWISH-GREEN STONES.

Division.	Name.	Specific gravity.	Hardness.	Refraction.	Dichroism.
I.	Zircon	4·6—4·7	$7\frac{1}{2}$	Double	Very feeble
	"Oriental chrysolite"	3·9—4·1	9	Double	Distinct
	Demantoid	3·83	7	Single	Absent
	Chrysoberyl	3·63—3·78	$8\frac{1}{2}$	Double	Feeble (yellowish and greenish)
II.	**Topaz**	3·50—3·56	8	Double	Distinct
	Epidote	3·47—3·5	$6\frac{1}{2}$	Double	Strong (green, yellow, brown)
	Idocrase	3·35—3·45	6	Double	Distinct (green and yellow)
	Sphene	3·35—3·45	$5\frac{1}{2}$	Double	Distinct
	Chrysolite	3·33—3·37	$6\frac{3}{4}$	Double	Feeble (green and yellowish-green)
III.	Hiddenite	3·17—2·20	$6\frac{3}{4}$	Double	Feeble (pale green and dark green)
	Andalusite	3·17—3·19	$7\frac{1}{2}$	Double	Strong (yellow, green, red)
	Tourmaline	3·1	$7\frac{1}{4}$	Double	Strong (yellow and green)
IV.	**Beryl**	2·67—2·76	$7\frac{3}{4}$	Double	Distinct
V.	**Moldavite**	2·36	$5\frac{1}{2}$	Single	Absent
	Glass	Variable	5	Single	Absent

Of the stones included in the first division of this group, chrysoberyl is most frequently met with: it is characterised by great hardness, being capable of scratching topaz, and often by the possession of a milky sheen. "Oriental chrysolite" is also capable of scratching topaz, but is much more strongly dichroic than is chrysoberyl. Zircon of this colour is rare; it has a strong adamantine lustre, and is far denser than any other stone in the division, so that an exact determination of the specific gravity of this stone is sufficient to establish its identity. Demantoid is the only singly refracting stone included in this division.

In Division II. topaz is characterised by its hardness, and is the only stone in this division which is capable of scratching quartz. The characters of many of these minerals have been considered already; chrysolite is harder than sphene, and much less dichroic than epidote or idocrase. Not infrequently the specific gravity of chrysolite is exactly the same as that of methylene iodide, the stone will therefore sink slowly as the liquid is warmed or rise to the surface as it is cooled, the contact of the vessel with the warm hand being sufficient to cause the stone to rise. "Oriental chrysolite" is much heavier, much harder, and much more strongly dichroic than is true chrysolite.

Division III. includes hiddenite, andalusite, and tourmaline; all three are dichroic, but andalusite is most strongly so, and is characterised further by one of the dichroscope images being red. Andalusite and tourmaline scratch quartz, but hiddenite does not.

The variety of beryl known as "aquamarine-chrysolite" is recognised by its low specific gravity and feeble dichroism.

Moldavite is singly refracting, and is distinguished from artificial yellowish-green glasses only by its lower specific gravity.

14. GREEN STONES.

Division.	Name.	Specific gravity.	Hardness.	Refraction.	Dichroism.
I.	Zircon	4·6—4·7	7	Double	Very feeble
	"Oriental emerald"	3·9—4·1	9	Double	Distinct (green and brown)
	Demantoid	3·83	7	Single	Absent
	Alexandrite	3·68—3·78	8½	Double	Strong (green, yellow, red)
II.	Diamond	3·50—3·52	10	Single	Absent
	Epidote	3·47—3·50	6½	Double	Strong (green, yellow, brown)
	Idocrase	3·35—3·45	6½	Double	Distinct (green and yellow)
	Sphene	3·35—3·45	5½	Double	Distinct (yellow, green, reddish-brown)
	Chrysolite	3·30—3·37	6¾	Double	Feeble (green and yellowish-green)
III.	Diopside	3·2—3·3	6	Double	Feeble
	Dioptase	3·29	5	Double	Feeble
	Apatite	3·2	5	Double	Feeble
	Hiddenite	3·17—3·20	6½	Double	Distinct (pale green and dark green)
	Andalusite	3·17—3·19	7½	Double	Stron (yellow, green, red)
	Tourmaline	3·1	7¼	Double	Strong (yellow and bluish-green)
	Fluor-spar	3·1	4	Single	Absent
IV.	**Emerald**	2·67	7¾	Double	Distinct (green and bluish-green)
V.	**Moldavite**	2·36	5½	Single	Absent
	Glass	Variable	5	Single	Absent

In the first division the green variety of corundum, known as "oriental emerald," is very rare. Zircon and demantoid are uncommon, and dark green chrysoberyl (alexandrite) more frequent. The latter is characterised by its strong dichroism and the possession of red as a second colour. Zircon, although doubly refracting, is practically not dichroic at all, while demantoid differs from all three in being singly refracting.

The only singly refracting stone in the second division is diamond. For the distinguishing features of epidote, idocrase, sphene, and chrysolite the reader is referred to the remarks appended to previous tables. Epidote, always of a rather dark green colour, differs from the other stones in that one of the images it gives in the dichroscope is of a dark brown colour. Under certain circumstances, however, it may be difficult to decide whether a stone is idocrase or epidote.

Diopside and chrysolite are sometimes almost precisely the same, both in colour and specific gravity, and in such cases one has to rely on the difference in hardness. Chrysolite is capable of scratching a crystal of diopside, but a cut diopside of course is not; a crystal of diopside may conveniently be kept at hand for this purpose. Dioptase is always very deeply coloured, and never perfectly clear. Fluor-spar is singly refracting. Apatite is usually of a dark green colour tinged with blue. Andalusite and tourmaline are the most strongly dichroic stones of this division, the former shows a characteristic red colour in the dichroscope, and the latter a bluish-green. Both scratch quartz, while the distinctly but less strongly dichroic hiddenite does not.

The true emerald falls into Division IV.; stones of similar colour, such as " oriental emerald," hiddenite, and alexandrite, cannot therefore be mistaken for it. The specific gravity of much fissured emeralds is lower than that of quartz, and such stones would therefore fall naturally into division V.; but this is never the case with faultless stones. The true emerald, however, is sufficiently characterised by its wonderful green colour; and small variations in the specific gravity are of no consequence for purposes of determination.

Moldavite, like artificial glass, is singly refracting, and is sometimes difficult to distinguish from glass, although it is, as a rule, harder and less heavy.

Alexandrite and green andalusite are very similar both in the colours of cut stones and in those of the dichroscope images; but besides the difference in the specific gravity, which is considerable, there is a difference in hardness, alexandrite being capable of scratching topaz while andalusite is not. Zircon is always recognisable by its strong adamantine lustre and high specific gravity, which latter character distinguishes the stone from diamond. Alexandrite, tourmaline, emerald, and moldavite, the green stones most commonly met with, are sufficiently distinguished by their specific gravity alone, each falling into a different division. The means whereby they may be distinguished from artificial glass have been given already in the remarks appended to previous tables.

B. TRANSLUCENT AND OPAQUE STONES.

In the distinguishing of translucent and opaque stones, we are obliged to dispense with the aid afforded in the case of transparent stones by the character of the refraction, and to rely in a large measure upon the specific gravity. In dealing with opaque stones, however, more use can be made of the character of hardness, since there is less fear of damaging such stones by scratches. The translucent and opaque stones here considered are classified, according to their colour and lustre, into eight main groups, each of which embraces five divisions, into which fall stones of different specific gravities. The main groups are :

1. White, faintly coloured, and grey stones.
2. Blue stones.
3. Green stones.
4. Black stones.
5. Yellow and brown stones.
6. Rose-red, red, and lilac stones.
7. Stones exhibiting more than one colour.
8. Stones with metallic lustre.

1. WHITE, FAINTLY COLOURED, AND GREY STONES.

Division.	Name.	Specific gravity.	Hardness.
III.	Jadeite	3·33	$6\frac{1}{2}$—7
IV.	Nephrite	3·0	$5\frac{1}{2}$—6
V.	Chalcedony	2·6	$6\frac{1}{2}$
	Opal	1·9—2·2	6
	Glass	Variable	5

The stones of this group are distinguished by their specific gravity.

Jadeite has almost exactly the specific gravity of liquid No. 2, and nephrite that of liquid No. 3, so that they remain suspended in these respective liquids, or in some cases slowly sink. Cut jadeite and nephrite can usually be distinguished by the difference in specific gravity, and sometimes also by a difference in hardness. Rough specimens may be distinguished by the difference in fusibility, for fine splinters of jadeite fuse even in an ordinary candle-flame without the application of the blowpipe.

Chalcedony is both harder and heavier than opal, and glass is invariably softer than chalcedony and heavier than opal.

2. BLUE STONES.

Division.	Name.	Specific gravity.	Hardness.
I.	Chessylite	3·8	$3\frac{3}{4}$
III.	Lazulite	3·1	$5\frac{1}{2}$
	Bone-turquoise	3·0—3·5	5
IV.	Turquoise	2·6—2·8	6
V.	Agate (artificially coloured)	2·6	$6\frac{1}{2}$
	Lapis-lazuli	2·4	$5\frac{1}{2}$
	Glass	Variable	5

Chessylite is distinguished from all other blue stones by its very dark colour, high specific gravity, low hardness, and by the fact that it effervesces when brought into contact with a drop of hydrochloric acid.

Lazulite and turquoise, and specially turquoise, are always lighter in colour than chessylite, and turquoise is never very brilliant. The difference in specific gravity is sufficient to distinguish these two stones one from another, and the characters which distinguish them from bone-turquoise have been detailed under the special description of that substance.

Lapis-lazuli is always of a dark blue colour, which has sometimes a more or less pronounced tinge of green. It frequently exhibits yellow, metallic specks of iron-pyrites and encloses patches and veins of calcite. Its hardness and specific gravity readily distinguish it both from the artificially coloured blue agate ("false lapis-lazuli") and from all the other stones of this group.

Turquoise and lapis-lazuli are sometimes imitated in glass; the means whereby such imitations may be recognised will be found under the respective descriptions of these stones in Part II. of this work.

3. GREEN STONES.

Division.	Name.	Specific gravity.	Hardness.
I.	Ceylonite	3·8	$7\frac{1}{2}$
	Malachite	3·7—3·8	$3\frac{1}{2}$
II.	Chloromelanite	3·4	$6\frac{1}{2}$—7
III.	**Jadeite**	3·33	$6\frac{1}{2}$—7
IV.	**Nephrite**	3·0	$5\frac{3}{4}$
	Prehnite	3·28—3·0	$6\frac{1}{2}$
	Turquoise	2·6—2·8	6
V.	**Prase**	2·65	7
	Chrysoprase	2·65	7
	Plasma (and heliotrope)	2·6	$6\frac{1}{2}$
	Jasper	2·6	$6\frac{1}{2}$
	Amazon-stone	2·55	6
	Opal	1·9—2·2	6
	Glass	Variable	5

In Division I. malachite is recognisable by the fact that it effervesces when brought into contact with hydrochloric acid; it is also characterised by a peculiarity of structure, being built up of curved concentric layers which are alternately lighter and darker. Ceylonite is of a dark blackish-green colour, almost black in fact; it is harder and heavier than any other stone in this group.

Nephrite and jadeite have figured already in Table 1. Chloromelanite is nothing more than a ferruginous, and therefore rather darkly coloured and heavy variety of jadeite, possessing otherwise all the features characteristic of that stone.

Prehnite is intermediate in density between nephrite and turquoise, and floats in liquid No. 3. It is capable of scratching felspar, but nephrite and turquoise are not. Nephrite and prehnite are both characterised by a fibrous structure; the green of prehnite has usually a pronounced tinge of yellow, while that of nephrite inclines more to grey. Turquoise, on the other hand, is never fibrous in structure.

The first four of the stones which constitute Division V. of this group are all varieties of quartz. Prase is of a dark leek-green colour, and chrysoprase of a pale apple-green; plasma and jasper are of a pure green colour, which is always dark in shade. The colour of true chrysoprase is so characteristic that it is difficult to mistake any other stone for it, except artificially coloured apple-green chalcedony, which, to all intents and purposes, is chrysoprase. Prase, plasma, and green jasper, though scarcely distinguishable when cut and polished, are easily recognised in the rough, or when thin sections are examined under the microscope. All three have about the same value as ornamental stones, and their distinguishing features are not therefore of very great practical importance. Prase is slightly harder and denser than is plasma or jasper. It is usual to apply the term jasper to stones which are perfectly opaque, and plasma to those which are slightly translucent. Plasma with red spots is known as heliotrope.

Amazon-stone is of a bluish-green colour, which is never very dark in shade. In hardness it is a whole degree lower than the varieties of quartz and is easily scratched by any of these. It possesses a distinct cleavage, the existence of which is very evident in rough stones, and is indicated in cut specimens by the presence of numbers of straight cracks.

Green opal (prase-opal) of the colour of prase is not very common, and is characterised by its very low specific gravity.

Glass is distinguishable from all the members of this group by its low degree of hardness.

4. BLACK STONES.

Division.	Name.	Specific gravity.	Hardness.
I.	**Hæmatite** Ceylonite	4·7 3·8	$5\frac{1}{2}$ $7\frac{1}{2}$
II.	Diamond	3·50—3·52	10
V.	**Obsidian** **Jet**	2·5—2·6 1·35	$5\frac{1}{2}$ 3—4
	Glass	Variable	5

In Division I. hæmatite is possessed of a metallic lustre and a red streak, while ceylonite is sufficiently distinguished by its great hardness and high specific gravity.

Black diamond is characterised by still greater hardness and by the brilliant lustre possessed both by natural crystals and by cut stones.

Obsidian and black glass are of very minor importance; they cannot be distinguished from each other by mere inspection, but require a microscopical examination of thin sections.

Jet feels warm to the touch and can be cut with a knife; the characters in which it differs from vulcanite have been given already under the description of jet.

5. YELLOW AND BROWN STONES.

Division.	Name.	Specific gravity.	Hardness.
I.	Iron-pyrites	5·0	$6\frac{1}{2}$
V.	**Carnelian** (and sard) Natrolite Fire-opal **Amber**	2·6 2·2—2·3 1·9—2·2 1·08	$6\frac{1}{2}$ $5\frac{1}{4}$ 6 2—3
	Glass	Variable	5

Iron-pyrites differs from all the other minerals of this group in the possession of a high specific gravity and a metallic lustre.

Carnelian varies in colour from yellow to yellowish-brown and reddish-brown; when of a pronounced chestnut-brown colour it is known as sard. It frequently exhibits alternating bands of different colours. Opal, though similarly coloured, is never banded, and is less hard and less dense than is carnelian. Natrolite is of an isabel-yellow colour inclining to brown; it has but little lustre and is always fibrous in structure. Amber feels warm to the touch, acquires a strong charge of electricity when rubbed, and can be cut with a knife; it is thus easily distinguished from glass.

Glass is always heavier than natrolite or fire-opal, and is readily scratched by carnelian.

6. ROSE-RED, RED, AND LILAC STONES.

Division.	Name.	Specific gravity.	Hardness.
II.	Rhodonite	3·55	$5\frac{1}{2}$
IV.	Lepidolite	2·8—2·9	2—3
V.	Rose-quartz	2·65	7
	Jasper	2·65	7
	Carnelian	2·6	$6\frac{1}{2}$
	Fire-opal	1·9—2·2	6
	Glass	Variable	5

Rhodonite is rose-red, but of a darker shade than rose-quartz, which is less dense, harder, and more lustrous than rhodonite.

Lepidolite is of a lilac shade and may be scratched even with the finger-nail, and still more readily with a knife.

Jasper is perfectly opaque and ranges in colour from dark red to brownish-red. Carnelian is translucent and usually of a darker or lighter shade of yellowish-red. Fire-opal is sometimes very similar in colour to carnelian, but is lighter and less hard.

Glass is softer than any member of this group with the exception of lepidolite.

7. STONES EXHIBITING MORE THAN ONE COLOUR.

Division.	Name.	Specific gravity.	Hardness.
I.	Malachite	3·7—3·8	$3\frac{1}{2}$
V.	Riband-jasper	2·6	$6\frac{1}{2}$
	Agate	2·6	$6\frac{1}{2}$
	Heliotrope	2·6	$6\frac{1}{2}$
	Amber	1·08	2—3
	Glass	Variable	5

The curved concentric layers of which malachite is built up appear, in section, as bands coloured alternately light and dark green, the latter, indeed, so dark as to be sometimes almost black. It is distinguished from the other minerals of this group by its high specific gravity and small degree of hardness ; and can be identified unmistakably by the fact that it effervesces when touched with hydrochloric acid. The green solution of the mineral thus obtained imparts a blue colour to the flame of a spirit lamp.

Riband-jasper is opaque, and is characterised by a banded structure, the bands being straight, and coloured alternately green and brownish-red. Agate is always more or less translucent, the bands of which it is built up show great variety of arrangement and marked contrast in colour.

Heliotrope is the name given to dark green chalcedony (plasma) spotted with red. Amber sometimes exhibits spots and clouds of a brown or yellow colour ; it is distinguished from the other stones by the characters enumerated in preceding tables.

Glass of variegated colours is sometimes met with, but is not likely to be mistaken for any of the stones included in this group.

8. STONES WITH METALLIC LUSTRE.

This group comprises iron-pyrites and hæmatite (including iserine): these minerals are respectively yellow and black in colour, and have been dealt with in Tables 5 and 4.

C. STONES WITH SPECIAL OPTICAL EFFECTS.

These optical effects are so characteristic of the stones which exhibit them that the consideration of other distinguishing features is almost superfluous.

1. **Stones exhibiting a chatoyant star.**—Star-sapphire, star-ruby and "star-topaz." These all belong to the species corundum and are generally referred to as star-stones or asterias. Having a hardness of 9 they are capable of scratching topaz. The specific gravity of each is about 4. They are respectively blue, red, and yellow in colour, while in other features they are identical.

2. **Stones exhibiting a chatoyant band.**—Girasol-sapphire, girasol-ruby, "girasol-topaz," adamantine-spar ; cymophane, cat's-eye, tiger-eye, and hawk's-eye ; moon-stone and chatoyant obsidian.

The four first mentioned stones, like those under the preceding division, belong to the mineral species corundum, and possess all the features characteristic of that mineral, including great hardness. Adamantine-spar is characterised by its small degree of trans-lucency and its hair-brown colour, features which distinguish it from the other three stones, which are only slightly clouded. The remaining stones are all softer and specifically lighter than corundum.

Cymophane or oriental cat's-eye is very similar in appearance to ordinary quartz-cat's-eye, but differs from it both in hardness and specific gravity, the former being $8\frac{1}{2}$ and 7, and the latter 3·7 and 2·65 in the two minerals respectively. The greater lustre and transparency of cymophane are usually sufficient to distinguish it from quartz.

Moon-stone resembles cymophane in the possession of a band of chatoyant light, but differs from it in being colourless and almost transparent, much lighter (sp. gr. = 2·6) and softer (H = 6).

Tiger-eye and hawk's-eye, like quartz-cat's-eye, have the characters of quartz, namely, a specific gravity of 2·65 and a hardness of 7. Both possess a markedly fibrous structure, but tiger-eye is of a bright golden yellow colour and hawk's-eye dark blue. Cat's-eye never exhibits the magnificent golden lustre characteristic of tiger-eye, the light reflected from it being more milky and opalescent in character.

The sheen of chatoyant obsidian is always less brilliant than that of the other stones of this group, from which it is also distinguished by a lower density (sp. gr. = $2 \cdot 5 - 2 \cdot 6$), and a lower degree of hardness (H = $5\frac{1}{2}$).

3. **Stones with a metallic sheen.**—Under this head come hypersthene, bronzite, bastite, and diallage, all belonging to the pyroxene group of minerals. Their hardness is rather less than 6, and their specific gravity varies between $3 \cdot 3$ and $3 \cdot 4$. The metallic reflection of hypersthene is copper-red in colour, that of bronzite is bronze-yellow, green, or brown, while that of bastite and diallage ranges from green to brown. Hypersthene is readily identified, but it is less easy and of but little practical importance to distinguish between the remaining stones. Their distinguishing features have been pointed out in the special description of these stones.

4. **Stones flecked with metallic shining points.**—Avanturine-quartz and sun-stone (avanturine-felspar) are flecked with specks exhibiting a red metallic sheen. They are distinguishable by their difference in hardness, the hardness of avanturine-quartz being 7 and that of sun-stone .6. The artificial avanturine-glass is a close imitation of these stones, the metallic reflection being given by the enclosure of small octahedra of metallic copper. These crystals, with their regular triangular faces, are distinctly observable when the glass is examined with a lens, and their presence serves to distinguish the imitation from the genuine stone. Avanturine-quartz possessing all the essential characters of the ordinary red variety, but of a green or blue colour, occurs as a rarity.

5. **Stones exhibiting a play of variegated colours.**—Precious opal, iridescent quartz, labradorite. Opal is usually white, less commonly yellow or red, rarely black; the play of variegated colours extends over areas of varying size. It has a hardness of 6 and a specific gravity which ranges from $1 \cdot 9$ to $2 \cdot 2$, features which serve to distinguish it from water-clear, iridescent quartz, with a hardness of 7 and a specific gravity of $2 \cdot 65$.

Labradorite is dark grey; the play of colour is confined to one surface, and frequently to straight bands running across this surface. It has a hardness of 6 and a specific gravity of $2 \cdot 7$. In rough pieces of labradorite a perfect cleavage in one direction is always noticeable. It would be impossible to mistake labradorite for opal, or *vice versâ*, but it is possible to confuse precious opal and iridescent quartz, although the characters mentioned above are sufficient to distinguish one from another. Labradorescent felspar is very similar to labradorite, but its play of colour is less fine.

APPENDIX

PEARLS AND CORAL

PEARLS.

THE NATURE AND FORMATION OF PEARLS.—We now come to the consideration of pearls, those objects which, on account of their beauty and costliness, may well rank next to the most splendid jewels. They are products of the life and activity of certain molluscs, the insignificant-looking inhabitants of warm seas and of the rivers and streams of many temperate regions; they thus differ in an important way from precious stones, but like the latter have been used from time immemorial for every kind of decorative purpose. In form they are spherical, ovoid, or pear-shaped, or sometimes quite irregular; they are never transparent, but at most only translucent; they vary considerably in size, and, as a rule, are colourless. Their beauty depends largely upon the peculiar lustre of their surface. Though to appreciate this beauty it is by no means necessary to be familiar with the minute structure and mode of origin of pearls, yet a knowledge of these is an aid to the comprehension of their characteristic features. Before beginning the consideration of these features, therefore, we will describe the mode of origin of the pearl.

A substance which stands in the closest relationship to pearls, and which, moreover, has derived from them its name *mother-of-pearl*, is also much used in decorative work. It has a lustre exactly similar to that of pearls, and frequently exhibits a more or less marked and beautiful play of colours. It forms the inner coating of the shells of many bivalve molluscs, and a mass of similar nature occurs also in the shell of certain univalve molluscs. As the formation of pearls by univalve molluscs is a rare phenomenon, and without significance from the point of view of pearl-fishers, we will confine our attention to the pearl-forming bivalves.

The thin outermost layer, the periostracum or so-called " epidermis," of the shell of any bivalve mollusc, consists of a horny material known as conchiolin. Beneath this comes the shell proper, consisting of two layers which differ in structure. The outer or prismatic layer is formed of minute prisms of calcium carbonate separated by thin layers of conchiolin; the inner forms the internal part of the shell, and is built up of alternate layers of calcium carbonate and conchiolin arranged parallel to the surface. The laminated internal layer is what is known as nacre or mother-of-pearl, and varies in thickness in different molluscs. The laminæ of which it is built up consist of that variety of calcium carbonate which is known to mineralogists as aragonite. The calcareous prisms, which form the middle layer of the shell, consist, on the other hand, of calcite, another modification of calcium carbonate which is softer and lighter than aragonite.

The laminæ, of which the pearly or nacreous layer of the shell is built up, are small compared with the size of the shell, and overlap one another something like the tiles on the roof of a house. This finely laminated structure is the cause of the peculiar lustre which characterises mother-of-pearl, a lustre which is exhibited by all substances having the same structure, that is to say, all substances which are built up of transparent, overlapping laminæ.

The laminæ which form the nacre or mother-of-pearl layer of the shell do not lie in planes parallel to the surface of the shell, but are always more or less bent and curved. Their edges intersect the inner surface of the shell, and produce a very fine striation, which can sometimes be seen with a simple lens, but which usually requires the help of the compound microscope. These striæ or furrows take zig-zag or quite irregular courses, sometimes indeed forming small closed rings; the distance between them averages $\frac{1}{3000}$ inch, but varies within small limits. It is to these striæ that the play of colours so characteristic of mother-of-pearl is due, while the peculiar lustre of the substance is due to its laminated structure, as has been already explained. This play of colours, then, is quite independent of the presence of pigment of any kind. It is due to purely physical causes, the fine striæ so acting upon the rays of ordinary daylight or candle-light as to split them up into their coloured constituents; these reach the eye singly, and so produce the sensation of colour. That this is the true explanation is proved by the fact that the same play of colours is to be seen upon sealing-wax after it has been pressed upon the natural surface of the mother-of-pearl layer, or, better still, upon a section of this layer cut obliquely to the surface, and has thus received an impression of the striæ.

The body of a bivalve mollusc is produced into two lateral flaps, the so-called mantle, which lie in immediate contact with the inner surface of the shell. The different parts of the shell of the mollusc are secreted by the mantle, the cells of which have the power of separating out the calcium carbonate dissolved in the water in which the animal lives. Different areas of the mantle have somewhat different functions in this respect: thus the edge of the mantle secretes the periostracum, the so-called "epidermis"; the outer surface lays down the calcareous laminæ, of which the nacre is composed; while the prismatic layer, between the periostracum and the mother-of-pearl or nacre, is secreted by a narrow zone round the margin of the mantle.

This, then, is the process of shell-formation which goes on under ordinary conditions, and so long as these obtain no pearls are produced. The formation of a pearl is the response of the mollusc to the stimulus afforded by a local irritation of the mantle. Being unable to eject the cause of the irritation, the mollusc obtains relief by enveloping it with a deposit of mother-of-pearl substance. The rounded aggregation of mother-of-pearl substance so produced is then known as a pearl.

That the formation of pearls is an abnormal occurrence in the life of a mollusc is shown by the fact that among the pearl-forming molluscs, only about one in thirty or forty is found to contain pearls. Moreover, the observations of pearl-fishers all point in the same direction; for they state that there is little prospect of finding pearls in a well-formed, normal shell, and that the shells most likely to contain pearls are those which are irregular and distorted in shape, and which bear evidence of having been attacked by some boring parasite. That the formation of pearls is caused by some disturbance of the normal conditions of life may, therefore, be regarded as a well-established fact; but the exact causes which bring about this secretion are not in all cases satisfactorily explained.

The nucleus of many pearls is a tiny grain of sand, and in such cases it is obvious that this foreign body set up an irritation of the mantle and caused an abnormal secretion of calcium carbonate, in the same way as a particle of dust in the eye causes a copious flow of water in that organ, or as the presence of a trichina (flesh-worm) in a muscle-fibre causes the latter to secrete a calcareous cyst around the intruder. Many observers, following

Möbius, the author of a valuable work entitled " The True Pearls," consider the formation of pearls to be due most frequently to the irritation caused by the presence of a grain of sand. Of fifty-nine pearls examined by Möbius himself, and obtained both from sea and from fresh-water molluscs, a certain number were found to possess a nucleus consisting of a crystalline, granular, calcareous substance, but that of the majority was brown in colour and of organic origin, being possibly the remains of small intestinal worms, while in no single case was the nucleus found to consist of a grain of sand. Not only is the formation of pearls actually caused by the presence of parasites in the mollusc, but also by the attacks of water-mites, small fishes, boring sponges, and worms, which penetrate the shell from without, by the growth of algæ, and even by the eggs of the mollusc itself.

Pearls formed by different parts of the mantle often differ in shape and appearance. For example, a pearl formed in the inside of the soft part of the mantle, perhaps in response to the irritation caused by a parasite of some kind, will be more or less perfectly spherical, and will lie free in the mantle. If, however, the pearly matter is laid down around the orifice made by some boring external parasite, the result will be a wart-like protuberance. In the former case is produced a pearl proper, which can be used as an ornament without preliminary treatment ; in the latter, the so-called *button* or *wart-pearls*, which are very irregular in shape, but, notwithstanding this, are detached from the shell and utilised in various ways as *fantasy-pearls*. In exceptional cases these button-pearls are hollow and contain a beautiful spherical pearl, lying freely in the cavity.

The number of pearls found in a single mollusc varies according to circumstances. If the mantle is irritated at one spot only, then only one pearl is formed ; if at several spots, then several pearls will be formed ; and in exceptional cases a single shell may contain a large number. Among remarkable cases of this kind is that of a pearl-oyster from the Indian Ocean, which contained eighty-seven pearls of good quality ; while in another from Ceylon sixty-seven of various sizes were found. As a general rule, the greater the number of pearls found in a single shell the smaller they are.

The first person to point out that the structure of pearls is identical with that of the molluscan shell was the French naturalist Réaumur (1683–1757). This structure can be best made out by examining under the microscope a thin section of a pearl taken right through its centre. It will be seen to be built up of concentric coats like an onion. Each of these concentric layers consists of overlapping laminæ, exactly like those which build up the mother-of-pearl layer in the shell of the mollusc. This concentric structure points to the fact that the secretion of calcium carbonate was not continuous, but that there were longer or shorter intervals of rest, coinciding, perhaps, with certain seasons of the year, when growth also was arrested. Thus, each concentric layer corresponds to a period of growth, and each interruption between neighbouring layers to an interval of rest. These concentric coats are sometimes visible to the naked eye, but, as a rule, they are of microscopic thickness. When a pearl is raised to a red-heat, the concentric coats peel off and the laminæ separate from each other. Much the same thing happens in the case of pearls which have been worn for a long time strung together to form a necklace. At the spot where each pearl is perforated, the concentric layers begin to fall off as scales, so that the orifice through which the string passes becomes gradually wider and wider. The substance of pearls has a hardness of between 3 and 4 on Mohs' scale, so that being comparatively soft they cannot be expected to resist a large amount of hard wear.

The majority of pearls, and certainly all the most beautiful, are formed in this way, and with the exception of the nucleus consist wholly of layers of nacre. Not infrequently, however, pearls are met with in which the nucleus is surrounded by a dark layer corresponding with the periostracum or "epidermis" of the shell; enclosing this is a layer showing a columnar or fibrous structure, which agrees in every respect with the prismatic layer of the shell, while the external layer only consists of finely laminated mother-of-pearl or nacre. Such a pearl, therefore, has the structure of a molluscan shell, but the layers are arranged in the reverse order, periostracum inside and the nacreous layer outside. In some cases the nacreous layer is entirely absent, and the outermost layer is constituted by the prismatic layer or by the periostracum, the pearl then being of a dark brown or black colour, without lustre and, therefore, without value. Not infrequently also there are several nacreous layers, separated from each other by prismatic or conchiolin layers.

One can easily see the connection between these differences in structure and the processes by which the pearls were formed. If a pearl arises wholly in that region of the mantle which secretes mother-of-pearl, as is generally the case, it will consist wholly of mother-of-pearl substance, the nature of which has been already described. A pearl formed in this way does not, however, remain indefinitely in the same position. From one cause or another it may be brought into contact with that part of the mantle which secretes the prismatic layer, when it will become invested with a layer of this description, or with the extreme edge of the mantle, when a layer corresponding to the periostracum of the shell will be deposited upon it: If the object, which eventually becomes the nucleus of the pearl, lie first in contact with the edge of the mantle, a layer of material corresponding to the periostracum will first envelop it. If the pearl during its growth moves slowly inwards it becomes coated successively with a prismatic and a nacreous layer, while if it move back again these same layers will be again laid down, but in the reverse order. In this way is attained great variety in the arrangement of the concentric coats of pearls, this variety depending solely upon the way in which the pearl moved about within the shell of the mollusc.

The pearl is not only identical with mother-of-pearl in structure, but also in **chemical composition, hardness, and specific gravity.** Like that substance it consists of that modification of calcium carbonate which is known as aragonite. Besides calcium carbonate, there are always present small amounts of other inorganic substances, and, in addition, up to 12 per cent. of conchiolin, the organic material of which the periostracum of the molluscan shell is formed. Layers of conchiolin alternate with layers of calcium carbonate, binding the whole together. The specific gravity of fresh, white, brilliant sea-pearls varies between 2·650 and 2·686. The hardness is nearly 4; it varies somewhat in different pearls, but is always rather less than that of mother-of-pearl. Owing to the admixture of conchiolin, both the hardness and specific gravity of pearls are rather less than those of aragonite.

As a result of their composition pearls dissolve readily in acid, even in acetic acid, with the evolution of carbon dioxide, which causes a brisk effervescence. Upon this is founded the story that Cleopatra, the Egyptian queen, at a banquet dissolved a priceless pearl in vinegar and drank the solution. In ordinary table-vinegar, however, the acetic acid is too weak to dissolve completely a pearl even of small size in the time that a banquet might be supposed to last, so that the story is probably apocryphal. Moreover, pearls do not dissolve completely in acid, the calcium carbonate only is extracted and the conchiolin left behind as a scaly, soft, somewhat swollen, but still shining mother-of-pearl-like mass, which has the form, size, and colour of the original pearl, but upon which the acid has no further effect.

Pearls are also affected by perspiration from the skin, and if they are much handled or worn for long in contact with the skin they gradually lose their lustre and much of their beauty. Old, much-worn pearls never possess the freshness and beauty of newly-fished maiden-pearls so-called. Not only do pearls, which are strung together, suffer from the rubbing of one upon another, and from the friction of the string, but the organic constituent, like all other animal substances, in course of time completely decays. An example of the way pearls are affected by the lapse of time is furnished by the state of those found in the grave of a daughter of Stilicho, a Roman statesman and general. The pearls had lain in the grave from the year 400 to the year 1544, a period of eleven centuries, and when brought to the light of day they fell instantly to dust. In this respect, therefore, pearls are in no way comparable with the unchanging precious stone, which preserves its brilliancy and lustre through age after age.

The perishable nature of pearls, as much a result of their softness as of their organic origin, is the more regrettable, seeing that when once the outer surface of a pearl is damaged its beauty is irrevocably lost. A precious stone which has sustained serious injury can be restored to all its original beauty by re-cutting and re-polishing, but not so with a pearl. These beautiful objects, therefore, need to be handled with great care, in order to preserve the surface layer in its natural condition for as long as possible. This outer layer when discoloured or damaged may, indeed, be sometimes peeled off, a perfect but smaller pearl being thus obtained. This operation, however, requires all the care of a skilled artist, and even then is seldom completely successful.

The **surface** of a pearl, like that of mother-of-pearl, is not perfectly smooth, but shows many irregularities, elevations, and depressions, delicate ridges and grooves, and so forth ; these are all of microscopic dimensions, and, as we shall see further on, have an important bearing on the appearance of the pearl.

The surface especially exhibits a peculiar **lustre**, which is not very brilliant, but beautiful and delicate, and which defies verbal description ; it is known to jewellers as the " orient " of a pearl, corresponding to the " fire " of a diamond. This pearly lustre is due, as in mother-of-pearl itself, to the laminated structure already described. The not wholly transparent, but very translucent layers lying near the surface allow some light to pass through, which is reflected outwards again from the deeper layers. This light reaches the eye in company with that reflected directly from the surface, and the two together produce the impression which we have learnt to call a pearly lustre. The thinner the calcareous laminæ are the more beautiful is the lustre, and the more valuable the pearl.

Individual pearls differ considerably in lustre ; those formed by marine molluscs are far superior to the pearls formed by the fresh-water pearl-mussel, which, compared with the former, appear dull and lifeless. Pearls which are unusually brilliant are also somewhat harder than more ordinary specimens, this character depending upon the more or less intimate association of the single layers.

As we have already seen, the lustre and brilliancy of pearls disappear with the lapse of time, and these objects, therefore, undergo a constant depreciation in value. Many efforts have been made to discover a means whereby the freshness and beauty of maiden-pearls may be restored, but in vain. Any attempt to remove the outer coat of a pearl, whose lustre has been dimmed by time, is doomed to disappointment, for the underlying coat is usually as dull and lustreless as the eye of a dead fish. It is, therefore, very rarely that a dull pearl can be improved by peeling off its outer coat. Attempts to restore their pristine beauty to old and faded pearls have been made by immersing them in the sea for long periods, by allowing them to be picked up and eaten by hens and doves, and in other foolish and irrational ways, but unsuccessfully. The inimitable freshness and delicacy of maiden-pearls once lost is lost for ever.

No pearl is completely transparent, but among different specimens there are many degrees of **translucency**. Different qualities of pearls are described, as in the case also of diamonds, as being of different " waters," and the difference between them depends upon the amount of light transmitted in each particular case.

The **colour** of a pearl has an important bearing on its value. Those used for ornaments are mostly white, yellowish-white, or bluish-white, more rarely reddish- or blackish-grey. A pearl with a perfect pearly lustre, or, as the jewellers say, a " ripe " pearl, has the colour of the mother-of-pearl layer in the shell in which it was formed, but each pearl has sometimes a certain individuality as regards colour. The pearls formed by the true pearl-oyster (*Meleagrina margaritifera*) are white, and it is these and the silvery, milk-white pearls which are most valuable. The smaller the dimensions of the microscopic irregularities in the surface of a pearl the finer will be its appearance, for on these rugosities of the surface depends the scattering of the incident light and the gleaming white colour of the pearl. The fine colour of " ripe " pearls is due partly also to the fact that they consist wholly of colourless nacre. Should there be present a nucleus consisting of the substance of the prismatic layer, it shines through the strongly translucent nacreous layer, making the pearl appear dull and dark, and this is specially the case when the outer pearly layer is thin. Such grey or brown translucent pearls are described as being " unripe." Of a large and beautiful Indian pearl it was said that it rolled about on a sheet of white paper " like a globule of quicksilver," surpassing even the metal itself in lustre and whiteness. Silvery, white, transparent pearls of this description are classed as pearls of the finest water: they always possess a thick outer nacreous layer. Many true pearls, however, are slightly tinged with yellow, or are even of a pronounced yellow colour, this being more frequently the case with those from the Persian Gulf than with the pearls from Ceylon. These yellowish pearls are much esteemed in Asia, India, China, &c., being considered to be less perishable than the white. It has been said that white pearls, if enclosed in the shells of decaying molluscs, acquire a yellow tinge, but according to special research in this direction this is not, or at any rate not always, the case. Pearls with a faint bluish tinge are also frequently met with, this colour being the same, as is also the case with yellowish pearls, as that of the mother-of-pearl layer of the shell in which such pearls were formed.

Beautiful black pearls are sometimes found in molluscs from the South Seas and the Gulf of Mexico, having been formed probably near the border of the mantle. They are the hardest of all pearls, and when of a beautiful and uniform colour and perfect form are worth almost as much as pearls of the purest white. Such black pearls are used in Europe in mourning jewellery. Intermediate between white and black are lead-coloured pearls, which are not uncommon. Reddish-brown pearls containing some iron come from Mexico. The hammer-oyster (*Malleus*) from the Gambia Islands yields pearls with a bronze-like sheen. Not infrequently greyish-brown pearls, in which the nacreous layer is absent, are found in the fresh-water pearl-mussel, *Unio margaritifer*. In the fan-mussel, *Pinna nobilis*, are found light and dark brown pearls, in some of which also the nacreous layer is absent, the outer coat consisting of a substance corresponding with the prismatic layer of the shell. The same shell, however, may contain garnet-red pearls, in which the pearly nacreous layer is present, and which are highly prized both by the Hindoos and by the Jews. Pale, rose-red pearls with delicate white wavy lines, like the most beautiful pink velvet, come from the Bahamas. Pale blue pearls are often met with in the edible mussel (*Mytilus edulis*); greenish-white and pale rose-red pearls in *Spondylus gædaropus*; violet in the ark-shell (*Arca noæ*); purple in *Anomia cepa*; and lead-coloured in *Placuna placenta*.

Dull white pearls, in which the beautiful lustre of typical pearls is absent, are probably produced by all molluscs, the shells of which have a white inner surface. Such pearls are found in the pilgrim-shell (*Pecten jacobæus*), the giant-clam (*Tridacna gigas*), in many varieties of the common fresh-water mussels (*Unio* and *Anodonta*), in the razor-shell (*Solen*), and many others. Dull white pearls have indeed been found in the edible oyster (*Ostrea edulis*) in spite of the absence of mother-of-pearl in its shell; and it has been related by a dredger how he found a pearl in an oyster he was eating, and obtained for it 22 thaler (66s.). The occurrence of pearls in certain univalves has been mentioned already. The large West Indian *Strombus gigas*, and the East Indian *Turbinella scolymus* yield very beautiful rose-red pearls, in which, it is true, there is no mother-of-pearl layer, and which, therefore, are not true pearls. They are distinguished from the latter by the fact that their colour, like that of the univalve shells in which they originate, gradually fades away with the lapse of time.

Some pearls exhibit the colour-effects characteristic of mother-of-pearl, but only to a slight degree and of very pale bluish, greyish, and reddish shades. In such pearls the outer layer of mother-of-pearl substance is not continuous over the whole surface, but is confined to small, irregularly bounded areas separated by areas from which it is absent. In addition to the elevations and depressions usually present on the surface of a pearl, there are also delicate and irregularly curved grooves, which pursue either approximately parallel courses or form closed curves of irregular form. The colours exhibited by such pearls are due, as in mother-of-pearl, to physical causes connected with the structural peculiarities of the surface.

The value of a pearl, and the uses to which it is applied, are considerably influenced by its **form**, and in this respect there is a certain amount of variety among pearls. They may be perfectly spherical, more or less ovoid, or pear-shaped. Pear-shaped and elongated ovoidal pearls are referred to as *pear-pearls*, and the former more especially as *bell-pearls*, while spherical pearls are known as *pearl-drops* or *pearl-eyes*. Ovoidal pearls sometimes contain two nuclei, each of which is invested by its own series of concentric coats, only the outermost coats of the pearl enclosing both nuclei. We have evidently, in such cases, two originally separate pearls which have become enclosed in a common coat, and thus formed a single ovoidal pearl.

Pearls of very irregular form are known as *baroque pearls* ("barrok pearls"), and are specially abundant in the fresh-water pearl-mussel. These also are used as ornaments and for other purposes, but are less valuable than those of a more regular form. As extreme examples of irregularity in form may be mentioned two pearls described by the Parisian jeweller Caire, one of which resembles in form the head of a dog, and the other the Order of the Holy Ghost.

The **size** of pearls is very variable. One of the largest known is the property of the Shah of Persia; it is pear-shaped in form, and is 35 millimetres long and 25 thick. A still larger one formed part of the famous collection of pearls and precious stones of Henry Philip Hope, and is figured and described by B. Hertz in his catalogue (London, 1839) of this collection. This pearl weighs 3 ounces (troy), or about 454 carats; it is irregularly pear-shaped in form, measuring 2 inches in length, $4\frac{1}{2}$ inches in circumference at its thicker end, and $3\frac{1}{4}$ inches at its narrower end, and is thus almost as large as a hen's egg. For a length of about $1\frac{1}{2}$ inches this gigantic pearl is of a fine bright "orient," the remainder being of a fine bronze tint or dark green shaded with copper colour. A portion of the shell on which it grew is left adhering to it, but this of so fine an "orient" and so well polished that it is scarcely recognisable as such. In the Austrian Emperor's crown there is a large pearl weighing 300 carats, but it is of medium quality only. A pearl brought to the Spanish Court from Panama in the sixteenth century is said to have been as large as a pigeon's egg.

Admittedly the most beautiful of large pearls is one in the museum of Zosima in Moscow, which has received the name " La Pellegrina." It was found in India, is perfectly spherical, of a pure white colour, and almost transparent, and weighs 28 carats. More remarkable than any hitherto mentioned is the " Great Southern Cross," which consists of nine large pearls of a pure white colour and beautiful lustre, naturally joined together to form a cross over an inch in length. This beautiful natural object was found in 1886 in a pearl-oyster off the north-west coast of Western Australia. It was shown at the Colonial Exhibition in London in 1902, and is valued at £10,000.

The pearls of ordinary, every-day occurrence are very much smaller than the exceptionally large specimens described above. Special terms are used for pearls of particular sizes : thus those with the dimensions of a walnut or thereabouts are termed *paragon-pearls*, and those of the size of a cherry as *cherry-pearls*. *Piece-pearls* are smaller, but not too small to be handled and dealt with separately, each exceeding a carat in weight. *Seed-*, *shot-* or *ounce-pearls* are dealt with in the trade only in parcels ; and the same is the case with *sand-* or *dust-pearls*, the largest of which are no bigger and sometimes even less than a grain of millet. Fine Indian pearls are usually from one and a half to three times the size of a pea.

THE APPLICATION OF PEARLS.—This differs in nowise from that of precious stones, which is mainly for purposes of ornament. Pearls have been valued as ornaments from the earliest ages, and the favour in which they were held, especially by the Romans, is evidenced by the writings of ancient authors.

Although pearls and diamonds are alike in the purpose to which they are devoted, they differ very widely in that while the latter need to be cut and polished to fit them for use as ornaments the former need no preliminary treatment, for they leave the hand of nature with a beauty which cannot be enhanced by artificial means. Polishing adds no lustre to the surface of a dull pearl, nor can the form of an irregular pearl be made more regular by grinding without destroying its lustre.

Pearls are set in various ways, but never *à jour*, because of their imperfect transparency. Fine pearls of large size are often mounted with a border of small diamonds or coloured stones, and, on the other hand, a border of small pearls makes an effective setting for a fine diamond or other precious stone. More frequently, however, pearls are bored and worn in strings and ropes. The perforation is easily performed, the substance of pearls being comparatively so soft, but as we have seen already the pearly laminæ are very apt to scale off around the perforation. To attain the most beautiful effect possible in a string of pearls, only such as associate well in form, size, and colour should be strung together. It is by no means necessary that each pearl should be the exact counterpart of all the others, for small differences between individual pearls do not affect the beauty of the *tout ensemble* of a pearl necklace. For this reason, it is usual when choosing one pearl from a string to cover over the adjacent pearls in order that their proximity may not prejudice or enhance the effect of the pearl to be chosen.

The fantastic forms often taken by baroque pearls make it possible to convert them with slight additions and alterations into caricatures of men and things. A large collection of objects of this kind, among which are some pearls of unusual size, is preserved in the " Green Vaults " in Dresden. One represents the figure of a Court dwarf, whose body is formed of a suitably-shaped baroque pearl, the size of a hen's egg. A proof that popular taste for articles in the rococo style has not yet died out is furnished by the fact that baroque pearls are sometimes even now treated in the same way.

Not only button-pearls, which are found attached to the shell, but also the equally irregular fantasy-pearls are sometimes of sufficient beauty to admit of their employment in jewellery. They usually have a hemispherical form when detached from the shell, and are frequently cemented together by their flat surfaces in pairs and worn in ear-rings, or strung together for necklaces. The absence of lustre on the flat surface of such pearls serves to distinguish them from pearls which, though formed free from the shell, are yet hemispherical in form.

The **value** of fine pearls is quite comparable with that of the costliest gems, and enormous sums have been paid for large pearls of singular beauty. As in the case of precious stones the value of pearls varies with their size, form, and the general beauty of their appearance. The more perfect the form of a pearl the more valuable does it become, and other things being equal a pearl of irregular form is considerably less valuable than one which is perfectly regular. Arranged in order of the degree of esteem in which they are held, we have: first, perfectly spherical pearls; secondly, those of an equally symmetrical pear-shaped form; and, finally, ovoidal or egg-shaped pearls. A pearl of the " first water " must possess, beside a symmetrical form, a smooth surface and a perfect " orient," the latter, a feature which depends upon the existence of a finely laminated structure; it must be free from blemishes and fractures, very translucent, and possessed of a fine white colour and a perfect pearly lustre. Provided the lustre is good, fine black pearls, as also those showing deep shades of red, yellow, and other colours, are as costly as those of the purest white. Pearls of even the most beautiful colour and perfect form if they are lacking in " orient " are comparatively valueless.

The prices of exceptionally large or beautiful pearls are subject to no fixed rules, and depend rather upon the eagerness of the purchaser and the length of his purse. The prices of pearls of ordinary size, such as are bought and sold every day, are governed by the laws of supply and demand, and the same general principles apply as in the case of precious stones. The relation between the size and the price of a pearl is in moderately close agreement with Tavernier's rule; that is to say, the price of a pearl varies with the square of the weight, the usual unit of weight being the " pearl-grain " ($= \frac{1}{4}$ carat). A pearl of unit weight will be worth from 2s. to 10s., according to the quality; the appended table of prices applies to pearls of a quality such that a pearl of unit weight is worth 6s.

Weight in "pearl-grains."		Value in shillings.
$\frac{1}{3}$	. . . . .	$\frac{1}{3} \times \frac{1}{3} \times 6 = \frac{2}{3}$
$\frac{1}{2}$	. . . .	$\frac{1}{2} \times \frac{1}{2} \times 6 = 1\frac{1}{2}$
$\frac{2}{3}$	. . . .	$\frac{2}{3} \times \frac{2}{3} \times 6 = 2\frac{2}{3}$
1	. . . .	$1 \times 1 \times 6 = 6$
2	. . . .	$2 \times 2 \times 6 = 24$
3	. . . .	$3 \times 3 \times 6 = 54$
4 (= 1 carat)	. . .	$4 \times 4 \times 6 = 96$

To convey an idea of the relative sizes of pearls of different weights, it may be mentioned that one weighing 3 carats has approximately the size of a pea.

The price of a string of carefully matched pearls is more in proportion than that of a single pearl would be, for the reason that there is often considerable difficulty in finding a sufficient number of pearls of appropriate size, quality, form, and colour. Considerable time is often needed to make up the required number, during which those already procured and paid for lie unused and depreciating in value. Möbius states that in his time (the end of the 'fifties) a string of from seventy to eighty three-carat pearls was worth from 4000 to 6000 thaler, that is to say, about 70 thaler (old German thaler = 3s.) for each pearl. This was approximately twice the price current at that time for a single pearl of the same size and quality.

In conclusion, it will be interesting to note the value of some of the more famous pearls. That in the Hope Collection was valued at £12,500. At the valuation made in 1793 of the French Crown jewels, a round maiden-pearl weighing $27\frac{5}{16}$ carats, and of magnificent lustre, was valued at 200,000 francs (£8000); while 300,000 francs was the value attached to two well-formed, pear-shaped pearls of very beautiful "water" which together weighed $57\frac{11}{16}$ carats; and 60,000 francs to four differently shaped pearls the combined weight of which was $164\frac{6}{16}$ carats. Another pear-shaped pearl weighing $36\frac{10}{16}$ carats, and therefore much larger than the one first mentioned, was valued at 12,000 francs only, on account of its being flat upon one side. At the International Fishery Exhibition held at Berlin in 1880, the Berlin jewellers exhibited a string of yellowish Indian pearls worth £4000, a string of white pearls from Panama which cost £5000, and a string of black pearls from the Pacific Ocean which was valued at £6000. The value attached to the "Great Southern Cross" pearl found off the north-west coast of Western Australia in 1886 is £10,000.

PEARL-FISHING.—Though as we have seen there are many molluscs which occasionally produce pearls, there are only two species which produce these objects in numbers sufficient to make the systematic collection of them a profitable industry. By far the more important of the two is the marine pearl-oyster *Meleagrina* (= *Avicula*) *margaritifera*, which inhabits the warm seas of many tropical regions. The other and less important mollusc is the fresh-water pearl-mussel *Unio* (= *Margaritana* = *Alasmodon*) *margaritifer*, and a few near relations inhabiting the streams of northern regions, or, at any rate, of extra-tropical countries. By far the largest number of pearls, and those also of the finest quality, are, and have always been, obtained from the pearl-oyster, which in addition supplies the bulk of the mother-of-pearl for industrial purposes. Only a small number of pearls, generally of poor quality, are obtained from the pearl-mussel.

The Pearl-Oyster.—According to the opinion of the majority of conchologists the salt-water pearl-forming molluscs from almost all regions of the world belong to one and the same species. Individuals from different regions do, indeed, show differences in the size and thickness of the shell, in the roughness of the exterior, the colouring of the inner surface, &c., but these differences are not of specific importance. A small, thin-shelled form from which no mother-of-pearl is profitably obtained is sometimes distinguished from the large thick-shelled *Meleagrina margaritifera* by the name *Avicula margaritifera*, but there are many transitional forms between the two, so that they cannot be sharply separated.

The pearl-oyster, like the common oyster, lives with large numbers of its fellows, forming the so-called oyster-banks. These lie usually from 3 to 5 fathoms, occasionally from 6 to 10 fathoms below the surface of the water, rarely any deeper. The bank has a foundation of calcareous material; very often, indeed, it is built on a coral-reef. The molluscs are not free but attach themselves firmly to any suitable object by means of the beard, or byssus, a bundle of tough horny threads, which reach the exterior through a hole in the hinge line of the shell. The pearl-oyster banks are inhabited also by corals, univalve molluscs, and many other marine animals; the temperature of the water in which the whole community lives is never much below 25° C. (= 77° F.).

The pearl-oysters are brought up from the sea-bottom by divers, who descend into the depths, in some cases, with no artificial appliances to aid them in their difficult and dangerous calling. The provision of the best and newest divers' apparatus makes their descent into not too great depths comparatively easy and safe, and renders a longer stay under water possible. Pearl-fishing is not a profitable industry in every place where the pearl-oyster is to be found, and, moreover, the individuals from which numbers of pearls are obtained do not always supply in addition mother-of-pearl of good quality. The best mother-of-pearl known, which is worth from £80 to £150 per metric ton (= 1000 kilograms), is obtained from the pearl-oysters found in the sea surrounding the Sulu Islands, between the Philippines and the north point of Borneo; comparatively few pearls are yielded by the pearl-oysters found in this region. On the other hand, the pearl-oysters inhabiting the Gulf of Manar, off the island of Ceylon, which yield a very large number of the finest pearls in the world, have shells so thin that they are useless in the mother-of-pearl industry.

These pearl fisheries in the Gulf of Manar, on the north-west coast of **Ceylon**, also known as the fisheries of Aripo, after an old fort, are more important than any other The fishery is not confined entirely to this gulf, a small number of pearls being obtained also from the Coromandel Coast, lying opposite on the mainland of India. The sea in this district is well sheltered by the islands and by sand-banks lying to the north, so that the pearl-oysters are undisturbed by buffeting waves. The most important banks lie between 8° 30' and 9° north latitude, at a distance of three miles from the coast; the largest are two miles long and two-fifths of a mile wide. The banks extend for a length of ninety miles along the coast, and the furthest out are about twelve miles from the shore. The best shells lie at a depths of from 18 to 40 feet beneath the surface of the water. Pearl-oysters have been brought up by divers from this spot for time immemorial, and much the same methods as were adopted in the time of the Romans, and even earlier, are still employed. Since the earliest times these pearl-fisheries have been under Government control, first native, then Portuguese, then Dutch, and finally English. The head-quarters of the divers in these districts is Kondachchi, and during the fishing-season, six weeks in March and April, when the sea is quietest, the place is inhabited by from 15,000 to 20,000 people. These, drawn from all parts of India, include divers, fishers, shark-charmers, merchants, and so on, who help to people this strip of shore, which at other seasons of the year is entirely unoccupied.

As many as 300 boats, each carrying ten divers, row about the fishing-ground, the boundaries of which are accurately marked out under the superintendence of the authorities Each boat can collect in one day on an average 20,000 oysters, and a yield of two or three shillings' worth of pearls per thousand oysters is sufficient to make the thing pay, while a haul which yields half as much again is considered good. The oysters are seldom opened directly they are landed, but are safely secured and allowed to rot, the atmosphere being pervaded during the process with an indescribably evil smell. The pearls are collected as they fall out of the decaying masses, and are there and then sorted according to size by means of sieves provided with meshes of various sizes. Many are bored and sold on the spot. The number of pearls suitable for ornaments is but a small proportion of the total yield. Those which are not adapted for ornaments are used in India and elsewhere in the East for medicinal purposes, serving, for example, as a costly substitute for the ordinary shell-lime used in the preparation of betel, a luxury which only the richest can afford. The pearl-oyster of Ceylon is small, no larger than the palm of the hand, and the shell itself is so thin that although the inner surface is extraordinarily lustrous and beautiful it has no value as a source of mother-of-pearl.

Pearl-fishing is not restricted in this district to the Gulf of Manar, but is carried on also in Trincomalee, on the east coast of Ceylon, and at other places, all, compared with the Gulf of Manar, unimportant. No part of a district is fished oftener than once in six or seven years, this arrangement giving the fishing-grounds ample time to become repopulated, by the development of young individuals. If an oyster-bank is allowed to remain much longer than seven years many dead individuals are found in it, so that this period appears to be the normal limit of their life.

The pearl-oyster banks in the **Persian Gulf** are also of great importance, and have been known and fished since ancient times. They are situated chiefly on the Arabian side, and are wholly controlled by the Arabs, who do not brook any interference with their rights. The methods they employ are exactly the same as those adopted in Ceylon. Very productive banks are situated in the neighbourhood of the Bahrein islands on the Arabian coast (about 26° North latitude), and further south, skirting the Pirate coast for a length of seventy geographical miles. At both places the banks lie at a depth of about 40 feet. Oysters, from which beautiful pearls are obtained, are found also at a greater depth off the Persian coast opposite, one such place being situated between the islands Kharak and Gorgo, north-west of Bushire. The pearl-oysters of the Persian Gulf are double the size of those of Ceylon, thicker and also smoother on the outside. The pearls found in this region have a yellowish colour as compared with the pure white of Indian pearls, but in other respects they are in no way inferior.

Pearl-oyster banks appear to be scattered over the whole of the **Red Sea**, except the most southerly part, and at several places flourishing fisheries have been established. One such is situated near the island of Dahalak, not far from Massaua, and another near the Farsan islands, which lie just opposite, off the Arabian coast. Pearls of an inferior quality are obtained also from the sea near Jedda, west of Mecca, in Arabia. The pearl-oysters of the Red Sea yield a large quantity of excellent mother-of-pearl.

Every part of the **Indian Ocean** yields pearl-oysters, but the fisheries have not the importance of those already mentioned. Pearls of small size and inferior quality are obtained from the Gulf of Cutch, on the north coast of the Kathiawar peninsula, and from the sea near Kurrachee, on the western mouth of the Indus; while pearls of rather better quality come from the coasts of the Mergui Archipelago, off the coast of Lower Burma. The Sulu Islands have been mentioned above; from them and from the neighbouring Tawi-Tawi Islands pearls equal to Indian are obtained. The pearl-oysters of this region are, however, more valuable as a source of mother-of-pearl. The shells are very large, averaging $\frac{3}{4}$ pound in weight, and the largest weigh as much as 2 pounds. They are remarkable not only for their size but also for the purity and lustre of the mother-of-pearl layer. In reference to the fact that many of these shells reach the market through Macassar, they are known as Macassar shells. Pearls are also obtained from oysters found off the coasts of New Guinea and the neighbouring island groups, especially the Aru Islands.

The pearl and mother-of-pearl fisheries of the north-west coast of **Western Australia** have constituted for the last quarter of a century one of the most valuable assets of the Colony. The value of the pearls exported in 1896 was estimated at £20,000 and that of pearl-shell at £30,000. Two definite varieties of the pearl-oyster are found off these coasts: the larger inhabits the north-west coast as far as Exmouth Gulf, in latitude 22° S.; while the smaller is confined to Sharks Bay, in latitude 25° S. The largest and finest pearls are yielded by the larger variety; those obtained from the smaller shells are perfect in form and lustre, but are of a bright golden- or straw-yellow colour, and find a readier sale in India and China than in Europe. The smaller variety is, or was formerly, the more abundant, and the oysters are obtained by dredging; while those belonging to the larger variety are collected by diving.

According to Möbius, the whole of the **Pacific Ocean** is a pearl-sea, for the inhabitants of most of the islands north and south of the equator have been observed by sea-farers to wear pearls and mother-of-pearl as ornaments, and to use fish-hooks fashioned out of mother-of-pearl.

South of the equator the pearl-oyster is known to occur in the vicinity of the Solomon, Society, and Marquesas Islands; also in the Low Archipelago, south of which lie the small Gambier Islands, particularly important as a locality for pearl-oysters. North of the equator these molluscs are found near the Marianne Islands and the Marshall Islands; while from the Sandwich Islands are obtained pearls of small size and inferior quality. Those from the latter islands are, however, not of marine but of fresh-water origin; the mussels in which they were formed inhabiting among other streams the Pearl river, distant fourteen miles from Honolulu in the island of Oahu.

On the west coast of Central America and of Mexico there are extensive oyster-banks, which were fished by the original inhabitants even before the discovery of the new world, especially near Tototepec, in the Mexican State of Oajaca. The Spaniards reaped a rich harvest from both the Gulf of California and the Gulf of Panama, and even now both pearls and mother-of-pearl are obtained from the same parts. In the Gulf of Panama, the neighbourhood of the Archipelago del Rey and of Taboga is rich in pearl-oysters; these are the Pearl Islands (Islas de las Perlas) of the Spanish conquerors, but the banks in the neighbourhood are now almost exhausted. On the coast of Costa Rica the Gulf of Nicoya is mentioned.

The islands of Cubagua and Margarita in the **Caribbean Sea** on the east side of America were once noted for their pearl-fisheries. The pearls found there surpass all others of American origin in size and beauty; but these so-called "occidental" pearls are never quite equal to the "oriental" or Indian. Though often larger they are usually less perfect in form and more lead-coloured in tint. The oyster-banks surrounding these islands are now completely exhausted; and New Cadiz in Cubagua, the town founded by Diego Columbus, the son of the discoverer, in 1509, once a busy centre of the pearl-fishing industry, is also deserted. From the Colombian coast between Rio Hacha and Maracaibo beautiful pearls are now obtained in greater numbers than from the west coast. These pearls originate, however, in another mollusc, namely, *Avicula squamulosa*, the shell of which, though beautifully lustrous, is too thin to be of any value as a source of mother-of-pearl. In the West Indian Sea the island of St. Thomas is mentioned as a locality for the pearl-oyster, but it is of little importance.

Möbius estimates that about 20,000,000 marine pearl-oysters are fished annually, and of these about 4,000,000 contain pearls. Even on the supposition that from every thousand pearl-oysters only one fine pearl is obtained, the yearly yield of costly specimens would be 20,000, and when the table of prices quoted above is referred to it becomes obvious that such an average yield allows of a considerable margin for profit. Moreover, the enormous quantities of shells supplied yearly to the trade, as a source of mother-of-pearl, are worth at least as much as the total annual yield of pearls. In spite of the millions of pearl-oysters taken every year from the sea, there is apparently no exhaustion of the banks. Although the fishing of certain spots has had to be abandoned because of the exhaustion of the banks, yet this has made no appreciable difference in the total yield.

Many attempts have been made in the Dutch East Indian seas to establish pearl-oyster banks, just as the development of edible-oyster banks is commenced by planting a number of animals at a suitable spot.   Although the colony of animals thus planted may thrive and grow, it does not follow that pearls will be formed in the individual oysters, for to provoke the attack of a boring parasite, or the entrance of a grain of sand, or other cause of irritation is at present somewhat beyond the control of man.

The Pearl-Mussel.—Compared with the marine pearl-oyster, the fresh-water pearl-mussel as a pearl producer is of very subordinate importance.   The variety inhabiting rivers resembles the common fresh-water mussel very closely, especially in the corrosion of the shell near the hinge line, but is somewhat larger.   It is estimated that one pearl will be found in every hundred mussels, and that one per cent. of the pearls so found are of good quality.   River-pearls of even the best quality often possess a lead-coloured tinge, or are lustreless and of a greyish-brown colour in consequence of the absence of the nacreous layer; they are never equal to pearls of marine origin.   As in the case of the marine pearl-oyster it is useless to expect to find pearls in well-grown, regularly formed shells, and even in distorted and abnormal shells they are often sought for in vain.

The pearl-mussel inhabits rivers in all parts of the world, but in contrast to the pearl-oyster is more abundant in temperate than in warm countries; its favourite habitat is in streams and small rivers of clear, fresh water.

It is absent from the southern countries of Europe and from the Alpine regions, but is abundant in **Germany** in the many water-courses which drain the Bohemian and Bavarian forests and the Fichtelgebirge, Erzgebirge, and Riesengebirge.   Specially remarkable for the number of their pearl-producing inhabitants are the Ilz and the Regen in Lower Bavaria; the Oelschnitz above Berneck, and the Perlenbach in the upper reaches of the Main; the Elster and its tributaries in Saxon Voigtland especially in the neighbourhood of the town of Oelsnitz; the Queiss and the Juppel in Silesia; the Moldau above Frauenberg and its tributary the Wattawa in Bohemia.   For centuries the pearl-mussels found in these rivers have been turned to the best possible account by the Government of the different countries, especially by that of Saxony.   The yield has always been small and is gradually diminishing both in quantity and quality.   In the year 1893 the total yield was 55 pearls; in 1894 only 13; and in 1895 there were 68 found, of which 21 were bright, 22 half bright, and 25 dull and useless.

The famous collection in the "Green Vaults" at Dresden shows, however, that at one time beautiful pearls were obtained from the mussels inhabiting the rivers of Voigtland. A necklace preserved in this collection has been valued at 3000 thalers; it consists of 177 pearls obtained from the river Elster.   For a necklace of pearls from Voigtland, said to have been the property of a duchess of Sachsen-Zeitz, 40,000 thalers (£6000) was once offered.

Pearls have also been obtained from true pearl-mussels inhabiting certain streams in the north of Germany; for example, the Wipperau, Gerdau, and Barnbeck on the Lüneburg heath, between Celle and Uelzen.   From *Unio crassus*, another species of mussel, have been derived the pearls occasionally found in the Tapps-Aa near Christiansfeld on the northern border of Schleswig, in the neighbourhood of the Rheinsberg, and in the lake near Lindow in the province of Brandenburg.

The pearls of **Britain** were mentioned by Tacitus and by Pliny, and a breast-plate studded with British pearls was dedicated by Julius Cæsar to Venus Genetrix.   We find a reference to Scotch pearls as early as 1355, in a statute of the goldsmiths of Paris, and in the reign of Charles II. the Scotch pearl trade was sufficiently important to attract the attention of parliament.   After languishing for years, the pearl-fishing industry of Scotland was revived in 1860 by a German named Moritz Unger, who visited the country and bought up all the pearls he could find in the hands of the peasantry, thus stimulating the search for more. It is estimated that the produce of the season's fishing in 1865 was worth at least £12,000. This yield, however, was not maintained; the rivers were over-fished, and the industry was discouraged as it tended to interfere with the salmon fishing, and in some cases to cause damage to the banks of the stream. At the present time a pearl is found now and again by an occasional fisherman.

The Scotch rivers which have yielded pearls are the Spey, the Tay, and the South Esk, and to a lesser extent the Doon, the Dee, the Don, the Ythan, the Teith, and the Forth.

In North Wales the Conway was at one time celebrated for its pearls; and it is related that a Conway pearl, which it is believed now occupies a place in the British crown, was presented to the queen of Charles II. by her chamberlain, Sir Richard Wynn. In Ireland the rivers of the counties of Donegal, Tyrone, and Wexford have yielded pearls. It is said that, in England, Sir John Hawkins, the circumnavigator had a patent for pearl-fishing in the Irt in Cumberland.

The pearl-mussel is abundant also in Sweden and Norway from Schonen and Christiansand as far north as Lapland; and in the north of Russia, from the sources of the Don and the Volga to the White Sea. The rivers of these regions yield a certain number of pearls, among which are many of good quality.

A pearl-mussel which differs in no essential particular from the European *Unio margaritifer* is found in **North America,** and is specially abundant in the New England States, but yields very few pearls. On the other hand, there are to be met with in the river-system of the Mississippi a number of species of the genus *Unio* from which many pearls are obtained. The first European discoverers of this region in the sixteenth century found immense numbers of pearls, the largest being the size of a nut. The occurrence of the fresh-water pearl-mussel in the Sandwich Islands has been noted already.

The pearl industry of eastern Asia and particularly of **China** is of peculiar interest. Pearls are greatly esteemed by the Chinese as ornaments, and for that reason have been eagerly sought for centuries. Pearl-producing mussels are said to inhabit some of the rivers of Manchuria and East Siberia, but to what genera and species they belong is not exactly known. The pearl-mussel which inhabits the water-courses near Canton and Hu-che-fu further to the south is *Cristaria plicata*. This mollusc possesses a peculiar interest in that for centuries it has been experimented upon by the Chinese in their attempts to induce it to form pearls in response to an artificial stimulation. Thousands of Chinamen make this a regular occupation, but their efforts are never quite successful. The manner in which they proceed is to insert into the carefully opened mussel without injury to the animal a small hemispherical object, or a thin image of Buddha in tin, which they place between the mantle and the shell. These objects when invested with a layer of nacre acquire a pearly appearance. After remaining inside the shell for a period ranging from 10 months to three years, their nacreous coat is from $\frac{1}{10}$ to $\frac{1}{3}$ millimetre thick, and the objects can be utilised for purposes of ornament. They are removed from the shell, to which they have become firmly attached, and mounted in a suitable manner.

Other similar attempts have been made to induce by artificial means the formation of pearls, such as, for example, by the introduction of a grain of sand or of small spheres of mother-of-pearl, but never very successfully. It is related that a method was known to Linnæus, which he had described in writing, but the details have never become known.

Not only have attempts been made to induce the formation of natural pearls by artificial means, but no efforts have been spared to produce less costly substitutes which shall resemble genuine pearls as closely as may be. With the consideration of this subject we shall close.

IMITATION PEARLS.—One of the best imitations of a pearl is furnished by a polished sphere of mother-of-pearl, but it differs very essentially from a natural pearl inasmuch as the coats of which it is built up are not concentric. In 1680, or possibly even earlier, in 1656, Jacquin, the Parisian rosary maker, discovered a means whereby imitation pearls, which reproduce the beautiful pearly lustre of genuine pearls, may be manufactured. His method is still employed, and on it depends a flourishing industry. The first step is the production of hollow, thin-walled glass beads of "girasol," a colourless, easily fusible glass manufactured for the express purpose. In form these may be spherical, ovoid, or pear-shaped, or they may be made to resemble baroque pearls. The inner surface of these beads is then coated with a silvery-white material obtained from the scales of certain fishes, for example, from the white-fish and the bleak (*Alburnus lucidus*). This material lies just beneath the scales, from which it is separated by shaking the same with water. The microscope reveals the fact that it consists of numberless minute, irregular, rhombic plates. One pound of the substance is yielded by seven pounds of fish scales, to provide which from 18,000 to 20,000 fishes are necessary. This silvery-white material, when mixed with a solution of isinglass, yields a thin, glutinous pulp, known in the trade as "essence d'Orient." It is introduced into the hollow glass balls, over the inner surface of which it is spread uniformly. When dry, this inner coating of silvery-white material gives the beads very much the appearance of real pearls, so that even an expert may be deceived at the first glance. In order to make them more substantial, the beads are filled with wax. When carefully made, they resemble very closely good Indian pearls, and are much worn in place of these, although on account of the care necessary in their manufacture they are not at all cheap. Less carefully made beads are employed in the cheaper articles of jewellery, and though they imitate real pearls less perfectly, yet the beautiful pearly lustre is always reproduced with more or less fidelity.

Very beautiful artificial pearls, with a lustre like satin, are sometimes made from the incisors of the Dugong, a whale-like, aquatic mammal belonging to the group which includes sea-cows. It inhabits the sea in the neighbourhood of the Dahalak Island, which lies in the Red Sea off Massaua, already mentioned as a pearl-fishing station. Imitation pearls of this kind are not, however, frequently met with.

In recent times the so-called opaline glass has been used for the manufacture of imitation pearls, the resemblance to real pearls being given by a careful treatment with hydrofluoric acid.

Black pearls can be imitated very successfully in hæmatite, as we have already seen under this mineral. A polished ball of hæmatite often resembles a black pearl very closely, especially when not too highly polished. It is readily distinguished, however, by its high specific gravity and by the fact that it feels cold to the touch. Red spheres cut from the shell of the great West Indian univalve mollusc, *Strombus gigas*, have a lustre which is somewhat pearl-like, but they are more easily passed off as coral than as pearls.

CORAL.

Red or precious coral is a material almost as important for decorative and ornamental purposes as are precious stones and pearls. It constitutes the substance of the calcareous axial skeleton of the coral polyp, *Corallium rubrum*, a lowly organised animal belonging to the class Anthozoa. The Mediterranean Sea is the principal habitat of this coral; and not only is it fished almost exclusively by Italians, but the working of the rough material is for the most part in the hands of the same people, so that we are dealing with what is practically an Italian industry.

Corallium rubrum has been sometimes known by other names, such as *Corallium nobile*, *Isis nobilis*, &c., but these terms are no longer employed. This coral is not a solitary organism, but forms branching colonies. Each colony is supported by an axial rod of red calcareous material, the so-called coral, and this is invested by a layer of soft, living material known to zoologists as the cœnosarc. At intervals along the branches are situated the individual polyps, embedded, as it were, in the cœnosarc, with the material of which their bodies are continuous. The cells of the cœnosarc have the power of separating out calcium carbonate from the sea water, in which the coral lives, and this forms the substance of the axial skeleton of the colony. From this the cœnosarc can be peeled off "like the bark of a willow twig in spring," leaving it a clean, red, branching rod, the coral of commerce. It is proposed, first, to consider the structure and life-history of a colony of *Corallium rubrum* in some detail, and afterwards the methods employed for collecting coral and its manufacture into ornamental articles.

The Coral Skeleton.—The calcareous skeleton of a colony of *Corallium rubrum* is red—more rarely white or black—in colour and arborescent in form. It is attached firmly by a disc-shaped foot to any suitable object in the sea, such as a rock or a large stone. Colonies have also been found fixed to cannon-balls, bottles, shells, or other corals, and in one case a human skull. The disc-like foot affords a firm base for the whole structure. It cannot penetrate the rock or other object to which it is attached as do the rootlets of a plant, but any depressions, furrows, or cracks in the surface are filled up with calcareous material, which thus cements, as it were, the two together. The main axis and its lateral branches are not straight, but curved, like the trunk and branches of a tree or shrub. The former seldom exceeds a foot in length and an inch in diameter. From a single disc-like foot there may grow out, not one, but several independent colonies, which are then usually of small size. This is especially the case with the corals off the coast of Provence.

The growth of a coral-colony is not affected by gravity in the same way as is that of plants; it always grows in a direction perpendicular to the surface to which it is attached, regardless of its inclination to the vertical. If attached to some object on the bottom of the sea, its direction of growth will be vertical and upwards; if to the vertical face of a rock it will grow out in a horizontal direction; and when attached to the roof of a rock cavity, it grows vertically downwards, this being, indeed, a direction commonly taken.

The main axis of the skeleton tapers gradually to a blunt point, so gradually, indeed, that a short length of it may appear perfectly cylindrical. It may commence to branch quite near the foot or at a distance of some centimetres away from it. The primary branches may bear secondary branches, and these, again, produce lateral offshoots, and so on. These lateral branches, like the main stem, do not follow a straight course, but twist and turn about in a more or less irregular manner; they also terminate in irregularly blunted points. The branching follows no fixed law, but the branches spread as much as possible, and never arise two at the same level on the parent stem.

The angle at which the branches are inclined to the parent stems varies considerably. It is often between 40° and 50°, but may be obtuse, so that the branch is directed backwards, or, on the other hand, so acute that it runs close beside the parent stem and may actually fuse with it, only to separate again after a short distance. Such an intergrowth may take place also between branches of the same colony which have originated at different spots, or between branches of neighbouring but independent colonies.

Though two branches never originate at exactly the same level on the parent stem, the difference in level between them amounts, as a rule, to only a few millimetres, though it may be several centimetres. The branches are usually crowded together at the attached end of the parent stem, and are less numerous towards the free end. At the point where a branch originates, the parent stem is somewhat flattened, so that its outline in section is oval instead of circular. The same flattening may be observed also in other parts of the stem where there is no obvious reason for it. This is often considered to be due to some temporary disturbance in the economy of the colony.

The general form of a coral-stock, the system according to which it branches, and the actual direction of the branches vary according to the locality in which it grows, its depth beneath the surface of the sea, and so on. Colonies which have grown under similar conditions usually resemble each other in form, so that we may reasonably conclude that the form taken by a colony depends upon the conditions under which it grows. So characteristic is the form of coral-stocks from different districts of the Mediterranean that an expert confronted with a collection of corals from the same locality has no difficulty in naming at once the place from whence they came. Corals from the Algerian and Tunisian coasts, from Sicily, and especially from Sciacca, from Spain, and from Provence, show remarkable differences in this respect, differences which are important, inasmuch as they render the coral more or less suitable for certain purposes, and therefore more or less valuable.

The furrowed surface of precious coral is another of its characteristic features. These fine furrows run in a direction either parallel to the length of the stem and its branches or in more or less of a spiral. When a furrow reaches the point of origin of a branch, it either passes to one side of it or divides into furrows, which enclose the spot, and which frequently unite again after a short course. These furrows are always more numerous towards the base of the stem, since a certain proportion disappear in their course from the base towards the apex. The distance between adjacent furrows is always small, never less than $\frac{1}{4}$ millimetre and never more than $\frac{1}{2}$ millimetre.

Another equally striking feature of a piece of natural coral is the presence of small, circular, shallow depressions, measuring at most two millimetres in diameter. They may lie so close that their edges touch, or, on the other hand, they may be separated by a space of a centimetre. They mark the spots where grew the individual polyps of the colony of which the piece of coral was the axis.

These characteristic ridges and depressions are an invariable feature of the natural surface of precious coral. When absent, it is quite certain that they have been removed by polishing or by some other artificial process. Besides the depressions in the surface of coral, there may be noticed also small pits no larger than a pin-prick. These, which are frequently absent in perfectly fresh coral, have been caused by marine organisms, such as boring-sponges and boring-worms. Dead coral is frequently so much bored and eaten away by such creatures that it is useless for commercial purposes.

A piece of coral which has not been attacked by boring animals appears perfectly homogeneous, compact, and solid, and free from internal cavities. It may occasionally enclose foreign bodies of various kinds, which have by some chance found themselves in such a position as to become enveloped by the calcareous material secreted by the colony, of which the piece of coral formed the axis. The fractured surface of a piece of fresh coral is uneven and splintery. In many cases, when a transversely fractured surface is examined with the naked eye or with a lens, it becomes obvious that the piece of coral is built up of thin, concentric layers, the whole mass, indeed, consisting, as it were, of a number of hollow tubes fitting closely one inside another. This structure is more clearly demonstrated by the examination under the compound microscope of thin, transverse sections; and one can make out, in addition, the fact that each concentric layer is built up of numberless fine fibres, the general direction of which is radial, that is to say, they run outwards from the common centre towards the periphery. These fibres have an extraordinary power of double refraction, in which respect, and in others to be mentioned presently, they agree with the mineral species calcite, to which they are probably to be referred. The concentric structure of a piece of coral is also demonstrated very clearly when the latter is ignited, the concentric layers separating from each other and peeling off.

The observation of thin, transverse sections of coral under the microscope also discloses the fact that the concentric layers are coloured alternately bright red and white. In very thin sections the red colour is scarcely apparent at all, only appearing in slices of a certain thickness. The precise shade of colour of coral is different in different specimens. That from which the cœnosarc has been newly stripped ranges in colour from pure white to the brilliant tint of red lead. Pure white coral is rare, and the absence of colour is said to be the consequence of a diseased condition of the organism. Yellow coral is also rare. In Italy, the home of the coral industry, special terms are used to distinguish coral of different shades of colour. Thus, first comes pure white (*bianco*), next a fresh, pale, flesh-red (*pelle d'angelo*), then pale rose (*rosa pallido*), then bright rose (*rosa vivo*), which is followed by "second colour" (*secondo coloro*), red (*rosso*), dark red (*rosso scuro*), and finally the darkest red of all (*carbonetto* or *arciscuro*). It is unusual to find different colours or different shades of colour in the same piece of coral, this being usually of one uniform tint in all its branches.

Red coral when reduced to a fine powder is pale reddish in colour, the shade being more pronounced the deeper the colour of the piece, and *vice versâ*.

The death and decay of the living portion of a coral-colony is accompanied by a change in colour of the skeleton, that is to say, of the red substance commonly known as coral. Coral which has lain at the bottom of the sea in muddy water for any considerable length of time is almost sure to assume a more or less dark brown or black colour, and is said by the Italians to be "burnt" (*bruciato*). Some of the black coral of commerce is, however, something quite different, and will be considered later. In exceptional cases dead coral, instead of becoming black, turns white or yellow. An immense amount of dead coral is rendered useless for industrial and ornamental purposes by the attacks of boring worms, sponges, and other marine organisms.

The black or brown colour of a piece of dead coral does not always extend over the whole of its surface nor penetrate to its innermost layers. There may be black patches and spots here and there, or it may be red outside, but quite black inside, or the reverse may be the case, while occasionally pieces of coral are met with in which the core and the external layer are black and the intermediate layer is red, so that a cross-section shows a central black spot, surrounded by an inner red and an outer black ring. It is sometimes stated that the original colour can be restored to coral which has turned black by allowing it to lie in water and then exposing it to the sun. The investigations which have been made do not, however, tend to support this statement.

The substance of coral consists for the most part of calcium carbonate, which, as we have already seen, is probably present in the form of calcite. This is impregnated with a small amount of organic material, the presence of which accounts for the fact that coral becomes black when heated. The specific gravity of coral is very near that of calcite, much nearer than to that of aragonite, the other crystallised modification of calcium carbonate. The specific gravity of pure calcite is 2·72, while that of precious coral, irrespective of colour, lies between 2·6 and 2·7; the values found by Canestrini, for example, are 2·671 and 2·68. Precious coral is rather harder than calcite, being placed between 3 and 4 on Mohs' scale, but rather nearer to 4, so that we may write $H = 3\frac{3}{4}$. This greater degree of hardness is no doubt due to the admixture of foreign material. Coral is soft enough to be easily worked with a knife or file, or turned on the lathe, but it is not hard enough to admit of a very brilliant polish, the material depending for its beauty more upon its fine colour.

The chemical composition of coral is given by the following analysis by Tischer:

	Red coral.	Black coral.
Water (H_2O)	0·550	0·600
Carbon dioxide (CO_2)	42·235	41·300
Lime (CaO)	48·825	48·625
Magnesia (MgO)	3·240	3·224
Ferric oxide (Fe_2O_3)	1·720	0·800
Sulphuric anhydride (SO_3) . . .	0·755	0·824
Organic matter	1·350	3·070
Deficiency, &c.	1·325	1·557
	100·000	100·000

From this can be calculated the following constituents:

	Red coral.	Black coral.
Calcium carbonate ($CaCO_3$) . . .	86·974	85·801
Magnesium carbonate ($MgCO_3$) . .	6·804	6·770
Calcium sulphate ($CaSO_4$) . . .	1·271	1·400
Ferric oxide (Fe_2O_3)	1·720	0·800
Organic matter	1·350	3·070
Water (H_2O)	0·550	0·600
Phosphates, Silica, &c., and deficiency .	1·331	1·559
	100·000	100·000

Earlier analyses give similar, though somewhat varying, results; it is clear therefore that, broadly speaking, coral consists of calcium carbonate, with a small amount of magnesium carbonate. The proportions in which these two constituents are present are not always the same; young coral contains only about 1 per cent. of magnesium carbonate, while older material may contain as much as 38 per cent. The greater the amount of magnesium present, the harder does coral become, and the extent to which its hardness exceeds that of calcite probably depends upon the proportion of magnesium carbonate present in it. We learn also from the analyses quoted above that the differences in the composition of red and of black coral are quite unessential, the chief being that black coral contains a larger proportion of organic material, which also probably differs in character from that present in red coral.

The colour of black coral is no doubt due to the presence of this organic material ; it has, indeed, been referred to the presence of manganese dioxide, but this substance was not detected in the above analysis. It has also been suggested that the action of hydrogen sulphide upon red coral might result in a change of colour from red to black ; but this requires proof. Attempts to refer the red colour of fresh coral to the presence of inorganic constituents have been equally unsuccessful. It has been said to be due to the presence of iron oxide, of which Tischer found 1·720 and other chemists up to 4·75 per cent. This, however, is not very probable, seeing that the red colour is destroyed on ignition, just as is the black. The red colouring matter is thus presumably organic in nature, as is the pigment of variously coloured univalve and bivalve shells, and the change of red coral first to black and then to dirty yellow mark different stages in an oxidation process.

The Living Coral.—As already stated, the branching axis of a living coral-stock is invested by the cœnosarc, a layer of soft, red, living material, with a surface like velvet, and a thickness of less than a line. In the substance of the cœnosarc are embedded calcareous spicules, which can be felt by pressing a portion of it between the thumb and finger. They are so small, however, that their form can only be made out by examining thin sections under the microscope. The cœnosarc extends beyond the ends of the branches of the skeleton, and the blunt prolongations of the branches so formed are soft and flexible, and can be cut through with a sharp knife, while the portion containing the calcareous skeletal rod cannot be so treated. The foot of young colonies is invested with cœnosarc, just as are the trunk and the branches, but in old stocks, not only the foot, but the lower part of the stem and the lower branches, are bare and often much corroded and eaten away. When a branch of living coral is allowed to dry in the air, the cœnosarc assumes the appearance of dry, rough skin of a brick-red or red-lead colour, raised here and there into wart-like protuberances. From the central orifice of each protuberance radiate eight short grooves, which divide it into eight wedge-shaped portions, and give the surface of the wart the appearance of an eight-rayed star.

These little protuberances mark the spots occupied by the individual polyps of which the colony is built up. Nothing more than what has been described can be seen of the polyps when a branch of living coral is examined in water which has been disturbed or is in motion, and the branch appears of a uniform red colour. When the water has come to rest, however, one may watch the wart-like prominences gradually expand and open, and the white cylindrical bodies of the polyps, each with eight white, pinnate tentacles come into view. The position of each polyp is marked in the skeleton by a shallow depression, to which attention has been directed already. The polyps respond readily to external irritation ; no matter how slightly the water be disturbed, or how softly one of their number be touched, each one is instantly retracted into its pocket-like depression in the cœnosarc, and then reassumes its original aspect of a wart-like protuberance. It may be some hours before the polyps may again be seen in a fully expanded condition, and even then they expand, only to retract again on the slightest disturbance of the surrounding medium. When fully expanded, the coral-polyps look like white starry blossoms on a coral-red background, and, indeed, formerly the coral-stock was regarded as a plant of which the polyps were the flowers. The true nature of the organism was first recognised, in the year 1723, by the French physician and naturalist, Peyssonel, whose perspicacity was not, however, recognised by his brother zoologists.

Into the single body-cavity of each polyp project eight radial partitions, the outer ends of which are united to the body-wall and the inner to the stomodæum or gullet. This opens to the exterior in the mouth, which is surrounded by eight tentacles. The nourishing of the polyp is performed by the ingestion of food into the body-cavity. The rapid and continual motion of the tentacles induces currents in the sea-water which sweep small organisms of all kinds into the mouth, down the gullet, and into the body-cavity of the polyp, where they are digested, forming a white milk-like fluid. This circulates in a complicated system of tubes throughout the cœnosarc, so that all members of the colony share equally, and none is better nourished than another. The fine grooves so characteristic of the surface of natural coral are due to this tube-system; they correspond to vessels lying in the innermost part of the cœnosarc, close to the skeleton.

Reproduction takes place in two ways, by budding and by the development of eggs. By budding, new individuals in an already established colony are formed, while from each egg arises a perfectly independent daughter-colony. The polyps of a single stock are usually all male or all female, but occasionally polyps of both sexes may be found in the same colony, though, as a rule, on different branches. The fertilising cells of the male are discharged into the water and eventually find their way into the body-cavity of a female. The eggs of the latter after fertilisation develop into small oval larvæ scarcely visible to the naked eye, which escape through the mouth of the parent, and for a time swim about freely in the sea. After a time each larva attaches itself to some suitable object on the sea-bottom and gradually assumes the form of an adult polyp, which by repeated budding forms a colony.

The first stage in the development of the polyp after the fixation of the larva, is the appearance of a tiny knob or swelling upon the free end. This becomes gradually larger and larger, and, as calcareous spicules appear in its substance, assumes a red colour, finally becoming transformed into a perfect adult polyp. This transformation is accompanied by the deposition of calcium carbonate in a circular area of the surface of attachment of the polyp, and the formation of the foot, the organ of attachment of a coral-colony. During the development of the colony, calcium carbonate is continuously separated out from the sea-water and deposited in the living cœnosarc in the form of spicules. These become embedded in a dense calcareous, cement-like substance and thus the hard, axial skeleton of the colony is formed. This continually increases in diameter by the deposition of fresh layers of calcium carbonate, and gives off new lateral branches with the development of new polyps. The foot also, which is invested by cœnosarc, increases in circumference proportionately with the increase in size of the colony. The laminated structure of the coral skeleton points to the fact that the deposition of calcareous matter does not proceed uninterruptedly, but that periods of activity alternate with periods of rest, these periods being possibly seasons of the year. Thus each layer of calcareous material corresponds to a period of activity, and the interruption between successive layers to a period of quiescence. The coral-skeleton grows also in length as well as in diameter, for fresh material is always being deposited at the free ends of the stem and branches.

At an early stage in its development the coral-colony consists only of one polyp, but, by a process of budding, multiplication of the polyps and the formation of a larger or smaller colony is effected. The new polyps arise at various spots in the cœnosarc as knob-like swellings, which gradually unfold, take on the characters of the adult, and perform their share of the work of nutrition and reproduction. The process suggests the formation and unfolding of a leaf-bud, and for that reason is known to zoologists as budding or gemmation.

Not only from a scientific but also from an economic standpoint it is important to know the period required by a coral-colony to attain its full growth, but there is much diversity of opinion upon the point. The length of the period probably varies with the conditions under which the colony lives, and more especially with its depth beneath the surface.

In the opinion of many experts a coral-stock reaches its full size only after a period of thirty years, but others maintain that well-grown stocks are to be found on coral-banks which have been fished very much more recently than thirty years previously. Thus at the beginning of the nineteenth century the fishing of the coral-banks on the north coast of Africa was abandoned, in consequence of war, for a period of four years, and when fishing was again commenced, an unparalleled amount of coral was harvested, many pieces of exceptional size being found.

Near Vico Equense, in the neighbourhood of Sorrento, in the Bay of Naples, is a coral-bank situated six miles away from the coast, on which the coral, at a depth of 60 feet, is supposed to require eight years to attain its maximum size, while at greater depths it requires still longer. The coral-bank which stretches along the coast of Sicily, from the Point of Faro to a point many miles south of the town of Messina is divided into ten sections, one of which is fished every year. A period of ten years therefore elapses between consecutive fishings of each of these sections, and this is sufficient to admit of the coral-stocks reaching their full size. A rich yield of coral was obtained from a bank still further south, near San Stefano, which had not been fished before within the memory of man. Notwithstanding the fact that the bank had remained undisturbed for centuries, the coral-stocks were no larger, and only about one-third thicker than those known to have developed within a period of ten years. It may be concluded from this that a coral-stock continues for a time to grow in thickness after it has ceased to grow in length.

The fact that the development of a coral-colony is greatly influenced by the conditions under which it lives is pointed to by the observations of coral-fishers in the Bay of Naples, among other regions. The coral formed off the west side of the bay is more beautiful and regularly formed than that obtained off the opposite coast near Sorrento; a difference which is attributed to the fact that the coast near Sorrento on the east consists of limestone rocks, while the islands of Nisida, Procida, Ischia, &c. on the west are constituted of volcanic tuffs, which are obviously more suitable for corals than the former.

The discovery of the conditions most favourable for the development of fine coral has been, and is, the subject of much experimental study, but no very valuable result has yet been obtained.

The polyp, *Corallium rubrum,* which forms precious coral is placed by systematists in the sub-kingdom Cœlenterata, class Anthozoa, sub-class Alcyonaria or Octactinia, all the members of which have eight tentacles and eight mesenteries.

Precious coral, as we have seen, forms the skeleton of small isolated colonies, but the reef-building corals, by whose industry are reared the coral-reefs and islands (atolls) of the Pacific Ocean and other warm seas, do not differ essentially in their organisation from precious corals, the chief difference being the possession of six mesenteries and of six, or some multiple of six, tentacles. Those corals which agree with the reef-building corals in this respect, constitute the other division of the class Anthozoa, namely the sub-class Zoantharia or Hexactinia. This sub-class comprises three orders of corals: the Madreporaria or stony corals, which includes most of the reef-building corals; the Actiniaria or sea-anemones, which are destitute of a calcareous skeleton and remarkable for their gorgeous colouring; and the Antipatharia, including the "black corals," the skeleton of which is horny.

The Distribution of Coral : Coral-banks.—Our attention must now be turned to the distribution of coral in nature, to the manner in which it is collected, and to some aspects of the coral-industry.

The colonies formed by *Corallium rubrum* are always found growing in groups, which are known as coral-fields or coral-banks. The shrub-like branches of living coral form with sea-weeds submarine forests, which afford food and shelter to numberless marine creatures. The coral-stocks are situated usually in clefts, crevices, or cavities in the rocks near the shore. They prefer a steep face of rock directed towards the south and never settle upon rocks which face north, though they are sometimes found in situations the aspect of which is east or west. The true precious coral, *Corallium rubrum*, is probably confined to the Mediterranean Sea and its inlets, and the red coral found in other localities belongs, as we shall see in passing later on, to another species.

The depth at which precious coral is found varies between wide limits ; very little grows at a depth less than 3, or greater than 300 metres. At depths such as the latter the development of the colonies is slow ; they never reach a large size and are always pale in colour. The depth most favourable for the growth and development of coral-colonies lies between 30 and 50 metres, but varies according to locality, the best grown corals in the Straits of Messina, for example, being met with at depths of from 120 to 200 metres.

A coral-field once discovered is not a perennial source of coral, but after being fished for a longer or shorter period becomes exhausted. Banks, which at one time were productive, are now exhausted through over-fishing or other causes ; while in some cases they have to be abandoned, usually on account of the roughness of the sea at that particular spot, and the consequent danger to the fishing-boats. The deficit in the total yield occasioned by the exhaustion of previously fruitful fields is usually compensated for by the discovery of fresh banks. The coral-producing portions of the Mediterranean Sea will be separately treated in some detail below ; they include the coasts of east Algeria and of Tunis, the west coasts of Sardinia and Corsica, part of the south and of the west coasts of Sicily, and the Straits of Messina from whence coral-banks stretch along the whole of the west coast of Italy, the coast of Provence, the whole of the Mediterranean coast of Spain, and finally in the neighbourhood of the Balearic Islands. The yield of coral from the Italian coasts of the Adriatic Sea is very meagre, and very little more is found off the Dalmatian coasts opposite : the stocks are so small and scarce as hardly to repay the searcher for his trouble. A small amount of coral is found further east in the sea round Corfu and Cyprus, and at various isolated spots off the coast of Asia Minor, but these localities are all unimportant.

The largest amount of coral is obtained from the coasts of **Algeria** and **Tunis**, the yearly yield from these regions being 10,000 kilograms. The coral-banks stretch eastward from Cape Ferro (Cap de Fer), a little west of Bona, to Cape Bon, and from thence southwards as far as the neighbourhood of Sfax in the Lesser Syrtis. An exhaustive search for coral has been made on the west coast of Algeria, west of Cape Ferro, but hitherto in vain. At places where coral-banks exist they are fished for a distance of six or eight miles out to sea and at depths varying from 90 to 900 feet, but the coral obtained at great depths is paler and less brilliant. In the districts mentioned above the coral-fishing industry has been carried on for centuries ; it has flourished and declined, and at times has almost reached a standstill, owing to the passive neglect or active opposition of the barbarian rulers of the coast. The headquarters of the fishing-fleet was formerly the island of Tabarca, which lies near the coast and very near the prolongation of the boundary line between Algeria and Tunis. The island is still of importance, as also is the island of Galita, lying a little further from the coast. The most important centre, however, at present is La Calle, a town on the neighbouring Algerian coast, where the industry is promoted in every possible way by the French Government. Other places in the same neighbourhood where abundance of coral is to be found are Vieille-Calle or Bastion de France, a fort erected in former times for the protection of coral-fishers; Cape Rosa, a little to the west of La Calle; further to the west the Gulf of Bona, on which Bona itself stands; then Calle-Traversa and other places; and still further in the same direction Cap de Garde and Cap de Fer, which constitute as far as is known at present the western boundary of the coral-producing stretch of these seas. Towards the east we have the coast of Biserta; the neighbourhood a little to the south of Cape Bon, near Kelibia; and further to the south Mansuria (Sidi Mansur), which lies to the north of Sfax, opposite the Kerkenna Islands in the Gulf of Cabes. The coral found on the African coast is distinguishable from that found at other localities, and specially from Sicilian coral, by certain peculiarities of form. The main stem of the stock is almost perfectly straight, rising up like a column, and bearing upon its sides perfectly straight branches, some pieces being like a hand with outstretched fingers. Pieces of coral of this form are much sought after as they can be worked with very little waste of material.

A large amount of coral has been obtained in recent years from the coasts of **Sicily**. Also from the neighbourhood of the small islands Linosa and Pantellaria south of Sicily, and from the sea between Malta and Cape Passaro, the southernmost point of Sicily. The most important localities for coral lie, however, near Sciacca, a little to the west of Girgenti, where coral-fishing has been carried on since the middle of the 'seventies; on the west coast near Trapani; and in the vicinity of the neighbouring Ægadean Islands. Near Sciacca there are three banks of different sizes, and at an average depth of about 200 metres (148–221 metres), which are remarkable in that all the coral-stocks are dead, and the skeleton in many cases has turned black. The process is of course progressive, and since the discovery of the banks in 1875 a gradual increase in the proportion of black and red coral has been observed, the deterioration being noticeable as early as the beginning of the 'eighties. Moreover, the old stocks not being replaced by young ones, the bank is quickly becoming exhausted. It is the presence of a thick layer of mud which has proved fatal to the corals of these banks, for the organism never thrives unless living in clear, still water. This covering of mud may be traced to the violent submarine volcanic eruptions which took place at intervals during a period of three months in the year 1831 in the sea between Pantellaria and Sciacca. To these eruptions was due the appearance of the small crater-island known as Graham (= Ferdinandea = Julia Island), now washed away by the sea, and the mud which killed the corals was probably laid down over great stretches of the sea-floor in the form of fine volcanic ash. The coral-stocks of Sciacca are so gnarled and distorted that, from the commercial point of view, they are of little use, since to work them into any of the objects ordinarily made of coral involves a considerable loss of material.

There are coral-banks in the neighbourhood of Ustica and the Lipari Islands (Lipari, Vulcano, Stromboli, Basiluzzo, &c.), small islands lying to the north of Sicily. They are moderately productive, but the stormy seas render the work of fishing difficult or impossible. They are less important than the coral-banks in the Straits of Messina, which extend from Cape Faro, the north-east point of Sicily, for a distance of six miles, that is to say, to a point three miles beyond Messina and opposite Chiesa della Grotta, while a few corals are found even as far south as San Stefano.

The opposite **Calabrian coast**, especially the neighbourhood of Scilla and Palmi, is famous for the beauty of colour of its corals, which on this account are specially valuable. This coast is productive as far north as Cape Vaticano and Tropea and the Gulf of San Eufemia, and in the south in the neighbourhood of Altafiumana, on Cape dell' Armi, and of

Melito. On the east coast coral is found off Capes Spartivento and Bruzzano, and off Cape Rizzuto, in the Gulf of Squillace, and on the eastern margin of the Gulf of Taranto, off Cape Santa Maria di Leuca.

In the **Bay of Naples** several coral-banks are known. They are situated five or six miles from the shore, in the neighbourhood of Capri ; near the small island of Nisida, between Pausilipp and Pozzuoli ; in the neighbourhood of Cape Miseno ; around the island of Ischia ; between Naples and Vico Equense ; and near Castellamare, on the promontory of Sorrento.

The coral-fisheries next in importance to the North African have been for a long time those in the waters surrounding the islands of **Sardinia** and **Corsica**, the fishing being confined almost exclusively to the west coasts. The islands of San Pietro, to the south of Sardinia, with the localities of Carloforte, San Antioco, and del Toro must also be mentioned ; while further north there is the Cape San Marco, and the stretch of coast between Bosa and Alghero. A still richer locality for coral is the Strait of Bonifaccio, between Sardinia and Corsica. It is obtained on the Sardinian side from Asinaro, Castelsardo, Longosardo, and from the Maddalena and Caprera islands. On the Corsican side it is found in the neighbourhood of Bonifaccio ; and also along the whole of the western coast of the island as far north as Cape Corso, for example, in the Gulf of Propriano (Gulf of Valinco), and at many other places. A little coral is found on the east of Sardinia, near Cape Corallo, but none on the east of Corsica.

A certain amount of coral is obtained from the islands of Elba and Giglio, and from that part of the **Tuscan coast**, between Monte Argentaro in the south and San Stefano in the north, opposite to which these islands lie. Here also lies Alsidonia (= Ansidonia), famous even in Pliny's time for its coral-fishery. Another coral-producing part of the Tuscan coast stretches from Cecina, near Livorno, in the south to La Spezia in the north. Monte Nero, near Livorno, was at one time a somewhat important centre, but fishing appears now to be discontinued.

There are coral-banks, though only of minor importance, on certain parts of the **French coast** ; in the neighbourhood of the Hyères, near Toulon, on the coast of Provence ; on both sides of the bay of St. Tropez, south of Cannes ; and a little further to the west, near Point Riche, east of the mouth of the Rhone. French coral is usually short and thick ; the foot of a stock frequently bears a large number of branches, so that the whole stock looks like a tuft of hair.

The whole of the **Spanish coast**, from the French border to Gibraltar, forming parts of the provinces of Catalonia, Valencia, Murcia, and Granada, is fringed with coral-banks, the yield of which is not without importance. The localities deserving of special mention lie quite in the north ; they are situated near Cabo de Creus, in the Gulf of Rosas, and in the vicinity of Cape Bagur, of Cape Sebastiano, and of Palamos, all near latitude 42° N. The seas surrounding the Balearic Islands are also productive of coral. The broad foot in Spanish coral-stocks supports several branching stems growing up like columns, and the coral itself is often of a particularly dark-red colour.

Pliny and other ancient writers, and also certain modern authors, state that precious coral is to be found in other districts ; for example, in the Red Sea and Indian Ocean. It does not seem to exist in those parts of the ocean at the present time, however, although reef-building corals abound. It is possible that true precious coral (*Corallium rubrum*) is really confined to the Mediterranean, but other seas are inhabited by many corals, which, though belonging to different species, are yet very like *Corallium rubrum*, and yield coral which is used for similar purposes. One of these, *Corallium lubrani*, is said to furnish the coral which for some time past has been obtained near the Cape Verde Islands, especially from the neighbourhood of the Island of São Thiago, and also of that from the Canary Islands. The coral-banks near São Thiago lie at a depth of from 90 to 190 metres, and at a distance of from 400 to 1000 metres from the coast. The fishery was established in the 'sixties by Antonio Lubrano, an Italian, from whom this coral takes its name. Coral of a red colour, though lighter in shade than precious coral, is found near the Sandwich Islands. It ranges in colour from pale rose-red to white, and the branches are sharply pointed, which is not the case with Mediterranean coral. The material, which at the present time figures in the trade as Japanese coral, is probably formed by a polyp of the same species, known, however, as *Corallium secundum* (Dana). This differs in no essential particular from *Corallium johnstoni* (Gray), found in the neighbourhood of Madeira. These and all corals other than those living in the Mediterranean are so unimportant from a commercial point of view that they need no further consideration.

Coral-Fishing : Application of Coral : Trade.—The methods adopted for coral-fishing are unique, and cannot be compared with those employed in any other kind of fishing. Coral-fishers pursue their occupation during the six summer months, and only in exceptional cases all the year round. The arrival of the autumn storms makes their trade too dangerous, and the ships then return to harbour laden with their spoils, to return to the fishing-grounds in the following spring.

These ships are constructed specially for coral-fishing, and are all of the same pattern in external form and in general equipment, but of various sizes. They are very solidly built, seaworthy, fast-sailing boats of 6 to 16 tons burden, and adapted for rowing when necessity arises. The largest measure from 13 to 14 metres in length, $3\frac{1}{2}$ in breadth, and $1\frac{1}{2}$ in depth. They are manned by a crew of from 6 to 12 men, who work hard for 18 hours a day for miserable wages. There are just a few quite small boats engaged in coral-fishing, with a capacity of less than six tons, and manned by no more than two or three men.

The fisheries lie, as a rule, from four to six nautical miles out to sea. Nearer the shore, where the depth of water is at most only ten metres, a small amount of coral is collected by divers; but the largest and most beautiful coral grows only at the depths which are inaccessible to the diver, even when provided with every possible appliance.

For fishing up the coral from these greater depths, there is in use all over the Mediterranean a special instrument, which in all probability has been employed by coral-fishers for centuries, and is known to the Italians by the term "ingegno," and to the Provençals as "engin."

Its construction and method of use are almost identical in all parts of the Mediterranean. Two massive beams of oak, with tapering ends and a length of from $2\frac{1}{2}$ to less than 1 metre, according to the size of the boat to which the instrument belongs, are bound firmly together crosswise. In order to make this sink in the water, a heavy weight is attached to the centre of the cross, or its four arms are let into a centre-piece of iron. The end of each of the four arms is grooved, and in each groove is fastened a strong line 6 to 8 metres in length, while a fifth, still longer line, is attached to the central point of the cross. These lines carry the catching apparatus proper, which consists of a number of very coarse, four-cornered nets, made of loosely twisted hemp-string of the thickness of a finger, and with a mesh several centimetres in size. Each net is gathered together at one end and bound firmly, so as to form a tassel-like bundle of string open at one end, similar to the mops used for swabbing a ship's deck. The length of the nets vary with the size of the "ingegno" to which they are attached, but may measure 2 metres, or even more. Each line has a certain number of nets attached to it at suitable distances apart, and there are about thirty or forty on each "ingegno." Between these hang similar but finer and closer-meshed bags, which are commonly made of old sardine-nets.

The "ingegno" is attached to the ship by a long rope, and in fishing is thrown over-board. In its descent through the water the netting-bags open, and when the sea-floor is reached, branches of coral, as well as other animals, plants and stones, become entangled in their meshes, and as the boat moves on are torn up. Such objects are caught chiefly in the wide-meshed nets, the largest of them remain there, but the smaller fall through and are again caught by the small-meshed nets.

The manipulation of the heavier "ingegni" is very arduous, especially when performed for long hours under the burning summer sun of the north African coast, or indeed of any other part of the Mediterranean. In the largest boats the "ingegno" weighs upwards of two hundredweight, and is worked by a winch, but in the small boats these instruments are of less size and are hauled about with no mechanical aid. The nets often get so inextricably entangled with objects on the sea-floor, that a special appliance is provided for hauling up the "ingegno" in such cases. The use of this even does not always loosen the instrument from its moorings, so that the fishermen are often obliged to abandon the whole of the gear, including the rope which attaches it to the boat, a proceeding which involves a loss of 200 francs, if the "ingegno" is a large one.

Each time the "ingegno" is thrown out it is allowed to remain a certain length of time in the water, the fishermen meanwhile controlling its movement along the sea-bottom in various ways designed to increase the catch. When hauled up, whatever has been caught in the nets is picked out, and the latter, which naturally are apt to be much torn, are repaired in readiness for another cast. The mending of the nets involves the expenditure of a large amount of time, and in one working-day, under average conditions, the "ingegno" cannot be let down and hauled up more than from seven to fourteen times. Small boats return to harbour after their day's work, but the larger ones remain at sea, cruising about from bank to bank, and only returning to harbour for provisions or repairs.

Coral-fishing is an almost exclusively Italian industry; nearly all the boats are built in Italy and winter in Italian harbours. The fishing fleet in the 'eighties included 260 large, and 200 small boats. The most important harbour is Torre del Greco, near Naples, from which 300 boats set out every year. Next comes Santa Margherita, east of Genoa, on the Riviera di Levante, which harbours 49 boats, though 50 years ago there were 200 boats at anchor there; then Alghero and Carloforte in Sardinia with 19 each, then Trapani with 8, Livorno with 6, and Messina with 3. The number of boats which respectively make their headquarters at these different harbours varies from time to time, but not to any great extent.

The most productive coral-banks lie within French domains on the North African coast, and no efforts have been spared by the French Government to establish a coral-fishing industry in Algeria. So favourably are Italian coral-fishers treated, that a considerable number have now settled in La Calle and other African harbours, from whence about 100 boats, all flying the French flag, though manned by Italians, annually set forth. The only coral not obtained by Italian fishers is the comparatively small amount found off the coast of Provence, which is fished by Frenchmen, and that collected by Spaniards, off the coast of Spain, who employ about 60 small boats.

The amount of coral collected yearly by one boat varies greatly according to circum-stances and to the locality at which the fishing has been carried on. The coral obtained from different localities differs not only in amount, but also in quality, and not infrequently the one compensates for the other. A boat working on the African coast collects on an average 150 kilograms per annum of coral worth 75 francs per kilogram; on the Sardinian coast a total weight of 190 kilograms, worth 50 francs per kilogram, will be collected annually, while in the neighbourhood of Corsica is obtained 210 kilograms of material valued at 45 francs per kilogram.

The total weight of coral collected during the last decade by boats flying the Italian flag amounted to not less than 56,000 kilograms, the value of which was 4,200,000 francs. In Algeria the yearly yield amounted to 10,000 kilograms, and was valued at 750,000 francs. The 60 Spanish ships brought in about 800,000 francs' worth, or 12,000 kilograms. The amount collected by vessels other than Italian boats is estimated to have been 22,000 kilograms, of the value of 1,550,000 francs; so that, all sources considered, there must have been collected every year of that particular decade on an average 78,000 kilograms of coral, of a total value of 5,750,000 francs (£230,000).

Rough coral before being placed on the market is sorted, and there is often a considerable difference between the mean market values of different classes of material. There is also a very striking discrepancy between the price of rough coral and that of finished ornaments.

The different qualities of rough coral are as follow :

i. *Dead or rotten coral.* This includes the disc-like foot of the coral-stock and also the lower portion of the main stem. The foot is often found still clinging to the stone to which the colony was attached; both it and the base of the stem are so encrusted with animal and vegetable growths of various kinds that it is impossible to judge of the quality of the coral beneath. The purchase of this class of material, at a price of from 5 to 20 francs per kilogram, is of the nature of a speculative transaction, for the removal of the unpromising outer crust sometimes discloses very valuable pieces of coral. The broad foot-plates are not infrequently worked into small dishes and bowls.

ii. *Black Coral.*—This includes coral in which the change of colour is not merely superficial but extends through the whole or a large part of its substance. When of good quality it is worth from 12 to 15 francs per kilogram, and is used for mourning ornaments. Black coral of quite another kind will be mentioned further on.

iii. *Ordinary Red Quality.*—In this class is placed red coral of all kinds, irrespective of shape and of form and size; it embraces alike whole stocks and broken fragments. The price ranges from 45 to 70 francs per kilogram, according to the character of the coral.

iv. *Selected Pieces.*—Pieces of coral of exceptional size or beauty constitute this class. They are sold by weight either separately or in parcels, and fetch as much as, or even more than, 500 francs per kilogram.

Among the factors which determine the price of a single piece of coral, colour is the most important. According to the caprice of fashion, now this shade of colour, now that, commands the highest price. Thus, at one time bright-red coral found most favour, but in Europe at the present time the coral most admired is that of a fresh rose colour, known to the Italians as *pelle d'angelo.* This same shade stands first also in the regard of the inhabitants of East India and China, the countries which receive the largest exports of coral. Well-formed pieces of coral of this colour, even though of small size, will fetch 100 francs or more. The taste for coral of this shade is not universal however, the Arabs, for example, still prefer the bright-red shade.

The **working of coral** is for the most part also an Italian industry, very little being worked in Spain or in France. It is very common, however, for coral which has been worked in Italy to be sent to France and Spain to be set, sometimes with diamonds and other precious stones, in articles of jewellery. There are about sixty workshops in Italy for the manufacture of coral ornaments and articles of various kinds. These are exported to all parts of the world and their manufacture gives employment to about 6000 workpeople. The centre of the coral-working, as of the coral-fishing industry, is Torre del Greco in which are forty workshops giving employment to 3200 persons, of whom 2800 are women. Other places at which the industry is established are Genoa, Naples, Livorno, Trapani, and, to a less extent, Rome.

A staple branch of the coral-working industry is the piercing of pieces of coral of all shapes and sizes; these being threaded on a string and used as necklaces, bracelets, rosaries, &c. When the coral is fashioned into beads, they are either spherical or ovoid in form—in the latter case being known as " olives "—large, medium, or small in size, with or without facets. Faceted beads are less in demand now than at the beginning of the nineteenth century. " Arabian beads " are from $1\frac{1}{2}$ to 2 centimetres in length; they are bored through lengthways but not otherwise worked, and are threaded to form long strings, which are much worn in the East as girdles. Beads of this description are often bored crosswise.

Italians are very skilful in the art of carving coral, and in the production of beautiful cameos and articles carved to represent trees, animals, figures, and other objects; they know how to utilise the small irregularities of the surface of coral to produce the greatest possible effect. Objects carved in this way are either set separately in brooches, pins, &c., or in rows in bracelets and necklaces. The ends of small branches are often polished and mounted in their natural form in ear-rings and pins, or utilised for the decoration of various other objects.

Pieces of coral of sufficient size supply material for the handles of sticks and umbrellas, and even of still larger objects. Pieces of fine quality are often carved, which add considerably to their intrinsic value. The carved coral handle of a sunshade belonging to the Queen of Italy is worth £360.

The value of worked coral depends not only upon the quality of the coral, but also upon the artistic worth of the workmanship. The price of a necklace or bracelet varies with the number and size of the beads and with their uniformity of colour. At the International Fisheries Exhibition held at Berlin in 1880, a coral necklace was exhibited which was valued at £6000.

The **uses** to which coral is put in Europe are by no means insignificant, but the material is employed to a much greater extent in India and China, the two countries to which the largest proportion of the total annual yield of coral is sent.

In Europe coral ornaments are worn, for the most part, by children; they are in general use only in certain parts of Italy, Austria, and Hungary, in Poland, and specially in Russia. In Turkey, however, coral serves not only for the personal adornment of men as well as of women, but also for mural decoration and the ornamentation of pipes, weapons, harness for horses, and various other articles. It is used to a large extent over the whole of north Africa, especially in Morocco, and also in Arabia, but is not much esteemed in Egypt.

Coral ornaments are as much in favour with Persians as with Japanese or Chinese. They are very generally worn by Chinese men and women, and incredible sums are often paid for coral buttons of large size and fine quality, intended for the decoration of mandarins' caps. The demand for coral is largest, however, in India, and several million francs' worth is imported annually to Bombay, Calcutta, and Madras. It is worn in this country in the form of necklaces, bracelets, anklets, and other ornaments; it is used for rosaries and charms, and is often offered to the dead, with the belief that it has the power of preventing the occupation of the body by evil spirits.

A moderately large amount of coral is exported to America, especially to South America, and also to Australia. The taste for coral for ornamental purposes would appear to be confined to partially civilised peoples, for attempts to substitute coral for glass beads in dealing with uncivilised tribes have been wholly unsuccessful, the more glittering and much cheaper glass being in every case preferred to coral.

Genuine coral possessing a considerable intrinsic value is of course subject to imitation, and a large amount of **imitation coral** of various kinds is sold at very low prices. Some of the substances used for the manufacture of imitation coral-beads are red gypsum, which, however, can be readily distinguished from genuine coral by the fact that it does not effervesce when touched by acid, and can be scratched even with the finger-nail ; bone, burnt and coloured red ; powdered marble mixed with isinglass and coloured with cinnabar or red-lead ; and even red sealing-wax.

The black coral which has been previously mentioned represents the first stage in the decomposition of precious red coral. The **black coral,** to be now briefly described, is black by nature, and constitutes the skeleton of the coral known to zoologists as *Antipathes spiralis* (Pall.), belonging to the order Antipatharia. The shining pitch-black, branched skeleton of the stock formed by this coral may reach a length of 2 feet, and a thickness of some inches. It is formed not of a calcareous, but of a horny substance, and single pieces of this kind of black coral can therefore be moulded to form armlets and such like. The material is found in the Indian Ocean, and is known in that region by the name of " akabar." It is much esteemed there, and often constitutes the substance of which the sceptres used by native kings and princes are made, hence the term king's-coral, which is also applied to it Black coral of a similar kind is found in the Mediterranean, where it is known as " giojetto."

On the Cameroon and Gulf coasts, **blue coral** was formerly fished and worked into ornaments, which were much prized by the negroes. It is known to the natives as " akori," and to zoologists as *Allopora subviolacea*. It has disappeared from the West African markets for a long period, and therefore needs no further consideration.

APPENDICES TO THE NEW EDITION

SYNTHETIC GEMS

This appendix, by C. Robert Castor, is excerpted from the Kirk-Othmer Encyclopedia of Chemical Technology *and is reprinted with the permission of the publisher, John Wiley & Sons, Inc., New York.*

FROM earliest times there have been efforts to reproduce gemstones synthetically, although only in recent years has this been possible. Today, large numbers of synthetic gems of many different types and colors are being used in the jewelry industry, and new synthetics or new growing methods are being developed and refined periodically. Moreover, the art of growing crystals is being spurred by still another consideration. This is the need for solid-state materials for lasers and masers in which impurity ions (for example, as in ruby, garnet, and emerald) can be made to amplify light and microwave signals, respectively. Research in this direction has already resulted in new crystals, some with considerable beauty, that do not exist in nature at all.

For an understanding of the subject of synthetic stones it is important, first, to define several terms that are commonly used to describe gem materials. This need is demonstrated by the story of the star ruby.

The natural "asteriated" or "star" ruby, found at the highest quality in Burma, is one of the rarest and costliest of all gems. These natural stones have the same chemical composition and crystal structure as clear rubies, but, in addition, they contain numerous microscopic needles of titania, TiO_2, scattered through the body of the crystal in a symmetrical, three-directional pattern. Incident light from a point source, falling on the gem, is scattered by these needles and reflects back to the surface of the stone as a six-rayed star.

In 1947, a way was found to synthesize star ruby; thus, in like fashion, star sapphire has been reproduced. Each has essentially the same chemical and crystal properties as the natural gem. Each has the same fine, needle-like titania inclusions that produce the six-rayed star effect. Since the chemical and crystallographic properties of natural and synthetic stars are alike, they share the same hardness, color, and optical properties. As a result, the only major difference is in rarity. Synthetics, thus, are far less expensive than mined gems of equal beauty, and they have fewer imperfections than the natural ones. Indeed, the character and habit of the imperfections are used to distinguish between natural and synthetic stones.

In addition to the natural and synthetic star stones, there are at least two types of imitation or simulated forms. In one, a natural or synthetic stone that does not contain the correctly oriented titania needles is cut "en cabochon" (dome-shaped with a flat base) and then scribed on the base with three fine lines 120° apart (like a three-directional diffraction grating). These lines scatter incident light and cause a star to appear, but the effect is limited. Such a stone must be called an imitation because it does not adequately reproduce the optical properties of the natural star. A second type of imitation, found in costume jewelry, etches the familiar star shape on the back of an inferior material (usually glass, and called "paste" in the trade). In both types, the star look is sometimes enhanced by providing a mirror back.

Natural or genuine stones are those found in nature. They are cut and polished as found. Certain stones, such as zircon and opal, may also be treated to bring about changes in color or other properties.

Reconstructed stones are aggregates or fused masses of small fragments of natural stones. These were the forerunners of synthetic stones but are only of academic interest today.

Synthetic stones are man-made materials with chemical, physical, and optical properties that are essentially identical with those of their natural counterparts. Various types of synthetic stones are now being made commercially.

There has been a good deal of semantic confusion between the terms artificial, imitation, simulated, and synthetic. They cannot be used interchangeably without causing ambiguity. In the condensation of the Federal Trade Commission ruling which guides nomenclature, published by the American Gem Society, is this rule: "The term synthetics cannot be used for any other material than that which possesses the same physical, chemical, and optical properties as the genuine stone which it emulates."

Materials

Corundum. The first and most important group of gemstone materials to be synthesized was the corundum family of ruby and sapphire. Corundum is α-alumina, Al_2O_3, which crystallizes in the hexagonal form. Pure corundum crystals are transparent and water-white, and are called white sapphire. A few percent of chromic oxide, Cr_2O_3, as an impurity in the crystal, produces what is identified as ruby. Corundum crystals containing small amounts of iron compounds and titania become blue sapphire. Other sapphire colors, including black sapphires, result from coloring the basic corundum with other metal oxides.

Spinel. When speaking of synthetic gems, the term "spinel" usually refers to a magnesia–alumina crystal of the composition $MgO.Al_2O_3$, which crystallizes in a cubic form. As in the case of corundum crystals, the wide variety of colored spinel stones results from the addition of small amounts of other metal oxides as colorants. Pure spinel is transparent and water-white.

Titania. This tetragonal rutile form of titanium dioxide, TiO_2, is unique among the synthetics in that its natural counterpart is seldom, if ever, found in pure enough form to be of value as a gem material. Titania, thus, constitutes a new gem which, in its pale yellow form, is unrivaled in its dispersive power and fire. Its principal disadvantage as a crystal for jewelry use is its relative softness.

Strontium Titanate. In somewhat the same vein as titania is strontium titanate, $SrTiO_3$, a clear, transparent, water-white stone that is sold under the trade name of Fabulite. Relatively soft, as is titania, it has achieved some popularity in the jewelry industry because of its brilliance and modest cost compared to diamond.

Diamond. Many investigators have tried to develop a reproducible process for synthesizing diamond crystals, and considerable progress has been made in recent years. Present technology involves the application of enormous pressures on graphite in the presence of heat and a catalyst. This breakthrough in crystallography was first achieved by scientists at General Electric and has since been repeated elsewhere.

Man-made diamonds thus produced are now being marketed for industrial cutting. At this writing, however, none has been made of a size or clarity to warrant use in jewelry.

Emerald. The costliest of all natural gems, emerald has been the object of many attempted syntheses. The earliest report of synthesis is that of Ebelman (1848) who obtained small hexagonal prisms by heating powdered natural emerald in fused boric acid. More successful experiments by Hautefeuille and Perrey (1888, 1890) resulted in the growth of emerald prisms 1 mm in length. The I. G. Farbenindustrie did experimental work between 1911 and 1942 and achieved small-scale production of synthetic emerald crystals that were marketed under the trade name of Igmerald. Synthetic emeralds have been grown in the United States for about 20 years by C. F. Chatham using a process which has not been divulged. They are probably grown from a molten flux. Two more types have recently become available commercially. One, referred to as the Gilson emerald, is manufactured by Pierre Gilson, Pas de Calais, France, and is probably grown from a molten flux. Another, synthesized by W. Zerfass, of Idar Oberstein, Germany, is believed (1) to be grown hydrothermally. Others (2), however, have concluded it is flux-grown. Properties of these emeralds have been described by Schlossmaker (3) and also by Liddicoat (4). A process for coating synthetic emerald (probably hydrothermally) on preformed stones of natural beryl was developed by J. Lechleitner in Austria. These stones are referred to as "Emerita" (5). Most recently, Union Carbide Corporation, Linde Division, has introduced and described a synthetic emerald grown hydrothermally on seed plates of natural beryl (6).

The Synthetic Gem Industry

Several experimenters attempted the synthesis of ruby and sapphire during the nineteenth century, but none was successful commercially. At the turn of the century, small quantities of reconstructed rubies appeared on the European market.

In 1904, however, the Verneuil flame-fusion process for making synthetic corundum was announced (7), and this effectively halted all manufacture of reconstructed stones. The Verneuil process has since been used, with only minor modifications, in the growing of millions of carats of sapphire, ruby, and spinel. More recently, star sapphires, star rubies, titania, single-crystal tungstate phosphors and even single-crystal refractories such as tungsten have been grown.

Originally, synthetic corundum and spinel crystals were important mainly as gem materials and as jewel bearings for watches and precision instruments and meters. In their mechanical applications, synthetic crystals are superior in quality and better in price than natural materials.

American Industry. Except for a time during World War I when crystals were grown in the United States to meet military needs, European sources provided the major supply of synthetic corundum and spinel from the invention of the Verneuil furnace in 1904 until the advent of World War II. Then, with normal European supplies cut off and crystals demands soaring, the United States undertook again to establish its own facilities. Although details of equipment design and process control were trade secrets closely guarded by the European makers, American industry set out to develop its own technology and to grow synthetics on a large scale. Led by Union Carbide Corporation, Linde Division, the work was completed after only 18 months at the beginning of World War II.

Since then the American crystals industry has expanded many times over and made substantial contributions to the technology of crystallography. The ability to make synthetic star ruby and star sapphire in blue, white, and black shades is an invention of Linde Division scientists. American work in synthesizing diamond, emerald, and other crystals has been of significant importance. Process development has also progressed in this country.

Manufacture and Properties

Synthetic crystals made by the Verneuil or flame-fusion process are unicrystalline and are called "boules." This name derives from the ball-shaped crystal obtained by Verneuil in the early days. Today, however, a corundum boule is a single crystal of α-alumina that may have a diameter of more than 1 in. and a length of 18 in. or more. Maximum sizes are dependent on the material being grown; thus, ruby and white sapphire are capable of forming bigger boules than either blue or black sapphire. Oxygen and hydrogen are used to fuel Verneuil furnaces, and growth takes place at controlled temperatures of 3700°F. Heat of this magnitude leaves thermal stresses which must be relieved adequately if the crystal is not to be subject to cracking later on.

Spinel crystals are approximately $1/2$ in. in diameter and up to 4 in. long; titania crystals are somewhat smaller. The many colors of crystals in synthetic corundum and spinel are possible with the addition of small quantities of metal oxides to the material used in their manufacture. This is called "doping" the crystal.

Titania boules as obtained from the furnace contain slightly less oxygen than corresponds to the formula TiO_2 and are black and opaque. They are subjected to a separate heat treatment in an oxidizing atmosphere that satisfies the oxygen requirement and yields clear material.

Asteriated sapphire and ruby is grown in boule form much the same as clear corundum. Star stones, however, must contain a titanium compound, the precipitation of which by suitable heat treatment causes the star effect.

Table 1 gives the properties of corundum, spinel, and titania crystals. The asteriated variety of sapphire and ruby are included in the corundum group.

The compressive strength of corundum is 300,000 psi. Other mechanical properties are:

c-axis orientation	30°	45°	60°	75°
elastic modulus in flexure, psi, $\times 10^6$	55	51	50	56
modulus of rupture, psi, $\times 10^3$	100	78	65	94

For sapphire, the Te point (temperature at which the electrical resistivity becomes 1 MΩ-cm) is 1231°C parallel to the c axis and 1214°C normal to the c axis. The resistivity of titania changes markedly according to whether or not oxygen is present; indeed, at high temperatures it can be used for the detection and even quantitative estimation of oxygen. Values in different atmospheres at 1150°C are as follows:

atmosphere	Air	O_2	N_2	93% N_2–7% H_2
resistivity, Ω-cm	30	43	8.1	0.13

The following table shows the change in resistivity of titania in an oxygen atmosphere with change in temperature:

temperature, °C	500	800	1000	1300	1550
resistivity, Ω-cm	1,900,000	3200	380	18	2

Table 1. Properties of Synthetic Crystals

Property	Corundum	Spinel	Titania
formula	Al_2O_3	$MgO.3^1/_2Al_2O_3$	TiO_2
crystal structure	hexagonal	cubic	tetragonal
mp, °C	2030	2030–2060	1825
sp gr	3.98	3.61	4.25
refractive index	$\omega D = 1.769$	$\eta D = 1.727$	$\omega D = 2.616$
	$\epsilon D = 1.760$		$\epsilon D = 2.903$
chromatic dispersion	$\omega F - \omega C = 0.011$	$\eta F - \eta C = 0.012$	$\omega F - \omega C = 0.155$
	$\epsilon F - \epsilon C = 0.011$		$\epsilon F - \epsilon C = 0.205$
infrared transmission,[a] %	83[b]	85[b]	66[h]
infrared limit of transparency, Å	57,000[c]	53,000[g]	54,000[i]
sp heat at 25°C	0.18		0.17
coefficient of thermal expansion, $\times 10^{-6}$	6.7[d,e]	5.9[j]	9.19[e,j]
	5.0[d,f]		7.14[f,i]
dielectric constant	7.5–10.0	8–9	170[e]
			86[f]
hardness, Mohs	9	8	7–7.5
Knoop	1525–2000	1175–1380	900–1000
water absorption	0	0	0
chemical resistance	unattacked by common acids or NaOH; unattacked by HF below 300°C	unattacked by common acids or NaOH; slightly etched by HF after 65 days at room temperature	resistant to attack by common acids and alkalies

[a] Loss largely due to Fresnel's reflection.
[b] For 5-mm thickness, at 10,000 Å.
[c] 30% transmission, 5-mm thickness.
[d] At 50°C.
[e] Parallel to c axis.
[f] Normal to c axis.

[g] 30% transmission, 5-mm thickness. Also exhibits absorption band at 29,000 Å.
[h] For 2.54-mm thickness, at 10,000 Å.
[i] 33% transmission, 2.54-mm thickness.
[j] At 40°C.

Preparation of Powder.   The powder used as starting material in the manufacture of corundum is prepared by the calcination of ammonium aluminum sulfate (alum, $NH_4Al(SO_4)_2.12H_2O$). For spinel a mixture of alum and ammonium magnesium sulfate, $(NH_4)_2SO_4.MgSO_4.6H_2O$, is used. Since materials of adequate purity for boule making cannot be purchased commercially, they must be manufactured under carefully controlled conditions, using special purification techniques. The purified sulfates are obtained by precipitation from aqueous solutions. Spectrographic analysis is used to control quality in the various steps of preparation, but the quality of boule powder can be determined positively only by growing a boule. Impurities such as iron compounds, magnesia, and silica in concentrations as low as a few parts per million can be detected in a clear sapphire boule immediately by the unaided eye.

Powder used in the manufacture of ruby crystals is prepared by adding chromic sulfate solution to the uncalcined alum in sufficient quantity to give from 0.5 to 6.0% chromic oxide in the calcined powder. The lower concentration of chromic oxide results in the growth of a pink-tinted crystal, while the higher concentration produces the dark ruby required for watch bearings (because the thin wafer section from a light ruby is not easy to see). Similarly, the blue color of sapphire is derived from comparable quantities of the oxides of iron and titanium, green from cobalt, and golden or "topaz"

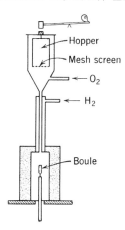

Fig. 1.   Typical Verneuil crystal-growth apparatus.

from nickel and magnesium. The popular deep blue spinel is colored by an oxide of cobalt, and "aquamarine" spinel gets its color from a complex colorant mixture containing small amounts of nickel, cobalt, vanadium, and titanium oxides.

When colored sapphire and spinel crystals are desired, the colorant metal salt solution is added to the alum before it is placed in the calcination furnace. Uniform distribution of the colorant in the powder is assured because the alum dissolves in its water of hydration during the early stages of calcination in gas-fired muffle furnaces. Shallow fused quartz dishes, each charged with 2 lb of alum, are placed directly in a hot furnace and calcined at 1000–1100°C.

After cooling, the calcined material is in the form of a light friable cake, which is then screened to obtain the fine powder used in the boule growth apparatus.

Titania powder is prepared by calcining hydrolyzed titanium tetrachloride for several hours in an oxidizing atmosphere at a temperature of about 500°C. Extremely pure titanium tetrachloride is required to obtain titania crystals of a desirable very pale yellow color.

Growing Flame-Process Crystals.   The basic oxyhydrogen-flame process for growing gemstone crystals has changed little since it was first developed by Verneuil. A typical Verneuil crystal-growth apparatus is shown schematically in Figure 1. The powder used to grow the crystals is contained in a hopper equipped with a fine-mesh screen bottom. During the growth cycle the hopper is tapped with a hammer, causing the powder to feed intermittently into the oxygen stream which flows down through the center tube of the diffusion-type oxyhydrogen burner. Hydrogen is fed to the flame through an annular passage surrounding the central powder-oxygen tube. The tip of the oxyhydrogen burner discharges the flame into a cylindrical ceramic furnace. Such a ceramic furnace shell is usually made in two halves for easy removal of the crystal boule, and a small rectangular slot is cut into one of the halves for viewing the boule during the growth process. The boules are grown on a ceramic pedestal which is centered in the refractory furnace and supported by a table equipped with a vertical screw adjustment.

At the start of the boule-growth process, the rate of powder flow is adjusted higher, and the flame intensity lower, than for the final boule-growth condition. The powder-feed rate is controlled by the frequency and/or the amplitude of the hammer blow. Flame characteristics are controlled by the oxygen-hydrogen ratio and the actual volumes of these gases fed to the flame. The powder falling through the flame builds up as a sintered mass on the top of the ceramic pedestal and, with favorable flame conditions, a single rodlike crystal soon begins to emerge from the mass. By careful control of the flame, and by lowering of the boule, this single crystal is made to grow out of the sintered mass until it is about $^1/_4$ in. long and has the diameter of a match stick. At this point, the crystal-growth conditions are changed so that a small ball is made to form on top of the rod which progressively broadens to resemble a small mushroom. When the diameter of this crystal "mushroom" has increased to standard boule diameter, the growth conditions are adjusted to generate a uniform-diameter cylindrical section. These final conditions of powder feed, flame character, and boule-lowering rate are maintained until the boule has attained the desired length. The growth process is then stopped, and the boule is allowed to cool within the furnace. As a general rule, clear, water-white sapphire boules are easier to grow than colored ones. When a high concentration of coloring agent is present, fusion becomes more difficult and the boule is more susceptible to cracking.

Frequently, the use of sapphire and ruby for a particular application is limited by the size of the article which can be formed from a half-boule since unannealed boules split into two pieces. Annealing of corundum boules at high temperatures has yielded encouraging results on the problem of shaping large, one-piece articles from sapphire. It is now possible to anneal whole boules as large as $^3/_4$ in. in diameter and several inches long so completely that they can be sawed, drilled, and polished without fracturing. The annealing process is carried out in a specially designed oxygen-gas-fired high-temperature furnace, at a maximum temperature of about 1950°C.

Star Sapphire and Ruby. Synthetic star sapphires and star rubies are grown in boule form, using the Verneuil flame process. Star gems contain a titanium compound, preferably titania, which may be added in concentrations of less than 1% to the powder from which the crystal is grown. The synthesis of star gems up to this point is very similar to the manufacture of ordinary blue sapphire boules.

The star effect emerges in the course of a special heat treatment in which the boule material is heated to a temperature between 1100 and 1500°C, causing the titanium compound to precipitate as fine needles along prominent crystallographic planes of the crystal. When removed from the furnace, the crystal is cloudy. It is then ready to be cut and polished *en cabochon,* making certain of proper orientation so that the star is centered in the finished stone. A movable six-ray star is visible when the gem is cut and polished with the *c* axis of the crystal normal to the base of the stone.

Industrial Fabrication

Of the synthetic gem crystals, sapphire is the only one that has found widespread industrial use. Industrial sapphire has a Mohs hardness of 9; the only practical abrasive for shaping it, therefore, is diamond, which has a Mohs hardness of 10. Since diamond is expensive, American industry has attempted to reduce the amount of diamond required in fabricating sapphire articles. The development of single-crystal corundum rods was an important advance in this respect.

In making jewel bearings for watches and other instruments from split corundum boules, the common practice in European gem centers was to slice the boule into thin, half-moon wafers, to saw these wafers into tiny squares, and then to grind the squares into circular discs. The advantages of starting with a cylindrical crystal rod of about the diameter of the jewel bearing are obvious. Only one slicing operation is required to arrive at the point reached by the many cutting and grinding operations on a boule.

The availability of sapphire in long-rod form permits developments not possible with boule sections. Although single-crystal corundum exhibits remarkable strength and rigidity at high temperatures, a corundum rod can be bent into a helix if the temperature is raised near the melting point. This bending phenomenon is related to the crystallographic orientation of the rod in that it is a combination of slippage on the basal plane and actual crystal-lattice distortion. The ideal orientation to the c axis for bending a rod has been found to be 45°, with the plane of bending containing the c axis and the growth axis.

The availability of lengths of corundum rod also permitted, for the first time, the observation and study of the phenomena of flame polishing. A cylindrical rod about $1/10$ in. in diameter can be given an excellent polish by slowly moving it through an oxy-fuel gas flame at a rate which allows the molten surface to heal over all of the grinding marks. A flame-polishing operation is comparatively inexpensive and fast compared to diamond polishing.

Manufacturing Emerald

The development of new and advanced techniques for growing crystals has contributed substantially to the ability to synthesize new varieties in recent times. One significant area where this is so is the refinement of hydrothermal technology to the point where a successful synthetic emerald can be produced commercially. The hydrothermal process is far more intricate than the growing of simple quartz crystals. Synthetic emerald is produced hydrothermally when chromiferous beryllium aluminum silicate crystallizes from an aqueous solution on a seed plate at high temperature and

Table 2. Comparison between Synthetic and Natural Emeralds[a]

	Natural emeralds	Synthetic emeralds	
		Flux-melt	Hydrothermal
refractive index range	1.57–1.59	1.56–1.57	1.57–1.58
birefringence	0.005–0.007	0.003–0.005	0.005–0.006
sp gr	2.68–2.77	2.65–2.67	2.67–2.69
fluorescence, uv short, 2537 Å long, 3650 Å	none, to distinct red	variable, depends on flux; none, yellow to green, or dull red to bright red	bright red
residual color through Chelsea filter[b]	none, to bright red (rare)	usually bright red; varies with flux to no red	bright red
inclusions and microstructures	2- and 3-phase inclusions, gas, liquid, salt crystal; inclusions of enstatite, mica, pyrite, or halite crystals	wisp or veil-like 2-phase inclusions, solidified flu and gas; phenacite inclusions; possibly seed-plate discontinuity	2-phase inclusions, liquid and gas; occasional phenacite inclusions; possibly seed-plate discontinuity
infrared spectrum	three OH bands[c] in region of 3700, 3600, and 1600 cm^{-1}	no OH band	single OH band[c] near 3700 cm^{-1}

[a] Union Carbide Linde data from this laboratory and reference 5.

[b] An optical filter whose absorption complements that of emerald.

[c] Tentative conclusion; requires verification with other specimens of known origin of natural and synthetic hydrothermal emeralds. However, any emerald of hydrothermal origin would be expected to contain OH groups (water and/or hydroxyl), giving rise to OH bands in the infrared region of 4000–1500 cm^{-1}.

pressure. This is believed to approximate the natural process in contrast to the flux method in which the beryl, alumina, and silicate with a little chromium added have been dissolved under no pressure at all.

A high-pressure "bomb" or autoclave is used to contain the solution under the appropriate heat and pressure while seed plates are suspended in the upper—and cooler —area to attract the emerald ingredients that are picked up from the lower—and hotter —area by circulating solutions. The significant differences between the synthetic emeralds grown in this fashion from the flux-melt product is that hydrothermally produced stones generally match the inclusions and infrared fluorescence of natural stones while the others do not. In particular, the characteristic wisp inclusions seen in flux-melt stones are not found in the hydrothermal type. Table 2 shows the comparison between natural, flux-melt, and hydrothermal emeralds and illustrates the greater degree of similarity attached to the hydrothermally produced synthetic.

The hydrothermal synthetic emerald is now (1966) being scaled up for volume production, and there may be some modification to the process. In general, however, seeds are cut parallel to a pyramid face, drilled through one end to admit a bit of platinum wire, and then are hung on a rack and suspended in the solution. Growth is rapid at the outset but diminishes in pace with time. As a result, it has been found that it is necessary to recycle the growth process a number of times from start to finish before enough thickness is achieved to get a rough of adequate size for cutting. Stones weighing more than $2^1/_2$ carats have already been produced, and still larger ones are in prospect.

Bibliography

"Gems, Synthetic" in *ECT* 1st ed., Vol. 7, pp. 157–167, by A. K. Seemann, Linde Air Products Co., A Division of Union Carbide and Carbon Corp.

1. E. J. Gubelin, *Gems and Gemol.* **11**, 139 (1964).
2. E. M. Flanigen, D. W. Breck, N. R. Mumbach, and A. M. Taylor, *Gems and Gemol.* **11**, 259 (1965). Kurt Nassau, *Lapidary J.* **18**, 42, 313, 386, 474, 483, 588, 690 (1964).
3. K. Schlossmaker, *J. Gemmol.* **9**, 104 (1963), cited.
4. R. T. Liddicoat, E. J. Gubelin, and R. Webster, *Gems and Gemol.* **11**, 131 (1964).
5. R. J. Holmes and G. R. Crowingshield, *Gems and Gemol.* **10**, 11 (1960).
6. F. H. Pough, *Lapidary J.* **20**, 56 (April 1966).
7. A. Verneuil, *Am. Chim. Phys.* **3**, 20 (1904).

General References

1. R. E. Hopkins and B. J. O'Brien, *J. Opt. Soc. Am.* **39**, 1061 (1949).
2. L. Morker, "The Synthetic Stone Industry of Germany," *Field Information Agency, Final Rept., No. 1001* (1947).
3. F. H. Pough, "The New Linde Synthetic Emerald," *The Jewelers' Circular—Keystone* (August 1965).
4. N. P. Rooksby, *J. Roy. Soc. Arts* **94**, 508–525 (1946).
5. G. O. Wild and H. Biegel, *Gemologist* **16**, 67 (1947).
6. U.S. Pat. 2,488,507 (Nov. 15, 1949), J. N. Burdick and J. W. Glenn.

C. Robert Castor
Electronics Division
Union Carbide Corp.

THE CULTURED PEARL

This appendix is adapted from The Cultured Pearl *by Norine C. Reece published by Charles E. Tuttle Co., Rutland, Vermont and Tokyo, Japan.*

ORIGIN

ONE of the most famous industries of Japan, and deservedly so, is certainly one of the most romantic. Back in 1893, when Kokichi Mikimoto succeeded in cultivating and producing a pearl known as the "shell" pearl, he had completed the first step in what was to become a lucrative business, but it is questionable if even he envisioned the beauty and delight he was eventually bringing to the whole world.

Until the achievement of cultured pearls, all pearls were simply the result of an irritant accidentally entering the oyster's shell and blindly making its way to some spot in the tissue where it would be covered with layers of nacre and eventually discovered as a pearl in the searches of the divers for these coveted gems. The art of introducing an irritant into the oyster so that the oyster would live and, over a period of years, transform the irritant into a pearl was the main problem that confronted the pioneers of what is today's cultured-pearl industry.

There was the additional, pressing problem of ascertaining the *type* of irritant upon which the oyster would most willingly build a pearl of value. The experiments and research, and the concomitant disappointments, involved in reaching a solution would have broken the hearts and spirits of many men less determined than the now-famous founders of the industry. Once these initial difficulties were resolved, the infant industry could move unsteadily ahead into the realm of production.

There are no artificial pearls. There are true pearls, and there are pearl beads—synthetics artificially manufactured and marketed as "simulated pearls." These latter are beads that have been coated to produce the general outward appearance of pearls, but they lack the deep luster and iridescence of true pearls. A simple comparison of true pearls with pearl beads reveals the character of each, the warmth and fire of a pearl and the cold glitter of a pearl bead. Cultured pearls are as genuine as those found by divers in South Sea waters or elsewhere. They are produced as the result of a controlled operation—artificial insemination, if you like—but are genuine pearls as much as babies born as the result of artificial insemination are genuine babies. They are in no way synthetic or artificial.

When one begins even a superficial study of the production of cultured pearls, the painstaking care, prolonged endeavors, and the financing of the venture necessary to bring these gems to perfection seems almost beyond belief. The very nature of the production means much delicate handicraft from its inception over a long period of years.

With only minor exceptions, the operations involved in producing the cultured pearl are entirely handwork. The industry requires a prodigious initial outlay of capital plus the financial ability and mental capacity to endure a long waiting period before any monetary return is realized. In addition to these financial and human requirements, the industry requires the coöperation of nature, the ability to outwit the wilder manifestations of nature, and the fortitude and solvency to rise from the blows inflicted by natural disasters such as earthquakes, tidal waves, typhoons, and "red tides." This red tide gains its name from the appearance of the sea; the water seeming to turn dark red from the influx of plankton, the natural food of the oyster, in a poisonous form, deep orange in color.

THE PEARL OYSTER

Beds of the pearl-building oysters, the *Pinctada martensii,* lie off the coast of Mie Prefecture, southern Honshu, in the Pacific Ocean. These oysters are not edible per se. These natural oyster beds, from which formerly all the oysters used in culturing pearls were secured, constitute one of Japan's most valuable natural resources and are under the control of the Mie Prefectural Fisheries Union. If the union did not exercise control over the oyster beds, an asset of Japan comparable to the nationally supervised fishing grounds, nothing would exist to preclude their complete spoliation by selfish interests. Oysters from these beds are taken only in late June and early July, and again in September each year, and then under union supervision. The oysters are procured by *ama,* or divers, and taken to a central market where they are auctioned to the pearl cultivators. The proceeds of the auction are divided between the union and the divers; approximately thirty per cent to the union and seventy per cent to the divers.

SEEDING

What happens next in the life of a pearl oyster depends on the age of the oyster. None younger than two years are seeded, as the mortality rate of the seeded young oysters is too great. This hand seeding constitutes the *only* difference between a cultured pearl and a natural pearl.

Finding a nucleus upon which an oyster would build a marketable pearl was the second greatest difficulty encountered by the pioneers in developing the cultured pearl. Just a few of the questions involved were: finding a substance upon which the oyster would deposit nacre; finding a substance which the oyster would tolerate and not eject; finding a substance which had the proper physical and chemical characteristics; and, finally, finding all of these qualifications, and more, combined in a substance relatively inexpensive and available in adequate supply. Experiments proved that oysters will build pearls upon bits of silver, glass, steel, and some types of shell, but a calcareous seed is especially suitable. On a hardness scale of 10, 10 representing a diamond, 3.5 to 4.0 represents a pearl. As this comparison indicates, pearls are relatively "soft" and can be easily drilled. This is because they are largely calcareous, but only by intensive study of the composition of pearls and almost endless experimentation did the pioneers finally find a satisfactory seed. Great credit is due Mr. Tokichi Nishikawa, patentee of the Nishikawa process, for his contributions to the solution of this problem. He did not, however, live to see the widespread adoption of his method by the industry.

Since the most satisfactory seed to produce a cultured pearl should be calcareous, the use of the present nucleus is especially harmonious, as it combines that qualification with the same specific gravity as nacre. The trade terminology for seed is "nucleus,"

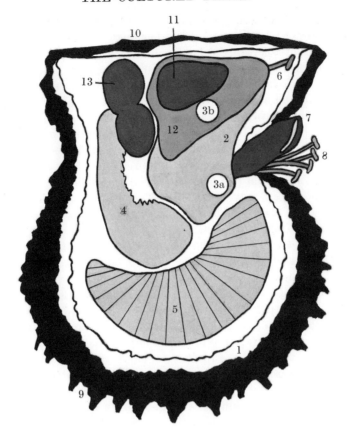

DIAGRAM OF OYSTER

1.	Mantle	7.	Foot
2.	Gonad	8.	Byssus
3a.	*Fukuro* (seeding area)	9.	Shell
3b.	*Ukashi* (seeding area)	10.	Hinge
4.	Adductor muscle	11.	Liver
5.	Gill	12.	Stomach
6.	Mouth	13.	Heart

and the only current source of nuclei is the pig-toe clam shell from the Mississippi Valley in the United States. Before World War II, some shells from the Yangtze River in China furnished material for part of the nuclei used, but trade with that area of China is suspended at present, and the Mississippi Valley clam shell is now used exclusively.

The procuring of clam shells for use as nuclei grew with the expansion of pearl farming and has become an additional and important facet of the pearl industry. Where formerly this enterprise was only another phase of the business of the individual pearl farmer, today, with the enlargement of the cultured-pearl business, it has expanded into a centralized industry. These shells are brought to Japan and processed for use by a factory in south Osaka which has access to differing grades of sand used in polishing the nuclei. The shells are first cut into strips, then into cubes, and finally spherically shaped and sand-polished, in varying sizes. Thus the cultivator can buy the sizes desired for any particular operation. The nuclei are bought in wholesale lots, from which he selects the exact nuclei he wishes to use. Nuclei are prepared in sizes from approximately 2.5 millimeters to 7 millimeters. Smaller nuclei are required for seeding younger oysters, as they cannot tolerate the larger sizes. Three- and four-year-old oysters are seeded with the larger nuclei to produce the larger pearls so much in demand.

After securing the oysters and nuclei, the next step is seeding the oysters. This process is fascinating and almost unbelievably intricate in some of its phases. Twenty-four hours before seeding takes place, the oysters to be seeded are brought in from the open water. On the day of the seeding operation, basket after basket of oysters is taken from the water and the oysters placed in dry containers on the shaded dock. After being left in the open air for thirty minutes or so, the shells begin to open. As fast as this happens a wooden peg is inserted in the opening and the oysters delivered to the seeders. Some oysters may be still "tired" from the winter hibernation period and the shells may not open readily. When this is obvious, those oysters are returned to the sea for another twenty-four-hour resting period, then again brought to the dock. The seeders are both men and women who have served a lengthy apprenticeship for this work, for upon the dexterity and delicacy of their operation depends in large part the mortality rate of the oysters.

To assist in explaining the process of seeding, the diagram of the oyster presented here shows only thirteen points of primary interest in this phase of pearl cultivation. This may be an oversimplification, but is done for the sake of clarity and to facilitate understanding. The mantle (1) is precisely what its name suggests, the coat of the oyster covering the entire body, and is the manufacturer of the oyster's shell. It is white, shading from brown to gray to black toward the outer edge. For each twelve to fifteen oysters seeded, one oyster dies to furnish the graft tissue required in the operation. The fringe of the mantle is cut away from the edge of the shell. In many cases this is then treated with an antiseptic, the colored portion is trimmed off, and the small strip of living tissue remaining is cut transversely into twelve to fifteen sections, each approximately one-eighth of an inch square. If properly treated and handled, this tissue, or epithelium, will retain life for as long as two hours.

With these segments of tissue in front of him, the operator takes one of the pegged oysters, rests it in or on a metal clamp before him, and replaces the wooden peg with a retractor. Controlling the action-motivating muscle or foot (7) of the oyster with a depressor, he makes a tiny channel into the body of the oyster (3a and/or 3b) and then inserts the nucleus in one of two ways. By one method, *saki okuri*, he slips a section of the graft tissue down the channel, then inserts the nucleus to lie immediately above the graft tissue; by the second method, *ato okuri*, he reverses this procedure and inserts the nucleus first, then the graft tissue to lie over the nucleus. In either method, the cells of the tissue (which are on the inner side) must lie next to the nucleus. Both systems are used, and each appears to be equally successful. After the insertion of the nucleus and the graft tissue, the main body tissue is smoothed back, the depressor and retractor removed, and the oyster returned to a small container of sea water immediately. Shortly thereafter it is transferred to a basket and suspended in the bay. On the sketch, 3a represents a small area (*fukuro*) in the gonad of the oyster where seeding is done, because of its accessible location. The placement of the nucleus there does not interfere with the reproductive activities of the oyster. The other marked area (3b) is a free area (*ukashi*) between the liver and the skin of the oyster (the mantle in turn lies over the skin); this likewise is a convenient, accessible area in which to plant the nucleus.

Seeding begins very shortly after the industry returns to Ago Bay in the spring, and the cultivators have been preparing oysters for seeding since November, while they were in the warmer waters of the southern regions. The *Pinctada martensii* is dioecious, the male and female oysters being distinct, but the complete transposition of sex from male to female and vice versa in these oysters is known to take place. Studies of this conversion are being carried on continuously, but the change within specific time limits, stabilized percentages of change from one sex to the other, and many other attendant factors are not yet conclusively established. During the winter period in the south, the oysters pass through a comparatively inactive period, called in the industry "hibernation," and during this period they become very sluggish. They are subjected to frequent examination and those which show only a very slight development of ova or sperm are closely packed in rows in wire baskets and the baskets placed on the floor of the sea. This process is called *yokusei,* an arresting of further development of reproductive activities and the absorption within the body of the oyster of the few ova or sperm which may have been present. These oysters are then ready for seeding almost immediately upon the return of the industry to home waters in the spring. It is believed that these oysters are the so-called immatures of the sex-conversion process, never completely developing either male or female characteristics.

When the spawning season arrives, oysters having ascendant male characteristics at that time furnish sperm to fertilize the ova of oysters having ascendant female characteristics to produce spat. The cultivators call both sperm and ova "eggs" indiscriminately, but the male and female agents must and do exist individually. Within twenty-four hours after fertilization, the shadowy outline of the eventual oyster is present—this has been microphotographed—and twenty to twenty-five days later the spat has developed.

During the seeding, if an oyster is found with the gonad distended with eggs, it is not seeded but is returned to the water for artificial spawning. This artificial spawning is induced by the administration of a mild stimulant—a very slight change of temperature or a very slight alternation in the salinity of the water is sufficient—and after a week or ten days of rest, subsequent to spawning, the oyster is brought out of the water again and seeded. This artificial spawning is known as *ran-nuki* and is a very important adjunct of the seeding process, another potential source of young oysters.

Seeding is performed more easily after spawning than at other times, for the tissue of the oyster is more tender then, and also the byssus (8), which is composed of the filaments by which an oyster clings to its supporting surface, is almost completely shed during the spawning season. This removes a slight hindrance to the process of seeding.

The eventual harvest of pearls is directly related to the skill and ability manifested in the seeding operation, for a misplaced nucleus will produce no pearl. If the seeding has been properly performed, in simple terms the following physiological process begins immediately: the epithelium (living graft tissue of the mantle) continues life, and in seven to ten days its living, growing cells have formed a "pearl sac" around the nucleus. Then continuing its natural function, the secretion of nacre, it deposits overlapping segments of calcareous material around the nucleus, thus achieving the formation and growth of the pearl.

With maximum care and deftness, and with the oyster in the best possible physical condition, it still sustains an operational shock from the seeding. The baskets of seeded oysters are kept in waters near the home farm for four to six weeks for recovery from shock and rebuilding of tissues and any damaged shell. At the end of that time, the baskets are withdrawn, the shells examined, and any dead oysters removed. The shells of the healthy, living oysters are cleaned of moss, barnacles and other marine growths, each one by hand, put into fresh wire baskets, and suspended from the huge wooden rafts for their growing period.

To digress slightly at this point, it should be noted that at this time the pearl cultivator has been in business for several months with all the money going out and nothing coming in; unless he is going to cultivate only the smallest pearls, he has no prospect of an appreciable income for at least another two years. But he is committed to the expenditure of much more money! As the oysters are seeded, the farmer must be ready with many, many containers for them, and large rafts from which to suspend the containers; he must be prepared to guard his holdings from natural enemies and possible "pirates" of the trade; he must sustain his share of the cost of watchmen and searchlights; he must be able to perform the frequent cleaning of the shells, and the renovation of the baskets at each cleaning; he must be prepared to move his holdings south in November and north in April. It is practically impossible for a pearl farmer to remain in business without at least a small motor boat, and that constitutes another heavy financial investment; but the rafts have to be towed through the bay, employees have to be transported to the rafts for various duties, and the farmer must have facilities to move his holdings hurriedly in case of emergency. All of these requirements have to be met, but one begins to understand that pearls are not just the result of simply planting nuclei in oysters and returning two or three or four years later and collecting the harvest.

GROWTH OF OYSTERS

The size of pearls desired, and/or the financial ability of the grower to endure a lengthier waiting period, determines the years of growth allowed the oyster. Small pearls from small nuclei in small oysters can be harvested after one season's growth, from May to January of the following year. Up to a maximum of four years, the longer the oyster is permitted to work, the larger the pearl that will be harvested, subject to certain uncontrollable factors. For instance, some oysters refuse to work at all (only nature knows why) and leaving them in the water for years will produce no pearl. There is no distinctive outward marking of the shell of the *Pinctada martensii* indicating sex, and there is no indication whether an oyster will be a worker or a non-worker, as for instance with the drone bee. Oysters are seeded without any attempt at sex distinction and do or do not produce pearls as chance would dictate, without the possibility of imposition of human control other than careful placement of the nucleus. Then, too, the longer an oyster is permitted to work, the greater is the chance that the pearl will go off-round and become baroque, which while beautiful does not have the intrinsic value of a perfect spherical pearl. After five years of growth, the pearl begins to lose its luster. And when pearls become too large, some oysters eject them and they are lost, so that all the labor and investment have gone for nothing. The cultivators are working on devices to outwit this maneuver of the oyster, but suitable protection without attendant disadvantage is not easily designed. Placing a nylon net or mesh wire of sufficient fineness to retain the pearl in the basket has a tendency to form a barrier to the oyster's food; the small openings clog with barnacles and moss much more quickly, retarding the growth of the oyster and the pearl. Under the free suspension method, there is no hope of saving the ejected pearl. Eventually some adequate arrangement to prevent these losses will be evolved, but no complete protection is available now. At present, constant care and cleaning and occasional testing are the surest methods of determining when the full harvest can be made most profitably.

Once the initial investment has been made and the first year's seeding accomplished, each year thereafter sees additional seeding (and additional investment). After expiration of the first full growing season for the size of pearls desired, a recurring annual harvest and annual income is assured, barring unforeseen disaster.

However, it is amazing how few pearls of a whole year's harvest are marketable, and of those it is even more amazing how few are perfect in symmetry, luster, and color. Possibly forty per cent may have some marketable value, but perfect gems constitue not more than five to ten per cent of the entire harvest.

LUSTER, COLOR, AND WEIGHT

There is as yet no final and authoritative scientific definition of luster in pearls. The components of a pearl are calcium carbonate, constituting about ninety-five per cent of the pearl, and protein, the remaining five per cent. During the warm weather, which is the active growing period of the oyster and the pearl, the oyster is feeding steadily and the protein is much richer than in winter, when the activity of the oyster lessens as it enters the period of hibernation. The reflection of light from the crystals of calcium carbonate combined with the protein produces the prismatic gleam and play of refulgence that we call luster. Oysters in cold water deposit a leaner, thinner protein in the building of the pearl and this thinness induces a greater reflection of light so that luster is then at its maximum. Much study remains to be done before a definitive scientific explanation of luster can be stated with finality. The sorting of pearls by color is entrancing. Color in pearls cannot be humanly controlled—it is a gift of nature—and when the final color sorting is made, interest and enthusiasm are at their height. It is believed that differing areas in the bay may account for some of the differing colors in pearls, based on the fact that a majority of oysters harvested from a specific locality have been found to contain pearls of similar color, but this has not been authenticated.

The laboratory recognizes six main color divisions: white, cream, pink, green, gold, and black. There are known to be many, many *gradations* of colors in pearls, but these are so subtle that only the finest experts of the industry can distinguish many of them. To the inexperienced eye, possibly three or four colors may be distinguishable, and sometimes not that many. Apart from white, yellow, and "black," which are clearly and obviously recognizable, an inexperienced buyer should seek expert advice from representatives of the industry.

The rarest of all cultured pearls is the "rainbow," and to find and harvest a rainbow pearl even once in three or four years is phenomenal. It is literally a gift of the gods, of totally unpredictable occurrence. It is an exquisitely beautiful pink-white pearl and, as its name indicates, seems to be permeated by every color of the rainbow. And the bounty of the giver is seemingly boundless, for with its ethereal beauty go magnificent size and perfection.

Following the rainbow, other shades follow in finest gradation from white through the pinks, creams, and yellows down to the "black" pearls, which are really variations of color from silver-blue to gunmetal. One of the loveliest and most difficult to obtain in any appreciable quantity is the perfect pearl of silver-blue hue. Its rarity, of course, greatly enhances its value.

Buyers and wearers of pearls are developing an appreciation of the nuances in colors. This is wonderfully self-satisfying to the owner and a source of great gratification to the industry. The pale pinks and creams are very flattering to certain skin tones, and the gold and deep creams are coming into their own. On some skins, their elegance is superb.

Studies of the building of pearls have revealed that occasionally, for reasons not yet completely established, organic matter will be deposited on the nucleus at some stage in the development of the pearl and in the covering of that matter, perfect symmetry may be lost and a baroque pearl formed. Another cause of the formation of symmetrically imperfect pearls is improper placement of the nucleus, so that in the development of the pearl, one side of the filled pearl sac will rub into the body of the oyster, forcing concentration of the deposit of nacre over the remaining areas, thus producing an off-round or baroque pearl. Baroque pearls are *not* diseased pearls nor the product of diseased oysters. The singular beauty of these pearls is beginning to be understood, however, and many exquisite items of jewelry are being made from them.

Weight, too, is a factor of value in pearls. The specific gravity of nacre and the nucleus is the same, 2.65 to 2.69. Thus two pearls of equal size and perfect symmetry should be equal in weight. If two pearls of equal size and symmetry differ in weight, usually the lighter will be found to have a layer of organic matter and, although spherically perfect, will have less intrinsic value. Pearl weight is calculated in *momme* (about three-fourths of an ounce), and heavy, perfect pearls are extremely valuable. Pearls come in all sizes, colors, and shapes, and of varying weights, and each demonstrates a beauty that is not measurable in terms of money alone to the owner and wearer.

PURCHASE AND CARE

Most purchasers need advice and assistance in making selections, and the experts of the cultured-pearl industry are glad to render this service. Every nation fixes its own import duties on the products of other nations, and the purchaser should consult the laws of his own country for information on such charges. In most countries, pearls strung in wholesale form (without clasps) usually carry less duty imposition than those with clasps.

A little information is furnished here concerning the proper care of pearls. When the thread upon which pearls are strung has become soiled, the pearls and thread may be washed. This is best accomplished by lining a long shallow container with an old turkish towel, pouring into the container a quantity of tepid, mild soapsuds (Ivory soap is very suitable), and immersing the strand for six to ten minutes. The strand may be extended to its full length and rolled back and forth over the towel, but do *not* hold pearls in a handful and scrub. Rinse thoroughly in clear tepid water, dry thoroughly, then rub each pearl very lightly with a soft piece of chamois or velvet just touched with lanolin or very pure, high-quality vegetable oil, to restore polish.

To restore the high lights to pearls which have not been worn for a period of time, make a soft cream of Tripoli powder and pure olive oil. With a velvet or chamois cloth, wipe each pearl gently with this cream, rinse in clear, tepid water, and dry carefully on a soft cloth.

Pearls are comparatively "soft" jewels. They cannot be knocked around or harshly treated without being damaged. When not being worn, they should be kept in padded velvet cases or between layers of cotton.

INDEX